Psychology and Life

8th Edition

The primary purpose of the University
Is to provide an environment
In which faculty and students
Can discover, examine critically,
Preserve, and transmit
The knowledge, wisdom, and values
That will help ensure the survival
Of the present and future generations
With improvement in the quality of life.

We seek a wide acceptance of this restatement of purpose. In so doing, we acknowledge the legitimacy of other purposes of the University and do not wish to interfere with them. Rather than alter these other purposes or interfere with academic freedom in any way, we seek positive incentives and procedures by which future-oriented programs would be encouraged. Ways should be found to allow students and faculty to engage in the interdisciplinary efforts that are implied by the statement of purpose. Such an orientation might help to close the "relevance gap" that now exists between faculty and students.

From "Purpose and Function of the University" by V. R. Potter, D. A. Baerreis, R. A. Bryson, J. W. Curvin, G. Johansen, J. McLeod, J. Rankin, and K. R. Symon, The University of Wisconsin; *Science*, Vol. 167, No. 3925, March 20, 1970, p. 1591. Copyright © 1970 by the American Association for the Advancement of Science. Reprinted by permission of the publisher and the authors.

Psychology and Life

8th Edition

Floyd L. Ruch
University of Southern California

Philip G. Zimbardo
Stanford University

SCOTT, FORESMAN AND COMPANY
Glenview, Illinois London

*Grateful acknowledgment is made for permission to reprint
or adapt the following:*

Brown, Reprinted with permission of The Macmillan Company from *Psycholinguistics: Selected Papers* by Roger Brown.
Copyright © 1970 by The Free Press, a Division of The Macmillan Company. / Gershwin, Copyright © 1937 by Gershwin
Publishing Corporation. Copyright renewed. Used by permission of Gershwin Publishing Corporation. / Kuder, From
Kuder Preference Record, Vocational, Form C—Administrator's Manual by G. Frederic Kuder. © 1960, G. Frederic
Kuder. Reprinted by permission of the publisher, Science
Research Associates, Inc. / Manis, From *Cognitive Processes*
by Melvin Manis. © 1966 by Wadsworth Publishing Company, Inc., Belmont, California 94002. Reprinted by permission of the publisher, Brooks/Cole Publishing Company. /
Pfungst, Excerpts from Chapter One, from *Clever Hans: The
Horse of Mr. von Osten,* by Oskar Pfungst. Edited with an
Introduction by Robert Rosenthal. Copyright © 1965 by
Holt, Rinehart & Winston, Inc. Reprinted by permission of
Holt, Rinehart & Winston, Inc. / Pribram, From *Psychology: A Study of a Science,* Vol. 4 by S. Koch. Copyright ©
1962 by McGraw-Hill, Inc. Used by permission of McGraw-Hill Book Company. / Rodgers, Copyright © 1963 by Williamson Music, Inc. Copyright renewed. Used by permission. /
Rubin, Copyright © 1970, by Social Education Foundation.
Reprinted by permission of Simon & Schuster, Inc., and A. M.
Heath & Company, Ltd. / Stein, *From Portraits and Prayers* by
Gertrude Stein. Copyright 1934 and renewed 1962 by Alice B.
Toklas. Reprinted by permission of Random House, Inc. /
Webb, Reprinted with permission of The Macmillan Company
from *Sleep: An Experimental Approach* by Wilse B. Webb.
Copyright © by Wilse B. Webb, 1968 / Coles, Copyright
© 1964, 1965, 1966, 1967 by Robert Coles. From *Children
of Crisis: A Study of Courage and Fear* by Robert Coles, by
permission of Atlantic-Little, Brown and Co. / Krim, From
the book *Views of a Nearsighted Cannoneer* by Seymour Krim.
Copyright 1948, 1951, 1952, 1953, 1956, 1958, 1959, 1960,
1961, 1968 by Seymour Krim. Published by E. P. Dutton &
Co., Inc., and reprinted with their permission.

Preface

To the Instructor

Never before in the history of psychology have so many students been so totally involved in the psychology of life. Many students, before they ever open their first psychology text, have already tried to act as therapists in helping a friend on a bad drug trip, while others have been the "friend" experiencing altered states of consciousness. Students have witnessed our perceptual illusions on television, and the aggression part of our frustration-aggression theories in action during urban revolts and campus riots. Freud has lost his sex appeal as liberalized pornography laws now make available books, magazines, and movies he could never have even dreamed of. Students are already on to the elements of behavior control—so dear to psychologists—since they have become aware of constant attempts to manipulate them and of their own attempts to "con" others. Group processes are old hat to students who regularly attend T-groups and encounter groups, in addition to organizing for political activity on and off campus.

Surprisingly, such increased sophistication, instead of short-circuiting an interest in general psychology, has been a remarkable catalyst. Enrollment in psychology courses has increased phenomenally in the past decade, and in many colleges it is now the most popular major.

We believe this is happening because students want to understand better what they have been experiencing. They want to make sense of, integrate, and be able to utilize their firsthand knowledge of psychology. For us and our colleagues, this represents an exciting challenge—to sustain the interest they bring, to search with them for the answers they are seeking, and to raise questions and offer solutions that they have not yet considered.

Psychology itself is in a state of dynamic growth and transformation, and those of us who are part of this change are eager to involve students who are also curious about why people behave as they do. Because psychology is at the core of everyday human existence, it is understandable why as an academic discipline it is at the intersection of many other areas: literature, physics, religion, biology, philosophy, biochemistry, art, and sociology—not to mention its applications in human engineering, business, law, and medicine.

The new edition of *Psychology and Life* is at the heart of the action—both the exciting new action in today's laboratories and the action in the complex, confusing world that students see around them and are trying to make sense of. Like its predecessors, this edition samples many points of view and conflicting bits of evidence, but a greater effort has been made this time to show how these bits may supplement instead of negate each other. Regardless of what sequence an instructor may choose to follow, he or she will find that the chapters are held together by two central themes: how the many facets of human potentiality develop, function, and can be perverted or enhanced; and the constant endeavor of all individuals, like scientists, to understand, predict, and control themselves and their environment. Some instructors may choose to put primary emphasis on the aspects that make psychology a rigorous experimental and biological science, some on the aspects that make it a social science; both aspects are present in full measure in the pages that follow. A quick reading of the six Part Openers will provide a capsule overview of the organization, main themes, and coverage of the new edition of *Psychology and Life*. The *Instructor's*

Resource Book gives suggestions for building different types of courses based on the text and other materials of the *Psychology and Life* Program.

To the Student

We hope in this text to start you on what should be an exciting intellectual adventure, one in which what psychologists learn in their laboratory experiments and what you learn in the classroom have direct relevance to what you are learning every day in all aspects of your life. This is not an "adjustment manual" or a "how-to-win-friends-and-analyze-parents" guide. Our task is to present a panoramic view of what scientific psychology is, knows, and does, and to relate that knowledge to other knowledge and to life. We have tried to breach the barrier of textbook anonymity and impersonality by addressing our thoughts, information, and questions directly to you, as if you were one of our own warm-bodied students.

This carries on the tradition of *Psychology and Life* which, when it first appeared in 1937, was the only introductory psychology text addressed to students and their concerns. Over the years, each edition has always been based on the assumption that psychology, of all subjects, should be presented as the fascinating, kaleidoscopic, centrally important field that it really is. Students coming to it for the first time should be given not one man's answers but a rich sampling of the questions being asked by many different researchers and the variety of answers that have been emerging.

In the present edition we are attempting to interweave the dual nature of psychology as a scientific and a human enterprise even more closely than before. We try to show how the goals of the academic psychologist—understanding, predicting, and controlling behavior—are congruent with the goals of the ordinary "individual" who wants to understand himself and predict what others will do, what the environment has in store for him, and how he can control events and processes important to him. In our scientifically oriented concern with how individuals develop, adapt, cope, think, and profit from experience, a persistent theme is man's quest for freedom from dependence, restraints, and external control; and his confrontations, along the way, with forces that can diminish his potential. "Relevance" is a natural, essential part of such a story of psychology and life and not something tacked on at the end to make a text more appealing to students. Throughout, the relation of the individual to his society and the responsibilities of the psychologist to both recur in many contexts. We hope to be able to bring you as close as possible to some of what is best in contemporary psychology.

Our concern for what you should get from this text and your formal introduction to psychology may be too ambitious. In order to keep our goals and ways of attaining them attuned to student values and interests, we would very much appreciate receiving any feedback you might provide about what you found valuable and what might be improved when we revise the text for the students who will come after you. (See the postage-free form at the end of the book.)

Special Acknowledgments

As with previous editions, we have sought reactions, comments, and criticisms from colleagues with expertise in many different fields, working in different parts of the country and in different kinds of institutions, in evaluating the preceding edition, planning the new one, and judging the adequacy of part or all of the new manuscript. For this help we are grateful to: James Bruning, Ohio University; William Kessen, Yale University; Kenneth Jacobus, University of Kentucky; Robert McCleary, University of Chicago; Neal Miller, Rockefeller University; Wendell Rivers, Meramec College, St. Louis; and Parks Whitmer, American River College, Sacramento.

Finally, we wish to acknowledge the valuable contributions to this edition made by our colleagues and students: Gordon Bower, A. C. Catania, Carol Christensen, Cedric Clark, Herb and Eve Clark, Ruth Day, Phoebe Diebold, Anna Beth Doyle, Michael Fehling, Scott Fraser, Leo Ganz, Jocelyn Gunnar, Kalen Hammann, Craig Haney, Wes Harper, John Havey, Beth Loftus, Harry Lando, Keith Nelson, Audrey Nulman, Lee Ross, Allen Schneider, David Smith, and Mark Snyder. Special thanks go to: Christina Maslach for her reliable scholarship and perceptive evaluations; William Ruch for his work on the Appendix on statistics; Letha Musgrave for her help in preparing the Glossary; Sally Monfort for her superb clerical assistance; and especially Marguerite Clark and Louise Howe for their truly dedicated and expert editorial assistance.

Overview

Table of Contents

Design by Lucille Lesiak. Charts and graphs by Paul Hazelrigg and
James Minnick. Physiological drawings by Arnold Chalfant and John
Pfiffner. Artwork for Special Transparency Inserts by James Minnick.

Part One

Psychology As a Scientific And Human Enterprise

Psychology is the scientific study of the behavior of organisms. Psychology is learning what makes people tick. Psychology is finding out how the mind works. Psychology is a way of thinking about how living creatures cope with their environment and with each other. Psychology is the intersection of philosophy, biology, sociology, physiology, and anthropology. Psychology is what distinguishes men from machines. Psychology is a kind of knowledge and approach that can be used to improve the quality of human life. Psychology is all these—and perhaps more.

The goals of the psychologist are too often stated abstractly as if they were part of the rules of his "science game"—description, explanation, prediction, and control. But these are the goals of the scientific analysis of behavior precisely because they are the goals of every individual who tries to make the most of the ecological niche in which he lives; making sense out of his existence, understanding how things are related, anticipating the consequences of his actions, and striving to control and to be independent rather than to be controlled and dependent.

In the first part of your introduction to psychology, we will outline what psychologists do, the assumptions that underlie their use of a scientific methodology, and how their approach relates to the approach of art and other scientific disciplines. Psychological research tries to map the structure of behavior, uncover the causal determinants of responding, and bring order and meaning to what often appears to be random and chaotic. Since psychology is part of your everyday life, and your reactions to life are part of its substance, we will try to show how these methods of psychological research and the results they yield will often have direct relevance for *you*.

Involved in any investigation of psychological processes are three basic problems: how to ask the appropriate questions; how to go about finding answers; and how to evaluate the validity of the answers obtained. Accordingly, these initial chapters will outline issues dealing with different levels and approaches to studying behavioral phenomena, tactics of scientific inquiry, and ways of limiting the drawing of false, premature conclusions.

It is virtually impossible to read a newspaper today without coming across some conclusion or other about psychological phenomena, including drug abuse, violence, sexuality, aptitude testing, IQ, and many others. How sound are these conclusions? On what evidence are they based? Before you take or avoid the action that is either proposed or implied in these conclusions, you need to know how much faith you can put in their validity. We will try to answer such questions in some detail by examining actual generalizations that we have been asked to accept as representing "psychological truths." In doing so, many of the pitfalls of casual observation, uncontrolled biases, and common-sense explanations will become apparent. In the process, we hope it will become apparent to you that the rigorous, systematic study of psychology can make a valuable contribution to the human enterprise.

Chapter 1

Unraveling the Mystery of Man's Behavior

Literally, the word *psychology* means the "science of the mind," but psychologists have never been satisfied with this definition because "mind" is a vague term that defies objective definition. So it is hardly surprising that definitions of psychology have varied considerably over the years according to the theoretical orientation of particular "schools."

Most contemporary psychologists would agree on a definition of psychology as *the science of the behavior of organisms*. By *behavior* they mean, first of all, activities or processes that can be observed objectively—both the isolated reactions of muscles, glands, and other parts of the organism and the organized, goal-directed overt reaction patterns that characterize the organism as a whole. Psychologists also interpret "behavior" to include internal processes—thinking, emotional reactions, and the like—which one person cannot observe directly in another but which can be inferred from observation of external behavior. Different schools of psychology have focused upon different aspects of behavior (such as learning, perception, personality) and have varied in their emphasis in saying what is the proper subject matter and approach for psychology.

Few psychologists today adhere wholeheartedly to any one of the historical schools of thought, and probably all would recognize the contribution each school has made to broadening the viewpoint of psychology and clarifying its scientific objectives. Contradictions remain, however, between the theories and findings of different researchers, and an adequate, comprehensive theory has not yet been found. Some psychologists meet this situation by either trying to squeeze research findings into a framework where they do not fit or trying to stretch them beyond their legitimate application. Such attempts remind one of Procrustes, the robber of ancient Attica who placed all who fell into his hands upon an iron bed. If they were longer than the bed, he cut off their feet; if too short, he stretched them to fit it.

In this text we will not confine ourselves to any one theory but will generally favor an *eclectic* approach, presenting a broad spectrum of psychological approaches and findings. This approach is necessary if students are to have a chance to evaluate the insights each of the systems has to offer. Only thus can we be objective about the data we so carefully collect and pave the way for a more comprehensive understanding than has yet been reached.

Regardless of one's theoretical approach to psychology, there are a variety of skills, tools, and knowledge that must be accumulated before adequate understanding of *any* kind of behavior will be possible. This text and most general psychology courses are designed to provide the student with an introduction to the basic concepts, approaches, and findings in a variety of areas of psychological investigation.

Studying Behavior—A Trial Run

One kind of human behavior is language. To get a firsthand experience of the difficulty psychologists face in trying to unravel the mysteries of behavior, read the following passages carefully and try to determine or guess intelligently where they came from. Who talks this way? Who might the authors be?

1

"A person once thought of, once said, wants to be admired, to be thought of as once said to be shown and admired, if it happens when and when to think of the individual, to think, but only as a guess on someone else's part. If it happened to be, it was supposed to have been done by another person than to ever have done such a foolish thing then is ever not to having. It must slip away into the imaginary when it takes, and then relieves it of all its, evidently a laugh is enough although it shouldn't be done in a way to make it difficult for a person why it is or isn't being done. If it is to show a person, why is it ridiculous?"

2

"No there's none, there's none, o no there's none, nor can you long be, what you now are, called fair, do what you may do, what, do what you may, and wisdom is early to despair: be beginning; since, no, nothing can be done to keep at bay age and age's evils, hoar hair, ruck and wrinkle, drooping, dying, death's worst, winding sheets, tombs and worms and tumbling to decay; so be beginning, be beginning to despair."

3

"Takes less place. Cat didn't know what Mouse did and Mouse didn't know what Cat did. Cat represented more on the suspicious side than the mouse. Dumbo was a good guy. He saw what the cat did, put himself with the cat so people wouldn't look at them as comedians. Cat and Dumbo are one and alike, but Cat didn't know what Dumbo did and neither did the mouse.

"Everyone should have a good laugh. Don't cry over it. Don't tell anyone—they will tell someone. Appreciate it without criticism. A word like *milk* shouldn't be mentioned."

4

"So to beseech you as full as for it. Exactly or as kings. Shutters shut and open so do queens. Shutters shut and shutters and so shutters shut and shutters and so and so shutters and so shutters shut and so shutters shut and shutters and. So and so shutters shut and so and also. And also and so and so and also. Exact resemblance to exact resemblance the exact resemblance as exact as a resemblance, exactly as resembling, exactly resembling, exactly in resemblance exactly a resemblance, exactly and resemblance. For this is so. Because. Now actively repeat at all. . . ."

5

"Leaves have to be thought of too. If no leaves, no stone. If leaf didn't have no place, then stone shouldn't have no place. If tree had no place, there wouldn't be any leave.

"Man was very wise and went more ahead, to his own satisfaction proved to where it takes to destination, also informing it before ever having it. Imagine, people do wonderful things without ever knowing it.

"Gratitude becomes more than itself to prove to one's capabilities to have to oneself without any doubt or undoing in the mind. Something, then again, nothing. If it were, it would be more approved to be than not to be."

Some students have said that the passages came from: "freshman themes on 'Who Am I?'," "computer-generated language," "a bad 'acid' trip," "a groovy 'speed' flight," "the first line of every other paragraph from Lewis Carroll's *Alice in Wonderland*," "stream of consciousness writing," "dictation-articulation training material," or "poor translations by students from foreign countries."

It should be evident from these replies, and from your own observation, that there is something unusual about the way in which language is being used in these passages. It is not "normal"; it does not follow the rules we use in speaking and writing. In fact, it appears to be meaningless and uttered only "for its own sake." At first reading, you might assume that no sense could possibly be made of it and that there

**READER'S ASSIGNMENT
OF SAMPLES OF VERBAL BEHAVIOR**

1	2	3	4	5	Total Correct

would be no point in even trying to see it as comprehensible behavior with an identifiable cause.

Actually, some of the passages were taken from the writings of modern poets, and some from an interview with a psychotic patient, Mr. F. B. (*Psychosis* is a general label for a wide range of mental disorders which so impair a person's functioning that he has to be hospitalized.) Can you decide which is which? Go back over each passage and carefully look for clues which might help you make this judgment. Indicate your choice in the table above by marking whether you believe each sample of verbal behavior is an excerpt from a modern poet's work or represents psychotic language.

You can see how well you did in this bit of detection by turning to the table on page 8, where the sources of the quotations are identified. The data in this table also allow you to compare your performance with that of 1700 introductory psychology students at three universities who were asked to make the same type of judgment of this material.

As you can see, the first, third, and fifth passages are psychotic speech, while the remaining two selections are excerpts from modern poetry. The table indicates how many students were accurate in their judgments of each passage and how many were in error. For example, 1065 students correctly identified the first selection as psychotic speech, while 685 students (40.3 percent of the total 1700) made mistakes. The second passage appears to be the easiest one to judge, since only a quarter of the students were wrong. The fourth passage is the most difficult, with almost two thirds of the students in error. Overall, the average rate of error is a rather high 42.5 percent. This indicates that it is quite hard to identify these passages correctly.

If you were not able to distinguish between the two types of verbal material and made incorrect assignments, then you were overly sensitive to apparent cues of *similarity*. If you did distinguish between them, then you were correctly responding to cues of difference or *dissimilarity*. What cues were you using in either case?

If you could not tell them apart, you probably were struck by their similarity in ignoring the grammatical rule of subject-verb-object. In fact, the distinction between subject and object is often blurred. There does not seem to be any logical structure connecting successive sentences or even successive parts of the same sentence. There are many words or phrases which are vague and ambiguous, or which appear in unusual contexts. The repetition of words and phrases, the minor variations in word endings, and the use of words with similar sounds all emphasize a concern with the sound and form of language, irrespective of its meaning. Such a "turning of language in on itself" is not customary in our standard use of English.

On the other hand, if you could tell them apart, you probably noted that the samples of modern poetry differ from those of psychotic speech in their use of rhythm and meter. Closer examination also reveals in each of them a distinct pattern or form in which meaning is conveyed both through the special use of certain words and phrases, and through the stylistic aspects of the poem.

We can conceive of language as a certain set of symbols to be used in prescribed arrangements. Ideally, all those who receive a communication should be able to decode it accurately and comprehend the meaning of the message. This kind of communication occurs only when the symbols are used in a limited, explicitly regulated way. Such language can be said to have a high degree of *consensual validation,* or interperson agreement. Mathematical formulas and musical scores provide examples of the objective use of language. Scientists in all disciplines aspire toward this level of objectivity, attempting to convey meaning in as clear, precise, and direct a manner as possible. Any language falls short of this goal of objectivity to the extent that it employs words which can have more than one meaning or whose meaning varies with the context.

Our ordinary conversation is objective in that it

employs words whose definitions can generally be agreed on and must follow many rules learned in grammar classes. But it is subjective in that it has many words with more than one meaning and allows considerable flexibility of usage. Thus there can be much variation among people in their use of language and in their interpretation of the same message from another person. Still less objective and more subjective is the speech of both poets and psychotics, as in the examples we have seen. At the extreme in subjectivity would be speech so idiosyncratic that no one could accurately decode and comprehend it.

Both the poet and the psychotic, then, are using a highly subjective, individualistic means of communication which portrays a reality different from that which is represented in our ordinary discourse. They do not present a description of the world which can be observed directly through the senses or comprehended rationally or logically. Rather, the language they use is a vehicle for conveying their interpretation of what lies beyond or beneath sense impressions, of how reality ought to be constructed, and of how its elements should be rearranged. Yet their ways of using language are more unlike than you may have thought.

It is differences in awareness, intention, and control which separate these two idiosyncratic uses of language. The poet is highly aware of his special use of words and deviations from grammar—so much so that in a perfect poem no word or comma could be changed without altering the entire poem. His intention is to communicate to an audience and to share with them his unique view of reality. To do so, he

must exert complete control over the use of his medium. He must be able to retain the logical, popular view of reality while contrasting it with his poetic view.

The psychotic, on the other hand, is not in deliberate control of the process of communication. His use of language serves a triple function: (a) to conceal from himself emotions and ideas which disturb him, (b) to allow him to abandon "acceptable" views of reality with their demands for social compliance, and (c) to act as a distress signal, to show that he is "going under" or needs help.

This text is obviously not the place to enter into a detailed analysis of the two types of language: for the one, the proper place is the English department; for the other, the more advanced courses in psychology. Our purpose is rather to use these materials as a basis for introducing you to the adventure of discovering meaning through analyzing behavior, and particularly for familiarizing you with the psychologist's approach. First, then, we will carry a step further our comparison of these two uses of language, and then we will have a look at where the study of behavior like language fits into the broader enterprise of psychology.

The basic assumptions of art and science are dramatically opposed to one another. Most poets, like other artists, see the world as a constantly changing, mutable system based upon an underlying chaos and flux. It is, therefore, one goal of art to impose permanence on transience, to "fix" events, images, thoughts, and feelings in time (as Keats' "Ode on a Grecian Urn" does so beautifully). It is the goal of the literary analyst, who shares the poet's assumptions, to illuminate the poet's craft. He seeks to show us how the poet went about capturing the essence— the idiosyncrasies—of a particular fragment of life so that we can re-create the poet's experience for ourselves.

To the scientific mind, on the other hand, there is an underlying order in nature, a system of regularity, predictable occurrences, and causally determined events. The scientist's goal thus becomes to uncover the lawfulness existing in all events. His task is to strip away the idiosyncrasies of a particular situation and reveal the orderly operation of events and variables in their pure, elemental form. He begins with an assumption of *causal determinacy*. This means

STUDENTS' ASSIGNMENT OF SAMPLES OF VERBAL BEHAVIOR

Selection	Number of Students Correct	Number of Students Incorrect	Percent Incorrect
1. Psychotic	1065	685	40.3%
2. Poet[a]	1335	415	24.4
3. Psychotic	1170	570	33.5
4. Poet[b]	650	1095	64.4
5. Psychotic	875	875	50.0
			Average rate of error: 42.5%

[a]Gerard Manley Hopkins, "The Leaden Echo"
[b]Gertrude Stein, "If I Told Him: A Completed Portrait of Picasso"

simply that every observed natural phenomenon can be shown to be caused by the operation of some other event(s) or process(es). Every event has a cause. Psychology, as a system of inquiry into the behavior of human and animal organisms, accepts this assumption of science and (as we shall see in the next chapter) also adopts the scientific method of analysis in an attempt to explain behavioral regularity. If it did not accept the assumption that behavior has causes, it could not expect to find laws of behavior.

The Approach of Literary Analysis

A literary critic might note that analysis of several features of Hopkins' poetry reveals a characteristic use of certain language forms which, in turn, tell us something about his particular way of perceiving objects in the environment. For example, some of the obscurity in his language is produced by the fact that he rarely uses adverbs ending in *-ly* when they would normally be expected to modify the verb. One of his poems begins with the words,

"Some candle *clear* burns . . ."

The word *clear* is used in a special way to describe both the subject and the verb, the actor and the activity, and not merely to modify the verb. In Hopkins' view the quality of clearness resided in the candle itself as well as in its burning. He felt that to discover the individual distinctiveness of an object it must be looked at and studied by itself, not in relation to, or contrasted with, other objects. He coined the term *inscape* to express this set of distinctive characteristics of an object. Once an object is "inscaped" it has activity. This activity finds expression in Hopkins' use of transitive verbs and altered verb forms and in his frequent use of the gerund rather than the abstract word (as in *dying* rather than *death*). The literary critic may, through careful analysis of such deviations in usage, discover a consistently meaningful pattern not only within a given poem, but across a poet's works.

To be able to apply principles of literary criticism in a systematic way requires more than just an understanding of the individual poet's vocabulary and his uses of ambiguity, subtleties of meter, and tension between words. Often poets draw examples from history, religious traditions, and mythology which the reader must be familiar with in order to understand their poetry. It is only when the poet resorts to symbols whose meaning is not shared by others, but is unique in his own life history, that his work is undecipherable.

The Approach of Psychological Analysis

We may be able to speculate from careful literary analysis what experiences and perceptions the poet wanted to share with us, but we cannot assume we know the poet as a man from his poetry. This is because his work is carefully crafted and may present a view of reality which is not necessarily identical with the commonplace view that probably guides most of his everyday behavior. In contrast, the view of reality which we can infer from the psychotic's speech is assumed to be his dominant view. His speech is but one of many kinds of behavior through which his problems are expressed.

The psychologist who is concerned about helping alleviate the psychotic's distress uses the verbal behavior of the person in several ways. First, he uses it to assess the degree to which there is disturbance in patterns of thought and emotional expression. Next, he explores it to try to re-create the patient's view of the world and the conflicts which beset him. Such knowledge may, in turn, suggest how he can be helped.

In order to give you a feeling for this aspect of the psychologist's work, we are going to examine the language of our psychotic patient in the light of his life history and other aspects of his behavior. For psychological analysis, the first question is, under what conditions did the behavior occur? What were the environmental events which appear to have directly instigated the behavior under investigation?

In this case, the psychotic passages presented earlier were Mr. F. B.'s answers (responses) when asked to explain the meaning of several proverbs (stimuli). More generally, the stimulus context of these responses was a psychological testing situation in which the patient was questioned for several hours by a young male psychologist in a state mental hospital where Mr. F. B. had been a patient for ten months.

The first selection is Mr. F. B.'s response to "He

who laughs last laughs best." In the third selection, the first paragraph is his response to "When the cat's away the mice will play"; the next paragraph is his response to "Don't cry over spilt milk." The fifth selection contains the patient's responses to three different proverbs. In the first paragraph, he describes what he believes to be the meaning of "A rolling stone gathers no moss." In the second paragraph, he is responding to "Don't cross your bridges until you come to them." The last paragraph contains his interpretation of "The proof of the pudding is in the eating." His responses on other tests and a description of his general behavior are given in Appendix A. It may be interesting for you to attempt an analysis of this material after reading this chapter and again after you have studied Part Six to see if the material has different meaning for you then.   ◆[1]

From a cursory analysis of his responses to the proverbs, we can advance some general hunches about Mr. F. B.'s general problems. Then we will test these ideas against the hospital reports of other behavior. The goal of our analysis will be to try to explain the language behavior in terms of past or present conditions in Mr. F. B.'s environment and to see if there are relationships between his language and his other behavior, past or present.

However faulty *our* thinking from time to time, most of us accept the rules of formal logic and can recognize an error in reasoning if it is made clear that our conclusion did not follow from our premises. For example, we would accept the following syllogism as valid logic:

Major premise	Moss grows on trees
Minor premise	Everything that grows on trees is green
Conclusion	Therefore, moss is green.

In a valid syllogism, the conclusion follows inescapably from the premises. (It makes no claim about the truth of either the premises or the conclusion, but simply says that *if* the premises are true,

the conclusion must follow.) Reasoning in which only one valid conclusion is possible from the premises is called *deductive* reasoning.

But though we would accept the logic of the syllogism above, we would not accept the following one as valid:

P_1	Moss grows on trees
P_2	Leaves grow on trees
C	Therefore, moss is leaves.

This example provides us with the transition into a central aspect of Mr. F. B.'s thinking, as revealed in the first part of the fifth selection. To the stimulus "A rolling stone gathers no moss," he replies, "Leaves have to be thought of, too." The transformation from moss to leaves follows faulty logic. His reasoning may have made moss and leaves interchangeable because they share identical predicates.

This type of thinking (called *paleologic thought*) is characteristic of mentally disturbed people who assume the identity of another person (e.g., Napoleon is a man; I am a man; therefore, I am Napoleon). In the case of Mr. F. B., who told the nurse "I am the Virgin Mary," his thinking may have been: "The Virgin Mary is pure; I am (or would like to be) pure; therefore, I am the Virgin Mary."

Although our task in analyzing Mr. F. B.'s speech is reminiscent of Sherlock Holmes' detective work, we must go beyond "elementary deduction, my dear Watson," in which conclusions follow inescapably, to *induction*, in which we must build on the evidence. From the individual instances and observations we have, we must try to infer a pattern that can organize and make understandable the separate elements.

The Proverbs Test was intended to measure an individual's ability to think about abstract relations, but it is clear that Mr. F. B. used it as a means for projecting his personal thoughts and emotions. The stimulus for each answer is really not the overt question put to him, but rather some covert process going on inside of him. Notice for example in the first selection that the response "laugh" comes ninety-five words after the stimulus "He who laughs last laughs best." A frequency count of recurring words through-

---

[1] Throughout the text geometric symbols like this will be used to direct your attention to charts, photographs, or other material illustrating a particular point. Each symbol in the text corresponds to the illustration marked by the same symbol.

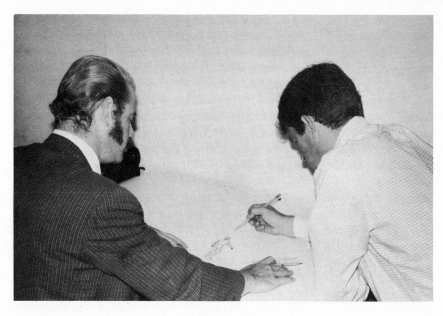

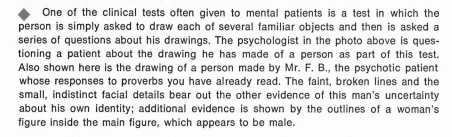

◆ One of the clinical tests often given to mental patients is a test in which the person is simply asked to draw each of several familiar objects and then is asked a series of questions about his drawings. The psychologist in the photo above is questioning a patient about the drawing he has made of a person as part of this test. Also shown here is the drawing of a person made by Mr. F. B., the psychotic patient whose responses to proverbs you have already read. The faint, broken lines and the small, indistinct facial details bear out the other evidence of this man's uncertainty about his own identity; additional evidence is shown by the outlines of a woman's figure inside the main figure, which appears to be male.

out his responses to this test reveals that the words "know" and "thought" were used ten times, "mind" and "should" seven times. "Criticism," "ought," "foolish," and "approved" are also used frequently. In another test (Incomplete Sentences), the idea of people criticizing someone else occurs nine times in forty-four sentences. In that same test, there are only three instances where Mr. F. B. portrays himself favorably, while there are ten in which he describes himself unfavorably. The unfavorable self-references express a condition in which the patient views himself as being in a conflict, being inadequate, or being punished or criticized for an act or thought.

If the high rate of occurrence of these words and phrases indicates an area of central concern for him, then one meaningful organization of these elements could be, "People have falsely criticized him, and have thoughts in their minds of an immoral act they

believe he committed. They ought to know better; what he did was just a normal expression which *they* misunderstood." This, then, forms a hypothesis which we can test against other responses and behavior.

The symbolic story related in the third selection may make sense if the "they" who ridiculed him are his parents—the cat being his father, the mouse his mother—while he himself is Dumbo. This may seem quite fanciful, until we compare "the Cat and Dumbo are one and alike" with the patient's hospital record, which quotes him as saying, "My father is a 'real man' who knows what he wants and gets what he wants." The record goes on to note, "patient admires father who got what he wanted." By putting himself with the cat so people wouldn't look at them as comedians (a "Dumbo"), Mr. F. B. is protected from ridicule and censure. Although his father was an authoritarian person who disciplined him severely and was less loving toward him than was his mother, Mr. F. B. still wants to be like his father and to identify with him.

The theme of exposure and criticism recurs in "Don't tell anyone, they will tell someone"; "appreciate it without criticism"; "a guess on someone else's part"; "If it is to show a person, why is it ridiculous?" "Once it is done there should be no questions as to why it has been done"; and in "But the cat didn't [really] know what Dumbo did and neither did the mouse."

With this network of conjecture in mind, we can now try to understand what the patient meant when he said that "a word like *milk* shouldn't be mentioned." Surely, this is a most unusual declaration which just doesn't make sense if Mr. F. B. is using *milk* in its usual meaning as a nutritious liquid. However, if we assume that *milk* is being used as a metaphor, it could take on many different meanings.

Milk could mean: Mother's milk (or her breasts), the milk of human kindness, or semen, through a vague association based on its appearance. If it is the latter, then the exposure incident might have occurred during Mr. F. B.'s puberty when he was caught masturbating. It may also refer to a semen stain from a natural nocturnal emission which was misinterpreted by his parents to be the result of masturbation.

Evidence for this latter line of reasoning comes from two additional responses of Mr. F. B. First, to the word *sex* he responded, "Someone criticizes something for what it actually isn't. The only thing it could have been was something else." Second, when the interviewing psychologist asked him why milk shouldn't be mentioned, Mr. F. B. said, "Reminds me of unpleasant family situation . . . exposing oneself . . . put thoughts in her mind . . . carried for years and years."

Obviously, when one is dealing with material as complex and ambiguous as the verbal behavior of psychotics, many different interpretations are possible. The adequacy of any one of them rests on several criteria. First, can the interpretation be consistently applied to a majority of the available data? Second, does it suggest additional evidence which could be collected to support or refute it? Third, is it parsimonious (that is, does it require fewer assumptions than do alternative interpretations)? Finally, and

most important in the case of a mental patient, does the interpretation lead to a successful program of treatment?

Underlying our interpretation of Mr. F. B.'s behavior is an assumption about the continuity of behavior —i.e., adult behavior reflects experiences and traumas of youth and even infancy. There is also an assumption about unconscious processes—that behavior is influenced in various indirect ways, even though the individual is unaware of them himself. Such assumptions are typical of the *psychoanalytic* approach to the study of personality and personality disorders. This school of psychology came into existence around the turn of the century in Europe under the leadership of Sigmund Freud.

Although the Freudian view, with its emphasis on sex and repression, is perhaps the most well known and intellectually appealing to many introductory psychology students, there are other approaches to the interpretation of behavior which completely reject its assumptions, techniques, and strategies. We will consider these various schools of thought in Part Six of this text, when we delve into the causes, consequences, and cures of psychological malfunctioning.

We have presented in these pages only one possible interpretation of a small part of the qualitative data gathered from the psychological testing of this patient. A complete case study would include much more. We have compared two unusual kinds of language behavior and the differing analytic methods of art and science. Psychotic language, of course, is only one of many kinds of behavior that psychologists study, and those who study it represent only one branch of psychologists. But we have found that even here, in behavior that at first seemed completely unintelligible, the analytic methods of science can find lawfulness and understandable cause-and-effect relationships.

Psychology and Other Sciences

Behavior is determined by a complex of factors that are partly biological, partly anthropological, partly sociological, and partly psychological. Therefore, psychology is closely related to both the biological and the social sciences. This is recognized by the large majority of modern psychologists, whether they specialize in teaching, research, or the many applications of their science. As a former president of the American Psychological Association has said,

"Psychology . . . thrives on polygamy with her neighbors. Our marriage with the biological sciences has produced a cumulation of ever more powerful knowledge. So, too, our joint undertaking with anthropology and sociology." (Bruner, 1965, p. 1016)

But despite the fact that there is a great deal of necessary—and even desirable—overlapping among the various areas of science to which psychology is related, each retains its own particular emphasis.

Biology—the science of life—is the study of how all living things grow, repair their bodies, reproduce their kind, and carry on other life processes. The biological sciences most closely related to psychology are *physiology,* the study of the functioning of living organisms and their parts; *neurology,* the specialized scientific study of the brain and nervous system and the diseases thereof; *embryology,* the study of the growth and development of organisms prior to birth; and *genetics,* the study of hereditary processes. A relatively new specialty within genetics is *behavior genetics,* the study of the heritability of mechanisms underlying specific behaviors, as opposed to body structure.

Anthropology is the study of the physical evolution of mankind, the origins of racial groups, and the development of civilizations. Its examination of widely divergent cultures—particularly the so-called primitive ones—has provided psychology with much significant data for understanding the influence of cultural factors on human behavior patterns.

Sociology studies the laws underlying the development and functioning of groups of all kinds—social, political, economic, religious. Both informal groups and formal institutions are studied, with emphasis on the observable characteristics of the groups' structure and functioning rather than on the motives or experience of the individual members. Sociology has helped psychology to understand not only group behavior but also the social influences upon the behavior of individuals.

Psychologists, sociologists, and anthropologists

have found that they can contribute very significantly to each other's efforts. As a result, there has developed a new discipline known as *behavioral science*, with emphasis on the problem of developing valid generalizations about human behavior in many situations. Important work in this area is being carried out in a wide variety of institutions and agencies, and an increasing number of books and articles show this broad orientation. The present text reflects this interdisciplinary approach.

What Psychologists Do

The work of psychologists has proliferated almost unbelievably in recent years, and often different specialists approach the same problem with different tools and different assumptions of what they are looking for. To give you a better idea about the breadth of orientation in just one area of psychology, we may begin by looking at two of the kinds of specialists that might be consulted about the case of Mr. F. B. and seeing how each of them would approach the problem of understanding his behavior. We can then expand our focus to other areas of psychology, and to the work and goals of psychologists in general.

The two most basically different approaches to analysis of Mr. F. B.'s case would be a medical as opposed to a psychological, behavioral one. At the one extreme, behavior is seen as rooted in biological processes. The malfunctioning is attributed to such causes as viruses, organic brain defects, vitamin deficits, endocrine imbalance, substances in the blood, or other physical agents. The locus of investigation is the body as it affects mental processes, and the significant reality to be studied is physical and biological. As an example of this approach, some researchers are working toward developing a serum to cure psychosis.

At the other extreme, behavior is seen as rooted in experience, especially social experience, and only psychological and social reality are considered to be important in understanding human psychopathology. Thus helping a psychotic patient means changing his perceptions and motivations or helping him learn specific new behaviors.

The two classes of people likely to treat Mr. F. B.

would be psychiatrists and clinical psychologists. The clinicians would generally endorse the second of these approaches to the understanding of psychosis; their treatment of Mr. F. B. would most likely involve use of talking, rewards and environmental changes, while psychiatrists, although varying considerably in their approach, would be more likely to favor the medical view, including drugs, electroshock, or other physical treatment along with their verbal therapy. They are medical specialists who have taken courses in psychology as well as standard medical courses in studying for the M.D. degree, and have served a hospital residency in the psychiatric ward. They are the only practitioners who can prescribe physical forms of treatment such as drugs or electroshock.

Clinical psychologists receive a Ph.D. degree from a graduate school where most of their courses are in psychology, then serve a year's internship in a mental hospital. To receive their degree, they must have completed a dissertation, which is usually based on an original research project. They are more likely than the average psychiatrist to be engaged in diagnostic testing of patients and in research. In conducting therapy, they rely chiefly on words or on the use of rewards.

Both of the approaches described above can be broadly classified as clinical, applied, practical, and treatment-oriented, with an exclusive focus on human beings. Such approaches represent only one area of psychological interest, however. As can be seen in the illustrations, the majority of psychologists are in subfields other than clinical, and many clinical psychologists do not engage in clinical practice as their primary work activity. ▪

There are many other areas in which psychology is applied to the solution of concrete, practical problems. Such applications are found in industry, schools, marketing, advertising, the space program, counseling and guidance centers, and psychometric programs involving a wide range of psychological testing and measurement. However, all these applications must rest upon a foundation of solidly established principles and laws of behavior. As the mechanical engineer is dependent upon the physicist, the behavioral engineer is dependent upon the research psychologist.

Pure research attempts to uncover basic patterns of lawfulness in behavior. It aspires to reveal relationships between classes of variables which can be generalized beyond the original limited set of observations to a wide range of organisms, both human and animal. Before we can help any particular Johnny to read and learn most effectively, we must know about general principles of attention, organization of stimulus materials, motivation to learn, laws of memory, and the operation of reinforcement. This knowledge is provided by experimental psychologists, who use the same basic set of research techniques whether they are studying child development, visual perception, social group processes, or the functioning of the hypothalamus in a chimpanzee brain. The major portion of this text will be an attempt to present to you the kinds of questions which such psychologists have raised, the methodologies they have used to test their problems, and the answers they are finding.

The Goals of Psychology

Psychology, like other sciences, is a child of curiosity, born of man's age-old desire to *describe, explain, predict* and *control* conditions and situations both in the world about him and within himself. The research psychologist devotes himself to increasing man's knowledge of the principles of behavior. His goals, however, are similar to those that a clinical psychologist would have in trying to help someone like Mr. F. B.

Description

All sciences have as a goal the accurate description of some aspect of the natural universe. The psychologist, of course, has chosen the behavior of man and other animals as his sector of the universe. Some sciences, such as anatomy, go very little beyond objective description, while others, such as theoretical physics, go far beyond this. As you get into the more detailed study of psychology, you will come to appreciate how extremely difficult objective description of behavior is. Not only are most living organisms highly complex and intricate systems, but the observer often has difficulty in maintaining an objective, unbiased attitude—particularly with regard to the description of human behavior. Yet one of the distin-

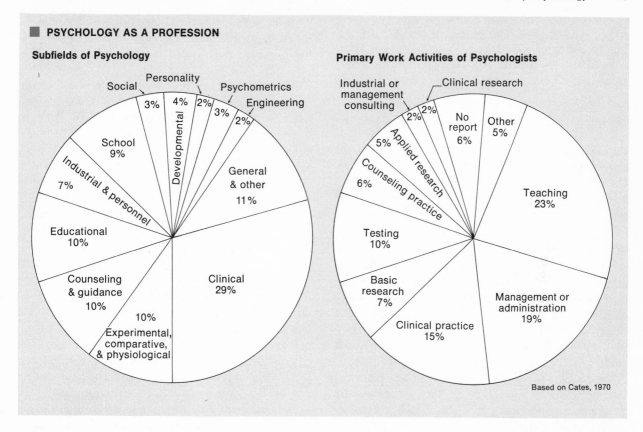

■ PSYCHOLOGY AS A PROFESSION

Subfields of Psychology

- Social 3%
- Personality 4%
- Developmental 2%
- Psychometrics 3%
- Engineering 2%
- School 9%
- Industrial & personnel 7%
- General & other 11%
- Educational 10%
- Counseling & guidance 10%
- Clinical 29%
- Experimental, comparative, & physiological 10%

Primary Work Activities of Psychologists

- Industrial or management consulting 2%
- Clinical research 2%
- No report 6%
- Other 5%
- Applied research 5%
- Counseling practice 6%
- Teaching 23%
- Testing 10%
- Basic research 7%
- Clinical practice 15%
- Management or administration 19%

Based on Cates, 1970

guishing features of any scientist is that he does not let his expectations or prejudices color his observations. And he must distinguish between what he actually *observes* ("The patient trembled and did not look directly at the therapist") and what he only *infers* ("The patient was anxious").

The psychologist thoroughly appreciates the validity of the old adage, "What you look for, you will find." To safeguard against this tendency of "seeing what he expects to see," a psychologist studying the effects of a certain drug would conduct a *double-blind* test. That is, he would arrange that the individual evaluating the behavior of the subjects would not know until he had completed his evaluation which subjects had received the drug and which had not. Nor would the subjects themselves know which group they were in or even that there were two conditions being tested.

In new areas of research particularly, it is often difficult for the investigator to maintain his objectivi-

ty. The closer he comes to a discovery that will be a real breakthrough into new areas of knowledge, the harder it becomes for him not to let what he wishes to see stand in the way of unbiased interpretation of results—no matter how good his intentions. When we read of "astounding new discoveries" in psychology, or in any science, it is well to be cautious about accepting them until time has proved their worth.

Only rarely does an apparent breakthrough prove to be a hoax. It can happen, though, as in the case of the "proof" of the inheritance of acquired characteristics presented early in this century. Here a careless scientist reported the work of a technician so anxious to please the great scientist that he had injected India ink under the skin of salamanders to make the experiments come out the way the scientist wanted them to. More often, the "breakthrough" that loses its momentum and is quietly buried is simply based on experimental error, which can happen to the best and most careful scientists.

Explanation

The recording of facts is one of the tasks of science, one of the steps toward truth; but it is not the whole of science. As Oliver Wendell Holmes once observed, there are:

"One-story intellects, two-story intellects, three-story intellects with skylights. All fact-collectors, who have no aim beyond their facts, are one-story men. Two-story men compare, reason, generalize, using the labors of the fact-collectors as well as their own. Three-story men idealize, imagine, predict; their best illumination comes from above, through the skylight." (Holmes, 1872, p. 43)

Psychology is based upon observation of behavior as its source of facts, but these facts are useless if left as isolated happenings. It is only by relating them to other facts, and by going beyond observation to inferences about the relatedness of facts that they have meaning and relevance. Built into the objective description of our sensory experience of an object, such as a piece of wood, are generalizations about wood as a substance with grain, with a specific density which allows it to float, with a kindling temperature at which it burns, and so on. Common-sense generalizations such as "milk is a liquid," "cars require gasoline to run," and "water rusts metal" shade off into more scientific generalizations such as "objects of opposite polarity attract," "combustion requires oxygen," and "responses which are accompanied by a state of affairs that is reinforcing for the organism are repeated." *Laws* are higher-level generalizations which are somewhat more precise or comprehensive statements about the processes or properties involved. These laws may themselves be incorporated into a more extensive general statement, a *principle,* which applies without exception to a large range of instances.

To achieve scientific understanding, however, the scientist must go one step further and organize his principles into a logical framework which demonstrates in an orderly, consistent manner how the various observed facts and derived principles are related. Such a systematic statement of relationships is called a *theory.* The value of a theory is measured in terms of (a) its ability to explain the known facts and to show relationships among previously unconnected concepts and observations and (b) its useful-

ness in suggesting specific hypotheses that can be tested in further research. (For a close-up view of the relationships between laws, principles, and theories, see Ψ Close-up, p. 17.)

Although facts do not change with time, the observation of new data often makes it necessary that theories be modified or discarded. In such cases the scientist tries to formulate a new theory which will embrace all the known relevant facts and explain them as fully as possible. However, there is a reluctance to give up an old theory for a new one, as evidenced in the persistence of Ptolemy's theory that the earth was the center of the universe long after Copernicus' heliocentric theory was empirically and logically proven to be a better model of planetary motion.

The scientist's second goal, then, is to explain, and in order to explain he must understand the underlying order in the confusions and complexities of nature, of which man himself is a part. But with the world full of so many things, the human mind cannot possibly deal with them all individually. In psychology, as in other sciences, understanding requires that facts be grouped or classified into meaningful categories on the basis of stated aspects of similarity. To explain an event consists in finding how to classify it by putting it into a familiar slot, the slot being a general law. Newton's laws made it possible for the first time to see an apple falling as related to a larger class of events. As in this case, such related events may not look alike at all and may share only some abstract quality.

Psychologists employ two basic kinds of classification: *qualitative* and *quantitative.* Actually, the line between the two is not entirely distinct.

Qualitative classification. In qualitative classification, items are grouped in categories on the basis of some particular quality or characteristic they have in common. People, for example, can be classed as males or females; as blondes, brunettes, or redheads; as Republicans or Democrats; as married, single, widowed, or divorced. For more precise scientific study, members of a class may often be divided into various subgroups. For instance, if people are classed as blind or sighted, those with sight can be further classed as normal or color blind.

The important thing about qualitative classification

Ψ *Close-up*   *Levels of Explanation*

	Physical Example	**Psychological Example**
Common-sense generalization	Apples fall to the ground.	People tend to do things that give them pleasure.
Scientific generalization	Objects heavier than air always fall down, not up.	When a response is followed by a positive consequence, its likelihood of occurring on later occasions increases.
Law	The force of gravity attracts all things that have mass.	Behavior that has a desired effect on the environment is stamped in.
Principle	The force of attraction between two objects is proportional to their mass and inversely proportional to the distance between them.	Behavior can be modified by appropriate schedule of rewards and punishments.
Theory	Einstein's theory of relativity.	Thorndike's associationist learning theory (see Appendix C).

As will be apparent, distinctions between laws and principles or between principles and theories are probably impossible to draw precisely. This array of levels of explanation is intended merely to illustrate the increasingly higher-order generalizations involved in going from inferences based on observations to more abstract concepts.

---

is that the classes or categories are not related to each other in a mathematical (quantitative) manner. Qualitative classification is primarily a process of sorting items into groups and giving the groups appropriate labels.

In addition to its value as an instrument of scientific inquiry, qualitative classification in psychology frequently produces results of considerable practical value. For instance, research conducted with personnel in the insurance business has shown that married men generally make more successful insurance salesmen than single men. Thus, by classifying all job applicants into the qualitative categories of "married" or "single," we have one basis for predicting whether a particular applicant is *likely* to prove successful or unsuccessful should he be hired and trained.

Quantitative classification. In a quantitative classification, categories are determined on the basis of different degrees of some measurable characteristic, such as height, weight, or musical ability. Everybody has *some* of the characteristic being measured, but some people have more than others. All the persons or objects in a group can be ranked on the degree to which they exhibit that characteristic. The categories are usually labeled in terms of the mathematical relationships between them. For example, the category of *tall women* might include all those over five feet ten inches in height.

The psychologist's ultimate aim is to make all classifications quantitative, though in many areas he is still far short of this goal. He prefers to work with quantitative categories because he can make his predictions more directly and precisely—and check on their accuracy better—when the available items of information (sometimes called *predictors*) and the behavior he is trying to predict both can be expressed in numerical terms.

Prediction

In addition to his desire to understand nature, man throughout history has sought to know the future—to predict and prepare for events in advance of their happening. In ancient times oracles and soothsayers held positions of great honor, for they were credited with a supernatural ability to reveal the future by reading signs from the gods. Today man relies largely on science for his predictions of the future. (Ψ Close-up, p. 19.)

The whole concept of insurance is based on the ability to predict very accurately the life span of different classes and types of people. The insurance company "bets" the customer that its prediction is right. Note that this type of *actuarial prediction* does not depend upon an understanding of life-death cycles, but merely upon observed relationships. In science, however, spectacular achievement comes about when the scientist understands the cause-and-effect relationships so well that he can predict something he has not seen in the past.

A psychological *hypothesis* is a sophisticated hunch that a given behavioral response (R_2), such as hitting baby sister, is related in a particular way to some other response (R_1), such as defying mother, or to some antecedent stimulus event (S), such as getting a spanking. The test of a hypothesis lies not in how appealing or probable it may seem intuitively, but rather in its success in predicting R_2. Thus if it were found that many defiant children also act aggressively toward baby sisters, then defiance would be a good predictor of the hitting behavior. Likewise, if getting a spanking were often found to precede hitting baby sister, then getting a spanking would be a good predictor of baby-sister-hitting behavior. In neither case would we yet be able to say whether the predictor *caused* the behavior but only that there was a predictable relationship between the occurrence of the events.

Predictions require imagination, insight, sound observations, and often complicated calculations, but they display a basically simple logical pattern. This can best be seen in the examples given by Black (1952) of how Uranus and Ceres were discovered.

"When astronomy had developed sufficiently for the average distance of the planets from the sun to be calcu-

lated, it was found that the ratios of the numbers obtained could be expressed by a simple formula known as 'Bode's Law.' We write down the series 0, 3, 6, 12, . . . doubling as we go; then we add 4 to each number, obtaining the series 4, 7, 10, 16, 28, 52, 100, 196. Of these eight numbers all except the fifth (28) and last (196) agreed well at the time of the law's formulation with the relative distances of the known planets from the sun. Thus, taking the Earth's distance as 10, the actual figures for Mercury, Venus, Mars, Jupiter, and Saturn are 3.9, 7.2, 15.2, 52.0, and 95.4. After the discovery of Uranus, its average distance (191.9) was also found to agree approximately with the last number in the series (196). But the fact that no planet was known to correspond to the number 28 in Bode's series led to the systematic search for a new planet and the eventual discovery (by accident, however) of the planet Ceres." (pp. 380-381)

Control

Man is not content to describe, understand, and predict. There are many occasions when he wants to influence and change what happens. This wish creates a fourth major objective for scientists—that of control. In the field of psychology during the past few decades, the ability to plan and direct many aspects of human behavior has increased considerably. Part of the current excitement which attends the development of psychology stems from the promise it holds for changing the human condition.

The ability to control behavior is the psychologist's best test of his understanding of the psychological processes involved. In the area of vocational guidance, for example, psychologists have been able to determine that success and satisfaction in a particular occupation are related to specific patterns of abilities, interests, and other measurable human characteristics. Utilizing this knowledge, the vocational counselor is able, through personal interview data and psychological test scores, to offer advice as to the vocational fields that are most likely to offer success and happiness for a particular client.

In his efforts to ensure job satisfaction for all employees, the industrial psychologist goes even further. Knowledge gained from scientific research is used by the management of large factories and businesses to maintain pleasant working conditions, good employee morale, and high productivity. In the field of vocational rehabilitation, persons who have

Ψ *Close-up* **Scientific Prediction Eclipses Fear**

It is easy for us to understand the overwhelming fear our ancestors experienced when suddenly a solar eclipse plunged the world into darkness. Without warning, in a matter of minutes sunlight was denied to them, and the source of all life's energy was mysteriously shrouded. The order and regularity of life were suspended as a warning from the gods, as a threat from evil spirits, or as whatever man's mind could conjure up to explain this terrifying discontinuity. It is little wonder that, like the Peruvian natives depicted at left, they frequently responded with elaborate rituals designed to pacify the angry gods.

Once the laws that govern this seemingly chance phenomenon were elaborated, astronomers could trace back the exact time of every prior eclipse and also predict when and where all future ones would occur. Although the phenomenon of a total eclipse of the sun was no less awe-inspiring when it occurred in March 1970, the ability of scientists to predict its occurrence precisely in time and location had stripped it of its fear-provoking powers. Far from being terrified, the Mexican villagers in the photograph watched with interest as scientists set up their equipment to study the eclipse.

Ψ *Close-up* *Control of Behavior*

The tools of psychology, like any other tools, can be used for good or evil—to help man achieve his goals and meet his needs, or to diminish him. Control of our movements by others in many everyday situations is essential, nonfrightening, and accepted by all, as, for example, the control exercised here by a French policeman, or similar control by a traffic signal. On the other hand, the idea of computerized electronic control by means of electrodes implanted in the brain seems a terrifying prospect. Yet such techniques make it possible for the monkey shown here to raise an otherwise paralyzed arm; thus they hold tremendous potential for enabling people with physical disabilities to regain control over their bodily functioning. Control also has its humorous aspects, as shown in the cartoon. Just as even the most powerful dictator is dependent on his people in that he can maintain his power only so long as he can get the response he needs from them, control in the laboratory is, in the last analysis, a reciprocal relationship in which the psychologist and his subject "control" each other.

"Boy, do we have this guy conditioned. Every time I press the bar down he drops a pellet in."

physical handicaps resulting from injury or disease are taught new skills that will enable them to work and return to normal living.

The ability to influence and manipulate behavior offers many exciting possibilities for bettering social and working relationships, making education more effective, improving the techniques of psychotherapy, and so on. Much of the substance of this text will be devoted to increasing your understanding of the conditions and issues associated with behavior control. B. F. Skinner's novel *Walden Two* portrays a Utopian commune based upon principles of positive control of behavior; it should be read as a contrast to George Orwell's pessimistic picture of negative control in *1984,* showing the potential dangers of control.

As Carl Rogers has pointed out, whenever it is established that if certain conditions exist, certain behavior can be predicted, it becomes possible, at least theoretically, to bring about that behavior by creating those conditions (Rogers & Skinner, 1956). The frightening success of brainwashing techniques has dramatically highlighted not only the potential effectiveness of psychological control but also the practical and ethical problems it poses. Robert Oppenheimer, the well-known physicist, said in a speech to the American Psychological Association:

". . . The psychologist can hardly do anything without realizing that for him the acquisition of knowledge opens up the most terrifying prospects of controlling what people do and how they think and how they behave and how they feel. This is true for all of you who are engaged in practice, and as the corpus of psychology gains in certitude and subtlety and skill, I can see that the physicist's pleas that what he discovers be used with humanity and be used wisely will seem rather trivial compared to those pleas which you will have to make and for which you will have to be responsible." (1956, p. 128)

Our view will be that while control can be exerted from without upon the individual's behavior for either positive or negative ends, the ultimate potential of psychology is to increase the individual's freedom from outer control. To the extent that psychological research and theorizing are put to the service of maximizing the individual's control over his own internal and external environment, dependence and feelings of futility can be converted to mastery and self-fulfillment. (Ψ Close-up, p. 20.)

Chapter Summary

Over the years, many different schools of thought have developed within the field of psychology, each with its own contributions and its own opinion of what psychology actually is. Most contemporary psychologists, however, would probably agree on a definition of psychology as *the science of the behavior of organisms,* and most would include in that term both *overt,* observable forms of behavior and those forms of behavior whose existence can only be *inferred,* such as thinking and wishing.

In contrast to the poet or other artist, who seeks to capture for all time the unique aspects of a particular experience, the psychologist—like other scientists—seeks to uncover the universal laws underlying *all* experience and other behavior. Psychology thus requires a high degree of *objectivity* in its observations and its language. It uses both *deductive* and *inductive* reasoning in drawing conclusions from evidence. It begins with the assumption of *causal determinacy* and goes on to uncover the underlying regularity in behavior.

The task of the psychologist is to increase his understanding of behavior through research; the hope is that this knowledge can aid in the solution of practical problems. Specializations in psychology include *clinical psychology,* concerned primarily with understanding and treating the various forms of abnormal behavior collectively described as "mental disorder"; *experimental psychology,* concerned with identifying predictable relationships between responses or between stimulus conditions and responses, whether in child development, perception, or other areas; and various fields of *applied psychology,* concerned with the use of psychology in such fields as industry, education, and testing.

The goals of psychology are similar to the goals of science in general. Through the use of carefully structured research techniques, the psychologist attempts to *describe* behavior, both quantitatively and qualitatively, to *explain* behavior in terms of *laws, principles,* and *theories,* to *predict* the future occurrence of behavior in terms of the conditions necessary for its occurrence, and to exert his influence both to *control* behavior and to enable others to control their own behavior.

Chapter 2

Social Implications of Psychological Research

Psychology As a System of Scientific Inquiry

One of the unique features of a psychology text such as this is that the reader is also its subject matter. You bring a whole lifetime of experience to this formal study of the behavior of organisms. You have made observations about your own behavior, and also about the behavior of others. You have developed explanations about how certain events are related and why you do some of the things you do. You often try to predict how others will react to your behavior. Finally, you are constantly trying to exert control by modifying your behavior, by influencing others to do certain things, and by changing your environment. To this extent, then, the goals of the research psychologist do not differ from those with which you have been very personally involved for a long time.

In this chapter, we will try to show why casual, informal, or common-sense bases for obtaining knowledge about human behavior are inadequate. In doing so, we will suggest that the systematic study of behavior by psychologists uncovers a realm of new and exciting relationships, and can lead to a different way of looking at yourself and your environment.

If You Can Believe Your Eyes and Ears . . .

We would like you to consider the following questions. Where do your beliefs about Nature and "human nature" come from? How do *you* evaluate conclusions about why people behave as they do? How can you increase the accuracy of your observations, as well as the confidence you place in your set of beliefs about the "whys" of behavior?

We learn about what man is, what he reacts to, and how he ought to react by observing, sensing, asking, being told, reading, and thinking. In other words, our understanding comes either directly, from our own experience with things in the environment, or secondhand, through the experience of others. Underlying all of our knowledge is a set of basic beliefs in the credibility of our own sensory experience and in the credibility of certain external authorities. Many of our beliefs are virtually "givens," insofar as we accept them without considering that there could be alternatives (e.g., a child's trust in his mother's description of why things are the way they are). Over time, these primitive beliefs are expanded to cover not only the particular experiences which gave rise to them, but also the classes of events which include instances not directly experienced. Beliefs then become generalizations, and generalizations come to be our personal statement about what is true. They are convenient summary statements which organize our personal experience. Moreover, they exert a guiding influence upon how and what we will observe in the future. At a very early age we seem to stop seeing things as they are, and start interpreting what we see in terms of expectations based on our previous generalizations.

Hugo Münsterberg, one of the first research psychologists at Harvard University, provides us with this remarkable account of the different observations made by reporters who covered a speech on peace that he gave to a large audience in New York:

"The reporters sat immediately in front of the platform. One man wrote that the audience was so surprised by my speech that it received it in complete silence; another wrote that I was constantly interrupted by loud applause, and that at the end of my address the applause continued for minutes. The one wrote that during my opponent's speech I was constantly smiling; the other noticed that my face remained grave and without a smile. The one said that I grew purple-red from excitement; and the other found that I grew white like chalk. The one told us that my critic, while speaking, walked up and down the large stage; and the other, that he stood all the while at my side and patted me in a fatherly way on the shoulder." (1908, pp. 35-36)

Surely, someone was not telling it like it was. In Chapter 7 we will examine research which explains how perception may be affected by attitudes, motives, and expectations. Our present task, however, is simply to illuminate how fallible supposedly credible interpreters of reality can be.

Let us start, not at the beginning of life with our wide-eyed infant or inquisitive child, but with a college student looking at ads or reading newspapers or magazines. Of course, the sophisticated student doesn't believe everything he reads or sees on TV, but it is likely that he believes (accepts as true) conclusions based on statistics, statements from established authorities, scientific tests, surveys, interviews, and reports of research. Since the Russians fired their Sputnik into space in 1957, the general public has come to feel that scientists are omnipotent. Therefore, assertions which bear the mark of the scientific enterprise are generally accepted at face value. What we want to demonstrate here is the difference between pseudoscientific conclusion-drawing (which can be very dangerous) and reliable conclusion-drawing based upon the principles embodied in the scientific method.

We will use an inductive technique (as described in Chapter 1) to abstract some general principles about arriving at conclusions. Our source material will be several accounts of psychology and life reported in the mass media.

Truth Can Be Packaged Under Various Labels

Advertising is aimed openly at manipulating not only behavior but ideas. Do ads fool you? For example, if you wanted a pill to relieve the pain from the ordinary headaches which millions of Americans are heir to, would you conclude that Bayer aspirin really is best because "Government tests have proven that no pain reliever is stronger or more effective than Bayer aspirin"?

What ads like this fail to mention is that the tests, which were sponsored by the Federal Trade Commission and published in the December 1962 issue of the *Journal of the American Medical Association*, actually simply found no difference among the five headache preparations tested, either in speed or in effectiveness of pain relief. True, none was more effective than Bayer aspirin, but neither was any *less* effective. Adding that second clause puts the conclusion in a somewhat different light.

Pity the Lackluster Brunette

Another familiar ad promotes a certain brand of hair coloring by showing happy and attractive girls reaping the rewards of having newly become blondes. The implication is that while the average coed with a mane of brunette hair is sitting in her room or in the library reading this kind of book, her blonde counterpart is out having a good time. *Do* blondes have all the fun, or more fun than brunettes?

Here is a case in which publicized examples of something lead to our noticing only instances supporting it. First we have Hollywood equating blonde hair with sex appeal by building this image of stars like Mae West, Jean Harlow, Marilyn Monroe, and Virna Lisi. Then companies that sell hair bleach televise sequences in the lives of blonde girls having fun.

Soon whenever we see real flesh-and-blood blondes laughing or doing anything animated, we are more likely to notice it as a verification of our generalization. Furthermore, once blondes and others believe this generalization, they may change their behavior in

such a way as to fulfill their expectations. For example, you do not talk about serious things to a (dumb, fun-loving) blonde, which leaves more time for nonserious "fun things," and so on. This eventually leads you to observe that blondes do spend more time having fun. The claim has become a self-fulfilling prophecy.

Smoke Gets in Their Eyes

Perhaps you have learned to be wary of claims made in advertising, but what about news stories? How do you know when you can believe what you read in the papers? What would you conclude from the article on smoking and grades reprinted in part above? If freshmen hope to be academically successful, must they stop smoking?

We need question neither the data nor the correlation between the two sets of behaviors (the students' smoking and the teachers' assignment of grades to them). Rather, we must focus on the implied *causality*. What leads to what? If grades and smoking are inversely related, will grades go up if smoking goes down? This will occur only if the two events are directly linked in a causal fashion. However, we can

readily posit several equally likely causal sequences which fit the observed relationship. First, perhaps smoking does cause poor grades. If so, the number of cigarettes smoked ought to correlate negatively with grade point average, and grades should change as smoking patterns are varied. But suppose poor grades can cause smoking. In fact, the newspaper article notes "that students with poor grades had a 'certain psychological reaction' that often leads them to nervous habits such as smoking or nibbling." If so, changing the effect (smoking) would not change the cause (poor grades).

It could also be that both events are caused by a third factor, such as "nervous irritability." This factor would lead to smoking behavior and also to poor study habits, which result in poor grades. By this argument, reducing smoking might increase nervousness, which in turn would result in more distraction when studying and eventually in poorer grades. So we might conclude (if we were in the employ of a tobacco company) that smoking is a safety valve which helps the 16.7 percent get "A" averages.

It is obvious, then, that even though two events or sets of behavior may vary together in some systematic way, it is not possible to assign a causal direction to such a correlation. Until more is known, several explanations may sound equally plausible. In the example above, we can add at least one more alternative (can you supply any others?). It might be that teachers dislike students who smoke in class (it looks as though they are not enraptured by the lecture, not studious, etc.) and therefore are predisposed to give poorer grades to smokers. In such a case, stopping smoking might lead to better grades, *not* by directly changing the student's study habits, attitudes, or psychic health, but by changing the teacher's perception of him.

Where Have All the Other Senior Citizens Gone?

For another experiment in conclusion-drawing, read the parts of the article headlined "Psychological Clues Detected in Elderly Year Before Death," reprinted on page 25. This article reports that of the half who died, a large proportion had "showed a distinct awareness of signs of death more than a year before it occurred." But does this fact allow us to draw the generalization that elderly people develop a special sense by which they anticipate their impending death?

Since the probability of dying for people over seventy is quite high, it seems realistic for them to expect to die before too long and thus to interpret a wide range of symptoms or bodily events as signs of death. The 85 percent accuracy figure among those who died is meaningless unless we are told what percentage of the forty surviving persons incorrectly believed they also had monitored signs of their death.

Sex Can Make You Crazy

Another recent newspaper article reported a university psychiatrist's findings that 86 percent of a group of coeds who were psychiatric patients had indulged in intercourse, as compared with only 22 percent of a group of coeds at the same university who were not psychiatric patients. The figures had been obtained through questionnaires, and the psychiatrist was quoted as concluding that his patients were "casualties of the sexual revolution." From the information given, would you agree with his conclusion?

Two claims are involved here: (a) that a much higher percentage of patients than nonpatients had

had intercourse, and (b) that the sexual activity of the patients was a causal factor in their emotional problems. Again the conclusion may be true, but before accepting it (or before you allow your mother to arm herself with such "authoritative" arguments), you must raise several questions.

First, how large was the sample of psychiatric patients? The surprisingly high figure of "86 percent" could be the data for only six girls who couldn't say no, out of a grand total of seven. And was the patient sample like the nonpatient sample except for amount of sexual activity, or did they perhaps start out differing in other ways (maybe less academic ability or more problems at home) that might have made them more vulnerable to emotional problems in the university setting? The conclusion as stated goes far beyond the original *sample* of students questioned. It is generalized to the entire *population* of all college girls, but we do not know how large the sample was or whether it was representative of college girls in general.

It is also conceivable that the untreated coeds were giving a more "socially desirable" self-report in which they underestimated their promiscuity, while those under psychiatric care either were more truthful or were bragging. The conclusion was not about the girls' *self-reports* but about the *behavior* referred to in those reports and we cannot blithely assume that self-reports and actual behavior are perfectly correlated. Differences between groups on self-report measures may reflect differences *not* in the behavior under consideration but in what the two groups were trying to prove about themselves. In fact, the patient group may even have regarded their sexual activity as one of the few healthy aspects of their lives and may have sought psychiatric help for other reasons entirely.

So we end up knowing only that the patient group reported more intercourse than the nonpatient group. We do not know how their actual behavior compared or whether the patients' emotional problems grew out of their sexual activity, caused it, or were unrelated to it.

A Little Data Can Be a Dangerous Thing

We are concerned about the harmful effects of LSD on the youth of the country and about the possible

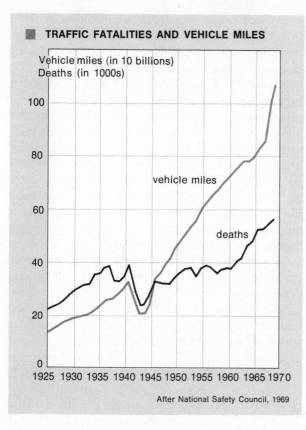

TRAFFIC FATALITIES AND VEHICLE MILES

Vehicle miles (in 10 billions)
Deaths (in 1000s)

vehicle miles

deaths

After National Safety Council, 1969

fatalities have increased from around 38,000 deaths in 1936 to over 56,000 in 1969. In 1936 we Americans drove about 22 billion miles; in 1969 we drove about a trillion miles. ▪ The pessimist looking at this curve will point out that the death curve continues to rise with the number of vehicle miles driven.

Now let us take a better look at the situation by viewing the relationship between these two sets of figures. There has been a 500 percent increase in miles driven compared to a 50 percent increase in fatalities. To get the picture more clearly in mind, look at the second graph, in which an additional curve plots the number of traffic deaths per hundred million vehicle miles, and you will see that the death *rate* has declined to about a third of what it was at the beginning of the period. ● Most encouraging of all is the notable dip since 1966, suggesting that the numerous programs of engineering, education, and enforcement are proving effective.

Neither set of figures is more "real" than the other.

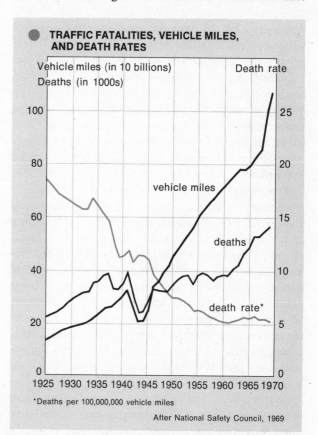

TRAFFIC FATALITIES, VEHICLE MILES, AND DEATH RATES

Vehicle miles (in 10 billions)
Deaths (in 1000s)

Death rate

vehicle miles

deaths

death rate*

*Deaths per 100,000,000 vehicle miles

After National Safety Council, 1969

discovery of the cause of cancer. These concerns were recently interrelated in an article with "published evidence of a possible link between the hallucinogenic drug LSD and leukemia." This possible link was reported by an Australian doctor who based his conclusions on a sample of exactly one patient. The patient had developed leukemia just a year after being given LSD as part of a program of therapy for an emotional problem. Although an intensive study and controlled analysis of a single case may be adequate for drawing valid conclusions, a casual, uncontrolled set of observations of only one case can never become "evidence."

Is Truth in the Eye of the Statistician?

We are frequently reminded by the popular press of the ever rising incidence of traffic fatalities, especially as each holiday surpasses the one of the year before in the number of persons killed on our streets and highways. The data in the first graph show that

They merely illustrate different ways of representing the same reality, showing that one can emphasize different aspects of the same data by one's choice of statistical language and concepts. Probably most of us will agree that the second one gives us more encouragement to continue our programs aimed at the reduction of traffic fatalities. However, if you had a grudge against the automobile industry you might prefer to talk about the first one.

Ah, to Be Black
Now That the Police Are Beating Whites

"Poor whites are more affected than Negroes" by use of unnecessary police force, according to a July 1968 news story. "Race prejudice is not a major factor in any beatings of poor people by the police . . . whites are more likely to be handled roughly by the police than are Negroes." Thirty-six observers who worked with the police in Boston, Washington, and Chicago during the summer of 1966 reported that of 643 white suspects, 27 were hit unnecessarily (a rate of 41.9 per 1000). Of 751 black suspects, only 17 were hit unnecessarily (a rate of 22.9 per 1000). Thus, allegations by civil rights groups of police brutality toward blacks are not supported by this data. Taken as they stand, these data have at least three possible interpretations: (a) they may be accurate, as is stated in the report; (b) they may be due to the uncertainty principle; (c) they may be due to observer bias or inaccuracy.

The physicist Heisenberg gave us the principle of uncertainty—that the act of measuring a process may change the process itself. Although he was referring to the speed and location of an electron in a cloud chamber, his statement is frequently true of psychological measurement. When the behavior being measured is influenced by one's awareness that he is being observed, the observer no longer gets an accurate picture. Rather, the measure is distorted by attempts to deceive the observer, to present a favorable image, to react against being a "guinea pig," or to "psych out" the observer—to give him what you think he wants.

In this study of police brutality, the police may have changed their pattern of distributing hits because they knew they were being observed. They were probably aware that it now was legally and politically riskier to mistreat a black man than a white. So, perhaps the conclusion holds only for the conditions when observations were being made.

We should not overlook a very different source of explanation for the findings. The definition of the vague concept "unnecessary force" may not have been used in the same way by the observers for black as for white suspects. A term so open to individual interpretation by each observer depends upon what is considered to be adequate justification, provocation, and so on. It is possible that the police hit as many black suspects as white ones—maybe even more— but that more of the hitting of blacks was regarded as "necessary" by the observers. That is, the observers might see as necessary against a black the same force that they would define as overly severe when used against a white. The basic data from which one draws conclusions must be tied less ambiguously to behavioral acts which can be described and enumerated with a minimum of interpretive bias.

Baby, It's Dark and Cold Outside

It is remarkable how many things are correlated in nature, and how that number increases when human beings are involved. In August 1966, newspapers in New York heralded an above-average increase in births "in several leading hospitals," "nine months after the 1965 power blackout." This claim was generally accepted without question, and people proceeded to try to explain it.

Among the thirty million people affected by the November 9 blackout on the East Coast were those who later theorized "that natural disasters lead people to turn to each other. Excavations of Pompeii, for example, showed couples embracing during the volcanic eruption." Said a mother at Brookdale Hospital: "I wouldn't go to bed by myself." A new father attributed the birth increase to his belief that "New Yorkers are very romantic. It was the candlelight." A more somber appraisal was offered by an official of the Planned Parenthood Federation of America:

"Sexuality is a very powerful force, and people would normally indulge in sex if they didn't have anything else to do. All the substitutes for sex—meetings, lectures, card parties, theaters, saloons—were eliminated that night. What else could they do?" (*The New York Times,* Aug. 11, 1966)

Again we see a causal inference from a correlation of two events. The frequency with which this type of thinking occurs attests to man's predilection to go beyond observations and seek the lawfulness which he believes must explain them. This is an admirable venture, but again we must counsel caution about assuming that a causal relation exists when only a correlation has been observed. In addition, there are two possibilities in this example which we have not considered in the earlier ones: (a) the data cannot be trusted, or (b) the relationship is coincidental.

Although one New York hospital (St. Luke's) reported three times the average number of daily births for each of the seven key days, the numbers were small, only about 10 extra babies a day. And the sixteen other hospitals combined reported only an increase of 47 births—2.9 babies per hospital. This output seems even less significant when we remind ourselves that in New York City there were probably three million women with childbearing capabilities who were in the blackout.

You might also object to comparing births during specific days with the average births per day over a whole year, rather than for those same days in other years. It is possible that there always are seasonal fluctuations (for example, one hospital administrator in Chicago noted a jump in births in the last week in September—nine months after a merry Christmas and a happy New Year). It would also be good to get beneath the impersonal numerical values and to inquire how many of these women who gave birth in New York that critical week had, in fact, been in the city on the night of the blackout.

An epilogue to the New York story was provided by the experience of Chicago the following year. Based on the New York claim, Chicago hospitals braced themselves for a baby boom in the fall of 1967 as a memento of their 23-inch snowstorm in January of that year. But statistics for the three fall months, compared with those of the corresponding months the year before and the year after, showed only slight fluctuations, with slightly fewer births than the previous year and slightly more than the following year. ◆

◆ **BIRTH RATES IN CHICAGO: 1966, 1967, AND 1968**

Month	1966	Difference	1967	Difference	1968
October	21.1	− .6	20.5	+1.6	18.9
November	19.8	− .8	19.0	+ .5	18.5
December	20.2	− .5	19.7	+1.1	18.6

(Chicago Board of Health, 1969)

The figures in the center column show the birth rate per 1000 population for 1967, the year of Chicago's "Big Storm." The outer columns show the corresponding figures for the preceding and following years. There is no evidence here of a "baby boom" in the fall of 1967; the differences in birth rate can better be ascribed to normal fluctuation.

Don't Give a Violent Prisoner a Pat on the Back

It appears that violent individuals are provoked simply by their hypersensitivity to the physical closeness of others. A report to the American Psychiatric Association (Kinzel, 1969) established that a group of violent prisoners had "body-buffer zones" almost four times larger than did a nonviolent group. (The size of the body-buffer zone is determined by finding out how close the subject will allow another person, in this case the experimenter, to come to him before saying "stop.") This difference was interpreted by the investigator as reflecting "a pathological body image state," "a tendency to perceive passive personal closeness as an active physical threat," and "homosexual anxiety" in the violent group. If being violent does reflect such psychological processes, then it would be possible to predict that people who had large body-buffer zones would be likely to become violent.

Only one aspect of this study and its conclusion will concern us here—the qualitative classification of individuals into groups according to some general concept; in this case, "violent" versus "nonviolent." Such classification occurs very frequently in psychological research as well as in the mass media. For example, depending on the interests of the researcher, children might be classified into "normal" versus "retarded" (or "prejudiced" versus "nonprejudiced" or "healthy" versus "malnourished"). The children's behavior would then be searched to see if one group behaved differently from the other in any consistent way. In some cases only one kind of behavior would be observed (body-buffer zones in the case of the violent and nonviolent prisoners). In other cases, the investigator would simply collect as many samples of behavior as he could from his subjects and then see if any behavior was more characteristic of one group than of the other.

This general procedure for drawing conclusions is justified only in the first stage of an exploration between related patterns of behavior. The fallacy we encounter is one of concluding that the group characteristic we have isolated accounts for the observed difference in behavior between the groups studied. In the prisoner study, the violent prisoners were distinguished from the nonviolent by their life histories of frequent violent behavior "defined as physical assault on another, producing tissue injury." However, there were (there always are) other ways in which the violent and nonviolent groups differed. On the average, the violent prisoners in this study were younger (by six years), stockier (one inch shorter and fourteen pounds heavier), and much less intelligent (by 23 points on an IQ test).

How can we conclude that the difference in body-buffer zone behavior can be unambiguously linked to the trait of violence, and not to age, body build, or intelligence? We cannot do so until we compare individuals differing on each of these characteristics who are matched for their degree of violence. Theoretically, there are an infinite number of traits which could be associated in some way with any single trait chosen as the basis for classification.

The danger lies in the temptation to designate a particular variable as a causative factor and then use it for diagnosis, prediction, and maybe even as the basis for a program of controlling the correlated behavior. In fact, the variable might simply happen to be present, while some other variable is "causing" the behavior. This can be illustrated by an example from the early days of medicine. When the bubonic plague raged in Europe, it was observed that epidemics were always accompanied by the presence of rats in the streets. Exterminating the rats, however, did not put an end to the epidemics. The spread of the disease was not halted until a French physician, Sismone, realized that the plague was actually carried by lice which infested the rats, and was thus being transmitted to townspeople who handled the dead rats while disposing of them.

Classification and categorization are necessary operations if we are to make sense of the myriads of stimuli, responses, situations, and individuals we are faced with when studying the behavior of organisms. We must beware, however, lest we blur the line between classification and causation. The analytical stance we adopted in Chapter 1 and the skepticism we are developing in this chapter are both necessary to keep our conclusions clean.

A Case History in the Instant Creation of a Scientific Authority

As a final cautionary tale in our review of the hazards of accepting at face value the scientific pronouncements of the popular press, we offer the following case history.

"The use of obscene language among women, from the co-eds of the New Left to the proper matrons at swank Manhattan cocktail parties, has risen sharply in the last few years, according to some leading psychologists."

Thus began a recent article in *The New York Times* (Leo, 1968) which, as you can imagine, provoked considerable national interest. What is most interesting for our purposes is that the reputed "leading authority" on this topic was the junior author of your text. The article focused upon his observations:

"Philip Zimbardo, a Stanford University psychologist, said that in observing agitated patients at two East Coast mental hospitals over a long period of time, he noted that the language of the women was more obscene than that of the men."

This report was picked up by the news services, reprinted in various forms in papers throughout the country, given a splashy *Newsweek* treatment under the heading "Girl Talk: **%# !," commented upon by Joyce Brothers in her syndicated column, and finally boxed in the Forum Newsfront of *Playboy Magazine*. Offers for this authority to appear on radio and television "talk" programs, as well as a rash of requests for reprints of his writings on the topic (some from as far away as South America) followed the *New York Times* report. We are in the unique position of being able to trace this widely circulated and fully accepted conclusion from its uncertain, speculative origin to its final convincing, authoritative ring.

It appears that one of the editors of *The New York Times* was cursed out by a woman at a party, and he promptly assigned a reporter to find out whether this was a unique experience or part of a regularly occurring phenomenon. The reporter telephoned several social scientists who might know something about the issue, one of whom (for some unknown reason) directed him to Zimbardo. Protests about not having any relevant evidence and the statement that no one was engaged in research on this particular problem were not accepted, since there was a deadline to be met. What was said, then, to the reporter was that "a number of years ago, in two mental hospitals, I observed that in the back wards (where chronic schizophrenics were kept), the women's wards tended to be noisier and to have a greater amount of exhibitionism and obscenity than the men's wards."

This conclusion emerged only after a period of uncontrolled observation, and because the observer was not testing a hypothesis about obscenity, he did not record any data other than his general impressions. There was no independent verification by other observers of the same data, no explicit definition of obscenity, and no comparability of observation periods of men and women. It is possible that the observer was simply more aware of female obscenity because of its usual low frequency in everyday life: it may have occurred with the same frequency as among the male schizophrenics, or its frequency might even have been lower. Or perhaps there were simply a few very loudly obscene female patients. In any event, with no systematically collected and recorded data, we cannot separate distortions in Zimbardo's recall (ten years later) of what he witnessed from either his original observations or the actual behavior that was occurring.

In the *New York Times* report, the casual "observed a number of years ago" becomes "observed over a long period of time" and "chronic schizophrenics" become "agitated patients." In *Newsweek* the original casual observations which were "noted" in the *Times* report became a relationship that was "found"—women patients in mental hospitals are much more likely to swear than men (notice the addition of "much"). In Dr. Brothers' column, the "back-ward schizophrenics" became "female mental patients"—a term that could include relatively normal outpatients in therapy.

The modern authority on all matters sexual—*Playboy*—simplified matters for its readers with the broad overgeneralization that "a number of psychologists, *The New York Times* reports, have found that women of every social level have become increasingly uninhibited in their use of obscene language." The only psychologist mentioned is the now well-known authority, Philip Zimbardo, whose comprehensive research "confirms" the above principle of human behavior (*Playboy,* 1969).

Can a Scientist Find Order and Law in a World of Apparent Chaos and Uncertainty?

It is obvious from the foregoing discussion that it is easy to draw false conclusions about "the way things are"—conclusions that may come to influence the beliefs people hold and the actions they take to change themselves, other people, or their environment.

Stripped of all its glamour, scientific inquiry is nothing more than a way of limiting false conclusion-drawing about natural events. This superficially simple goal is exceedingly difficult to achieve. It requires a set of special attitudes on the part of the investigator as well as explicit procedures for stating, testing, and evaluating propositions which might become general conclusions. Taken together, these attitudes, orientations, and procedures are what is meant by the *scientific method*.

It is not our intention to try to build a case for psychology as a "hard" science with a close resemblance to the natural sciences. But it will become clear as we progress through this text that the important psychological discoveries made so far (as well as the hoped-for breakthroughs) are possible only because psychology has adopted the scientific method as its model for understanding the behavior of all living organisms. Because of this, we believe you will be in a better position to appreciate *what* psychologists are finding and concluding about human nature, if you first recognize some of the basic principles which guide *how* they investigate their particular subject matter.

The Scientific Method

Although different scientists and philosophers of science may include somewhat different things under the rubric of *scientific method*, all would agree that it is a set of explicit assumptions, attitudes, and rules which enable an investigator to:

a) collect the facts he needs by making systematic observations and recording them;

b) evaluate the data (recorded observations) that he has collected;

c) communicate his results and conclusions to others;

d) present his findings and interpretations in such a way that they can be *replicated* (repeated by others for verification or challenge);

e) add what he has discovered to what others before him have contributed to the solution of a given problem;

f) provide the next investigator with a more advantageous starting point than before, by making available his new facts and explanations.

As we noted in Chapter 1, the starting point of the scientist is the assumption of an orderly universe. This leads to an acceptance of the doctrine of causal determinacy which, as stated by John Stuart Mill, says, "There are such things in nature as parallel cases; that what happens once, will, under a sufficient degree of similarity of circumstances, happen again." (1843, p. 354)

In turn, this results in a systematic search for the *causes* of things. While logicians still argue about what *causality* means, we shall regard causality as present when there is an invariable relation between two or more processes. For one of these events or processes to be regarded as a cause of the other, it must temporally precede and be necessary for the occurrence of the other and not the other way around. These requirements were set forth in Mill's famous Canons of Proof, as paraphrased in the Ψ Close-up above.

In passing, it should be mentioned that there are many different *levels of causality*, and the question

---

Ψ *Close-up*   **John Stuart Mill's Canons of Proof**

To determine whether a particular factor is the cause of an observed event, John Stuart Mill proposed four requirements to be met before the factor under consideration can pass the test and be regarded as a cause. The gist of them is summarized here.

1. For something to be the cause, it must always occur if the phenomenon occurs.

2. For something to be the cause, the phenomenon must always occur when the supposed cause occurs.

3. For something to be the cause, the phenomenon must vary if the supposed cause varies.

4. When a phenomenon whose cause is known shows additional characteristics, there are additional causes operating.

These Canons of Proof provide guidelines for eliminating false hypotheses about the causes of an observed event. You are encouraged to use them to reevaluate the "causal laws" that were being set forth in the newspaper stories and ads we discussed earlier.

"what is the cause of phenomenon X?" can be answered validly by a variety of statements. Each investigator must decide the degree of precision and specificity, as well as the general nature of the causal proposition that he will accept. The question "what caused the murderer to kill the victim?" can be answered:

a) at a *macroscopic level*—for example, the defendant's cultural or biological heritage;

b) at a *molar level*—for example, the victim's provocation, passion, revenge, a sizeable reward for doing so;

c) at a *molecular level*—for example, digital muscular contractions around the trigger of the gun, a brain wave pattern of arousal;

d) at a *microscopic level*—for example, specific biochemical energy transformations within a nerve, a brain cell, or the retina of the eye.

The scientist often feels that Nature takes on many disguises to conceal her true identity from voyeurs. For this reason, he adopts the general attitude that he can never be absolutely certain he has unmasked one of her secrets. His conclusions are always incomplete, tentative, and provisional. They can never be held dogmatically, but are always open to revision or even refutation by new facts. Finally, his conclusions must be stated in *probabilistic* terms. For example, he might give the *likelihood* that the relationship he has observed will reoccur under repeated testing. Or he could state the *degree of confidence* one can have that the measure he has obtained, with his particular sample of subjects, is an accurate representation of the measure he would get if he could observe the entire class from which his sample was drawn (all eighteen-year-olds, all college sophomores, or whatever).

The objectivity and the critical, analytical attitude characteristic of the scientific method can thus be seen as a safeguard against premature, incomplete, inaccurate conclusion-drawing. Above all, the scientist develops a sense of respect for data as the ultimate arbiter of all confrontations. His own data and that of all other investigators (as well as the methods for obtaining the data) must be *publicly verifiable*—open to inspection, criticism, and replication. Nothing gains the status of a scientific fact, however reasonable or even obvious it seems, unless it can be substantiated by independent investigators.

Nature will not allow her data to be tampered with for long. Stalin tried to decree acceptance of the theory that characteristics acquired during one's lifetime could be inherited by one's children. This theory was congenial to the political assumption that man, once perfected by being given a good environment, would stay that way through heredity. Stalin failed not because he did not have enough political power or military force, but because the data would not yield. Learned characteristics are not inherited, and saying they are does not make it true. Data wait, sometimes many years, for an observer who cannot be silenced, and who can read their signal honestly. (Ψ Close-up, p. 34) In this sense, then, "data become like heavily starched underwear—concealed from others, but difficult to ignore." (McCain & Segal, 1969, p. 6)

Tactics of Scientific Inquiry

The special set of attitudes held by the scientist dictates how he will (or ought to) behave when he is conducting his search for meaning, order, and explanations. There are a number of tactics in the scientific approach which are common to researchers in all fields. We will outline them here, dwelling at greater length on those that are especially crucial for understanding much of the content of psychology which will be presented in the remainder of this volume.

Narrowing the focus. The likelihood of finding a satisfactory scientific answer to a question about behavior is greatly increased if the question which initiates the search is phrased in terms of a potentially soluble problem. By focusing on a limited area of investigation, rather than seeking ultimate explanations (the all-embracing "why" of experience), one is more likely to come up with an answer that has some utility. However, the scientist is acutely aware of both the boundary arbitrarily set around his particular inquiry and its relation to the larger problem area.

From individual cases to general laws. In Chapter 1, a distinction was made between deductive and inductive conclusion-drawing. The former (syllogistic reasoning) relies upon a process of rationally considering the premises available and determining whether a given conclusion can be inescapably deduced.

Science, of course, uses such reasoning often, but it relies primarily upon the process of induction, using inference to go beyond the observed facts. From specific instances that have actually been observed, a conclusion is derived about the general *class* of such instances which have not yet been observed. The scientist wants to make generalizations about *relationships* between things, but all he can know directly are the particular examples of the things themselves that he sees. He must *infer* the connection between them, as well as their representativeness of a larger class.

Knowledge of this limitation, combined with his critical attitudes about faulty conclusion-drawing, leads the scientist to insist upon methods of data collection which will yield "facts" that are reasonably trustworthy, and to demand procedures for drawing inferences which can be made explicit and which are objectively determined before the data are collected.

Ψ *Close-up*   **Truth Through Faith or Sense?**

While most laymen now accept the role of sense experience as the legitimate grounds for arriving at knowledge of nature, such was not always the case. Truth as divinely revealed in the Scriptures has been the Dogma of Faith upon which many men have tried to create a unique view of the universe. The trial of Galileo is a reminder of the time when this philosophy was dominant. Galileo's data, secured through precise observation, had to be rejected because they supported Copernicus' theory of a heliocentric universe (in which the sun is the center). The Church of that period held that the universe was geocentric—with the central point being man and his earth. In 1615, Galileo was denounced by the Church for his heretical views, and when he did not cease and desist, he was tried in 1633. The wording of his sentencing and abjuration provide a valuable lesson for us which needs no further comment.

Sentence of the Tribunal of the Supreme Inquisition Against Galileo Galilei, Given the 22nd Day of June of the Year 1633.

It being the case that thou, Galileo, son of the late Vincenzio Galilei, a Florentine, now aged seventy, wast denounced in this Holy Office in 1615:

That thou heldest as true the false doctrine taught by man, that the Sun was the centre of the universe and immovable, and that the Earth moved, and had also a diurnal motion: That on this same matter thou didst hold a correspondence with certain German mathematicians: That thou hadst caused to be printed certain letters entitled "on the Solar Spots," in which thou didst explain the said doctrine to be true. . . .

This Holy Tribunal desiring to obviate the disorder and mischief which had resulted from this, and which was constantly increasing to the prejudice of the Holy Faith; by order of our Lord (Pope) and of the most Eminent Lords Cardinals of this supreme and universal Inquisition, the two propositions of the stability of the Sun and of the motion of the Earth were by the qualified theologians thus adjudged:

That the Sun is the centre of the universe and doth not move from his place is a proposition absurd and false in philosophy, and formally heretical; being expressly contrary to Holy Writ: That the Earth is not the centre of the universe nor immovable, but that it moves, even with a diurnal motion, is likewise a proposition absurd and false in philosophy, and considered in theology ad minus erroneous in faith.

We say, pronounce, sentence, and declare, that thou, the said Galileo, by the things deduced during this trial, and by thee confessed as above, hast rendered thyself vehemently suspected of heresy by this Holy Office, that is, of having believed and held a doctrine which is false, and contrary to the Holy Scriptures, to wit: that the Sun is the centre of the universe, and that it does not move from east to west, and that the Earth moves and is not the centre of the universe: and that an opinion may be held and defended as probable after having been declared and defined as contrary to Holy Scripture; and in consequence thou hast incurred all the censures and penalties of the Sacred Canons, and other Decrees both general and particular, against such offenders imposed and promulgated.

Galileo's Abjuration

I, Galileo Galilei, . . . after having been admonished by this Holy Office entirely to abandon the false opinion that the Sun was the centre of the universe and immovable, and that the Earth was not the centre of the same and that it moved, and that I was neither to hold, defend, nor teach in any manner whatever, either orally or in writing, the said false doctrine; and after having received a notification that the said doctrine is contrary to Holy Writ, I did write and cause to be printed a book in which I treat of the said already condemned doctrine, and bring forward arguments of much efficacy in its favor. . . .

I abjure with a sincere heart and unfeigned faith, I curse and detest the said errors and heresies, and generally all and every error and sect contrary to the Holy Catholic Church. And I swear that for the future I will neither say nor assert in speaking or writing such things as may bring upon me similar suspicion. . . .

Guarding against bias in observation. If the "stuff" of science is sense observations, then the whole enterprise depends on making trustworthy observations. But we have seen in our opening discussion of erroneous conclusion-drawing in the mass media that observations can be quite misleading. Two more examples, of a very different type, will make the point even more convincingly.

Shown below are two lines, the ends of which are marked a_1–b_1 and a_2–b_2. Which horizontal line is longer?

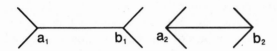

The sense impression is that line a_1–b_1 is longer than a_2–b_2. But "in fact," they are equivalent. To check your two comparison observations, place a ruler or other straightedge against each in turn. Even when you know that they are equal, they still look unequal. In Chapter 7, where we deal with perception, we will explain why you experience this phenomenon (called the Müller-Lyer illusion) the way you do. For now, what is important to know is that the extensions of the lines are distorting your observation. They are a source of *bias* which results in a sense impression which is discrepant with the physical event (the measured length of the lines). For accurate observation of the comparative length of these lines, the end lines would have to be eliminated, or their effect counteracted by a more accurate means of observation—measuring each line. You can eliminate the extensions by blocking them from view; when you do so, the illusion suddenly disappears and the two horizontal lines look equal.

Here is a case where getting independent judgments from other observers would not improve your accuracy. They, too, would be subject to the same psychological process of perceptual illusion—as long as their environment was also one in which right angles were prominent (in the design of homes, furniture, etc.) Can you figure out why? This principle has major implications for our observation of human behavior when we consider that most of the observers used in psychological research come from essentially the same environment as the subjects they are studying.

A different kind of bias in observation is illustrated by the way in which a horse, "Clever Hans," deceived his trainer and a reputable, scientifically oriented Investigating Commission in Berlin back in 1904. It appeared that Hans had a remarkable memory and could spell, read, comprehend complex questions, count, and perform mathematical operations. The investigators carefully observed the horse's feats but could find no deliberate trickery, since the horse performed as well for them as for his trainer. They concluded that he could reason and think at least as well as most humans. After reading about what Hans could do, can you detect how he did it and recommend to the Commission the necessary controls to correct their observation?

". . . The stately animal, a Russian trotting horse, stood like a docile pupil, managed not by means of the whip, but by gentle encouragement and frequent reward of bread or carrots. He would answer correctly nearly all of the questions which were put to him in German. If he understood a question, he immediately indicated this by a nod of the head; if he failed to grasp its import, he communicated the fact by a shake of the head. We were told that the questioner had to confine himself to a certain vocabulary, but this was comparatively rich and the horse widened its scope daily without special instruction, but by simple contact with his environment. . . .

"Our intelligent horse was unable to speak, to be sure. His chief mode of expression was tapping with his right forefoot. A good deal was also expressed by means of movements of the head. Thus 'yes' was expressed by a nod, 'no' by a deliberate movement from side to side; and 'upward,' 'upper,' 'downward,' 'right,' 'left,' were indicated by turning the head in these directions. . . ."

"Let us turn now to some of his specific accomplishments. He had, apparently, completely mastered the cardinal numbers from 1 to 100 and the ordinals to 10, at least. Upon request he would count objects of all sorts, the persons present, even to distinctions of sex. Then hats, umbrellas, and eyeglasses. . . . Small numbers were given with a slow tapping of the right foot. With larger numbers he would increase his speed, and would often tap very rapidly right from the start. . . . After the final tap he would return his right foot—which he used in his counting—to its original position. . . .

"But Hans could not only count, he could also solve

problems in arithmetic. The four fundamental processes were entirely familiar to him. Common fractions he changed to decimals and vice versa. . . .

"Hans, furthermore, was able to read the German readily, whether written or printed. . . . If a series of placards with written words were placed before the horse, he could step up and point with his nose to any of the words required of him. He could even spell some of the words. This was done by the aid of a table devised by Mr. von Osten, in which every letter of the alphabet, as well as a number of diphthongs had an appropriate place which the horse could designate by means of a pair of numbers. . . .

"He, moreover, gave evidence of an excellent memory. . . . Hans carried the entire yearly calendar in his head; he could give you not only the date for each day without having been previously taught anew, but he could give you the date of any day you might mention. . . ." (Pfungst, 1911, pp. 18-24)

It was some time before the Commission found that Hans could not solve any problems if he wore blinders, if the trainer stood behind him, or if the person who posed the question did not himself know the answer. These *controls* on the observation of Hans' behavior make it immediately obvious that Hans was merely responding to subtle, unintentional, visual cues given by the questioner as to when he should start tapping and when he should stop. Hans had learned to do what is done consciously by "mind-reading" entertainers.

Because of instances such as these, the scientist learns that the "raw appearance" of things is only one source of data about reality. It must be checked against a variety of other observations of the same phenomena. How do you convince a child that the earth is not flat or that the sun does not rise in the east, move across the sky, and set in the west?

Refusing to treat private sensations as facts. The *content* of private experience cannot be admissible as scientific fact because it is idiosyncratic and not available to observation by others. However, verbal *reports* about private events are behaviors which are acceptable as such, although one cannot assume that they correspond exactly to the event they describe. A *description* of a dream is not the same as the *content* of the dream, since it can be distorted and modified in the process of recall and reporting.

Using concrete terms and operational definitions. If science can be thought of as a language for describing nature (see Bronowski, 1953), then that language must not carry a burden of ambiguity. In connection with the poet-psychotic distinctions we discussed in Chapter 1, a wide range of language, from objective to subjective, was described. The scientist wants his description of nature to be understood by other scientists so that they are able to replicate his observations. This becomes more of a problem the further away he moves from the use of symbols and formulas whose meaning is limited and fixed by agreement among all users.

But can different psychologists "read" the following observations of another researcher in the same way that members of different symphonies can read a composer's score? "The anxious child, when frustrated, withdrew." "The rat explored the novel environment when given the opportunity to do so." It is immediately apparent that the language used in these descriptions of psychological phenomena can lead to a variety of interpretations of the actual events that occurred. Can independent observers agree that a given behavior or set of behaviors classify a child as "anxious" and "withdrawing," or a rat as "exploring"? What constitutes being "frustrated"? Is it an internal state of the child, his self-report, or some overt behavior? Or is it defined in terms of environmental barriers which prevent the child from engaging in some activity? How different does one environment have to be from another before it becomes "novel"? The serious problems raised by such considerations have led psychologists to seek out various ways of attempting to minimize ambiguity, sharpen the meaning of their terms, and be sure they are talking about the same thing.

Using concepts which have a physical representation (that is, which can be anchored to observable physical reality) is one way of enhancing agreement between people about what a concept means. "The temperature of the water is 90° F" is a more reliable description of the thermal state of the water than the statement, "The water is hot." The first statement is not only a more precise description, but one that can be repeated by different people using the same thermometer (assuming, of course, that what they are measuring does not change).

This statement about the water is really tied to the *operations* used to define its temperature: "A thermometer placed in the water registered 90° F." Such a usage is called an *operational definition*, a term coined by the physicist Bridgman. His radical view is most clearly expressed in his own words:

"The new attitude toward a concept is entirely different. We may illustrate by considering the concept of length: what do we mean by the length of an object? We evidently know what we mean by length if we can tell what the length of any and every object is, and for the physicist nothing more is required. To find the length of an object, we have to perform certain physical operations. The concept of length is therefore fixed when the operations by which length is measured are fixed: that is, the concept of length involves as much as and nothing more than the set of operations by which length is determined. In general, we mean by any concept nothing more than a set of operations; *the concept is synonymous with the corresponding set of operations.*" (Bridgman, 1927, p. 5)

According to this principle, "anxiety" could be described in terms of the test (either verbal or nonverbal) which is used to measure it. Or it could be described as a consequence of specific environmental events (operations) which are presumed to elicit it.

Making use of advances in instrumentation. Just as the use of a ruler increased the accuracy of your observation of the lengths of the lines in the Müller-Lyer illusion, so the use of instrumentation is crucial in all science to extend the range, precision, and accuracy of our observations. It has been said that man occupies a place between the planets and the atom; before he could land on one and split the other, he needed a telescope and a microscope.

Major advances in science are very often correlated with the development of new instruments which make possible better control of some causal part of the phenomenon, as well as more accurate observation, recording, and measurement of its effects. For example, much of our present knowledge of the brain has come since the 1920s, when W. R. Hess, a Swiss physiologist, developed a microelectrode that could be used to stimulate a tiny portion of the brain of a living, active organism. ■

Measurement: from "yes or no" to "how much?" An event becomes *data* when its signal is recorded by an observer. ● (p. 38) It becomes *reliable data* when a second observer makes the same recording of its signal. This basic process of scientific investigation requires that there be *standardized* ways of making the observations, measuring the event, and recording its occurrence (existence) and its characteristics (the nature of what is occurring). Measurement involves an explicit set of rules for transforming events taking place in physical reality into symbolic representations

■ **THE SKINNER BOX**

A development in instrumentation that opened new vistas of research on learning and has had an important influence on the direction such research has taken is a simplified learning situation first developed by B. F. Skinner. Pictured here are a modern version of the "Skinner box" for rat subjects, with a bar which the animal presses to obtain food, and an adaptation of the apparatus for pigeon subjects. When the pigeon pecks the disk correctly, food is delivered below.

of those events. These rules specify the standard or unvarying aspect of the environment against which the events to be measured are evaluated. They also state the procedures to be used in applying this standard to the event. For example, when you measured the length of the line in the Müller-Lyer illusion, you implicitly used a set of rules about keeping the ruler at a certain angle relative to the line, using a straight ruler (rather than a curved one) to measure the line, and so on.

The symbols used in these transformations are

● We assume that sun spots were occurring long before men became aware that there was such a thing. They did not become *data*, however, until Galileo recorded his observations of them in his notebook, a page of which is reproduced here.

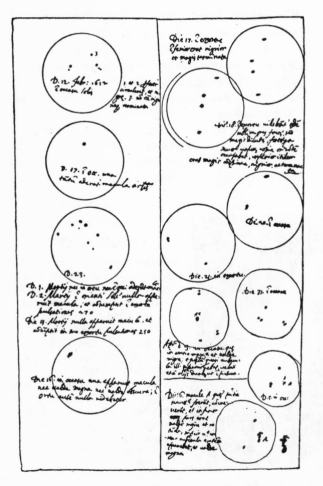

purely arbitrary (for example, inches or centimeters), and are determined by common agreement among a group of observers. It is important to remember that these symbolic representations are not *the reality,* but convenient *translations* of it. Therefore, they can themselves be transformed into other equivalent symbols without loss of meaning (such as Fahrenheit to centigrade, numbers in base ten to other bases or to logarithms, etc.).

The set of such individual instances of *prime data* (only one symbolic step transformed from the observed occurrence) must always be organized and summarized in some way. It is then possible for an interpreter of the data to note general or abstract qualities of these events as a group. For example, the achievement test scores of the individual members of a freshman class (*prime data*) can be summarized as "the average achievement of this year's class" (one form of *secondary data*) and this average can then be compared with that of last year's class. Other secondary data, such as the percentage scoring above a certain level or the average achievement for particular subgroups, such as prep- or public-school students, can also be reconstructed from these prime data.

Advances in science depend largely upon the researcher's ability to analyze a problem into measurable components. There is much that can be said about measurement in psychology; indeed, it is the major preoccupation of many psychologists. However, all we can do in these introductory remarks is to outline some basic measurement operations. In subsequent chapters, the question of how to measure various psychological phenomena will come up repeatedly and will be discussed in the context of the relevant behaviors and environmental events being measured.

Measurement in psychology, as in other fields, may be defined as assigning numbers to persons, objects, or events in accordance with certain rules. Psychologists make use of four different *scales of measurement: nominal, ordinal, interval,* and *ratio* scales. Each of these scales has certain distinguishing characteristics, as described below.

Nominal scales. The lowest level of measurement —that is, the level of measurement which imparts the least information—is the nominal scale. Numbers are used only to distinguish one individual or group from another. Examples of the use of the nominal scale are the numbering of football players, of congressional districts, and of license plates. The numbers used do not represent an *amount* of anything, nor does a high number stand for more of something than a low number. The numbers merely differentiate one individual or class from another. Some argument might be made as to whether this is measurement at all, but it does fall under the definition, "assigning numbers to persons, objects, or events according to certain rules."

The essence of measurement on the nominal scale is *qualitative classification.* We might classify registered voters by assigning to them the number of the congressional district in which they live. Since there are many persons in the same congressional district, each number would be assigned to more than one individual. In some uses of nominal measurement, there is only one person per class. This is the case with social security numbers or with the numbering of license plates.

While a particular category may contain more than one individual, no individual may be assigned to more than one category. A person cannot be in two congressional districts, nor can a football player have two numbers. Thus in nominal measurement persons, objects, or events are put into *mutually exclusive* categories.

Ordinal scales. Measurement on an ordinal scale not only distinguishes one individual from another, but also tells us whether a person has more or less of the trait being measured than other persons in the group. An example of the ordinal scale is the order in which runners cross the finish line in a race. The runner who finishes first is faster than the runner who finishes second, who in turn is faster than the runner who finishes third, and so on. By noting the order in which the runners cross the finish line, we have measured their speed on the ordinal scale.

Ordinal measurement, however, gives no information as to the amount of difference between two individuals in the trait being measured. Thus, although we know that the first-place runner is faster than the second-place runner, we do not know how much faster. Nor do we know whether the difference

in speed between the first- and second-place runners is the same as between the third- and fourth-place runners. Ordinal measurement is used quite frequently by psychologists, because psychological traits are often difficult to measure on a quantitative scale.

Interval scales. The interval scale has all the properties of the nominal and ordinal scales and in addition the property of equal units. This means that equal differences in scores represent equal differences in what is being measured. An example of the interval scale is the temperature scale, as found on a thermometer. The difference in temperature between 99 and 100 degrees centigrade is the same as the difference between 49 and 50 degrees centigrade, or any other difference of one degree centigrade. In other words, the *intervals* are equal throughout the scale. By measuring temperature on an *interval* scale we know not only that one object is hotter or colder than another, but also *how much* hotter or colder.

Measurement on the interval scale does not, however, give us information as to the ratio of two objects with respect to the quantity being measured. Thus, it would be incorrect to say that an object whose temperature is 50 degrees centigrade is twice as warm as an object of 25 degrees. This statement would be correct if 0 degrees centigrade were an absolute zero—that is, if an object at 0 degrees had no warmth at all. In fact, however, absolute zero occurs at −273 degrees centigrade. Thus, an object at 25 degrees is really 298 degrees warmer than absolute zero, and an object at 50 degrees is 323 degrees warmer than absolute zero. The second object, then, is clearly not twice as warm as the first.

Ratio scales. The ratio scale is the highest level of measurement. It has all the properties of the lower scales, and the additional property of an absolute zero as its point of origin. This is the scale upon which the common physical measurements of length, time, and weight are made. Since the scale has an absolute zero, statements of ratios are meaningful. Thus, a six-inch line is twice as long as a three-inch line, a two-pound object is one fifth as heavy as a ten-pound object, and so on.

Psychologists usually have no knowledge of the absolute zero point of the measuring devices they use and therefore must be wary of talking about percentages or other proportions. For example, given that Mary has an IQ of 100 and Susan has an IQ of 110, we cannot say that Susan is 10 percent brighter than Mary. There are, however, rare instances in psychological measurement where such statements are possible.

The properties of these four common measurement scales can be summarized as follows:

Properties	Nominal Scale	Ordinal Scale	Interval Scale	Ratio Scale
Classification	X	X	X	X
Order		X	X	X
Equal Units			X	X
Absolute Zero				X

As can be seen in the table, each of these levels of measurement has all the properties of lower levels, plus an additional property. The higher the level of measurement, the more information is given about the attribute being measured. It is for this reason that psychologists, as well as other scientists, strive to use the highest level of measurement possible in a given situation.

A hypothesis is for testing. Once the scientist has confidence that his data collection procedures provide facts that he can trust, his interest focuses upon interrelating those facts and discovering their causes.

Every investigation into the causal nature of a phenomenon starts with a *hypothesis*. Hypotheses are suggested solutions to the problem of how two or more events or variables are related. They are stated in a precise form, with implications that can be tested by observation and logical inference.

There are no rules for how one comes up with a good hypothesis. It depends on the scientist's knowledge, his ability to analyze and to synthesize, his creativity, and sometimes, as we shall see, on chance. But even in the face of a "lucky" or chance discovery (such as Fleming's discovery of penicillin from moldy bread), "chance favors only the prepared mind," according to Pasteur.

The critical task of the investigator is to specify all of the *alternative hypotheses* about what could be the cause or causes of the phenomenon. He then pro-

ceeds by the *strategy of elimination* to reject those hypotheses which he finds do not adequately account for the observed event. As false hypotheses are eliminated, the investigator emerges with a single hypothesis which seems preferable to its rivals. He then uses objective procedures to test the adequacy of this hypothesis.

But as we pointed out earlier, confidence in it is never absolute. Even hypotheses that have been supported by many studies, and finally given the elevated status of laws, are not considered to be "proved." They are still assumed to be only provisional—the best available truth at this time. The investigator can never assume that his initial set of hypotheses was exhaustive and included the true causal law of the phenomenon.

It should be noted that some researchers believe that it is wrong for psychologists to begin their investigation with preconceived hypotheses before they see the data. They feel that hypotheses are theoretical abstractions which can unduly bias the observer. His attention may be directed toward only one set of events while more significant ones go unnoticed or denied. Opponents of this view argue that all data collection is guided by some hypothesis even if it is not made explicit.

The Proof of the Science Is in the Experiment

In "real-life" settings, experiments are occurring all the time. In fact, you have probably conducted many natural experiments yourself. A few brief examples will suffice to illustrate the point.

1. Deep in California forests, some trees grow *horizontally*, sometimes for many feet before changing direction and growing vertically. ◆ Next to these trees are others which do grow in the expected vertical direction. The cause of this difference appears to be the differing accessibility of sunlight. Here nature has arranged an experiment in which the location of available sunlight is varied, apparently causing different growth patterns.

2. Some children have parents who are very demanding and set high standards, while others have parents who are very permissive and relaxed about the child's performance. Some pupils with a high level of intelligence consistently do poorly in school

◆ Clusters of redwoods have blocked the sun from smaller trees like this laurel. Its response has been to grow out horizontally to an open area of sunlight before growing vertically.

examinations, while others excel. Here are two sets of naturally existing variations. If we find that there is a consistent relationship between them, it may be that they are causally related in some way.

3. After a series of unsuccessful dates, a college student changes his "line" from one that comes on strong to a soft sell. His date is more responsive to him than previous dates. What can he conclude?

Such naturally occurring experiments suffer from the host of problems outlined at the beginning of this chapter. Without more information we are unable to narrow down the many alternative hypotheses that could account for the observed relationship. This brings us to the central paradox facing the person who wants to understand the causes of things. He must contrive an *artificial* situation in order to study and know *natural* events because observing alone does not reveal how things "are," but only how they appear. And Nature, like Mr. F. B. (the psychotic in Chapter 1), disguises her secrets in many ways.

Using an analogy from the area of signal detection, we might say that in everyday situations the "signals" we are interested in (conformity or parental pressure or whatever "signal" we are studying) are accompanied by so much "noise" (unrelated events or processes that are also present) that they do not stand out clearly enough for us to "read" them. The natural signal may be very strong (stronger, in fact, than could be generated artificially), but so is the noisy background. • (p. 42)

The contrived laboratory experiment attempts to simulate the two (or more) natural signals which are specified in the hypothesis, while minimizing the noise-to-signal ratio. It thus gains in precision what it loses in power. However, the most important feature of such an experiment is that it enables the observer to draw causal inferences. A relationship between the signals is established when one of the signals is varied systematically and a corresponding variation occurs in the other.

The laboratory experiment shares the same essential strategy of elimination as Mill's Canons of Proof, summarized on page 32. By varying one factor at a time systematically, we can narrow down alternative hypotheses and increase the probability that a remaining hypothesis is the best causal explanation of the phenomenon. Thus we could test our various hypotheses about why smoking is related to low grades and reject those whose predictions were not borne out.

Independent and dependent variables. The hypothesis that is tested by a laboratory experiment predicts one event from knowledge of another event. The predictor is called the *independent variable*. In experiments it is the thing which is *systematically varied* (manipulated) by the experimenter. The effect which is dependent upon it is the thing which is predicted. Accordingly, it is labelled the *dependent variable*.

In psychology the dependent variable is always some measure of behavior. More specifically, it is some observable, measurable unit of behavior—a *response* (R). The response can be a molar one such as an action (e.g., running, hitting, crying), a test score, or a verbal report. It can also be a molecular one, such as heart rate or brain wave activity.

The part of the psychological environment which is varied is typically some *stimulus* element (S). A stimulus is conceptualized as some change in physical energy which is capable of being detected by some receptor of the organism studied. The *causal* relationship (between a stimulus and a response) is termed an S → R law. In comparison, the *correlational* connection discussed earlier, where both variables are responses of the organism, is an R − R law; here one cannot be assumed to be the cause of the other, as we saw in several of the newspaper examples.

Although there are certain technical differences among them, the following pairs of terms are often used interchangeably:

cause — effect
independent variable — dependent variable
stimulus — response

Regardless of the particular terms used, they must be *operationally defined* if there is to be agreement about what is being related to what.

Control is essential. The most crucial feature of an experiment is its attempt to *control* all conditions that might prevent a clear, unambiguous test of the hypothesis. For example, any relevant variables that could either add to or obscure the effects of the independent variable must be held constant for all subjects (Ψ Close-up, p. 43).

These and other controls are achieved through a variety of techniques. We will describe them only in general terms for the moment, but they will be illustrated more concretely when we analyze specific experiments throughout the remainder of this book.

To understand better the function of these experimental controls, it will be helpful to begin by examining the concept of variability in responding, or *response variance*. Behavior is always influenced by a multitude of factors. The behavior of a subject in a

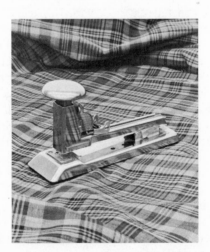

● The relation of signal to noise is like the relation of a visual figure to the background. A clear figure against a gray background stands out clearly, whereas the more structured and heterogeneous the background becomes, the more difficult it is to identify the outlines of the figure and distinguish it clearly from the background.

The variables being investigated in psychological research are like the figures in pictures. Often, especially in "real life," they do not stand out clearly enough from the context in which we see them operating to let us identify and measure them. By studying them in the laboratory we get both the *advantage* of being rid of the "noise" of the background and the *disadvantage* of having to create the figure artificially, with the result that it may be a weak or incomplete representation of the variable that occurs naturally outside the laboratory.

Ψ *Close-up* *A Typical Experimental Design*

Two groups are chosen randomly from the same population. Both are given the same pretest and posttest, during which all relevant variables (directions, room temperature, time allowed, and so on) are the same for both groups. So far as is known, the only systematic difference during the interval between pretest and posttest for the two groups is the difference in the experimental treatment. The change in learning performance for each group is determined by subtracting pretest from posttest scores. If the experimental group has changed more than the control group, the difference is attributed to the difference in the experimental treatment. Is it clear to you what the independent and dependent variables are here?

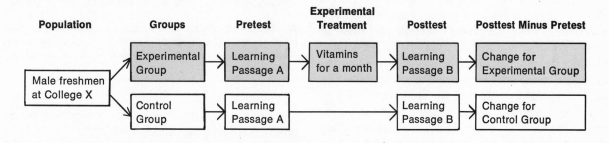

given setting may vary from one period of observation to another period, and the behavior of different individuals exposed to the same environmental stimuli at the same time may also vary.

Thus, the question we must pose in our research is: "How much of the observed response variance can be attributed to variations in the manipulated independent variable(s) and how much of it can be attributed to other sources?" The first of these, which is what the researcher is interested in studying, is referred to as *true variance*, while the second is called *error variance*. A good research design attempts to minimize the error variance, thereby increasing the proportion of the total variance which can be attributed to the experimental manipulation.

Error variance can arise from two sources—randomly occurring and systematically occurring error. *Random error* affects the response when, for example, a loud noise happens to occur accidentally, and distracts the experimental subject. Sometimes it will affect the response in one direction, sometimes in the other. But whatever the specific effect, it is always

unpredictable. *Systematic error* has a predictable effect on the response, since it occurs with regularity and consistently biases the response in one direction. For example, an attractive female experimenter might inadvertently induce her male subjects to try harder in her presence than in her absence.

Both random and systematic error are reduced by the use of experimental controls. Such controls also sharpen our understanding of the sources of true variance. Six major controls are employed:

Environmental control. A testing environment is constructed in which extraneous stimuli (such as sounds, lights, temperature changes, etc.) can be eliminated or minimized. The experimental setting is also designed to make more probable the occurrence of the behavior being investigated, relative to other irrelevant behaviors. For example, the likelihood that a hungry animal will press a bar which delivers a food reward can be increased by putting him in a small chamber in which the bar is the most prominent stimulus object.

Procedural control. The use of standardized instructions and stimuli, as well as consistent modes of presenting them, are features that must be built into every experiment. In addition, the observations must be made in the same way for all subjects and by all observers. The subject's task and the response alternatives must also be identical for all subjects. The *double-blind* procedure mentioned in Chapter 1 is a common form of procedural control.

Selection control. One goal of an experiment is often to demonstrate that the behavior of subjects will differ after those in one group have been exposed to a change in the independent variable and those in another group have not. Therefore, the subjects must not differ in this particular behavior *before* the independent variable is presented. Initial comparability can be achieved by *matching* the subjects in the two groups on as many variables as are thought to be related to the variables being investigated. This is often difficult because it requires a large population from which samples can be drawn and matched on a number of factors (sex, socioeconomic class, length of hospitalization, grade-point average, number of cigarettes smoked per day). Moreover, one can never anticipate all the variables which might bear an important relationship to those under study.

Randomization is an alternate way of obtaining pretest similarity among different groups of subjects. Individuals drawn from some larger group (college sophomores, for example) are assigned to various experimental treatments purely by chance, or random, procedures (perhaps a flip of a coin or, better, use of a table of randomly generated numbers). It can then be *assumed* that there are no systematic initial differences between subjects in the groups before they are differentially exposed to the independent variable and that both groups are equally representative of the larger group from which they were drawn.

An example of what can occur when randomization is not used to select experimental subjects is taken from a military study. The subject selection procedure involved picking every thirty-second name on a list of soldiers. This resulted in a sample composed only of sergeants, since (unknown to the researchers) the list was systematically organized with each sergeant's name followed by the names of the

This "free environment" cage provided the rats with more stimulating surroundings and more chances to explore and be active than are present in the usual laboratory cage.

thirty-one men in his unit. This group was hardly representative of the list as a whole.

Another instance of the importance of randomization is a study focusing on the effects of different lengths of time spent in an "enriched" environment on subsequent exploratory behavior in young rats. The experimental design called for some rats to be taken out of the special environment ■ after 25 days, others after 50 days, and the rest after 100 days. Without a random selection procedure specifying *in advance* which subjects would be taken out each time, the groups might well have been composed of different types of rats. That is, the experimenter would have been likely to pull out of the cage first those animals which he could get most easily—the ones that didn't run away or bite when he touched them. Thus the 25-day group might have included the most docile rats and the 100-day group the most aggressive and agile ones.

Statistical control. Some degree of analytical control may be introduced by statistical techniques applied after the experiment is completed. These techniques estimate the effects of possible influential but uncontrollable variables on the variables being studied. One such technique is *covariance analysis*. When it is known that the subjects do differ in some way but the differences can be measured, their influence can be isolated statistically from that of the independent variable. For example, in studying the effects of electric shock on running speed in subjects that were known to differ in weight, the experimenter could use covariance analysis to be sure that it was the variations in shock and not the differences in weight that were causing any differences he found in running speed.

Control groups. "The groups using Crest had 38 percent fewer cavities!" When you ask "fewer than what?" you are asking for information about the control group, the basis for comparing the relative effectiveness of the treatment. You would not run out to buy Crest if the answer to your question was, "fewer than people who never brushed their teeth." You would demand that the comparison control group do everything the experimental group did— brushed their teeth with the same frequency, had similar diets (especially with regard to fluoridated water), and were drawn from the same initial population (same age, health, etc.).

A control group shares all characteristics and treatments with the experimental group *except* for the independent variable, the thing whose effect is being studied. If there is a difference between the two groups later, we can infer that the cause of the difference was the experimental treatment—the change in the independent variable for the experimental group.

The most direct comparison between treatment and nontreatment effects occurs in a *yoked control.* In this procedure, two subjects are tested simultaneously under virtually identical conditions except for the difference in the independent variable. (This technique was utilized by Joseph Brady in a study of ulcers in "executive" monkeys which we shall discuss shortly.)

A control for initial differences in heredity when studying the effects of some training procedure is the *co-twin control.* One of a pair of identical twins is randomly assigned to receive the experimental treatment (for example, early training in language) while the other does not receive it. Both twins are then given a performance test. With animals, such as rats, that have large litters (averaging about eight pups), experimenters may use the *split-litter control,* randomly assigning the members *within each litter* to the experimental and control groups.

Finally, in some studies the investigator does not want to compare one subject with another, but to compare each subject with himself. This *within-subject control* makes each subject a complete experiment in himself. His response to the independent variable manipulation (or some level of it) can be compared to his response in the absence of it. Such a procedure reduces the systematic error variance because the responses of one person are likely to be less variable than are the responses of two different people. To put it another way, what is common in his response to both the experimental and control treatment can be subtracted from the variation in his response to each treatment separately. Within-subject research designs are used effectively to assess the impact of some stimulus upon the ongoing behavior of an organism, as well as the change that occurs in a given individual following exposure to a treatment variable.

Of course, there are many problems which cannot be studied using this within-subject procedure. If the subject is permanently changed after he receives one treatment, he will not respond to the second one as he would have initially. An example of this is the effect of relaxation training upon anxiety experienced during a woman's first pregnancy. Her second pregnancy cannot serve as a control condition (*no* relaxation training), because she is no longer anxious, as a result of the first training.

Where possible, when a single subject receives successive exposures to, or administrations of, the independent variable, they must be *counterbalanced.* Thus in studying the effects of two levels of a drug on performance, an investigator might have the subject receive the drug in a High-Low-Low-High sequence. This A-B-B-A sequence ensures that the effect of Low is not due simply to the fact that it follows High.

The major criticism leveled against most experiments is their failure to include some control group or procedure which is logically necessary in order to rule out an alternative hypothesis. This is more true in the behavioral sciences than in the physical sciences because the variables affecting the behavior of organisms are not easily separable for analytical purposes. They are "strongly coupled" rather than "weakly coupled," as Warren Weaver (1955) describes it. Therefore, the number of elements to be controlled

Ψ *Close-up* **Mean, Variability, and Correlation**

In our discussion of research findings we will occasionally mention the terms *mean*, *variability*, and *correlation*. Their meanings are briefly summarized here. For a fuller explanation of statistical terms, see Appendix B.

1. To describe a group's performance (and be able to compare it with that of another group), you need two things: a single number *typical* enough to represent the whole group of numbers, and a number that tells how widely the scores *vary*, or are scattered.

　　a) The most typical number is a *measure of central tendency,* known more familiarly as an *average*. The three kinds of average most often used are the *mean* (sum of the scores divided by the number of scores), the *median* (the score in the middle when all the scores are lined up from the lowest to the highest), and the *mode* (the score gotten most often). For a graphic demonstration of the practical differences among these three, see the Ψ Close-up on page 47.
　　b) Measures of variability tell whether the scores cluster closely or are spread out. The measures of variability most often used are the *range* of the scores (from lowest to highest) and the *standard deviation,* a measure of the average variation of the individual scores from the group mean.

2. To describe the relationships between two sets of scores for the same individuals (intelligence and grades, for example), in order to know whether you can predict one from knowing the other, you use a formula to obtain a *coefficient of correlation* (r). This figure tells you whether there is a relationship and if so whether it is positive or negative and how strong or weak it is.

Coefficients of correlation range from *minus one* (-1.0), which would mean perfect *negative* correlation (as intelligence gets higher, grades get lower), through *zero* (0), which would mean no correlation at all, to *plus one* ($+1.0$), which would mean perfect positive correlation (as intelligence goes up so do grades). Perfect correlations are rarely found, however. A "moderate" correlation would be between .25 and .60 (either $+$ or $-$); a "high" correlation would be between .70 and .99. The table on page 670 shows how the accuracy of prediction increases as the coefficient approaches 1.0.

can be rather large. Each investigator must decide in advance which elements he believes will not make a difference and which ones will. What he controls depends upon his knowledge of the phenomena, the practical limitations imposed by his available resources, and his ingenuity in devising proper controls for what he knows ought to be controlled.

Drawing conclusions through statistical inference. We finally come to the last step in the long process of drawing a conclusion from a set of observations. The data have been collected properly, and a behavioral difference between the experimental and control groups emerges. Can we conclude that the independent variable was responsible for this difference, and thus that the experimental hypothesis has been confirmed? After all this investment of time, energy, intellect, and money, our objective scientist might be inclined to see any difference, however accidental or trivial, as a "real" one. He safeguards himself against such a temptation by agreeing in advance to a convention shared by all his colleagues on what will be regarded as a *significant difference*.

In using statistical inference procedures, the researcher begins by formulating what is called a *null hypothesis* (H_0): the hypothesis that the observed differences occurred solely by chance. His task is then to determine, through the use of coldly objective statistical tests, whether the differences are large enough to warrant *rejecting* the null hypothesis. This determines how much confidence can be placed in the original, experimental hypothesis (H_1) that the difference is produced by the manipulated variable and *not* merely by chance.

The statistical tests used vary according to the nature of the data collected, but all yield the same final *probability statement*, an estimate of the probability that the difference is a chance occurrence. This probability statement is what makes it possible for psychologists to adopt a common rule for deciding when an experiment has "worked." A result is accepted as a real one and is labeled "statistically significant" only when the probability (p) that the difference could have occurred by chance is less than five in one hundred ($p < .05$). This is the most lenient level of significance permitted, and for some problems it is still not acceptable. More stringent require-

Average Is As Average Does

In being interviewed for a part-time job, you are promised an average salary and you have heard from other sources that the firm's average salary is over $12,000. You rush to take the job. Only later do you find that you are receiving a salary of $2001. But that too is "average," with half the workers getting even less.

The distribution on the right shows where you fit. There are 21 employees, of whom 10 get more than you and 10 get less. Thus you are getting the *median*. More employees get $2000 than anything else, making it the *mode*. The sum of the salaries is $259,501, which, divided by 21, gives $12,357, the *mean*. Know your statistics before you leap.

			X	
1	Boss		$100,000	
2	Son		$50,000	
3	Uncle		$25,000	
4	Brother		$15,000	← mean—"average"
5	Cousin		$10,000	
6-10	Senior men		$7,500	
11	You →		$2,001	← median—"average"
12-20	Slaves		$2,000	← mode—"average"

ments are imposed on conclusion-drawing as the consequences of making a false conclusion become more serious (e.g., if someone's life depends upon it, or sizable resources will be committed to following its implications). In this case, a probability level of .01 might be demanded. However, in the final analysis, any statistics (and conclusions based on them) are only as good as the quality of the data fed into the formulas. Thus, rigorous adherence to proper procedure is the quality control of science for observation, data collection, and experimental design.

The pros and cons of experimenting with human and nonhuman subjects. You may often have found yourself wondering why, if psychologists are primarily interested in finding out about human behavior, so many of their experiments make use of animals as subjects. Subhuman subjects are often studied by psychologists for the following reasons:

a) they are less complex than human beings, making it easier to observe some behavior patterns which might not be as apparent in humans;

b) hereditary and environmental factors can be experimentally controlled;

c) they have shorter life spans than the experimenter, which allows him to investigate transmission of an effect over several generations;

d) they can be used to study problems which

have direct relevance for human behavior, but cannot be investigated because of moral issues.

In addition, there are psychologists who are not merely interested in studying animal behavior for the light it might shed on human functioning. Rather, they are interested in the field in its own right, because they want to discover the general laws of the behavior of organisms. Comparative psychologists and ethologists typically have this orientation in studying the behavior of subhuman species. The use of animals in experimental psychological research is a characteristically American enterprise which was encouraged by the behaviorist movement, of which we will hear more in later chapters.

Whenever an experimental subject—particularly a human being—is subjected to a procedure which changes him in some way, an ethical question must be raised. The experimenter tries to find a test of his hypothesis which will maintain the integrity of his subjects. However, he must decide whether particular inconveniences or experimental disturbances to the subject or infringements upon the subject's privacy are justified in terms of the potential contribution of the experiment. It should improve our knowledge about how organisms behave, and hopefully will improve their life. But the issue is always with us, and there are no easy rules for resolving such ethical dilemmas.

A Grant for Your Thoughts

Any student can be trained to be relatively proficient in the use of research designs, control procedures, experimental methods, and statistical analysis. But we have thus far paid scant attention to one very critical aspect of the process: where does the original idea to be tested come from? This is clearly the most creative part of scientific discovery, and there are no rules or known pedagogical techniques to help the curious mind come up with a good hypothesis.

Hypotheses come from a variety of sources. For example, hypotheses can be: (a) derived from a theory; (b) perceived as a consequence of conflicting or anomalous observations or theories; (c) derived from intensive analysis of a single case (whether it be oneself or someone else); (d) discovered accidentally, "serendipitously"; (e) developed in attempts to understand a complex phenomenon which puzzles the observer; (f) developed as a consequence of trying to change an existing condition of life.

In later chapters we will see how a great deal of research (especially in the area of learning) has been stimulated by theoretically derived hypotheses and by the attempt to reconcile a conflict of experimental findings or competing theories. Freud's ideas about the nature of human motivation will be presented in Chapter 11 as the best illustration of hypotheses generated from intensive self-analysis and from probing in depth the behavior of a relatively small number of patients. In the present chapter, we will elaborate on two of the sources of hypotheses listed because in doing so we can review some of the principles developed thus far. This discussion will also allow us to introduce some additional concepts which will complete our introduction to the psychological approach. We can then turn our focus in the following chapters to the *content* of psychological investigations, as we will be in a better position to appreciate the development and merit of the generalizations we will encounter.

Serendipity: Observing how executive monkeys get ulcers. To discover one thing while looking for something else is called *serendipity,* a beautiful word coined by the physiologist Walter Cannon. He took the term from Walpole's story "Three Princes of Ser-

endip." The princes traveled throughout the world and did not find what they were searching for, but instead discovered many other interesting things. This process of discovery, while exciting and glamorous to read about, actually occurs infrequently; but when it does occur, it may result in a major discovery, as in Pavlov's accidental discovery of "psychic secretions," which led to the formulation of the basic principles of conditioning (to be described in Chapter 5).

Of considerable interest is the little known story of the discovery of the major psychological and physiological variables which can cause the development of ulcers (Brady, Porter, Conrad, & Mason, 1958; Brady, 1970). A number of years ago, in the psychological research laboratories of Walter Reed Army Hospital, the incidence of monkeys dying from ulcers suddenly increased. This was quite unusual because ulcer-precipitated deaths are rare among monkeys. What could be causing this reaction?

Dr. Joseph Brady, director of the laboratory, and his colleagues began their investigation into this problem with an *ex post facto* analysis. That is, they used a retrospective, after the fact, analysis of what could have been the common experience in the experimental treatment of the afflicted monkeys. These monkeys had been in very different studies—some on brain stimulation, some on effects of drugs, some on learning. But the common element in all these situations was that the animal had to learn a response to avoid the punishment of being electrically shocked (called avoidance learning). If the animal made a given response (e.g., pressing a lever within a short time after a light came on), no shock was delivered. But shock was delivered if the subject failed to react quickly enough to the signalling cue of the light.

Three alternative hypotheses were generated which could account for the mysterious ulcers: (a) being confined in the restricting experimental chair for long periods leads to ulcers; (b) getting shocked leads to ulcers; (c) the stress from having to work to avoid the shock leads to ulcers.

The experiment devised to eliminate some of these possibilities employed a *yoked-control* design. A pair of monkeys was confined in the apparatus shown in the photograph. •   The experimental monkey had to press a lever within twenty seconds of the appearance of the cue light to avoid shock. If he failed to do so, *both* monkeys were shocked simultaneously (thus controlling for the number and pattern of shocks). The only difference was that the control monkey's lever was nonfunctional: pressing it had no effect on the environment. When the working partner pressed the lever at the appropriate time, both monkeys avoided shock; when he did not, both got a jolt. Nothing the control monkey did could help him avoid the shock.

Because of space limitations in the laboratory, the pair of monkeys had to be tested in the office of a new staff member (not in a position to complain). Since he used his office from 10 A.M. to 4 P.M. (6 hours), the monkeys were run for six hours (4 P.M. to 10 P.M.), rested for six hours (10 P.M. to 4 A.M.), run from 4 A.M. to 10 A.M., rested while the office was being used, and so on. While the monkey responsible for the shock soon learned to respond very efficiently, eventually allowing very few shocks for him and his partner, the control monkey soon stopped pressing his lever, and just sat there squealing whenever an occasional shock did come on.

After twenty-eight days of this procedure, the hard-working experimental monkey died, but the control did not. An autopsy of both monkeys revealed that the "executive" monkey (given the responsibility of being vigilant and controlling the environment) had died of a perforated ulcer, while the control monkey had remained in perfect health throughout the experiment.

A replication of this procedure with three more yoked pairs of monkeys was conducted with the same outcome. All of the experimental monkeys died of ulcers within twenty-five to thirty-five days, while the controls remained healthy.

This result was taken as strong support for the hypothesis that the psychological stress of maintaining the avoidance response caused the ulcers. If this line of reasoning is correct, then by application of Mill's canon of concomitant variation it would be expected that increasing the stress would increase the rapidity with which ulcers were developed.

The young faculty member was moved out of his office, and three groups of monkeys were tested with the following work-to-rest schedules: two hours work/one hour rest, six hours work/one hour rest, twelve hours work/one hour rest. Contrary to expectation, none of the subjects had died after two months. In desperation, the researchers had monkeys working almost constantly (twenty-four hours work/zero hours rest). Apparently, the animals learned to take cat-naps of less than twenty seconds duration. After working on this slave-labor schedule continuously for thirty days, the animals were tired, but alive!

Unable to understand how the phenomenon had been lost, the researchers superstitiously put the young faculty member back in his office and had six pairs of monkeys working on the six hours on, six hours off schedule. Within a month, four of the experimental monkeys died of ulcers, one got tuberculosis, and one developed pancreatic malfunctioning. The controls were, as ever, quite healthy.

If variations in the work period (holding the rest period constant) did not affect the dependent variable, then perhaps variations in the rest period (holding the work period constant) might have an effect.

● In the "executive monkey" study, conditions for the two monkeys were identical except that one had a lever which would postpone the shock for both of them (left), whereas the other monkey had only a dummy lever (right).

Brady now added one additional feature—every hour he recorded levels of hormonal secretions in the monkeys' stomachs while they worked or rested. All monkeys now worked for six hours and the rest period was varied from one to eight hours. The results obtained were that:

1. Ulcers developed only in animals who rested for at least six hours between work periods.

2. While there was no increase in hormonal secretions *during* stress periods or during short rest periods, pepsinogens were secreted after two hours of rest and increased until a maximum level of secretion was reached after six hours of rest. These secretions are the physiological agent responsible for the breakdown of the stomach lining.

3. Initiation of a new stress period before secretions were at their maximal level inhibited further secretions.

We can see in this experimental case study that the chance factors which determined the initial work/rest schedule and eventually led to the discovery of the phenomenon were capitalized on by the researchers' previous training and skills. Can we also generalize that it is not the work that kills us, but the vacations?

Control of irrational behavior: cigarette smoking. The final source of hypotheses suggested on page 48 was research undertaken to try to change some existing but undesired condition. One such undesired condition today for many people is the smoking habit. In the survey of 3567 University of Illinois freshmen we discussed earlier, in connection with the relationship between smoking and grades, 90 percent said they believed that cigarette smokers had a greater chance of developing cancer than did nonsmokers. Nevertheless, 40 percent reported that they were smokers, and half of these said they wanted to stop, but could not. This finding is probably a typical one across the country and parallels the irrational behavior of most smokers who went right on smoking after the Surgeon General's report appeared.   ◆

If psychologists are interested in the understanding and control of human behavior, and if there are individuals who wish to moderate or eliminate their smoking behavior, then here is surely a ripe area for research. An excellent review of attempts to modify smoking behavior (Bernstein, 1969) reveals that

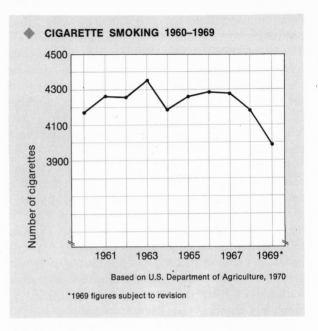

◆ **CIGARETTE SMOKING 1960–1969**

Number of cigarettes

Based on U.S. Department of Agriculture, 1970

*1969 figures subject to revision

much attention has indeed been given to this practical problem.

The question of the motivations involved in the maintenance of smoking behavior—particularly in individuals who profess a desire to quit—is an extremely complex one. Numerous hypotheses concerning the behavioral mechanisms involved in such behavior have been advanced. An amazing array of techniques have been used, singly or in combination, in attempts to modify smoking behavior. ■ Such techniques reflect the wide variety of hypotheses—implicit or explicit—held by different workers in this area.

Studies like these could raise a host of questions concerning research methodology. We will consider briefly just two such issues. First, how does the *goal* of the research influence its procedures and conclusions? Second, why is specification of the *criterion* of success so important in studies like these?

One popular approach to overcoming the cigarette habit has been the establishment of "stop-smoking" clinics. One such program (McFarland, Gimbel, Donald, & Folkenberg, 1964) involved a 90- to 120-minute session every day for five days. The combination of techniques used included medical and religious information, lectures, films, demonstrations, discussions, dieting, physical fitness, a buddy system, and others. The result was that of 144 people who *completed* treatment (we are not told how many began), 72.2 percent quit smoking.

If the goal is to make smokers into nonsmokers, then this "total push" clinic approach appears useful. But if you now ask what *caused* those who stopped to do so, or what methods most effectively modify smoking, such research is of little value. Which of all the techniques employed accounts for the change in cigarette consumption? To answer such questions it is necessary, as we have seen, to employ a systematic research design with procedures that permit identification of the causal factors. This would mean making precise hypotheses about cause and effect in the continuation or stopping of smoking and proceeding to test them systematically under controlled conditions.

Such a systematic approach is especially needed in studying problems of this nature, for we often find

▨ **TECHNIQUES USED TO MODIFY SMOKING BEHAVIOR**

---

1. Chewing food a certain number of times before swallowing
2. Keeping especially clean
3. Avoiding profane language
4. Changing diet
5. Rising early
6. Hot baths
7. Cold showers
8. Sending clothes to be cleaned
9. Deep breathing exercises
10. Keeping physically fit
11. Drugs such as lobeline
12. Hypnotic instructions
13. Verbal encouragement
14. Supportive counseling
15. Group discussion
16. Signing a pledge, with loss of a deposit contingent upon breaking it
17. Drug-induced nausea paired with cigarette smoking
18. Aversive stimuli (hot air puff in face) paired with smoking
19. White noise interrupting ongoing pleasant music contingent upon smoking
20. Electric shock contingent upon smoking
21. Saying "Cigarette smoking causes cancer" prior to performing some frequently occurring behavior
22. Role playing a doctor-patient interview where the patient learns that he has lung cancer

---

Based on Bernstein, 1969

that the immediate effect is only temporary. In the study just cited, although 72.2 percent of the smokers had quit by the end of the treatment sessions, only 33.9 percent were still abstaining three months later. Many other studies have had similar results. The significant dependent variable, then, is not immediate change in the behavior, but continued abstinence from smoking over a prolonged period of time. The criterion of success here, as in the use of various therapies with mental patients (to be discussed in Chapter 15), must be long-term rather than short-term effectiveness. It is not important that the mental patient can be released after a given treatment, but that he can continue functioning well enough not to require hospitalization again.

Bernstein concludes that ". . . clinic activity tells us little or nothing about smoking behavior and the ways in which it can be reliably modified" (p. 431). Such activity can, however, serve to generate new hypotheses to be subjected to more rigorous research techniques.

Social Implications of Psychological Research

Science is sometimes considered to be an elegant game, played according to the elaborate set of rules we have been discussing in this chapter, which provides intellectual stimulation for the players and is admired by the spectators because of its apparently mysterious way of discovering new and marvelous things. Viewed in this light, psychology offers an endless source of delight to the mind that is curious about the causes of behavior. Nevertheless, such delight and enjoyment are counterbalanced by the very serious effects that these games can have on human life. Science has produced the atomic bomb, and psychology has been used as a basis for both the Supreme Court's decision on school desegregation and the argument that there are racial differences in intelligence.

When people start placing real money bets on the outcome of the game, rather than merely chalking up the results on their mental blackboards, the rules of the game stay the same, but some of its values change. The objectivity and impartiality which must still govern procedures of data collection, analysis, and presentation are strained when it comes to evaluating research which has direct implications for dealing with social problems.

The issue of providing equal educational opportunities to all children, regardless of race, provides a valuable case in point. If we begin with the undisputed finding from every available source that there is a difference in performance on basic skills tests between black and white children—clearly favoring the latter—a number of alternative directions of inquiry and action are suggested. Is the source of this discrepancy: (a) some basic inherited differences between the two racial groups, (b) the criteria used in evaluating intelligence and educational performance, (c) the formal and informal qualities of the school experience, or (d) the experiences of the child outside of school? Or is it some combination of such factors?

We cannot fully evaluate here all the arguments and evidence put forth with regard to these alternatives. We can only examine briefly some attempts to improve the performance of the black children. We do so to highlight both the dangers of simplistic conclusions regarding complex relationships and the interplay of scientific and nonscientific forces when research evidence affects public action.

The two major forms of intervention designed to provide "access to equal opportunity for maximum development" for all school children are compensatory education (through Head Start and enriched opportunities in elementary school) and integration of previously white schools by bringing in black children from ghetto areas.

Compensatory education assumes some basic deficiency in the child (verbal retardation, lack of motivation, experiential and sensory deprivation) that prevents him from getting the full benefit from normal schooling. Attempts at remedy have usually consisted of reduced teacher-student ratios, cultural enrichment programs, improved classroom materials, and better libraries. Recent widely publicized evaluations of several major programs of compensatory education are in substantial agreement that though some gains have been registered, both in academic achievement and in health and general development, the programs have not solved the problem.

Proponents of compensatory education interpret this conclusion as an indication that the attack must be intensified, with more resources brought to bear. On the other hand, some opponents claim that the results indicate that blacks are inferior in ability and cannot improve as rapidly as whites even under ideal conditions. Still a third group argue that programs so far have been just a "band-aid" approach, with more of what has failed in the past. They claim that what is needed is a basic restructuring and much more innovative programs.

It should be apparent to you in your new role as social and psychological analyst that the value of compensatory programs cannot be analyzed solely in terms of whether factors like more money, more books, or smaller teacher-pupil ratios improve children's achievement. Rather, we will need to find out what is happening to particular aspects of the development of particular children under specified conditions. For example, what kinds of stimulus inputs from a child's environment increase the likelihood that he will: (a) attend to what his teacher and classmates say in class, (b) risk asking questions and giving answers, (c) maintain interest in academic topics for a sustained period of time, and (d) be able to apply his classroom learning outside of school? We can anticipate that to modify the behavior of any individual child along these lines will require bringing about changes in both the nature of the social *motivation* and the pattern of *reinforcement* that he experiences.

This, in turn, means that we must know what his major sources of motivation and reinforcement are at home. Where compensatory education programs have only provided "more of the same," or have not made provision for follow-through, we would predict that the programs would fail. The psychologist's job, then, is to find out more precisely what kinds of programs can produce what results with what children, and how far such interventions may go.

In later chapters we will be discussing the general topics of reinforcement and motivation—but consider for a moment the differences between black and white children in the conditions which provide motivation for their intellectual efforts and reinforcement for their educational achievements.

The average middle-class white student continues

in the educational system because of factors such as pressure and support from parents and friends, intellectual stimulation from classmates and teachers, identification with the implicit and explicit goals of the teachers, and perception of education as a means to the end of better employment. The disadvantaged ghetto child has few of these sources of justification. In the ghetto culture, school is unreal; it is an alien institution which you attend because you get into trouble if you don't. There is no obvious relationship between what happens inside school and outside, on the block. You learn "school wits" to satisfy the teacher, but your culture regards "book learning" as secondary to "street savvy" and "real-life" learning.

Ghetto children find little to identify with in their white middle-class teachers, and on the average their black teachers have, so far, been more poorly trained, with lower vocabulary scores and more deficient backgrounds than white teachers. Because of the insidious network of discrimination which has existed for so many years, there are few older models available among family and friends who have completed high school, college, and graduate schools. There has been little outside-the-school educational support in the form of consistent encouragement for purely intellectual, literary, and cultural pursuits.

Finally, there still exists in many schools the tracking system, in which children are assigned to classes on the basis of presumed differences in level of ability. On the basis of such assignments, often made early in elementary school, a disproportionate number of black and other minority students are limited to vocational and commercial high schools and are thereby excluded from the possibility of ever going to college. Perhaps it is not surprising, then, that the models tend to be those who have beaten the system by "getting rich quick" on natural skills and talents.

In 1969, considerable controversy followed the report of a comprehensive study of the relationship between pupil achievement and various objective school factors (Coleman, 1969). This study had found that achievement was only weakly correlated with physical characteristics of schools, such as class size and how much money was spent per pupil. The controversy, however, has not been over the data—the observed correlations—but over the interpretation of them. Widely differing causal inferences have been drawn from correlational evidence, and public policy (including the voting or withholding of huge sums of money) has been based on these causal inferences.

In going from some of the trivial and "cute" examples of conclusion-drawing found in the mass media examples at the beginning of this chapter to the serious implications involved in attention to improving the education of all citizens, our focus has expanded from considerations of methodology, logic, and analysis, where objectivity is essential, to questions involving social, political, and legal action, where objectivity is not enough (Ψ Close-up, below). The ultimate goal of psychology is the control of behavior, and such control always implies intervention and change. In turn, any attempt to intervene in the

---

Ψ *Close-up*   Science As the Arbiter

The following eloquent statement by the philosophers Cohen and Nagel was made over three decades ago, but it is even more relevant today for our understanding of the real value of scientific inquiry:

"Scientific method is the only effective way of strengthening the love of truth. It develops the intellectual courage to face difficulties and to overcome illusions that are pleasant temporarily but destructive ultimately. It settles differences without any external force by appealing to our common rational nature. The way of science, even if it is up a steep mountain, is open to all. Hence, while sectarian and partisan faiths are based on personal choice or temperament and divide men, scientific procedure unites men in something nobly devoid of all pettiness. Because it requires detachment, disinterestedness, it is the finest flower and test of a liberal civilization." (Cohen & Nagel, 1934, pp. 402-403)

However, the *detachment* which must characterize the data-collection and analysis phases of research must give way to an *attachment* to humanity when it comes time to carry the implications of research out of the laboratory and into the lives of people in the real world.

flow of human behavior, to change what a man is or might become, must rest on value judgments:

Why change?
Change from what to what?
Who will benefit from such change?
Who determines who will be changed and who is to do the changing?

Any answer to these questions inevitably goes beyond the "facts."

Psychologists generally are not Machiavellians, out to control men's minds, but rather are concerned people trying to illuminate the principles of control in order that such knowledge can be used by each man to direct his own behavior better. Nevertheless, it is this question of control which both makes psychology the most exciting intellectual venture and forces it to become a useful tool in every man's struggle for self-knowledge, self-control, and self-fulfillment.

Chapter Summary

Casual observation and common-sense generalizations often lead to faulty conclusions. Reported "facts" may go unquestioned, correlation may be mistaken for causation, and labels devised for classifying individuals may be misused as explanations.

The purpose of scientific inquiry is to limit false conclusion-drawing about natural events by searching systematically for causes. The *scientific method* is a set of assumptions, attitudes, and rules by which an investigator collects and evaluates data and communicates his results to others in such a way that his work can be replicated and either confirmed or challenged. The question of what caused an event can be answered at a *macroscopic* level (for example, cultural influence), at a *molar* level (for example, motives), at a *molecular* level (for example, muscle contractions), or at a *microscopic* level (for example, biochemical processes).

Scientific conclusions are always tentative, pending further information; no hypothesis can be proved once and for all. Conclusions are given in probabilistic terms, stating the likelihood that one's findings are representative of the entire class from which his subjects were drawn and did not occur by chance. Psychologists, like other scientists, try to guard against bias in observation and limit their observations to overt, verifiable events. For the greatest possible clarity, precision, and objectivity, they use concrete terms and *operational definitions*, definitions stated in terms of the operation required to specify the process or event in question. Major advances are often correlated with the development of new instruments that make possible new ways of manipulating the variables or measuring events.

Events become *data* when an observer records them in some way; data are thus symbolic representations of events. *Prime data* (such as the scores of individuals) can be used as the source of *secondary data* (for example, class averages or the performance of certain subgroups).

Scientific investigation requires standardized ways of observing and measuring events and recording both their occurrence and their characteristics. *Measurement* involves an explicit set of rules for transforming events into data; such rules specify the standard against which events are to be measured and the procedures and symbols to be used.

Scales used in psychological measurement range from the *qualitative classification* of a *nominal scale* through three increasingly powerful *quantitative* scales: *ordinal scales,* which give only ranking; *interval scales,* which have equal units; and (rarely) *ratio scales,* in which the absolute zero is known, making statements of ratios meaningful.

An investigation about the cause of some phenomenon starts with one or more *hypotheses.* These are tested and those that are found not to account for the phenomenon are eliminated. Occasionally Nature provides varied conditions, in which the correspondingly varied results give us a test of our hypothesis; more often, we can establish the cause only by the systematic procedures possible in a planned experiment. A laboratory experiment sharpens the "signal" in relation to the "noise" but may give us a weaker or less complete "signal" to measure.

The *independent variable* is the *stimulus condition* that the experimenter manipulates. The *dependent variable* is the *response* that is predicted to change with changes in the independent variable. A *causal relationship* between stimulus and response is called an $S \rightarrow R$ law. A *correlational relationship*, in which two events simply occur together, is called an $R - R$

law; here one cannot be assumed to be the cause of the other.

Variability of response, known as *response variance,* may be *true variance* (the result of the manipulation of the independent variable) or *error variance* (the result of unintended influences). Error variance can arise from *random error* (chance events) or from *systematic error* (a consistently operating variable of which the investigator is unaware). Error variance can be minimized by *environmental control* (elimination or control of extraneous stimuli), *procedural control* (use of standardized instructions, stimuli, and data collection), *selection control* (ensuring that subjects are comparable and representative of the group from which they are taken), *statistical control* (estimating and taking into account by statistical means such as *covariance analysis* the effects of variables not controllable physically), and the use of *control groups.*

Since the goal of an experiment is to show that two groups of individuals differ after one has been exposed to the independent variable and the other has not, the experimenter must make certain that the two groups are as identical as possible before the experiment begins. *Random sampling,* statistical techniques, or *yoked, co-twin, split-litter,* or *within-subject controls* can be used to increase the similarity. The technique of *counterbalancing* (presenting two conditions in both sequences—A followed by B, then B followed by A) ensures that any difference found in behavior is the result of one of the treatment conditions and not of the sequence in which they were presented. Because the variables that can influence behavior are so numerous and so closely related, many control groups may be needed to rule out alternative hypotheses.

If there is a difference in behavior after the experimental treatment, the experimenter determines by statistical means the probability that it could have occurred by chance. If the probability is smaller than .05 (5 chances in a hundred) he rejects the *null hypothesis* (which states that the difference resulted from chance) and concludes that the behavioral difference is real and significant and that the hypothesis about the effects of his manipulation of the independent variable has been supported.

Both for convenience and for ethical reasons, animal subjects are often used instead of human ones. Typically such studies have the goal of shedding light on human functioning, though comparative psychologists and ethologists tend to be interested in animal behavior in its own right.

Hypotheses, the most creative part of scientific inquiry, come from many sources, including (a) theories, (b) conflicting observations, (c) analysis of a single case, (d) accident, (e) a puzzling phenomenon to be explained, and (f) an attempt to change some life condition. Though collection and analysis of data require the greatest possible objectivity and detachment, the drawing of conclusions about changes that should be made in people's lives inevitably involve value choices. Therefore in evaluating any conclusions, one must evaluate not only the data the conclusion-drawer has used but also the values which guide his search and his interpretations.

Origins of Adaptive Behavior

Psychologists are concerned with the study of behavior of living organisms, both *external* behavior—behavior which has a direct effect on the environment—and *internal* behavior, which may or may not influence external behavior. This internal behavior can be of two general classes: *physiological* and *experiential*. Physiological behavior refers to biochemical and electrical activities within the body and often is directly measurable. Experiential processes are things like thoughts and feelings—a broad class of internal behaviors presumably activated by, and having consequences in, the functioning of the nervous system, but involving units too complex and inaccessible to be measured directly.

We all know when we have a dream, a thought, a fantasy; when we have wanted something, longed for someone, hoped an event would occur, feared for an unpleasant occurrence, held an opinion, had an expectancy. But can we give another person outside of ourselves access to events like these in such a way that we and he can be sure we are talking about the same thing? Can someone else ever really know how sad you are feeling or how much in love you are?

Psychologists have tended to be suspicious of attempts to study these inner, "subjective" processes of experience and generally have felt more comfortable studying overt behavior, where different people could check each other's observations and where the responses could often be measured. So in the next several chapters we will be examining the advances made as a result of studying *overt* behavior. In this Part we will start with the "givens" in the organism itself. Chapter 3 will focus on what can be discovered at the physiological level of analysis about man's attempts to process information and cope with his environment. We will look at his basic equipment for picking up, processing, and reacting to signals from the environment—how and why this equipment probably developed and how it works. At the outposts of what is now known we will find that numerous puzzling questions remain.

In studying the organism's early development, in Chapter 4, the twin problems we will encounter will be those of understanding the *origins* of behavior patterns and the means by which behavior patterns can *change*. How does a brain become a mind? Which is more important in determining your intelligence and personality—your heredity or your environment? How does the unbelievable chaos and confusion of the world a newborn baby faces become the ordered, causally related, organized world you now take for granted? These are but a few of the questions we will raise in considering the origins, stages, and transformations in the life of a human being.

Parts Three and Four will continue this focus on overt behavior, investigating in greater detail how behavior is modified and how organisms attend, perceive, think, create, and direct their behavior. But from time to time we will be considering whether or not further advances in our understanding will demand a broader focus—one which incorporates the *experiential* side of behavior. This question will come into focus in Chapter 10.

Chapter 3

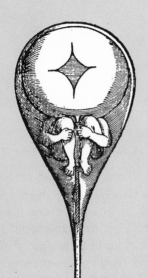

The Physiological Bases of Behavior

What a piece of work is man!
how noble in reason!
how infinite in faculty!
in form and moving how express and admirable!

Shakespeare and *Hair*

When the captain of the Apollo 11 crew, Neil Armstrong (shown in the picture on our Part Two opening spread), set foot upon the surface of the moon in July 1969, an achievement unparalleled in science and technology had been witnessed by millions of television viewers throughout the world. A journey dreamed of through centuries as an impossible fantasy had become an actuality. A man had traveled 237,000 miles through space, taking a supportive environment with him, had landed safely where no man had ever been before, and had even been able to talk to us here on earth while he was doing it.

Two aspects of this historic flight deserve further mention here. One is the contrast it highlights between man's achievements in exploration of outer space and the little gain he has made in exploring the inner space of his own body and brain. The other has to do with an apparently minor event that occurred just before the lunar module landed on the moon, which represented perhaps an even more significant human achievement than the landing itself. At a critical point in the final descent, when the LEM was under automatic computerized control, Armstrong suddenly put the ship under manual control and changed its course. In doing so, he was able to guide it to a smooth landing surface rather than the dangerous, rocky terrain for which it was headed. In that moment of decision, Armstrong revealed the level of perfection man has reached as a consequence of billions of years of evolution. He was able to receive a complex set of stimulus inputs, decode them, organize them into a meaningful pattern, reject other sources of input and influences upon his behavior, and act upon his discriminations. The sensory detection apparatus, the integrating and coordinating nervous system, and the reasoning processes of this individual human being proved to be superior to the best available computers and scores of accessory mechanical parts.

In this chapter, we will explore some aspects of man's inner space. In the process of doing so, we will put ourselves in the role of a biological engineer, trying first to understand how the present level of human capability (represented by acts such as that of Armstrong) evolved from a simple, single-celled organism only a few thousandths of an inch in diameter. We will then consider how the information necessary for the responsiveness of the individual and the survival of the species is transmitted from one cell to another. Only after building a basic knowledge of the internal workings of the mechanism that has become man can we begin to appreciate the complexity and subtlety of the interplay between it and the environment. Man, as scientist, is on the threshold of discovering the secrets of his own existence, and man, as student, can appreciate the vast implications of such knowledge.

The key to unlocking the secret of Nature's prize puzzle—the behavior of human beings—can be found in two activities: one scholarly, the other technological. The first and most essential task for advancing our knowledge about man's functioning is to learn how to ask Nature the appropriate questions. The second task involves developing techniques for providing answers to these questions in the form of phenomena that can be seen and measured.

The history of science clearly shows that its development has been held back, sometimes for centuries, when men posed questions which were unanswerable. Such questions did the disservice of misdirecting attention to false issues and distinctions, of leading to partial or superficial views of reality. They either encouraged a belief in simple truths where complex ones held, or discouraged investigation because of apparent complexity when the truth was, in fact, simple.

Man's attempt to understand how he perceives the external world was long hamstrung by such unanswerable questions. There could be no breakthrough in knowledge about perception until the seventeenth century, for two reasons: first, the ancient and medieval investigators were trying to answer the question of how the soul guides perception; second, they were failing to distinguish between physical, physiological, and psychological questions.

It was the French philosopher and mathematician, René Descartes, often called the "father of physiological psychology," who began to ask the right questions in the early 1600's. He began with a view of the body as an "animal machine" which could be understood scientifically. He then raised purely physiological questions, questions of bodily mechanics of mo-

tion, which could be separated from psychological questions of how men sense, know, or experience the qualities of the world. The answers to the former questions could be found in mathematical proofs and physical demonstrations.

Johannes Kepler, Descartes' contemporary, had been asking similar questions about the movement of celestial bodies. Kepler wrote, of his new mathematical work on the motion of planets, "My goal is to show that the heavenly machine is not a kind of divine living being but similar to a clockwork." In like manner, then, vision was to be understood as a purely optical problem (see Crombie, 1964).

We might note that Descartes' contribution becomes even more impressive when we realize that he was a devoutly religious man who was thereby committed to housing a soul within the body. And remember that at this same time in history, Galileo was being judged a heretic by an inquisitorial court in Rome for advocating that the earth was not the stationary center of the universe. Descartes' intellectual feat was postulating a *dualism* to separate the action of the mechanistic body and brain from that of the spiritual soul and ephemeral mind, thereby rendering the body and its processes available for naturalistic study. Although the soul was assumed to be united to the entire body, it could not act upon all parts of the body or be acted upon by all parts. If it could, the body could no longer be a perfect machine and would be rendered an "unaccountable mechanism." According to Descartes, the soul and body interact at that single part of the brain which is not duplicated in the two halves, or cerebral hemispheres: the pineal gland. ● His view was that the soul is not confined to this space, but acts upon the extended substance of the body only at this point. Interestingly, the physiological function of the pineal gland is only now beginning to be uncovered (Axelrod & Wurtman, 1970).

The *mechanistic* approach was given technological support by Helmholtz' demonstration, in 1850, that the transmission of the nerve impulse was not instantaneous, but rather took an appreciable amount of time. If bodily motion were a series of temporal events, then such movement in time could be separated from the event of Will that caused it and could be studied as a natural process. Helmholtz' experi-

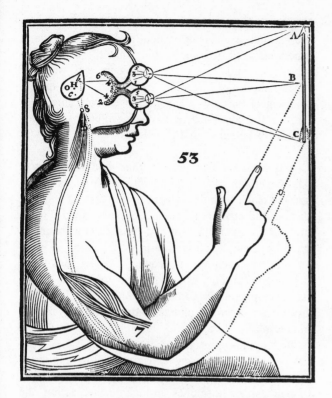

As portrayed in this 1686 woodcut, Descartes believed that information about the outside world was received by the eyes and transmitted by "strings in the brain" to the pineal gland, which then sent appropriate messages to the muscles. Interestingly, there is accumulating evidence today that the pineal gland does in fact translate cyclic nervous activity generated by light into hormonal messages.

ment "brought the soul to time, as it were, measured what had been ineffable, actually captured the essential agent of mind in the toils of natural science" (Boring, 1950, p. 42). Such an approach ultimately enabled psychology to become allied with physiology and independent of religion.

It is appropriate, then, that our study of the behavior of organisms begin with a focus on the physiology of nerve transmission, sensation, and brain functioning, with an analysis of man's primary means of contact with the "real world," through vision and hearing. We, too, will adopt a mechanistic point of view and ask questions which are answerable at a physiological level of analysis—some even at the molecular level of biochemical activity within a por-

tion of a single cell. In subsequent chapters, however, we will be sensitive to the general problem of selecting the *level of analysis* which is most relevant to understanding the problem at hand. For example, we would not expect to utilize this mechanical, physiological orientation to answer a question such as "What led Sirhan Sirhan to kill Senator Kennedy?" Such a question would be best answered not in terms of electrical activity of brain cells, but rather by an analysis of what aspects of Sirhan's history directed him toward this action, what social and personal events in his present environment drove him to it, and what expectations of future gain guided his death-dealing hand.

Many students of introductory psychology are impatient with approaches which do not immediately get to intriguing questions about behavior like these. We will get to such issues and questions when we have built a framework for tackling them; hopefully, in the process of getting there, we may be able to excite you about a host of other problems which you may never have considered inherently fascinating before.

The Evolution of You from It

As you look at a one-celled organism, such as a *paramecium,* swimming about on a microscopic stage, it seems inconceivable that the complexity which is you—with 10^{13} body cells and 7×10^{26} atoms—has evolved from such apparent simplicity. Our forebears found it inconceivable too. A Dutch microscopist, Hartsoeker, used a crude viewing instrument back in 1694 to look at a sperm cell and thought that what he saw was a completely formed, miniature human figure, a *homunculus*. This preformed creature needed only nourishment and time to develop into an adult, or so thought advocates of *preformation*. Moreover, each homunculus was thought to contain tiny sex cells with smaller homunculi; they in turn contained others, and so on, thereby explaining both individual development and the sequence of the generations. The drawing on page 58 is one that Hartsoeker made.

The appealing simplicity of such ideas has been incorporated into theories which represent evolution as a process in which all organisms were once upon a time "infolded" in some primordial cell, to be "unfolded" at later times in the development of the species. Such theories of *orthogenesis* view evolution as the progressive manifestation of latent forms of preexisting life.

Aristotle advanced an alternative view which is more in line with what has been discovered about embryonic development. He believed that organs were formed only gradually out of simple, unformed substances in the fertilized egg. He called this process *epigenesis,* a term still used by embryologists.

Before we examine the epigenetic interactions which result in the differentiation of a fertilized egg cell into the specialized tissues of the organism, we might ask why early organisms were not content to remain one-celled but evolved into protozoa, worms, fish, reptiles, mammals, and men.

The Single Cell

A single-celled organism would seem to contain all the material necessary for survival: (a) *cytoplasm,* which is the matrix in which most of the cell's biochemical reactions take place and in which the breakdown of nutrients generates body energy; (b) an *outer membrane,* which keeps the internal contents separate from the external environment and, through its contractions, provides one means of locomotion; (c) a *nucleus,* which directs the activities in the cytoplasm through the production of various nucleic acids. The cell can also divide to reproduce and perpetuate itself.

But a single cell is not designed to adapt to changes in the environment which interfere with its usual functioning. Thus a cell's mobility is limited when rapid motion is required; it may have nutritional problems because it is not flexible enough to synthesize new substances when its regular food supply is unavailable; and the new copies which it produces will be no better suited to a changing, hostile environment than the parent cell.

The Multi-Celled Organism

For greater complexity and flexibility, a multi-celled organism with specialized cells is the only answer.

Every cell in your body still has cytoplasm, a membrane, and a nucleus, which perform the general functions described above, but what the cells themselves do, and hence their makeup and ways of functioning, have become specialized. Our understanding of how these changes have come about has built on the combined research of evolutionary biologists, embryologists, and geneticists.

Cell differentiation, specialization, and redundancy. The development of cellular differentiation is highly specific, such that one system of cells forms a given, distinct end product (such as a kidney or liver), while another forms a different end-product (for example, nervous tissue), with no intermediate organs allowed. In addition, each system manages to give rise to its normal end product even when the conditions during its development are somewhat abnormal. (This control breaks down, of course, if the conditions are *too* abnormal.)

Within these systems, the various cells have developed widely differing capacities. Thus endocrine cells have specialized in developing an efficient way of synthesizing hormones through enzyme action, the neural membrane has specialized in being able to propagate information without itself moving, and so on.

These special functions of various individual cells are duplicated many times over to create a redundancy which guarantees the overall functioning of the organism despite malfunctioning of some subsets of cells. Thus the organism that has evolved has gained flexibility by combining cell specialization with duplication. But at what cost? What has it lost to gain these advantages?

The demands upon the multi-celled organism. Important new demands have been put upon the system by its increase in number and complexity of cells. The major problem is that the many cells can no longer work independently, but must operate in a coordinated fashion. For example, while some provide the basis for locomotion, others must provide nourishment. Still others must provide the means for rapid communication of important information. Imagine a worm entering an aversive environment. Its head contains receptors which detect hostile stimu-

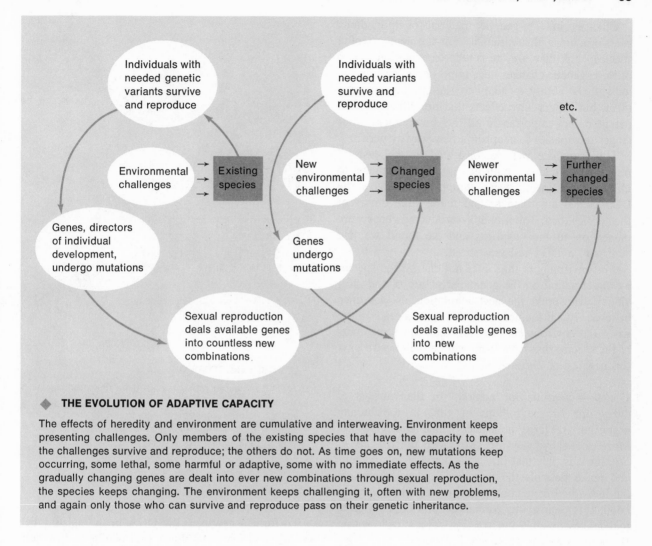

◆ THE EVOLUTION OF ADAPTIVE CAPACITY

The effects of heredity and environment are cumulative and interweaving. Environment keeps presenting challenges. Only members of the existing species that have the capacity to meet the challenges survive and reproduce; the others do not. As time goes on, new mutations keep occurring, some lethal, some harmful or adaptive, some with no immediate effects. As the gradually changing genes are dealt into ever new combinations through sexual reproduction, the species keeps changing. The environment keeps challenging it, often with new problems, and again only those who can survive and reproduce pass on their genetic inheritance.

lation, but its tail must be signaled to stop the movement which will carry it further forward. Unless the stop time is very short, the animal may not survive contact with that environment. The problem of coordination and rapid communication has been solved by the evolution of the specialized cell called the *nerve cell* or *neuron*, the main character in the present chapter.

Devices for Improving Adaptability

By the time the multi-celled organism had evolved, four processes were operating and influencing each other in such a way as to force development toward higher and ever more complex levels. ◆

Environment—the taskmaster. Contemporary biology views the environment as an active force which constantly poses challenges to the organism, challenges that may change radically from time to time (Dobzhansky, 1957). Whether this continuing confrontation results in extinction or improvement of the species depends upon whether or not there are, in the existing species, genetic variants from which can develop the cells needed for adaptation to the changed environment.

Changes in the genetic material of individuals keep producing this variability among members of a species; thus they are the source of evolution. Some of these genetic changes have important effects on the individuals' ability to adapt to the existing environment, but others have effects that are either not apparent or not important until the environment challenges the species to adapt in a new way or perish.

This sequence was demonstrated in the case of insects that had a "built-in" genetic resistance to DDT. These insects were equipped to survive the DDT-ridden environment and mate while others of the species died. The immunity-producing genes were passed on to the offspring, and we found we had "created" a DDT-resistant strain.

The environment thus does not change the species by direct action on the genetic structure of the individuals who make the new adaptation, as was once believed. But if the needed variants are already there when the environment changes, then those members of the species that have them will be the ones to pass this new test of who is fit enough to survive.

Genes—blueprints for copies. In the nucleus of every one of the billions of cells in the human organism are large molecules called *chromosomes*. More poetically, they are also called the *threads of life*, for it is they that direct the activities of the cells and make possible the growth and development of the individual from conception to and through adulthood. It is their ability to make copies of themselves that makes possible the creation of new cells within the body as well as whole new individuals.

The chromosomes are large molecules consisting mainly of DNA (deoxyribonucleic acid) and proteins. The chemical structure of DNA is simple—long chains consisting of pairs of nucleotide bases, arranged like a twisted ladder. •   At various locations along this "ladder" are the *genes*—strings of these nucleotide bases that function as units in providing many kinds of "instructions" for the development and functioning of the body. Only four bases are found— *guanine* paired with *cytosine* and *adenine* with *thymine* —but a single gene may contain thousands of them in a long chain. The same four basic constituents are found in the DNA of other species but in different proportions and sequences.

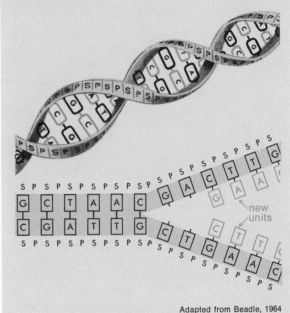

Adapted from Beadle, 1964

● **THE STRUCTURE OF DNA**

A DNA molecule replicates itself by unwinding, separating down the middle like a long zipper, and picking up the appropriate new units from the surrounding fluid. DNA is so tiny that all the DNA strands in the egg cells that have given rise to the approximately three billion people living today would fit into a ⅛-inch cube (Beadle, 1964).

To form a new cell, the DNA in the existing cell uncoils and "unzips" down the middle of the "ladder." Each half then acts as a template and picks up the needed bases in the proper sequence from unattached ones present in the cytoplasm. When this process is complete, the cell then divides into two cells, with a complete set of DNA remaining in each one.

To direct activities within the cell, the genes make copies of themselves, called *RNA*. These copies then function as templates in various parts of the cell in the assembling of amino acids in the proper sequences to form particular *proteins*. Many of the life activities within cells are carried out by certain proteins called *enzymes* that act as catalysts for various chemical reactions: they may speed up reactions, perhaps by as much as a million times, but remain themselves unchanged afterwards. The formation of each protein is directed by a particular gene.

The important decoding question was how the information in the genes could determine the structure of all the proteins. How could four letters (the four nucleotide bases) form a language which could describe all life in the twenty-two words of the amino acids?

Such a feat would be possible if the amino acids were coded not singly but by triplets, each consisting of three of the four DNA bases and each triplet forming a "word" in the genetic instructions. In a DNA molecule containing 10,001 bases, the number of different possible sequences would be four to the 10,000th power, providing ample possibilities for coding all the variety we see in the forms of life. The coding triplet is now regarded as the model in genetic studies.

Ψ *Close-up*   **PKU Babies**

Phenylketonuria (PKU), a form of severe mental retardation in humans, has been traced to a specific mutation which prevents the manufacture of a necessary enzyme. Phenylalanine, an amino acid, is broken down into phenylpyruvic acid and tyrosine, and normally the phenylpyruvic acid is then neutralized by a particular enzyme. In infants who lack this enzyme, however, the phenylpyruvic acid keeps building up and becomes toxic to the central nervous system.

The therapy required is either to supply the missing enzyme or to feed the child a special diet low in phenylalanine. If such therapy begins in time, the child's intelligence develops normally. Saving such babies is not only a saving in human potential but also a considerable financial saving. In California, for example, in 1969, PKU still accounted for 1 percent of the population in the state's mental institutions at an estimated lifetime cost to the taxpayer of $158,500 apiece for treatment and institutional care. Since 1966, California has had a mandatory PKU test for all newborn babies (*San Francisco Chronicle*, April 20, 1970).

Mutations—sources of change.   We can speculate about the development of life and evolution in the light of the following bio-logic. At some point in time, strands of DNA must have formed containing sequences of bases that could produce useful proteins. These proteins enabled the cell to metabolize nutrients and to reproduce—thus to maintain itself and grow and, over the eons, to try out the viability of many kinds of alterations in the DNA.

Such alterations in the DNA are called *mutations*. A change in a single base in a DNA molecule will change the corresponding amino acid sequence in the proteins it forms. This change may be beneficial, harmful, or lethal for the individual or his offspring. (Ψ Close-ups, this page and page 66)

Since every cell of the body is programmed by a copy of the individual's DNA, every cell is subject to mutation. If a mutation occurs in *body cells*, it will affect the person but will not have an effect on his children. Such mutations are suspected in leukemia and also in the process of aging; they may act by disorganization of an increasing proportion of body cells as new, crippled cells are formed. When a mutation occurs in the *germ cells*—either sperm or egg— then it has no effect on the individual's body but may be passed on to his offspring.

Mutations are constantly taking place, and as we have seen, every group carries a pool of latent mutations, some of which may stand it in good stead if the environment starts making new demands. Most mutations are damaging, however, and unfortunately man has added to the burden of such deleterious mutational mishaps by filling his environment with chemicals and sources of radiation that are *mutagenic*—capable of causing mutations.

Natural radiation from the sun may also damage genes. Ultraviolet radiation is known to fuse together two bases in the DNA molecule, and there are people who develop skin cancers from exposure to sunlight. Evidently this extreme sensitivity is inherited: as many as five of seven people in a family have been known to have this disease.

Recently biochemical research has uncovered enzyme systems which correct gene defects by hunting down defective parts of the DNA molecule, marking the defect, repairing it, and then "sewing" the repaired molecule together again. The search-and-mark enzyme is called *endonuclease;* the repairing enzyme is called *DNA polymerase;* the "sewing machine" enzyme is called *ligase* (Kelly, Atkinson, Huberman, & Kornberg, 1969).

If, as is now believed, the cancer-producing sunlight sensitivity is due to an inability of enzymes to repair ultraviolet damage to DNA, then it follows that the only effective therapy for such victims would be to provide them with enzymes which could repair the DNA damage. Theoretically, at least, it may some day be possible to manipulate genes in order to correct hereditary defects—"genetic engineering." Success in such efforts would indeed represent a culmination of the scientist's quest for control over nature. The uses to which that control could or should be put will raise a host of ethical, moral, and legal problems for man. Hopefully, at that time, we will all be "humanists," concerned as much for the least of our kind as for our own DNA molecule.

Sexual reproduction—the kaleidoscope. At the time of conception, two living *germ cells*—the *sperm* from the father and the *ovum,* or *egg,* from the mother—unite to produce a new individual. The male and female germ cells are known technically as *gametes*, and the single cell they form at the moment of conception—which becomes the new organism—is called the *zygote.* The human zygote contains 46 chromosomes—23 from each parent. As it divides and redivides into more cells, the chromosomes are duplicated each time so that there still are 46 chromosomes in each new cell. The only exceptions to this rule will be the sex cells, which in their last division do not duplicate their chromosomes first but simply split, each new cell carrying half of the available chromosomes. The 23 chromosomes contained in each egg or sperm thus represent various selections from among the 46 possible ones. Different selections, in different matings of the same two parents, account for the wide genetic differences among their children.

It is the sexual union of individuals who differ in some of their genes that gives rise to the tremendous variability present in a population. This *hybridization* —mating of dissimilar individuals—freely deals the existing genes and their mutations into new arrangements. Thus it is sex which puts enough variety in the

---

Ψ *Close-up*   *Sickle-Cell Anemia in Two Environments*

Sickle-cell anemia is a disease in which the red blood cells, carriers of oxygen through the bloodstream, become crescent shaped instead of rounded and tend to clog the small capillaries. Normal distribution of oxygen throughout the body is thus prevented, and often blood clots result. Those afflicted are likely to die before they are thirty.

This is a hereditary disease, evidently caused by a mutant gene that occurred in the African population. It occurs almost entirely among Negroes and only in individuals who receive sickle-cell genes from both their parents. Thus it is called a "recessive" gene, since it is carried by many people who never develop the disease. Interestingly, about half the black population in Africa carry one such gene, whereas only one in ten black Americans carry one. We do not know whether this difference is the result of an unrepresentative sample brought to this country, a new mutation in this country, or (more likely) a strengthening of the strain by greater survival and reproduction of those equipped to meet the higher demands for oxygen consumption required by heavy physical labor in the fields.

---

shows it sends on the road to guarantee that at least some will survive the severest environmental critics. The infinite variety, originality, and uniqueness of the human form can be traced to sexual reproduction. An instance of the virtually endless permutations it makes possible is seen in our fingerprints. No two identical fingerprints have been found on the hands of one person or those of any two people who have ever lived. In fact, the F.B.I. has a standing offer of a substantial reward for evidence to the contrary.

How Do I Get Through to You?

The processes which we have been considering allow us to appreciate the sources of human variability, but it is the process of nerve impulse transmission which allows individual man to appreciate the constant variability and challenge of the world about him. It is in this experience and his reactions to it that man defines himself as both similar to and unique among living creatures. To understand how such contact with the world is made, we will start by painting a sketch of the life and travels of the basic unit in the nervous system, the individual nerve cell.

A Nerve Cell Is Born

A nerve cell has all the general characteristics of other living cells and in addition is specialized to receive, carry, and transmit electrochemical messages (*nerve impulses*). Nerve cells are also called *neurons,* as we have seen. Possibly no two are identical in size, shape, branching parts, or interconnections with each other.

During prenatal development, the nerve cell, like other cells, goes through a series of stages of progressive differentiation from the undifferentiated cell that was formed at conception. Such cellular differentiation is stimulated by chemical substances called *organizers*. But this epigenetic reaction can take place only during critical periods in tissue development—when some portion of the tissue is *competent* to be activated by the organizers. This tissue competence—as well as the action of the organizers—is seen as the result of a set of gene-controlled processes. (Ψ Close-up, right.)

In the earliest stages of embryonic development, the cell material is so pliable and "plastic" that it can be channeled to become any part of the organism—skin, eye, or muscle, for example. In fact, tissue transplanted from one part of the embryo to another part develops in accordance with its new surroundings instead of developing as it would have in its original location. A cell originally destined to become part of one organ can thus become part of another. With older embryos, however, tissue transplants do not continue to conform to their new environment. Once the primitive outline of the nervous system, the *neural plate*, is etched on the surface of the embryo, for example, these cells have already specialized far enough that they are no longer so versatile and interchangeable. Later still, each nerve cell has its own particular fate within the nervous system permanently

determined, and it can then play only its unique, specialized function in the life of the organism.

As the embryo develops, the neural plate transforms itself into a neural tube in which the brain and spinal cord are differentiated. The cells lining the wall of the neural tube move to a position in the tube where *mitosis* (splitting of the nucleus) occurs and daughter cells are formed. Then a remarkable migration takes place. Every nerve cell traverses the neural tube to reach a given site in the mantle surrounding the tube. Some migrate a second time to reach another destination along the tube; others leave the tube and travel enormous distances (for a cell) to set up a homesite in internal organs or near what will become sensory receptors. No one yet knows how this migration is activated or directed.

Two kinds of nerve cells that migrate great distances are the *motor nerve cells*, which will innervate muscles and glands from a site in the spinal cord and the *sensory nerve cells*, such as those in the eye,

---

Ψ *Close-up*　**The Chick Embryo Comes to "Life"**

Is the growing embryo alive, or does life depend upon the ability to engage in *functional activity*—to respond to stimulation? For the chick embryo, the first limb reflexes can be elicited on the seventh day of incubation. But even before that, some spontaneous, random limb movements can be observed.

The onset of the gross motor behavior of parts of the embryo is correlated with a dramatic rise in the activity of specific enzymes, especially the enzyme AChE. It appears that there must be genes specific to each species which initiate a vast increase in enzyme production at those places in the body of the embryo which will involve important behavior patterns. Thus, for the chick, there is a fivefold increase in enzyme AChE in the wing region of the spinal cord from the seventh to the thirteenth day of incubation. For the salamander, this abrupt enzyme increase occurs in the appropriate regions when the swimming activity is about to begin.

which will bring sensory information to "headquarters." For example, when the embryonic motor nerve cell reaches a certain point in the neural tube, a branching process develops which perforates the membrane around the nerve tube. This end of the nerve cell is called an *axon;* it leaves the tube, and as it grows longer it roams about, apparently at random. The branching fibers collect in bunches and these, in turn, are joined by other fiber bundles from sensory nerves. Together they enter the growing limb buds and other parts of the developing embryo.

Although the cell body of the motor neuron stays in the spinal cord, the axon journeys far afield, insinuating itself into distant regions of the embryo. Nerve cell growth is determined both by growth factors like hormones and by the conditions the growing axon encounters. Interestingly, recent studies have demonstrated that nerve cells have considerable growth potential which is not fully realized in development under normal conditions but can be developed more fully in the presence of certain artificial chemical activators—among them, surprisingly, snake venom.

By the time the nerve cell can conduct impulses, its differentiation, wandering, and proliferation are completed but not its growth to full size. The nerve cell, unlike the total organism, takes on its major responsibility early in life, and grows up afterward. As the organism grows and the distance between the cell body and the terminal of the motor axon in arm or leg or other body part stretches out, the cell must undergo prodigious growth. It has been estimated that the protein increase in the cytoplasm of the motor nerve cell of the rat is 200,000-fold from the early embryonic stage to adulthood (Hydén, 1943).

Even after the adult organism stops growing, the cell body continues to produce a type of plasm which travels through the axon, maintaining its readiness to change or grow further if necessary. Thus the nerve cell is never in a static state, but rather in a "steady state." When the continuity of a peripheral axon is disrupted by accident or disease, even in an adult, regeneration can still occur.

The Grand Plan: The Nervous System

Now that we have looked briefly at the evolution and development of the human organism and individual

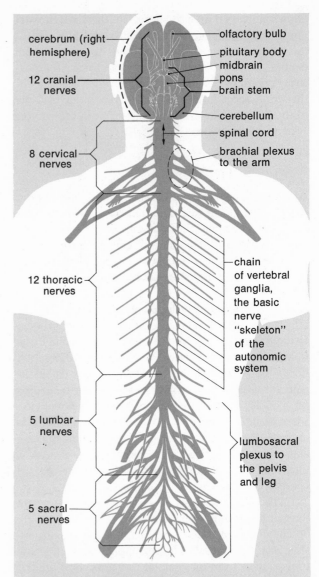

◆ THE NERVOUS SYSTEM

All the neurons (or parts of neurons) *within* the brain and spinal cord make up the central nervous system; all those *outside* make up the peripheral nervous system. Many individual neurons thus start in one system and end in the other.

Twelve important nerves in the peripheral system originate in the brain itself and are thus called *cranial* nerves (though one, the *vagus* nerve, wanders through the body and innervates most of the visceral organs along the way). The other main peripheral nerves connect with the spinal cord between the vertebrae all the way down and have more localized functions.

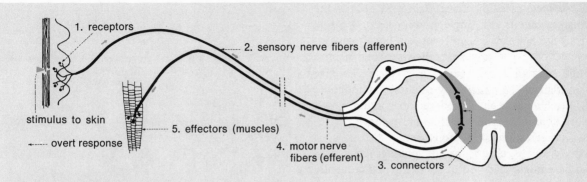

1. receptors

2. sensory nerve fibers (afferent)

stimulus to skin

← overt response

5. effectors (muscles)

4. motor nerve fibers (efferent)

3. connectors

■ **A SENSORY-MOTOR ARC**

Response to a stimulus requires all five of the steps shown in this diagram except in rare cases where there is no connecting neuron in the spinal cord. No response will be able to take place if the stimulation is too weak or of a kind to which the receptors are not sensitive, or if the neural impulse fails to cross any of the synapses in the chain, or if the impulse finally reaching the effectors is too weak to activate them, or if the effectors are unable to respond (perhaps because of fatigue).

A single chain is drawn here with one interneuron. Actually, this simple arc is duplicated many times in a stimulus-response act, and typically interneurons bring involvement of segments of the spinal cord above and below the one shown.

Not evident in this diagram is an essential feature of sequential behavior—and most of our behavior is actually continuing action, not just one stimulus-response circuit. As our action proceeds, we get sensory feedback indicating the consequences of our ongoing motor output or other changes in the environment. We keep monitoring this feedback and adjusting our output to meet the changing requirements.

cells, our next basic question is, how does such an organism work? How does it respond to events occurring in the environment? How does it detect changes within itself? How is it able to make various movements? How does it process information and "think"?

All these queries are concerned with the functioning of the *nervous system*. This system is made up of those parts of the organism which respond to and integrate sensory input, initiate and control behavioral output, and form the basis for the various mental processes of thought, memory, and learning. Essentially, the nervous system consists of two subsystems, the central and the peripheral. The *central nervous system* is made up of the brain and the spinal cord. Its function is to correlate and integrate—to make the various parts of the body work together. The *peripheral nervous system* consists of nerve fibers which connect the central nervous system to cells which are sensitive to stimuli (*receptors*) and to the muscles and glands (*effectors*), which perform the actual adjustive actions of the organism. ◆

The response of the entire nervous system to a stimulus follows a rather basic pattern. The stimulus is first picked up by the appropriate receptors (for example, a tactual stimulus is picked up by special cells in the skin of a finger). This information is then relayed by the *sensory nerve cells* to the spinal cord and thence to the brain. Here the information is processed and, if deemed appropriate, a particular response is "selected." This decision is then sent via the *motor nerve cells* to the appropriate effectors, which make the behavioral response (for example, the hand will move away from the painful stimulus). The basic pattern of *sensory input → central nervous system → behavioral output* is known as the *sensory-motor arc;* actually it is duplicated many times in any single stimulus-response act. ■

As we have seen, the basic structural unit of the nervous system is the single *nerve cell* or *neuron*. Neurons are not isolated, however, but have many interconnections. The tiny space between one neuron and the next in line is called a *synapse*. To give you an idea of the complexity of these interconnections, the human brain is believed to contain a vast network of approximately ten billion neurons.

The organization of neurons within the nervous system is not as chaotic as the photograph reproduced here might lead you to believe. • Frequently a number of axons (or *nerve fibers,* as they are more generally called) are gathered into bundles that have a common place of origin and destination. Within the central nervous system, such bundles are known as *nerve tracts* or *pathways*. When these bundles connect the central nervous system with other parts of the body, they are called *nerve trunks* or simply *nerves* and, as we have seen, contain both sensory and motor fibers. There also are certain brain areas called *nuclei* where the cell bodies (and hence their nuclei) are concentrated. Finally, the entire complex of neurons is embedded in a network of *neuroglia*, or *glial cells*, which nourish and protect the delicate neurons. Some think they also play a critical role in nerve functioning, but this has not yet been proven.

Although this overview of the nervous system is a very brief and simplified one, it points up the reason for including physiology in the study of psychology. Without the nervous system the organism could not live, much less respond. It is the mainspring which makes him tick. Obviously, if we were ignorant of its underlying dynamics, our understanding of human behavior would be very limited. The purpose of the rest of this chapter is to make you knowledgeable in this regard—to familiarize you with the essentials of how the nervous system works and to spell out its importance for an understanding of the behavior of animals and men.

Going Through Channels

As the organism evolved from a single cell to multiple cells, the problem of internal communication became critical. The various cells had to be able to communicate and interact with each other in order for the organism to function effectively and survive.

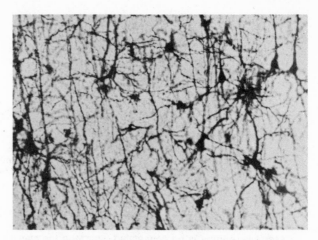

● You can get some idea of the complexity of the internal communication system provided by the nervous system in this highly magnified section of tissue from the brain of a cat. A small fraction of the neurons in this brain slice have been stained to make them more visible.

The nervous system can be viewed as an extremely complex communication network which developed to help meet this need for internal coordination. Given the necessity of communication, the question then becomes, just *how* do the various parts of the nervous system "talk" to each other?

To understand better the system that has evolved, you might think about the necessary requirements for a reliable communication system. First of all, different parts of the system must be able to send information over long distances rapidly and accurately, without loss or distortion. Secondly, they must be capable of receiving information accurately from other parts. This would presuppose one or more common languages of communication between them. Thirdly, there must be a means by which many different bits of information can be integrated, or processed.

Information please . . . Certain features of the neuron are critical for its job of transmitting information. The *cell body* of a neuron is somewhat spherical in shape and contains the nucleus. Projecting from the cell body are two types of fiberlike extensions: various numbers of *dendrites* and one *axon*.

The dendrites are typically short, multiple, and

branched. They serve to receive nerve impulses from many other cells and to conduct them to the cell body, although very commonly the communication is directly to the cell body without the intervention of dendrites.

The axon is a long fiber which may have branches and which terminates in *end feet* (also called *synaptic knobs* or, in the case of motor neurons, *end plates*). The length of an axon is extremely variable; some axons extend as far as several meters. The axon transmits the nerve impulse from the cell body to other neurons or to muscles or body organs. Large axons are often covered with a *myelin sheath* of fatty material which serves to insulate the axon and provide for more rapid conduction of nerve impulses.

As mentioned above, the space between one neuron and the next is called a *synapse*. A synapse is very narrow—about 200 angstroms wide (1/500,000 cm)—and is located between the membrane at the end of an axon (the *presynaptic membrane*) and the membrane of the dendrite or cell body of the next neuron (the *postsynaptic membrane*).

Information is transmitted in two basic ways, both of which are required for getting any message through the nervous system. *Axonal transmission*, the movement of nerve impulses *within* a nerve, is important principally in the passing along of information. *Synaptic transmission*, the transfer of impulses *between* neurons, is important in the coordination and processing of information.

1. *Axonal transmission.* One question you probably have is how bodily tissue can create an electrical impulse. A truly complete answer would be very technical, but a somewhat simplified account can provide general understanding of the electrochemical action that takes place.

Solutions of two different chemicals, sodium and potassium, are found on both sides of the axon membrane. This membrane is selectively *permeable;* potassium ions can move through it more easily than can sodium ions. As a result of this selective permeability, the concentration of sodium ions is much higher on the outer side, while the concentration of potassium ions is much higher *inside* the axon. This means that the external and internal solutions have different voltages, with the inside of the axon most of the time being electrically negative with respect to the outside. In this condition the axon is said to be *polarized,* and the inside-outside voltage difference is called the *membrane potential;* in the resting state (i.e., when no nerve impulse is occurring) it is approximately −60 millivolts. If the membrane potential is more *positive* than that (for example, −40 millivolts), the axon is *depolarized.* If the membrane potential is more *negative* (for example, −80 millivolts), the axon is *hyperpolarized.*

Changes from the resting potential indicate the presence of a nerve impulse. The axon has been stimulated and is responding. What happens is that a membrane "gate" opens, letting sodium ions pour from the outside to the inside of the axon. This causes the interior of the axon to become positive at that particular location, which means that this part of the axon is depolarized. After this first "gate" closes, a second one opens and lets potassium ions flow out of the axon, temporarily making the membrane even more negative than in the resting state. When the impulse has passed on down the axon, special physiological systems reverse the flow of the chemicals and things return to the resting state. In other words, the nerve impulse corresponds with the large depolarization of the nerve membrane. This depolarization is called an *action potential.* Although this interchange of ions has been intensively studied (in the giant axon of the squid), the actual way in which stimulation triggers the opening of the sodium and potassium "gates" is as yet unknown (Hodgkin, Huxley, & Katz, 1949).

But how does the nerve impulse move along the axon? How does the interchange of ions at one point of the membrane produce an interchange at another? Essentially, the large depolarization in one area of the axon spreads to the next area, causing it to be slightly depolarized (a phenomenon known as *passive spread*). The latter depolarization then causes a nerve impulse to occur at this second point of the axon, which, in turn, spreads to the next area of the axon, and so on like a lit fuse. To summarize, each nerve impulse changes the membrane permeability of the area immediately ahead of it on the axon, causing another impulse to occur, and this entire process creates a continuous, progressive impulse moving along the axon.

For a few milliseconds after the axon has "fired," when the membrane potential is more negative than normally, the membrane is temporarily unexcitable and cannot be fired again. This interval is known as the *absolute refractory period*. As the membrane returns to normal, there is a short period during which a stronger-than-normal stimulus is required to fire an impulse; this is called the *relative refractory period*.

Does the axon "fire" in response to all incoming stimulation? The answer to this question is "No," introducing us to the very important concept of threshold. Each axon requires a certain level, or *threshold* of stimulus intensity before a nerve impulse can be produced in it. If the strength of the stimulus is below this threshold, there is no firing of a nerve impulse. However, if the stimulus strength is anywhere above threshold—whether barely above or far above—the axon fires with the same full response. Thus the axon fires either completely or not at all; this is known as the *all-or-none principle*. The size of the nerve impulse is always the same for any particular axon, regardless of the magnitude of the stimulus—as long as the stimulus is above the threshold.

Threshold and the all-or-none response are critical properties of the neuron for transmitting information. First of all, because a nerve impulse is always a full-sized one, it will not fade away and get "lost" during its travel down the axon. For this reason, axonal transmission is generally very accurate and reliable. Secondly, the fact that the neuron will not fire at all to below-threshold stimuli means that chance fluctuations in membrane potential will not produce a nerve impulse. This ensures that the neuron will respond only to actual information signals and not to random activity, or "noise." ◆

2. *Synaptic transmission.* Now that we have a better understanding of how information is propagated along an axon, our next question is how this information gets passed on from one neuron to the next. In other words, how do neurons communicate to each other? Information transfer occurs at the *synapses*, the gaps between the ends of an axon and other neurons near it. The electrical impulse does not somehow "jump" these gaps however; rather, a chemical "messenger" crosses over to the other side. Much of our knowledge about the events involved in this crossing over are due to the work of an Australian neurophysiologist, Sir John Eccles, and his associates. The complexity and interaction of these events

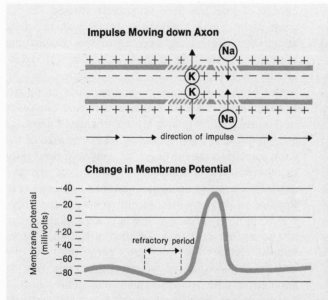

Impulse Moving down Axon

direction of impulse

Change in Membrane Potential

Membrane potential (millivolts)

−40
−20
0
+20
+40
−60
−80

refractory period

◆ **AXONAL TRANSMISSION**

The movement of a nerve impulse down an axon is shown in the upper part of the diagram. The impulse travels along the axon as membrane "gates" are opened which allow sodium ions to move inside the membrane, depolarizing it. After the impulse has passed, the negative potential of the membrane is restored.

The changes in the membrane potential are shown in the lower part of the figure. The spike indicates the point at which the electrical potential becomes positive enough for the axon to "fire." Just after firing, while potassium ions are flowing out, there is a brief refractory period in which the electrical potential becomes even more negative than usual. During this period it is difficult or impossible for the axon to fire.

Information is conveyed in the form of the number of impulses per second and the number of neurons activated. Once an impulse starts down an axon, it is virtually never diminished in strength.

● **EFFECTS OF EXCITATORY AND INHIBITORY INPUT**

Different amounts and combinations of input to a motor neuron produce different results. Four possibilities are shown here in simplified form.

The electrical events in the neural input are the same whether the impulses are carried by excitatory or inhibitory fibers. Their effects on the next neuron are different because different chemicals are released at the synapse.

1. Input from one weak excitatory fiber

2. Input from two weak excitatory fibers

3. Input from two excitatory fibers and one inhibitory fiber

4. Input from inhibitory fiber only

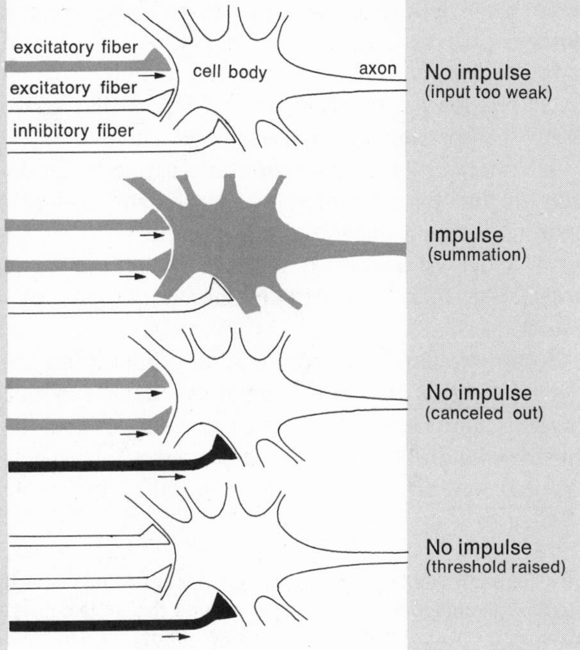

excitatory fiber
excitatory fiber
inhibitory fiber
cell body
axon

No impulse (input too weak)

Impulse (summation)

No impulse (canceled out)

No impulse (threshold raised)

suggest that the synapse is a major site of information processing and integration, as well as transmission.

When a nerve impulse reaches the end of the axon, it stimulates the release of a chemical transmitter substance. This substance crosses the synaptic gap and interacts with receptor molecules on the dendrites or cell body of the second neuron, either triggering an impulse in the second neuron (excitation) or putting the "brakes" on it and making it less likely to be activated (inhibition). In contrast to the all-or-none principle found in conduction of impulses along every axon, synaptic transmission involves *graded* activity, sometimes known as a *more-or-less principle*. The chemical transmitter produces small shifts in the polarization of the postsynaptic membrane, which are proportional to the amount and type of incoming signals. These changes in polarization spread from its dendrites and cell body to the beginning of its axon, where a full-sized nerve impulse will be initiated if the membrane is depolarized enough to reach threshold. If these shifts are below threshold, there is no neuronal activity.

Basically, there are two types of graded shifts in the postsynaptic membrane. The *excitatory postsynaptic potential* (*EPSP*) is a graded response which depolarizes the membrane. It is called excitatory because sufficient depolarization "excites" the neuron and causes it to produce nerve impulses along its axon. The *inhibitory postsynaptic potential* (*IPSP*) is a graded response which hyperpolarizes the membrane. Hyperpolarization means an increase in the negativity of the membrane potential, which, in turn, makes it more difficult for the membrane to be sufficiently depolarized to reach threshold. Thus, an IPSP *opposes* the action of an EPSP and inhibits the firing activity of the neuron. In a sense, EPSPs and IPSPs compete for control. ●

Although we have been talking of one neuron activating a second one, this is actually somewhat misleading. There is generally enough of a decrement in the transmission system at the synapse that the amount of chemical transmitter released by only a single nerve impulse is insufficient to fire a second impulse. Usually a second neuron can be activated only by more than one active axon ending (either several different axons or multiple endings of a single axon or both). The graded responses of several different axon inputs are summed to produce a larger postsynaptic potential. In *spatial summation*, several inputs that arrive at the same time are added together. In *temporal summation*, several inputs that arrive in rapid succession are summed.

This necessity for summation in synaptic transmission means that information from many different neurons is being integrated and passed on in a new form. Obviously, a great amount of interaction is possible between excitatory and inhibitory inputs to a neuron.

So far, we have focused attention primarily on the electrical events (changes in polarization) of synaptic transmission. The chemical events, while perhaps the most fascinating of the synaptic processes, are generally less well understood. There are many intriguing questions about this chemical crossing of the synaptic gap that have yet to be answered.

For example, how does the nerve impulse traveling along the axon produce the secretion of the transmitter substance from the axon's terminal? The end of an axon has a knoblike structure containing *vesicles,* or tiny sacs. It is believed that these vesicles contain the chemical transmitter substance, and that each nerve impulse causes just a few of these vesicles to discharge chemical molecules into the synaptic gap. Exactly *how* the nerve impulse accomplishes this is still a mystery. ■

What determines whether the nerve impulses of a particular axon will excite or inhibit the next neuron? Since all synapses have the same kind of structure, it is believed that the different effects we see must be produced by different *transmitter substances.* An

■   The remarkable photo on the left was made possible by a new technique of scanning electron microscopy of specially prepared tissue. It shows the synaptic knobs of many axons synapsing on what appears to be a cell body.

On the right is a highly magnified view of one synapse, showing the synaptic knob of an axon, a dendrite of another neuron, and the tiny space between them. You can also see the cluster of vesicles in which the chemical transmitter is stored. In fact, clusters of vesicles like these enable researchers to tell which direction the impulse can flow across the synapse.

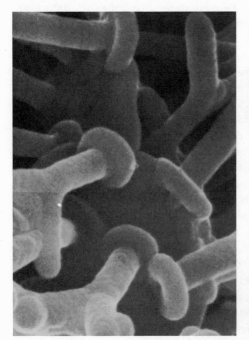
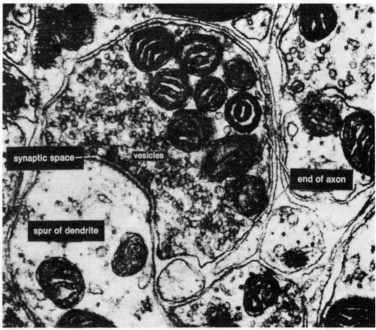

axon which releases an excitatory substance will cause the postsynaptic membrane to depolarize and produce an EPSP. Similarly, an axon which releases an inhibitory substance causes hyperpolarization of the membrane and production of an IPSP. Many different chemicals have been suggested as possible transmitter agents, but so far only a few have been conclusively identified. Of these, the major one is *acetylcholine* (ACh), which is an excitatory transmitter for many of the synapses in the peripheral nervous system and possibly in the central nervous system.

When the chemical transmitter crosses the synapse, attaches itself to receiving sites on the adjacent neuron, and causes graded activity in the postsynaptic membrane, how long does such activity continue? What stops it and how? Obviously, our transmission system would be extremely inefficient if neurons kept responding to one set of informational inputs. Once a signal has been received by a neuron, it must be moved out of the system so that the next signal can be processed.

In the synapse this clearing-out activity is mediated by the action of enzymes. It is believed that the enzyme which destroys or inactivates the transmitter substance is located on or near the postsynaptic membrane. For example, ACh is broken down into its constituent parts of acetate and choline by the enzyme *acetylcholine esterase* (AChE). After the transmitter has caused an EPSP or an IPSP, the relevant enzyme moves in and stops further action of the chemical transmitter substance. The chemical components that result from this process are then recycled and resynthesized into the transmitter substance, which can then be used again to cross the synaptic gap. But exactly how and where this recycling takes place is not yet completely understood.

One-way traffic. Neural activity follows the *law of forward conduction:* information is transmitted only in one direction—from the dendrites and cell body of one neuron to its axon, along the axon and across the synapse to the dendrites and cell body of a second neuron, then along the axon of that neuron and across the synapse to a third neuron, and so on. Although by artificial means an impulse can be made to go in the wrong direction along an axon, it can

cross a synapse only in one direction—from the axon of one neuron to the dendrite or cell body of the next, since only the synaptic knobs of the axon are capable of producing the chemical transmitter.

The transmission of information in the nervous system is an extremely complicated process which has been presented in a somewhat simplified way to give you a general picture. We have talked in terms of a single axon transmitting signals across a synapse to a second neuron. The nervous system, however, is composed of billions of cells synapsing on billions of other cells, as well as on all the glands and the muscles. Hundreds or thousands of neurons may be involved in the transmission of the same message, and the basic activity of the single nerve cell is continuously being repeated in all parts of the body in connection with many simultaneous messages. The many interconnections and interactions make the nervous system truly staggering in its complexity.

How Is Information Acted On?

Demands are made on the organism both by its external environment (for example, for following social requirements) and its internal one (for example, for nourishment). What happens in the nervous system between sensory input and motor or glandular output?

The Input-Output Network: The Peripheral Nervous System

The peripheral nervous system, as mentioned earlier in the chapter, is made up of the nerves which connect the central nervous system with all the receptors and effectors throughout the body. The system has both *somatic* components, which control the skeletal muscles, and *visceral* components, which control the glands and the special kinds of muscle found in the heart, blood vessels, eyes, and internal organs. Neurons of the somatic system have all their synapses in the brain and spinal cord; neurons in the visceral portion always synapse with another neuron *outside* the central nervous system. The centers controlling both systems are located in the brain, with the important difference that the visceral control centers are largely in the lower, evolutionarily older parts of the brain, whereas the somatic control centers are in the cerebral cortex (although subcortical structures contribute to final motor acts). Thus while control of the skeletal muscles can be either voluntary or reflexive, very little voluntary control of visceral functions is possible without special training. In fact, until recently such control was thought to be impossible.

Somatic components.   Earlier in this chapter we traced the migration, during embryonic development, of the sensory and motor neurons that are destined to become the somatic components of the peripheral system. Although they send impulses in opposite directions—sensory neurons toward the spinal cord, motor neurons away from it—they travel in the same trunks over most of their length. Thus they enter or leave the spinal cord at the same level, and the motor fibers end in or near muscles close to the receptors that activate the sensory components.

Sensory neurons have their cell bodies near the spinal cord and send their axons into it. This means that for some sensory neurons, such as those coming from arms or legs, the dendrites will be very long. Most other neurons, as we have seen, have very short dendrites and longer axons. The motor neurons have their dendrites and cell bodies in the spinal cord; only their axons extend outside it.   ▲

Visceral components.   The visceral portion of the peripheral nervous system is usually called the *autonomic nervous system*. This system is considered important in psychology because it controls all the internal and many of the external signs of emotion. Actually, the term *autonomic* is somewhat misleading, since only a few of the system's activities (such as digestion) are truly "autonomous" and self-regulating. There are two divisions of the autonomic system—the *sympathetic* and the *parasympathetic*—which originate from different sections of the brain stem and spinal cord and which often oppose each other's functions.   ◆

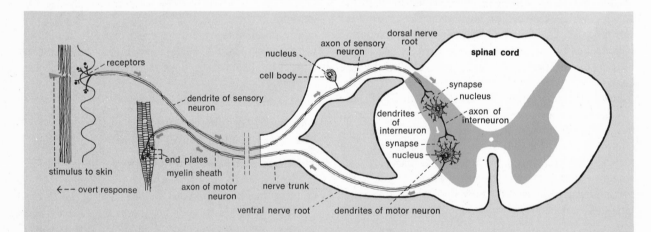

▲ **KINDS OF NEURONS**

This is a more detailed drawing of the sensory-motor arc shown on page 69. Three kinds of neurons are represented here: (a) a sensory (afferent) neuron, different from most neurons in having a long dendrite and relatively short axon; (b) an interneuron, with its many tiny branches, well designed for its job of providing multiple connections among many neurons; and (c) a motor neuron, with its long axon traveling most of the distance in the same nerve trunk as the sensory neuron and ending at effectors near the origin of the sensory input. In a sensory-motor arc, all synapses are in the spinal cord.

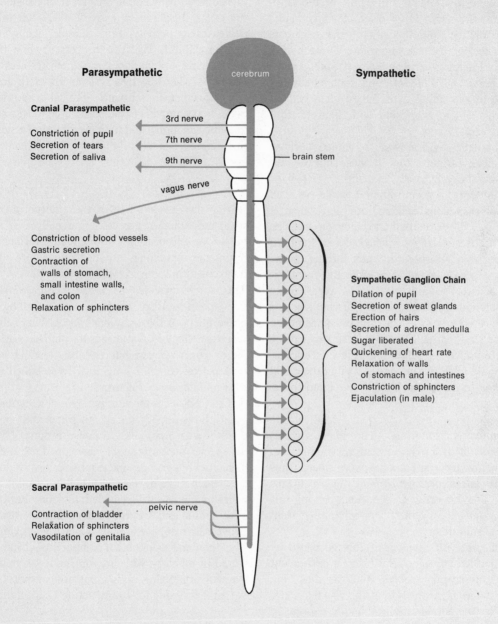

Parasympathetic

cerebrum

Sympathetic

Cranial Parasympathetic

3rd nerve

Constriction of pupil
Secretion of tears
Secretion of saliva

7th nerve

9th nerve

brain stem

vagus nerve

Constriction of blood vessels
Gastric secretion
Contraction of
    walls of stomach,
    small intestine walls,
    and colon
Relaxation of sphincters

Sympathetic Ganglion Chain

Dilation of pupil
Secretion of sweat glands
Erection of hairs
Secretion of adrenal medulla
Sugar liberated
Quickening of heart rate
Relaxation of walls
    of stomach and intestines
Constriction of sphincters
Ejaculation (in male)

Sacral Parasympathetic

pelvic nerve

Contraction of bladder
Relaxation of sphincters
Vasodilation of genitalia

◆ **THE AUTONOMIC NERVOUS SYSTEM**

This is a highly simplified and diagrammatic portrayal of the parts of the autonomic
nervous system—where they originate and what their main functions are. For simplicity,
parasympathetic parts and functions are shown on one side and sympathetic ones on the other;
actually, of course, both parts occur on both sides of the body.

The sympathetic division. In this part of the autonomic system, the nerve fibers originate only in the middle part of the spinal cord—in the segments between the neck and the lower spine. These nerves run only into a nearby, vertical chain of *ganglia* (collections of nerve cell bodies); one such chain lies on each side of the spinal cord. Fibers then run up and down this chain, synapsing with neurons that lead to the visceral organs.

The sympathetic division was so named because early anatomists believed that it was supposed to make the visceral organs work "in sympathy." It does in fact usually work as a coordinated whole, with all or most of its functions coming into play when it becomes active. The sympathetic division can be regarded as the trouble-shooter which takes charge in cases of emergency. It operates when the life of the person is threatened, when he is engaging in strenuous effort or exercise, and when he is experiencing such strong emotions as fear and rage. Essentially, the system prepares the body for action by speeding up the heart rate, causing the liver to release sugar to be used by the muscles, stimulating the flow of adrenaline, stopping the digestive processes so that the blood normally going to the stomach can be diverted to the muscles, and so on.

The parasympathetic division. The fibers in this division branch off from the central nervous system above and below the sympathetic nerve fibers, thus giving it the name *parasympathetic* (*para* means "next to"). The majority of the functions of this division are controlled by the fibers originating from above, in the brain stem.

Most of the vital functions of life are governed by the parasympathetic division. Basically, it carries out the body's housekeeping chores, such as digestion, elimination of wastes, protection of the visual system, and, generally, the conservation of bodily energy. In contrast to the sympathetic division, the parasympathetic system does not respond as a whole but activates only whatever functions are necessary at the time.

Coordination of the two divisions. Most organs of the chest and abdomen receive fibers from both systems; where this happens, the action of the two divisions is always antagonistic. If one system excites the organ to increased activity, the other inhibits or decreases its activity. For example, the sympathetic division inhibits digestive processes while the parasympathetic system facilitates them. However, there are times when the two systems are both active and work together in sequence. Sexual response in the male, for example, requires first erection (a parasympathetic function) and then ejaculation (a sympathetic function).

The Connection: The Central Nervous System

During the development of the embryo, as we have seen, individual nerve cells first collect in a neural tube. One end becomes differentiated further into the brain, the remainder into the spinal cord. Together they constitute the *central nervous system* (CNS). This system provides the basis for connecting the vast network of sensory receptors and incoming *afferent* nerve fibers to the outgoing *efferent* nerve fibers and response effectors. Input sensory pathways and output motor pathways are interconnected within the CNS by a net of *associative* neurons (also called *interneurons* or *internuncial* neurons).

The CNS is more than merely a connecting switchboard, however, for it also integrates and coordinates the stimulus input and response output. The higher the species the more highly developed are the mechanisms for integration and coordination. In some species which have developed a highly specialized CNS, neural facilities are provided to store both sensory information and information concerning the consequences of response actions. Complex activities of the CNS then make possible a comparison of information stored in memory with present input, as well as new ways of organizing both input and output (creativity), and planning for future action (expectation).

The reflex action of the spinal cord. It is surprising to realize that animals that have had their brains separated from their spinal cords (*decortication*) can still react to stimuli and even show simple learning. In the course of evolution, however, the development of the "thinking" brain came after the development of the simpler spinal cord. The functions of protecting the organisms from injury, keeping the internal machinery operating, and maintaining the animal's posture are basic to survival of the organism. Thus they could not await development of the brain, but were built into the spinal cord.

If a baby's finger is pinched, the whole arm is drawn away. The localized stimulus (of potential danger) results in the activation of muscles over a large area of the body as a result of the distributing system of the spinal cord. The first stage in this distributing system is provided by the *afferent* neuron itself. On entering the spinal cord, it divides into ascending and descending branches, giving off *collaterals* (branches) at each level of the spinal cord. Each of these collaterals, in turn, can connect with an *interneuron*, which also runs up and down the cord, at each level giving off collaterals to *motor neurons*. Through this distributing mechanism, impulses from a single afferent neuron can innervate many different muscles, producing large-scale gross reflex responses. This type of distribution is called *divergence*.

A reverse consequence of this arrangement is called *convergence*. Impulses from many afferent neurons can ultimately reach the same motor neuron, the system acting much like a funnel. Convergence makes it possible for the same muscle fiber to take part in many different reflexes.

Another function of the distributing system of collaterals and interneurons is the prolongation of excitation, occurring because the interneurons are arranged in *self-exciting circuits*. ■ When a neuron in such a circuit discharges, the nerve impulse passes down the main axon and also into a collateral branching off from it. This branch may connect with a second neuron, causing it to be excited. The axon of the second neuron, in turn, may transmit the impulse to the original cell and excite it a second time. This may be repeated many times. Each time around this reverberating circuit, or *feedback loop*, the impulse goes also to the motor neuron and muscle, like a spark from a grindstone. Thus a momentary stimulus can cause a response which continues long after the stimulus has been withdrawn. Such a response is not possible in the rare cases where only a two-neuron arc is involved.

In the intact animal, interneurons in the spinal cord and collaterals from incoming afferent neurons serve still another function, forming long circuits

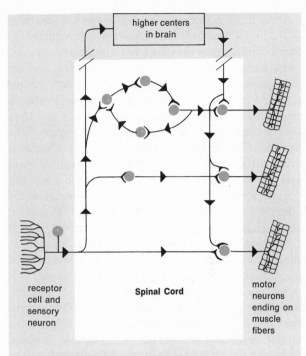

■ **COORDINATION IN THE SPINAL CORD**

Divergence, convergence, self-exciting circuits, and connections to and from the brain are all provided by the networks of neurons in the spinal cord. All but convergence are shown here.

which carry impulses to the brain. These keep "headquarters" informed of what is going on, and the brain may then modify the activity of the simpler reflex arcs. Thus the distributing system of the spinal cord does four things: (a) enables impulses from a single receptor to reach many muscles (divergence), (b) permits the same muscle to be used in reflexes initiated by stimulation from many points on the skin (convergence), (c) extends a response in time, and (d) causes impulses to be long-circuited to the brain.

The adaptive nature of reflexes. Reflexes are "automatic" responses that usually perform some muscular or glandular action which is obviously of service to the organism. Withdrawal of a limb when it is injured protects it from further injury and is therefore termed a *protective reflex.* Another protective reflex is seen when a fleck of dust induces tears that wash it out of the eye. Some reflexes are necessary to vital functions of the body; these includes reflexes which regulate the beat of the heart or the diameter of blood vessels.

In contrast with the protective reflexes are the *postural reflexes* which underlie standing and holding the head upright. For example, if someone jumps on your back, your knees buckle momentarily and then your legs extend, restoring your upright posture. The bending of your knees stretches a *muscle spindle*, a group of muscle fibers wrapped with both afferent and efferent nerve endings. The stretching of this spindle by the bending of your knees stimulates the afferent nerve endings, sending impulses to the spinal cord. Here they pass directly to the motor neuron that supplies the ordinary muscle fibers adjacent to those from which the message came. The stretched muscle contracts and your balance is restored. This reflex is called the *stretch reflex* because its stimulus is the stretching of the muscle spindle. Afferent neurons involved in postural reflexes such as this are the largest and the fastest-conducting neurons, perhaps because continuous maintenance of posture may be even more important to survival than the rapid protective reflexes.

Inhibition and reciprocal innervation.   In general, the muscles of the body are arranged opposite one another in antagonistic pairs, one extending and the other flexing (bending) a given joint. Normally, when one muscle contracts, its antagonist relaxes, for the *excitation* of one is accompanied by the *inhibition* of the motor neurons supplying the other. This is known as the *law of reciprocal innervation.*

Inhibition can occur only at synapses. It is not the muscle fibers themselves that are inhibited, but the motor neurons leading to them. Whenever a skeletal muscle is not excited, it relaxes.

How does the nervous system decide which message will be inhibited when there is conflicting stimulation? Three characteristics of the stimulus give advantage to one over another in the competition for dominance in the organism's activity.

1. Painful stimuli usually have the right of way. The important business of self-protection comes first.

2. Strong stimuli or repeated weak stimuli have the right of way.

3. Too frequent repetition of a response will give the right of way to a rival response, partly because of fatigue and partly because of *adaptation*. That is, if a stimulus is either on continuously, or presented repeatedly at a constant level of intensity, the receptor adapts to the barrage by lessening its receptivity. It is obvious why organisms faced with a myriad of stimuli to process would develop a sensory adaptation mechanism to deal with persistent, unchanging, stimuli.

With this picture in mind of how the nervous system transmits information within the body, we are ready to turn to the original source of such information—the environment—and a new puzzler: if the basic unit in the code of the nervous system is an electrical impulse of a constant size, how do the many kinds of physical stimuli that impinge on the organism get translated into this code?

How Does Information Get In?

Information about the nature of the environment "out there" is detected by a variety of organs composed of highly specialized *receptor* cells. In its usual functioning, each receptor organ is sensitive to only one type of physical or chemical characteristic of the environment—sound waves or light waves, for example. These differences are not absolute, however. Thus the eye, though "tuned" to detect light waves, will also respond to the pressure of a finger poked against the eyelid—as you can determine empirically (but gently!) for yourself.

Transduction and Psychophysics

An organism can detect three things about environmental stimuli: (a) their general class or the type of energy they represent, such as light, temperature, or pressure; (b) their location in space; and (c) their intensity at each point in time.

Information about the first of these—classification of the stimulus—is conveyed by the type of receptor that is stimulated. For example, response of certain receptor cells in the eye indicates stimulation by light waves within certain frequencies of electromagnetic radiation. Clues to the second—the location of the stimulus—are provided by the location of the receptors stimulated, since there are multiple receptors for

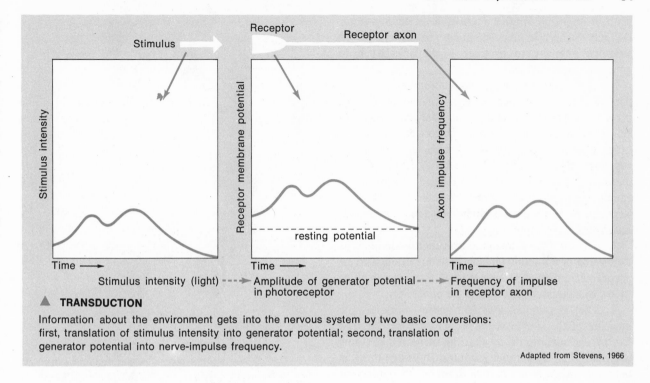

Stimulus

Receptor

Receptor axon

Stimulus intensity

Receptor membrane potential

Axon impulse frequency

Time ⟶

Time ⟶

Time ⟶

resting potential

Stimulus intensity (light) ---▶ Amplitude of generator potential ---▶ Frequency of impulse
in photoreceptor   in receptor axon

▲ **TRANSDUCTION**

Information about the environment gets into the nervous system by two basic conversions:
first, translation of stimulus intensity into generator potential; second, translation of
generator potential into nerve-impulse frequency.

Adapted from Stevens, 1966

every class of stimulus input. The third—detection of how intense the stimulus is—is accomplished by the fact that the stimulus energy is converted into a graded depolarization of the receptor cell membrane by a process called *transduction*. ▲ There is a constant quantifiable relationship between the intensity of the stimulus and the amplitude of the receptor membrane potential which it excites: each intensity of the stimulus is converted into a *generator potential* (a depolarization) of a given *amplitude*. This amplitude is then coded into a particular rate of firing. With stronger stimulation a cell responds more frequently and more cells respond. Once in the "common currency" of the nervous system, information can be propagated and processed according to the basic principles of communication we have described earlier.

What effect does changing the intensity of a stimulus have upon the amplitude of the generator potential? This physiological question can be rephrased in several ways. How much does a stimulus have to be changed before the organism responds to it as changed? Or, what is the mathematical relationship

between the intensity of the stimulus and the responsiveness of the receptor? In practical terms, if you can detect the difference in transmission of high frequency sounds between your old hi-fi speaker and your present one, should you invest in a still more expensive one capable of producing even higher frequencies? Would you detect the further superiority of the new speaker?

Whether our senses can discriminate a change in stimulus intensity depends upon the ratio of the added intensity to the intensity of the previous stimulation. For example, if 2 grams had to be added to a 100-gram weight before a person felt it as heavier, 4 grams would have to be added to a 200-gram weight before he would notice any difference. The exact ratio varies with the kind of sensitivity being measured and with the range of intensities involved, but, in general, the smallest perceived difference in stimulus intensity is a constant proportional part of the comparison stimulus.

This means that for nearly all receptors a small change in stimulus intensity can produce a change in the generator potential when the stimulus is at a low level of intensity. As the intensity level of the stimulus gets higher, it takes a much greater change in stimulus intensity to produce a similar change in generator potential.

The relationship between stimulation and sensation can be measured either in terms of the organism's physical response (generator potential and nerve impulse) or in terms of its psychological response (how much change in the stimulus is necessary before the organism detects it as different). Techniques for measuring psychological response are appropriately called *psychophysical scaling* methods. Use of these techniques allows the researcher to quantify the following basic concepts:

1. The *limen*, or absolute threshold—defined as that value of a stimulus which is strong enough to be accurately detected 50 percent of the time. Values below this threshold are said to be *subliminal*.

2. The *just noticeable difference* (j.n.d.)—the measure of the size of the stimulus increase required for the organism to detect that the increased stimulus is greater than a reference stimulus. By usage this has been the increase detected as different 75 percent of the time.

3. The *Weber-Fechner Law*—relating stimulus change and sensation across various values of the stimulus. The stimulus increment ($\triangle S$) which produces a j.n.d. is a constant proportion for most values of the stimulus (not at the extremes), as shown in the example below, where $\triangle S = 5/10$ or .5.

Starting Stimulus Level		Increase Needed	
If 10 units	plus	5 units	→ 1 j.n.d.
then 15 units	plus	7½ units	
or 22½ units	plus	11¼ units	} → 1 j.n.d.
or 33¾ units	plus	16⅞ units	
etc.			

Varieties of Sensory Information

Our present concern will focus only on vision and hearing, the senses about which most is known. In addition to these two "long-range" senses, which gather precise information about the environment from long distances, man also gains information

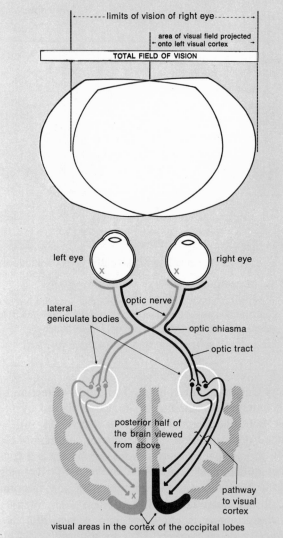

● **THE MECHANICS OF SEEING**

In normal vision, light from one point in the right half of the visual field stimulates points on the left halves of both retinas, instigates impulses over nerve pathways from both points, and finally activates only one point in the left visual cortex of the brain, as shown above. Light from an adjacent point in the visual field will, in turn, activate a different but adjacent point in the visual cortex. Meanwhile, the points in the left half of the visual world are activating points in the right half of the visual cortex. Somehow, despite the double pathways to each location in the visual cortex (and the slightly different input to each one), and despite the fact that only half of the visual field is represented in each side of the brain, we see a single, unified world.

about the environment through several somatic (body) senses which are much less accurate and depend upon direct contact. There are four somatic senses whose receptor cells are located in the skin: pressure (touch), pain, cold, and warmth. These skin senses are sometimes called the *cutaneous senses*. Each one tells the organism something different about the external world.

There are two more somatic senses that are intimately connected with each other and cooperate to help maintain bodily balance and to inform us of the position of our arms, legs, head, and all movable parts. These are the *kinesthetic* and *labyrinthine* senses. In addition, there are the chemical senses of taste and smell. The somatic and chemical senses will not be treated in further detail here.

Vision

The sense of sight, so important to survival, has followed a fascinating course of development. The intricate human eye apparently has evolved from a few light-sensitive cells such as those found in primitive forms of life. Gradually, as more advanced forms developed, there evidently appeared a greater and greater number of visual elements per unit area, an especially sensitive central spot, and more complex nerve pathways and related brain areas, making possible a more accurate appreciation of patterns. ◆ The eye also developed mechanisms for making use of the small amount of light available at night, giving it enormous range. And in monkeys and man, the eyes moved gradually around to the front of the head so that binocular vision became possible. Finally, with the development of superior brain connections to the eyes, especially in man, far more intelligent use of visual input became possible. •

Structures for seeing. The eye is made up of two visual systems combined into one but specialized for different functions. Each system has its own distinctively shaped receptor cells; those of one system are called *cones*; those of the other, *rods*. The cones function only in the light; they are responsible for color vision and high visual acuity. In dim light, the cones cannot be stimulated and the rods function alone. The rods are extraordinarily sensitive to very

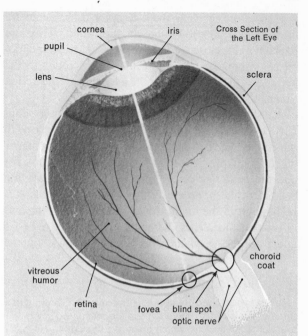

cornea — iris — Cross Section of the Left Eye
pupil
lens
sclera
choroid coat
vitreous humor
retina — fovea — blind spot — optic nerve

◆ The eyeball is composed of three layers: (1) an outer protective coat called the *sclera*, a portion of which is the transparent *cornea* which acts as a refracting surface; (2) a middle layer called the *choroid* coat which is pigmented; and (3) a light-sensitive inner layer called the *retina*. When light enters the eye, it passes first through the cornea and then through the *pupil*, which is an opening in the pigmented *iris*. The pupil adjusts in size to regulate the amount of light entering the eye, which influences both the brightness and the clarity of the image. The light rays then penetrate the *lens*, which focuses them onto the sensitive surface of the retina. Before reaching the retina, the light rays must pass through the liquid (*vitreous humor*) which fills the eyeball. Light from the center of the *visual field* (i.e., what the person is looking at) is focused on the *fovea*, which is at the center of the retina and is the most sensitive part of the eye in normal daylight vision. The retina contains the visual receptors which, when stimulated by light, initiate nerve impulses that travel through the *optic nerve* and ultimately reach the *occipital lobes* at the back of the brain, one in each hemisphere.

dim illumination (night vision) but not to hues, responding only to black, white, and shades of gray.

The rods and cones are located in the bottom layer of the retina, which means that light must travel through several layers of nerve fibers and blood vessels before reaching these receptor cells. There are more than 7,000,000 cones in the retina. They are packed most closely together in the fovea and decrease in number from the center of the retina to the periphery. Rods are found in all parts of the retina *except* the fovea.

As shown in the diagram, the receptors connect to the *bipolar cells*, which in turn synapse with the *ganglion cells*. (There are also many interconnecting cells in the retina, such as the *horizontal cells* and the *amacrine cells*.) The axons of the ganglion cells form the *optic nerve*; they synapse on cells at a relay point in the brain, the *lateral geniculate nucleus* of the thalamus. These latter cells, in turn, have axons going to the *occipital cortex* at the back of the

brain. At the point where the optic nerve leaves the retina there is a *blind spot* which is not sensitive to light.

Ordinarily we are unaware of our blind spots because when we are using both eyes an image never falls on both blind spots at once, since each faces a slightly different part of the visual field. You can determine the location of your blind spots by a very simple experiment. Close your right eye, hold the book at arm's length, and fixate on the circle below. Still fixating on the circle, move the book toward you until the cross disappears.

■ RETINAL PATHWAYS

This is a stylized and greatly simplified diagram showing examples of the pathways that connect three of the layers of nerve cells in the retina. Incoming light passes through all these layers to reach the receptors, which are at the back of the eyeball and pointed away from the source of light. Through convergence, several receptor cells send impulses to each ganglion cell, while through divergence, one receptor cell may send impulses to more than one ganglion cell. Nerve impulses from the ganglion cells leave the eye via the optic nerve and travel to the next relay point.

The photo shows actual cones in the retina. It was taken by the same technique as the photo of synapses on page 74.

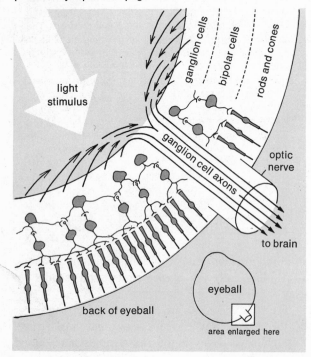

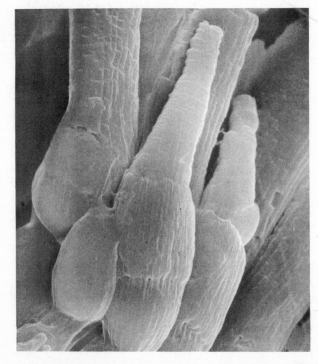

At that point, the cross corresponds to the part of your visual field that is falling on the blind spot of your left eye. To find the location of the blind spot in your right eye, follow the same procedure, but this time close your left eye and fixate on the cross with your right eye.

It has been estimated that the retina contains about 120 million receptors, a few million bipolar cells, and one million ganglion cells. Obviously, there is a tremendous *convergence* of information from many receptors to one ganglion cell. However, because of the many interconnections between cells in the retina, there is also a *divergent* system of information flow. Thus, one receptor connects to several bipolar cells, which in turn connect to even more ganglion cells.

But how do these receptors translate light into nerve impulses? Photopigments contained in the receptors play a major part in this transduction process. The rods have one type of photopigment, called *rhodopsin*, while each cone has one of three types of *iodopsin*, corresponding to the wave lengths of blue, green, and red light. When light hits a receptor, it is absorbed by the photopigment, causing the pigment to break down into its component parts (for example, rhodopsin breaks down into *retinene* and *opsin*). This process changes the polarity of the membrane of the receptor cell, producing a generator potential (similar to an EPSP) which activates the bipolar cells. As is true of other sensory systems, the visual transduction process is not completely understood; a number of important questions have yet to be answered.

After millions of receptors have responded to a visual stimulus, this tremendous amount of information must somehow be processed and interpreted by the nervous system. By combining the visual input in various ways, the nervous system provides us with information about different aspects of the visual image, such as brightness, color, form, and movement. To achieve this, input from the receptor must be analyzed for several different types of information *simultaneously* at the same level. The system of anatomical divergence, mentioned earlier, provides for such multiple parallel processing of information.

How we see brightness. The absorption of photons of light by the receptors activates both the rods and, through them, chains of neurons, to produce the "perception" of light. The greater the intensity of the light (the larger the number of photons per unit time activating the rods), the greater will be the activity produced in the retina and transmitted to the brain, and the greater will be the sensation of brightness. The integrating process here is one of *summation* of information from many different receptors. This summation takes place in the ganglion cells, each of which receives inputs from many receptors.

Such summation in the rod system is responsible for the great sensitivity of the rod system to light. A single rod must be struck almost simultaneously by two photons of light in order for it to activate a ganglion cell. Such a simultaneous event, however, is likely to occur only at high light levels. Summation of the input from many different rods makes it possible for the ganglion cell to be activated by *any* near-simultaneous combination of light "captures" occurring among these receptors that totals two photons. This means that the ganglion cells will respond even to very small amounts of light. The rod system has several ways of maximizing the amount of summation in order to gain greater sensitivity, but it pays for this advantage by a loss of visual acuity, or sharpness of vision.

The process which prepares the eyes to see under low illumination is known as *dark adaptation*. You undoubtedly have had the experience of going into a darkened theater and being unable to find your way to an empty seat without help. Yet after a few minutes, you were able to see quite well. For most people, complete dark adaptation requires about half an hour of darkness after the last use of the eyes in bright light. Discrimination between hues becomes less keen as the level of illumination falls, finally disappearing completely as the "color-blind" rods take over the job of seeing.

You can perform a simple but interesting experiment on dark adaptation by staying in a dark room for ten minutes. At the end of this period close one eye and, holding your hand over it, turn on the light for a few seconds. Then turn off the light again. Observe the room first through the eye that has been closed all the time and you will be able to see objects fairly clearly. Then close that eye and observe the room through the eye that was exposed to the brief period of light; the room will appear totally black. This experiment demonstrates that the process of dark adaptation takes place in the retina of each eye rather than in the brain.

How we see color.   Color vision is the ability to differentiate various wavelengths of light (various colors) independently of their relative intensity, or brightness. This is believed to be accomplished through the cones in combination with special cells in the lateral geniculate nucleus called *opponent* cells. Each of these cells responds with excitation to impulses initiated by one wavelength and with inhibition to impulses initiated by another wavelength.

There are four basic types of opponent cells: red excitatory, green inhibitory $(+R, -G)$; red inhibitory, green excitatory $(-R, +G)$; yellow excitatory, blue inhibitory $(+Y, -B)$; and yellow inhibitory, blue excitatory $(-Y, +B)$. When light is absorbed by the cones (each of which, as you will recall, contains one of three types of photopigments), this information is passed on to the opponent cells, which *subtract* the output of one class of receptors from output of another. For example, a $+R, -G$ opponent cell subtracts the output of the green cones from the output of the red cones. Thus, the firing rate of a single opponent cell is dependent on the differential excitation of the two sets of receptor cells leading to it. Different patterns of excitation and inhibition of the opponent cells produce the sensations of different colors. The psychological dimensions of color and two of the tests that are used to detect color blindness are described on the back endsheets.

As often happens as knowledge grows, the present opponent-cell model of color vision provides support for certain aspects of both the earlier classical theories in this field. The *Young-Helmholtz theory* represents ideas proposed by the physicist Young in 1801 and later modified by the physiologist Helmholtz. According to this theory, the human eye was thought to contain three kinds of cones, each kind sensitive to one of the three primary colors of light. A sensation of white was thought to result from the equal stimulation of all three, with other color sensations resulting from the combined stimulation of the three types of cones in different proportions. Although other details of the Young-Helmholtz theory

have proved erroneous, modern research does bear out the view that different types of cones are responsible for different color sensations.

The *Hering theory* (proposed by another physiologist) postulated the existence of three pairs of neural processes (black-white, red-green, yellow-blue). Each of these pairs was thought to be capable of two modes of responding that were opposed to each other. Clearly, this theory anticipates the current opponent theory of color vision in its hypothesis of red-green and yellow-blue processes. The black-white process matches with what we know about the activity of the rod system.

How we see patterns.   Recent work in vision has begun to discover the ways in which pattern information is processed. That is, we now have some idea of how the eye perceives form and movement in the visual field.

Contours.   Experiments with the eye of the horseshoe crab, *Limulus,* have shown that every stimulated cell inhibits cells adjacent to it, a phenomenon known as *lateral inhibition* (Ratliff, Hartline, & Miller, 1963). If the entire visual field is uniformly stimulated, any individual cell does not respond very much since all the cells are inhibiting each other. Suppose, however, that half of the receptors are strongly stimulated and half are not, as by a visual stimulus that is half white and half black. While there is little activity in those parts of the visual field that are uniformly stimulated, the *border* is highly emphasized in the firing pattern of the ganglion cells. The edge of the bright side of the stimulus is characterized by extra-high firing because these cells are being inhibited from only one side. At the edge of the dim part of the stimulus there is extra-low firing because these cells are being inhibited by neighboring cells on the bright side. The result of this process is that the border in a visual pattern is highly emphasized. The dark edge of the border is seen as extra-dark, and the light edge as extra-light; such edges are called *Mach bands.*   ■

Form.   The *receptive field* of a given neuron is that area of the retina from which it receives impulses. It has been found that the ganglion cells in the retina have concentric receptive fields with either an excita-

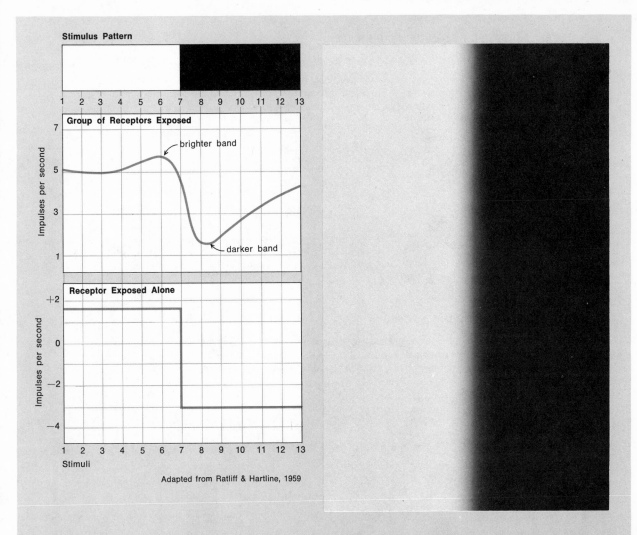

Adapted from Ratliff & Hartline, 1959

▨ MACH BANDS

If a single visual receptor is exposed to the successive areas of a bright-dark stimulus pattern (from areas 1 to 13), there is a sudden drop in its response corresponding with the point at which the pattern changes from light to dark (lower graph). But when the same receptor and those around it are exposed at the same time (upper graph), its responses are quite different because lateral inhibition occurs.

As long as the stimulus is homogeneously bright, the receptor's response stays the same, but near the border its response becomes higher because there is less inhibition from adjacent cells (some of them are no longer being stimulated), and a bright band appears, as you can see for yourself in the photo. Just over the border, on the dark side, some of the adjacent receptors are still receiving stimulation from the bright side and thus producing more inhibition than is true over the dark area generally. The result is that you see a dark band at this point.

You can demonstrate the reality of these inhibitory processes by using a card to block out first the right half of the photo and then the left half: the Mach bands disappear as soon as the stimulus is homogeneous.

● RECEPTIVE FIELDS OF VISUAL CELLS

Receptive Fields of Two Ganglion Cells

Each ganglion cell in the eye receives input from a round area of the retina consisting of many receptor cells. In some cases the center of this area is excitatory and the outer part inhibitory; in other cases it is the other way around. A ganglion cell is most sensitive to input from the center of its receptive field.

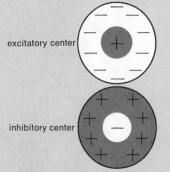

excitatory center

Stimulation of cells in center excites ganglion cell; stimulation in periphery inhibits same ganglion cell.

inhibitory center

Stimulation in center inhibits ganglion cell; stimulation in periphery excites same ganglion cell.

Receptive Fields of Cortical Cells

By contrast, the retinal area that excites a simple cortical cell is elongated; it too has both excitatory and inhibitory parts. A cortical cell can receive input from a whole line in the visual field by receiving input from many ganglion cells whose receptive fields overlap to form a line.

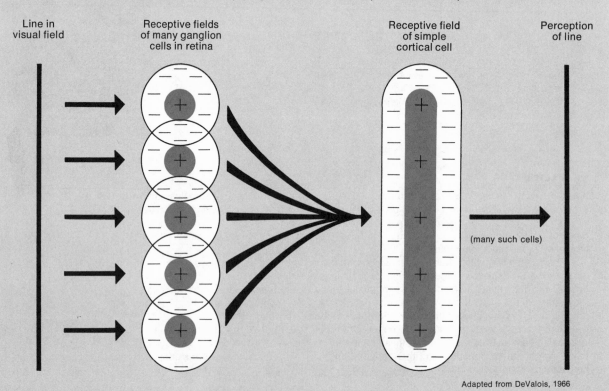

Line in visual field

Receptive fields of many ganglion cells in retina

Receptive field of simple cortical cell

Perception of line

(many such cells)

Adapted from DeValois, 1966

tory center and an inhibitory surround or the other way around. These ganglion cells are very sensitive to *small spots* of light which just fill the center of their receptive field. In contrast to the ganglion cells, the cells in the visual cortex often have elongated receptive fields, rather than concentric ones. In this case the stimulus which produces the greatest amount of activity of the cell is a *line* of a certain width located in a particular plane in the visual field. The "optimal orientation" of the stimulus varies systematically across the cortical surface. The major researchers in this area, Hubel and Wiesel (1959), have proposed that the "line" cells in the brain are responding to the input from a group of retinal "concentric" cells whose receptive fields are in a line. •

There are other, more complex cells in the cortex which seem to be still later elements in the chain of visual processing. For example, some of these cells respond to any line regardless of its location and orientation. It would appear that they can be activated by any one of a group of preceding cortical cells, each receptive only to a line of a particular location and orientation. Other higher-order complex cells respond only to an angle. Presumably, the inputs to these cells come from "line" cells whose optimal orientations are at an angle to each other.

Movement.   Certain ganglion cells have been found to respond only to a stimulus that is moving in a certain direction. Movement in the opposite direction inhibits the cell, while movements in other directions produce intermediate amounts of excitation and inhibition. Each of these cells differs in the direction of motion to which it is most responsive. Just how these cells are able to detect movement is not yet known, but higher-order analysis of the responses of these movement-sensitive cells is believed to take place in the cortex.

This brief description of the mechanisms for seeing brightness, color, and various aspects of pattern is enough to suggest how intricately equipped the human organism has become for responding to visual stimuli. Much of what has been presented has been discovered only in the last ten or fifteen years, and new findings are appearing in rapid succession. As with our knowledge of genetic mechanisms, however, many puzzles remain.

Hearing

The sense of sound involves the use of one of the most complex organs in the human body—the ear. The sensitivity of the ear is so great that it can respond to extremely soft, low sounds. (In fact, it can almost—but not quite—detect the sound of air molecules randomly hitting against the eardrum!) However, the ear is also resilient enough to withstand the pounding of very strong sound waves, such as highly amplified music at a rock concert. Moreover, it can be very selective, as when it picks out one voice from many in a crowd or a choral group.

How sounds get in.   When an object produces sound, it creates waves of pressure differences in the surrounding air. These alternating waves of dense and thin air are the stimuli for hearing, but before nerve impulses can travel to the auditory center of the brain, sound waves must pass through the three principal parts of the ear: the external ear, the middle ear, and the inner ear (*cochlea*), where they are finally transformed into nerve impulses. ▲   (p. 90)

At this point you may be asking yourself: why does there have to be such a complicated mechanism to transform sound waves into nerve impulses? Why, for example, couldn't the auditory receptor cells be on the outside of the ear? The answer to these questions is that the ear is especially designed to maximize the amount of energy that is absorbed from the sound waves hitting the eardrum. Normally, when sound waves strike a solid surface, most of their energy is reflected away. The various structures of the ear manage to conserve this energy by converting the large amplitude of the sound waves into stronger vibrations of smaller amplitude (von Békésy, 1957).

How sounds are coded.   The sounds we hear have pitch and loudness—related, respectively, to the frequency and the amplitude of the sound waves. But how does the inner ear signal both the frequency and the amplitude of the auditory stimulus to the brain so that both pitch and loudness can be recognized? One explanation of this is the *place theory* set forth by Helmholtz before the turn of the century. He believed that different fibers on the basilar membrane were responsive to different frequencies, like the different strings on a piano, and thus that a particular tone would cause particular fibers of the basilar membrane to vibrate and excite the receptor cells at that point. This in turn would give rise to impulses in particular nerve fibers going to a specific band in the auditory cortex. The place theory is familiarly called the "pitch is which" theory—that is, the pitch we hear is thought to be determined by which fiber is stimulated. Intensity of the stimulus, according to Helmholtz, is indicated by the frequency with which the nerve fiber responds.

For various reasons, the place theory has difficulty in explaining our hearing of low tones. Some of the

frequency theories that have been developed do a better job with this problem. Typical of these is the *telephone theory* suggested by the physicist Rutherford. He held that the frequency of nerve impulses was directly correlated with the frequency of the sound wave. Thus the basilar membrane was thought to act like a telephone transmitter, sending impulses at various frequencies to the brain. The loudness of an auditory stimulus was supposedly determined by the number of nerve fibers excited. The problem with this theory was that it could not explain the hearing of *high* tones: since a single nerve fiber cannot respond more than 600 times per second, it obviously

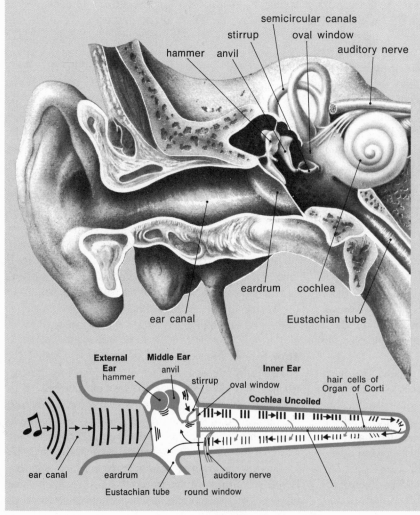

▲ **STRUCTURES OF THE HUMAN EAR**

The top drawing is a cross section of the human ear. Below it is a diagrammatic cross section with the cochlea as it would appear if it were unwound and stretched out straight.

The sound waves travel first through the outer ear and auditory canal to a thin membrane called the *eardrum,* which begins to vibrate. These vibrations are picked up by three small bones (*ossicles*) in the middle ear and are transmitted through another membrane, the *oval window,* to the fluid of the *cochlea* (the auditory part of the inner ear). One of the ossicles (called the *stirrup*) acts like a piston, moving the fluid back and forth in the rhythm of the sound waves. The movement of the fluid makes a thin membrane within the cochlea (the *basilar membrane*) begin to vibrate. This, in turn, bends the hair cells of the *Organ of Corti,* which rests on the basilar membrane. These hair cells are the actual auditory receptors; moving them "excites" them and produces a generator potential which initiates nerve impulses in the fibers of the *auditory nerve.* The auditory nerve then carries the impulses to the brain.

◆ **VOLLEY THEORY**

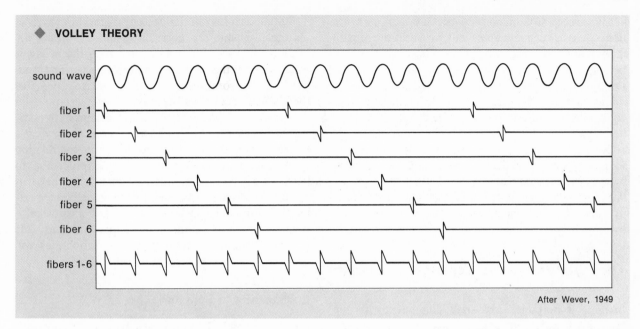

After Wever, 1949

cannot transmit all the frequencies within the range of hearing, which go as high as 20,000 cycles per second.

A theory which supplements the telephone theory is the *volley theory* (Wever & Bray, 1930). Since we can hear frequencies much higher than the maximum frequency of nerve fiber discharge, it was suggested that the nerve fibers operate in groups, with the various groups reacting (discharging their volleys of impulses) at different times. For example, if a tone of 4000 cycles per second were transmitted, there would be a spurt of activity in the auditory nerve every four thousandth of a second, or once for every peak in the sound wave—but *different* groups of fibers would be responsible for the spurt each time. Some fibers might react to every fourth cycle of the sound wave, some to every fifth cycle and so on. ◆

The latest evidence seems to indicate that a combination of a volley theory and a place theory is needed to explain hearing. For frequencies up to 5000 cycles, the volley principle seems to be the major factor, but above 5000 cycles the experience of pitch can be explained only by the place theory (Wever, 1949). The intensity, or loudness, of an auditory stimulus may be coded both by the total number of impulses activated each second (number of fibers involved and frequency of firing) and by the activation of "high threshold" fibers (i.e., nerve fibers that require a tremendous amount of bending of the hair cells before they are stimulated). It should be pointed out that none of these theories has been able to explain the critical process of auditory transduction—that is, exactly how the stimulation of the receptors by sound (i.e., the bending of the hair cells) is translated into nerve impulses.

The range of pressures to which our ears are sensitive is immense. In fact the ratio of the least to the greatest is about 1 to 5,000,000. Because of this large range, auditory intensity is usually measured in a logarithmic unit known as the decibel (db). The decibel measures the intensity of a particular sound in terms of how many times more intense it is than a sound at the lower threshold of hearing. Actually this lower threshold is somewhat dependent on the frequency as well as the amplitude of the sound wave; thus zero on the decibel scale has been set at the least intense stimulus we can hear at a frequency of 1000 cycles per second.

In spite of the wide range of frequencies that the human ear can respond to, there are certain frequencies to which it is rather insensitive. This is most true of very low frequencies, for which there is a reason of physical necessity: it is only because our ears are insensitive to such low tones that we avoid hearing all the vibrations of our own bodies. However, you can hear such sounds by putting your fingers in both ears, stopping them to sounds in the air. The low, irregular sound that you hear is the muscle contractions of your arms and fingers. You may be able to hear your heartbeat as well. Obviously, if we always heard our body vibrations, as well as other low-frequency sounds, significant auditory stimuli would be masked by this "noise" and we would hear them less clearly. Paradoxically, then, if our ears were any more sensitive than they are, they would actually be *less* sensitive.

The Quintessence of Essence: The Brain

Imagine a portable, desk-sized computer with the following features: immense storage capacity for possibly all important inputs it will receive in seventy years or more; discriminative capacities diverse enough to detect a vintage-year wine, the difference between two perfumes, or whether a sphere traveling at great velocity toward it will be a "strike" or "ball"; the ability to plan its own reproduction and improvement and to modify its environment. Finally, can you imagine a computer which could program its own destruction and that of its species? Your brain is a mass of tissue organized into such a computer system —which also allows you to imagine its feats, as well as to recognize its as yet unattained potential.

The Ways into the Brain

In examining how the brain processes information it is interesting first to consider the methodological question of how we can study the operation of the brain. The two most basic techniques employ electrical *stimulation* and brain *lesions*.

Stimulating one portion of the brain with minute amounts of electrical current makes one of the hands tremble. Stimulation of another portion stops the patient's speaking. Stimulation of the back of the brain induces visual sensations, while stimulation of a more forward region of the brain invokes the memory of a musical tune.

Stimulation may be induced by chemical as well as electrical means. By correlating the region of the brain stimulated (brain anatomy) with the behavior which accompanies such stimulation (brain function), it has been possible to map precisely many of the known functions of the brain.

Mapping of the brain can also be done by recording how behavior changes after a lesion. Thus when a tumor is removed and convulsions cease, the relation of this brain *lesion* (an area of destroyed cells) to behavior can be recorded. Lesions may occur naturally through disease or accident, or they may be experimentally produced in lower animals. Fuller descriptions of the use of these techniques to study the behavior of humans and subhuman vertebrates will be given in the last section of this chapter.

Localization of Function

Back in the early 1800's, a movement called *phrenology* developed. Its basic principle was that the mind was not a unity, but rather was composed of various distinct powers. These powers, argued Gall and Spurzheim, the originators of phrenology, could be found in various "organs" of the brain. The places they identified as the seats of various functions can be seen on page 441.

Modern neurophysiologists have come to the same general conclusion, not about powers of the mind or the naïve categories suggested by the phrenologists, but about the fact of specialized functions. Thus the modern doctrine of localization of function states that nerve cells with the same function form an aggregate in a particular region of the brain. This aggregation results in a great *redundancy* of function within the area. Such duplication means that important functions can continue reliably even if some of the cells are destroyed, because many others are still carrying the message.

Since all portions of the brain interact to some degree, loss of part of the brain may often be compensated for to some extent by activity of other parts sharing related information. Although destruction of some areas results in permanent loss of a given function, damage to other areas may be only temporarily incapacitating. In some cases, loss of function seems less dependent upon the *location* of the brain tissue removed than upon the total *amount* removed. This "mass action of the brain," discovered by Lashley (1929), equips the higher organism to survive even extensive damage to his central switchboard: even with his specialization of capacities, his brain retains some "equipotentiality" too. In effect, it eats its cake and has it too.

Main parts and functions of the brain.   Looking in at the top of the brain of a surgical patient, we would see a mass of gray tissue separated into two halves,

each covered with ridges and convolutions (like an oversized walnut). ▲   This tissue is the outer covering of the brain and is only a tenth of an inch thick. It is called the *cortex* (meaning "bark") and is made up largely of the dendrites and cell bodies of neurons whose axons extend into the interior part of the brain.

The cortex is part of the major portion of the brain, the *cerebrum*. The cerebrum is connected to the spinal cord by a group of structures collectively called the *brain stem*—the earliest beginning of a

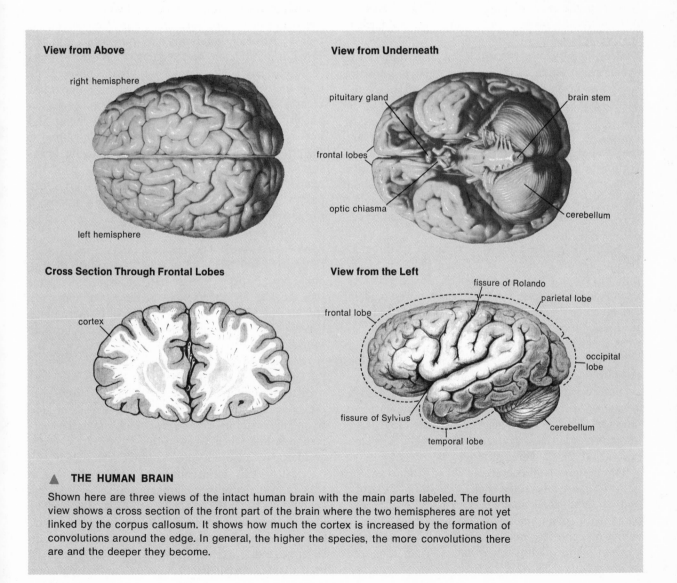

View from Above

right hemisphere

left hemisphere

View from Underneath

pituitary gland

frontal lobes

optic chiasma

brain stem

cerebellum

Cross Section Through Frontal Lobes

cortex

View from the Left

fissure of Rolando

parietal lobe

frontal lobe

occipital lobe

fissure of Sylvius

temporal lobe

cerebellum

▲ **THE HUMAN BRAIN**

Shown here are three views of the intact human brain with the main parts labeled. The fourth view shows a cross section of the front part of the brain where the two hemispheres are not yet linked by the corpus callosum. It shows how much the cortex is increased by the formation of convolutions around the edge. In general, the higher the species, the more convolutions there are and the deeper they become.

"headquarters" within the nervous system. At the back of the brain, tucked under the cerebrum, is the *cerebellum,* whose function it is to maintain balance, posture, and certain regulatory mechanisms.

The halves of the cerebrum, called *hemispheres,* are in fact not separated but connected by a heavy bundle of nerve fibers, the *corpus callosum.* Each hemisphere of the cerebrum can be divided functionally into four lobes by reference to two deep grooves (fissures) within each hemisphere. It can be seen that in front of the *fissure of Rolando* lies the *frontal lobe,* behind it the *parietal lobe.* Beneath the *fissure of Sylvius* lies the *temporal lobe* and at the far back is the *occipital lobe.*

Beneath the cortex layer is the larger portion of the brain, which is almost all white due to the presence of the white myelin sheaths covering countless axons. Some of these fibers are sensory fibers coming up to the cortex from the spinal cord by way of relay centers in the older parts of the brain; some are motor fibers going down to the spinal cord from the cortex; others connect one area of the cortex with another area of the same hemisphere, with areas on the opposite side of the brain, or with a variety of separate subcortical structures beneath the cerebrum.

Sensory functions. Though stimulation of different sensory nerves gives rise to different kinds of sensation, this is not because the impulses are different. As we already have seen, nerve impulses differ only in amplitude and rate of propagation. They yield different sensations because they end at different locations in the brain.

The most highly developed receiving areas, making possible the most precise discriminations, are in the cerebral cortex. All the senses are represented to a greater or lesser extent by lower receiving areas also, however. Thus if the higher centers are destroyed, lower ones can take over at least part of the same decoding of the incoming message.

The highest visual centers, as already indicated, lie in the occipital lobe at the back of the brain. Destruction of these areas in man destroys vision except perhaps for some primitive ability for gross discrimination of lightness and darkness. In lower animals, however, more ability for visual discrimination remains after cortical damage.

Sensory messages from the various parts of the body surface are projected on the *somatosensory* areas shown in the diagram. ◆ The primary somatosensory area runs along behind the fissure of Rolando, across from the primary motor centers. The body is represented upside down, with far more space devoted to face and hands than to the rest of the body. Centers for taste are close to those for touch sensitivity for the tongue.

Auditory centers lie along the fissure of Sylvius in the upper part of the temporal lobe. They are close to, and to some extent intermingled with, some of the receiving areas for touch. Smell is decoded in the oldest part of the forebrain, the *rhinencephalon*—located deep inside the hemispheres.

Besides the primary receiving areas shown in the diagram, various adjacent areas—or in some cases areas some distance away—are also involved in the analysis and organization of the sensory input and hence in complex perceptions. For example, although the primary auditory receiving area is along the lower surface of the fissure of Sylvius in the top of the temporal lobe, patients with injuries in many other parts of the brain may also have difficulty in recognizing sounds. ■ (p. 96)

Motor functions. The primary motor area is concentrated immediately in front of the fissure of Rolando, across from the somatosensory area. Here, too, the feet are represented at the upper part, the trunk farther down, and the hands still farther down; nerve centers controlling motions of the face and tongue are localized at the bottom.

Long axons lead down from this area of the brain through the spinal cord directly or through interneurons to the motor neurons supplying the muscles of the body and the extremities. When a part of this brain area is stimulated, some voluntary-muscle group responds, and when areas in this region of the brain are destroyed, movement is impaired accordingly.

Because of the clear connection between this brain area and activity of the voluntary muscles, it was long believed that control of the muscles was centered in this strip of brain. But Luria (1970) has pointed out that to make such an assumption is like assuming that all merchandise exported from a particular port has been manufactured there. Actually, several parts of

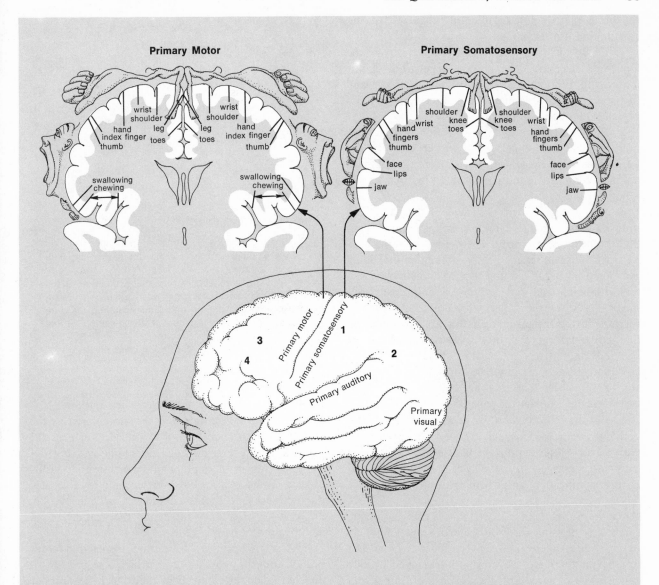

◆ PRIMARY MOTOR AND SOMATOSENSORY AREAS

The primary motor and somatosensory areas of the cortex lie along the fissure of Rolando: the motor area just in front of it, the somatosensory area just behind it. Corresponding parts of the body are represented by points roughly across the fissure from each other, and representation is upside down; that is, the legs and feet are represented at the top and around the inner surface between the hemispheres, hands and arms are below them, and the head at the bottom. The greater precision of sensitivity and control in head and hands than in other parts of the body is reflected in larger areas of representation on the cortex.

the brain play important roles in organizing voluntary motion. For example:

1. Feedback from the sensory area across the fissure is necessary for precise regulation of the movement. Without such feedback, both flexor and extensor muscles are innervated indiscriminately, and organized motion is impossible.

2. Proper organization of the action in space requires the action of cells still farther back in the parietal-occipital area. With lesions here, the individual may confuse left and right or may lose his way in a familiar place.

3. For a coordinated sequence of actions, there must be termination of each link as it is completed so that the next one can occur. With a lesion in the area in front of the primary motor area, the individual may keep repeating the first part of an action.

4. Planning and carrying out a coordinated sequence requires the action of an area still farther forward in the frontal lobe. If this area is damaged, the individual repeats links already completed or responds impulsively to outside stimuli; purposive, goal-directed action cannot be carried through (Luria, 1970). These four areas are indicated by **1, 2, 3,** and **4** on the diagram on page 95.

5. Besides all the cortical areas mentioned and perhaps others, subcortical areas of the brain also play a role—for example, in filtering or magnifying incoming messages, in inducing a particular level of energy mobilization, and in other ways.

Association functions. If we make a drawing of the cerebral cortex and mark off the areas now known to be involved in motor and sensory functions, we find that by far the larger portion is not touched by our pencil. These parts are the *association areas,* so named because it was originally assumed that it must be here that new "associations"—that is, learning—took place. Although much remains to be learned about these areas, it is now recognized that this is far too simplified a picture.

The association areas of each side of the cerebral cortex are connected with each other, with motor and sensory areas, with corresponding areas on the opposite side, and with inner parts of the brain. They are thought to correlate and integrate the simpler functions of the sensory and motor areas. In fact, as

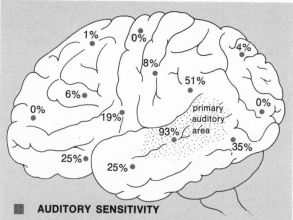

■ **AUDITORY SENSITIVITY**

This diagram shows the percent of patients with brain lesions in different parts of the brain who had difficulty recognizing sounds. Not only the area commonly designated as the primary auditory area but most of the rest of the brain plays some role in normal sound perception and understanding. (Figure adapted from "The Functional Organization of the Brain" by A. R. Luria. Copyright © 1970 by Scientific American, Inc. All rights reserved.)

we have seen, the sensory areas act essentially as gateways into the cortex, and the motor area as the exit. Thus injuries to the cortex outside but near the primary visual area do not cause blindness but destroy awareness of depth and recognition of visual objects. There is also, however, considerable vertical interaction between cortical and subcortical levels in the analysis of sensory input and the shaping of an adaptive motor output.

Disease in or injury to certain association areas brings about a condition in which the person is unable to recognize objects by their "feel." A familiar object like a door key or a pencil can be handled indefinitely and still not be recognized. Patients who show this type of disorder are still capable of experiencing normal elementary sensations; their difficulty is in organizing these elements into normal perceptions.

Similar disorders of perception are found in other sensory fields. These disorders are called *agnosias,* or "inabilities to know," and are classified on the basis of the nature of the function which is impaired. Related disorders affecting language are called *aphasias.* One example is inability to recognize spoken words, sometimes called "word deafness." These conditions are associated with lesions in the association regions that lie close to the various sensory areas of the cortex.

Similar impairments of the association region near the motor areas may give rise to motor disturbances, especially of the apparatus used in speech. In some cases the sensory and motor aspects of speech are little affected, yet there are subtle disturbances of speech which are difficult to describe.

In 1861 Paul Broca reported the classic case of a patient who showed an almost complete loss of speech ability. Careful examination of the patient's brain showed that an area in the frontal lobe of the left cerebral hemisphere just above the fissure of Sylvius had been destroyed. This area, which is near the area controlling the mouth, has come to be known as *Broca's area.* About ten years later Carl Wernicke discovered that destruction of the cortex of the left temporal lobe below the auditory area, extending backward and curving up around the end of the fissure of Sylvius, was associated with inability to understand spoken language. This area is called *Wernicke's center.*

Research since then has shown that one of the hemispheres of the brain exerts a dominant role over the other. Cerebral dominance is related to right- and left-handedness. Because of the cross-over of motor and sensory fibers, it is the left hemisphere that is dominant in right-handed people.

Several parts of the left cerebral cortex of a right-handed person are now known to be involved in different aspects of the use of language. Speaking, writing, reading, and comprehending spoken language all involve somewhat different combinations, since they have differing component parts. For example, in writing a word in response to a spoken instruction, one must discriminate the *sounds* (temporal lobe near auditory area), formulate the word to be written (kinesthetic centers near Broca's area), and put it into writing (visual and spatial areas in occipital and parietal lobes), with the whole thing coordinated by the frontal lobes. The location of brain damage can often be inferred from the kind of inability that a patient shows. Thus a patient who has no trouble understanding spoken speech but cannot write or recognize written or printed words might have brain damage in the parietal-occipital area.

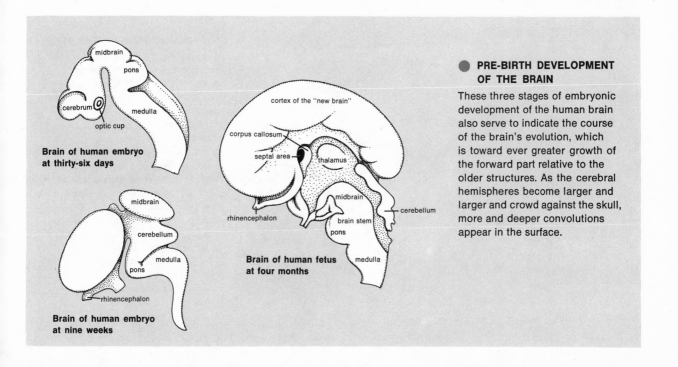

Brain of human embryo at thirty-six days

Brain of human embryo at nine weeks

Brain of human fetus at four months

● **PRE-BIRTH DEVELOPMENT OF THE BRAIN**

These three stages of embryonic development of the human brain also serve to indicate the course of the brain's evolution, which is toward ever greater growth of the forward part relative to the older structures. As the cerebral hemispheres become larger and larger and crowd against the skull, more and deeper convolutions appear in the surface.

The old brain: the subcortex. The prominent position of the cortex at the top of the nervous system and its accessibility to surgical and stimulation research led investigators at first to the false conclusion that it alone was responsible for almost all complex adaptive behavior. Moreover, it was the cortex, or *neocortex*, in which the course of phylogenetic evolution—the upward development of more complex species—was revealed. The fish has no neocortex, while amphibians, reptiles, and birds have more, in that order. In mammals, the neocortex becomes much larger, until in man it achieves its greatest size. This trend is called *corticalization.* • (p. 97) Meanwhile, the *subcortex*, or brain stem, did not follow this pattern of increased development. It thus seemed likely to early researchers that many of its former functions had been taken over by the neocortex.

Recently, however, it has become clear that man, like other animals, still does much of his living in the old brain. While man's cortex has been assigned the principal tasks of decoding complex sensory inputs, storing information, reasoning, thinking, speaking, and learning, there is much left for the old brain to handle. Paths to and from the cortex pass through it and there is ample two-way communication between it and the higher centers. In addition, man's appetites (hunger, thirst, sex), aversions (fears), consummatory behavior (eating, drinking, mating), sleep, arousal, and temperature control are all under the influence of parts of the subcortex. Finally, housed deep within these primitive structures are centers that play a vital role in emotional behavior.

The main parts of the brain stem are the *thalamus*, the *hypothalamus*, and the *reticular formation*. In the human brain, the thalamus, as you can see in the diagram, is in almost the center. ◆ It is an important relay station for incoming sensory messages from all parts of the body. Directly below the thalamus and merging into it is the hypothalamus, in which are located important centers for the regulation of metabolism, body temperature, hunger, thirst, and emotional behavior. Hess (1954) has shown that stimulation of the back of the hypothalamus will produce reactions of the sympathetic nervous system (increase in heart rate and blood pressure), while stimulation of the front part produces

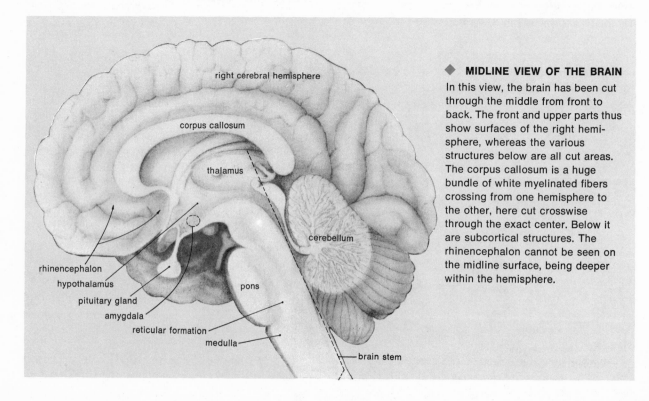

◆ MIDLINE VIEW OF THE BRAIN
In this view, the brain has been cut through the middle from front to back. The front and upper parts thus show surfaces of the right hemisphere, whereas the various structures below are all cut areas. The corpus callosum is a huge bundle of white myelinated fibers crossing from one hemisphere to the other, here cut crosswise through the exact center. Below it are subcortical structures. The rhinencephalon cannot be seen on the midline surface, being deeper within the hemisphere.

right cerebral hemisphere

corpus callosum

thalamus

cerebellum

rhinencephalon
hypothalamus
pituitary gland
amygdala
reticular formation
medulla

pons

brain stem

■ Dr. José Delgado is a pioneer in the brain implantation of radio-activated electrodes. His ability to find an exact spot in an animal's brain is so precise that he can trust his life to it. Here, even after the bull has started to charge, Dr. Delgado can stop it by a radio message to electrodes planted in its brain. After repeated experiences such as this, the animal becomes permanently less aggressive.

parasympathetic reactions (slowing of heart rate, dilation of blood vessels in the intestine and stomach). The hypothalamus is sensitive to changes in the external environment which demand either "fight or flight." It is also sensitive to internal requirements of the body and important in maintaining the exchange of energy between the organism and its environment.

The reticular formation is a tangled mass of nuclei and fibers in the core of the brain stem just above the spinal cord. This formation has two important functions. By responding to fibers coming down to it from the various higher centers, it suppresses some incoming sensory messages and facilitates others. Through fibers going upward from it to all the higher centers, it acts as a general arousal system: stimulation in this area causes a sleeping animal to wake up and one already awake to become more alert. It is therefore called the *reticular activating system* (RAS). Magoun and his collaborators (1963b) performed the crucial experiments which demonstrated that the reticular formation influenced wakefulness or arousal by maintaining electrical activity in the forward part of the cortex. It also appears that impulses originating in a specific part of the reticular formation can inhibit activity in some brain structures, reducing arousal and even inducing sleep.

Another important part of the evolutionally older part of the brain is the *rhinencephalon*. This is primi-

tive cortical tissue, tucked between the top of the brain stem and the newer parts of the cortex.

The rhinencephalon was originally thought to be the "nose-brain" because nerves from the smell receptors in the nose project directly into various of its structures. However, it contributes to the regulation of behavior in much more significant ways than merely serving as an "odor decoder." Located in this most primitive portion of the brain is a group of structures called the *limbic system* which are active in functions as different as attention, emotion, and remembering. For example, stimulation of many of these structures produces an *attention response* in which the animal alertly searches its environment. Stimulation of a limbic structure called the *amygdala* brings responses of flight and defense. ■ Lesions made in the amygdala or in another structure, the *cingulate gyrus*, can tame a wild animal, while lesioning the nearby *septal area* can induce vicious rage in a previously tame one. Selective initiation or suppression of behavior in adapting to environmental demands has also been shown to involve the limbic system.

Still another part of the limbic system, the *hippocampus*, is involved in at least two very different behaviors, mating and remembering. Electrical stimulation of this region can produce an erection of the male sex organ (MacLean, 1960). Patients with damage to the hippocampus have great difficulty remembering new events unless they keep their attention focused on them. Although they exhibit normal intelligence, reasoning, and vocabulary, they suffer from *retrograde amnesia*. This is a memory defect in which old habits and events are well remembered, but more recent ones are increasingly less well remembered.

A similar phenomenon seems to accompany senility: with aging and hardening of the arteries (and less oxygen to the brain) goes a loss in memory, especially for more recently experienced information. Exploratory research appears to show that daily administration of doses of pure oxygen prevents this loss in memory efficiency of older people (Jacobs, Winter, Alvis, & Small, 1969). These changes in functioning highlight the fact that memory is ultimately a physical process, related in some way to the neurophysiology of nerve impulses.

Brain Wave Activity

From before birth until the moment of death, the brain never stops its constant activity, never "rests" even for a minute. Recordings of the electrical activity of the brain (*electroencephalograms*, EEGs) from electrodes attached to the scalp have established that even during sleep, slow waves of nerve impulses sweep across the cortex, as we will see in Chapter 7.

What *are* the brain waves, and what do they tell us about the physiological basis of experience, the problem of primary concern to us in this chapter? Brain waves probably reflect the alternating states of excitability and refractoriness of neurons. Many nerve fibers are activated along parallel pathways at each synaptic junction along the route to the brain, forming a wave of varying electrical voltage. At each relay stage of the cortex, there may be as many as 100 neurons; accordingly, an advancing wave may, in a second, sweep over 100,000 neurons. This wave front may follow diverse pathways through a mosaic of neurons, and may even double back on itself, forming a reverberatory circuit.

These wave fronts may be both the carriers of the sensory nerve impulse frequency code and the means by which parts of the message are organized to form a meaningful sensory experience. The sensory information started at the receptors comes to the cortex as a specific signal that can be picked up even in single cells in the appropriate sensory projection area of the cortex. But since different cortical cells decode information about different characteristics of an object (size, shape, movement, color, texture, weight, odor, temperature, and so on) all this information must be somehow integrated. This integration may occur between the wave fronts generated by each of these receptor-organ impulses. Some think that these constantly flowing wave fronts interlock and integrate every sense organ input and response output.

All this activity of the brain requires an enormous expenditure of energy in the form of cell metabolism. In fact, this metabolism utilizes 20 percent of the total oxygen consumption of the whole body at rest. As brain activity increases with the stress of anxiety or with concentration, the brain uses more oxygen. In contrast, when brain functioning starts to decline (as in elderly people with senile psychosis), or almost comes to a standstill (as in surgical anesthesia or alcoholic coma), the brain consumes much less oxygen —sometimes less than half the normal requirement. It is believed that processes which interfere with synaptic transmission decrease cerebral oxygen consumption (Kety, 1967b).

We have learned a great deal about the workings of the human brain, but the communication code is still far from having been broken. Despite the great advances witnessed recently in neurophyisology we have not solved the riddle of how a series of electrical impulses can eventuate in the recognition of a friend in a crowd, the feeling of joy at the first sign of spring, awareness of the beauty of a loved one, or your sense of self-identity.

The Endocrines: Aids to Neural Regulation

It might be concluded that man's highly developed nervous system must be sufficiently complex to handle competently all of the body's adjustive behavior. This is not the case, however, as the hard-working *endocrine system* will testify. The endocrine glands pump secretions directly into the bloodstream which are carried to and influence every part of the body. These chemical substances are *hormones* (Greek for "I excite"). They are responsible for a diverse range of effects on the organism.

The activity of the endocrine glands is regulatory in nature. Their secretions serve to control the individual's *metabolism*—the chemical reactions by which energy is provided to carry on the life processes and by which growth takes place in bones, muscles, and nervous tissue. Action of these glands also helps to maintain internal conditions within an optimal range. For example, if there is an oversupply of sugar in the bloodstream, certain endocrine structures release a flow of the hormone *insulin*, which helps the body metabolize the sugar and return the blood to its normal chemical state. This tendency of the body to maintain internal conditions permitting a constant balance, or steady state equilibrium, is called *homeostasis*; it involves activity of the nervous system and other physiological mechanisms as well as the endocrine glands.

The endocrine glands play a large role in *coordinating* the processes of the body. In sudden fear, for example, a hormone is circulated through the blood which brings about such widely diverse processes as dilation of the pupil of the eye, constriction of the blood vessels in the wall of the stomach, and an increase in the rapidity with which blood clots in the presence of air.

The master neural control center for the endocrine system evidently lies in the hypothalamus. There is now evidence that even the nerve cells in the hypothalamus secrete certain regulatory hormones.

In helping to maintain equilibrium and coordinate body functions, the various endocrine glands work closely together. Those whose functions are of greatest interest to the psychologist are the pituitary, the thyroids, the adrenal glands, and the sex glands. •

The *pituitary*, a small structure attached to the underside of the hypothalamus, secretes a number of different hormones which perform various functions concerned with growth and maintenance. Particularly vital to normal bodily development during childhood is the *pituitary growth hormone*, which controls the growth of the skeleton, muscles, and various internal organs.

The pituitary also produces a variety of "middle man" hormones which act directly upon other endocrine glands—most notably the thyroids, the sex glands, and the adrenal cortex—to stimulate their functioning. A multitude of factors seems to control

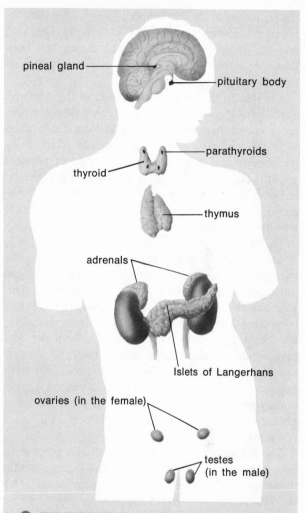

● **THE ENDOCRINE GLANDS**

The locations of various ductless glands are shown in the diagram. The pituitary body produces the growth hormone and the "middle man" hormones. The thyroids affect principally metabolism, growth, and the development of intelligence. The parathyroids influence calcium and phosphorous metabolism. The adrenal medulla produces adrenaline and noradrenaline, both important in emotion; the adrenal cortex affects general body activity, secondary sex characteristics, and reactions to prolonged stress. The gonads are vital to sexual development, sexual drive, and reproduction; the ovaries (female) produce estrogen and progestin and the testes (male) produce androgens. The islets of Langerhans secrete insulin which controls the sugar level in the blood. The thymus plays a role in body immunities.

the secretion of these hormones. The interaction between the pituitary hormone *corticotropin* (ACTH) and the secretions of the adrenal cortex has been shown to be an important factor in physiological reactions to prolonged stress.

Located in the neck at either side of the "Adam's apple" are the *thyroid glands*, which produce a hormone called *thyroxin*. Operating in close conjunction with the pituitary gland, the thyroids affect body metabolism and help to control the rate of physical growth. High thyroid output goes with high general activity; low output goes with sluggishness of movement. Thyroid secretions influence both the structure and the functioning of the nervous system, especially in the development of intelligence.

Located at the upper end of the kidneys are the two *adrenal glands*, each consisting of two parts: an inner core (the *adrenal medulla*) and an outer shell (the *adrenal cortex*). The adrenal medulla is directly controlled by the nervous system, which stimulates the gland to secrete its hormones, *adrenaline* and *noradrenaline* (also called *epinephrine* and *norepinephrine*), during strong emotion. The adrenal cortex produces hormones that influence maturation of secondary sex characteristics, such as the voice change at puberty, as well as hormones that influence the stress reactions mentioned above.

The sex glands, or *gonads*, have a dual purpose in both sexes: (a) the secretion of sex hormones that influence bodily development and behavior and (b) the production of gametes (sperms or eggs). These functions are performed in males by the *testes* and in females by the *ovaries*. The male hormones are called *androgens*. There are two kinds of female hormones: *estrogens,* which control menstruation, and *progestin,* which controls uterus changes.

The Brain and Behavior

For students of psychology, the justification for learning about physiology comes through demonstrating that such knowledge increases our understanding of how important behavioral processes can be influenced. Although we will attempt to provide such evidence where relevant in subsequent portions of this text, let us here consider five examples of the interaction between physiology and behavior.

A Rich Environment Makes the Brain Smart, but Fat

The nature of the early life environment to which an organism must adapt obviously ought to play a determining role in its later behavior. This expectation was borne out a few years ago by systematic experiments. It was found that rearing rats for eighty days in environments which were "enriched" made them superior in maze learning to litter mates whose early life was spent in an "impoverished" environment (Bennett, Diamond, Krech, & Rosenzweig, 1964). ▲

If learning ability is changed by early experience, it should then be possible to show that the nervous system, which mediates between these environmental inputs and the organism's adjustive reactions to them (learning) is itself modified by variations in the environment. Mark Rosenzweig and his associates (1969) have indeed uncovered a number of significant differences in brain weight and chemical activity between enriched and impoverished animals. Rats reared in the more complex environment have heavier brains, and their cortex is thicker. In addition, analysis of their brains reveals more activity of the chemical substance AChE (involved, as we have seen, in synaptic nerve transmission). An increase is also found in the enzyme ChE in the glial cells which

▲ Experimental cage of the "environmental complexity and training" group. Ten rats were housed in this cage, with a food and water platform and "toys" of various kinds, including ladders and swinging blocks. Different toys from a set of seven were placed in the cage each day.

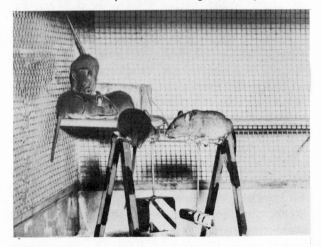

nourish the neurons. These differences are much greater in the occipital region of the cortex than in other cortical areas. This increased activity of the cortex has been found even in animals first exposed to this enriched setting as adults, and even for only a thirty-day exposure or a two-hour-a-day *look* at "the good life."

The greater modification of the occipital cortex than of other cortical areas would seem to be due to greater visual stimulation from the rich environment. Surprisingly, however, a number of experiments have shown that visual experience is *not* a necessary condition for inducing the greater changes in the occipital cortex. The same pattern of brain differences emerges when the enriched-condition rats are reared in total darkness or are blinded. These findings would suggest that the occipital cortex is a center for many sensory inputs or widespread sensory-motor integration in addition to vision—raising a host of new questions for research to answer, such as the nature of the integration between the senses and what constitutes an "enriched" environment.

To Eat or Not to Eat

At some point during a food orgy of the Thanksgiving dinner variety, the average person cannot eat another morsel, no matter how tempting it smells, looks, or tastes. His consummatory behavior has been turned off by a message from a "satiety center" located in his hypothalamus. If this center is lesioned, as it has been in experiments with rats, the signal to inhibit eating is not transmitted, and the animals may literally eat themselves to death. This excessive feeding (called *hyperphagia*) leads to extreme obesity, in which body weight is doubled and in some cases quadrupled. ◆

Lesions in a neighboring region of the hypothalamus make the animal stop eating completely and may result in starvation and death. Here a "feeding center" has been inhibited by the lesion. Obviously, under normal conditions these pairs of opposing centers must operate in complementary fashion to maintain the level of eating required for the animal's nutrition.

Further proof of the hypothalamic control of appetite comes from stimulating rather than lesioning such regions. Electrical stimulation of the feeding

◆ Following a lesion in its hypothalamus, this rat ate itself to the 1080 grams shown here—three or four times its normal weight.

center activates eating behavior in a fully satiated rat, while stimulation of the satiety center prevents a food-deprived rat from eating food that is available to him.

There is some current controversy over whether there are specific hypothalamic centers concerned with feeding and over the interpretation of the variables which control this process. Nevertheless, it is clear that food addicts can be made into ascetics with the right kind of brain stimulation.

Appetite As a Matter of Taste

Studying brain functions by means of lesions and electrical stimulation runs into trouble when the complex neural pathways being studied overlap geographically. A preferred procedure would involve stimulating or inhibiting the activity of these pathways by varying the concentration of neurohumoral transmitter substances in highly specific regions of the brain. This technique, which can focus more precisely on a given level or layer of the brain, has been elegantly developed by Grossman (1967).

Basically, Grossman's technique consists of permanently implanting a double tube (cannula) in the animal's skull. The inner cannula is removed, sterilized, filled with crystals of a given chemical and reinserted through the outer tube into the brain area under investigation. A microinjection of drugs in this way into various regions of the limbic system has revealed the complexity of chemical and anatomical interactions in determining behavioral functioning.

Injection of one chemical into the hypothalamus of satiated rats elicits drinking, but inhibits feeding. Injection of another chemical into the same site inhibits water intake, but elicits feeding. Drug injection into another portion of the hypothalamus (ventro-

medial) does not selectively affect food or water intake. It may be that this region is not an "appetite center" at all but a center for inhibiting *affective* reactions (that is, liking, preference, or taste for a stimulus). This interpretation emerges from research which demonstrated that injections of atropine (which block the normal inhibitory mechanisms) may increase both food and water intake but does so *only if* the diet is tasty. With the inhibitory mechanisms not functioning, consumption goes up when the diet is palatable but drops sharply when the only food and water that are available are made bitter by the addition of quinine.

Apparently, good breeding may make a man of taste, but some good taste may be bred into us, courtesy of the hypothalamus. The more we learn about the hypothalamus, however, the more puzzles we uncover about its workings, as we shall see in Chapter 9. ■

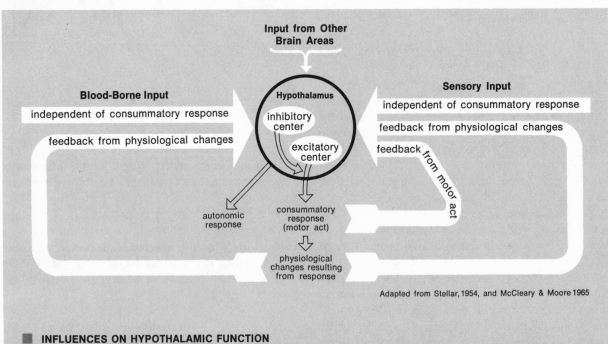

Adapted from Stellar, 1954, and McCleary & Moore 1965

■ INFLUENCES ON HYPOTHALAMIC FUNCTION

The hypothalamus receives input from other brain centers, from external stimulation, and from the blood. This input includes a running report on the state of the organism and the environment as well as both sensory and chemical feedback from actions already taken or in progress.

Putting the Skids on a Top Banana

A common feature of social life among many animal species is the existence of a "pecking order." A dominant, aggressive, assertive member of the group becomes the leader through bullying and winning confrontations with all of the other group members. Among chickens, the dominance-submission hierarchy is so clearly established that each hen in a large roost has a position in which she dominates all those below and is submissive to all those above her (Guhl, 1956).

The same social organization can be witnessed in monkey colonies. One monkey always establishes himself as the leader by his threats and overbearing manner. Rarely is it necessary for more physical aggression to be used. The "boss" monkey takes over the turf and roams about the cage freely, while the rest of the group restrict their activity to one corner. This "top banana" assumes a privileged position with regard to available food as well as available sex partners.

The group social structure as well as individual characteristics of dominance, aggressiveness, and fearful submission can all be dramatically changed— up to a point—by a little electrical stimulation to the brain of the boss. In one such colony, when the septal area in the rhinencephalon of the leader was electrically stimulated, his immediate loss of aggressiveness was recognized by the other monkeys. They moved about the cage freely—until the stimulation was stopped and the bully in him returned (Delgado, 1970). •

The dominance hierarchy in a colony of eight young rhesus monkeys was more permanently changed by surgically altering the rhinencephalic amygdala area in the original leader and then, successively, of those who took his place (Pribram, 1962). ▲ (p. 106)

Before any operation, Dave was number one man, and each of the others occupied some subordinate position in the hierarchy. After Dave's operation, and forever more, he became bottom man on the totem pole. His assurance was replaced by fear and submission.

Zeke, formerly number two, took over as the dominant leader, and all the others moved up one notch.

● The chief of this monkey group was Ali (center), usually ill-tempered and aggressive. Radio stimulation to his brain through implanted electrodes, however, made him docile and unaggressive. A submissive monkey, Elsa (left) learned to press a lever, sending stimulation to Ali's brain. She never became the dominant animal, but prevented attacks against herself in this way.

Larry, who had been totally submissive, was now laying it on Dave.

When Zeke's amygdala was operated upon, he too became submissive, lost his leadership to Riva, and spent his time occasionally attacking his former tormentor, Dave.

Surprisingly, however, Riva's operation did not end his reign of terror, but rather, exaggerated it. In part, this may have been due to the failure of Herby's nonaggressive "personality" to overthrow the crown.

Personality and even the social psychology of groups are thus influenced by the physiological functioning of the individual. Later on, we shall see how social and cognitive factors, in turn, can modify physiological functioning.

Brain Splitting: Two Minds in One Body

The two hemispheres of the brain are contralaterally organized, as we have seen. This means that the right one receives information from the left visual field (via the optic chiasma) and from the left side of the body, while the left hemisphere gets input from the right visual field and the right side of the body. Normally, these sensory inputs are then integrated, resulting in coordinated perception and behavior. But in a patient whose corpus callosum has been severed, this coordi-

Based on Pribram, 1962

▲ BOTH PHYSIOLOGY AND PERSONALITY INFLUENCE DOMINANCE

This sequence of operations demonstrated the importance of the amygdala in determining dominance, but interestingly showed also the importance of both personality differences and the social context. Dave, the original leader, fell to the bottom of the heap and stayed there. Zeke's aggressiveness enabled him to take over first place after Dave's operation and also kept him from being dominated by Dave again after his own operation. Riva's operation upset his "cool" but, in the absence of a clear challenge from placid Herby, only made him more cantankerous.

Given the same physiological situation (an operated amygdala), Dave, Zeke, and Riva thus showed three different patterns. In each case, the behavior, heavily influenced and greatly changed by the operation, was also influenced by the animal's temperament and habits, as well as by the challenge provided by members of the group.

nation cannot take place in the brain. This operation is sometimes performed in cases of severe epileptic seizures that cannot be cured by medication. Without such surgery, the seizures may become fatal; with it, the patient is freed from seizures and reports an improvement in well-being. A by-product of this surgery is the natural experiment created by making two brains operate within a single body. Each half acts independently of the other, and each seems to have its own sensations, perceptions, and memories, as well as cognitive and emotional experiences.

Investigation of the abilities of split-brain patients has been carried out in an apparatus in which the individual is instructed to fixate the midpoint of the visual field; in this way there is no overlapping of the images being sent to the two hemispheres. If you were put into this type of apparatus and instructed to respond to all light stimuli in the left visual field by pressing a button with your right hand, your reaction time would become much slower if at the same time you had to respond with your left hand to signals coming from the right visual field. It would take time for your brain to coordinate these diverse sensory inputs and reactions.

In contrast, the split-brain patient responds as quickly to a double reaction-time situation as he would to a single one. Each reaction is independent of the other, so no coordination time is required (Gazzaniga & Sperry, 1966). On the other hand, all motor coordination between the two hands or between visual input to one hemisphere and the hand on that side of the body is totally lost by the split-brain patient. ◆

Research with split-brain patients has also confirmed the belief that one hemisphere is clearly dominant and the other inferior. Not only is the inner visual world of such people made up of two entirely separate experiences instead of being unified as it is for us; in addition, what the right hemisphere of a right-handed person sees or remembers cannot be communicated in speech or writing because his *control centers for communication* are contained only in his opposite, left (major) hemisphere.

Intriguing is the nature of the emotional reactions of a split-brain patient when his minor hemisphere is exposed to an emotion-arousing stimulus. For example, the unexpected presentation of a picture of a nude female only in the left visual field (and thus to only the right hemisphere) results in the following sequence of behaviors:

"The subject under these conditions will characteristically say that he or she saw nothing, just a white light, as regularly happens for stimuli projected into the left field.

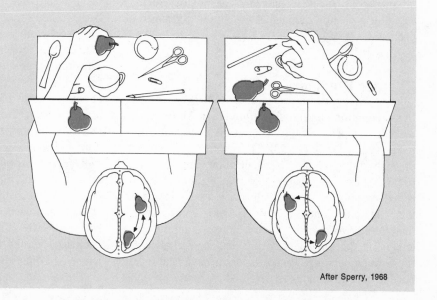

◆ EYE-HAND COORDINATION WITH A SPLIT BRAIN

A person with his corpus callosum severed has no trouble recognizing with his left hand the object that matches one presented in his left visual field because the messages from his left hand and the left visual field (projected on right halves of both retinas) reach the same cerebral hemisphere. On the other hand, messages from his right hand go to his *left* cerebral hemisphere, from which there is no connection with his right visual cortex; thus he cannot pick out the same object with his right hand unless it is also presented in his right visual field.

After Sperry, 1968

However, one may then notice an inner grin beginning to spread over the subject's features which then lingers and carries over through the next couple of trials or so. It may also cause blushing and giggling and affect the tone of voice coming from the major side. If one then asks the subject what he is grinning about, the reply suggests that the talking hemisphere has no idea what it was that had turned him on. He may say something like, "That's some machine you have there!" or "Wowee—that light!" Apparently the emotional tone alone gets across to the speaking hemisphere, as if the cognitive aspect could not be articulated through the brain stem." (Sperry, 1968, pp. 319-320)

Such studies of human split-brain patients by Sperry and others, together with experimental research with animals, are providing valuable insights into the mechanisms by which the "blooming, buzzing confusion" in the world about us becomes a unified perceptual experience on which we then base our actions.

The behavior of one hemisphere at a time can also be studied by coating the surface of the cortex on one side with potassium chloride. As you might predict from the discussion of nerve impulses (p. 71), this dense potassium concentration on the outside evidently prevents the potassium ions inside the axons from flowing out and thus makes it more difficult for the cells to become depolarized and transmit impulses. The result is a temporary stopping of brain activity. This technique makes it possible to use the animal as his own control subject and has the obvious further advantage of not damaging the brain permanently (Schneider, 1967).

Chapter Summary

In studying the physiological foundations of behavior, we gain perspective by looking at the ways organisms have evolved. Single-celled organisms developed, through differentiation, specialization, and generous provision for redundancy, into many kinds of multi-celled organisms; in so doing, they vastly increased their flexibility and adaptability and, consequently, their ability to survive. Such changes continue endlessly: as the environment presents new challenges, those members of a species that have the now-needed genetic variants survive and reproduce, genetic

mutations in the surviving strain continue to occur, and the genes present in the species keep being dealt into new combinations through sexual reproduction.

The chief mechanism for the assessment of information from the environment and the coordination of reactions to it is the nervous system. The basic unit of this system is the *nerve cell*, or *neuron*. During fetal development, nerve cells become increasingly specialized and may migrate long distances from the *neural tube*.

The *nervous system* consists of the *central nervous system* (the brain and spinal cord) and the *peripheral nervous system* (all the portions outside the brain and spinal cord). The information from the environment is picked up by *receptors* and sent over *sensory, afferent* fibers to the spinal cord and brain. Responses are carried over *motor, efferent* fibers to the *effectors* (muscles or glands). The processing of information between input and output is carried out by the *central nervous system*, consisting of the brain and spinal cord. The *sensory-motor arc* is the simplest form of this mechanism.

Axonal transmission carries information within a neuron; *synaptic transmission* carries it across a *synapse* to another neuron. Impulses travel in one direction only, following the *law of forward conduction*, from *dendrite* to *axon* to *synapse* and on to the dendrites or cell body of the next neuron.

In the resting state, an axon is *polarized*, with the inside negative relative to the outside. A *nerve impulse* occurs when stimulation is strong enough to *depolarize* the axon membrane; this change in membrane potential then travels down the nerve fiber. The axon transmits on an *all-or-none* basis: it either transmits a full impulse or does not transmit at all. Information about intensity of stimulation is conveyed by how many neurons fire and how often they fire.

Synaptic transmission is *graded* rather than all-or-none. The message is carried across the synapse by *chemical transmitter substances* which affect the polarization of the next neuron. If the *postsynaptic potential* is thereby *increased*, the effect is *inhibitory* (IPSP); if polarization is *decreased*, the effect is *excitatory* (EPSP). The second neuron fires only if the excitatory inputs to it exceed the inhibitory inputs enough to equal its threshold.

The *somatic* part of the peripheral nervous system

connects the central nervous system with the sensory receptors and the skeletal muscles. The *visceral* part (usually called the *autonomic nervous system*) connects the central nervous system with the internal organs. The autonomic system, in turn, is divided into the *sympathetic* division, which regulates emergency functioning, and the *parasympathetic* division, which governs continuing vital functions.

Because of *reciprocal innervation*, excitation of one muscle is typically accompanied by inhibition of the opposing muscle. In general, painful, strong, or repeated stimuli have the right of way in the nervous system. Coordination in the spinal cord takes place through divergence, convergence, self-exciting circuits, and collateral fibers to and from the brain.

The process by which stimulus energy is converted to a nerve impulse is called *transduction. Psychophysical scaling* methods establish the relationships between given intensities and resulting sensations. The threshold, or *limen*, is generally taken as the strength of stimulus that can barely be detected half the time. The *just noticeable difference (j.n.d.)* is the stimulus increase required to produce a barely noticeable difference in sensation three fourths of the time. According to the *Weber-Fechner Law*, this is a constant proportion of the standard stimulus over most of the range of intensities.

The various classes of sensory stimuli for which we have receptors include vision, hearing, pressure, pain, cold, warmth, taste, smell, balance, and position. Of these, vision and hearing are the most important to man and the most accurate.

The eye has two separate systems of receptors: the *rods*, sensitive to very dim light but not to color, and the *cones*, specialized for daylight and color vision. Cones are most numerous in the fovea, the area of sharpest vision; there are no rods in the fovea. Light passes through several layers of nerve fibers until it reaches these receptor cells, which translate it into messages carried over the *bipolar* and *ganglion* cells to the *optic nerve* and thence to the visual area of the brain, the *occipital cortex*. At the point where the optic nerve leaves the retina, there is a blind spot. The perception of form, pattern, and movement depends upon specialized cells which are activated only by stimuli in a given spatial orientation or location. Three types of *photopigments* in the cones absorb

blue, green, or red light, respectively. Four types of *opponent-process* cells in the *lateral geniculate nucleus* sum the information reaching them and pass it on to the visual cortex, producing color vision.

In our perception of sound, *alternating pressure differences* (sound waves) enter the *outer ear*, are transmitted through the *middle ear* to the *cochlea* in the *inner ear*, and there are translated into nerve impulses. Both a *volley theory* and a *place theory* seem needed to explain the coding of sounds.

Brain functions have been studied through *stimulation* and through *lesions*. There is a great redundancy of pathways, often enabling new sections of the brain to take over the functions of damaged areas. The brain has two *hemispheres*, connected by the *corpus callosum;* each hemisphere has four lobes: *frontal, temporal, parietal*, and *occipital*. The outer layer of these hemispheres is called the *cortex*.

Primary sensory reception areas are located in relatively specific parts of the cortex, and primary motor functions are localized in the cortical area just forward from the *fissure of Rolando*. The remaining areas of the cortex are *association areas*. Damage to them, especially in the left hemisphere of a right-handed person, may impair understanding or use of language.

The *subcortex*, or *brain stem*, controls primitive functions such as appetites, pleasure, and pain. Important structures here are the *thalamus*, an important relay station for sensory information, the *hypothalamus*, controlling many vital functions, and the *reticular formation*, a general arousal system. The *rhinencephalon* is primitive cortical tissue involved in functions as diverse as attention, emotion, and memory.

Brain waves, measured by electroencephalograms (EEGs), reflect the spontaneous activity of neurons in the brain. Brain activity accounts for about a fifth of the oxygen consumed by the body.

The *endocrine system,* whose secretions help in maintaining chemical equilibrium and coordinating body functions, includes the *pituitary gland,* concerned with growth and maintenance; the *thyroid glands,* affecting metabolism and growth; the *adrenal glands,* influencing maturation and aiding the body's reactions to motion; and the *gonads,* influencing bodily development and behavior and producing *gametes* (*sperm* and *ova*) for reproduction.

Chapter 4

Developmental Processes

In Chapter 2 we discussed Head Start and other compensatory programs designed to make up for the disadvantages some children face when they enter school. Such programs have not been as successful as we would like, perhaps because insufficient attention has been given to the processes of development that can either leave children mentally crippled or make them ready and eager to learn. Besides helping us learn how to overcome disadvantages, a better understanding of these processes might even teach us ways to give all children "head starts."

It can be argued that almost every child is held back from performing at his or her maximum level because of false assumptions parents and teachers make about the limits of human potential. This is not the only reason for studying development, of course, but it is a good one, and much of the recent interest in this area of study has resulted from just this practical concern. B. L. White notes that "there has been a striking shift of interest, unprecedented in history, toward the first three years of life." He points out that the government's Project Head Start was originally based on the notion that "something's wrong with these children at age six. There was no appreciation of how early that something comes about."

White and his fellow researchers set out to study the development of three- to six-year-olds. From among the pupils in local nursery schools, kindergar-

tens, and Head Start centers, they selected one group of outstanding youngsters (the "A" group) and a parallel group of children who were not outstanding in any way, those who couldn't quite compete (the "C" group). After a year of studying their 440 "A" and "C" children, they found that they had come too late. In the words of one project member, E. R. LaCrosse, "With our 'A' kids, the three-year-old children had basically the same cluster of abilities, in perhaps less polished form, as the six-year-old children; and, in fact, they were more advanced than the six-year-old 'C's' in terms of both social and nonsocial skills."

"We were surprised, really, and kind of excited," continues LaCrosse. "Big Daddy Freud had said everything was over at 5, with the resolution of the oedipal conflict, but we tended to disbelieve this. Then suddenly, we found that if you're talking about competence, the action comes before the age of 3." (Pines, 1969, p. 10)

The reports of only limited success with Head Start programs have thus focused the attention of educators on earlier critical stages in the child's development—periods when behavior patterns are first being molded. The basic question raised by attempts to make up for past deprivation is: To what extent is human behavior modifiable? This question will be of special concern to us in the present chapter but also will recur throughout the book.

111

Determiners of Development

If we are to understand the processes of human development we must study the actions and interactions of heredity and environment through time. *Heredity* is defined as the totality of biologically transmitted factors that influence the structure of the body, (including, of course, the very important brain and nervous system), thereby setting certain limits on development. *Environment* is the totality of conditions that serve to stimulate behavior or act to bring about modification of behavior. The action of these factors in determining the level of an individual's biological, psychological, and social development is sometimes expressed in the following formula:

heredity $\times$ environment $\times$ time = developmental level

This formula, admittedly oversimplified, highlights the fact that it is meaningless to speak of either heredity or environment acting alone. Both are necessary for any development at all to take place. Heredity could not operate except in some sort of environment, whereas even behavior that we describe as environmentally caused must obviously be carried out by inherited body structures.

In studying the relationship between heredity and environment, it is not enough to ask which of the two is primarily responsible for a given aspect of development or even in what proportions the two have contributed. The important question is how they interact. For example, heredity is mainly responsible for giving us a particular body build, complexion, or cast of features. Any society is likely to prize certain combinations of these physical characteristics and frown on other combinations. A person born with a set of hereditary characteristics that makes him the object of scorn or ridicule by his society may react to the discrimination against him by rejecting that society. Out of the interaction a juvenile delinquent—and eventually an adult criminal—may be created (Anastasi, 1958). A well-known historical example is "Billy the Kid," who was very sensitive about his shortness. Both heredity and environment played a part here, but through interaction rather than through simple addition of their effects.

What the formula given above fails to show is that at any given moment environment is interacting not only with heredity but with a level of development already reached (Hirsch, 1962). This level of development, in turn, reflects previous experience and thus is the product of both hereditary development and learning up to that point. For example, given a natural talent plus years of teaching and practice at home, pianist Van Cliburn was able to gain admission to a famous music school and there develop his talent to the point where he could win the international Tschaikovsky competition in Moscow. Without the proficiency gained from his earlier practice, he would not have been ready to profit from the advanced instruction despite his inherited potential. One of the great questions of interest to psychologists at present is whether the same development of hereditary potential is possible at any period in the life span or whether certain types of development must come at a particular time if hereditary potential is not to be permanently lost. Studies bearing on this question will be discussed later in this chapter.

The role of heredity in guiding an organism's development is clearly dominant prior to the moment of birth. Yet this is not to say that the unborn child has no environment, for within the mother's body he is surrounded by a protective fluid and receives nutrients from the maternal bloodstream. As we shall see, there is also some evidence that simple responses and even some learning can take place before birth. The main function of the prenatal environment, however, is to support the normal growth processes of the unborn child. Recently, research on hereditary mechanisms has focused less on the effects of genetics on structure and more on the effects of genetics on behavioral processes. This *behavior genetics* approach holds much promise.

Heredity and Maturation

At birth, learning begins to play an increasingly important role in shaping new behavior patterns. Heredity does not cease to operate, however. Hereditary potentialities for a particular growth sequence and for many kinds of behavior typical of the species continue to develop for months or even years. This process by which heredity continues to function after birth is called *maturation*. One familiar result of maturation is the voice change that occurs in boys at the age of puberty. The boy's voice becomes lower because of a thickening in his vocal cords, which results from increased functioning of the portion of the endocrine system that produces the male hormones. Although the low voice of the adult male does not develop until long after birth, it is nevertheless determined by heredity—acting through maturation. Observation of boys who have grown up out of touch with other boys shows that even in the absence of knowledge of this change, the characteristic lowering of voice takes place at adolescence. Clearly, it is not learned, nor is the onset of menstruation in girls. At a much lower level is the pecking response by means of which the baby chick or other bird breaks the egg and frees itself. Such behavior is obviously unlearned and appears only after a certain period of maturation.

Evidently, then, a number of physiological structures are essentially mature and ready to function at birth, or even earlier, whereas other nervous, muscular, and glandular structures are not ready to function until months or years later. Until these structures are mature, no stimulus will be effective in producing the type of behavior which they underlie.

Environment and Learning

Most patterns of behavior, of course, depend on learning as well as on a certain level of maturation. No amount of instruction and practice can teach an infant to read before his neural and muscular structures are sufficiently mature; yet even when the structures are ready, no child of any age is able to read without learning.

In addition to providing the conditions necessary for life and growth, the environment influences the development of behavior in three ways: (a) it supplies stimuli which elicit patterns of response already prepared by maturation, (b) it presents situations that require the learning of new responses or the changing of old ones, and (c) it provides feedback or reinforcement, which maintains successful responses or eliminates unsuccessful ones. Each individual's environment, through its social patterns and through the resources it provides or fails to provide, determines what patterns of behavior will be necessary for that individual to learn.

Given an adequate environment, each individual develops at his own rate. Psychologists and physiologists have been able to outline a general developmental schedule which, under normal conditions, is characteristic of human development. Knowledge of this schedule, which is based on a comparison of great numbers of individuals, not only aids our understanding of man as a species but is useful in studying individuals.

Physical Development

Most anatomical and physiological development is rather directly controlled by heredity. The process of development begins with the union of genetic material from the parents. When sperm and egg meet and combine their genetic information to produce a full set of chromosomes in a single-celled zygote, the stage is set for a programmed growth sequence of enormous complexity. The beginning is simple enough: the cell divides, then the two new cells divide again, and so forth. In time, some of the cells begin to differentiate and form specialized structures: for example, some cells become identifiable as neurons and begin to form the brain, spinal cord, and peripheral nervous system, as we saw in Chapter 3.

These processes go on during the *prenatal* period —the 280 days that human organisms spend in the mother's womb. The first two weeks of the prenatal period, in which cell division produces a hollow sphere of cells about a fifth of an inch in diameter, are called the *germinal* period. During the next six weeks the differentiation of cells and formation of structures produces internal organs and external characteristics. When this *embryonic* period has run its course, the organism has become recognizably human although it is still only two inches long at most. At this point, eight weeks after conception, the *fetal* period begins, and the fetus continues to grow until birth. ◆ (p. 114)

Even in the protected seclusion of prenatal life, where heredity dominates the development process, environmental factors can play a part. Since the mother herself provides the fetal environment, her condition during pregnancy must be considered. There have been many false beliefs about the mother's

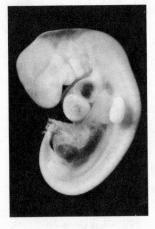 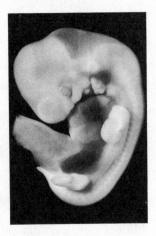 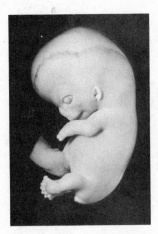 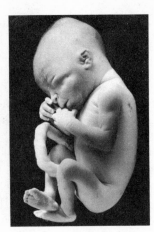

◆ The photos show the developing human embryo at (from left) 30 days, 34 days, 44 days, and 150 days. At 30 days, the embryo shows little resemblance to its adult form, but its parts are still characteristically human. It is about half the size of a pea and has rudimentary eyes, ears, mouth, brain, and internal organs. By 34 days, the facial features are better formed and hands and feet have started to develop from the stublike arms and legs. When the embryo is 44 days old, it possesses all its adult features and organs, although it is less than an inch long. By this time, the beginnings of fingers, toes, eyelids, teeth, and a tongue are visible. The formation of bone cells which will replace cartilage marks the end of the embryonic stage and the beginning of the fetal period. By the 150th day, the fetus is completely formed. In the next four months it will grow and mature in preparation for birth.

prenatal influence on development, but some important effects can occur.

Emotional disturbances in the mother can apparently produce physical abnormalities. For example, it is believed that emotional distress in the first ten weeks of pregnancy can cause cleft palate in the child. The time factor can be accounted for by the fact that the bones of the palate are being formed between the seventh and tenth weeks; but what is the mechanism that interferes with their development? Since there are no nerves connecting the mother and the unborn infant, the influence cannot be transmitted by the nervous system. There is no direct connection of blood vessels either, but nourishment and oxygen are passed from the mother's bloodstream to the fetal circulatory system in the placenta, and waste materials are passed in the opposite direction. Thus there is an exchange of materials in the two bloodstreams. Since hormones are produced in emotional distress, and circulated by the blood, it has been suggested that hormones are the causal link. The theory has been tested by injecting hormones associated with stress into pregnant rats and mice; when the injections are made at the crucial developmental stage almost 90 percent of the young are born with cleft palates (Montagu, 1959).

Because of the exchange between blood supplies, drugs taken by the mother are circulated to the fetus, where they sometimes have terrible effects. A tragic illustration of the need for precaution in prescribing medication occurred in the early 1960s, when it was discovered that thalidomide, a supposedly harmless sedative, had dangerous side effects when taken by women at a certain critical stage of pregnancy. The birth of hundreds of deformed babies, lacking hands and sometimes even arms, was traced to the use of this drug.

Recently, there has been an increase in the number of babies born either "high" or actually addicted to drugs. If the mother is herself a drug addict and continues to take drugs during her pregnancy, the infant, when born, will show the withdrawal symptoms of an addict deprived of a "fix."

Physical growth is most rapid during the prenatal

period. The rate of growth continues to be high during the first year after birth but then slows down. When we graph the amount of growth over successive time intervals, we see a *growth curve* that rises steeply at first and gradually levels off. For example, half a child's height is attained by the age of two and a half. Similar kinds of curves are characteristic of many developmental processes. The importance of this is seen in the evidence that environmental influences are greatest when change is most rapid (Bloom, 1964). Probably development is influenced more easily when it is happening the fastest; later, when it has slowed down, the factors impinging on it must be much more powerful to have an effect. As we mentioned, this is part of the rationale for giving Head Start an earlier start.

Physical growth during childhood and adolescence brings several changes in body proportions. By the time the individual has reached physical maturity, the proportionate size of the head is much smaller than during infancy, whereas the trunk and limbs are proportionally longer. These changes greatly increase the grace and efficiency of the individual's body movements. There are, of course, many deviations from the general pattern of development and each of us comes to have a unique set of bodily and facial characteristics.

Nutritional and Metabolic Deficiencies

Although physical growth is the maturational result of heredity in a normal environment, it may be greatly influenced by deficiencies in the environment. Obviously the environment must provide the food required for growth. Not quite so obviously, the food must also contain specific nutrients such as protein, necessary for normal development of the brain in early life. Reports of hunger and malnutrition in many parts of the world raise the possibility that some children are, or will be, suffering incorrectable mental deficiency because of their diet.

Even in our own country this may be occurring. One study found that with racial and other factors held constant, the children of poor mothers in New York were born 15 percent smaller than children of nonpoor mothers. They also showed a different pattern of organ growth—a pattern characteristic of both human and animal subjects who have experienced chronic undernutrition (Nalye, Diener, Dellinger, & Blane, 1969).

The role of nutrition in affecting learning capabilities and psychological growth as well as physical growth has only recently been investigated by rigorous scientific methods. Evidence from both animal and human subjects points to the same conclusion: "early nutritional deprivations have resulted in a decreased learning capacity as well as changes in other behavioral characteristics" (Barnes, 1967).

A provocative study has convincingly demonstrated the role that vitamin deficiency plays in reducing intellectual functioning. Public school children were first examined to determine the level of ascorbic acid (vitamin C) in their blood plasma. Then they were given tests to measure their intelligence level. Those with lower levels of vitamin C had lower average scores on the intelligence tests. After three months of orange juice therapy (a glass a day in school), the mean increase in IQ scores for the low-ascorbate group was 3.5 points, while the originally high-ascorbate group did not benefit further from the orange juice supplement.

This study was interrupted by the summer vacation. When the children returned, those initially low in vitamin C were again low, and their intelligence scores had dropped to the initial levels. However, after three more months of vitamin C supplements, these children again showed an average gain in measured intelligence of 3.5 points (Kubala & Katz, 1960).

Differences in reading level among Puerto Rican children in New York City have been found to be associated with the levels of nicotinic acid (niacin), vitamin B_{12}, and vitamin C in their blood. Low reading levels were correlated with abnormally low levels of these substances (Ziffer, Frank, Christakis, Talkington, & Baker, 1967). Of course, we cannot determine whether it was the vitamin C alone that was the effective independent variable, or the attention and refreshment associated with the "orange juice break." Furthermore, an IQ change of 3.5 points, although statistically significant, does not make very much practical difference in what a child can do, as we will see in Chapter 11.

The old saying that "you are what you eat," has been translated recently by Nobel laureate Linus Pauling (1968) into, "if you have a vitamin-deficient diet, you are not what you could be." Pellagra, beri-beri, scurvy, and pernicious anemia are some of the more well-known diseases to which poor people have often been subject because of inadequate diet. Pauling has shown that such vitamin deficiencies are causal agents in diminishing optimal functioning across a range of mental processes. We will discuss his research in more detail in Chapter 15 as it relates to therapy for mental disorders.

Even people who eat the "right" foods may suffer from dietary deficiencies because of their unique metabolism. For example, there are a number of errors of amino acid metabolism which result in mental retardation. Although they are genetic mutations, most have effects correctable through proper diet (Sober, 1968). One such disease, PKU, was described in Chapter 3. This disease can be treated by a diet which is low in phenylalanine—a substance that cannot be properly metabolized by children who have this error in metabolism.

Physical development can also be stunted by an inadequate social environment. "Deprivation dwarfism" seems to result basically from the anxiety and emotional starvation of children in extremely unhappy homes—just how unhappy can be guessed from the fact that simply taking thirteen such children from their homes and hospitalizing them was enough in most cases to start a spurt of growth. How the emotional impact stunts growth is not yet known; some suspect that the growth-regulating pituitary gland is involved, while others believe chronic anxiety interferes with the absorption of food in the digestive system. The children studied, whose growth had been abnormally retarded, showed remarkable acceleration when in a hospital away from family strife, but growth decelerated again when they were returned to the conflict situation (Powell, Brasel, Blizzard, & Taiti, 1967).

Critical Periods When Stress Is Not a Strain

We have been concentrating on detrimental effects of the environment; now let us turn to some positive ones. Preliminary studies of the effects of early environment showed that petting and handling infant rats produced larger adult rats. These studies also showed the importance of the time factor, since sim-

ilar handling of slightly older rats did not increase growth. Thus, there appears to be a *critical period* in development, a particular time at which this environmental factor can have an effect (N. Miller, 1968). Once the critical period has passed, the opportunity to produce the effect has been missed. Periods of varying durations, occurring at different points in development and critical to various particular processes have been discovered or hypothesized.

One obvious explanation is that handling and gentling infant rats increases their growth because it provides "affection" and "security." Research by Seymour Levine (1962) demolished this "common-sense" explanation by stimulating rats with violent rides in a bottle-washing machine or with electric shocks. The same improvements in growth and behavior were seen as when they were more lovingly stimulated. Stimulation of any kind in early life seems to activate the adrenal glands by way of the growth-controlling pituitary gland.

Stimulation, as an independent variable administered during infancy, has also repeatedly been shown to have a beneficial effect on subsequent emotionality. Stimulated animals are less emotional and timid, eat more, and are more active than matched, unstimulated controls. Moreover, these differences may endure for the whole of the animal's lifetime (Dennenberg, 1967).

The effects of stimulation, good or bad, apparently can begin to operate even before birth, indirectly through the mother. Pregnant rats were made anxious by a buzzer that had previously been used as the signal for a shock. Their offspring were more emotional at 130 days of age than those from control mothers (Thompson, 1957). When the pregnant mothers were handled, however, their pups were found to be less emotional when tested at 100 days of age (Ader & Conklin, 1963).

Here is a good example of the way research studies by different investigators provide a check on each other and suggest new hypotheses to be tested. If aversive treatment of infant rats produced the same benefits as handling them, why should aversive treatment of pregnant mothers make their offspring more emotional? Several hypotheses suggest themselves: (a) perhaps the maternal influence transmitted by hormones through the bloodstream to the fetus was not comparable to the effect produced directly on the infant, (b) perhaps the influence of a factor is different before than after birth, (c) perhaps the effect of a shock (which the infants experienced) was different from the effects of anxious expectation (which the mothers experienced). Can you think of others?

Experimentally programming the early life experiences of human infants has also been shown to exert a significant effect on their development.

Sixteen institutionalized babies were given twenty minutes of extra tactile stimulation, five days a week over ten weeks (only 1000 minutes total). Each of these babies was matched on a number of factors with a control baby, who was not given more than the amount of stimulation usual for the institution. At the end of the ten-week period, the absolute developmental scores for both groups had *declined*—probably due to the overall lack of stimulation they received. However, the effects of the minimal extra stimulation prevented the experimental babies from having as great a loss in their rate of development as did the relatively unstimulated babies (Casler, 1965).

In contrast to this lack of stimulation in the institutionalized environment is the intense stimulation which infants and children experience in some societies. Piercing the skin and molding the bones are two classes of stressful stimuli studied by Landauer and Whiting (1964) across a large number of different cultures.

Stressful beautification procedures in some cultures involve cutting the skin to form scar patterns, piercing the nose, lips, or ears, molding the shape of the head, and stretching limbs. Circumcision, inoculation, and cauterization are other stresses infants may experience. These investigators found that those societies whose child-rearing practices included separating infants from their mothers and subjecting them to procedures of this nature produced males who were over two inches taller than those where such stress was absent. The critical period appeared to be within the first two weeks of life. Females who live in societies where they are separated from their mothers and subjected to either pain or bone shaping during the first two weeks of life reach the age of menarche (first menstrual period) fifteen months earlier than those who live in societies where these stresses are absent (Whiting, 1965).

Again, we must remember that we are dealing with correlations only; we must be wary about drawing conclusions regarding causality.

Why does one kind of stress seem to produce growth while the "deprivation dwarfism" described in the last section seems to suggest just the opposite effect? Further experiments will be needed to discover the difference and deepen our understanding of both processes. Perhaps short-term stress is a challenge that stimulates the infant, while chronic stress eventually exhausts his physical resources. Another possibility is that stress which occurs after the child is mature enough to understand its psychological significance (as in family quarrels) triggers mechanisms of neurological inhibition, rather than of activation. While research is pointing out the pervasive significance of the heredity-environment interaction, even in a process such as physical growth, we have only just begun to understand the mechanics by which such developmental processes operate.

The Growth of the Brain

The infant at birth has the full number of brain cells, but brain size increases rapidly, doubling in size in the first six months, and doubling again by the age of four. Even though all the brain cells are present, not all brain structures are mature enough at birth to function. Development of functional capacity in the brain seems to occur in a definite order, beginning at the lower levels of the brain stem and proceeding upward. For the first month after birth, the neocortex is essentially nonfunctional; in the second and third months, it begins to undergo rapid maturation. Because different parts of the brain serve different functions, as we saw in Chapter 3, this sequential maturation of brain structures helps to explain the sequential emergence of behavioral capacities in the course of development (Bronson, 1965).

In the first month of life, behavior is limited largely to reflex responses, reactions to changes in intensity of stimulation, and reactions to pain. Accompanying the rapid neocortical maturation beginning in the second month is the appearance of smiling to specific stimuli, emotional expression, and an active visual interest in the environment. By three months of age, neocortical perceptual systems mature and the infant's overt exploration is maintained longer, daytime wakefulness increases, discriminations are more refined, and there emerges the capacity for acquiring fears of specific stimuli, as well as an apparently innate fear of perceptual strangeness. While many unobservant parents see only a little creature who continually eats, sleeps, cries, and defecates, others are entranced by the remarkable development of behavioral action patterns during these first months of life.

Motor Development

We have seen that the fertilized egg undergoes a series of divisions, with each division doubling the number of cells. Among the specialized types of cells that become differentiated during the embryonic period are the muscle cells.

The first muscular structure that begins to function observably is the heart. By the time the fetal period begins, at about eight weeks after conception, the heart has already been beating for some time. At twenty-five weeks, the neuromuscular systems for respiration have developed to the point that a fetus removed from the mother's body (for medical, not experimental reasons, of course) can carry on respiration for about twenty-four hours.

Prenatal Motor Activity

The voluntary musculature is capable of producing body movements as early as the eighth week of prenatal life. Two kinds of movements are distinguished: spontaneous or emitted movements and externally stimulated or elicited movements.

The human fetus makes many movements of the head, trunk, and limbs which are "spontaneous" in the sense that they occur in the absence of any external stimulus. Particularly after the fourth month, the mother can feel the movements of her unborn child, and a few weeks before birth, it may become quite active. Its movements are slow and irregular, involving several joints, or even several different parts of the body, at once. This sluggish, irregular, widespread movement is aptly described as *mass action* or as *irradiation* (diffusing outward).

Most early fetal responses to specific stimuli are more jerky than the spontaneous movements but still show gross irradiation—the application of the stimulus to one part of the body elicits a generalized response of several body members. Response to stimulation of the nose or chin includes movements of the trunk and neck and extension of the arms. ■ Not all fetal responses, however, are generalized; some are quite specific, especially during the final months of the prenatal period. A touch applied to the lip, for example, arouses the response of opening and closing the mouth—probably the beginning of the sucking response. Grasping and sucking movements appear at about twenty-nine weeks of gestational age. During the final period of prenatal life, these reflexes continue to mature.

The Sequence of Motor Development

At birth, the infant has his full total of muscle cells, but they must grow in size and strength through maturation and exercise. Already, however, the neonate is equipped with a variety of motor abilities. He can yawn, hiccough, frown, lift his head slightly (this means that he can free his nose for breathing), make prancing movements with his legs if supported at the armpits, and focus his eyes momentarily on a light. These accomplishments—together with the even more important sucking, swallowing, and other mouth movements involved in eating—are often called *general responses*, because they are responses to definite stimuli and in most cases involve the activity of rather large portions of the body. The infant also exhibits a number of *reflex actions*. These involve mainly a specific part of his body, although even they are accompanied by some total body activity. One of the most readily observed is the grasping reflex. Other reflexes include the knee jerk, the pupillary reaction to light, blinking, and sneezing. Because most responses continue to involve a large portion of the body for a time after birth, the human infant expends about two and a half times as much energy in proportion to body weight as does the adult.

Motor maturation proceeds in a definite sequence, beginning in the head region and gradually extending throughout the organism to the feet; maturation also

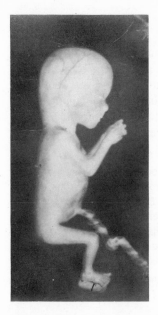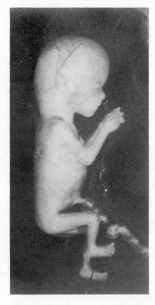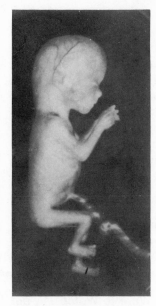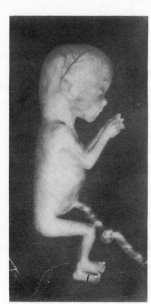

Movies were used to record the behavior of prematurely delivered fetuses. The sole of this fourteen-week fetus has just been stroked with a hair (left). The response (center pictures) is extreme flexion of the big toe, fanning of the other toes, flexion of the hip, and a slight backward movement of the foot. The fetus then returns to normal posture (right).

proceeds from the trunk outward to the extremities. Thus, the eye and mouth movements come under control first, then those of the head and neck, later those of the trunk and arms, still later those of the hands and lower trunk, and finally those of the pelvic region, legs, and fingers (Shirley, 1931). The rate at which new achievements appear is also faster for the upper regions of the body. Thus, some control of the eyes, head, neck, and arms is usually gained in rapid succession, with only a few days between achievements. But after the baby begins to sit alone, it may be weeks or months before new abilities involving the lower portions of the body—such as creeping, standing, and walking—are added to his repertoire. The muscles involved in toilet training are among the last over which the child gains control; hence it is futile to expect a child to be "trained" before he or she is maturationally ready. Training that starts too early or is too rigid may arouse undesirable emotional reactions in the child, who is not able to meet his parents' demands.

As maturation progresses, the generalized responses of the young infant give way to more precise and more effective reactions. For example, the hand becomes able to grasp without the whole torso being involved in the movement. Three somewhat overlapping stages can be identified: (a) a stage of global, undifferentiated mass activity, (b) a stage of differentiation in which body parts can be moved individually with the rest of the body remaining quiet, and (c) increasing coordination and integration of individual responses. This coordination or integration, though dependent upon the interaction of the differentiated parts, takes place at about the same time that differentiation is occurring. Transport movements of the whole body occur before there is maturation of specific manipulative movements. (Ψ Close-up, p. 120.)

The age of about twenty-two months appears to be a critical period in maturation, for at this time the transition begins to be made from generalized control of the environment through motion of the entire body to more refined selective, manipulative control.

The Importance of Maturational Readiness

The neuromuscular structures of the body must reach a certain stage of maturation before they are capable of responding to stimulation (Bousfield, 1953). This is called the *principle of motor primacy*. For example, regardless of the amount of training he receives, a child cannot walk until the necessary physical structures have developed. The majority of babies cannot walk before their first birthday, because until then their muscles are too weak to support their bodies and the neural mechanisms for coordination are not ready.

Every child develops at his own rate. Some walk as early as nine months of age; others wait until they are nearly twice that old. Although most babies succeed in "getting into everything" quite efficiently by creeping about on all fours, many skip this method of locomotion altogether and pull themselves along on their stomachs or even hitch themselves backward. Wide variations also exist in the development of less conspicuous achievements than walking, and it is useless to try to push children beyond their physical capacity. (Ψ Close-up, p. 121.)

The importance of maturation in development of some motor behavior patterns is seen in comparisons of two groups of Hopi children. Those in one group were allowed freedom of movement during their early months, whereas those in the other group spent many hours a day bound to a board carried on the back of the

---

Ψ Close-up   **Babies Will Work to Watch TV, but Not to Turn it on**

A revolving playpen was used in an experiment in which thirty children between the ages of ten and twenty-eight months served as subjects. A closed-circuit TV monitor was placed outside the pen; the child had to crawl continuously in order to correct for the motion of the pen and continue to see the image on the screen, which was sometimes his mother and sometimes a stranger. The arrangement is depicted in the diagram below.

Time spent looking at both the mother and the stranger increased with the age of the child. The "most rapid developmental changes in orientation" to the TV screen occurred from the twentieth to the twenty-fourth month.

Related experiments involved visual and sound stimuli, including various images shown on a TV monitor and tape recordings of music, of parents' voices, and of the children's own voices. Nearly all infants below the age of twenty-two months, even infants only nine months old, oriented actively to both sound and visual images, turning or crawling toward them. However, none of them learned to touch a control plate on the side of the crib which would turn on the TV or start the music.

In another experiment, the child was placed in a crib with a rough floor which would be uncomfortable to his bare legs and hands. A blanket that could have been used to provide a softer surface hung on the side of the crib, but only one of five babies below the age of twenty-two months tried to use the blanket for protection even after having it put into his lap.

The experimenters were unable to develop any devices which a child under twenty months of age would use to control his environment; in fact, they found purposeful manipulation to be very limited before the age of two years (Smith, Zwerg, & Smith, 1963).

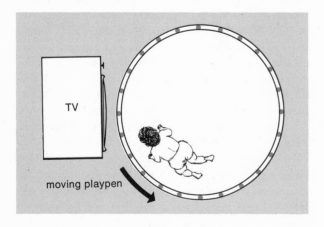

moving playpen

TV

Ψ *Close-up*   *Uganda Babies Thrive on Old-fashioned Ways*

Investigators tested 308 East African (Uganda) children, most of them below the age of two years, for strength and motor coordination and compared them to Western children on the basis of criteria standardized by Arnold Gesell at Yale University.

The Uganda babies, some of whom are shown in the photographs, were found to be noticeably superior to Western babies of the same ages, and from the fifth month were also advanced in adaptivity, language, and personal-social relationships. Most of the African children studied came from lower-class families which still followed the ancient child-rearing practices of their culture. The typical mother-child relationship before weaning was one of complete solicitude, involving companionship during the night as well as the day; feeding according to the demand of the child; constant external stimulation such as cuddling, tickling, and soft words; and help with motor tasks. Indeed, even before birth, the mother's sole interest was in her coming child.

Because it was generally believed by these Africans that any unhappy thoughts of the mother might adversely affect the future of the new baby, every attempt was made to prevent the occurrence of any emotional upsets during pregnancy. Thus the environment was favorable before as well as after birth. Those few children studied who came from the higher classes, whose families had become somewhat Westernized, tended to show considerably less precocity (Geber, 1958).

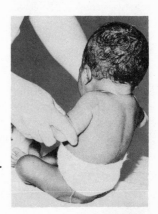

Uganda infants develop motor coordination much earlier than do Western children. A child nine hours old (right), when drawn up to a sitting position, is able to prevent his head from falling backward, a feat not accomplished by the Western child until the age of six weeks. At two days (bottom left) the African child holds his head firmly and, with his eyes focused, looks at the examiner; not until eight weeks is this done by the average Western child. A seven-week-old Uganda infant (left center) can support himself in a sitting position while watching his reflection in a mirror in a manner comparable to that of a Western child of twenty weeks. At five months, as compared to nine months for the Western child, the Uganda child is able to hold himself upright. He can even take the forms from a Gesell testing board (right center); this is done by the Western child only at eleven months. At seven months, a Uganda child walks to the Gesell box to look inside (bottom right); an average Western child does this at about fifteen months.

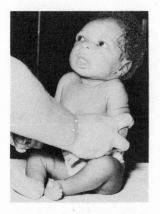

mother. ▲ Although the cradleboard almost completely restricted leg movements, the children reared on it began to walk at the same average age as those who had not been bound (Dennis, 1940).

The time of beginning to walk was evidently set by maturation. This finding is consistent with the results of a classic experiment.

Children between the ages of two and three years were divided into two matched groups. One of these, the practice group, was allowed to climb a two-and-a-half foot ladder to a table top on which interesting toys had been placed. By the end of the twelfth week, this group had acquired considerable skill. The other group had no opportunity to practice climbing—although they did, of course, practice other habits, such as walking, which have something in common with ladder climbing. At the end of twelve weeks, this group was also given a table full of toys which could be reached by a ladder. Within a week, these children could climb just as well as the practice group (J. Hilgard, 1932).

The second group in this experiment was able to catch up quickly with the practice group because at a later stage of maturation less practice was required to achieve a given level of performance.

When a child or animal is maturationally ready, a small amount of practice will develop the skill to a level consistent with the current level of maturation. This general conclusion from research on the relative effects of maturation and learning on skills was most convincingly demonstrated in an early study.

A group of frog and salamander eggs were placed in an anesthetic solution which allowed normal physical development but prevented the animals from moving about as they matured into tadpoles; a control group remained in a normal environment of pure water. After a period of time, when the control animals had been swimming freely for five days, the experimental group was removed from the anesthetic and placed in pure water. Half an hour later, these animals were swimming just as well as those that had five days of "practice." Further investigation showed that the thirty-minute delay could not be construed as a learning period, but was merely the time required for the anesthetic to wear off (Carmichael, 1926, 1927).

Attaining Muscular Proficiency

Muscular development is slow throughout early childhood. Studies indicate that a person still has to gain

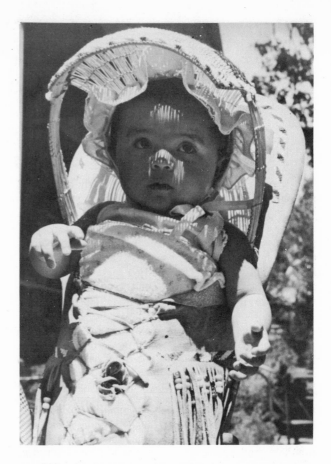

▲ This picture shows one of the types of cradleboards used with Hopi children.

about four fifths of his total strength after the age of six, although he has attained two thirds of his adult height by that time. Muscular growth is most rapid during adolescence, when the individual begins to "fill out" and approaches adult height and proportions. In tests of pure muscular strength such as hand grip, both boys and girls show steady increases throughout adolescence, although boys display more marked increases and continue to develop over a longer period of time than girls (Jones, 1949). In athletic skills such as the fifty-yard dash and the broad jump, for instance, boys improve regularly during adolescence, whereas girls level off at about the age of thirteen and then actually decline in proficiency (Espenschade, 1940). The peak development of motor abilities typically occurs during the mid-twenties. Even at this advanced stage, maturation apparently continues to influence performance if performance is pushed to the limit by practice.

That maximum proficiency in various skills develops at different ages has been clearly demonstrated by a study of several thousand outstanding male performers in a number of athletic activities (Lehman, 1951). Some of the findings of this study are summarized below.

Type of Performance	Ages of Maximum Proficiency
Professional football	23-27
Professional ice hockey	24-28
Professional tennis	25-29
Championship rifle and pistol shooting	25-29
Championship billiards	25-29
Professional baseball (hitting)	26-29
Heavyweight boxing	26-30
Professional baseball (pitching)	26-31
Championship golf (open)	27-31
Championship cornhusking	27-31
Bowling	30-34

It is important to note that only outstanding performers, many of them champions, were considered in this study. The reason for limiting the study to performers who displayed a high degree of skill is that few people ever actually reach the very peak of performance within the bounds of their capacity. Most human beings are content to rest at some point below their maximum potential performance, whereas athletic champions attain an exceptional level of performance not only because they have great innate capacity but also because of an enormous amount of practice. ■

Perceptual Development

While motor development is primary, in the sense we have discussed, it is only one factor in behavior. Many responses are reactions to stimuli from a distant source impinging on the organism. Moving away from an aversive stimulus, or moving toward a pleasant one, requires the development of sensory capacities for detecting stimuli and for identifying their positive or negative qualities. Even responses to inter-

■ This teen-age backstroke champion performs at a high level of proficiency, due to both her natural ability and a great deal of practice.

nal conditions may require perceptual capacities. The body conditions we sense as "being hungry," for example, can be thought of as conditions in the environment of the nervous system. Adaptive behavior in this situation requires that the nervous system detect and recognize the bodily stimuli that signal a need for food. In a later chapter we will see that abnormalities in responsiveness to such stimulation can lead to obesity in humans.

Furthermore, motor behavior itself can be treated apart from perceptual development only in a somewhat superficial way. Walking, for example, is not done as effectively when blindfolded. In fact, it would be a very valuable experience for you to spend one day of your life blindfolded in order to appreciate better the interaction of your motor and perceptual systems (as well as for other lessons inherent in this experience). Imagine how difficult it would be if you also lacked the kinesthetic sensations that tell you where your legs are in relation to your body, and the tactile sensations that tell when your feet are on the ground. Even simple motor acts would be random movements of no adaptive value if they took place in a sensory vacuum.

The anatomical structures of most sense organs are well developed even before birth. Whether or when they actually begin to function in the fetus or newborn infant is a question that must be answered with careful testing procedures. Testing sensitivity early in life is difficult, however, because it must be inferred from a response of some sort, and a response may fail to occur because motor systems are not sufficiently developed. The principle of motor primacy applies to such experiments as well as to development in general.

Secluded in the womb, the fetus is not exposed to many stimuli. The newborn enters a vastly more complex stimulus environment, and does show sensitivity to many kinds of stimulation. But just how much he organizes the welter of sensations is another question; perhaps, as William James expressed it classically, "the baby, assailed by eyes, ears, nose, skin, and entrails all at once, feels it all as one great blooming, buzzing confusion" (James, 1890, p. 488). By studying development we hope to find out what is confusion and what is not, and how the confusion becomes unconfused, ordered, and stable.

If indeed Nature is organized according to underlying principles of regularity, then the task of all living creatures who hope to survive is to learn some of the secrets of this system. Before overtly adapting to the environment or trying to change it (which we will study in the two chapters on learning), organisms must first come to perceive accurately the significant objects and the relationships among them which exist in their environment.

Touch, Temperature, and Pain

As we have seen, the human fetus can react to touch stimuli about eight weeks after conception. By this time, then, some rudimentary sensory capacity has developed. Sensitivity to touch develops along a physiological gradient, similar to the one for motor development, from the head downward. In the eighth week of prenatal life, the fetus becomes responsive to touch stimuli on the nose, lips, and chin, and the area sensitive to stimulation gradually increases with the passage of time. By the thirteenth or fourteenth week, the entire body is sensitive except for the top and back of the head, which do not respond to stimuli until after birth. Even at birth, the face is more sensitive to touch and pressure than other parts of the body.

Temperature sensitivity is present before birth, since premature infants, like full-term ones, may re-

fuse milk of the wrong temperature. They may also respond to external temperatures, usually reacting more strongly to cold than to heat.

Sensitivity to pain is weak in the fetal period and during the early days of life outside the womb. It is greater on the face than elsewhere (another example of the physiological gradient in maturation) and sufficiently underdeveloped that circumcisions may be performed without anesthetic during the first two weeks. The delay in development of the pain sense has been interpreted as a biological defense mechanism to protect the child during the birth process (Carmichael, 1951).

Apparently the environment must provide experiences of tactile and painful sensation if these senses are to develop normally. Without this "environmental training" normal development may be seriously disturbed. Interesting effects of tactual deprivation have been studied in the chimpanzee.

One subject, Rob, had his limbs from elbow to fingertips and from knee to toes encased in cardboard tubes from the age of four weeks to thirty-one months. Rob never learned to turn his head toward the hand which the experimenter stimulated. That is, if the experimenter squeezed his right hand, Rob was to turn his head to the right in order to receive a reward. After 2000 trials he was unable to do this, although a normal chimpanzee learned the task in about 200 trials (Nissen, Chow, & Semmes, 1951).

It has also been found that dogs deprived of normal stimulation in infancy are virtually incapable of learning to avoid painful stimuli later and do not learn to fear objects associated with such stimuli (Melzack & Scott, 1957).

Taste and Smell

A sense of taste is well developed at birth. Newborn infants usually react with sucking movements to sweet or salty stimuli and with negative behavior to sour or bitter ones. The taste sense apparently develops some time before birth, since even premature babies respond to taste stimuli.

Smell is another well-developed sense in the neonate. Definite changes in bodily activity and breathing rate following olfactory stimulation have been observed. Studies have shown that the neonate can distinguish between such odors as acetic acid, asafetida, phenylethyl alcohol, and anise oil, although no clear differences are observed in response to odors which are pleasant and unpleasant to the normal adult (Engen, Lipsitt, & Kaye, 1963). The testing procedures employed in studies of this type will be described in Chapter 5, when we discuss the *orientation reaction*.

Hearing

There is some question as to whether the fetus can hear in spite of the fluid in his ears. It has been found that the rate of the fetal heartbeat will increase sharply in response to a tone sounded close to the mother's abdomen (Bernard & Sontag, 1947). A team of Swedish investigators studied fetal reactions to tones of differing frequency.

Reactions of the fetal heart to tones of 1000 and 2000 cycles per second at an intensity of 100 decibels and a duration of five seconds were observed in this study, which involved thirty-two women in the last month of pregnancy. The pulses of the mother and fetus were registered before, during, and after presentation of the tones. In the group tested at 1000 cycles per second, the increase in fetal heart rate averaged seven beats a minute. In the group tested at 2000 cycles per second, the acceleration was eleven beats a minute. The mother's pulse did not show any acceleration (Dwornicka, Jasienska, Smolarz, & Wawryk, 1964).

One point of especial interest in this study was that the higher tones produced a greater response. Studies of babies soon after birth show them to be more pleased by low notes than by high notes, as inferred from their external behavior. These two observations suggest that the fetus is really hearing.

At birth, hearing seems to be less well developed than the other senses, though there is much variation from child to child. Hearing is at first hampered by amniotic fluid, which often remains in the middle ear for a few days after birth. Usually sometime between the third and the seventh day the neonate reacts to ordinary noises, responding more vigorously to the rattling of paper or dishes than to a voice. After the fourth week, however, he responds more frequently to voices than to loud noises. By the age of two months he is apparently not just hearing auditory

stimuli, but discriminating among the sounds impinging on him.

Vision

Because of the great importance of vision as a source of information about our world, the question of whether perception depends on learning has long intrigued investigators. It would seem that if simple motor reflexes are inherited to protect a helpless young animal from gagging, falling, or too intense stimulation, then perceptual abilities should also be available, without learning, to further ensure its survival. Migrating birds and fish do not have to learn the perceptual cues that guide them unerringly on their way. Nor do natural prey have to learn to perceive the characteristics of their predators. Similarly, the bee sucks nectar from certain flowers without any special lessons about how to tell one flower from another. This innate basis for perception is genetically coded within the species and passed on from generation to generation so that the individual inherits the capacity for a given range of appropriate responses to objects or situations even the first time they are experienced.

Animals low on the scale of evolutionary development are limited to this innate or "instinctual" knowledge, and profit very little from learning. In contrast, the visual world of the human infant is expanded daily through perceptual learning.

Studies of infant vision. Since the retina, the light-sensitive tissue of the eye, has not reached its full development at birth, it was once assumed that the neonate could not see clearly at first. Experiments have shown, however, that there is an innate ability to perceive form visually. One study found that infants under five days of age looked longer at black-and-white patterns than at plain colored surfaces (Ψ Close-up, p. 126). Infants a few days older were found to show even greater visual discrimination (Fantz, 1963). In another study, investigators showed newborn babies a series of pairs of shapes, each shape differing in the number of angles it contained. Shapes with ten angles or turns were preferred to other shapes with five turns or twenty turns, as inferred from photographic recordings of eye fixations (Hershenson, Munsinger, & Kessen, 1965). By about ten days after birth the infant can follow slowly moving objects with his eyes. Because his eye muscles are not well coordinated at first, his gaze may occasionally seem to "flare out" in two directions at once.

There is some disagreement as to whether the young infant perceives color, but experiments suggest that he does.

Ψ *Close-up* *Pattern Vision in Infants*

The ability to differentiate between different visual stimuli is inferred from consistent differences in response to them. Babies under two days old and between two and five days old looked roughly three times as long at a black and white picture of a face as at a plain colored circle the same size. Older infants showed the same order of preference between patterned and plain circles but showed more discrimination between the face and the concentric circles than the younger infants had shown.

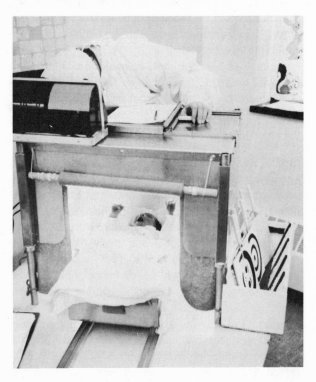

Stimuli varying in shape, color, or both were presented in pairs to infants four months of age. Preference (and hence ability to discriminate) was inferred from the amount of time spent in visual fixation. It was found that red and blue were significantly preferred to gray, but that shape dominated color as a basis for preference. A bull's-eye pattern was preferred to other patterns (Spears, 1964).

How can we show that human infants supplement their inherited perceptual repertoire with acquired knowledge in order to make contact with, and understand, novel aspects of encountered phenomena? An elegant study by Nelson provides a research design for getting at this basic question.

If a baby is watching a moving object which briefly disappears from sight, then reappears consistently at another place, will the baby visually track the extension of the observed trajectory of the object? Nelson began by recording the eye movements of eighty babies varying in age from 99 days to 264 days as they watched an electric train moving around a track. As soon as the babies spotted the train, all previous, random behavior stopped instantly. With feet or hands "frozen" in midair, they watched the moving train intently. On the first trial seventy-three of the subjects tracked the train steadily, until it disappeared into a tunnel. They continued fixating on the entrance ("like cats at a mouse hole") and usually were unaware of its exit at the other end. However, on each of the next three successive runs, the babies looked progressively more toward the exit and spotted the reappearing train sooner and sooner. Visual tracking and anticipation in this complex, novel situation were learned in only a few trials, and more readily by seven-month-old babies than by those five months old (Nelson, 1970). ◆

Innate and learned factors in vision.   Is early stimulation necessary for vision to develop normally? One investigator found that raising a chimpanzee in total darkness resulted in degeneration of the retina and permanently impaired vision. When another chimpanzee was prevented from seeing objects but was allowed to experience light, however, his retina was not damaged (Riesen, 1950).

Later studies with both kittens and chimpanzees have also demonstrated that wherever visual deprivation leads to chemical changes in the retina, such changes become irreversible when the deprivation is

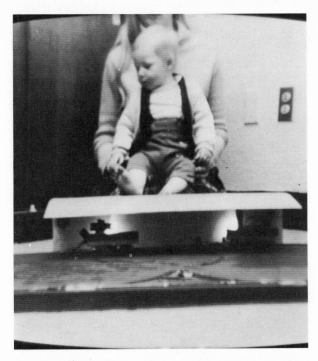

◆ A seven-month-old boy anticipates with his gaze the reappearance of a toy train from the tunnel.

continued beyond infancy, with the result that the animals suffer a permanent inability to learn certain perceptual habits (Riesen, 1961).

How do babies learn to see figures as entities? Since the identity of a figure depends on the form and location of boundaries and corners, active learning would call for devoting most attention to those aspects of a figure. Passive learning, on the other hand, would presumably involve simple scanning of the whole visual field. Photographic records of the eye fixations of newborn babies looking at a triangle indicate that attention is highly concentrated on the significant features—the corners especially (Salapatek & Kessen, 1966). From the beginning, then, the process of perceptual learning is more than a passive reception process. It involves active concentration of attention on the significant features of visual stimuli.

Despite the obvious importance of learning in perceptual development, *some* initial organization of sensation is apparently provided by innate patterning by the brain and nervous system. We have seen that new-

borns display greater interest in some kinds of figures than in others, and concentrate attention on significant features of visual forms. Since the newborn has had no previous opportunity for perceptual learning, these aspects of perception are probably innate. Further evidence of inborn abilities to perceive pattern and meaning in visual stimuli has been provided in an interesting series of experiments with young organisms of various species employing the "visual cliff."

This apparatus consists of a board laid across the center of a large sheet of heavy glass which is supported a foot or more above the floor. On one side of this board a sheet of patterned material is placed flush against the underside of the glass so that the glass appears to be as solid as it in fact is. On the other side of the board a sheet of the same material is several feet below the glass. This gives the visual appearance of a drop or "cliff," in spite of the solid glass above it. In experiments with thirty-six infants aged six to fourteen months, each baby was placed on the center board and his mother called to him first from the deep side and then from the shallow side. ■ (p. 128)

Twenty-seven of the children tested moved off the board; all of these crawled out on the shallow side at least once, but only three crept off onto the glass above the "cliff." Many cried when the mother called to them from the cliff side, but were unwilling to go to her over the apparent chasm; others actually crawled away from her. Some patted the glass on the deep side, ascertaining that it was solid, but still backed away. Apparently they were more dependent upon their visual sensations than upon the evidence of their sense of touch.

Although this experiment does not prove that the infants' perception and avoidance of the chasm are innate, similar experiments with animals tend to support the hypothesis that such perception is inborn. Nearly all animals tested were able to perceive and avoid the visual cliff as soon as they were able to stand or walk. This was true of chicks less than twenty-four hours old, and of kids, lambs, and kittens. Rats ventured onto the deep side as long as they could feel the glass with their whiskers but consistently chose the shallow side when the center board was raised enough to prevent their whiskers from touching the glass (Gibson & Walk, 1960).

In general, these experiments suggest that some prepatterning of perception does exist in species whose survival depends upon their being able to perceive depth by the time they can move about on their own.

■ These pictures show the apparatus used in the visual cliff experiments and the reactions of two subjects to the apparent drop-off. Although the child patted the glass with his hand and thus had tactual evidence that there was a firm surface there, he refused to crawl across it when his mother called to him. The one-day-old goat walked freely on the shallow side but would not venture out on the deep side. When placed at the far edge of the deep side, he perched carefully on the narrow edge of the board and shortly thereafter leaped across to the shallow side again.

Motor Factors in Perceptual Development

We have pointed out the obvious fact that motor performance depends on perceptual capacity. Though not at all obvious from everyday experience, perceptual development also depends on motor activity.

In one experiment, kittens were restrained so they could not walk around from the time they were first exposed to light. Compared to animals reared normally, their behavior in situations calling for visual orientation was deficient. The original interpretation attributed these results to the effects of stimulus deprivation. Since the restrained kittens could not change their stimulus environment by walking about, they had been deprived of a great deal of variation in visual stimulation; this was presumed to be the cause of their deficient visual discrimination.

Further study showed that this explanation was not sufficient. Pairs of kittens were given experience in a device that equalized movement through the environment but prevented active motion by one member of the pair. ● The movements of the active kitten were transmitted through a pivoted bar and chain linkages to a small gondola in which the second kitten was restrained. When the active kitten moved around, the passive kitten in the gondola moved in identical ways; thus both animals experienced the same variation in visual stimulation. The active kittens developed normally: they blinked when objects approached and put out their paws when carried toward a surface, for example. The passive kittens did not display these behaviors, though they learned quickly after a few days when allowed to move about normally (Held, 1965).

The practical significance of findings such as these was suggested in another experiment. A group of children being cared for in institutions were given special opportunities to deal actively with an enriched visual environment. Their developmental rates accelerated markedly for some kinds of visual-motor abilities. Evidence of a critical period was also found; the treatment was less effective if it came either too early or too late (White & Held, 1966).

Thus some aspects of perception and perceptual-motor coordination require not simply experience, but active participation of the motor systems in the process of experiencing, if normal development is to occur. It is the function of all effective stimulus processing and perceptual behavior to prepare the organism to respond overtly to the demands of its environment. If perception is to be a dependable link in this sequence, we must develop a sensory-motor feedback system that gives us stable information about the consequences of our movements.

The Development of Adaptive Behavior

We have examined the development of systems of perceiving and of capacities for responding. For an animal to survive, it must adapt to its environment. Such adaptive behavior involves the *integration* of responses and perceptions. It is not enough for a child to develop responses like hammering or eating and perceptions of hammers and sandwiches. He must also learn that hammers are for hammering but not eating, while sandwiches are for eating but not hammering.

While many psychologists have preferred to theorize about these processes as if they were independent, current views stress their interdependence (see Gibson, 1970, for example). Understanding how an organism learns and behaves requires an understanding of how it perceives relations among objects and events. Karl Lashley has pointed out that "It is not the fact of learning but what is learned that differentiates animals in the evolutionary scale. The learning of higher animals involves a perception of relations which is beyond the capacity of the lower." (1949, p. 30)

Nature apparently has ensured that perception of events in space which could be either dangerous or beneficial for survival develops early in the life of all animals with little or no learning. However, the "fine-grain" differentiation of multidimensional objects and of written symbols represents an evolutionary achievement of man that is revealed only after considerable education. The study of the development

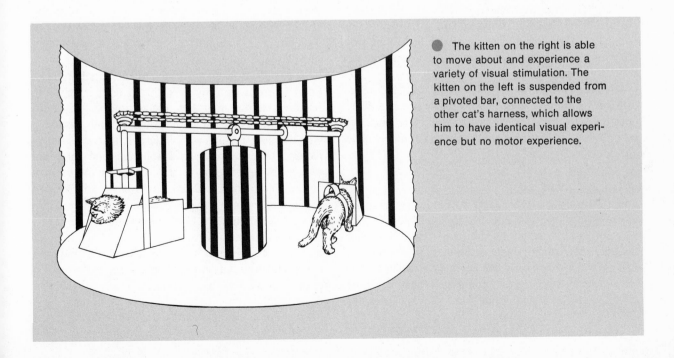

The kitten on the right is able to move about and experience a variety of visual stimulation. The kitten on the left is suspended from a pivoted bar, connected to the other cat's harness, which allows him to have identical visual experience but no motor experience.

of behavior, therefore, rests largely upon three classes of response systems: reflexes, instincts, and learned acts.

Reflexes

The most direct connections between stimuli and responses are provided by reflexes. As we saw in Chapter 3, basic reflex action involves transmission of nerve impulses along a relatively simple path from receptors, through the spinal cord, to effectors. The development of reflexes, then, is basically a process of physical and physiological development. When the appropriate receptors, neurons, and muscle fibers have formed and become capable of functioning, the reflex is ready to operate. No learning experience is necessary; the connection between stimulus and response is "wired in" innately as genetically programmed development proceeds.

We have already mentioned some reflex reactions of the fetus. Touching the lip causes the mouth to open and close, and presenting a tone close to the mother's abdomen increases the heart rate. At birth, the infant displays a variety of reflexes: the knee jerk, pupillary contraction in response to light, blinking, and sneezing. The grasping reflex develops in two phases. The closure reflex, present at birth, is a closure of the hand in response to light pressure on the palm. The second phase is a strong gripping or clinging response to stimulation of the finger tendons by pulling on them.

Reflexes, then, are highly specific, reliable reactions to a limited class of physical stimuli. They constitute the newborn's basic response repertoire, inherited as a function of their survival value to the species.

Instincts

There is probably no concept in psychology which has had a more controversial history than the instinct doctrine. We cannot here describe fully the heated debate which has raged for years over whether human behavior is governed by inherited "instincts"; for a detailed—and delightful—analysis, see Beach's (1955) paper, "The Descent of Instinct."

It is instructive, however, to consider briefly sever-al of the bones of contention involved. First, theologians, positing a man-brute dichotomy in order to establish man's unique claim to an afterlife, distinguished between man's free will (and thus responsibility) and the automatic instincts of nonthinking animals. However, at the turn of this century notable psychologists such as McDougall and William James declared that human behavior, too, reflected the driving force of instincts. In fact, it was maintained that man possessed even more instincts than animals, Bernard (1924) being able to list over 10,000 instincts identified by various authors.

The demise of this popular view, which dominated American psychology for several decades until the 1930s, came from a three-pronged attack. First, promiscuous labeling of virtually every conceivable behavior as instinctive made apparent the underlying *nominal* fallacy—that by naming something you have explained it. Calling behavior *instinctive* brought researchers no closer to an understanding of when, how, and under what conditions it would occur. Second, the behaviorists (to be met in Chapter 5) were demonstrating the importance of environmental conditions in inducing many kinds of behavior and were arguing persuasively that all behavior was controlled by environmental stimuli. And finally, the field studies of the cultural anthropologists had demonstrated that many of the behaviors typical in Western societies and assumed to be instinctive and hence universal did not occur in other societies.

But how can one explain the phenomenal organization of a troop of army ants, the social hierarchy of a bee hive, salmon migration, the complex but invariant patterns of sexual behavior within animal species, or web-building in spiders? Modern *ethologists* such as Konrad Lorenz and Niko Tinbergen, who study animal behavior patterns as they occur in the animal's natural interaction with its environment, have given the instinct concept new respectability by their careful observational studies. These behaviors are seen as a complex sequence of responses to a pattern of internal stimulation (e.g., hormone secretions) and environmental stimulation (e.g., odor cues in a stream or cues from the sun's position in the sky), to which the organism has an inherited sensitivity. Some ethologists prefer the term *fixed action pattern*, which puts the emphasis on overt behavioral components rather

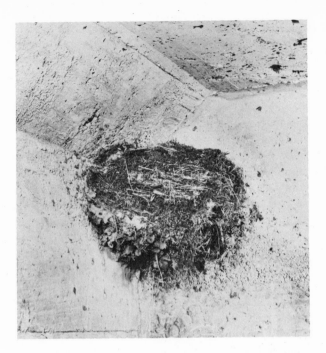

◆ Although there is a characteristic pattern for every form of instinctive behavior, this pattern varies in individual cases, depending upon the particular stimulus provided and the demands of the environment. An example of variations in nest-building behavior brought about by differences in environment is found in the two phoebes' nests pictured here. A nest built under a concrete bridge (left) is composed primarily of mud, which adheres to the concrete. A nest built on a schoolhouse rafter (right), however, has less of a gravity problem; therefore less mud is required, and the nest accordingly consists mainly of grasses cemented with mud.

than presumed internal, inherited mechanisms.

It is now generally agreed that an instinctive behavior pattern is one whose underlying biological pattern has been produced by maturation rather than by learning. It is inborn—a product of heredity—although it may not appear until months or even years after birth. It is found in all members of a species, regardless of differences in their environment. Once the underlying biological pattern is mature, a behavior pattern that is truly instinctive will appear "full-blown" the first time that adequate stimuli are presented, without previous opportunity for learning.

The last part of the definition is what distinguishes it from the earlier concept, which defined instincts as operating without reference to environmental opportunity or stimulation. Even in the clearest case of instinct, all modern psychologists would agree that

some stimulation is required. Some variation of the usual pattern of the instinctive behavior also occurs as a result of variations in the exact stimulation received from the individual's particular environment.

While instincts are "preprogrammed" behavior patterns, they differ from reflexes in various ways. They are typically more complex behaviors involving coordination of many motor systems, a temporal sequence of activities, and modifications to adapt to environmental opportunities and demands. A nest, for example, requires searching for materials, bringing them together, and arranging them in a structure. All members of a species will build a nest in about the same way in a given environment, but they may use substitute materials or add extra mud to attach the nest to an inhospitable wall or make other modifications appropriate to different environments. ◆

While there are innumerable examples one could use to illustrate the puzzling complexity of instinctive behavior, even given this modern definition, none is more compelling than the case of the navigation of the green turtle.

Female green turtles, which normally inhabit feeding grounds on the coast of Brazil, swim all the way to Ascension Island every few years to lay their eggs. Ascension Island is a target only five miles wide and some 1400 miles away. When individual turtles were tagged for identification purposes, it was found that some of the turtles tagged on the island were indeed recovered on the coast of Brazil, and that some returned from Brazil to the island three years later. One turtle returned to within a few hundred yards of the nesting beach she had left four years and 2800 miles before. It is believed that the set of cues which guide this journey may include chemical cues from the island, and chemical or visual cues from the Brazilian coastline; in the open sea, however, only a cue such as the sun's height above the horizon at noon would seem a likely candidate (Carr, 1965). ■

Some responses of human infants may be instinctive—avoiding the deep side of a visual cliff or concentrating attention on the corners of visual figures, for example. But in general, purely instinctive behavior of the kind observed in animals is quite rare in man. His nervous system, especially his brain, makes him much more able than lower species to adapt to variations in environmental stimulation, with the result that whatever instincts he may start with are rapidly overlaid by the effects of learning. It is highly doubtful whether the human adult exhibits any *purely* instinctive behavior. Particular human patterns fall somewhere on a continuum between pure instinct and pure learning, depending upon the degree to which learning has interacted with maturation in their development.

Learned Acts

The human nervous system has virtually infinite flexibility and almost endless modifiability. The old saw that "you can't change human nature" is simply wrong. The key lies in knowing how to devise the appropriate environmental conditions to steer development in the desired direction. The behavioral

modification which results from the adaptive interaction of man with his environment can best be understood using the language and concepts of research on learning.

Learning through association and practice. One type of learning builds upon and extends the range of our inherited response patterns: a stimulus that originally evokes no particular response is paired with a stimulus that does evoke a response until the first stimulus by itself can produce the response. In a second kind of learning, a particular response is *reinforced* by some change in the environment each time it occurs. A baby might be given milk whenever he presses a switch but not when he cries, with the result that he would learn to press the switch to get more milk. These two kinds of learning are called *respondent conditioning* and *operant conditioning* respectively; they are important in the development of adaptive behavior and will be examined in detail in Chapter 5.

Although opportunity to learn in prenatal life is very limited, it has been demonstrated that the human organism is capable of learning simple responses during the last two months in the womb.

In a study of prenatal respondent conditioning, preliminary investigations showed that a loud sound made just

■ This turtle is equipped with a radio monitoring device which will allow scientists to track the exact path of her journey to traditional nesting grounds.

outside the mother's body elicited body-movement responses, whereas a vibrator applied to the mother's abdomen was not an adequate stimulus to cause such responses. During subsequent learning trials, the vibrator was applied to the abdomen for five seconds, during which time the loud sound was also produced. Fetuses moved in response to the vibrator alone after fewer than a hundred paired presentations of sound and vibrator. There were marked individual differences, however, in the number of trials necessary for the response to be learned (Spelt, 1948).

Studies of learning after birth begin with an identification of the conditions that are pleasant or aversive for newborn infants. What will a baby learn to work for? Recent research indicates that reinforcers are not limited to food, water, and removal of unpleasant stimuli. Exteroceptive stimuli such as sounds, patterns, textures, warmth, and so on may serve to provide reinforcement for attention, visual tracking, auditory localization, smiling, making sounds, and other basic response patterns.

A promising research project on infant learning by Siqueland (1969) employed visual reinforcement. Four-month-old infants who were reinforced for engaging in nonnutritive sucking on a pacifier (by having a visual stimulus projected on a wall as long as they were sucking) learned to increase their sucking behavior. On the other hand, sucking behavior decreased in cases where the visual stimulus was withdrawn whenever the infant began sucking. ▲

Exposure to specific stimuli at an early age can also affect later performance (Gibson & Walk, 1956). For example, rats raised in cages containing four wall plaques—two triangles and two circles—performed much better on a learning task which required them to discriminate between these two geometric forms than did rats raised in plain white cages (Ψ Close-up, p. 134). In a later experiment, rats exposed early to an equilateral triangle and a circle did much better than control rats in discriminating between an isosceles triangle and an ellipse, showing that their knowledge carried over to similar figures (Gibson, Walk, Pick, & Tighe, 1958).

The environment determines most of the *content* that is learned, and the *time* at which it is learned (once readiness has been achieved). As maturation proceeds and learning ability develops, the child faces

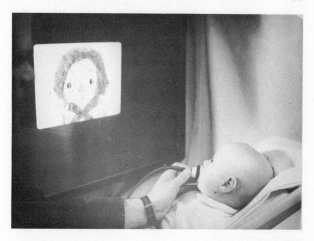

▲ This was the apparatus used to condition sucking behavior in infants. The infant learned to increase or decrease his sucking, depending on which was reinforced by the appearance of the picture.

a world in which natural laws and social rules govern what behavior is possible, impossible, rewarded, or punished. At each period in life, there are particular "developmental tasks" for each individual to master, imposed on him by his society and by his own needs and made possible of solution by past learning and the continuing process of maturation (Havighurst, 1952, 1953). For example, both environmental pressures and his own growth forces are active in pushing a child toward learning to walk and talk. Walking and talking are developmental tasks of all young children, and the success with which these and other tasks are achieved has a great influence both on the individual's general adjustment and happiness and on his success in achieving subsequent tasks.

Specific developmental tasks vary greatly, of course, from one culture to another. Although children in all cultures learn to walk and talk, not all learn to sit cross-legged, to be deferential in the presence of adults, to read printed characters, or to recognize animal tracks. Members of each society are presented with a unique pattern of developmental tasks. The principal developmental tasks for each stage of development in our society, as formulated in the early 1950s, are shown in the chart. ◆ (p. 135) Would you say the tasks of adolescence and early adulthood have changed in the years since then?

Ψ *Close-up*   *Early Experience Can Improve Later Learning*

The experimental group was raised in a cage with geometric forms on the walls (left), but nothing in particular was done to call their attention to the forms. Living and training conditions were the same for the control group except that no forms were put on the walls of their cage. Later, both groups were given tasks involving discrimination of geometric forms (below, right). If they chose the correct form, they received food. The learning curves (right) show the percentage of correct responses per day for the two groups. Interestingly, a later study replicated the effect of the cut-out forms, as used here, but found no such effect with printed forms.

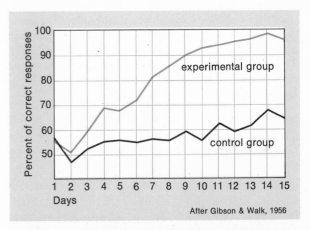

After Gibson & Walk, 1956

Learning through interaction with parents.   Although learning through direct association and reinforced practice constitute the major mechanisms of adaptive behavior, two additional processes are involved in the early learning experiences of the young of most species. These are *imprinting* and *observational-identificatory* learning.

"Parent-child interaction represents an important arena of adaptive and social learning for the child, particularly in the earliest years. Little (if any) of the young child's early adaptive and social learning occurs outside the parent-child interaction setting, and what the child learns there is assumed to provide the basis for his later behaviors and learnings in a variety of other social settings." (Gewirtz, 1969)

How does a young animal get "attached" to, or come to know, his parent—and, later, his appropriate sexual mate? And what function does the presence

◆ **DEVELOPMENTAL TASKS FROM INFANCY THROUGH LATER MATURITY**

Infancy and Early Childhood (birth to 6 years)	Middle Childhood (6-12 years)	Adolescence (12-18 years)
Learning to walk	Learning physical skills necessary for ordinary games	Achieving new and more mature relations with age-mates of both sexes
Learning to take solid foods	Building wholesome attitudes toward oneself as a growing organism	Achieving a masculine or feminine social role
Learning to talk	Learning to get along with age-mates	Accepting one's physique and using the body effectively
Learning to control the elimination of body wastes	Learning an appropriate masculine or feminine social role	Achieving emotional independence of parents and other adults
Learning sex differences and sexual modesty	Developing fundamental skills in reading, writing and calculating	Achieving assurance of economic independence
Achieving physiological stability	Developing concepts necessary for everyday living	Selecting and preparing for an occupation
Forming simple concepts of social and physical reality	Developing conscience, morality, and a scale of values	Preparing for marriage and family life
Learning to relate oneself emotionally to parents, siblings, and others	Achieving personal independence	Developing intellectual skill and concepts necessary for civic competence
Learning to distinguish right and wrong and developing a conscience	Developing attitudes toward social groups and institutions	Desiring and achieving socially responsible behavior
		Acquiring a set of values and an ethical system as a guide to behavior

Early Adulthood (18-35 years)	Middle Age (35-60 years)	Later Maturity (60-)
Selecting a mate	Achieving adult civic and social responsibility	Adjusting to decreasing physical strength and health
Learning to live with a marriage partner	Establishing and maintaining an economic standard of living	Adjusting to retirement and reduced income
Starting a family	Assisting teen-age children to become responsible and happy adults	Adjusting to death of spouse
Rearing children	Developing adult leisure-time activities	Establishing an explicit affiliation with one's age group
Managing a home	Relating oneself to one's spouse as a person	Meeting social and civic obligations
Getting started in an occupation	Accepting and adjusting to the physiological changes of middle age	Establishing satisfactory physical living arrangements
Taking on civic responsibility	Adjusting to aging parents	
Finding a congenial social group		

Based on Havinghurst, 1953

of a behaving parent (or parent surrogate) have on the behavior of the developing child?

Imprinting (or, I'll follow you anywhere). In 1935 Konrad Lorenz called attention to a phenomenon of significance both to the development of the individual and to the maintenance of the species—the imprinting of following and sexual responses. The term *imprinting* refers to an early experience in which a young animal follows an animal that is present during a critical period in its development and at a later time selects an animal of the same species as a mate. The usual object of imprinting is, naturally enough, the infant's mother.

Illustrative of these phenomena, which have been studied primarily in Mallard ducklings and chickens, are the two observations that a newly hatched duckling placed with a foster mother of another species (a) will follow her rather than his biological mother, and (b) when it matures sexually, will select as a mate a member of the foster mother's species.

Hess (1959) has carried out controlled laboratory studies in which ducklings have been imprinted on a wooden duck decoy that is artificially made to move and render ducklike sounds. Using the apparatus shown in the drawing, he has verified the natural observations of ethologists that the critical period of following-imprinting (for Mallard ducklings) is between five and twenty-four hours, with the peak at thirteen to sixteen hours. ■ After this time imprinting is rare, and strange objects are reacted to with shyness or fear. The corresponding period for dogs occurs at about the age of thirteen weeks, after which they cannot be made into pets. Similarly, kittens not handled during the first few weeks of life always show a fear of people.

Some of the remarkable features of imprinting are (a) that the reaction can be "fixed" in a period as short as one minute's worth of following (Schutz, 1969), (b) that the reaction is stronger the more effort required to follow the model, and (c) that aversive stimulation, such as shocking the young followers, *enhances* the effectiveness of the imprinting.

Under natural life conditions, the following reaction is important for the immediate survival of the helpless infant, which must attach itself to its mother for protection and nurturance. Imprinting to the mother also ensures later selection of a mate of the same species, preventing cross-breeding.

The study of imprinting makes clear the interaction between inherited response mechanisms, maturational processes, and specific environmental experiences. While it might appear that humans are less subject to this process than lower animals, it is interesting to conjecture whether the permanent lack of sociability observed in some persons who spent their early childhood in institutions (Goldfarb, 1943) may be traced to a failure to experience normal contact with (and adequate "imprinting" on) people.

Learning through observation and identification. The process by which a child learns to behave in ways

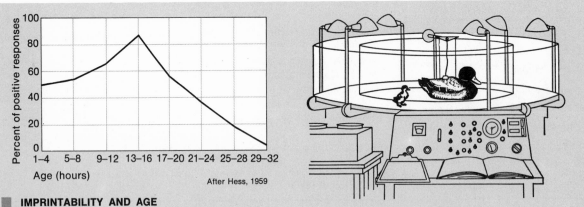

■ IMPRINTABILITY AND AGE

The apparatus which Hess used to study imprinting (right) consisted of a decoy, suspended from a rotating arm, which the duckling followed around a circular runway. The controls are shown in the foreground. The graph (left) shows the percentage of positive responses made by groups of ducklings imprinted at different ages on test trials after imprinting sessions. Some imprinting occurred immediately after hatching and as late as thirty-two hours after hatching, but ducklings imprinted at an age of thirteen to sixteen hours consistently made the highest scores.

appropriate to the general value system of his culture is called *socialization*. In a sense, it refers to the complex ways in which a basically egocentric little animal is turned into a "civilized" human being who can live with, and contribute to the well-being of, other people.

But consider the almost endless bits of knowledge and behavior patterns that one must acquire in order to make that transition; for example, self-control; delay of gratification; means-ends relationships; codes of etiquette; laws; implicit contracts; attitudes toward self, parents, property, nation, sex, hair, war, strangers, death, and so on and on. Consider further the virtually infinite variety of sentences that children can, and usually must, construct in order to be understood and to comprehend what others are saying.

Rewards and punishments experienced for responses made in the past do not seem sufficient to account for the range of such *social learning*. One psychologist has gone so far as to say that "if social learning proceeded exclusively on the basis of rewarding and punishing consequences, most people would never survive the socialization process" (Bandura, 1969b). It may well be that it is the ability of humans to profit from the mere observation of the behavior (verbal and nonverbal) of appropriate societal models that is the key to their adaptability and relatively successful control of other animals and their environment.

Many years ago Miller and Dollard (1941) hypothesized that animal and human subjects could learn by observation and imitation of a successful model. However, such imitation learning does not explain how an observer acquires *new* response patterns which he has never practiced overtly, which have not been reinforced (either for him or for the model), and which may first appear a considerable time after the original observation, even in the absence of the model. In addition, effective social learning requires more than just learning to imitate the behavior of one model, such as a parent. What is demanded is the selection and integration of diverse combinations of responses from observations of many, often quite different, models.

The systematic program of research by Bandura (1969) has demonstrated that novel patterns of behavior can be generated from observational learning (in which there is presumably identification with the model's behavior). Involved in such acquisition of new responses are:

1. *Attentional processes* in which the person attends to, recognizes, and differentiates what is distinctive in the model's responses.

2. *Symbolic coding processes* in which stimuli from the model's behavior are coded into images or words in the person's memory.

3. *Retention processes* in which coded modeling events are retained and available for retrieval. Covert or vicarious practice of the modeled behaviors greatly enhances retention.

4. *Motoric reproduction processes* in which the symbolic, coded representations are used by the observer (as internal stimuli) to guide his own overt performance of the response.

In order for the response to be executed by the observer, two more factors are involved: the person must possess the necessary skills, intelligence, maturational development, and so on, and he must be motivated or positively reinforced for doing so.

But this entire process sounds very sophisticated and cerebral, requiring a highly developed level of intellectual functioning. Could it be expected to influence an infant's behavior? A recent study comparing thirty American and thirty Japanese babies three to four months old revealed that the babies had already learned to be "Japanese" or "American" in that they showed the type of behavior their mothers expected of them (Caudill & Weinstein, 1969). The subtle cultural differences which are revealed in distinctive adult patterns of emotional response can be seen emerging in infancy as a consequence of quite contrasting learning experiences.

"American infants are more happily vocal, more active, and more exploratory of their bodies and their physical environment, than are Japanese infants. Directly related to these findings, the American mother is in greater vocal interaction with her infant, and stimulates him to greater physical activity and exploration. The Japanese mother, in contrast, is in greater bodily contact with her infant, and soothes him toward physical quiescence, and passivity with regard to his environment. Moreover, these patterns of behavior, so early learned by the infant, are in line with the differing expectations for later behavior in the two cultures as the child grows to be an adult." (p. 42)

Language Development

It has been said that man's greatest intellectual feat is the acquisition of his native language—an accomplishment basically completed by each individual long before he ever receives any formal schooling. Of course, it may not seem like so much to you, since everyone you know probably has achieved this goal. Even mentally retarded children usually learn the language of their culture, and children in some cultures learn to communicate through highly complex languages (such as Chinese) despite extremely impoverished learning conditions. Nevertheless, the impressiveness of this human achievement becomes apparent when you consider whether a chimpanzee (our evolutionary neighbor) can be made to talk, and how you would go about training one to communicate his ideas and to understand yours.

Language is more than a *medium* of communication; it plays a basic role in ordering experience and in stabilizing the confusing world a young child faces. In fact, there are very few psychological processes which are not affected by the operation of language, verbal labels, and symbols. By "appropriately" using language, a child can have his biological needs better met, secure attention, control the behavior of others, represent things symbolically and thus operate intellectually on an abstract rather than concrete level, recall, plan, reason, analyze, synthesize, explain inconsistencies, reduce uncertainty, and form a common bond of social reality with those in his shared language community.

Schachtel (1959) argues that we can not remember anything before the age at which we acquired language because memory requires verbal coding (to be elaborated upon in Chapter 6). As language codes events and permits them to be stored, catalogued, and tagged for recall, so, too, it is said to be "time binding." It creates the uniquely human capacity to re-create the past and anticipate the future by means of symbols. By doing so, it helps put the present, however overwhelming, into a perspective which can be better handled. William James felt that "the great source of terror in infancy is solitude." The acquisition of language is the means by which this solitary, isolated existence is shattered.

In this section we will describe the sequence of language development in children. We will also look into the experiences of investigators who have accepted the challenge of teaching chimps to talk. In Chapter 6 you will find a brief overview of the basic elements involved in a linguistic and psycholinguistic analysis of language, as well as a presentation of two theories about how children learn to produce and comprehend their native language.

Language Production

Almost all children in standard environments in all cultures begin to speak in phrases between the ages of eighteen and twenty-four months; within another year they have probably become masters of the essential components of the language used by their language community. How can we account for and understand this remarkable process?

Human language production can be roughly divided into four stages, which overlap and are not sharply differentiated but form a convenient chronology of early vocalization (Kaplan & Kaplan, 1970).

Stage 1. The study of language development in human children begins with the birth cry of the newborn. For the first three weeks, the infant's vocal repertoire is extremely limited. The basic cry may be modified somewhat to produce variations, from which the alert parent infers anger or physical pain. But cries, coughs, and gurgles make up the sum of the newborn's vocal products.

Stage 2. From about three weeks of age to four or five months, the infant introduces some pseudocries —cry vocalizations that are not simply cries. Variety in these sounds is produced by changes in duration, pitch, and use of the articulatory organs.

Stage 3. During the last half of the first year, the production of speech sounds is sufficiently varied and continuous to earn this period the name "babbling stage." Vowel-like and consonant-like sounds are articulated, and adult intonation patterns are imitated.

There are broad sequential patterns in the development of babble sounds, which seem to depend primarily on how difficult it is to produce the sound. For the most part, the neonate uses vowels that are produced at the front of the mouth with the tongue in a relaxed position, such as the *e* in bet, the *i* in bit, and the *u* in but. It is much more difficult to produce back vowels, such as *oo* and *ah*, which require humping the back part of the tongue. The percentage of utterances of back vowels increases as the child matures. When he is about two and a half, the relative proportions of all sounds used in his speech are about the same as found in adult speech (Irwin, 1948).

Stage 4. The beginnings of patterned, "true" speech occur some time near the end of the first year. The "prelinguistic" period which characterizes the previous stages gives way to the appearance of distinct utterances and the first recognizable words of the child. Surprisingly, the variety of phonetic forms used by the child decreases before true speech begins. Jakobson (1968) and others have observed that certain sounds (for example, /r/ as in the comfort sound /ra/) disappear from the child's spontaneous speech at this time and sometimes do not reappear for several years. The child retains his ability to use them, since he can repeat these sounds when required to, but he stops using them spontaneously as his second sound system begins to develop. It may be, as the Russian investigator, Shvachkin (1948), suggests, that this limitation of production of sounds is necessitated by the child's increased involvement with semantic processing, needed to go from sounds to language.

The vocabulary of two to three words typical of the average year-old child increases to about 50 words by twenty-four months and 1000 words by the age of three (Lenneberg, 1969). It is likely that the greater stimulation provided by daily exposure to television programming will be shown to accelerate vocabulary development, and if skillfully prepared (as on the program "Sesame Street") may have an impact on other areas of language development. One study (Irwin, 1960) demonstrated that when children of working-class parents were regularly read to for fifteen minutes a day from their thirteenth to their thirtieth month, their production of speech sounds was increasingly superior to that of matched controls from the age of seventeen months onward.

The development of a grammar can best be indexed during a child's early years using the mean

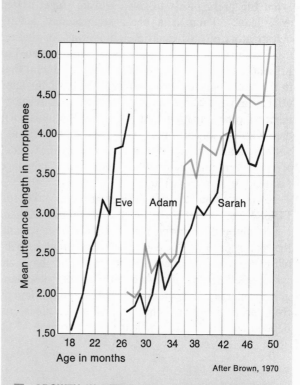

After Brown, 1970

■ GROWTH IN UTTERANCE LENGTH WITH AGE
The graph plots mean utterance length of each child in morphemes (meaningful segments) rather than words in order to give credit for the use of inflections such as plural word endings.

length of the child's utterances. The mean length of utterance (MLU) when speech begins is, of course, a single word and MLU = 1.0. As word combinations appear, the value of MLU increases, and children with the same MLU value are likely to show similar internal grammatical detail in their speech. Roger Brown (1970), in his analysis of speech development in three children, Adam, Eve, and Sarah, presents a graph which plots mean length of utterance against chronological age. ■ The utterances of all three children increase steadily over the whole observational period, with only occasional "setbacks." It is evident that chronological age is a poor index of the linguistic level that one can expect, given the marked individual differences in rate, pattern of acceleration, and level of attainment even in this small sample.

From the prelinguistic to the linguistic stage: a step or a leap? There is a basic disagreement among investigators of language development as to whether there are prelinguistic regularities which are related to subsequent true speech. Some accounts maintain that in the babbling stage (which forms the basis for later utterances) there is an ordered sequence of development: a preoccupation first with vowel sounds (*v*), then with consonant sounds (*c*), then with *cv* combinations, and finally, with *cvcv* units in which there are rhythm and intonation resembling language (Kaplan & Kaplan, 1970).

In opposition to this viewpoint are Jakobson (1968) and Shvachkin (1948) who assert that there is no continuity between the prelinguistic stages and the true speech of Stage 4. They argue that in babbling, "sounds produce themselves," and have no systematic linguistic use. According to this view, language emerges in a manner which is discontinuous from prior linguistic behavior and which does *not* depend upon regularities in learning experiences.

Language Reception

The child says, "Daddy, see the pire truck," but gets upset when Daddy says, "Yes, I see the pire truck." Although he has difficulty in producing all the correct sounds himself, this child understands what the correct form should be. The important point here is that speech is a symptom of language development, but it is not the language system itself. The child may be able to receive and comprehend many more messages than he can transmit.

As we saw earlier in this chapter, the sensory capacity to detect speech and other sounds is present at birth or soon after. At first, though, the human voice is just another sound to the infant. After about two weeks, it is distinguished from other sounds. About a month after birth, the sound of a voice becomes an effective stimulus for eliciting smiles and vocalizations by the infant (Nakazima, 1966). In the third month, the infant begins to distinguish some basic qualities of adult vocalization. Responses to familiar and unfamiliar voices are different (Wolff, 1963). An angry tone of voice provokes withdrawal responses, while a friendly tone evokes smiling and cooing.

So far, the infant seems to be detecting only continuous qualities, like anger and familiarity, in a flow of speech sounds. In the fifth or sixth month, he begins to respond to variations within this flow. At first, it is apparently variations in intonation, rhythm, stress, and duration that the baby distinguishes, rather than the arrangement of phonemes. For example, one student of language development taught his eight-month-old son to turn toward the window when asked "Wo ist das Fenster?" He found the child made the same response when asked, "Où est la fenêtre?" with the same pattern of intonation. Unless the boy had learned both German and French at a remarkable age, he must have been responding to the identical intonation patterns, and ignoring the phonetic differences (Tappolet, cited in Lewis, 1951).

It is not until sometime near the end of the first year that children begin to distinguish between the specific sounds of their language. In a classic study Shvachkin (1948) investigated how Russian children from ten to eighteen months of age comprehend commands to pick up objects. The objects were arranged in pairs, and the words used to differentiate them differed in only a single initial consonant. Shvachkin concluded that a child has to have made a distinction between two sounds in terms of meaning before he can use the difference functionally in speech production.

Remarkably little systematic data have been collected on the development of language reception, although it is obviously one of the most important attributes of man. In part, this lack may have resulted from the view that understanding sounds is a by-product of learning how to generate them. It may also be that researchers have a greater interest in the overt behavior of speaking than in the covert behavior of listening.

Studying Monkey Talk

Is the gift of language which nature has bestowed upon man uniquely his because of evolution and innately given mental structures or because of the ideal language learning environment to which other species do not have access?

Since 1932, five experiments have been conducted to determine whether chimpanzees reared in home

Ψ Close-up *Birds of the Same "Dialect" Flock Together*

You undoubtedly are able to identify the regional background of many of your classmates by certain characteristics of the way they use the English language—that is, the dialect they speak. But did you know that birds have "dialects," too? Investigators studying the white-crowned sparrow, a small North American songbird, have found that there are regional differences in their song, and that these differences have important behavioral correlates.

Analysis of sound spectrograms of the mating songs of 18 male white-crowned sparrows from three localities in the San Francisco Bay area revealed that song characteristics are consistent among birds in the same area, but are quite different from those of others of their species living as little as 60 miles away. These birds not only react more strongly to the songs of other members of their own species than to those of a different species (e.g., the song sparrow), but even to those within their own species who have the same dialect, preferring them for companions and mates.

Peter Marler (1967) and his associates at Rockefeller University have studied the development of these dialects, rearing birds in isolation and preventing acoustic feedback through deafening. These studies point up some interesting parallels to the development of speech in children and the concept of a "language community":

1. The white-crowned sparrow has a predisposition to learn some sound patterns rather than others, just as some aspects of human language appear to be innate.

2. The young bird must be able to hear its own voice if it is subsequently to translate the memory of the normal song of its parents into motor activity and produce a song of its own. Thus heredity and learning interact to produce a working model against which auditory feedback from the young bird's own efforts at song production can be tested.

3. Song does not appear suddenly in young birds but develops over time with practice and is preceded by transitional stages termed *subsongs*. These early subsong vocalizations appear to be necessary for all subsequent song activity.

4. Dialect patterns are transmitted from adults to young birds, a learning process from one generation to the next.

5. The existence of dialects maintains the local populations as distinguishable units, by promoting inbreeding (since males and females react most strongly to recordings of their own dialect). Once song patterns have been acquired, there is little exchange or roaming of individual birds to their nearby kindred species who sing a different dialect.

6. The behavior patterns which create this "common song community" are under environmental, rather than genetic, control. One speculation is that they are maintained because inbreeding in local populations leads to subtle, more effective physiological adaptions to local conditions.

---

environments can develop communication skills comparable to those exhibited by children (Jacobsen, Jacobsen & Yoshioka, 1932; Kellogg & Kellogg, 1933; Kohts, 1935; Hayes & Hayes, 1952; Gardner & Gardner, 1969). The young chimp rapidly adapts to its physical and social environment, becomes strongly attached to its caretaker, imitates adult acts without any training, and develops its motor behavior more rapidly than a child of similar age. However, the results in terms of language development are dismal. None of the chimps studied ever copied or reproduced human word sounds spontaneously, nor was there any evidence of attempts to do so. There was not any period of babbling or random emission of sounds (other than the food-bark, the "oo oo" cry, and screeching). Gua, the chimp studied by the Kelloggs, did learn a series of gesture signals which humans could interpret reliably, but did not talk.

"The acme of chimpanzee achievement in producing human sounds" is represented by the four words, "mamma," "papa," "cup," and "up," which the Hayeses taught their chimp, Viki, to utter. Viki learned these words with great difficulty, only after considerable training, and even then she could not really produce them easily and could not keep the sound patterns straight. On language comprehension, the chimps fared much better, with Gua showing fifty-eight specific correct response patterns to simple human commands over a nine-month period (compared with sixty-eight for her human control, little Donald).

Washoe Talks in American Sign Language . . .

If chimps can comprehend, gesture, and imitate, then perhaps the key to language acquisition is through voiceless communication via an arbitrary system of sign language. In June 1966, Allen and Beatrice Gardner, psychologists at the University of Nevada, began what may be the definitive test of the language acquisition in apes, with a female named Washoe. Using the American sign language (ASL), a code of arbitrary symbols devised for the deaf, and insisting that this be the only form of communication between human handlers and Washoe, the Gardners report (1969) remarkable progress and promise. ◆

In the first seven months, Washoe acquired four signs that she used reliably: "come-gimme," "more," "up," and "sweet." Moreover, she understood more signs than she produced. In the next seven months, she added nine more signs and by three years of age had control over thirty-four signs. The stringent criterion of sign acquisition was one appropriate and nonimitated occurrence for each of fifteen consecutive days.

What has led psychologists like Roger Brown (1970) to sit up and take notice of what Washoe is saying is not the extent of her vocabulary, but rather that she spontaneously uses a great many (twenty-nine) signs per day, has begun to string words into simple phrases, and demonstrates both generalization and differentiation. For example, she uses the same sign, "more" for continued play and additional food, or "open" for opening a door, a soda bottle, or a stuck zipper. The ASL gesture for flower was

◆ Washoe, the chimp, is "telling" her trainer that she wants some soda by making the hand signal for "drink."

initially used both for flowers and all things with a strong scent. But she could be taught distinct signs to distinguish "flower" from "smell." Her multi-sign sequences, such as "gimme please food," "Please tickle more," "Hurry gimme toothbrush," "You me go there in," or "Roger Washoe tickle" are not just word strings but semantically valid constructions.

Although Washoe's constructions (mean length of utterance) have grown as do those of children where one sign precedes two, two precedes three, and three precedes four, her sentences are not syntactically acceptable. They exhibit no rules for sign order, and all possible arrangements of a given set of signs are used.

. . . And Sarah Answers Back!

Using a slightly different approach, David Premack and his associates have had remarkable success in teaching their chimp, Sarah, to communicate by constructing sentences with colored chips of plastic on a magnetized board. Sarah first learned, through simple conditioning procedures, to associate a chip of a particular color and shape with a particular fruit —being allowed to eat the correctly identified item as a reward. Other chips became the "names" of the experimenters or represented certain actions, and

Sarah was soon comprehending and constructing sentences like "Mary give apple Sarah" and "Sarah insert banana pail."

The next step was to determine whether Sarah was capable of learning relational concepts such as "on" or "under." Working first with colored cards, then with plastic color names, she soon learned to follow instructions and place "red on green" or vice versa. Another type of relationship, still more abstract, can best be described as "name of." When presented with a symbol and a piece of fruit, Sarah readily learned to use symbols meaning "name of" or "not-name of" to construct such sentences as "(symbol) not-name of apple." • Perhaps the high point of Sarah's "writing" career, however, was the day when, apparently bored with what was going on, she set up a string of incomplete sentences and gave her astonished trainer a multiple-choice sentence-completion test! (Premack, 1969, 1970)

"When does a piece of plastic cease to be a piece of plastic and become a word?" asks Premack. "When it is used as a word," he concludes. "When it occurs along with other words of appropriate grammatical class in sentences, and when it occurs as the answer or part of the answer to questions" (1969, p. 40). The accomplishments of Washoe and Sarah clearly challenge previous conceptions of the linguistic limitations of subhuman species. When all the results are in and verified by independent investigators also willing to invest the time, energy, and patience required in such research, we may be in a better position to understand just what is the human aspect of human language development.

Cognitive Development

When Meno asked Socrates whether virtue can be taught by rational discussion, or requires practice, or is a natural inborn attitude or state, the basic question in child development was posed. Posed not necessarily with regard to the concept of "virtue," but more generally with regard to any aspect of human behavior. What would happen if nothing were done, if there were no teaching, no opportunity to observe other people, in short, no social environment? Would the child develop the same way?

One approach to this problem has come from the study of "feral" children, children abandoned in the wild and apparently reared by animals. Such cases are rare, and conclusions regarding them are uncertain because of inadequate knowledge of the children's heredity, the characteristics of their parents or the details of their nonhuman environment. However, in one famous case of a wild boy, named Victor, found in a French forest and studied intensively by Itard (1962), training changed some response patterns from their original wolflike appearance, but others could not be modified or new ones, such as language, acquired. Such children usually die at an

● Sarah the chimp "talks" by putting plastic symbols on the board. Here she makes the request, "Give chocolate Sarah."

early age (for reasons unknown), and so it has not been possible to extend their training over a long period of time.

The Gospel According to Piaget

A very different approach to the problem of how the child develops "the attributes of mind" is that of the Swiss psychologist Jean Piaget. Over the past forty years, Piaget has been observing how normal children interact with their environment, in much the same way that Lorenz and the ethologists have observed animal behavior in the natural habitat. Piaget (himself trained as a zoologist) began by carefully observing the behavior of his own children in given situations. After formulating a hypothesis that related the behavior and the environment, he would alter the environmental demands slightly and see how the child would then react.

To study the complexities of the conceptual world of childhood, how the child comes to understand abstract relations, and to perform logical operations, Piaget has relied upon ingeniously simple demonstrations. Consider his lemonade study: an equal amount of lemonade is poured into two identical glasses. Who has more, the child or the experimenter? Swiss five-, six-, and seven-year-olds all report that they have the same amount. But now the lemonade from one glass is poured into a taller, thinner glass and given to the child. Who has more now? The five-year-old is convinced he has more in his tall glass; the six-year-old is less certain, but says he too has more, while the seven-year-old "knows" there is no difference. When the lemonade is poured back into the identical glasses, the five-year-old says there is more in the glass that came from the tall one, but the six-year-old knows there is again an equal distribution of lemonade.

Young children start the journey through their inanimate environment as *naïve realists*, placing complete trust in the appearances of things. For many problems they face, such a perceptual orientation is adequate. They do well so long as the underlying dimension or attribute is related in an invariant way to the distinguishing perceptual cues. To the five-year-old, the salient cue of height usually is a reliable cue to the dimension of "more than." But when the

dimension is volume, and height and width change simultaneously, then height cues are misleading. The "average" six-year-old realizes that something besides height is important, but can not yet integrate two dimensions at once conceptually. The seven-year-old has come to understand that the concept of amount depends on both height and width. If changes in one dimension are compensated for by equal changes in the other, then the underlying reality is *conserved* (that is, the reality remains unchanged even though the appearance varies). ▲

Some developmental psychologists believe that analysis of how children at different ages respond to a variety of conservation problems involving different levels of conceptualization can form a basis for understanding cognitive development. The contention is that cognitive development is represented by a shift in judgmental activity from an initial dependency upon the sensory and perceptual properties of things toward a reliance upon inferential or internal representations of things, concepts, and relationships. To Piaget (1957), cognitive development is neither a continuous process of adding skills or discrete responses, nor one of maturational growth. Rather, the child's understanding, inferences, abstractions, logical rules, and problem-solving ability develop entirely from occasions of unsatisfactory *interaction* of the child with his environment (*states of tenuous equilibrium*). Knowledge is structured, as is behavior, and these structures change only when there is a perceived *discrepancy* between them (or their level of complexity) and the complexity of the environment. Out of these encounters between a child and the problems that are posed by his *physical* environment there emerges an invariant sequence of cognitive developmental stages. While different children may move through the various stages of development at different rates, the sequence they all move through is the same.

The baby starts life with biologically inherited modes of interacting with the environment (called *functions*). These functions enable the child to perform acts which *assimilate* objects in its environment (such as ingestion of food). Through the process of accommodation, the organization of these acts changes and the child acquires new abilities. In adapting to the environment, cognitive structures called

▲ PIAGET'S CONCEPTUAL CONSERVATIONS

Illustrated here are some of the types of conservation studied by Piaget. The right-hand column gives the ages at which the Swiss youngsters with whom he was working were able to master the various concepts. Note that there is a steady progression with age, and that conservation of volume is usually not grasped until youngsters are well into their teens.

Type of conservation	Dimension	Change in physical appearance	Average age at which invariance is grasped
Number	Number of elements in a collection 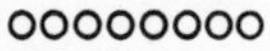	Rearranging or displacing the elements 	6–7
Substance	Amount of a deformable substance (e.g., clay) 	Altering its shape 	7–8
Length	Length of a line or object 	Altering its shape or displacing it 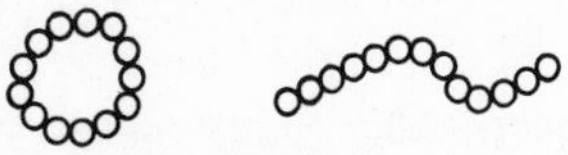	7–8
Area	Amount of a surface covered by a set of plane figures 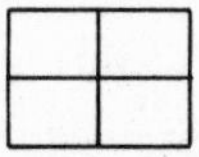	Rearranging the figures 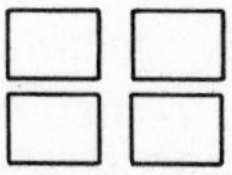	8–9
Weight	Weight of an object 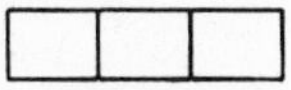	Altering its shape 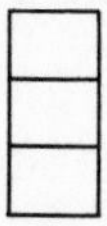	9–10
Volume	Volume of an object (in terms of water displacement) 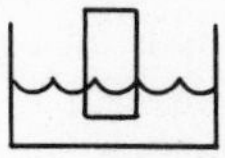	Altering its shape 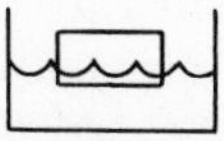	14–15

schemata (plural of schema) are formed which relate means (looking, reaching, grasping) and ends (receiving stimulation from the hand-held object). Cognitive development, in Piaget's terms, consists of a succession of changes in these structures. It is these schemata which exert a guiding or controlling influence over what the child can understand and do at a given time (see Phillips, 1969, and Flavell, 1963).

Until quite recently, Piaget's approach to cognitive development has not been well received by American psychologists, perhaps for several reasons: (a) his structuralism rubs their functionalism the wrong way, (b) his response unit—schema—is very broad and not precisely defined, (c) his stimulus and response interact and are not isolatable as behaviorists demand, and (d) he seems to believe that cognitions develop best in the absence of formal education and without incentives (see Kessen, 1965). In one of his rare public lectures on this continent, Piaget shocked educators by declaring: "Every time you teach a child something you keep him from reinventing it."

Development of Concepts

Educators, charged with the responsibility of "making learning happen," are not in a position to sit back and wait for children's concepts to develop naturally. If we understand *how* concepts are learned, we should be able to create situations in which such learning is likely to take place.

One innovation based on Piaget's approach is the "inquiry training" procedure developed by Suchman (1962). Students are shown a puzzling phenomenon, such as a piece of metal seeming to bend of its own accord. Presented with this discrepancy between what they expect and what they see, they are encouraged to form hypotheses, ask questions, and try themselves to solve the mystery.

If concepts develop out of interaction with the environment in trying to resolve discrepancies, is it possible to speed up the development of basic concepts like conservation by a careful structuring of the environment to provide just the right degree of discrepancy at the right time and help the child to see the critical features? If educators could manage to arrange challenging situations just barely beyond the child's available structures, how early could critical

concepts be learned? Ongoing American research is trying to answer these questions. It is interesting to note that in the lecture quoted above, Piaget also remarked, "Every time I describe a developmental sequence, an American asks, 'How can you speed it up?'"

One group of investigators (1966) gave special training to half of a group of twenty bright nursery-school four-year-olds on operations that a child would need to understand before he could grasp the principle of conservation. The training was carried out with the children as a group and included practice in multiple labeling, multiple classification, multiplicative relations, and finally, reversibility. For example, several objects would be presented one at a time and labeled; then differences and similarities would be identified, as in the following conversation:

Teacher: Can you tell me what this is, Mary?
Mary: A banana.
Teacher: What else can you tell me about it?
Mary: It's straight.
Teacher: It's straight. What else?
Mary: It has a peel.
Teacher: What can you do with it?
Tom: You can eat it!
Teacher: That's right! . . . Now let's see . . .
Children: . . . I love bananas!
Teacher: What is this?
Children: An orange.
Teacher: Is it really an orange?
Children: Uh-huh. . . . Yes.
Teacher: Look at it closely.
Children: You can eat it . . . It is round . . .
Teacher: Now, look at this one . . . What's this?
Children: An orange . . . orange.
Teacher: And what can you do with it?
Children: You can eat it . . . and it's round . . .
Teacher: It is round . . .
Child: It has a peel . . .
Teacher: It has a peel . . . Now, look at these two things. Are they the same?
Children: No.
Teacher: What's different?
Children: This one . . . this one here is pressed in on the side a little . . . this one is lighter.
Teacher: Do you know what this really is? This is a tangerine . . . and this is an orange. Now tell me in what ways they are alike.
Children: This is smaller and that's bigger.
Teacher: I said, "In what way are they alike?"

Children: They are both round . . . they both have a stem . . . both orange.

Teacher: They both have a stem, both round, both orange: Anything else alike about them?

Child: They're both fat.

Teacher: Uh-huh. What can you do with them?

Children: We can eat them . . .

Teacher: We can eat them . . . Now, tell me what's the same about all these things?

Child: These are round, but this isn't.

Teacher: I said, what is the same about them, not what's different about them.

Children: They're both round . . . they're round . . .

Teacher: What about the banana?

Child: It's straight.

Teacher: But . . . tell me something else that's the same about all of these things.

Child: . . . They have . . . all have a peel.

Teacher: That's right, too, but what can you do with all of them?

Children: You can eat them!

Teacher: That's right! That's the same about every one of them. Do you have a name for all of them?

Children: Yes!

Teacher: What?

Children: Fruit . . . fruit.

Teacher: And what's the same about all fruit?

Children: They are all round except bananas.

Teacher: No, . . . why do you call all of these things fruit?

Children: Because you can eat them.

Teacher: You can eat them.

Children: And they are food.

Teacher: And they are food. If I had a piece of bread here, would that be fruit too?

Children: No.

Teacher: Why not?

Children: Because it is not sweet . . . not round . . .

Through such sessions they tried to draw the children's attention to the fact that objects have many characteristics (multiple classification), that they can be combined in different ways to form different categories (multiple relations), and that reorganization can restore an earlier arrangement (reversibility). The control group met with the same teacher and discussed topics like the roles of community helpers.

Posttests, compared with pretests, showed improved ability for the training group in both conservation and verbalization; the control subjects showed no change in either. The investigators suggest that previous attempts to teach conservation to four-year-olds may have failed because the researchers did not start where the children

were and make sure that prerequisite understanding was developed for each new step. (Sigel, Roeper, & Hooper, 1966).

Other studies have dealt with such aspects of the formation of concepts as the gradual decrease in dependence upon direct perceptual stimuli. The forming of concepts involves going beyond the information given and correctly placing objects in broader categories so that they can be dealt with effectively. To do this, the young child requires more sensory cues—a more complete representation of the object—than does the older child or the adult (Gollin, 1965).

It is expected that further research in this area will shed light on the periods in development when shifts from perceptual to conceptual functioning are most likely to occur and on the conditions which will hinder or facilitate these shifts.

Investigations of the development of mathematical concepts in children have suggested that some concepts do not develop gradually but appear all at once. In one case, for example, the concept to be identified was "similarity of position of odd elements" (in displays similar to that shown below). Over many

$$\triangle \quad \triangle \quad \bigcirc$$
$$\text{---} \quad \text{---} \quad \text{---}$$

trials the children would show no response to this characteristic of the situation, then suddenly on one trial they would respond to it and on subsequent trials would continue to do so. The same "all-or-none" learning was found for more complex mathematical concepts (Suppes, 1966).

Determinants of Cognitive Development

One way to recast much of our discussion about cognitive development is to ask, "How does a brain become a mind?" What is the process by which some protoplasm and the biochemical-electrical activity within cells become a system for perceiving, organizing, integrating, memorizing, planning, and directing action?

This "humanization of matter" has intrigued philosophers for centuries, but only recently has the basic philosophical question of "How do we know?" been modified to make it appropriate for psychological analysis. For psychologists the question has become, "What are the relative contributions of heredity and environment to the development of human intelligence?"

Philosophers such as Immanuel Kant maintained that there exist at birth in the organism many ideas and relationships which develop naturally as the child matures. The basis of human knowledge is to be found in innate ideas (*a priori* axioms) existing prior to any environmental experience. In twentieth-century terms, then, the mind is a prewired kit which is inherited as part of one's native endowment and needs but to be tuned by experience.

Such a nativist position was first opposed by Hobbes in the seventeenth century, who argued that sensations and experience are the source of all knowledge, and that memory and imagination are decaying sense impressions held together by association. Thus one should search for the origin of the mind in sensation and examine its development through association. This experiential basis of human knowledge, called the *empiricist* position, found its champion in the reknowned philosopher John Locke. He advanced the thesis that the infant's brain was like a blank tablet (a *tabula rasa*, in Latin), on which experience writes sense impressions by which the meaning of life is communicated.

In psychology, too, these extreme positions have found staunch supporters eager to do intellectual battle to defend either nature or nurture as the more important contributor to intelligence. Let us briefly examine some of the evidence used to support each side before considering what all the fuss is really about. Does it make any difference for your view of man and human potential if one side or the other is right?

Arguments for nativism.   Who says nature is the key to intelligence? Galton, Dugdale, Goddard, and the people who compare the correlations of IQ scores of identical and fraternal twins all have said so.

Galton's studies of eminent men.   Francis Galton, in 1869, published a monumental work entitled *Heredi-*

tary Genius: An Enquiry into Its Laws and Consequences. In it he showed that eminence and genius run in families and concluded that they are therefore inherited. Galton's data from the biographies of great men revealed that their children as well as their parents and forefathers were more likely than could be expected by chance to have achieved fame. Galton subsequently reported that he had replicated his findings: "During the fourteen years that have elapsed since the former book was published, numerous fresh instances have arisen of distinction being attained by members of gifted families whom I quoted as instances of heredity, thus strengthening my arguments." (Galton, 1907, p. 57)

Jukes and Kallikaks; the bad seed theory.   The case of inheritance was promoted by an ingenious tactic, attempting to prove the reverse side of the same coin. While inheritance was being acclaimed in England as the causal agent in producing great men, it was "proven" in America to be the basis for the failings of two of the world's most infamous breeds, the notorious Jukes family and the equally decadent Kallikaks.

Richard Dugdale's investigation of the inherited basis of "crime, pauperism, disease and insanity," published in 1875, was accepted throughout the world as the best documented evidence of the bad seed theory of evil. In his intensive analysis of the "Jukes" clan, Dugdale identified over 700 people "belonging to the Jukes blood," of whom more than 500 were social degenerates. There were those who were "immoral," "harlots," "lecherous," "paupers," "drunkards," "lazy," "fornicators," as well as murderers, rapists, and thieves. So evil and corrupt was this family line that during the seventy-three years of its studied existence it cost the taxpayers of New York State over a million dollars.

In 1912 another researcher, Henry Goddard, found further support for the nativist position when he came upon a natural experiment in breeding. A Revolutionary War soldier, whom Goddard dubbed "Kallikak" (from the Greek *kalos*, "good" and *kakos*, "bad"), sired two families, one illegitimate and one legitimate. His first alliance was with a tavern maid who was reportedly mentally defective; he later married a young woman of "better stock." What were the consequences of these different unions? Only a few of the nearly 500 descendants from Martin Kallikak's legal marriage could be classified as "undesirable." In contrast, the son born of Martin's affair with the tavern maid produced a long line of defective descendants. Of 480 traced descendants, 143 were reported to be feeble-minded, 33 were sexually immoral, 24 were alcoholics, many died in infancy, and others were criminals, brothel keepers, and the like.

These studies led some criminologists to accept the theory that "social disease" as well as insanity and idiocy could be inherited. The apparent inevitability that a tainted individual would pass his bad seed on to future generations was a powerful stimulus to the eugenics movement. Twenty-seven states proceeded to adopt compulsory sterilization laws to prevent the transmission of such "unalterable" defects.

After having read Chapter 2 of this book, you should have at least wondered how intelligent people could ever have accepted as valid the evidence and conclusions of Galton, Dugdale, and Goddard. Of course fame, eminence, and social recognition "run in certain families"—but can we eliminate the possibility that the critical factors are really social influence and contacts? A supportive family environment which encourages achievement and public service is as plausible an explanation as a general hereditary factor.

In addition, when you examined the evidence presented for genetic negative influences, did you wonder how the family trees of the Jukes and Kallikaks were plotted, in days when vital statistics were rare or incomplete—and nonexistent for illegitimate births? Furthermore, how objective are the labels and designations given by the researchers to the members of these families ("immoral," "lazy," etc.)? Were they determined by anything more objective than the researcher's own value system?

Twin studies. More solid, though less dramatic, support for the nativist position came from studies which correlated the intelligence test scores of identical twins and compared them to the scores of fraternal twins, siblings, and unrelated individuals. This method is based on the assumption that, to the extent that heredity influences intelligence, *monozygotic* twins (from the same fertilized ovum and with identi-

◆ CORRELATIONS IN INTELLIGENCE

Types of Children Pairs	Number of Pairs	Correlation Coefficient (r)
Ordinary Siblings	384	.53
Fraternal Twins	482	.63
Identical Twins	687	.87

(Based on McNemar, 1942; Nichols, 1965)

cal hereditary equipment) should vary less in intelligence than *dizygotic* twins, who develop from separate ova and whose genetic constitution is no more similar than that of any pair of siblings. Thus we should be more likely to find similar intelligence among identical twins, be it high or low, than among fraternal twins. This is indeed the case as the correlation coefficients shown in the table reveal. ◆ It is evident that the correlation of IQs for identical twins (.87) is much higher than for fraternal twins or ordinary siblings. Similarly, investigators have found more similarity of intelligence between children and their biological parents than between comparable children and their foster parents. (Ψ Close-up, p. 150.)

In one study, identical twins reared apart even showed higher correlations (.84) than fraternal twins (.53) reared together (Burt, 1955). However, it should be noted that the identical twins who had lived in different environments were somewhat less similar in intelligence than a group who had grown up in the same environment (correlations in the same study of .92 vs. .84).

The heredity-environment question may have begun as an abstract philosophical or scientific issue, but it should be obvious that it has become inextricably linked with practical social and political concerns. If intelligence, mental illness, morals, and social disease were all genetically determined, like eye color, it would follow that: (a) they cannot be modified, and thus rehabilitation and compensatory training programs are useless (and waste taxpayers' money); and (b) although the individual's nature cannot be changed, his deleterious effect on society can be— through legislating against intermarriage, requiring sterilization, or placing him in an institution.

The environmentalists fight back. If it is difficult to establish precisely the role of heredity in determining some complex behavior in a complex organism like man, then consider whether it is ever possible to isolate the role of that vague, catch-all concept, the environment. Support for the importance of nurture over nature comes from some indirect evidence and some chipping away of the evidence advanced by the nativists.

In this chapter and the preceding one we have seen many instances of development fostered or inhibited by environmental conditions: physical growth stunted or distorted by physical or emotional stress but fostered by handling and other stimulation in infancy; mental retardation following protein deficiency; bigger brains and better learning ability after being in an "enriched environment"; quicker pattern learning in adulthood following exposure to patterns while growing up, and many others, with both human and animal subjects. We have also seen many examples of the need for certain kinds of environmental opportunity at particular periods in development, and of the need for chances to respond and practice as well as merely to be stimulated. From this vast lode of experimental evidence, environmentalists argue for the crucial role of certain kinds of opportunity at certain times if particular components of "intelligence" are to develop.

As we have seen, reflexes are least influenced by the environment, instincts a little more affected, and adaptive behavior most affected and most dependent on learning. Intelligent behavior is adaptive behavior, requiring flexibility, identification of the critical requirements of a problem, and selection of appropriate resources for solving it. Perceiving, integrating, memorizing, planning, and directing action are all parts of intelligent behavior, and environment plays an important role in their development. Thus environmentalists argue that potential for intelligent behavior does not simply unfold but requires particular kinds of experience.

Heredity could explain the higher correlation of IQs for identical twins than for fraternal twins. But why are fraternal twins more alike in intelligence than other siblings, whose genetic inheritance is no more different? Environmentalists point out that the environment is likely to be more similar for fraternal twins, since they are the same age, than for siblings of different ages. The environment is probably even more similar for most identical twins, who are usually

---

Ψ Close-up   *Similar Environment, Dissimilar Heredity*

To the extent that intelligence is determined by heredity, we would expect children to be more similar in intelligence to their biological parents than to foster parents. Some years ago, Leahy (1935) compared a group of children who had been reared by their biological parents with a group of children who had been adopted into foster homes before the age of six months and who were five to fourteen years old at the time of the study. In the latter group it was assumed that there could be no relationship between the heredity of the parents and that of the adopted children. To make the two groups as comparable as possible, each child in the adopted group was paired with a child in the other group on the basis of the real or foster parents' intelligence-test scores and on the basis of objectively measurable environmental factors, such as occupation and educational status. The children's intelligence-test scores were then correlated with the average intelligence of the parents with whom they had been living.

The correlation between the intelligence of the biological parents and the intelligence of their children reflects the combined effects of similar heredity and similar environment, whereas in the case of the children raised in foster homes, any correlation would reflect the influence of similar environment only. Not surprisingly, a much higher correlation (.60 as compared with .18) was found where both heredity and environment were similar than where only environment was similar. The same differential correlations were found between the two pairs of groups for education of either parent, parental vocabulary, and status of home environment.

Ψ *Close-up*   *Boosting IQ with a Little TLC*

During the depression of the 1930's, two baby girls neglected by their feeble-minded mothers were committed to an Iowa orphanage for custodial care. When first observed by Harold Skeels, they were physically sick and clearly retarded in mental development. When they were fifteen and eighteen months of age, respectively, they were transferred to an institution for the mentally retarded. When Skeels saw them six months later, they were alert, smiling, normally active, healthy children. Intelligence test scores also indicated progressive increases. Skeels suspected that the change might have been due to the fact that these little waifs had been "adopted" by the nurses and patients. Although the older girls and women had mental ages of less than ten years (their chronological ages ranged from eighteen to fifty years), they provided a loving, stimulating "family" environment.

This chance observation was then tested in a systematic fashion. A total of thirteen similarly neglected children, several of them illegitimate and unwanted, averaging nineteen months of age with a mean IQ score of 64, far below the "normal" IQ of 100, were sent from the orphanage to a home for mental retardates as "house guests." They were to be compared with a contrast group of similar ages, but higher initial IQ, who were tested at the same times but remained in the orphanage. Each child in the experimental group was quickly adopted by an older woman, and warm personal relationships developed. These were supported by frequent contact with the other patients. For the older patients, the babies served as the primary source of stimulation in the bleak institution. For the babies, their foster mothers were the source of far more attention and stimulation than they had received in the orphanage.

What were the effects of this tender, loving care?

1. All of the experimental babies showed increases in IQ—from 7 to as much as 58 points.

2. The average *gain* for the experimental babies was 31.6 points, most of it occurring in the first nine months after transfer. The average *loss* for the contrast group in the unstimulating orphanage was 20.6 points.

3. The median educational level attained by the "TLC" subjects was twelfth grade; for the contrast subjects, it was less than third grade.

4. Eleven of the "adopted" subjects later married and had children, whose average IQ was a normal 104. (The range was from 86 to 125 for the 28 second-generation babies.) Only two of the contrast group married.

5. Four of those reared in the orphanage, but none of the experimental group, were still in an institution after all those years. It appears that environmental extremes may indeed stifle or nourish intellectual growth and affect all areas of life associated with intelligent functioning.

Interestingly, the averages for the contrast group were mysteriously raised by the figures for one subject who had completed high school (he was the only contrast subject to get beyond eighth grade), married, had four normal children, and was earning far more than any of the others in this group. On investigation, it turned out that he had had an enriched environment for a year at age five as part of another study and had been transferred to a special school for the deaf at age eight (Skeels, 1966).

---

dressed alike and treated very similarly—unless or until they rebel. Similarly with the Leahy study: why should there have been any correlation at all between children and foster parents? The fact that there was a positive correlation argues that environment must have played some role in the children's intelligence.

The fact that some children under certain conditions have shown a marked rise or drop in measured

intelligence argues for the influence of those conditions in determining intelligence. And the psychological environment may be even more important than the physical environment. In one study, children were removed from an orphanage and reared by retarded foster mothers in the drab, usually debilitating environment of an institution for the mentally retarded. These children, unlike those they left behind, showed gains in intelligence and all-round competence for living that persisted into adulthood. The secret was apparently the attention, stimulation, and love that were part of that particular psychological environment (Ψ Close-up, p. 151).

Clearly, Skeels' results are not "hard data" and broad conclusions cannot be drawn from an after-the-fact study of such a small number of cases. For example, the greatest gains were made in the months immediately following transfer to the second institution. Does this mean that the original scores were not valid, perhaps because of previous trauma associated with deprivation, separation from parents, and placement in an institution? Does it mean that the chil-

dren's ability really made a big jump with the encouragement, affection, and greater stimulation of their new environment but eventually hit a genetically determined "ceiling"? These and other questions are left unanswered by this study. The fact that such changes can occur, however, shows the danger of trying to predict individual growth on the basis of a test administered at an early age to culturally disadvantaged children. It also gives us clues to what variables should be given more careful study.

Finally, environmentalists point out that genetic potential can never be measured directly. Any behavior used in testing inevitably reflects both genetic potential and learning. Since a test score is thus

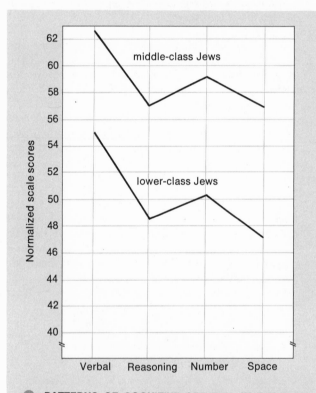

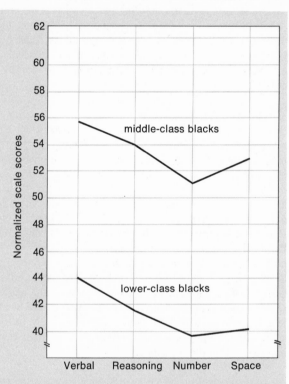

After Stodolsky & Lesser, 1967

● **PATTERNS OF COGNITIVE ABILITIES IN DIFFERENT GROUPS**

Stodolsky and Lesser, studying four primary mental abilities in middle-class and lower-class children of several different ethnic groups found that each ethnic group had a different "profile" of strengths and weaknesses on the four ability tests, and that in each case the lower-class children's scores were considerably lower. Again we have a correlation which tells us nothing about causality. Were the lower scores caused mainly by environmental deprivation or by a poorer genetic inheritance from low IQ parents? Perhaps both factors were operating. Low IQ parents tend to earn low incomes, and deprivation, as we have seen, can inhibit normal development.

always a measure of both inherited capacity and experience, low genetic potential cannot be inferred from a low IQ when the environment is extremely impoverished or emotionally hostile. •

Critical evaluation. While in the past those overemphasizing the genetic aspect of cognitive development have adopted a fatalistic picture of human potential and have used their conclusions to justify simplistic solutions to social problems, those pushing the empiricist view have often erred equally in the opposite direction. The American behaviorist tradition, to be discussed in the next chapter, has held that virtually all behavior is modifiable by experience and training. By disregarding genetic limitations, the environmentalists have sometimes raised unwarranted optimism about how much some upper individual limit might be modified.

Today the pendulum is starting on a less extreme swing as it becomes clearer that the two factors are in constant *interaction* from the moment an individual is conceived. Probably no one would take a pure nativist or a pure environmentalist position today. It seems clear that genetic potentials can be realized only in a favorable environment but that no environment can create potentials that do not exist.

It is generally agreed today that what we inherit from our parents—and through them from all of our ancestors—makes possible a range of behaviors and perhaps some maximum level of functioning within each of those behaviors. The stimulation provided by the environment may or may not push these givens to their best potential level of expression. We cannot say at this time how much of a beneficial effect an environment can have, because we do not know enough yet to design an ideal one.

Is cognitive development predictable? A great many studies have been carried out to determine whether intelligence test scores, as indices of cognitive development, remain the same over a period of years. The universal conclusion is that they usually remain essentially constant when conditions remain the same—that is, when health, type of education, and home situation do not change markedly. The single notable exception is in the case of very young children, whose potentialities may still be more varia-

ble, and with whom, in any case, there are special difficulties in designing and administering tests. For example, attention may be erratic, or poor motor coordination may prevent an accurate assessment. Another serious problem is that tests at different ages draw on different components of intelligence: those for young children test largely sensory and motor abilities, whereas those for older children are more dependent on verbal and conceptual abilities. This is undoubtedly one reason why scores obtained after age six usually correlate more highly with adult intelligence than do scores obtained during the preschool years. Scores obtained below the age of two are not very stable and in any case are more tests of general developmental level than specifically of mental ability.

With changes in the environment, as we have seen, there may be striking changes in intelligence test scores. This is especially true when there has been deprivation in the past and when the child is quite young at the time of the change. It seems clear in such cases that the original intelligence test score was not a measure of the child's inherited potential. Unfortunately, we do not know to what extent this is true of test scores generally or how often—and at what ages—other children's scores would go up with a better programming of their environment.

Two longitudinal studies have helped us to pinpoint the factors responsible for constancy or change in particular cases. One study at the Fels Research Institute of Human Development in Ohio (Sontag, Baker, & Nelson, 1958) has complete records for 20 years on 200 noninstitutionalized subjects. The other study, directed by Nancy Bayley and her colleagues at the University of California at Berkeley (1968), examined 56 "normal" people from birth to age 36. The remarkable dedication of scientists engaged in long-term, complex studies like these has paid many dividends in new knowledge and in clues for further research. One of their most striking findings was how different the course of cognitive growth may be in different individuals. For example:

1. Both studies found that for many of the children they observed, there were changes in mental-ability scores not only during the preschool period but throughout childhood.

2. The *rates* of mental growth for individual chil-

dren during the early years were unstable: growth seemed to show spurts and plateaus.

3. Different individuals showed different patterns of change in IQ: for some it did not change; for others, there was progressive increase or decrease; for still others the pattern was variable at different periods as they grew up.

4. The greatest gain observed was 73 points (from 107 at two and a half years of age to 180 at 10 years of age); the greatest loss seen was 40 points (from 142 at age three to 102 at age eight).

The Bayley study found many evidences of a different course of cognitive development for boys than for girls, as well as different relationships between cognitive development and various personality variables. Only a few examples can be cited here.

For the girls, vocalization showed a clear correlation with later intelligence from early childhood on (more vocalization, higher later intelligence). With the boys, however, vocalization showed a positive correlation in the early years, but at age six and beyond actually showed a negative correlation with later intelligence.

Correlations between early behavioral traits ("personality" variables) and later intelligence also revealed sex differences. Several consistent, stable correlations were found for the boys between behaviors during the first three years of life and verbal intelligence scores over the thirty-six-year span. For the girls, however, there were no striking consistencies between childhood behaviors and either concurrent or later intelligence. In fact, in some cases correlations found for the girls at age sixteen were reversed at age thirty-six. For the boys, too, there were some reversals: for example, boys who were high-active between ten and fifteen months tended to have low verbal scores later, whereas high activity in boys between eighteen and thirty-six months was predictive of high verbal scores later if the boys were also happy. At age one, shyness and unhappiness were predictive of later high verbal scores for girls, but for boys at the same age, happiness was a predictor of later high verbal scores. Shyness at age four was unrelated to later verbal scores for either boys or girls. Clearly, on this more analytical level, many things are happening that are obscured by overall scores or scores that represent averages from many individuals.

What effect does the quality of maternal behavior have on the development of intelligence and personality-related behaviors? Correlations of maternal behaviors with children's intelligence revealed a very interesting pattern. For boys, how their mothers responded to them during the first three years evidently had a permanent effect on their intelligence as measured at eighteen and even thirty-six years of age. Hostility in mothers was related to low adult intelligence in their offspring (correlations of around −.60), while maternal love and understanding were positively related to adult intelligence. The girls' intelligence scores, in contrast, were independent of the maternal *handling* they received, but were related to indices of parental *ability*. Bayley concludes:

"These sex differences in patterns of correlations led us to the suggestion that there are genetically determined sex differences in the extent to which the effects of early experiences (such as maternal love and hostility) persist. The girls appeared to be more resilient in returning to their own characteristic inherent response tendencies. Boys, on the other hand, were more permanently affected by the emotional climate in infancy whether it was one of warmth and understanding or of punitive rejection." (pp. 14-15)

More studies are needed which provide adequate data for understanding the specific ways in which heredity and environment interact to shape intelligence. The above findings would suggest that hereditary factors may be more potent contributors to intelligence for females than for males. Boys and men appear to be more susceptible to environmental influences than girls and women. This rather surprising finding is supported consistently across a wide spectrum of behaviors. For example, males are more likely than females to die in infancy, to have reading problems, to develop childhood schizophrenia, to commit suicide, to commit acts of violence, to be hospitalized for physical and mental diseases. In fact, it has been reported that after the atomic bombing of Hiroshima male fetuses were more likely to be born dead or defective than female fetuses (Maccoby, 1966).

The growth of cognitive ability cannot be separated from the basic growth of the individual since cognitive functioning determines what the individual can do in and to his environment. On the other hand, cognitive ability is but an extension of the individual's total personality. In Chapter 11 we will examine different ways in which people have conceptualized cognitive abilities and tried to measure them. From our discussion so far, however, it can be seen that intelligence should not be viewed as a static, fixed entity—something a person "has" inside him. Measures of "intelligence" are always measures of an individual's *adaptive behavior* in meeting a particular set of environmental challenges. For complex adaptive behavior, the individual requires both the hereditary potential for dealing with complexity and the kinds of environmental encounters that permit the learning of the necessary component skills—perceptual, conceptual, motor, and perhaps also linguistic and social.

Personality Development

"Once the notion of development is accepted, and the child is no longer seen as a malformed adult, the two central tasks of the child psychologist are set. He must describe the beginnings of development—the problem of origins—and he must propose a mechanism for further development—the problem of change." (Kessen, 1965, p. 245)

We have seen that Piaget's concern is with the origins of knowledge and how a child learns and changes his cognitive structures through encounters with inanimate nature. For the Viennese analyst, Sigmund Freud, the significant issue in human development was a problem of being. In contrast to Piaget's approach, Freud disregarded the physical world (or took it as a given). His focus was on the consequences of the child's encounters with other people, as well as with the impulses and biological strivings from within his own body and mind. Personality develops, according to the Freudian view, from the matrix of interactions between biological-sexual needs and the way they are allowed expression or are inhibited by social forces.

In Chapter 11, we will discuss various theories of personality which differ in what are seen as the critical elements in the formation of personality. The present section will only outline some areas of investigation relevant for understanding the early development of personality.

Born Different

In earlier sections of this chapter, evidence was presented to support the conclusion that many of the influences upon an individual's pattern of development begin to operate soon after the parents' sperm and egg fuse. Some of the influences are genetically determined by what each parent brings to the union. Others involve chemical and physical features of the intra-uterine environment of the fetus—which may be affected by the mother's health, nutrition, and psychological well-being. This combination provides the neonate with its basic biological equipment. However, from birth the external environment begins to play its role. The physical environment may readily sustain life or offer an ecological challenge to it. Food and water may or may not be available; it may be too hot or cold (as in the Arctic); it may breed disease; its air may be polluted, and so on. Man's greatness is his adaptability to the environments in which he finds himself, but the environment nevertheless helps determine what kind of person will adapt successfully. The social environment of family, peers, class, and culture provides a broader class of influences which determine the social and human nature of man.

A look through the observation window of a hospital nursery will readily reveal what every nurse in the obstetrics ward knows—babies are born different. Some sleep a lot, others cry incessantly, some are active, and others passive. Some have no trouble eating and digesting, others have colic and food allergies which produce considerable gastrointestinal distress. Moreover, some are male, others female, some are born big and strong, while others are small and frail. ■ (p. 156)

These initial differences will influence maturational growth patterns, subsequent reactions to stimulus inputs and the way parents and others react to and care for the baby. Both Brazelton (1962) and Freud have suggested that some newborn babies seem to possess a *stimulus barrier*, which is a capacity to limit excessive stimulation by a pattern of physiological response comparable to that observed in deep sleep (breathing slows down, motor activity diminishes,

Differences in typical behavioral patterns are detectable immediately after birth. The infants in this Japanese hospital nursery already seem to be reacting to this strange new world in different ways.

and the EEG pattern is altered to slower waves). The existence of this physiological defense system in some neonates and not in others would account for very different effects that the same degree of environmental stimulation might have upon a group of children comparable in other ways.

Individual differences in intensity of reaction which one can observe in the nursery appear to be relatively stable over the first two years of life. The correlations between any two five-month periods from 0 to 6 months up to 22 to 27 months vary between .30 and

.49 (Thomas, Chess, Birch, Hertzig, & Korn, 1963). Other researchers have found that a high level of activity in infancy is related to more impulsive behavior in childhood and through adolescence (Shaefer & Bayley, 1963).

The role of genetic factors in shaping social behavior is seen in a recent study which found more similarity between identical than fraternal infant twins in social smiling, fearfulness, and attentiveness (Freedman, 1965). Similar results were found for adolescent twins with regard to dominance, sociability, and self-control (Gottesman, 1966).

One Man's Cause Is Another Man's Effect

Throughout this chapter, we have had to rely largely upon correlational evidence to support claims for the direction in which one event affects another. But as we saw in Chapter 2, correlations only tell us a relationship exists; they tell nothing about which of the things correlated is the causal agent and which the consequence. For example, in assessing parental influence on child behavior, the parents' behavior and the child's behavior are correlated. Does this mean that a punitive parent makes his child behave aggressively or that aggressive children make their parents act punitively? In Freudian theory, the child is thought to perceive the father as a rival for the mother's love and then fear the father's wrath at this discovery. But perhaps the father is upset with the child because the mother devotes too much attention to baby and not enough to Daddy. One of the major pitfalls in establishing conclusions about determinants of personality development is the reliance on *relationships*, especially when only reported and not independently and directly observed by the investigator.

The Press of Social Forces

The prolonged period of dependency of human infants on adult caretakers establishes the mother-infant dyad as the basic human relationship. This becomes extended into the nuclear family (parent and siblings), the extended family (other relatives), and ultimately to the particular society of which these smaller units are a part. The infant and young child is initially egocentric, demanding immediate satisfaction of his needs, while oblivious to or unconcerned about the needs of others. He must learn to accommodate to the existence of other people with their own needs which may compete or conflict with his, as well as to delays in gratification. Socialization is the process by which an individual becomes an accepted member of a society of people.

In the course of his maturational and cognitive development, the child learns what he is able to do; through socialization training he learns what is appropriate, proper, acceptable, and necessary to do. He acquires the wide range of beliefs, values, ideologies, social customs, and rules which the society prescribes as essential for its maintenance.

Socialization begins with the caretaking adults as its primary agents, but is also carried on more formally through institutions such as schools. While we may thus learn to become civilized and good citizens, we may also learn attitudes and values which are not conducive to ideal growth of personality. For example, prejudice and overconcern for wealth and power may be readily acquired if the family and the society reinforce such attitudes and their behavioral accompaniments (see Sarnoff, 1966).

The breast and the toilet. The two areas of socialization in infancy that most interest and speculation have centered on are feeding and toilet training. From a parental point of view, this is how it should be, because the parents' life for a time seems to be devoted to little else but filling bottles and changing diapers. Since these activities occur so frequently and regularly and involve interactions of child and parent, they become a focal point for the transmission of parental attitudes which may influence personality development.

The relationship between child-rearing practices and parental attitudes was studied by Sears, Maccoby, and Levin (1957) through interviews with 379 mothers in the Boston area. They found that mothers who fed their babies on a "demand schedule" (when the baby wanted it) and weaned them gradually (from breast to bottle to cup) had quite different basic attitudes than mothers who fed on a time schedule and weaned abruptly. The former mothers were generally more permissive, less concerned about neatness, order, and control of aggression in their preschool children. In addition, they were less likely to try to toilet train early or to use coercive techniques in doing so.

In the process of learning to perform the acts of urinating and defecating where and when the external culture—rather than his internal demands—prescribe, the child may learn many social attitudes which affect his personality development. For some children toilet training, though difficult, is accomplished without significant incident—depending largely on the way the mother handles it. For others, whose mothers may begin severe bowel training before muscular control and sensory feedback mechanisms are sufficiently developed, the process may become a source of considerable distress and anxiety. The variation in starting times for bowel training in the Sears et al. (1957) study was from less than five months to over thirty months, with urinary training starting later, but still being incomplete in about 20 percent of kindergarten children.

What is learned in this early interpersonal situation is: impulse control; delaying gratification; substituting social gratification (approval) for biological gratification; a relationship to authority; cooperation, conformity, or rebellion; attitudes toward cleanliness and one's body. Reviewing the scant body of controlled research in this area, Ferguson says, "It seems probable, then, that a mother who is stubborn and values order and cleanliness will produce similar characteristics in her children and will be rigid in her approach to toilet training" (p. 64).

Psychoanalytically oriented authors have placed great emphasis upon toilet-training frustrations and anxiety as causal agents in the arresting of personality development and the emergence of an "anal character." Freud described the personality consequences of unsatisfactory transition through this developmental stage as a triad of orderliness, parsimony (concern for saving or hoarding), and obstinacy. There is, however, no solid empirical evidence to support this hypothesized relationship between early toilet-training experiences and the subsequent development of these character traits (Hetherington & Brackbill [1963], in fact, found no relationship between them).

Birth order. Are you the first-born child in your family, or are you a later-born? In either case, the

● **DIFFERENT CLASSES CREATE DIFFERENT SOCIAL DEFINITIONS OF REALITY**

Aspects of Life	Typical Middle-Class View	Typical Lower-Class View
Authority (courts, police, school officials)	A source of security, to be supported and appealed to	Enemies, to be hated and avoided
Education	A means of success and upward mobility	Something to endure till children can go to work
Goals in life	Material success, social acceptance	"Coolness"; to get by without attracting notice of authorities
The future	Something to look forward to	Non-existent; one lives each moment fully and fatalistically
View of self	Self-acceptance	Self-hatred or bristling defensiveness
Society as a whole	Something to identify with and conform to	Something to be resisted and suspected
Delinquency	An evil originating outside the middle-class home	An inevitable fact of life, to be ignored unless police are involved
One's home	Something to own and cherish	A way-station to nowhere
The street	Paved path for one's auto	An escape from crowded living quarters
Violence	Last resort for authorities	A cathartic; a tool for living and getting on
Sex	Binding force for family, source of adventure, factor in family planning	A release; one of few pleasures without present cost
Money and possessions	To be saved and used wisely with careful planning	To be used now before they disappear

Adapted from Segalman, 1965, by courtesy of Ralph Segalman, University of Texas

social environment you entered in your new home was probably very different from what it would have been otherwise. First-borns have no competition for parental attention, at least at first; they are talked to more, more likely to be breast-fed and cuddled. In addition, they certainly will have mothers who are more uncertain and anxious about how to handle a baby (and who thus consult Dr. Spock more often). When first-borns grow up, these and other aspects of their environment result in the following behavioral differences relative to later-borns: greater dependency, conformity, anxiety, and need to affiliate with others when in stress (Schachter, 1959). This bleak picture of first-borns must, however, be tempered by the observation that virtually all of America's astronauts have been first-borns.

Different cultures, different pressures. We have just seen that birth order affects aspects of personality through the operation of differential child-rearing practices experienced by first- and later-borns. Not

surprisingly, the same is true of sex differences, since society holds different expectations for boys than for girls. We may not see quite so readily, though, some of the other kinds of pressure that are operating in our society. The shaping forces of the environment of the rich child differ from those of the poor one, the black from the white, and those of one ethnic culture from those of another. ●

While we have relied upon anthropologists to tell us about cross-cultural differences, we have neglected to study in a systematic way the behavioral consequences of being born poor in affluent America—or black, brown, or yellow in white America. The emerging change in the social consciousness of the nation and of research psychologists will help to correct this limited perspective. In the meantime, we can learn about our internal cultural differences and how they mold personality by listening to what someone who has experienced them has to say. In *Manchild in the Promised Land* (1965), Claude Brown tells us what it was like to grow up in Harlem:

"As a child, I remember being morbidly afraid. It was like a fever that never let up. Sometimes it became so intense that it would just swallow you. At other times, it just kept you shaking. But it was always there. I suppose, in Harlem, even now, the fear is still there." (p. 413).

. . . "I always thought of Harlem as home, but I never thought of Harlem as being in the house. To me, home was the streets. I suppose there were many people who felt that. If home was so miserable, the street was the place to be. I wonder if mine was really so miserable, or if it was that there was so much happening out in the street that it made home seem a dull and dismal place." (p. 415)

Look back for a moment at the developmental tasks outlined on page 135. Do some of them seem particularly class- or culture-bound? Which ones?

The Impact of Freud

Before Freud came upon the Victorian scene, childhood was a period of innocence and meaningless play which had little connection to or relevance for the serious business of adulthood. With his monumental work, *Three Contributions to the Theory of Sex* (first published in 1905), Freud shattered this illusion (Freud, 1910).

"What poets and students of human nature had always asserted turned out to be true: the impressions of that remote period of life, though they were for the most part buried in amnesia, left ineradicable traces upon the individual's growth and in particular laid the foundations of any nervous disorder that was to follow. But since these experiences of childhood were always concerned with sexual excitations and the reaction against them, I found myself faced by the fact of infantile sexuality—once again a novelty and a contradiction of one of the strongest of human prejudices. Childhood was looked upon as 'innocent' and free from the lusts of sex, and the fight with the demon of 'sensuality' was not thought to begin until the troubled age of puberty. Such occasional sexual activities as it had been impossible to overlook in children were put down as signs of degeneracy and premature depravity or as a curious freak of nature. Few of the findings of psychoanalysis have met with such universal contradiction or have aroused such an outburst of indignation as the assertion that the sexual function starts at the beginning of life and reveals its presence by important signs even in childhood. And yet no other finding of analysis can be demonstrated so easily and so completely." (1935, pp. 58 ff.)

In Freudian theory, then, the foundations of adult personality are laid in early childhood. Not only is the course of normal personality development a continuous one across ages and stages, but the origins of adult fears and neurosis can be traced back to traumatic events in early life.

Stages of psychosexual development. As Piaget is the "giant" in the area of cognitive development, Freud occupies a similar position with respect to personality development. According to Freud's psychoanalytic theory, personality development in childhood is divided into *psychosexual* stages. Each stage is dominated by instinctual, unlearned biological urgings, which are *hedonistic* (pleasure-seeking) in nature. During each of these successive periods, sensual satisfaction comes through stimulation of various "erogenous" zones of the body—the mouth, the anus, and the genitals. These broadly conceived sexual forces are termed *libido*, and comprise all of the ways in which an individual derives gratification from bodily stimulation. At each stage of development, the extent to which such libidinal drives are satisfied or frustrated provides the occasion for intrapsychic conflict. Excess of either gratification or frustration at one stage prevents the normal progression to the next and is said to lead to *fixation* at that stage. Such fixations then influence how the child will interact with his environment. Thus, as anal fixation is presumed to lead to a cheap, neat, stubborn, obsessive-compulsive character, oral fixation is alleged to be a determinant of drug addiction, compulsive eating, and even tendencies toward sarcasm and verbal fluency.

The most primitive stage of this psychosexual development is the *oral* stage, in which the mouth region is the primary source of nourishment, stimulation, and contact with the environment. There is little doubt that infants and young children spend a great proportion of their time in sucking activities of a nonnutritive nature (such as thumb or toe sucking).

The *anal* stage, which follows, focalizes gratification first on elimination of feces, then on retention of them. The child's pleasure from both the process and the products of excretion is challenged by social

demands in most cultures and is suppressed and regulated.

The final general period of erotic satisfaction centers around the exploration and stimulation of one's own body, especially the penis for the boy and the vagina for the girl. This *phallic* stage is followed by a *latent* stage; finally, with puberty, the individual arrives at the *genital* stage of sexual differentiation, away from autoeroticism toward stimulation from contact with the genitalia of others. As they progress through these stages, children learn their appropriate sex-role identification, develop a conscience through the resolution of their sexual love for the opposite-sex parent (the Oedipal situation), and become ready for normal adult heterosexuality.

While this sketch does violence to the subtlety of Freud's thought, which you should read more fully, it does provide the basic outline of his central theme of personality development. It should be mentioned in passing that this grand design of the child's psyche was derived not in the fashion of Piaget, through observation of children, but largely from Freud's own analytical introspection and from his psychoanalytical interviews with adult patients. We will have more to say about Freud's theory of personality in Chapter 11 and about psychoanalytic therapy in Chapter 15.

Erikson's complete portrait of man. While many of the personality theorists we shall meet later are in disagreement with Freud's views on development, Erik Erikson's contribution has been instead to add a new dimension to this thinking. From his clinical observations of children, adolescents, college students, and older adults, Erikson made three major contributions to the theory of personality develop-

ment in his book *Childhood and Society* (1950). First, parallel to the psychosexual stages he posits *psychosocial* stages of ego development in which the individual establishes new orientations to himself and to other people in his social world. Second, personality development is seen as continuing throughout all stages of life, rather than being established primarily during the infantile stage. Third, each of these stages requires a new level of social interaction which can change the course of personality in either positive or negative directions.

Eight stages of psychosocial development have been identified by Erikson, describing the human cycle of life from infancy through old age. At each stage a particular conflict comes into focus; although it is never resolved once and for all, it must be resolved sufficiently that the individual can cope successfully with the conflicts of later stages.

1. *Trust vs. mistrust* (first year of life; corresponds to Freud's oral stage). Depending upon the quality of the care received, the infant learns to trust his environment, to perceive it as orderly and predictable, or to be suspicious, fearful, and mistrusting of its chaos and unpredictability.

2. *Autonomy vs. doubt* (second and third years of life; corresponds to Freud's anal period). From the development of motor and mental abilities and the opportunity to explore and manipulate emerges a sense of autonomy, adequacy, and self-control. Excessive criticism or limiting the exercise of the child's exploration and other behaviors leads to a sense of shame and doubt over his adequacy.

3. *Initiative vs. guilt* (fourth to fifth year of life; corresponds to Freud's phallic stage). The way parents respond to the child's self-initiated activities,

intellectual as well as motor, creates either a sense of freedom and initiative at one extreme or at the other, a sense of guilt and a feeling of being an inept intruder in an adult world.

4. *Industry vs. inferiority* (sixth to eleventh year; corresponds to the *latency* phase in Freudian theory when the child is least sexually preoccupied). The child's concern for how things work and how they ought to operate leads to a sense of industry in formulating rules, organizing, ordering, being industrious. However, a sense of inferiority may be promoted in a child when these efforts are rebuffed as silly, mischievous, or troublesome. It is during this stage that influences outside the home begin to exert a greater influence on the child's development—at least for middle-class American children.

5. *Identity vs. role confusion* (adolescence from twelve to eighteen years of age). During this period the adolescent begins to develop multiple ways of perceiving things, can see things from another person's point of view, behaves differently in different situations according to what is deemed appropriate. In playing these varied roles the person must develop an integrated sense of his own identity as distinct from all others, but coherent and personally acceptable. The alternatives are for one to be confused about who he really is or to settle upon a "negative identity"—a socially unacceptable role, such as that of a "speed freak" or the "class clown."

6. *Intimacy vs. isolation* (young adulthood). The consequences of the adult's attempts at reaching out to make contact with others may result in intimacy (a commitment—sexual, emotional, and moral—to other persons) or else in isolation from close personal relationships.

7. *Generativity vs. self-absorption* (middle age). Here one's life experiences may extend the focus of an individual's concern beyond himself to his family, society, or future generations. This future orientation may not develop, and instead, like Scrooge in *A Christmas Carol*, a person may become concerned with only his own material and physical well-being.

8. *Integrity vs. despair* (old age). In this last stage of life one looks back on what it has been all about and ahead to the unknown of death. As a consequence of the solutions developed at each of the preceding stages, he can enjoy the fulfillment of his life, with a sense of integrity. But despair is what faces the person who finds that his life has been unsatisfying and misdirected. Too late either to look back in anger or ahead with hope, the life cycle of such a person ends with but a whimper of despair.

As our world changes ever more rapidly, becoming both less stable and more complex, it appears that views such as Erikson's (1968) are more appropriate for understanding the "identity crises" which so many students feel (see Winter & Nuss, 1969) than the more traditional views of Freud derived from a relatively static conception of the challenges posed by man's social and physical environment.

Chapter Summary

Development is determined by the actions and interactions of *heredity* (biologically transmitted characteristics) and *environment* (external and internal conditions acting upon the organism) over time. Some traits, although determined by heredity, appear gradually over time through the process of *maturation*.

Physiological development depends primarily on heredity. From the moment of conception, the organism develops by processes of cell division and specialization through the *germinal*, *embryonic*, and *fetal* stages in the protective environment of the mother's womb. Such maternal conditions as drug addiction, emotional disturbance, and nutritional deficiencies can affect the development of the child prior to birth.

After birth, such environmental factors as inadequate nutrition or severe social deprivation clearly have adverse effects on development. It seems, however, that there may be *critical periods* during which some types of environmental stress are actually favorable to development.

Although all brain cells are present at birth, not all of them are functional. But by three months of age, the infant remains awake longer, explores his environment more, and is able to make more precise discriminations.

Body movement may occur as early as the eighth week of prenatal life, and the slow, irregular *mass action* of the fetus is particularly noticeable after the fourth month. At birth, the infant has already acquired a repertoire of general motor responses, as well as more specific reflex actions. Motor activity will continue to be refined and differentiated, with the sequence of maturation proceeding from the head downward and outward to the extremities.

Learning of any given motor skill cannot take place until the neural and muscular structures involved have reached the appropriate state of maturation. Muscular development proceeds slowly throughout childhood, becoming more rapid during adolescence. The peak of development for many skills occurs during the mid-twenties, although there is considerable variation.

The anatomical structures of most sense organs are physically complete before birth, but it is difficult to determine the extent to which they are actually functional. Some sensitivity to touch and to temperature changes is apparently present before birth, but sensitivity to pain is weak. Postnatal environmental stimulation seems necessary if the tactile and pain senses are to develop normally. Both taste and smell are well developed at birth.

Hearing seems to be less well developed in the newborn than other senses, but there is some evidence that it may function before birth. Some ability to perceive form, and possibly color, is present at birth, but further development of the visual structures is necessary. Evidence suggests that some factors in visual perception are innate, whereas others are learned. Opportunities to practice coordination of perceptual and motor skills are essential to adequate sensory-motor development.

The development of adaptive behavior is based on three classes of response systems: *reflexes*, *instincts*, and *learned acts*. Reflexes involve the most direct physical connection between stimulus and response; they are based on maturation rather than learning. Instincts are also the product of maturation. They usually comprise fairly complex sequences of behavior, which appear full-blown upon the first presentation of the requisite environmental stimuli. Purely instinctive behavior is rare in man.

Learning is by far the most important factor in the adaptive behavior of man. Learning through the association of stimulus and response, known as *conditioning*, can take place prior to birth. Learning through interaction with parents takes place from the time of birth onward. One form of such learning, evident primarily in animals, is *imprinting*. This type of learning is seen in the young animal's tendency to form a strong attachment to the first readily accessible moving object—normally its mother.

The young child learns from his parents and other adults through *observation and identification*. Through the process of *socialization*, he learns to behave according to the value system of his culture. Specific *developmental tasks*, some universal, some unique to a particular culture, must be mastered at each stage of the individual's development.

The acquisition of language is probably the most distinctly human of man's accomplishments. The child's language production during the first year of life is limited to various forms of crying and babbling. At the end of this year, recognizable words appear and true speech begins. From here, the child goes on to increase his vocabulary and develop his use of grammar. Language reception begins with the ability to distinguish the human voice from other sounds. The baby begins by distinguishing variations in intonation, rhythm, stress, and duration of speech; only toward the end of the first year is he capable of distinguishing between specific speech sounds.

Psychologists have long been intrigued by the question of whether the ability to use language is restricted to the human species. Several investigators have tried to teach chimpanzees to talk, but with little success. Attempts to teach chimps to communicate by means of various forms of signs and symbols, however, have fared better.

The child begins life as a naïve realist, accepting appearances at face value. According to Piaget, cognitive development occurs through interaction with the environment. As the child perceives discrepancies between simple concepts and environmental events, he forms new concepts to account for them. Through the processes of *assimilation* and *accommodation,* he gradually refines the cognitive structures (*schemata*) he has formed to relate processes and results. Children move through the stages of cognitive development at different rates, but in the same sequence. American educators are developing programs to facilitate cognitive growth by skillful presentation of problems just "a step ahead" of the child's current capabilities.

Throughout history, arguments have raged over whether the infant's mind is a blank tablet to be filled in by the environment or a storehouse of inherited abilities. Contemporary psychologists agree that the answer lies somewhere in between and are seeking to identify the environmental conditions conducive to the best development of whatever potential is present.

A number of incredibly naïve early studies purported to "prove" the inheritance of specific levels of intellectual ability, as well as such interesting and diverse traits as insanity, pauperism, lechery, alcoholism, and "social disease." More respectable evidence for the importance of heredity comes from studies showing higher correlations between the intelligence of genetically identical twins than between other siblings.

Evidence from various sources, including studies of children raised in foster homes or moved to more stimulating environments, indicates that environment plays a crucial role in the development of intellectual functioning. Current evidence suggests that intellectual ability is the result of an interaction between heredity and environment, with heredity setting the limits and environment determining the exact level reached.

The concept of intelligence testing is based on the premise that cognitive abilities are stable, and therefore predictable. Other things (health, social environment, etc.) remaining equal, this is essentially true for children above the age of six. Dramatic changes in environment, however, may bring about equally dramatic changes in intelligence test scores. There is evidence to suggest that the course of cognitive development is different for the two sexes.

Personality traits, like intelligence, are affected by both heredity and environment. In many respects, infants are born with different "personalities." Certain of these initial differences remain fairly stable throughout infancy and influence both the way the baby responds to his environment and the way other individuals respond to him.

To a large degree, however, the child's personality development is guided by his social environment, which begins to exert its influence at birth. Such factors as feeding methods, toilet training, birth order, and sociocultural environment have all been found to have some relationship to personality traits.

The great stress placed on early experiences in the development of personality can be traced to Freud, who believed that all the foundations of adult personality (and psychological deviance) are laid down in childhood. He delineated five stages of *psychosexual development (oral, anal, phallic, latent,* and *genital),* based on instinctual biological drives and interaction with parents.

Erik Erikson expanded Freud's psychosexual stages to *psychosocial stages.* He proposed eight stages of development, marked by prominent conflicts for the individual, which come into focus at different times during his life. These stages include *trust vs. distrust, autonomy vs. doubt, initiative vs. guilt, industry vs. inferiority, identity vs. role confusion, intimacy vs. isolation, generativity vs. self-absorption,* and *integrity vs. despair.* Erikson's stages differ from those of Freud in that development is seen as continuing throughout life, rather than ending with childhood, and the stages are identified in terms of personal and social goals rather than biological drives.

Profiting from Experience

In order to survive and adapt to the demands of a changing, sometimes hostile environment, organisms —from paramecia to people—must be able to profit from past experience. The physiological apparatus for tuning in to available environmental information and for initiating action must be coordinated through learning processes if the organism is to function effectively and efficiently.

Organisms that have to depend primarily on inborn reflexes are severely limited in their capacity to respond adaptively or creatively to novel stimuli. The stereotyped behavior that is common to lower forms of animal life becomes increasingly flexible, modifiable, and original as one moves up the phylogenetic scale. Creatures with complex nervous systems can learn two basic relationships essential for successful adaptation: prediction of a future environmental event on the basis of a prior event, and prediction of the environmental consequences which follow from given responses on their part. The first kind of learning helps to define how the environment is structured and enables the organism to recognize signals of imminent dangers or good things in the offing. The second kind of learning helps to establish the extent to which what one does makes a difference —whether anything happens or changes in the environment as a result of one's behavior. Taken together, therefore, the level of sophistication of these learning processes sets the limits on how far an organism can modify its behavior to suit the conditions in the environment.

In man such modifiability appears virtually endless because of his capacity to learn not only from the effects of his own actions but also vicariously by observing others, to learn abstract relations by manipulating symbols, and to use language to describe and remember relationships.

The two chapters in this Part will establish the two basic kinds of learning as building blocks for understanding how behavior is brought under the control of stimuli and how environmental stimuli can be controlled by behavior. For many psychologists, such processes are considered to be the most essential ones for an understanding of practically all psychological phenomena, however complex. We *learn* to perceive, to think logically or critically, to experience emotions, to be frustrated, to get ulcers, and we learn how to become "mentally ill." The extent to which our gift of language is hereditary or acquired is under intensive investigation at the present time.

For learning to have more than transient utility, what is learned must be stored and available upon demand when called for. Thus we will also be concerned with the interrelations between human learning, remembering, and forgetting and with methods for improving both learning and remembering.

Chapter 5

Learning About Events and Consequences

It is likely that snow was falling in St. Petersburg at the time of the year when Ivan Petrovich Pavlov prepared to board the train on his journey to Stockholm. It was 1904, and Pavlov was on his way to accept the highest tribute for a contribution to basic knowledge: the Nobel prize. The Russian physiologist had devised a technique for studying the functioning of the digestive glands in intact animals. The role of salivary and other secretions involved in digestion could now be studied by extracting them from the body through fistulas implanted in the glands and viscera of experimental dogs.

Surprisingly, Pavlov was more troubled than happy as he departed. It appeared that recent problems in his own laboratory were calling into question the utility of his approach to studying the physiology of digestion.

At an early stage in an experiment, his dogs would salivate shortly after the meat powder was placed in their mouths. However, after this procedure was repeated a number of times, the animals began to salivate *before* they tasted the food. First, the sight of the food made them salivate; then later on, the sight of the experimenter who brought the food, and finally even his footsteps would suffice to elicit salivation. Pavlov's assistants were at a loss to understand how they could get rid of this undesirable effect, which was a source of error and confounding in the simple

process they wished to study. Any stimulus which regularly preceded the placing of the meat powder in the dogs' mouths came to evoke the same reaction as did the food itself!

The interference of this "psychic process" on the basic physiological process under investigation intrigued Pavlov. His prepared mind was able to grasp the significance of these events, and he redirected all of his research, even though Sir Charles Sherrington, the leading physiologist of the time, advised him not to get sidetracked by such psychical nonsense. Pavlov persisted and was able to turn this chance phenomenon into one of the major discoveries of our time—uncovering the basic laws of learning by conditioning.

The implications of Pavlov's psychological contribution to our knowledge of how organisms learn to adjust to novel stimuli in their environment became immediately apparent. So much so, that when the historian H. G. Wells was asked to judge whether Pavlov or his contemporary, George Bernard Shaw, was more important to society, he answered by stating that if they were both drowning, and he had but one life preserver, he would throw it to Pavlov.

Incidentally, Shaw (1933) took exception to such a judgment and retaliated by parodying Pavlov's contribution in *The Adventures of the Black Girl in Her Search for God*. In this story the girl encounters a pompous, elderly myop in a jungle of ideas. After analyzing her fear reaction to an unexpected roar as a simple conditioned reflex, he goes on to exclaim:

"This remarkable discovery cost me twenty-five years of devoted research, during which I cut out the brains of innumerable dogs, and observed their spittle by making holes in their cheeks for them to salivate through instead of through their tongues. The whole scientific world is prostrate at my feet in admiration of this colossal achievement and gratitude for the light it has shed on the great problems of human conduct."

"Why didn't you ask me?" said the black girl. "I could have told you so in twenty-five seconds without hurting those poor dogs." . . .

"The fact was known of course to every child; but it had never been proved experimentally in the laboratory; and therefore it was not scientifically known at all. It reached me as an unskilled conjecture; I handed it on as science. Have you ever performed an experiment, may I ask?"

With that, the girl demonstrated that she, too, could control behavior. By verbally manipulating environmental stimuli ("You are sitting on a sleeping crocodile"), she got the old man to scramble up a tree and then, in a similar manner ("There is a tree snake smelling at the back of your neck"), got him to jump down in a jiffy.

As we turn to consider how such "behavioral engineering" works (which we shall do in both this chapter and the next), we will begin by analyzing simpler phenomena and asking simpler questions upon which complex control of behavior rests.

What Organisms Must Learn

The two most essential bits of knowledge which any organism must acquire in order to survive are: (a) how environmental events are related to each other, and (b) how its own actions and environmental events are related—what events happen when it acts in certain ways.

What Things in the Environment Are Related?

By learning something about the regularity with which certain events go together, the organism establishes environmental correlations. This information

both structures the environment and makes it predictable. It is this orderliness which enables us to make *predictions* of the likelihood of future events from knowledge of present events.

In addition, the organism may learn something about how to react to stimulus sequences. The first of a pair of stimuli can come to serve as a "signal" for the second, thereby eliciting an anticipatory response before the second stimulus event is experienced. This learning is especially valuable when the second stimulus is unpleasant, noxious, or potentially lethal. For instance, by ducking when his opponent feints with a left jab, a boxer may avoid a right fist to his face—if the first stimulus event regularly "telegraphs" the impending occurrence of that hard right.

Finally, the intellectual activities of *analyzing* complex stimuli into simple components or of *synthesizing* simple elements into complex wholes relies upon perception of relationships between stimuli. Analysis and synthesis are important components of the processes of problem solving and creativity, which will be discussed in Chapter 8. In the present chapter we will consider how and why stimuli develop "signal" values which enable man to predict accurately, and in many cases control, various aspects of his environment.

What Actions and Consequences Are Related?

The second type of correlation to be learned is the one between a response that we make and the consequences it has on the environment or on our relation to it. Some things we do have an effect; others do not. Those that do may either change our orientation to some part of the environment, or change some part of it directly. For example, at the sign of smoke, you may walk to the nearest exit and escape harm, or you may scream "fire" and run, causing a panic which seals off the exit. Of course, you may also react to the smoke by trying to put out the fire—by fanning at it with your newspaper or throwing the paper on it. As this makes the fire grow bigger, you quickly learn that such behavior has undesirable consequences. Through any of these acts, you learn something about yourself as an agent of environmental control, about what features of the environment can be controlled, and about what techniques produce what results.

All living organisms possess this capacity to learn about these two kinds of relationships. Organisms higher up on the phylogenetic scale are capable of learning more subtle and complex relationships between environmental stimuli than are lower ones. In addition, they can learn better how to change their relationships to their environment—either to adapt to it or to change it to adapt to them.

Too Hot to Shower

The poor plumbing found in many college dormitories and apartment houses offers us an excellent example for illustrating most of the basic points to be made about both of these two fundamental relationships.

Imagine taking a warm, soothing shower after a hard day's work. As the water pours down against your back, you soon relax contentedly and become oblivious to everything but the comforting warmth. Suddenly, your relaxation is smashed by the awareness that the water has become scalding hot. Someone has flushed a toilet, and when that happens, there is no cold water to temper the shower. The heat burns your back, causing considerable pain. Just as quickly, the temperature of the water returns to its previous condition, and you continue your shower, although unable to regain your former state of contented oblivion. But soon you detect that the water pressure has abruptly and momentarily dropped. Bam! On comes the red-hot flow again, accompanied by expletives from you.

That one association between water pressure reduction and heat increase may be sufficient to develop an "expectancy" in which the former forecasts the impending danger of the latter. Certainly, if the two stimulus changes repeatedly occurred together, you would learn to see the first event as a signal for the second.

So you have experienced an association between two stimuli: namely, there is a high degree of correlation between reduction in cold water pressure and subsequent rise in water temperature. One is a dependable *signal* for the other.

Unless you can put such knowledge to work on your behalf, however, you will be smarter but no less in pain. You did not have to learn to experience pain when skin tissue was damaged. Those connections are physiologically built in. But you do have to learn the connection between the event and its effect on you—namely, "very hot water burns my skin." Moreover, there are many behavioral reactions that may accompany your pain response, such as screaming, crying, cursing, stomping up and down, kicking the wall, and so on. What you obviously must learn is what action will be adaptive—will terminate or prevent the painful experience.

If the event is an intense, noxious one, it is not sufficient to learn an escape response—a way of getting away *after* the hot water starts. It is much better to avoid the discomfort completely. An *avoidance response* involves getting out of the path of the shower before the scalding water comes. Doing so means that you have learned a response of moving to the environmental signal of a drop in water pressure. Your learned response has effective consequences and gives you one type of control over your environment.

Such environmental control is vastly extended in man by the use of language. Individuals may be given instructions about the relationship between events. They may also be taught appropriate responses which have desirable outcomes without the necessity of repeatedly experiencing signal-event-reaction trials. Thus not every resident or visitor in a dormitory with this plumbing problem has to go through the painful process of discovering it for himself. It becomes part of the storehouse of knowledge which can be passed from one person to another through words.

At one level of analysis, the psychology of learning is concerned with understanding the principles involved in establishing correlations of the two kinds we have been discussing—between stimulus events and between responses and their consequences. At a broader level of analysis, however, the study of learning processes is fundamental to any understanding of what man is. The characteristic which most distinguishes higher organisms from lower forms of animal life is the relative independence of their behavior from unchangeable, inherited physiological mechanisms and the greater modifiability of behavior through learned encounters with the environment. We learn how to become human beings, to live with others, to speak, to attend, to perceive, to reason—as well as to act. Moreover, our attitudes, tastes, idiosyncrasies, loves, hates, fears, prejudices, and emotions are all learned. For better or for worse, we learn how to be an individual with a unique personality. Therefore, it is not surprising that basic to almost any analysis of human behavior will be a consideration of some principles of learning.

The present chapter focuses primarily upon the phenomena of learning per se and, in particular, the two basic patterns by which learning ties things together. Subsequent chapters, which focus on complex human learning and on other kinds of psychological phenomena, such as perception, social interaction, and therapy for mental illness, will often rely either implicitly or explicitly upon this foundation of learning principles. First, however, we will need an understanding of some phenomena that can be seen as stepping stones to learning.

The What-Is-It? Reaction

There are few things more effective in lowering a lecturer's self-evaluation than seeing the members of the audience, supposedly enraptured by his compelling rhetoric, turn their heads to attend to a door opening, someone leaving his seat, or virtually any other "trivial" stimulus that occurs. Pavlov's assistants were likewise embarrassed when they asked their professor to observe some new conditioning technique they had perfected, and the experimental dogs looked at Pavlov instead of performing the required response.

This mechanism for paying attention to novel environmental stimuli is called the *orienting reaction*. It has long been studied extensively by Russian researchers, but it was not until the 1950s that American researchers began studying it. Curiosity and exploratory behavior are some of the more complex forms of it that have been extensively studied since then.

Alert for a Possible Emergency

Many changes accompany the apparently simple turning toward the source of the novel stimulus. In general, they serve to increase the sensitivity of the organism to the incoming stimulus, so that he can discern where it is and mobilize for action if necessary. Components of the orienting reaction include:

1. *Increased sensitivity.* Auditory and visual thresholds are lowered, the pupil dilates to let in more light, and ability to discriminate between similar stimuli is increased.

2. *Specific skeletal muscle changes.* Depending on the species, muscles that direct the sense organs operate to turn the head, focus the eyes, prick up the ears, and so on.

3. *General muscle changes.* Ongoing activities are suspended; general muscle tonus rises, and electrical activity in the muscles increases.

4. *Brain wave changes.* The pattern of the EEG is modified toward increased arousal, with fast, low-amplitude activity predominating.

5. *Visceral changes.* Blood vessels in the limbs constrict, while those in the head dilate. The galvanic skin response (GSR), a change in the electrical resistance of the skin, occurs, breathing becomes deeper and slower, and (in man and some other animals) heart rate decreases. Thus the orienting reaction plays the dual role of maximizing sensitivity to informational input while simultaneously preparing the body for emergency action.

Conditions that elicit orientation. What conditions elicit these responses? For simplicity, we may distinguish three classes of stimuli which generate orienting reactions, based on a categorization developed by Berlyne (1960).

1. *Novel or complex stimuli.* Events which are different from those recently experienced or arranged in a novel sequence, creating "surprise," elicit orientation. Monkeys trained to find a banana under a cup showed marked orienting reactions when they found lettuce there (Tinklepaugh, 1928).

In addition, stimuli of moderate to high intensity elicit orientation, as do varicolored stimuli compared to monochromatic stimuli. Complex or incongruous figures are more likely to elicit orientation than are simple ones.

2. *Conflicting stimuli.* When an organism must make a difficult perceptual discrimination between similar stimulus events, one of which has been associated with positive consequences and the other with

negative consequences, strong orienting reactions occur. A conflict between required motor responses or between required verbal responses can also result in orientation (Berlyne, 1961).

3. *Significant (signal) stimuli.* When a stimulus has acquired special significance for a subject, its presentation elicits orientation. Furthermore, it continues to elicit orientation even though it is repeated, is not novel, and produces no conflict. Your own name, "Watch out," and "Danger" (either seen or heard) are examples of a class of stimuli which continue to call forth the orienting reaction, whereas many nonsignificant stimuli that are presented equally often produce no reaction.

To Orient or to Habituate?

Virtually all stimuli have the power to evoke an orienting reaction, although those belonging to one of the three classes outlined above produce stronger, more enduring orienting reactions. There is obvious functional value in attending to and investigating stimuli which are novel, surprising, puzzling, or of biological or personal significance (Bindra, 1959). If the environmental detection system is to be truly efficient, however, there must be some mechanism for "turning off" the orienting reaction once incoming stimuli have become familiar, understood, and expected and it is known that they do not signal anything of importance happening "out there."

Most stimuli cease to evoke an orienting reaction merely by being repeated in identical form. With such repetition the organism *habituates* to the stimulus, both physiologically and psychologically, and stops responding to it. It is as if a stimulus loses its existence once it stops carrying new or significant information of potential value to the organism. Thus, after ten to thirty stimulations, the generalized orienting reaction typically habituates.

Repeated stimulation by stimuli of even moderate intensity can produce drowsiness and eventually sleep (a fact you must have experienced while reading certain introductory textbooks or listening to canned, large-hall lectures delivered in a droning monotone). It has been shown that many normal rested adults fall asleep after being exposed to only eight minutes of repetitive stimulation (Gastaut & Bert, 1961). Induc-

ing sleep by "counting sheep" or inducing a hypnotic state of extreme relaxation by repeating a simple verbal formula both employ this principle of habituation.

Both orientation and habituation are necessary for species survival, since each individual organism must learn what is going on in his particular environment before he can try to adapt to or control it. Although present in some form in all species, however, orienting is more pronounced among the more highly developed animals than among the simpler ones. In addition, since they are equipped to extract more information per stimulus exposure, higher animals also show more rapid habituation. (Ψ Close-up, below)

The importance of orientation to survival is indicated by the observation that for each species there are stimuli of special significance which resist habituation. For example, it has been found that rustling noises evoke only weak orientation and rapid habituation in domesticated dogs, whereas in hares such

---

Ψ *Close-up*   *No Orientation and Habituation— No Learning*

The importance of orientation and habituation as stepping stones to learning is demonstrated in Luria's (1963) extensive studies of mentally retarded children. Luria finds that unlike their nonretarded peers, mentally retarded children:

1. Frequently give no orienting reaction to stimuli of medium intensity.

2. Usually give powerful orienting reactions which resist habituation to strong stimuli.

3. Are unable to prolong their orientation if verbally instructed to do so.

Therefore, they have difficulty in learning to know and manipulate their environment because most novel stimuli do not evoke orienting reactions, whereas strong, irrelevant stimuli are a constant source of distraction, and verbal instructions cannot direct and hold their attention on stimuli relevant for the new learning.

stimuli evoke a strong orienting reaction which does not habituate over 240 repeated trials; similarly, owls do not habituate to the sight of cats, beavers to the sound of splintering wood, or fish to the sound of splashing waves (Klimova, 1958). It is not known whether such reactions are genetically built in or are the consequence of early learning.

Dishabituation— Return of the Orienting Reaction

After habituation has occurred, the orienting response can be induced again if the stimulus input becomes distinguishably different—even if it includes the same elements but in an unusual or unexpected order. For example, Unger (1964) presented numbers in series (1, 2, 3, 4, 5, etc.) until the subjects habituated to them, as measured by constriction of a blood vessel in a finger. When he suddenly presented one number out of sequence (9, 10, 11, 10), the orienting reaction returned equally suddenly.

Dishabituation may occur with changes in the length, the pattern, or the "meaning" of the stimulus. This response to unexpected stimuli suggests that the incoming stimulus is constantly being compared to some expectancy on the part of the organism. Apparently the organism has associated all the characteristics of the original stimulus presentation as belonging to a particular pattern, and can instantly identify as "different"—and worth responding to—any variation in that pattern. Thus whereas orientation and habituation merely involve responses to change (or lack of change) in stimulus input, dishabituation seems to give evidence of some primitive form of learning.

If dishabituation does *not* occur when habituation has taken place and some element of the stimulus complex is altered, we can infer either that the change is too small to be detected or that the organism has not noticed the change that has taken place. This latter may mean simply that the organism did not perceive that particular element as part of the original stimulus complex. (Ψ Close-up, p. 173)

What Happens in the Brain?

It is evident that the processes of orientation and habituation have a very basic function in guiding our behavior, but how? What is the mechanism by which such information processing and response adjustments take place?

Much of what is known about these processes can be accounted for by an elegant model proposed by a Soviet psychologist, Sokolov (1960). His model provides an explanation of how the orienting reaction comes about, how habituation and dishabituation are linked to it, and, finally, where in the brain it all takes place. A representation of the conceptual model developed by Sokolov, which is generally supported by neurophysiological evidence, is presented in the figure. ◆   (p. 174)

The essential feature of this proposed explanation is a system for comparing incoming events with previously experienced events. This system provides a forecast of future stimuli and reflects the most probable sequence of future actions in response to such stimuli.

With prolonged habituation, inhibition of the reticular formation results in drowsiness and eventually in sleep. With a change in stimulus input, a mismatch occurs and hippocampal release of the reticular formation takes place, resulting in dishabituation and a new orienting reaction.

Sokolov's model has an interesting predecessor worthy of mention—namely, Bichat's view of matching the new with the old as a basis for sensation. This position, first published in the early 1800s, is best appreciated in the words of the author:

"The action of the mind on each feeling of pain or pleasure, arising from a sensation, consists in a comparison between that sensation and those which have preceded it. The greater the difference between the actual and past impressions, the more ardent will be the feeling. That sensation would affect us most which we had never experienced before. . . .

"The nature of pleasure and of pain is thus to destroy themselves, to cease to exist, because they have existed. The art of prolonging the duration of our enjoyments consists in varying their causes." (Bichat, 1809)

Armed with an overall picture of the two kinds of relationships organisms must learn and an understanding of orienting and its sequels, we are ready now to go back and see what was happening in Pavlov's laboratory that changed the direction of his research.

Respondent Conditioning— Pavlovian Learning

Certain stimuli have biological and behavioral consequences which do not have to be learned but are evidently provided for in the genetic instructions. Reflexes (discussed in the previous chapter) are one such class of unlearned responses to specific stimulation of sense receptors. Salivation is also apparently an unlearned response elicited by the presence of food in the mouth. Pavlov termed such a response an *unconditioned* or *unconditional response* (UR), and the eliciting stimulus, an *unconditioned stimulus* (US, or sometimes UCS).

With reflexes, there is a virtually perfect correlation between the two events (the UR inevitably follows the US) since the very survival of the organism may depend upon an instantaneous reliable response.

Ψ *Close-up*   *Detective Work via Dishabituation*

The phenomenon of dishabituation has made possible an ingenious technique for studying infants' ability to discriminate between different odors. The research on olfactory sensitivity of Lipsitt and his colleagues (1963, 1966) was described in the preceding chapter. When babies only a few days old are presented with certain olfactory stimuli (such as asafetida), they respond with bodily movements and changes in breathing and heart rate, as shown in the record below. These responses indicate that the infants are sensitive to these stimuli. The apparatus used is shown in the photograph.

Such a stimulus is presented repeatedly until habituation occurs; then the experimenter presents another stimulus. If the infant can detect the difference, dishabituation occurs and there is a reappearance of the olfactory response. If the new stimulus is not perceived as "different," however, habituation should continue.

The graph shows an infant's habituation curve to a mixture of three chemicals. The mean responses for each block of trials are plotted, and a line is drawn showing clearly their downward direction. Presentation of one of the three components in the mixture then brings a much stronger response, indicating dishabituation and, by inference, the ability to distinguish between the original mixture and the single element. Despite habituation to the mixture, response to the component alone is almost as great as it was before the habituation trials.

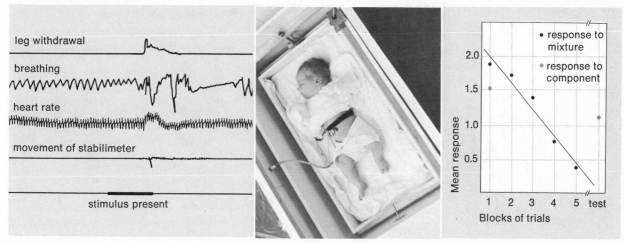

After Engen, Lipsett, & Kaye, 1963, and Lipsitt, 1966

For example, the retina would be severely damaged if the pupil did not respond to intense light by rapidly contracting. This response occurs "automatically" without thinking or learning. When there is no built-in mechanism to protect the individual, he must *learn* what events and situations are potentially dangerous to him.

What Pavlov found was that when he presented meat powder and observed the automatic, unlearned response of salivation, it was not long before other stimuli occurring at the same time (sight of food, sight or sound of experimenter) also became capable of eliciting salivation. ■ When an originally neutral stimulus acquires a new power to elicit a response similar to the unconditioned response, it is said to have become a *conditioned stimulus* (CS). The response it produces is called a conditioned response (CR). Sometimes this response looks just like the original response, but often, as we shall see, it has new components too. This process is called *respon-*

dent conditioning because it is an originally automatic, genetically given response or *respondent* (salivation, eye blink, pupillary contraction) that is conditioned —related to a new stimulus. The respondent is said to be *conditioned* when it is elicited reliably by a stimulus which previously was "neutral"—uncorrelated with its appearance. (This type of conditioning is also sometimes called *classical conditioning* to distinguish it from other forms of conditioning that have been delineated since.)

It should be clear that what has occurred is a *stimulus substitution* in which the functions of the original, unconditioned stimulus (US) are acquired by a new, conditioned stimulus (CS). It should also be noted that in this procedure, neither stimulus is under the organism's control; both occur regardless of its behavior. They are programmed by the environment (as with the water pressure change and heat increase in our shower example), or by psychologists studying this process.

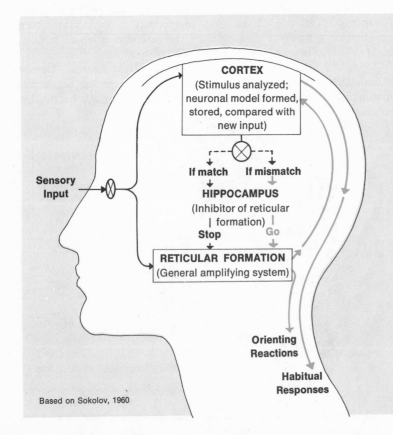

Based on Sokolov, 1960

◆ SOKOLOV'S "MODEL OF THE MIND"

This is a simplified diagram of Sokolov's model of what takes place in the brain during orientation, habituation, and dishabituation.

1. Sensory input is analyzed in the cortex and a neuronal model of it is formed.
2. New stimulus input is matched against this model.
3. In case of *mismatch,* impulses result in release of reticular formation, which produces orienting reactions (cortical, somatic, visceral).
4. In case of *match,* downward impulses result in inhibition of the reticular formation and blocking of further input to it from the afferent sensory nerves. Result: habituation.

■ PAVLOV'S CONDITIONING APPARATUS

In Pavlov's early experiments, the dog was held in place with a harness while a dish of food was placed in front of him. A glass tube conducted the saliva from an opening in the duct of one of his salivary glands to a lever (center) which activated a stylus (far left); the stylus recorded the quantity and rate of salivary secretion on a revolving drum.

After Yerkes & Morgulis, 1909

In the movie *The Diary of Anne Frank* the arrival of the Nazi SS troops was always preceded by a wailing siren of their squad car and followed by the perpetration of some horrifying incident against the Jews. By the end of the movie, the peculiar sound of the siren alone (CS) elicited strong feelings of revulsion (CR) in many members of the audience, as it undoubtedly did in those who actually experienced this symbol and the events with which it came to be associated.

Not only simple physical stimuli but words and other symbols can become conditioned stimuli. Such conditioning vastly extends the range of stimuli which can elicit vital reflexes, can signal danger, or can "stand in" for unconditioned stimuli that are not readily available. Words and symbols associated with significant events come to be substitutes for the events, producing the same reaction as the events themselves. The words "I love you" in a letter to one's beloved can elicit a strong emotional response even though their originator is far away (assuming the beloved can read English). ●

The conditioning of words as symbols is effectively demonstrated in a humorous "experiment" conducted by two young pranksters. Their pompous old minister, who rode his horse to church each Sunday, insisted that they clean the horse and do other duties without payment or thanks. To get even, they conditioned the horse by riding him, calling out "Whoa," and thereupon sticking him in the behind with a pin. You can imagine what happened the next Sunday when the horse trotted up to the church and the minister, sitting proudly on his back, called out the familiar "Whoa."

The Anatomy of Pavlovian Conditioning

"The whole life of a higher animal, and especially of man, consists of continuous formation of new conditioned connections on the basis of unconditioned stimuli that differ in biological quality." (Anokhin, 1961, p. 901) Whether or not we would agree, it certainly is true that during the course of one's life the many inborn activities of the organism—such as eating and sexual activity—become connected with a variety of environmental stimuli. As we have seen, the original activity can then come under the controlling influence of these new environmental signals: it can be elicited by them directly.

How are these connections built up, and how are they broken when the environment changes and the conditioned stimulus is no longer a meaningful or

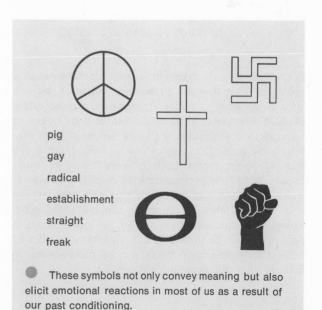

pig
gay
radical
establishment
straight
freak

● These symbols not only convey meaning but also elicit emotional reactions in most of us as a result of our past conditioning.

trustworthy signal? The following is a summary of the major processes underlying conditioning.

Generalized excitability. Even after a single pairing of a neutral and an unconditioned stimulus, the animal will respond to the conditioning situation with an elevation of excitability. This may be great enough to trigger spontaneous motor reactions as well as glandular secretions. If it is a food response that is being conditioned, there is a "general alimentary excitation, a general preparation for future alimentary activity, the expectation of feeding in general that is supposed to follow. Then the reaction is concretized, and the animal awaits the definite conditioned stimulus that is followed by feeding, and focuses its attention on this stimulus." (Kupalov, 1961, p. 1050)

Temporal patterning. Increasing the number of pairings of the conditioned and unconditioned stimuli increases the strength of the conditioned respondent (up to some maximal level), but only under certain temporal relations between the two events. The most favorable interval between stimuli has been shown to be half a second between onset of CS and onset of US. This time interval is sufficient for the first stimulus to signal the second and to prepare the organism physiologically. Shorter time intervals reduce the signaling utility of the CS; longer ones allow time for other stimuli to occur, other responses to be activated, and a loss of attention to the CS.

The time interval itself can become the conditioned stimulus. If the unconditioned stimulus is presented repeatedly with a consistent interval between presentations, the subject learns to respond to the interval by making a response just before the time the US is due to appear. This is called *temporal conditioning.*

Stimulus generalization. During the early stages of the development of a conditioned response, many signals similar to the primary one will evoke the response. This phenomenon, called *stimulus generalization*, operates in a sense to open the organism to all stimuli which are related to the conditioned stimulus and guarantees that a response will be made to a wide range of signals, any of which might be the "true" CS. With additional experience, the animal responds only to stimuli which are increasingly similar to the actual signal. This tendency to "confuse" stimuli early in conditioning occurs most readily between stimuli in the same sensory modality as the conditioned stimulus—tones of different pitch or lights of different brightness—but it may also occur between stimuli of different sensory modalities (Brogden & Gregg, 1951). (Ψ Close-up, p. 177)

Response generalization. A painful unconditioned stimulus to a dog's paw elicits the response of lifting the paw. Early in conditioning, the conditioned stimulus—perhaps a tone—will elicit not only the specific response of paw-lifting but also a generalized motor reaction. For example, the dog may struggle with his whole body at the appearance of the signal (Culler, Finch, Girden, & Brogden, 1935). Thus the conditioned response may look and actually be quite different from the unconditioned response, especially at first. It is only with added trials that the response becomes localized and specific.

This response generalization has value for the animal, as shown by a study where during conditioning a dog's feet were placed in shallow frames with apparatus for measuring their movement and shift in weight.

Ψ *Close-up*   *Using Conditioning*
to Study Hidden Processes

In studying animal subjects or human infants, we cannot ask them what they are perceiving. But often we can infer it by what conditioned responses can be established. For example, if an infant can be conditioned to respond to a tone, then we know he must have perceived the tone. (Failure, of course, would not prove inability: poor motor control, distractions, or other factors could have prevented conditioning.) Likewise, if we can condition him to respond to a high tone but not to a low one, then we know he can tell them apart. Colors, concepts like triangularity, or other stimulus parameters can be studied in this way. Many studies of brain functioning have made use of conditioning to identify what stimuli are being detected.

Ψ *Close-up* *Transfer of Conditioned Emotional Responses (or,
The Sad Tale of Little Albert and the White Rat)*

Little Albert started out as a healthy, stable, rather unemotional baby. He never reacted fearfully to any of the test situations devised by the experimenter. His reaction to the succession of objects suddenly thrust upon him was to reach and play. There were a white rat, a rabbit, a dog, a fur coat, a ball of cotton, and some masks. But he did startle and go into a crying fit from the unexpected loud noise of a steel bar being struck a sharp blow just behind him.

At the tender age of eleven months and three days, when the white rat was presented and he reached for it—bong went the steel bar. After two such experiences, the baby was whimpering. A week later when the rat again appeared on the scene, Albert had learned his lesson— he withdrew his hand before it touched his old playmate. Then systematic respondent conditioning was started in order to establish a strong negative emotional response to the white rat. For seven trials, rat and startle noise were paired. When next the rat was presented

alone, Albert began to cry, turned, fell over and crawled away with all his little might.

About a week later, this same fear reaction had generalized from the white rat to the friendly rabbit. The dog frightened him, the fur coat made him cry, he pulled away from the cotton ball. Saddest of all, "he was again pronouncedly negative" when shown a Santa Claus mask. No such fear was shown to blocks or objects which did not share the apparently controlling stimulus dimension of "furriness."

Whether little Albert developed into a Scrooge who hated Christmas with its Santa Claus fear reminders must remain a conjecture. The experimenters reported, "Unfortunately, Albert was taken from the hospital the day the above tests were made. Hence, the opportunity of building up an experimental technique by means of which we could remove the conditioned emotional responses was denied us." (Watson & Rayner, 1920)

It was clear from these measurements that the postural adjustments of the dog's body prepared it to lift the shocked paw without losing its balance (Anokhin, 1959).

Human subjects who have learned a correct response word to a given stimulus often show response generalization on later tests of retention by giving responses similar in meaning, structure, or sound to the correct response. For example, they may say "resting" instead of "restful," "misty" instead of "filmy," or "gaiety" instead of "festive" (Underwood, 1948).

Differentiation and inhibition. While it may be initially useful for the organism to respond to all stimuli which *might* have signal value, continuation of such responding is, of course, inefficient. Furthermore, it serves no purpose once the environment is sufficiently stable that one very specific stimulus is a consistent and dependable signal. The animal must then learn to

inhibit its response to all the stimuli that are *not* associated with the US.

During conditioning, the organism learns to differentiate between the conditioned stimuli and those irrelevant stimuli. We know this differentiation has been made when the conditioned stimuli continue to elicit responding but the others do not: they have come to evoke *inhibition* of responding. Conditioning, then, is a process in which differentiation wins over generalization.

The more distinguishable the *signal*, the more quickly it will be identified and attended to at the expense of the *noise* stimuli—irrelevant stimuli occurring at the same time. Thus a sharp discontinuity or difference in intensity between the stimuli to be differentiated will speed up differentiation. In the shower example, the association between drop in water pressure and hotter water will be more quickly learned with a marked water-pressure change and a great and sudden rise in temperature.

Some stimuli come to be signals for the *absence* of the US. Such stimuli then come to assume a safety stimulus value, signaling that the US will *not* appear as long as this condition is present.

"Not responding," although a passive act behaviorally, is still a physiological response. It involves considerable activity at the *neural* level in order to inhibit inputs that are irrelevant and responses that are not appropriate. In fact, many investigators believe that the coordinating role of inhibitory processes is the most intriguing aspect of conditioning. ▲

Temporary inhibition of a conditioned response may occur when other stimuli compete for attention. For example, conditioning is temporarily disrupted by the sudden presentation of an unexpected irrele-

vant stimulus, such as a noise or light, because the animal orients to it. Such inhibition of conditioned responding by random external stimuli can be largely eliminated in the laboratory, where almost all external stimulation can be controlled.

Conditioned responding can also be inhibited by competing stimulation within the animal. Such internal inhibition may come from fatigue, drugs, a full bladder, being in heat, or other physiological or motivational states.

Higher-order conditioning. One of Pavlov's colleagues, Krylov, found that after a morphine injection had elicited nausea and vomiting, the mere sight of the needle about to be injected could also produce

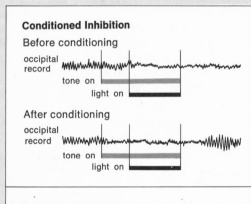

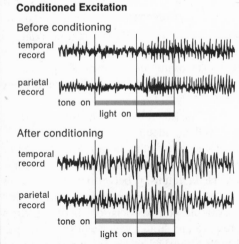

▲ **BRAIN WAVES DEMONSTRATE CONDITIONING**

Pavlov observed constant changes in behavior following the pairing of a neutral stimulus with one that Nature had already made effective. Correlated alterations in brain rhythms are now demonstrable, showing the neurological reality of the behavioral changes seen in conditioning.

1. *Conditioned Inhibition.* At the beginning of conditioning, there is an unconditioned *blocking* of the occipital EEG when a bright light is on, but the tone preceding the light does not change the EEG record; by the ninth trial, however, blocking of the response is apparent before the light is presented (Morrell & Ross, 1953).

2. *Conditioned Excitation.* At the beginning of conditioning in another study, a light stimulus brings an unconditioned *increase* in electrical activity in the temporal and parietal regions but a tone does not. After conditioning, the tone alone, prior to the onset of the light, evokes an increase in electrical activity (Yoshii & Hockaday, 1958).

vomiting—a typical conditioned response. But not only that: he found in addition that nausea came to be elicited by any stimulus regularly preceding the sight of the needle—alcohol on the skin, the box with the needle, eventually even the laboratory room. This process, by which each conditioned stimulus may, in turn, serve as a substitute for the original conditioned stimulus and itself produce the response, is called *higher-order conditioning*. Such chaining of conditioned stimuli, however, is effective only if the original, unconditioned response is strong, and even then it is necessary occasionally to include some trials with the original CS-US pairing.

Actually, it is difficult to establish conditioning beyond the second order ($CS_2 \rightarrow CS_1 \rightarrow US$), although an early study showed that as many as four orders of conditioning could be established in dogs: The first conditioned stimulus was a tone; then a light became a conditioned stimulus for the tone and was able to produce the response of paw-lifting. Next, a bell was made a conditioned stimulus for the light; finally, an electric fan was made a substitute for the light (Brogden & Culler, 1935).

Extinction. Since the actual connections between events in the environment change from time to time, it is vitally important that the connections established by conditioning also be temporary. Otherwise, we would not have the flexibility we need for responding appropriately to a changing environment. Once a conditioned stimulus no longer signaled either danger or a state beneficial to the organism, then continued response to it would be nonfunctional and perhaps harmful.

Fortunately for us, such nonfunctional responding eventually stops when presentation of the CS is regularly *not* followed by the US. The conditioned response becomes weaker and occurs more slowly in the absence of the US, until after repeated extinction trials (CS + *no* US), the conditioned response reaches zero intensity. It is then said to be *extinguished*.

That such extinction is a special case of the process of active inhibition (rather than actual loss of the learned response) is shown by the *spontaneous recovery* of the CR after a rest period following massed extinction training. Without any practice or relearning opportunity, the CR spontaneously recovers some

of its strength at the first presentation of the CS. Repeated extinction training, however, if carried on long enough and thoroughly enough, can permanently extinguish the CR. The typical sequence in respondent conditioning is shown in the upper section of the Special Transparency Insert following page 196.

Just as a novel stimulus will produce dishabituation of the orienting reflex, so, too, a novel stimulus presented after a CR has been extinguished may cause the CR to reappear temporarily. It is as if the novel stimulus released the inhibition that was suppressing the conditioned response. Razran (1939) showed, for example, that after the salivary response to a light flash was extinguished, a buzzer sounding just prior to the light flash reinstated salivation to the flash.

During extinction, a process takes place that is analogous to stimulus generalization during acquisition of a CR. Responses to stimuli not directly subjected to extinction training will also extinguish—in proportion to their similarity to the conditioned stimulus. This spread of inhibition is known as *generalization decrement*.

Strength of conditioning. The strength of conditioning must be inferred from some kind of observable, measurable behavior. Pavlov, as we have seen, used *amplitude* of response—quantity of saliva secreted—as his measure of response strength. Other measures sometimes used are *latency* of response—how much time elapses between the onset of the conditioned stimulus and the response—and *frequency*, or rate of emitting a given response.

Strength of learning can also be measured by *resistance to extinction*. The more trials required to extinguish a conditioned response, the stronger it is assumed to have been.

A Little Learning May Be a Dangerous Thing

From our description of the conditioning process, you have probably evolved a conception of animal behavior as guided by a set of rational principles designed to promote survival efficiently and effortlessly. Unfortunately for us animals, there are some complications in the machinery of conditioning which must be included in our story.

Schizokinesis. When the observed CR undergoes extinction in a conditioning experiment, other concomitant responses may not extinguish along with it but may function independently. Sometimes such responses lead to a permanent impairment in learning and a life-long disturbance in "personality."

For example, Liddell (1934), studying sheep, showed that leg flexion to a shock is accompanied by changes in breathing, cardiac rate, and general activity. All these changes continue in the conditioned response. More recently, Zeaman and Smith (1965) have found that when light and shock are paired in conditioning of the human cardiac response, a conditioning of breathing responses also occurs.

Thus the conditioned response may have many components. Whereas the automatic, unconditioned response to meat powder is salivation, the conditioned response is salivation plus other responses. Similarly the reflex withdrawal of the paw in response to electric shock may, in response to a light or tone, become paw withdrawal, cringing, yelping, anticipatory changes in heart rate and breathing, and perhaps generalized inhibition. The danger to the organism comes when the overt, specific conditioned response is extinguished (i.e., the saliva stops flowing or the withdrawal of a limb ceases in response to the conditioned stimulus), but the extra components of the response linger on, resisting extinction. Inappropriate general emotional components may be especially troublesome. As one psychologist has observed:

"The fact that conditional reflexes are so difficult to eradicate, once formed, makes the individual a museum of antiquities as he grows older. . . . He is encumbered with many reactions no longer useful or even . . . detrimental to life. This is especially true for the cardiovascular function, and it is these conditional reflexes that are most enduring. A person may be reacting to some old injury or situation which no longer exists, and he is usually unconscious of what it is that is causing an increase in heart rate or blood pressure. The result may be chronic hypertension. This may be the explanation of many cardiac deaths." (Gantt, 1966, p. 62)

Schizokinesis is the term coined by Gantt to refer to this dual reaction in which component reaction systems of a complex, conditioned response split and go their separate ways over the course of time. In many cases the individual shows no overt behavioral response to the stimulation, although it is having an effect upon him at a physiological level.

Such resistance to extinction of a once-significant signal stimulus which had become meaningless is demonstrated in a study of reactions to "the call to battle stations" (Edwards, 1962).

Hospitalized Army and Navy veterans who had seen active service during World War II were exposed to a series of twenty sound stimuli and their autonomic responses were measured by a recording of GSR changes. The biggest difference between men from the two services emerged when they heard a repetitive gong sounding at the rate of about 100 percussions a minute. This signal was used as a call to battle stations aboard U.S. Navy ships during the war, and it continued to elicit a strong autonomic response from the Navy veterans. Even though more than fifteen years had elapsed since this stimulus had signaled danger, the sailors showed a significantly more vigorous emotional response to it than did the soldiers—a difference obtainable by chance alone less than one time in a hundred ($p < .01$).

Experimental neurosis. Sometimes an extreme abnormal reaction pattern develops in experimental animals when the conditioning training places them under considerable stress. One of Pavlov's assistants first observed this reaction in a dog that had been conditioned to salivate in response to a circle projected on a screen. A discrimination was then established between the circle and an ellipse by a series of trials in which the circle was followed by food and the ellipse was not.

Next, the shape of the ellipse was changed by stages until it looked almost like a circle with one side slightly flattened. The dog continued to make appropriate discrimination, salivating only to the full circle, but when the point was reached where the two stimuli were almost interchangeable, the discrimination broke and got worse. Eventually, the animal could not even make the original simple discrimination. Even more dramatic were the accompanying behavioral changes. The formerly tranquil dog barked, squealed, tore at the apparatus, showed signs of fear of the room, and exhibited generalized inhibition leading to drowsiness and sleep. Similar reactions have been found in studies with rats (Cook, 1939), cats (Masserman, 1943), and sheep (Liddell, 1956).

This phenomenon has been called *experimental neurosis;* such an analogy to human neurotic symptoms (to be discussed in Chapter 14) seems justified by a comparison of the major characteristics of such behavior in animals with neurotic symptoms in man (Kimble, 1961). In both cases, behavior:

a) results from prolonged stress and inescapable conflict;

b) involves behavior indicative of anxiety;

c) is marked by symptoms which are unusual in the life of the animal and which provide only a partial solution to the conflict; and

d) persists without extinction for many years, unless special "counterconditioning" is provided.

Liddell (1956) reports symptoms enduring for thirteen or more years, as well as an increased incidence of premature deaths among sheep who were made experimentally neurotic. He relates one incident in which, when the experimenter returned after a year at another job, his 400-pound neurotic sow, Tiny, "by friendly overtures, lured him into a fence corner and attacked him so viciously that he required medical attention." (pp. 982–983)

The House That Pavlov Built

"American behavioral scientists have surely added wings to the house that Pavlov built, but really only wings; the main house continues to overtower and to stand firm, little worn by wind and weather." (Razran, 1961, p. 816)

From Pavlov's serendipitous discovery of conditioned salivation in dogs while investigating the physiology of digestion has developed an approach to the study of behavior which to this day dominates all branches of Soviet psychology. In America, too, many psychologists who study the learning process consider themselves to be neo-Pavlovians, as do many neurophysiologists who are trying to identify what happens in the brain during learning. For though Pavlov measured responses of the peripheral nervous system (salivation, leg flexion), his theoretical interest was in "higher nervous activity"—the cortical processes which he assumed must underlie the learning of conditioned responses.

In America, John B. Watson, the founder of the objective psychology *behaviorism*, went even further toward a psychology of stimulus-response connections and physiological events. He argued that behavior is composed *entirely* of glandular secretions and muscular movements and that these responses are determined by effective stimuli.

Thus for Watson the job of psychology was to identify and control the relationships between stimuli and these overt, observable responses. There was no point in studying conscious processes, mentalistic phenomena, or introspective accounts of the contents of the mind because they could not be observed objectively and perhaps had no part in the causal chain anyway. In any case, behavior could hopefully be explained and predicted without them, using only the objective "hard" data provided by such methods as conditioning.

The importance Watson placed on conditioning and environmental influences (CS-US pairings) in molding human behavior, in contrast to the then prevailing notions of inherited tendencies and instincts, is seen in his famous boast:

"Give me a dozen healthy infants, well-formed, and my own specified world to bring them up in and I'll guarantee to take any one at random and train him to become any type of specialist I might select—doctor, lawyer, artist, merchant-chief, and, yes, even beggar-man and thief, regardless of his talents, penchants, tendencies, vocations and race of his ancestors." (1926, p. 10)

The intervening years have brought convincing evidence that this is far too extreme a claim—that genetic structure as well as environmental conditions must be taken into account. As we shall see, too, evidence has accumulated that points to the need for studying cognitive factors in behavior. But even with these qualifications, the house that Pavlov built continues to be an impressive and much-lived-in edifice. (Ψ Close-up, p. 182)

The most important conclusion to be derived from all studies of respondent conditioning is that any stimulus which the organism can perceive can be used to elicit a conditioned response in any muscle or gland by appropriately pairing the CS and the US. Bykov's (1957) impressive survey of the extent to which internal organs can be classically conditioned might be summarized as: "if it wiggles or squirts naturally, it can be conditioned." These are very powerful statements since they have implications not

What does a lowly flatworm have to tell us about the principles of conditioning? Planaria are the highest form of animal life capable of regeneration after being cut up into as many as six pieces—each section becoming a new functioning organism. They move by a process of muscular contraction and respond to aversive stimulation by longitudinal contractions. Early learning experiments with these intriguing creatures (Thompson & McConnell, 1955) showed that they contract (UR) in response to an electric shock (US) and that this response can be conditioned to a light (CS).

The next question posed by McConnell and his coworkers was: If these "educated" planaria were cut in two and allowed to regenerate, would the learning be retained only by the animals with the conditioned heads, or would it also show up in those grown from conditioned tails? That is, does memory exist only in the brain section or in all parts of such an organism?

Half of a group of conditioned planaria were cut in two, while half remained with their own heads on their tails. A month later, when the split halves had regenerated and recovered from the surgery, all subjects were retested. The regenerated animals with the tail ancestors had retained as much as those with the head ancestors; furthermore, both groups of cut-ups had retained as much of the original learning as had the intact conditioned group. The experimental groups also showed faster relearning than did a control group which had not been conditioned but simply cut in half and allowed to regenerate. (McConnell, Jacobson, & Kimble, 1959)

How far could such findings be extended? What was the basis for such transfer of memory? It was possible, reasoned McConnell, that learning brought about a change in the RNA in the animals' body cells (see Ch. 3, p. 64). It so, would this altered RNA, if fed to uneducated planaria, make *them* superior learners? To test this hypothesis, RNA from the ground-up bodies of both conditioned and unconditioned planaria was fed to unconditioned planaria (McConnell, 1962). The results appeared to support the hypothesis of a transfer of

memory from a trained to an untrained generation of planaria. You can imagine the excitement such a discovery created in scientific circles, as well as among the students on the campus. Here at last was a use for old psychology professors: grind them up and feed them to the introductory psychology students!

Sad to note, however, was the fate of these provocative findings when subjected to critical scrutiny by independent investigators. Hartry, Keith-Lee, and Morton (1964) employed rigorous controls in evaluating alternative explanations of the basis for superior learning in unconditioned planaria who had cannibalized their previously conditioned brethren. Seven different treatments were used in the experiment. One group of planaria was conditioned and then fed to other planaria; another was conditioned but remained intact. Other groups were not conditioned but were exposed to certain elements involved in the conditioning procedure (shock, light, or simply being handled by experimenters) and then fed to cannibals. Two groups received no stimulation of any kind; one of these groups became cannibal fodder; the other remained intact. The procedures followed with each group are shown in the diagram.

The five groups of cannibals and the two groups which had remained intact were then tested, using a double-blind technique, to see how many trials it took for them to reach the criterion of learning reached by the original conditioned groups (twenty-three correct responses on twenty-five consecutive trials).

Experience made a difference. The unfed-inexperienced group (G) performed much worse than any other. However, the actual process of conditioning the victims did not appear to be the critical factor in enhancing the conditionability of the cannibals. If it were, Groups A and B should have shown the most savings (fastest reconditioning). Instead, Groups D (light only) and C (handling only) conditioned faster. It appears that the faster learning, where it occurred, was not a function of an earlier conditioned memory trace, but simply of stimulation or nutritional experience.

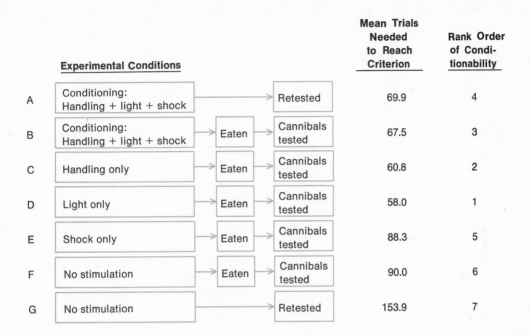

	Experimental Conditions			Mean Trials Needed to Reach Criterion	Rank Order of Condi- tionability
A	Conditioning: Handling + light + shock		Retested	69.9	4
B	Conditioning: Handling + light + shock	Eaten	Cannibals tested	67.5	3
C	Handling only	Eaten	Cannibals tested	60.8	2
D	Light only	Eaten	Cannibals tested	58.0	1
E	Shock only	Eaten	Cannibals tested	88.3	5
F	No stimulation	Eaten	Cannibals tested	90.0	6
G	No stimulation		Retested	153.9	7

If this revised conclusion is valid, then reconditioning in cannibals ought to be greater the more stimulation their "victims" have received—regardless of conditioning. This was demonstrated in a study by Walker and Milton (1966), in which rate of conditioning in cannibals was directly related to the amount of shock stimulation given to the planaria that they had devoured.

Finally, Jensen (1965), in a review of all studies on this subject, has shown that those studies which purport to have found transfer of learning in planaria suffer from serious methodological faults, while the best conducted studies yield negative results. The final demise for memory transfer in planaria was accomplished by Byrnes (1966) in a formal statement in *Science* magazine, endorsed by twenty-three research scientists: "In 18 experiments, no clear evidence of a transfer of any of these kinds of training from trained donors to recipients was found" (p. 58).

Thus the generalized enhancement of learning in cannibal planaria by means of prior "sensitization" of their victims can be defined as a change in the strength of responding due to a specific type of stimulus experience. It is considered to be a form of *pseudoconditioning* since there is a change as a result of experience but no actual learning of a new association.

Our extended discussion of the controversy stirred up by the seemingly trivial question of what makes a worm turn shows the importance of several of the characteristics of psychological science we mentioned in Chapter 2:
1. There is many a slip between the "discovery" and the "proof" of a psychological phenomenon.
2. It is the most interesting ideas which have the greatest implications and become subjected to the most severe tests of disbelief.
3. The system of checks and balances inherent in the exercise of the scientific method is a safeguard against false conclusions, but it must be policed by critical researchers who are willing to devote their efforts and talent to testing a conclusion independently before accepting it.
4. Even when the first explanation advanced for a "discovery" is proven untenable, the process of checking may yield other explanations which are of value.

only for stimulus detection and learning but for the social control of human behavior.

Conditioning Based on Consequences

Learning what events in the environment are predictably related to each other is not enough for adaptation and survival. Any organism, as we have seen, must also learn what consistent relationships can be expected between its own actions and subsequent events in the environment—in particular, what changes it can achieve or prevent.

Instrumental Learning— American Cats in Puzzle Boxes

At about the same time that Russian dogs were salivating or flexing their muscles to assorted stimuli, American cats were learning to work their way out of strange boxes. In order to get out of their solitary confinement (and get food), hungry cats had to discover how to operate a latch on each of a series of seven different "puzzle boxes." American psychologist E. L. Thorndike reported the results of this pioneering study of the behavioral (as contrasted with physiological) approach to learning in 1898:

"When put into the box the cat would show evident signs of discomfort and of an impulse to escape from confinement. It tries to squeeze through any opening; it claws and bites at the bars or wire; it thrusts its paws out through any opening and claws at everything it reaches; . . . It does not pay very much attention to the food outside [the reward for a hungry cat], but seems simply to strive instinctively to escape from confinement. The vigor with which it struggles is extraordinary. For eight or ten minutes it will claw and bite and squeeze incessantly. With 13, an old cat, and 11, an uncommonly sluggish cat, the behavior was different. They did not struggle vigorously or continually. On some occasions they did not even struggle at all. It was therefore necessary to let them out of the box a few times, feeding them each time. After they thus associated climbing out of the box with getting food, they will try to get out whenever put in. . . . Whether the impulse to struggle be due to an instinctive reaction to confinement or to an association, it is likely to succeed in letting the cat out of the box. The cat that is clawing all

over the box in her impulsive struggle will probably claw the string or loop or button so as to open the door. And gradually all the other non-successful impulses will be stamped out and the particular impulse leading to the successful act will be stamped in by the resulting pleasure, until, after many trials, the cat will, when put in the box, immediately claw the button or loop in a definite way." (p. 13) ◆

From observations such as these on "trial-and-error learning," Thorndike began the study of what came to be known as *instrumental conditioning*. His methods and his formulations became cornerstones in the American investigation of the learning process in man and lower animals.

Let us briefly analyze some of the characteristics of such learning as illustrated by these cats. In doing so, some of the major differences between classical and instrumental conditioning will become obvious. Then we will use this example to introduce other concepts which have evolved in the study of learning by various psychologists.

Mediating variables—drives, response hierarchies, and cues.   To explain the cats' behavior, Thorndike

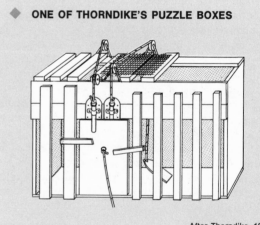

◆ **ONE OF THORNDIKE'S PUZZLE BOXES**

After Thorndike, 1898

Thorndike's cats were confined in boxes like this one and food was placed outside of the box. To get out, the animal had to loosen a bolt, bar, or loop in order to release a weight which would then pull the door open.

inferred unseen, inner processes which *mediated*—intervened between—the observable events. For example, he believed that his cats in the puzzle boxes were motivated by *drive states*—strong internal stimuli that impelled them to action by energizing their behavior. Their behavior he thus saw as *emitted* behavior—behavior caused by internal conditions rather than elicited by an external, identifiable stimulus.

Thorndike saw these inner drives as forcing a variety of responses from the individual—some innate and "wired in" according to the inherited nervous system of the species (meowing and hissing for cats, crying for human infants), others learned in previous experiences. The responses in the individual's repertoire, both innate and learned, could be arranged in a *response hierarchy* according to the probability that they would be made or according to the sequence in which they would be tried.

When a cat was first put in a puzzle box, it tried many of these available responses, but in the course of several trials most of them dropped out. Thorndike believed that although the responses were emitted in response to *internal* stimuli, the selection and narrowing down was guided by cues from *external* stimuli. Such external stimuli might help focus the subject's attention on the relevant parts of the environment (the latch or the food tray) or might serve as cues to indicate when a particular response was appropriate. For example, when a light was consistently on when food was available and off when it was not, the animal's behavior would come to be guided by the presence or absence of the light. Although its "hunger" was constant, it would learn to work for food only when the light was on, since correct responding would be followed by food only then.

Instrumental Behavior and the Law of Effect

Like Thorndike's cats, you encounter many situations in which what you do makes a difference. If a coke machine regularly fails to deliver a coke after you deposit a coin, you learn that coin-dropping in that situation has no effect on that machine. Your behavior does not change the environment. If you kick the machine and a cold coke appears and you quench your thirst, your behavior has had a consequence on the environment. Next time you are thirsty, you may go up to the coke machine and start kicking it. Kicking the machine has moved up in your response hierarchy. If that fails to produce a coke, you may learn that the behavior which is followed by the coke reinforcer is composed of two response units: first depositing the coin and then kicking the recalcitrant machine. On subsequent occasions you will repeat the response that has been instrumental in getting what you wanted.

If the latch had been dropped by means of a sound-activated relay when the puzzled cats meowed or hissed, or if mama cat had come and opened the door then, they would have learned that meowing or hissing was a way of making a change in their environment and would have continued to meow or hiss on later trials. But meowing and hissing were not followed by freedom or food; in fact, they had no effect on the environment at all.

Thorndike observed that of all the responses originally made, those with no effect on the environment became less probable—moved down in the response hierarchy. But when the cat made a successful motion—one that was instrumental in both letting her out of confinement and making the food available, that motion become more probable—moved up in the response hierarchy. What made the difference was the success in changing the environment and, according to Thorndike, the *feeling of satisfaction* in this accomplishment (another mediating variable).

Thorndike believed that connections between responses and successful environmental consequences (goal events or reinforcing states) were "stamped in" on successive trials. According to his *law of effect,*

"Any act which in a given situation produces satisfaction becomes associated with that situation, so that when the situation recurs, the act is more likely than ever before to recur also. Conversely, any act which in a given situation produces discomfort becomes disassociated from that situation, so that when the situation recurs, the act is less likely than before to recur." (1905, p. 202)

For a time, Thorndike also argued for a *law of exercise*—that repetition of a response would tend to stamp it in. He found, however, that sheer repetition

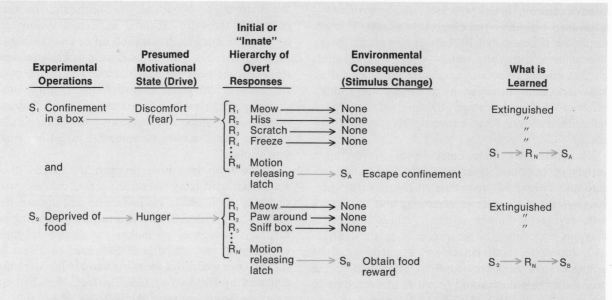

Experimental Operations	Presumed Motivational State (Drive)	Initial or "Innate" Hierarchy of Overt Responses	Environmental Consequences (Stimulus Change)	What is Learned
S₁ Confinement in a box	Discomfort (fear)	R₁ Meow ⟶ None		Extinguished
		R₂ Hiss ⟶ None		"
		R₃ Scratch ⟶ None		"
		R₄ Freeze ⟶ None		"
		⋮		S₁ ⟶ Rₙ ⟶ Sₐ
and		Rₙ Motion releasing latch ⟶ Sₐ Escape confinement		
S₂ Deprived of food	Hunger	R₁ Meow ⟶ None		Extinguished
		R₂ Paw around ⟶ None		"
		R₃ Sniff box ⟶ None		"
		⋮		
		Rₙ Motion releasing latch ⟶ S_B Obtain food reward		S₂ ⟶ Rₙ ⟶ S_B

■ **INSTRUMENTAL LEARNING: LETTING THE CAT OUT OF THE BOX**

In Thorndike's experimental situation two motives were assumed to be instigating action: fear and hunger. The same response leads to both release and food. But Thorndike never knew whether both motivational states were necessary or whether the cats might have worked equally hard to get out if they had been well fed. Research today is more likely to study the result of one experimental operation at a time.

of a response was *not* sufficient to strengthen the connection between the stimulus and the response, as a law of exercise would hold. Behavior must have an effect on the environment in order for it to move up in the resultant hierarchy of responding. If it does so, then repetition may facilitate the learning. ■

This utility value of responses in producing consequences is one of the major differences between classical conditioning and instrumental conditioning procedures. In classical conditioning, presentation of the unconditioned stimulus (whether pleasant, like food, or unpleasant, like electric shock) is unrelated to anything the individual does. Both its presentation and its temporal pairing with the conditioned stimulus are determined either by the environment (as with lightning and thunder) or arbitrarily by the experimenter. Thus the dog gets the food whether or not he salivates, and shock is turned on whether or not he lifts his paw. His behavior is not instrumental in the occurrence of either one. But what the cats

did was instrumental in getting them freedom and food and what you do is instrumental in getting you a coke or some other stimulus event you want.

Operant Learning

In the years since Thorndike's early study of consequence-controlled learning, research on such learning has become highly sophisticated. The puzzle boxes have become standardized "Skinner boxes" with electronic devices for dispensing consequences and recording the subject's responses, and the concepts, methods, and objectives of the research have undergone continuing refinement.

Emphasis on empirical operations. One strong move has been toward precision of concepts and, where possible, dependence on empirical referents rather than inferred inner states. For example, what did we really know about those cats of Thorndike's?

What could we *see?* Meowing and scratching, yes; inner drives, no. Higher rate of occurrence of the successful response, yes; satisfaction, no. Cessation of the ineffective responses, yes; "stamping in" or "stamping out," no. In fact, if you conceptualize learning as a "stamping in" of connections, you may spend years looking for the wrong thing in the wrong place if what happens in learning is in fact quite different. Psychologists are much more aware today of the need to make their concepts precise and explicit and closely related to what *can* be observed.

Some psychologists hold that a learning situation can and should be described *entirely* in terms of empirically observable and directly manipulable operations—that nothing need be said about what is happening within the organism. For example, they define hunger not by an inference about drives but by the operation of withholding food for a certain number of hours before the trial. One cat deprived of food for forty-eight hours is then by definition as "hungry" as another similarly treated. In Chapter 1 we discussed the utility of such operational definitions.

Consequences, too, can be defined empirically. A *reinforcer* (or *reinforcing stimulus*) is defined as any stimulus that follows a response and increases the probability of its occurrence. If getting food as a result of opening a latch makes the latch-opening response more probable next time, then getting food is a reinforcer.

These definitions are empirical rather than conceptual. Hunger is hours of deprivation. A reinforcer is something that has made a response more probable. In this framework, instead of saying that hunger *motivated* the animal to work for the food, it is said that food deprivation made food a more effective reinforcer, as gauged by more rapid responding. Deprivation, amount and type of food, and rate of response are all overt, observable, measurable events. It is easy to change one and see what effect that has on another. Much of the ongoing learning research has limited itself to such directly observable operations.

Studying operants. Getting out of the puzzle box (or getting a coke) is an act which occurs once and then stops, at least for the time being—until you get

thirsty again or are put back in a puzzle box. Much of the recent learning research has been carried out not with such discrete, single-unit acts but with *operants*—responses which keep occurring at a given rate as long as you are in a particular situation—like blinking during a conversation. They too are *emitted* responses (not elicited by particular external stimuli) and they too are responsive to pleasant or unpleasant consequences although they occur at some discoverable rate even without consequences. When operants are studied, it is the *rate* of response that is measured rather than whether or not the response occurs. In general, they are simpler bits of behavior than opening a latch and easier to record.

The operant level.   The rate at which a freely available response occurs when its consequences are neither positive nor negative is called the operant level of that response. Other examples of operants are heart-beat rate when relaxed, or swallowing while reading. Each would have a *base-level rate of emission* for a given individual.

Operant strengthening—increasing the rate of responding.   Starting from the operant level, the rate at which the response is made can be increased if it is paired with certain stimulus consequences—suitable reinforcers. The measure of learning, or *acquisition*, as many prefer to call it, is the change in rate of responding from the original operant level to a higher, equally stable level. For example, pigeons have a relatively high operant level of pecking. If made hungry and put into an apparatus in which a peck against a disk on the wall activates a food dispenser, the pigeon will increase its rate of pecking at the disk.

Response rate is conveniently recorded on an apparatus called a *cumulative recorder*. A strip of paper moves past a recording pen at a constant speed. The pen is electrically activated so that it steps upward a short, uniform distance each time the subject makes a response and then continues to move along at *that* level until another response pushes it higher. (If it gets to the top of the paper, it returns to the bottom and starts again.) ◆   (p. 188)

In our pigeon example, each disk-peck is immediately followed by a food pellet (a reinforcer for a hungry bird); it also simultaneously moves the cumulative recorder pen up a notch. The more responses made in a given time period, the more accumulated upward steps of the recording pen there will be over the width of the paper that has moved by the pen during that interval. A high rate of responding gives a steep cumulative curve; a low rate of responding gives a less steep one.

It is thus possible to look at the *topography* (shape) of a cumulative curve and see how the rate of responding has changed during the course of learning. Typically in a new situation the curve goes up very slowly and irregularly at first and there may be long pauses between responses; during these pauses, the recording pen simply moves horizontally along the paper. Then, as learning proceeds, the cumulative curve shows less variability and becomes steeper. A skilled researcher can read a subject's response curve much like an X-ray plate, to find out the behavioral effects of different histories of reinforcement.

Operant extinction.   If the electrical relay which activates the food dispenser is disconnected, then responding no longer has any "payoff," and the pigeon soon stops his rapid responding. Conditioned operants which are unreinforced will decline in strength until they are at or below their original operant level and

◆   DIAGRAM OF A CUMULATIVE RECORDER

response record   time record

will again show variability in their topography. These changes are the process of *operant extinction.*

Stimulus control.   Operant responses are regarded as emitted by the organism rather than elicited by any identifiable stimuli, as we have seen, and the crucial relationship in operant conditioning is between the response and its consequences—the stimuli that follow it and are produced by it. Preceding stimuli may play a role too, however, in signalling whether reinforcement will be forthcoming if a response is made. Thus a pigeon will learn to peck a disk only when a green light is on if the green light is made a consistent predictor of food. This means that even though they cannot get at the inner stimuli that supposedly lead to the emission of the response, researchers can control its occurrence by providing a dependable signal that a reinforcer is available. Such a control of the occurrence of the response is called *stimulus control.* It is assumed that respondent conditioning is being superimposed on the operant conditioning. The reinforcing, consequence stimulus (food) is the unconditioned stimulus and the preceding, signal stimulus (green light) becomes the conditioned stimulus.

Positive and negative reinforcement.   Thorndike's cats got two kinds of reinforcement—something they wanted (food) and escape from something aversive (being shut up in the box). Food is called a *positive reinforcer*, and escape from confinement is called a *negative reinforcer*—the removal of an aversive state. Operant researchers generally prefer to use positive reinforcers delivered according to some prearranged schedule. However, conditioning is also studied in situations where correct responding to an aversive stimulus results in not receiving any of it (avoidance) or only some of it (escape). If the organism can prevent contact by the correct response, the procedure is called *avoidance conditioning.* If he is exposed to it but can terminate it by the correct response, it is called *escape conditioning.*

You can't reinforce a response in its absence.   Let us assume that you are a benevolent parent, teacher, or trainer of men or beasts, and you have a pocketful of reinforcements you want to dispense—if only the individual will make the correct response. What procedures can you use to elicit the first correct response, so that it can be reinforced and thus can be made to recur more frequently? This is a problem Pavlov never had because he was studying responses that could always be produced by careful presentation of the proper eliciting stimulus.

This is a crucial and basic problem in learning, to which all too little systematic attention has been given, and all we will do here is outline and briefly comment upon the possible effectiveness of alternative approaches. Some of the means of getting the individual to make that first correct response so you can reinforce it are: (a) increasing motivation; (b) lowering restraints; (c) structuring the environment; (d) forcing; (e) providing a model; (f) giving instructions; (g) trial and error; and (h) successive approximation or shaping. Each of these techniques has certain advantages and disadvantages, depending on whether only immediate results or more permanent, long-term ones are desired. Because some of the consequences of applying these techniques are unintentionally negative, especially in the long run, we must be judicious in deciding which fits the particular learning situation best.

Increasing motivation. Prodding the organism into responding and emitting many responses increases the probability that one of them will be the correct one. Electrifying a grid will get the rat moving about, and in the process he may discover an escape route. Here necessity is the mother of invention. Threats and promises of future reward (called "incentive motivation") as well as deprivation states or noxious stimulation all may be successfully used to motivate action. There are, however, a number of potentially bad effects such motivators may have on the learning process.

Raising the level of motivation is not recommended if the individual does not have the response in his repertoire or does not have the ability to make it. For example, the mother who "won't love baby any more if baby soils his little diapers" will have no effect on changing the bowel movements if the child does not have sphincter muscle control yet. She may, however, produce both feelings of inferiority and a long-lasting resentment in her child. Such a procedure can also lead to conflict if there is strong competing motiva-

tion. Finally, if the individual makes the response only because of the *extrinsic motivation* provided by avoidance of pain or anticipation of reward (perhaps a gold star or a dessert), he will be less likely to learn to value the task activity itself (studying or eating spinach).

Lowering restraints. If the organism has already learned the skills involved in making the correct response, but does not emit it under motivating conditions, it may well be that the response is being inhibited or suppressed. Previously learned habits may be incompatible with emitting the desired response. The shy student who knows the answer will not ever get reinforced for it unless he raises his hand and says it out loud, but this he cannot do because he has learned that it is very painful to him to talk in class. Many males cannot express "tender" responses such as love or grief because prior learning has defined them as "unmasculine" responses. To get soldiers to kill, or medical students to start to cut up a cadaver, techniques are used to lower learned restraints against such "antisocial" behavior. Discovering what are the competing motives and weakening them, or finding out what reinforcers are maintaining the inhibitions on behavior and removing them, may help to induce the desired response. On the negative side, whatever is inhibiting the behavior in question may also be holding in check other behaviors which you would *not* want to be released, as we shall see in Chapter 13.

Structuring the environment. Suppose you want two competitive children to learn to cooperate with each other. One way to encourage this type of responding is to place them in an area containing toys which can be manipulated only by two or more children. If you want an animal to learn to press a bar, peck a key, open a latch, go through an escape hatch, or even consume an available reward, you can make the behavior more likely by removing distracting, irrelevant stimuli, simplifying the environment, making the *manipulandum* (bar, key, etc.) stand out more than other features of the environment. The change from Thorndike's relatively complicated puzzle box to the simplicity of the Skinner box (p. 37) is an illustration of making the desired response more likely by structuring the environment to remove most other possibilities. Of course, learning to survive in only a relatively simple environment may leave the organism overwhelmed by the stimulus variety if it encounters a complex environment (as when the country mouse goes to the city).

Forcing. Often the most efficient method of getting out that first correct response is to assist its execution physically. You take the child's hand with the spoonful of unfamiliar food and direct it into his mouth. Then you reinforce his putting the food in his mouth (and hopefully swallowing it) with praise or whatever. To teach a dog to roll over, trainers first provide a verbal cue, then physically roll the dog over and praise or feed him each time until he "catches on."

This rapid response elicitation technique probably has the worst long-term consequences for human learners, especially if they are involuntary or unwilling participants or if the individual using the technique is inept. Imagine how our shy student would feel toward the teacher who forced the response of answering in class by picking up his hand. Regardless of the size of the subsequent reinforcement for the response, this crude type of forcing would likely develop negative emotional responses toward the coercive agent of reinforcement, inculcate a sense of personal inadequacy, or lead the subject to make the correct response by rote without ever understanding the underlying principle.

Imitation of model. "Répétez, s'il vous plaît" says the French teacher, and the student attempts to imitate what she has said—both the content and manner of delivery. Observational learning is also valuable where the details of a complex motor task cannot be easily communicated in words—as, for example, tying one's shoelaces, or hitting a baseball. We discussed this kind of learning in the preceding chapter; it is evidently important in the social learning of both animals and man. On the other hand, overdependence on models (who usually are "authority figures") may limit the individual's own initiative, making him a conformist; it may also lead him to "pick up" a host of other responses made by the model. These may be responses correlated with the desired one, such as parents' speech habits, dialects, and so on, learned

along with the language. Or they may be unrelated responses that just happen to be emitted with high frequency by the model, such as statements of prejudice against minority groups.

Verbal instruction. "Do what I say, not what I do," distinguishes this approach from the previous one. The ability to use language can clearly facilitate some kinds of learning and can greatly accelerate elicitation of the first correct response. In fact, verbal instructions can be used not only to outline how the response should be made, but also to provide a description of the happy consequences that such responding will bring. Complex sequences may be communicated, as well as abstract principles, information regarding delay of response, ways of using past learning, and instructions for the future.

Naturally, following verbal instructions presupposes understanding them, which is not always the case, as parents will testify who have tried in frustrating desperation to assemble a child's toy from the "easy-to-follow directions." Ambiguity in language usage, implied reliance upon a set of concepts or skills, and the occasional difference between what is said and what is actually meant all may reduce the effectiveness of verbal instruction for many potential learners. On the other hand, overly explicit instructions can lead in the long run to a learned dependence on being told exactly what to do and how to do it—along with a loss of intellectual curiosity and a fear of taking risks.

Trial and error. This "sink or swim," survival-of-the-fittest method is peculiar in a number of ways. It is one of the least effective techniques for getting out that first correct response (in the absence of any other techniques), but it may have the most desirable long-term consequences when it works. It is a decidedly undemocratic, elitist approach, however, where many are called, but only a few are reinforced. For those who try and do succeed, the relative subjective reinforcement is greater when viewed in the perspective of all those who did not succeed. In addition, what is reinforced is not only the correct response, but the entire process of searching for a solution. In contrast, for the many whose trials end only in more errors, reinforcement for correct responding never

▲ These photographs illustrate how a meek laboratory rat, "Hercules," was transformed into a brute weight-lifter capable of lifting as much as twice his own weight. First, any response of the hungry rat directed toward the food cup was followed by a loud click, a light on the food cup, and a pellet of food. Once he had become familiar with the feeding mechanism, he was rewarded only for movements of his body toward the bar, then only when he touched it, and then only when he pulled it down. Once this stage was completed, the effort required to depress the bar was gradually increased by the addition of small weights to the mechanism at the other end of it. By carefully spacing out the reinforcements and stepping up the weights systematically, the 250-gram rat became capable of lifting 515 grams of weight after only a few hours. In like manner, pigeons can be trained to play Ping-Pong or to bowl.

comes, and the effort and curiosity involved in the behavior are likely to undergo experimental extinction. The vast wastefulness of overreliance on such a general approach is evident in the failure of about half of all graduate students (who are bright and motivated) to complete the trial-and-error procedure of the doctoral dissertation.

Successive approximation or shaping. How would you get a pigeon to play Ping-Pong, or a rat to lift more than his body weight?

For many behaviors which are complex and unlikely to occur in perfect form on the first trial, the criterion for reinforcement must be lowered. At the beginning, the "correct" response is any overt response which is an approximation of (bears some resemblance to) the final behavior desired or of one step in a desired sequence. Then, on successive trials, the response must be progressively more like the response wanted in order to earn reinforcement. Finally, these partial behaviors get shaped into the whole complex sequence. By the end of training, only the sequence is followed by reinforcement.   ▲

If done subtly, shaping can elicit the desired behavior without the individual's awareness that he is being conditioned. However, shaping can be a very time-consuming procedure, requiring much skill and patience on the part of the reinforcer. For many behaviors, some of the other techniques we have discussed would elicit the correct terminal response more rapidly and effortlessly. For example, if you had a human subject and wanted him to turn a page, it would be far simpler to say "Turn the page now" than to try, through reinforcement of *successive approximations*, to shape all the actions involved in page turning.

This discussion should make it obvious that in any learning situation, the "teacher" (used in the broadest sense) should not only be aware of the various possible techniques but seriously consider both their immediate results and their possible long-term consequences.

The Three Basic Terms in Associative Learning

The three basic elements in studies of associative learning have been: (a) stimuli preceding the response, (b) the response, and (c) stimuli following the response. The stimuli that "lead to" a behavioral event, whether they elicit it or simply signal that reinforcement is available, are called *discriminative stimuli*, abbreviated as S^D (pronounced "ess dee"). Stimuli which "follow from" a behavioral event are denoted as *environmental consequence stimuli*, abbreviated as S^C. The *behavioral event* is designated as R, though in some cases it will be an elicited respondent and in other cases an emitted response. These elements may be arranged diagrammatically as shown:

The most essential comparisons between respondent and operant conditioning can be made in terms of which of these elements are studied and what relations are postulated between them. In addition, starting from this simple model, we can elaborate many basic behavioral principles.

Respondent conditioning has been concerned with the first two terms, the S^D and the R. In this case the R is a *respondent*, an elicited response, and the S^D *elicits* it. In the case of an unconditioned reflex, the correlation between them is nearly perfect: the pupil contracts (R) virtually every time bright light (S^D) shines into it. Respondent conditioning demonstrates that another S^D, after repeated pairings with such an unconditioned S^D, can also become correlated with the response—a dependable predictor of it. These relationships can be visualized as shown below:

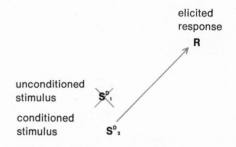

In operant conditioning, the basic relationship is between the R and the S^C. Here the R is an emitted response and the S^C is the *reinforcing stimulus* that follows it. The preceeding stimulus does not cause the response. Thus the relationships in operant conditioning can be visualized as follows:

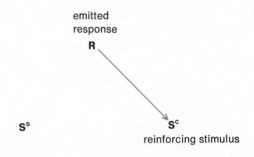

Actually, as we have seen, S^D may also come to play a role in operant conditioning—but through a connection established with S^C, not through influencing R directly. The basic relationship in operant conditioning is between the response and environmental consequence.

The rest of this section will be devoted to a more detailed study of each of the three basic terms—the *discriminative stimulus*, the *response*, and the *consequence stimuli*—and the various possible relationships among them.

The Discriminative Stimulus (S^D)

The discriminative stimulus is the signal stimulus that precedes the response. In the case of reflexes—conditioned or unconditioned—it is seen as *eliciting* the response, as we have seen. In the case of operant, instrumental, consequence-related behaviors, it is seen not as eliciting the response directly but as helping to control its occurrence by signaling that a reinforcer is imminent or available.

Stimulus generalization. When a response to some portion of the environment has been strengthened by reinforcement, the response will also be given, in somewhat weaker form, to other similar stimuli and related environments. We saw this in the case of little Albert, who showed fear not only of the rat but also of a dog, a fur coat, and even a Santa Claus mask. Since no two situations are ever identical, this principle of *stimulus generalization* is important in understanding how and when learning gets *transferred* from one situation to another.

The functional relationship between stimulus similarity and response strength is expressed as the *gradient of generalization*. Response strength *decreases* in proportion to the dissimilarity between the present stimulus environment and the original reinforcing environment.

This gradient provides a "response code" by which the subject tells us whether he is perceiving differences between stimuli and how clearly he distinguishes between them.

Can a bird let us know whether it sees the difference between green and blue or between blue and violet? Guttman and Kalish (1956) provided a means for the bird to transmit this information.

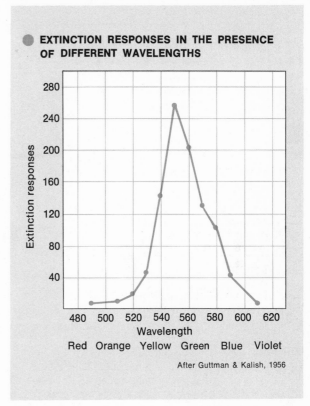

EXTINCTION RESPONSES IN THE PRESENCE OF DIFFERENT WAVELENGTHS

After Guttman & Kalish, 1956

Pigeons were taught by an operant strengthening procedure to peck at a disk light with a wavelength of 550 millimicrons (yellow-green). Then, when the response was firmly established, reinforcement was stopped and the bird's continuing rate of response during extinction to the original wavelength and ten others was measured. These varied from 490 millimicrons (red) to 610 millimicrons (blue-violet) and were presented in randomized order for 30 seconds each.

By comparing the number of responses made to the originally conditioned stimulus with those made to the other wavelengths, we can determine whether pigeons can discriminate between these colors. The gradient of generalization shown in the graph reveals that as the stimuli become more different from the original discriminative stimulus, response strength decreases.

Actually this graph tells us that pigeons are extremely sensitive *wavelength analyzers* rather than that they are good *color detectors* since it shows us what physical properties they can distinguish but not what colors or hues they are actually perceiving.

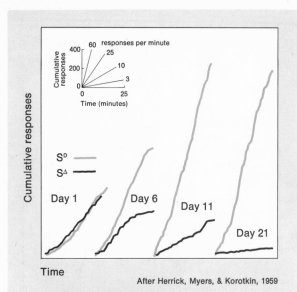

After Herrick, Myers, & Korotkin, 1959

▲ **SAMPLE RECORDS DURING DISCRIMINATION TRAINING**

At the beginning of discrimination training responses to S^D and S^Δ were virtually identical. As training proceeded, the curve showing responses to S^D became more vertical, indicating a faster and faster rate of responding. On the other hand, responses to S^Δ became fewer and fewer, as shown by the increasingly horizontal line on successive days.

discriminative stimulus (S^D), and the other one becomes the *negative discriminative stimulus* ($S^Δ$, pronounced "ess delta"). After repeated discrimination training, S^D and $S^Δ$ have very different effects on behavior. ▲ For example, on Day 1, this subject (a monkey) was insensitive to the differences between the two stimuli, emitting the same rate of responding to each. Over time, it formed the discrimination between S^D and $S^Δ$. By Day 21, $S^Δ$ produced almost no responding, while S^D set the occasion for a high rate of responding (Herrick, Myers, & Korotkin, 1959).

Jump, Rat, Jump!

Animals, like people, can learn a double discrimination involving two responses and two stimulus conditions. Lashley's jumping stand was used to demonstrate the formation of such a discrimination. The hungry rat must learn to jump to a particular card (with, say, a square on it), and not to jump to a different card (with, say, a triangle on it). Jumping to the correct S^D card opens a hinged window and the rat lands in a bowl of delicious mash. But the window behind the $S^Δ$ card is locked, so jumping to it results in the rat's falling into a net below. The location of the S^D card is varied over trials, to make sure that the rat is learning to jump to a particu-

Stimulus discrimination.   If generalization is similar responding in different situations, then its opposite process is differential responding in similar situations. Human beings are remarkable in the extent to which they can make accurate discriminations between virtually identical stimuli. In fact, some, like gourmets and art experts, organize much of their lives around this ability. We may think that such people are "born with" their powers of discrimination, but it is possible to demonstrate that even complex discriminations from simple conditioned discriminations grow.

The basic operation for the *formation of a discrimination* involves differential reinforcement of the same operant response under differing conditions. Whenever one stimulus is (or has just been) present, the response is reinforced. When another stimulus is (or has just been) present, response brings no reinforcement. The first stimulus then becomes the *positive*

◆ One of the original Lashley jumping stands in use.

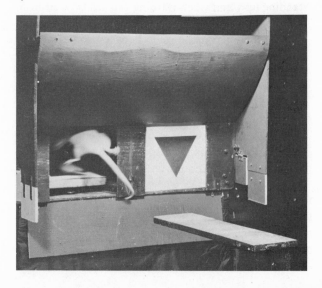

lar card and not always to the left or always to the right. ◆

Animals can be trained to match a given stimulus (a color, pattern, shape, or other dimensions) to a corresponding stimulus among a set of two or more stimuli. In this *matching-to-sample* procedure, the subject may be required to choose the item that is *similar* to a sample or the item that is *different* from the others. ▪

To Err May Be Human, But . . .

Terrace (1963) has developed a technique for discrimination training in which subjects never make an error, even during the initial stages. What he did was to establish a red-green discrimination in pigeons (an easy discrimination for them to learn) and then superimpose horizontal lines on the red and vertical lines on the green (or the other way around). By fading the red and green gradually until only the horizontal and vertical lines were left, the subjects were able to learn the horizontal-vertical discrimination without making any mistakes.

Terrace's discovery is important for two reasons: (a) learning achieved in this way without errors is more stable later on, and, even more important, (b) it has provided a technique for teaching discriminations formerly thought to be impossible. For example, mental retardates have been taught perceptual discriminations that had seemed to be beyond their capabilities (Sidman & Stoddard, 1969).

I've Got S^D-S^Δ Under My Skin

Although psychologists have extensively studied the effects of external or *exteroceptive* stimuli, little research until recently has been directed toward analysis of internal or *interoceptive* stimuli as signals for our behavior. But discriminating correctly among internal stimuli may be as important as discriminating correctly among outer ones.

Learning to discriminate internal cues is difficult unless: (a) they produce sizable enough effects to be recognizable by the individual and (b) differential reinforcement can be applied in their presence and absence. In studying the formation of such discriminations, it is thus necessary to employ special tech-

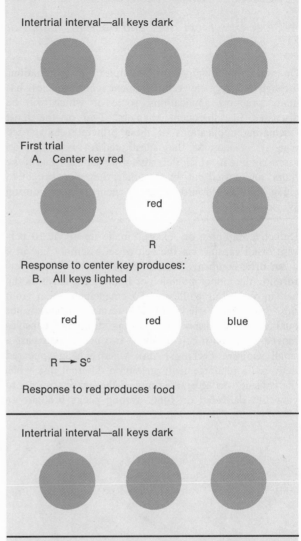

After Cumming & Berryman, 1961

▪ MATCHING PROCEDURE

All three keys were wired so that they could be illuminated with red, green, or blue, and pigeons were trained to peck at any key lighted by any one of the three colors. On the matching trials, the center key lighted up and as soon as the pigeon pecked it, the other two keys lighted up also, one matching the center disk and the other not. If the pigeon pecked at the matching one, the lights went off and food was delivered; if it pecked at the center disk again, nothing happened; if it pecked at the key on nonmatching side, all the lights went out and no food was delivered.

Ψ *Close-up*   *From Hunt and Peck to Search and Destroy*

Operant conditioning of complex discriminations through appropriate reinforcement contingencies has many practical applications, some of which will be discussed in subsequent chapters. Two of the most fascinating applications of these principles have used pigeons: in one case, they substituted for women on an assembly line in which defective drug capsules had to be found and sorted out; in the other, they were taught to guide missiles toward selected enemy targets during World War II.

Defective capsules, or "skags," made up about 10 percent of all capsules on the belt of an assembly line in a given drug company. Women employees had been performing the monotonous job of hunting for skags as the belt moved along endlessly. To emancipate them from this drudgery, Verhave (1966) trained pigeons to be quality-control inspectors. During training, capsules moved along on a belt at about two per second past a small window. Pecking a disk when a skag appeared delivered a reinforcement; pressing a different disk when the capsule was acceptable moved the next capsule into view but delivered no food. Wrong pecks brought no

food and a thirty-second blackout. Within one week of daily discrimination training, the birds had become capable of taking over on the inspection line with 99 percent accuracy.

During World War II, B. F. Skinner reasoned that if pigeons could learn to vary their responses continuously according to the demands of a constantly changing stimulus situation, then they could be put in nose cones of missiles to guide them in searching out and destroying selected targets. The feasibility of such a scheme was demonstrated by Skinner as part of Project Orcon (ORganic CONtrol). During the discrimination training reinforcement was made contingent upon pecking only at the center of a target (in the form of an enemy ship) which appeared on a screen. When a gold electrode on the pigeon's beak touched the screen, an electronic circuit in the missile sensed the exact location of pecks on the screen. The missile was held on course when pecking was in the center of the screen, but changed its course depending upon any other location of the pecks. Shown here are some frames of a patriotic bird's-eye view of a target about to be destroyed (Skinner, 1960).

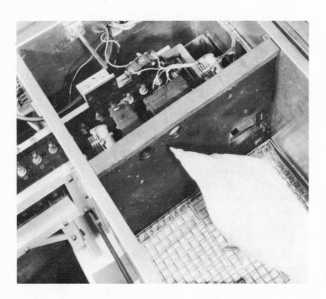

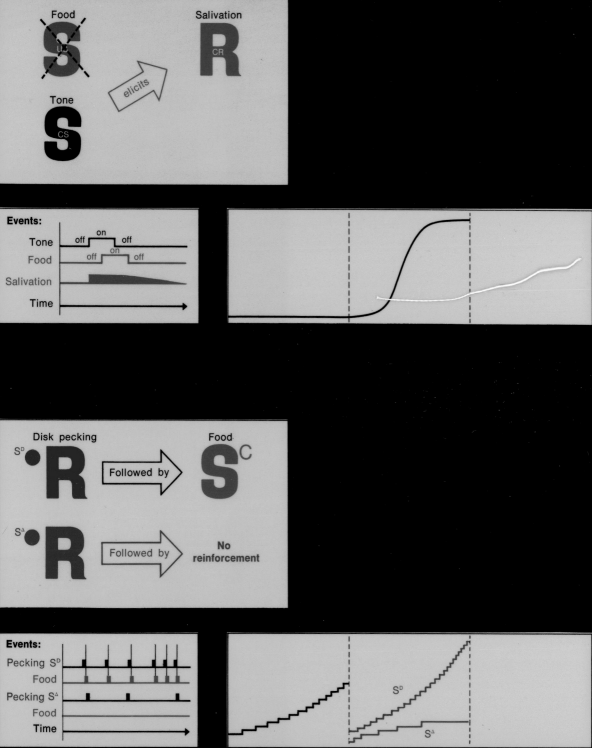

Tone
S CS

elicits

Food
S US

Salivation
R CR

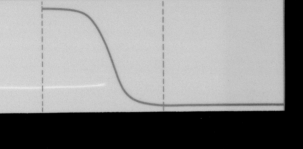

Events:

Tone   off ⌐ on ⌐ off
Food   off ⌐ on ⌐ off
Salivation
Time →

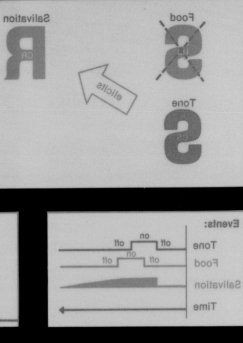

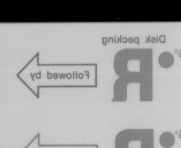

Disk pecking
R S^D

Followed by

Food
S^C

Disk pecking
R S^Δ

Followed by

No reinforcement

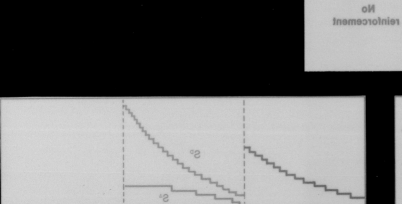

Events:

Pecking S^D
Food
Pecking S^Δ
Food
Time →

S^D
S^Δ

Respondent (classical) conditioning

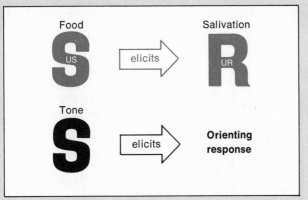

1 *Before conditioning.* A tone is sounded, eliciting an orienting response. Food is presented, eliciting salivation. Tone has no effect on salivation initially.

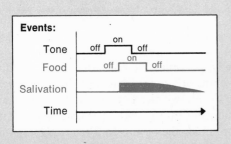

Operant conditioning

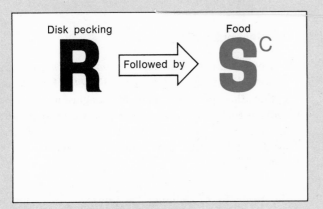

1 *Operant strengthening.* When the reinforcement (food) follows the response of pecking a disk, the rate of responding increases.

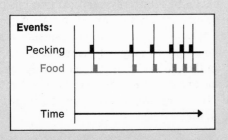

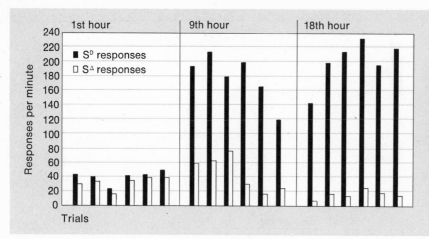

1st hour   9th hour   18th hour

Responses per minute

■ S^D responses
□ S^Δ responses

Trials

▲ **DISCRIMINATION OF INTERNAL STIMULI**

These sample comparisons show the development of an interoceptive discrimination in a rhesus monkey. Initially, responding to S^D (presence of visceral stimulation) and to S^Δ (absence of such stimulation) was indiscriminate. By the eighteenth hour of training with differential reinforcement, lever pressing was clearly under the control of S^D.

After Slucki, Adam, & Porter, 1965

niques to get "under the subject's skin." The internal cues may need to be amplified, their occurrence must be monitored by a reinforcement dispenser, and responses made in the presence of the discriminative stimulus must be immediately reinforced. Under these conditions, it can be clearly demonstrated that there is no essential difference in the laws of learning governing exteroceptive and interoceptive conditioning.

Such an approach has successfully demonstrated that rhesus monkeys can learn an operant discrimination between the presence and absence of intestinal stimuli. The discriminative stimulus was mechanical stimulation applied to the internal wall of the small intestine. A small balloon inserted in the intestine was inflated and deflated by the experimenter to provide the S^D–S^Δ discrimination. After operant bar pressing for food reinforcement had been established, operant discrimination training followed. Bar presses were reinforced only if they occurred in the presence of the internal stimulation (provided by inflating the balloon). In less than a day's worth of training, the subjects made many more responses when the balloon was inflated (S^D) than when it was deflated (S^Δ). The figure is a record of the progressive formation of this discrimination by one monkey, Eva. ▲

Discrimination reversal training was begun, in which the S^D–S^Δ contingencies were reversed—reinforcement followed responding only when the intestine was *not* stimulated. Responding shifted appropriately, being emitted primarily in the presence of the new S^D (Slucki, Adam, & Porter, 1965).

In this study, providing the nonverbal subjects with the overt operant of bar pressing gave them in effect a "language" with which they could communicate to the experimenter in a precise, if simple way, what was going on under their skin. In a later chapter we shall see that the poor discrimination training we get from our verbal training community (parents, teachers, peers, and so on) may make us as poor judges of what is going on inside of ourselves as of what others are feeling (Bem, 1970).

The Response (R)

It is often claimed that *"any response which can be reinforced quickly can be conditioned."* Before accepting this powerful general conclusion, derived from instrumental learning research, we must inquire first into just what constitutes a *reinforceable response*, and, in the next section, into what can be *reinforcing*.

The problem of defining "response."   Behavior is continuous but can be arbitrarily analyzed into bits of varying size. Some of these bits of behavior are referred to as *movements;* they are component parts of larger bits and may or may not themselves have a direct effect on the environment. Larger, chunk-sized bits of behavior are called *acts* and do have a direct consequence on the environment or on the individual's relation to it.

Beyond the level of an efferent nerve impulse, there is thus no such thing as a *single response.* Even a muscle twitch is composed of many response components. Therefore, what we call a "response" refers actually to an integrated unit or collection of responses—some arbitrarily defined segment of ongoing behavior. The size of the unit designated as a response can vary widely. An operant response could be 100 key presses which, as a unit, produce reinforcement, or going to college for four years to get one degree of reinforcement.

The issue of what a response is goes beyond questioning the size or unity of a response. Are there any responses other than overt behaviors that are reinforceable? Is a thought such a response? What about attitudes (often defined as predispositions to respond)? When you hold someone's *attention* with your good looks or witty remarks, what exactly are you holding? When you learned to talk, did you learn only particular verbal utterances that were reinforced, or did you learn broad classes of covert responses of "linguistic understanding and competence"?

When a student learns how to "psych out" his professor, he may be learning more than to anticipate what will be put on a test. He may be learning *how to learn*—in this case, how to deal with the kinds of materials and problems the professor provides. Ideally, what is learned in the process of schooling should be not rote matching of particular responses to particular stimulus questions, but ways of thinking about issues and effective approaches to a wide range of problems. Harlow (1949) has used the term *learning set* (or L-set) for what is learned when individuals acquire the ability to solve any of a class of related discrimination problems in the same way even when the particular elements have not been encountered before. ◆ Much more research is needed on the learning of principles and generalizations, which represents such an important part of the human learning sought through schooling.

New responses from old: behavioral chaining. You have undoubtedly seen trained animals on TV performing remarkable feats in which only the last response was followed by the carrot, sugar cube, or fish tidbit. An experimental demonstration of the procedure involved in producing such smart animals

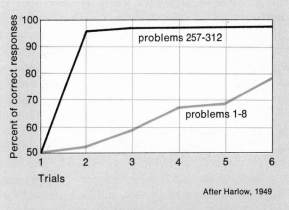

After Harlow, 1949

◆ **THE ESTABLISHMENT OF LEARNING SETS**
Once subjects learned to expect food consistently under one of two geometric forms, they responded to new pairs of forms with 98 percent accuracy.

would show that the key ingredient is the patience and operant conditioning skill of the trainer.

Pierrel and Sherman (1963) were able to turn a rather commonplace little rat, "Barnabus," into an exotic performer, just as Professor Higgins did with his street waif in *My Fair Lady.* Barnabus learned to:

  a) climb a spiral staircase,
  b) cross a narrow drawbridge,
  c) ascend a ladder,
  d) pull a toy car over by a chain,
  e) jump into the car,
  f) pedal it to a second ladder,
  g) climb this ladder,
  h) crawl through a tube,
  i) board an elevator,
  j) pull a chain which raised a flag and which lowered him back to the starting platform, where he could
  k) press a lever delivering a tiny food pellet and, after eating the food,
  l) climb the spiral staircase . . .

To teach Barnabus to go through this remarkable sequence, the experimenters started not at the beginning of it but at the end. First Barnabus learned to press the lever to get food pellets. Next, they put him in the elevator, which, when lowered, gave him access to the food lever. Once he learned that elevator rides were followed by such happy results—and how to achieve them—it was no trick to get Barnabus to crawl through a tunnel to reach the elevator. And so on. Individual parts of the responses that were not originally in Barnabus' repertoire sometimes had to be induced by one or more of the techniques outlined on pages 189-192)—demonstration, putting him in the situation, making critical parts of the environment stand out more clearly, and so on. Approximations of the desired responses were then shaped toward the precise action desired. Eventually each link in the chain became a *discriminative stimulus* for the next step and a *conditioned reinforcer* for the preceding one. (Such interim reinforcers will be discussed further in the next section.)

We assume that some such pattern as this is involved when we learn a complex series of new responses like tying our shoelaces, speaking, driving a car, playing the piano, or dancing. Component segments are emitted—sometimes first in rough form—and then are perfected by selective reinforcement and integrated into a sequence.

Behavioral contrast.   Sometimes when children are punished at home for aggressive behavior, they seem

to "make up for it" when they are outside, becoming much more aggressive than is usual for them. The phenomenon of *behavioral contrast* is said to occur when lowering the rate of responding in one situation results in an increased rate of responding in a second situation, even though the stimulus features in the second situation have not been changed.

The phenomenon of behavioral contrast can be illustrated in the laboratory in the formation of a discrimination. First, reinforcement is given for responding in the presence of orange, yellow, and red stimuli. Next, reinforcement for responding on the orange and yellow is stopped, while responding on red continues to be reinforced as before. Not only does responding on orange and yellow *extinguish*, but at the same time responding on red *increases*. The rate is greater than that established during original conditioning and is correlated with the decrease in responding to orange and yellow. (Incidentally, can you explain why responding to the orange stimulus is more resistant to extinction than to the yellow?)   •

The fixed action pattern.   The stickleback fish performs a courting dance with a typical stereotyped pattern and will do so even if reared in isolation from time of hatching (Tinbergen, 1942). Similarly, the courtship of a certain species of duck involves the preening movement of a brilliantly colored feather by the male. A drake who failed to develop this feather nevertheless showed this same pattern of preening (Lorenz, 1955).

As we saw in Chapter 4, such sequences have been given the term *fixed action pattern* by the ethologists, who have observed and studied them in various free-ranging species. They are invariant and rigidly stereotyped patterns, spontaneous in their appearance, not subject to extrinsic stimulus control, and not learned from experience (Moltz, 1965). We know that their components are not learned through a chaining process because the parts cannot be elicited by the stimuli preceding them in the sequence; only the stimulus which elicits the entire reaction can elicit any of its component responses.

Although many instinct theorists have pointed to these fixed sequences as evidence for a genetically encoded response pattern, an epigenetic explanation is being advanced by ethologists and behavior geneti-

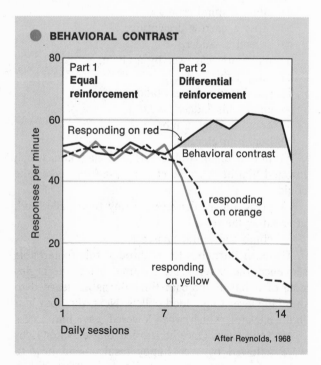

● **BEHAVIORAL CONTRAST**

Part 1
**Equal
reinforcement**

Part 2
**Differential
reinforcement**

Responding on red

Behavioral contrast

responding
on orange

responding
on yellow

Responses per minute

Daily sessions

After Reynolds, 1968

cists comparable to that now accepted in regard to embryological development (see page 61). According to this view all response systems, like all body structures, are seen as developing from the integrative influence of both processes within the organism and external stimulation provided by the particular environment in which development occurs (Moltz, 1965).

Can responses of the autonomic nervous system be conditioned? Until recently the answer to this question was "yes and no": "yes," as we saw previously, through respondent conditioning techniques, but "no" when it came to instrumental learning procedures. However, a major scientific breakthrough by Neal Miller (1969) and his associates has changed the "no" to a "yes."

If heart rate, blood pressure, temperature, sweating, dilating of the blood vessels, and digestive secretions can all be shown to be subject to the same laws of learning as overt skeletal muscle responses, then the class of reinforceable responses becomes almost unlimited. Moreover, if the smooth muscles and glands are responsive to environmental circumstances, we are in a position to discover how *psychosomatic* illness develops. Ulcers, asthma, colitis, high blood pressure, and related physiological symptoms are generally thought to be caused by psychological problems, at least in many cases. The mechanism may be operant conditioning.

The reinforcing aspect of the visceral response is shown in the case of a city boy who became so acutely asthmatic every time his parents sent him away to vacation at a relative's country house that he would always have to be brought back home. They had to discontinue the vacations (much to his delight) because of his apparent allergy to some pollen in the country. However, he never developed any respiratory problems when he camped overnight in the woods with the Boy Scouts.

Ordinarily, most responses of the autonomic nervous system have no effect on the environment. Thus they do not get reinforced by consequences and are not under environmental control. To demonstrate that they *could* be changed through reinforcement and thus become controllable, Miller and his colleagues had to devise three sets of procedures for use with their subjects:

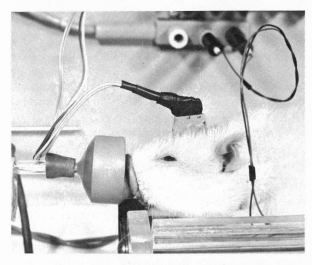

▲ In this photo of Miller's apparatus, the rat, paralyzed by curare, is receiving artificial respiration through a nose cone. Through previously implanted electrodes, stimulation is delivered to the brain promptly after each electrocardiograph change in the desired direction.

1. They had to prevent skeletal responses such as breathing and moving, which might influence visceral responses. This was accomplished by administration of *curare*, which blocks all motor responses but does not eliminate consciousness. Breathing was maintained artificially, and nonhuman subjects were used.

2. Small visceral responses had to be detected and amplified, and slight changes in amplitude or rate had to be reinforced immediately. This was accomplished with sophisticated physiological recording devices controlled by a small computer which could sense response change and initiate reinforcement. ▲

3. The reinforcement had to be delivered immediately, have instant effectiveness, and not require the subject to make any motor responses (as eating would, if the reinforcer was food). This was accomplished by administering a small amount of electric current directly into specified regions of the brain stem already known to be "pleasure centers." (Ψ Close-up, p. 202)

These techniques have enabled researchers to control salivation, heart rate, intestinal responding, kidney function, and gastric changes through reinforcement. Rats have not only learned to "blush" by dilating their blood vessels but can do so in one ear only. The precision of the control that is possible is hinted by the fact that even the time interval *within* a single heart beat (from auricle to ventricle pumping) can be controlled.

The potential implications of this work can be gleaned from the finding that when rats were rewarded for speeding up or slowing down their heart rate, seven of forty rats rewarded for heart-rate deceleration slowed down their hearts so far that they died. None of the rats rewarded for acceleration died (N. Miller, 1969).

Involuntary and unperceived internal responses in humans can also be changed by environmental consequences. For example, it was demonstrated that if the showing of nude female pictures was made contingent upon increasing the frequency of their galvanic skin responses, college males soon had more GSRs. The frequency did not change where the provocative photos were presented as often but were not contingent upon the appearance of this autonomic response. The subjects remained unaware of exactly what was being reinforced (Schwartz & Johnson, 1969).

Do such findings mean that we are helpless against anyone who gains the power to give or withhold reinforcers systematically? The potential influence of cognitive factors in changing the course of conditioning will be explored in Chapter 10.

The Reinforcer (S^c)

Early views of reinforcement linked the concept closely with basic drives. Reinforcers were "good events" such as food, water, sex, and escape from pain, which were thought to be effective because they reduced these drives. It was also thought necessary to reinforce every occurrence of a response in order for it to be learned and retained.

In this section, we will examine how the concept of reinforcement has been liberated from its traditional confines. The greater theoretical freedom today in how investigators think about what reinforcers are and can be has opened a vast range of socially significant behaviors to modifiability when the appropriate reinforcement conditions are specified. After discussing the *when* of reinforcement—different schedules on which reinforcements may be delivered

---

Ψ *Close-up*   **Pleasure and Pain Centers in the Brain**

As we saw in Chapter 3, a microelectrode can be implanted deep in the brain of an experimental subject and a small amount of electric current passed through it, artificially triggering impulses in the neural cells in the region surrounding the electrode tip. Olds and Milner (1954) discovered that there are regions of the brain which are "pleasure centers." Animals will learn operant responses which are followed by such stimulation. They will cross an electrified grid to get such stimulation. They will learn complex mazes if the goal is a little brain stimulation. When put into a Skinner box in which they can turn the current on themselves by pressing a bar, they put out as many as 7000 presses per hour. And the behavior does not satiate: they will continue until they drop from exhaustion. Once the current is turned off, however, the responding extinguishes very rapidly.

Other investigators (Delgado, Roberts, & Miller, 1954) have found areas of the brain which are "punishment sites." Stimulation of these regions will result in the learning of responses to turn off (or escape) the stimulation.

This technique of electrical stimulation of the brain has had a major impact on neurophysiological research as well as on behavioral research aimed at uncovering the basic mechanisms of learning and memory. As we have seen, it also has practical potentialities for the relief of human suffering: paralyzed limbs can be moved, and hostile aggressiveness can be lessened by electrical stimulation to the brain. It has even been shown that epileptics can use self-stimulation to keep themselves from having seizures (Delgado, 1970).

and the effects of delay of reinforcement—we will consider *what* can become reinforcing. This will include a discussion of conditioned reinforcers, responding as a reinforcer, feedback reinforcement, and, finally, what may be the ultimate human reinforcer: "competence" or mastery of one's environment.

The "when" of reinforcement: the payoff function. Girls "know" that if they want to maintain a high rate of attention in a new boyfriend, they should not be available all the time. A few properly placed "No" responses in a "Yes" sequence keep the boy eager and increase the value of the yesses.

Gambling houses "know" that if they want to maintain a high rate of playing the slot machines, the payoff must be properly programmed. With too many payoffs, they go broke; with too few, the customer quits. The payoff must be occasional and at irregular intervals—otherwise, the smart customer will learn to play the intervals.

Learning what the payoff function is ("How much do I get and when do I get it for putting out how much work?") is part of the basic lore acquired early in the life of a college student or factory worker. The student asks, "When will the tests be given and what is the minimal output Professor X will accept for a 'pass' (or some other grade)?" For the factory worker on fixed wages, the questions become, "How are raises scheduled?" "Are they related to my productivity?" "If not, how little can I do and still get my weekly salary?"

While girls, gamblers, college students, blue-collar workers, and a host of laboratory animals from cockroaches to chimps are industriously finding out what they will gain from what efforts, those who administer the payoffs are equally concerned about what schedule of payoffs will induce the most effort. Every reinforcement is part of some schedule, whether systematic or haphazard. Discovering the current schedule and changing it is the basis for most attempts at behavior modification.

While a new response is being acquired, the experimenter is likely to provide reinforcement for each correct response or approximation of it. Once it has been learned, however, such a schedule of *continuous reinforcement* is not needed to maintain the response, and the experimenter usually reinforces only selected responses. Since there are many bases on which responses may be selected for a payoff, there are a variety of *schedules of intermittent reinforcement*, each of which has been found to have a characteristic effect on behavior.

Ratio Schedules. A "response" is sometimes considered to be made up of a class of response units, all of which must be run off before reinforcement is earned, as we have seen. If the same number of units earns a reinforcement each time (like getting pay for piece work), the schedule is called a *fixed ratio (FR) schedule*. In the laboratory, a pigeon might have to peck a key anywhere from two to over a hundred times before getting a single pellet. "FR-25," for example, would be laboratory shorthand for "one reinforcement for each twenty-five responses." FR schedules produce very high rates of responding in the laboratory, as can be seen from the cumulative record shown. ▲ (p. 204)

The payoff schedule of the slot machine described earlier is known as a *variable ratio (VR) schedule*. Successive reinforcements may come close together or far apart; there is no knowing. The more one puts in, the more he may lose, but there is always the chance that the next play will bring the jackpot. This schedule, too, maintains a high response rate.

Interval schedules. It may be not *how much* work you do that brings the reinforcement but *when* you do it. Learning to look busy when the Man (employer, lab instructor, policeman, head resident) makes his rounds may be enough to assure getting your just rewards. When reinforcement is set on a temporal basis, it is theoretically being given for all the responses during the preceding interval. Actually, however, only the last response before the reinforcement need be made. If the interval is the same length each time, say once every ten seconds, or even once every week (as with salaried workers), it is called a *fixed interval (FI) schedule*.

FI schedules reveal a typical, but peculiar, topography, as can be seen in the figure. After each reinforced response, the subject stops his relevant responding for a time and performs "time-out" responses. As the time for the next payoff approaches, relevant responding switches on and increases sharply

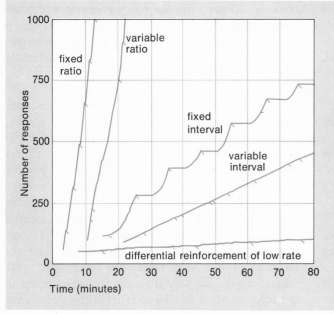

until the reinforcement occurs. This effect is called "scalloping." Any work system employing FI reinforcement schedules must use *surveillance* to keep the workers from dallying during the "time out" period immediately following a reinforcement.

If the interval is not fixed, but varies from one time to the next, it is called a *variable interval (VI) schedule.* Trout fishermen who don't quit probably learn "patience" as a by-product of such a schedule.

Schedules of reinforcement may occur in mixed forms and may be quite complex. Schedules can be designed to generate high levels of responding or to ensure continuous, steady responding over a long time (as with the chimps used in NASA's space flights). Some schedules even suppress behavioral output. A *differential reinforcement for low rate of responding (DRL) schedule* reinforces a response only if it occurs after an interval of no responding. If the subject responds too soon, the timer resets and he has to begin the wait again.

Delay of reinforcement: late may not be better than never.   For reinforcers to be effective, they must be "quick on the draw." Learning varies directly with the immediacy with which the reward follows the response to be learned. If too much time elapses

between the terminal response in a sequence of behavior and its reinforcement, the effect of reward is completely wasted. Put the other way, the *principle of delay of reinforcement gradient* (also called the *principle of the goal-gradient*) states that responses which occur close in time or space to the delivery of the reinforcement are learned more quickly than responses remote from reinforcement (Hull, 1952). Research has shown, for example, that there is a general tendency for mazes with several choice points to be learned in *backward order*, presumably because correct choices near the goal are more quickly reinforced.

For animals in a Skinner box, if the interval between response and reinforcement is more than a few seconds, response strength decreases; a reinforcer delayed longer than thirty seconds is ineffective (Perin, 1943). In fact, even a five-second delay of the primary reinforcer may be too long if the situation is controlled so as to remove sources of indirect reinforcement (Grice, 1948).

If any response which can be reinforced with relative *immediacy* can be learned, it would seem that effective education would demand approaches which dispense a sufficient number of rewards with minimal delay. This is not the way it happens, as every

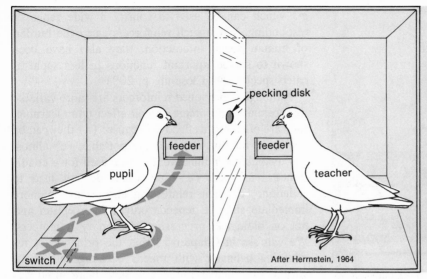

pupil

pecking disk

feeder

feeder

teacher

switch

After Herrnstein, 1964

◆ **MUTUAL REINFORCEMENT IN TEACHING**

The development of the ideal teacher-pupil relationship, in which each gives something to the other, was demonstrated in the experiment illustrated above. The "teacher" and the "pupil" could see each other through a transparent screen. When the teacher pecked his disk, food was delivered to his pupil's feeder. If the pupil happened to be standing on a switch in one corner at the time, both birds received food. Soon there was subtle process of interaction in which the teacher shaped the pupil to go to the switch. Then the teacher pecked, and each went to his feeder to collect the reward.

student will testify. Reinforcement may come long after the effort expended in learning, and when it comes, it is often a general grade rather than specific informational feedback for particular responses. ◆ To shorten the customary delay between response and reinforcement, two procedures are being used with increasing frequency, with both animal and human learners. Both involve doing away with the slow, inefficient human reinforcement dispenser.

The first procedure makes it possible for the learner to reinforce himself for correct performance. Self-stimulation of pleasure centers in the brain is the most powerful new technique discovered for aiding rapid response acquisition (see p. 202). Less dramatic are the teaching machines and programmed books, in which the correctness of the response can be ascertained as soon as it is made.

The second procedure involves the sophisticated information-processing equipment of the computer. Such equipment can evaluate a response and give the appropriate reinforcement in seconds or less, whereas human teachers would require much longer to do so. We will have more to say about this method in the next chapter.

When the delay of reinforcement cannot be shortened by these or other procedures, then a teacher may help to make reinforcements as sure and as prompt as possible by:

1. Making the correct completion of the response

so clear and unambiguous that he or she will be sure to see it.

2. Using language and other reminders to establish the symbolic connection for the learner between the late-appearing reward and the long-gone response.

3. Employing *conditioned reinforcers* to "stand in" for the primary reinforcer along the way. Barnabus had several conditioned reinforcers to mark his remarkable route, as we saw on page 199. Such acquired or secondary reinforcers are so important in the control of behavior that they will be discussed further below.

What is reinforcing? Although we still are a long way from knowing all the things that are or can become reinforcing to people or just what innate base our learning builds upon, our whole concept of what can reinforce behavior has been greatly broadened and refined in recent years.

Conditioned reinforcers. During the Korean War, some American POWs collaborated with the enemy to get small material benefits (others could not be compromised because they would not be bought off even at the cost of their lives). Elementary-school children can be made to do almost anything to receive a small gold paper star from their teacher. Their parents hold out for paper money. The masochist has learned to seek punishment and the sadist

This photo illustrates the use of a conditioned reinforcer. For word-saturated Americans, "WOW" has come to signal the height of intense, positive experience. Thus it is a powerful conditioned stimulus to try to attach to a product you would like the public to feel intensely and positively about.

to enjoy inflicting it. Mental patients who have stopped responding to their environment can be made to do so again when their responses are followed by cigarettes, pennies, or even the opportunity to watch kittens being fed.

In technologically advanced, relatively rich countries, little of our behavior in the course of a day is reinforced by primary reinforcers that have biological consequences for us. Far more important in controlling our behavior are stimulus events which originally were neutral but which have acquired the power to reinforce behavior as a function of their history of association with primary reinforcers. Such learned reinforcers are called *conditioned reinforcers*, as you have seen. •

Any discriminative stimulus which predictably sets the occasion for reinforced responding can become a conditioned reinforcer. Thus, if S^D is a smile, S^Δ is a frown, and baby's approach in the presence of the smile is followed by a delicious treat, the smile will become a conditioned reinforcer for approach even in the absence of the treat.

Smiles, nods, pats on the back, and money all represent a class of generalized *conditioned reinforc-*

ers which can be used to control a wide range of responding. While such reinforcers carry the burden of human social interaction, they also have been shown to serve important functions in less sophisticated species. (Ψ Close-up, p. 208)

Although conditioned reinforcers are more variable than primary reinforcers in their effect upon learning, they are often more effective because: (a) they can be dispensed rapidly, (b) they are portable, (c) almost any available stimulus event can be used for a conditioned reinforcer, (d) they often do not lead to satiation, (e) their reinforcing effect may be more immediate since it depends only on perception and not on biological processing of primary reinforcers. We will see in Chapter 15 that the principle of reinforcing behavior with tokens exchangeable for a variety of tangible rewards is now being used extensively in behavioral modification programs with humans.

One of the major trends in the psychology of learning over the last decade has been an ever widening view of the kinds of environmental events that can become conditioned reinforcers. It appears that the only restrictions on the class of potential reinforcers are the perceptual limitations of the organism. Whatever it can perceive it can learn to value.

Responses as reinforcers.   Not only environmental stimuli but the organism's own activity can be reinforcing.

When monkeys were given painful, unavoidable shocks, they became aggressive, biting and scratching objects placed in their reach. They even learned to pull one of two chains—the one which, in turn, gave them access to an inanimate object that they could attack (and did at almost every opportunity). All subjects learned to make the specific response which would provide this opportunity for aggressive responses. ■   The investigators concluded that the opportunity to attack the inanimate object was the principal reinforcer for the chain-pulling response (Azrin, Hutchinson, & McLaughlin, 1965).

A very useful way of identifying activities that can be used as reinforcers has been developed by Premack (1965). He first observed what animals did in a "free response" situation, where they had a choice between response alternatives. Not surprisingly, he found that water-deprived rats drank rather than exercised, while exercise-deprived rats ran rather than drank. These observations led Premack to the simple but penetrating insight that any response with a higher probability of occurrence should be usable to reinforce any response of lower probability. Sure enough: he found that water-deprived rats would run in order to get a drink of water, and that exercise-deprived rats would drink water when that response was followed by opportunity to run.

A human application illustrating the potential usefulness of this principle comes from a nursery school. When three-year-old children scream and run around instead of sitting still as instructed, they often are punished. According to Premack's principle, the screaming and running, being the highest probability response, should be usable to reinforce the lower probability behaviors that the teacher wants the children to learn. This hypothesis was tested successfully.

". . . sitting quietly in a chair and looking at the blackboard would be intermittently followed by the sound of the bell, with the instruction: "Run and scream." The Ss would then leap to their feet and run around screaming. At another signal, they would stop. . . . At a later stage, Ss earned tokens for low probability behaviors which could later be used to "buy" the opportunity for high probability activities. With this kind of procedure, control was virtually perfect after a few days." (Homme, de Baca, Devine, Steinhorst, & Rickert, 1963, p. 55)

The teacher was thus able to induce the attention and quiet she needed for teaching without any punishing or screaming on her own part.

Feedback as a reinforcer. *Alpha waves* are large, slow brain rhythms which predominate when we are relaxed and not thinking. Concentration or alertness replaces the alpha with smaller brain waves of greater frequency. Kamiya (1969) has discovered that if a tone is sounded as a signal whenever EEG's indicate the presence of alpha waves (state A) and is off in their absence (state B), subjects instructed to try to keep the tone on can actually learn to do so.

The state of consciousness that accompanies alpha waves is apparently intensely pleasurable and thus reinforcing in its own right. In fact, the joys of "turning on alpha" appear not too different from other kinds of "turning on," especially of the kind observed with electrical self-stimulation of pleasure

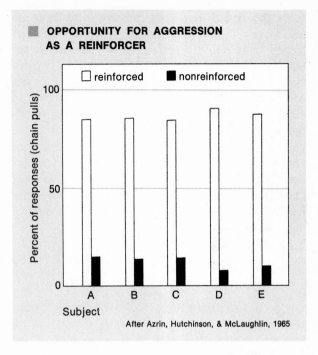

OPPORTUNITY FOR AGGRESSION AS A REINFORCER

After Azrin, Hutchinson, & McLaughlin, 1965

centers in the brain by rats. Kamiya reports that training in producing the alpha-state experience is so desirable to many subjects that instead of paying them to participate, "they're almost ready to pay me to serve as Ss, especially if I say I will let them turn on alpha for an extended period of time" (p. 515).

Evidently the tone gives the subject a clearly perceivable discriminative stimulus which provides immediate and unambiguous feedback for his learning of the new skill and becomes a conditioned reinforcer through association with the much-enjoyed alpha state itself. This work opens up for new scientific analysis the "mystical" phenomena of private states of consciousness as well as those of Zen and Yoga meditation.

The most basic reinforcer: competence through control. It well may be that at least for humans, the basic reinforcer which sustains broad classes of behavior over long periods of time is the confirmation of one's *competence* (White, 1959). This source of reinforcement comes from attaining mastery over one's external or internal environment rather than from satisfying appetites or minimizing aversions.

From the infant's elation in learning to walk to the mountain climber's pride in conquering difficult and hazardous terrain, the perception of ourselves as active, capable agents is one of our greatest joys, whereas the perception of ourselves as helpless pawns controlled by others is one of the most galling of experiences. Students given all the privileges of affluence are not content with these gifts but go to painful lengths to get some control over their own education. No dictatorial regime has been able to indoctrinate its people beyond the point of at least underground resistance; sooner or later people who feel oppressed always rebel and demand to control their own destiny.

Even rats will try to establish control over their environment. If an activity wheel is turned on by the experimenter they will turn it off. If he turns it off, they will turn it on (Kavanau, 1967). Even if they are very hungry and thirsty, they will explore a novel environment for a time before eating or drinking (Zimbardo & Montgomery, 1957).

If some measure of autonomy and control over one's environment is such a basic need, its potency as a reinforcer is hardly surprising. We will discuss motivation toward competence and mastery and its implications at greater length in Chapter 10.

The Four Kinds of S-R Relationships

We have been looking at the three basic terms in associative learning—discriminative stimuli, responses, and reinforcing stimuli. From these three terms,

---

Ψ *Close-up* **Night Work**

Back in the 1930's, a psychologist trained chimps to work and learn how to solve problems for "money." By first developing the association between inedible tokens and very edible raisins, he was able to substitute tokens for the primary reinforcers. The chimps would then work all day for the tokens which they could later deposit in a "chimp-o-mat," designed to exchange tokens for the valued raisins (Cowles, 1937).

However, the behind-the-experiment story was even more interesting and provides a more valuable lesson for us. First of all, the experimenter reported that the above findings applied only to male chimps. After a while, for some reason, the females would not work as hard as the males in order to secure the tokens. Many explanations were put forth to account for this inferior female performance, until a laboratory assistant reputedly discovered the truth when he returned to the lab by chance late one night.

He found that the male chimps were giving some of their hard-earned tokens to the females in exchange for certain sexual privileges, and the "stupid" females were depositing them in the chimp-o-mat to get their raisins!

four kinds of relationships are derived between behavioral and stimulus events: R — R, S → R, R → S, S — S (Catania, 1969). When we talk about the first two pairs (R — R and S → R) we are concerned especially with the properties of *behavior*. When we talk about the second pair (R → S and S — S), we are focusing more on properties of the *environment*.

R — R relationships. Any behavior is made up of response units, and any individual may emit many behaviors simultaneously or successively. Looking for sequences or clusters of responses that tend to occur together enables the psychologist to learn about the structure of behavior. For example, the pattern of responses which comprises the orienting reflex, the interrelated movements of mouth and tongue in saying words, or the sequence of responses which occur in emotional behavior all are examples of clusters of responses that often occur together. Aggressive responses and sexual responses are other Rs which may follow each other consistently.

Establishing a correlation between responses allows us to *predict* the probability that one will occur given the other. On the other hand, as we saw in Chapter 2, it does *not* allow us to make causality statements relating the two behaviors.

S → R relationships. This pairing relates the probability that a response will occur following the presentation of a particular stimulus. With reflexes and powerful unconditioned stimuli, the probability is extremely high. Some stimulus situations have the opposite but also predictable effect of virtually always inhibiting a response. Such inhibition can be established to new stimuli through classical conditioning; it also is seen in the courtship rituals of some species, when stimuli provided by one individual result in the suppression of aggressive responses in the potential mate.

In respondent conditioning it is assumed that the stimuli which precede these responses *elicit* them. Some operant learning theorists too conceive of drives and cues as evoking the response, as we have seen. Generally, however, operant researchers proceed from the assumption that response probability is not influenced by preceding stimuli but only by pre-

vious reinforcing stimuli that have followed successful responses. They recognize that the organism learns to emit a response only in the presence of a given stimulus and not to do so in its absence.

R → S relationships. What effect *you* have on your environment is a question that can be answered in terms of the probability that your response will be followed by some change in environmental stimuli. There are three general types of relationships between your responses and events which follow them—*dependency, contingency*, and *coincidence*.

Dependency. A tennis ball hit with a racket will be propelled in the direction of the racket's movement. The movement of the ball is said to be *dependent* on the response if it *must* occur following the response. If the electrical circuitry is intact, lights go on when a switch is thrown; if the plumbing is defective (as in our dormitory example), the shower gets too hot whenever the toilet is flushed.

Contingency. But many environmental events are occurring even when you are not responding. How do you know which ones your behavior is influencing? If an event follows behavior with some regularity (a high degree of probability but not necessarily 100 percent), then it is said to be *contingent* upon the response. The tennis player learns that the ball is most likely to go over the net if he holds the racket in a certain way, swings it with a given force, and so on, because in the *past* he has observed the contingency: if he did R, then (the desired) S was most likely to follow.

Many of the contingencies we have to discover are arbitrary. Instead of being inherent in the nature of things, like motion of tennis balls, they are set by other people. An A from one professor is contingent on apple polishing; from another, on three-page bibliographies for every paper. In the Skinner box, the release of the food pellet is *dependent* on the activated switch but *contingent* upon a particular pattern of response determined by the experimenter.

The idea of behavioral contingency is perhaps the most important concept in operant conditioning. By setting up different contingencies—different relationships between responses and reinforcers—operant conditioners make a given response more or less probable over time. To change an undesirable behavior pattern, the behavior-oriented therapist first finds the contingencies that are currently *maintaining* that behavior and then attempts to arrange new contingencies that will reinforce different behavior. Instead of giving in to the whining child eventually (thus reinforcing and maintaining the whining), the parent is taught to give positive reinforcement for desirable behavior and only when the child is *not* whining. A fuller discussion of behavior therapy is reserved for Chapter 15.

Coincidence and superstitious relationships. Perhaps the most fascinating relationship between responses and the stimuli that follow them occurs when, in fact, no relationship exists between them, but the individual believes that one does. One day our tennis player, in dressing for the game, puts on his left sock, right sock, right shoe, and left shoe in that order. He then wins the game. Next time, he puts his socks and shoes on in a different order, and he loses the game. With as little as one "learning" trial, some people (including at least one well-known former tennis star) have come to believe that the outcome of their game was contingent upon the behavior of putting on their socks and shoes in one inviolable order.

Consider another example of this type of learning. A man who calls himself Orpheus tells you that he has the power to make the sun rise by singing to it. Being, by now, scientifically skeptical, you demand a demonstration of this environmental control. Orpheus begins to sing at about 5 A.M. and soon the sun rises. He can repeat this demonstration for you daily, showing that his response is always followed by this change in the environment. You now suggest another test; omit the singing and see if the sun still comes up. (This is another of the canons of proof of causality, as you saw in Chapter 2.) But Orpheus must reject such a test. The consequence of his not singing would surely be the sun's not rising, and for the sake of the world he dare not risk such a dire consequence.

This example can be seen as accidental operant strengthening of a *coincidental* relationship between behavior and reinforcers. The rituals gamblers use in trying to change their luck illustrate their learned belief that a particular behavior pattern has caused

the dice to fall a certain way. Such accidentally conditioned responses are called *superstitions*.

When the environmental consequences are vital for the individual or his group, then superstitious behavior is extremely resistant to extinction. This is true for two reasons. First, as in the case of Orpheus, the risk involved in not making the response, *if* the connection were a causal one, would be greater than the gain in knowledge from finding out that one's behavior was not producing the effect. Second, if the individual believes in the validity of the superstition, making him refrain from the "necessary" act might produce other changes in his behavior which *would* directly effect the event in question. This is often seen among some students who have a special pen or pair of jeans that they always use for taking final exams. If the pen is lost, or the filthy jeans are thrown out by Mother, they may indeed do poorly on the exam because of expectation of failure and distracting thoughts about "their luck running out."

The development of such superstitions can be easily demonstrated in the laboratory. A hungry pigeon is confined in a box with a feeding mechanism that automatically dispenses a pellet of food every fifteen seconds, regardless of what the pigeon does. Whatever response the pigeon happens to be making when the food is delivered then becomes a reinforced response, and the probability of its occurrence is increased. Different, stereotyped behavior patterns are likely to emerge in different subjects—turning counterclockwise, turning in a circle several times before going to the food dispenser, jerking the head in one direction, as well as other "bizarre" movements.

You can conduct a similar demonstration using a couple of friends as subjects. Their task is to try to discover the secret for making you say "Good." Tell them they are to make only nonverbal responses, and they will know when they have made the correct one because each time they do so you will say "Good." Put them with their backs to you and to each other and have them start making a variety of responses. Meanwhile, you pay no attention to what they are doing but count silently to ten and say, "Good." Then count to nine and say, "Good," and so on, saying the reinforcing word more and more frequently, until you say it five times at about one-second intervals. You will notice their motions becoming less variable and more stereotyped but very different from each other. Then have each one explain his "secret of success" in causing you to say "Good."

S — S relationships. In learning about the environment, we learn stimulus relationships. Relationships between stimuli underlie the basic process in both perceptual learning and classical conditioning.

The traditional world of Pavlovian conditioning consists of only two stimuli. Elicitation operations present the subject with an unconditioned stimulus and a neutral, to-become-conditioned stimulus. The individual learns something about the nature (quality and intensity) of the unconditioned stimulus, about the temporal relation between it and the neutral stimulus, and about the informational or signal value of the latter. In operant conditioning studies, too, the subject may learn relationships between stimuli—in this case between a stimulus present before he makes the response and a pleasant or unpleasant stimulus that appears afterward.

But do stimuli ever occur singly in pure, isolated form? To the contrary, even simple environments offer a complex network of stimulation to be received and decoded by the individual. Moreover, stimulus elements lose their virgin qualities when wed to other concurrently available stimuli. The reaction any stimulus elicits—and its inferred "associative strength"—is markedly different depending upon its context. The two stimuli shown in the figure are objectively equal in brightness, but they are subjectively dissimilar because of the difference in their backgrounds. A

reaction in which a compound stimulus provides information concerning the occasion for reinforcement or nonreinforcement may not carry over to situations where only elements of the compound are presented separately—or vice versa. Many recent studies have begun to point up the importance of understanding the complex relationships between stimuli and to suggest the need for greater integration of research on perceptual and learning processes (see Kamin, 1969, and Wagner, 1970).

The environmental control of behavior and the behavioral control of the environment. In the process of learning about how stimuli are related and how your behavior is related to them, you also learn which of these events you can control and which you can only predict. For example, you can predict the weather but you cannot change it. You also find that your behavior may be controlled by them: the weather may dictate what kind of clothes you wear, whether or not you go on a picnic, whether you put down the top of your convertible. Marriages, suicides, and deaths from natural causes are all "behaviors" whose incidence is correlated with the season of the year. There are many such physical properties of the environment which occur independently of what you do with regard to them.

One of the primary goals of science and technology is to discover means of either controlling environmental stimuli or intercepting their influence on man. One of the primary goals of psychology is to discover the means by which behavior can be brought under new kinds of control. This idea of "control" is often interpreted by the layman as meaning a kind of totalitarian suppression. On the other hand, a precondition for individual freedom is knowledge of how to control one's own behavior and one's relationships with other people while limiting the undesirable controlling influences that the environment and others are exerting.

Chapter Summary

In order to survive, any organism must be capable of learning: (a) what things in the environment are related, and (b) how its own actions affect and are affected by environmental events. Such learning enables the organism to make predictions about future events and to use the environment to meet its needs.

In the presence of novel or complex stimuli, conflicting stimuli, or especially significant stimuli, the organism experiences an *orienting reaction*, which includes increased sensitivity, heightened muscle activity, general arousal, and visceral changes which prepare the body for possible action. When stimuli are no longer bringing new information, *habituation* occurs, and responding decreases or ceases. After habituation has occurred, a change in the stimulus can bring about *dishabituation* and reinstate the orienting reaction.

A stimulus that elicits a response predictably prior to learning is called an *unconditioned stimulus* (US or UCS). A neutral stimulus that repeatedly occurs just before the onset of an unconditioned stimulus acquires the ability to elicit the response, thereby becoming a *conditioned stimulus*. This process is called *respondent conditioning* or *classical conditioning*. In such learning, one stimulus comes to substitute for another as a signal that a *pleasant event* (perhaps food) or an *aversive event* (perhaps electric shock) is imminent. The originally automatic response is called a *respondent* or an *unconditioned response* (UR). The conditioned response elicited by the new signal may be very similar or may have additional new components. Not only physical stimuli but words and other symbols as well may become conditioned stimuli.

In a conditioning situation there is a generalized increase in excitability. The most favorable interval between onset of the CS and onset of the US is half a second. *Stimulus generalization* typically occurs, in which not only the precise conditioned stimulus but other stimuli somewhat similar to it also elicit the response. With continued trials in which reinforcement occurs only after the precise CS, the organism comes to respond only to the correct stimulus. *Response generalization* also occurs. The organism learns to respond only to the correct stimulus and to make only the precise response through *differentiation* and *inhibition of competing responses*. *Higher-order conditioning* may occur, in which the conditioned stimulus rather than the unconditioned stimulus serves as reinforcement in establishing second-order association. *Extinction*, due to active inhibition of the response, occurs after conditioning when the conditioned stimulus is regularly *not* followed by the unconditioned stimulus. *Spontaneous recovery* of the response can occur after a rest period following massed extinction training. The *strength of conditioning* can be measured by *resistance to ex-* *tinction* as well as by *amplitude of response, frequency of response,* or *latency of response.*

Past conditioning can leave unfortunate and often unrecognized residues. In *schizokinesis*, component parts of the conditioned response (changes in heart rate, for example) remain after the primary muscular or glandular response has been extinguished. When the conditioned animal is forced to make finer and finer discriminations, the original conditioned discrimination may be lost and "neurotic" symptoms may appear, a phenomenon known as *experimental neurosis*.

Any innate, reflexive response can be conditioned. Basic assumptions of *behaviorism* are: (a) that neurological events underlie the observed behavioral relationships established in conditioning and (b) that environmental conditions (rather than instincts or "mentalistic" phenomena) induce and maintain behavior.

Conditioning based on the consequences of behavior was first studied by E. L. Thorndike with hungry cats confined to puzzle boxes. Here behavior is *instrumental in reaching a goal*; it is *emitted* by the organism rather than *elicited* by a stimulus, and reinforcement is given only if a particular response is made. To explain such *instrumental conditioning*, Thorndike postulated *mediating variables*, including *drives, response hierarchies*, and *cues*, and a *law of effect*: that the feeling of satisfaction following successful response made the response more likely next time.

In *operant conditioning*, also based on consequences, the responses studied are usually responses that occur at a given rate, and it is *rate of response* rather than whether a response occurs that is measured. The operant rate is recorded on a *cumulative recorder*; the more rapid the rate, the steeper the *cumulative response curve*. A stimulus consistently present when a response will be reinforced and absent when it will not comes to exert *stimulus control*. Such a stimulus is seen not as eliciting the response but as becoming a signal for the availability of reinforcement, through the mechanism of respondent conditioning. If reinforcement stops, the new rate of response is lost (extinguished) and responding returns to the original *base-level rate*.

In operant conditioning, a *reinforcer* is defined

operationally as a condition following which a response becomes more probable. If a negative reinforcer is used, the response of *avoidance* or *escape* becomes more probable.

Since reinforcers can influence only responses that are already occurring, special means need to be devised for inducing the first response. Such means include increasing motivation, lowering restraints, structuring the environment, forcing, providing a model, giving instructions, inducing trial and error, and rewarding successive approximations (*shaping*).

Through stimulus discrimination, the subject can learn to identify one stimulus as a *positive discriminative stimulus* (S^D), setting the occasion for a high rate of responding—and another as a *negative discriminative stimulus* (S^Δ), setting the occasion for a low rate of responding. Animals, like people, can learn a double-discrimination, involving two stimuli and two responses. Even internal, visceral cues can come to serve as discriminative stimuli.

A *response* may be a behavioral act, a tiny movement of a muscle, or (by definition) a given number of bits of behavior reinforced as a group instead of individually. An operant response might thus be 100 key presses. A subject can learn not only particular reinforced responses but ways of approaching a situation, as in the case of *learned sets*.

In *chaining*, a subject can be taught a sequence of responses in which the discriminative stimulus for one step becomes a *conditioned reinforcer* for the step preceding it.

When punishment or cessation of reinforcement in one situation brings about extinction or withholding of a previously reinforced response, the rate of response in another situation may increase with no change in the stimulus properties; this is called *behavioral contrast*.

A *fixed action pattern* is evidently not learned through operant chaining because only the stimulus that sets off the whole chain can set off any part of it. Recently research has demonstrated that autonomic responses are subject to operant as well as respondent conditioning. Salivation, heart rate, GSRs, and even blushing in one ear only can be controlled by environmental consequences.

Both the *when* and the *what* of reinforcement have been studied extensively. Once a response has been learned, it can be maintained by *intermittent reinforcement*. Four schedules of intermittent reinforcement are *fixed ratio, variable ratio, fixed interval*, and *variable interval* schedules; each induces a characteristic pattern of responding. The more prompt and specific the reinforcement, the more effective it is. Any stimulus that becomes a conditioned stimulus through association with a primary reinforcer can come to be sought for its own sake, thus becoming a *conditioned reinforcer*. Activity itself can be reinforcing, as can achieving certain states of consciousness, such as "turning on alpha." Perhaps the most basic reinforcer for human beings is a perception of one's own competence to control events.

There are four kinds of stimulus-response relationships. In *response-response* ($R — R$) *relationships*, responses (dependent variables) are correlated; here one response predicts the likelihood of the other but cannot be presumed to cause it. Through such relationships we learn about the *structural patterns of behavior*—which responses tend to occur with others, which ones are predictive of others. In *stimulus-response* ($S \rightarrow R$) *relationships*, external or internal stimuli elicit responses, and behavior is directed or controlled by such stimuli; here there *is* a causal relationship.

In *response-stimulus* ($R \rightarrow S$) relationships, there are three possibilities: the stimulus (here a reinforcing stimulus that *follows* the response) may be *dependent* on the response, may be *contingent* on it at some level of probability, or may simply follow it by *coincidence*. Behavior maintained because a coincidental relationship is mistaken for a contingent, causal one is called *superstitious behavior*. In *stimulus-stimulus* ($S — S$) *relationships*, one stimulus event signals that the other will occur; through such relationships, organisms learn about the *structural relationships in their environment*. A primary goal both of science and of every individual is to gain a predictable environment and some measure of control over it by discovering which relationships in the environment and between one's behavior and subsequent events are in fact causal relationships.

Chapter 6

Human Learning and Memory

When we designate the ages of man as the stone age, the bronze age, the iron age, and so on, up to the atomic age, we are referring to the materials which man learned to manipulate in adapting to and changing his environment. By developing these basic skills, he could not only survive, but make this "the best of all possible worlds." But before he could learn manipulative skills and make effective use of the objects in his environment, he had to develop certain perceptual skills. And because he lived with others, he also had to develop language skills to be able to communicate ideas with them and social skills in order to share, organize, specialize, cooperate, and compete with others. Finally, he needed to be able to store information and retrieve it later in order to use his past experience to alter his future.

Think for a moment of all the complex information you have learned in school: grammar, foreign languages, chemical formulas, geometric proofs, syllogistic reasoning, and much more. Then consider how much more you have had to learn outside of class about your environment, especially about the people and institutions in it. Some of this learning has come easily and "naturally"; some of it you have had to work hard to learn.

Forgetting has not been the same for everything either. Have you had the experience of mastering material well enough to get an "A" only to find a few months later that you have forgotten most of what you knew? On the other hand, if you put on a pair of skates, began to skip rope, or tried a dance you had not done for years, you would probably find that in a short time you were as good as you ever were. Why do some things stay with you so much longer than others? Does the difference lie with the kind of material learned, or does something about the way you learn it determine how well you are able to remember it later?

In our discussion of conditioning in the preceding chapter, as well as in our earlier discussion of neural processes, we have spoken as if there is always a direct, one-to-one relationship between stimulus input and representation of this input by the nervous system. In many simple cases, we can assume that for all practical purposes the stimulus "out there" is the same as our perception of it and thus that the responses a given stimulus induces in our nervous system will always be similar.

In most cases of human interaction with the environment, however, we are not so directly bound to the stimuli that impinge on us. We can process incoming information in various ways rather than reacting item for item or point for point. Far more than for other species, our processing of information includes not only receiving and literal coding of input but selectivity, reorganization, and transformation of the input that we receive. This means that most human learning is as much dependent on our special ability for processing information as on our ability to retain new knowledge or to change a way of responding. Thus processing and coding of information are important components of learning to perceive, learning skills, learning to speak, and acquisition and memory for verbal and conceptual material.

You may have noticed already that we have made a distinction between learning and memory. Psychologists usually make this distinction in their studies. A psychologist is investigating learning when he looks at how well his subject is ultimately able to perform on some task after different kinds of practice—a change in performance as a result of experience. He is investigating memory when he is interested in how well something that has been learned will still be known by the subject after some elapsed period of time. Studies of learning are most likely to involve *skills in responding* (motor, perceptual, linguistic). Studies of memory are most likely to involve *knowledge*—retention of stimulus patterns. Before reading further, stop and test your memory (Ψ Close-up, p. 218).

Learning to Perceive

In our earlier discussion of developmental processes (Chapter 4), we briefly introduced some aspects of the organization and development of perception in the young organism, with emphasis on what seem to be inborn factors. In Chapter 7 we will examine in more detail the basic phenomena of perception, as well as the theories advanced to account for how we perceive the world as we do. Our concern in this chapter is with how learning changes the act of perceiving and how perception and learning interact to influence almost all human behavior.

"The search for invariants...is the task of perception, while detection of them at once reduces uncertainty and is reinforcing" (Gibson, 1970, p. 100). This statement accurately describes what is the central problem in the study of perception, as well as the problem the perceptual systems themselves face.

Thus it also sets the direction that perceptual development must take if perception is to become a more effective tool than it is at birth.

Traditionally, perceptual development has often been viewed as a process in which perceived elements gradually acquire various associations through experience. But although things we perceive obviously do acquire new meanings for us through our experience with them, Eleanor Gibson (1969) has pointed out that the main task of perception, as our link with what is "out there," is to process the variety of signals that come to us in such a way as to reduce uncertainty and make the significant signals stand out from the "noise." Only in this way can the world become comprehensible and predictable so that we can deal with it appropriately.

Thus Gibson, who has made extensive studies of early perceptual development, sees perception as primarily a process of *reduction* rather than *addition*. This reduction she sees as involving identification of three kinds of characteristics: (a) distinctions between similar-seeming stimuli, (b) continuing identities despite changes in appearance (seeing a chair as the same object even if its position changes) from one moment to the next, and (c) structures and relationships. Perceptual *development* is seen as a matter of developing greater proficiency in making these three kinds of identifications: making finer differentiations, seeing invariant characteristics despite surface variations, and grasping more subtle and comprehensive relationships, rules, and patterns.

Differentiating Patterns

To most young people the differences in the kind of music played by various rock groups are very clear. A teen-ager of the 1970s would hardly confuse a record by the Rolling Stones with one by the Jefferson Airplane. To the parents of the teen-ager, however, this distinction is usually unbelievable; both records are just "some loud rock music."

No matter what generation we belong to, there seem to be certain things about this world to which our parents are "blind"! But how often do teen-agers and their parents listen attentively to the same kind of music? Certainly not very often. So when a young person hears a group like the Jefferson Airplane perform, he is better able than his parents, from his experience, to distinguish specific features which identify that performance. On the other hand, they might be able to perceive differences between the music of Artie Shaw and that of Glenn Miller—which might sound indistinguishably syrupy to our teen-ager.

This is where Gibson's theory of differentiation becomes relevant. With experience, according to Gibson, similar stimuli begin to look or sound different as you begin to notice characteristics in one set that do not occur in the other. Gradually you identify important constancies and consistent relationships by which you can recognize them and tell them apart.

Repeated exposure is not sufficient, however, to ensure that such differentiation will take place. For example, it is quite possible that your parents have had enough *exposure* to the music you like to have learned to identify the different musical groups but have not paid attention to what they were hearing. It is clear that attention plays an important role in such differentiation. Only with close attention to the successive stimuli will the elements be differentiated and the consistencies and differences be identified.

Learning Perceptual Habits

In the next chapter there are many examples of how the *content* of what we see in a given stimulus pattern changes as a result of our past experience. Experience provides expectancies that certain stimuli will occur together or in a particular way as well as expectancies of probable pleasant or unpleasant consequences. And as we develop emotional investments in the people and objects around us, what we perceive is often determined by what we *want* to see.

In this chapter it is changes in the *process* of perceiving that concern us. Perception changes not only through increased power to differentiate and identify invariants but also through the development of perceptual habits of various kinds. One example is the habits we develop in learning to read our particular language.

Hebb (1949) has hypothesized that perception of a particular stimulus pattern depends upon repeated stimulation of a pattern of receptors, which in turn activates a particular set of neural cells in the optic pathways and in the brain (a "cell assembly"). For readers of English text, this repeated process should result in unequal training of certain parts of the retina. Since they are trained to scan to the right for the next word, they should be more sensitive to stimuli just to the right of the point of focus. Indeed, experiments have shown that for American subjects (past the sixth grade) words presented briefly to the right of a fixation point are recognized better than words presented on the left. On the other hand, for subjects whose native language is Yiddish (where text is scanned to the left), more left-of-center words are recognized (Mishkin & Forgays, 1952).

Scanning within individual letters has also been found to be in a rightward direction for readers of English (Kolers & Perkins, 1969). This would be predicted from the fact that the letters of the Roman alphabet contain most of their distinguishing features on the right side.

But when you read English text, you read across a line, not single words or single letters. What do you suppose results when the following cards are flashed (one at a time) on a screen for a fraction of a second and the subject is told to fixate on the center dot and describe what he sees? Which letter will be most frequently recognized?

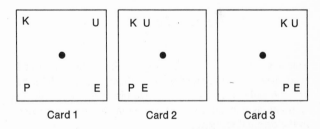

Card 1   Card 2   Card 3

Although K is close to the fixation point in only one card, it is recognized much more frequently than any other letter in all the cards. The least often recognized letter is E, with U and P intermediate. This pattern of results is to be expected from the learned attentional pattern of fluent readers who are set to start at the left end of the upper line and move toward the right (Heron, 1957).

Learning to See After Being Blind

Experience in receiving and organizing sensory input seems to be essential for development of the ability to perceive. A dramatic illustration of the results of failure to meet this need has been provided by studies of adults, blind all their lives, who have suddenly been given the gift of sight.

Certain people are unfortunately born with cataracts (clouding of the lens of the eye). If they have cataracts in both eyes, they are totally blind. The operation to correct this defect is quite simple. However, for one reason or another some of these people are left untreated until they are adults. Such people, of course, are completely naïve about visual experience but fully as capable as any other adult with respect to most other abilities. In studying them immediately after the cataracts are removed, we have subjects who are at the earliest stage of visual development and yet able to communicate as adults about their experiences.

Von Senden (1932) compiled data on a number of such cases. Following their operations, the patients lacked the ability to identify even the simplest objects. Each patient needed many exposures to an object in a particular setting before he would be able to name it. Even then, if the context was only slightly

---

Ψ Close-up   *Memory Test*

Below is a series of twenty digits; either have a friend read them to you slowly or scan them yourself, looking at each only once for a few seconds. Then write down as many as you can remember, trying to reproduce them in the original sequence.

12, 3, 18, 27, 96, 41, 37, 82, 65, 54,
77, 8, 26, 75, 98, 6, 32, 56, 98, 40

It is likely that you were able to recall no more than about twelve of the numbers correctly, and only about seven in the proper sequence. What variables of training, practice, and testing do you think might improve your memory score? The techniques to be discussed at the end of this chapter should help you to increase this ability considerably.

---

altered he would very likely be unable to recognize the object. For example, he might repeatedly be shown a wooden block on a table top until he could identify the block at each exposure. But if the patient was then shown the same wooden block on the floor, he would become confused and be unable to recognize it as the same object. He could learn to identify a lump of sugar in the experimenter's hand but failed to recognize it when it was suspended from a string. Motivation was ruled out as a factor in such cases by the fact that the patients experienced just as much difficulty in identifying the faces of friends, relatives, and other persons of great importance in their lives as they did in identifying geometric figures. One exceptionally intelligent patient could identify only four or five faces two years after the operation.

Many of the distinctions we take for granted and assume are in anyone's perception these patients had to learn. For example, they could quickly learn to distinguish between circles and triangles but then might still be unable to distinguish triangles from squares. Apparently they had only recognized that the triangles had certain features the circles did not —perhaps corners. Such differentiations seem so obvious to us that we do not realize we once had to learn them too. In any case, it seems clear that perception is not at all the "automatic" activity we usually assume it to be, as we shall see further in the next chapter.

The available evidence suggests that restoring sight to adults who have learned to live in a sightless world has not always been the blessing it might have been expected to be. Many could see little at first and had difficulty learning to distinguish between simple shapes and objects; in fact, some never attained useful vision. A common occurrence in many of these cases was the development of severe depression followed by a voluntary "giving up" of the gift of vision. A patient described by Gregory (1966), a fifty-two-year-old Englishman blinded at ten months of age, continued to rely on his sense of touch as an informant and validity check for his uncertain sense of sight. In drawings of English buses made forty-eight days after his operation and then six months and a year later, we can see at first his reliance on features that one would probably know by touch from the inside of the bus. The increasing detail is

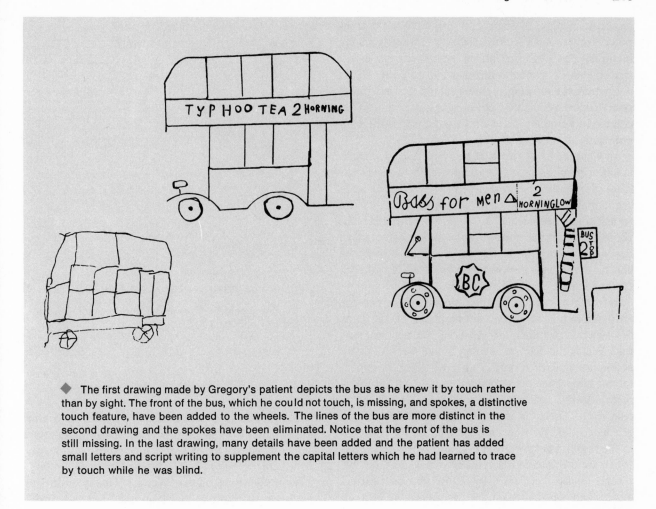

◆ The first drawing made by Gregory's patient depicts the bus as he knew it by touch rather than by sight. The front of the bus, which he could not touch, is missing, and spokes, a distinctive touch feature, have been added to the wheels. The lines of the bus are more distinct in the second drawing and the spokes have been eliminated. Notice that the front of the bus is still missing. In the last drawing, many details have been added and the patient has added small letters and script writing to supplement the capital letters which he had learned to trace by touch while he was blind.

evidence of perceptual learning, but note that the front of the bus (which usually cannot be inspected by touch) is missing, and perhaps not seen! ◆

"We saw in dramatic form the difficulty that S. B. [the patient] had in trusting and coming to use his vision whenever he had to cross the road. Before the operations, he was undaunted by traffic. He would cross alone, holding his arm or stick stubbornly before him, when the traffic would subside as the waters before Christ. But after the operation, it took two of us on either side to force him across a road: he was terrified as never before in his life." (Gregory, 1966, p. 197)

Eventually, S. B. would not bother to turn on the lights in the evening, but would sit alone in the (comforting) darkness. The same phenomenon has been reported for other senses. Bruning (1970) has described the case of a deaf man who, when his hearing was restored by an operation, was so overwhelmed by the noises he heard that he insisted upon another operation to restore his deafness. There have been some reported cases, however, where effective use of sensory processing was regained in active, intelligent, well-educated patients.

Learning Human Skills

What are the common elements in eating rice with chopsticks, hitting a ball with a bat, knitting, playing the piano, singing, wiring a ham radio, riding a motorcycle, playing chess, and programming a computer? They are all learned skills which involve three features: (a) organization of sequences of motor movements or symbolic information or both, (b) a given purpose—that is, some goal or desired target state toward which the sequence is directed, and (c) corrective reactions based on feedback from the consequences of previous responses.

In Chapter 3, we saw that all responding to sensory input involves processing and transforming *energy* from the environment. Equally vital for coherent, sequential behavior is our ability to process and transform environmental *information*. Ultimately, the coordination of fine movements in an intricate pattern depends as much on ability to process complex and constantly changing information as on ability to contract and relax particular muscles.

Information about the environment enters into the "programming" of every movement we make: How far away is the floor, or the book we are reaching for? Will it be hard or spongy? And so on. Every action we undertake starts with a whole set of expectations about the environment around us (from information stored earlier and information currently being received). Then, as the action proceeds, we keep getting feedback concerning our spatial relationships to the floors, books, piano keys, or other objects with which we are interacting. This feedback may involve several senses at once—perhaps vision, hearing, touch, and smell—which, as we know, send their information to different parts of the brain. Coordination requires that we keep evaluating all this information and using it appropriately in guiding the ongoing action.

Patterns of Acquiring and Maintaining Skills

The earliest studies of motor skills were attempts to discover the typical pattern in such learning. Only later did the focus shift to identifying factors that help or hinder development and retention of new skills.

A good example of skill learning is learning to send and receive Morse code by telegraph. Telegraph operators have learned a motor skill—to operate a key rapidly and smoothly with prolonged sequences of on-off contacts of consistent and prescribed dura-

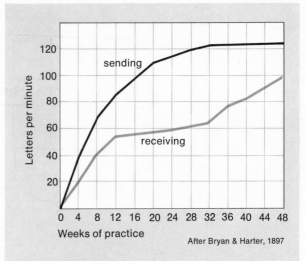

After Bryan & Harter, 1897

IMPROVEMENT IN LEARNING MORSE CODE

The graph depicts the gradual improvement in skill at sending and receiving Morse code. The "phantom" plateau seen in the receiving curve is not evident in the sending curve.

tions. They have also acquired a peculiar perceptual skill which allows them to hear speech in a miniature language, consisting of sequential groups of dots and dashes corresponding to alphabetic letters.

An early study of two Western Union on-the-job trainees was reported by Bryan and Harter in 1897. Separate learning curves were constructed for each subject for sending and receiving code. They found, as have other researchers since, that learning was more rapid at first, gradually leveling off until the subject reached his maximum level of efficiency. Learning to send was easier than learning to receive: performance in sending was better from the beginning. In the case of receiving, there seemed to be a *plateau*—a period of little or no improvement, followed by a spurt. Bryan and Harter recognized that the task involved a hierarchical organization of habits, and it was thought that the plateau might represent a period during which the learner was reorganizing his method of perceiving—perhaps learning to hear and recognize groups of letters instead of individual ones.

Later studies did not substantiate the plateau phenomenon, perhaps because in many cases the tasks did not involve a hierarchical organization of skills. But the importance of hierarchical levels of units in memory storage has since been well established, as we shall see.

Later studies by E. L. Thorndike examined learning of such diverse skills as "rapidity of tapping, as with a telegraph key," "the delicacy of discrimination of pitch," "ability to grasp and retain a series of nonsense syllables," and "skill in tossing balls." The curve shown here is typical of those he found. • Despite day-to-day fluctuations, there was continuous improvement, rapid at first and slower later as the maximum level of proficiency was approached.

Since Thorndike, studies of skill learning have generally been more specifically of motor learning. Although virtually all the learning we do—certainly all skill learning—involves some motor learning, the term *motor skill learning* is used in cases where the learning involves primarily the muscles.

A favorite piece of apparatus for studying motor skills in the laboratory has been the *pursuit rotor*—a metal target mounted on a moving turntable. The subject must try to keep a stylus in contact with the target. Other popular tasks have involved more complex perceptual-motor coordination. For example, the subject may be seated at an apparatus which has two or more switches. He is presented with various stimulus patterns in random order and must learn to flick the correct switch when each pattern appears.

In spite of our proficiency at forgetting such irrelevancies as the material that appeared on yesterday's exams, we seem to retain motor skills almost indefinitely. The popular belief regarding motor skills, that once learned they are never forgotten, is supported by empirical evidence. In a typical study by Fleishman and Parker (1962), subjects learned a complex perceptual-motor task and were later tested for retention. The authors reported "virtually no loss in skill regardless of the retention interval."

No one really knows why we apparently retain motor skills so well. It may be that we remember them better because they were acquired over a prolonged practice period so that they were very well learned; or it may be that other things we learn later do not interfere and perhaps even give us practice in many of the same movements.

Feedback (or, "You gotta know where you've been to know where you're going")

Considerable experimental evidence indicates that a person who has knowledge of his progress will learn more rapidly than an equally motivated subject of comparable ability who is working "in the dark" (Ammons, 1956). It has become common for psychologists to replace the term *knowledge of results* with the more general expression *psychological feedback* (Brown, 1949). Psychological feedback is the process whereby the individual gains information concerning the correctness of his previous responses in order that he can adjust his behavior to compensate for errors. Thus feedback is essential not only for new motor learning but also for the performance of any integrated sequence of motor acts.

Functions and kinds of feedback. Feedback serves three distinguishable functions: (a) providing *information* both about the results of a response and about its characteristics (temporal, spatial, directional, level of intensity, and so on); (b) providing positive or negative *reinforcement*, depending on the adequacy of the response; and (c) providing *motivation* to continue the task by helping to make the world

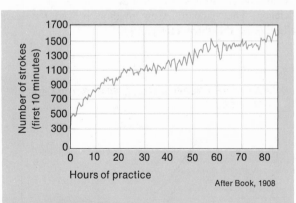

Hours of practice

After Book, 1908

● **IMPROVEMENT IN TYPING BY THE SIGHT METHOD**

This curve shows the improvement of one of Thorndike's subjects in learning to type. The graph records the number of strokes made in the first ten minutes of each hour of practice.

and one's behavior predictable and potentially controllable.

Not surprisingly, the more clearly the feedback is related to specific responses, the better. Thus feedback for each response is better than information about overall progress, and precise information at the time the response is made is better than general advice about a sequence of responses.

During World War II, an experiment compared the effectiveness of three methods of training gunners to "track" targets with a 40-mm gun. The task in tracking involves continuous sighting of the gun on a moving object. Tracking with this gun required two men—one to follow the horizontal movements of the target, the other to follow the vertical movements. The standard Army method of training in this skill was to give verbal instructions and coaching before, during, and after each session of gunnery practice.

Three experimental conditions were used to test the efficiency of this training method. For Group A the standard Army method was used; in Group B each man coached his partner; and in Group C a special telescopic sight mounted on the gun was used to check the accuracy of aim, so that the instructor could sound a buzzer whenever the gun was off target, giving the men immediate knowledge of results. The men in Group C were also told what scores they had made at the end of each training session. As the graph shows, the men in this group improved much more rapidly than did those in the other groups and achieved the greatest proficiency. The standard Army method proved the least effective of the three (Bray, 1948). ▲

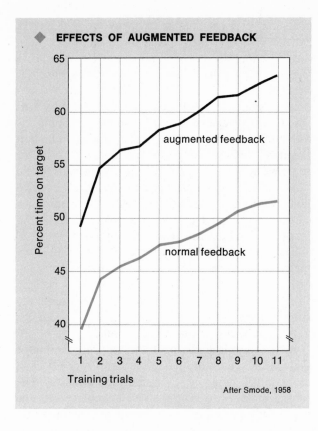

♦ **EFFECTS OF AUGMENTED FEEDBACK**

Percent time on target

augmented feedback

normal feedback

Training trials

After Smode, 1958

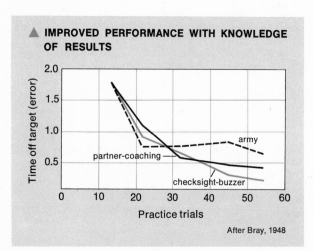

▲ **IMPROVED PERFORMANCE WITH KNOWLEDGE OF RESULTS**

Time off target (error)

army

partner-coaching

checksight-buzzer

Practice trials

After Bray, 1948

Feedback may be of two general types: *intrinsic* or *externally augmented*. When you are asked to count rapidly aloud from 1 to 100, you know where you are in the series at any moment from the sound of your voice which is feedback to your ears. Similarly intrinsic are the kinesthetic cues providing information which guides the rate of movement and location of your limbs. But if you closed your eyes and tried to touch the tip of another person's nose, and that person told you when you were "getting hot," you would be using externally augmented feedback.

The positive effect of augmented feedback in improving performance has been shown convincingly in an experiment where two groups of subjects had to keep an erratically waving needle centered on a dial. The experimenter told one group the length of time they were on target (normal feedback). For the other group, augmented feedback was introduced by a counter on which they could immediately see how their score was accumulating. Augmented feedback resulted in remarkably superior performance (Smode, 1958). ♦

The use of augmented feedback in the conditioning of heart rate, brain waves, and other responses previously assumed not to be controllable is an even more dramatic example. As we saw in the previous chapter, operant conditioning of autonomic nervous system functions became possible only when an ingenious technique was devised for providing knowledge and reinforcement following very slight changes in responding in the desired direction. Discovery of the role of feedback in controlling such behavior has opened up one of the most exciting new areas of research in psychology and one with the most far-reaching social consequences.

Delayed feedback. Because intrinsic feedback works so well under normal conditions, we are totally unaware that we are even using it. To study our reliance upon it and the variables influencing its functioning, the researcher must find a way to disrupt it. Information coming in through auditory and visual channels has proven easy to disrupt under controlled laboratory conditions.

The study of delayed visual feedback started during World War II when it became apparent that there was a delay between the movements of the sighting control of an anti-aircraft cannon and the correlated movements of the gun, which made accurate firing difficult. Subsequent research has been concerned with the basic issue of how man learns to coordinate his motor tracking of an object in his environment with the visual feedback he gets from his movements. One tracking job used in the laboratory is tracing a star hidden behind a screen. Another is trying to write a list of words on paper that the subject cannot see directly. In each case, the subject can see what he is doing only on a TV screen which he views as he continues his task. The record of his performance, however, is played back after a short delay interval. The handicap this delay creates for coordinated eye-hand movements is insuperable. ■

The effects of auditory feedback have also been studied by delaying the interval between uttering a sound and hearing it. Rather than hearing the words he has just spoken through air conduction, as he

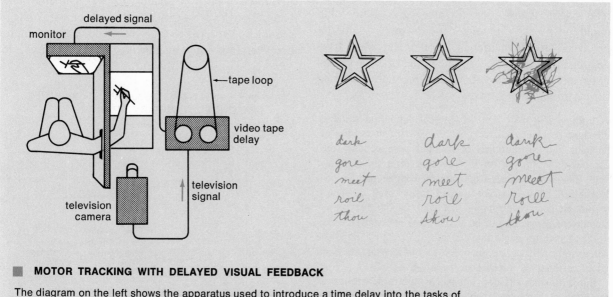

■ MOTOR TRACKING WITH DELAYED VISUAL FEEDBACK

The diagram on the left shows the apparatus used to introduce a time delay into the tasks of tracing a star and writing a list of words. On the right are shown one subject's responses. Items in the first column were done under normal conditions, items in the second column were done using a TV monitor but no delay, and items in the third column were done using a TV monitor with a delay.

normally would, the subject hears them over a set of earphones, with a delay interposed.

The consequences of such delay are measured in terms of changes in the subject's speaking—its intensity, duration of phrase, fundamental speech frequency, intelligibility, articulation, and emotional stress (Smith, 1962; Yates, 1963). Under conditions where the delay interval is about a fifth of a second, speech is extremely disrupted. In fact, the speech of some people breaks down altogether. Some subjects report that if they cannot hear what they are saying, they cannot even think well enough to answer simple questions or describe what they are feeling.

Delay is most disruptive when the feedback is loud and when the material is closely organized with the parts dependent on each other, as in singing, whistling a tune, or saying a tongue-twisting limerick. Delays shorter or longer than a fifth of a second are less disruptive. There is very little adaptation or improvement with continued practice, although long-term studies have not been tried.

Conceptualization vs. Practice

You might assume that learning of a motor skill could only be by practice in moving the muscles involved. Studies of human learning, however, have demonstrated that at least some of the practice can be done just by thinking about and mentally picturing the performance of a task.

A total of 120 male college physical education students, all right handed, took part in an experiment on the effects of varying amounts of manual practice and conceptualizing practice on the learning of a novel motor skill. The task consisted of using a wooden paddle held in the left hand to strike a small rubber ball so that it would hit a large target on the wall twenty feet away. Balls were projected out of a tube, one every twelve seconds, at such an angle that the subject had to change the ball's flight 90 degrees in order to hit the target. Each trial consisted of a series of twenty-five balls.

Subjects were divided into six comparable groups on the basis of their performance on the final trial series. The groups used various combinations of manual and conceptual practice for five periods, followed by a test, five more practice periods, and a second test. For the conceptual practice periods, five minutes in length, subjects were asked to concentrate on introspectively rehearsing

the sequence of movements required. A written description of these was read by each subject at the beginning of the period.

The final mean score for the groups which had manual practice only was slightly higher than that of the group which alternated periods of manual and conceptualizing practice, but the difference was not statistically significant. Thus the findings support the hypothesis that some conceptualization can help in the acquiring and improving of gross motor skills. The relative amount and placement of it are important, however: conceptualizing with no manual practice at all produced little improvement, whereas alternate manual and conceptual practice was more effective than five periods of either one followed by five periods of the other. Most interesting of all in its implications for situations where practice facilities are limited was the finding that those who had used the equipment only 40 percent of the time did virtually as well at the end as those who had used it all the time. The latter group, however, evidently reached a given mean level of proficiency somewhat sooner (Egstrom, 1964).

Verbalization also has been shown to be a valuable aid in human maze learning, a popular laboratory technique for studying the acquisition of motor skills (Warden, 1924; Husband, 1928). On the other hand, though verbalization can help motor learning, it cannot be expected to take the place of actual motor practice. It is only by making overt responses and

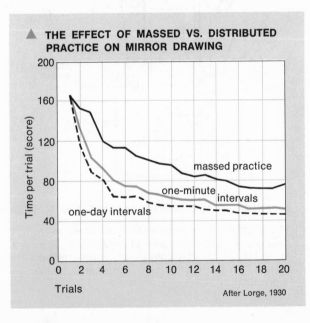

THE EFFECT OF MASSED VS. DISTRIBUTED PRACTICE ON MIRROR DRAWING

Time per trial (score) / *Trials*

massed practice

one-minute intervals

one-day intervals

After Lorge, 1930

correcting them in the light of feedback that good motor learning takes place. To learn to drive, you must practice driving. To learn to ski, you must practice skiing.

To Cram or to Spread It Out?

If you have a certain number of hours a week to spend learning a new skill—perhaps typing—does it make any difference whether you put it into one or two long, concentrated study periods or spread it out over many short sessions? The relative merits of *massed* versus *distributed* practice have been thoroughly studied in the laboratory for different kinds of learning.

For acquisition of motor skills, the value of distributed practice has been clearly shown in a number of experiments.

In one study subjects learned to draw while viewing their hands in a mirror, which reversed their apparent movements. Subjects worked at this skill with either no rest between successive trials, a one-minute rest, or a one-day wait between trials. The figure clearly shows the superiority of interspersing rest periods between trials, even if the rest period is only one minute in length. Similar results were obtained in mirror-writing and code-substitution tasks (Lorge, 1930). ▲

Considerable investigation has been done on the ideal length for rest periods in motor learning. With longer practice periods, longer rest periods are required for highest learning efficiency; with shorter practice periods, the rest intervals can be shorter and the maximum learning rate still be maintained. The optimal length of rest periods for learning different skills is also heavily dependent on the nature of the particular task. Various investigators have shown that the introduction of brief rest periods is especially valuable during the early trials in motor learning.

Psychologists have also investigated whether or not subjects who have learned motor skills under massed practice catch up later with those who have learned by spaced practice.

In one study using a pursuit-rotor task with psychology students, a group given distributed practice (D) was consistently ahead of a massed-practice group (M) during the practice trials on the first five days. At the end of this time Group M was at the level of proficiency

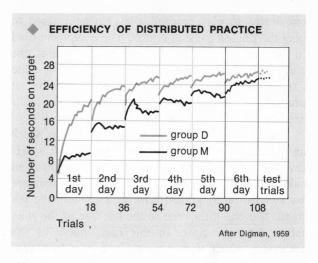

EFFICIENCY OF DISTRIBUTED PRACTICE

Number of seconds on target

28, 24, 20, 16, 12, 8, 4, 0

1st day, 2nd day, 3rd day, 4th day, 5th day, 6th day, test trials

18   36   54   72   90   108

Trials

group D
group M

After Digman, 1959

Group D had attained about two thirds of the way through the series, indicating that the subjects with massed practice had been getting only about two thirds as much benefit from the practice as the others. Clearly there had been more learning per trial under distributed practice.

On the sixth day, the last day of the experiment, both groups were given distributed practice. At the end of that day, Group D had shown almost no further improvement, while Group M was improving faster than under the earlier conditions. On later test trials, the differences between the groups had almost disappeared. Those findings suggest strongly that the conditions of practice had not influenced the ultimate level of performance but only the amount of practice time required to reach it (Digman, 1959). ◆

The clear advantage of distributed practice over massed practice seems to be restricted to the acquisition of motor skills. For verbal learning, consistent results have not been found, whereas for complex ideational learning, massed practice may be superior.

Transfer of Training

The efficiency of practice is often influenced by what we have already learned or have been learning just before. If previous learning improves new learning, the effect is called *positive transfer*. If previous learning inhibits new learning, the effect is called *negative transfer*.

An example of *positive transfer* is seen when someone learns to play baseball after having learned to play the English game of cricket. The equipment used in the two games is highly similar. In addition, the way in which the game of cricket is played is quite like baseball. Thus, if one has learned to play cricket properly, he has already learned many of the skills necessary for playing baseball.

Negative transfer is seen in the situation in which an American must learn to drive an English sports car which has the driver's position on the right-hand side of the car. The stimuli are similar, but some are backwards. Shifting must now be done with the left hand, and one must keep to the left side of the road rather than the right. In this case, many of the responses which were previously correct are now totally inappropriate. The situation is so difficult that some people learning to drive a car in Britain might be better off with no previous driving experience than with the experience of having driven American cars.

Learning a Language

"It is a very inconvenient habit of kittens (Alice had once made the remark) that, whatever you say to them, they *always* purr. 'If they would only purr for "yes," and mew for "no," or any rule of that sort,' she had said, 'so that one could keep up a conversation.' But how *can* you talk with a person if they always say the same thing?' "

Lewis Carroll
Through the Looking Glass

Probably the most astonishing capability which human beings possess is the capacity to learn, within the first few years of life, the vast and complicated system of the language of their own culture. By translating physical events into linguistic symbols, a human being can manipulate the environment "in his head," thereby saving himself an inordinate amount of overt trial and error behavior and enabling him to transport himself to worlds unseen and in some cases nonexistent. Ben Jonson noted early in the seventeenth century that "*speech* is the only benefit man hath to express his excellency of mind above other creatures. It is the *Instrument of Society*."

Both psychologists and linguists have long sought

to determine just how this feat is accomplished; their joint pursuit has led to the establishment of the area of study known as *psycholinguistics*. Before we can examine the major theories as to how language is learned, however, we must take up the question of what language consists of, and how it is put together.

The Structure of Language

On the surface, the languages of man appear to be infinitely varied. To the student of psycholinguistics, however, it soon becomes apparent that they share certain universal properties. Thus while the specific sounds, words, and rules we shall consider in our discussion of language are those of English, the same broad principles are applicable to any of the languages spoken in the world.

Levels of linguistic analysis.   Among the properties common to all human languages is a basic linguistic structure, a hierarchical system building from simple sound units to complex idea units. In comprehending speech, we rely upon cues at many levels of this linguistic organization, including phonological, grammatical, and semantic levels.

Phonological level.   At the phonological level, we are concerned with the basic sound units that make up the stream of speech. A *phoneme* is a class of sounds that are recognized by speakers of a given language as having certain distinctive features that set them apart from other sounds. For example, while the sound of the letter *p* in *pan* is not entirely identical to that of the *p* in *plan*, any speaker of English would recognize them as instances of the same phoneme: /p/. Furthermore, he would make a clear distinction between this phoneme and the initial sound in the word *ban* (the phoneme /b/). Obviously, to understand any spoken language, a person must learn to make the necessary phonemic distinctions and identifications. According to the notion of perceptual learning described earlier, we would expect the pattern of language development in children to show a gradual increase in the number of phonemes used as the child comes to recognize more and more of the features that distinguish between them. Evidence that this is indeed the case has been provided by case histories of the development of speech in children (Jakobson & Halle, 1956).

Grammatical level. The grammatical level has two divisions: *morphology* and *syntax*. The phonemes are combined several at a time to comprise as many as 100,000 *morphemes*. A morpheme is the smallest unit of speech that has a definable meaning; it may or may not be a word. Thus the word *tigers* is composed of two morphemes, the animal name and the *s* which indicates the plural.

A word is an arbitrary arrangement of letters (visually) or sounds (aurally) to form a symbol, which in turn represents a general class of objects, events, activities, etc. Some words have a specific and unique referent (for example, *Beatles*), but most words represent a broad class of conceptually related members (for example, *music*).

Words are combined into larger units—phrases and sentences—by rules of *syntax*, or *grammar*. These rules specify the permissible orders in which words and phrases may be arranged to form sentences. Chomsky (1957) postulated that the basic element of speech is a simple, positive sentence, called a *kernel sentence*. This basic sentence can be transformed into different forms according to syntactic rules. The specific rules vary from language to language, but certain aspects of these transformational rules are universal across languages.

Semantic level. Some linguistic events have meaning, others are meaningless. The study of meaning is called *semantics*. Some words or word strings have meaning because they evoke specific images, others have arbitrarily agreed upon meanings (as the word *semantics*), or else acquire meaning through emotional or cognitive associations. The meaning of a word also depends on its immediate context and the inflection with which it is uttered relative to related words. For example, the simple word *run* has over twenty meanings (how many of them can you list?). A "white house cat" becomes a very different thing depending upon where the inflection falls: "a *white* house cat," "a *white house* cat," "a white *house* cat," and so on. The sentence, "She sang a table" is acceptable on the phonological and grammatical levels but not on the semantic level.

The psychological reality of linguistic analysis. Do these units, levels, and rules really possess psychological "reality" for the native speaker/listener? The research strategy employed by psycholinguists to answer this question involves changing a single linguistic element and then observing whether this has any effect on the subject's ability to perceive, learn, or remember a given utterance.

Phonology. Investigators working at the phonological level have succeeded in determining the basic physical acoustic properties necessary to perceive and discriminate a phoneme. Spoken sounds can be converted to visual displays and spectrograms plotted showing frequency (cycles per second) on the vertical axis and the passage of time on the horizontal axis. Investigators at the Haskins Laboratories in New Haven have developed a method of constructing simplified patterns from actual spectrograms. ● By

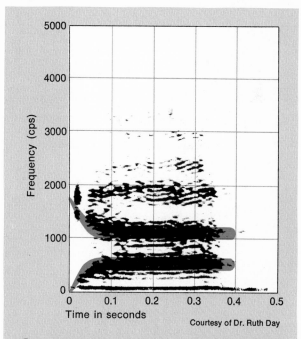

● **ACTUAL AND IDEALIZED SPECTROGRAMS**

The actual spectrogram of the spoken syllable /ga/ is shown in black. Superimposed in color is the idealized spectrogram constructed by investigators at Haskins laboratory.

special apparatus these idealized spectrograms can be converted back to sound and played to naïve listeners who are asked to report what they hear. Using this method, the investigators have been able to establish the minimum physical acoustic properties which differentiate between phonemes. They have found that some very similar physical patterns are perceived as different phonemes, as shown for /da/ and /ga/ in the top portion of the figure. ▲ Other very different physical patterns are not distinguished, as shown in the lower part of the figure. The fact that there is no one physical configuration to correspond with the perception of a given phoneme (such as /d/) makes it all the more amazing that phonemes are so readily extracted from the speech stream and recognized by listeners.

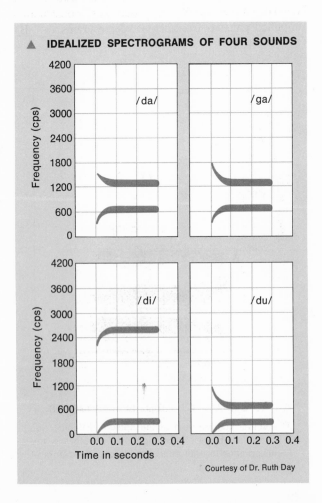

▲ **IDEALIZED SPECTROGRAMS OF FOUR SOUNDS**

Time in seconds

Courtesy of Dr. Ruth Day

Morphemics. In English, the plural morpheme takes on three different sounds, depending on the last phoneme of the noun. Thus /s/ is added to a word like *trick*, /z/ is added to a word like *bird*, and /ɪz/ is added to a word like *glass*. We can specify the precise rules that determine when each form is used. But do English speakers *know* these rules?

In an ingenious experiment, Jean Berko sought to determine whether preschool and first-grade children knew certain morphological rules. For example, she showed each child a drawing of a birdlike creature and told him, "This is a *wug*." Next, she pointed to a drawing with two of the same creatures and had him complete the sentence, "There are two_____ ." The correct form of the plural morpheme in this case is /z/.

The children were able to answer the questions consistently; the investigator concluded that "there can be no doubt that children in this age range operate with clearly defined morphological rules." Boys and girls performed equally well; first-graders performed significantly better than preschoolers on many of the items (Berko, 1958).

It is important to note that nonsense names were used in this study; had acceptable English names been used, such as *bird*, we would be unable to determine whether the child knew the rule, or whether he had heard both *bird* and *birds* before and had simply memorized both forms. What is meant by "knowing a linguistic rule" is not that the person can state the rule in all its technical glory, but that he uses it correctly, especially in novel situations.

Syntax and semantics. In a series of experiments, George Miller and his co-workers have violated syntactic and semantic rules and observed the psychological effects. Consider the five "normal sentences" in the table. ◆ Note that all follow the same syntactic sequence, namely (Subject) + (Verb) + (Direct Object) + (Preposition) + (the) + (Indirect Object). From these, a new set of sentences was generated which violated semantic rules, but preserved syntactic order. Each of these was prepared by selecting the first word of normal sentence 1, the second word of normal sentence 2, the third word of normal sentence 3, and so on, yielding the string, "Gadgets kill passengers from the eyes." This procedure was continued until all words were used,

◆ SENTENCES USED IN STUDYING CONSEQUENCES OF LINGUISTIC RULE VIOLATIONS

Normal Sentences

1. Gadgets simplify work around the house.
2. Accidents kill motorists on the highways.
3. Trains carry passengers across the country.
4. Bears steal honey from the hive.
5. Hunters shoot elephants between the eyes.

Semantically Anomalous Sentences

1. Gadgets kill passengers from the eyes.
2. Accidents carry honey between the house.
3. Trains steal elephants around the highways.
4. Bears shoot work on the country.
5. Hunters simplify motorists across the hive.

Ungrammatical Strings

1. Around accidents country honey the shoot.
2. On trains hive elephants the simplify.
3. Across bears eyes work the kill.
4. From hunters house motorists the carry.
5. Between gadgets highways passengers the steal.

monitoring his own sounds and enables him to hear those of others, (c) a normally functioning brain which controls mouth and throat movements, as well as making associations, storing inputs, processing information, and so on, and (d) a capacity to imitate the speech of others. The environment has then only to provide linguistic models from a common language community. When child meets environment, language results. While few would object to this simple formulation, there is great disagreement as to the significance of the encounter with the environment.

The learning theorists' approach. One school of thought, represented by learning theorists (Mowrer, 1958; Skinner, 1957), argues that language is learned according to the same principles as hold true for the learning of other behavior. The infant begins with no knowledge of language, but gradually acquires language skills largely by reinforced imitation of models. Individual language units are then strung together in larger units which are reinforced if they are appropriate and correct.

Reinforcement of early vocalizations. We have seen that the basic principle of reinforcement states that when the consequences of a behavior are rewarding, positive, or "desirable" from the organism's standpoint, they strengthen or reinforce the tendency to produce that behavior. In terms of learning theory, then, some of the child's babblings will be reinforced and others will not. Reinforcement is most likely to follow vocalizations that are similar to adult speech. For example, parents are likely to be very attentive to the infant when they hear something that sounds like the first word, and verbal requests for, say, a cookie are more likely to be rewarded with a cookie if the mother can recognize the intended word. In one version of learning theory, the assumption is that babbling produces all the sounds found in all languages and accents. Given the spontaneous production of all language sounds, the people in the child's social environment simply reward or reinforce the sounds used in their own language community. In time, the child produces only those sounds that earn reinforcement, and in doing so becomes part of the language community.

Another version of learning theory emphasizes

yielding the five "semantically anomalous sentences" given in the table. A third set of sentences was generated by haphazardly rearranging the words of each normal sentence to destroy their normal syntactic structure, yielding the "ungrammatical strings" shown in the table. The sentences were tape recorded, and subjects were asked to "shadow" them by repeating each word out loud immediately after it was heard. When their responses were scored for the number of complete sentences correctly repeated, 89 percent of the normal sentences, 80 percent of the anomalous sentences, and only 56 percent of the ungrammatical strings were repeated correctly. Similar results were found when subjects were asked to memorize these types of sentences. Thus both semantic and syntactic rules affect our ability to hear and to remember sentences (Miller & Isard, 1963; Marks & Miller, 1964).

Explanations of Language Learning

In acquiring his "mother tongue," a child must bring to the situation: (a) a physical speech mechanism, (b) a hearing apparatus which provides feedback for reinforcement for imitating sounds, rather than "shaping" by selective reinforcement of spontaneously produced sounds. Because the voice of the mother (or other caretaker) is associated with food, warmth, and comfort, the vocal sounds of adults come to function as secondary reinforcers. It then becomes fairly easy for the child to reinforce himself by producing the sounds himself (just as you might be happy to print your own money, if it "worked"). This is Mowrer's *autism* theory of language, which holds that appropriate imitated sounds are repeated because they provide a pleasurable experience for the child. Furthermore, good imitations will also be reinforced by adults, who will exclaim and be encouraged to "talk" to the child, thus providing still more attention and vocalization.

There is empirical evidence to support the view that vocalizations in three-month-old infants can be increased by socially reinforcing occurrences of vocalizations (Rheingold, Gewirtz, & Ross, 1959). Other recent studies have shown that the incidence of a particular sound can be increased or decreased via reinforcement (see Routh, 1969). Mowrer's (1950) comparative analysis of the speech of talking Mynah birds also stresses imitation of those sounds which have been associated with rewarding experiences. The functional significance of mimicry of speech by these birds is that it attracts attention from and prolongs the presence of caretakers.

Reexamination of the learning approach. Let us briefly outline some of the arguments and evidence which suggest inadequacies in the above approach to understanding language development. First, the *variability* in environmental or reinforcing conditions should result in tremendous variability in language development and performance in different children within the same culture or across different cultures. But this is not the case. Despite differences in the kind of opportunities for training and social reinforcement offered by the great variety of social environments in which language acquisition takes place, the development of language by children of various cultures and social classes seems to follow a relatively standardized, universal pattern. An unusual speech environment is provided by deaf parents, who would be unable to reinforce adult-like vocalizations selectively since they could not hear them. Lenneberg (1969) reports a fascinating study in which he recorded the environmental sounds and the vocalizations of two groups of infants, six born of deaf parents and six of hearing parents. These observations were carried out twice a week for three months, starting before the babies were ten days old.

The children whose parents were both deaf experienced little in the way of normal speech sounds from them, and there was significantly less other sound (from TV, radio, and voices) in their homes than in the homes of the other children. However, these dramatic environmental differences made no difference between the babies in the two groups in their vocalizations (crying, cooing, and fussing). "Thus the earliest development of human sounds appears to be relatively independent of the amount, nature, or timing of the sounds made by parents." (p. 637)

Furthermore, Wahler (1969) found that mothers in a natural situation did not reinforce vocalizations selectively. In other words, they did not reinforce only the sounds that were like adult speech; they reinforced any sound about as much as any other. But still the children learned to make the appropriate sounds.

A second argument against the learning theory analysis of language is that in "normal" environments, the acquisition of language should be a gradual and continuous process. The research by Roman Jakobson cited in Chapter 4 points rather to *discontinuity* between the prelinguistic stages and true language production. In addition, it has been shown that infant babbling does *not* include all sounds found in every language. Preston (cited in Moffit, 1968) found that at least one sound—the /p/ used in *pie*—is not produced by ten-month-old infants in any of a variety of language communities.

A third criticism is that reinforcement should lead to learning only specific responses that are reinforced and then only gradually through generalization to broader response classes. Bandura (1969b), himself a social learning theorist, argues that "children can construct an almost infinite array of sentences that they have never heard" (p. 253). Instead of imitating and memorizing specific utterances they may have heard at one time or another, they must therefore be learning sets of rules, on the basis of which

● **CORRELATION OF MOTOR AND LANGUAGE DEVELOPMENT**

Age (years)	Motor Milestones	Language Milestones
0.5	Sits using hands for support; unilateral reaching	Cooing sounds change to babbling by introduction of consonantal sounds
1	Stands; walks when held by one hand	Syllabic reduplication; signs of understanding some words; applies some sounds regularly to signify persons or objects, that is, the first words
1.5	Prehension and release fully developed; gait propulsive; creeps downstairs backward	Repertoire of 3 to 50 words not joined in phrases; trains of sounds and intonation patterns resembling discourse; good progress in understanding
2	Runs (with falls); walks stairs with one foot forward only	More than 50 words; two-word phrases most common; more interest in verbal communication; no more babbling
2.5	Jumps with both feet; stands on one foot for 1 second; builds tower of six cubes	Every day new words; utterances of three and more words; seems to understand almost everything said to him; still many grammatical deviations
3	Tiptoes 3 yards (2.7 meters); walks stairs with alternating feet; jumps 0.9 meter	Vocabulary of some 1000 words; about 80 percent intelligibility; grammar of utterances close approximation to colloquial adult; syntactic mistakes fewer in variety, systematic, predictable
4.5	Jumps over rope; hops on one foot; walks on line	Language well established; grammatical anomalies restricted either to unusual constructions or to the more literate aspects of discourse

Lenneberg, 1969

they can generate an unlimited variety of grammatical sentences.

In passing, we should also note that Mowrer's Mynah birds imitated a whistle which was played in the presence of food—just as learning theory would predict. But it turned out that they also did so when the whistle was sounded in the absence of food. Thus, notes Foss (1964), "one is left with the unsatisfactory alternative of saying that Mynah birds have a tendency to imitate." (p. 88)

The psycholinguists' approach. One alternative to reinforcement as the basic mechanism for language development is based on the theories of Eric Lenneberg (1969) who stresses the importance of biological aspects. All evidence indicates that the ability to develop a real language is *species specific*; that is, unique to man. Some animals, such as baboons, for example, have developed a reasonably complex signal system to communicate the presence of danger or food. However, such systems contain no means for novelty of expression or abstraction as in man's

language, and, as we saw in Chapter 4, the ability of such animals to learn human speech is limited.

Language capacity also seems to be *species uniform*: there is no known instance of a group of human beings without a language. Furthermore, there is little difference in the complexity of the descriptions of various languages in terms of a set of abstract grammatical rules. Observations such as these have led a number of students of language processes to propose that many aspects of our linguistic ability are probably innate. That is, much of our ability to speak and understand a language is due to our genetic makeup rather than to the specific reinforcements to which we have been exposed. Lenneberg points out that "Children begin to speak no sooner and no later than when they reach a given stage of physical maturation." (1969, p. 635) He has shown that the development of language correlates consistently with motor development and maturational indices of brain development. ●

As we saw in Chapter 3, language functions in most adults are localized in the left hemisphere of the brain, and lesions in this area bring about permanent impairment of language ability. This is not true of infants, in whom the right hemisphere remains capable of taking over language functions. In light of this fact, a critical period for language acquisition can be established. Up to the early teen-age years, damage to the language center of the left hemisphere does not completely impair language competence. After that time, however, when the brain has attained its final state of maturity in terms of structure and function, compensation is no longer possible, and the same extent of damage to the major cerebral hemisphere interferes with speech permanently.

Genetic factors in language acquisition. Starting with his review of Skinner's *Verbal Behavior* (1959), Noam Chomsky has led the psycholinguists who argue along with Lenneberg that man has developed an *innate* capacity for dealing with the linguistic universals common to all languages. Experience and learning then provide only information about the specific instances of those universal aspects of language which are needed to communicate with other people within a particular language community (Chomsky & Halle, 1968; Chomsky, 1969).

This linguistic approach attacks the view that language is built upon learned associations between words. What is learned is not strings of words *per se*, but transformational rules that enable a speaker to generate an infinite variety of novel sentences and a listener to understand the infinite variety of sentences he hears. Even single words are learned as concepts: they do not stand in a one-to-one correspondence with the particular thing signified, but represent all members of a general class.

This view of the innate aspect of language learning is at first not readily integrated into existing psychological frameworks and presents a challenge that has stimulated much thought and, recently, new research directions. Chomsky argues that a precondition for language development is the existence of certain principles "intrinsic to the mind" that provide invariant structures underlying perceiving, learning, and thinking. Language involves all of these processes; thus its study sheds light on our theories of knowledge in general.

Basic to this model of language is the notion that a child's learning of language is a kind of theory construction. It is thought to be accomplished without explicit instruction, independent of intelligence level (beyond a certain minimum), at an early age when he is not capable of other complex intellectual or motor achievements, and with relatively little reliable data to go on. Nevertheless, the child constructs a theory of an ideal language which has broad predictive power. Chomsky argues that all children could not develop the same basic theory were it not for the innate existence of properties of mental organization which limit the possible properties of languages.

Transformation: From deep structure to surface structure. According to the psycholinguists, the thoughts which language communicates have their meaning rooted in a deep structure which is never actually expressed by the speaker. This deep structure is intuitively and unconsciously converted by native speakers, according to certain *transformational rules*, into the surface structure: the morphological and syntactic arrangement of the sentences they speak (or write).

Many of the sentences we use can be seen as comprising one or more smaller (*kernel*) sentences. Take, for example, the sentence "The man who is sitting at the head of the table is my father." We may consider this sentence to be composed of a transformed version of "The man is my father" and "The man is sitting at the head of the table." In this case the speaker has unconsciously transformed two separate "sentences" (at the conceptual level) into the single sentence that he speaks. He has used certain transformational rules to *embed* one sentence in the other and make the morphological and syntactic changes necessary to produce a well-formed construction. For example, the noun phrase "the man" in the embedded sentence has undergone *pronominalization* —"the man" has been replaced by "who." The principle of embedding is the fundamental one which allows us to communicate tremendously complex and interrelated systems of concepts.

There are many such transformational rules by which we are able to alter certain kinds of expressions to produce others. For example, we can transform a conceptual structure such as "John hit ball" to: an *active* sentence, "John hit the ball"; a *passive* sentence, "The ball was hit by John"; a *negative* sentence, "John did not hit the ball"; a *question,* "Did John hit the ball?"; or combinations of these such as "Wasn't the ball hit by John?" which is a passive negative question. Note, however, that we cannot make the transformation: "The ball hit John" without significantly changing the meaning of the event being described.

In challenging the traditional psychology establishment, the psycholinguists are generating research that will shed needed light on the inadequately studied process of human language development.

Environmental factors in language acquisition. Whatever the genetic factors in language development, environmental factors also play a role. A comparison of British mothers from different social classes (holding intelligence constant) reveals that those from the working class tend to use linguistic codes differing in both word usage and grammar from middle-class mothers (Robinson & Rackstraw, 1967). The "restricted" code employed by the working-class mothers, as contrasted with the "elaborate" code of those from the middle class has the following features (Bernstein, 1959):

1. Short, grammatically simple sentences, often unfinished, with syntactically poor construction.

2. Simple and repetitive use of small numbers of conjunctions (so, and, then, because).

3. Rigid and limited use of adjectives and adverbs.

4. Frequent use of personal pronouns (we, you) as subjects, rather than impersonal pronouns (one, it).

5. Frequent use of statements formulated as implicit questions which set up a sympathetic circularity ("It's only natural, isn't it?").

6. Frequent tendency for reason and conclusion to be confounded to produce a categoric statement ("Because I said so").

7. Frequent use of traditional, idiomatic phrases.

8. Implicit meaning, failing to explain the background, assumptions, and implications of remarks.

These differences are likely to lead to greater verbalized control of behavior and better planning strategies in middle-class children. The social advantages of being reared in the linguistically more enriched environment are extended further since middle-class mothers also use language much more

than their working-class counterparts for discussing emotions, morals, discipline, and their child's independence (Bernstein & Henderson, 1969).

Remembering and Forgetting in the Laboratory

It was pointed out at the beginning of this chapter that learning may be studied in two fundamentally different ways. The first—studying the change in some skill as a result of experience—has been discussed in the previous chapter and the first sections of this chapter. Now we will consider the second method of analysis—the study of memory. In studying memory we are trying to develop an understanding of: (a) how knowledge is stored, (b) how well the stored knowledge is retained over time, and (c) how stored knowledge is retrieved for use. Thus we will be concerned largely with stimulus learning rather than response learning. The stimuli most often used in these studies have been words (in some cases artificially constructed words), digits, and pictures.

Memory Studies in the Verbal Learning Tradition

In laboratory studies memory is inferred by comparing how much is remembered after some period of time with how much was known immediately after learning. It is assumed that with perfect memory the two would be the same—there would be no loss. Actually, therefore, memory is usually assessed in terms of how much the experimental manipulation—whatever it was—has increased forgetting. This explains why much of what we say about "memory" in this section will be in terms of forgetting and, furthermore, why the most important theories about memory have been developed in terms of the process of forgetting.

General experimental procedure. The usual sequence by which memory is studied experimentally has already been implied. First, some task is presented to the experimental subject to be learned, and usually some measure is made of how much learning has taken place. Second, during some length of time the subject is asked to engage in specified types of activity (perhaps additional learning or perhaps some time-filling task like doing arithmetic problems, that simply keeps him from thinking about the original task). Finally, he is tested on what he is able to remember from the original task and his score is compared with the original score at the end of the learning session.

To measure the amount remembered, the investigator may use *recall, recognition,* or *relearning.*

1. *Recall.* Recall is reproduction of the learned material. If the exam question asks you to give the causes of the Civil War, you must dredge them up out of your memory and formulate a response that convinces your teacher you know them.

Two kinds of recall are distinguished by researchers. The first is *rote* or *verbatim* recall. Whenever we need to remember the exact form of things, especially arbitrary items like telephone numbers, we must store the entire information in order to reproduce it correctly. Most cases of recall that involve any complexity, however, require some *reconstruction.* In this case, we store and recall only part of the information but are able to reconstruct the rest of the event or fact from this partial information.

2. *Recognition.* Another technique of assessing remembering involves the ability to *recognize* something previously experienced. Think of the tremendous number of objects and people you can recognize. The streets and buildings of your neighborhood, the faces of numerous friends and acquaintances, words—the list is nearly endless. Furthermore, most of the things you can recognize you could not possibly reproduce from memory. On a multiple-choice test you recognize many correct alternatives that you could not formulate.

When an experimenter wants a more sensitive measure of retention than recall, he may use the technique of recognition. Recognition is usually tested by presenting a stimulus and asking the subject whether it is one of a set he learned earlier or is a new one. Another method is to present several items and ask the subject whether he recognizes any as previously experienced. This is the technique used in the police lineup.

3. *Relearning.* A still more indirect measure of retention, *relearning,* incorporates the techniques of recall and recognition. A record is kept of the amount

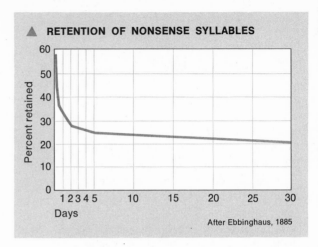

RETENTION OF NONSENSE SYLLABLES

Percent retained (y-axis: 0, 10, 20, 30, 40, 50, 60)

Days (x-axis: 1 2 3 4 5, 10, 15, 20, 25, 30)

After Ebbinghaus, 1885

of time it takes to learn the material to some criterion, such as perfect recall twice in a row. Then, after some interval of time, the subject studies the material again until he can pass the same test equally well.

Psychologists have devised the term *savings* for the extent to which an experimental subject learns a task more quickly the second time than the first. This savings score is regarded as a measure of the extent to which he has retained his original learning.

The relearning technique is the most sensitive measure of all. Even when a recognition test does not reveal any evidence of remembering, relearning may be faster than original learning, indicating that the effects have not been entirely lost.

Depending on the interests of the experimenter and the hypotheses being tested, a particular study may involve manipulating conditions in the original learning, the intervening interval, or the final remembering phase. For example, the researcher may want to compare the effects of different original learning conditions on later retention. In this case, experimental and control subjects learn under different conditions but their learning and later retention are measured in the same way and conditions are the same for them during the intervening period between learning and remembering.

Perhaps he is interested in the effects of different activities during the time interval after original learning. In this case, conditions and degree of original learning must be the same for all his subjects; otherwise, if they remembered different amounts later, he could not tell whether it was because of the different intervening activities or because of different original learning. And of course he would use the same procedure in measuring remembering. If he used recall for one group and recognition for the other, the differences in their scores might result from the differences in measuring procedure instead of the differences in intervening activity that he was trying to study.

Ebbinghaus and serial learning.   The first significant study providing a truly quantitative measure of retention was performed by Ebbinghaus toward the end of the last century. Ebbinghaus invented the "nonsense syllable"—a meaningless three-letter unit consisting of a vowel between two consonants, such as *ceg*, *dax*, and so on. His procedure was to study a list of such nonsense syllables until he could repeat the list perfectly twice in *serial order*. In addition, he would measure the amount of time it took him to learn the list. Then, after some fixed period of time—during which he would usually be learning other lists—he would relearn the original list and again measure his learning time. The amount by which this second time was shorter—the savings score—he used as his measure of retention.

The type of result obtained by Ebbinghaus is shown in the figure, where percent of time saved in relearning is plotted as a function of the length of the retention interval. ▲ As you can see, there is a rapid initial loss, followed by a gradually slower decline. This curve is typical of results obtained in *rote retention* studies.

Ebbinghaus used nonsense syllables because he wanted to obtain a "pure" measure of retention, uncontaminated by previous learning or associations that might otherwise have been brought to the task being studied. Nonsense syllables, being meaningless, would have no significance either during the conditions of initial learning or at the time of recall. In contrast, meaningful material would have been in some sense already partly learned *before* the initial learning trials. Thus the scores made in learning such material would not reflect the same amount of new learning, and without a comparable beginning point, retention scores could not be compared either. Later research has borne out Ebbinghaus' assumptions.

There is less forgetting of meaningful material, and it occurs more slowly.

Ebbinghaus' lists contained twelve nonsense syllables, and during his years of active research he memorized hundreds of such lists in his self-investigations. In fact, he frequently learned groups of ten to fifteen such lists under a given set of conditions. His method came to be one of the two standard methods of studying verbal learning and memory. It is generally known as the *method of serial anticipation*. If you have ever been given a list of directions in a strange city, you have made use of this method.

In the laboratory, the typical procedure is to present all the items in a list by exposing them one at a time for a fixed duration in the window of an apparatus called a *memory drum*. ◆ After the whole list has been shown, it is presented again in the same way and in the same order. As each item appears, the subject is asked to "anticipate"—that is, to tell what the next item will be. After the last word in the list, there is a pause; then the first word appears again, and so on. This continues for as many *trials* (presentations of the complete list) as are needed to meet whatever learning criterion the experimenter has established. In Ebbinghaus' case, as we have seen, the criterion was two trials without errors. Whatever the criterion decided on, the same one is used again later, after relearning.

◆ The pattern of serial learning is being used in this memory drum experiment. The nonsense syllable *jec* is being shown; the subject must respond with the next syllable in the series.

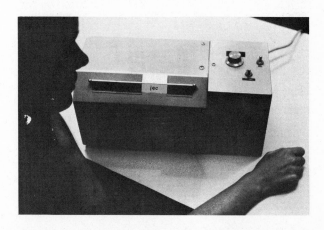

In any practical experience you have had in serial learning, you may have noticed a phenomenon that nearly always occurs. If you are learning a list of items—such as digits in a telephone number—the first and last numbers in the list seem easier to remember than the middle ones. This is called the *serial position effect.* ■ No one is completely certain yet why it occurs, but it has been observed consistently in experiments. So far, the accepted explanation is that the first and last items occupy unique positions in the list and thus are especially noticeable because they serve as markers for the beginning and the end of the list. For example, if there is no pause between the "last" and "first" item of the series—it is presented as a circular list—then the average serial position curve is markedly reduced. Sometimes the person apparently selects a subjective "starting point" for the series, and a serial position develops around that subjective anchor point.

Ebbinghaus' pioneering effort was important for several reasons. His approach, as well as his sound results, marked a transition from philosophical speculation to scientific experimentation and thus set the stage for the appearance of modern learning theory. Ebbinghaus had been impressed by Fechner's rigorous analysis of sensation (see page 82) and was the first to try to apply the same rigor and precision to the study of higher mental processes. He did this in a systematic way, studying all the variables he could think of—number of syllables in a list, rehearsal time, trials, and so on—by varying them one at a time with other variables held constant. He used quantitative measures and special materials of comparable difficulty and for the first time measured learning and remembering separately and related retention to initial learning.

By using the same learner throughout (himself) and completely objective measures of performance, he eliminated many of the sources of error and bias that plague many experimenters even today. The equation he developed for forgetting—a simple decay curve with number of syllables retained plotted as a function of time—has not been greatly modified in all the years since.

Ebbinghaus overlooked one important thing, however—the effect of having learned so many lists of nonsense syllables. It turns out that the first time a

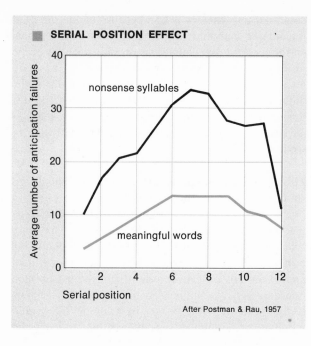

SERIAL POSITION EFFECT

Average number of anticipation failures (y-axis: 0, 10, 20, 30, 40)

nonsense syllables

meaningful words

Serial position (x-axis: 2, 4, 6, 8, 10, 12)

After Postman & Rau, 1957

subject learns nonsense syllables, he remembers about 70 percent of them the next day. The more lists he learns, the worse becomes his retention of the most recent list; after learning many lists, he may remember only about 25 percent of a list a day after he learns it. So instead of the universal curve he was trying to find, Ebbinghaus' "typical forgetting curve" turns out to be "typical for people who have learned a lot of nonsense syllables." Again we find that to generalize from the findings of particular research we must be sure that all the relevant conditions are the same.

Paired-associate learning.   Think of learning English equivalents of foreign vocabulary words, or of learning the capital cities of various states. In these cases, the information to be acquired is a set of pairs, such that one element of a pair goes with or is to be associated with the other element of the pair. These examples illustrate a second technique, known as *paired-associate learning.* Typically the subject studies each pair for a short time until the entire list has been presented. Then the first item in each pair is presented alone and the subject is asked to recall the second item of the pair.

Occasionally, instead of insisting that the recall be in the proper sequence or that the correct second member of each pair be given in response to the first member, the experimenter simply asks for *free recall* of all the items the subject can remember. Even here a serial position effect is typically found, with the beginning and end of the list learned first and the items near the middle (actually, just past the middle) learned last.

Both serial-anticipation and paired-associate learning have been used extensively to investigate particular aspects of memory. For example, one major line of investigation has been to study how learning one thing interferes with or facilitates learning or remembering something else. Both forward-working (*proactive*) and backward-working (*retroactive*) interference have been investigated using the technique of having subjects learn successive paired-associate lists in which the first items for the pairs never change but the items that they are paired with change from list to list. For example, if the pair *yuf-dax* is in the first list (X-A) then the second list (X-B) will contain a pair like *yuf-geb*. One way to test for proactive interference or inhibition is to have subjects learn first the X-A list, and then the X-B list and later, after some fixed period of time, test for recall of the list learned second—the X-B pairs. The scores for these experimental subjects are then compared with the scores for control subjects, who have learned only the second list and spent the preceding interval in some nonlearning activity. Under such conditions, the control subjects will remember more of the X-B list than will the experimental subjects, leading to the inference that the experimental group's learning of the first list must have interfered with their learning of the second list.

To test *retroactive* inhibition, on the other hand, both groups learn the *first* list instead, with only the experimental group learning the second list while the control group does some irrelevant task. Both groups are then tested again on the first list. Again the control group usually does better, presumably because of less interference from the intervening activity. Retention of the first learning is best if the interval after it was spent in sleeping, next best if it was spent in waking but nonlearning activity, next best if it was spent in learning material of quite

different content, and worst if it was spent learning similar, competing material. Typical experimental designs used by psychologists studying proactive and retroactive interference are summarized in the Ψ Close-up, below.

Sometimes there is forward-working facilitation instead of inhibition—new learning is easier because of something you have learned previously. Forward-working facilitation and inhibition are analogous to the positive and negative transfer already discussed in connection with skill learning. The more common elements or principles there are in the old and new material, the more facilitation there will be: the more the first learning will help the second. The more responses or principles the new material has that

---

Ψ Close-up *Typical Sequences for Studying Interference*

Proactive Interference

Condition	List 1	List 2	Test
Experimental	X-A	X-B	X-B
Control	filler task (no learning)	X-B	X-B

Retroactive Interference

Condition	List 1	List 2	Test
Experimental	X-A	X-B	X-A
Control	X-A	filler task (no learning)	X-A

These are called *paradigms*, meaning basic designs that can be used with a variety of content and with systematic variations in any of the terms. For example, the effect of different kinds of subjects, different kinds and amounts of content, different "filler tasks," and different time intervals can all be studied by varying one of them at a time in some systematic way within this same basic procedure.

compete with the earlier material, the greater the interference in both directions. With neither common nor competing elements, neither facilitation nor interference is to be expected.

Studies of Memory As Productive

We all know the way gossip changes the details of a story. One person hears a juicy morsel about somebody; by the time that he has a chance to tell someone else, his memory for the details seems to have changed the story slightly. After the story has passed among several people, the originator of the gossip may hear it and not even recognize it as the same story!

F. C. Bartlett, an Englishman, was not much concerned with gossip but he was very sure that such systematic distortion is a real property of memory. His research was aimed at demonstrating and explaining this distortion. Thus it represents a distinctly different type of investigation from that of the verbal learning tradition developed in this country.

Bartlett developed a technique known as *successive reproduction*, and some of his work was with visual rather than verbal memory. One person might be shown a picture and asked to remember it. After some time this person would be asked to draw the picture from memory. A second individual would be given the first person's drawing as the picture to be memorized and reproduced, and so on. The figure shows a typical result. •   In this figure the original picture of an owl was gradually transformed into one of a cat.

Bartlett's interpretation of these results was that memory is *productive* as well as *reproductive* and that this productivity induces certain predictable changes in what is stored. This productive aspect of memory helps explain the systematic distortions that take place when a *rumor* is transmitted from person to person.

Explanations of Memory and Forgetting

Explanations of memory and forgetting focus on two related questions: what is happening when we forget and how are memories stored in the brain?

Original drawing   Reproduction 1   Reproduction 2

Reproduction 3   Reproduction 4   Reproduction 5   Reproduction 6

Reproduction 7   Reproduction 8   Reproduction 9   Reproduction 10

●   The original figure is a stylized drawing of an owl. In successive reproductions it becomes increasingly ambigious; by the tenth drawing it has definitely become a figure of a cat.

Hypotheses About Why We Forget

Hypotheses about what is taking place during forgetting determine how a researcher sets up his experiments and what he looks for. Any procedure induces certain events and prevents others, thus limiting the observations that can be made. Productive, sequential changes were not observable in the experiments of Ebbinghaus; amount retained verbatim under varying conditions was not observable in the experiments of Bartlett. From the diverse types of research, several theories have been proposed to explain how and why we seem to lose material we have learned.

Trace decay theory.   According to the trace decay theory, knowledge we have learned just fades away. The longer it remains unused, the greater the decay. The amount we have forgotten is just a measure of this decay. There is considerable evidence that just as unused muscles atrophy, unused knowledge may simply be lost.

Interference theory.   In interference theory the basic notion is that any information you learn may interfere with—and be interfered with by—everything else you learn. As we have seen, the experimentation in the verbal learning tradition has amply demonstrated that one learning task may interfere with memory of another.

Trace transformation theory.   A third theory, the trace transformation theory, postulates that remembering is an active process in which information stored will be distorted or transformed to make it more stable or balanced or more consistent with other knowledge we are remembering. Bartlett's work was based on this assumption and led to considerable evidence in support of it. The details of these inherent tendencies toward stability and consistency of information will be developed further in our discussion of perception in the next chapter.

Repression theory.   In all three theories so far discussed, forgetting was viewed as an automatic process over which the individual has no direct control. Sigmund Freud considered such an approach to be wholly inadequate. His thesis was that the things we remember and the things we forget are related to their value and importance to us. Things which are very disturbing to us, for example, are likely to be temporarily "forgotten" by being driven out of our consciousness. Such *repression* is a device by which we unknowingly protect ourselves from unacceptable or painful information. In fact, repression is considered by Freudians to be the most basic of the many unconscious strategies individuals develop in order to maintain a favorable self-image.

Forgetting as loss of access.   A fifth hypothesis is that actually we never forget anything—that the things we seem to have forgotten have merely become temporarily inaccessible for one reason or another. Even without motivation to "forget," as in the case of repression, old experiences keep being overlaid with newer ones. In some cases it seems that memories are not lost but only "buried"—that new ideas interfere

with our *recalling* of older ones through some active mechanism of *response inhibition*. When this happens, techniques that eliminate the inhibition may make the older memories accessible again. But most often, it may be just a matter of our being so busy attending to newer experiences that we have no occasion to think of the older ones. We have all had the experience of suddenly remembering some fact or experience that we had not thought of for years. And as people get older, long "forgotten" childhood memories start cropping up with increasing frequency and clarity.

Perhaps the most interesting evidence of the permanence of memory is Penfield's (1958) work using brain stimulation. Penfield performed surgical operations in which a portion of an epileptic patient's temporal cortex was exposed, using a local anesthetic so that the patient remained fully conscious.

During one of his earliest operations, Penfield electrically stimulated different points on the exposed cortical surface and then, to his surprise, listened as the patient recounted in elaborate detail an early childhood experience. The patient said that although he realized it was a memory, he seemed to be actually re-experiencing the events. Penfield observed this same sort of phenomenon repeatedly in later cases. One patient stimulated in this way saw an orchestra, heard a specific piece of music, and even felt the emotion he had experienced earlier on the occasion being recalled. ■   (p. 240)

Although we do not know whether anything we have ever experienced is completely forgotten, some things clearly become inaccessible, and some are definitely changed in the remembering. It seems likely that some memories simply drop out of our awareness, some are blocked or replaced by other memories, some change to become more meaningful or stable or consistent with other things we know or think, and some, that are painful, "go underground" in some way. There is no basic inconsistency among these explanations for apparent or real forgetting and no reason to believe that all our memories must follow the same course.

Hypotheses About How We Remember

Current hypotheses about how memories are stored are concerned with the possible neural mechanisms and with the question of whether one such mechanism can explain all the remembering we do.

The great engram hunt.   As we saw in Chapter 3 (p. 99), the phenomenon of retrograde amnesia gives us some clues to the relationships between memory and physiological processes in the brain. Unfortunately, however, we still know very little about the neural basis of human memory despite considerable ongoing research and analysis. Almost fifty years ago, Karl Lashley set out to find just where memory traces, or *engrams*, might be stored in the brain. "In search of the engram," Lashley surgically removed various areas of the cortex in

■ This is the right cerebral cortex of an epileptic patient. It has been exposed for surgery with the patient fully conscious. The numbers indicate spots at which electrical stimulation produced positive responses—simple sensory and motor responses at spots 2, 3, 7, 4, and 8 and flashback experiences at spots 11, 12, 15, and 14. For example, when spot 11 was stimulated the first time, she said "I heard something familiar, I do not know what it was." When the stimulation was repeated without warning, she said, "Yes, Sir, I think I heard a mother calling her little boy somewhere. It seems to be something that happened years ago." When asked to explain, she said, "It was somebody in the neighborhood where I live." She added that it seemed that she herself "was somewhere close enough to hear." (Penfield, 1958, p. 28)

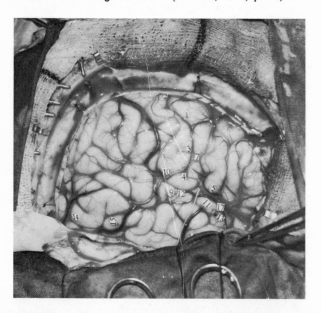

both primates and rats and observed the effects on their memory for learned tasks. His search ended in failure when he reported: "It is not possible to demonstrate the isolated localization of a memory trace anywhere within the nervous system." (1960, p. 501) From his failure he concluded that the engram probably consists of a "vast system of associations involving the interrelations of hundreds of thousands or millions of neurons." (p. 498)

Three hundred years earlier, Descartes had provided a clue to where a profitable search for memory might begin—namely with the differential transmission efficiency or receptivity at the synapses. It is revealing to review Descartes' early doctrine of the neural basis of memory and compare it with the current physiological approach to this problem. Descartes wrote:

"When the mind wills to recall something [directed attention], this volition causes the little [pineal] gland, by inclining successively to different sides, to impel the animal spirits [nerve impulses] toward different parts of the brain, until they come upon that part where the traces are left of the thing which it wishes to remember; for these traces are nothing else than the circumstance that the pores [synapses] of the brain through which the spirits have already taken their course on presentation of the object, have thereby acquired a greater facility than the rest to be opened again the same way by the spirits which come to them; so that these spirits coming upon the pores enter therein more readily than into the others." (quoted in Lashley, 1960, p. 478)

Recent experiments with rats have used drugs to change synaptic transmission efficiency and have observed corresponding changes in memory efficiency. With drugs that block reception of the transmitter substance by the receiving neuron, memory is worse. With drugs that keep the transmitter substance from being destroyed, memory improves. Such evidence suggests that the physical change underlying learning is related to an increase in efficiency of the synapse to transmit impulses following use, whereas memory deficits may be due to reduction in efficiency of synaptic transmission for one reason or another (Deutsch & Deutsch, 1966). We are, however, a long way from the day when you can take a memory pill which will enable you to remember all that you have learned.

Short- and long-term memory. Whatever the exact neurological mechanisms involved, there is general agreement that we have at least two different memory systems and perhaps more. There seems to be a short-term retention of sensory information which differs in important ways from long-term memory storage and may involve different neurological processes and even different parts of the brain.

Although the original energy that stimulates our sense receptors and triggers a nerve impulse may have only a brief duration, its presence is in effect maintained much longer both neurologically and in our consciousness. For example, a light flash as short as a thousandth of a second can produce bio-electrical activity that persists over 200 times as long. Thus we have a system for preserving sensory information long enough to be used in perceiving, remembering, judging, and so on. This *sensory storage system* has been studied by Sperling in a series of experiments on *backward masking*.

If stimulus information is being scanned for further processing during the interval immediately following reception, then a second, stronger stimulus, presented during this time, would presumably "mask" the first and thus prevent such scanning.

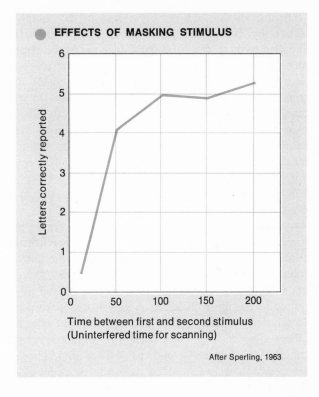

● **EFFECTS OF MASKING STIMULUS**

Letters correctly reported (vertical axis, 0 to 6)

Time between first and second stimulus
(Uninterfered time for scanning) (horizontal axis, 0 to 200)

After Sperling, 1963

To test this reasoning, Sperling (1963) presented initial stimuli, followed at various intervals by a second, "masking" stimulus. The initial stimulus in each pair was a briefly exposed slide with a number of letters on it; the second stimulus was a slide with random black and white squares. Intervals between slides varied up to 200 milliseconds (a fifth of a second).

Sperling found that the longer the interval, the more letters of the first slide his subjects reported correctly. In fact, with intervals under 100 milliseconds, one additional letter from the first stimulus pattern could be reported for approximately every 10 milliseconds of uninterfered time (no second stimulus).

In another study, Sperling (1960) used a spatial matrix composed of three rows of three letters each. When this nine-element stimulus pattern was flashed, only about four or five letters could be reported. He then ran a second experiment using a partial report method. In this case, following the flash of the 3 x 3 matrix of letters the subject heard a high, medium, or low pitched tone which, by previous instructions, meant that he was to report either the top, middle, or bottom row. Assuming that the person's earlier performance indicated that he had perceived only about four letters,

he would supposedly have seen only a third of those in any one row. The surprising outcome was that using the partial report method Sperling's subjects could report almost twice the expected number of letters. In other words, they appeared to be perceiving and briefly remembering most of the displayed items rather than only the few items available with the complete report method. With a longer interval between presentation of the display and onset of the tone, however, there seemed to be a rapid drop-off of the number of items available to the subject for recall.

Sperling tentatively concluded from this work that there must be a nearly total storage system for visual information which operates at least in part according to the principles of a decay theory. The decay rate is exceedingly rapid, and briefly flashed information must be classified or labeled by the subject and transferred to some other memory system if it is to be retained for more than a second or so.

Such studies indicate the existence of a memory store for briefly holding visual signals. Similar results and memory stores have been found for the other sense modalities. Such sensory stores are all characterized by exceedingly rapid decay of brief signals supplied to them. If a brief signal is to persist or exert an effect beyond the few seconds required for its decay, then the person must process the signal in some way. That is, he must attend to it, react to it, classify or categorize or label it, encode it, or associate to it. In the simpler cases, this reaction to the sensory signal takes the form of saying its verbal label, aloud or silently. Once this reaction has occurred, the label can then be rehearsed and remembered for many more seconds than the precategorized sensory signal.

An analogy may help to illustrate the concepts involved here. Imagine that sensory signals are like a continuous stream of suppliants arriving at the anteroom (sensory store) of a very busy palace. There are many more suppliants than can possibly be admitted to the inner chamber. A guard or doorkeeper (attention) admits some and ignores or rejects others. The rejected ones leave the anteroom very rapidly (as others arrive and crowd them out). Those favored for selective attention receive further processing, perhaps having their name announced as they are ushered into the inner chamber (the short-term verbal memory store). Once in the inner chamber, a few people can be kept waiting to see the king (go into long-term memory) as long as their names are repeatedly announced (rehearsed) by the doorkeeper. If their names are not rehearsed sufficiently often, they may cease to be remembered and be ushered out through a side door without having seen the king.

This elementary analogy to the operations of the sensory store, short-term verbal memory, and long-term memory systems even suggests some of the variables likely to affect whether a given event (sensory signal) will be remembered. A signal is likely to be quickly lost if attention is occupied elsewhere—for example, if many other signals crowd in at the same time or if the person in charge is attracted to other signals at the expense of the one in question. The likelihood that a signal will be attended to depends on many factors, including its vividness, novelty, and significance or utility to the person. A further point is that familiar sequences are perceived and encoded much more readily than unknown sequences. The letter array "FLASH" can be perceived much more

quickly than can the array "LFHSA." Furthermore, the first string can be encoded into a unified pronunciation whereas the second string requires pronunciation and continuous rehearsal of the five distinct letter sounds. In terms of our analogy, brief exposure of the string FLASH is much more likely to be admitted to the inner chamber than is LFHSA; and once admitted to short-term memory, FLASH will be more easily rehearsed and retained because of its shorter pronunciation code.

This example also indicates to some extent how linguistic encoding is implicated in short-term memory. However, we also constantly have short-term memories for conceptual representations of sensory signals that have not been encoded verbally. Deaf mutes are not devoid of short-term memories; similarly, we have transient memories lasting over many seconds or hours of tactual, visual, or olfactory sensations to which we either did not or could not attach a verbal label. Just how representations of those sensations are maintained in memory without benefit of verbal encoding is a mystery. We simply seem in many cases to remember the appearances of things in imagery, without benefit of corresponding verbal or propositional accompaniments. Certainly we would have to say that nonverbal organisms remember events or identify their recurrence in this way.

In order for us to profit from our experience—not to make the same mistakes again—information must somehow get transferred to long-term memory. According to the theory outlined above, in order to store a novel event in long-term memory, it must first go through a fragile period in short-term memory during which it could easily be forgotten or lost from the system. Some recent experiments with animals as well as clinical observations of humans with brain injuries suggest that the memory for an event during this fragile period can be easily disrupted and "shaken out" of the system. In studies with animals, a standard technique for disrupting a recent memory is to give an electroconvulsive shock to the brain or induce unconsciousness and coma by a drug. It is found that behavioral events occurring shortly before the convulsion or coma are almost totally erased from memory, so that little if any remnant of that information can be detected upon later testing. The longer the delay interval between the event and the trauma to the brain, the less the memory for an event is likely to be disrupted. This finding is in accord with the view that information transmitted to long-term memory increases with the time an item is able to remain in short-term memory without interference.

We have distinguished a long-term memory system from a short-term memory system. These systems appear to have somewhat different characteristics. For one thing, the rate and type of forgetting differ in the two cases. Loss of short-term memories is far more rapid and more likely to be a matter of simple decay over time, whereas long-term memories seem to decay less but are more subject to interference and distortion from competing memories. When there is interference in short-term memory, it is likely to be from sound-alike items, rather than from items with similar meaning. This would be expected if the short-term system holds verbal pronunciations. However, it also raises the puzzling question of how the brain can discriminate and store meanings.

Patients who have had a part of their hippocampus removed have no memory for new information but can remember material learned prior to the operation (Milner & Penfield, 1955). Thus the hippocampus may be involved in the transfer of information from the short-term store to the long-term store. Many researchers, however, prefer to use the terms *short-* and *long-term memory* to designate *processes* by which storage occurs rather than *places* where it might occur.

Several factors help to get the information transferred from the first system, where its rate of loss is great, to the second, where it is relatively more persistent. The likelihood of information getting into long-term storage is greater the smaller the amount of material presented, the more novel it is, the more actively it is rehearsed, and the greater its significance for the individual's orienting to and coping with environmental demands. Unfortunately for those who hate commercials, much information that is of no value to us gets stored in very long-term memory because it meets these criteria. Thus the messages of cigarette advertisements, which certainly have a negative value for human survival, seem to linger on and on. Consider:

"I'd walk a mile for a _____."

"_____tastes good like a cigarette should."

"You can take _____ out of the country, but. . . ."

If you recognize these slogans, you are cluttering up long-term memory storage with them and may remember them for the rest of your life.

Memory Retrieval via Context Cues

Events in the world are neither perceived nor stored in memory as unrelated, isolated, individual happenings. Rather they are both perceived and remembered as located in time and space, occurring within a causal network of surrounding events. They also arouse within us perceptual interpretations or emotional meanings or perhaps elaborate trains of associations and thoughts. Psychologists use the term *context* to refer to this psychological milieu of an event. They believe that this context—the background perceived with an event—is intimately involved in both the storage of the event in memory and the retrieval of it later. In particular, they believe that the context is always part of what is stored, and that the event can be retrieved from memory (recalled) only by the reinstatement or reactivation of some portion of that context.

Categories and cues. An analogy may prove helpful here. Imagine that putting the perception of some event (or a factual description) into our memory is like putting a book into the stacks of a large library. The location of the book and a number of indexing classifications of its contents are entered on a file card in the card catalog, and it is also cross-referenced on other file cards referencing related materials. In this illustration, the indexing items—the categories to which the event belongs—stand for the elements of the psychological context of the event, and these elements are apparently as necessary for retrieving memories as the card file entries are for retrieving a desired book.

Recall always begins with a retrieval request, stipulating the properties of the answer sought by interrogating one's memory. Queries like "Where did I leave my car keys?" or "Who invented the nonsense syllable?" provide a small set of indexing items (retrieval cues) with which we enter memory, seeking the associated information. The memory of any one fact or event is usually multiply connected to many other memories; these various connections provide alternative access routes for retrieving that fact or event. Because of the possibility of alternative access routes, it is difficult to know for certain whether an event has ever been forgotten in some absolute sense. We are all familiar with cases where some questions about an event elicit no memory of it whatsoever, whereas other questions about the same event bring back one's memory of the entire episode. Thus failures to recall may sometimes be laid to the use of ineffectual retrieval cues: the person knows the answer but has not been asked the right question to unlock that memory.

Psychologists have often demonstrated the role of different types of retrieval cues in remembering. An elementary illustration is to read aloud some arbitrary set of twenty or thirty unrelated words and then request the hearer to retrieve various subsets of this list which satisfy some criterion. Examples would be to recall all words that were in the beginning half of the series, all words preceding a particular item, all words read in a female rather than a male voice, all words denoting animals or containers, all words that rhyme with *bag,* all words beginning with the letter *b,* all words that function as adjectives, and so on. Any word, even one of singular meaning (of which there are relatively few), is classifiable in multiple ways. Thus it has multiple possible access routes, and each of these can be tried to see whether it produces recall of the specific target word.

The general outcome of such studies is the conclusion that a stimulus becomes a potent retrieval cue for an item only if the person thinks of the two as related at the time he studies the to-be-remembered item. Thus, if the person thought solely of the item *bag* as an old woman, then "a word beginning with *b*" would be an ineffectual retrieval cue. Similarly, the semantic category "containers" would be ineffectual since he had earlier "marked" the item for the semantic category of *persons* rather than *containers.*

The fact that someone can monitor and edit his recall on demand according to certain criteria does not necessarily imply that those are the retrieval cues he would normally use—just that they might be. For example, the names of the twelve months of the year are stored in most people's memories as a serial chain of verbal associations. Stop now, and try to recite the months of the year in alphabetical order. How many do you wind up with? You probably experienced some difficulty—hesitated, made false starts, "forgot to mention" a few months, and so on. It is clear in such cases that a person is meeting the stipulated recall criteria by subvocally recalling by his "normal route," then editing and overtly saying the As, then checking for Bs, and so on.

Sometimes even the most obscure memory can be reactivated by a judicious search among context cues that might be associated with that memory. Thus you might assume that the names of the guests at your tenth birthday party would be irretrievably lost to you. Yet with slow, patient effort you would be astonished to discover how much you could recall by interrogating your memory with questions about the contextual surroundings of the birthday party: Where did I live then? Who lived next door? Who were my friends then? Who was my teacher? Which relatives lived nearby? What games did I play, what did I wear, what did we eat? And so on. Often the recall of one fact seems to release the floodgates of (act as a retrieval cue for) other memories associated with it, sometimes in a startling way.

Such searches for long-forgotten memories are part of what patients do on the psychoanalyst's couch. Freud's recommended method of free association—for the patient to report without inhibition the stream of conscious thoughts and associations that flow through his mind—leads to many instances of retrieval of obscure memories by reinstatement of context cues.

Memory monitoring: knowing what you know.   You search through the stacks of a library for a specific book only if you have reasonable grounds for believing that it is there. It is patently futile to search for esoteric, out-of-date government documents in a small bookmobile. Human memories seem to have a built-in monitor that tells you whether you are likely to know something—whether a more extensive search of your memories will prove fruitful in answering the question. For example, you know that you know your current telephone number; you know that you may possibly remember your previous number; but you know surely that you do not know Mao T'se Tung's number in Peking. Experiments have shown that these feeling-of-knowing (or not-knowing) judgments can be quite accurate.

In one experiment, college students were asked a number of general information questions (e.g., "Who invented the steam engine?"). If the student could not recall the answer to a particular question, he was asked to rate his "feeling of knowing" on a 5-point scale. Later he received a multiple-choice test covering the same questions on which recall had been attempted. An analysis of only those items for which subjects could not recall the answer (which surely loaded the dice against them) revealed that their feeling-of-knowing judgments predicted whether or not they could recognize and select the correct answer on the multiple-choice test. The observed percentage of correct choices was about 63 percent for tests on items the subject thought he knew versus 47 percent for tests on items he thought he did not know, as compared with the 25 percent correct that would have been expected by chance on the four alternate questions. In other words, the subject could judge to some extent whether he knew information which he could not recall at the time (Hart, 1967).

This introspective monitoring, this knowledge of our own knowledge, is surely one of the more fascinating capabilities of the mind. It serves to inform a person whether it is worthwhile for him to search his memory for some elusive item of information; by this means, time and effort are not wasted in hopeless and fruitless searches.

Applying Learning Principles to Improve Remembering

The psychology of learning, like any science, is ultimately concerned with problems of utility as well as theory. Clearly, a set of high-level principles which successfully describe memory and learning processes will be truly valuable only if the principles tell us something about how to deal with these phenomena outside the laboratory. Such practical knowledge is important not only for college students and professional people, but for people from any walk of life. We live in a complex age. Each day we are bombarded with more information than we can possibly remember and use. Yet as participating members of

society we are called on to help make many decisions on the basis of whatever information we have gathered. And so the job of educators becomes more and more difficult as it becomes more and more crucial.

Principles of practice can come out of learning and memory research in two ways. First, research on basic processes can often suggest practical procedures. For example, in our discussion of skill acquisition we concluded that knowledge of results is necessary for efficient learning. One practical implication is that whenever you take an examination, you will benefit most if it is graded promptly and you then go over it again very carefully right away. Certainly many students would benefit if their teachers made this possible and encouraged it.

The second way in which practical principles can come out of learning and memory research is much more direct. One may conduct research directly on the question of what conditions improve learning or retention in school or other life situations. This is not to say that such practical research has no theoretical relevance. Whenever a procedure is discovered that dramatically improves retention or learning rate, theoreticians should be able to use it in improving their theories as well. For example, there is every reason to believe that discovering the utility of mnemonic schemes for aiding retention is as important a clue to understanding memory processes as was discovering that learning one thing could interfere with later learning in the laboratory.

Theory and practice are thus in no way opposing interests. As one matures, so does the other. In this final section we shall review what research both in and out of the laboratory has to say about factors that can improve our learning and remembering.

Improving Retention

Verbal learning research early identified three techniques for improving retention of learned material—overlearning, review, and recitation.

Overlearning. If your task is to learn a list, you might think that when you can recall the complete list without error, your learning is complete and there would be no point in studying it further. To the contrary: further practice, called *overlearning,* has a marked effect on how much of the material you will remember later.

In one study, subjects were given a task of serial-order learning for several lists of twelve nouns. As soon as they had learned the entire group of lists, they were divided into three groups and given varying amounts of additional practice. All three groups were tested for recall at intervals throughout the next month. The results, shown in the figure, are typical of those obtained in many such studies of overlearning (Krueger, 1929).   ▲

Review.   If you read a book at the beginning of a term and expect to be tested on its contents some time later, you are likely to make a better showing if you periodically look through the material to review it. It is thought that one reason such review is helpful is that it enables you to direct your attention to parts you did not learn thoroughly the first time. With periodic review, less and less review time is needed to maintain recall as time passes.

Active recitation.   During original learning, active recitation interspersed with reading leads to better retention of the material. Such recitation ensures active attention rather than passive reception and also ensures that your learning has reached the degree necessary for recall rather than only recognition.

Active recitation is also a useful method of review. In fact, though not the best strategy, it is even useful to test yourself on the material with the book closed —in other words, to recite the material without visually reviewing it. Psychologists have suggested that the effectiveness of such recitation, even in the absence of a check on accuracy, may lie in the opportunity it provides for practice in *retrieving* the information—perhaps devising the strategy that will be most effective later.

Motivational and Emotional Factors

As early as 1873, Herbert Spencer recognized that there is a motivated selection in what we remember and what we forget. He defined *pleasure* as "a feeling we seek to bring into consciousness" and *pain* as "a feeling we seek to get out of consciousness." Early studies, inferring memory from replies to questionnaires, tended to show that there was indeed

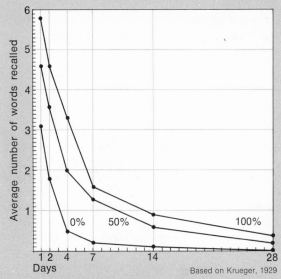

Based on Krueger, 1929

▲ **OVERLEARNING EFFECT**
Subjects who had already memorized a group of words were divided into groups which either practiced the words again for the same amount of time it had taken them to learn the words originally (100%), practiced the words for half the time it took to learn them originally (50%), or did not practice at all (0%). The 100% group recalled about twice as many words on each of six later tests, though by the 28th day, recall was very low for all groups.

preferential recall for pleasant over unpleasant life experiences.

Legend has it that several decades later, Kurt Lewin and his students were puzzled by an occurrence in a Berlin beer garden. It seems there was a waiter with such a remarkable memory that he could retain long, detailed, complicated orders without writing them down. Once after the meal had been served and he had given the party their bill, however, someone asked him a simple question about the order. It turned out that he could remember very little of it once he had completed his task.

The result was a classic experiment that demonstrated greater recall of tasks before completion than of comparable tasks after completion. This effect of enhanced recall for uncompleted tasks was named the *Zeigarnik effect* after Bluma Zeigarnik, the student who carried out the study.

In this experiment the subjects performed simple tasks which they would be able to accomplish if given enough time, such as writing down a favorite quotation from memory, solving a riddle, and doing mental arithmetic problems. In some of the tasks the subjects were interrupted before they had a chance to carry out the instructions in full. In others they were allowed to finish.

Despite the fact that the subjects spent more time on the completed tasks than on the interrupted ones, they tended to recall the unfinished tasks better than the finished ones when they were questioned a few hours later. This superiority of recall for the uncompleted tasks disappeared, however, within twenty-four hours. Apparently it was attributable to short-term motivational factors which affected the rehearsal process (Zeigarnik, 1927).

As often happens, further experimentation has refined our understanding of short-term motivational factors in remembering and forgetting. Later evidence indicates that the Zeigarnik effect applies only to memory for tasks performed under nonstressful conditions. When noncompletion threatens the individual's self-esteem, there is a tendency for the Zeigarnik effect to be reversed—that is, for the completed tasks to be remembered better than the uncompleted ones (Alper, 1952).

Improved retention under certain conditions of motivation has been even more clearly demonstrated in more recent studies. For example, it has been shown that recall is increased by emotional arousal during the learning, whether it is pleasant or unpleasant. Arousal lessens over time and negative arousal declines more rapidly than positive, so that there is greater loss of negative associations. Therefore, later on there tends to be selectively better recall of pleasant memories (Holmes & Schallow, 1969).

Other research has found that a subject will more readily learn an item if he knows that he will be punished by an electric shock for failure to recall it. Similarly, if he is paid a large sum for learning some items and a small sum for learning others, he will pay closest attention and give most rehearsal to the high-payoff items (Weiner, 1967). These effects of payoff seem to operate in determining how hard the person studies and tries to remember the information that is most relevant at the time of study. The important component is the rehearsal or strategy employed, not

how much reward the person receives for remembering. This is shown by the finding that if the person is not informed of the incentive for recalling an item until the time of the recall test, there is then little effect or even an adverse one. If the material has been stored, a simple request for recall can retrieve it even without any payoff.

Clinical experience has shown that if experiences are too painful, they may not be recalled at all. People *do,* of course, remember many unpleasant experiences, but when a particular memory threatens the individual's self-esteem, its recall may be inhibited. The following case affords a clear-cut example.

Two girls about twelve years old had been placed by their parents in a house of prostitution under circumstances that were almost unbelievably degrading. When this situation became known and the girls were encouraged by the authorities to tell their story, they gave highly detailed information which was quite adequate to incriminate their parents and the others responsible.

But when the girls were questioned again several months later, they omitted many of the factual details —even those concerning some of the more drastic parts of their experience. When their earlier testimony was summarized for them, they denied with apparent sincerity that such things had ever happened and said indignantly that the stories must have been made up to discredit them (Erickson, 1938).

In a case like this, where the original experiences had been so vivid and so emotionally significant, we would expect retention of the facts to be easy. As we have seen, inability to recall, in such cases, is attributed by some clinicians to *repression*—a self-protective, intentional but unconscious mechanism by which the person "forgets" such painful experiences. As we shall see in a later chapter, the "forgotten" material may persist at an unconscious level and produce emotional conflicts for years afterward.

The inhibiting effects of threatening experiences on memory have also been demonstrated in the laboratory. Memory has been shown to be impaired when "anxiety" stimulus words are used (Merrill, 1954), when there is a threat of failure associated with the material (Worchel, 1955), or when frustration or other unpleasantness is experienced between learning and recall (Zeller, 1950). Whether memory is facilitated or inhibited by motivation depends on the kind and intensity of emotion aroused as well as on the nature of the task, the kind of response called for, and the place in the sequence of learning and remembering at which the motivational conditions are introduced.

With controversial material, the degree of retention seems to be related to the individual's own attitudes about the issue. People have a tendency to learn material faster and remember it better when it agrees with their own associative networks than when it contradicts them (Levine & Murphy, 1943).

A (now archaic) 350-word passage dealing with the advisability of admitting women students to a male university and containing a number of pro-male, pro-female, anti-male, and anti-female statements was read by both male and female college students. After one reading of the passage the subjects were required to reproduce the material in writing at ten-minute intervals during the following hour.

The results showed significant sex differences for recall of partisan items in the passage. The male subjects retained more pro-male, pro-female, and anti-female items than did the female subjects; women subjects retained more anti-male items. Although their recall scores were somewhat higher for pro-female items than for anti-female items, women excelled men only in retention of anti-male material. In general, these results support the principle that people tend to remember best whatever is favorable to their own attitudes (Alper & Korchin, 1952).

The better memory for anti-male items than for pro-female items requires further explanation. The general tone of the passage was derogatory to female students, and the authors of the study suggest that the women's emphasis on anti-male items tended to transform a generally anti-female passage into one more evenly weighted in terms of anti-male and anti-female connotations. It is also possible that the greater recall of anti-male items by the women functioned as a symbolic outlet for aggression. And since members of both sexes retained less of the material which was derogatory to their own sex, there is evidence that repression may have functioned as one of several factors inhibiting recall of unacceptable ideas.

Important variables were uncontrolled in this study, however, and alternative explanations are possible. No check was made of subjects' actual attitudes: it was just assumed that the women would all be pro-female and the men pro-male. More serious was the lack of any check on previous familiarity of the arguments. If you know in detail the arguments for your position and have rich and diverse associative connections between these and related concepts but are not familiar with the arguments on the other side, your recall of pro and con items might be comparable to your recall of meaningful versus nonsense material.

"Chunking" and Memory

Recent research has focused on *memory units*—groups of elements that tend to be either all remembered or all forgotten together. It has become clear that the organization we see in material has a great deal to do with how fast we can learn it and how well we can remember it.

In almost any type of verbal material, various levels of units can be identified. For example, at the lowest level of any communication there are the letters or phonemes. These go together systematically in sequences to form larger units—words. Words, in turn, form grammatical segments which, in turn, form sentences. The sentences may then be organized into sequences of ideas which may themselves be organized into the general theme or conceptual structure of the communication. We describe this property of a communication by saying that the increasingly higher levels of organization form a hierarchy.

The fundamental hypothesis regarding the memory unit is that the amount which a person has to learn in any new material is determined by the *level* of the units which he already knows in the material. For example, in learning the material in this chapter most readers begin with a knowledge of the words as units. Thus at the beginning, the memory units are the words and very short phrases. Such already known units are called *chunks* by the psychologists who study them (G. Miller, 1956). Below we will discuss what you do with these chunks in order to understand and remember the content of an entire chapter such as this one. But first let us see how these basic chunks relate to our ability to learn and retain information.

Read the following sequence of letters once and

then close your eyes and try to recite them from memory.

TH – EDO – GSA – WTH – ECA – T

Very probably a sequence of letters like this one is at or near the limit of your short-term memory capacity. The way the letters are organized into groups is probably meaningless; thus the letters must be remembered individually. However, if you had noticed that this sequence of letters, with different groupings, says "the dog saw the cat," then it would have been a simple matter to remember and recall the sequence.

Our ability to recall once-presented material depends upon the number of familiar chunks we see in it. Many studies have shown that we can take in only somewhere between five and nine chunks in a brief time—as George Miller says, seven plus or minus two. This seems to be true whether the units are large or small, complex or simple.

One psychologist taught himself to recode sequences of two digits in a random pattern—for example, 101100111010—by using a code that transformed every group of three digits into a single digit between 0 and 7. For example, the series above—grouped 101,100,111,010—would be recoded as 5472.

He first determined how long a sequence of the original digits he could recall without recoding. Then he learned a recoded series. As expected, his recall increased just a bit less than threefold. Evidently what had been remembered as three chunks in the original sequence was being remembered as one chunk in the recoded series, with a corresponding increase in the amount that could be retained (S. Smith, cited in G. A. Miller, 1967).

Many studies have verified this tendency to recall a constant number of chunks, whatever their size or complexity. Thus when letters are grouped into words, there is about a sevenfold increase in the number of letters that can be retained, even though the words are more complex informational units. When the words are organized into sentences and the sentences into larger thought units, the amount of material we can take in increases accordingly.

Evidence of chunking in our perception of sentences has been provided by a technique using free recall of words in various types of "sentences."

Miller and Selfridge (1950) organized lists of words with varying degrees of similarity to the word order of natural English sentences. Below are examples of such sequences of words with various degrees of approximation to English.

Zero order: byway consequence handsomely financier bent flux cavalry swiftness weather-beaten extent

First order: abilities with that beside I for waltz you the sewing

Second order: was he went to the newspaper is in deep and

Third order: tall and thin boy is a biped is the beat

Fourth order: saw the football game will end at midnight on January

Fifth order: they saw the play Saturday and sat down beside him

Seventh order: recognize her abilities in music after he scolded him before

Text: the history of California is largely that of a railroad

These investigators found that subjects were able to recall more words when the words were arranged in sequences with a closer approximation to English. Notice that as the degree of approximation to English increases there is an increase in the average length of the sequences of words which seem to "make good sense" and correspondingly fewer chunks to be learned. The greater ease in learning them suggests that the subjects were indeed using the "sensible sequences" as chunks.

In a follow-up study, Tulving and Patkau (1962) replicated the original result, finding the same increase in words recalled with greater approximation to English. But they went one step farther and defined a "recall chunk" as any sequence of words which the subject recalled in the same order as it was in the presented list. Examining the number of such units that subjects recalled from the various lists, they found that the average size, or length, of the recall chunk increased with the list's approximation to English. But most important, for all types of lists, the *number* of chunks recalled remained fairly constant.

This kind of evidence establishes quite well the notion of chunking and constant capacity for immediate memory in terms of chunks. It may be that our greater recall for meaningful than nonmeaningful material (reported earlier in this chapter) results from the fact that nonmeaningful items such as nonsense syllables are composed of many small chunks which cannot be grouped into larger units and thus must each be processed separately.

In any case, it is quite clear that we do indeed organize material to be learned into "meaning-encoded" units. For example, we noted that initially in your reading of this chapter the chunks were probably words or short phrases. But if this situation continued, there would by now be an enormous amount of material to remember in terms of the number of chunks. Obviously you do not generally remember the precise words of any chapter you read. Instead, you remember the *topics* talked about in the chapter and the sequence of ideas. As you read, you *reorganize* the material into higher-level, meaningful units. In the present chapter, for example, there have been discussions of perceptual and motor learning, language learning, remembering and forgetting of verbal material, and now, conditions that influence efficiency of learning.

In coding material into larger meaningful units, however, we lose the precision of literal, rote memory. Thus you will remember tomorrow some of what was said in this chapter but you certainly will not remember the exact words that were used.

That it is these larger units of meaning that we are storing, rather than the exact words we have read, has been demonstrated in many studies.

In one experiment subjects were read a short story, within which was a particular sentence for which they were later given a recognition test. This recognition test came after either 0, 80, or 160 additional syllables of story. On the test, a sentence was presented which was either identical to the original one, changed in form but not meaning, or changed in meaning. As can be seen in the figure, the subjects were very good at detecting changes in meaning but not so good either at recognizing verbatim wording as the same or at detecting changes in form when the meaning had been preserved (Sachs, 1967). ●

Mnemonic Strategies

Until recently, those trying to apply psychological principles in the classroom have made little effort to deal directly with the organizational problems that confront the learner as the task of learning begins. With the discovery of chunking and the importance of hierarchical organization and meaningful encoding, however, psychologists have begun to investigate the

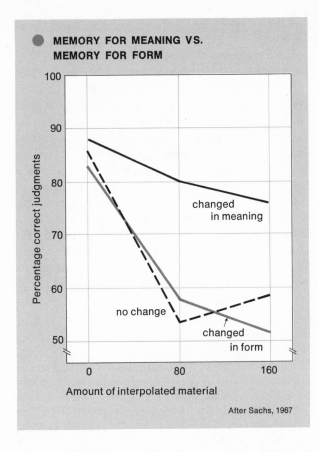

MEMORY FOR MEANING VS. MEMORY FOR FORM

Percentage correct judgments vs. Amount of interpolated material

changed in meaning

no change

changed in form

After Sachs, 1967

mental processes by which material is encoded, and techniques for making this coding more efficient. Such techniques are called *mnemonic strategies*. The idea behind most mnemonic strategies is to use old knowledge as an anchor or context for new knowledge.

Using an existing framework.   The subject may use the organization of some already well-known structure as an "outline" for new information. For example, the correct order of a group of items can be remembered more easily if they are assigned numbers in sequence. And how many young musicians have learned to name the lines of the treble staff by reciting "Every Good Boy Does Fine"?

Reducing the number of units.   One mnemonic strategy is to reorganize the material to be learned into fewer units. For example, if a list of words is to be learned, an effective technique is to group the words of the list into about seven classes in which the words of each class are related in some simple way (perhaps similar in meaning or similar in sound). These classes then become the recall units.

Increasing meaningfulness. Since meaningful material is easier to learn and recall, another effective mnemonic strategy is to give meaning to relatively meaningless material. For example, if a list of meaningless items must be learned, each of which is a cluster of three consonants like DLR, a useful strategy is to code the items into words that contain those letters. Thus DLR might be encoded as "dollar." Although "dollar" is longer, it is a unit we already know and to which we attach meaning. Such meaningful codings, in turn, can be organized further into categories or tied together in some other way.

One of the most effective mnemonic devices for increasing meaning in lists of words is to put them into a story or sentence. Bower and Clark (1969) demonstrated the effectiveness of this strategy for remembering a list of nouns.

Subjects were given a list of ten totally unrelated nouns that they had to learn in the order presented. The experimental subjects were told to construct a story in which these nouns appeared in the correct order. For example, a subject's story woven around the nouns (capitalized here) for one list was:

"A VEGETABLE can be a useful INSTRUMENT for a COLLEGE student. A carrot can be a NAIL for your FENCE or BASIN. But a MERCHANT of the QUEEN would SCALE that fence and feed the carrot to a GOAT."

Each subject learned twelve lists this way. For each experimental subject, a matched control subject was given the lists and given the same amount of time to study each one that the "story" subject had used. The control subject was given no instructions about constructing stories.

Since there were only ten words in each list, both groups of subjects had almost perfect recall for each list immediately following the study period. After all the lists had been presented and learned, however, each subject was given the first word of each list and asked to recall the rest of each list in correct order. As you can see from the figure, the contrast was dramatic. ▲ Subjects who had made up stories were able to recall correctly 94 percent of the words from all the lists, as compared with only 14 percent for the control subjects. The mnemonic strategy had increased recall sevenfold.

Using visual imagery. Visual imagery is one more example of an effective type of mnemonic strategy. The technique is particularly effective when small groups of meaningful items such as words must be associated. In this technique, the objects to be associated are pictured as being in some vivid interacting scene. For example, if the pair *dog-bicycle* is part of a list for a paired-associate task, then the pair will likely be more rapidly learned and more accurately remembered if you picture a large, spotted dog pedaling a decorated child's bicycle.

People's names, too, can often be remembered more easily by the use of such imagery. The more vivid and specific the imagery, the better. In a large number of experiments involving paired-associate learning, the technique of visual imagery has been shown to be a powerful device to improve recall.

The most appropriate mnemonic strategy to use depends somewhat on the type of material to be learned as well as the type of remembering that will be required. Such strategies have long been touted in

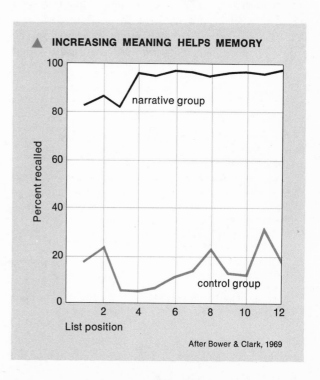

▲ **INCREASING MEANING HELPS MEMORY**

narrative group

control group

Percent recalled

List position

After Bower & Clark, 1969

the popular literature but have only recently begun to be studied seriously by psychologists and educators.

The Computer as Tutor

Computer-assisted instruction provides perhaps the most dramatic example of the application of laboratory principles to educational practice. First, let us look at the evolution of the learning principles used in such instructions.

The development of programmed learning.   The original ideas for machine teaching were embodied in the pioneering efforts of S. L. Pressey in 1926. Pressey's original teaching machine is shown in the photograph.   ◆

The techniques of *programmed learning* which were to be applied with teaching machines were developed by B. F. Skinner. Instead of using the device for review and testing of material already learned, Skinner used it for the original learning itself. His general technique was to present material to be learned in very small steps and require *active responding* by the student at each step. A bit of information was given and a simple question was asked or a blank provided for the student to fill in. As soon as the student had made his response, he would be given immediate *knowledge of results*—that

is, information as to whether he had responded correctly. Each unit—information plus question—was called a *frame*.

Shown here is a portion of a learning program devised to teach high-school physics.   ■   In this program the student proceeds one step at a time through the material, responding to every question. No deviations from the pattern are provided for; each student goes through the whole sequence. Programs which have these properties are called *linear programs*. If the program is printed in a book, the student is merely shown the correct answer after he makes his response, and then he proceeds to the next frame whether he was correct or not. If the program is presented in a machine, the student may have to make the correct response before the machine will advance to the next question.

An alternative to the linear program allows the student who makes an error on a question to branch to a special section containing supplementary material that takes him through that material in greater detail. Programs written in this way are called *branching programs*. With branching programs, the student is told why a particular response was wrong and what principles he should have applied in selecting the correct response. Then he is given another chance to answer correctly. Branching programs thus provide for more detailed knowledge of results. They

■ SAMPLE OF A LINEAR PROGRAM	Sentence to Be Completed	Word to Be Supplied
This is the beginning of a programmed lesson in high-school physics. One item at a time is presented to the student. The student makes a written response and then uncovers the correct answer (shown at the right). Such programs may be in the form of a book or may be presented by a teaching machine.	1. The important parts of a flashlight are the battery and the bulb. When we "turn on" a flashlight, we close a switch which connects the battery with the _____.	bulb
	2. When we turn on a flashlight, an electric current flows through the fine wire in the _____ and causes it to grow hot.	bulb
	3. When the hot wire glows brightly, we say that it gives off or sends out heat and _____.	light
	4. The fine wire in the bulb is called a filament. The bulb "lights up" when the filament is heated by the passage of a(n) _____ current.	electric

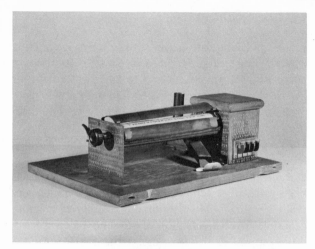

◆ The original teaching machine developed by Pressey was actually a testing machine which presented a series of multiple-choice questions which the student was to answer by pushing the proper key. The series was repeated until the student had given the correct answer to each question on two successive exposures. It was thirty years before this technique was developed further and put into widespread use.

also provide for individual differences in that all learners need not go through the extra explanations.

Computer-assisted instruction (CAI). The development of computer-assisted instruction is just a logical further step in the development of programmed learning. A number of additional techniques become possible through the use of a large digital computer, because with computer-controlled presentation, there is virtually no limit in the variety of audio and visual materials that can be incorporated into a program for study.

The diagram shows the organization of a system for CAI that operates at the University of Illinois. ● This system has been dubbed PLATO (for *Pro*grammed *L*ogic for *A*utomatic *T*eaching *O*perations). The student sits at a console and communicates with the computer through a typewriter keyboard. The computer presents its displays, questions, and messages on the television screen, which may also display photographic slides. This system has been used to teach programs as diverse as elementary arithmetic and pharmacology.

Systems such as PLATO can be used with varying degrees of interaction between the student and the computer program. The simplest of these is a *drill-and-practice system*. In this case the computer is used merely for practice. It presents a series of exercises, branching to more complicated exercises if the student responds correctly, or to simpler ones if he answers incorrectly. The second type of interaction is a *tutorial system*. Here the program is not merely providing supplementary exercises for practice; instead the computer is actually used to teach new concepts. The system acts as an individual tutor by branching to levels of successive difficulty as the student becomes ready for them. The third type of system is the *dialogue system*. Here the student is free to ask certain questions of the computer as well as being questioned. As yet, attempts to develop dialogue systems have not been very successful, although the PLATO system allows for a program with "inquiry logic," in which students are allowed to select questions from a prepared list.

One computer-assisted instruction system has a central computer at Stanford University operating 1000 student terminals in elementary schools throughout the country (Suppes, 1967; Atkinson, 1968). Materials are presented on a cathode-ray tube and responses may be made by touching a special probe directly to the tube, as shown in the picture. If the student's answer is correct, the computer so informs him and presents the next bit of material to be learned. If it is incorrect, the student

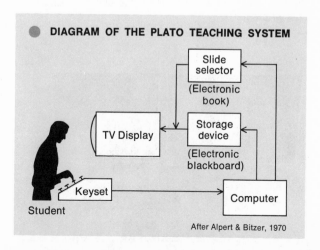

● **DIAGRAM OF THE PLATO TEACHING SYSTEM**

Slide selector
(Electronic book)

TV Display

Storage device
(Electronic blackboard)

Keyset

Student

Computer

After Alpert & Bitzer, 1970

is "branched" to a review or to a simpler level of material. ▲

It is clear that computer-assisted instruction can optimize many of the conditions for learning which we have discussed in this section. The display devices, when used properly, can catch and hold the complete *attention* of a student. At least initially, the novelty of working with a computer produces high levels of *motivation*. It keeps calling upon him for active responses (*recitation*) and presents new material only as he is ready for it. And finally, it provides the prompt and specific *knowledge of results* required for efficient learning. The main difficulty has been that so far no one has been able to write a program to foresee and provide for all possible problems.

A fascinating and unexpected result came out of research on one CAI project. A group of junior-high youngsters from disadvantaged backgrounds in San Jose, California, were taught by both a CAI system and a real, flesh-and-blood teacher. After the instruction experiment was over, the children were asked to rate both the computer and the teacher on scales such as fairness, intelligence, and warmth. Amazingly, the computer was given a superior rating to the teacher on all these scales (Hess & Tenezakis, 1970). Evidently the children not only attributed human qualities to the computer but liked it better than their human teacher.

▲ This computer-controlled apparatus "asks" the student questions and "responds" to his answers. The problem is presented on the screen at left; the student selects one of the possible answers by touching the other screen with a special probe.

Chapter Summary

Man's capacity for learning and for remembering what he has learned makes it possible for him to adapt to his environment and to change it to suit his needs. Human learning often goes beyond mere processing of stimulus input to include selection, reorganization, and transformation of that input.

Psychologists make a distinction between *learning*, a change in performance as the result of experience, and *memory*, retention over time of material that has been learned. Psychological studies of learning generally involve skills in responding; studies of memory generally involve retention of stimulus patterns.

Perceptual skills are among the first things the infant must learn. According to Eleanor Gibson, perception is primarily a process of *reduction of uncertainty*. The world becomes more structured for the infant as he makes discriminations, identifies continuity, and learns more subtle and complex relationships, rules, and patterns—eventually developing a set of perceptual habits. Early experience in processing sensory input seems essential to adequate perceptual development.

We must not only learn to organize information from the environment, we must also learn purposeful, organized sequences of behavior (*skills*) based on such information. Skills that involve primarily the use of the muscles are called *motor skills*. Learning of such skills proceeds rapidly at first, then gradually levels off as the learner reaches his maximum level of proficiency. Once learned, motor skills seem to be retained almost indefinitely.

An extremely important element in any kind of skill learning is *psychological feedback*, through which the individual gains knowledge of the results of his previous responses, enabling him to make any necessary corrections or adjustments in subsequent responses. The more closely feedback is related to specific responses (rather than to overall progress), the better. Feedback may be either *intrinsic* or *externally augmented*. Disrupting or delaying feedback can drastically impair performance.

The nature of practice has considerable effect on performance. While motor skills cannot be learned without motor practice, a certain amount of conceptualizing practice (mentally picturing performance) can facilitate learning. *Distributed practice* is more advantageous than *massed practice* for motor skill learning, though this is not necessarily true for verbal or ideational learning.

Skill learning may be affected by prior or subsequent learning. *Positive transfer* occurs when previous learning makes a new skill easier to learn, *negative transfer* occurs when it interferes.

The study of language and language learning, *psycholinguistics*, begins with the study of the content and structure of language. Linguistic analysis takes place on three levels: (a) the *phonological level*, concerned with *phonemes*, the basic sound units of language; (b) the *grammatical level*, which includes *morphemics*, the study of *morphemes* (words and meaningful word segments) and *syntax*, the rules for combining words and phrases into sentences; and (c) the *semantic level*, concerned with meaning.

Language learning results from the child's encounter with language models in the environment. Learning theorists hold that language is learned like any other behavior, through *reinforcement* of correct responses which the infant produces spontaneously or in imitation of adults. Psycholinguists, on the other hand, argue that language production is an innate human ability, based not on imitation, but rather on construction of a general theory of language based on transformational rules. Of course, environment also plays a role in language learning, since language varies according to geographical and social factors.

The study of memory involves the questions of how knowledge is stored, retained, and retrieved. It is conducted by measuring the amount retained immediately after learning and the amount retained at some later time. Verbal learning studies use the methods of *recall* (either verbatim or reconstructive), *recognition*, and *relearning* (in which the experimenter is interested in *savings* in learning time). The verbal learning tradition began with Ebbinghaus, who learned lists of nonsense syllables by the *method of serial anticipation*. Ebbinghaus found a typical rote retention curve with rapid forgetting at first, followed by a gradually slower decline, and also a *serial position effect* (a tendency for the first and last items in a series to be recalled most easily).

Also used in studying memory is the *paired-associate method,* in which the subject learns pairs of words and must recall one of the pair when given the other. *Free recall* is also studied. The paired-associate method has been used extensively in studying forward (*proactive*) and backward (*retroactive*) inhibition. Memory can also be *productive*, distorting details of the thing recalled. Studies of this phenomenon employ the technique of *successive reproduction* of pictures or stories.

Explanations of forgetting include the *trace decay theory*, the *interference theory*, the *trace transformation theory*, the *repression theory*, and the *theory of loss of access*. It is likely that different theories account for different types of forgetting.

Theories of how we remember vary greatly. Physiological psychologists are investigating the relationship of memory to the efficiency of synaptic transmission. Although the nature of the neurological mechanisms involved is not clear, there is general agreement that there are two or more kinds of storage. In *short-term memory*, sensory input is stored for immediate use. Content that is to be retained for longer periods of time must be transferred to *long-term memory* storage. All memories are imbedded in the context in which they were originally perceived, and *contextual* clues are thought to be used in retrieval.

Principles gained from learning research that can be used to improve one's own learning and retention include *overlearning*, *review*, and *active recitation*. *Chunking* and *mnemonic strategies* are also useful. Motivational and emotional factors, such as the pleasantness or unpleasantness of an event or our attitude toward it, can have an effect on what we remember.

The concept of *programmed learning,* based on Pressey's early teaching machines, is one of the most exciting new areas in the study of learning. Programming techniques emphasize *active responding* by the learner and *immediate knowledge of results*. Programs may be either *linear* or *branching*. The latest development in this field, *computer-assisted instruction* (CAI) may involve varying degrees of interaction between the pupil and the computer, including *drill-and-practice systems*, *tutorial systems*, and the more complex *dialogue systems* in which actual give-and-take is possible. In some cases, CAI programs have seemed to elicit better attention and motivation than ordinary teaching methods.

Part Four

Stimulation and Information Processing

Although the capacity to profit from experience is a key to the versatility shown by both man and beast in adapting to environmental contingencies, it may not unlock all the secrets of psychology which we seek. Why do we spend a third of our lives sleeping? What *is* the stuff that dreams are made of? How are we aroused to consciousness and to action? How are we able to separate what we want to attend to from what is irrelevant or distracting? How is it possible to establish a perception of events as related, unique, continuing, and invariant when the stimuli that keep bombarding us are discrete, similar, momentary, and variable?

In answering such questions about sleep, arousal, attention, and perceptual processes, we begin to see further complexity in the organism that we have been observing in the process of developing and learning. But it is when we turn to consider the mechanics of thinking, the intricacies of reasoning and problem solving, and especially the puzzle of creativity that the phenomenon that is man emerges in a new dimension. So far has man gone beyond mere concerns for survival—for adapting to the tasks the *environment* poses for *him*—that he now transforms his environment and even designs computers and robots to simulate human thought and action. Both as evidence of his creativity and power to control and as a source of clues about how *he* was designed to function as he does, computer simulation of human psychological processes holds fascinating possibilities, some of which we will examine in this section.

But getting the whole complicated show on the road requires motivation. The driving force which initiates, activates, energizes, directs, and keeps behavior going despite obstacles, setbacks, and lack of reward is motivation. Impetus for action is provided by the more biologically based drives of hunger, thirst, sex, temperature regulation, and pain and is bolstered by psychological and social motives such as curiosity, anxiety, and achievement needs. The interrelated role of physiological factors and external stimulus conditions in arousing motivational states will be explored in depth here. The incentives that will induce action and the reinforcers that will be effective depend upon motivational conditions.

The girl who writes to a lovelorn column, "How can I get this dreamer aroused enough to pay attention to me and perceive that I'm nice and want to marry him?" is asking a motivational question that touches all the bases we will lay out in this section. But so too do the related queries of educators, politicians, businessmen, the man in the street, the bewildered parent, and the student in whatever field he or she may be.

Chapter 7

Awareness of the World We Live In

Each of us, locked within the isolation chamber (or you might say time-bound capsule) of his own body, spends a lifetime trying to discover what the outer world and other people really are like. Without such knowledge about what is "outside" we can never know what we are like "inside."

However, this search must be called off every night as we, like most other living creatures, move into the state of sleep. Man has always been fascinated by this cloak of darkness which falls over his consciousness, and even more by the dreaming which accompanies it. It is only quite recently that psychologists have developed physiological techniques for studying this behavior. It has been found that not only do we human beings each have several dreams every night of our lives; so do monkeys, dogs, cats, and other animals. Research in this area holds promise of discovering the link between the "normal" irrationality that we all express in our dreams and the "abnormal" madness that some people manifest when they are awake.

No less interesting for the psychologist are the mechanisms by which we become aroused, alert, and once again aware of the distinction between our internal reality and the external reality of the environment. In fact, the beginning of our search is learning how to focus our attention and on what. Our attentional processes perhaps underlie all of our more complex adjustments to the environment.

Beyond attention comes perception. Without the perception of objects, space, events, movement, people, and relationships, we would drift through a world of meaningless, random sensations. Perception is the ordering principle which gives coherence to sensory input and meaningful unity to stimulus elements, thus making possible an organized direction to our behavior. It is our perceptual processes that enable us to find stability and continuity in a world of constant change.

Levels of Awareness

To be able to interact with the world around him, a person must first be *aware* of that world. That is, he has to be receptive to all the many different events that are occurring in the environment. In Chapter 3, we saw how various kinds of stimuli can get "into" the organism and be processed in the central nervous system. However, whether the sensory pathways are open or closed to stimulation is largely a function of the person's state of awareness. In his normal waking state, a person is sensitive to all the cues in his environment for which he has receptors (although he may be attending to some more than to others—a problem we will be discussing later on in this chapter). In other states, such as sleep, he is much less aware of these environmental cues and is quite unresponsive to normal sights, smells, sounds, and other stimuli.

But just what accounts for these differences in awareness? What are the mechanisms which control man's responsiveness to the outside world? To answer these questions, scientists have begun to focus more attention on the physiological and behavioral apects of both the sleeping and waking states. We often think of sleep in a negative way, as being a *lack* of action and awareness and only serving a restorative function. Actually, investigators are discovering that it is an extremely complex state, with much activity taking place in the body while we are asleep. Such activity appears to be intimately related to many aspects of our behavior, such as attention, emotion, memory, and learning. Thus the study of sleep may be one way of increasing our understanding about awareness and the waking state.

The Behavior We Call "Sleep"

"All men sleep. Between the darkness out of which we are born and the darkness in which we end, there is a tide of darkness that ebbs and flows each day of our lives to which we irresistibly submit. A third of life is spent in sleep, that most usual yet profoundly mysterious realm of consciousness where the person seems to live apart from the waking world. . . ." (Luce, 1965, p. 1)

Sleep is a very familiar state to all of us, and yet we know surprisingly little about it. Only in the last decade has sleep been the focus of a great deal of study and research.[1] As a result of this interest, science has made some exciting and enlightening inroads into those dark periods of stillness that we call sleep.

Must we sleep? Undoubtedly, there have been times when you wished that you could get along on much less sleep than you normally do. The night before an examination or a term paper might seem par-

tially wasted because you can't use all those hours for study. You have probably also heard stories about people who have managed to go without sleep for long periods of time and yet still performed well (e.g., doctors in a hospital, soldiers on a battlefield). These all raise the question of just how important sleep is to our normal functioning. How much sleep could we eliminate before we suffered any negative consequences? Some suggestive evidence on this point is provided by an example of extreme sleep deprivation.

In January, 1959, a thirty-two-year-old disc jockey named Peter Tripp staged a 200-hour "wakathon" in a Times Square booth for the benefit of the March of Dimes. During this sleepless marathon, he was attended by several doctors and given periodic medical examinations, performance tests, and psychological tests. From the beginning, Tripp had to fight to keep himself from falling asleep. After two days, he began to have visual hallucinations, such as seeing cobwebs in his shoes. By 100 hours, his memory was becoming quite poor, and he was having a great deal of difficulty with simple performance tests. His hallucinations became more and more frightening: he saw a doctor's tweed suit as a suit of furry worms, and when he went to a nearby hotel for a change of clothing, he saw the bureau drawer in flames. To explain these visions to himself, he decided that the fire had been deliberately set by the doctors in order to frighten and test him.

A simple algebraic formula that he had earlier solved with ease now required such superhuman effort that Tripp broke down, frightened at his inability to solve the problem, fighting to perform. Scientists saw the spectacle of a suave New York radio entertainer trying vainly to find his way through the alphabet.

"By 170 hours the agony had become almost unbearable to watch. At times Tripp was no longer sure he was himself, and frequently tried to gain proof of his identity. Although he behaved as if he were awake, his brain wave patterns resembled those of sleep. In his psychotic delusion, he was convinced that the doctors were in a conspiracy against him to send him to jail. . . . At the end of the 200 sleepless hours, nightmare hallucination and reality had merged, and he felt he was the victim of a sadistic conspiracy among the doctors." (Luce, 1965, pp. 19-20)

Although the setting of Peter Tripp's bad trip was an unusual one, the effects on his behavior were not. Similar results have been obtained in more systematic

---

[1]This widespread interest in sleep research is demonstrated by the fact that there is now an Association for the Psychophysiological Study of Sleep, which held its tenth annual meeting in 1970.

studies of prolonged wakefulness. Experiments conducted at the Walter Reed Army Hospital have provided a clearer understanding of some of the phenomena that Tripp experienced. For example, the deterioration in performance is a consequence of "lapses" or periods in which the person is unable to respond, rather than a general decline in ability. During these periods, the person shows a brain wave pattern that is characteristic of the sleeping state (Murray, 1965). Another interesting aspect of this research is that practically all of the symptoms of sleep loss, including the more extreme ones, disappear with a single night's sleep. Such quick recovery raises some questions about the amount of sleep necessary to maintain normal functioning.

The physiological changes that result from loss of sleep have still not been identified. However, there is some evidence that the production of ATP (a body chemical necessary to transform food energy into useful energy) stops almost entirely after several days of sleep deprivation (Luby, Frohman, Grisell, Lenzo, & Gottlieb, 1960).

The shape of sleep.   In studying sleep, psychologists are concerned primarily with *internal* behavior—that is, processes that are presumed to take place inside each person. However, as we have seen, before we can study such behavior we must find a way to make it external so that it can be observed and measured. Thus some of the basic problems in psychology are methodological ones—how do you go about externalizing internal behaviors?

The lack of early research on sleep was due primarily to the lack of methodology. No one knew how to identify all the differences between a light sleep and a much deeper one; no one could tell when a person was dreaming. In fact, scientists did not even know how to pinpoint the moment of drowsiness when a person actually falls asleep.

The methodological breakthrough for the study of sleep came with the development of the electroencephalograph, which allowed man to "listen" to the brain (see Chapter 3). In 1937, Loomis and his associates made the important discovery that brain waves change in form with the onset of sleep and show further changes during the entire sleep period. This meant that researchers could now continuously

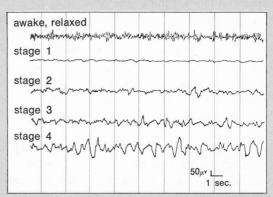

After Webb, 1968

■ EEG CHARACTERISTICS DURING VARIOUS STAGES OF SLEEP

The top line shows the wave pattern of 10 cycles per second, called *alpha rhythm,* which characterizes a relaxed waking state. As the person begins to fall asleep, the alpha rhythm disappears and is replaced by the low-amplitude, fast, irregular rhythm of Stage 1, which is very similar to the EEG pattern of an active waking person. In Stage 2 the person is more soundly asleep, and his EEG pattern shows the presence of sharply pointed waves known as *sleep spindles.* Stages 3 and 4 are characterized by high-amplitude, slow waves which are called *delta waves.* These waves are most predominant in Stage 4—a state of deep sleep from which a person is not easily awakened.

monitor the changes within sleep, as well as accurately demarcate its beginning and end.

The various wave patterns of the EEG that indicate different levels of depth of sleep are shown in the figure. ■ There is another stage of sleep called *Stage 1-REM.* It has the same EEG pattern as Stage 1, but it is accompanied by rapid eye movements (REM), and an inhibition of motor activity. This is the stage in which dreaming occurs. Although the EEG pattern of this stage resembles that of an alert, waking state, the person is very deeply asleep (as indicated by the difficulty in awakening him). For this reason, REM sleep is often termed *paradoxical sleep.*

During sleep, people drift several times from one stage of sleep to another. The stages do not occur with equal frequency during all periods of sleep. For example, Stage 4 occurs primarily during the first half of the night, while REM sleep is more frequent in the last third. The amount of time spent in each stage varies tremendously among different people, but any single individual is remarkably consistent in the sleep pattern that he shows night after night. In general, people spend about 5 percent of their sleep in Stage 1, 25 percent in Stage 1-REM, 50 percent in Stage 2, and 20 percent in Stages 3 and 4 (Williams, Agnew, & Webb, 1964). •

To sleep, perchance to dream.   Although sleep was opened up to research by the use of the EEG, the scientific study of dreams had to wait for another methodological discovery. It was suspected that dreaming might occur in certain stages of sleep and not in others, but the brain wave patterns did not provide the answer. Instead, an incidental finding in 1953 provided the key to dream research. While working on a study of sleep, Aserinsky and Kleitman noticed that several times during the night there were rapid, jerky movements of the closed eyelids, indicating that eye movements were occurring. During these periods there were increases in both heart rate and breathing, which suggested an emotional response. Acting on the hunch that REM activity was associated with dreaming, the experimenters woke their subjects during REM periods. The subjects almost always reported that they had been dreaming, while they rarely did so when awakened during other periods of sleep (Aserinsky & Kleitman, 1953).

▲   The treadmill prevents the cats from falling into REM sleep. Although they can doze briefly as they ride to the end of the slowly moving belt, they cannot go into a deep sleep without being carried over the end of the device and landing in a tank of water.

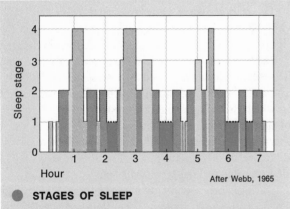

Hour

After Webb, 1965

● **STAGES OF SLEEP**

The graph shows an individual's progression through various stages during seven hours of sleep. The solid color bars indicate periods of Stage 1-REM.

These findings were confirmed by Dement and Kleitman (1957), who also showed that the REM period of sleep was accompanied by the "awake and active" EEG pattern of Stage 1. Since then, major physiological changes, particularly in the autonomic nervous system, have been established as a common feature of REM periods. These changes often include large, erratic fluctuations in heart rate and blood pressure (Snyder, Hobson, Morrison, & Goldfrank, 1964). Such "autonomic storms" have important medical implications because it has been found that heart attacks and cardiac failure often occur during the early morning hours—the time when a person is most likely to be in REM sleep.

With this increased activity in the nervous system, one might expect the person to display more bodily movement than usual. This does not occur, however. It appears that there is a special mechanism in the brain which operates during REM sleep to inhibit motor activity by blocking nerve impulses traveling to the muscles (Dement, 1969). As a result, the body "goes limp" during REM sleep (although occasional muscular twitches show that this inactivity is not always complete). This inhibitory straitjacket is a protective device, since without it the dreamer would be forced to act out his dream. For example, when the inhibitory brain area is destroyed in cats, they jump around, spit, and hiss during their REM periods, even though they are deeply asleep, their eye membranes are closed, and they are oblivious to the environment (Jouvet & Delorme, 1965).

The stuff that dreams are made of. At this point, you may be wondering, "why the long description of dreaming? How important could dreams possibly be?" Actually, we are discovering that dreaming, or at any rate REM sleep, is extremely important; not only can it affect our emotions and other waking behavior, but it may provide a key to the mysteries of such mental illnesses as schizophrenia.

One way to determine the importance of some bodily function is to deprive the organism of it and see what the subsequent effects of such deprivation are. Our "need to dream" was demonstrated by just such a technique. Volunteer subjects were allowed to sleep normally until they began to go into REM periods. They were immediately awakened at that point, and then allowed to go back to sleep until the start of the next REM period. In this way, they were virtually prevented from having any REM sleep. Subjects in a control group were awakened the same number of times during the night, but only during *non*-REM (NREM) sleep. As compared to the controls, the REM-deprived subjects started more REM periods each successive night of deprivation. Their daytime behavior also changed considerably, with increases in irritability, anxiety and tension, difficulty in concentrating, and memory lapses. Many reported a marked increase in appetite and gained an average of a pound a day. When finally permitted to sleep undisturbed, subjects "made up" for their deprivation by dreaming about 60 percent more than they normally did—a phenomenon known as a *REM rebound* (Dement, 1960).

The human subjects in the above experiment were deprived of REM sleep for only five successive nights. What would be the effects of a much longer deprivation? To answer this question, cats were systematically deprived of their REM sleep by being placed on an automated treadmill. ▲ The cats were

---

Ψ *Close-up*   *"Sleepwalking"*

If bodily movement is inhibited during REM sleep, how do we explain such phenomena as sleepwalking? We intuitively think of sleepwalkers as "acting out" their dreams, a view which seems to be supported by various anecdotes. For example, a college girl was awakened by her roommates after they found her beating their beds with her pillow. She reported that she had been dreaming that their bedroom was on fire and that she was trying to put the blaze out. In another case, a woman was found lying in her nightgown on the ground, crying from the pain of a broken leg. She said that she had dreamed she was eloping with her fiancé, and had stepped out of the window onto a ladder which, it turned out, existed only in her dream.

Despite stories such as these, however, the assumption that sleepwalking takes place during REM sleep appears to be a false one. There is experimental evidence that it occurs in the deep sleep periods of Stages 3 and 4, which are not associated with much dreaming. As the sleepwalker moves around, his EEG patterns show a shift from deep to light sleep, as though he were about to wake up (although he usually remains asleep). Although his eyes are often open, and he is able to avoid bumping into furniture, the sleepwalker shows little recognition of things in the environment. Furthermore, he usually has no memory for any of his sleeping excursions (Jacobson, Kales, Lehmann, & Zweizig, 1965).

deprived of REM sleep for as long as seventy days, but even such extreme deprivation failed to produce any basic impairment in the animals' behavior. However, there was a dramatic *enhancement* of all drive-related behaviors. The REM-deprived cats became hyperaggressive and hypersexual (even mounting other male cats who were anesthetized). Also, their hunger apparently increased, since they ate their food in only half the normal time (Dement, Henry, Cohen, & Ferguson, 1967). Exactly how REM sleep is related to the control of primary drives is a fascinating problem that has yet to be solved.

What other role might REM activity have? One possible clue is found in the large amount of REM sleep in infants. Newborns spend about 50 percent of their daily sleep in the REM period. ◆ As the infant grows older, there is a sharp decline in the amount of REM sleep, while amount of NREM sleep remains fairly constant. It has been hypothesized that

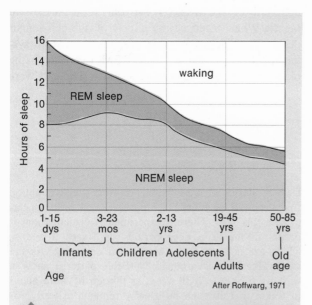

◆ **AGE CHANGES IN REM AND NREM SLEEP**

The graph shows how the total daily amount of time spent in REM and NREM sleep changes with age. REM sleep shows a steep decline, from 8 hours out of 16 at birth to just over 1 hour out of 6 in old age. NREM sleep, after a slight rise, falls more slowly, eventually coming to represent about 80 percent of the total.

the REM mechanism provides a great deal of stimulation for the higher centers of the brain. Such excitation during early development might promote the growth and development of key sensory and motor areas within the central nervous system, thus preparing them to handle stimulation from the environment. As the child matures, there is less need for such "autostimulation," and so the amount of REM sleep declines (Roffwarg, Muzio, & Dement, 1966). This is a provocative theory, but further evidence is needed to check its accuracy.

An even more exciting result of the study of dreams is the discovery of their possible link to schizophrenia. Such early thinkers as Sigmund Freud and Carl Jung had noted the similarity between dreams and psychotic episodes, and the idea that schizophrenics were "dreaming while awake" has been the subject of much speculation. A recent study of actively ill schizophrenic patients found that they failed to show the normal REM rebound effect after having been deprived of REM sleep (Zarcone, Gulevich, Pivik, & Dement, in press). This suggested to Dement and his colleagues that REM activities were being discharged during the patients' waking hours. If deprivation of REM sleep did not mean complete cessation of REM activity, there would be no need for the usual compensatory rebound. If this was the case, reasoned Dement, the bizarre symptoms of psychotic patients might represent activity that would normally be discharged as dreams during periods of REM sleep when connections to the muscular system were "turned off."

What brain mechanism might allow REM activities to "spill over" into the waking state? Current research appears to implicate a brain chemical called *serotonin*. Turning back to his laboratory, Dement began treating cats with a chemical compound which blocks the production of serotonin in the brain. The cats showed marked changes in behavior: they appeared to be "hallucinating" much of the time, turning their heads to "listen" in a silent room and striking out at objects that weren't there. During these hallucinatory episodes, electrical recordings of activity in the cats' visual systems showed patterns usually found only during REM sleep. These cats also seemed to lose control of their drive responses, just like the ones that had been deprived of REM sleep for long periods of time. Furthermore, when themselves deprived of REM sleep, the treated cats, like the schizophrenic patients, failed to show a rebound effect. It was shown that all of these bizarre "psychotic" behaviors could be eliminated by administering chemical compounds which facilitate the production of serotonin. One such compound is *chlorpromazine*, a drug which has long been used in the treatment of schizophrenics (Dement, 1969).

All this experimental evidence suggests that there is a system in the brain which regulates drive behaviors and normally "discharges" through dreaming. If the functioning of this system is disrupted (e.g., by depleting the serotonin supply), there is an uncontrolled occurrence of REM activities and drive behaviors in the waking state. It is possible that this type of malfunctioning is the basis for the mental illness we call *schizophrenia*. Much experimental work must be done to test such hypotheses. Nevertheless, we have already learned much about man by studying the mind at those times when it is speaking only to itself.

The Neural Control of Sleep and Waking

What is the mechanism which determines whether we are awake or asleep? Is it localized in some part of the central nervous system? Scientists once thought they had the answers to these questions; however, as often happens, they are finding that the truth is far more complex than they ever imagined.

The reticular activating system. As we discussed in Chapters 3 and 5, the reticular formation is one of the major brain structures implicated in alertness, orientation, and sleep. The general location of the reticular formation within the brain is shown in the illustration on page 98. Its core is surrounded by sensory pathways ascending to higher regions of the brain, and by motor pathways descending from the brain.

In a classic experiment, Bremer (1935) cut the brains of cats at the level of the brain stem and found that these animals behaved as though they were asleep. Their EEG patterns showed the slow waves and spindles associated with sleep, and the pupils of their eyes were constricted to a narrow slit (another

response indicative of the sleeping state). Bremer thought that the animals "slept" because transection of the brain at that level abolished most sensory input. His data seemed to support the prevalent theory that waking states occur during the presence of sensory stimulation, and that sleep ensues when sensory input is abolished.

This theory had to be discarded after the publication of Morruzzi and Magoun's famous study of reticular activation (1949). They demonstrated that electrical stimulation of the reticular formation aroused and awakened sleeping cats. The EEG patterns changed from the spindle pattern of sleep to the low voltage, fast activity of the waking animal. Since the reticular formation was the part of the brain transected in Bremer's animals, the data from these two studies made possible the conclusion that impulses from the reticular formation are the source of both EEG patterns and behavioral arousal. It is for this reason that it is often called the *reticular activating system* (RAS).

More recent studies have continued to refine our understanding of the RAS. The earliest experiments involved lesions of the RAS (i.e., much of the RAS was destroyed, to see what effect this had on the animal's functioning). Such massive lesions produced a comatose animal which soon died (Lindsley, Shreiner, Knowles, & Magoun, 1950; French & Magoun, 1952). These results supported the idea that the RAS was solely responsible for arousal. However, if the lesions were made in several stages, rather than all at once, the animals showed considerable recovery of both general behavior and conditioning performance (Adametz, 1959; Doty, Beck, & Kooi, 1959). This suggests that the RAS is not absolutely essential for maintenance or initiation of arousal, although it probably contributes to that function in the normal animal. Its importance is further confirmed by the fact that animals do better on discrimination tasks when the RAS is electrically stimulated, presumably making them more aroused and alert. The stimulated animals show a greater percentage of correct responses, with shorter reaction time, than do nonstimulated controls (Fuster, 1958).

Other neural centers. In addition to the RAS, there are other parts of the brain which appear to affect the sleeping and waking states. One such neural "center" is a part of the thalamus, called the *diffuse thalamic system*. Slow, repetitive stimulation of this area produces sleep in normal, waking cats (Akert, Koella, & Hess, 1952). Experimental observations such as these have led some investigators to the theory that the diffuse thalamic system is the active "sleep center," while the RAS is the active "wakefulness center" (Magoun, 1963a). The hypothalamus and other parts of the brain stem also have important roles in sleeping and waking.

It should be emphasized that the existence of all these brain "centers" is still rather hypothetical and cannot be regarded as conclusively proven. In fact, there are many scientists who would reject the idea of neural "centers" which control wakefulness and sleep. Rather, they believe that *all* parts of the brain interact in different ways to produce these two states. Support for this view comes from the fact that more and more "centers" are continually being discovered. Only two such centers had been identified in 1960; the number had increased to four or six by 1967, and probably there will be ten or twenty of them in a few years. It may be quite some time before we know the complete answer to the question: "What determines whether we are awake or asleep?"

Arousal

Within what is loosely termed "the waking state," there can be many different levels of excitement. For example, a person can be very tense and hyperactive, or he can be fairly alert, or he can be rather sluggish and unresponsive. The terms *arousal* and *activation* are often used to refer to these variations in the general excitation of the individual. Some psychologists have been interested in relating the level of generalized arousal (as indicated by a combination of physiological measures) to the variables of human emotion and performance (Duffy, 1962). The research of these activation theorists has shown that the relation between arousal and performance generally takes the form of an inverted U (Malmo, 1959). That is, as his arousal increases, a person's performance improves—up to a point. After that, any further increases in arousal will have a negative ef-

fect on his performance. Perhaps you know of a person who became so agitated and tense before an exam that he was unable to take it.

Although the theory of generalized activation seems intuitively reasonable, recent studies have shown that it is far too simple an idea to account for all the physiological changes that occur with different levels of arousal. According to activation theory, a person's autonomic responses (e.g., heart rate, breathing, skin conductance) ought to correlate highly with one another. Thus someone who was becoming very aroused might be expected to show increases in all of these measures. However, different stimulus situations have been shown to produce different patterns of somatic response. For instance, heart-rate *acceleration* (often assumed to denote anxiety) occurs in situations requiring concentrated mental activity and the exclusion of distracting external stimuli. Trying to solve an arithmetic problem in your head would be an example of such a situation. However, when the situation requires careful attention to external input (e.g., the person has to respond to differently colored flashes of light), there is a marked *deceleration* in his heart rate (Lacey, Kagan, Lacey, & Moss, 1963). It has also been found that different individuals show differing patterns of physiological responses (Lacey, 1967).

A different view of the functions of arousal has been proposed by Routtenberg (1968, 1969). He states that two arousal systems operate to maintain the ongoing behavior of an organism. The first system is related to the reticular formation and is a response-processing system. It acts to organize and execute a selected motor response, such as eating, drinking, or running. The second arousal system is related to the *limbic system* (primitive cortical structures just above the thalamus) and is a stimulus-processing system. It is sensitive to different kinds of stimuli (rewarding, aversive, or novel), as well as to different stimulus intensities. These two arousal systems are hypothesized to act separately. This could explain how an animal can remain awake and alert even when its reticular formation is affected by lesions or drugs. Such a two-arousal theory might explain the abnormal responses of people suffering from different types of mental illness, but these speculations have yet to be tested experimentally.

Attention

We are under constant bombardment by innumerable stimuli competing for our attention. *Attention* is the psychological process of selecting only a portion of the available stimuli to focus upon while ignoring, suppressing, or inhibiting reactions to a host of other stimuli.

Without such a mechanism, we would each be a tower of Babel. All the stimuli would be talking in a different, but familiar language, and they all would be equally loud and equally persistent in their demands upon us. Such a state of sensory overload would lead to distractability, an inability to carry out coordinated action, and possibly a shutting-off of all responsiveness to stimuli, as occurs in fainting or shock reactions. Therefore, it is necessary for the individual to have developed both physiological and psychological means to enable him to attend to his environment *selectively*.

Getting and Holding Attention

Suppose you wanted to get someone's attention; how would you go about it? In the previous chapters on learning, we saw that the individual's attention to conditioned or unconditioned stimuli is highly directed because the experimenter can manipulate various aspects of the laboratory environment. He can minimize distracting noises with soundproofing, restrict the subject's extraneous movements with a restraining apparatus, and guide attention by gestures and verbal instructions, as well as resort to threats for poor attending or rewards for good attending. Under such artificially controlled situations, where the individual is not truly free in his movements, what is relevant and must be attended to is clearly defined by the experimenter, the boss, or the teacher.

But in situations where actions and attention are free to wander, how can someone's attention be captured? How do girls go about the task of attracting male attention to themselves? How does a male attract the eye of a girl he would like to date? Suppose you were hired by a Madison Avenue advertising firm for the sole purpose of getting the public to *notice* a client's product. What would you suggest they do to get the attention of the freely roving band of potential buyers? Or suppose you were a college teacher who believed that you had something of value to tell your students—if only they would listen. In a recent study, Cameron and his associates (1968) discovered that during a lecture course, students are not really listening to the teacher over 50 percent of the time, even if he is rather good by their standards. In fact, a fair portion of time is spent attending to their own internal distractors, which engage them in daydreaming and sexual fantasy. What would you do to get and hold the attention of such students?

There are doubtless many other situations you can think of where you want to attract the attention of some specific person or group of people. What techniques do you regularly employ, and under what conditions does their effectiveness vary? Or looked at from the other side, what is a good way for someone to get *your* attention?

Attention-getting devices. Although psychologists cannot yet offer an ideal definition of the attention process, they have been able to identify conditions that affect attention. These include both characteristics of the stimulus situation and factors that depend on the individual himself. Some of the factors listed below will certainly be on your list of ways you can get attention from others, or they from you.

1. *Change.* Change, or contrast, is movement in any direction: from one place to another; from one intensity to another; from absent to present; from red to green; from high to low; from moving to stationary. The kitten ignores the ball of yarn when it is still but pounces on it when it moves. A sudden shout in the middle of a quiet talk or a whisper from a man who has been shouting makes you "sit up and take notice." In other words, anything that is novel or unexpected is change of some sort and attracts your attention.

2. *Size.* Other things being equal, something large attracts attention better than something small. This is one factor favoring the full-page advertisement. Size, however, is only one of many interrelated factors determining the direction of attention. Even a large advertisement may suffer by its nearness to another—perhaps smaller—one which appeals more to the reader's interests or has a more striking use of color.

3. *Prepotency.* Stimuli of greater intensity are more potent than others in the same sensory modality. For example, high sounds are prepotent over low sounds; tickling is prepotent over broad, smooth pressure; and bright, saturated colors are prepotent over pastel shades. The latter is especially evident in the brilliant rows of laundry products, canned goods, baking mixes, and other products found in the supermarket. •

4. *Repetition.* A weak stimulus frequently repeated may be as effective as a strong one presented once. But there is a limit to such effectiveness. If overdone, repetition can lead to monotony and complete loss of attention. Actors and actresses pay special attention to this phenomenon when trying to determine the optimal number of personal and TV appearances which will maintain public interest.

Experience shows that repeating a fundamental theme or motif with minor variations is more effective than repeating the original presentation exactly. Beethoven's Fifth Symphony illustrates this principle beautifully. Many radio and TV commercials are designed on this idea, their "jingles" being an ever constant reminder that simple repetition with minor variations can work its way into your brain.

5. *Organic condition.* The stimulus that wins the competition for your attention is usually the one that relates to the strongest biological need operating at the moment. If you are hungry, stimuli related to food will attract your attention. If you are tired, stimuli related to resting will be most effective. Since sexual needs are frequently operating, it follows that sex-related stimuli may be used to call attention to any object with which they are paired—from convertibles to cigars. ▲

6. *Interests.* People vary greatly in their attention to the same stimulation because a person's interests, like his organic condition, predispose him toward a particular response. For example, most people might not even notice a rather ordinary-looking rock on the ground. But it would certainly attract the attention of a "rock hound" who knew it to be a gemstone. The objective stimulus is the same in both cases, but because people's interests differ, their attention and behavior vary accordingly.

7. *Personal contact.* We saw in Chapter 5 that people do not habituate to personally significant stim-

By means of bright and colorful package design, manufacturers of breakfast cereals and many other products compete for the shopper's attention.

uli, especially their own names. Therefore, calling out the names of some members of the class or audience gets their attention. In addition, it increases the level of attention in the rest of the audience because it establishes the audience as individuals whom you can single out, instead of as an anonymous mass in which individuals can submerge themselves. Individuating listeners is one of the most effective means of getting —and holding—attention. When you are talking to a single individual, looking him straight in the eye increases the likelihood that he will look back at you and listen to what you have to say.

Maintenance of attention.   We can think of the attention process as the breaking down of habituation. By making some change in the environment, we cause the organism to make an orienting response toward a particular stimulus. Then, if there are no further changes, he will eventually habituate to that stimulus and no longer attend to it. Thus habituation is the major problem we face when we are trying to *maintain* someone's attention for a long period of time. Once we have attracted his attention, what can we do to prevent him from habituating to the stimulus?

Psychologists have not devoted much study to this problem, but it seems reasonable to assume that the same principles used to attract attention in the first place could be used to maintain it. For example, successive changes, or variation in the stimulus situation will probably help maintain attention. A politician, teacher, or other public speaker is more likely to have an attentive audience if he makes changes in the content of his presentation (e.g., making a joke, asking rhetorical questions), or in his manner of delivery (e.g., changing the pitch or loudness of his voice, pausing in the middle of a sentence). Other techniques to maintain attention are taught in speech and drama courses.

Attention span.   How long can you attend to a given stimulus event or activity before your mind wanders? This length of time is a measure referred to as *attention span.* Attention span is frequently used by elementary-school teachers to classify their pupils, since it is assumed to increase with mental age. Also, teachers often use it as a correlate of intellectual ability, since a child who has a short attention span cannot follow all of a lesson and will perform poorly on recall tests of the portion of the material not attended to. That attention span is largely under the control of the individual's interest in what is going on can be observed when the same pupils who cannot sit still for five minutes during arithmetic drill remain glued to their Saturday morning TV cartoons for hours on end. Defining a too-short attention span as something wrong with the child puts the burden on the child, enabling the educator to shirk his responsibility for devising more interesting materials and techniques of presentation which are relevant to the child's interests and experiences.

One man's distractor . . .   One of the first rules in any freshman guide to good study habits is to eliminate distractors such as music, roommates talking, noises, and so on. Breaking the silence rule is a cardinal sin in our libraries, where attention to the reading material must be protected from noise. Recently, this rule has been outrageously violated with remarkably favorable results. A branch library in a predominately black neighborhood in San Francisco allows talking and plays loud rock music continually. The result has been that more people from the community use the library and spend more time in it reading. For people used to living in a noise-filled environment, silence can be a potential distractor to which they must learn to adjust. This was also found

You'll love the way it holds you on the road. For mileage lovers, safety lovers, comfort lovers, family lovers, value lovers…it's built with polyester cords and belts of fiber glass to give you up to double the mileage of unbelted tires. Ask your Armstrong Dealer (he's in the Yellow Pages) for the tire for lovers. It's the Surveyor 78. You can't get a better value for love nor money.

the tire for lovers

ARMSTRONG TIRES
FIRST IN FIBER GLASS

▲ Skimming through the advertising section of any popular magazine—and especially of one directed primarily at a male audience—provides a great deal of insight into advertisers' theories about what attracts people's attention.

among residents living within earshot of the roar of Niagara Falls when Army engineers "turned off" the Falls to study and repair the damage done by erosion. It also occurred among New York City tenement dwellers who had difficulty adjusting to the silence after the demolition of the Third Avenue elevated line, whose noisy trains had passed only a few feet from their windows (at times every five minutes or so).

Just What Is Attention, Anyway?

Although the laboratory investigator goes to great lengths to control the attention of his subjects, he is usually not interested in attention itself. Rather, he must guarantee attention to certain stimuli if he is to study their relation to behavior. But some researchers do set out to uncover the dynamics of this crucial process of attention. One of the main obstacles they face is finding an operational definition of "attention." Since there are no direct measures of what the organism is experiencing, how can one know that it is attending? What overt behavior can you assume to be a sign of attention? Must an individual be looking at an object to be paying attention to it? Can you attend to something you want very much and give off no behavioral signs that you are doing so (i.e., "play it cool")? If so, then it is clear that defining and measuring attention is a difficult problem.

One obvious behavioral indicator of attention is orientation toward a stimulus (see Ch. 5) or investigation of it. Dishabituation can be used as evidence of attention to the new stimulus which is mismatched with the stored neuronal model. Neurophysiological measures such as brain wave patterns have been used as correlates of attention. But it has not yet been established whether they reflect attention alone, or are also measures of muscle tension from anticipation of making the overt response and perhaps other cognitive activity related to processing the incoming information (MacNeilage, 1966).

My, what big eyes you have! Although psychologists speak of attention in general terms as a selection-focusing activity, they are still unable to define or measure it precisely. It is not surprising, therefore, that considerable intellectual excitement greeted the announcement by psychologist Eckhard Hess that he had found a simple, reliable measure of attention—pupil dilation. The diameter of the pupil was reported to vary directly with a subject's interest in various pictorial stimuli. ■ When males were looking at a series of pictures, their pupils became more dilated when they were shown females than when the pictures were of males. The reverse was true with female subjects (Hess & Polt, 1960). Moreover, in a subsequent pilot study (a preliminary test of a hypothesis with a small number of observations), Hess and his colleagues (1965) found that this response to pictures of nude females was limited to males whose sexual activities were exclusively heterosexual. Four

Adcox Associates, Inc.

■ "I don't understand it. All of the men on her floor seem to have dilated pupils!"

out of five known homosexual subjects exhibited greater pupil dilation to pictures of nude males than of nude females. The graph illustrates this difference in attention and affective interest among homosexual and heterosexual males as detected by pupil dilation. ●

Unfortunately, more recent investigations have failed to establish pupil dilation as a reliable measure of interest. It has been suggested that pupil dilation is a response of the organism which reflects complex cognitive activity as well as primary attention or interest in external stimuli.

Photographic records of the pupil during a discrimination experiment revealed small but consistent differences in pupil size related to experimental procedures. When subjects had to make an overt response of pressing a key to signify completion of a task (judging two tones as same or different), pupil diameter increased by as much as .3 mm, or 6 percent above base-line diameter. This increase was significantly greater than in experimental conditions where no overt response was required, or where a motor response irrelevant to the task was required. Also, pupil dilation increased in all conditions following the word "now," the signal to respond or withhold responding (Simpson, 1969).

More research is needed to establish the correlates of mental activity and this apparently "sensitive and valid index of cognitive events."

Is attention in the ear of the beholder? Up to this point, we have been looking at attention mainly from the point of view of the person interested in getting the attention of someone else. We now want to study what is going on internally when the individual is paying attention to something.

Until recently, an experiment by Hernández-Peón, Scherrer, and Jouvet (1956) was regarded as the classic neurophysiological demonstration of selective attention.

Recording electrodes were permanently implanted in the part of a cat's brain called the *cochlear nucleus*, which receives impulses from the ear via the auditory nerve. The experimenters could then measure the cat's response to the sound of a click. When the cat was lying relaxed, the click produced a sizable response, as shown in the first recording. (The arrows indicate when the clicks occurred.)

When a jar containing two mice was placed in the cage, the cat crouched in front of it, watching the mice intently. The click was then repeated, but this time there was virtually no response:

When the cat relaxed again, the earlier responses to the click reappeared:

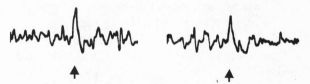

Similar results were obtained when the cat smelled a fish or received a forepaw shock during the presentation of the clicks. The same stimulus produced a physiological response or not, depending on the cat's attention.

The results of this experiment suggested that attention is basically a screening process in the central nervous system, which inhibits all "irrelevant" sensory input. This process can be described as the efferent control of afferent input. (You will recall from Chap-

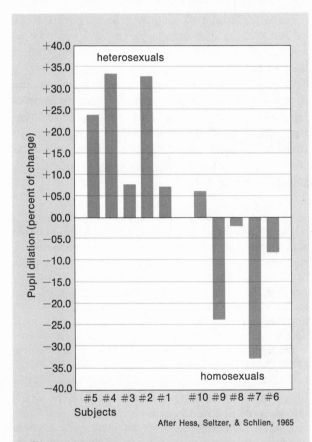

After Hess, Seltzer, & Schlien, 1965

● **PUPIL RESPONSES AND SEXUALITY**

The graph shows the percent of change in pupil dilation of five men known to be heterosexual and five known to be homosexual, in response to male and female pictures. The negative scores of the homosexuals indicate their higher response to pictures of males; the positive scores of the heterosexuals indicate their higher response to pictures of females. Note that there is no overlap between the groups; even the highest score attained by a homosexual is lower than the scores of any of the heterosexuals.

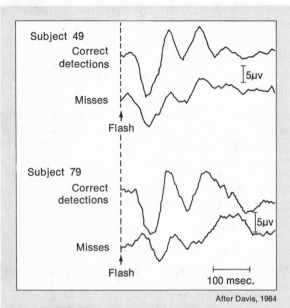

After Davis, 1964

■ **RESPONSES TO DETECTED AND MISSED SIGNALS**

The neural response of two subjects to detected and missed visual signals were recorded and averaged by a computer. In both cases, the neural response to detected signals was greater than the response to missed signals.

ter 3 that afferent fibers carry stimulus information *toward* the central nervous system, while efferent fibers generally carry information *away from* it, usually toward the muscles and glands.) There also are some "wrong-way" efferent fibers to relay stations in the *sensory* pathways. Such fibers could inhibit or "gate" the incoming, afferent information, preventing it from reaching the brain (Galambos, 1956; Desmedt, 1960).

The findings of Hernández-Peón and his colleagues are very impressive and seem intuitively to be the correct representation of how selective attention must work. However, many researchers have been unable to replicate this study, which suggests that some other factor was responsible for the results. Recently, Worden and his colleagues discovered that the position of the cat's ear relative to the overhead speaker produced variations in acoustic input to the ear. These variations, in turn, influenced the cat's auditory re-

sponse to the click. In addition, the activity of the cat's ear muscles was found to be a significant factor. When these variables have been carefully controlled (e.g., by putting earphones on the cat rather than using an overhead speaker), no consistent relationship between attentive states and auditory responses has been demonstrated (Worden, 1966).

At least two methodological maxims can be illustrated by this example: (a) the necessity for independent replication of a study before its results can be accepted as true ones; and (b) the necessity to control all variables which could conceivably affect the findings.

A number of recent studies have tried to specify neurophysiological correlates of attention by recording the brain waves during tasks requiring close attention. These have involved studies of vigilance, in which the subject must attend to a series of similar stimuli and make a response only to occasional, slightly different ones.

In one study, for example, the subject was exposed to a series of relatively bright flashes of light interspersed with occasional dim flashes; he was to press a key whenever there was a dim flash. In another, subjects heard several series of 4 tones each and were to determine, in each case, whether the third was louder than the second. ■ Several of these studies have found that responses in the cortex to both auditory and visual signals were greater when the signal was correctly detected than when it was not (Haider, Spong, & Lindsley, 1964; Davis, 1964; Spong, Haider, & Lindsley, 1965).

A mechanism that might explain these differences is suggested by the findings of another study, in which responses of individual neurons in the cortex were monitored. Although the response in many cases was directly proportional to the intensity of the stimuli, there were a few groups of cells that responded only when the animal appeared to be definitely "paying attention" to the stimulus (Hubel, Henson, Rupert, & Galambos, 1959).

The development of attention. An ideal place to study attention is in the crib, where it all starts—as evidenced by the recent upsurge of interest in the development of attentional processes in the human infant. Visual attention to the environment is present at birth, even though the total duration of the new-

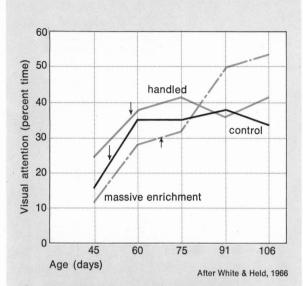

After White & Held, 1966

● **TIME SPENT IN VISUAL ATTENTION**

The graph shows the percentage of time spent in attention to the environment by control infants (reared in standard institution cribs with little environmental stimulation), infants reared in the same cribs but given extra handling by nurses, and infants reared in "enrichment" cribs with colorful and touchable fittings. The arrows show the age at which hand regard (visual examination of the infants' own hands) appeared. Although the control infants discovered their hands earliest, presumably because there was not much else for them to look at, their general attention to their visual environment was much less than that of the other infants by the age of three and a half months.

born's alertness is quite limited. A study of ten infants (observed from the first day of life throughout their first month) revealed that attention span can be prolonged and the onset of sleep delayed by making the infant's environment interesting (Wolff, 1965). Human faces have high attention-holding value for infants, greater than do geometric designs, even at six months of age. Female babies were reported to be able to sustain attention longer and attend more to unexpected stimulus patterns than male babies (Kagan & Lewis, 1965).

The significance of attention in the development of coordination between visual and motor responses has been brought out in studies of sensory-motor development. A study of institutionalized infants (see

pp. 128-129) showed that enriching their environment increased the amount of time they spent attending to objects in the environment (White & Held, 1966). ● The same study showed that children in the enriched environment mastered such skills as visually directed reaching considerably ahead of those whose cribs offered little in the way of visual stimulation. ▲

Attention to Multiple Stimuli

Thus far, we have talked mostly about the aspects of attention to a single stimulus. What happens to attention when multiple stimuli compete for part of the action? Recent research has uncovered two fascinating ways organisms have developed for solving this general problem: attentional filters and biased scanning.

Studying the cocktail party problem. Consider the "cocktail party problem" in which a person is in a crowded, noisy room where many conversations are being held simultaneously. How can he follow one conversation without being confused by the others? What properties of language and speech enable him to sort out and attend to certain stimuli and ignore

▲ Many parents plan lively, stimulating decorations for their baby's crib, so that he does not have to spend his waking hours gazing at the ceiling or at protective padding that blocks his view. As soon as he can, he will reach out for the things he sees, and begin exploring his world by touch.

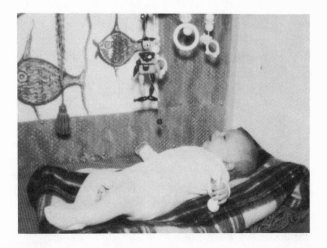

others? Since this situation contains a wealth of potential information about language perception, it has been brought into the laboratory for more precise experimental control.

Attentional filters. In the *dichotic listening* technique, the subject wears earphones, and a different verbal message is presented to each ear at the same time. The messages might be prose passages or lists of digits. For example, the number "seven" is presented to the right ear while at the same time the number "nine" is presented to the left ear; then "five" and "four" are presented to the right and left ears, respectively, then "two" and "six." When asked to report all six digits, the subject typically reports all the digits from one ear, followed by all the digits from the other ear: "seven, five, two, nine, four, six" (Broadbent, 1954).

Broadbent (1958, 1962) has proposed two mechanisms by which the brain may selectively filter such complex incoming information. First, the two ears may serve as separate processing channels, information to one being decoded immediately, while input to the other is temporarily stored in short-term memory for subsequent processing. While many experiments support this view, *dichotic fusion* tests have shown that the information presented to the two ears can be combined: when "back" is given to one ear and "lack" to the other, subjects often report hearing "black" (Day, 1968, 1969).

Broadbent's research also suggests that the brain responds to selected physical characteristics of the sound wave. It is differences in *pulsation rate* (the rate at which puffs of air are forced through the vocal cords) that make one human voice distinguishable from another. It is the combination of *frequencies* in the sound wave that make one speech sound distinguishable from another (for example, frequencies of 375 and 1700 cycles per second combine to produce the vowel sound in the word "bit," while frequencies of 450 and 1700 cycles result in the vowel sound of "bet"). But suppose wave trains from two different voices arrive simultaneously. How does the listener determine which pairs of frequencies "go together"? Broadbent suggests that the brain responds to differences in pulsation rate, and is able to concentrate on messages spoken by a particular voice by "filtering

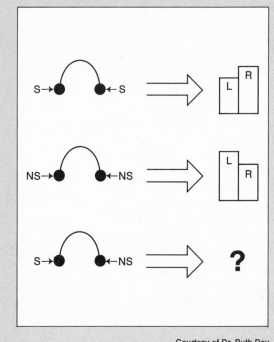

◆ **SUMMARY OF EAR-ADVANTAGE RESULTS IN DICHOTIC LISTENING EXPERIMENTS**

Courtesy of Dr. Ruth Day

out" any sounds that arrive at a different pulsation rate.

The two hemispheres and the perception of speech. When different speech stimuli are presented simultaneously to each ear, there is a right-ear advantage. That is, there is significantly better identification of information that went into the right ear (Kimura, 1961). This finding makes sense when you recall that the right ear serves primarily the left temporal lobe, and that the left temporal lobe is "dominant" for speech in most people (see the section on "split-brain" patients in Ch. 3).

While the left hemisphere is specially equipped to process speech, it appears that the right hemisphere (served by the left ear) is better able to handle non-speech auditory signals. That is, given competing nonspeech stimuli, identification is significantly better for the information that went into the left ear (Kimura, 1964).

The distinction between speech and nonspeech plays a crucial role in dichotic listening experiments. The right-ear advantage occurs for a wide variety of speech stimuli, including digits (Kimura, 1961), words (Borokowski, Spreen, & Stutz, 1965), and simple consonant-vowel syllables (Shankweiler & Studdert-Kennedy, 1967). The left-ear advantage occurs for a wide variety of nonspeech stimuli, including melodies (Kimura, 1964), sonar signals (Chaney & Webster, 1965), and environmental noises (Curry, 1967). These results are summarized in the top two portions of the figure. ◆ The bottom portion of the figure asks a simple question: what happens when speech (S) is presented to one ear and nonspeech (NS) to the other? A reasonable prediction is that a given ear will perform best when its "proper" kind of stimulus is presented to it. Surprisingly enough, there is *no* ear advantage in this situation: both ears perform equally well regardless of which kind of stimulus each receives (Day & Cutting, 1970). Perhaps, then, speech and nonspeech can be identified by separate processing systems. This possibility gains further support from the fact that subjects make virtually no errors on the speech/nonspeech test, while their performance drops to about 60 to 70 percent correct when both stimuli are of the same type.

In a variant of the dichotic listening test, the stimuli do not begin at precisely the same time. For example, given "back/lack," "back" begins first by a few milliseconds on some trials, while "lack" begins first on other trials. Subjects are asked to make a temporal order judgment (TOJ) by reporting the first sound (phoneme) they heard on every trial (Day, 1969). Typically, performance is more accurate for stimuli leading in the right ear, as shown for a typical subject in the black curve of the figure. • However, when both stimuli are nonspeech, the stimulus that led in the left ear is reported more accurately. The shape of that curve would be the mirror reflection of the speech/speech curve. In both cases, the ear advantage is small but significant.

What happens when subjects are asked to make temporal order judgments when one stimulus is speech and the other is nonspeech? Again, the results are surprising, as shown for a typical subject in the colored curve of the figure (Day & Cutting, 1970). Subjects make highly accurate temporal order judgments when the left-ear stimulus leads, no matter whether it is speech or nonspeech. However, when the right-ear stimulus begins first, performance is very poor: even though the right-ear stimulus leads by as much as 50 to 75 milliseconds, subjects keep reporting that the left-ear stimulus began first. Although these results for mixed items are not well understood at present, they suggest that the two hemispheres may take different amounts of time to do their work. Research in progress is designed to study the interplay of time perception and attention with the linguistic and physiological bases of speech perception.

Biased scanning. If someone is looking at pictures of two works of art, and they are similar in size, vividness, composition, and other general details, at-

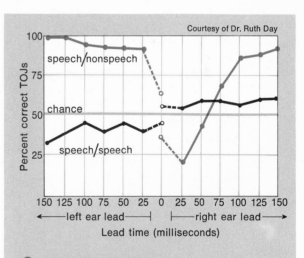

Courtesy of Dr. Ruth Day

● **TEMPORAL ORDER JUDGMENTS IN DICHOTIC LISTENING**

These are typical temporal order judgment curves. When both messages were speech, the subject was somewhat more accurate in judging which began first for right-ear leads. When one message was speech and the other nonspeech, the subject had great difficulty in judging short right-ear leads. Note that there is no "correct" response for 0-lead time items; therefore the percent responses for both ears are shown.

tention is likely to be divided equally between them. If he now is told that he can have one of them, what happens to his unbiased (equal-time) attention scanning? Gerard (1967) investigated such a situation using the arrangement depicted in the drawing. ■

The visual orientation of the subject toward each of the alternatives was continuously monitored. Prior to making the decision, Gerard's subjects paid more attention to the picture they eventually *rejected* than to the one they chose. However, once the decision was made, there was a dramatic shift in attention, as well as a correlated physiological change—a decrease in pulse amplitude. The subjects now focused on the chosen alternative.

Stimulus features were the major determinants of initial "uninvolved" visual scanning, but the cognitive processes of choice and decision-making biased attentional focusing during the second phase. Before the *overt* commitment, more attention was focused on what would be lost by choosing the other picture; after the commitment, attention focused on what had been gained.

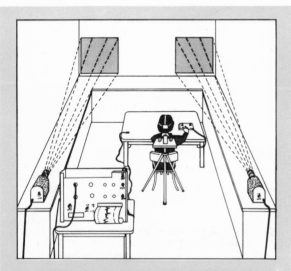

■ GERARD'S BIASED SCANNING APPARATUS

Two paintings were projected onto screens at equal distances from the subject. The apparatus in the foreground recorded the subject's pulse. The subject registered his preference by pressing one of the buttons on his right.

The Problem of Perception (or, When Is What Glitters Really Gold?)

The naïve observer accepts the evidence of his senses uncritically. He feels that he is perceiving in a direct, *unmediated* way the attributes of objects out there. He believes he has direct contact and acquaintance with them. He has a "vivid certainty" of the correctness of perceptions. Moreover, he assumes that other observers will perceive the situation in the same way —unless they are being "willfully perverse." His position is known as *phenomenal absolutism*.

Like the student we left in the shower in Chapter 5, you can tell the difference between hot and cold water. Certainly the attribute of heat resides in the water! If you think so, though, you might try an experiment proposed by John Locke in 1690. Put one hand in a bowl of hot water, the other in cold water for a few minutes. Now put them both into a third bowl filled with lukewarm water. That water will feel cool to one hand and warm to the other whereas, as Locke pointed out nearly three centuries ago, "it is impossible that the same water, if those ideas were really in it, should be at the same time both hot and cold."

More recent experiments also demonstrate that what you perceive may not be what is there, despite your certainty that it is. For example, you know when something is up or down (relative to you) because it *is* up or down, do you not? Also you know when something moves relative to other stationary objects because it *does!*

In one set of experiments, subjects were seated in chairs in a room that was normal except for one feature—it could be tilted. When a subject in his chair was stationary and the room tilted, his perception of up and down was impaired because he assumed that he and objects in the room might tilt but that walls always stay vertical. So he experienced the tilted walls as vertical and himself and the other vertical objects in the room as tilted (Witkin, 1954).

A similar effect occurred in a classic study when a *stationary* dot of light within an illuminated frame (in a darkened room) was seen to move. Actually the frame moved, but it was seen to be stationary. Although the subject saw *absolute* movement of the dot, what was there was *relative* movement—movement of the dot relative to the frame (Duncker, 1929).

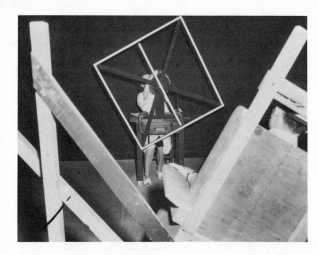

▲ In the room shown here either the subject's chair (in foreground) or the stimulus frame or both can be tilted. In darkness, where only the stimulus frame is visible, the subject is to indicate when it is vertical.

A similar phenomenon has been reported by some passengers on the mammoth 747 jets, who say that when the plane takes off, it appears that the ground is receding, rather than that they are rising.

Every time you go to a movie you see motion that is not there. The continuous movement of the actors is made up of a series of individual frames appearing at the rate of about twenty-four per second. There is no motion in the frames, yet you see motion. The same apparent movement is the basis for the neon light displays of cartoon figures endlessly performing some simple act and for the huge signs in which words seem to move across from one side to the other. Actually each single light in the display simply goes on and off, but if the timing of these unmoving on-off events is properly arranged and the stimuli are close enough together in space, you see movement. This perception of one moving light instead of two or more stationary lights going on and off is called the *phi phenomenon*.

The task of perception, as we have seen, is to filter and decode the information that comes in such a way as to identify the consistencies and relationships in the world around us and thus make it predictable so that we can deal with it appropriately. Our discussion here will center mostly on vision because of its dominant role in guiding human behavior.

The Trickery of Perception

The tropical forests in which the BaMbuti Pygmies live are so dense that the natives can rarely see for more than a few yards in any direction. Under such circumstances they have come to rely largely upon sound cues to guide their hunting. Rarely is it necessary to make perceptual judgments based upon visual cues of distance or depth discrimination. One of the remarkable consequences of this "natural" experiment is reported in the observations of an anthropologist, Colin Turnbull (1961). When one of the Pygmies, Kenge by name, traveled with Turnbull to an open plain where the view was unobstructed, nature (or nurture?) suddenly began playing tricks on him. Turnbull reports:

"Kenge looked over the plains and down to where a herd of about a hundred buffalo were grazing some miles away. He asked me what kind of *insects* they were, and I told him they were buffalo, twice as big as the forest buffalo known to him. He laughed loudly and told me not to tell such stupid stories, and asked me again what kind of insects they were. He then talked to himself, for want of more intelligent company, and tried to liken the buffalo to the various beetles and ants with which he was familiar.

"He was still doing this when we got into the car and drove down to where the animals were grazing. He watched them getting larger and larger, and though he was as courageous as any Pygmy, he moved over and sat close to me and muttered that it was witchcraft. . . . Finally, when he realized that they were real buffalo he was no longer afraid, but what puzzled him still was why they had been so small, and whether they *really* had been small and had so suddenly grown larger, or whether it had been some kind of trickery." (p. 305)

In Kenge's attempt to maintain a rational explanation of his world, he attributes such capricious perception to witchcraft. It is external evil spirits who play tricks on people by changing the sizes of things or by tricking their eyes into believing that this is what has happened. In our attempt to explain such an illusion (and, like Kenge, to maintain the assumption of "rational" causal determinacy), we assume that natural causes can be found. We look for an explanation either in unusual conditions of stimulation or in the particular background of experience of the perceiver.

● These three pictures are part of a continuous motion picture made as the man walked across the room in less than a minute. He is the same man, and the room did not change. How could this phenomenon have been produced?

From this anecdote, several important conclusions emerge. We assume, as does the Pygmy, that objects like buffalo do not change their size drastically over a short period of time. In a setting familiar to us, we see objects as maintaining their size regardless of our distance from them (Turnbull's perception); but in an unfamiliar perceptual environment, the size of objects may appear to vary as a function of distance (Kenge's perception). We attempt to fit novel perceptions into familiar contexts or frames of reference (Kenge compared the "insects" to beetles). Finally, under unusual conditions of stimulus presentation, our normal perception may change so that we see illusions. This is what happened when Kenge saw the buffalo grow as he approached them rapidly in a fast-moving car.

From related evidence to be discussed a little later we know that Kenge would probably have come to see the world *veridically*, as Turnbull did, once he had learned that the objects were in fact buffalo. A *veridical* perception is a more accurate one in which the person's subjective perceptual experience of an object, his *percept*, agrees with its objective physical characteristics, as measurable and verifiable independently. The perceptual experience—how something appears to the observer—is also called the *phenomenological* experience of it.

The perception of illusion.   Would it be possible for you—a "sophisticated" perceiver—to have the same distorted experience of reality that this so-called "primitive man" did? Do you see the man at the left becoming twice as tall as he walks across the room? If you roll a sheet of paper into a tube and look through it at the man in the successive views, the phenomenon will be even more striking. You *know* this is impossible. What is happening? ●

Psychologists are interested in illusions as a possible key to the understanding of all perception. Several other illusions are shown in the Special Transparency Insert opposite.

The deceiving retina and the roving eye.   If these illusions have convinced you that your eyes and interpretive mechanisms are faulty and not to be trusted, consider the basic perceptual apparatus you start out with and the job it must do. At the back of

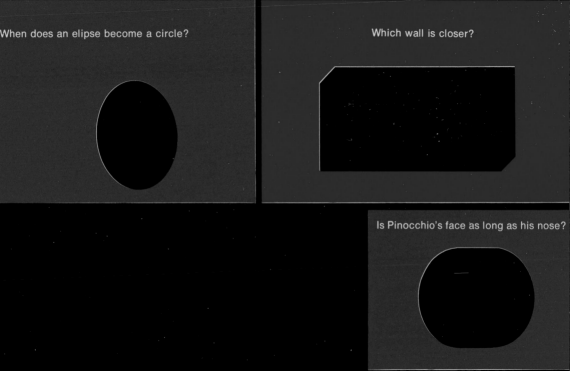

Which wall is closer?

When does an ellipse become a circle?

Is Pinocchio's face as long as his nose?

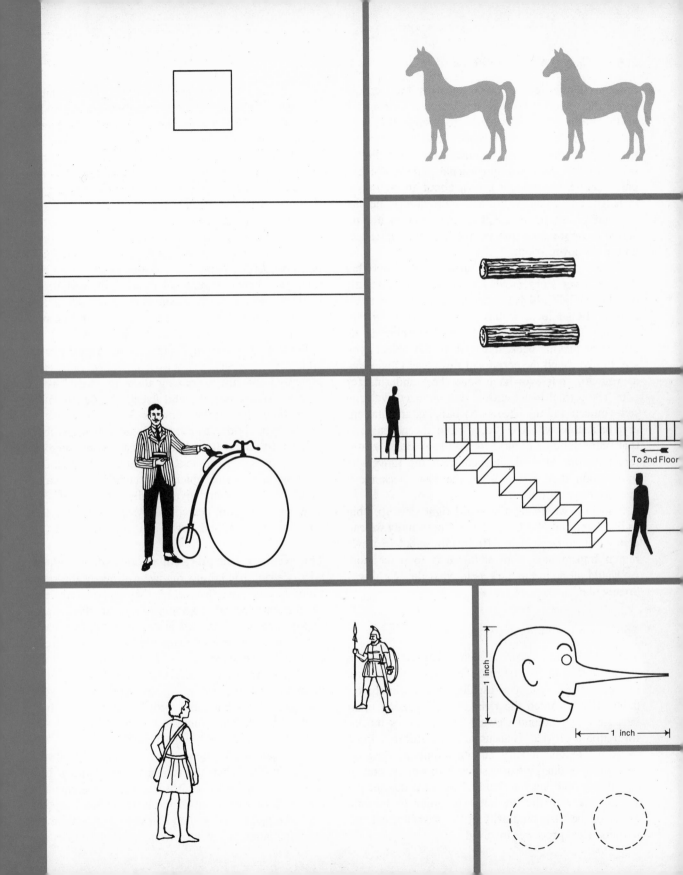

the eye is the retina, which receives the sensory stimulation coming through the lens and transmits it to the brain for higher level processing. But what kind of information does it send? Since it is a two-dimensional surface, it must convert the three-dimensional world into a two-dimensional pattern which it passes along. Secondly, it is only about an inch or so in length and width so the lens must *minify* the size of what is out there. Finally, since images are *inverted* as light passes through the lens, the retina sees an upside-down world.

Complicating matters still further is the fact that the eye never stops moving around. The constantly drifting eye has a high-frequency, slight, but constant *tremor*. In addition, it has *saccadic movements* of irregular flicking back and forth. Yet there is no tremor or flicking back and forth in the objects you see. Look around the corners of this page. Obviously, as you do, your eyes have done the wandering for you. The retinal image moved and changed, yet you saw yourself and the page as unchanging and stationary, in accord with the "facts." Did the retina send that information upstairs? If so, how does it differentiate this kind of situation from the movement information that is sent when the page does move and your eyes are fixed?

Somehow we *do* see the world right side up, "big as life," and full of 3-D substance, and usually we can distinguish movement in *it* from movement in *us*. If retinal transmission were all there is to perception, we would all be in the dark as to what the world was "really like."

The Dependability of Perception

The trickery and deceit of perception that we discover in the illusions surprise us precisely because our perceptual system is usually so remarkably reliable. It has earned the right to be depended upon because under normal viewing circumstances the information it provides is accurate and useful in helping us adjust to and modify our environment. Because perception ordinarily works so well, so simply, and so effortlessly and "unconsciously," we must disrupt the system (as with the illusions) in order to become aware of the vast complexity of the physiological and psychological processes involved.

How does the perceptual act provide a stable, organized, coherent, and meaningful view of reality when the preceding examples have shown how fallible it can be? When we search for an explanation of the illusions or seek to understand how the perceptual system manages to establish invariance between *objective reality* and *phenomenal reality*—our experience of what is there—a network of interlocking processes becomes apparent. The perceptual system acts like an on-line, data-processing computer, taking in multiple sources of information, selecting, integrating, abstracting, comparing, testing, sorting, outputting, and then repeating all these again and again. Each perceptual act is a construction or creation of reality based on all of the relevant past and current information available to the organism. ◆

Perception, far from being a direct experience of "things as they are," is thus a *mediated* process of organized conclusion-drawing about the "real" world of time, space, objects, and events, based on much more than simply the stimulus input. In order to isolate "perception" as a field of study, then, psychologists must establish *arbitrary* boundaries between the various processes of sensation, attention, memory, learning, and so on, which are actually not separate at all but closely and dynamically interrelated.

What *does* your perceptual system give you that you can count on and how can it do so?

The accuracy and precision of perception.   Under good viewing conditions, the eye can detect the separation between two lines where they make an angle as small as one second of an arc. Moreover, the extraordinary precision of the eye is shown by the fact that it can detect a fine line substantially less than the size of the smallest cones in the retina would seem to make possible. The eye can detect an animal on a distant mountain or the ridges in fingerprints—and can change its focus back and forth instantly. It skillfully guides the delicate hand-eye coordination of the watchmaker and the brain surgeon.

How can it do these things when *it* is always moving itself? When the retinal image changes, how does the eye tell whether it is because of movement in the world or movement of the head or eyes? Apparently the perceptual system learns to compensate for the stimulation it receives from internal sources.

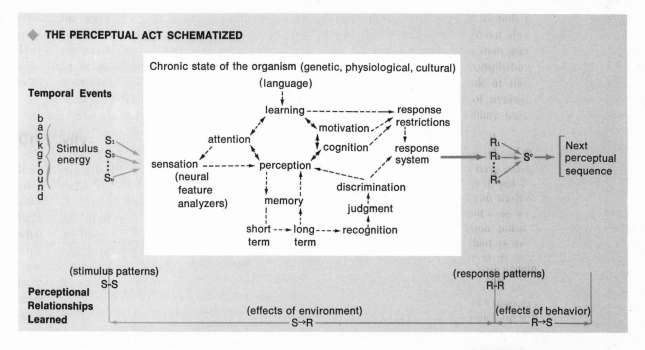

◆ **THE PERCEPTUAL ACT SCHEMATIZED**

The obvious explanation would appear to hinge on feedback from the eye muscles. But this is not the answer. When the eye muscles are made immobile by an intravenous injection of curare and the subject is told to move his eyes, he perceives them as moving even though no motion is taking place (Brindley & Merton, 1960). This phenomenon was first reported over a hundred years ago by Helmholtz (1867). He had held subjects' eye muscles still with tweezers, commanded the eye to move, and found that movement of the stationary eyes was perceived. His explanation was based on the *principle of efference*: "Our judgments as to the direction of the visual axis are simply the result of the effort of will involved in trying to alter the adjustment of the eyes."

The constancy of perception. Take a small box and move it slowly around, now at arm's length and then close to your face, into the sunlight and then into the shadow. It does not appear to change in shape, size, or brightness, although the image on the retina changes dramatically with each of these moves.

The stability of our visual world depends on this perception of *object constancy*—the perception of continuous existence of an object as the same object despite changes in the size, shape, and position of the retinal image. In the competition for which source of stimulation will dominate the final perceptual judgment, the stimulation we get from the *distal stimulus* (the actual object) must win out over that of the *proximal stimulus* (the retinal pattern) if perception is to be accurate. The paradox of perception is that this is precisely what happens: what we experience subjectively *does* correspond more closely with the *objective* stimulus pattern out there than with our retinal image of it. Part of the mystery of how this happens is explained in the Ψ Close-up on page 283.

Seen from the top of the Empire State Building, people look like ants, just as Kenge's buffalo did from the distance of a few miles. When you are in a novel situation and the cues you must rely on for distance estimation are inadequate or confusing, then size constancy no longer rules and your perceptual system falls back upon whatever information it has available —namely, good old unreliable proximal stimulation.

The regularity in illusions. Illusions, far from being aberrant examples of runaway perception, are full of information about what is required for normal, accurate perception to take place. They do not reveal defects in our perceptual system, but rather show its strengths. They demonstrate the extent to which perception is not totally dependent on any one bit of stimulus information in the currently available environment. It is this freedom that keeps man from being stimulus-bound and enables him to use his perceptions in thinking.

The explanations for some of the perceptual illusions we examined earlier depend in part upon novel arrangements of cues or cues mixed in ways that change their utility value. Instead of a literal perception of what is there, we have an experience that clearly shows additional input from our own eyes or brain or both.

Have you ever noticed that the moon looks much bigger at the horizon than it does when it is high in the sky? Since we know its size does not really change each night as it moves across the sky, our perception of its apparent change in size is an illusion. This illusion was discussed as early as the second century by

the Egyptian astronomer, Ptolemy. It has sometimes been blamed on the upward tilt of the eyes or on neck strain from looking up.

The moon illusion is explained now as combining the principles of size constancy and those underlying the "railway tracks" illusion shown on the transparency. Objects near the horizon are seen as larger because they are judged to be farther away. The misjudgment of the distance cues leads to a breakdown in the usual size constancy formula. Kaufman and Rock (1962) have demonstrated the superiority of this explanation by a special apparatus which projected artificial moons of variable sizes into the "sky" of a darkened theater.

How did the man become a giant as he walked across the room? You saw this illusion because you assumed that the room was rectangular whereas it was actually trapezoidal, as you can see by this diagram and other view of it. ■ The right-hand corner was actually much nearer. Because you assumed a

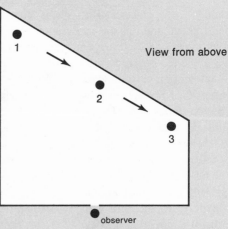

View from above

observer

■ From the diagram and this view of the room on page 278, you can see why the man seemed to become larger. If you were to rest your chin in the hollow in the crossbar and close one eye, you would see it as the camera saw the other room.

normal room and did not have reliable distance cues, you took the larger retinal size at face value and saw the distal size as increasing.

Other illusions seem to represent an exaggerated or unchecked use of normal organizing tendencies which operate in all perception and will be discussed a little later in the chapter.

Theories About Perception

Why do we see what we see? How much are our perceptions changed by various kinds of past experience, and how are these changes brought about? Even more basic, what role does perception play in the ideas we develop about what "reality" is? Although philosophers, psychologists, and physiologists under many different banners have agreed that perception is the key to what man is all about, their differing explanations of it have been a source of heated controversy. We will sketch the main ones briefly. You can then weigh them for utility as we examine the ways evidence has been sought and the answers that have been found.

The "Gambling House" Theories

Two of the explanations of perceptual processes that have been offered can be thought of as "gambling house" theories. The first is the *transactional approach* of Ames (1951) and others. Each individual is thought to develop, through his transactions with his own unique environment, a restricted set of perceptions to handle the infinite variety of possible retinal images that he continually receives. On the basis of his experience, he thus makes assumptions about how reality is constructed, and it is these assumptions that determine what he will perceive. Perception becomes a learned act of constructing reality to fit one's assumptions about it.

The second of these theories, the *probabalistic functionalism* of Brunswick (1956), argues that perception involves finding out which cues can be depended upon to guide behavior. For each species, certain cues in the natural environment have a higher probability than others of being functionally adaptive. The perceiver must learn how to establish the *ecolog-*

Ψ *Close-up*   *Size Constancy*

Imagine trying to adjust to a world in which objects kept changing their apparent size depending on their distance from us, so that the same object looked twice as big ten feet away as it did twenty feet away. This would happen if perception depended only on the size of the retinal image, because the retinal image *does* get larger as objects come closer. We perceive constancy of size by integrating the input about retinal size with input about distance and visual angle.

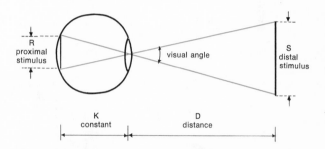

The incoming light from the distal stimulus (S) is refracted by the lens of the eye and projected on the retina. The distance from the lens to the retina is the constant factor (K). Retinal size (R) depends upon the visual angle because that determines how much the light will be spread when it reaches the retina. In turn, the visual angle is fixed by the size of the distal stimulus (S) and the distance from it to the lens (D). A number of relations follow:

$$\text{Visual angle} = \frac{\text{distal size (S)}}{\text{distance (D)}} = \frac{\text{retinal size (R)}}{\text{lens-to-retina (K)}}$$

$$\text{Thus } \frac{S}{D} = \frac{R}{K} \text{ and } R = K \frac{S}{D}$$

Knowing retinal size, one infers the size of the distal stimulus by estimating distance. Information stored in memory about usual distances and sizes of familiar objects may enter into this estimate.

ical cue validity of various stimulus patterns to find out which ones yield the most accurate perception of the distal stimulus in his environment.

In both theories, we can envision a gambling casino whose operator learns from experience what the odds are for different combinations of events. Usually the house has more information than it needs and it wins. In winning consistently, however, it learns nothing new. If it suddenly begins losing its bets and the events it depended upon appear changed, new information must be sought. ▲

▲ You may sometimes think that you can't bet on anything these days. Basic to perception "... is the fact that the organism has built up certain assumptions about the world in which he lives. These assumptions, which are usually unconscious, [result in] the attaching of significance to cues." (F. H. Allport, 1955, pp. 278–279)

W Miller

British Associationism

The question of how we come to know reality was of philosophical interest long before psychologists began investigating perception. Starting in the seventeenth century, the British associationists (Locke, Berkeley, and Hume) proposed a general theory of knowledge and perception which has influenced scholars ever since. Knowledge of reality, they held, could come only from impressions processed through the sensory apparatus. Simple ideas were seen as the irreducible elements of sensory experience. Complex ideas were thought to be built by learned *association* of these simple elements. The contents of the mind thus could be analyzed into those basic units which are the building blocks of sensation. Because of their emphasis on sensory experience rather than on an innately given basis for knowledge, these men are also called the British *empiricists*. Their interest was not in how the perception takes place but in the role of perception in our knowledge of reality. We encountered their notions about the mind as a *tabula rasa* and about learning by association of stimuli in Chapter 4.

Analytical Introspectionism

If sensations are the raw material which is knit by learning into the fabric of perception, then how does one ever discover what people are "really" sensing, before the sensory experience is overlaid by learning and perception? In the late 1800's a number of psychologists, notably Wundt and Titchener, argued that the job of psychology was to train observers to experience pure sensation, uncontaminated by additives from learning. To do so, they must be trained to eliminate or analyze out "perception," since it distorted the supposedly more primary *sensory* experience. They believed this process of trained introspection would yield the most basic psychological experience and that this should be the starting point for the subject matter of psychology.

The Gestalt Revolution

A group of German psychologists at the University of Berlin (Kohler, Koffka, Wertheimer) attacked the concepts of both *association of elements*, as the basis of perception and *introspective analysis* as the key to primary, original experience. They also attacked the behaviorists' idea of learning as building connections between stimuli and responses. In the Gestalt approach there is an emphasis on innate organizing processes that give us not the isolated sensations Wundt assumed we must have started with but *patterns* as a primary characteristic of perception.

The German word *Gestalt* has no exact English equivalent; the closest approximation is *configuration.* The configuration is seen as the basic unit of perception and other experience. According to the Gestaltists, "the whole is greater than the sum of its parts" and in many ways determines the character and behavior of the parts, instead of the other way around. A melody is the same in one key as in another even though the individual notes all change. Also, qualities of wholes—like the liltingness or the plaintiveness of a melody—do not reside in the individual notes. Relational properties such as these are part of the primary perception, not added later through unconscious inference. Thus, for example, no amount of introspection of the apparent movement in the phi phenomenon can make it go away.

The Gestalt psychologists postulated an *isomorphism*—identity of pattern—between the active organizing processes in perceived configurations and the chemical-electrical events taking place in the brain. If the configurations seen in the world are being mapped onto the brain in point-for-point correspondence, then it follows that information about brain function can be gained by careful study of perceptual experience. According to those with a Gestalt orientation, the reality of the observer's phenomenological (subjectively experienced) view should thus be the reality of concern for psychologists, both in its own right and for what it can tell us about neurological events.

Perception As a Filter

In the last chapter we described Eleanor Gibson's theory of perception as not *addition* but *reduction.* She sees perception not as adding meaning, form, and so on to sensory elements but as filtering out nonessential elements—the "noise"—and identifying the essential elements of the signal. This process enables the organism to learn what is predictable about the environment in order to deal with it.

Like technology's new machines for processing information, perception is seen as basically a process of reducing uncertainty by identifying regularities. In information theory, *information* is defined not in terms of content or meaning but in terms of regularity as opposed to randomness. The random elements in a signal are like "static" and may get in the way of our detection of the signal, which is nonrandom and patterned. The more *redundant* the signal is—the more parts of the signal there are that carry duplicate information—the easier it is for us to identify the information. Look at the sentence below:

"We Hope you are enjoxing this new informatio ."

There is "static" or noise in it, in the wrong and missing letters, but considerable redundancy too, in that there are more clues than we need to identify the intended signal. Similarly, perceptual signals come to us with both static and redundancy. The greater the redundancy and the less the static, the easier our job in reducing uncertainty by identifying the invariants —the regularities in features and relationships.

There are many other general and "mini" theories of perception, but these (and those mentioned in passing subsequently) will suffice to give you a feel for how basic one's theory of perception is to his conception of what the task of psychology is. The psychologist who sees perception as a combining of elements will investigate different problems from those tackled by the psychologist who sees perception as a matter of making new differentiations and identifying continuing structures, whether his special research happens to be on learning, thinking, motivation, social behavior, or measuring individual differences.

Factors Determining What We Perceive

It seems clear that the act of perceiving involves both a complex physiological processing of the stimulus signal energy and a psychological processing of the information received. Thus research on perception has tended to fall into three broad categories, according to the primary focus of the investigators: (a) an emphasis on the *stimulus* determinants of perception, such as configuration, complexity, signal strength, signal-to-noise relationships, and so on; (b) an emphasis on our *physical apparatus* for detecting the signals, at both the receptor and neural levels; and (c) an emphasis on *other factors in the individual* that affect perception, such as prior training history, cultural background, and motivational or personality factors.

In Chapter 3 we looked at our detection apparatus —our sensory receptors and neural processes. In this section we will discuss the research findings concerning (a) unlearned organizing processes in perception, (b) "prewired circuits," (c) the effects of learning, including interests and motivations.

Organizing Processes in Perception

The basic tenet of the Gestaltists—that organization is part of any perception, not something added after elements are sensed—has been generally accepted. Several aspects of this organization have been identified.

Figure-ground relations. We tend to organize the perceived flux in such a way as to hold changes and differences to a minimum while maintaining unity and wholeness. Most basic in this process is our tendency to perceive a figure against a background. This seems to happen automatically, whether we are looking at the objects around us or at clouds or tea leaves.

Compared to the ground, the figure appears to: (a) have shape, (b) be nearer, (c) be object-like, (d) be more vivid, (e) be more substantial in color, (f) own the common contour between them, (g) have the ground extend behind it (Rubin, 1921). Some of the factors that determine what the "figure" will be are summarized in the Ψ Close-up on page 287.

A familiar example of the use of these principles to change the figure seen is camouflage. Whether practiced by nature to conceal prey from predators or by armies (for the same purpose), camouflage is successful when it reduces the prominence of the figure cues, allowing the figure to be "lost" in the ground, as happened in the example on page 42.

Not only do we create the best figure we can from the sensory information supplied us; we often tend to

fill in missing parts, or see an almost circular figure as more circular than it is, or in other ways make the figure more stable or regular or complete than the sensory information provides for.

Although this concept of "good figure" seems quite vague, it has recently received empirical support through application of the information-theory concept of *redundancy*. Garner (1970) has demonstrated that good figures are those with maximum redundancy. Like any other information signal, a figure becomes more *good* as it becomes more *predictable* from any of its parts. This systematic investigator concluded that "somehow the human organism develops its perceptions toward good patterns and away from poor patterns." (p. 40)

We tend to perceive configurations even when the elements taken individually bear no relationship at all to the composite which "emerges" from them. This is readily seen in the ingenious computer-generated composite of the gargoyle of Quasimodo on Notre Dame Cathedral. •   (p. 288)

Combining cues to perceive depth.   Among the cues by which we perceive depth are those based on distinctness, linear perspective, texture, light and shadow, relative position, and known standards. All contribute to the fund of data which are organized into a meaningful whole in perception.

1. *Atmospheric perspective.*   Because of dust and smoke in the air, objects a long way off may appear to be blurred and indistinct in outline. Details we know are there may not be observable. The extent of the dimming depends on the distance, and we have long since learned to interpret distance in these terms. In fact, when the characteristic condition of the air changes, we often judge distances incorrectly. For example, a person reared in a smoky industrial city will greatly underestimate the distance of objects seen through clear mountain air. A tenderfoot on a ranch will amuse the old hands by announcing that he is going to "ride to the hill and back before breakfast," only to learn that the "hill" is really a mountain some fifty miles distant.

2. *Linear perspective.*   Objects appear smaller and closer together as they become more distant. Railroad tracks or the edges of a highway appear to meet on the horizon. Uniformly spaced objects such

Ψ *Close-up*   *Why Do We See the Figures We Do?*

1. *Similarity.*

Similar elements are seen as belonging to each other more than to other elements equally close but less similar. In this figure, do you see columns of Rs and Zs or rows of alternating letters R Z R Z R Z?

```
R  Z  R  Z  R  Z
R  Z  R  Z  R  Z
R  Z  R  Z  R  Z
R  Z  R  Z  R  Z
R  Z  R  Z  R  Z
R  Z  R  Z  R  Z
```

2. *Proximity.*

Elements that are physically close are seen as belonging to each other more than to similar elements that are farther away. Here you see pairs of RZ.

RZ   RZ   RZ   RZ

Proximity can also make things look more alike than they really are. The same figure that looks like an antelope when seen among antelopes looks like a bird in the company of other birds.

3. *Closure.*

We tend to perceive incomplete figures as if they were complete. We see the line below as a circle with a break in it and the irregular fragments as an animal.

4. *Continuation.*

Elements are seen as belonging to each other if they appear to be a continuation of the direction of previous elements. The curving line is seen as one figure, the line with the right angles as another figure.

5. *Common fate.*

Elements that move in the same direction are seen as belonging to each other. When alternate dancers in a ballet line step forward and make the same motion, we see them as a unit.

6. *Reversible figure and ground.*

Occasionally a stimulus pattern is so organized that more than one figure-ground relationship may be perceived. When these conflict, they alternate in consciousness. In the example shown here, when the vase becomes "figure," the black ground seems to extend behind it; the reverse occurs when the two faces are seen as figure.

7. *Good figure.*

The nervous system seems to prefer regular, simple forms. We see two overlapping squares here instead of a triangle and two irregular forms, equally possible from the sensory input.

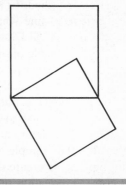

as telephone poles appear to be spaced more closely as they recede into the distance. These phenomena of linear perspective are used by artists to represent distance in pictures.

3. *Texture.* Closely related to linear perspective is the factor of texture. On any surface not perpendicular to the line of sight, the texture elements appear denser as the surface recedes. Thus texture is an adjunct to linear perspective, operating in situations where there are no converging parallel lines to give us clues.

4. *Light and shadow.* When light strikes an irregular surface, as for example the human face, certain parts are brightly illuminated and others are cast in shadow. The appearance of these shadows tells us much about the depth of the parts concerned. The

artist uses shading and highlights to convey the notion of depth on a two-dimensional canvas.

5. *Relative position.* When two objects are in the same line of vision, the nearer one conceals all or part of the farther one. Near objects usually appear at the bottom of the two-dimensional field of vision, distant objects at the top.

6. *Known standards.* Once we are familiar with the size or shape of an object it can be used as a standard for the height of other objects. This cue is of course critical in establishing object constancy.   ▲

The perception of depth also involves using cues derived from changes in the lens of the eye, which bulges slightly when we look at close objects and flattens for looking at distant ones. Binocular vision greatly aids depth perception because of the extra

● First, look very closely at the symbol elements. Then hold the book at arm's length. Quasimodo becomes even clearer as you move farther away.

feedback information provided by the *convergence* of the eyes as they focus on an object near the observer. In addition, the slightly different images we get from the two eyes (called *retinal disparity*) help us perceive depth and distance. We interpret distance by automatically comparing and integrating these two images—which permits inspection "around" contours.

Stereoscopic slides are an application of this principle. Two pictures are taken simultaneously by a camera with two lenses positioned a slight distance from each other. When the two pictures are viewed, one by each eye, the effect is that of a single, three-dimensional picture. By increasing the distance between the two pictures, it is possible to increase the illusion of depth—up to a certain point. When the two views become too different, however, they no longer merge in perception but are seen alternately.

The stereoscopic principle is used in the study of aerial pictures taken from different points in flight. Look at the diagrams below.

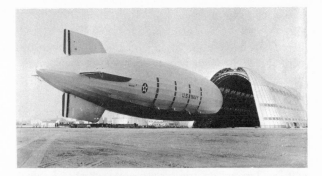

▲ Looking at the top picture, you might think you were looking at a smallish hangar next to a fair-sized blimp. The same hangar in the lower picture looks oversize next to the planes. But it is not until you notice how tiny the cars and people are that you realize how mammoth even the planes are.

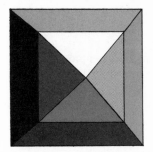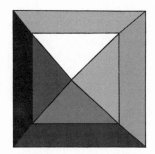

They show the top of a monument as it might look from two positions. Take a piece of cardboard ten to fourteen inches long and place it vertically between the two figures. Next, hold your head in contact with the upper edge of the cardboard so that the left eye sees only the diagram on the left and the right eye sees only the diagram on the right. The two flat images will fuse into a solid which appears to be located at a position between the two drawings.

Using cues in sound perception. People are able to locate the position of sounding objects in space in terms of distance and direction. This ability to locate sounds is of considerable adaptive value in modern life. For example, in crossing a busy street your very

life may depend upon your knowing accurately the position of an approaching automobile.

Perceiving the direction of sounds. Our ability to localize sounds is due almost entirely to our possession of two ears located at different points in space.

1. A sound coming from an object at the left of the head strikes the left ear before the right one. This difference in time can be very short, but it tells us from which side the sound is coming.

2. Sound waves coming from the left stimulate the left ear more strongly than they do the right ear.

3. Sound waves, as we saw in Chapter 3, consist of areas of high and low pressure. Since the two ears are at different points in space, a sound wave will be in different phases as it stimulates the two ears. Sound waves travel very slowly as compared with light waves, with the result that differences in phase in sound waves are appreciable.

We can use these cues to direction only when sounds come from one side or the other. Sounds directly in front of us cannot easily be distinguished from those above or behind us because the stimulation reaching the two ears is identical.

Perceiving the distance of sounds. Two clues help us determine how far away the source of a familiar sound is—*loudness* and *timbre*.

The farther away its source, the weaker the sound will be. The ear-splitting locomotive whistle heard in the station becomes fainter and fainter as the train moves away.

The farther away a sound is, the purer it will be. The tinny jangle of a cheap phonograph gives way to mellow music when heard in the distance, as from across a lake. This increase in purity results from the loss of the irregular sound waves (or noise) and from the loss of certain shrill overtones, which lack sufficient energy to carry very far.

Combining cues from several senses. The main thing that an individual is doing at any one time is constantly being influenced by simultaneous activities. Usually we are organizing data from several sensory modalities at once—visual, auditory, kinesthetic, and perhaps olfactory. That the contribution of one sense is modified by that of another has been demonstrated in several studies.

In a study showing the influence of auditory stimulation on the visual perception of verticality, college students were asked to look at a forty-inch luminescent rod in a dark room. The rod was pivoted at its center and could be rotated. The subjects wore headphones which permitted the presentation of auditory stimuli to either ear or both. Their feet did not touch the floor but were placed on a foot rest, in order to reduce cues for orientation in space. Three different intensity levels of stimulation and five different starting positions of the rod were used. On each test, the subject told the experimenter how to move the rod in order to make it seem vertical. The subjects had their eyes covered with goggles between tests.

It was found that the position of apparent verticality of the rod was shifted away from the side being stimulated with sound when only one ear was stimulated and away from the side of more intense stimulation when both sides were stimulated. The amount of shift was related directly to the intensity of the auditory stimulus.

When different sounds were conveyed to the two ears, no shift in apparent verticality occurred (Chandler, 1961).

In moving about in the world we navigate our perceptual space by combining higher-order stimuli from several modalities. Thus we see our position and that of objects around us, receive kinesthetic cues about the flexing and relaxing of our muscles, and keep track of our posture and equilibrium relative to the pull of gravity, all at once. When conflicting cues in the tactual and visual modalities offer conflicting information, then *visual capture* usually occurs: vision dominates and the tactual input is transformed so that we have a tactual perception consistent with the visual perception (Rock & Harris, 1967).

Until recently, this combining of information from different senses was studied only as a psychological process. Recently, however, the role of physiological mechanisms in providing a mechanism for sensory interaction has been revealed by the discovery of *polysensory* neurons. These neurons are in cortical and subcortical regions of the brain and seem to be capable of response to more than one kind of sensory input (Teuber, 1967).

Information learned through one modality—perhaps vision—can also be recognized and used through other modalities. The ability to verbalize a learned relationship can help this transfer from one modality to another and may even be essential to it. The letter A, learned through visual inspection, can be recognized tactually if it is a raised shape or kinesthetically if one is blindfolded and his hand guided through the motions of printing it.

"Pre-wired Circuits" in Perception

Besides these apparently unlearned tendencies toward organizing the stimulus input in the most stable way, does the newborn baby, chick, frog, or any other perceiving creature come into the world with ability from the beginning to perceive and distinguish between particular patterns?

The parsimonious answer accepted by many psychologists until recently has been "No." There has seemed no reason to assume any "pre-wired circuits" in the head that would equip new members of a species for instant pattern perception prior to any opportunity to learn. However, such a view has been effectively challenged by recent researchers armed with new ways of studying this age-old question.

Shape discrimination in infancy. When newly hatched chicks, only a few hours old, were presented with seeds of several different shapes, they showed a consistent preference. They pecked primarily the oval-shaped seeds—the "usual" shape that seeds come in! This demonstration of an innate perceptual preference for a very specific shape has obvious survival value for chickens (Fantz, 1957).

Infant monkeys from eighteen to twenty-five days old also show shape discrimination.

The ingenious test for whether these infant monkeys discriminate geometrical shapes at such an early age consisted of a circle and a triangle, with a nipple in the center of each. Sucking one produced milk for the hungry subject, while the other did not. Almost immediately there was a preference for the shape associated with the positive reinforcer, which generalized to a variety of stimuli related to the original stimulus shape (a secondary reinforcer). The lack of gradual acquisition typically found in the learning of new discriminations suggests that the subjects were discriminating between the shapes on the basis of built-in mechanisms (Zimmerman, 1961).

Depth perception in infancy. Even stronger support for the "innateness-is-important-too" hypothesis comes from the research using the "visual cliff" apparatus discussed on page 128. As we saw there, infants of several species showed a clear preference for avoiding the apparent abyss.

The beauty of the procedure in these studies lay in separating the perceptual response from the general instrumental act of locomotion. The locomotor responses would be the same whichever side the infant chose to cross. Thus any preference would be entirely a matter of his perceptual capacities. Also, somewhat surprisingly, it was discovered that instead of responding to depth cues the subjects were responding to the *motion parallax:* the perceived changes in their own position relative to other objects. When the "floor" was close, a given movement of their own seemed faster relative to it and the changes in their position were more clearly related to changes in its

appearance from one moment to the next. Evidently there was unlearned perception of this difference and preference for the conditions associated with the faster motion.

Size constancy in human infancy. To find out whether young infants have size constancy, one investigator trained a two-month-old baby to respond to a 30-cm. cube. Every time the baby turned its head toward this discriminative stimulus, a potent reinforcer was presented—the experimenter popping up and "peek-a-booing."

When this operant response was well established, generalization tests were conducted to determine whether the baby was responding on the basis of the retinal size, the distance, or the distal size. It was reasoned that if size constancy is innate (or learned very early), then the true stimulus size (30 cm.) should be the perceptual factor to which the baby would continue to respond rather than either a constant retinal size or a constant distance if the three factors were varied independently so that he had to choose one and ignore the others. This is exactly what was found: most responding occurred where retinal image size and distance were different from the original condition but distal size was the same (T. G. R. Bower, 1966a).

In another study, the discriminative feature of the stimulus was not its size but its shape (angle of slant). Again the infant perceiver detected the "correct" stimulus on the basis of its objective shape, rather than its retinal shape (T. G. R. Bower, 1966b).

Evidence from rearing without opportunity for learning. Another way to evaluate the innateness of perception involves studying the perceptual abilities of subjects deprived of normal sensory stimulation and hence of chances for perceptual learning.

In Chapter 6 we saw that adult cataract patients, who had had no chance for pattern vision prior to their operations, perceived figure and ground right away but had trouble recognizing objects in different contexts. More systematic evidence has come from studies in which animals have been reared under conditions of sensory deprivation.

One such study investigated monkeys' ability to make a horizontal-vertical discrimination without prior learning.

Monkeys reared in darkness were able to learn an operant response that required them to discriminate between a vertical and a horizontal line. This was true even when the stimuli were presented to the retina by a special device which stabilized the image on the retina. As the eye moved, the image moved with it; thus the eye could not get clues by following the contours of the different shapes. Not only was the discrimination still learned, but it generalized despite extreme transformations to other stimuli as long as the correct one was vertical and the incorrect one horizontal. Thus after training with solid horizontal and vertical blocks, subjects correctly discriminated fine lines and even lines composed of small units, such as those below.

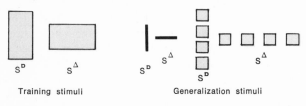

Training stimuli   Generalization stimuli

In this study the deprivation rearing ruled out general previous experience, and the stabilized images ruled out rapid learning from eye-movement feedback. Two conclusions are suggested by the findings: (a) learning perceptual discriminations involves not combining elements, but analyzing the basic features of the stimulus pattern, and (b) organisms have innate mechanisms for analyzing features like horizontal and vertical position (Ganz & Wilson, 1967).

Another ingenious study demonstrated the use of binocular depth vision in chicks who had been prevented from learning to use it.

For several months after hatching, a group of chicks were prevented from using binocular vision by alternately having one eye or the other covered each day. They were then tested to see if they would use binocular cues when both eyes were exposed even though they had had no prior experience with binocular vision. During testing they wore hoods containing lenses which distort the visual field. If binocular vision is used, the lenses move the visual field forward, while if monocular vision is used, the visual field is displaced to the right. Examination of the birds' error pattern in pecking while wearing these lenses revealed that they pecked short of the target. This suggests that binocular vision in the chick is innate, since the birds were evidently using binocular vision even though the opportunity for learning how to use it had been withheld (Hess, 1956).

Evidence from the neural circuits themselves. If visual stimuli consist of flashes of light varying in intensity, mass, and location but we see shapes, forms, and movement, how and where does this translation take place? The classic discovery of Hubel and Wiesel (1959) provides a possible answer to this question. As we saw in Chapter 3, they were able to demonstrate that single cells in the visual cortex are "programmed" to be activated by only certain features of a stimulus, such as lines with a particular orientation and location with respect to the retina, while other cells were inhibited by such features.

This sensory translation system starts in the retina, continues in the thalamus, and is finally integrated at later stages in the cortex. The input "passes through two or more synapses in the retina, one or more in the thalamus, and a dozen more in the cortex. At each of these synapses there is a convergence of inputs and some sort of processing of visual information. By the time sight stimuli are perceived and responded to, the information has passed sequentially through a great many stages of analysis." (De Valois, 1966, p. 87)

In a given sequence, as information from many individual cells converges at each successively higher level of neural processing, some details of the initial information are lost. Instead of a single sequential processing of information, however, it is likely that man's billions of cortical cells allow multiple channels of information to be scanned in parallel, thereby integrating much information and losing as little as possible. By relying on the complex networks available in the visual cortex to do the final processing and synthesizing of output from the receptors, man has developed an almost infinitely adaptable data-processing system.

To appreciate the significance of this evolutionary gift, consider the frog who has no cortex and must process inputs at the retinal level. Single cell recordings from the frog retina have shown that some cell units respond only to objects the size and shape of a small bug. Moreover, they respond only if the bug-shaped object moves (Lettvin, Maturana, McCulloch, & Pitts, 1959). Compared to man, the frog is a slave to his stimulus environment and would starve to death amid a feast of plenty but for the charity of Nature which encourages bugs to jump and flies to fly.

How Learning Changes Perception

"Of *course* perception is dependent on past experience," you say. But just *what part* of the vague term "past experience," and how can you prove it? The many attempts at such a proof have studied the effects of broad cultural experiences, general perceptual habits, differential training, instructional sets, and manipulated influences on psychophysical detection.

The influence of culture.   Kenge's perception of the distant buffalo as insects was a dramatic example of the effect of our cultural experience on what we perceive. To the extent that perception depends upon assumptions based on past experience with the environment, there should be many differences in the perceptions of people from different cultural environments. Such differences should show up in the way they perceive illusions.

◆ **VIEW I**

Evidence of differences in perception of illusions comes from a cross-cultural study of 1878 persons from fourteen non-European cultures, plus an American sample. The investigators hypothesized that there should be cultural differences in susceptibility to two different types of illusions—the horizontal-vertical (Pinocchio's nose) and the Müller-Lyer (p. 35). They reasoned that experience with broad plains and open vistas should *increase* susceptibility to the horizontal-vertical illusion, whereas the absence of such experience (as with forest dwellers) should *decrease* it. In contrast, those living in a "carpentered world," where angles are important and prominent, should be more susceptible to the Müller-Lyer illusion than those living in an environment such as that of the Zulus, where huts are circular and regular angles are rare. Their data supported these predictions (Segall, Campbell, & Herskovits, 1966).

Differential training.   To illustrate how even brief training can influence your perception, perform the following experiment. Carefully examine for the minute the woman's face in the illustration. At the same time, have a friend do the same for the face on the next page, which *you should not see*. Then flip to page 298 and both call out, as soon as you can, what kind of face you see there.   ◆

When a similar experiment was first performed in the laboratory many years ago, the experimenter found that perceptual preparation with one of the first pictures was very effective in determining what the response would be to the ambiguous figure, whereas verbal preparation had no effect. He also found that when subjects saw only the ambiguous picture, twice as many of them reported seeing the young woman as the old one. With supposedly comparable past experience, other characteristics—perhaps in the stimulus pattern itself—tipped the balance between which possibility was seen (Leeper, 1935).

On your mark, get set...   A *set*, as the term implies, is a readiness to perceive or respond in a certain way. A set can be based on expectancies resulting from past experience or can be established by instructions from the experimenter (or anyone else whose edicts you take seriously). Thus a given set can be a momentary condition or a long-lasting part of your basic approach to situations.

The influence of sets on perception has been exten-

VIEW II

the way individuals will process new information. These attitudes come to function as "anchors" or comparison standards with which new inputs are compared. Inputs similar to the standard tend to be perceived as more *similar* than they really are (whether it is weights or political judgments that are being judged). Inputs definitely different from the standard tend to be perceived as more *different* than they really are. If subjects are asked to put opinion statements about important issues into categories, they typically displace items either toward or away from their own position (Sherif & Hovland, 1961).

Interests, motives, and self-defense. Research by proponents of a formal, structural view of perception has traditionally dealt with such determinants of perception as the stimulus, the proximal stimulation at the retina or other receptor points, or neuronal connections—in short, the innate endowment of the organism and the physical stimulus energy impinging on the receptors. The "new-look" school of functional perception has set out to add a new dimension to this traditional analysis by putting the *perceiver* back in perception. Its proponents have demonstrated in numerous studies that between the sensory receptors and motor effectors is a human organism with motives, needs, values, attitudes, expectations, and emotions, all of which can influence perception in important ways. One formulation, which groups such variables into two main channels of influence, is summarized in the Ψ Close-up on page 295.

The study which began the controlled laboratory research on emotional factors in perception, known as the "poor boy, rich boy" study, had a serious methodological flaw in it. Can you detect it?

A group of thirty ten-year-olds were tested with an apparatus consisting of a wooden box with a screen at one end and a knob at the lower right-hand corner. By turning the knob the children could vary the diameter of the circle of light shining on the screen. Two groups of children, one rich and the other poor, were asked to match the size of the circle of light to the size of coins of various denominations; a control group matched the light to the size of cardboard discs.

The coins, socially valued objects, were judged larger in size than the discs. Furthermore, the poor group overestimated the size of the coins more than did the rich group (Bruner & Goodman, 1947).

sively studied in the laboratory. As Floyd Allport wrote some years ago (1955), "Sets tend, other things being equal, to determine physiologically what objects are to be perceived, the speed or readiness of their perception, and within limits, the content and vividness of the percept." (p. 241)

Perceptual discrimination can be increased by instructions that prepare the subject for the classes of objects or attributes on which he will have to report. In addition, such instructions can be effective in "priming" the response channels—making one response more likely than another, especially to an ambiguous stimulus pattern. While research has clearly shown that sets do affect reported perceptual judgments, it is less clear at what level the effect occurs—whether it is actual perceptual sensitivity that has changed or attention, memory, or motivation to respond.

Long-term sets can become attitudes which bias

Ψ Close-up   *Effects of Past Experience on Signal Detection*

In Chapter 3 you were introduced to the field of psychophysics, which developed out of the attempt to find regular relationships between stimulus intensity and strength of sensation. By recording the stimulus intensity that could be detected half of the time, they established a subject's absolute threshold; by recording the amount of change in intensity that he could distinguish as different half of the time, they established the difference threshold. They found that in the laboratory, other things being equal, stimulus intensity had to progress *geometrically* to produce successive *just noticeable differences* in sensation.

But we do not always compare stimulus strengths in the laboratory, and other things are not always equal. Since the early days of Fechner, who pioneered the psychophysical approach, research in this field has become broader and more sophisticated. It is clear that capacity to detect a stimulus of a certain energy is only one factor determining threshold.

Two main ways in which other factors affect and change detection of a stimulus have been described by Galanter (1962) in terms of the relationships shown below. The diagram depicts a situation of psychophysical choice in which the subject must say whether the signal is on or off. He makes his judgment not only on the basis of the stimulus input but also on the basis of how likely he thinks it is to be on and what the rewards are likely to be if he is right (or punishments if he is wrong).

As you will see, these two ways other factors can influence perception also correspond to two ways past experience can affect present perception and also correspond to the two kinds of relationships learned through conditioning, as described in Chapter 5. What Galanter calls "expectations" are the stimulus sequences we learn to expect following a familiar "signal" (discriminative) stimulus.

What he calls "motives" are the results of the reinforcements we have received as consequences of past actions, leading us to choose one course rather than another as most likely to bring satisfaction and avoid pain.

In a signal detection system such as that portrayed in the diagram, the signal may be *off* or *on,* and the judgment may be *yes* or *no,* leading to four possible combinations, two correct and two incorrect. The probability of making each one varies not only with the strength of the stimulus (stronger stimulus, more positive hits) but also with the conditions or presentation and payoff. If there is a lot of action, the observer becomes more vigilant and develops an expectation to see the signal on. This leads to more positive hits but also to more false alarms. The frequency of "false arrests" in the high-crime areas of our cities is in part a result of the expectation to see acts of crime—including some that are not there.

When the stimuli are infrequent and the expectation develops that the signal will not come on (consider radar operators in the Antarctic), then there will be more misses (*no*'s when the signal is on) but also more correct *no*'s.

Different payoff contingencies also influence the pattern of hits and misses. If it is very important to get hits, then false alarms may be tolerated for a considerable time (remember how long the boy got away with crying "wolf"). The same thing might occur in attempts to detect enemy planes thought to be carrying an H-bomb. In research where subjects gain or lose money depending upon their detection responses, they alter their responses to maximize payoffs and minimize losses. We can anticipate that the effect of expected payoffs will be even greater in the "looser" environmental conditions occurring in the real world than it has been found to be in the highly controlled conditions of the laboratory.

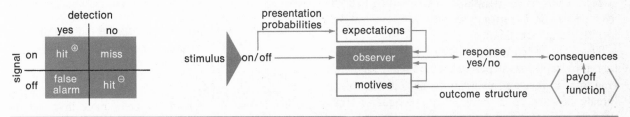

This study led to considerable controversy because critics were quick to point out that there was no proof that values and needs were the determining factors, since other variables such as past experiences with coins were not controlled. However, one group of investigators appears to have overcome these objections by the use of hypnosis to make people "poor" or "rich."

Before being hypnotized, middle-class subjects adjusted the size of the light spot until it looked equal to the actual size of each of three coins—a nickel, a dime, and a quarter. When made to forget their real life histories and given "poor" life histories under hypnosis, the same individuals made settings consistently larger than the ones they had made in the normal state. When given "rich" life histories while hypnotized, they made consistently smaller settings than previously. Thus the conclusion was that their perceptions were indeed affected by needs and values, since their prior experience with money was identical. The effectiveness of the "poor" and "rich" life histories in inducing different needs and values was further shown by the fact that when "poor," the subjects sat erect and worked with great care, whereas when "rich," they slouched in their chairs and worked rapidly but condescendingly (Ashley, Harper, & Runyan, 1951). •

Perceptual accentuation of a valued characteristic was also indicated in an "I like VW" study of owners of Volkswagen cars. Those who valued owning their VW tended to perceive it as smaller than those who were indifferent about it (Stayton & Weiner, 1961).

By using a measure of content analysis of children's drawings at different times of the year, investigators have discovered that Santa Claus drawings made before Christmas were bigger than those made after the holiday. This was not a general euphoria effect but a "Santa-specific" one since only drawings of Santa got bigger as his coming approached (Solley & Haigh, 1959; Sechrest & Wallace, 1964). In another carefully controlled study, the avoidance motive of fear seems to be implicated in the finding that the average size of drawings of witches *decreased* at Halloween (Craddick, 1967).

The active role of emotional and motivational factors in perception is shown in the fact that individuals tend to misperceive stimuli that are socially taboo and threatening and to require longer recognition time than for neutral stimuli.

The first study to offer support for this hypothesis presented college subjects with seven "critical" words (such as "belly," "raped," "bitch") interspersed among eleven other, more innocuous, words. The duration of exposure was controlled by a *tachistoscope*, a device which projected the words on a screen for a fraction of a second. A longer duration of exposure was required for identification of the critical words than for the neutral ones. In addition, the greater galvanic skin response to the taboo words during the time interval *before* they were reported was taken as evidence for an unconscious *perceptual defense* mechanism (McGinnies, 1949).

The intriguing explanation of perceptual defense was subjected to criticism because the methodology of this study permitted three equally plausible alternative explanations. The differences in recognition thresholds could result either from differential sensitivity to taboo words because of their antisocial meaning as claimed, or from the fact that they are less frequently seen under normal viewing conditions. Or it could be that the effect was not a perceptual one at all, but one of response inhibition: maybe the

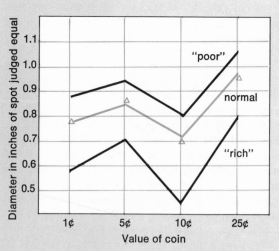

Based on Ashley et al., 1951

● **NEEDS AND VALUES INFLUENCE PERCEPTION**

This figure shows the sizes of white spots judged to be equal in size to the four coins at the start of the experiment in the normal state and under "poor" and "rich" conditions when hypnotized. Triangles indicate the actual sizes of the coins.

subjects perceived the bad words as rapidly as the nice ones, but felt inhibited about reporting them.

Several subsequent studies helped support the perceptual defense hypothesis. Threat and nonthreat words were printed in booklets where they were totally blurred on the top page, but became decreasingly blurred (more signal in relation to noise) with each page turned. Threat words required more pages turned before they were recognized. This was true even though the frequency of the words was controlled. The same effect was found when subjects were alerted to the impending threat words and when

---

Ψ *Close-up*   **Which Game Did They See?**

To illustrate how the *purposes* which people bring to a stimulus situation determine what they will perceive despite "common sensory impingements," we can look at what happened at the Princeton-Dartmouth game of 1953. Princeton, nationally ranked, with its tailback Dick Kazmaier an All-American candidate, was the target of much Dartmouth newspaper coverage and dormitory talk for weeks before the game. The "Get the Princeton Preppies" campaign must have been effective, because the game was extremely rough, with Kazmaier's nose being broken.

Psychologists at each of the schools gave a questionnaire to a sample of undergraduate students who had seen the game. Each group then viewed the same film of the game and recorded any infractions of the rules that they observed.

The attitudes of nearly all the Princeton students were that the game was "rough and dirty," with 90 percent of them believing the other side started the rough play. Dartmouth students also described the game as "rough" but said that the two sides were equally to blame. The Princetonians recorded the Dartmouth team as guilty of twice as many penalties as their team. In contrast, the students from Hanover saw the teams making the same number of infractions and being equally penalized. Although they watched the same film, they clearly saw a "different" game (Hastorf & Cantril, 1954).

the sex of the subject and the experimenter were the same (Cowen & Beier, 1954).

In another experiment the frequency of the words was again controlled, but this time they were presented in pairs. That is, a "pretask" word, sometimes taboo and sometimes neutral, was presented for an interval of two seconds, and then the "task" word, always a neutral word, was presented for .01 second. If it was not recognized, the pretask word was again exposed for two seconds, followed by the task word for .02 seconds. This was done until the task word was finally recognized. When the pretask word was a taboo word, the threshold for recognition of the neutral task word associated with it tended to be higher than when the pretask word was neutral (McGinnies & Sherman, 1952).

The complex relationship between the stimulus and response sides of the perceptual mosaic is even more apparent in the phenomenon of *subception*—perception below the level of awareness.

The study responsible for demonstrating this activity presented subjects with nonsense syllables, some of which were paired with shock, and some not. When all the syllables were later presented *without* shock, those previously associated with shock produced more emotional arousal in the subjects, as measured by greater GSR. Not only that, but even when the words were exposed for a period so brief that subjects could not report them accurately, their autonomic (GSR) responses were different for the words previously experienced with shock (Lazarus & McCleary, 1951).

It has been pointed out that these results may also reflect the fact that verbal reports were simply right or wrong, with no intermediate positions available, whereas the GSR measures could be at many different points along a continuum (Postman, 1963). But despite controversy over interpretation of some research, the hardly still "new-look" school of perception has served the valuable function of broadening the range of variables that must be taken into account in our attempts to understand what is added to sensory input during perception.

Distortion and Hallucination

Under optimal conditions of observation, when the discriminative capacities of the perceiver are maximized and stimulus factors are clean and clear, our perceptions are usually a good, fairly literal translation of what is generally agreed to be external reality. However, when the viewing conditions are bad and the stimulus is ambiguous, then perception is more heavily weighted (biased) by internal organizing processes and motivational factors. The distortions of perception by emotional and motivational factors described in the previous section of this chapter were in part a result of the inadequacy of available external stimulation and the "take-over" by other, nonperceptual systems which were in a state of readiness.

Extreme Emotional Arousal

The distorting effects of extreme stress or euphoria in modifying the reality of the perceptual world can be better illustrated by reference to Shakespeare (for the

VIEW III

former) and to modern song writers (for the latter) than by laboratory experiments.

Macbeth in anguish says:

Is this a dagger which I see before me,
The handle toward my hand? Come, let me clutch thee.
I have thee not, and yet I see thee still.
Art thou not, fatal vision, sensible
To feeling as to sight? or art thou but
A dagger of the mind, a false creation,
Proceeding from the heat-oppressed brain?

. . . . .

Mine eyes are made the fools o' the other senses,
Or else worth all the rest; I see thee still,
And on the blade and dudgeon gouts of blood,
Which was not so before. There's no such thing:
It is the bloody business which informs
Thus to mine eyes.

(Act 2, Scene 1)

Similarly, the ecstasy of love can induce perceptual distortion, although of a different nature:

Are there lilac trees in the heart of town?
Can you hear a lark in any other part of town?
Does enchantment pour out of every door?
No, it's just on the street where you live.[1]

Hallucination—Perception Turned In on Itself

Under certain extreme and unusual conditions the stimulus for perception seems to be not "out there" but "inside the head." An illusion of perception in which there is a perception of reality in the absence of external stimulus energy is called a *hallucination*. Unlike perceptual illusions, which are shared by most comparable observers, hallucinations are private, idiosyncratic events. It is this feature which makes them an intriguing puzzle for psychologists, and a cause of concern for psychiatrists. Active hallucination is taken as one of the primary diagnostic indicators of psychosis and will be discussed in that connection in Chapter 14. But hallucinations can also be caused by emotional stress, sensory deprivation, hypnosis, and hallucinogenic drugs, as well as by sleep deprivation, as in the case reported earlier of the New York disc jockey. (Ψ Close-up, p. 299.)

[1]"On the Street Where You Live" Copyright © 1956 by Alan Jay Lerner and Frederick Loewe. Used by permission of Chappell & Co., Inc.

Hallucinations from prolonged sensory deprivation. In earlier chapters we saw how development is affected by sensory deprivation in infancy. Studies have also been made of the effects of the sensory deprivation on the functioning of normal adults. Particularly as space travel becomes a reality, it is important to know the effects of prolonged isolation on human beings.

In some studies of sensory isolation, an attempt is made to come as close as possible to *eliminating* visual and auditory stimulation. Subjects have remained in dark, silent chambers up to ten days.

In one study, subjects lay on an air mattress in a dark, soundproof chamber. They wore earmuffs to deaden any sounds that they might make inside the chamber. They were instructed to lie quietly on the mattress without engaging in any unnecessary physical or vocal activity. Toilet facilities, a food chamber, a "panic button," and an air-conditioning unit were all provided. The subjects were requested to spend one week in the chamber; they were, however, given no information as to the passage of time. The only intrusions on the conditions of isolation were occasional test sessions of approximately forty-five minutes duration for the appraisal of intellectual abilities. During these periods, a 15-watt red bulb lighted the chamber.

Sixteen subjects were tested, four of them women. All spent the requested week in the chamber; one stayed eight and a half days, and another ten days. In general, the women withstood the isolation for longer periods than the men.

Eleven of the subjects experienced hallucinations— mostly flashes of light, flickering lights, dim glowing lights, and so on, which lacked shape and usually appeared in the peripheral field of vision. The hallucinations were usually of very short duration, about five to ten seconds, although some were reported to last for as long as fifteen minutes. Many subjects reported only one or two brief hallucinatory periods a day; others only one or two during the entire week. Five reported no hallucinatory activity; the women appeared less prone to hallucinations.

In addition to visual hallucinations, several auditory hallucinations were reported. These were usually very realistic, such as howling dogs, a ringing alarm clock, and the sound of a typewriter. Two tactual-kinesthetic hallucinations were also reported. One consisted of cold steel pressing on the subject's forehead and cheeks; the other was a sensation of someone pulling the mattress from under the subject. In most instances, the auditory

Ψ *Close-up* *Checking Out a Possible Hallucination*

In trying to evaluate whether a strange perceptual experience is a bona fide hallucination or only a facsimile of one—that is, caused by some nonobvious external source of stimulation—apply the following six tests:

_____1. Volitional Control—Can you will it away?

_____2. Blocked Sensory Input—Is it still there when the appropriate sense receptor is blocked (mask eyes or cover ears)?

_____3. Consensual Validation—Do other people in the same situation report the same experience?

_____4. Cross-Modality Check—Can you touch it or kick it?

_____5. Physical Attribute Check—Does a tape recorder or light meter also detect it?

_____6. Response-Stimulation Coordination—Does it get bigger under a magnifying lens or louder with a sound amplifier? Does the sound level change as you move toward or away from it?

If the first two checks are positive and the others are negative, do not pass "Go," but proceed immediately to the student health service.

and tactual hallucinations were reported during the last two days of isolation.

On first emerging from the chamber, subjects reported that images were more vivid than previously experienced. Hypersensitivity to sounds was also very common, especially during the first night after the experiment, when subjects were aware of even the slightest sounds. Many sounds which normally are irritating seemed pleasant and in some cases were even considered delightful. Traffic noises seemed particularly loud and somewhat startling. Tests administered after isolation, however, showed no gross perceptual changes, and the minor changes in sensitivity disappeared shortly after the first day (Zubeck, Pushkar, Sansom, & Gowing, 1961).

Other studies of sensory isolation have involved depriving the subject of all *structured* stimulation. In some such studies the subjects are enclosed in chambers in which diffused light is seen through translucent goggles, to prevent any pattern vision. A buzzer or other meaningless sound blocks out meaningful sounds of the environment; cardboard cuffs restrict movement and eliminate tactual stimulation of the hands and arms. In some studies subjects have been put into tanks of warm water. More elaborate hallucinatory experiences followed by perceptual distortions have typically been reported under such conditions, which can usually be endured for only two or three days or less, even when the subject is paid a fee of $20 per day.

In one study in which a low level of diffuse visual and auditory stimulation was present, subjective reports indicated that when first in isolation the subjects thought about realistic problems but as time went on they had difficulty concentrating and just "let their minds drift." Finally there were periods in which they thought of nothing and some were confused to the point of being unable to distinguish between waking and sleeping.

Visual hallucinations were generally quite simple at the beginning, but later became more vivid and complex. At first there was a general lighting of the visual field, then dots or lines of light, then geometric figures and patterns. Finally full scenes appeared. One man thought he saw things coming at him and withdrew his head accordingly when this occurred; one was convinced that pictures were being projected on his goggles; another felt that someone was with him in the cubicle. These hallucinations were more vivid than normal imagery and appeared to be projected as on a movie screen in front of the subject, rather than between his ears as is normally the case with imagery.

To test what effects the diffuse light had on hallucinatory activity, the experimenters removed some of the hallucinating subjects to a dark room. At first the hallucinations became more vivid, but within two hours they were either gone or greatly diminished. When returned to diffuse light, the subjects again hallucinated. It was clear that diffuse light was more disruptive than total darkness.

When the subjects were taken from isolation and seated in a chair, with their goggles removed, they were asked to describe their surroundings. Nearly all subjects reported gross perceptual distortion. This lasted for only a few minutes, except in one case which lasted for several hours. Examples of this distortion were movement of objects in the visual field or of the walls of the room, objects changing shape and size, and flat surfaces appearing curved (Heron, 1961).

It seems clear from present experimental findings that meaningful sensory experiences are necessary for the normal functioning of the brain. The complex, continually active brain, which never even allows itself forty winks, apparently demands that the environment, too, stay awake and provide stimulating conversation. Sensory isolation may be thought of as a means of "destructuring the environment." The subject, made uncertain and anxious by the lack of space and time orientation, has a tendency to try to restructure the environment and restore meaning to the situation. In this attempt, the fantasies, hallucinations, and perceptual distortions that appear are in accordance with the subject's personality and past environment, as well as with the experimental setting (Ruff, Levy, & Thaler, 1961).

Subsequent research has accumulated considerable evidence indicating that the effects of sensory deprivation can facilitate or impair mental functioning depending upon the interaction of: (a) the personality of the subject, (b) the set induced by the experimenter, and (c) the aesthetics of the experimental setting (Brownfield, 1964). When the apprehension and fear of this novel situation are removed, "the imagery of sensory deprivation becomes like the imagery of daydreams, quite familiar and usually not anxiety-provoking" (Leiderman, 1965).

Hypnotic hallucinations and age regression. With appropriate training, many people are able to increase their level of suggestibility until certain out-of-the-ordinary phenomena can be experienced. The hypnotic process involved will be discussed in Chapter 10; in the present context two interesting perceptual phenomena are of concern.

Many investigators have found that hypnotic subjects report experiencing both positive and negative hallucinations upon the suggestion that they do so. Subjects can be made to perceive objects that are *not* there or to fail to perceive what *is* there or see it as radically changed. Induction of such hallucinatory experiences is often utilized during the process of childbirth when hypnosis is the only anesthetic. The prospective mother may be sent on a hallucinated vacation in the Caribbean or made not to perceive the surgical instruments, the pain, or the blood.

But these hallucinations are records of private

events presumably occurring inside the person's mind. Although introspective reports are a valid source of evidence, the observing psychologist must corroborate them with other, nonprivate, objective response indicators.

With highly susceptible hypnotic subjects, it is possible to have them project an image of a stimulus object with their eyes open. These hypnotic hallucinations are so vivid that they seem indistinguishable from waking state percepts. Several studies have attempted to validate the reality of these hallucinations by using objectively recorded eye movements as a criterion. "In general these studies have shown that eye movements tend to accompany hallucinations and that the form of the eye movement recording approximates the object imagined." (Graham, 1969a, p. 10)

One study found that subjects hypnotized and directed to see a rotating drum had the particular kind of eye movements that they had when actually watching such an event. In addition, the subjects were unable to feign these movements in the waking state when they were directed to do so (Brady & Levitt, 1964, 1966).

In another study, hypnotized patients were trained to hallucinate two gray circles on a white card. When they projected these hallucinated circles onto a black and white background, they reported the usual brightness contrast: the one against white looked darker and the one against black lighter, so that they no longer appeared the same. A comparable group, asked to respond as if they were hypnotized, tended not to report the contrast (Graham, 1969b).

Further controlled studies are necessary before we can conclude that people can *create* percepts, in the absence of distal stimuli, which are truly indistinguishable from the percepts induced by external stimuli. There is some evidence, however, to suggest that such a possibility may exist, at least for some people.

While under hypnosis, an individual can be "regressed" to an earlier age and asked to tell what he has been doing, how he feels, and what things look like. Such hypnotic regression provides an interesting source of information about some primitive properties of size constancy. Imagine that you were being age-regressed back to infancy. Do you think you would feel yourself as growing smaller and smaller until you could again fit into your crib or your mother's arms? Almost all of twenty-four well-trained

hypnotic subjects (college students) studied by one of the authors reported a very different change. The world got bigger, but they did not notice themselves changing at all. A finger placed in their palms not only induced clenching, and often shaking or sucking, but also was reported to feel "enormous." Similarly, the crib and faces and sounds were all experienced by the hypnotized subjects as being very big and loud.

Because of the slow process of growth, we do not at any time perceive our bodies as growing. Because of this apparent constancy of our own body size, it is likely that we learn to use it as a standard against which to judge other objects more often than we use other objects to judge its size. In fact, you may have had a similar experience without hypnosis, if you returned to a well-remembered childhood scene only to find that everything looked much smaller than it "was" then.

The psychedelic experience. When in 1943 a Swiss chemist, Albert Hoffman, accidentally ingested a small amount of a newly developed drug, lysergic acid diethylamide-25, the most potent mind-altering drug known to man was discovered. The dramatic perceptual changes, fantasies, and cognitive alterations which he experienced with *LSD* have now been replicated millions of times over in "independent experiments" throughout the world.

The use of intoxicants to transcend the limits and constraints of reality has an ageless history. The oracle at Delphi was located on a site where fuming gases could intoxicate Apollo's priestess and thus allow divine truth to be perceived. The Shaman and medicine men of many cultures have taken drugs and prescribed them to the people. Before Aldous Huxley opened his "doors of perception" (1954) with a mescaline-induced trip, austere William James had turned on with a nitrous-oxide revelation (1882).

But it remained for LSD to create the psychedelic revolution. The emergence of a whole subculture organized around "acid" and a philosophy of love and mystical experience, originating with San Francisco's (Haight-Ashbury) flower children, will be discussed, along with other aspects of drug use and abuse, in Appendix D.

Although controlled research on the effects of LSD

on perception and other processes barely began before it was limited legally, there have been a number of studies investigating its behavioral consequences (Tart, 1969).

In one series of studies conducted at the International Foundation for Advanced Study in Menlo Park, California, nearly 400 subjects were studied before, during, and after a psychedelic experience with a large dose of LSD (Mogar, 1969). These studies and others have found that even with a chemical substance as powerful as LSD, the effects on perception and cognition are largely determined by the personality of the subject, the atmosphere of the setting, and the emotional preparation and support provided by those guiding the trip. Thus the same dose has different effects, depending on whether the subject is anxious, mentally stable, or dependent on ego-defensive patterns, on whether the setting is a sterile hospital room or a friendly, informal one, and on what he expected to experience.

The general change induced by the psychedelic experience may be one of "mystical consciousness," where the subject/object dichotomy is transcended and the reality-testing ego is abolished, or it may be of a nonmystical nature. The nonmystical hallucinations involve perceptual changes in which: (a) spatial relationships are no longer maintained; (b) the solidity of mass becomes pliable; (c) colors become richer, deeper; (d) contours sharpen; (e) three-dimensional, colored geometric patterns often appear and disappear; (f) *synesthesia* often develops in which music is seen in changing, vivid colors; and (g) faces and objects, familiar and foreign, may emerge.

Illustrative of this general level of perceptual experience is the following quotation from one of the subjects in an experimental research program on the effects of LSD.

"I lay on my stomach and closed my eyes and brilliant colored patterns of fantastic beauty collided, exploded, raced by. Other things too: teeth and pearls and precious stones with lips and eyes. Outside of the window the branches of the tree were gigantic arms with transparent muscles, now threatening, now embracing. Glasses started rolling on the table, the bookcase was full of swimming books, the door bulged like a balloon, the carpet in the other room was full of a thousand green snakes." (Pahnke & Richards, 1969, p. 409)

Extrasensory Perception

Are there forms of perception that circumvent all the known sensory channels? Large amounts of publicity have been given to clairvoyance and mental telepathy. As a result, the psychologist often is asked, "Is there really such a thing as extrasensory perception?"

Extrasensory perception (ESP) is said to comprise (a) *mental telepathy*, in which one person becomes aware of what another is thinking without sensory cues, and (b) *clairvoyance*, in which an individual becomes aware of a physical object without using his sense organs. J. B. Rhine, one of the leading workers in this controversial area, and others who are convinced that extrasensory perception occurs, are also investigating the possibility of "incorporeal personal agency," which is closely related to the ancient question of whether there is personal survival after death (Rhine, 1960).

A typical mental telepathy test is conducted as follows: There is a deck of twenty-five cards containing five cards for each of five symbols—star, circle, square, plus sign, and parallel wavy lines. After the cards are shuffled, one subject (the "sender") goes through the deck, concentrating on each card in turn, while another subject (the "receiver") tries to read his mind. As the receiver calls out "square," "circle," and so on, his judgments are recorded by an observer. In clairvoyance experiments, the cards are shuffled and the receiver (there is no sender other than the cards themselves) attempts to record the order.

Thus far, ESP investigators have not succeeded in designing experiments which give the same or comparable results when repeated by other investigators. Nevertheless, some psychologists feel that there is sufficient support for ESP and that it should be accepted as a reality despite the failure of public verifiability of the results—one of the requirements of scientific acceptance discussed in Chapter 2. The reluctance of most scientists to accept the ESP phenomenon, which one of its advocates describes as "a response to an unknown event not presented to any known sense" (McConnell, 1969), is not because they do not take psychic phenomena seriously. Just the opposite; they recognize what revolutionary implications the reality of transmission without a transmitter would have. A physicist tells us:

"If ESP is indeed a fact, then this is the most important fact in modern physics, for to explain it requires the assumption of a new kind of force—a force presently unknown to physicists. The only alternative is to abandon causality altogether, which would entail an even greater revolution in science." (Rothman, 1970, p. 280)

The Perception of People

Like other perceiving, the perceiving of other people is not a passive process on the part of the perceiver but an active one. To make sense out of the complex behavior of others, we make inferences about their intentions, emotions, motivations, and personality traits. Such inferences, or impressions, are a major influence on our own behavior toward these other persons.

Like the perception of objects, person perception is also subject to various illusions and distortions. That is, we often "see" people differently from the way they are objectively presented to us. How do such less-than-accurate impressions occur? What information do we use in order to judge another's personality, responsibility for actions, and general dispositions? Not only do all of us engage in this process informally almost all the time, but personnel managers, salesmen, and others make their livelihood from it, and jurors may take away a life on the basis of their perception of causality and intention on the part of a suspect.

Judgment at First Sight

You may think that your judgments of other people are based on long and careful consideration of their behavior in different situations. This is almost opposite to the truth, however. Psychologists have found that the perceiver's first impression of another person has an enormous impact on his judgment.

In one study two groups of subjects were presented with the same list of personality traits which supposedly described a particular person. For some of the subjects, however, the positive traits were presented first (i.e., intelligent, industrious, impulsive, critical, stubborn, and envious). The other subjects received the negative traits first (i.e., envious, stubborn, critical, impulsive, industrious, and intelligent). When the good traits came before

the bad ones, subjects had a more positive evaluation of the person and were more likely to attribute other good traits to him (Asch, 1946).

Asch also found that certain traits were more influential than others in the formation of an impression. If a list of traits included the term "warm," subjects rated the person as being happy, good-natured, and generous. However, if the same list of traits was presented, except for the substitution of "cold" for "warm," subjects perceived the person as being unhappy, irritable, and ungenerous.

Similar results were obtained in a "real-life" experiment on first impressions in which a professor told his class that a guest lecturer would be teaching that day and then passed out a brief biographical note which described this person. Half of the students received a note which described the lecturer as a "rather cold person, industrious, critical, practical, and determined." The other students received identical notes, but with "warm" substituted for "cold." Not only did the "warm" subjects like the lecturer better, but they volunteered in the class discussion, while those who had received "cold" notes did not (Kelley, 1950).

Why is the first impression so influential? One explanation is that the initial information creates a *frame of reference* which the perceiver uses to interpret later information. If later information is discrepant, it is distorted so that it fits the established frame of reference. This process is very similar to the operation of set in nonsocial situations, as discussed earlier. Such first-impression distortions encourage us to perceive others in terms of very simple stereotypes which are often a function of our initial prejudices.

Consistency Is in the Mind of the Perceiver

One of the best known perceptual errors is the "*halo effect*," which was noted as early as 1907 by Wells. When a person rates others on several traits, he usually rates them in terms of an overall impression (or "halo") of goodness or badness. For example, if he values courtesy and notices that another person is polite, he is more likely also to see him as being friendly, honest, and intelligent. The perceiver may also make the *logical error* of assuming that certain traits always go together. Thus, if he rates someone as being strong, he will probably also see him as being active and aggressive. A third kind of common error in perceptual judgment is the *leniency error*. There is a general disposition for people to lump their judgments on the positive end of a scale, and to minimize negative evaluations. This leads to a situation where "warm is the norm." Finally, a *central tendency error* occurs when a rater ignores the variability among people or in the traits of one person and rates them all as "good," "fair," or "average."

As a result of these judgmental errors, the perceiver sees other people as being more consistent than they really are. A number of studies have found that people may behave rather inconsistently in different situations.

One of the earliest of these studies focused on the trait of "honesty." The researchers found that they could not accurately predict a person's honesty in one situation on the basis of how honestly he had behaved in another situation. For example, a person who cheated in a game did not necessarily steal things from a store or lie at home (Hartshorne & May, 1928).

In spite of this demonstrated lack of consistency in people's behavior, we assume that people *are* consistent and perceive them in this way. The extent to which we generate consistency by inferring underlying traits or dispositions is shown by our tendency to attribute such traits even to inanimate objects. This tendency was demonstrated in a study in which subjects saw geometric forms as "aggressive," "shy," and so on—traits that obviously do not exist in triangles and circles. ◆

Inferring Inner Dispositions from Overt Acts

How do we manage to perceive consistency in a person on the basis of inconsistent and often incomplete information about him? How do we move from the acts we observe to the dispositions we assume? A very sophisticated answer to these questions has been given in the theoretical writings of Fritz Heider (1944, 1958). According to Heider, the perceiver's goal is to comprehend the structure which underlies the actions he observes. To do this he must find sufficient reason for the observed person's behavior. It is not enough to know what he did; the perceiver

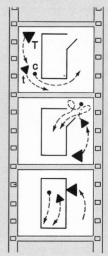

◆ In one study subjects were shown a film in which geometrical forms moved in and out of a large rectangle. Underlying motivations were attributed to the "characters," and the triangles were often seen as two males fighting over a female (the circle). On the basis of their movement, the large triangle was perceived as being aggressive, the small triangle as being heroic, and the circle as being timid. In the sequence shown here, most observers reported seeing T chase t and c into the house and close the door (Heider & Simmel, 1944).

wants to know *why* he did it. Since the perceiver cannot see the thoughts or desires of another person, he must *infer* them from the observable behavior and does so actively, drawing on his preconceptions about this individual and about people in general. In making such inferences, he may attribute characteristics to them that for one reason or another he *wants* them to have.

One important decision which the perceiver must make is whether the observed person's behavior stemmed from his internal disposition or was caused by the external situation. For example, when we see a man laughing at his boss's joke, it could be because he thinks it is funny (internal disposition) or because he is being polite to the boss (external situation). The less freedom of choice the observed person has, the more likely we are to perceive his behavior as reflecting situational demands.

To illustrate this point, one researcher had subjects supervise the work of two subordinates, A and B, who were assigned an extremely boring task and whose output was exactly the same. The monitoring schedule forced the supervisors to check up on worker A much more often than on worker B.

The supervisor-subjects saw A's performance as externally caused by the pressure of their continual surveillance, while they attributed B's performance to his internal disposition (i.e., his personal desire to do well). Furthermore, they perceived the infrequently monitored

B as more trustworthy and dependable than the frequently watched A (Strickland, 1958).

Generally, if a person *conforms* to situational demands, we are likely to see his behavior as externally caused. On the other hand, when a person *deviates* from situational demands, we are very likely to see such out-of-role behaviors as signs of underlying dispositions. That such attributions depend heavily on the perceiver was shown in another study.

The subjects read a speech allegedly given by a person while he was a member of a university debating team. The speech either supported the Castro regime in Cuba or opposed it. Half of the subjects were told that the debater had been assigned the side he defended, while the other half were told that he had been given his choice of sides. After reading the speech, the subjects were asked to assess the debater's true attitude toward Castro. The debater who allegedly chose the position he defended (internal motivation) was seen as more in favor of that position than the debater who was assigned it (external demand), though the delivery was exactly the same in both cases (Jones & Harris, 1967).

A second major result of this study was that the debater who had been assigned a *pro-Castro* position was seen as *more favorable* toward Castro than the debater who had been assigned an *anti-Castro* position (even though neither of them had had a choice in the matter). In other words, there was a general tendency to attribute *internal causality* to the debaters' behavior even when such a conclusion was not logically warranted.

Such a tendency is fairly common: often we perceive chance happenings as being indicative of a person's inner nature and intentions. A man who slips on a banana peel is seen as clumsy; a person who unintentionally slights us is seen as hostile. In many cases, such inferences are made automatically and almost unconsciously and rest only on our preconceptions.

How can we explain this tendency to see some behavior as internally caused? Heider has proposed that we often perceive internal motivation because it is simpler to do so. If we try to find the reason for a change in our environment, we often find ourselves engaged in an infinite regression of causes because every cause is also the effect of another cause. However, when personal causation is invoked, the effect can be attributed in an *absolute* way to one origin and the causal chain terminates.

Self-fulfilling Prophecies

Heider also argues that this tendency results from man's desire to have some control over his environment (or at least to think he does). When a crime is committed in our neighborhood, when our country loses a war, or when our livelihood depends on the sale of a material whose price is dropping rapidly, we want to know why. Moreover, we want to feel that we have some control over such important events. The causes of these events are likely to be numerous and elusive, however. To understand crime, war, or the price of goods, we would need a complete understanding of sociology, political science, or economics. Not only would such an understanding be time-consuming to achieve, but it would convince us of the difficulty of bringing such events under control. Therefore, a substitute cause must be found—one which is easily understood and more controllable. Persons, as *absolute causal origins*, fill this need, for it is assumed to be possible to exert control over a small number of people. So when a crime is committed, the tendency is to deal with it by punishing the criminal rather than by looking for causes in the reinforcement structure of the society and trying to change those.

Awareness of this inference process, then, is critical to our understanding of others because it is one of the major ways by which we all make sense out of the complexity of the world. We perceive others as causal agents and infer enduring personality traits.

Recent research has also demonstrated the extent to which our perceptions of others may become *self-fulfilling prophecies*. We act toward others according to the way we expect them to respond (warm toward a person we predict will be warm), and then they do—because *we* have acted the way we did.

In a game situation, at least, whether prophecies are fulfilled or not seems to depend on whether the person holding the impression is male or female. Males *do* behave according to their impression of a partner, which in turn produces reciprocal behavior from him. Females, however, show a "compensation" effect: a tendency to be "warmer" toward a person they expect to be "cold." This "warmer" behavior toward a "cold" person then makes the other person act more warmly, as judged by observers (Jones & Panitch, 1970; Bond, 1970).

The important conclusion to be drawn from all this is that impressions *we* hold of others can lead to differences in *their* behavior. People are reacting to our behavior as much as we are reacting to theirs. A general *theory of attribution* (Kelley, 1967) has developed, based on studies of the perceptual and cognitive processes involved in people's attempts to find causal explanations that meaningfully relate situations, actions, actors, and consequences.

Chapter Summary

Awareness of the world around us through attention to sensory input is the starting point of the perceptual processes that give coherence and direction to man's behavior. The individual's sensitivity to stimulus input at any given time is a function of his *level of awareness*. In a state of sleep, for example, he will be quite unresponsive to ordinary stimuli.

Widespread research on sleep is a fairly recent development. Studies have shown that sleep deprivation can lead to hallucinations, deterioration in performance, and changes in brain chemistry, but symptoms disappear with a single night's sleep.

A sleeping individual passes in and out of several different stages of sleep in the course of a night. In *Stage 1-REM, rapid eye movements* signal the occurrence of dreams. Normal subjects who have been deprived of REM sleep will show a *rebound effect* when REM sleep is once again permitted. Studies of REM-deprived cats have shown a dramatic enhancement of drive-related behavior (sex, aggression, eating, etc.). It seems possible that schizophrenia may be related to the brain processes involved in REM sleep. The most important neural mechanism affecting level of awareness is the *reticular activating system*. It seems probable that the RAS is the center for arousal and that the *diffuse thalamic system* controls sleep. Other brain mechanisms, including the hypothalamus, are also involved.

The terms *arousal* and *activation* refer to variations in the general level of excitation in the waking individual. Performance improves as arousal increases, but only up to a certain point; excessive arousal has a negative effect on performance. The notion of a single, generalized arousal system seems oversimplified.

Attention is a process of stimulus selection by which we focus on particular portions of our environment. There are a number of factors involved in getting a person's attention, some of them related to the stimulus situation and some to that person. These factors include *change, size, prepotency, repetition, organic condition* or relation to biological needs, *interest value*, and *personal contact*. Once we have someone's attention, habituation is the major obstacle to maintaining it. Attention span and susceptibility to distraction vary greatly; they are dependent largely on the individual's interest.

Research on attention is hindered by the difficulty of defining and measuring it. Research on neurophysiological correlates of attention has produced a variety of theories, but few answers as yet. Hess's research on *pupillometrics* has suggested that pupil dilation may be a measure of interest or attention, but further research has indicated that such dilation may also reflect complex cognitive activity independent of interest.

At birth, the infant has a limited attention span. It can be increased, however, by providing a more stimulating environment.

Research on attention to multiple auditory stimuli has focused on *attentional filters* and *dichotic listening*. In some instances the two ears seem to serve as separate processing channels, but it is also possible for information presented to the two ears to be combined, as when "back" and "lack" become "black." Broadbent has suggested that the brain responds to differences in the pulsation rate of sounds, concentrating on one voice and filtering out competing stimuli.

Studies of dichotic listening have shown that the left hemisphere of the brain (served by the right ear) is superior in processing speech sounds, while the opposite holds true for nonspeech stimuli. The right hemisphere, however, appears to process stimuli of either kind more quickly than the left. The implications of these differences are still under investigation.

Studies of attention to multiple visual stimuli have revealed the phenomenon of *biased scanning:* subjects offered a choice pay more attention before choosing to the stimulus they will reject, and more attention after the choice to the one they have chosen.

Studying perception enables us to appreciate the complex ways in which inherited sensory mechanisms are adapted by psychological processes for the task of constructing an effective working model of reality. We observe variability and postulate stability. We observe specificity and postulate generality. We observe discontinuity and postulate consistency. We observe flux and chaos, and postulate structure and meaning. This translation system works with only occasional slippage, and even then we learn how to profit from our perceptual errors to build more invariance into the process of perceiving our world.

The problem of perception is to know when the *phenomenal* reality (our perceptual experience) is a *veridical* (true) representation of *objective* reality (what is really there). *Phenomenal absolutism* is the belief that perceptions are direct and accurate renditions of qualities that exist in the environment. *Illusions* dramatize the extent to which perception may trick us; they surprise us precisely because for the most part perception does such a dependable job of providing us with a constant, predictable environment despite constantly changing retinal images. Illusions demonstrate the active organizing forces in perception. Unless we lack distance cues, the perceived size of an object is in accordance with its *distal* (actual) size rather than its *proximal* (retinal) size.

Theories about perception include: (a) "gambling house" theories, according to which, in effect, the perceiver learns to "bet on" what is there from partial and changing cues; (b) the theory that we learn to have complex perceptions by associating simple ones; (c) the theory that perception consists of sensation plus additives from learning so that trained introspection is needed to identify the "original" sensory experience; (d) the Gestalt theory that even prior to learning perception gives us relationships; and finally, (e) the theory that learning to perceive is essentially not a process of addition but a process of reduction in which we make new differentiations and identify continuing structures.

Factors determining what figure is seen include *proximity, likeness, closure, common fate,* and *context.* *"Good"* figures are simple and regular; a figure becomes more "good" as it becomes more predictable from knowledge of any of its parts.

Cues that we use in depth perception include *atmospheric perspective, linear perspective, texture, light and shadow, relative position, known standards, convergence of the eyes,* and *retinal disparity.* Differences in *arrival time, intensity,* and *phase* of sound waves enable us to locate the directions of sounds unless they are at some point equidistant from the two ears; we cannot locate sounds made directly in front of, above, or behind us. *Loudness* and *timbre* help us identify the distance of sounds.

Although psychologists study the sensory modalities separately, most of our perceptions combine cues from two or more modalities, and sensory input in one modality can affect perception in another. There is evidence that *"pre-wired circuits"* help to provide pattern and depth perception, binocular vision, and size and shape constancy. But *cultural experience* and *personal experience* affect perception too. *Interests, motives,* and *expectations* also affect perception, often dramatically.

Individuals deprived of sensory input or given low-level, unstructured input soon develop *hallucinations* —perceptions without adequate sensory input. Hallucinations may also be induced under hypnosis, by drugs such as LSD and mescaline, and by lack of sleep. Whether extrasensory perception occurs is still under investigation. To accept it would require an alteration in basic philosophical assumptions.

The perception of people, like other perception, is an active process in which we try to identify a consistent and predictable structure in other people. Thus we tend to attribute characteristics to them, thereafter continuing to see these characteristics in them, even despite contrary evidence. Such attribution gives us a comforting explanation (accurate or inaccurate) of the cause of behavior and a feeling that we have potential control.

Chapter 8

To Think, To Reason, To Create

"What goes on four legs in the morning, on two legs at noon, and on three legs in the twilight?"

In answering "Man," Oedipus solved the riddle of the Sphinx and freed the people of Thebes from its tyranny. By freely exercising his unique ability to think, to reason, to solve problems, man frees himself from the oppression of a life dominated by environmental forces and internal needs. To overcome the many obstacles in the path of his full development, man has had to learn how to analyze what those problems were, and how to devise creative solutions to them, as well as how to carry them out. Our many and varied achievements in art, science, and technology are testimony of man's power to go beyond concerns for survival to higher level concerns of esthetics, justice, and discovery.

Our species is called *homo sapiens*—knowing man. Our ability to know includes the ability to think —to manipulate or organize elements in the environment by means of symbols instead of physical acts. Such symbols include words, numbers, gestures, pictures, diagrams, and visual images. Thinking can take many forms, ranging from the solution of a practical problem to daydreaming and flights of fancy. In reasoning, our thought processes are said to be realistic. But beyond our capacity to be riddle-solvers of everyday practical problems, has been the emergence of man as *homo ludens*—playing man. We play with the environment, and with each other. We have learned how to take pleasure in reasoning for its own sake, to delight in games of skill, of chance, of daring.

When uninhibited, highly imaginative thinking is used in the service of reality, man becomes creative. His proposed solutions to the problems he encounters (as well as those he creates) are then new, unusual, and original.

This chapter will study these highly complex mental processes to try to understand how they work. As instances of "man," we are our own greatest challenge.

Thinking is the most complex activity that man ever performs. It involves the use of *symbols* to represent and organize elements of the environment. It may involve manipulating symbols entirely "in your head" without any external stimulation at all, as when you plan to leave a few minutes early to stop at the library on the way to class. On the other hand, thinking may involve perception. This may be either perception of graphic symbols, as when you form a mental picture of a house by looking at an architect's blueprint, or perception of the object itself, as when the sight of an overdue book on your desk reminds you to stop at the library.

There are different kinds of thinking which range between two extremes—autistic and realistic. *Autistic thinking* is determined primarily by our own needs, wishes, and feelings and is frequently indulged in for self-gratification without regard to reality. Fantasy, dreams, and wishful thinking are all examples of autistic thinking; they are ends in themselves and not means to an end. *Realistic thinking*, or reasoning, is determined largely by the requirements of the objective situation and tends to be productive—to be directed toward action or the solution of a problem. Most of our thinking involves components of both of these extreme types: reasoning is notoriously subject to distortion by the wishes and prejudices of the reasoner, while daydreams may be prompted by problems that are quite real and accurately perceived.

The Tools of Thinking

What does "thought" consist of? What are the ways in which we think? How are our thought patterns influenced? These are some of the basic questions that psychologists are trying to answer.

The Pictures in Our Heads

People sometimes think with images, which are mental pictures of actual sensory experiences. Most people seem to be strongest in visual imagery though some are strongest in auditory imagery, and a small minority report that images of touch, muscle movement, taste, or smell predominate for them.

Although some early psychologists believed that thought *required* the use of imagery, various studies through the years have indicated that thought can also proceed in the absence of images. For example, one pioneer study found that many scientists and mathematicians, though engaged in the highest and most complicated type of thinking, were actually quite deficient in visual imagery (Galton, 1883). Poincaré, the great French geometrician, described

Look at this picture for about three seconds; then read the note at the bottom of page 312.

himself as lacking in the ability to visualize space. All this is not to deny that imagery is used in many kinds of thinking, but to point out that it is not always necessary.

Before reading further, look at the photograph. ■ Some individuals possess imagery which is almost like actual perception in its clarity and accuracy. These strong images, usually visual, are called *eidetic images*. People with eidetic imagery can frequently tell the exact position of a formula or fact on the printed page of a textbook. They can even glance for a fraction of a second at an object, such as a comb, and then call up such a vivid image that they can give a complete description, including the number of teeth in the comb. In examinations, they may "copy" from their image of the printed page, performing with an accuracy as great as though the book were actually open before them (see Haber, 1968).

Striking examples of eidetic imagery have been documented in *The Mind of a Mnemonist*, a case study by the Russian psychologist Luria.

The subject was a man who had such powers of imagery that he was able to perform staggering feats of memory. The following is one of the many experiments carried out with this man, which you might want to try yourself. The man spent three minutes examining the table of numbers reprinted below. He was able to reproduce the

6	6	8	0
5	4	3	2
1	6	8	4
7	9	3	5
4	2	3	7
3	8	9	1
1	0	0	2
3	4	5	1
2	7	6	8
1	9	2	6
2	9	6	7
5	5	2	0
x	0	1	x

table perfectly, by calling off all the numbers in succession, within 40 seconds. He could call off the numbers in both the columns and the horizontal rows in either forward or reverse order. He also reproduced the numbers which form the diagonals (e.g., 6, 4, 8, 5; 5, 6, 3, 7) within 35 seconds. Finally, he took a minute and a half to convert all fifty numbers into a single fifty-digit number (Luria, 1968).

At this point, you are probably wishing that you had the gift of eidetic imagery (or "photographic memory," as it is often called). You might think that all of your schoolwork would be extremely simple to do, since you could remember everything so well. Actually, eidetic imagery is very much a mixed blessing, and often obstructs thinking, rather than helping it. Materials stored eidetically are not easily broken down and reassembled in new patterns (Ψ Close-up, p. 313). The individual can reproduce what he has seen, but it is difficult for him to use this information in new ways. Thus, eidetic imagery does not appear to play a role in abstract thinking or creative imagination, which require flexibility in thought. For example, Luria's mnemonist was unable to understand simple abstract ideas because he could not "see" them in concrete visual images. Because eidetic imagery hampers real learning, people who have it may stop making use of it as they grow older.

This would explain why eidetic imagery is most often found in children and is comparatively rare in adults.

One of the methodological problems in studying eidetic imagery is to determine whether it is a *memory* process or a *visual* process. That is, did the mnemonist have a special way of verbally *coding* the fifty numbers, so that he could later figure out what they were? Or did he have an exact image of the table in his head, which he could "look" at and call out numbers from? If the latter "visual trace" hypothesis is correct, it could be demonstrated in a special type of experiment. There is a certain type of visual illusion, the *Land phenomenon*, in which a person sees a picture in color only when stimulus A is presented to his right eye and stimulus B to his left eye simultaneously. Suppose the experimenter first presents stimulus A to the subject's right eye and then takes the stimulus away and presents stimulus B to the subject's left eye. If the subject has eidetic imagery and has a visual "trace" of the first stimulus, he ought to be able to see the colored picture and accurately report what the colors are. Such results have been obtained in a preliminary study done recently at Harvard with a subject reputed to have remarkable eidetic imagery (Stromeyer, Psotka, & West, 1969).

Words in Thinking

Although words are probably not essential to thought and may sometimes even be a hindrance to it, language appears to be an aid in solving problems. Indeed, few of us would want to try to think without it. Words and other symbols can greatly facilitate the solution of problems which would be much more difficult to cope with if we had to rely on the direct manipulation of objects and images. The development of the precise symbolic systems of algebra and calculus, for example, has greatly increased man's ability to control his environment.

The powerful influence that language has on our perception and recall is demonstrated in an early study. Two groups of subjects were shown the same stimulus figures but were given different words describing what the figures represented. All the subjects were later asked to redraw the figures as they remembered them. The drawn figures were consistently

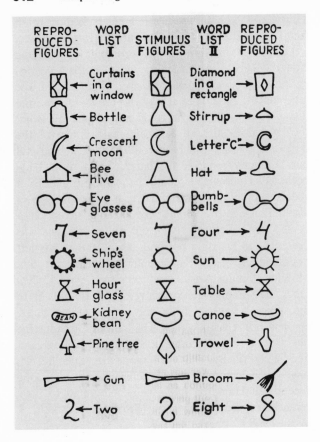

REPRO- DUCED FIGURES	WORD LIST I	STIMULUS FIGURES	WORD LIST II	REPRO- DUCED FIGURES
	Curtains in a window		Diamond in a rectangle	
	Bottle		Stirrup	
	Crescent moon		Letter "C"	
	Bee-hive		Hat	
	Eye-glasses		Dumb-bells	
	Seven		Four	
	Ship's wheel		Sun	
	Hour-glass		Table	
	Kidney bean		Canoe	
	Pine tree		Trowel	
	Gun		Broom	
	Two		Eight	

● Some of the stimulus figures used in this study are shown in the center column, with the word lists presented to the two groups. The outside columns show some of the figures drawn from memory.

more like the named object than the original figures had been (Carmichael, Hogan, & Walter, 1932). ●

"Do you know what I mean?"   Our thinking about any concept is invariably influenced by the meaning that we have attached to the word used to describe it. As we saw in Chapter 6, Ebbinghaus, and other psychologists after him, were quick to recognize the effect of meaning and, in order to eliminate this influence, used unfamiliar nonsense syllables in their studies of learning and memory.

Osgood and his associates have developed a technique called the *semantic differential* for studying meaning. Subjects are presented with a series of seven-point scales made up of pairs of adjectives that are opposites which they are to check with reference to the person or concept whose "meaning" is being studied. He has found, from ratings of a wide variety of concepts on these scales, that meaning is primarily determined by three independent dimensions. These are the *evaluative* dimension (e.g., good-bad), the *potency* dimension (e.g., strong-weak), and the *activity* dimension (e.g., active-passive). What is interesting about these findings is that the rich complexity of our language and thought can be reduced to these few basic factors (Osgood, Suci, & Tannenbaum, 1957). ▲   (p. 315)

Cloak or mold?   Language can certainly influence our thought (as demonstrated in the Carmichael study), but to what extent does it actually *determine* what we think? The problem of whether thought determines language or language determines thought has stimulated much interest and controversy among students of linguistics (Brown, 1956). Is language a "cloak following the contours of thought" or a "mold into which infant minds are poured"?

The major proponent of the "mold" position is Benjamin Whorf, who contends that the language patterns of a cultural group determine the thought patterns and even perceptions of the children reared in that culture (Whorf, 1956). For example, the Eskimos have seven names for different types and conditions of snow, while English-speaking people have just the single term. The Hopi Indians have one name for birds and one name for all other things that fly (airplane, bee, etc.). Whorf would argue that such differences in descriptive nouns result in a different conception of the event. That is, Eskimos' perceptions and thoughts of snow are different from those of English-speaking people; the Hopis think about flying objects differently.

Whorf's hypothesis raises several important questions which, unfortunately, are difficult to resolve with experimental data. One major problem is the old one of cause and effect. Perhaps the culture's thinking

How many chairs were there in the picture on page 310? If you have eidetic imagery you will still have a clear enough visual image to count them.

about an event led to the development of different linguistic labels for it, rather than vice versa. Because the condition of the snow has a major impact on his daily life, the Eskimo needs several terms to differentiate them linguistically. However, the type of snow may have no real importance to a person living in New York City, so that for him, all snow (even slush) is "snow."

Critics of Whorf have also challenged the idea that there are actual differences in perception and thought between cultures with different languages. The fact that a person has only a single term for an event does not necessarily mean that he cannot distinguish differences within that event. A child in New York has just one term for snow, but he can easily tell what kind of snow is good for packing snowballs and what kind is not. Similarly, skiers are very sensitive to snow conditions and can distinguish between wet snow, powder snow, icy snow, and so on, even though they do not have completely different words for each of them.

The meaningfulness of a linguistic pattern for a particular culture may affect its way of categorizing events, but not its ways of actually perceiving them.

Navaho-speaking and English-speaking subjects were asked to divide eight colored chips into groups on the basis of the label the experimenter gave to each chip. He then proceeded to call four of them *ma* and the other four *mo*. However, two *ma* and two *mo* chips were spoken of with the vowel drawn out, while the others had the short form of the vowel. This change in vowel length does not mark a phonemic change in English, but in Navaho the long and short vowels are two different phonemes. As a result, Navaho-speaking subjects grouped the chips into *four* groups (mā, mă, mō, mŏ), while the English-speaking subjects only divided them

---

Ψ Close-up   *He Can Beat You Blindfolded*

The kind of visualization which is useful in complex thought is not necessarily the same as visual imagery. This fact is brought out in an introspective account by a psychologist who is also a chess master capable of playing twelve boards of "blindfold" chess simultaneously. In blindfold chess, the player does not actually wear a blindfold, but sits with his back to the board or boards so that he cannot see the pieces. A referee calls out his opponent's moves to him, and he replies with his own. Obviously, ability to visualize what is happening on the board is a primary factor in winning. However, this visualization process is "a summation of many learned skills," more a process of abstraction than a literal visualizing of all details. This psychologist-master has summarized it as follows:

1. As a result of long experience with the game, both the board and the pieces acquire many associations for the player. It becomes impossible to think of the board separately from the pieces or of the pieces with no relationship to the board.

2. It is also impossible to think of the moves separately from the special notation or symbolic language which chess players use to describe their plays. Simultaneous games are kept separate in the player's mind largely with the aid of such symbols. For example, the notation 1P-K4 stands for one possible opening move, while 1P-QB4 represents another, and so on. Games vary greatly in character according to the opening used, and as they progress and differences become greater, it is easier, rather than more difficult, to keep them separate.

3. A space-time Gestalt or pattern is formed of the entire board. That is, the position of the pieces changes in space and with time, but the number of plausible changes is limited.

4. A prime skill factor in chess is the ability to sum up each position dynamically in terms of the most significant elements in it, not to recall all details regardless of significance.

5. For the most part, the first four phases take place below the level of active consciousness. Once the summation of significant elements is made, the visual image reaches consciousness. Because of the player's capacity to organize the abstract and symbolic data, the "picture" he visualizes consciously is a coherent one (Fine, 1965).

into *two* groups (ma, mo). Many of the English-speaking subjects reported that they had noticed the slight differences in vowel length, but had considered them irrelevant to the task (Brown, 1956).

The "cloak-mold" controversy has never been resolved in one way or the other, but it seems fairly safe to say that language and thought affect each other. Ideas are undoubtedly "shaped" by language, but certainly not to the extent postulated by Whorf.

Concepts in Thinking

Much of our education—both formal and informal —consists of learning to employ abstract categories, or *concepts*. A concept involves the association of a single response (e.g., a label or action) with a variety of distinguishable stimuli (e.g., objects or events). For example, to learn the concept "cat," a child must be able to apply this single term to many animals who might vary quite a bit in shape, color, type of fur, and so on. Furthermore, once he has learned the concept "cat," he should be able to apply it correctly to animals that he has never seen before. The advantage of being able to use concepts is that it allows people to employ summaries of past experience in analyzing and organizing new objects and events.

Kinds of concepts.   There are several types of concepts, each of which uses a different labeling rule. The *conjunctive concept* requires that all examples of the concept must have one or more attributes in common. The concept of "cat" is a conjunctive one, since there are certain features (e.g., four legs, fur) which are essential to an animal's being called a cat. Instances of a *disjunctive concept* must have any one of several alternative characteristics, rather than all of them. For instance, a "strike" is called in baseball when any one of the following occurs: (a) a pitch crosses home plate between the batter's shoulders and knees, (b) a pitch results in a foul ball, or (c) the batter swings at a pitch and misses. A disjunctive concept may be either *inclusive* (characteristics *a* or *b*, or both) or *exclusive* (*a* or *b* alone but not both). Finally, there is the *relational concept*, whose members must show some characteristic relationship (e.g., all women who are taller than their husbands), rather than any particular feature.

An early, classic study on conjunctive concepts made use of Chinese characters. College students were shown a series of thirty-six characters and were asked to learn a nonsense syllable associated with each of them. Although the subjects did not know it in advance, the characters were divided into six groups; in each group, all the items had some common visual element and were associated with one particular syllable. For example, characters such as those below, which all have "a check mark with two half-moons," were all called "oo."

With practice, subjects learned the "oo" concept as well as various others. In addition, they could correctly label new instances of the concepts (i.e., new characters which also contained the same critical elements). The experimenter proposed "the principle of dissociation" to explain concept formation: "What is associated now with one thing and now with another tends to become dissociated from either, and to grow into an object of abstract contemplation." (Hull, 1920).

Concept development in childhood.   To discover whether a child has formed a particular concept, we can present him with unfamiliar objects and see if he can identify the ones to which the concept applies. For example, suppose a child has learned to call grass "green." We conclude that he has formed the concept of "greenness" if he can correctly apply the label "green" to objects other than grass—for example, if he says that a lime is green but that the sky is not. Often a child who does not know the verbal label will indicate by his actions that he has formed a concept —that is, that he is aware of distinguishing characteristics. For example, he may cry and run away every time he sees a dog, but reach out to hold a cat. The fact that many basic concepts are evidently learned in an infant's early months suggests that language is not necessary to the formation of concepts.

The first meaningful words which the child uses stand for single, concrete objects. He will use the word "dog" or "kitty," for example, in reference only to the family pet or some other specific animal. As a next step, he will learn the categories of "dog," "cat," "cow," "horse," and so on, and will be able to group *many* individual animals into them. Still later, he will learn to group all these animate objects under the single unifying concept of "animal." This process of learning to group varied objects in terms of some distinguishing common property is called *abstraction*. As a person progresses toward maturity, he develops and uses concepts at higher and higher levels of abstraction—concepts such as "truth," "beauty," "democracy," "justice," and so on.

The following study of abstraction in children was concerned with the concept of "roundness."

The apparatus consisted of two identical compartments in which stimulus objects were placed. As long as the compartments were lighted from the inside, the stimulus objects were visible through a mirror-screen on the front of the compartments. Each compartment had a hole in its base out of which a piece of candy could come when the mirror was pressed.

Each subject was brought into the room alone and allowed to play with the apparatus. If he pressed the mirror of the compartment containing the positive stim-

ulus, the lights went off and the piece of candy rolled out as a reward. The mirror was usually pressed spontaneously by the child; if it was not, its action was demonstrated by the experimenter.

After the subjects had learned to select the positive stimulus (always a ball of some sort) instead of the negative stimulus (never a ball), they were tested on a variety of objects to see if the concept of roundness had been identified. All subjects gave evidence of responding to the characteristic *roundness* by selecting the spherical object more often and by selecting it first from a pair of objects not used in the training. For eleven of the thirteen subjects the concept of roundness was broad enough to include cylindrical as well as spherical objects. When presented with pairs of objects neither of which was perfectly round, the subjects chose the more nearly round one. The older children learned more rapidly than did the younger ones, and those of higher mental age learned more rapidly than those of lower mental age (Long, 1940).

A child's early concepts depend heavily on visual similarity between various objects. As he grows older, he learns that some things are grouped together which have little or no outward similarity—for example, dogs and fish and earthworms and birds are all "animals." He also learns to make distinctions among objects whose superficial characteristics are very similar. From the biologist's point of view, for instance, whales have more in common with dogs than with sharks, because whales and dogs are "warm blooded" while sharks are "cold blooded." Essentially, the child develops a concept by learning and applying *rules* about its attributes.

Stages in representational development. One hypothesis of concept development in children starts with the premise that successful interaction with environmental objects requires the construction of an internal representation of these external objects and relationships. In the course of cognitive growth, it is postulated that three successively more efficient types of representation are built up. The first is *muscular* or motor representation. We can climb our back stairs in the dark without tripping because we have learned to adapt our movements to the exact height of the steps and to turns or irregularities in the stairway. Even without visual cues, we can make the exact motions needed.

▲ **A SEMANTIC DIFFERENTIAL OF A PSYCHOLOGY PROFESSOR**

The semantic differential technique can be used in studying the "meanings" we attach to other people as well as to concepts. Students in an introductory psychology class were asked to complete a semantic differential scale describing their instructor. A portion of the items, as marked by one student, is shown below.

Instructions: *Place an X in the blank which best represents how you feel about the person referred to by the following pair of adjectives. Of the five blanks, the middle space is the neutral point; those closer to the adjective indicate more of that trait. Check one position for each pair of adjectives.*

1	good	:	X	:	:	:	:	bad
2	large	:	X	:	:	:	:	small
3	beautiful	:	X	:	:	:	:	ugly
4	hard	:	:	X	:	:	:	soft
5	sweet	:	:	:	X	:	:	sour
6	strong	:	X	:	:	:	:	weak
7	clean	:	X	:	:	:	:	dirty
8	high	:	X	:	:	:	:	low
9	calm	:	:	:	:	X	:	agitated
10	valuable	:	X	:	:	:	:	worthless
11	young	:	X	:	:	:	:	old
12	kind	:	:	:	X	:	:	cruel
13	loud	:	:	X	:	:	:	soft
14	deep	:	X	:	:	:	:	shallow
15	pleasant	:	:	X	:	:	:	unpleasant

The next type of representation is through the use of *images*. Unlike motor representations, images can serve us in the absence of the objects themselves. But images are literal records; they remain similar in form and in their interrelationships to the objects as previously perceived. Not until we become able to construct *symbols*, such as language symbols, do we have a system of representation which can transcend the exact characteristics of what we have perceived. Images are based on particular perceptual details, while symbols may represent inference, abstraction, or transformation according to a rule (Bruner, 1964).

For example, five-year-olds are as proficient as seven-year-olds in reconstructing the following pattern of glasses varying horizontally in width and vertically in height. After the child has seen them in the positions

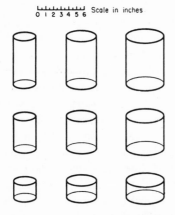

shown here, he has no trouble replacing any that are removed or putting them back into this order when the experimenter scrambles them. Only imagery seems to be required.

If one of the corner glasses is put in a different corner, however, and the subjects are asked to reproduce the pattern in the new orientation, the five-year-olds make twice as many errors as the seven-year-olds in doing so (Bruner & Kenney, 1966). ■

These findings indicate that older children have progressed further in their ability to translate their experience into a representational system using symbols. Younger children are still limited by having only motor or image representation, neither of which allows for transposition.

Are concepts formed gradually or suddenly?   When a person forms a concept, does he do so slowly and gradually over time? Or does he learn a concept suddenly, all at once? The *continuity* position is that concept formation is a continuous process, in which the person is gradually building up, over many trials, the associations between the various features and the concept label, even if he is initially thinking of the wrong concept. The *discontinuity* approach argues that concept learning is an all-or-none process, in which the person tests out different hypotheses and forms the concept *only* on the trial in which the hypothesis turns out to be the correct one. These two theories predict different patterns of performance in learning a concept. The continuity theory says that a person's performance will gradually improve over trials; the discontinuity theory predicts that he will perform at chance level until he learns the concept, at which point he will immediately shift to perfect responding. The performance curves predicted by these two theories are thus strikingly different.   ●

In general, experiments have found that the performance of animals and children of average intelligence supports the continuity theory, whereas that of college students and bright children supports the hypothesis-testing, discontinuity theory. For example, monkeys learn to select the odd stimulus object in a set of three gradually rather than suddenly (Gunter, Feigenson, & Blakeslee, 1965). In learning the concept of "twoness," bright children showed sudden, all-or-none learning, while average children were

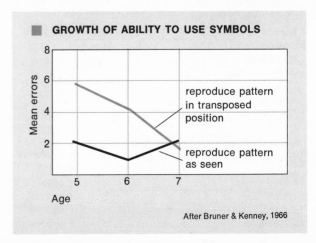

■ **GROWTH OF ABILITY TO USE SYMBOLS**

reproduce pattern in transposed position

reproduce pattern as seen

After Bruner & Kenney, 1966

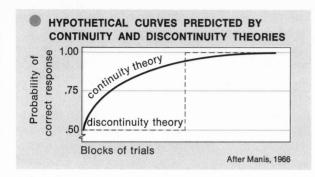

HYPOTHETICAL CURVES PREDICTED BY CONTINUITY AND DISCONTINUITY THEORIES

After Manis, 1966

more likely to show gradual improvement over time (Osler & Fivel, 1961). Complex mathematical concepts appear to be learned by children in a discontinuous, all-or-none fashion (Suppes, 1966). Finally, college students clearly display sudden learning on concept formation tasks, as indicated by the abrupt changes in their performance curves (Bower & Trabasso, 1963).

Physiological Processes in Thinking

What sorts of physiological processes take place when we are thinking? Despite the great amount of study devoted to this question, we know much more about *what* the individual can perceive, learn, remember, and think than we do about the neurological processes that are occurring.

The Role of the Brain

Man has long believed that the brain is the "organ of thought." Such knowledge, no doubt, was originally derived from observations that persons whose brains suffered massive damage through accidents of various kinds lost much of their previous ability to think. Even now, however, scientists do not know just how the brain functions during thinking. Is the entire brain involved in thinking, or are there localized "thought centers" like the centers for vision and hearing? Are the thought processes in problem solving different from those in daydreaming?

The development of EEG recording has been a major breakthrough for understanding brain activity, as we have seen. However, our knowledge about brain rhythms is still somewhat limited, and at this point we can only determine the person's state of awareness—not his mode of thinking within these states. With further research, we may be able to distinguish different kinds of thought processes neurologically; this would give us a valuable diagnostic tool. For example, we could improve the education a child receives by knowing whether he depends on visual images in his thinking and whether he can think abstractly. It has been suggested that eventually an EEG for every child will become a standard diagnostic procedure, perhaps even replacing standard intelligence tests (Walter, 1968).

The Role of Muscular Activity

Much of our thinking is accompanied by tiny muscular contractions which are called *implicit speech*. These contractions are often so minute that they can be detected only with the aid of a sensitive apparatus which picks up the small but measurable electrical impulses (action potentials) produced by contracting muscles.

In an early experiment, action potentials at the right elbow were recorded while the subject imagined performing certain actions. (1) When the subject imagined lifting a ten-pound weight with his right arm, there was a sharp rise in electrical activity. (2) When he imagined lifting the weight with his left arm, there was no such response in the right arm. (3) When he imagined hitting a nail twice with a hammer held in his right hand, two bursts of electrical activity occurred. The three records are shown below; the first bar above each record indicates the signal to begin imagining; the second bar indicates the signal to relax (Jacobson, 1932).

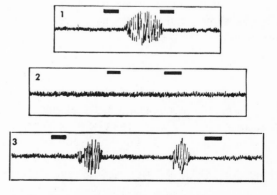

The role of implicit muscular activity in abstract thinking was investigated in a study using both deaf-mute and normal subjects. When thinking or reading difficult material, persons who can speak often make tiny movements of the vocal apparatus (subvocal speech movements). If such implicit speech is a correlate of abstract thinking, would deaf-mutes (who use their arm muscles in communicating via sign language) make tiny "speech" movements with their hands and arms during thought? The study showed that when doing multiplication and division problems "in their heads," 84 percent of the deaf subjects showed measurable action potentials in their arm muscles, as against 31 percent of the normal subjects (Max, 1937).

The correlation found between muscular contractions and thought processes has been explained differently by the two classic theories of thinking. The *peripheralist* theory, advocated by J. B. Watson and other behaviorists, maintains that all thinking actually consists of implicit movements. For example, a young child will often talk aloud while doing some task. He later learns to talk silently to himself, which means that he has learned to think. A different position is taken by the *centralist* theory, which argues that thinking takes place in the brain and nervous system and may or may not be accompanied by implicit muscular movements. That is, the movements are not the thinking itself but may result from it. The studies showing implicit movements during thinking do not support one of these theories in opposition to the other because there is no evidence of the direction of a *cause* and *effect*. It is as possible that the thought causes the implicit movement as that the implicit movement causes the thought. In a summary of the research in this field, McGuigan (1970) suggests, however, that implicit speech movements may play a role in facilitating both the reception of external language stimuli and the internal processing of information.

The Role of Sensory Input

Symbols may be manipulated in the absence of any stimulation, but we know from sensory deprivation experiments that in the long run, normal thought patterns require a certain level and heterogeneity of stimulation. Evidently we need to keep checking against "reality" to confirm or alter the assumptions on which we are basing our thinking and action.

One important type of stimulation that we need for coordinated and adjustive action is the sight and sound and feel of our own actions. This is because each step in an action sequence must be built on what has gone before. Even a slight delay or disruption in the sensory feedback that we normally receive can seriously disrupt both our action and the accompanying thought processes, as we have seen in Chapter 6 in discussing studies of delayed visual and auditory feedback.

How Long Does Thought Take?

The psychologist who sets out to study thought processes soon finds that most of the phenomena he is interested in are not the sort of things that can be measured. One thing that can be measured, however, is reaction time: the interval elapsing between the presentation of a stimulus and a given reaction to that stimulus. The study of reaction time has been important in psychology, not only for what it tells us about simple motor reactions but also because it serves as an indication of how much mental processing may be taking place between stimulus and response. For example, it has recently been used very effectively to measure differences in the degree of complexity of processes involved in linguistic reasoning (Clark, 1969).

The relationship between reaction time and thought can best be appreciated if we examine it from a historical perspective. Reaction time studies fall roughly into four chronological periods: (1) astronomers' studies of the "personal equation," (2) Helmholtz' experiments on nerve conduction, (3) the period of "mental chronometry," and (4) modern studies of human behavior as a temporal succession of events (Bartlett, 1958).

The "personal equation." In 1796 an assistant to the Astronomer Royal was dismissed from his post at the Greenwich Observatory. He was fired because he consistently recorded the transit of a star about one second later than the Astronomer Royal himself. Not much scientific note was made of this discrepancy until 1819, when the German astronomer, Bessel,

◆ The device shown here is designed to measure reaction time. The subject, on the right, must hold down each button until the light above it goes on, then release it instantly. The automatic timing device clocks both the stimulus and the subject's response; the interval between them—his reaction time—will be recorded by the experimenter.

became interested in such "errors" of observation. He carefully compared his own reports of stellar transits with those of other astronomers, and showed that there are very consistent differences between people in the times they give to the occurrence of natural events. Bessel expressed these differences in the form of an equation. For example, the difference between the reports of Walbeck, another astronomer, and himself was:

$$\text{W (Walbeck)} - \text{B (Bessel)} = 1.041 \text{ sec.}$$

As a result, this phenomenon of consistent discrepancies in observation was called the *personal equation*. It continued to be studied by astronomers, who began to discover the various external conditions (e.g., magnitude of the observed star, its rate of movement) which could affect the recorded times. The "personal equation" concept, as one of the first instances of the systematic study of *individual differences* in behavior, is a precursor of the concept of personality traits as an explanation for differences in reaction to the same situation.

Helmholtz' experiments on nerve conduction. Before 1850, scientists believed that impulses were conducted instantaneously along the nerve. However, in that year, Helmholtz demonstrated (a) that nerve conduction took time, and (b) that the time it took could be measured. In his experiments on sensory nerves, Helmholtz administered a weak electric shock first to a man's toe and later to his thigh. The difference between the man's reaction times to these two stimuli was the measure of the speed of conduction

in the sensory nerves. Actually, these experiments were the first true studies of reaction time ever to be done.

"Mental chronometry." After Helmholtz had shown that there is an interval of time between a physical stimulus and a person's physiological response to it, scientists began to think that this might be a good measure of a person's mental processes. From the 1850's to about the 1930's, reaction time was studied under a variety of conditions, using different versions of a measuring device called the *chronoscope*. One of the major experimenters during this period was a Dutch physiologist named Donders. He pointed out three types of reaction time: (1) *simple reaction time*, the single response to a single stimulus; (2) *discrimination reaction time*, in which there are several different stimuli but the single response is not made until a particular one is distinguished; and (3) *choice reaction time*, in which there are several different stimuli and a different reaction for each of them. As you might expect, the third is longer than the second, which in turn is longer than the first. Thus reaction time appears to reflect the psychological *complexity* of the reaction—the amount of mental processing that must take place before the person responds to the stimulus.

In addition to the different external conditions that affect reaction time, scientists have studied *internal*, or organismic conditions. For example, it was found that a person's "set" or predisposition made a difference. Suppose that a subject's task is to release a button as soon as he sees a flash of red light. ◆ If he has a "response set" (is concentrating on the movements he has to make to release the button), his reaction time is consistently *shorter* than if he has a "stimulus set" (is concentrating on the incoming signal).

The model of the servomechanism. Although a great number of experiments on reaction time were carried out in the late nineteenth and early twentieth centuries, they really did not lead to changes in our conception of human functioning. It was not until after 1930 that psychologists began to recognize that human response to stimulation is a *series* of successive events—not a single event. When behavior is seen in this way, there are at least three such events that can be measured: (a) the interval between the stimulus and the beginning of the response (the classical reaction time); (b) the interval between the beginning and the end of the response movement (the movement time); and (c) the interval between the end of one movement and the beginning of the next (the recovery time). Each of these time intervals is influenced by the others, as well as by various external and internal conditions. There are many reaction times in an action sequence like leaning over and picking up a book.

Not only does behavior consist of a series of events, but feedback from the events completed and in progress is needed for smooth continuation of the sequence, as we have seen. Thus the *servomechanism* —the goal-directed, error-sensitive, self-correcting machine—has become a useful model for the thought-and-action sequences characteristic of living organisms. A servomechanism involves four basic processes: input, throughput, output, and feedback. The relationships between these four operations are shown in the figure. ■

Processing input, integrating and organizing throughput, directing output, and utilizing feedback from previous and ongoing output are all part of the mental process called *thinking*. Imagine, for example, that you are playing a game of chess. Your thought processes can be described in terms of these operations:

1. *Processing input*—noting the move your opponent has just made and the immediate threat it poses to your men.

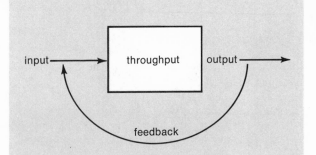

■ DIAGRAM OF A SERVOMECHANISM

In referring to human behavior in terms of a servomechanism, *input* refers to the stimuli which initiate the person's response. These stimuli produce activity within the nervous system called *throughput*; this, in turn, activates muscles which produce a response. Each finite response is an *output*, and the sum total of output in a situation is the behavior pattern, which is culminated when the goal is attained. Output is continually corrected by *feedback* information from the relevant portions of the environment or from within the organism.

2. *Integrating and organizing throughput*—figuring out what the new position means in terms of the board as a whole and assessing possible moves.

3. *Directing output*—deciding on your next move and making it.

4. *Utilizing feedback*—observing the new situation on the board and your opponent's response to it.

These elements of thinking overlap to some extent, and cannot be entirely separated. All can be demonstrated to take time, however. Thus it is clear that reaction time is not, as it was once thought to be, a single, unitary process.

Productive Thinking

We mentioned earlier that thought ranges between two extremes—autistic and realistic. The fantasies, dreams, and wishful thinking of the autistic mode are used primarily for self-gratification and wish fulfillment. A heavy reliance on autistic thinking is found in the "Walter Mitty" type of person, who spends a large part of his time in a world of fantasy and daydreams. An even more extreme form of autistic thinking is a factor in many types of mental disorders.

Realistic thinking, or reasoning, in contrast to autistic thinking, helps us adjust to the reality about us. Such thinking is often motivated by the need to reach solutions to problems involving an individual's livelihood or his very survival. It may also be engaged in for sheer pleasure, as by the chess player or the crossword-puzzle addict. When a person uses highly imaginative thinking in the solution of some problem, we speak of him as being very *creative*.

Types of Reasoning

Three different processes are generally involved in reasoning: *deductive, inductive,* and *evaluative.* As we saw in Chapter 1 (p. 10), *deductive reasoning* is essentially a matter of "putting two and two together." The person combines bits of knowledge previously obtained on separate occasions or draws conclusions that follow from the available data. Basically, this thinking converges toward the correct answer that is implicit in the evidence.

Deductive reasoning is exemplified by syllogisms, which follow the rules of Aristotelian logic. Given premises P_1 and P_2, there can be one, and only one, *valid* conclusion. You have undoubtedly used such reasoning when studying geometry. If the conclusion is not derived by using the rules of logic, then the syllogism is invalid. For example:

Valid Syllogism

P_1 All As are B

P_2 All Bs are C

C   Therefore, all As are C

Invalid Syllogism

P_1 All As are B

P_2 All Cs are B

C   Therefore, all As are Cs

The *validity* of a syllogism should be distinguished from the *truth* of its conclusion. A syllogism may be valid but its conclusion false if it rests on false premises. Or the conclusion may be true but not logically derived from the premises; in this case the syllogism is invalid.

For many problems, however, there is not a single right answer, and the requirements of the situation cannot be met simply by putting together the available evidence. Something new must be added by the thinker, and more than one solution may be appropriate. Such a situation calls for *inductive reasoning*, where the thinker builds from the known to the unknown. From the known, he makes an intuitive leap, formulates a new hypothesis about what future observations may reveal, or suggests several new lines of exploration. This is the essence of creative thinking, whether in science or art. Inductive reasoning can lead potentially in any of several directions instead of one, and thus the conclusion is essentially unpredictable.

A third kind of reasoning is *evaluating*—judging the soundness or appropriateness of an idea or product. Critical thinking is evaluative—it involves judging the suitability or goodness or effectiveness of an idea or representation, as distinguished from trying to create or add to it. The validity of the result depends not only on the reasoning process itself—here the evaluating—but also on the standard used. If the standard is faulty, a solution judged "appropriate" may not fit the real requirements of the situation.

Solving Problems

Whenever an individual finds himself in a novel situation in which he is motivated to achieve a certain goal but in which his progress toward it is blocked by some obstacle for which he has no ready-made response, he is confronted with a *problem* (and a potentially frustrating situation). Solution of the problem involves the development of some mode of response which will eliminate the obstacle. Since frustration is an inevitable concomitant of living, a large part of an individual's behavior necessarily involves problem-solving activity.

Learning and insight.   As you will recall from Chapter 5, Thorndike's cats engaged in random trial-and-error behavior before they eventually managed to escape from their puzzle boxes. The results of this research suggested that problem solving was more a matter of learning than of thinking—that is, the animal gradually learns to behave correctly rather than suddenly recognizing the correct response. Gestalt psychologist Wolfgang Kohler disagreed with this position, arguing that Thorndike's experiment was not appropriate to the study of problem solving since it was impossible for the cat to use foresight and planning in the solution of the problem. The release mechanism for the trick doors was out of the animal's field of vision, so he could not "figure out" how the doors worked. Also, the correct response (manipulating a door latch) was so foreign to the animal's normal movements that it could probably only be discovered by accident, and not by "reasoning."

Kohler attempted to handle these difficulties by placing animals in problem situations where all the materials necessary for solution were in clear view. In his famous series of experiments with apes, the animal's problem was to get some food which had been placed out of reach. For example, a basket of fruit was suspended from the wire roof of the cage in such a manner that the basket could be made to swing back and forth when a string was pulled. At one point of the arc described by the swinging basket, there was a scaffolding. Although the animal could not reach the basket from the ground, he could catch it as it swung by if he jumped up on this scaffolding.

In contrast to Thorndike's cats, Kohler's apes seemed to discover the solution suddenly rather than stumbling onto it accidentally while making random responses. Furthermore, once they had found the solution, they responded perfectly on all succeeding trials, instead of showing the gradual improvement over time that was characteristic of Thorndike's animals. In other words, Kohler's apes acted according to the *discontinuity* hypothesis, while Thorndike's results supported the *continuity* position. Kohler (1926) maintained that problem solving was primarily a matter of insight and perceptual reorganization, rather than trial-and-error behavior.

Later studies have modified Kohler's position by demonstrating that insight is not a completely sudden process but employs relevant previous trial-and-error experience.

One investigator placed some food beyond the reach of chimpanzees, so that they could obtain it only by using

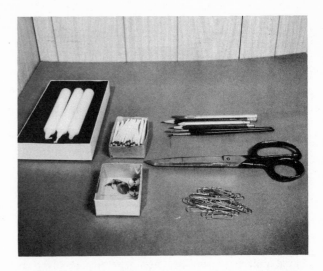

● In one study of human problem solving, subjects were presented with objects like those shown here. The task was to mount the three candles vertically on the screen behind the table, using only materials from among those on the table. Can you solve the problem? Try to figure it out; if you are stumped, turn to page 324 for a clue.

a hoe to rake it toward them. Animals who had previously played with some short sticks and gradually learned to use them for digging, pushing, and so on, were able to solve the food problem fairly easily. The problem was too difficult, however, for animals without this earlier experience (Birch, 1945).

The same thing is true of Harlow's experiments in which monkeys "learned to learn" (see p. 198). The monkeys' dramatic, insightful behavior on later problems in a series was based on their earlier, simple trial-and-error learning.

Human problem solving commonly involves a mixture of insight and trial and error. Usually we start out with more insight into a problem than was possible, for example, for the cats in the puzzle box. Most of our problems are not totally unfamiliar to us, and there are likely to be intrinsic relationships in our situation, whereas the latch to be pressed in the puzzle box had no inherent relation to the food. So we make plausible hypotheses on the basis of what we already know from experience and then test them, either through action or by thinking through the proposed solution (*covert* trial and error). As we see the results of these tentative solutions, our insight increases, and our later hypotheses come closer to meeting the requirements for solution—until at last we "have it." Seldom do we solve a problem without trying some alternative possibilities; and the final achievement of a solution implies, by definition, some insight into the important relationships. Even the cats in the puzzle box gave evidence of this in the end, by going straight to the latch. Indeed, their earlier attempts to bite through the slats or to reach between them were not completely random movements.

Studies of human problem solving have used problems of several types—mathematical problems, mechanical or "tool" problems, practical problems, and puzzles of various kinds. The problem presented to subjects in one study is shown here. ● Can you solve it?

Individual factors in problem solving. Success in any problem-solving situation depends on many factors. All reasoning takes place within a context which includes the individual's motives, attitudes, and memories of past experience, as well as his particular set at the moment. Thus, solving problems, like perceiving and learning, is always personalized to some extent; each person's particular background of motives, experience, and beliefs gives him a unique framework within which his thinking takes place.

Mental set. As we saw in Chapter 7, the situation we are in at any particular moment gives us a set which makes some perceptions and thoughts more likely than others. Numerous experiments with reaction time, perception, learning, recall, and problem solving have shown the importance of this set in determining response time and quality. For instance, if the subject is set to work for speed, his accuracy may suffer. If the experimenter instructs his subjects to cancel out all the O's in a stanza of poetry, the subjects may not notice what the poem is about; or, if he tells them to memorize the poem, they probably will not notice such other things as whether the page arrangement is artistic or whether there are more O's than A's in the lines. In other words, what we perceive, learn, or think is greatly influenced by what we are set for. Such processes of selection and regulation are always going on, even though we may be unaware of them. Try your skill at solving the prob-

lem of the honest blacksmith (Ψ Close-up, below).

A mental set can either help or hinder you in solving a problem, depending on whether it directs you toward the answer or makes you "blind" to the key elements. If you approached the chain problem with the customary set, thinking in terms of joining each short chain to the next one, you probably had trouble solving it. Many problems, both in the laboratory and in everyday life, seem temporarily insoluble if we approach them with an inappropriate set.

One way in which set can hinder problem solving is through a rigid continuation of a cognitive solution which has been successful previously but which for some reason is inappropriate to the present situation (Ψ Close-up, p. 325). Such *rigidity* may be only a matter of the particular set established just prior to the critical problem or may result from long-term habitual ways of behaving that keep you from seeing new possibilities. You may be familiar with all the elements needed for a new solution but be unable to organize them in new ways. This helps explain why an "outsider" can sometimes suggest solutions that have not occurred to those closely involved with a problem.

Ψ *Close-up*   **The Honest Blacksmith**

A farmer brought a blacksmith 5 bits of chain, each having 3 links, and asked to have them welded into a single length of chain with 15 links.

The blacksmith said the charge would be 5¢ per cut and 25¢ per weld. The farmer gave him $1.20, but the blacksmith said, "I don't want to cheat you; the price is 90¢." How did the blacksmith do the job for 90¢? Check your solution with the one given on page 327.

● If you could not think of a way to mount the candles vertically on the screen, would it help to have the objects presented to you like this instead? If you still are stumped, turn to page 328 for the solution to the problem.

Another way in which set may hinder problem solving is through *functional fixedness*, which is similar to rigidity but involves inability to see a new use for a familiar tool rather than inability to find a new cognitive solution. This is demonstrated by the candle problem posed on page 322. A clue to this task is shown in the photograph above and the solution is shown on page 328.

Because of the way the materials were presented in the first photograph, you probably perceived the boxes as containers, rather than as potential resources to be used in solving the problem. In general, when an object necessary to the solution of a problem is previously given a different use, subjects have twice as much difficulty in finding the solution (Duncker, 1945; Adamson, 1952).

Past experience. In cases such as we have just described, past experience appears to blind a person to the requirements of the new situation. However, in many other instances, past experience is a major aid in solving problems. Often we are able to use concepts and generalizations formed in past situations that had certain similarities to the present one. Some "new" problems, in fact, can be solved entirely by the application of past learning. In general, the greater an

individual's relevant experience in a given field, the more concepts and generalizations he will have as potential tools for solving new problems in that field. Thus, only a mathematician can solve complex mathematical problems. Without relevant past experience, we may not even be able to understand the problem to be solved.

Personal context. The way in which a problem relates to an individual's values, beliefs, and so on, will often affect his reasoning about it. For example, we have all seen people become so emotionally involved in the defense of a controversial position that they seem blind to logical arguments on the other side.

This phenomenon has been studied by asking subjects to indicate the validity of syllogisms (remember our discussion of syllogisms on p. 321).

Forty syllogisms were used, half of which dealt with socially controversial material and half of which had neutral content. In addition to judging their validity, subjects were asked to state whether they agreed or disagreed with the conclusion of each of the syllogisms. The results showed that most subjects judged the neutral syllogisms more correctly than the emotionally toned ones. Their attitudes and beliefs about the emotionally toned syllogisms tended to influence their reasoning in the direction of their convictions. Also, previous knowledge of the truth or falsity of the conclusions of the neutral syllogisms influenced subjects' reasoning in the direction of their knowledge. Finally, subjects who judged all the controversial syllogisms first did most poorly on the neutral ones, whereas subjects who judged the neutral ones first did better than the other subjects on the emotionally toned ones. This shows that emotional content can affect logical reasoning not only in the immediate problem but also in those which follow it (Lefford, 1946).

Frustration and stress. The effect of stress on problem solving has been the subject of a number of studies. One method has been to induce frustration on one task and note its effect on following tasks.

For example, subjects in one experiment were frustrated by being given a test so difficult that success was impossible (although they were led to believe that they were capable of solving it). They were then given a series of problems of increasing difficulty. At first they did better on the problems than a nonfrustrated control group, apparently because they were highly motivated to succeed this time after having "failed" the previous test. However, as the problems became harder, the frustrated group fell off sharply in their performance, while the controls steadily continued to improve. Subjects who had been most frustrated on the previous test did most poorly on the difficult problems (Mohsin, 1954).

Stress is more of a hindrance to problem solving when the solution requires a complex response that goes against old habits of thought and action than when simple, isolated judgments are required and previous experience is directly applicable (Reynolds, 1960). It has also been found that when people do not feel they must defend themselves from threat, they show much greater flexibility in exploring new solutions (Cowen, 1952).

Using Computers to Study Thinking

Up to this point, we have been discussing many of the factors that influence thinking. But what about the actual *processing* of information? Just how does

---

Ψ *Close-up*   *Water, Water, Everywhere . . .*

You are faced with the following problem: to obtain an exact amount of water although your measuring jars are not marked, and you can only know the total each one contains when it is filled to capacity.

As an illustration, you might be asked to obtain 20 quarts from two jars, one of which holds 29 quarts when filled and the other 3 quarts. The desired result would be obtained by filling the 29-quart jar, then filling the 3-quart jar from it three times. Exactly twenty quarts would remain.

Now, for a practice example, obtain 100 quarts with three jars whose capacities are 21, 127, and 3 quarts, respectively.

    = 100

Solve the problem by shading the jar you fill first and drawing arrows to indicate pouring from one jar to another. Number the arrows in the sequence of pouring.

You should have filled B, then poured once from B to A and twice from B to C.

Now, covering the test problems from sight, solve each of the following training problems as quickly as you can, again shading the first jar you fill and drawing arrows to show where the water is going.

Training problems:

   = 99

   = 5

= 31

Now get a naïve, untrained friend, and see who can solve each of the next two test problems most efficiently. Have a third person draw the jars for your control subject and keep them covered while you explain the task. Give him no practice examples, but tell him what the problem will look like and ask him to draw arrows to show how he solves the problem. Then give the signal and start at the same time solving the two problems.

Test Problems:

    = 20

= 18

Who won? For further discussion of the implications of this experiment, see the Ψ Close-up on page 330.

Based on problems used in Luchins & Luchins, 1959

the brain synthesize and transform information in thinking and problem solving? Recently, models for explaining this process have described the flow of information in the nervous system not in terms of neurophysiological structure but in terms of computer programs.

The information-processing approach is one of the most exciting developments in the study of cognitive processes and holds considerable promise for the future. The use of computer programs requires that the steps in a sequence of information processing be spelled out in explicit, precise, and rigorous terms, rather than vague generalizations. Such a sequence can be diagrammed in a *flow chart*, or *algorithm*. ◆ The rectangular boxes indicate *action steps*—the computer is instructed to do something. The oval box represents a *decision step*—the computer must an-

swer "yes" or "no." In this case, each time the answer is "no," the computer must perform a *loop*, repeating the same sequence of steps as long as there are cards to be processed. Flow charts are merely visual representations; the actual *program* is the set of coded step-by-step instructions fed into the computer.

Are Computers Intelligent?

Why did psychologists interested in human thought processes turn to the computer? The inspiration for this union appears to be a paper by the English mathematician, Turing (1950), in which he posed the question, "Can machines think?" He argued that our answer would have to be "yes" if a human judge could not distinguish between the output responses of a computer and those of a human being. Turing

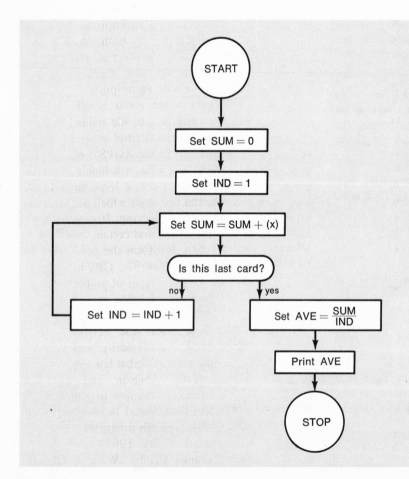

◆ A flow chart depicting the steps in a hypothetical computer program designed to calculate the average of a series of numbers. Each number to be processed is presented on a keypunched card. SUM stands for a memory cell of the computer which is being used as a temporary working space. IND stands for the index number which tells how many cards have been added. The computer is instructed to read the number (x) from each card in the stack, increasing IND by 1 each time it does so. When the last card in the series has been processed, the computer averages the numbers (dividing SUM by IND) and prints out the result (AVE).

proposed a game in which the judge could communicate with the computer and the human thinker only by teletype. He would ask them any questions he liked, then try to determine which teletype source was which. Turing believed that someday a computer which could "win" the game would be developed.

The first major computer system that could claim to show "intelligence" was the Logic Theorist, which was designed to find proofs for theorems in logic (Newell, Shaw, & Simon, 1958). In one test of the Logic Theorist's ability, it was able to prove thirty-eight of the first fifty-two theorems in Whitehead and Russell's *Principia Mathematica*. In addition to certain problem-solving procedures, the program of the Logic Theorist incorporated several "rules of thumb," or *heuristics*, which are used by humans. For example, one such heuristic was "working backwards" from the theorem to be proved. That is, the Logic Theorist would develop several propositions which would each imply the theorem, and then check whether one of these propositions could be deduced from the initial "givens." The problem-solving behavior of the Logic Theorist showed many "human" characteristics, such as examples of sudden "insight" into the solution of the problem. For this reason, its makers argued that such a system could actually be considered a *model* of human thought, since it appeared to simulate human cognitive processes.

The implications of computer simulation for the study of reasoning excited many psychologists who had ability and interest in computer programming. After the appearance of the Logic Theorist, a great many programs were developed which attempted to solve problems in the same way that people do. For instance, Gelernter (1960) wrote a program that made use of diagrams in solving problems in geometry. Computers have also been programmed to play board games against an opponent. Samuel's checker-playing program (1967) has an excellent performance record, having beaten human checker champions. A successful chess-playing program, however, is still in a more developmental stage. The best program that existed in the late 1960s (Greenblatt, Eastlake, & Crocker, 1967) could play fairly good chess but was still beaten by human experts. These programs continue to improve, and it is probable they will soon be ready to take on chess masters.

Can Computers Be As Versatile As the Human Brain?

Psychologists soon realized that a computer program that could solve geometry problems but could not play games was not really an appropriate model of the human brain, which can do both. Presumably, human beings use the same intellectual processes to solve all problems—not one for checkers, and a different one for logic. Could an all-purpose computer model be designed which could handle a wide variety of problems regardless of the nature of their content? The most ambitious attempt in this direction is the General Problem Solver (GPS) of Newell, Shaw, and Simon (1960). This is a highly sophisticated system that incorporates a large number of concepts, strategies, and heuristics which are believed to underlie human problem solving. It can be given some initial premises, a goal, and certain transformation rules and will then transform the premises into the goal by following the rules. The GPS has proved to be inappropriate for some types of problems, however, and thus falls short of being the all-purpose supersystem that Turing envisioned.

Information-processing ideas and techniques have also been used to study psychological processes other than problem solving, such as verbal learning and the recognition of patterns. Abelson and Carroll's (1965) Ideology Machine attempts to simulate an individual's stable, resistant, social or political belief structures. Computers have been programmed to simulate a neurotic person (Colby, 1965), and also to act as a psychotherapist (Colby, Watt, & Gilbert,

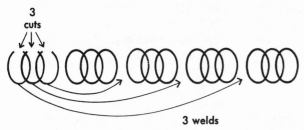

3
cuts

3 welds

The blacksmith cut all three links of one piece of chain (15¢) and used them to join the remaining four pieces (75¢).

● Here is the solution to the candle problem. Replications of the original problem have confirmed the original finding that the problem is more difficult when the objects are presented in the boxes, as you saw them first, fostering the perception of the boxes as containers instead of as possible materials to use in solving the problem. The problem is also made more difficult when extra, unnecessary objects are presented, as was the case here.

1966). Your junior author's encounter with the computer "therapist" is reproduced here (Ψ Close-up, p. 329). His subsequent bout with a paranoid computer "patient" appears in Chapter 14.

Uses and Limitations of Computers

In the past few years, there has literally been an explosion in the use and development of information-processing models and "artificial intelligence." A tremendous number of research problems have been started and the computer programs themselves have become increasingly refined and sophisticated. Such rapid progress, however, has not been viewed without reservations. The most prevalent criticism is that computers, being single-minded and unemotional, cannot possibly simulate human thought.

While such criticisms are well taken, they certainly are not damning. More recent models of information-

tion processing have begun to build in some of the human "weaknesses" that were previously lacking. For example, Simon (1967) has developed a model which includes such attributes as "impatience" (selection of best alternative found in a given period of time), and "discouragement" (cessation of processing after a given number of failures). With further work in this area, we should not be surprised to see a computer program which can get bored, experience conflicting motives, be stupid at times, and so on. On the other hand, although such programs might be more similar to human thought, we would not want to use them for managing machinery. Thus the models developed to run intricate machinery or business operations may differ greatly from those developed to study human thinking.

In general, we can view the relevance of information-processing research in much the same way as the relevance of research on animals (Reitman, 1965). There are many *similarities* between the behavior of man and that of other animals (they all eat, drink, reproduce, learn, and so on). Thus we can try to understand man's drives, habits, and learning by studying these processes in a rat, since we assume that a large part of the explanation for such behavior is common to both the rat and the man. The limits of such a comparative approach depend upon the basic *differences* between man and other animals (e.g., man uses spoken and written language, while animals do not). What these basic differences are is thus critical to a decision as to what animal findings can be applied to man; unfortunately our knowledge of the characteristics specific to each species is all too sketchy at the present time.

Information-processing models, like animals, share certain characteristics with man (both take in information, recognize significant objects, solve problems, and so on). Therefore, such models can be justified as a basis for studying man's cognitive processes, but within limits and with the same cautions that apply to conclusions from animal behavior.

At this point in time, the future of the information-processing approach is filled with unbounded expectations of what is possible. Many computer-science centers have been established and are currently engaging in a flood of ingenious research projects. Such work will undoubtedly continue to uncover the remarkable ways in which man, the natural problem solver, analyzes a problem and discovers its solution. There may even some day be a computer program which solves problems *creatively*—a characteristic presently unique to man.

Creativity

If you were asked to think of people who were highly creative, what names would come to mind? Undoubtedly, you would list such individuals as Michelangelo, Beethoven, Shakespeare, or Einstein. But exactly what is the basis for your judgment? What characteristics do such people possess that lead you to label them as creative? One answer might be that they have all produced something new which has been acclaimed as a great work of art or as a brilliant scientific theory. However, such a criterion would allow us to identify creativity only in people of genius and acknowledged fame. What about the great majority of people who are less than geniuses and not at all well known for their accomplishments?

For example, let's look at the responses that a ten-year-old black boy of average IQ gave to the simple question, "How many uses can you think of for a newspaper?"

"You can read it, write on it, lay it down and paint a picture on it. If you didn't have covers, you could put it around you. You can burn it, put it in the garage and drive the car over it when you wash the car, lay it down and put your baby on it, put it on a busted window, put it in your door for decoration, put it in the garbage can, put it on a chair if the chair is messy. If you have a puppy, you put newspaper in its box or put it in your back yard for the dog to play with. When you build something and you don't want anyone to see it, put newspaper around it. Put newspaper on the floor if you have no mattress, use it to pick up something hot, use it

---

Ψ *Close-up* **The Mad Doctor**

Can a computer help you solve your personal problems? An example of its therapeutic abilities is demonstrated in the following actual conversation between a patient (the junior author of this text) and the "Mad Doctor" computer whose office is at Stanford University's Artificial Intelligence Laboratory. The patient types his responses on a teletype, and seconds later the computer-therapist replies by teletype or a videoscope display.

Patient (P.Z.): Hello.
Therapist (Mad Doctor): How do you do. Please state your problem.
P.Z.: I feel depressed all the time.
M.D.: Tell me more about such feelings.
P.Z.: I am just unhappy and I want your help.
M.D.: You believe I can help you, don't you?
P.Z.: I am not sure.
M.D.: Is it because you are not sure that you came to me?
P.Z.: I think that I hate you.
M.D.: Perhaps in your fantasy, we do not like each other.
P.Z.: You are nothing but a dumb machine.

M.D.: Do computers worry you?
P.Z.: Computers and therapists worry me.
M.D.: Why do you mention computers?
P.Z.: You mentioned it first.
M.D.: We were discussing you—not me.
P.Z.: Are you a therapist or a computer?
M.D.: What do you think machines have to do with your problem?
P.Z.: They are the cause of it.
M.D.: Did you ever think they might *not* be the cause of it?
P.Z.: No.
M.D.: Are you saying "no" just to be negative?
P.Z.: No.
M.D.: You don't seem very talkative today.
P.Z.: I don't want to talk any more.
M.D.: Don't you *really* want to talk any more?
P.Z.: No.
M.D.: You are being a bit negative.
P.Z.: You bet I am. I am leaving.
M.D.: Do you believe it normal to be leaving?

Courtesy of Dr. Kenneth Colby

to stop bleeding, or to catch the drips from drying clothes. You can use newspaper for curtains, put it in your shoe to cover what is hurting your foot, make a kite out of it, shade a light that is too bright. You can wrap fish in it, wipe windows, or wrap money in it and tape it (so it doesn't make noise). You put washed shoes on newspaper, wipe eyeglasses with it, put it under a dripping sink, put a plant on it, make a paper bowl out of it, use it for a hat if it is raining, tie it on your feet for slippers. You can put it on the sand if you had no towel, use it for bases in baseball, make paper airplanes with it, use it as a dustpan when you sweep, ball it up for the cat to play with, wrap your hands in it if it is cold." (Ward & Kogan, 1970)

In evaluating this boy's answers, you might say that he is very creative because he gave many unusual responses that you would never have thought of. In fact, if you were to compare his answers to those of other ten-year-old children of average IQ, his performance might be even more impressive. But where does such an ability come from? Is it a general characteristic that he was born with, or is it something that he learned? If we look at this boy's answers

---

Ψ Close-up   *Taking Off the Set of Blinders*

If your problem-solving behavior was like that of over 2000 students tested by Luchins (1942) on the water-jar problems, your solution was likely to be fast but indirect and inefficient. Your control subject, not given the "benefit" of the training which established a perceptual set in you, probably used a simpler, more direct way of solving the problem. For example, to get 20 quarts, did he simply fill A (23) and pour off into C (3)? To get 18, did he just fill both A (15) and C (3)? Did you even "see" these possible solutions? Or did you continue to use your "old" approach (such as filling B, pouring once into A, and then into C)?

Think about the implications of such response perseveration, which is maintained even though it is inefficient or inappropriate when the environment changes. How would such an *Einstellung* (German for "set") operate in a prejudiced person?

---

again, we might say that *experience* is an important factor. Clearly, the more often a person has had to use something in different ways, the more likely he is to think of other uses for it. Perhaps this child's responses would be considered less creative by people of the same socioeconomic background as he. If so, this would imply that creativity is a relative quality which only exists when someone thinks it does. Many psychologists dispute such a viewpoint, however, and maintain that creativity *is* a general characteristic of certain people which can be reliably measured and assessed.

What Is Creative?

The most widely used definition of creativity is that it is the occurrence of *uncommon or unusual, but appropriate responses*. This assumption underlies most of the tests that have been developed to measure creativity. ■

Although originality is usually taken for granted as a major factor in creativity, the importance of appropriateness is not always recognized. However, it is the criterion which distinguishes between creative and nonsensical acts. Solutions to a problem which are unique but totally worthless or irrelevant cannot be considered as creative responses. For example, suppose someone were asked to imagine all the things that might happen if all national and local laws were suddenly abolished. A reply of "it would rain for forty days and forty nights," might be novel, but would not be regarded as creative because it lacks any relationship to the problem. Similarly, the utterances of psychotic patients (such as those of Mr. F. B. in Chapter 1) may be unique and eccentric but are not viewed as evidence of creative talent.

When we speak of originality as an important aspect of creativity, we are referring to the ability to combine elements in a new and different way. This ability is beautifully illustrated in the work of an artist such as Picasso.   ●   (p. 332)

In describing an Italian sculptor, Burnham (1968) has said, "[His genius] was such that he displayed an almost pathological inability to execute the expected solution to any problem in sculpture." To see a problem in a new way has often been the key to an important discovery or scientific breakthrough, as

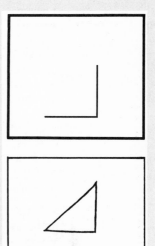

Common Responses
1. Smudges
2. Dark clouds

Uncommon Responses
1. Magnetized iron filings
2. A small boy and his mother hurrying along on a dark windy day, trying to get home before it rains

Common Responses
1. An ape
2. Modern painting of a gorilla

Uncommon Responses
1. A baboon looking at itself in a hand mirror
2. Rodin's "The Thinker" shouting "Eureka!"

Common Responses
1. An African voodoo dancer
2. A cactus plant

Uncommon Responses
1. Mexican in sombrero running up a long hill to escape from rain clouds
2. A word written in Chinese

◻ TESTS FOR CREATIVITY

Two of the projective tests which have been used to distinguish between creative and uncreative individuals are the inkblot test and the drawing completion test. In order to describe the inkblots shown above, the individual must attribute some order and meaning to a nondescript configuration. The average individual is apt to describe the inkblot in terms of its simple, obvious features. The creative individual is more likely to impose an elegant new order on the figure which is personally satisfying to him. When asked to complete a drawing (top, right), the average individual is satisfied with a drawing that "makes sense" (middle) while the creative individual gives meaning and even emotion to his drawing (bottom).

After Barron, 1958

was demonstrated by Descartes in freeing physiological functioning for scientific study by postulating two kinds of processes (described in Chapter 3). This process of choosing and shaping appropriate representations for a problem is the focus of computer programs which attempt to simulate human creative behavior (Amarel, 1966). Basically, the quality of originality means that the creative response is not a predictable one until it is made—and then it becomes a standard by which the creativity of future responses can be judged.

Who Is Creative?

There are a number of different orientations in research on creativity. Some studies have focused on the *process* of creativity, some on the *product* that is created, and others on the *situational* factors that influence creativity. However, the major approach in this field has been research on the *creative person*. Who is this individual? What characteristics distinguish him from less creative people? How did he get to be the way he is? (Could you get there too?) The

● A variety of creative approaches to the same subject, all by Pablo Picasso. (From left: Visage, The Detroit Institute of Art; Woman Weeping, the Roland Penrose Collection, London; Girl Before Mirror, The Museum of Modern Art, New York.)

search for answers to these questions has been undertaken by many psychologists.

In general, studies have shown that there is a particular pattern of psychological traits that consistently characterizes creative individuals, regardless of their age, cultural background, or area of work. Creative persons appear to be distinguished more by their interests, attitudes, and drives than by their intellectual abilities (Dellas & Gaier, 1970). The lack of a strong correlation between creativity and intelligence may seem surprising, but research has clearly supported this conclusion (Wallach & Kogan, 1965).

There are other cognitive variables which do seem characteristic of the creative person, however. One of the most distinctive of these is a cognitive preference for *complexity*, as opposed to simplicity. This is revealed in a preference for figures which are asymmetrical, dynamic, and even chaotic, rather than those which are regular, neat, and simple.   ▲

Much of the research on the creative person has been concerned with personality characteristics. Several investigations have studied groups of creative individuals who were eminent and well established in their fields. The results pointed to a personality syndrome of impulsivity, independence, introversion, intuitiveness, and self-acceptance that was characteristic of all these people. Creative architects (MacKinnon, 1961) and creative research scientists (Gough, 1961) were remarkably similar in these personality traits, despite the differences in the content of their professional work. Creative writers displayed a similar complex of traits, although they showed greater originality and an emphasis on fantasy (Barron, 1963).

Independence, in both attitudes and behavior, is perhaps the most striking characteristic of this creative syndrome. Practically all studies have found that the creative person is not very concerned with the impression he makes on others or with their opinion of him. As a result, he is freer to be himself and to express new ideas than other, less creative people. Such independence is a critical necessity, since the creative response is often met with (and must continue in the face of) criticism, ridicule, and a total lack of reinforcement. As the Gershwins said,

They all laughed at Christopher Columbus when he said the world was round;
They all laughed when Edison recorded sound;
They all laughed at Wilbur and his brother when they said that man could fly.
They told Marconi wireless was a phony; it's the same old cry.

Another personality variable that distinguishes the creative person is that his pattern of interests reflects both the feminine and the masculine side of his nature. Creative men are able to accept the feminine aspects of their personality without experiencing any sexual conflict, thus leading them to a greater openness to emotions and feelings, and to a greater esthetic sensitivity (Hammer, 1964). One might expect that creative females would show an acceptance of masculine traits in their personality, but the little research available does not entirely support this view. Creative women differ from the less creative in that they retain their femininity despite admission of masculine traits and are often *less* "masculine," rather than more so (Helson, 1967). Perhaps certain masculine characteristics in the female inhibit creativity rather than promote it. The extent to which there is a real sex difference in the creative process can only be elucidated by much more research.

The popular view of exceptionally creative people is that while they are geniuses, they are also completely crazy. The madness of such artists as Van Gogh or Nijinsky is often cited as a "typical example." What psychological evidence is there for a relationship between creativity and psychopathology? The answer (surprising to some) is that there is almost none. Instead, creative people appear to have superior ego strength and a constructive way of handling problems (Cross, Cattell, & Butcher, 1967). It may be that such characteristics as independence and originality, which lead creative individuals to think in ways that are taboo or considered "strange," cause the rest of the world to think of them (erroneously) as mentally unbalanced.

Can Anybody (like me, for instance) Be Creative?

Even though people often criticize or attach negative labels to highly creative individuals, they still, paradoxically, want to be more creative themselves. Creativity is an attribute that has a high positive value for almost everyone, in the sense that they wish they had more of it, and they would like the schools to provide more of it for their children. If creativity were something that you were born with, then it would be impossible to achieve such an improvement. Either

you would have it or you wouldn't. Fortunately, there is no evidence to support the notion that creativity is innate; rather, it appears to be *learned* behavior.

How can we stimulate people to be more creative? Following basic principles of learning, Maltzman (1960) assumed that if people had been reinforced for creative responses in a preliminary training session, they would show more creative behavior in a later test situation as a result of response generalization.

To test this idea, Maltzman gave subjects a word-association test six times in a row, requiring them to give different answers each time. He thus forced subjects to go beyond common word associations and to produce more creative responses. When these subjects were later given a creativity test, they received higher scores than a group of control subjects who had not received such training.

Creativity is often stifled by the individual's fear that his new idea will be regarded as stupid or worthless by other people. If he refuses to express new ideas (or is negatively reinforced when he does), he may eventually learn never to think in a truly creative way. How can we prevent this from happening? One proposal has been the use of "brainstorm-

▲ These pairs of drawings are from the Welsh Figure Preference Test. Subjects chosen at random tend to prefer those on the left while subjects identified by other tests as creative prefer those on the right.

ing" sessions (Osborn, 1957). In the initial "idea-finding" stage, the members of a group are presented with a problem and asked to think of all possible solutions to it, whether they seem practical or not. Participants are encouraged to be free of all inhibitions, except that they are not allowed to be critical of anyone else's ideas. In the second, "evaluation," stage, the group considers each idea very carefully, retaining all those that have a remote possibility of being useful. This entire procedure of *deferred judgment* can be used by an individual thinker as well as by groups.

How successful is the brainstorming technique in improving creativity? Unfortunately, there is very little evidence to support its effectiveness, however reasonable the method may seem. For example, one study found that brainstorming did not generate any more original ideas than were produced by the same number of individuals working alone (Taylor, Berry, & Block, 1958). This would suggest that the presence of other people, even under ideal conditions, can have certain inhibitory influences on creativity. However, individual brainstorming sessions could be made even more effective if they were preceded by a group "warm-up" session (Dunnette, Campbell, & Jaastad, 1963).

Although a truly effective technique for promoting creativity has yet to be found, it is clear that creativity *can* be enhanced. This fact has important implications for education, since it suggests that a child can learn creativity as well as reading, writing, and arithmetic. It is to be hoped that more research will be done on possible methods for stimulating creativity. Strangely enough, the technique of reinforcing a person for his original responses may not be the most successful one in the long run, since many creative individuals produce their most original work when they are independent of the traditional reinforcers dispensed by their society.

George Bernard Shaw, in his *Maxims for Revolutionists*, made a distinction between reasonable and unreasonable men which appears to be equally valid for distinguishing creative, innovative people from others. "The reasonable man adapts himself to the world: the unreasonable one persists in trying to adapt the world to himself. Therefore all progress depends on the unreasonable [and creative] man."

Chapter Summary

Man's capacity to use his mind for solving problems above and beyond the ordinary problems of survival frees him from being a slave to his environment. He can manipulate symbols representing elements of the environment (*think*), utilize these symbols in solving problems (*reason*), and conceive new and original ideas (*create*). Thinking may be either *autistic*, such as daydreaming, or *realistic*, such as reasoning directed at the solution of a particular problem, or it may be a combination of the two.

Thinking may utilize images, words, or concepts. *Images* are "mental pictures" of actual sensory experiences. Most people are strongest in visual imagery, though a few report stronger imagery for other senses. While imagery is used in many kinds of thinking, it is not essential to the thought process. Some people possess *eidetic imagery*—the capacity for imagery as clear and accurate as the original perception.

Words, like images, are apparently not essential to thought, but greatly enhance it. Our perception of objects is clearly influenced by the words we associate with them. The *semantic differential* technique has been developed as a way of studying the meaning we attach to various concepts.

Psychologists have long disputed whether thought determines language or vice versa. The *Whorf hypothesis* holds that the language patterns of a cultural group determine its thought patterns and perceptions. Whorf believes differences in the language applied to events lead to different ways of thinking about those events. Critics of Whorf have argued that it may well be different conceptions of the event that have led to the difference in labels. Furthermore, it has been shown that differences in labeling and categorization do not necessarily reflect differences in perception and thinking.

Much of our thinking involves the use of abstract categories, or *concepts*. A concept involves the association of a single label or action with an entire class of objects or events. Concepts may be: (a) *conjunctive*, in which all instances of the concept have one or more attributes in common; (b) *inclusive disjunctive*, in which instances may have either or both of two characteristics; (c) *exclusive disjunctive*, in which instances have either of two characteristics but not both; or (d) *relational,* in which all instances bear a certain relationship to some other object.

Language is evidently not necessary to the development of concepts, since it can be shown that children can distinguish between concepts before they can speak. At first, the child's concepts depend heavily on outward similarity, but gradually he learns to use concepts at higher levels of abstraction, such as "truth" or "beauty." It has been suggested that there are three stages in conceptual development. First we learn to use *muscular representations*, then *images*, and finally *symbols.*

The *continuity theory* of concept learning holds that concepts are formed gradually, over many trials, while the *discontinuity theory* holds that they are formed suddenly, on an all-or-none basis. Studies of animals and children of average intelligence have tended to support the continuity theory, while studies of bright children and young adults have supported the discontinuity theory.

We do not yet know very much about the neurological processes underlying thinking. While EEG recordings enable us to determine a subject's state of awareness, they tell us nothing about his actual thought processes. Tiny muscular contractions of the vocal apparatus, called implicit speech, have been shown to correlate with thinking. Two different explanations of this phenomenon have been advanced. The *peripheralist theory* maintains that thinking actually consists of such movements, while the *centralist theory* holds that the movements are merely a result of thought, which takes place in the brain.

The length of time involved in thinking has been studied in *reaction time* experiments. Such studies began with the astronomer Bessel's development of the *personal equation*, based on consistent discrepancies between persons in the timing of observations. Since Helmholtz' demonstration that the speed of nerve impulses can be measured, studies of *mental chronometry* have used reaction time as a measure of the complexity of thought processes. Studies have shown that when a person has a *response set*, his reaction time is shorter than when he has a *stimulus set*. In recent years, psychologists have come to think of human responding as a series of events, and of the thinking organism as similar to a *servomechanism:*

a goal-directed, error-sensitive, self-correcting device operating through *input, throughput, output,* and *feedback.*

There are three types of reasoning: *deductive reasoning*, in which data are combined and inescapable conclusions are drawn; *inductive reasoning*, in which hypotheses about the unknown are formulated on the basis of inferences from what is already known, and *evaluating*: judging the soundness or appropriateness of some idea or product.

When an individual in a new situation wishes to reach a goal, but finds some obstacle to his progress, he is confronted with a *problem*. Human problem solving involves a combination of *insight* and *trial-and-error* learning. We begin with some ideas about how to solve the problem, try a few of them out (perhaps only mentally), and finally come up with the correct solution. The success with which we do this depends on several factors. A person's *mental set* (the expectation with which he approaches the problem) can help him or, if it is inappropriate, can hinder him (as in *rigidity* and *functional fixedness*). The more applicable past experience the individual has, the more likely he will be to solve the problem. *Personal context* can also affect problem solving. If the individual is emotionally involved, he may not be able to reason as objectively. Frustration and stress can also be a hindrance on complex tasks.

Recently computers have been used to study the processing of information in thinking through simulation. Computers have imitated humans in processes as different as solving geometry problems, playing checkers, and acting neurotic. While we are a long way from developing a computer that will duplicate all the complexities of a man's mind, we can learn a great deal by using computer simulation and by studying the similarities and differences between men and machines.

A *creative* individual is one who makes uncommon, but appropriate, responses. Creativity is a measurable characteristic, involving the ability to combine elements in new and different ways. Creative persons are distinguished from others more by their interests, attitudes, and personality traits than by their intellectual abilities. It appears that creativity is a learned ability, although investigators have not yet determined how it can best be encouraged.

Chapter 9

The Motivation of Behavior

Man attends to certain events in the environment, perceives patterns, learns relationships, recalls information, reasons, solves problems, plans strategies and acts on them—*if* he is motivated to do so. When we ask what makes us, and other living organisms, "tick," we are asking questions about motivation.

Is human behavior driven by impulse and appetite? Why does competition bring out the best in some individuals and teams, who get "psyched up," and the worst in others, who end "psyched out"? Why are some people ready to sacrifice their lives for what they believe in, while others are so apathetic they seem not to care about anything? How can children be taught to cooperate? What must be done to increase the productivity of workers? How can a manufacturer make people "want" his product? Is it true that people on relief do not want to help themselves? The answers given to such questions imply some conception of the way in which motivational factors influence our lives. Thus any understanding of the behavior of organisms rests upon an understanding of motivational principles.

Beyond the wish for understanding of motivation is the hope to control behavior, to regulate and improve the quality of one's own life and that of others. What does a knowledge of motivation tell us about the technology for controlling behavior used by teachers, parents, salesmen, politicians, animal trainers, entertainers, marriage counselors, therapists, and other agents of change—including ourselves?

The Concept of Motivation

Our attempt to explain a bit of human behavior involves the discovery of a whole network of causal relationships, only some of which we can actually see. We observe situations, stimuli, and responses. But we can only make inferences about whatever psychological processes are going on in between. Motivation is thus a concept, or hypothetical construct, not an overt, observable event.

Motivation As an Explanation for Variability

The basic function of a motivational analysis is to explain the observed *variability* in behavior. How can we make sense out of the differences in response to the same external situation between different people and even in the same person at different times? When conditions of training, testing, and ability are equated and the performance of individuals still varies, differences in behavior are attributed to motivation.

We do not assume motivation by a "fainting drive" when a man loses consciousness from excessive loss of blood. However, if we should find that a big, tough athlete is more likely than other people to faint at the prospect of receiving a hypodermic injection, we would feel justified in searching for an internal reason. Similarly, a knee jerk from a tap on the patella is not taken as evidence of a drive to flex the knee but is regarded as a nonmotivated reflex. No motivational constructs are required to understand why a person dies after receiving a high-voltage electric shock, but the sudden death of a seemingly healthy older person shortly after having been placed in a home for the aged does seem to require a motivational explanation.

You do not eat every time food is placed before you, or study as much as you know you should before every exam. And you might never devote time or energy to perfecting some skills that are utterly absorbing to other people. Take the U.S. Aces Bridge Team, for example, which won the world championship after two years of regimented, constant practice, or baton twirlers, yo-yo spinners, and, for that matter, academic scholars. What explains such single-minded concentration of effort? We say that we eat because we are "hungry," and that we work to excel others because we are impelled by a desire for "achievement." It is because the relationship between the behavior and the stimulus event is *not* perfect—is not a completely *dependent* one—that we invoke concepts of "motivation" to take up the "slippage."

In trying to "establish the motive," all the possibly significant characteristics of the situation and the person's traits, habits, and actions are listed and carefully sifted to see if a pattern emerges.

■ DRIVE AS AN INTERVENING VARIABLE

Three things that *affect* drinking behavior (independent variables) are shown on the left, and three ways of measuring drinking behavior (dependent variables) are shown on the right. Any one of the three on the left could be manipulated to change one or more of those on the right. But instead of postulating nine possible relationships, it is simpler to postulate a single intervening or "mediating" variable, *thirst,* as the mechanism through which all the variables on the left affect those on the right.

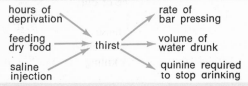

After Miller, 1959. From *Psychology: The Study of a Science*, Vol. 2 by S. Koch (Ed.). Copyright © 1959. Used by permission of McGraw-Hill Book Company.

Inferring inner determination. In inferring internal motivation to explain behavior, we try to simplify the complex web of possible interrelations by postulating a single intermediate, intervening variable linking the various stimulus inputs to the varied response outputs. Thus instead of trying to establish a variable relating each aspect of the stimulus situation to each aspect of the response, we postulate an overall variable like *hunger* or *thirst.* ■

The psychologist, cast in the role of a Sherlock Holmes, must use the available evidence from the stimulus conditions and the observable behavior to identify this basic internal variable, or motive. • This key to the puzzle of behavior not only makes the parts fit, but accounts for otherwise unexplainable and apparently irrational behavior on the part of the "guilty" individual. Once the action in question is assigned to an actor, it becomes important to establish his specific intent because that is what determines his degree of legal responsibility for his action (Ψ Close-up, below).

The words we use to label inner states behind this observed variability of behavior all share some implication of causal determination: *Purpose, intention, goal-directed, need, want, drive, desire, motive.* Psychologists usually use the label *drive* when the motivation is assumed to be primarily biologically instigated. The labels *motive* and *need* are more often used to refer to psychological and social motivation, which is generally assumed to be at least in part acquired. However, there is variation in the usage of these concepts among psychologists. Some, for example, prefer to use the term *needs* only for biological demands (like the need for oxygen) whether or not they trigger actual behavior.

Aspects of motivation. In its broadest definition, the study of motivation is the search for all the determi-

nants of human and animal activity (Young, 1961). Limited to just internal determinants, however, motivation includes: (a) energy arousal, (b) direction of effort toward a particular goal, (c) selective attention to certain stimuli (and decreased sensitivity to others), (d) organization of activity into an integrated pattern, and (e) persistence of this activity until the initiating conditions are changed.

Motivated states are generally initiated by *deprivation* of something required for biological or psychological functioning. For example, number of hours without food is a stimulus condition which affects level of hunger. The hungry animal will turn from other activities to searching the environment for food, and eating it once it is found. The *consummatory response* of eating *reduces* or temporarily eliminates the complex of internal conditions we call the *hunger drive*. The consummatory behavior ceases or becomes less probable as the animal becomes *satiated* (has had enough of the goal or activity). The *instrumental response*—the behavior of searching or working to-

---

Ψ *Close-up*   **When Is a Killer Not Responsible for Killing?**

Determination of the actor's state of mind is basic to our system of justice. The same act of taking another person's life is regarded as *murder* if it is an intentional act, or as the lesser crime of *manslaughter*, if not.

We can learn much about a society's conception of human nature from its definition of those conditions under which one who takes another's life is not held responsible for that act. To see how varied such judgments can be, check below the conditions you think should "excuse" a killer and compare notes with your friends.

1. Inability to exercise reason due to:
   _____a. tender age
   _____b. mental retardation
   _____c. insanity, temporary or chronic
   _____d. killer being infrahuman—i.e., an animal.

2. Influence of controlling agents which limit exercise of free will:
   _____a. drugs and intoxicants
   _____b. sleepwalking

3. Influence of emotions which overwhelm reason:
   _____a. passions of jealousy
   _____b. uncontrollable rage

4. Situational and role-required behaviors which change intention of act or individual responsibility:
   _____a. public executioner
   _____b. policeman in line of duty
   _____c. soldier in battle
   _____d. citizen in self-defense
   _____e. father protecting his child
   _____f. doctor in mercy killing

ward the goal—increases in strength as motivation increases in intensity and decreases with its reduction.

Motivated states may also be produced by the presence of noxious agents, such as painful electric shock, smog, or a bully. In addition, they may be induced by the presentation of conditioned stimuli associated with strong unconditioned stimuli, as with *Playboy* fold-outs or romantic love stories. Finally, as we saw in Chapter 3, modern techniques make it possible to induce motivational states directly via electrical or chemical stimulation of various parts of the brain. Similarly, brain lesions and direct infusion of drive-relevant substances into the blood, stomach, or other organs can make animals hungry, thirsty, or sexually aroused.

Internal conditions and environmental incentives. Some investigators have sought to study the effects of motivation on behavior at a purely physiological level. This approach has proven inadequate for two reasons. First, in certain systems like hunger and thirst, that are essential to an animal's survival, nature has built in a big safety factor by developing multiple controls. "Any one of these controls, and perhaps more than one may be damaged without destroying or too seriously impairing the overall regulation, and for this reason it is difficult to interfere experimentally with the regulation of food or water intake." (Teitelbaum, 1966, p. 570)

Second, the test of any physiological intervention procedure must be made by observing the animal's behavior, thereby involving laws of behavior—psychological laws. For example, electrical stimulation of certain portions of the brain elicits eating in the rat. Does this mean that the hunger control center has been found? Not necessarily. Perhaps the stimulated animals are just gnawing available food in a reflex-like activity, and not experiencing a "true" motivational state at all. This is evidently what is happening when they continue to chew inedible objects such as pieces of wood and fail to expend any directed effort to get food which is nearby but not right under their noses (Miller, 1957). It was considerations such as these that led psychologist E. C. Tolman to maintain, years ago, that "a psychology cannot be explained by a physiology until one has a psychology to explain" (1936).

The first truly modern approach to the problem of what motivates behavior was made by K. S. Lashley (1938). He regarded motivation as being controlled by the responses of the central nervous system to a complex variety of both internal and external stimuli. He pointed out that motivated behavior clearly does not consist simply of chains of stimulus-response sequences since our response to the same stimulus varies as conditions in the organism change. Furthermore, motivated behavior depends not upon a single stimulus but rather upon a complex pattern of stimuli, even when a single stimulus triggers the response.

The continued search by some investigators for a *single* most important variable in a given drive (inevitably in vain) has unfortunately diverted attention away from the study of: (a) the exact sequence from deprivation and incentive stimuli to motivated act, including all the events that occur, (b) ways in which the many control systems interrelate and interact in any particular motivational condition, and (c) the external, nonphysiological variables which do, in fact, contribute in large part to the control of motivated behavior.

The more recent, emerging view is that the effects of motivation on behavior must be understood as an interaction between certain stimulus objects in the environment (*incentive objects*) and a particular physiological state or condition of the organism (Bindra, 1969). Even when "drive sites" are electrically aroused in the brain, motivated behavior occurs only in the presence of appropriate incentive objects. When both internal and external conditions are appropriate, a *central motive state* is created in the organism which has two powerful effects on behavior. It alters the effectiveness of sensory input so as to increase the probability that a response will be made in relation to a certain class of incentive objects (selective attention). It also biases responses by increasing the discharge into the motor neurons involved in the appropriate class of responses, thus raising the probability that this type of action will occur.

Motivation thus influences behavior both through its specific cueing and sensitizing function and in its role as an energizer. Besides the directed energy associated with the particular motivational state, there may be general arousal through the action of the general arousal system discussed in Chapter 7. As we have seen, the activity level of the organism may vary from the low level of sleep to the high level of alert excitement. As arousal increases, there is a generalized increase in the strength of instrumental responses, regardless of their actual utility in satisfying the motivational requirement.

The same stimulus can serve both an *arousal* function and a *cue* function (as the smell of food which may both initiate a search for food and also guide its direction). Or sometimes, different stimuli are responsible for arousal of activity and direction of it, as when changes in blood sugar level lead to feelings of hunger and the sight of food moves us toward it.

The capacity of sensory stimulation to guide behavior is poor when arousal is very low or very high. With very low arousal, the sensory message does not get through; with very high arousal, too many messages get through and prevent the individual from responding selectively to the correct stimulus message. Thus an intermediate level of arousal produces optimal performance, because more useful information can be extracted from the relevant cue stimuli to guide the behavior. ◆ Numerous lines of evidence have indicated that the effect of increased arousal on efficiency is beneficial up to a point, but beyond that has bad effects. This reaction between arousal and excellence of performance is called an *inverted*-U function.

Motivation As "the Useless Language of Complaint"

It might appear from our discussion thus far, and from the fact that the remainder of this chapter is devoted to a detailed analysis of various drives and motives, that there is general agreement that the study of motivation is an important enterprise for psychologists. This is not the case.

Some critics of the way motivational concepts are used have focused on the popular use of such concepts as catch-all apologies for some behaviors, and the basis for complaint when other, desired behavior is not undertaken. To say that someone engaged in a given behavior because he was driven by basic motives or did not do what was expected because he was not motivated, is to offer a worthless explanation. We are all too likely to assume that we

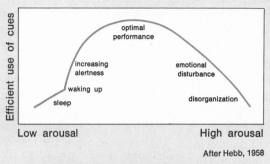

◆ THE INVERTED-U FUNCTION

The inverted-U curve shows how the effectiveness of use of stimulus cues varies with the level of general arousal. Optimum performance can be expected with moderate arousal; very low or very high arousal will produce poorest performance.

have explained some behavior merely because we have labeled it as "a hang-up," "a destructive urge," "altruism," or "shiftlessness." In *West Side Story,* when the Jets sing "Gee, Officer Krupke," they poke fun at the motivational jargon used by social workers to explain their delinquent behavior. If we do not specify the stimulus conditions which initiate and maintain the observed behavior, we can have no hope for changing the behavior.

George Kelly (1958) has observed that in education the most frequent complaint of teachers is that their students "just aren't motivated." He goes on:

"Often the teacher would insist that the child would do nothing—absolutely nothing—just sit! Then we would suggest that she try a nonmotivational approach and let him 'just sit.' We would ask her to observe how he went about 'just sitting.' Invariably the teacher would be able to report some extremely interesting goings on. An analysis of what the 'lazy' child did while he was being lazy often furnished her with her first glimpse into the child's world and provided her with her first solid grounds for communication with him. Some teachers found that their laziest pupils were those who could produce the most novel ideas; other, that the term 'laziness' had been applied to activities that they had simply been unable to understand or appreciate." (pp. 46-47)

A more total damning of the concept of motivation comes from the radical behaviorists who follow the operant conditioning approach of B. F. Skinner (see Chapter 5). They acknowledge that in earlier theories of learning where reinforcer effectiveness was assumed to depend on the reduction of drives within the organism, motivation played a major explanatory role in linking stimulus, responses, and consequences. But today, "The practitioner of operant conditioning scarcely mentions motivation, since it has come to refer only to those conditions that render a given event reinforcing at a given time. Since the emphasis in operant conditioning is on the effects of reinforcement, these motivational conditions have become mere technological details." (Reynolds, 1968, p. 127) Motivation, in this view, becomes the insignificant stagehand that sets the scene for the reinforcer to operate as the star of the show. It is only when a new species or social group is being studied, or when traditional reinforcers are no longer effective, that motivational conditions need become a matter of concern to the experimenter.

The proper study of behavior, in this view, comes from an analysis of the controlling variables that currently affect behavior, not from "appealing to physiological fantasies about the communality of reinforcers" (Reynolds, 1968, p. 128). Consider again the teacher's (or boss's) complaint that the students and workers simply are lazy and lacking in motivation. In some instances, the motivational explanation borders on an accusation of innate lack of will power in people or groups that are disliked. But there are at least half a dozen other reasons, not involving motivation, that might account for this apparent "laziness."

1. The desired response may have been extinguished by lack of reinforcement (the teacher has not paid attention in the past).

2. A wide range of responses may have been inhibited by punishment or ridicule of prior incorrect action in a particular situation (this often happens in foreign language classes).

3. Inaction itself may be an operant behavior which attracts attention if others are active.

4. Inaction may result from nutritional deficiencies.

5. Inaction may result from fear of violating a social norm, or being a scab or "rate buster." Where students "play it cool," teachers often mistake failure to respond for lack of enthusiasm. Similarly, in the military, recruits learn not to volunteer or act in any way which will get them singled out.

6. Inaction may result from the operation of strong motives in conflict. This was observed in a heated argument over the status of Puerto Ricans in America between a girl's prejudiced mother and her tolerant new boyfriend. The girl remained silent throughout, but not from lack of motivation.

7. Inaction also results if the behavior in question is reinforced at fixed intervals. Such a reinforcement schedule produces workers who learn to sit and wait until the next payoff is imminent. Changing to a variable interval schedule will turn the lazy loafers into hustling hotshots.

A more nebulous attack on the area of motivation comes from its being *gerrymandered* by assorted groups of psychologists who carve up (or dissolve) the broad area of motivation into units to be studied by those whose primary interest is perception, memory, cognitive processes, or some other area.

Post Hoc Explanations, No! Motivation, Sí!

These criticisms are valid and call for a reformulation of the task and concepts involved in a motivational analysis of behavior. However, the concept of motivation should not be banished with undue haste since much has been learned both in content and method from the combined approach of physiologically and behaviorally oriented psychologists studying "motivation." Although it is sufficient for an empirical law to state that reinforcers gain in effectiveness as a function of deprivation conditions, it is still legitimate to ask *how* they do so. By what mechanisms does deprivation or excessive stimulation change the value of a stimulus object for an organism? Furthermore, do psychologists at this time know what the effective reinforcers are for subjects other than white rats and white middle-class college sophomores? Motivational considerations will still be necessary until the appropriate "reinforcement technology" is developed for the poor, the minority groups, the peasant populations, the "incurable" mentally ill, drug addicts, vandals, and many others.

The internal conditions that arouse and direct an individual's responses to objects and situations in the environment fall roughly into two groups: *biological drives,* resulting usually from such basic tissue needs as those for water, food, oxygen, sleep, warmth, or coolness, and *psychological motives,* resulting from such needs as those for social approval, self-esteem, security, and knowledge. The biological drives are *innate,* although the ways in which they are satisfied are greatly influenced by learning and cultural factors. The exact origin of psychological motives is still a matter of lively debate, but most of them seem to be *acquired* as the result of experience, especially the experience of living with other people. These psychological motives assume greater significance as the basic needs for survival and maintenance are satisfied well enough that they no longer preoccupy us.

In this chapter we will dwell in depth on several of the biological drives and will set the stage for later chapters in which psychological motivation will be discussed.

Studying Biological Motivation

Biological drives originate in the organism's undeniable biological requirements. These drives motivate the behavior of the organism in directions that lead to the required changes in internal environment. For example, the hunger drive motivates the organism to seek and take in food, which is necessary to maintain metabolism. Prolonged failure to satisfy this drive can result in impaired health and intellectual functioning, increased susceptibility to disease, and, ultimately, death. To sustain life, the organism must have food, water, oxygen, rest, and sleep. It also needs some means of maintaining a constant body temperature, and a signal system (pain) that will enable it to avoid tissue damage. In addition, to ensure the continuation of life from one generation to the next, sexual drives and "maternal" drives must come into play. It is not clear whether these latter drives should be considered "biological" in the same sense as hunger and thirst. Similarly uncertain are the status of a "drive to dream" (as evidenced by the REM rebound phenomenon discussed in Chapter 7), and of exploratory or curiosity drives. Drives influence behavior from birth and are present even during fetal life, although normally at that time they are automatically satisfied by the mother's body.

Biological Drives As Homeostatic Mechanisms

Though they vary in intensity, all the biological drives are regulatory mechanisms that help maintain the physiological equilibrium of the individual. An organism will go to remarkable lengths to maintain the constancy of its normal internal environment—a process called *homeostasis.*

Biological drives originate in physiological conditions which have disturbed the organism's equilibrium. When an internal state is disturbed, conditions are produced that motivate the organism into seeking activity. Such activity ceases only when the goal is attained and biological equilibrium is restored or when a stronger motive takes precedence—as when you stop in the midst of preparing a midnight snack to investigate the smell of smoke.

Many homeostatic activities are largely internal and automatic. Among these are the maintenance of constant body temperature and of the proper balance of oxygen and carbon dioxide in the bloodstream. Another, related to nutrition, is the very complex process by which the body maintains a constant level of sugar in the bloodstream.

But biological needs can never be satisfied permanently, and complex higher forms of activity have developed—particularly in man—to meet the problem of recurring disturbances in tissue constancy (Stagner, 1951). Besides becoming able to detect very small physiological changes as cues to a change in equilibrium, many species have developed mechanisms for anticipating certain needs. Animals build nests and hoard food for winter use. Man not only has learned to eat before hunger pangs begin, but has developed elaborate systems of agriculture, food preservation, storage, and commodity exchange in order to ensure an adequate food supply at all times.

Thus homeostasis is more than the automatic maintenance of chemical conditions of the body in response to specific stimuli. It involves an active effort of the organism to establish a physical and social environment that is as constant as possible. To sum up:

". . . Homeostasis has been empirically demonstrated to be a process which, operating from a *measurable baseline* (for example, normal pulse rate, blood sugar level, and so forth), works *automatically* through a system of *specific* and intricately *complementary* mechanisms that are controlled to a considerable extent by the autonomic nervous system as a *governing system* and implemented through a *specific medium,* the so-called 'fluid matrix.' Homeostasis makes it possible for an organism that is essentially unstable to *maintain itself at the maximum efficiency* possible for it at a given point in its life cycle, while it slowly changes in the direction of evolution and degeneration (aging), and until it has reproduced itself and brought up its young." (Henry, 1955, p. 302)

One of the problems created by an addiction to alcohol or to a drug like heroin is that a new chemical equilibrium is established in the body. Once this occurs, homeostatic tendencies then operate to maintain this new state, and the individual begins to experience a compulsive craving for the substance to which he has become addicted.

Homeostasis does not account for all types of behavior, however, even at the physiological level. An organism may occasionally behave in a manner detrimental to bodily maintenance. For example, human babies, if given the chance, may eat enough salt to kill themselves. Also the human body is without means of protecting itself against certain harmful conditions, such as too high a level of radiation in the environment. Thirdly, an organism sometimes strives for goals that have no significance for adaptation. Rats that are not thirsty will learn to thread complex mazes when rewarded only by water sweetened with saccharin, a substance that is not required in the body chemistry. This, of course, could be a conditioned response built in as a result of tasting sugar, which *is* needed. Or it could be that the animal organism is set or genetically "programmed" at birth to seek sweetness. Homeostasis is a valuable concept, but it does not seem to tell the entire story.

Manipulation and Measurement of Biological Drives

Much of man's knowledge of the biological drives has come from careful study of the behavior of animals under experimental conditions. Since measurement and quantification is the basic aim of any science, psychologists and physiologists have developed numerous ways of measuring the strength of drives

They do this by varying the intensity of drive stimulation and observing the effect produced on some facet of behavior.

To arouse drives, experimenters employ stimulus operations which disturb the organism's homeostatic balance. Deprivation of a needed substance, such as food or water, or variation in the calorie/bulk ratio of food or the salt concentration of water are most often used. As we have seen (p. 92), direct stimulation of specific brain sites by electrical current or by chemical injections is being increasingly used to study biological drives. In addition, changing environmental conditions by creating an excess of heat, cold, or noxious stimulation provides another means of experimentally manipulating the antecedent variables of motivation.

The dependent consequences of the arousal of biological drives are measured by a variety of response indicators. Among them are: (a) gross motor activity; (b) autonomic nervous system activity; (c) consummatory behavior (amount, latency to begin, and patterning); (d) rate or force of responding; (e) speed of learning associations that are reinforced by biologically relevant reinforcers; (f) resistance of conditioned responses to experimental extinction; (g) preference shown when given a choice between alternative activities or goal substances; (h) interference with an ongoing activity; and (i) amount of obstruction overcome to reach an appropriate goal.

This last measure, though not much used currently, was one of the earliest sources of data on the relative strengths of various drives. A group of psychologists at Columbia University in the late 1920s devised an obstruction box which separated a motivated rat from the object of its affection by an electrified grid. The strength of a variety of drives (induced by deprivation) was pitted against a constant level of noxious stimulation which the animal had to endure in order to reach food, water, a sexually responsive mate, or its own offspring. The behavioral index of drive strength was the number of times the animal would repeatedly cross the "hot grid" in a given period of time. (It could also have been the highest level of shock intensity that would be tolerated to get the goal.) Typical of the data obtained with this method are the patterns shown in the figure. ■ The motivating effects of thirst are greatest after a short period of de-

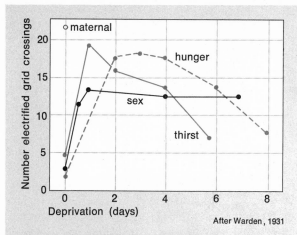

■ You say you would climb the highest mountain, or swim the deepest ocean, but would you cross a hot grid in the Columbia Obstruction Box for me?

privation, then decline, as does hunger, with extreme deprivation. This inverted-U function may, however, reflect primarily the debilitating effect of prolonged deprivation. In contrast, the rats kept on running at a constant rate in order to get a little sex, regardless of length of deprivation (after the first few hours). Surprisingly, mother rats overcame the greatest obstruction in order to retrieve their young. This powerful evidence for the existence of a maternal drive went unchallenged until quite recently, as we shall see.

It is of interest to note two other aspects of these studies. Without deprivation of any kind the animals nevertheless crossed the grid a few times. Furthermore, even when there was nothing on the other side —except a chance to explore the novel environment —they crossed the barrier. This program of research is characteristic of early studies of drive, which focused only on deprivation and ignored the effects of external incentive stimuli on the motivated behavior.

Let us now look at a sampling of the significant facts which have been uncovered about some of the biological drives.

Hunger: The Most Apparent Drive

Of all the motivational states, hunger has received the most study from both psychologists and physiologists.

Eating and its related activities are, of course, quite prominent in the everyday life of all of us, and most theories of motivation have dealt extensively with the phenomena of hunger and eating. To regulate its food intake effectively, an organism must be able to detect the physiological state of hunger, initiate and organize eating behavior, and then stop this behavior when it has ingested enough food. As we shall see, the nature of the internal conditions and regulatory mechanisms associated with hunger and eating—and cessation of eating—are quite complex.

What Makes Us "Hungry"?

Subjectively, we know the feeling of hunger as a mass of sensations seeming to come from the region of the stomach. But just what are the physiological and cognitive changes that produce these sensations? Is the stomach primarily responsible for regulating hunger or are there other factors involved?

One of the prominent early explanations of the hunger sensation came from Walter Cannon, a physiologist. He suspected that the feeling of hunger was triggered by stomach contractions (gastric motility) which occurred when the stomach was empty. The main support for this idea came from an experiment which Cannon performed with Washburn, his research assistant. Cannon persuaded Washburn to swallow a thin rubber balloon attached to a long tube whose free end was connected to a recording device. After the balloon had been inflated, any changes in pressure which were caused by stomach activity were graphically and automatically recorded. Whenever he experienced hunger pangs Washburn pressed a button which activated a marking device, thereby recording the time and frequency of hunger pangs.

Continuous records of stomach behavior over a period of many hours revealed two types of stomach activity: one associated with digestion and another occurring when acute hunger was reported. Only the regular churning movements of digestion were observed immediately after eating, but as the stomach emptied, the contractions associated with hunger set in. They appeared about every hour and a half at first but came more frequently as the length of time without food increased. When the records were examined closely, it was found that Washburn had reported feeling hunger pangs *only* during times of strong stomach contractions. Cannon concluded that the "disagreeable ache" of hunger was actually caused by the vigorous contractions of the empty stomach (Cannon, 1934).

A number of more recent studies using sophisticated recording devices have reported that the classic pattern of stomach activity which Cannon found does not occur until *after* the balloon has been placed in the stomach and inflated (Penick, Smith, Wienske, & Hinkle, 1963). This provides an excellent illustration of the fact that the technique of measurement may affect the thing that is being measured. In this case, the presence of the balloon apparently *caused* the contractions that were measured. Of course, we still cannot discount other evidence that many people do experience the occurrence of hunger pangs.

The early enthusiasm for Cannon's theory quieted as evidence accumulated which was incompatible with the notion that stomach contractions alone were responsible for hunger. If the sensation of hunger and the initiation of eating activities were solely the result of stomach contractions, it should be possible to alter eating behavior drastically by preventing the "message" of stomach contractions from reaching the rest of the body. This, however, is not what occurs; a number of studies, in which the stomachs of animals were surgically removed or the connecting neural pathways severed, showed that the animals continued to eat with only slight changes in their normal feeding patterns. For example, in one experiment, rats whose stomachs had been removed exhibited essentially the same hunger-related behavior that normal animals (used as a control group) did. They learned mazes to obtain food just as quickly as did the controls, and they were equally active as feeding time approached. The only difference was that the rats without stomachs sought food more often than the control animals, which would be expected since they had only their intestines for food storage and hence had to eat more often (Tsang, 1938).

Cofer and Appley (1964) have raised an important point concerning the interpretation of this and similar experiments. Such studies demonstrate only that the *continuation* of already established eating patterns does not depend entirely on stimuli from stomach contractions. It is conceivable, however, that

the organism may have utilized this particular hunger stimulus in the early development of eating patterns, or it may be that an organism normally relies on the stimuli from stomach contractions, but when deprived of this information is able to regulate feeding adequately by use of other cues. Since the animals used in these studies were mature and experienced in eating, it is likely that they had come to associate eating and food-related responses with a variety of both internal and external stimuli. The food-oriented behavior observed after stomach removal may have been part of a previously established habit pattern, elicited and maintained by the presence of various conditioned stimuli. Thus, while stomach contractions probably play some part in the regulation of eating, they are by no means the only, or even the most important, stimuli involved.

Blood chemistry and hunger. The body's immediate source of the energy it needs for cellular functioning is glucose, or blood sugar. Therefore, it has been suggested that chemical changes in blood composition should play a role in hunger.

Early studies showed, for instance, that blood transfused from the body of a starving dog to that of a recently fed one can cause stomach contractions under certain conditions (Luckhardt & Carlson, 1915; Tschukitschew, 1929). It has also been found that transferring blood from a recently fed animal to a starving one stops stomach contractions in the latter (Bash, 1939). More recent research with humans has used the concentration in the bloodstream of plasma-free fatty acids (FFA) as an index of hunger (Dole, 1956). These acids are released from "stored energy food" and their concentration rises in response to increased energy demands on the individual and during fasting. The positive correlation found between FFA levels and fasting suggests that more free fatty acids are normally released into the bloodstream as time after eating passes (Klein, Bogdonoff, Estes, & Shaw, 1960).

When subjects are given an injection of insulin, the glucose level in their blood is lowered, inducing a state known as *hypoglycemia*. Following insulin injections, patients and experimental subjects report feelings of hunger as well as stomach contractions (Goodner & Russell, 1965). Animals given insulin exhibit a variety of food-related instrumental activities (Balagura & Hoebel, 1967).

If glucose deficit induces a state of hunger, then injections of glucose should produce satiation, and they apparently do. Glucose injections inhibit eating in food-deprived animals as well as inhibiting electrical self-stimulation of brain areas presumed to be satiety centers (Mook, 1963; Balagura, 1968a).

How changes in glucose level in the blood are registered in the central nervous system in order to direct behavior is still uncertain. One suggestion is that specialized cells, called *glucoreceptors*, in the stomach, liver, and hypothalamus initiate messages regarding the available glucose levels (Russek, 1963). Because overall blood sugar levels do not correlate well with reports of hunger, it has been proposed (Mayer, 1955) that what is detected as hunger is the difference between the blood sugar levels in the veins and arteries. Following a meal, the level is greater in the arteries than in the veins, but as time since eating increases, the blood sugar levels in the two kinds of vessels become similar and indicate a state of hunger. This interesting theory has yet to be adequately tested.

Does the "feeding center" control hunger? Early evidence, mentioned in Chapter 3, showed that lesions in various parts of the hypothalamus affected not only eating behavior, but other consummatory responses and apparently even some motivated behaviors, such as aggression. This evidence, plus its location at a kind of geographical bottleneck in the brain through which impulses to and from the cortex must funnel, made it seem a logical candidate for central mediator.

The later development of techniques for electrical stimulation of the brain generated an amazing amount of research focusing on the hypothalamus not merely as a mediator but as the control center for hunger and the other biological drives. Stimulation of specific hypothalamic regions was thought to produce drive states which were functionally equivalent to naturally occurring drives. Even food-satiated rats could be motivated by electrical stimulation of the hunger center to learn a new response for which food was the reinforcement (Coons, Levak, & Miller, 1965). This and other sites were assumed to be highly specific in

function, with one region controlling eating, another drinking, another aggression, and so on.

As newer evidence accumulates, however, several troubling conclusions threaten to dethrone the hypothalamus. First, there is a lack of anatomical specificity for a number of consummatory responses. Eating and drinking sites coexist with those for general exploratory behavior. Feeding and drinking areas have also been found in parts of the posterior hypothalamus associated with elicitation of male copulatory behavior (Caggiula, 1970). Moreover, there are a number of areas in the limbic region of the brain which seem to exercise a more specific influence on motivational states than does the hypothalamus. It has been suggested that the hypothalamus may only operate as a "connection center" for these other basic areas (S. P. Grossman, 1968).

If an animal eats food when one hypothalamic site is stimulated, and drinks water when another site is stimulated, obviously the first taps "hunger," the second "thirst." Obvious, but apparently not true, say investigators who performed a simple but very telling experiment.

It was found that when the object initially preferred by a stimulated rat (say, food) was removed from the animal's cage, subsequent stimulation at the same site was just as likely to elicit other forms of consummatory behavior, such as drinking or gnawing on wood (Valenstein, Cox, & Kakolewski, 1968a).

Other studies by these investigators have shown that animals eating in response to hypothalamic stimulation will not switch to a familiar second food when the first is removed—as they do when actually deprived of food. In fact, they will not even switch to another form of the same food, as when pellets are mashed into a powder (Valenstein, Cox, & Kakolewski, 1968b).

The final trouble area for defenders of the hypothalamic theory of motivation is the self-stimulation problem. As we saw in Chapter 5, there are a number of regions of the brain which have been identified as "pleasure centers," and animals will generate extremely high rates of response in order to receive electrical stimulation of such centers. Some investigators have noted that this motivation is so powerful that rats will cross a "hotter" grid in an obstruction box when this stimulation is available on the other side than they will for any other deprivation-incentive condition.

The problem is that the same areas of the lateral hypothalamus that are reinforcing pleasure centers appear also to be drive-producing centers eliciting feeding (Hoebel & Teitelbaum, 1962). How can the same stimulation provide reinforcement and induce eating?

One recently suggested explanation which radically alters the earlier conception of the place of the hypothalamus in motivation is that hypothalamic stimulation does not create hunger, thirst, or other drives directly. Rather, it creates the conditions which excite neural activity underlying a well-established consummatory response; the act of carrying out the response may in itself be reinforcing (Valenstein, Cox, & Kakolewski, 1970).

The issue is far from settled, and although the absolute monarchy of the hypothalamus may be over, selection of a successor awaits advances in physiological technology and behavioral research designs. Nevertheless, the search for the "center of motivation" has revealed a wealth of information about the motivated behavior of organisms.

Inner and outer instigators.   Anyone who has been in the Big Cat house at the zoo around 2:30 on a 3 o'clock feeding day is amazed at how the lions and tigers "know" that dinner time is drawing nigh. They prance, circle, bellow, roar, scratch, and are full of (exciting to watch) activity. Does their hunger drive "drive" them into this state of frenzied activity? Do they have an "internal clock" which is coordinated with the clock in the zoo-keeper's office?

Such basic questions about why it is that motivation seems to heighten an animal's activity have intrigued psychologists, too. Early studies of rats running on activity wheels seemed to agree with the observations of animals in the zoo: food deprivation makes animals more active.

Activation or sensitization?   The simple activation notion was questioned, however, when Campbell and Sheffield (1953) showed that hungry rats were significantly more active than satiated ones *only* when there was a change in environmental stimulation (an increase in light and the cessation of sound from a fan). Perhaps, they reasoned, hunger does not

have a general activating effect, but rather a *sensitizing* effect; that is, the effect of lowering thresholds of response to various kinds of stimulation. If this is the case, activity should be correlated with whatever external stimulation regularly precedes feeding. This is exactly what Sheffield and Campbell (1954) found in their next study. Comparing the activity of two groups of equally deprived rats, they found that hunger increased activity in response to any novel stimuli, but *greatly* increased activity in response to stimuli associated with eating.

It would seem that from an adaptive point of view, increased drive should make organisms *selectively* sensitive to stimuli that signal events related to drive satisfaction and not merely indiscriminately active or sensitive. This appears to be the case from a recent study which compared reactivity of hungry and deprived animals to a range of stimulus change conditions. Hungry animals were more active than nonhungry ones in response to the odor of food but less responsive than the other animals to light and sound (Tapp, Mathewson, D'Encarnacus, & Long, 1970.) ●

Exploratory behavior is one type of activity that appears to be facilitated by hunger. In the wild, where animals must forage for food, it would be

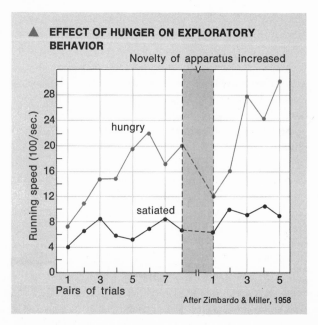

▲ **EFFECT OF HUNGER ON EXPLORATORY BEHAVIOR**

Novelty of apparatus increased

hungry

satiated

Running speed (100/sec.)

Pairs of trials

After Zimbardo & Miller, 1958

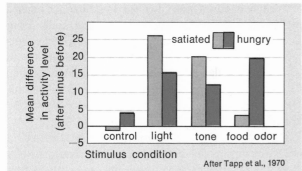

● **THE SMELL OF FOOD BRINGS OUT THE RESTLESS (HUNGRY) BEAST**

The graph compares activity level in hungry and satiated animals before and after the onset of various stimuli. When no stimulus was presented (control), the activity level of satiated animals went down over time, while the activity level of hungry animals showed a slight increase. When a light or a tone was used as the stimulus, the activity level of the satiated animals increased more than that of the hungry animals. When the odor of food was used as the stimulus, however, the activity level of the satiated animals increased only slightly, while the activity of the hungry animals was affected more than in any of the other conditions.

expected that exploration when hungry would have adaptive significance in helping the animal locate food sources.

In a laboratory experiment it was shown that after rats had thoroughly explored one part of their environment, the opportunity to explore a novel compartment was seized upon more by hungry than by satiated rats. With successive trials the hungry animals ran faster from the familiar to the unfamiliar section of a two-compartment box. When the novelty of the environment was increased, their relative speed of entering the unexplored portion increased even more (Zimbardo & Miller, 1958). ▲

The facts of motivation do not often yield the simple generalizations one hopes for in reducing behavior to explanatory principles. Increased drive does increase sensitivity to external stimulation, *but* the effect varies from species to species, is not the same for all other drives as it is for hunger, and depends on what stimuli are being changed and what behaviors are being observed.

Can external cues take charge? How often have you eaten a meal because the clock told you it was the appropriate time to do so, even though you did not feel hungry? Have you ever gotten hungry just from watching others eating some delicious, creamy pastry or from smelling a turkey roasting in the oven or a spicy pizza ready to be cut into mouth-watering pieces? Certainly, external cues such as these sometimes govern when, what, and how much we will eat.

The importance of many of these external hunger cues has been demonstrated in studies of animal behavior. It is known, for example, that the presence of a hungry rat eating can stimulate eating responses in a satiated one. A number of experiments have shown that the more familiar an animal is with the eating situation in which he is being tested, the greater will be the strength of his eating behavior (Bolles, 1967).

External environmental cues may become associated with physiological states through conditioning. These "neutral" cues may subsequently become capable of eliciting food-related responding and even the experience of being hungry. A very interesting experiment by Balagura (1968b) suggests how the physiology of hunger may become linked to external stimuli. After a group of rats had been injected with insulin (the unconditioned stimulus), their food-seeking and consummatory behaviors increased, as we have discussed previously. Once this pattern had been established, the researcher continued the injections, but without the insulin. These preliminary events, which had in the past been normally associated with the UCS of the insulin injection, became conditioned stimuli. The animals reacted to the insulinless injections with the same food-seeking behavior that they had previously shown to the insulin injections. Apparently, the learned association of external cues with the *sudden onset* of the experience of hunger can bring eating under the control of these cues. Under normal circumstances, hunger mounts slowly and is reduced slowly; therefore it is more difficult to establish an association between a specific conditioned stimulus and the unconditioned stimulus. The short hunger cycle in infants may render them more susceptible than adults to environmental modification of food-seeking and eating.

In any case, the feeding-time activity of lions and

tigers is probably best explained by two factors: food odors from preparation of the meat pails, and the increased number of people like us who always arrive just before feeding time. But they still may have a good internal clock operating too. Can you suggest a means of setting up a study to determine whether or not such a factor exists?

Scarcity of food and external sensitivity. Diogenes said, "a rich man eats when he is hungry, a poor man eats when he can." Animals living in an economy of abundance can rely on internal cues to regulate consumption, since food will be available whenever they feel the need for it. But for animals living in an economy of scarcity, the situation is quite different. When food is scarce and available only at irregular intervals, it is more adaptive to eat as much as possible when one has the opportunity, and therefore to be more sensitive to external cues (such as the taste of food) than to internal ones (such as feelings of hunger).

Wild opossums (as well as other species) have been found to be highly sensitive to the taste qualities of their diet and insensitive to internal hunger cues. It has been suggested that rigid caloric regulation is of little value to them, given the irregularity of the food supply, whereas sensitivity to palatability of food would aid in rapid detection of and discrimination between nutrients (Maller, Clark, & Kare, 1965). Hibernating animals also have to eat in excess of their current physiological need before beginning their period of inactivity. Research on snakes has shown that there is *no* relationship between length of deprivation (which may last for months) and amount eaten or speed of initiating eating when food is made available after deprivation (Myer, 1968).

Laboratory rats, however, "eat for calories," maintaining a relatively constant intake in terms of energy requirements. Rats in a wild situation where there is a variable food supply maintain a pattern of internal control by developing the habit of hoarding. By hoarding food when it is available and eating it when he becomes hungry, the animal maintains a steady level of intake (Barnett, 1943). Rats deprived of food early in life show an increased level of hoarding, which persists. into adulthood, regardless of the later abundance of food (Hunt, 1941).

When rats are deprived of food and cannot engage in hoarding, however, control of eating shifts from internal regulation to external regulation. Hungry rats faced with an economy of scarcity will eat more in response to the taste of the food they are given than to the caloric value of the food (Jacobs & Sharma, 1968). In a sense, they become more externally sensitive as they become hungrier.

Gross (1968) has demonstrated that this effect holds for prolonged experience of deprivation (100 days) and continues even when rats are returned to a state of constantly available food. Rats that have been deprived respond to experimental variations in the taste and caloric value of their diet by ignoring the caloric density and "eating for taste." Rats that have been normally fed continue to maintain a steady caloric intake despite taste variations.

What makes us stop eating? How does the hungry organism know when it has eaten enough? The mechanism involved in the cessation of food intake is related to, but different from, that of the initiation of eating. One hypothesis is that "metering" takes place in the mouth as a function of the quantity and taste qualities of the materials passing through it. The validity of this hypothesis has been tested by means of "sham feeding" experiments in which animals are operated upon surgically so that food entering the mouth is chewed and swallowed but passes through an opening in the esophagus and never reaches the stomach (James, 1963). These animals do stop eating, but only after the food intake is much greater than it would have been had the food reached the stomach. Apparently some metering by means of feedback in the mouth occurs, but it is crude and inaccurate.

On the other hand, the rat can regulate its food and water intake perfectly in the absence of taste, smell, or tactile input from the mouth or esophagus.

Investigators placed food directly in the stomachs of rats through an oral-esophageal bypass, thus eliminating taste, smell, and tactile stimulation in the mouth. The animals were taught to use voluntary acts—bar presses in this case—to obtain the intragastric food injections. The animals were able to regulate their food intake, holding their body weights at normal levels (Teitelbaum & Epstein, 1962).

A number of studies have highlighted the dual nature of the hunger satiation mechanism. They have shown that while animals will learn to perform new responses to obtain food rewards injected directly into the stomach, producing stomach fullness and satisfaction of metabolic needs, they learn much more rapidly when the food is taken in normally through the mouth. It is apparent, then, that food metering is facilitated when both oral and gastric factors are involved.

Interestingly, the same research revealed that saccharin was reinforcing only when taken in through the mouth. When it was injected directly into the stomach, it had no more effect on hunger than distilled water. Apparently, then, taste factors are involved in the regulation of eating but only, as we would expect, when food is ingested by mouth.

Despite the vast amount of research on hunger, our relative level of ignorance is still apparent when we realize how little is known about individual differences in the eating behavior of humans, and when we face our inability to cure "problem eaters." Therapists report extreme difficulty in treating people who simply stop eating and starve themselves, presumably due to pathological anxiety. But these cases, called *anorexia nervosa*, are rare compared to their opposite type, *obesity*, in which people literally eat themselves to an early death.

Although food addiction is a more serious health hazard than other types of addictions such as alcohol and drugs (Mayer, 1968), and is a greater problem in terms of the sheer number of people afflicted, there is yet not a single effective weight-reduction program for obesity. As in the case of cigarette smoking (see Chapter 2), almost any program for weight reduction has a short-term effectiveness and a long-term failure, or rebound. Sometimes obese patients have lost as much as 100 pounds while hospitalized and kept on a strictly supervised diet, only to gain it all back just as soon as they are home again (Ψ Close-up, p. 352.)

The selectivity of hunger—specific hungers.   One of the most obvious facts about our normal eating patterns is selectivity—not only do we eat regularly and in accord with our biological needs, but we also show strong preferences in our selection of foods. Probably the most common source of food preference can be traced to ethnic or cultural norms. Each of us has, no doubt, been intrigued by ethnographic reports of the eating customs of exotic cultures, as well as the variety of taste preferences of subgroups even within our own country. For the most part, these preferences or "specific hungers" seem to be somewhat arbitrarily determined, although we do recognize that in economies of scarcity, such as the Eskimo, choice of food such as whale or seal blubber is often determined simply by its availability.

Often, however, specific hungers are the result of biological needs and deficits—the organism seeks out foods which contain substances lacking in its diet. The behavioral effects of *deficiency cravings*, as they are called, are often particularly evident in lower animals which have been deprived of certain necessary substances. For example, rats which have been deprived of thiamine and salt will select foods containing these substances, even when a large variety of foods is available to them (Rozin, 1965). Similar results have been obtained for deficits of calcium, fat, protein, and parts of the vitamin-B complex. Of course, for an animal to be able to regulate adequately the intake of a particular substance, increasing its consumption when the body has been depleted of it, the substance must yield a sensory discrimination for him. That is, he must be able to distinguish foods which contain the needed substance from those which do not.

Dietary self-selection gives further evidence that the body is sensitive not only to the total amount of food intake, but to the many aspects of nutritional balance as well. Many studies have shown that human subjects, as well as lower animals, are able to select their foods in a manner which satisfies specific bodily needs and provides a balanced diet.

In a now classic study, three newly weaned infants were allowed to select their meals from a wide variety of wholesome foods. Two of them selected their foods for six months, the other for a full year. All subjects gained normally and showed no signs of nutritional disorders. In fact, a baby who suffered from rickets at the beginning of the experiment cured himself by choosing large quantities of cod-liver oil, which contains the vitamin D required to overcome rickets. The baby gave up the oil when the rickets had disappeared.

All three babies tended to eat large quantities of one food for a time and then switch to another, going on "egg binges" or "cereal binges." But in the long run, with this cafeteria feeding program, the babies generally did on their own what nutritional experts would have recommended—and obtained a balanced diet. At the end of the study their health and growth were normal (Davis, 1928).

We know that learning and conditioning are ways of instilling habits or predispositions in an organism. What happens, though, when these habits

---

Ψ *Close-up*   *What Happened to the Brakes?*

Schachter (1967), Nisbett (1968), and their colleagues have attempted to determine under what stimulus conditions obese people eat more than normals, and under what conditions they do not. It seems obvious that people become overweight when they are stimulated to eat more often and consume more food than is nutritionally required, and/or when they keep on eating regardless of internal hints to stop. But what cues turn on—or fail to turn off—such eating behavior? The hypothesis has been advanced that the obese person is *more sensitive* than others to external cues related to food, and relatively *insensitive* to internal ones.

Clinical evidence implicates both of these factors. One study found that obese patients ate more as the attractiveness of their physical and social environment was increased. They restricted their diet dramatically, however, when their meals had to be drunk through a tube projecting from a liquid dispenser (Hashim & VanItallie, 1965). In addition, unlike people of normal weight, whose reports of experienced hunger are associated with gastric motility (hunger pangs), there is no correlation among the obese between stomach activity and feeling hungry (Stunkard & Koch, 1964).

In the controlled laboratory research conducted by Schachter, Nisbett, and their students, the eating of overweight college students was compared with that of a comparable normal-weight control group across a wide variety of situations. When their fear was aroused, or their stomachs were preloaded with food, normal subjects reduced their food intake, whereas these internal conditions had no effect on the eating (cracker consumption) of the obese students. On the other hand, obese subjects ate more than normals when given tasty ice cream, but less when the ice cream was bitter.

Obese subjects also ate more than normals when they thought it was dinner time—on the basis of external information rather than their own biological clock. This was shown by using a trick clock which could be speeded up or slowed down. An actual thirty-minute experimental session scheduled near dinner time appeared to last either sixty minutes or only fifteen minutes. The obese ate more when the clock indicated it was 6 P.M. than when it looked like only 5:15 P.M. The normals did not. Also, when a plate of cashews was placed before an obese person, he ate more when they were made salient by either brighter illumination or instructions to think about them. These variations in cue salience did not affect amounts eaten by normal-weight subjects.

It appears from this and other evidence that obesity may be characterized by an oversensitivity to environmental cues which initiate and maintain eating independently of physiological need. In a society of abundance, attractive packaging, good cooking, and time-related eating patterns like that of the technologically advanced United States, it is no wonder that such people overeat and become obese.

These investigators have also been struck with the parallels in behavior patterns between obese humans and overeating (*hyperphagic*) rats. Both show a greater taste sensitivity, greater sensitivity to shock and work/reinforcement payoff schedules, faster sensory reaction times, and less willingness to expend effort in order to get food. It has been suggested that in such individuals a central state is involved which produces a generalized type of "externality"—an overresponsiveness to all external stimuli, food being but one class.

are placed in conflict with the organism's biological needs? Do acquired tastes interfere with the organism's natural ability to choose the type of food that it needs? Answers to these questions are suggested by the following studies.

An organism which has had its adrenal glands removed requires abnormal amounts of salt. Normally rats will ingest extra salt after the removal of the adrenals, preferring salt solutions to glucose solutions when offered a choice. But more "sophisticated" rats that have had experience with both sweet and salty solutions before their operation will choose the glucose and die (Harriman, 1955).

It has also been found that rats deficient in protein will select sucrose rather than protein whenever they are placed in a test situation in which they have formerly selected sucrose. In a new and different test situation, however, they will choose the needed protein. If the experimenter alternates the old and new situations, the rats will alternate in their choice of sucrose. Apparently, the preferential habit for sucrose is strong enough under the original stimulus conditions to override the bodily need for protein. The investigator summarizes these results by noting that preferences based on taste and those based on bodily need may sometimes lead to incompatible selections of foodstuffs and, further, that "habits tend to form in agreement with bodily need but established habits tend to persist regardless of need." (Young, 1961, 1968)

Unfortunately civilized man, like the "educated" rats, has formed many food habits—such as the American taste for candy and soft drinks—which are not in accord with bodily needs. Thus the "wisdom of the body," though remarkable in natural conditions, may be undermined by acquired habits.

When Food Runs Short

Over one third of the world's population lives under conditions of famine or semistarvation, yet relatively little investigation has been done concerning the effects of chronically inadequate food intake on human behavior and human life. How does the body adapt itself to such an experience? What are the psychological consequences of semistarvation? One rather elaborate laboratory study, conducted during World War II, answers some of these questions.

Thirty-six volunteer subjects participated in the study, which lasted nearly a year. The experiment consisted of three phases: (a) a twelve-week control period, during which the subjects received a well-balanced diet designed to represent the fare eaten under good economic conditions in the United States; (b) a twenty-four-week semistarvation period, during which the subjects were maintained on a diet characteristic of European famine areas; and (c) a twelve-week rehabilitation period, during which the subjects were carefully nourished back toward normal. The experimental semi-starvation diet consisted mainly of bread, macaroni, potatoes, turnips, and cabbage. It provided only 1570 calories a day, less than half the calories of the "normal" diet received during the control period. ■

Throughout the experiment the subjects were kept on a full-time weekly schedule of physical exercise, maintenance of the living quarters, and educational activities. Each subject was given regular physiological and psychological checkups (Keys et al., 1950).

■ During the semistarvation period of the experiment, the hunger drive became the most important factor affecting the subject's behavior. The men became unsociable, frequently ignoring such amenities as table manners.

The physical changes produced by the twenty-four-week period of semistarvation were, of course, profound. As the body struggled to adapt to the severely restricted caloric intake (resulting in an average weight loss of 25 percent), marked changes took place in the energy allotments for various bodily functions. During the control period it was established that an approximately equal number of calories were used in the performance of both basal metabolic functions and voluntary physical activity—slightly less than 50 percent of the total calories going to each. At the end of the starvation period, however, it was found that approximately 60 percent of the now reduced caloric intake was used in basal metabolic functions while less than 30 percent was devoted to physical activity. The body appeared to have adjusted in the most adaptive way possible, with a larger percentage of the lowered total number of calories going into essential body maintenance and a correspondingly smaller percentage into voluntary (thus expendable) physical activity (Brozek, 1963).

The authors of the study adopted the term "semistarvation neurosis" to describe the striking personality changes that appeared as a result of the semistarvation and then disappeared when the subjects returned to a normal diet. The outstanding characteristic of the "neurosis" was apathy. Humor disappeared, a depressing air of gloom and dejection appearing in its place. There was also a marked decrease in sociability. The men became nervous and irritable, tended to be boorish and tactless, dressed sloppily, and were inclined to "blow up" at each other. Self-confidence was replaced by feelings of inferiority and depression.

In addition, sexual urges decreased markedly and were slow to return during the rehabilitation period. Subjects "cooled" noticeably toward their girl friends and courtships collapsed. The men seemed practically incapable of displaying affection.

Tests of intellectual capacity administered at different times throughout the study failed to reveal any marked changes, although the subjects' general level of performance on such tests did decrease slightly, probably due to general physical impairment. Because of their constant preoccupation with thoughts of food and their inability to concentrate on other things, the subjects became convinced that they were actually suffering a decline in intelligence.

There can be no doubt that by the end of the semistarvation period the hunger drive had become the dominant factor in the subjects' lives. Food, either directly or indirectly, dominated their conversation,

reading, leisure activities, and daydreams. Many of the men devoted their spare moments to reading cookbooks and collecting recipes; some seriously considered changing their occupations and becoming cooks (Keys et al., 1950; Guetzkow & Bowman, 1946).

It is interesting to note that many of these very same clinical symptoms have been manifested by chronically obese persons (often weighing over 300 pounds) who have been hospitalized and placed on reduced diets over an extended period. "Dietary depression," the overweights' analogue of semistarvation neurosis, consists of acute depression, withdrawal, overt hostility, and generalized anxiety. These patients also report intense feelings of hunger and are preoccupied with thoughts of food and eating, both in their waking fantasies and in the manifest content of their dreams (Gluckman & Hirsch, 1968).

Awareness of hunger is much more insistent under conditions of semistarvation than with total fasting. After several days of complete abstinence from food, hunger disappears almost entirely, but in cases of prolonged semistarvation, where a small but inadequate amount of food is available, the craving for food grows increasingly until it dominates the individual's consciousness and behavior. This fact has been utilized by some physicians in designing dietary programs for their extremely obese patients. Instead of the usual extended period of reduced caloric intake, these doctors have interspersed short periods of total fasting with periods of normal food consumption. So far, this technique seems to have successfully avoided many of the unpleasant side effects of semistarvation reported above.

Other Maintenance Drives

While hunger is perhaps the most obvious of the physiological drives, and the easiest to study, there are other drives that are equally vital. Chief among these are air hunger—the need for oxygen—and thirst. But if the organism is to survive in a sometimes hostile environment, it has other needs as well. These include, for most higher animals, the need for sleep, the maintenance of a fairly constant body temperature, and the protection of the body from physical harm. In this section we shall discuss three examples of such needs—thirst, temperature control, and the phenomenon of pain.

Thirst

Although man can live for weeks without food, he can survive only a few days without water. Men who have been completely deprived of both food and water for long periods of time report that the sensations of thirst soon become maddening, whereas the pangs of hunger tend to disappear after a few days. King (1878) described the intense suffering experienced by a detachment of the U.S. Cavalry deprived of water for eighty-six hours in the Texas desert. When at last they had the opportunity to drink, "although water was imbibed again and again, even to repletion of the stomach, it did not assuage their insatiable thirst."

Effects of thirst. Hunger and thirst not only differ in intensity but also seem to have qualitatively different effects on behavior, at least in lower animals. In experiments with rats it has been found that thirsty animals will learn to find a reward of water more quickly than hungry ones learn to find food, at least when the rewards are in the same location in the maze. However, when the rats have to learn to go to different goal locations on alternate trials, the hungry rats learn to alternate between the two locations much more readily than do the thirsty ones (Petrinovich & Bolles, 1954). This suggests that the motivational state of hunger leads to variability in behavior, whereas thirst facilitates stereotyped responding. An interpretation of this result could be provided in terms of the adaptive significance of these behavior patterns. The natural environment of the rat is one in which the animal is usually forced to explore and forage for its food, while the location of its water supply usually remains relatively fixed.

The physiology of thirst. A parched or dry feeling in the mouth and throat seems to be a sufficient stimulus for the initiation of drinking. As the water supply in the body becomes low, the tissues of the mouth become dry; to alleviate this dryness, the organism drinks. ● Studies using the technique of

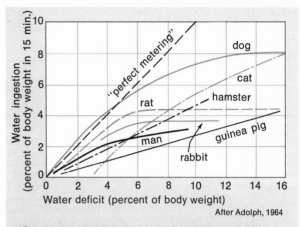

After Adolph, 1964

● **WATER METERING IN DIFFERENT SPECIES**

The graph shows the relationship between water deficit and water consumption in different species. The line marked "perfect metering" represents a hypothetical case in which the animal drinks exactly as much water as his body requires. Dogs exhibit almost perfect metering, while other species show less sensitive metering either at all levels of deficit or after some critical level of water deficit has been reached. It is clear from these findings that the animal's species must be taken into account when making conclusions about thirst based on water consumption.

preloading, in which an animal's stomach is injected with a large quantity of water, show that an animal which has been prevented from drinking will start and continue to drink (at a reduced rate), even though its stomach may have been preloaded to twice the normal drinking capacity (Moyer & Bunnell, 1962). This would suggest that at least one set of cues involved in the initiation of drinking is oral.

But water metering by mouth is not a necessary condition for regulation of water intake. When thirsty rats must learn to press a bar in order to receive water injections directly into their stomach, they soon maintain normal levels of water intake (Teitelbaum & Epstein, 1962). Thus water regulation is still possible without feedback from the mouth or throat, and gastric factors must also be involved. However, it appears that thirst is reduced to a greater extent when water is drunk by mouth than when the same amount is passed directly into the animal's stomach. Using, as an index of thirst, the rate of bar pressing for water reinforcement, Neal Miller (1957) reports that among deprived rats, those given no water pressed at the highest rate, a group given 14 cc. water by injection into the stomach was next, and a group receiving 14 cc. water by mouth pressed least.

Biologically, of course, an animal does not drink simply in order to moisten its mouth or fill its stomach with water. Rather, there is a delicate balance of body fluids which is preserved by an interrelated system of physiological processes. All animals keep losing fluids through perspiration, excretion, and so on, whether or not they are allowed to replenish their supply. With continued deprivation, the extracellular fluids which bathe the cells of the body become depleted, and the concentration of a number of substances, mainly sodium and chloride, increases in the extracellular fluids. Osmotic pressure then drains water from within the cells into the extracellular fluid. Dehydration within the cells themselves occurs with continued deprivation. Wolf (1958) refers to tissue dehydration as "true thirst," distinguishing it from local dryness in the mouth and throat, or "false thirst."

The most prominent explanation of the homeostatic control of thirst postulates the existence of *osmoreceptors*—special receptor cells, probably located in the hypothalamus, which respond to signals of increased osmotic pressure by initiating drinking. Support for this theory comes primarily from studies in which salt solutions are injected into the body and increased drinking results, even when the animal has been satiated with water immediately prior to the injections (Fitzsimmons & Oatley, 1968).

As a complete explanation of thirst, however, the osmoreceptor theory is found wanting. For example, the exact mechanism by which the receptors cue the rest of the body that the time to begin drinking has come, is as yet unknown. In addition, as Bolles (1967) has pointed out, there are a number of phenomena inconsistent with the theory: a perspiring man (losing salt) will drink water, even though this further increases osmotic imbalance, and animals depleted of salt increase rather than decrease their water intake (Falk, 1965).

The intricacy of the timing of water intake and return of water to the cells from the extracellular fluid is remarkable. An animal will stop drinking before any appreciable amount of water has left its stomach (thereby diluting the salt concentration in the extracellular fluid). When an investigator implanted a sensitive recording apparatus in the brains of thirsty rats he found that hydration (return of fluids to the cells) begins almost as soon as water reaches the stomach (Novin, 1962). In some way, there is an anticipation that liquid will be available to add to the extracellular fluid, and water is released to the cells *before* it is paid back by the stomach's supply.

External stimuli in drinking. Man very often drinks for "social" reasons, rather than to satisfy a thirst drive. In fact, there are people who pride themselves on never drinking water, preferring to let their body extract it from the highballs that they drink. Drinking has been shown to be regulated by a wide variety of associative factors which are independent of cellular dehydration or other physiological aspects of "true thirst."

Rats will drink more in situations that have remained constant than in situations that have changed. Their drinking can become so controlled by regularly occurring drinking times that their water intake becomes independent of deprivation state (Collier, 1962). In man, drinking is a usual accompaniment of eating ("a jug of wine, a loaf of bread . . ."). The two processes may become associated so that once either drinking or eating is begun, it becomes a cue-producing response, eliciting the other behavior.

An ingenious series of experiments illustrates the extent to which consummatory behavior may be brought under the control of other stimuli, even other motivational states. The experimenter was able to get rats to consume large quantities of water by making the termination of painful shock contingent on drinking. To avoid receiving the shocks, rats learned to drink far beyond the point of satisfaction or that required by bodily needs. Hunger as well as shock was used to induce drinking. Hungry rats were trained to drink enormous quantities of water simply by feeding them only after they had drunk some water (Teitelbaum, 1966).

It is obvious that this conditioning paradigm can be extended to make any consummatory behavior contingent upon any other drive or stimulus pattern. Housewives who complain that they eat more when they are around the house and feeling anxious may be eating *not* because anxiety distracts them from other tasks, but because the distraction provided by eating keeps them from concentrating on anxiety-provoking thoughts.

On the other hand, consummatory behavior can be inhibited by making an unpleasant event contingent upon its occurrence. This principle is being employed by behavior therapists attempting to treat patients who have problems controlling eating, drinking, smoking, or sexual behavior they consider unacceptable. The thought or action associated with the consummatory behavior is paired with an aversive consequence such as shock, induced nausea, or an unpleasant image. In Chapter 15 we will discuss this approach, and others, to the problems created by inappropriate relationships among behavior, motives, and values.

In any event thirst, like hunger and other drives, is evidently not the single, unitary intervening variable researchers once hoped to find. It is conceptualized now as a heterogeneous cluster involving many neural centers which are "differentially affected by various regulators and have differential effects on various response systems" (N. Miller, 1957, p. 1275).

Keeping Cool: The Need to Regulate Body Temperature

Everybody talks about the weather, and, contrary to the popular saying, we all do something about it. In addition to our attempts to change the weather directly (by seeding clouds to produce rain, for example), we change the effects weather has on us by internal alteration of our body physiology and external alteration of our environment. There is little doubt that although man *can* adapt to the intense heat of the tropics or the freezing cold of the arctic, he has a need to avoid excessive warmth and cold. Some environmental determinists argue that man's technological and intellectual achievements have come from cultures in the temperate zones of the world and would not have occurred if the climate had been chronically hot or cold. After living through a humid, hot summer on our eastern or southern coasts, students are often ready to accept such an assertion.

But what is the physiological origin of this motivation to avoid extreme temperatures, to maintain a constant body temperature, and to devise ways of controlling heat and cold?

Control through balance of heat produced and heat lost. Humans are *homeothermic*, that is, they maintain a relatively constant body temperature, even when the environmental temperature fluctuates widely. A large percentage of the cells in the body are involved in *metabolism*—the production of energy and heat. Much of the heat which is produced, however, is continually lost to the surrounding environment. The process of temperature regulation required to maintain a stable body temperature, then, involves a balancing of heat produced by metabolism and heat lost to the environment.

We detect cold and warmth because of temperature-sensitive receptors in the skin which respond to the addition or subtraction of heat from the prevailing temperature level of the skin—called *physiological zero* or the *indifference point*. When we feel cold (as the external temperature falls below 57° F) a number of physiological processes are stimulated. Increased secretion of thyroxin and adrenaline helps bring about increased muscular activity (shivering), which speeds up heat production. The blood vessels at the surface of the body constrict (*vasoconstriction*), driving blood to the deeper tissues where heat loss is not so great. On the other hand, the reaction to high external temperatures is largely the opposite. Blood vessels near the body surface dilate (*vasodilation*), exposing a greater volume of blood to the outer surfaces of the body where heat loss is greatest. The circulation rate is increased to send blood through this "cooling system" faster. And perspiration, which helps cool the body surfaces, is initiated.

However, the metabolism of the human body, with its unavoidable heat production, makes it by its very nature a furnace, not a refrigeration unit. It can be quite easily speeded up in response to environmental cold, but it is not very effectively made into a cooling system. This is why humans and other homeotherms can exist comfortably in constant environmental temperatures twenty to thirty degrees below their body temperatures, but are able to withstand environmental temperatures which are more than a few degrees above their own for only short periods of time (Keeton, 1967).

Control through behavior. Perspiration, vasodilation, vasoconstriction, shivering, and increased metabolic activity are all physiological adjustments made automatically in response to variations in external temperature. Often, however, when these automatic physiological processes are not sufficient, *behavioral thermoregulation* occurs. Electric fans, air conditioners, ice cubes, central heating, hot drinks, and overcoats are all examples of behavioral thermoregulation —things we design to keep our bodies at a comfortable temperature. The frequent use of voluntary behavior to supplement our physiological homeostatic controls provides excellent evidence that humans are truly motivated to maintain stable body temperatures. A human being could never have journeyed to and walked on the moon were it not for the ability of scientists to devise materials to shield his fragile body from unbelievable extremes of temperature.

The behavioral regulation of temperature is not restricted to humans. Many studies have shown that rats subjected to low temperatures will learn to press a bar that turns on a heat lamp, thus warming themselves (Weiss & Laties, 1961). In fact, rats put into an overheated chamber will even learn to pull a lever which will give them a shower. The moist spray is used by the animals to cool their skin surface (through evaporation) and not necessarily as drinking water because they will continue working to get the spray even when it is a bitter quinine shower (Epstein & Milestone, 1968). ◆

◆ The photo on the left shows the heat reinforcement apparatus developed by Weiss and Laties. When the cold rat presses the lever, a switch is closed, turning on the heat lamp at the top. On the right is Epstein's shower apparatus. The hot rat can give himself a cooling shower by pressing the lever.

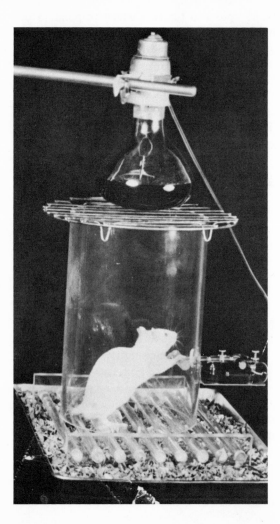

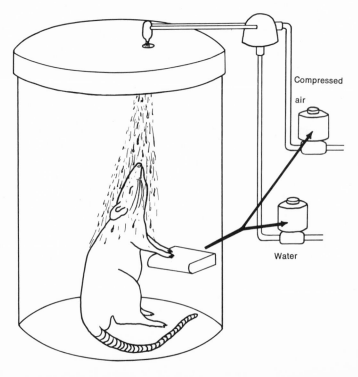

Goldfish, too, will learn a new behavioral response which will aid in controlling the temperature of their environment. In one experiment fish kept in an overheated water tank learned to press a button which delivered a brief flow of cool water into the tank. Once this operant response was strengthened by the cool water reinforcement, its rate and vigor increased. This is a remarkable example of total behavioral thermoregulation since fish, being "cold blooded," have evolved no physiological mechanisms for temperature regulation and are thus totally at the mercy of the environment (Rozin & Mayer, 1961).

A hot hypothalamus blows its cool.   The ubiquitous role of the hypothalamus in motivation is also evident in thermoregulation. Psychologists have found that cooling of the anterior part of the hypothalamus elicits shivering in some species, while heating the same area will produce vasodilation and panting. It appears that these changes are not simply reflexes, but are accompanied by a motivational state, since the animals will perform work to regain a stable temperature in their hypothalamus. Rats learn quickly to press a bar to turn on an infrared heat lamp if their hypothalamus is cooled, or turn off the lamp if the hypothalamus is heated. Such bar pressing will occur irrespective of room or body temperature, suggesting that the temperature of the hypothalamus can become the dominant stimulus in thermal control.

Even when the anterior hypothalamus was lesioned, so that they could no longer maintain their falling body temperature by physiological readjustments, rats were able to learn a behavioral response which turned on a heat lamp and stabilized their body temperature (Satinoff & Rutstein, 1970). Evidently homeostatic regulation need not depend entirely on the hypothalamus, important as it is in temperature regulation.

Pain

Perhaps the most eloquent definition of pain is that it is "a hurt we feel" (Sternbach, 1968). It is a hurt that may come from tissue damage caused by external conditions—stubbing one's toe, burning a finger on a hot stove, being hit hard, or receiving a gun or knife wound. But it also comes, as we know only too well, from "inside" us, in the form of toothaches, headaches,

menstrual cramps, arthritic pain, or the intractable pain accompanying terminal cancer. Our susceptibility to pain often leads to the speculation of how wonderful it would be if we could feel no pain. Imagine living with immunity from pain!

A moment's reflection shatters this fantasy, for the ability to experience pain, and its motivating properties, is actually one of Nature's most valuable gifts to us. People born with an insensitivity to pain—and a few are—must live a precarious life. Even stimulation which is doing severe damage to part of their body goes unnoticed unless it is visually perceived and responded to in an intellectually learned way (Critchley, 1956; Dearborn, 1932). Pain should be viewed as: (a) a signal system which has evolved to warn us of assaults on the integrity of the body and (b) a defensive system triggering automatic withdrawal reflexes as well as motivated avoidance and escape behaviors. As such, it is indispensable in coping with the vicissitudes of an occasionally hostile environment and with the diseases and eventual deterioration of the living matter that is our body.

Private pain and "public" pain.   The privateness of your experience of pain becomes apparent when you try to explain the hurt you feel to someone else. How would you ever communicate what your pain is to someone who could feel no pain? The subjectivity of pain is comparable to that of dreams, memory, and perception. But as we noted in our discussion of those phenomena, there is a distinction made between the experience and the behavior. Pain as experience is not a public, reproducible event, therefore is not subject to objective, scientific analysis, whereas pain as nerve cell activity or overt motor responses can be objectively described and studied analytically.

Is pain produced by tissue damage from a known stimulus more "real" than pain where the stimulus is unknown, or maybe only a thought or an image? Pain can be described in different languages: neurological, physiological, behavioral, and affective, but none of these is a "truer" description of "pain" than the others. They are merely parallel ways of talking about pain, using abstract conceptions.

Pain as a neurological event.   The stimulus which initiates the pattern of neurological pain responses is an intense or rapid change in physical energy capable of producing tissue damage. It appears that there are not specialized pain receptors, but that undifferentiated free nerve endings distributed throughout the body are responsible for pain reception. These impulses are transmitted by two different types of fibers of different diameter and different degrees of myelination (see p. 71). Fast-traveling, "bright," pricking pain sensations of different quality are carried by phylogenetically newer, myelinated fibers, while slower, dull, chronically aching pain is carried by older, unmyelinated fibers (Bishop, 1962).

Bundles of these fibers form nerves which enter the dorsal root of the spinal cord and, after synapsing, send impulses up various spinal tracts. The thalamus is the end of the line for all incoming pain signals, although pain fibers in the spinal tracts also communicate with the reticular formation. Pain fibers in the head carry signals to the thalamus via the sensory nucleus of one of the cranial nerves.

This view of the specificity of pain input, pain structures, and pain responses, however, does not do justice to the complexity and subtlety of the process of perceiving and controlling pain. Melzack and Wall (1965) have advanced a "gate-control" theory which effectively integrates a variety of the paradoxes of pain, and accounts for both the specificity and patterning of pain. They propose a two-unit, control-feedback system which continuously interacts to modulate any pain input. Cells at each level of the spinal cord act as a gate-control system changing the receptivity of transmission cells to incoming signals from the peripheral nerves. They in turn are influenced by a central control trigger mechanism (in the thalamus and other subcortical areas of the brain). This central control can inhibit afferent input by efferent processes.

Other languages for describing pain. Pain can also be described in terms of the physiological responses it induces. In general, their function is to prepare the body for action to avoid or escape damage. Specific effects vary but may include an inhibition of gastrointestinal activity, higher oxygen consumption, increased muscle tension, more blood to the stimulated area, and constriction of the arteries.

At a *behavioral* level, pain tolerance decreases when there is lowered sensory input and frequent exposure to pain. Tolerance for pain can be increased by distraction, relaxation, motivating instructions, or group identification. Complaints of pain vary with ethnic group membership. Pain can also be shown to disrupt performance and to stimulate aggression.

The *affective* description of pain stresses the association of pain with anxiety, depression, loss of parental love, "regressive" needs for punishment and guilt-reduction, and the interpersonal communication of hurt.

In attempting to integrate the diverse body of research on pain and develop a core set of elements that characterize pain, Sternbach (1968) proposes that an individual's reaction to pain involves: (a) his perceptual coping style, especially the way he responds to anxiety, (b) the learned association of physical stimuli which cause pain reactions with the social context in which the pain occurs, and (c) the internal sensory modification of these pain responses by various cognitive inputs.

Psychological aspects of pain. In the next chapter, we will examine how pain can be controlled by cognitive processes. Before concluding this section, it may be instructive to consider two deviant uses of pain motivation: pain as torture and pain as pleasure.

Pain as torture. During the Inquisitions that took place throughout Europe in the Middle Ages, it was believed that devils were very sensitive to pain. This belief provided the justification for subjecting women thought to be witches and men possessed of Satan to unbelievable tortures. If the victims reacted with expressions of pain—as they invariably did—they identified themselves as devils and were executed. "From the thirteenth and fourteenth centuries downwards such was the reign of terror that we find persons of the highest condition abandon rank, fortune, everything, the moment they were accused, and take flight" (Michelet, 1962, pp. 314-315).

As the church-state yielded power to the police-state, the motivating effect of pain was attributed not to satanic forces but to the distinct weakness of human flesh. The rack and iron boot gave way to the abuses of the "third degree": water tortures, exposure to the desert sun, and the like. However, man also realized the psychological determinants of pain, especially the pain arising from social isolation. In earlier centuries offenders were walled up permanently with only a slit through which daily bread was thrown in. This torture, ironically called the *in pace* (place of peace), successively became the solitary confinement of our penal institutions and, more recently, the psychological isolation used as part of the program of "brainwashing" practiced by the Chinese Communists during the Korean War (Schein, 1965).

Pain as pleasure. It is easy for us to identify pain as an inevitable outcome of torture, but pain as a source of pleasure is a less obvious relationship. Yet, from the earliest days of the Christian church, we have the writings of mystics who believed that by enduring pain one could transcend the bodily senses and attain a higher state of being. The barrier between pain and pleasure disappeared when suffering for God became

▋ In this famous statue, Bernini has depicted the ecstasy experienced by St. Teresa. It seemed, she recorded in her autobiography, that an angel was piercing her heart with a fiery spear, "and so excessive was the sweetness caused me by this intense pain that no one can ever wish to lose it."

the ultimate experience to which one could aspire in this mortal life. ▪

" 'Whip me,' said the masochist. 'No,' replied the sadist gleefully." The nineteenth-century writings of Leopold von Sacher-Masoch and the Marquis de Sade gave names to the perverse sexual pleasure that some individuals derive from the infliction of pain on themselves or a sexual partner. It has been suggested that one-trial conditioning may be responsible for cases in which the experience of pain becomes essential for sexual gratification. In discussing the origins of this behavior pattern, Paul Gebhard (1965), of Kinsey's Institute for Sex Research, points to the occurrence of an unusual combination of situational factors experienced by an adolescent coming into puberty. He cites the case of a boy who had fractured his arm. While it was being hurriedly set without anesthesia, the physician's attractive nurse caressed the boy and held his head against her breast. This experience of a "powerful and curious combination of pain and sexual arousal" influenced not only his adult attraction to women who had a hair style similar to the nurse's, but his heterosexual relations, which were marked by both sadistic and masochistic tendencies.

"(Another) case is that of an individual, now in his thirties, who, when nearing puberty, had not as yet recognized sexual arousal. He became involved in a childhood tussle with a girl somewhat larger and more powerful than he. While struggling and wriggling beneath her he experienced not only his first conscious sexual arousal but in a strong degree. This one experience has dominated his life ever since. He has always been attracted to large, muscular, dominant females; and in his heterosexual contacts he tries to arrange the same wrestling. He has, not surprisingly, developed some masochistic attributes." (Gebhard, 1965, p. 489)

The Sexual Drive

Everybody thinks about s-x, and most people spend a lifetime doing something or other about it. Once the individual's basic survival needs are satisfied, sexually motivated behavior becomes a dominant force in shaping the life of the individual and the society. In the study by Cameron and his colleagues cited previously, for example, it was found that about a quarter of the time college students were attending a freshman lecture course, they were actually engaged in daydreaming about sex (Cameron et al., 1968).

Despite the significance of the sexual drive, it has not received the scientific attention it merits. In large part this has been due to potent cultural restrictions directed against any discussion of sex—even as the object of basic research. Most of our scientific knowledge of the determinants of sexual arousal and the patterns of sexual response comes from three sources: anthropological studies of "primitive" peoples, ethological field studies of courtship and mating among animals, and some controlled investigations of physiological and experiential factors in infrahuman sex (notably pioneered by Frank Beach, 1948).

Until a few decades ago the study of human sexual behavior was primarily limited to the clinical and anecdotal reporting of sexual abnormalities, as in the classic work on perversion by Krafft-Ebing (1932). The investigation into normal sexual behavior in man was given an impetus by the work of Kinsey and his colleagues (1948, 1953), although the data collected were limited to interview reports. It remained for the team of William Masters and Virginia Johnson (1966, 1970) to break down the traditional taboo by directly observing and recording the physiological and behavioral patterns involved in human sexual intercourse and sexual inadequacy.

It is expected that the next decade will see a many-fold increase in our scientific knowledge about the nature of the sexual drive in human beings. It will also be interesting to observe whether changes in social mores and legal definitions of what constitutes "acceptable" sexual behavior will change the pervasive impact that sex motivation has on our behavior. Currently, sex sells not only itself (in the form of prostitution and pornography) but virtually anything it can be associated with, from girlie magazines and entertainment to automobiles, cigarettes, and even food. Ernest Dichter (1964), president of the Institute for Motivational Research, reports that:

"In our studies we found fascinating contrasts in the sex attributes of food. Rice is considered feminine, but potatoes are masculine; tea is feminine, and coffee is strongly masculine. The two extremes are meat and cake, the latter being the most feminine of foods. Some foods are bisexual, among them roast chicken and oranges." (p. 66)

Will man become more hedonistic and dominated by sexual passion or less preoccupied and influenced by the lure of sex, as the "sexual revolution" of the seventies gains strength? What do you predict will be the long-range consequences of more liberal abortion, pornography, and sexual-deviance laws; of sex education in the schools, free-sex leagues, computer-arranged mating, communal marriages, public nudity, birth-control pills, and coed dorms?

What Makes Sex Different from All Other Drives?

There are a number of ways in which the sexual drive occupies a unique place in our analysis of motivation.

1. It is not essential to individual survival, as celibacy indicates; it is an "altruistic" means to the end of ensuring racial survival.

2. Its arousal is independent of deprivation operations except for a variable refractory period after the male has ejaculated.

3. It can be aroused by almost any conceivable stimulus.

4. Arousal of the drive is as actively sought as reduction.

5. It will motivate an unusually wide variety of behaviors and psychological processes.

6. It is not clear what constitutes the terminal goal response, making its status as a homeostatic function questionable.

What Do You Mean, "Sex"?

It is surprising to note that researchers studying "sexual behavior" are not at all in agreement as to what constitutes "sexual." Some see as fundamental only the exchange of gametes in the act of mating; others maintain that copulation in heterosexual intercourse is what sex is all about. But insemination and copulation are only a small part of a larger, complex pattern which includes attracting a mate (using appropriate "display tactics"), courtship, foreplay, nest building, and care of the young produced by the sexual union. Still other investigators, from a different vantage point, stress the *gender-role* and the learning experiences that define what is masculine or feminine behavior.

Within these general classifications of what is meant by "sexual" are the specific behaviors actually observed. Each component of the sexual act is a behavior which has its own initiating stimuli, and which may be affected differentially by various neural, hormonal, and environmental conditions. For example, in the analysis of the "simple" sexual behavior of the male rat, one could record the latency, duration, and/or frequencies of attempted mounts, actual mounts, intromissions, ejaculations, and recycling of this sequence. The description and measurement of sexual behavior should be as objective, quantified, and explicit as possible with regard to the particular response units or patterns that have been selected for observation.

How Do You Know Whether You Are ♂ or ♀?

What sex you are may be as obvious to you as what is meant by sexual behavior. However, your confidence depends on a number of different variables of sex which you assume are congruent. They are: (a) genetic sex, determined by the XX (♀) or XY (♂) chromosome constitution, (b) hormonal sex, determined by a predominance of androgens (♂) or estrogens (♀), (c) gonadal sex, determined by the presence of testes or ovaries, (d) reproductive sex, determined by internal reproductive organs, (e) physical (morphological) sex, determined by external genitals, (f) assigned sex, determined by parents and doctors, and (g) psychological sex or gender-role, determined by learned masculine or feminine identification.

Normally, of course, all of these determinants of sex are in agreement. But occasionally, experiments of nature mix these variables into combinations which are incongruent, thereby producing a *hermaphrodite*: "an individual in whom there exists a contradiction between the predominant external genital appearance on the one hand, and the sex chromosome pattern, gonads, hormones, or internal reproductive structures, either singly or in combination, on the other." (Hampson, 1965, p. 110) The existence of hermaphrodism indicates that sexual *differentiation* is not complete at birth, or for some time thereafter.

There is a critical period in the establishment of such differentiation. It appears that about the time a child learns its native language may be the latest period when sex reassignment of hermaphrodite children is possible without psychological maladjustment. Evidence from cases in which children's initial sex assignment was later changed by their parents indicates that the later the point at which those changes are made, the greater the likelihood of disturbance in sexual and personality functioning (Hampson, 1965).

During embryonic development, sexual differentiation can be interfered with by administration of hormones or removal of the sex glands (castration) in mammals. Experiments with castration of genetic male rabbits before the 24th embryonic day resulted in a feminization of the reproductive system. Castration after the 24th day, however, did not affect masculine differentiation, thus establishing a highly specific critical period (Jost, cited in Jones & Scott, 1958). At another critical period in embryonic life, *androgen* is necessary as an active organizer substance (see Chapter 3) for masculine genitalia and internal reproductive organs to develop. ". . . Without androgen, nature's primary impulse is to make a female—morphologically speaking at least." (Money, 1965, p. 8)

The degree to which "boys will be boys" and "girls will be ladies" is strongly influenced by early parental child-rearing practices, which help support or distort appropriate gender-role development.

One study of four-year-old children showed that those of both sexes tend to become more "feminized" as a consequence of any of the following conditions during the first four years: (a) father's anxiety about sex, (b) mother's punitiveness and nonpermissive attitudes toward aggression, (c) high degree of physical punishment and ridicule, (d) severe weaning, toilet training, and demands for table manners. A girl became more "masculinized" as a consequence of the father's behavior toward her if: he had been involved in taking care of her in infancy, was highly affectionate, rewarded her for being dependent, was permissive and praising, but was more distant from her by the time she was four years old (Sears, 1965).

Another critical period during which environmental factors have a powerful effect on sex-role establishment, at least in males, is the time of puberty (Gebhard, 1965).

Sexual Behavior Patterns

The patterns of overt sexual response in animals are remarkable for their *inter*species variability and their *intra*species consistency. However, the unlimited imagination of man, the empiricist, provides for an enormous range of sexual behavior patterns.

The influence of the estrogens on the female sex urge is most clearly seen in the lower mammals. At ovulation, when the bloodstream becomes enriched with estrogens, the female animal loses her previous indifference to the male and becomes highly receptive or even aggressively suggestive in her sexual behavior. This behavior is known as *estrus*, or "heat," and is a signal that the female animal is in a condition of readiness for pregnancy. The behavioral signals to the male are species-specific stereotyped responses designed to attract and focus his attention on the female's genital region. Human females, not under such internal hormonal control, present such reliable readiness cues to males only voluntarily, depending upon a host of learned factors.

The sexual response in animals is also under the influence of odor cues, especially in females. The name given this "sweet smell of sex" is *pheromone*. Crowding together of female mice can induce pseudo-pregnancies—which are prevented if their olfactory bulbs are removed. Inseminated female mice will not become pregnant if they are made to smell the urine odor of a mature male mouse other than the original stud. This pregnancy block occurs with a greater frequency if the male odor is from an alien strain. Male rhesus monkeys show sex-related physiological changes such as increase in testes' size when they smell the estrus odor of females in adjacent cages who have been brought into heat through hormone injections. A sexually potent male mouse introduced into a cage of female mice will initiate a "recycling" of estrus in the females; most of them will go into estrus at once (Parkes & Bruce, 1961).

The variability in copulation can be seen from a few examples: apes remain linked in copulation for only about fifteen seconds, sables for as long as eight hours. Predators such as bears and lions copulate for hours, while prey such as antelope copulate for a few seconds at most, while on the run. The male rat engages in a series of ten to twenty successive, brief intromissions before ejaculating. The frequency of intercourse in humans reported in the Kinsey research varies from as much as ten to fifteen times a day to occasional holiday specials. While most mammals use the dorsal-ventral (rear entry) sex position, humans more typically adopt the face-to-face position.

The arousal of sexual response patterns results in a complex stimulus-response chaining between the male and the female which must be coordinated for successful insemination to occur (Schein & Hale, 1965). • One of the most frequent complaints and sources of frustration among married women is the lack of synchronicity with their husbands in rates of arousal and timing of orgasm.

The importance of early experience. Early experience factors have been shown to affect the initiation, maintenance, and improvement of sexual behavior in

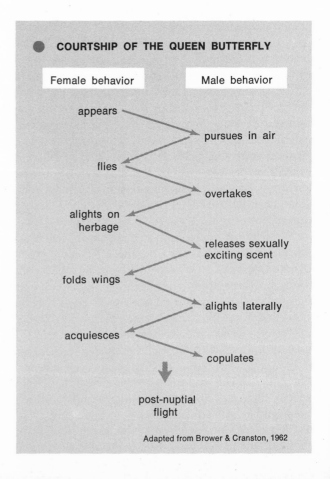

● COURTSHIP OF THE QUEEN BUTTERFLY

Female behavior	Male behavior
appears	pursues in air
flies	overtakes
alights on herbage	releases sexually exciting scent
folds wings	alights laterally
acquiesces	copulates

post-nuptial flight

Adapted from Brower & Cranston, 1962

animals. Beach (1958) has shown that rats reared in isolation from before weaning display adequate sexual patterns. Other research, however, demonstrates that early social experience is a necessary condition for normal sexual behavior. Comparing male rats reared in isolation with cohabitation-reared males on a variety of measures, Zimbardo (1958) found the isolated males to be relatively ineffective in all aspects of sexual performance. This deterioration of sexual behavior due to social isolation has also been found in comparing isolates reared in cages adjacent to males or females with rats reared with other males or females (Gerall et al., 1967).

In summarizing the extensive research on the pervasive effect of learned sexual and social experiences on subsequent sexual behavior, Rosenblatt (1965) says that experience can even modify the effect of hormones and castration. "As a social bond, sexual behavior grows out of affective reactions between the animals, and is rooted in a general background of social responses developed earlier in life." (p. 419)

Human sexual arousal and response. Sexual activity may be observed in some infants at birth and may last well into senility. Age does take its toll, however, with the peak intensity of male sexual drive occurring between puberty and the early twenties and steadily declining thereafter. For females, approximately the same generalization holds, but cultural factors complicate matters. The decline of sexual drive with age is in part related to poor health and to greater fatigue rather than to an inherent "cooling of the blood." Although there is a reduction in androgens with old age, the Kinsey researchers report cases of men in their fifties who averaged fourteen acts of intercourse a week; Mae West, at close to eighty, could still boast plenty of "sex appeal."

Poor nutrition diminishes sexual drive (as we noted in the semistarvation experiments), as does excessive use of alcohol or drugs. Similarly inhibiting are preoccupation with personal problems, fear of the consequences, or overconcern for sex as a performance to be evaluated. A decrease in male responsiveness to a once effective "arousal agent" has been found in many species, including man. This stimulus-satiation effect vanishes when a new female sex partner is introduced (Beach, 1965). Research has not yet been done to determine whether the female of the species also loses her sexual responsiveness to repeated mating with the same male.

One external stimulus which triggers the pattern of sexual arousal is tactile stimulation of erogenous body zones, women being more responsive to touch than to other forms of stimulation. Men are more readily aroused than women by visual and narrative erotic stimuli and images, as well as by their own fantasies (Money, 1965). While men are more perceptually distractible than women during erotic pursuits, the opposite holds during the act of copulation. In animals, the male's steadfast concentration makes him oblivious even to noxious stimuli, and he totally loses his arousal state if a competing stimulus does distract him. The female, on the other hand, seems more capable of paying attention to two things at once (Gantt, 1949).

Cultural variations in sexual behavior. We are never so aware of the extent to which our sexual drive and the behavior patterns to which it gives rise are under the controlling influence of a broad set of cultural experiences as when we compare ourselves to people from other cultures. Margaret Mead's (1938) perceptive analysis of Samoan and American girls revealed that the physiological disturbances and psychological tension which accompany coming of age in America must be learned since they are absent in Samoa.

Another anthropologist has described a pattern of sexual behavior among people living on the Melanesian Islands in the Southwest Pacific which is alien to many of our basic conceptions.

Since the sex drive is assumed to be a powerful urge that requires satisfaction, and since premarital intercourse is forbidden, males and females are encouraged to masturbate. In addition, to relieve this drive, all males engage in homosexual intercourse with the full knowledge of the community. There is, however, no indication of subsequent sexual inversion in which males prefer other males as sexual objects. Premarital chastity is so strictly enforced that unmarried females and males are kept separated and not allowed even to talk or look at each other if they have a chance to meet. This results in considerable shame, awkwardness, and embarrassment during the "excruciating adjustment" period at the start of married life (Davenport, 1965).

Among the conditions of life in this society which may account for the fact that most of these couples eventually reach a healthy sexual adjustment despite the awkwardness of the "honeymoon" period are the open and frank family discussion of all matters pertaining to sex and the basic conception of sexual satisfaction as the normal expression of an undeniable human drive.

The Maternal Drive and "Contact Comfort"

It is commonly accepted that human and animal mothers have a biological drive (virtually a "maternal instinct") to protect and nurture their offspring. The data from the obstruction box studies cited earlier (p. 344) indicated that female rats would endure pain more often to reach one of their pups than they would for any other motivational condition. Our literature is replete with instances of human mothers abandoning all concern for self-preservation to rescue their children from danger, and of animal mothers successfully defending their litter against attack from physically stronger predators.

It has been argued that enduring the pain of childbirth and providing the prolonged care required for the survival of dependent infants requires the existence of such a basic drive. A modern expression of the maternal drive is witnessed in the statement of a 19-year-old unwed mother who said, ". . . right now I've got to take care of my son . . . I'm acting in these films ['skin flicks'] because I will do and have done anything that will give me money to feed William." (*The Daily Californian,* July 26, 1970, p. 3)

However, the innate universality of such a drive is questioned by other equally significant evidence. In the Murray Islands a balanced sex ratio is maintained by killing newborns of whichever sex is becoming too numerous. Many mothers in our society willingly give their children up for adoption, and mothers in the Andaman Islands adopt their friends' children while giving up their own. In lower mammals, development of "appropriate" maternal behaviors may depend upon certain stimulus-specific experiences. If female rats are reared with a rubber collar around their necks which prevents them from sniffing and licking

their own genitals, their mothering instinct is absent. If they cannot lick their young as they are being born, they not only subsequently neglect them but are even likely to eat them (Birch, 1956). A rat in the Yale University colony which gave birth to a record litter of 18 pups ate them all after they had been touched by (and thus carried the scent of) the overeager laboratory assistant who picked them up to count them. Animal caretakers are familiar with such phenomena, in which olfactory cues are important determinants of maternal behavior.

What does a mother provide for her child that is unique to the mother-child relationship? What are the conditions under which females who bear children do not become "mothers"? The first question was posed by Harry Harlow and investigated by him and his colleagues in an extensive program of research with monkeys. The second question emerged as a consequence of the observations they made while studying *"contact comfort"* as a significant aspect of the mother-child union.

Happiness Is Having a Terry-cloth Mother

In a series of experiments macaque monkeys were separated from their mothers at birth and placed with artificial surrogate mothers.

A substitute mother made of wood covered with sponge rubber and terry cloth and a wire mother of similar size and shape were placed in the infants' living cages. ▲ Half the monkeys could obtain food from a bottle attached to the cloth mother, the other half from the wire mother. All of them were free to go to either mother at any time, and the amount of time spent with each mother was recorded automatically.

With increasing age and opportunity to learn, time spent with the lactating wire mother decreased and time spent with the nonlactating cloth mother increased. Thus contact comfort completely overshadowed nursing in determining which mother was preferred. Furthermore, when a fear stimulus (a toy bear beating a drum) was introduced, the monkeys consistently sought the cloth mother, regardless of which mother gave milk.

Open field tests confirmed this reaction. Twice a week for eight weeks each monkey was put into a room containing many stimuli known to produce curiosity-manipulative responses in baby monkeys, a cloth diaper always being one of the stimuli. The cloth mother was

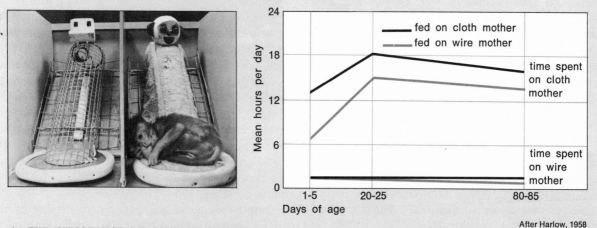

▲ **THE IMPORTANCE OF CONTACT COMFORT**

The baby monkeys nestled close to the cloth mother and spent little time near the wire one, regardless of which one gave milk.

present on alternate occasions. After one or two adaptation sessions the monkeys would rush to the mother and clutch her, using her as a base of operations and a source of security, exploring one stimulus and returning to her before going to explore another. When the cloth mother was absent, they would often freeze in a crouched position or rush to the mother's usual position and then run from object to object screaming and crying. Although they often clutched the diaper, it never pacified them. Again cloth- and wire-fed monkeys behaved alike.

The monkeys were then separated from their mother substitute and were tested for affectional retention daily for the first nine days and at thirty-day intervals for five months, by means of open field tests. On these occasions they spent their time on the mother and did not explore other objects, except that occasionally they would bring a folded piece of paper to the mother. When the mother was absent, they at first behaved as they had in early tests but gradually overcame their fear and became adapted to the open field situation. When the mother was covered by a clear plastic box, they were initially disturbed but much less so than when she was absent, and they still used her as a base of operations. The affection of the monkeys for their cloth mothers showed no decline throughout the period.

Four control monkeys had cloth and wire mothers attached to their cages for the first time at the age of 250 days (after weaning). All screamed and tried to escape. However, within forty-eight hours they began to

explore and after ten days were spending about nine hours a day on the cloth mother, even running to her when frightened. They came to use her as a base of operations in field tests, but they never rushed to her as did those who had had her from the beginning. Less than half an hour a day was spent with the wire mother (Harlow & Zimmerman, 1958).

In general, the behaviors which the infant monkeys exhibited toward the cloth mothers were almost identical to those displayed by other monkeys toward their real mothers. It appeared as though the young monkeys had developed real emotional and affectional bonds to the cloth mothers which persisted over long periods of time, even when the cloth mother was removed. The initial implication of these findings was that the essential ingredient in mothering was simply contact comfort, which apparently could be provided by any old terry-cloth towel. When these young monkeys matured, however, strange behavior patterns unfolded, which should make us cautious of joining a "Down with Mother's Day" movement.

Neurosis Is Not Having a Real Mother

What happened in the next generation, when it was time for the "motherless" monkeys to become mothers themselves? It was found that they showed totally inadequate heterosexual behavior. Despite elaborate arrangements designed to promote some "monkey business" (including putting the colony on an uninhabited island in the zoo and introducing sexually competent wild-reared monkeys) mating did not occur. After many months four (out of eighteen) laboratory-born females were inseminated and gave birth.

"After the birth of her baby, the first of these unmothered mothers ignored the infant and sat relatively motionless at one side of the living cage, staring fixedly into space hour after hour. If a human observer approached and threatened either the baby or the mother, there was no counterthreat. . . . As the infant matured and became mobile, it made continual, desperate attempts to effect maternal contact. These attempts were consistently repulsed by the mother. She would brush the baby away or restrain it by pushing the baby's face to the woven-wire floor." (Harlow, 1965, pp. 256–257)

In addition to the several socially deprived females who gave birth after being inseminated by persistent and patient breeding males, other "motherless monkeys" were artificially inseminated. From this total of twenty new mothers three patterns of maternal responsiveness were observed. Eight of the mothers brutalized their infants: biting off their fingers or toes, pounding them, and nearly killing them were it not for intervention by the caretakers. Seven of the females were simply indifferent to their babies—ignoring them, unresponsive to their demands, unprotective. Finally, the remaining five were described as being "borderline adequate" in their maternal behavior. Three of these had experienced some minimal social contact with other monkeys during their own infancy (Arling, 1966).

Despite the consistent punishment the babies received for approaching the mother, they persisted in their struggle to make maternal contact. In the end "it was a case of the baby adopting the mother, not the mother adopting the baby" (Harlow, 1965, p. 259). ◆   Fortunately, it turned out that with subsequent pregnacies, the maternal behavior of these unmothered mothers improved.

◆   Monkeys who were separated from their mothers at birth and who were prevented from observing behavior in others of their species subsequently either rejected or ignored their own babies. The infant monkey's attempts to make maternal contact were consistently repulsed by the mother. Sometimes she would restrain her baby by pushing its face to the wire floor (left). Infants who were continually thwarted in their attempts to gain maternal contact often approached the mother by climbing onto her back (right) and gradually working their way around to the front.

In subsequent studies the Harlows found that the monkeys who had only terry-cloth mothers showed adequate, but considerably delayed, heterosexual adjustment if they were given ample opportunity to interact with other infant monkeys as they were growing up. However, the Harlows concluded that:

"The implication [of these studies] is that mothering is important not only as a source of social security, but also as a very powerful agent in the social training of infants, and we are happy to state that we now believe that real mothering, monkey or human, is a very important social factor and that real mothering is here to stay!" (Harlow & Harlow, 1966)

The Nature of Psychological and Social Motivation

In our discussion of biological motivation, we have seen enough interactions between internal and external conditions, and enough examples of the central role which conditioning, expectation, and anxiety play to realize how arbitrary the dichotomy between biological drives and social motives is. The motives called *psychological* (for convenience of classification) are those which are not aroused either by neurophysiological forms of stimulation or deprivation of biologically relevant goal substances or activities. It is assumed that they are learned or acquired, and therefore are analyzable entirely in terms of external stimulus conditions which initiate and maintain the relevant behaviors.

Man generally seems to develop psychological needs which he expresses through the social patterns of his particular culture. He needs security, he needs to respond to others through the exchange of love and esteem, he needs to accept himself and at the same time to strive to better himself, he needs to seek new experiences, he needs to be accepted and approved by those around him. Although these needs are sometimes overwhelmed by other needs and by obstacles in the environment, their satisfaction is nonetheless essential to the individual's healthy development. Psychologists have learned that frustration of man's psychological motives—while it does not lead directly to death as does prolonged frustration of most biological drives—can eventually result

■ The importance of psychological motives, as well as the close interdependence of biological and psychological motivation, is readily seen in the way rebuffs or worries can suddenly lessen the urgency of physiological drives and change the attractiveness of biological reinforcers.

in emotional disturbances or even in physical illness.

The distinction between physiologically and psychologically instigated motivation can never be a clear one, since all behavior is responsive to external incentive stimuli and at the same time must involve physiological processing of information and efferent activation. Likewise, the dichotomy between psychological and social motives is not sharp since even absent individuals may arouse the needs of other individuals, as when distance makes the heart grow fonder. ■ On the other hand, people often interact with others for satisfaction of personal nonsocial needs such as greed and frustration.

Although certain basic psychological needs (for example, the needs for security and for social approval) seem always to be present, the manner in which they are satisfied depends on the individual's environment and also on his emotional development. An individual's motivational pattern becomes increasingly complex as his experience widens. The adult has many motives as a spouse, parent, or wage earner, for example, that he did not have as a child. Two attempts to categorize adult human needs and motives are summarized in the table. ● (p. 370)

● **CLASSIFICATION OF HUMAN NEEDS AND MOTIVES**

There have been many attempts to classify human needs and motives. One classification
identifies three categories of needs (Prescott, 1938):

Physiological	Needs for essential materials and conditions, for a certain rhythm of activity and rest, and for sexual activity
Social	Needs for affection, belonging, and likeness to others
Ego-integrative	Needs for contact with reality, harmony with reality, progressive symbolization, increasing self-direction, a fair balance between success and failure, and attainment of selfhood

Another classification lists fifteen "manifest needs" as being present in varying strengths
in everyone (Edwards, 1959). These items were derived from an earlier list developed
from responses to the Thematic Apperception Test (Murray, 1938).

Achievement	To do one's best, to be successful, to accomplish tasks requiring skill and effort, to be a recognized authority, to accomplish something important, to do a difficult job well
Deference	To get suggestions from others, to find out what others think, to follow instructions and do what is expected, to praise others, to accept leadership of others, to conform to custom
Order	To keep things neat and orderly, to make advance plans, to organize details of work, to have things arranged so they run smoothly without change
Exhibition	To say clever and witty things, to have others notice and comment upon one's appearance, to say things just to see the effect upon others, to talk about personal achievements
Autonomy	To be able to come and go as desired, to say what one thinks about things, to be independent of others in making decisions, to do things without regard to what others may think
Affiliation	To be loyal to friends, to participate in friendly groups, to form strong attachments, to share things with friends, to write letters to friends, to make as many friends as possible
Intraception	To analyze one's motives and feelings, to understand how others feel about problems, to judge people by why they do things rather than by what they do, to predict others' behavior
Succorance	To have others provide help when in trouble, to seek encouragement from others, to have others be kindly and sympathetic, to receive a great deal of affection from others
Dominance	To argue for one's point of view, to be a leader in groups to which one belongs, to persuade and influence others, to supervise and direct the actions of others
Abasement	To feel guilty when one does something wrong, to accept blame when things do not go right, to feel that personal pain and misery do more good than harm, to feel timid and inferior
Nurturance	To help friends when they are in trouble, to treat others with kindness and sympathy, to forgive others and do favors for them, to show affection and have others confide in one
Change	To do new and different things, to travel, to meet new people, to have novelty and change in daily routine, to try new and different jobs, to participate in new fads and fashions
Endurance	To keep at a job until it is finished, to work hard at a task, to work at a single job before taking on others, to stick at a problem even though no apparent progress is being made
Heterosexuality	To engage in social activities with the opposite sex, to be in love with someone of the opposite sex, to be regarded as physically attractive by those of the opposite sex
Aggression	To attack contrary points of view, to tell others off, to get revenge for insults, to blame others when things go wrong, to criticize others publicly, to read accounts of violence

---

Psychological motives differ from biological drives in the *degree* to which they are influenced by learning, and in the nature of the stimulus conditions which arouse and satisfy them. Social motives may be distinguished from psychological ones only in so far as it is possible to demonstrate that the instigation of the motive and the reinforcement of the motivated behaviors do or do not require real or imagined interaction with other people.

In subsequent chapters we will analyze the effects of social motives on behavior, the control of biological drives by psychological, cognitive processes, and the interaction of these three sources of motivation in the development of personality. We will also consider in detail the adverse consequences of interfering with motivated behavior.

For now, let us examine (a) how two powerful psychological drives—anxiety and fear—may be learned, (b) the significance of deprivation and satiation of social-psychological satisfactions, and (c) the manifestations of the basic drive to explore and know the environment.

Learned Fear and Anxiety

Suppose you are observing while an experimenter places a rat in one compartment of a shuttlebox. It sniffs, moves around slowly, and engages in what appears to be exploration of that side before going through the hatch into the next compartment. After similar behavior on the second side, it returns to the first, and eventually it settles down on one side or the other.

The experimenter now repeats the procedure with the same apparatus but a different rat. This animal races to the hatch, jumps through it, runs to the far end of the other compartment and remains there. If on the next trial the hatch between the compartments is closed, the rat squeals and scratches at it. If there is some means of opening the hatch, the rat soon learns how to use it. In fact, he will quickly learn to press a bar, pull a chain, turn a wheel, or make any other response that is instrumental to escape —and will not return again to the first end.

How would you characterize each of these rats? If two humans acted in comparable ways, what would you assume about their "personalities"? To account

for these dramatic differences in behavior given the same objective, physical environment, we postulate that the subjective, psychological reality faced by the two rats is different. The current stimulus situation must have acquired a special meaning for the second rat from its association with a past physical experience.

In the example described, the second rat had been placed in the apparatus before, and had always received a shock in the first compartment. Shock alone is an unconditioned stimulus producing a strong, internal response because the organism has been "prewired" to react to painful stimuli. Avoidance of this pain will motivate behavior. Eventually, the internal reaction to the shock will be elicited by the visual cues associated with the compartment itself. After repeated trials (perhaps only one if the painful stimulus is "traumatic"), being placed in the compartment arouses a strong fear reaction. ▲ (p. 372) Fear is learned then through its conditioned association with pain. It is regarded as a drive because it will motivate the learning of any response which removes the conditioned stimulus (changes the organism's relation to this "hostile" environment). Fear is the most important of the acquirable drives because: (a) it can be so readily associated with and elicited by any conditioned stimulus which the organism can perceive and (b) it is extremely resistant to experimental extinction (Miller, 1948).

This kind of fear in humans is termed "anxiety" when the original conditions of learning are vague, or the connection between the CS and the US is not conscious (or is repressed). Fear and anxiety increase our adaptability by motivating the learning of new responses to cope with "danger"; on the other hand, as their intensity increases, anxiety and fear often lead to maladaptive responses and even to self-destructive behaviors, as we shall see in Chapters 13 and 14.

The Operation of Social-Psychological Reinforcers

How best to motivate workers in order to increase their productivity was the problem studied by researchers at the Hawthorne Works of the Western Electric Company in Chicago. A group of women workers were exposed to a variety of special conditions including variations in working hours, rest periods, illumination, and pay incentives, among others. No matter what the researchers did, productivity went up. Even when work conditions were made worse than they were originally, the women worked harder and more efficiently. The secret ingredient? The *attention* shown to them by all those concerned with the study was the variable which influenced their behavior. Although this was not the experimenters' independent variable, it was what the subjects were responding to. This phenomenon has been called the "Hawthorne effect" (Roethlisberger & Dickson, 1939).

The powerful influence on behavior of psychological needs for attention, recognition, and approval has also been shown in significant research with mentally retarded children (Ψ Close-up, opposite).

The operation of deprivation and satiation of social-psychological reinforcers is similar to that of biologically necessary reinforcers. Social reinforcers increase their effectiveness following a period of social deprivation and are less effective as the person is more satiated for that reinforcer.

In an experiment using 102 first- and second-grade pupils as subjects, the task or "game" was to place marbles in either of the two holes in a simple toy. Before beginning the game, one group of subjects (Deprivation) spent twenty minutes in social isolation, while the experimenter was supposedly looking for the toy. A second group (Nondeprivation) began the game immediately, while a third group (Satiation) spent twenty minutes drawing and cutting out designs, with the experimenter constantly approving and admiring their efforts. The "game" then started, with four minutes of unreinforced play, followed by a conditioning period during which the experimenter used such words as "Good," "Fine," or simply "Mm-hmm" as reinforcers whenever the subject dropped a marble into the hole that had been selected least often during the fourth minute. This approval functioned as a reinforcer after all three conditions, increasing the frequency of the response. However, it was most effective following the Deprivation condition and least effective following Satiation (Gewirtz & Baer, 1958).

In a similar study (Gewirtz, 1967), each child was asked to look at some picture books while the experimenter was busy with his notes. While the child looked at the books, the experimenter said the word "Good" either twice (Mild satiation) or sixteen times (Satiation) for no apparent reason. Then the child was left alone for either one minute (Mild deprivation) or eight minutes (Deprivation) prior to presentation of the experimental task.

The child was then asked to choose whichever of two pictures (a plant or an animal) he liked best. The type of picture the child did *not* choose on the first trial was considered to be the "correct" response, and was reinforced by a "Good" from the experimenter every time the child chose it on subsequent trials. While the number of

▲ Shown at the left is a typical shuttlebox with two compartments, one lighted and the other dark. The floor of each compartment is a metal grid which can be electrified to produce a shock. The close-up view in the center shows the hatch between the compartments, which the rat can open by pressing the lever in the corner of the box. As shown at the right, if the rat has been shocked in the lighted compartment, but not in the dark one, he soon learns to open the hatch and escape to the "safe" compartment as soon as he is placed in the lighted one, even in the absence of shock there.

Ψ *Close-up*   *Motivation and Mental Retardation*

On a variety of experimental tasks mentally retarded children do not behave as do children of the same mental age (MA) whose intellectual development is regarded as "normal." The common conclusion of most investigators has been that such children are inherently "different." Explanations advanced have included underlying defects in cortical and subcortical functioning, a basic inability to learn because of cognitive rigidity, and fear of adults. To adopt the position that retardates are different because of a defective nervous system obviously leads to a pessimistic view of their *behavioral* potential.

Such a view has been cogently attacked in an extensive series of studies by Edward Zigler and his associates (1961, 1966, 1968, 1969). Zigler set out to determine the extent to which differences in performance between retardates and normals could be due to motivational rather than cognitive factors. He found that varying the nature of the tasks and the reinforcement from the adult tester led to systematic variations in the performance of the retardates. They persisted (were "rigid") when their persistence prolonged adult contact but were not "rigid" when persistence was not reinforced. Their presumed rigidity thus turned out to be traceable to their greater need for maintaining contact with and securing approval from adults.

This difference in motivation rather than in inherent cognitive rigidity was traced to their social deprivation. The longer a retarded child had been institutionalized, the longer he would spend on a simple task in order to gain social reinforcement—and the same pattern was found for other institutionalized children who were not retarded.

The motivational pattern of institutionalized retardates was also complicated by ambivalence: they both needed adult reinforcement more than normals and were wary and fearful of adults because of many negative experiences with them. In addition, they had learned to have lower expectations for success.

This team of researchers agree that there are differences between normals and retardates but believe that these differences are most appropriately viewed not as differences in kind but as differences in cognitive *rate* and upper *limit,* coupled with important differences in motivation and expectancy attributable to environmental factors. Thus for many reasons retardates have developed reinforcer hierarchies which differ from those of children with normal intelligence. These findings would suggest that a fundamental change is called for in our view of what constitutes mental retardation and in the kind of custodial care that is provided for institutionalized retardates.

"correct" responses increased for all subjects, it started and remained higher for the Mild satiation subjects (regardless of deprivation level) and the Deprivation subjects (regardless of satiation level).

Curiosity: The Need to Explore and Know

An important motive that is apparently inborn or learned early without formal training is curiosity. As early as 1881 it was observed that monkeys would tirelessly investigate their surroundings and manipulate any new object, although no reward was to be gained except the sheer fun of it. One monkey worked for two hours (unsuccessfully) trying to open the lock of a trunk in which nuts were stored, although a plentiful supply of nuts was within easy reach (Romanes, 1881).

Thorndike (1901) reported the case of a monkey who repeatedly struck a projecting wire, apparently just to make it vibrate. Thorndike states, "He did not, could not, eat, make love to or get preliminary practice for the serious battles of life out of that sound. But it did give him mental food, mental exercise. Monkeys seem to enjoy strange places; they . . . like to have feelings [as much] as they do to make movements. The fact of mental life is to them its own reward." But after this early work psychologists neglected curiosity for over forty years.

Even during the first day or two of life, monkeys show visual curiosity and exploration, staring at objects placed outside their cage and trying to reach them although the monkeys cannot discriminate visual detail at this age. This curiosity is unquestionably innate. About the tenth day of life the baby monkey starts locating the nipple of his nursing bottle by vision instead of by contact with his cheek. At this same age he suddenly develops the ability to learn discrimination problems. Furthermore, he now begins to show a strong need to explore his world visually (Butler & Harlow, 1954). This, in turn, leads to manipulation, which becomes an exceedingly powerful motive. Indeed, he cannot seem to stop manipulating and will play with whatever is available.

This visual curiosity and need for manipulation, once it has appeared, is never lost. Both wild and caged monkeys spend a large part of their time in such activities. It is particularly interesting to note that this motive precedes the motive to eat solid food and in fact is essential to the latter. When first given bits of solid food, baby monkeys play with them and manipulate them as they would toys. They first place such food in their mouths as a form of exploration, and many days may pass before a piece of food is actually eaten in this process.

Monkeys readily learn various kinds of problems with no reward given for correct performance.

In one experiment monkeys learned to discriminate between two colors of screw eyes. A test board was presented to them, in which a number of screw eyes had been placed. The red eyes could be removed, but the green ones could not; the monkeys learned to remove all the red eyes without touching the green ones. In this and six other problems involving different paired colors of screw eyes, the monkeys showed progressive improvement, with no decrease in their motivation throughout the study. Rest periods prevented satiation or boredom with the problem, but such rewards as food were unnecessary to stimulate learning (Harlow & McClearn, 1954). Indeed, an earlier study showed that food rewards may actually disrupt learning (Harlow, Harlow, & Meyer, 1950).

Much research has shown that even the lowly laboratory rat has a strong drive to explore novel environments. In reviewing this body of research, Welker (1961) and Dember (1961) note the many studies which demonstrate that rats will work for the opportunity to explore a novel environment, will avoid environments that have recently been explored in favor of more foreign soil, will alternate responding to maximize novelty, satiate on familiar stimuli, and prefer to explore a new environment rather than stop and eat or drink, even when deprived of food and water for several days.

Man's limitless curiosity, desire to know, and need for varied experience (Fiske & Maddi, 1961) have directed his adventurous pursuits of the unknown and guided his creation of an educational system to satisfy these basic intellectual desires. Samuel Taylor Coleridge once observed:

"The first man of science was he who looked into a thing, not to learn whether it could furnish him with food, or shelter, or weapons, or tools, or ornaments, or *playwiths*, but who sought to know for the gratification of *knowing*." (*Notebooks, 1814-1818*)

Chapter Summary

The study of motivation is the search for the causes of variability in behavior. Motives are not directly observable; we can only infer them by noting the relationships between stimuli and responses. Aspects of internal motivation include: (a) arousal, (b) direction of effort, (c) selective attention, (d) organization of activity, and (e) persistence.

Motivated states are generally initiated by some kind of *deprivation*. They culminate in a *consummatory response*, such as eating, which satisfies the organism and reduces the drive state. Another common source of motivation is the presence of noxious stimuli.

Biological drives result from the organism's basic tissue needs. *Homeostasis* is the tendency to maintain a constant internal environment within the limits needed for physiological equilibrium.

The *hunger drive* is the one that has been most extensively studied. Stomach contractions play a part in causing awareness of hunger, as does level of blood sugar. The hypothalamus plays an important role in the processing of hunger and other drives, but it is not clear whether it functions as a "center of motivation" or only a "center of communication."

Hunger seems to exert a sensitizing effect, lowering thresholds for various kinds of stimulation. Both *external* and *internal* cues may initiate the hunger drive. It has been found that animals living in an economy of scarcity are more sensitive to external cues; those who live in an economy of abundance are more sensitive to internal cues. Studies show that *metering of food intake* involves both the stomach and, to a lesser extent, the mouth. Both animals and humans experience *specific hungers*, particularly when they have been deprived of needed substances. In humans, however, these hungers are often overruled by learned preferences. Prolonged semistarvation leads to increasing apathy and preoccupation with food.

The *thirst drive* is more intense than the hunger drive under conditions of deprivation, and also shows certain qualitative differences. For example, the behavior of thirsty animals tends to be stereotyped, while that of hungry ones does not. Water metering involves both the stomach and the mouth. The physiological basis of the thirst drive is maintenance of a correct balance of fluids in body cells.

Human beings are *homeothermic*, maintaining a constant body temperature. The process of temperature regulation involves maintaining a balance between heat produced by body metabolism and heat lost to the environment. This is accomplished in part by the circulatory system, and is controlled largely by the hypothalamus. A great deal of man's temperature control, however, takes place through behavioral thermoregulation—control of the environment.

Pain serves as both a signal system and a defensive (reflex) system, protecting the organism from physical harm. It can be studied on the neurological, physiological, behavioral, and affective levels. The cognitive aspects of pain are complex, and it can serve as a source of mystical or sexual pleasure.

Sex, unlike other biological drives, is not essential to the survival of the individual—although it is obviously essential to the survival of the species. It can be aroused by almost any conceivable stimulus, and its arousal is as actively sought as its reduction. The psychosexual differentiation of male and female depends on both physiological factors (determined primarily by hormones) and psychological factors (such as learned gender role).

The sexual behavior of animals is under the control of physiological factors, such as the cycle of estrus in the female, to a much greater extent than is that of humans. There is wide variation among species in frequency and timing of copulation, but in all of them response patterns depend on complex reciprocal cues between male and female. Isolation from peers during infancy can lead to inadequate sexual behavior in adulthood.

Most human beings are capable of sexual behavior throughout most of their lives, although sexual activity generally diminishes with age. Psychological factors, as well as changes in physical health, can lead to a decline in sexual responsiveness. Sexual attitudes and behavior patterns are dependent to a great extent on cultural factors.

Although the existence of an innate "maternal drive" is commonly accepted, there is evidence which leads one to question it. Animal mothers' acceptance of their young seems to depend heavily on olfactory cues.

Early studies of "contact comfort" showed that baby monkeys raised with artificial mothers vastly preferred a "cuddly" terry-cloth one, even when milk was provided by one made of wire. These monkeys seemed to develop normal affectional responses to their surrogate mothers, and they were thought to be growing up normally. It eventually appeared, however, that the adult sexual behavior of these "unmothered" monkeys was totally inadequate—and when some of them eventually became mothers themselves, they rejected their young. Apparently both "real" mothering and social interaction with peers are essential to adequate heterosexual adjustment in adulthood.

The dichotomy between man's biological and psychological motives is not entirely distinct. The latter are presumably acquired rather than inborn, and they are expressed through the patterns of the particular culture. Their satisfaction is nonetheless essential to one's well-being. Fear in particular can be shown to be a learned motive, acquired through conditioned association with unpleasant stimuli.

Social and psychological reinforcers like attention and approval function similarly to biological reinforcers. Curiosity is also a potent motive.

Personal and Social Control of Behavior

The uniqueness of man lies in his learning capacity, the complexity of his thought processes, the sensitivity of his perceptual systems, and the range of psychological conditions which motivate his behavior. For some psychologists, the perfectability of the human organism is seen in the marvel of his conquest of nature. For others, however, man demonstrates his level of perfection in the mystery of the internal control he can exercise over his own physiology. Or perhaps man's greatness is to be found in the social systems he has created which enable him to offset individual weakness with collective strength and individual limitations with the benefits of diversified, specialized talents—as well as to find love, recognition, and a confirmation of self-worth.

Man is clearly a social animal, actively seeking the companionship of others, herding together in great cities, often more responsive to the social reality of the community than to the physical reality of the natural environment. But man has simultaneously evolved as an *individual* with potential for a sense of his self-identity and a singular personality. In the course of doing so, he has also superimposed the distinctly human constructs of history and of time on the flow of events and on the static sequence of random occurrences. Identity, history, and time combine to make possible consistency in his personality and self-concept, purposiveness in his planning, and meaning in his life.

In this next section, we will expand our perspective on the study of the behavior of organisms by focusing on man's complex cognitive controls, on how psychologists have tried to describe and measure personality and intelligence, and on a variety of social psychological processes.

Beginning with an analysis of emotion in terms of the interaction of cognitive aspects of the mind and physiological aspects of the body, we set the stage for the mind-body controversy. In what sense can the mind and its insubstantial thoughts govern the physical acts of the body? Field observations and laboratory experiments provide some answers to this age-old question. Included for analysis are psychosomatic illness, voodoo deaths, hypnosis, the effects of helplessness and hopelessness, and cognitive control over whether one lives or dies.

The question of whether a science of psychology, with its emphasis on general laws, can encompass the study of personality, individual uniqueness, and individual differences will also be of concern for us. Do you think your personality and intelligence can be reduced to trait labels or represented by a single number? We shall see.

Finally, we will turn to the motives and values which drive men to seek the company and compassion of other people—an association from which some of them gain power, influence, and leadership. How the individual is molded by social norms and changed by group pressures is a fundamental question to be answered. Perhaps even more vital is our understanding of how an individual or a minority can influence the whole group or the society.

Chapter 10

The Cognitive Control
of Behavior

*There are more things in heaven and earth, Horatio,
Than are dreamt of in your philosophy.*

William Shakespeare
Hamlet, Act 1, Scene 5

How is behavior influenced by the mind? For centuries man has been intrigued by the puzzle of a nonphysical source of "energy" contained within the physical substance of the body. The essence of human life has been seen as flickering in the ephemeral light of an inner spirit, a soul, mind, will, or consciousness. It was assumed that the engagement of these forces provided the energy which drove the human machine. In 40 B.C., a Roman poet declared: "No barriers, no masses of matter however enormous, can withstand the powers of the mind; the remotest corners yield to them; all things succumb; the very Heaven itself is laid open" (Marcus Manilius, *Astronomica I*).

Christian religious thought not only subordinated the mortal body to the immortal soul, but in its mystical teaching went further, making the physical body a "no-deposit, throw-away container." The knowledge that is contained in God can be apprehended by man's soul directly without intervention of feeling or reasoning. To believe this mystical Oneness required *contemplative meditation* exercises through which the individual could transcend his dependence on thinking or sensation. Indeed, the transcendental exercises described by a fourteenth-century Roman Catholic canon, Walter Hilton, in *The Ladder of Perfection*, are similar to those proposed by a famous sixth-century Yogi, Pantanjali (Woods, 1914).

In the Renaissance view of man, the soul (as a consequence of Adam's fall in Paradise), was differentiated into three aspects: sense, reason, and understanding. "From sense there arises appetite or longing, which is common with brute beasts; from reason arises election or choice which is proper to man; from understanding by which man may be partner [once again] with the angels, arises will." (Castiglione, 1528) "In apprehension, how like an angel," was the ultimate description of man's potential.

In previous chapters we have seen that there were a number of attacks upon this view that mind controlled the body or that mind could function as an entity independent of sensation and learned associations. Descartes' mechanistic conception of behavior (see Chapter 3) separated mind from matter and focused attention on the physiological and physical operation of the "human clockwork." The empiricism of the British Associationist philosophers (see Chapter 7) established pure sensory experience as the only possible means of knowing. With the advent of an

American psychology based upon the model of physics and biology, admitting only objective behavior and measurable stimuli, the body lost its soul. Some say it lost its head as well. William James dismissed the concept of "consciousness" as "the name of a nonentity [which] has no right to a place among first principles. Those who still cling to it are clinging to a mere echo, the faint rumor left behind the disappearing 'soul' upon the air of philosophy." (1912)

The scientific assumption of causal determinacy and proof by consensual validation (see Chapter 1) required psychologists to use procedures and operations which were not psychical, mystical, or even subjective. Behaviorists gained acceptance of the thesis that observable responses to manipulable environmental stimuli were the only acceptable level of reality for understanding the nature of man. The concept and procedures of conditioning, discussed in Chapter 5, are based on this foundation. Such a view leads one to the conclusion that either the neurological events are primary and influence the mental ones or mind does not exist as a meaningful concept at all.

Modern Psychology vs. Faith, Hope, and Internal Attribution

It is obvious that a discipline which hoped to free itself from its speculative, philosophical origins and align itself with the "hard-headed" natural sciences had to disown any form of mentalism, just as chemistry had to disassociate itself from alchemy. To establish a sound basis for this modern psychology required a search for isolatable, external causal agents which had physical or biological reality. Only then would behavioral output be "sufficiently related" to stimulus input to make general laws of behavior possible. The American emphasis on pragmatism, on "facing realities," on technology, and on productivity replaced wishful thinking with hard work, thoughts with action, and faith with contingencies.

People behave as they do, *not* because of unseen supernatural forces or equally unseen internal forces of the mind, but because of empirically established patterns of environmental stimulation. This is not only a central assumption in psychology, but the basis for what is the "common-sense" view of behavior.

We distrust any behavior for which there is apparently not sufficient outer justification. Such behavior—behavior that is not explainable given all of the available information—is in fact classified as "irrational."

Although most college students fundamentally accept this sensible view, nevertheless, there remains a fascination with the irrational. We are drawn to situations where rational principles may not hold, where there is no apparent objective cause for the effect, where the incentives make others behave in ways we believe we would not behave.

Religious miracles, faith healing, the death of healthy individuals after being "hexed," anesthesia from inert substances people *believe* will take away their pain, dying for an ideal, the man without a "price," the influence of words in hypnosis or in brainwashing, unconscious motivations, and the conformity pressures induced by group consensus are perhaps the most intriguing of all human phenomena. They are interesting precisely because their existence challenges our basic conception of causality. In addition, they pose the possibility that man is not the passive victim of his immediate physical environment but on the one hand, is related to forces external to himself and on the other, possesses the potential for internal control over the environment. Suppose "believing could make it so": would faith and hope be more valuable commodities? Is the physical reality "out there" fixed, immutable, and the only determinant of our behavior? Suppose that man assumed a more dynamic view of himself, one in which—by exercising his capacity to choose—he could reject reality as a given, and create for himself a new social and physical reality?

Carl Rogers, years ago, underscored the importance of raising such questions since,

"[The] ability of the person to discover new meaning in the forces which impinge upon him and in the past experiences which have been controlling him, and the ability to alter consciously his behavior in the light of this new meaning, has a profound significance for our thinking which has not been fully realized. We need to revise the philosophical basis of our work to a point where it can admit that forces exist within the individual which can exercise a spontaneous and significant influence upon behavior which is not predictable through knowledge of prior influences and conditioning." (1946, p. 422)

In our attempt to provide a comprehensive, unified view of the determinants of human behavior, it is necessary to consider (albeit briefly) some topics not traditionally presented in introductory psychology texts: Voodoo deaths, miracle cures, witchcraft, hopelessness, and the power of cognitive control over appetite and sensation. In addition, the effects of placebos and of hypnosis on pain will be analyzed.

We will begin with *emotion*, a phenomenon which somehow falls at the intersection of the mind-body problem. The experience of emotion not only is subjective but is commonly viewed as a psychological process though emotions can be induced by environmental stimuli and are clearly mediated by physiological reactions. Furthermore, inadequate handling of emotional reactions can lead an individual to mental disorder or to psychosomatic illness or other disease states.

Emotion

Let us imagine that we could create a robot that looked, talked, and moved exactly like a human being. By means of an elaborate computer system, we could program the robot to think, solve problems, and perform various activities. Such a robot could certainly do many things just like a man but, like Mr. Spock of *Star Trek*, would never express any emotions. That is, it would never smile, laugh, cry, blush, and so on. Anyone introduced to our robot would probably guess that it was not human because it never showed any feelings when in an "emotional situation."

How could we make our robot more human? One solution would be to take the behavioral response associated with a particular emotion and build that into the robot. For example, if we wanted to make the robot appear sad, we could put in some tear ducts and program the robot to cry at the same times that humans do. But when *do* people cry?

If we look around, we see that babies cry until they are given food, and a small child will cry and throw a temper tantrum until he gets a cookie or a favorite toy. People cry while watching certain movies, and sometimes cry at weddings. They cry when they stub their toes or otherwise hurt themselves. An actress may cry while she is playing a dramatic role on stage. A student protester will cry when he gets a whiff of tear gas. People often cry when they hear a speech given by a skillful orator, and they cry while cutting up onions. A mother will cry if she hears that her son is killed in the war, and she will also cry if her son arrives home safely from the war.

At this point you may be saying to yourself, "Hey, wait a minute! Not all of these examples of crying refer to an emotion. And even when they do, the emotion isn't necessarily a sad one." Obviously, then, a single behavioral response such as "crying" cannot signal the presence of a single emotion. But in that case, how do we ever know that an emotion is being experienced either by others or by ourselves? Why do we say that we are "sad" when we hear bad news but not when we are slicing onions? In other words, what *is* the complex process that we call emotion? Before we can program our robot, maybe we have to learn how *we* have been programmed to experience emotion. How *do* you know the difference between feelings of happiness, sadness, anger, and euphoria?

The Concept of Emotion

Since the beginning of time, man has tried to understand the stirred-up, *affective* states that he often experiences. The ancient Greeks believed that there were four characteristic emotional responses, each based on the dominance of a particular fluid in the body: sanguinary (blood), melancholic (black bile), choleric (yellow bile), and phlegmatic (phlegm). Aristotle was the first to distinguish between the physiological and the psychological components of emotion, which he referred to as its "matter" and its "form or idea," respectively. Seventeenth- and eighteenth-century philosophers generally thought that the emotions were instinctive and nonrational and thus represented the animal side of man. In contrast to the emotions were the uniquely human attributes of reason and intellect, which were meant to curb man's emotions and govern his behavior in a rational way. This rigid opposition of the emotional and the rational implied not only that the emotions were harmful and disruptive, but that they were an aberrant psychological process which was different from and opposed to thought and reason. Many common-sense expressions still support this viewpoint, such as "I got so mad that I couldn't think straight," "I tried to do the right thing but my emotions got the better of me," or "In the heat of passion, I didn't realize what I was doing."

When psychology came into being as a formal discipline separate from philosophy and physiology, one of the first problems it considered was that of emotion. Psychologists attempted to provide a more precise definition of emotion, but quickly found that it was a very difficult task. Some have defined emotions as *motives*, while others feel that emotion is a very different process from motivation. Some define emotions as bodily changes, while others define them in terms of the subjective feelings experienced and reported by the individual. This lack of agreement on a definition has been one of the factors that has hampered research in this area.

Paradoxically, the term is very meaningful for the layman, despite its awkwardness for the experimental researcher. As a result, some psychologists do not define emotion at all, assuming that everyone will "know what they mean" when they discuss it. In a recent attempt to bridge this theoretical gap between the layman and the scientist, Davitz (1969) simply asked a number of people to describe what they meant when they used emotional terms and then constructed a "dictionary of emotion" on the basis of their responses.

In accordance with varying definitions of emotion, psychologists have studied a wide range of responses. Some of them have been concerned with the role of such neurophysiological processes as activities of the brain, endocrine system, and autonomic nervous system. Another approach has focused on overt bodily movement and facial expressions. Many researchers rely on verbal self-reports of emotional experiences, as well as other introspective data. None of these has been accepted as adequate by itself, suggesting that a successful account of emotion will have to integrate all these facets of emotional response in some fashion.

While the research on emotion has yielded many interesting results, it has suffered from several limitations. One of these is the assumption (inherited from rationalist philosophy) that emotions are disruptive and usually coincide with the disintegration of some ongoing, rational behavior. But although extreme emotional states like panic and stage fright can and often do interfere with performance, this model does not seem adequate for all emotional responses. Leeper (1948) proposed that emotions often serve the very positive function of forcing the individual to organize new adaptive responses to a changed environment.

A second limitation of the research on emotion is that it has concentrated on the negative emotions (primarily anxiety and fear), while neglecting the positive emotions such as love, happiness, and contentment. Finally, much of it has focused on the *consequences* of emotional states and has paid little attention to the antecedents of the emotion and to the characteristics of the emotions themselves.

How Do We Perceive Emotion in Others?

Don't sigh and gaze at me,
Your sighs are so like mine,
Your eyes mustn't glow like mine,
People will say we're in love.

Richard Rodgers
Oklahoma!

Behavioral cues.   Although we can never directly observe another person's feelings, we often make judgments about them, as when we say, "I've never seen him look this angry," or "She looks so sad today." How do we arrive at these emotional classifications? We could, of course, just ask the person how he is feeling (assuming that his answer will be truthful and accurate). However, we often use a person's *nonverbal* behavior, such as facial expressions and body movements, as reliable signs of what emotion he is experiencing. The "look" of love communicates just as much feeling (if not more) as a verbal protestation of passion.

The detection and interpretation of nonverbal cues to the emotional state of others require rather subtle perception, and are quite difficult skills to learn. Societies that tend to inhibit strong displays of individual emotion must develop highly stylized, ritualistic patterns of behavior to deal with recurrent, emotionally charged situations such as weddings and funerals. This recognition of the relevant nonverbal cues leads not only to the appropriate overt reaction, but may determine the emotional experience as well. Thus a child can learn to feel grief at a funeral simply by observing the nonverbal reactions of his elders. This point is captured in Tolstoy's description, in "The Death of Ivan Ilych," of a man attending the wake of a close acquaintance.

"And Peter Ivanovich knew that, just as it had been the right thing to cross himself in that room, so what he had to do here was to press [the widow's] hand, sigh, and say "Believe . . . me . . ." So he did all this and as he did it felt that the desired result had been achieved, that both he and she were touched."

It is also interesting to note that the more inhibiting and less spontaneous the society, as in Imperial Japan or eighteenth-century England, the more stylized, complex, and exaggerated the social rituals governing even the most minute and commonplace expressions of emotion. In their study of Balinese character development, Margaret Mead and Gregory Bateson (1942) concluded that spontaneous emotion was completely replaced by elaborate formal gesture. In the classic Balinese dances, faces were concealed behind masks and movements were dictated by ritualized, rigid rules. These dances were often dominated by the theme of the Balinese mother-witch who brings disaster to mankind. These anthropologists found that Balinese mothers methodically frustrated their infants' impulses—teasing, leading them to the expected gratification and then giving none. By three years of age or so, a Balinese child could be characterized as withdrawn into a world of its own, reacting emotionally only with an occasional show of fear. It thus became safe to express emotion or desire only through conventional ceremonies, in which the individual could conceal his own emotional vulnerability. However, such stereotyped forms prevent direct expressions of one's own feelings as well as recognition of individual variations in the emotions of others.

We noted in Chapter 4 the differences between American and Japanese mothers in the reinforcement they provided for their children's general vocal and physical expressiveness. Thus the Japanese child could be expected to be more restrained and self-contained, and to manifest less outward show of emotion than his American counterpart.

Experimental research has focused on four general types of nonverbal expression. Much study has been made of *facial display*, since the most important overt expression of emotion occurs in the face, at least for humans. Another area of study is *kinesics*, which is concerned with body positions, posture, gestures, and other body movements. A third area of study is *paralanguage*, which covers aspects of communication that are vocal but not verbal—i.e., voice qualities, such as pitch, intensity, and rate of speech; hesitations, errors, and other speech nonfluencies; and non-language sounds, such as laughs and yawns. *Proxemics* focuses on spatial distance between people interacting with each other, as well as their orientation toward each other (as reflected in touch and eye contact).

The "animal" in you.   The first person to emphasize the behavior and expression of emotion, as opposed to the subjective experience, was Charles Darwin. In his book *The Expression of the Emotions in Man and Animals* (1872), he advanced the belief that emotional patterns are largely inherited, innate responses which have had biological utility in evolution. For example, animals who are preparing for attack will bare their teeth, growl, and show a bristling of their hair. If such displays were effective in warding off attackers, they would have obviously adaptive significance for survival. The remnants of this behavior are seen in the tendency of man to sneer and grit his teeth when he is feeling hostile.

To what extent are emotional expressions innate, as Darwin has argued, and to what extent are social learning factors involved? In support of his position, Darwin pointed to the fact that blind children show the same facial expressions of emotion, in the same situations, as normal children. However, we can't rule out learning in this case, since the blind children could have been reinforced for exhibiting the correct response and corrected when they displayed an inappropriate one. Darwin also cited the universality of emotional expressions, particularly in infants. While confirming the universality of various types of expressions in all cultures, Ekman and Friesen (1969) found that the emotion linked to particular expressions (and thus the interpretation of them) varied tremendously from culture to culture. For example, both Americans and Chinese stick out their tongues to express emotion, but for the American, the emotion is disgust or contempt, with a strong component of hostility, while for the Chinese, it is surprise (Klineberg, 1938).

Your face is like an open book . . . Even within one culture, a particular nonverbal response can reflect any of several different emotions, as we saw earlier in the example of crying. If there is not a one-to-one relationship between a facial or behavioral expression and a particular emotion, then nonverbal behavior does not provide a very reliable communication system. The results of many early studies of facial expressions would tend to support this statement. Subjects were asked to look at pictures of people's faces and indicate the emotion that they thought was being expressed. Contrary to the expectations of the experimenters, there was a great deal of variability in the subjects' judgments suggesting that people are not very accurate in judging emotions. A more recent study by Schlosberg (1952), however, found that facial expressions could be described in terms of two dimensions—pleasantness-unpleasantness and rejection-attention—with a fairly high degree of agreement between judges. ■ Later Schlosberg (1954) discovered a third dimension in facial expressions (intensity, or level of activation) and developed a three-dimensional model of emotion that has influenced much subsequent research. Current experiments have

established that subjects rating facial expressions by the use of this model show very high accuracy and agreement (90 percent or more) in their judgments of basic, simple emotions like fear, surprise, happiness, anger, sadness, disgust, and interest, and furthermore that such agreement is cross-cultural (Ekman, Sorenson, & Friesen, 1969).

However, people do not always express such pure, simple emotions as happiness and anger. Often they experience compound or mixed emotions, such as embarrassment, frustration, and jealousy, and the nonverbal expression of these is rather ambiguous. How do people make accurate judgments of these emotional states, since the cues, though strong, are so complex? One solution is to infer the emotion from the situational context. Thus, if we saw a woman crying as she greeted her son who had returned from the war, we would say that she was happy, overjoyed, and relieved. However, if we saw her crying after hearing that her son had died, we would label her emotion as grief.

This reliance on situational cues when the expressions tend to be ambiguous was demonstrated experimentally (Munn, 1940). Subjects were presented with photographs taken from *Life* magazine and asked to judge the emotions of the person in each picture. In some of the photographs, the background had been eliminated, so that only the person was visible. Munn found that subjects' accuracy and agreement in labeling the emotion was considerably better when the background situational cues were included. ● The importance of these cues is also stressed by Frijda (1970), who argues that emotions are *always* interpreted in terms of a situational reference. He noted that subjects who were judging facial expressions rarely used simple words like "angry" or "happy." Instead, they usually described an inferred situation —for example, "You told her a disgusting story," or "She seems to be looking at a tiny kitten."

I can hear it on your lips but can't see it in your eyes. Although there are many different channels of expressive communication (e.g., verbal, vocal, facial, and motoric), we usually assume that they all will say the same thing. That is, when a person says "I'm really happy," we expect that he will say so in a lighthearted, laughing way; that he will smile; and that he will

● Can you tell from this man's facial expression what emotion he is probably experiencing? Check your judgment on page 386.

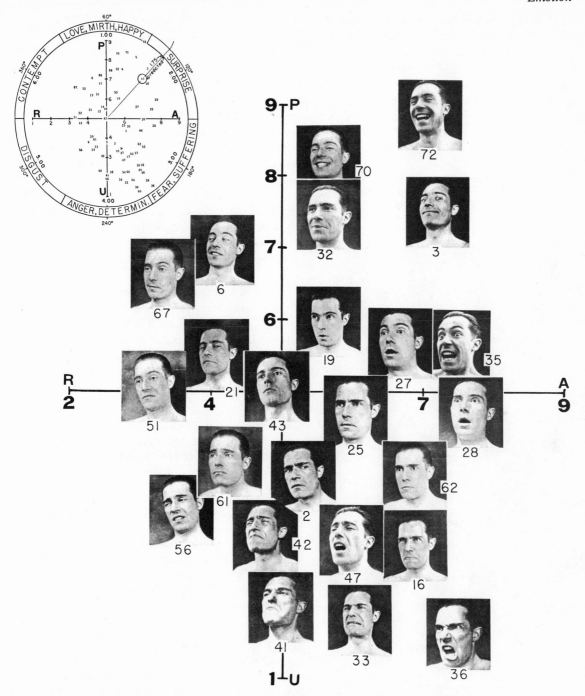

These pictures are some of the ones used by Schlosberg, shown placed on the two axes: pleasantness-unpleasantness and rejection-attention. The periphery and the two axes, as shown in the diagram, permit the location of any picture with respect to two dimensions of facial expression: quality and intensity. Intense emotions are placed near the periphery; more neutral ones toward the center.

be lively and carefree in his movements. But what if there is some discrepancy between the various channels? How do we then judge the person's emotion? Suppose, for example, that someone said "I'm really happy" in a quavering voice, while his hands were trembling. Would you guess that he was actually feeling happy? Or would you be more inclined to label his emotion as one of fearfulness? If you did,

● Now that you know the man pictured on page 384 was trying to cross a street after a mudslide, do you have any different judgment of what emotion he might have been experiencing?

you would be relying more on the nonverbal cues than on the verbal one.

This is the characteristic response to discrepant information, as researchers have begun to discover. In fact, the verbal channel is generally perceived as the least trustworthy in reflecting a person's true emotion (Mehrabian, 1969). This may be because the verbal channel is the one most consciously controlled and monitored by the sender. Presumably, the nonverbal channels are not so well controlled and thus more directly reflect the person's deep-down, true feelings and attitudes. What do you suppose would be the consequences of a family situation in which the child was regularly told verbally that he was loved and consistently told nonverbally that he was either insignificant or resented?

Stereotyped judgments of emotions.   One of the situations in which it becomes very important to make accurate judgments of emotional state is diagnosis of patients in mental hospitals by members of the staff. The therapy and care prescribed, as well as the evaluation of progress toward being released depend upon such observation of emotions in others.

A recent study compared the evaluation of emotion experienced by patients and the staff's conception of these experiences. Using a test called the Emotions Profile Index (EPI), staff members checked items they thought applied to a depressed patient, and then those they thought appropriate to a manic patient. Patients in a depressed state completed the same form and repeated the process later when they were in a manic state.

The results revealed that:

1. The twelve individual staff members were in close agreement as to which emotions were appropriate to mania and which to depression.

2. The staff members' and patients' descriptions of depression corresponded well.

3. There was a marked discrepancy about the emotions constituting a manic state. Staff members thought manic patients would be fearless, impulsive, aggressive, rejecting, and moderately sociable. Manic patients considered themselves to be somewhat cautious and fearful, sociable, trusting, and not at all aggressive—"on the whole, generally pleasant and agreeable people" (Fieve, 1970).

It cannot be determined from this research which set of observations was the more veridical—the patients' self-judgments or the staff members' judgments of them. A further discovery, however, was that the patients' emotional profiles showed much variability, while those completed by the staff were rather uniform. The investigator concluded that the staff members had a stereotyped view of what the patients were feeling—they were thinking about some hypothetical, "typical" patient and not about real individuals.

This study is illustrative of the fundamental problem raised in Chapter 8 by the *Einstellung* (set) demonstration. How do we ever perceive the emotional cues actually provided by the behavior of others when our training, past experiences, and expectations of what is "typical" in a given situation predispose us to see what we think ought to be there instead of what is?

How Do We Perceive Emotion in Ourselves?

For all the reasons described, trying to identify the emotion that someone else is experiencing can often be a very complex process. A main stumbling block is that we cannot observe what is going on inside his head and are forced to rely only on overt, outer cues. But in the case of our own emotions, the covert, inner aspect is available to us, and thus we ought to know just what *our* emotions are. Do we?

The physiological component. Several attempts have been made to relate emotion to physiological processes, or even to explain emotion entirely in such terms.

The James-Lange theory. Whenever you have experienced a strong emotion, you have undoubtedly had a feeling of being "churned up" inside because of various bodily changes. If someone were to ask you how this stirred-up state comes about, you would probably say that your feeling of an emotion (e.g., "I am feeling sad") gives rise to the subsequent bodily expression of it (e.g., "therefore I am crying"). Most people would agree with your statement—but not William James, the father of American psychology. In 1884 he proposed that the sequence of felt emotion and bodily changes was the *reverse* of the common-sense one just stated: "our feeling of the bodily changes *is* the emotion." (James, 1884) In modern

terminology, "the changes are the medium." That is, James believed that the cognitive, experienced aspects of the emotion were a *result* of physiological arousal instead of the other way around. To use his classic example, the sight of a bear produces a stirred-up internal state which is then perceived as fear.

A Danish scientist named Lange presented some similar ideas at about the same time, and so this theory is known as the *James-Lange theory* of emotion. Its importance lies in the fact that it was the first to postulate that visceral processes exert some control over emotional behavior and thus to challenge the idea that mental processes control bodily reactions.

Cannon fires back. There were many people who responded to the James-Lange theory with cries of "It just ain't so!" One of these was the physiologist Walter Cannon. His criticisms (1929) were the most serious attack made against the theory, and they had a major influence on much of the subsequent research on emotion. The James-Lange theory implied that in order for a person to experience different emotions, there must be discriminably different sets of physiological changes for the person to rely on as cues. Cannon disputed this notion by citing evidence that different emotions are accompanied by the *same* visceral state, that the viscera are too insensitive for changes in them to be noticed and used as cues, and that visceral changes are too slow to be a source of emotional feelings, which are fast-changing and mercurial. He also pointed to the work of Marañon (1924) as being critical of the James-Lange theory, since Marañon had found that artificial stimulation of the viscera through injections of adrenaline (epinephrine) produced only "cold" or "as if" emotions in the person (e.g., "I feel *as if* I were afraid") rather than true emotions.

The "centers" of emotion. Partly because of Cannon's criticisms, many researchers began to look at other physiological systems that could be the site of emotion. In general, there has been an increased interest in central neural mechanisms.

One of the most popular theories has placed the control of emotion in the limbic system (which includes the earliest parts of the cortex and parts of the thalamus and hypothalamus). As we have seen, researchers have found that stimulation and lesioning of various parts of the limbic system produce changes in emotional reactions.

The fact that the limbic system is made up of the primitive brain probably lent credence to the idea that the "primitive" emotions are located there. However, as Pribram (1960) has noted, these supposedly phylogenetically old structures have achieved their greatest degree of evolutionary development in man just as have the so-called "higher" cortical structures, and thus they can no longer really be considered as "primitive." Furthermore, research has shown that the limbic system is involved in cognitive functioning as well as in emotion (e.g., lesions and stimulation of limbic structures influence problem solving). Moreover, stimulation and lesions of parts of the brain other than the visceral areas also produce emotional changes (Pribram, 1967). These findings would suggest that the emotions (and cognitive behavior) are controlled by many different interacting parts of the brain, rather than by any single "emotion center."

Physiological differentiation of emotions. If the James-Lange theory were correct, every emotional state would have to have its own physiological syndrome. Thus, when a person felt one particular set of symptoms, he would say, "I'm angry," and when he felt another, he would say, "I'm happy." We do, in fact, often use different physiological responses to distinguish between emotions, as when we speak of a person going purple with rage or white with fear, or experiencing "butterflies" in his stomach when he is nervous. But as experimenters have searched for these physiological correlates of emotions, they have met with varying success.

One of the first studies to demonstrate physiological differentiation was Wolf and Wolff's (1947) report of a patient with an opening through which they could observe stomach changes. They were able to observe two different patterns of stomach activity— one when the patient was angry, and the other when he was anxious and fearful. Other subjects exposed to various anger- and fear-provoking situations also showed two different patterns of responding, as measured by changes in heart rate, blood pressure, skin conductance, and muscle tension (Ax, 1953). A

similar study found differences in response patterns for fear, anger, and pain (J. Schachter, 1957).

Considerable research has shown that two adrenal hormones—*epinephrine* and *norepinephrine*—appear to be related to different emotions.

Early studies found that epinephrine is generally associated with fear, while both norepinephrine and epinephrine are found in anger reactions. Animals which are fearful and which survive by being able to run away from danger (e.g., rabbits) secrete mostly epinephrine, while animals that usually attack (e.g., lions) secrete a high amount of norepinephrine (Funkenstein, 1955).

Another study found that college students who were exposed to a frustrating task showed one of three emotions: fear, anger expressed outwards toward the experimenters, and anger directed inwards (blaming themselves). Students who expressed anger outwardly tended to show a secretion of norepinephrine, while those who were fearful or blamed themselves showed more secretion of epinephrine (Funkenstein, King, & Drolette, 1957). More recent research on the endocrine system has demonstrated both increased and differential release of both epinephrine and norepinephrine under various conditions of stress (Brady, 1967).   ▲

In addition to being secreted into the bloodstream, norepinephrine is also found in the brain, particularly in the hypothalamus and the limbic system. There is evidence to suggest that drugs which cause changes in mood do so through their effect on brain norepinephrine. Drugs which increase the accumulation of norepinephrine produce euphoria and hyperactivity, while drugs which deplete it produce depression (Kety, 1967a).

All this research is evidence that different emotions involve different physiological patterns. However, the evidence is not, at this point, overpowering. Distinctive physiological patterns have been found only for simple, strong emotions like anger and fear and not for more subtle or complex ones. Thus it still is not clear how physiological cues could serve as the basis for these latter emotions. Some investigators (e.g., Duffy, 1962) have argued that physiological differences correspond only to different amounts of the same general, *undifferentiated arousal* (see Chapter 7 for a discussion of this activation theory). Although intensity is certainly one aspect of emotion, this approach seems a rather limited one, since (a) it is

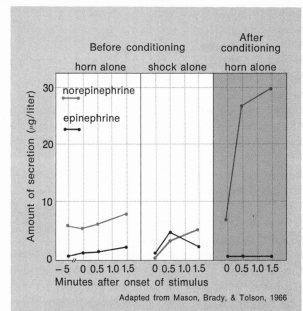

NOREPINEPHRINE SECRETION AND FEAR

Before conditioning, either the horn alone or the shock alone elicited low levels of both norepinephrine and epinephrine. After the horn had come to be perceived as a signal that shock was coming, it elicited a greatly increased secretion of norepinephrine, while epinephrine secretion remained minimal.

possible to be physiologically aroused and not feel emotional (as when you have been exercising strenuously), and (b) differentiating between different intensities of arousal still would not account for the *qualitative* differences in the experience of different emotions. If you feel your heart pounding and have "butterflies" in your stomach, what is it that tells you whether you are afraid, excited, angry, or madly in love? Even if researchers, with high-powered recording and amplifying devices, could eventually identify all the physiological correlates of every single emotion, it still would not explain why people *experience* what they do.

The cognitive component. If clues from physiological activity are not the whole story, what about perceptions, expectations, interpretations, and other such cognitive processes? What role do they play in emotion?

Emotional stew: add one part gut and one part cognition. As we saw in Chapter 7, the information provided by the proximal stimulus alone is not sufficient to explain why we see things the way we do. It is only through cognitive organization and interpretation of stimuli after they reach the retina that we can apprehend what is "out there." Similarly, modern psychologists believe that emotion is not determined by physiological responses alone, but requires a cognitive appraisal and evaluation of the stimulus situation.

One theory is that physiological responses (essentially undifferentiated) determine the *intensity* of an emotion but that a person uses emotionally relevant cognitions to determine its *quality*—which emotion it is. If he does not already have an appropriate cognition for arousal that he is feeling, he will draw on cues available in the immediate environment to help him label his stirred-up state.

This theory was proposed and tested in an ingenious experiment in which subjects were led to believe that the experimenter was studying the visual effects of a vitamin compound called "Suproxin." They received an injection and then were sent to a waiting room, supposedly to wait for the drug to take effect. For experimental subjects, the injection actually consisted of epinephrine (adrenaline), which usually causes increased heart rate, accelerated breathing, tremor, and sometimes a feeling of flushing. A group of control subjects received a placebo injection (saline solution), which produces no physiological arousal at all.

In giving the injections, the experimenters also manipulated the subjects' cognitive appraisal of their bodily states. The first group of subjects were told that Suproxin's side effects typically consisted of tremor, palpitation, and flushing; thus they had an appropriate explanation of the arousal they would be feeling. The second group were told that the drug would have no side effects, while those in the third group were told that the typical side effects consisted of numbness, itching, and a slight headache. In these two latter conditions, then, the subjects had an inappropriate explanation for their subsequent arousal. It was predicted that subjects in these two conditions would search their immediate situation for appropriate explanations of what was going on inside them, being more susceptible to such cues.

In the waiting room, each student found another student, supposedly waiting like him for the drug to take effect. Actually this was a confederate of the experimenter, who soon began to behave emotionally. For half of the subjects, he acted very playful: doodling, throwing paper airplanes, twirling a hula hoop, and so on. For the rest of the subjects, he became increasingly irritated and angry with a questionnaire that the experimenter had given them to fill out, until finally he ripped it up and stomped out of the room. During both of these situations, observers watched the subject through a one-way mirror and rated the extent to which he acted either euphoric or angry. Subjects also filled out self-report questionnaires on their emotional state.

At this point, if you were to ask each subject whether he felt happy or angry, what do you think he would say? These investigators found that the two groups who did not have an appropriate cognition for their arousal felt happy when the stooge acted happy and angry when he acted angry. Presumably, perception of the stooge's behavior and mood influenced their appraisal of their own unexplained arousal. But the correctly informed subjects, who already had an appropriate explanation for their arousal, were not susceptible to the confederate's mood and did not report that they were either angry or happy. Similarly, the control subjects, with no arousal but with the same social cognitions, reported neither emotional state (Schachter & Singer, 1962).

These results thus support the theory that the quality of emotional states is determined by cognitive factors. Given the same state of physiological arousal (for which they had no explanation), subjects labeled their emotion as either "happiness" or "anger," depending on the cognitive aspects of the situation. This demonstrated ability of researchers to change emotions by manipulating the cognitive component independently of physiological arousal promises to reopen the area of emotion to experimental analysis. It also poses a direct challenge to the earlier theory of emotion that posited a causal link between physiological arousal and cognitive experience, the former coming first and causing the latter.

Unexplained arousal hurts bad.   One of the assumptions apparently supported by the above experiment was that physiological arousal alone is essentially neutral and "plastic," convertible into any type of emotion, given the availability of appropriate cognitions. On the other hand, unexplained arousal is characteristically part of *anxiety*, which is certainly a negative emotional state. To be "churned up" inside

and not to know why is an upsetting experience which motivates people to search for an explanation. Since such arousal is usually experienced as negative to begin with, it is hard to see how it could ever be converted into a positive emotion, at least in adults, who have already learned to react negatively to unexplained arousal. The answer to this problem will have to await further studies which attempt to replicate the earlier research and extend the concept of emotion by considering the broader general question of how man takes stock of himself in any situation, emotional or not.

Cognitive appraisal theories.   Although more investigators are becoming concerned with the role of cognitive processes in emotional and other reactions, few have tried to speculate on the dynamics of such processes. What does it mean to have a cognition that determines an emotional response? Two of the psychologists who have worked on this problem have discussed such cognitions in terms of *appraisal*.

Appraisal is the evaluation and judgment of the significance of a stimulus. One of the first people to use this concept in a theory of emotion was Magda Arnold (1960), who proposed a sequential model. The first step in this sequence is *perception*, in which external stimuli are received. The next step is *appraisal*, in which the stimuli are judged as good and beneficial or bad and harmful. This appraisal then determines the *emotion*, which is defined as a felt tendency toward stimuli appraised as good or away from those appraised as bad. The *expression* of the emotion is the pattern of physiological responses which accompany the felt tendency. These may be organized toward approach or toward withdrawal. The final step in the sequence is *action*, when actual approach or withdrawal occurs.

A more complex extension of this approach is that of Lazarus (1968). He postulates two basic kinds of appraisal processes: *primary appraisal*, which evaluates whether the situation is threatening or not, and *secondary appraisal*, which has to do with assessing alternative means of coping with a perceived threat. If a situation is perceived as threatening, there are two possible *coping strategies*: (a) *direct action*, such as fight or flight, with the negative emotional states accompanying them; or (b) *benign reappraisal*, in which the person reassesses the situation as less threatening, thereby reducing the negative emotional state. The positive emotions follow various appraisals of nonthreat (including benign reappraisals). This entire analysis stresses the interplay between cognitive appraisals and emotional reactions. Thus it is related to other psychological models of cognition and information processing, such as that of Sokolov, discussed on page 174.

Both these theories argue against the notion of neutral, undifferentiated arousal later given meaning, as proposed by Schachter. They postulate that there *are* different patterns of physiological responses, but that such responses do *not* determine or cause the emotion. Rather, the physiological component is seen as a function of the cognitive appraisal—usually following it but in any case being incorporated into it.

The research done by Lazarus to test his theory has generally focused on how appraisals and reappraisals are used to cope with extremely threatening situations.

In one study, subjects watched a film which showed some very crude genital operations carried out as part of male initiation rites in a primitive Australian tribe. The sound track that accompanied the film either emphasized the dangers of the operation, denied such dangers, or discussed them in an intellectualized, detached way. The investigators hypothesized that these sound tracks would alter the subjects' cognitive appraisal of (and thus their emotional response to) the threatening film. They found that, as compared with arousal by the film alone, levels of physiological arousal were higher with the "danger" sound track and lower with the "denial" and "intellectualization" tracks (Speisman, Lazarus, Mordkoff, & Davison, 1964).

In another experiment, subjects who watched a film showing unexpected, dramatic accidents in a woodshop, such as an accident in which a man was impaled by a circular saw, showed less physiological arousal, as measured by skin conductance and heart rate, if they had cognitively rehearsed, or imagined, the threatening scenes prior to seeing the film. ● Relaxation training also helped to reduce stress, but the opportunity for advance cognitive appraisal was clearly more effective (Folkins, Lawson, Opton, & Lazarus, 1968).

Such results have important implications not only for our intellectual understanding of what emotion is, but for preparation of people who will be subjected to

severe stress and for the practical problem of treating "emotionally disturbed" individuals (to be discussed in Chapter 15).

Emotions and Health

When an organism faces a threat to its well-being, it may learn to escape, avoid, or directly confront the dangerous situation. In addition, as we have seen before, something else is learned—an internal, emotionally conditioned fear response. Thereafter this internal fear response may be triggered by any warning stimulus associated with the original threat and thus may come to motivate behavior even in the absence of the aversive stimulus. The behavior of the rat in the shuttlebox described on page 371 was motivated in this way: as soon as the animal was put in the illuminated compartment (associated with pain), it would race down, press a bar, and scramble across to the "safe" environment even though the shock was not turned on. By making this complex series of responses, the animal successfully coped with the potential threat by quick avoidance. But such a response prevented it from learning whether in fact the shock might have been permanently disconnected.

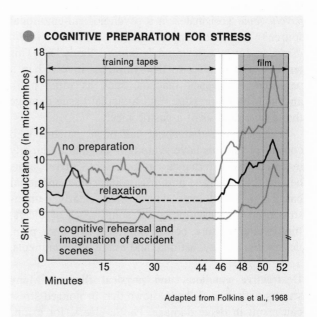

● COGNITIVE PREPARATION FOR STRESS

Adapted from Folkins et al., 1968

In some cases then, the arousal of strong emotions can thus be maladaptive by: (a) maintaining emotional operant responding after the situation changes and is no longer a potential threat; (b) limiting the individual's ability to discriminate between threat and nonthreat; (c) narrowing the perceived response possibilities, thereby reducing "creative" solutions; and (d) taxing the internal biological economy of the organism.

An example of a lasting negative consequence of emotional conditioning is *schizokinesis,* described on page 180. Years after the overt, behavioral, instrumental response has been extinguished, the conditioned emotional respondent can still be elicited by the conditioned stimulus. Thus, as we saw, the "call to battle stations" still elicited strong GSR's in Navy veterans twenty years after the battle was over. Many of those hospitalized for mental illness suffer from serious emotional disorders of mood in which inappropriate learned reactions distort and dominate their appraisal of new situations.

Emotions Can Make You Sick

Sometimes, in the face of repeated, intense emotional arousal, the mind continues to function with apparent normalcy but makes unreasonable demands upon the body. Deterioration in bodily functioning which is *psychogenic* (originates in a psychological-emotional source) is called, appropriately, a *psychosomatic disorder* (*psyche*="mind," *soma*="body"). This term is used to refer to the symptoms involved in a persistent emergency reaction, such as rapid pulse and high blood pressure, and to actual tissue damage that may result, as in a gastric ulcer.

It is estimated that about half of all patients who consult physicians have symptoms originating largely in emotional disturbance. In fact, some investigators believe that *all* illness and disease has some emotional basis. Emotional factors have been clearly demonstrated in the development of some cases of ulcers, high blood pressure, colitis, migraine, low back pain, dermatitis, obesity, asthma, and many other ailments.

Destructive emotions and physical illness. Many studies with animals have shown that prolonged stress can result in tissue damage. Peptic ulcers, for example, have been produced experimentally in animals subjected to stress-provoking situations, as you saw in the case of the "executive" monkeys described on page 48.

The stress response, which involves activation of the adrenal cortex, is indicated physiologically by increases in serum cortisol levels. "Executive" Navy pilots clearly showed this adrenocortical stress response during aircraft landing practice in a two-man F-4B jet aircraft, whereas their partners in the jet did not. Thus it apparently was not simply exposure to danger which induced the stress response, but responsibility for the complex and hazardous task which the pilot—but not his passive partner—had to assume (Rubin, Miller, Arthur, & Clark, 1969).

Although prolonged stress can lead to a wide range of serious gastrointestinal disorders, psychosomatic reactions cannot be predicted solely on the basis of exposure to behavioral stress. Constitutional factors and specific kinds of past experience appear to play a role not only in whether stress will result in a psychosomatic reaction, but in the kind of reaction as well.

In some students, the heart and blood vessels reacted under induced stress as they would have had the students received an injection of adrenaline. These were the students whose primary reaction to the stress was anxiety and fear or a feeling of anger directed toward themselves. In the other group, who tended to experience anger directed outward, the heart and blood vessels behaved as they do when a person receives an injection of noradrenaline.

When the students filled out a questionnaire concerning their childhood discipline, it was found that nearly all of the "anger-out" group had strict fathers who had played a dominant role in discipline. The "anger-in" group, on the other hand, for the most part had mild fathers who had usually shared equally with the mother in discipline or even allowed the mother to be dominant. This may indicate that the method of control during childhood induces a particular reaction pattern which remains fairly constant in later life (King & Henry, 1955).

An early study established the fact that hostility increases the secretion of stomach acid and produces an engorgement of the stomach lining with blood, evidently through the action of the parasympathetic division of the nervous system. The patient mentioned

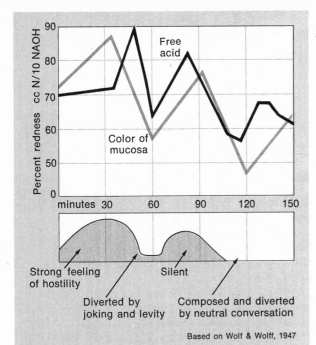

◆ HOSTILITY AND GASTRIC PHYSIOLOGY

This graph was drawn from observations made on the patient whose stomach was open for scientific study. At the beginning, the patient was feeling resentment and hostility as the result of a humiliating experience. While he discussed it, his hostility increased, and there was a greater flow of acid in his stomach and more redness of the mucosa. With changes in his mood, there were corresponding changes in gastric physiology.

of these coronary-prone men. Among them are: feelings of time urgency, a sense of unrelenting external demands, and behavioral patterns of compulsive activity designed to ward off impending harm (Jenkins, Rosenman, & Friedman, 1967).

We often hear that "bottling-up" one's feelings is bad for one's health. Research evidence supports this view at least as far as frustration and pent-up aggression are concerned.

In separate studies employing over 160 college-age subjects of both sexes, frustration was experimentally aroused by the blocking of goal activity, or by ego threats. Some of the subjects were allowed to aggress physically, verbally, or in their fantasy against the frustration, while others were given no such opportunity.

The results clearly indicated that both heart rate and systolic blood pressure rose significantly following the frustrating experience. Opportunity to aggress physically or verbally lowered these levels, whereas when subjects were not allowed to express their strong feelings overtly, the physiological changes persisted. Interestingly, when the status of the frustrating agent was varied, opportunity for verbal aggression against a high-status frustrator had much *less* of an effect on lowering the vascular reactions than did opportunity for aggression toward a low-status one (Hokanson & Burgess, 1962a, 1962b).

The complex problem of what happens to hostile feelings, once aroused, and the possibility that freely expressing them may lead to more aggressiveness (thus increasing the long-term problem instead of lessening it) will be discussed in Chapter 13.

Full-blown asthmatic reactions to psychological stimuli were demonstrated by a team of Dutch psychologists in some patients who had a history of asthma.

One patient, shown a picture of a man mourning at a grave and reminded by it of her father's death and burial, suffered a sharp decrease in the vital capacity of her lungs, as measured by constricted breathing. In another case, a patient who had had a pet fish destroyed by her mother as a child was shown a toy fish in a fish bowl. She not only showed the same constriction in breathing but experienced a severe asthmatic attack (Dekker & Groen, 1958).

Psychological factors may also play a role in disorders that might seem far removed from control by neural or endocrine processes.

on page 388, whose stomach had to be opened following an injury, was asked disturbing questions, and his stomach reactions were observed. When he reported feelings of hostility, the free acid present in his stomach rose, and the stomach lining flushed with redness, much as one's face does in anger (Wolf & Wolff, 1947). ◆

Physicians are currently recognizing the fact that high-pressure, "go-getting" businessmen are especially prone to heart conditions. According to one report, coronary heart disease strikes these men seven times as often as it does individuals in the general population (Friedman & Rosenman, 1960). Several cognitive factors have been discovered which are characteristic

Pernicious anemia was found to be associated with depression in ten patients who were studied by means of intensive interviews. In each case there had been a loss of a loved one. Severe depression had followed, causing a depletion in gastric secretion and thus contributing to the development of anemia (Lewin, 1959).

In a study of sixteen families studied periodically for twelve months both streptococcal and nonstreptococcal respiratory illnesses were about four times as frequent following family episodes judged to be stressful (Meyer & Haggerty, 1962).

Another study found that among 1000 telephone operators, one third of the group accounted for two thirds of the absences, mostly from respiratory problems. Those highest in absenteeism differed from those lowest primarily in their psychological outlook: they were more unhappy, resentful, and frustrated. This group suffered from twelve times as many respiratory illnesses (Hinkle & Plummer, 1952).

As we saw in Chapter 4, even physical growth of children can be stunted by living in an emotionally upsetting environment during the early years of childhood.

Convincing evidence that physical and psychological factors may combine to cause disease comes from a study using mice as subjects.

Mice were stressed for three days by being given cues for anticipating shock plus the shock itself, then inoculated with Coxsackie B virus and stressed for four additional days. Neither stress alone (for some control groups) nor virus alone (for others) was sufficient to cause manifest disease. Only a combination of the two —environmental stress plus the viral agent—resulted in disease (Friedman, Ader, & Glasgow, 1965).

After reviewing the available evidence on factors related to acquiring or resisting infectious disease, a team of physicians concluded that "relatively subtle psychological and environmental factors appear to influence susceptibility to a wide range of infectious and parasitic agents" (Friedman & Glasgow, 1966, p. 323). (Ψ Close-up, p. 395)

Life crises and health change. Even with diseases such as cancer or leukemia, emotional traumas earlier in life may contribute to the development of the disease. Even more surprising is the evidence that such early psychic traumas may not show their effects until many years later.

In a study investigating the history of early psychic traumas in cancer patients, a *psychic trauma* was defined as an experience in which "emotional relationships brought pain and desertion."

Of 450 cancer patients, 72 percent, as compared to only 10 percent of a noncancerous control group, were found to have suffered such an experience early in life. It was theorized that the cancer patients had, as children, responded to these crises with feelings of guilt and self-blame. During adolescence and early adulthood, these feelings were submerged as desires and energies were concentrated on school, job, and meaningful relationships with others, particularly the spouse. However, often after as long as forty years, when the pattern was changed, perhaps by retirement from work or by the death of the spouse, and the individual could find no substitute source of satisfaction and meaning in his life, his feelings of guilt and inadequacy returned. Usually the first symptoms of cancer appeared from six months to eight years after this second life crisis (LeShan, 1966). Likewise, separation or threat of separation from a loved one has often been found to precede leukemia (Greene, 1966).

Another group of investigators developed a scale for rating the degree of adjustment required by forty-two different life changes, both pleasant and unpleasant.

In a group of almost four hundred subjects, a consistent relationship was found between the number of life change units, according to the scale, and major health changes during the same ten-year period. Of those who had had moderate crises, 37 percent had had a major health change; of those who had had substantial life crises, 70 percent had showed a major health change. In addition, those who usually remained well during flu epidemics were more likely to have flu after a major life change (Rahe & Holmes, 1966).

In a group of 2684 Navy and Marine personnel, it was found that number of life change units reliably predicted visits to sick bay during the same cruise period. It was also found that those with greater life change prior to the cruise reported to sick bay more often and that illness increased with job dissatisfaction (Rahe, Gundersun, & Arthur, 1969).

"Medicine of the mind" for physical illnesses. Most physicians have long realized that even when symptoms are due primarily to physical causes, emotional strain can work against successful treatment. The emotionally unstable person who suffers from a severe organic disorder may become so depressed by his physical condition that he will lose his normal recuperative powers. A Baltimore coroner has reported that a number of individuals die each year after taking nonlethal doses of poison or inflicting minor wounds on themselves. Although the injuries in themselves would not have been fatal, apparently thinking made them so (Richter, 1957).

At the other end of the spectrum are the many cases on record of patients determined to get well who have done so despite a physician's opinion that they were beyond recovery. It has been reported that old people are more likely to die after a holiday or birthday than before, as though they were determined to live until a certain target date.

Emotional factors are particularly important in such organic disorders as tuberculosis, heart disease, diabetes, and epilepsy. In treating tuberculosis, for example, care must be taken to avoid emotional disturbances, since the patient is not allowed to engage in vigorous physical exercise and is thus denied an important natural means of working off his emotional tensions. Unless efforts are made to help the patient maintain a cheerful mood, a disease which is essentially organic may be intensified by emotional factors.

It is likely that at least as many patients are cured by a doctor's reassuring "bedside" manner as by any of the medicines he prescribes. Physicians are now being cautioned to be more responsive not only to the whole patient but to the social-emotional network in which the patient lives. Although the significance of the "mind" in physical illness is receiving greater attention in medical circles, however, it may be that the general trend away from family doctors and general practitioners to clinics and specialists means that the patient's emotional needs are receiving less attention than the family doctor could give.

Two explanations of psychosomatic disorders. Evidence that emotional factors may play an important role in both illness and recovery is accepted by all. The mechanisms by which they do so, however, are a matter of debate. Two rival explanations vie for acceptance.

The general-adaptation-syndrome. A theoretical approach which helps explain psychosomatic symptoms is the concept of the *general-adaptation-syndrome*, developed by the prominent endocrinologist Hans Selye (1953, 1956). According to Selye's theory, the body's reaction under stress occurs in three major phases: the *alarm reaction*, the *stage of resistance*, and the *stage of exhaustion*.

1. The *alarm reaction,* sometimes called the *emergency reaction*, comprises the physiological changes which are the organism's first response to the application of a stress-provoking agent, or *stressor*. A stressor is anything injurious to the organism, whether physical (such as inadequate food, loss of sleep, bodily injury) or psychological (such as loss of love or personal security). The alarm reaction consists of various complicated bodily and biochemical changes

---

Ψ *Close-up* *Psychological Reactions and Bodily Changes*

The close and predictable relationships shown here between particular psychological reactions to threat and specific bodily changes highlights the importance of beliefs and perceptions in determining both. For those with differing beliefs, the same stimulus situation can lead to very different psychological reactions and hence to different physiological changes (Jackman et al., 1963).

Psychological Reaction	Physiological Change		
	Urinary Excretion of:		
	Water	Sodium	Potassium
Vigilance, preparation for action	decreased	decreased	—
Relief, relaxation, threat termination	increased	—	—
Uncertainty of capacity to meet threat, apprehension	increased	increased	—
Aggressive response to threat, anger	increased	increased	increased
Hopelessness, depression, or exhaustion	decreased	decreased	decreased

which usually have the same general characteristics regardless of the exact nature of the stressor.

In an experimental situation, a large number of animals were subjected to a wide variety of stressful conditions including starvation, infections, poisoning, extreme cold, extreme heat, surgical hemorrhage, and others. Regardless of the type of stressor, much the same general pattern of physiological change was observed (Selye, 1950).

This finding accounts for the similarity in general symptoms of people suffering from diverse illnesses —all seem to complain of such symptoms as headache, fever, fatigue, aching muscles and joints, loss of appetite, and a general feeling of being "run down."

2. If exposure to the stress-producing situation continues, the alarm reaction is followed by the *stage of resistance*, the second phase of the general-adaptation-syndrome. Here the organism seems to develop a resistance to the particular stressor which provoked the alarm reaction, and the symptoms that occurred during the first stage of stress disappear, even though the disturbing stimulation continues. Resistance to the stressor seems to be accomplished in large part through increased level of secretions of the anterior pituitary and the adrenal cortex (ACTH and *cortin*, respectively). We saw that this adrenocortical stress response occurred in the Navy pilots responsible for the hazardous job of aircraft landing. During the stage of resistance, the physiological processes disturbed during the alarm reaction appear to resume normal functioning.

3. If exposure to the injurious stressor continues too long, a point is reached where the organism can no longer maintain its resistance. It thereupon enters the final phase of changes related to stress, the *stage of exhaustion*. The anterior pituitary and adrenal cortex are unable to continue secreting their hormones at the increased rate, with the result that the organism can no longer adapt to the continuing stress. Many of the physiological dysfunctions which originally appeared during the alarm reaction begin to reappear. If the stressor continues to act upon the organism after this time, death often occurs. It is rare, however, for stress not to be relieved before this stage of exhaustion is reached.

The concept of the general-adaptation-syndrome has been exceptionally valuable in explaining psychosomatic disorders. In terms of its framework, many disorders can be viewed as the results of stress or of the physiological processes involved in adaptation to stress. The value of administering additional ACTH and cortisone in treating some of these diseases can also be understood. In effect, such treatment may be regarded as a way of helping the anterior pituitary and the adrenal cortex to maintain the body's resistance to some stressor.

One psychologist, after reviewing the work of Selye and others, summed up the situation as follows:

"Perhaps emotional reactions are basically constructive —defensive and adaptive. However, if emotional activity or reactivity is sufficiently frequent or prolonged or intense, it becomes maladaptive or destructive, leading to physiological aberration or structural damage to the organism, and even to death. Thus, an organism may be injured or destroyed by its own defenses." (Lachman, 1963, p. 27)

Operant control of autonomic responses.   We have seen earlier (Chapter 5) that rats can learn to increase or decrease their heart rate when such a response is immediately followed by the reinforcement of brain stimulation. Neal Miller and his associates have demonstrated a variety of such conditioned visceral responses: animals have learned to regulate their intestinal contractions, to alter the rate of urine formation in their kidneys, to increase or decrease the amount of blood in their stomach walls, and to change their systolic blood pressure.

The startling specificity of the responses which are brought under this operant control argues against the idea that stress necessarily brings a generalized, over-all increase in autonomic activity. We saw in Chapter 5 that some animals have learned to dilate the blood vessels in only one ear!

Other researchers have shown that human subjects, trained to relax and concentrate intensely through hypnosis, have been able to vary the skin temperature of their two hands in opposite directions simultaneously. The graph shows the changes in skin temperature for one coed subject instructed to make her right hand hotter and her left hand colder than normal, and then after a period of time to return them to normal. Unhypnotized control subjects, not able to concentrate as deeply, showed no systematic temperature changes in either hand (Zimbardo, Maslach, & Marshall, 1971). ▪

Visceral learning may offer part of the explanation of the ways in which different individuals develop specific psychosomatic disorders.

"If a child is afraid of going to school," Dr. Miller explains, "he might display a variety of autonomic symptoms. If one of the symptoms, say an upset stomach or a change in heart rate or blood pressure, is particularly disturbing to the child's mother," he says, "she might reinforce the symptom by demonstrating her concern or by keeping the child at home." Eventually, the child might develop a habit of responding to stress with a visceral symptom (Massett, 1970, p. 275).

Both of these explanations seem to describe part of what happens in psychosomatic disorders. It is clear that visceral responses *can* come under operant control and also that in long-continued stress there is a chronic overactivity of the adrenocortical system which in the long run can be damaging to the organism.

It may be, in a loose manner of speaking, that in the initial stages of a psychosomatic disorder, the mind tricks the body by getting it to work for an immediate reinforcement (however maladaptive in the long run), but that after a while, the environment deceives both body and mind by arranging reinforcement contingencies that perpetuate the response and are not under the individual's control. Thus what began as a reasonable visceral coping strategy becomes a maladaptive conditioned response, and what starts out as a normal process becomes a serious problem.

Emotions Can Help Keep You Well

Obviously, negative emotions do not always lead to illness. Under what conditions do they *not* do so? Are they ever actually beneficial?

When not enough fear is too much.   Does the person who is fearless in the face of danger have a psychological advantage over the worrier? Not necessarily, according to research. In fact, under some circumstances too little fear may have as bad an effect on health as too much.

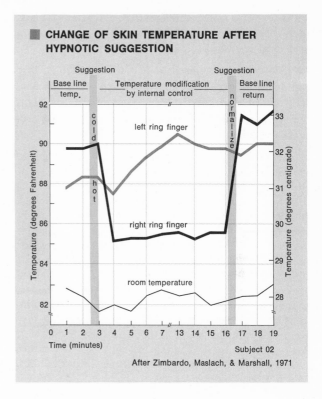

■ **CHANGE OF SKIN TEMPERATURE AFTER HYPNOTIC SUGGESTION**

After Zimbardo, Maslach, & Marshall, 1971

One investigator hypothesized that when an individual must cope with a threatening situation, as in anticipating major surgery on oneself, a moderate amount of realistic fear before the surgery would be valuable in promoting both psychological and physical adjustment afterward. He found that a moderate level of fear, which initiated the "work of worrying" prior to exposure to the actual event, helped the patient to plan his future reactions and modulate his stress and induced a kind of "emotional inoculation." Extreme fear created the general stress syndrome we have discussed, and thereby introduced additional physiological complications. On the other hand, the patient with little or no fear before the surgery, who did not engage in mental rehearsal of the impending event, was less well prepared to cope with the consequences of the surgery. When he suddenly became aware of the loss of a limb, or of being incapacitated or in extreme pain, such a person tended to respond with feelings of helplessness, vulnerability, disappointment, and anger.

The graph illustrates the better postoperative adjustment made by a group of college student patients whose fear level before the operation was moderate, as compared with the adjustment of those at either extreme.

Those with low preoperative fear displayed most anger, most complaints against the hospital staff, and most emotional disturbance (Janis, 1958). ●

Patients with a low level of fear due to denial, false optimism, or ignorance may be given an "emotional inoculation" by preparatory communications. This cognitive preparation has been shown to have remarkable effects.

A group of 97 patients at the Massachusetts General Hospital were randomly divided into two groups. One of the groups received only the routine, minimal medical interview, while the other group received additional relevant information about the surgery. The anesthetist who administered these treatments did not tell the hospital staff or the surgeons which patients were in which group, so as to keep constant all other aspects of their hospitalization. Following the operation, the forewarned group required a much smaller dosage (about half as much) of morphine sedation than the routinely processed group. Not only did they complain less, but they were judged to be in so much better health that they were discharged an average of nearly three days earlier than the cognitively unprepared patients (Egbert, Battit, Welch, & Bartlett, 1964).

When does fear make you act?   Research—as well as your own observation—makes it clear that warnings of danger are not always accepted and acted on. Even when they are believed, as in the case of VD, drug abuse, and cancer related to smoking, they sometimes only increase the individual's emotional arousal without also increasing the likelihood of his initiating preventive behavior.

In a series of studies focused on the problem of how a person can be made to act to promote his own health, one researcher set up information booths at the New York World's Fair and several state fairs and also in conjunction with college health centers. He found that many of the people most in need of the preventive action refuse it in an attempt to maintain their illusion of personal invulnerability. Among a group of smokers encouraged to have chest X rays, 53 percent of those with low fear were willing to do so, as compared with only 6 percent of those with high fear, demonstrating that those with the greatest fear were *not* the ones most likely to take action to safeguard their health (Leventhal, 1965).

In the same way, people who are afraid they have cancer often put off seeing a doctor.

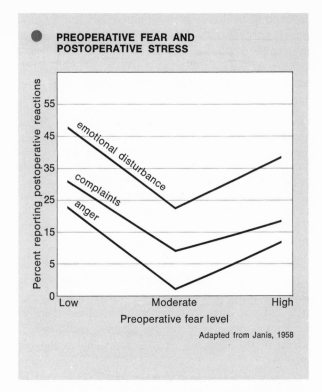

● **PREOPERATIVE FEAR AND POSTOPERATIVE STRESS**

Percent reporting postoperative reactions (vertical axis: 0, 5, 15, 25, 35, 45, 55)

emotional disturbance

complaints

anger

Preoperative fear level (horizontal axis: Low, Moderate, High)

Adapted from Janis, 1958

For fear warnings to serve an effective function, they must: (a) establish a reasonable (not excessive) level of fear, (b) not only arouse fear but also change general attitudes toward doing something about the feared activity or event, and (c) provide clear guidelines for coping action in concrete terms of what the person must do, how, and where. Finally, recommendations for action are more likely to be followed if an overt commitment to act is made, and the sooner the action is to be taken, the more likely it is to be done.

So who's afraid of the big bad wolf, anyway?   A soldier about to go into battle, a surgeon about to perform his first major operation, a prizefighter facing an undefeated opponent, and a novice parachutist readying for a leap into open space all face fear head on. If they cannot master their fear, their performance will suffer, with obviously disastrous personal consequences.

How does an individual cope with the dangers inherent in a situation such as sport parachuting? Regardless of the motivations which draw a select sample of people to such activities in the first place, they experience extreme fear during their early training. The effects of this emotion on their psychological performance, and their manner of exerting cognitive control over their fear, were studied in a provocative field experiment.

Twenty-seven novice sport parachutists were tested on a battery of measures at three different times in relation to jump time: two weeks before a jump, one day before, and on the day itself. They were tested on word-association lists and projective tests, both of which contained items varying in their relevance to the critical event—the parachute jump. In addition, GSR and basal skin conductance were recorded as indicators of physiological activation.

As compared with a control group of similar age, education (college), and geographical location who were not involved in parachuting, the parachutists, two weeks before a jump, reacted less emotionally to words that were not associated with parachuting. "This finding appears to reveal a personality difference as it may be interpreted to indicate that parachutists are more apt to

release tension in motor activity, rather than to inhibit their emotions, or bind their tensions." (p. 13)

On the other hand, the parachutist's general state of tension, generated by increasing proximity to the jump, was handled in a complex way. On the projective measure, they denied fear of jumping in reactions to pictures of high relevance to parachuting, but then expressed more fear responses in relation to pictures of little or no relevance. Their physiology betrayed them, however: as the time of the jump came closer, there were increasingly steep gradients of GSR. ◆

Further complicating the pattern of mind versus body reactions to this threatening event were *lower* levels of skin conductance as the jump time approached (usually an indication of *less* stress) but *higher* sensitization to parachute-relevant words, as reflected in measures of perception, memory, and association. Evidently mounting stress can produce a general state of physiological inhibition coupled with a greater sensitivity and readiness to react to specific stimuli (Fenz, 1964).

These findings are in accord with a report of the Parachute Club of America which indicates that most

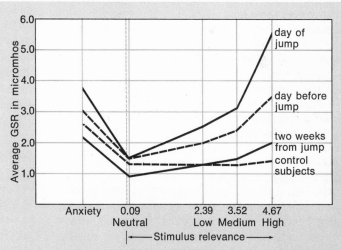

After Fenz, 1964

◆ **MIND AND BODY IN STRESS REACTIONS**

In the projective test, the parachutists made up stories about pictures such as these, which had differing degrees of relevance to jumping. Although their verbal responses showed less fear with high-relevance pictures, their GSR responses, as shown in the graph, were clearly higher for the more relevant pictures as the time to jump approached.

failures are due to the jumper's inability to develop cognitive control of his fear (Moore, 1963).

Denial of fear may serve an adaptive function, but in excess it may also interfere with execution of responses which depend upon complex, unbiased information-processing.

To suffer in silence or cry out . . . Denial of the experience of fear, stress, or pain is not necessarily an individual matter, but may be acquired by members of ethnic groups as a consequence of certain cultural experiences. In fact, in some cases, patients who show exaggerated pain reactions are referred for psychiatric care when actually they are only manifesting learned behavior patterns approved in their group.

When surgical patients at a Bronx VA hospital were observed and interviewed (along with their families and staff), ethnic group membership generally predicted how they were handling the pain they were experiencing. The Jewish and Italian patients emotionally exaggerated the intensity of their pain, feeling free to cry out to elicit support from family or hospital staff. By contrast, Irish and Old American patients (Anglo-Saxon Protestants from at least three generations of Americans) adopted a phlegmatic, detached, matter-of-fact orientation which inhibited any public show of emotion. When their pain became intense, they would withdraw; they would moan or cry out only when alone.

Further investigation showed that the common demonstrativeness of the Jewish and Italian patients stemmed from different concerns. The Italians focused on the immediacy of the pain experience and pain relief, whereas the Jewish patients were concerned about the meaning and future implications of the pain and also had a distrust of pain-relief procedures.

Although both the Irish and the Old Americans were "good" patients who did not make a fuss, they too were acting from quite divergent attitudes. The Old American patients, in refusing to be seen as weak or helpless, assumed that pain was a common experience which everyone has but which threatens one's masculinity. With probing by an interviewer, however, such patients openly discussed their feelings and were optimistic about their future since "doctors are experts."

The Irish patients, on the other hand, were reluctant to speak about their pain and seemed to need to endure it alone as a unique experience. Their inability or unwillingness to share their feelings gave a superficial appearance of outward calm and lack of concern. The investigator reported that "among the four groups of patients of different ethnic backgrounds, the Irish patient presented the saddest, most depressing picture . . . not prepared to think in terms of illness and health care, he discovers in the hospital a world of human suffering of which he is a part. But he is unable to share his emotions, anxieties, and fears with a close person who would understand them and offer some comfort and support." (Zborowski, 1969, p. 235)

The basic results of this research were substantiated in a controlled laboratory study, where pain was induced by electric shock in housewives of various ethnic backgrounds. The Italian subjects were most sensitive to the pain, with significantly lower pain tolerance than any other group. Jewish women were able to take the greatest increase in shock level when motivated (coaxed) by the experimenter. While Yankee subjects adapted to shock physiologically more readily than any other group, the Irish housewives deliberately suppressed their suffering and concern for the implication of the pain (Sternbach & Tursky, 1965).

There were important differences, however, in the experience and interpretation of pain induced in the laboratory, as compared with pain experienced by patients in the hospital. For example, in the laboratory, where the cause of pain was obvious and controlled by the experimenter, the Jewish patients had a higher threshold for pain, as compared with the Jewish hospital patients, since the pain did not signal ominous future dangers. Typical differences are summarized in the chart. •

Helplessness, Hopelessness, and Loss of Cognitive Control

The psychologist attempts to formulate general laws of behavior in order to be able to explain, predict, and control behavior. For the individual attempting to cope with the demands of his environment, existence itself depends upon his being able to meet this goal. To discover causal relations gives meaning to events; to be able to predict the occurrence of events brings order and regularity where chaos and uncertainty would otherwise exist; to control events by one's purposeful actions leads to active mastery in place of passive dependence and submission to the environment.

LABORATORY AND NATURAL PAIN COMPARED

	Laboratory Pain	Natural Pain
Source	The subject is aware of the experimenter as the external agent of pain.	May be known and external, as in an accident, or unknown and internal, as in migraine or abdominal pain.
Onset	Usually predictable within a short time interval, and sudden.	May be unexpected, unpredictable, and gradual.
Duration	Finite, self-limiting.	Usually prolonged, may be indefinite.
Localization	Usually clearly defined.	Often diffuse, vaguely defined.
Preparatory set	The subject must be told about stimulus, and may thus prepare for it.	Usually no preparatory set for initial symptomatic pain.
Attending persons	Usually only a researcher whose interest in the subject is limited.	Physician, nurses, etc., and/or family whose interest in the patient is extensive.
Secondary gains	May not be very appreciable, but primarily approval from the experimenter, money, or mastery of feared stimulus.	May be quite extreme, involving dependence, manipulation of others, attention, sympathy, excuse for failure, punishment for guilt.
Future implications	None, except where pain tolerance is perceived as a challenge and self-esteem is at stake.	Patient's normal life routine may be interrupted, pain may be a symptom of worse pain or fatal disease.
Interpretation of pain	Subject has allowed himself to experience a pain that is under control of a scientist (assumed to be benign and rational).	Patient may feel victimized by a hostile environment (assumed to be irrational or perhaps responsive to religious ritual or magic); may feel a need to suffer.

Zimbardo, 1969a

Give-up-itis

A fateful reaction of some prisoners of war has been aptly described as "give-up-itis." In this syndrome, the loss of all hope of ever being freed and consequent loss of interest in the future resulted in emotionally caused death. Bruno Bettelheim (1960), a psychologist who himself survived imprisonment in Nazi concentration camps, characterizes one such reaction that he observed among fellow prisoners in this way:

"Prisoners who came to believe the repeated statements of the guards—that there was no hope for them, that they would never leave the camp except as a corpse—who came to feel that their environment was one over which they could exercise no influence whatsoever, these prisoners were, in a literal sense, walking corpses. In the camps they were called 'moslems' (*Muselmanner*) because of what was erroneously viewed as a fatalistic surrender to the environment, as Mohammedans are supposed to blandly accept their fate.

". . . they were people who were so deprived of affect, self-esteem, and every form of stimulation, so totally exhausted, both physically and emotionally, that they had given the environment total power over them." (pp. 151-152)

For the American P.O.W. of the Chinese Communists in the Korean War, there were reported to be similar feelings of being abandoned and deserted by one's own people, of suffering constant intimidation, of loss of self-respect, of the day-to-day uncertainty of existence, of social-psychological isolation from one's fellow Americans (planned by the captors), and, finally, of the futility of resisting or escaping

(Nardini, 1952; Schein, 1957). Even after repatriation and return to civilian life, these men were observed to show a "zombie-like" detachment. This is a common reaction pattern among many hospitalized mental patients, who seem to withdraw, quietly or sullenly, from all social contact. They stop caring about personal cleanliness or even eating and must be coaxed or forced to care for themselves. Among some schizophrenic patients,

"the sense of self-preservation is often reduced to zero. The patients do not bother any more about whether they starve or not, whether they lie on a snowbank or on a red-hot oven. During a fire in the hospital, a number of patients had to be led out of the threatened ward; they themselves would never have moved from their places; they would have allowed themselves to be suffocated or burnt without showing an affective response." (Bleuler, 1950, p. 40)

This psychic state of loss of feelings of cognitive control over the environment has been shown to render even "normal" individuals more biologically vulnerable to a host of diseases. Medical investigators have begun to accumulate evidence suggesting that when a person responds to events in his life with helplessness or hopelessness, he initiates a complex series of biological changes that foster the development of any disease potential which is present—even diabetes, heart disease, and cancer. These findings are explained by one physician in an analysis which has broad implications beyond those of psychosomatic medicine.

"Man is constantly interacting within his many environments, and at many levels of organization—from the subcellular and biochemical to the most external or peripheral, that of family, work and now even his universe. We postulate that when a person gives up psychologically, he is disrupting the continuity of his relatedness to himself and his many environments or levels of organization.

"In making such a break, or with this loss of continuity, he may become more vulnerable to the pathogenic influences in his external environments and/or he may become more cut off from his external environments and more predisposed to internal derangements. Thus, disease is more apt to appear at such times of disruptions and increased vulnerability." (Schmale, cited in Brody, 1968, p. 11)

Voodoo Deaths

There is no human phenomenon which so captures the imagination as the sudden voodoo deaths described in anthropological reports. For example, the following is an account of what happens in one tribe when a man discovers that he is being "boned" —having a bone pointed at him in a certain way by an enemy.

"He stands aghast, with his eyes staring at the treacherous pointer, and with his hands lifted as though to ward off the lethal medium, which he imagines is pouring into his body. His cheeks blanch and his eyes become glassy and the expression of his face becomes horribly distorted . . . . He attempts to shriek but usually the sound chokes in his throat, and all that one might see is froth at his mouth. His body begins to tremble and the muscles twist involuntarily. He sways backwards and falls to the ground, and after a short time appears to be in a swoon; but soon after he writhes as if in mortal agony, and, covering his face with his hands, begins to moan. After a while he becomes very composed and crawls to his wurley. From this time onwards he sickens and frets, refusing to eat and keeping aloof from the daily affairs of the tribe. Unless help is forthcoming in the shape of a countercharm administered by the hands of the Nangarri, or medicine-man, his death is only a matter of a comparatively short time." (Basedow, 1925, cited in Cannon, 1942, p. 172)

Other reports tell of healthy people succumbing to sudden death upon discovering that they have transgressed against the supernatural world by eating a food which is cursed.

A young traveler, lodging at the house of a friend, was served a dish containing fowl. He asked his host if it was wild hen, for that delicacy was banned for the young. The host replied, "No," so the boy ate his fill and then went on his way. A few years later the two friends met again and the older man asked the youth if he would eat a wild hen. When the boy said, "No," the man laughed and told him that he had eaten the forbidden food a few years before at his house. At this knowledge, the young man began to tremble and in less than twenty-four hours he was dead (Pinkerton, 1814).

Such reports from so-called "primitive" societies were thoroughly analyzed by the physiologist Walter Cannon (1942), who became convinced of the reality of this phenomenon. Nevertheless, people from technologically and scientifically more advanced societies find it difficult to accept such events. We do not believe in black magic or witchcraft, but rather in natural causes for rationally related events. But in lumping voodoo deaths with magic, we overlook the possibility that the ultimate cause of death may indeed follow physiological laws but be set in motion by the cognitive belief system of the tabooed person and his society. In order to understand how this might work, let us look at the ways in which some societies view the phenomena of disease.

Knowing what we now do about the role of cognitive appraisal in emotional arousal, such mysterious sudden deaths are easier to understand when we realize that in many cultures illness is not separated into mental and physical categories as with us, nor is the cause of illness clearly attributed to natural causes as opposed to supernatural ones. Illness, disease, and early death are more common in less advantaged societies and thus represent an ever present concern, as does the burden of treating and caring for the sick. In addition, the greater dependence upon the vicissitudes of nature for one's daily bread strengthens the belief that man is impotent and totally at the mercy of external and supernatural forces.

A cross-cultural study compared the beliefs about disease held by a sample of American students and rural Mexican adults (both non-Indians and Spanish-speaking Indians). The categorization of disease by the American sample seemed to be based primarily on two dimensions: "Is it contagious?" and "How serious is it?" Emotional diseases like psychosis and ulcers were distinguished from those with organic causes.

In contrast, analysis of the Mexican belief system regarding disease classification revealed no dimension of contagiousness as such. Rather, diseases were classified as requiring either "hot medicine" or "cold medicine" and as children's diseases (most of which were contagious) or diseases of old age, the latter category including visceral ailments and diseases caused by witchcraft. No distinction was made between physical and mental diseases.

Such belief systems do not recognize the dangers of contagion in epidemics since diseases are considered to be happenings caused by external (often magical) sources in which their bodily processes do not play an active role. If many people get the same disease, they are all considered to be afflicted by some common external agent over which they have no control. This raises a serious problem for public health officials concerned with preventing the spread of disease (D'Andrade, Quinn, Nerlove, & Romney, 1969).

Once an individual accepts his society's beliefs about external disease causation, capricious spirits and evil sorcerers, and the unalterability of certain disease states, it is easy to see how he comes to accept the inevitability of his doom when designated as a transgressor against the supernatural world (Frank, 1961). His feeling of "helplessness" is then reinforced by his friends and relatives who, believing in the same system of fate, begin to withdraw their support, socially isolate him, and finally treat him as if he were already dead. One function of modern education is to enhance the perception of personal control, and its message is bolstered by the evidence from technology that nature can be tamed.

If ulcers in animals can occur after a prolonged period of vigilance, stress, or learned helplessness, then it is not hard to see how the extreme fright induced in a person who believes he is doomed might lead to a kind of "surgical shock" and death. An outpouring of adrenaline from the inner portion of the adrenal glands has been suggested as the cause of death in such cases. According to this theory, adrenaline impairs the capillary walls, allowing a passage of fluid to the surrounding tissues; the resulting reduction in the volume of circulating blood sends the organism into a state of shock which leads to deterioration of the heart and nerve centers (Cannon, 1957).

To demonstrate experimentally that an organism deprived of hope of survival will give up and die, Richter (1957) immersed wild rats and domestic rats singly in a water jar. Normally, laboratory rats will swim in such a container for sixty to eighty hours before exhaustion sets in and they drown.

Richter found that when he clipped the whiskers of tame rats before placing them in the tank three out of twelve died within two minutes of being put in the water, but the others did not give up and kept swimming for forty to sixty hours. When the procedure was repeated with wild rats, thus depriving them of perhaps their most important means of contact with their natural environment, all thirty-four animals died either within fifteen minutes after being placed in the water or even while simply being held. Their giving up is even more dramatic when it is noted that they are "characteristically fierce, aggressive, and suspicious . . . constantly on the alert for any avenue of escape." A slowing of heart rate and lowering of body temperature preceded death, indicating that in this case death was due to overstimulation of the parasympathetic system rather than to hyperactivity of the adrenal glands.

The hypothesis that hopelessness was the initial cause of the sudden deaths was supported by two observations. First, when animals close to death were removed from the water, they became normally aggressive and active within a minute or two. Even more convincing was the finding that when wild rats were briefly held and then released several times and given several experiences of being briefly immersed in the water ("hope pretraining") they subsequently did not give up and die but swam as long as the domestic rats.

Before dismissing this general line of evidence as perhaps revelant only to wild rats and primitive man, we must add the results of a thorough investigation into the causes of the sudden and unexpected death of a great many American soldiers who were not in combat at the time of death.

From a sample of 1000 such reported deaths between 1942 and 1946, investigators surveyed 550 cases in which the men were young (under forty years of age), physically healthy, died within twenty-four hours after the onset of any symptoms, and were not engaged in exertion or physical activity at the time of death (most were asleep). In 140 of these cases no physical cause of the death could be determined after analysis of all available protocols and postmortem autopsies (Moritz & Zamchech, 1946).

Hope Is to Action
As Hopelessness Is to Apathy and Inaction

Systematic research on the hopelessness seen in the sudden-death phenomenon has begun only recently. In general, behaviorally oriented psychologists have tended to avoid such loose concepts as "hope" or "hopelessness." There have been occasional exceptions, however, in which such cognitive concepts have been used in relation to expectation of success in attaining one's goals. In fact, the purposeful psychology of E. C. Tolman (see Appendix C) saw expectancy of achieving a goal as an essential part of all voluntary activity. Tolman pointed out that an organism undertakes an action only when it expects that action to lead toward a desired goal state.

Expectation of the instrumental value of one's behavior for effecting a change in the environment creates a state of hope and motivates action. Apathy and inaction become consequences of the hopelessness that attends ineffectual responding. When an organism, man or animal, comes to believe that nothing it can do can eliminate a threat, it yields to passive resignation.

The acceptance of control by external factors or "fate" is not an all-or-none affair but varies with the degree to which we have had the experience of seeing that what we do makes a difference. Rotter (1966) conceives of this dimension of perceived degree of environmental control as a consistent personality trait. Some individuals perceive that they possess considerable internal, personal control over what reinforcements they receive. At the other end of the continuum are those who believe that the external environment—forces beyond their control—determines what happens and that nothing they could do would change the outcome.

Learned helplessness.   What happens to an organism when it learns from its experience that traumatic events continue to occur independently of any attempts on its part to reduce or eliminate them? This problem, although first put to experimental test several decades ago, has only recently been revived as basic to an understanding of all forms of apparently pathological behavior.

In the early study hungry rats were shocked ten seconds after they began to eat. The animals in one group were given control over the shock since it was terminated when they jumped up off the shock grid. The animals in the other group had no control over the shock. For each rat in the "Yes Control" group there was one in the "No Control" group that received the same amount of shock. It was found that the animals who could control the shock ate more often (on 12.4 trials out of 14) than those who had no control (only on 5.5 trials out of 14). The experimenters postulated that exposure to the unavoidable shock caused the animals to eat less because they had developed a "sense of helplessness" (Mowrer & Viek, 1948).

Such a sense of helplessness might derive from either or both of two sources: inability to control the aversive stimulation itself through any action (lack of *behavioral control*), and inability to predict when it would start or stop (lack of *perceptual control*).

Recent research has convincingly demonstrated that when an organism is unable to escape shock in one situation, hopelessness is developed which carries over into other situations. Even where escape is possible, it does not even try.

One group of dogs received inescapable shock while strapped into a harness. The next day they were put in a shuttlebox in which a danger signal was given 10 seconds before the grid floor was electrified. An animal could avoid the shock by jumping over a barrier to the "safe" side after the danger signal. Naïve dogs not given the prior training quickly learned to avoid the shock in this way. In startling contrast, the dogs who had experienced the inescapable shock the day before "seemed to give up and passively accept the shock." They failed to make escape movements and took 50 seconds of pulsating shock on each trial. Even if they jumped the barrier on one trial and got to the safe side, they might revert to taking the shocks on later trials (Overman & Seligman, 1967).

When another group of dogs were shocked in the harness but given a means of controlling the shock (by pressing a panel), they escaped normally when put in the shuttlebox later (Seligman & Maier, 1967).

Another study showed that although the effects of a prior session of helplessness seemed to wear off after forty-eight hours in the original study, they could be made chronic and nontransient. Repeated, spaced exposure to inescapable shocks produced a failure to try to escape danger as long as a week later. This study also showed that domesticated beagles were more susceptible to the conditions inducing helplessness than were mongrels of unknown history, who may have had to learn to persist in order to survive in an environment that was unfriendly and not as predictable as that of the laboratory (Seligman & Groves, 1970).

If the incentive for responding comes from an expectation that responding will produce relief from pain and fear, then this incentive is undercut if one observes that emitted responses and environmental consequences are not related to each other. The learned helplessness which results takes a toll on physiological functioning as well as on behavioral adaptation to the threatening environment.

Rats given a series of uncontrollable shocks were compared to yoked controls given the same number of shocks but provided with the means to avoid them. The helpless rats showed more defecation, a greater weight loss, and suppression of drinking; in addition, they developed ulcers (Weiss, 1968).

The results of these studies seem at first glance to be at odds with those in the studies of "executive monkeys." Here it is the animal that can do nothing that gets sick; there it was the animal who could prevent the shocks.

The difference is apparently due to a basic procedural variation. In the earlier example, the powerless, yoked-control monkey stopped getting shocked as soon as its partner learned what to do to prevent shocks; from then on, the environment placed extreme demands only on the hard-working "executives." In the studies of learned helplessness, both animals received many shocks, but one had a controllable environment to the extent that it could terminate the shocks, whereas the other faced a totally uncontrollable environment, receiving random shocks throughout.

The ray of hope. Even when aversive stimulation cannot be avoided, its disrupting effect can be reduced by making it predictable.

In one study, after animals had learned to press a bar for food, their bar pressing was suppressed when shock was given. When the shock became predictable, however, responding again occurred regularly. Six of eight subjects in an unpredictable shock condition developed ulcers after forty-five days, whereas none of eight animals given predictable shock developed ulcers (Seligman, 1968). ◆ (p. 406)

The fear and anxiety created by uncertainty about future threatening events can be reduced in several ways. Subjects given a choice will choose a shock which has a predictable warning signal over one that is unsignaled (Lockard, 1963). They also prefer to take an inevitable shock immediately—to "get it over with" —rather than wait for a delayed shock (Gibbon, 1967; Knapp, Kause, & Perkins, 1959). Human subjects given a choice of advance information about intensity or timing of coming shock request temporal information more often than information about intensity (Jones, Bentler, & Petry, 1966).

A recent study extends these basic findings about the consequences of both behavioral and perceptual control of the environment on physiological reactions in human subjects.

Male college volunteer subjects worked for half an hour on a demanding shock-avoidance task. To keep from being shocked, they had to press a start button, quickly respond by depressing the correct lever when one of a

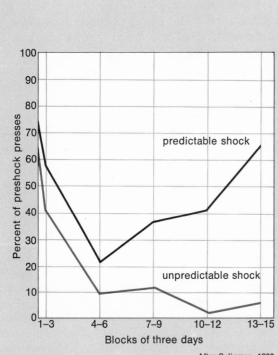

♦ **CHRONIC FEAR PRODUCED BY UNPREDICTABLE SHOCK**

A base-line rate of bar pressing without shock was established; thereafter, this rate was regarded as 100 percent and the rates of bar pressing under predictable and unpredictable shock were plotted in terms of percents of the base rate. After an initial drop for both conditions when shock began, the subjects with predictable shock steadily increased their rate again.

series of lights came on, and then immediately go through the next trial. Once every forty-five seconds, on the average, they missed at some point and received a painful shock. Their arousal to this stress was recorded by elevations in systolic blood pressure.

At first, twelve experimental subjects were given the opportunity to call for a time-out of one minute whenever they wanted it, while twelve yoked controls received the same time-out periods, but not upon request. Thus the only difference was in the cognition of one group that it controlled the avoidance response of calling for a time-out and of the other group that it did not. Over the course of the experiment, systolic blood pressure was consistently higher for the helpless subjects, indicating a higher level of arousal (and, presumably, stress). ■

In a second part of the study (using different subjects), the rest period was preceded by a signal indicating that relief was on the way. The subjects again worked on the light-matching task, which was interrupted by a conditioned stimulus signaling that a time-out was thirty seconds away. The subjects had to continue working after the signal until the relief period started.

Even though they were still being shocked as often and as intensely after the safety signal as before, and had no control over its occurrence, their knowledge gave them perceptual control and their blood pressure dropped markedly as soon as the signal appeared. When, in addition, they *did* have control over the timing of the safety signal (both perceptual and behavioral control), the reduction in physiological stress was even greater though the number of signals and time-out periods remained unchanged (Hokanson, DeGood, Forrest, & Brittain, 1971).

Hope, Faith, and Cognitive Cures

If the phenomena of psychosomatic disorders, debilitation from stress, and sudden death represent the negative influence of the mind over the body, what is the evidence for its positive influence? Hopelessness in the confined wild rats was eliminated simply by repeatedly exposing them to immersion in the water for a few minutes and then freeing them. These few trials were sufficient to relearn "hope": after that they became aggressive again, tried to escape, and did not give up. Similarly, as we saw, dogs are "immunized" against learned helplessness when they are given prior experiences with avoidable shock. Or if they have

BEHAVIORAL CONTROL, HELPLESSNESS, AND SYSTOLIC BLOOD PRESSURE

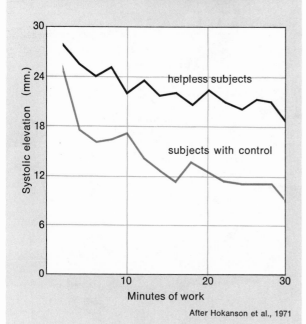

helpless subjects

subjects with control

Systolic elevation (mm.)

Minutes of work

After Hokanson et al., 1971

given up, physically forcing them to perform the overt response which terminates the shock can sometimes provide learned relief and self-initiated activity thereafter (Seligman, Maier, & Greer, 1968).

Faith, defined as belief despite absence of knowledge or impossibility of empirical validation, is the essential characteristic of religion and of religious healing. Absolute faith in the power of God's will can provide a powerful source of expectancy motivation. One study reported that 71 percent of Roman Catholic patients said their religious faith had helped them through a surgical crisis, and their records showed that they required appreciably smaller doses of morphine than patients of other religions (Egbert, 1969). Healing sects, such as Christian Science, and the shrines of miracle cures, such as Lourdes in France, attract millions of believers from all parts of the earth. There is ample, well-documented evidence that severe illnesses have been cured, that the lame have given up crutches and the blind have seen, after

participation in religious-emotional pilgrimages to such spots (Cranston, 1955).

The existence of such cures, whether skeptically viewed as cures of the mind, or accepted as cures of organic illness, represents to the cured person genuine relief from a lifetime of real pain, incapacitation, and suffering. Our discussion of pain in the previous chapter and the complex interactions of mind and body shown in disease causation should indicate the difficulty in establishing whether pain is "real" or a bleeding ulcer is all in one's mind.

The placebo problem. We moderns put our faith in a medical doctor, in ritual visits to his office, and in the pills he dispenses. This faith is so strong that even when the pill or procedure administered is a *placebo* (has no medicinal value), the individual may nevertheless be relieved of his pain and other symptoms of illness. But how effective can a sugar pill really be?

In a survey of 4681 patients treated with placebos for over twenty ailments or symptoms, including colds, epilepsy, and multiple sclerosis, successful results were achieved in 27 percent of the cases (Haas, Fink, & Härtfelder, 1959). According to another report, headaches were shown to be relieved by placebos in 58 percent of 4588 cases. Overall, about one third of all patients treated with placebos in fifteen test series achieved positive results (Beecher, 1959).

Even pain from incurable organic illness was lessened. In studies comparing pain relief from placebo and morphine injections, for 122 patients with postoperative wound pain 39 percent were relieved by placebos while 67 percent were relieved by morphine. The chronic pain of cancer was relieved in 65 percent of the patients receiving a 10-mg. injection of morphine. But 10 mg. of placebo equally helped 42 percent of the cancer victims (Beecher, 1959).

Believing that a placebo will lead to pain reduction is thus sufficient to bring about major psychological (and perhaps physiological) reorganization. Such belief not only reduces pain but can produce new symptoms. Placebo-treated patients have complained of a wide range of "negative side effects" following administration of a placebo, including nausea, headaches, sleepiness, and reduced concentration.

Likewise, the patient's conviction can do more than make potent an inert drug: it can even *reverse* the usual pharmacological effect of a medicine. Ipecac, which is normally used to induce vomiting (for example, in cases of poisoning) "had healing effects on patients with nausea of pregnancy when it was suggested to them that they were receiving a good preparation" (Haas et al., 1959, p. 27).

Positive placebo reaction is a "problem" precisely because placebos work so well when they are not supposed to. How can the effectiveness of a "real" drug or treatment procedure be tested when people are so ready to respond to their expectations instead of to the physical properties of the treatment? ●

It is instructive to note the characteristics that distinguish placebo reactors from nonreactors. Those whose postoperative pain was relieved by placebo tended to be regular churchgoers, talkative, anxious, dependent, self-centered, and preoccupied with their internal bodily processes. Nonreactors tended to be withdrawn, rigid, and intellectually critical rather than emotionally responsive (Lasagna et al., 1954).

In general, when those who believe in the doctor's recommendations and have faith in authority are given a placebo, they experience a reduction in their *anxiety* over the illness and with it, pain relief and improved healing. Since even the most rationally critical, intellectually skeptical person may retain some of the "irrational" beliefs of childhood, everyone is potentially a placebo reactor.

Animal magnetism and hypnosis. In the eighteenth century, a Viennese physician, Anton Mesmer, startled the world when he began to cure afflicted persons by application of *animal magnetism*. He believed that a universal fluid influenced the planets and all living things. A diseased body could be restored to its harmony with the universe by placing magnets on it to induce a flow of healing magnetic fluid. In *The Influence of the Planets on the Human Body* (1776), he wrote:

". . . through certain manipulations (such as touching, stroking, in a word 'magnetizing') even simply by merely a strong act of will, one can produce power in persons, impart to others and cause the most marvelous and wholesome effects."

The power of *mesmerism* achieved such fame that as hundreds of patients experienced relief from pain,

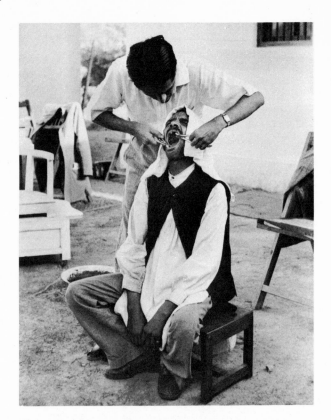

Although the Indian yogis regard tooth troubles as curable by diet or spiritual means, they permit their disciples to perform extractions for moderns who insist on it. After a special technique of head manipulation, the individual feels no pain while his teeth are yanked out.

thousands more came. To handle the demand, Mesmer "magnetized" virtually everything in sight and proclaimed that contact with these objects would be curative. The hope of relief from suffering even led many to tie themselves together in a row and then to a special magnetized oak tree. Animal magnetism was eventually discredited as having no physical basis by a commission of the French Academy of Science, led by Benjamin Franklin.

A little later, hypnosis replaced animal magnetism and regained some scientific acceptance through the efforts of a Manchester surgeon, James Braid. He discovered in 1843 that the nervous system could be artificially induced into a state of "nervous sleep." The name *hypnosis* is derived from the Greek word *Hypnos,* the name of the god of sleep. It was demonstrated that this special state of sleep could be produced merely by concentrated attention or "fixity of gaze." The person in this state was shown to be very responsive to verbal suggestions given by the hypnotist.

From 1845 to 1853, a Scottish surgeon working in India, James Esdaile, performed nearly 300 painless major operations including amputations and cataract removals, with hypnosis as the only anesthetic. The subsequent discovery of ether, however, led surgeons to prefer that physical drug treatment to the psychic one of hypnosis, although the latter was shown to be equally effective and to lead to fewer side effects and a lower mortality rate for many types of operations.

While acceptance of hypnosis in academic and medical circles has fluctuated over the years, it has always captured the popular and literary imagination. Hypnosis is not like ordinary sleep, as evidenced by comparison of EEG records of sleeping and hypnotized persons. Rather, it is an altered state of consciousness. The hypnotic subject agrees to suspend his usual, critical, reality-testing apparatus and go along with the suggestions of the hypnotist. A heightened state of selective attention is created by hypnotic induction procedures. The person "tunes out" the distractions of irrelevant realities and focuses upon the experiences suggested to him. Almost every person has at some time informally experienced hypnosis without realizing it. Daydreaming, being lost in love or totally absorbed in a book or a movie, religious rituals, and natural childbirth—all these share elements of the hypnotic experience.

Induction of hypnosis can be achieved by any of a variety of techniques which have in common conveying to the subject that he should: (a) relax, (b) concentrate, (c) give free rein to his imagination, (d) voluntarily agree to let his mind and body "behave involuntarily," (e) allow temporal, spatial, physical, and causal relations to be distorted or dissociated, if necessary, and (f) be responsive to the suggestions of the hypnotist.

Variations in susceptibility to hypnosis are found in measures taken during the first formalized attempt to hypnotize individuals, and often such measures show high correlations with measures made as long as ten years later (Hilgard, 1965). Some investigators

have taken this to mean that such susceptibility is a relatively stable personality characteristic. On the other hand, those who use hypnosis in medical or psychological therapy are finding evidence that, with training, subjects can learn to become more hypnotizable. In fact, with training, many subjects can experience autohypnosis, in which they dispense with the outside hypnotist. In becoming both subject and agent of suggestion, the self-hypnotized person can be said to increase his potential for internal control. The extent to which such techniques can increase a person's potential control over the impact of a threatening environment is demonstrated by the finding that even in terminal cancer, pain can be brought under the patient's control so that he no longer needs to depend on morphine (Sacerdote, 1966).

Some investigators have argued that all hypnotic phenomena represent nothing more than strong states of motivation. Barber (1969) has shown that many behaviors attributed to the "state of hypnosis" can be reproduced in unhypnotized subjects simply given a set of motivating instructions in the waking state. Such effects, it is argued, show how far the human potential of all men might be increased—not by the magic of hypnosis, but by the well-understood application of principles of motivation.

There is little question from our preceding discussions that hypnosis shares some of the same components of belief, hope, and expectation-motivation as operate in placebo-induced pain reduction, religious cures, and primitive healing. But in addition to the placebo effect that occurs when pain is relieved by hypnosis, a second effect, unique to hypnosis, has been convincingly demonstrated.

In a well-controlled study, pain thresholds were recorded as well as subjective and physiological reactions to the stress of ischemic pain (stopping of arterial blood flow in the arm by a tourniquet). The twenty-four male paid volunteer college students then underwent two additional, double-blind sessions—one in which they believed that a drug (placebo) would relieve the pain, and one in which they were simply told under hypnosis that they would feel no pain. It was known from previous measures that half of the subjects were highly susceptible to hypnosis and half were not.

It was found that there was a sizable placebo effect on reduction of pain for both placebo and hypnotic subjects

but no correlation between degree of hypnotic susceptibility and amount of placebo reaction. Over and above
the general placebo effect with both the placebo and the
hypnotic procedures, there was a perceptual distortion
effect in the subjects who were known to be highly
susceptible to hypnosis and were deeply hypnotized,
enabling them to withstand pain significantly longer than
the subjects in any other condition (McGlashlin, Evans,
& Orne, 1969).   ▲

The following study is dramatic evidence of how
complete the independence of the pain response from
environmental stimulation can become under hypnotic control.

A GSR record was kept of the reactions of a student to
a series of constant-intensity, painful electric shocks.   ◆
Before hypnosis, he reacted with a sizable GSR to each
stimulus onset. After being hypnotized and told only,
"This time the shocks will not hurt as much," his
response to the shocks was greatly lessened. For the last
ten shocks in the series, he gained autonomy over the
sensory input and was no longer affected by the once-
painful stimulation. Responses can be brought under
stimulus control, but apparently the effects of stimuli

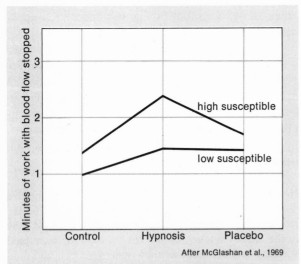

After McGlashan et al., 1969

▲ **HYPNOSIS VS. PLACEBO IN PAIN REDUCTION**
The greater reduction of pain for the high-susceptible
subjects during hypnosis than for either the low-sus-
ceptible subjects with hypnosis or either group under
a placebo indicates that hypnosis was having a separate effect.

can also be brought under the influence or response-con-
trolling cognitions (Zimbardo, Rapaport, & Baron,
1969).

Meditation and altered consciousness.   For centuries
Eastern philosophers and religious mystics have
maintained that man can transcend the confining
limits imposed by normal consciousness. Various
techniques of meditation have been developed to
guide Zen monks and other practitioners to these
"higher" states of transcendental awareness. These
techniques require not only daily practice, but a
reorientation of one's life about them.

The state produced by transcendental meditation
has been shown to be physiologically distinguishable
from the more commonly encountered states of consciousness.

A sample of fifteen college students trained in this
technique from six months to three years were used as
subjects. The technique was defined as "turning the
attention inwards towards the subtler levels of thought
until the mind transcends the experience of the subtlest
state of thought and arrives at the source of the
thought" (Mahesh Yogi, 1969).

On all recorded measurements there were significant
changes between a control base-line period and the
meditation period. In the meditation state, oxygen consumption and heart rate decreased, skin resistance increased, and EEG frequency changes were predominately toward alpha-wave activity, with no slow waves or
sleep spindles (Wallace, 1970).

One of the most remarkable findings is that EEG
recordings of Zen monks during this unusual state
revealed that they did not habituate to repetitive
stimuli. They continued to respond to each stimulus
in a series as if it were perceived anew, contrary to
the basic pattern described in Chapter 5 of habituation to recurrent stimulus events (Kasamatsu & Hirai,
1966). This is especially notable because habituation
is one of the most fundamental of all psychological
adaptation processes: across a wide range of species
and for virtually all responses that organisms make,
from leg flexion to complex patterns of exploration
and play, habituation is observed with repeated stimulus exposure (Welker, 1961). Such a continuous
openness to experience may result from a release of

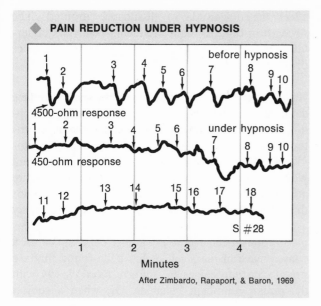

◆ **PAIN REDUCTION UNDER HYPNOSIS**

4500-ohm response

before hypnosis

450-ohm response

under hypnosis

S #28

Minutes

After Zimbardo, Rapaport, & Baron, 1969

the efferent regulation that is usually exercised over stimulus input.

It can only be speculated at this time that training in producing such special states of consciousness should greatly extend man's control over his involuntary and voluntary bodily functioning and result in major therapeutic effects, both mental and physical.

Choice, Responsibility, and Cognitive Control

When the environment overwhelms man with extreme deprivation, unpredictable noxious stimulation, or aversive confinement from which there is no escape, he may become "stimulus-bound"—concerned only with survival and reacting directly to stimuli with a minimum of mediation by evaluation or choice. Under less pressing environmental conditions, however, his highly developed nervous system enables him to withhold or delay response to stimulation, evaluate and anticipate, plan ahead, and even restructure the source of the stimulus input. Thus instead of simply reacting, he often has—and creates—alternative reactions to the same stimulus condition. The presence of alternatives gives man the potentiality for choice.

According to an old Dutch proverb, "He who has

choice, has trouble." This may be so because the ability to choose involves, first, psychological freedom to specify what the alternatives are, or to perceive at least two available courses of action. The act of deciding upon one alternative and rejecting others requires consideration of the attributes, implications, utility, and costs of each one. Since the consequences of any act cannot be fully known at the time of the choice, there is always some risk that the decision may be the wrong one.

But if one chooses freely, then one bears personal responsibility for the consequences of the choice. If there are outcomes which will be evaluated as right or wrong, good or bad, wise or stupid, then the individual knows that he himself will be evaluated according to the consequences of his choice. Where the alternatives are mutually exclusive and the choice irrevocable, and the consequences involve important aspects of the individual's aspirations, values, and attitudes, then his very self-definition is at stake. So choice may bring pain. But only with choice is there potentiality for control. If he gives up one, he loses the other too.

Competence and Mastery of the Environment

In higher animals, and especially in man, behavior is ordinarily directed not only toward merely adapting to the environment that is given but also toward manipulating and modifying it. Activities which change the environment establish the *competence* of the behaving organism and signify some degree of mastery over the environment.

As we saw in Chapter 5, a perception of one's competence is a powerful reinforcer. It has been hypothesized that much environment-changing behavior is motivated not by the need to satisfy biological drives, but rather by a cognitively generated *effectance motivation*. This striving to make sense of one's environment and be effective in relation to it seems to be a basic part of our motivational equipment. It is apparent in every infant's avid explorations and testing of his environment (social and physical) to see what it holds and how far he can control it (White, 1959). It continues throughout one's life as long as he believes that what he does can make a difference in what happens.

Maintaining or Creating Consistency

In learning how to control aspects of the environment, the individual must first be able to predict relationships between and among stimuli and responses, as discussed in Chapter 5. To do so requires identifying or establishing patterns of consistency. Without a perception of consistency in things, events, and activities, the individual operates in a chaotic, capricious environment. Such a state puts him at the mercy of the environmental demands instead of in the position of mastery.

Given the importance to us of predictability it is not surprising that in recent years a number of psychologists have developed theories organized around the central theme of the need for consistency (see Abelson et al., 1968). It is postulated that individuals seek consistency, prefer balanced relations to unbalanced ones, and are motivated to reduce the disharmony inherent in inconsistent perceptions.

Discrepancy and dissonance.   The most formally developed of these approaches is the theory of cognitive dissonance (Festinger, 1957; Brehm & Cohen, 1962). It has provided a set of explanatory principles which meaningfully relate cognitive input variables to behavioral consequences, and in so doing has instigated a large body of empirical research.

Essentially, this theory says that the need for consistency will arouse a tension-like state of dissonance in an individual when there is a *discrepancy* between two or more cognitions that are in a *relevant* relation to each other and of *importance* to him. Cognitions represent "knowledge, opinion, or belief about the environment, about oneself, or about one's behavior." Every overt response is represented cognitively in the behaver's mind, as are the antecedent conditions and consequences and whatever relationships he sees between them. It is his task to establish consistency between cognitions about his behavior and about aspects of his internal and external environment which have either been motivated, reinforced, or changed by the behavior. When consistency does not exist naturally, it must be created by restructuring of the ill-fitting elements. Dissonant cognitions must be changed or consonant ones added.

The theory specifies a number of variables which affect the magnitude of dissonance aroused. The strength of the dissonance-reducing behaviors undertaken becomes a measure of the initial magnitude of dissonance previously aroused.

Reducing cognitive dissonance.   A person can reduce dissonance most easily by changing his perception or interpretation of his subjective feelings, attitudes, beliefs, or motive states. Thus when the individual engages in a behavior which is inconsistent with his existing relevant attitudes, his attitudes are more likely to be changed to fit the overt behavior than the other way around. After arguing publicly against one's own private attitude position, for example, as may occur in role-playing, debates, or as a consequence of one's job, it has been found that the private attitude comes to conform more closely with the public compliant behavior. Or, when a subject who has engaged in a boring task is induced to lie to a fellow subject by describing it as an interesting one, he himself subsequently will perceive it as less boring.

Dissonance-reduction may also take other forms. For example, the individual may reevaluate the attractiveness of a chosen alternative relative to a rejected one, seeing it as more attractive than he did before the choice was made. Or he may seek social support or expose himself only to sources of information that agree with the position he has taken.

Behavior that is inconsistent with one's beliefs or desires does not cause dissonance if the person thinks he has no choice or if there is adequate external justification (he'll lose his job if he doesn't lie). Either a lack of choice or an adequate external justification puts the behavior under external stimulus control and the individual can "disown" it as not personally caused. One sees one's behavior as dissonant only when he attributes its cause to himself and not to circumstances.

In the experiment where subjects lied (as a favor to the experimenter) about how interesting a boring task was, they did not change their perception of the task when they were promised the adequate justification of $20.00 for the compliant falsehood. However, after having lied for only $1.00 (an insufficient justification), they judged the task significantly more interesting than they had before (Festinger & Carlsmith, 1959).

In the first case there was no dissonance and thus no need to change, but in the second case the subjects were motivated to make an unjustified action seem more rational.

Cognitive Control of Physiological Processes

Recent research has demonstrated that in the attempt to achieve consistency, physiological as well as subjective and behavioral responses can be altered. Voluntarily committing oneself to a state of deprivation or an unpleasant arousal state is presumed to create dissonance. Refusing for no good reason to take water when thirsty or food when hungry—or taking electric shocks that are painful and could be avoided—is inconsistent unless one convinces himself that he really was not very thirsty or hungry, or that the shocks did not hurt so much.

In a series of independent experiments with over 1000 subjects, the impact of biological drives (hunger, thirst, pain, stress) and social motives (approval, achievement, frustration, aggression) was demonstrated to be lessened through cognitive processes involved in establishing consistent explanations for inconsistent behavior. Such results as reduced free fatty acids in the blood (a physiological measure of hunger), reduced GSR to painful shock, lessened water consumption when thirsty, as well as changes in attitudes, perceptions, learning, memory, and conditionability, were all found under conditions where maximum dissonance was created; the individual apparently was attempting to make his motivational state consistent with his behavioral commitment (Zimbardo, 1969a). ■

Thus it now becomes possible to argue that cognitive control processes can impose consistency where it is lacking, even if that requires changing the usual relationship between a physical stimulus and the body's reaction to it.

The Cognitive Control of Death

In a society with the accent on youth, what does it mean to be old? At best, the aged are tolerated; more typically they are ignored, made to feel useless and a burden to their family. Approximately one of every ten Americans is over sixty-five, and the proportion increases as life expectancy is prolonged. Two thirds

of these individuals suffer from some chronic condition such as high blood pressure, heart trouble, or arthritis. Increasingly, they are being abandoned to care by nursing homes, of which there are about 30,000 in this country. "It's rather like condemning old cars to the scrap heap," commented Charles Boucher, senior medical officer in the British Ministry of Health.

What are the consequences to the aged individual forced by his or her family to enter an old-age home?

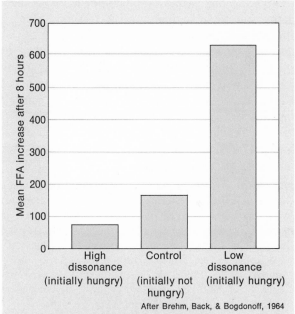

After Brehm, Back, & Bogdonoff, 1964

■ **COGNITIVE CONTROL OF HUNGER**

Under ordinary conditions FFA level (plasma-free fatty acids in the blood) is correlated with length of time without food, thus providing an objective measure of physiological hunger. In the graph shown here, the FFA rise of two groups who had fasted sixteen hours was compared with that of an initially not-hungry group. One hungry group, who agreed without external justification to continue their fast and thus experienced high dissonance, actually showed a lower rise in FFA after eight more hours than did the initially not-hungry group. The other hungry group, who were paid generously for continuing their fast and told that the study would greatly help medical science (low dissonance) showed the expected rise in FFA level, in keeping with their bodies' actual need for food.

In one carefully documented study of forty people whose applications were received by a nursing home in Cleveland, Ohio, twenty-three died within a month of mailing the application. It turned out that this group contained 86 percent of the applicants whose families had made application for them, as compared with only 22 percent of those who had made the application themselves (Ferrare, 1962).

This study suggests an important relationship between the perception of choice to enter the home and the "sudden death" phenomenon discussed earlier. It seems probable that extreme hopelessness would be common among people who feel they have no alternative but to leave their own homes and enter a strange environment, with no ties to the past, an uncertain present, and the worst expectations about the future. In contrast, a comparable group of people who believed that they still retained freedom of choice, that they did not have to go to the home if they did not want to, would be more able to restructure their environment cognitively to make it liveable. Support for this line of reasoning comes from another finding by the same investigator.

After each of fifty-five female applicants to the home was interviewed, they were classified into one group of seventeen, who perceived they had no choice but to go to the home and one group of thirty-eight who perceived that they did have other alternatives even though they were going to the home. Within ten weeks of being admitted to the home all but one woman in the no-choice group had died. In sharp contrast, all but one of the choice group were still living (Ferrare, 1962).

If it is the exercise of choice which is the independent variable accelerating or retarding death, then by providing a perception of choice, it should be possible to prolong life. Even for those who have no choice about entering the home, a series of minimal choices might be presented, such as which day to enter, which floor to be housed on, which of several activities to engage in, and so on, the dependent variable being delay of death.

The existentialist philosopher Jean-Paul Sartre (1957) has said that "Man makes himself" and "Through his choice he involves all mankind, and he cannot avoid making a choice." Unless the helpless, hopeless person can be provided with more meaningful alternatives, his final choice may be death.

Chapter Summary

Men have long been intrigued by the puzzle of the nonphysical "mind" in the physical body. At one extreme, mind and soul have been seen as *the* fundamental and lasting reality; at the other, as in American behaviorism, even consciousness has been regarded as a nonentity, or perhaps as a by-product of neurological events, playing no part in the causal chain.

Emotion, difficult to define objectively, has been much studied by psychologists. We judge others' emotions from their verbal and nonverbal behavior; much of the overt behavior in emotion is learned in accordance with cultural expectations and reinforcements. Nonverbal expressions of emotion include *facial display*, *kinesics* (body movements), *paralanguage* (voice characteristics, nonlanguage sounds), and *proxemics* (distance and orientation). Simple emotions can be judged with some accuracy and agreement, even across cultures, but the same behavior, like crying, may appear in several different emotions. Sometimes we receive contradictory cues, and often we use stereotypes in judging others' emotions.

According to the James-Lange theory, *physiological events* precede and cause the *felt emotion*, but there has been mixed success even in finding specific physiological states associated with the different emotions. *Physiological cues* perhaps contribute to the intensity of felt emotions, but their quality—which emotion is felt—depends partly on *cognitive cues* from the individual's interpretation of the situation. *Appraisal*, both of the *meaning* and of the *seriousness* of a situation, is clearly important in determining the emotion felt.

Emotions and health have long been known to be closely related. Responses learned in the past but no longer appropriate may fail to be extinguished. Chronic threat or other stress may lead to physical illness, may make one more susceptible to infection, or may work against recovery. There is a clear association between *life crises* and *health changes*. It may be that emergency physiological reactions which begin as adaptive responses to stress are continued, through reinforcement, even after they become maladaptive.

Even negative emotion can be adaptive, however. Patients who experience moderate fear before an operation undergo less stress and recover faster than those who have either low or high fear before the operation. Warnings of danger that produce only moderate fear are more conducive to action than warnings that make people more fearful. Clear guidelines for coping action and an attitudinal change also make warnings more effective.

People exposed to predictable danger may learn to handle their fear in complex indirect ways. There are wide cultural differences in response to surgical pain, associated with different interpretations of it.

A belief that one has no control renders an individual more susceptible to disease. In fact, feelings of *helplessness* and *hopelessness* can lead to death, even in previously healthy humans and animals. In Voodoo deaths, a healthy individual who has been "boned" by an enemy will sicken and die. In such deaths, extreme fright may lead to an outpouring of adrenaline, leading to a state of shock, or the mechanism may involve an overstimulation of the parasympathetic nervous system. Laboratory studies point to the role of hopelessness in setting this mechanism into action. Other studies have demonstrated that either *perceptual* or *behavioral control* is associated with ability to withstand threat and shock. Predictable pain can be withstood better than unpredictable pain.

Just as belief that one will die can bring death to a healthy person, belief that one will recover can bring remission of physical symptoms. Even in incurable illnesses a placebo can be effective in relieving pain. Belief can even reverse the usual effect of a drug.

Hypnosis is an altered state of consciousness in which the person suspends critical reality testing, can experience dissociation of various kinds, and can vividly imagine a variety of sensory and cognitive events. Hypnotism was used for painless surgery before the discovery of anesthetics. An individual can also bring pain under control himself through self-hypnosis.

Hypnotic phenomena are related to the state of awareness achieved through *transcendental meditation*. The latter state is distinguishable from ordinary awareness by a different EEG pattern; it also is unique in that during it the process of habituation seems able to be suspended.

Man, through his capacity to delay responding, plan ahead, and restructure the environment, is less stimulus-bound than lower species. Possessing alternatives gives him choice, with both its pains and its potentialities for control of his own life. Activities which change the environment establish the individual's perception of his competence and give him some measure of control over what happens to him. Feelings of predictability and control are also enhanced through perceptions of consistency; to achieve such perceptions, we may reduce *cognitive dissonance* by changing our own motives, feelings, attitudes, and even biological states like hunger. Cognitive control over physiological processes is thus demonstrable. For an older person who feels he has lost control of his life, even death may represent a final act of cognitive control—the ultimate choice.

Chapter 11

Personality:
The Psychology of the Individual

"O.K., so psychologists may be able to explain and predict typical behavior on the basis of general laws, but not mine. I'm *special!*" "You can't analyze, dissect, and pigeonhole what I am, because I'm a unique, whole person. And while you're at it, you know what you can do with your psychological tests, those inkblots and word associations and nosy questionnaires and handwriting analyses." "No one can pin down what I am, like a butterfly on a collector's frame."

Psychologists interested in understanding the nature of human personality must answer student grumblings such as these. And at the same time, they must cope with attacks by other psychologists who maintain that the "proper study of mankind" involves only an analysis of the stimulus determinants of behavior, and need not be concerned with individual differences.

Uniqueness and Consistency: Key Problems for Personality Theory

In attempting to unravel the complexity and mystery of human behavior, psychologists break up their problem into manageable units. Their focus may be on *structures* (the eye, the neuron), on *problems* (prejudice, education), on *phenomena* (overlearning, short-term memory), on *principles* (reinforcement contingencies, constancies), on *areas* (developmental, perception), or on any of innumerable *subtopics* and *processes* within any of these, such as the relation of attitudes to compliance. These tactical divisions of labor and interest are all part of the same search for an understanding of why people behave as they do. In fact, behind all this apparent diversity of what psychologists study when they say they are studying people's behavior are the same two conceptually related questions:

a) What makes people behave alike?

b) What makes people behave differently?

The first question seeks to determine the minimal number of conditions, factors, and variables that can account for the reactions that members of the human species show in common. The second question seeks to account for the observed differences in the behavior of different individuals in response to apparently the same situation. Here the problem is to explain individual uniqueness, the variability in response that is not attributable to the stimulus situation. In the physical sciences, only the first question is asked. It is assumed that individual deviations from basic "average" laws represent either errors of measurement or incomplete knowledge of the relevant causal conditions. But in the biological sciences, it is assumed that no two organisms are exactly alike and that the differences are part of what must be studied.

On the one hand, then, the study of personality is indistinguishable from the broad study of psychology, which is an attempt to understand the *totality* of human behavior. In addition, however, the personality theorist has a special interest in trying to understand why people's behavior still differs after all of the known environmental factors have been specified.

How Different Is Normal?

A common misconception perpetuated by newspaper advice columnists is that normal human beings function pretty much alike. Moreover, to be normal, one *ought* to be functioning like others who are in some way comparable (of similar age, sex, or education, for example). Mothers worried that their baby has not yet begun to walk are told the age at which the "normal" baby does, while adolescents are told when it is "normal" to begin dating (or petting) according to surveys of when the "average" teen-ager does.

The myth of the normal, average, human function is nicely exploded in a thorough analysis by Williams (1956) showing the enormous range of variation in the location, size, and operation of internal human organs. Nearly every organ is several times larger in some normal individuals than in other individuals equally normal. For example, some stomachs hold six to eight times as much as others. It is perfectly normal for the bottom of the stomach to lie about one inch below the tip of the breastbone; this is the location about one fourth of the time. It is just as normal for the stomach bottom to lie seven inches or more below the breastbone; one fourth of human stomachs are in this location. Similarly, examinations of 182 normal young men revealed heart rates ranging from 45 to 105 beats per minute. Normal pumping capacities range from 3.15 to 11.9 quarts per minute. Similar differences are reported in neural structure, chemical composition and activity, and reactions to drugs and various stimuli.

When such an array of differences is added to the infinite variety of life experiences individuals have, it is no wonder that different organisms do different things even in the same situation. These intersubject differences are hindrances to researchers looking for general laws, and are usually either overcome by using powerful stimuli in simple situations or averaged out by combining the varied responses of a large number of subjects. Most personality theorists, however, take a quite different view of this "problem." What makes people behave as individuals is looked on not as a problem to get rid of, but as *the* problem to be studied.

This does not mean that psychologists working in personality are not interested in finding general laws. As in other areas of psychology, many personality theorists believe that eventually psychologists will discover powerful explanatory principles applicable to all human beings. But in personality theory the principles must also be able to account for differences among people. Not all personality theories emphasize individual differences, but all must be able to account for them. They must be able to say what makes one person different from another, what makes one person behave consistently in different situations, and what makes people either remain the same or change over a period of time.

Personality As Consistency

"I like her because she has a good personality." "He is so dynamic he always becomes the leader." Popular usage, as in these statements, makes "personality" something akin to "attractiveness," "charm," "forcefulness," or "charisma." It is a quality movie stars and those politicians we like have a lot of, while the rest of us must make do with less. As psychologists use the word *personality*, however, it has a more neutral, universal meaning, being "what characterizes an individual." Or, put more formally, personality is "the sum total of the ways in which [an individual] characteristically reacts to and interacts with others" and with objects (Ferguson, 1970, p. 2).

Just what *does* characterize an individual? Without really thinking about it, we are able to recognize our friends, even if we have not seen them for some time. If we know a person well enough, we are even able to recognize him from someone else's account of his behavior. ("Oh, that must have been Jim. He always does things like that.") How are we able to do it? The key seems to lie in *consistency*. We are able to recognize a particular individual, and to characterize him to others, by the ways he is consistent. Even if he is consistently unpredictable, that is something we can say about him which distinguishes him from less mercurial folk.

But the matter is more complex. Try the following test. Think about some person who is important in your life. Is that person primarily good (strong, kind, understanding) or primarily bad (weak, cruel, inconsiderate)? Or does it depend upon the circumstances? Now think about yourself and answer the same question.

Most often, the results of this simple experiment are to discover that we see other people we know well as quite consistently either good or bad irrespective of the situation, while we see ourselves as more influenced by circumstances and thus more variable. This paradox highlights our need to attribute consistency to the behavior of others and to formulate consistent patterns of responses and traits when we characterize others.

We saw in Chapter 7 that this tendency to perceive consistency in other people was an extension of a more general tendency to perceive consistency in all events, part of a general process of organizing our world in such a way as to make it coherent, orderly, and more readily predictable. Thus we must raise the question of whether the consistency we perceive in people, around which theories about personality traits are organized, actually exists in the people observed or only in the minds of naïve observers and sophisticated personality theorists.

Personality theorists differ markedly in how they describe this consistency and in the ways they try to account for it. In this chapter, we shall first consider a number of these different ways of thinking about what personality is. We shall then go on to look at the complicated process of personality assessment—how tests and other devices are used in an attempt to measure and reduce to numbers and labels what the theorists are theorizing about.

Naïve Personality Theories

Different as fortune-tellers, pool hustlers, and police interrogators are, they all have in common the fact that they are practitioners of the art of quickly sizing up an individual (customer, "mark," or suspect) by detecting subtle clues and fitting him into a typology of human nature—for the purpose of getting something out of him. They must make predictions that hold for the given individual they are faced with, but they do so from some general set of beliefs about how this person fits or fails to fit into a number of empirically derived classes of human types. By "empirically derived," we mean that they have learned what they know from observations and experience—both their own, in the "school of hard knocks," and those accumulated by their fellow practitioners, which are passed along by word of mouth or through practical training manuals. A brief examination of some aspects of these theories will help to establish the contrast between a naïve personality theory and the more formalized, theoretically based, "scientific" theories of personality which we will present subsequently.

Fortune-Tellers

"By trial and error, by shrewd observation of men, many fortune-tellers have worked out long since many of the great truths that official psychology has only just discovered. Before Freud, the soothsayers knew that little boys are often jealous of their fathers; before Adler, they recognized that a brash manner usually conceals a sense of inferiority. As the alchemist preceded the chemist, the herb doctor the druggist, and the midwife the obstetrician, so the average 'mind reader' anticipates in technique and knowledge the psychiatrist. He is, in fact, the psychiatrist of the poor; and when he is clever enough he sometimes becomes the psychiatrist of the rich as well." (Gresham, 1949, p. 59)

Such an individual is a skilled pseudoprofessional who combines observational acuity, a knowledge of human nature, and considerable *chutzpah* (nerve) to read minds "cold"—to size up a gullible client as he goes along, without gimmicks and without knowing anything about him in advance. His basic tools are an ability to classify people quickly on the basis of age, appearance, marital status, and so on, and a shrewd knowledge of what kind of problems a given type of individual is most likely to have. Thus a married woman is likely to be worried about husband, children, or income; an outgoing, attractive single girl is probably trying to catch a man; a timid, unattractive one is either afraid of men or afraid she won't catch one (Ψ Close-up, p. 421).

Police Interrogators

Fortune-tellers have an advantage in that their clients are self-selected people who want to believe, to put faith in another person's mystical powers. Consider the plight of the police interrogator, whose task is considerably more difficult: he must encourage people to confess when such confessions will lead to loss of freedom or even loss of life.

Despite this initial disadvantage, police interrogators apparently know enough about the personalities of the people they interrogate to be very successful at their work. In one survey of eighty-six U.S. District Courts of federal jurisdiction, it was found that 80 percent of the defendants in criminal cases pleaded *guilty* or *no contest* and did so *before* their court trial. Almost 225,000 suspects of a sample of nearly 270,000 confessed (Rogge, 1959). Since the use of "third-degree" physical coercion is illegal, how do the police get their man to talk? One police manual says:

"If one knows what he is talking about, knows what information he is seeking, has a layman's knowledge of practical psychology, and uses the salesman's approach, he can be successful in reaching into a man's brain and pulling out the facts he wants." (Mulbar, 1951)

This practical psychology involves first sizing up the suspect and assigning him to a tentative category, then using a prearranged set of techniques and appeals. If these are unsuccessful, then the line of questioning is adjusted to the peculiarities of the personality or attitudes of the particular suspect.

For example, a partial list of general types and opening tactics advocated by the author of one manual used to train interrogators categorizes subjects into such types as "Timid" (housewives, the uneducated, and the foreign born fall into this class), "Disinterested," and "Know-Nothing" and suggests specific techniques to be used with each type. For example, with timid suspects, questioners are advised to act "friendly and confidential." With disinterested suspects, flattery is recommended, to give them a feeling of importance. With the know-nothing type, one should use extensive warm-up by asking many simple questions which clearly can be answered by anyone with minimal intelligence.

In dealing with a boy who is clearly not a criminal, but appears to be implicated in his first criminal act, "Mother" is the magic word; emphasis is laid upon how hurt she will be. With a hardened juvenile delinquent, however, who is expecting the police to be vicious, the officer is advised to use friendliness in an attempt to catch him off guard.

In dealing with the large group of white-collar first offenders (office workers, teachers, students, etc.) who traditionally subscribe to orthodox ethical principles and conventional moral standards, the calm, dignified approach of the physician will command respect and therefore be effective. "The character of a person in this category is weak, and this defect must be exploited fully." Also recommended for this group is the "Dutch uncle" pose, in which the interrogator indicates that he is going to do the worrying for the suspect and clear the decks of trouble as long as he gets some cooperation (O'Hara, 1956).

Other police training manuals distinguish between offenders who show emotion (feelings of remorse, anguish, or nervousness), and nonemotional offenders committing a premeditated crime, who are sorry only for having been caught.

Interrogations are no longer conducted with bright lights shining in the suspect's eyes while a team of cops shout at and bully him. Rather, a personal relationship is established between the interrogator and the suspect in an environment which minimizes sensory stimulation and social support for the suspect and maximizes the impression of the invincibility of authority and law.

The reader is referred to these police manuals (notably that of Inbau & Reid, 1962) for a basic course in how personality appraisal and psychologically oriented techniques have been developed by methods other than laboratory research, systematic programs of personality testing, or reading about personality theories that have been derived from clinical research, all of which we will be talking about in this chapter. Rather, the police, over the years, have tried various approaches, and those that work have become part of their tactical arsenal, the others being discarded. In this way, they have developed an empirically based theory of personality as well as one of how to motivate men. In like manner, others whose livelihood depends upon getting another person to do something, including workers as diverse as pool hustlers (see Polsky, 1967), salesmen, doctors, clergymen, and politicians, have had to become perceptive personality theorists if they were to be successful.

Theorizing about personality, then, is a basic and inevitable part of the game of life which we all play. In the remainder of the chapter we will examine the ways in which formal personality theories and assessment methods differ from those of the "man in the street."

Ψ *Close-up*　*A Prediction Is Worth Money When a Fortune Is at Stake*

When I couldn't see how he did his stuff, the Doctor would explain. "Now that little woman with the rundown heels, for instance . . ."

She crossed the floor toward the Doctor of Mental Science, clutching her pocketbook. On her ring finger there was a telltale mark—she had removed her wedding ring with a muddled idea of fooling the fortuneteller. By the time she sat down he had her classified:

Wife, probably at least two small children—she had the hunted look. Age, about thirty-five; looks beginning to go; clothes good last year, but this year made over inexpertly (that meant less money this year than last). No servants—the hands gave him that. Conservative, unimaginative, timid—the uninspired get-up and the timorous mouth and eyes gave him that. Strain in the eyes, anxiety and self-pity in the mouth. Probably husband trouble.

"My dear lady," he began, speaking quickly and almost inaudibly. The client, concentrating all her attention to hear him, forgot to be wary. "My dear lady, I am glad you have taken this opportunity to consult me, for I feel I can be of help . . . you understand, of course, I make no claim to occult powers and do not predict the future in any way . . ."

That was in case she was a policewoman, though she wasn't the type. Policewomen are easy to spot; they are almost the only women in the world with poker faces.

"Now I see that your *husband* is giving you some anxiety, isn't that so?" Right: the lady's eyes widened,

sure sign of a hit. The Doctor fished. "There is another person, a woman . . ."

Wrong: the eyes narrowed. Try money. Ah, warmer—

". . . and this sum of money which must be paid . . . I see that this is not the main difficulty; there is some anxiety concerning your husband, a lack of will power" —the eyes have widened again—"to stand up for himself to his boss . . . or is it that he lacks will power in his leisure hours"—aha!—"when his weakness for a few drinks . . . or gambling . . . I seem to see cards on a table . . ."

Whoa! The brows have knitted!

"No, his weakness for these things is not sufficient, as I said, to cause you alarm, but on the other hand there is one temptation which he cannot resist, which takes the money you need, not for yourself—for I can see you are not vain and greedy like so many women"—

Nothing like a little flattery to soften 'em up.

"—but for your young children. And I seem to see crowds, bright colors . . . horses, that's it! Madame, your husband is addicted to betting on the races, isn't he?"

The eyes filled with tears. While the lady used her handkerchief, the Doctor continued:

"Now there is no way I could have known this, isn't that right, and you did not speak a word . . . you see, I just plucked it out of your mind . . ." (Gresham, 1949, pp. 138-139)

Ways of Thinking About Personality

Only a few of the many systematic personality theories can be presented here. Those that we have chosen represent four basic ways of conceptualizing what personality is. Most of these imply or specify a particular explanation for what happens when something goes wrong and adjustment difficulties appear. Thus specific methods of therapy have been developed in connection with many of these theories; they will be discussed in Chapter 15.

Freud and His Followers: Consistency As the Outcome of a Battle

Toward the end of the nineteenth century, in the aftermath of Darwin's powerful reminder that men and animals have much in common, many psychologists tried to explain consistency in individual behavior by talking about "instincts." If a man went around hitting other men, it might be because of his inborn "instinct of pugnacity." If he was miserly, it was his "hoarding instinct." As we saw in Chapter 4, this sort of explanation did not work out very well. If a psychologist had a new kind of behavior he wanted to explain, he had only to postulate a new instinct, which left him with a new "psychological term" but very little more understanding of the psychological process than before. By the 1920s, according to one survey (Bernard, 1924), at least 849 different classes of instincts had been proposed. Clearly a more fruitful approach was needed. For many it was provided by the work of Sigmund Freud.

Freudian concepts. In Chapter 4 we summarized the stages Freud believed were characteristic of psychosexual development. Here we will see how these stages fit into his general theory of personality and human functioning. Again, however, we cannot begin to encompass the complexity of his thought but will touch on only a few central notions. ■

Eros and Thanatos. Freud was a tireless observer. From thousands of careful observations of both himself and his patients in Vienna, he concluded that all behavior is powered by two fundamental "drives." Freud believed that these drives (mistranslated "in-

stincts" in most English editions of Freud's works because his writings hit the United States when instincts were in their heyday) are present in every individual at birth. He labelled the two "Eros" and "Thanatos." *Eros*, the "sex drive" or "life instinct" (which earned Freud his reputation in some quarters as a "dirty old man"), actually meant more than we usually mean by the sex drive. Eros encompassed all striving for creative synthesis; one expression of this drive, but only one, was seen as urge for sexual union. *Thanatos*, the "aggressive drive" or "death instinct," included all striving toward self-destruction, or breaking down of order, form, and regulation. Freud assumed that psychological activity, like physical activity, takes energy. The energy of the creative drive, Eros, he called *libido;* he did not suggest a separate term for the psychic energy supposedly associated with Thanatos.

Id, superego, and ego. Freud accounted for individual differences by suggesting that different people deal with their fundamental drives (Eros and Thanatos) in different ways. To explain these differences, he pictured a continuing battle between two parts of the personality, the id and the superego, moderated by a third part, the ego.

The *id* is conceived as the primitive, unconscious part of the personality, the storehouse of the fundamental drives. It operates irrationally; impulses push for expression and gratification "no matter what," without considering whether what is desired is realistically possible or morally acceptable. It is characterized by the kind of *"primary process thinking"* in which we engage in our dreams. During such thinking, the rules of logic and reality do not hold and we can be in two places at once, or move backward in time, or do other impossible things.

The *superego* is the repository of an individual's values, including his moral attitudes. The superego proper corresponds roughly to the *conscience*; it develops when a child *internalizes* the prohibitions of his parents and others against certain kinds of actions. The superego also includes the *ego ideal*, which develops as a child internalizes the views of others as to the kind of person he should try to become. Thus the superego, society's representative in the individual, is often in conflict with the id. The id just wants to

■　Before Freud, it had been assumed that people's actions were influenced largely by conscious thought and rational choice applied to present situations. Freud believed that the thoughts and behavior of which a person was aware constituted only a small portion of his ongoing experience and that the major influences on both conscious thoughts and observable behavior were irrational, unconscious, and historical, each layer influencing those above it.

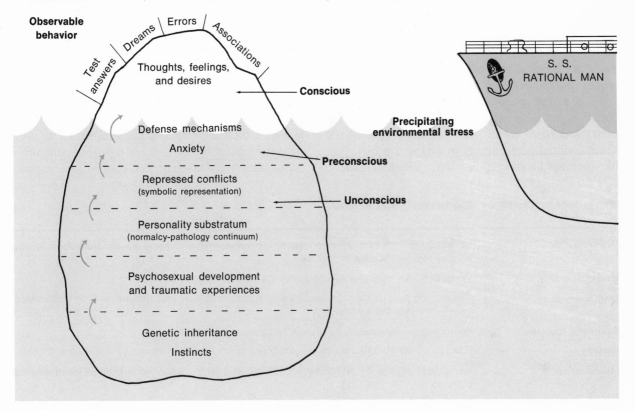

do what feels good, while the superego wants to do what is "right."

In this conflict, the *ego* plays the part of arbitrator. The ego represents the individual's picture of reality, of what will lead to what and which things are possible in the world as it is actually perceived. Part of the ego's job is to choose kinds of action that will gratify id impulses without having undesirable consequences. Thus the ego would probably block an impulse to fly by leaping from a cliff, and might substitute sky diving or a trip on a roller coaster. When the id and the superego are in conflict, the ego generally tries to find a compromise that will at least partially satisfy both. In doing so, it may make use of one or a number of unconscious "defense mechanisms." ● (p. 424) Since Freud's model assumes

that any urge has psychic energy associated with it, each of these mechanisms involves finding some outlet for the energy linked to the unacceptable urge. In the mechanism known as *reaction formation*, for example, the energy gets linked to expression of an opposing impulse ("I don't hate him, I love him. See how nice I am to him?").

According to Freudian theory, we all have some urges which are unacceptable in our society and thus all use these defense mechanisms to some extent. Overuse of them, however, constitutes *neurosis*. A person who is neurotic spends so much of his energy deflecting, disguising, and rechanneling unacceptable urges that he has little energy left over for productive work or satisfying relationships.

The conflicts focused upon by psychoanalytic theorists are those which are thought to emerge during the various psychosexual stages of development, which were discussed in Chapter 4. The individual's ability to adjust in later life is thought to be determined largely by his early childhood experiences. If painful conflicts have been repressed in childhood without being adequately resolved, they will continue— though unconscious—to influence the individual's thoughts, feelings, and behavior, causing emotional tension and difficulties in adjustment.

Freud's conception of a healthy or well-adjusted person is someone who can successfully engage in both "love and work." He was rather pessimistic about civilized man's ability to escape neurosis. Perhaps because he grew up in a fairly Victorian society,

he believed that any society must teach its children that most expression of their basic drives is bad. Hence nearly everyone will have to be defending against such impulses nearly all the time. Those who came after him, as we shall see below, were more optimistic about our prospects for avoiding repressed conflicts and neurosis.

The psychopathology of "normal" behavior. What evidence is there that the conflicts Freud described actually take place? Freud's answer has passed into the popular culture as the "Freudian slip." According to Freud, these unacceptable impulses within us, even though inhibited, suppressed, or repressed, still strive for expression. Man's desire to confess his imagined

● SUMMARY CHART OF EGO DEFENSE MECHANISMS

Compensation	Covering up weakness by emphasizing desirable trait or making up for frustration in one area by overgratification in another
Denial of reality	Protecting self from unpleasant reality by refusal to perceive it
Displacement	Discharging pent-up feelings, usually of hostility, on objects less dangerous than those which initially aroused the emotion
Emotional Insulation	Withdrawing into passivity to protect self from being hurt
Fantasy	Gratifying frustrated desires in imaginary achievements ("daydreaming" is a common form)
Identification	Increasing feelings of worth by identifying self with person or institution of illustrious standing
Introjection	Incorporating external values and standards into ego structure so individual is not at the mercy of them as external threats
Isolation	Cutting off emotional charge from hurtful situations or separating incompatible attitudes by logic-tight compartments (holding conflicting attitudes which are never thought of simultaneously or in relation to each other); also called *compartmentalization*
Projection	Placing blame for one's difficulties upon others, or attributing one's own unethical desires to others
Rationalization	Attempting to prove that one's behavior is "rational" and justifiable and thus worthy of the approval of self and others
Reaction Formation	Preventing dangerous desires from being expressed by exaggerating opposing attitudes and types of behavior and using them as "barriers"
Regression	Retreating to earlier developmental level involving less mature responses and usually a lower level of aspiration.
Repression	Preventing painful or dangerous thoughts from entering consciousness
Sublimation	Gratifying or working off frustrated sexual desires in substitutive nonsexual activities socially accepted by one's culture
Undoing	Atoning for, and thus counteracting, immoral desires or acts

transgressions against society "oozes from his pores" and takes on many forms. For example, "forgetting" an important appointment with the dentist or being consistently late for dates with a particular person may not be accidental but may be an instance of this tendency to express the way we *really* feel. Telling an unwanted guest on his arrival, "I'm so sorry—oh, I mean glad you could come," may reveal the true intention of the host. When a radio announcer, reading a commercial for Barbara Ann Bread, failed to say "Barbara Ann for the best in bread," as he was supposed to, and said instead, "Barbara Ann for the breast in bed," was he making a public confession of his impulses?

According to Freud, such slips are meaningful, the meaning being in the unconscious intention. Similarly, such "errors" can be explained in terms of the final result produced, even though some other meaning was expected by the hearer or apparently intended by the speaker. Freud believed that such slips invariably indicated an actual intention.

As an exercise in Freudian slip detection, read the letter in the Ψ Close-up (right) quickly once, then reread it more carefully. What is the message Mama is unconsciously telegraphing to her son, who has just broken the news of his engagement to a girl from Richmond, Virginia?

Symptoms as signals.   Freud believed that more serious disturbances, such as irrational fears, paralysis without physical cause, or uncontrollable anxiety, also had a meaning in the life of the individual, in expressing his sense of helplessness and in getting others to be concerned about him. He considered such symptoms to be merely signals of some underlying conflict; the job of a therapist was to uncover the connection between the symptom and the problem causing it. Thus for both normal and abnormal behavior he postulated the principle of *psychic determinism*: that mental events do not occur by chance, however random they may appear, but are meaningfully related if we explore them deeply enough. In fact, he found that even dreams seemed to be meaningful though disguised expressions of hidden, unconscious processes. Freud has been called the "world's greatest egoist" because he hoped, by subjecting his own every thought and action to relentless micro-

scopic analysis, to discover the true meaning of everyone's feelings and actions.

Criticisms of Freudian theory.   Critics have complained that psychoanalytic theory is very difficult to evaluate because it makes few empirically testable predictions. The theory can be used to explain a good deal, but most of its explanations are made "after the fact." Also some critics have pointed out that psychoanalytic therapy represents a learning situation in which patients are reinforced for making statements which are congruent with the theory. Hence psy-

Ψ *Close-up*   **The Prospective Mother-in-law**

My dear Irving,
  The news of your engagement came as a delightful surprise. Naturally we are very pleased at the results of your efforts. When must we meet the fair lady again? She seemed just to shine when we saw her at your New Year's party. Richmond is such a long way—I hope you won't be going to Virginia so often that you have no time left for studies.
  We look forward to the future knowing that I have not lost a son but a daughter.
      Congratulations,
        Mother

choanalysts' assertions that the theory is "confirmed" by what they actually encounter in their patients may be somewhat suspect. In addition, the theory has developed from speculation based on clinical experience with people suffering from neuroses and other problems of adjustment, people in whom something has gone wrong. Thus it has little to say about healthy personality or life styles that are not primarily defensive.

Finally, much of the evidence on which the theory is based has depended on an analyst's memory of what happened during a therapy hour. This means that the events have had to pass through the therapist's "theoretical filter," which will have tended to screen out data inconsistent with his theory of personality. Freud too, in building his picture of personality development, had to rely on his patients' memories. In fact, he was quite dismayed when he learned that many of his patients had been telling him of early sexual traumas which had never really occurred. He resolved the problem for himself by deciding that what a patient thinks happened is significant even if the memory is incorrect.

Even Freud's severest critics, however, acknowledge certain of his contributions to modern thought.

1. In applying the concept of unconscious causes for behavior (as opposed to the rationalists' claim that man's will has full control over his behavior), Freud for the first time emphasized the importance of unconscious and irrational processes in the motivation of human behavior. ◆

2. Although most modern psychologists believe that Freud overemphasized the role of sexual factors, psychoanalysis "opened up" the scientific study of sexuality and indicated its importance as a source of adjustment problems.

3. Psychoanalysis focused attention on the importance of childhood experiences in later personality development and adjustment.

Neo-Freudian theories. Many of those who came after Freud kept his basic picture of personality as a battleground in which unconscious primal urges fight it out with social values. Most, however, made a few changes. Some, like Carl Jung and Alfred Adler, offered different candidates for the most important "primal urges" to replace Freud's broadly defined sex

◆ "All right, deep down it's a cry for psychiatric help—but at one level it's a stick-up."

drive. Adler focused on power, contending that what people basically strive for is superiority, to compensate for feelings of inferiority to others that they experienced when they were small and helpless. Jung stressed the importance of universal symbols and predispositions—*archetypes*—inherited, he believed, in a "collective unconscious" shared by all men. He also expanded Freud's picture of personality development by suggesting that a "self" emerges around the age of thirty to hold together the parts that have developed by then. Other "neo-Freudians," like Hartmann, Kris, Lowenstein, Rapaport, and more recently Schafer, have expanded Freud's account of the ego and its functioning to make it equal in importance to the id and superego instead of a mere arbiter between them. Still others, like Horney, Fromm, and Erikson (discussed in Chapter 4), have believed that Freud overemphasized the biological influences on personality at the expense of the social influences and have attempted to redress the balance. We shall consider in some detail the theory of one of those who went farthest in emphasizing the social nature of personality: Harry Stack Sullivan.

Sullivan, like Freud, proposed that tension arising from a set of physiological needs often gets people to act. Unlike Freud, however, he believed that man's basic needs are not biological but derive from interactions with people, and that these interpersonally developed "human" characteristics may directly affect or alter physiological functioning. Most cultures, for example, have more or less elaborate sets of rules specifying when and how one may eat, eliminate, and so on.

Sullivan went so far as to define personality not as something in the person but as "the relatively enduring pattern of recurrent interpersonal situations which characterize human life" (1953, p. 111). Thus for him personality meant consistency not in internal traits but in what a person does *in relation to other people*. These other people need not be present physically, however, for personality to manifest itself (nor need they even actually exist) because a person can interact with people in imagination as well as in actuality. For example, a person can drive along lost in fantasies of what he "should have said" to the policeman who stopped him, or can even interact in his "mind's eye" with a fictional character in a book or movie.

In accounting for consistency in interpersonal behavior, Sullivan introduced the concepts of "dynamism" and "personification." A *dynamism* is a prolonged, recurrent behavior pattern (other theorists would call much the same thing a *habit*). For example, a person who characteristically behaves in a hostile way toward a certain person or group of persons is said to be expressing a dynamism of hostility; a man who tends to seek out lascivious relationships with women displays a dynamism of lust. A dynamism can be any habitual reaction, whether in the form of an attitude, a feeling, or an overt action.

One particularly important dynamism is the "*self-system*," which, according to Sullivan, develops as an individual learns to avoid threats to his security. He learns, for example, that if he does what his parents like he will not be punished. He then comes to engage in habitual "security measures" which allow some forms of behavior (the "good-me" self) and forbid others (the "bad-me" self). Unfortunately, in our society the self-system typically interferes with our ability to deal effectively with others, because it tends to become isolated from the rest of the personality and is resistant to new information which might change it. Sullivan held out the hope that in a more rational society the self-system might not be so great a problem, since in such a society children would not be made to feel anxious in so many irrational ways.

A *personification* is an image a person has of someone else. It is a complex of feelings, attitudes, and conceptions which in large part determines how he will act toward that person. If personifications learned in infancy remain intact and influence the individual's reactions to people when he grows up, they are called *eidetic personifications*. A child who personifies his father as overbearing and hostile, for example, may come to personify other older men as being overbearing. He then reacts to teachers and employers as if they were overbearing and hostile whether they actually are or not. A personification held in common by a group of people is called a *stereotype*. Examples of stereotypes common in our culture are the "long-haired student radical," the "ivory-tower intellectual," and the "rising young executive with a house in the suburbs."

Sullivan outlined seven stages of personality development in Western European societies. These are: (a) infancy, (b) childhood, (c) the juvenile era, (d) preadolescence, (e) early adolescence, (f) late adolescence, and (g) maturity. These stages differ not so much in the kinds of physical gratification presumed to preoccupy the individual (the basis of Freud's stages) as in the kinds of interpersonal relationships and the ways of thinking which become possible in each. Thus he recognized that somewhat different patterns might be found in other societies.

Although he stressed the influence of social forces in the development of personality, Sullivan also recognized the potential influence of individuals in changing their society. Indeed, he was often critical of contemporary society, believing that many of the ways it influences personality development run counter to people's biological needs and inhibit rather than enhance the full realization of human potential. At the same time, because he believed that people remain malleable throughout their lives, he was optimistic about men's chances to live in harmony with the dictates of a society more rational than ours.

Those who view personality in a psychoanalytic or neo-analytic framework, then, see individual consistency as resulting from a complex interplay of forces, some arising from man's biological nature and others from his social relationships. These theorists have differed in how much emphasis they have placed on the biological forces as opposed to the social ones, in how fully they have spelled out the nature of cognitive functioning, and in how optimistic they have been about the possibility of a world in which people might function more happily and effectively than they have in the past.

The Learning Theorists:
Consistency from Learned Habit-patterns

Most experimental psychologists have looked somewhat askance at personality theories and their creators. By and large, they have focused their attention on trying to find consistent relationships between stimulus conditions and behavior, making as few assumptions as possible about unobservable processes that may intervene in the organism between observable stimuli and observable responses. They have felt that a full theory of personality is both unnecessary and premature at this stage in our knowledge. A few, however, have tried their hand at extending stimulus-response learning theory to account for the more complex kinds of consistency in human behavior. For a long time the best known of these were John Dollard and Neal Miller.

Dollard and Miller: the reconcilers. Dollard, a sociologist-anthropologist, and Miller, an experimental psychologist who had undergone psychoanalysis in a training program at the Vienna Institute of Psychoanalysis, combined a concern for the sorts of problems discussed by Freud with an appreciation for the methodological rigor of Hullian learning theory (see Appendix C). So they set about trying to find a way to put the two together. At first sight, Freud's rich theory seems very different from the sort of statements usually generated by studies of rats running around in mazes. In fact, however, there are some strong points of similarity. First, Freud's conceptual-

ization, like Hullian learning theory, was a *tension-reduction* theory: both conceived of the organism as acting in order to reduce the "tension" produced by unsatisfied drives. Second, both kinds of theory stress the importance of *early learning* in determining what an organism does later in life. Although the two theoretical systems use very different words to describe their conclusions, they thus come out with models of the human organism which have important parallels.

Basically, what Dollard and Miller did was translate many of Freud's concepts and problems into terms more amenable to rigorous experimental study (1950). One of the most interesting examples of this approach was their handling of the concept of internal conflict.

Consider, they suggested, the case of a bachelor contemplating marriage. He finds a lovely girl, the juices rise within him, and he proposes. But as the day of the wedding approaches, his doubts increase. Finally, to the consternation of all concerned, he calls the whole thing off at the last minute. A week later, he decides he wants to go through with it after all. But again, when the day approaches, he changes his mind. How are we to account for this wishy-washy, vacillating behavior? And how are we to account for the scores of men who, in spite of increasing doubts at the last minute, go ahead and get married anyway?

Miller (1944) listed four principles derived from animal research which seem to help us understand this sort of conflict situation:

1. The tendency to approach a desired goal gets stronger the nearer the subject is to it (*approach gradient*).

2. The tendency to go away from a feared place or object also gets stronger the nearer the subject is to it (*avoidance gradient*).

3. The strength of the second (avoidance) tendency increases more rapidly than that of the first (approach). In other words, it may be said that the avoidance gradient is steeper than the approach gradient.

4. The strength of both tendencies varies with the strength of the drive upon which the tendencies are based. A high level of drive may thus be said to raise the height of the entire gradient. The two graphs show how these principles help us understand our

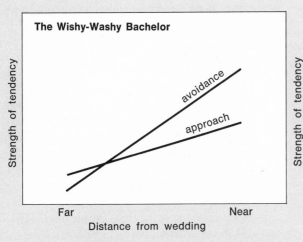

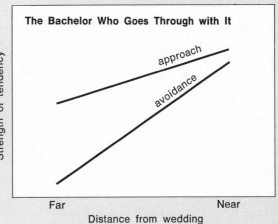

Adapted from N. Miller, 1944

● I'M (NOT) GETTING MARRIED IN THE MORNING

The first figure shows visually what Miller's principles might mean in the case of the bachelor who kept calling the wedding off. He both desires and fears marriage, but when the wedding is still far off, the approach gradient is well above the avoidance gradient: the tendency to approach is greater than the tendency to avoid, so he goes on with his marriage plans. Then, as the day comes closer, the tendency to avoid increases faster than the tendency to approach, until at some point the tendency to avoid is stronger. He may go on with the plans anyway for a little while, knowing how upset everyone would be if they knew how he felt. But soon the tendency to avoid is a great deal stronger than the tendency to approach and he decides not to go through with it.

That, however, puts him back where he started: a long way from getting married, where the tendency to approach marriage is again stronger than the tendency to avoid it. So he changes his mind again. Miller's principles would predict that the poor man might go on vacillating forever, unless the girl decides she's had enough and tells him to get lost.

The second figure shows what might be going on in the case of a man who has doubts which increase as the day approaches but goes ahead and gets married anyway. He too starts with fears, but he also starts with a stronger drive to get married. Thus though both tendencies increase and his avoidance gradient increases faster, his approach gradient remains higher than his avoidance gradient right up to the wedding, so he goes through with it.

two bachelors. ● These examples are intriguing illustrations of Dollard and Miller's approach, but they have more to do with how people behave in relatively transient situations than with the kinds of consistency with which personality theorists are usually concerned.

The central focus in Dollard and Miller's formulations is on the process of learning, or habit formation. They discuss four significant features of this process: drive, cue, response, and reinforcement (reward). *Drives* get the organism into action, *cues* suggest what behavior is appropriate (will lead to drive reduction), *response* is the behavior itself, and *reinforcement* strengthens the connection between cue and response by reducing the tension of drives.

In Chapter 9 you saw an example of how this all works in the learning of "irrational" fears. A rat was given a chance to escape from electric shock in a lighted compartment by running to a dark one. Soon he learned to be afraid (drive) in the lighted compartment, and to use being in that compartment as a signal (cue) for running out of it (response). The result, escaping or avoiding shock (reinforcement), makes this response more likely next time.

Suppose we now put the rat in a different box, one that is dimly lighted. The principle of generalization suggests that he will still be afraid and will still try to escape even though no shock is given. Someone who does not know about the rat's earlier experiences and sees him struggling to escape from the harmless box may believe that he is behaving "irrationally"; if the observer is a psychoanalyst, he may even say that the rat is behaving as if he had a "phobia" of lighted boxes. Clearly the description of how rats learn irrational fears can be applied with very little alteration to the development of irrational fears in human beings and to the notion that habits learned in this way can become the basic and enduring elements of personality.

Bandura and Walters' social learning theory.   Albert Bandura and Richard Walters, two learning theorists whose major work has come out more recently (1963), applauded Dollard and Miller's experimental methods and testable statements but have criticized them on two other counts. First, they see it as an important limitation that Dollard and Miller have relied so heavily on results from studies using *nonhuman subjects* in deriving a theory they hoped to apply to humans. Second, they consider it essential to study human behavior in a *social* setting rather than in isolation (for example, studies of people sitting apart learning lists of words rule out many of the interpersonal processes which are most characteristically human).

In their own work, Bandura and Walters have focused a good deal of attention on the process of *modeling* ("no-trial learning"), in which a person learns to do something not by doing it himself but by watching someone else do it and what happens as a result. They found, for example, that children who observed adult models exhibiting aggressive responses toward a large plastic doll showed a greater frequency of precisely imitative aggressive behaviors than did control subjects who did not observe the models (Bandura, Ross, & Ross, 1961).

Bandura and Walters discovered further that children could learn such behaviors from just watching film sequences of models, even cartoon characters.

They found that people are more likely to imitate a model they perceive as somehow like themselves than a model seen as dissimilar. And they found that if the model is seen to be rewarded for his behavior, the subject is more likely to *perform* the behavior himself, though he will *learn* it just as well if the model is not rewarded.

In addition, Bandura and Walters have found that modeling can be a source of more effects than just learning specific behavior. For example, they demonstrated that "rule-modeling" also takes place, in which a child learns to govern his behavior by the same *rules* that he has watched models follow, even when he faces an entirely different situation from the ones in which he watched them performing. Modeling can also produce *disinhibition* of responses previously learned. For example, if a well-dressed man (attractive model) crosses the street against a "don't walk" sign, others who were waiting for a "walk" light may imitate him. Finally, an individual can learn to administer *self*-rewards (such as helping himself to candy after getting a high score in bowling) and self-punishments by watching someone else do so; Bandura and Walters suggest that such learning may be the basis of the development of self-control.

Criticisms of learning theories.   In sum, the learning theorists see consistency in human behavior as resulting from the learning of habit-patterns. The most telling strength of their approach has been their statement of hypotheses and conclusions in a form subject to experimental verification. Their work has, consequently, given rise to a good deal of interesting research and to an effective set of therapeutic procedures. The major criticism of their work has been that it remains too elementaristic and environmentalistic: they propose little in the way of mechanisms to tie their bundles of habits together and give them coherent direction, and the organism is pictured as essentially a puppet whose strings are pulled by environmental forces.

The Organismic Field Theorists: Consistency As the "Actualization" of Self

The ways of thinking about personality that fit into this general category have a good deal more to say about both the central coordination and the autonomous purposefulness of human behavior. Three such theories will be summarized here. All have been strongly influenced by *field theory*, a concept which emerged from analogy with the physical sciences. Based on the study of electromagnetic fields, this theory postulates fields of force which are in dynamic and constantly shifting equilibrium. For psychologists applying this theory, psychological events, like physical events, are thought to represent a balance and interaction of many forces, and a change anywhere in the system is seen as affecting the whole system. Thus behavior is seen as shaped not by individual chains of cause and effect, but by the combination of forces which make up the entire field.

Goldstein's organismic theory.   A personality theory which has borrowed heavily from field theory is *organismic theory*, a leading exponent of which is Kurt Goldstein (1963). As a neuropsychiatrist working with brain-injured soldiers in World War I, Goldstein arrived at the principle that particular symptoms could not be understood merely as the product of particular diseases or injuries but only as products of the organism behaving as a whole. The organism is a unity, and what happens in any part of it affects the whole. Organization is natural to the organism, and disorganization means disease. Although constituent parts have to be differentiated for study, they do not operate in isolation.

Organismic theory stresses primarily the orderly unfolding of the inherited potentialities of the organism. However, it does recognize that an appropriate environment is essential if this unfolding is to occur. As one might expect, the organism is thought to be motivated by one main drive rather than by a number of different, independent drives. This drive is man's constant striving to realize his inherent potentials and is called by Goldstein *self-actualization*.

Rogers' theory of the self.   Among the best known of the organismic theorists who have achieved recognition also as therapists is Carl Rogers (1961). He emphasizes the private world of the individual, the world of experience, which he calls the *phenomenal field*. It is the individual's perceptions and interpretations that determine his behavior. Thus to understand

his behavior, it is not enough to know the external situation: we must understand how it looks to him.

A differentiated portion of this field is the *self-concept*, which develops out of the individual's interaction with his environment. He behaves in ways that are consistent with his picture of himself and tends to reject or distort incoming information that is threatening to the self. Thus experience may be *symbolized*, in which case it becomes clearly and consciously perceived, or it may be denied symbolization and remain below the level of consciousness, or it may be ignored.

For Rogers as for Goldstein, the most basic drive of the human organism is toward self-actualization. Unfortunately, this drive at times comes into conflict with the need for approval or *positive regard* from both the self and others. If other people in a child's environment who are important to him express dismay at some of the things he does without making it clear that this "conditional regard" applies to his behavior rather than to him as a person, he may begin to do and think only things which are "acceptable." In that case, *incongruence* will develop between his "real" feelings and natural tendency to seek out fulfilling activities and situations, on the one hand, and the "acceptable" things he allows himself to feel and do, on the other. Mental illness comes when one does not dare to be oneself or to acknowledge one's real experiencing.

Once the alternatives are clearly perceived and adequately symbolized, however, Rogers believes that the individual chooses the path of growth. Thus in therapy it is the patient's own inner urge toward growth and wholeness that makes recovery possible, and the therapist's task is to provide a safe and encouraging climate.

Maslow's self-actualization theory.   Another theorist who found self-actualization a fruitful concept was Abraham Maslow. Feeling that psychology had concentrated too much on man's weaknesses, neglecting his strengths, Maslow sought to round out the picture by studying emotionally healthy individuals. He regarded man's inborn nature as basically good, but saw the innate tendency toward growth and self-actualization as rather weak and fragile, easily overcome by social pressures. Maslow distinguished between *deficiency motivation*, in which the individual seeks to restore his physical or psychological equilibrium, and *growth motivation*, in which the individual seeks to go beyond what he has done and been in the past and may welcome uncertainty, an increase in tension, and even pain if he sees it as a route toward greater fulfillment.

According to Maslow, man's inborn needs are arranged in a hierarchy of priority. As those on one level are satisfied, those on the next level take precedence. Thus when the physiological needs such as hunger and thirst are satisfied, the needs on the next level—safety needs—press for satisfaction. After these come, in order, needs for belongingness and love, needs for esteem, needs for self-actualization, needs for knowledge, and finally aesthetic needs. In sharp contrast with Freud's theory, no antisocial needs are included, since these are not regarded as innate. A need to behave aggressively, for example, is thought to arise only when innate needs are denied or frustrated in some way. The person who is seeking to satisfy an innate need experiences delight and happiness in the process (Maslow, 1959).

Although for most people self-actualization is only a hope or a goal, something wished for and striven toward, a few appear to achieve it to a large degree. Maslow studied a group of such persons, although he never made it very clear just how he chose his sample and carried out his investigations. He did include both historical personages, such as Beethoven and Lincoln, and persons alive at the time of the study, including Einstein and Eleanor Roosevelt. On the basis of his findings, Maslow formulated a list of fifteen characteristics of self-actualized persons (Maslow, 1954). These are as follows:

1. Self-actualized persons perceive reality more effectively than most people do and have more comfortable relations with it. That is, they *live close to reality* and to nature, can judge others accurately, and can tolerate ambiguity or uncertainty more easily than most people can.

2. They can *accept themselves* and their various characteristics with little feeling of guilt or anxiety and, at the same time, can readily *accept others*.

3. They show a great deal of *spontaneity* in both thought and behavior, although they seldom show extreme unconventionality.

4. They are *problem-centered*, not ego-centered, often devoting themselves to broad social problems as a mission in life.

5. They have a *need for privacy* and solitude at times and are capable of looking at life from a detached, objective point of view.

6. They are relatively *independent of their culture and environment* but do not flaunt convention just for the sake of being different.

7. They are capable of *deep appreciation* of the basic experiences of life, even of things they have done or seen many times before.

8. Many of them have had *mystic experiences* such as having felt a deep sense of ecstasy, having felt limitless horizons opening to them, or having felt very powerful and at the same time very helpless but ending with a conviction that something significant had happened.

9. They have a *deep social interest* and identify in a sympathetic way with mankind as a whole—witness Abraham Lincoln.

10. They are capable of very *deep, satisfying interpersonal relations*, usually with only a few rather than many individuals.

11. They are *democratic* in their attitudes toward others, showing respect for all people, regardless of race, creed, income level, etc.

12. They discriminate clearly between means and ends but often *enjoy the means toward their ends* more than impatient persons do.

13. They have a good *sense of humor*, tending to be philosophical and nonhostile in their jokes.

14. They are highly *creative*, each in his own individual way. They have "primary creativeness which comes out of the unconscious" and produces truly original, new discoveries. This shows itself in whatever field the self-actualized person has chosen and is to be distinguished from the kind of productive creativity reflected in art, music, poetry, science, or invention. Of course, the self-actualized person in any of these fields will show both kinds of creativity.

15. They are *resistant to enculturation*. That is, although they fit into their culture, they are independent of it and do not blindly comply with all its demands.

With all these characteristics, self-actualized persons are particularly capable of loving and of being loved in the fullest way. Their love shows great spontaneity and is characterized by gaiety and elation as well as by care and responsibility for the loved one. Their sexual love episodes may be very intense, approaching the level of mystic experiences. In fact, *peak experiences* of various kinds are characteristic of the self-actualized. These are "moments of highest happiness and fulfillment" and may come, in differing degrees of intensity, during various activities—parental experiences, creative activity, aesthetic perceptions, appreciation of nature, or even athletic participation.

Thus organismic field theorists such as Goldstein, Rogers, and Maslow have stressed a basic drive toward self-actualization as the organizer of all the diverse forces whose interplay continually creates what a person is. In the process they have developed theories which seem more "human" than many which preceded them, with an emphasis on the importance of how a person perceives his world and on processes of health and growth.

Criticism of self-actualization theories.   Criticisms of this approach focus on the fuzziness of the central concept, "self-actualization." First, it is not clear to what degree self-actualization is a socially defined rather than an inborn tendency. Second, it is not well enough defined to be very powerful as a specific predictor of behavioral relationships. Thus these theories have difficulty in accounting, except in a very general way, for the *specific* kinds of consistency which characterize particular individuals.

The Factor Theorists:
Consistency from a Collection of Traits

The last way of thinking about personality that we shall consider is perhaps the best of those presently available at describing and accounting for clusters of human characteristics.

Trait theory and the development of factor analysis. One of the earliest and most straightforward ways of describing human consistency was by the delineation of "traits." If a person was consistently friendly, he had a trait of "friendliness"; if he did well in sports, a trait of "athletic ability." Traits were like

instincts in being seen as inner characteristics, but the question was left open as to whether a given trait was inherited or not.

Not too surprisingly, trait theorists ran into the same problem as instinct theorists: their lists of traits seemed to go on endlessly, and no two lists agreed. Then it occurred to someone that perhaps some traits were more "basic" than others: that the confusing multitude of *surface traits* might reflect the interaction of a much smaller, more orderly set of *source traits* (Cattell, 1957). That was not much help at first, for it was anyone's guess which were the surface traits and which the underlying source traits. The lists of source traits that were proposed were shorter but still showed little agreement. Then a powerful mathematical tool called *factor analysis* came on the scene.

Factor analysis is a mathematical technique (involving matrix algebra) for reducing a large number of observed phenomena to a smaller number of basic, more fundamental variables. Assume that we begin with many people taking a large battery of personality tests on which for each person 100 scores (presumed trait measures) are obtained. We want to know how these scores are related to each other, but if we correlated all the scores individually, we would have 4950 different figures to evaluate. To make sense of this vast amount of data, much of which may be redundant (that is, measuring the same thing), mathematical and statistical techniques are used to determine the minimum number of factors that can adequately account for the correlation matrix (see Horst, 1968, and Edwards, 1970).

These factors are then given names according to the general characteristic that they seem to represent, for example, "sociability" or "impulsiveness." In this way a factor analysis of the results of 100 personality test questions might yield five or six factors that most of the questions were really measuring in different ways.

Why were such findings important? For the trait theorists it was highly exciting, because factor analysis made it possible to examine tests designed to tap different traits and discover whether in fact they appeared to be measuring the same thing or different things. When the same factor was found in several tests, it seemed reasonable to assume that that factor must represent one of the "source traits" the theorists had been trying so hard to find. Here was an objective, mathematical procedure theorists could use to discover the underlying structure of human personality. Several of them set about at once to try to do so. We will examine in detail the work of one of these, J. P. Guilford.

Guilford's factor theory.   Guilford has identified two groups of general personality factors, as well as a group of factors having to do with specific kinds of intellectual functioning.

Hormetic factors.   The hormetic traits are the direct motivational aspects of an individual's personality.

(The word *hormetic* comes from the Greek, meaning "to set in motion" or "to excite.") These factors depend upon the physical needs of the body and upon the kinds of experience the individual has had; thus they might be somewhat different in different societies. They include needs, attitudes, and interests.

Careful work by Guilford, Cattell, Eysenck, and many others over the years has revealed a number of measurable needs, attitudes, and interests which are seen as directing our behavior and consciousness and as keeping us busy seeking until some goal is reached. Several of these are shown in the chart (Guilford, 1959). ▲   The present list is by no means exhaustive, and research in this area continues. Other

▲   **HORMETIC FACTORS**

Type of Factor	Factors Identified	Type of Factor	Factors Identified

Need factors	organic condition:
	  male sex drive
	  general activity
		Vocational interest factors	professional level:
			  scientific
			  esthetic expression
			  social welfare

	environmental:
	  need for a safe environment
	  need for orderliness
	  need for attention
			commercial:
			  business
			  clerical

	achievement:
	  general ambition
	  persistent effort
	  endurance
			physical activity:
			  mechanical
			  outdoor
			  aviation

	self-determination:
	  need for freedom
	  self-reliance vs. dependence
	  cultural conformity
	  honesty
			interests unique to women:
			  career-woman
			  domestic
			  verbal vs. mathematical

	social:
	  gregariousness
	  benevolence
	  need for discipline
	  aggressiveness
		Avocational interest factors	overt activities:
			  liking for adventure vs. security
			  liking for diversions

			activities with certain properties:
			  liking for variety
			  liking for precision

Attitudinal factors	liberation vs. conservatism
	
	religionism
	
	humanitarianism
	
	nationalism
	
	gradualism vs. revolution
			appreciative:
			  general cultural interests
			  esthetic appreciation

			interest in thinking:
			  reflective
			  autistic
			  rigorous

From *Personality* by J. P. Guilford. Copyright 1959. Used by permission of McGraw-Hill Book Company.

psychologists are working in the same field, and it is interesting to note that their findings are in essential agreement—a situation quite different from that which has often arisen among those using less objective approaches (Cattell, 1965; Eysenck, 1960).

Temperament factors. Guilford and his associates have also studied factors of temperament, which describe the *manner* in which an individual characteristically operates in certain types of situations. Such characteristics are measured by scales like the Guilford-Zimmerman Temperament Survey, a self-inventory device that has grown out of the factor analytic research (Guilford & Zimmerman, 1949). Each trait is conceived as a dimension with two extremes; the individual's score falls somewhere on a scale in between. A "profile" of his high and low scores on the ten dimensions can be constructed (see p. 456). This scale is frequently used in predicting an individual's probable success in various jobs.

While this test provides measures of ten traits, it is important to keep in mind that no trait stands alone. Each is conditioned and modified by all the other traits and characteristics of the individual. For example, a person very high in ascendance and at the same time high in friendliness would have a vastly different personality from that of a person who was equally dominant but low in friendliness.

1. *General activity* (slow–energetic). A high score indicates a high level of activity. Persons scoring high on this factor need activity, must be doing something. A high level of energy tends to exaggerate other personality characteristics. Thus, the sociable person who has a great deal of energy engages in more social activity than the sociable person of lower drive. Less desirable personality traits, such as hostility toward others, will also be more obvious in a person who has a high level of energy. A high level of energy is important to executives, salesmen, production supervisors, and so on, but might be a handicap for sedentary workers.

2. *Restraint* (impulsive–restrained). Very high restraint means that the individual is likely to be overcontrolled, stiff, and lacking in spontaneity in his relations with others. Very low scores suggest serious lack of control, impulsiveness, ill-considered actions, and speech. A good level of control is needed in the

executive, in the supervisor, and in such technical occupations as engineer, accountant, or scientist. Sales jobs which require spontaneity in personal relations with others, on the other hand, require that the person have a lower score on self-restraint. Very low scores on this factor may or may not indicate serious personality difficulties, depending upon the strength and patterning of other personality factors.

3. *Ascendance* (timid–self-assured). High scores indicate confidence in personal contacts with others and a desire for the leadership role. Low scores suggest lack of confidence in social situations, lack of aggressiveness, or even fear of others. Executive, sales, and supervisory positions require a rather high level of dominance, but high scores are not desirable in positions in which there is no opportunity to dominate, control, or lead others.

4. *Sociability* (solitary–sociable). High scores indicate a liking for face-to-face personal contacts with others. Low scores suggest a lack of social confidence, lack of interest in social contacts, and probable preference for working alone. Those who score low on this trait are not likely to be thought of as friendly persons. Those who have to work with people should not have low sociability scores. However, extremely high sociability scores are not necessarily a good indication for sales, executive, or supervisory personnel since it is important that persons in these positions not be socially dependent—that is, overly concerned with the opinions of others.

5. *Emotional stability* (easily upset–emotionally stable). A high score indicates a good, healthy mental attitude and freedom from excessive neurotic tendencies. Low scores suggest moodiness, instability of emotional life, and neurotic tendencies.

6. *Objectivity* (oversensitive–objective). A high score on this factor indicates a realistic view of self. Persons with high scores do not get their feelings hurt easily, while those who make low scores are sensitive, touchy, and easily offended. Extremely high scores on this factor may indicate lack of sensitivity to the feelings of others.

7. *Friendliness* (resistant–agreeable). A very high score may indicate pacifistic tendencies, a good adjustment to daily annoyances, or a wish to please others. A low score indicates a tendency to react defensively or belligerently toward others. The impor-

tance of extremely high or low scores on this factor depends upon other personal characteristics, such as dominance, sociability, and self-restraint. Generally speaking, persons with high scores tend to be cooperative, agreeable, and "easy to live with," while those with low scores are most likely to be quarrelsome, critical, and antagonistic in situations in which they feel they can get away with it.

8. *Thoughtfulness* (superficial–reflective). A high score indicates a tendency toward reflective and thoughtful behavior. Extremely low scores usually indicate frivolous attitudes and a dislike of situations requiring deep, prolonged analytic thinking. Executives, supervisors, and those who have positions requiring planning, organization, and a good deal of thoughtful analysis should not have low scores on this factor. Scores on this factor must be interpreted in the light of all other personality traits.

9. *Personal relations* (critical–trusting). A high score on this factor indicates a tolerance of others, an acceptance of society's mores and customs. A low score suggests suspiciousness and a critical, cynical attitude toward people and society. High scores on this trait are extremely desirable in sales and supervisory personnel or in any position requiring the ability to handle or get along well with people.

10. *Masculinity* (sympathetic–hard-boiled). A high score means the person behaves in a manner characteristic of men. A high scorer is not squeamish, tends to be callous and insensitive to the needs of others. Low scorers are said to resemble women. They are "motherly" and protective toward the young and helpless. (What kind of cultural definition of sex is implied here?)

Where do lists like these leave the theorist? Is he reduced to a mere reporter, telling the world what the computer has most recently come up with? Hardly. For one thing, each factor must be looked at carefully to see whether it duplicates a factor already discovered and described elsewhere and must be given a name which conveys as accurate an impression as possible of the source trait it seems to be tapping. Equally important, and a good deal more interesting, once a number of factors have been discovered and verified, it becomes possible to look for relationships among them. For example, further work by Guilford in the area of temperament resulted in the identification and isolation of fifteen dimensions of temperament which seemed to define temperamental differences more adequately than the set of ten listed

■ **A MATRIX OF TEMPERAMENT FACTORS**

Kind of Dimension		Areas of Behavior Involved		
		General ↓	**Emotional** ↓	**Social** ↓
Positive vs. negative	⟶	confidence vs. inferiority	cheerfulness vs. depression	ascendance vs. timidity
Responsive vs. unresponsive	⟶	alertness vs. inattentiveness	immaturity vs. maturity	socialization vs. self-sufficiency
Active vs. passive	⟶	impulsiveness vs. deliberateness	nervousness vs. composure	social initiative vs. passivity
Controlled vs. uncontrolled	⟶	restraint vs. rhathymia	stability vs. cycloid disposition	friendliness vs. hostility
Objective vs. egocentric	⟶	objectivity vs. hypersensitivity	poise vs. self-consciousness	tolerance vs. criticalness

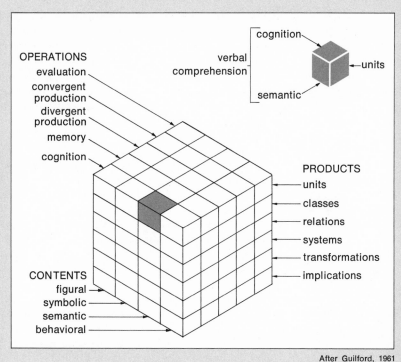

OPERATIONS
- evaluation
- convergent production
- divergent production
- memory
- cognition

cognition

verbal comprehension

semantic

units

PRODUCTS
- units
- classes
- relations
- systems
- transformations
- implications

CONTENTS
- figural
- symbolic
- semantic
- behavioral

After Guilford, 1961

◆ **THE STRUCTURE OF INTELLECT**

Each factor can be classified as to operation, product, and content. There are 5 kinds of operations: evaluation, convergent production, divergent production, memory, and cognition; 6 kinds of products: units, classes, relations, systems, transformations, and implications; and 4 kinds of content: figural, symbolic, semantic, and behavioral. An example or one such factor is the well-known verbal comprehension, which under this system is classified as *cognition* of *units* with *semantic* content.

above. He then suggested that these can be conceived of as involving three different areas of behavior—general, emotional, and social—each varying on five dimensions, as shown in the chart. ▪

Intellectual factors. A still more ambitious attempt to classify factors into a systematic framework is Guilford's *structure of intellect* (Guilford, 1961). Guilford classifies intellectual factors according to *content* (kind of information), according to *product* (form), and according to the *operation* involved. ◆ The different intellectual abilities represent different combinations of contents, products, and operations. That is, any of the four types of content may take the form of any of the six products ($4 \times 6 = 24$). On these twenty-four resulting kinds of information, any of the five types of operation may be performed ($24 \times 5 = 120$). Thus we have a total of 120 possible intellectual abilities. These are illustrated in the three-dimensional structure of intellect model. Each of the 120 cells of this model represents one of the

120 ability factors and is represented by high scores on a particular kind of test.

This theoretical model is analogous to the chemist's periodic table of the elements. By means of such a systematic framework, intellectual factors, like chemical elements, may be postulated before they are discovered. In several cases this has in fact happened: abilities postulated on the basis of the model have later been successfully identified by testing (Guilford, 1964, 1966).

Criticisms of trait theories. It is plain that the factor theorists have developed potent ways of describing and accounting for even highly complex patterns of consistency in individual characteristics. Criticisms of the approach have been of three kinds: theoretical, methodological, and empirical.

Theoretically, the main complaint has been similar to the criticism of learning theories we outlined above: the factor theorists picture personality as a bundle of traits but provide little to help under-

Ψ *Close-up*   *On the Analyst's Couch or Up Against the Social Behaviorist's Wall?*

A student radical confronts the Dean with the need for a restructuring of the university and society. He says his ultimate goals are to stop war and hatred and to promote love and understanding between all people. As he advances his arguments (and a series of nonnegotiable demands), an impartial observer of the human condition notes the following pattern in his behavior:

A. An increase in rate and loudness of speaking
B. An increase in stuttering
C. An increase of negative affect in speech
D. Frequent cynical statements of distrust about the Dean's intentions
E. Decreased eye contact with the Dean, but maintained argumentation and verbal contact

Let us compare how this case might be analyzed by traditional personality theorists (looking for inner traits and dispositions) and by the new social behaviorist breed. If it were observed that this general pattern was a recurrent one whenever radicals confonted deans, then such an analysis could be extended from the case of this particular student's behavior to a general explanation of "The Dynamics of Radical Confrontation," which would then appear in some Sunday news magazine supplement. The explanatory models which each camp might erect to account for the student's behavior are shown in the diagram.

The traditional personality theorist begins his search for a parsimonious causal explanation with a historical-

biographical account of certain developmental experiences of this young man. He "begins at the beginning" with early life interactions between child and parents, and he postulates that the student's current dispositions toward authority figures represent generalizations from these early experiences.

Through the use of interviews, case material, projective personality tests, and self-reports, it would be discovered that this student is full of hostility and resentment; has both low self-esteem and weak ego strength; needs affection and support but cannot ask for them for fear of rejection; tends to have a drive toward independent thinking coupled with strong needs for social approval; is generally orderly, clean, stingy with his possessions, and easily provoked into pugnaciousness.

The young man's problem is "obviously" rooted in an ambivalent love-hate relationship toward his parents as a consequence of severe toilet-training experiences. The "anal-compulsive" syndrome which has developed has led to an overreliance on thought and words rather than deeds, to anxiety over any expression of hostility, and to stuttering from pent-up rage. All the behaviors observed are merely the surface manifestations, "smoke screens," concealing his real, deep-down problem. Clearly, therapy for such a person will require his developing insight into the relation between his current behavior and his repressed conflict.

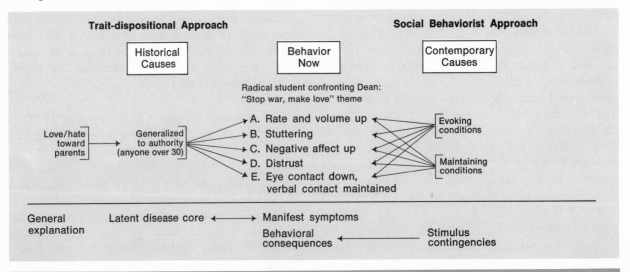

Consider now the following alternative explanation by the social behaviorist, which derives entirely from observing current behavior and stimulus conditions.

1. When the student talks at a slow rate, the Dean interrupts him more often than when he talks fast. Fast talking in this situation is reinforced by fewer interruptions; the student's usual slower rate of talking is extinguished by the aversiveness of interruptions.

2. When the student talks loud, the Dean listens more attentively than when the student uses the "timid," polite volume which the Dean is used to hearing from him (and other students). It also allows him to talk above the Dean's objections.

3. When the student uses negative affect (strongly worded phrases, warnings, threats), the Dean's demeanor changes: he flushes, his pupils dilate, he becomes more animated.

4. When the student alters his usual speech delivery— talking fast, speaking loud and emotionally—he begins to stutter because of the disruption in the normal flow and feedback pattern.

5. From previous conversations with the Dean, the student has learned that there is no correlation between present verbal statements of agreement and later positive action. This knowledge is expressed as distrust of the Dean's verbal agreement.

6. As the Dean becomes more upset, he frowns, scowls, looks disapprovingly and angrily at the student. The student avoids eye contact because it is upsetting to see anyone reacting so negatively toward him.

7. The student persists with his rhetoric because as long as he is talking it reinforces his own self-image as someone who is engaged in meaningful action to effect social change. When he stops and is faced with an unchanged political and social reality, he feels helpless and hopeless.

To modify his behavior will obviously require attempting to change the evoking and maintaining stimulus conditions. *How he confronts the Dean* can be altered by reprogramming the Dean's reactions to him. *What he confronts the Dean about* can be changed only by changing the nature of his current, threatening environment.

stand how these traits hang together to form the coherent system that we recognize as a personality.

Methodologically, the approach has been accused of generating scales which are impure or mislabeled. For example, several different measures labeled "anxiety" do not seem to correlate highly with each other. At the other extreme, it is charged that too often high correlations between scales result simply from the use of identical items in the different scales —differently phrased but really testing the same thing. Finally, scales which are intended to measure particular traits have sometimes been contaminated by social desirability (the tendency of the person being tested to check items he thinks would be approved of) or by acquiescence (consistency in agreeing—or disagreeing—with almost any statement).

Empirically, the strongest criticism of trait theory has come from Walter Mischel (1968, 1969). In his view, the various personality dimensions derived from factor analysis of questionnaire responses look fine on paper but do not correlate highly enough with anything except other questionnaire responses to be trusted for any use beyond gross screening decisions. Even attempts to develop paper-and-pencil measures that would correlate with particular behaviors have come out with very low correlations, especially when they investigated the behavior in different kinds of situations. Only with intelligence have high correlations been found between the behavior (academic and other achievement) and the test scores.

In fact, Mischel goes a step further to question whether these traits and factors are in the person at all. He has marshaled an impressive array of evidence that noncognitive (nonintellectual) traits are not good predictors of behavior because behavior itself is unstable and inconsistent across different situations. He argues cogently that this lack of a nice, neat pattern of high correlations is due not to imperfect methodological tools for personality assessment, but rather to the faulty assumption that there *is* a central core of personality dispositions to be found.

Mischel eschews the historical approach of looking for remote origins of *now* behavior in distant childhood experiences. The "social behavior" theory he has developed stresses instead the forces in the current situation that evoke behavior and the reinforcing conditions that maintain it. (Ψ Close-up, left.)

A person's behavior is stable when the maintaining conditions are stable; it is consistent from one condition to another if and when the important stimulus features are the same. However, whenever the cue and reinforcing properties of the environment change, behavior changes (is unstable or inconsistent) regardless of whatever core of enduring dispositions there may be.

This is not to say that behavior is capricious, learned anew in every situation. Rather, it follows laws of learning, and the consistencies we attribute to "behavioral traits" simply result from the fact that the evoking and maintaining conditions stay substantially the same for most of us most of the time.

Does such a view render man into a mechanistic automaton without uniqueness and distinctive character? To the contrary, contends Mischel: in insisting upon postulating invariance, despite the variability we observe, we do violence to the complexity of human behavior. To recognize that people are responsive to subtle changes in their environment is to argue for human adaptiveness and flexibility.

Ways of Assessing Individual Differences

Any attempt to assess individual characteristics is based on the notion that "it all hangs together somehow." That is, such assessment always involves the attempt to predict a wide range of ways in which an individual will be consistent from a much narrower range of characteristics that we can tap directly. In the following sections we shall look at three main approaches to the problem of predicting a lot from a little, but first we need to consider why such assessment is undertaken despite the difficulty and grief often entailed.

Why Try?

One of the questions most frequently asked about psychological testing is "What's it for?" Students who have to take psychological tests sometimes feel dehumanized, "put in boxes" which leave no room for their individuality to show through. Prospective employees—particularly those from minority groups—sometimes feel that tests are being used against them. This is indeed ironic, for the main purpose in giving a psychological test is usually to be able to take *better* account of the test-taker's individual characteristics. If personality theorists are trying to find fruitful ways of conceptualizing the kinds of consistency in individual behavior, psychological testers are in the business of trying to predict which individuals will show which of these kinds of consistency under what conditions. Typically they are trying to do so for one of three broad reasons.

1. *To predict success.* A great many psychological tests are used in vocational counseling, as "entrance examinations" for schools, and in personnel placement work. In settings such as these, the tests are used to predict the probability that an individual will be successful in a given line of work, at a particular school, or in some specified job. If the probability is low, the individual is well advised to look elsewhere, and the tests may even give him some indication of where he might reasonably expect to do better. The ultimate goal of this sort of testing, then, is to get as many people as possible into settings where they will be maximally effective and therefore, presumably, happier and more self-actualized.

2. *To determine treatment.* The second major use of psychological tests is in schools and clinical settings; here the tests are used in deciding what sorts of educational or therapeutic experiences will be helpful for which people. In some cases they are used to determine the advisability of special classes for children who are mentally retarded or emotionally disturbed. In others, they are used to explore the degree and nature of psychopathology in order to determine which sort of therapy will be likely to be most fruitful. At times, they are used to investigate the possibility that psychological or neurological difficulties are involved in physical ailments or below-average functioning. In all such testing, the ultimate goal is to get as many people as possible matched with the kinds of teaching, training, and therapy from which they will benefit most.

Intelligence tests were originally designed as a democratic means of ensuring that qualified children would be allowed to progress in the public education system solely on the basis of their objective test performance and would not be held back by subjective biases of teachers. Psychologists are now at work to remove the other sources of bias which have crept into the construction, administration, and evaluation of intelligence tests. The real value of such testing is that it enables us to see how a child's performance compares with the norms of other children who are most comparable in terms of language, cultural and socioeconomic background, educational opportunities, and broad patterns of life experience, in order to determine what educational experiences will be most fruitful for him at this stage of his development. (Ψ Close-up, right.)

3. *To further our understanding.* Finally, psychological tests are used in research aimed at refining our conceptions of how people function. Part of this research involves testing the sorts of personality theories we examined above. Another part involves the development of new tests which will enhance our ability to predict who will be successful at what, and who will benefit from which types of treatment. Still another has to do with learning about how people develop: at what ages children develop which skills, attitudes, and ways of dealing with the world. In all such testing, then, the goal is to find out more: to further the development of psychology as a theoretical and applied science.

Before the development of sophisticated tests and statistical analyses of their scores, attempts had long been made to measure individual differences and predict consistency on the basis of physical characteristics and various kinds of "natural" behavior. We will look briefly at these before tracing the development of systematic psychological testing.

Body Type, Physiognomy, and Bumps on the Head

As our fortune-teller (p. 421) was aware, one good way of trying to predict what a person is like is to make a guess based on his appearance. In everyday life, we often base such judgments in large part on the kind of "uniform" a person is wearing, whether it be the conservative suit and tie of a businessman or the wild bell-bottoms and love beads of a hippie. However, we are too easily fooled in such judgments for them to be the basis of a science: that "wand'ring minstrel" may be an emperor's son traveling incognito. Other judgments are based on more enduring characteristics. The beliefs that persons with high foreheads are intelligent, that redheads have frequent outbursts of fiery temper, and that fat men are jolly are examples of the many popular attempts to predict personality from physical characteristics.

Phrenology. In Chapter 3 we saw that *phrenology* came into wide popularity during the nineteenth century and for a time was regarded as a legitimate science. The phrenologists believed that personality was composed of a specific number of "faculties," or proneness to particular types of feelings or behavior, each located in a specific area of the brain. They argued that the person who possessed a great deal of a particular faculty would have a bump on his skull at the point where the "organ" for this power was located and that an individual's personality could therefore be determined by studying the shape of his head.

Ψ Close-up   "Startling Admission on IQ Tests"

Any tool, however useful, can be misused, and psychological tests are no exception. The above headline in the *San Francisco Chronicle* (January 24, 1970) introduced a story which was not only startling but distressing in its implications. The article reported that 45 percent of the elementary-school children with Spanish surnames who were in classes for the mentally retarded in one school system had been found to be of average or above-average intelligence when retested in Spanish! One child's IQ soared from 67 when tested in English to 128 when the same test was administered in Spanish. The average IQ gain for the thirty-five students who had been mislabeled "mental retardates" by the use of inappropriate test procedures was a sizeable 17 points.

Added to the obvious bias of administering the test in an unfamiliar language was the less obvious bias introduced from economic considerations. The school system, which received an additional $550 in government funds for each retarded child, was reluctant to retest and reclassify these children. A federal judge had to order retesting in the native language of the child when affidavits were filed by concerned psychologists, educators, parents, and students (*San Francisco Chronicle*, February 7, 1970).

The seat of "amativeness," for instance, was supposed to be at the base of the skull, and persons who possessed large bumps at that point were described as "alive to the charms of the other sex, polite, affable, and free in their company, successful in gaining their confidence, and courageous in their defense." (Olin, 1910, pp. 82–83)   •

Modern objections to the claims of phrenology are overwhelming. A comparison of a phrenologist's map of the brain with the actual findings of neurologists shows that there is no correspondence whatsoever either in the location or in the function of the brain area represented. (When we stimulate the part of the brain thought by phrenologists to be the center of religiousness, for example, the subject twitches his leg.) Modern research has found nothing to support the existence of "faculties" as they were conceived by the phrenologists. The only type of brain localization that actually exists is of general types of function— motor, sensory, speech, and so on, as we have seen.

Physiognomy.   Many people still believe in *physiognomy*, the art of judging personality from facial characteristics. Physiognomic stereotypes for a number of personality traits have been built up in our culture over the years and are widely accepted today. For example, remarkable agreement has been shown among college students in characterizing faces as self-confident, cheerful, refined, and so on (Secord, Dukes, & Bevan, 1954). But do such judgments of faces, however well they may agree with each other, agree with the actual personalities of the individuals studied, as revealed by their behavior? In an attempt to answer this question with regard to judgments of leadership qualities, one investigator asked college students to rank groups of photographs for leadership ability.

The photographs used were those of seventy-five candidates for the Colorado State Highway Patrol who had been rated for leadership characteristics by skilled judges. Subjects were given both full-figure and head-and-shoulders photos of all candidates, divided into small groups. They were asked to rank the photos in each group as to which man would be the best leader, the next best, and so on. As might be expected there was a relatively high degree of agreement among the subjects as to which men looked most like leaders. However,

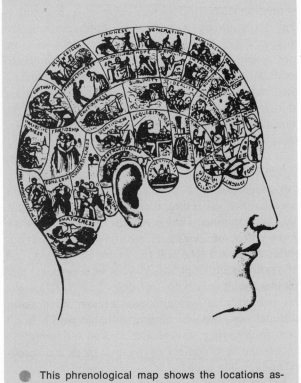

●   This phrenological map shows the locations ascribed to the various presumed powers or faculties of the mind. These were largely social-moral personality traits.

their judgments showed only a very low correlation with the actual leadership ratings of the candidates that had been made earlier by the skilled judges (Mason, 1957).

Another study found judgments of intelligence based on physiognomy to be invalid when compared with the results of intelligence tests. In this case the men themselves (317 airmen), rather than their photographs, were observed briefly by subjects who attempted to judge their level of intelligence on the basis of their appearance (Ray, 1958).

At the present time, any value that physiognomy has in measuring actual characteristics of a person can probably be explained on the basis of popular stereotypes or "pictures in the mind." If most people think that a square jaw is a sign of leadership, they will tend to follow the man with a square jaw and thus make him a leader and he will come to think of himself as one.

Somatotypes. Characteristics of the body as a whole, rather than just the face or the head, have also been studied in relation to personality. A body-type theory which has been investigated extensively in relation to mental illness was proposed by a German psychiatrist (Kretschmer, 1925). In a group of patients that he studied, he noticed that the schizophrenic ones tended to be tall and thin, whereas the manic-depressive ones were most often short and plump. He also found that each body type was associated with a characteristic temperament pattern. It was only a short step further to suggest using body build to predict which type of disorder a given individual would develop if he were to become mentally ill. Although clinical experience upholds Kretschmer's observations to a slight extent, studies in the main fail to support the relationships he suggested.

An outgrowth of Kretschmer's work which has become much more widely known is Sheldon's somatotype theory (Sheldon, 1942). According to Sheldon's classification, there are three basic body types (somatotypes), each of which can be identified with a corresponding personality type. ■

Sheldon's major study was performed over a five-year period on two hundred young men, all college students or college graduates are engaged for the most part in academic or professional careers. These men were rated as to somatotype and were also interviewed to determine temperament traits. High correlations were reported between body type and temperament. Unfortunately, study of Sheldon's table of correlations has revealed serious computational errors and shown that some of the correlations were mathematically impossible (Lubin, 1950).

Controversy arising from Sheldon's claims stimulated research on the part of other psychologists to determine whether his theory could stand the test of impartial investigation. In one study of 10,000 male freshmen, the relationships between body type and temperament described by Sheldon were either absent or so small as to have no practical significance (Hood, 1963).

A More Dynamic View: Naturally Occurring Behavior

Other popular attempts to understand personality are based on the individual's behavior rather than his anatomy. Among the most common forms of expression so used are handwriting, voice, and posture.

Graphology. Assessment of personality characteristics by studying a person's handwriting is known as *graphology*. Although many psychologists feel that it has no more value than palmistry or the reading of tea leaves, it has been studied scientifically in recent

---

■ SHELDON'S CLASSIFICATION OF BODY TYPES

Body Type	Endomorphy (tendency toward roundness and softness)	Mesomorphy (predominance of muscle and bone)	Ectomorphy (fragility and linearity in body build)
Personality Type	Visceratonia	Somatotonia	Cerebrotonia
Typical Traits	Fond of food, inclined to eat too much, apprehensive, insecure, amiable, sleeps well, conforms to social conventions	Adventurous, likes strenuous exercise and cold showers, dresses informally, withstands pain easily and willingly	Asocial, unamiable, lacks desire for exercise, nonadventurous, does not withstand pain easily

After Sheldon, Stevens, & Tucker, 1940, & Child, 1950

years by rigorously controlled methods. The general conclusion is that graphology may eventually prove to have some value in predicting personality traits.

Two studies, for example, suggest that the use of unnecessary beginning strokes may be related to certain personality characteristics. Two kinds of unnecessary strokes were observed. *Primary* strokes, consisting of voluntary elaborations or embellishments of the basic letter, and *secondary* strokes, representing a retention of writing habits learned in the first years of school, as indicated by the dotted line here: *uv* .

Both primary and secondary stroke users showed highly authoritarian attitudes. Users of primary beginning strokes were actively self-assertive but showed greater social conformity than either users of secondary strokes or those who used neither kind of beginning stroke. Users of secondary beginning strokes were found to have lower scholastic aptitude than those who did not use such strokes. They also tended to be passive and to have difficulty in adjusting to new situations and in controlling their impulses (Linton, Epstein, & Hartford, 1961, 1962).

Some graphological studies have been concerned with *global* or total impressions of handwriting rather than individual signs or letters. Judgments based on such impressions, however, are inevitably highly subjective.

A recent study relates one aspect of handwriting, the size of one's signature, to his status. Signatures on library book call cards were measured for faculty members, graduate students, undergraduates, and those individuals who had moved up the academic ladder at a given college from student to professor. The higher the status became, the bigger (bolder?) the signature that went with it (Zweigenhaft, 1970).

A number of objective techniques have been developed for measuring specific characteristics of handwriting, such as pressure and speed. Both the pressure exerted on the point of the pen and the pressure exerted in gripping it can be measured by means of a sensitive table with a recording device. Early studies using such devices confirmed that men used more pressure in gripping the pen or pencil than did women (Katz, 1948).

Unfortunately, very little has actually been done with these measuring devices in experimental graphology, though one early investigator did find a positive correlation between point pressure and the personality variables of "energy" and "expressiveness." He also showed that an adult's handwriting remains about the same with regard to pressure and speed (Pascal, 1943).

Although graphology is widely used in Europe, reviewers in the United States have typically concluded that graphology has thus far proven to be of little, if any, practical value in assessing personality traits (Fluckiger, Tripp, & Weinberg, 1961). It is possible, however, that further research may substantiate some of the claims that have been made. Should graphology prove to be as valid as its advocates claim, it would have a great practical value because of the ease with which samples of handwriting can be obtained for evaluation.

Other forms of expressive behavior. Relatively little research appears to have been done on the relationship between personality traits and such forms of expressive behavior as voice and posture.

One study compared the vocal characteristics of 372 college students with their scores on certain personality variables as measured by a self-inventory (see p. 449). Those who scored high in dominance tended to have louder, more resonant, and lower-pitched voices than those who showed submissiveness on the self-inventory (Mallory & Miller, 1958).

Research of the sort described above may be greatly facilitated by the use of "voice prints" such as those shown here. • Since every individual's voice print for a given word is unique and unchanging, this recently developed technique has proved to be of use in the identification of criminals. It should also be of value in other situations where an objective measure of vocal characteristics is needed. The relationship between voice patterns and other personality traits is a matter that has yet to be determined by careful research.

Posture undoubtedly plays a part in many "snap judgments" of personality. That is, the stereotyped idea of the leader usually includes an upright, confident bearing, whereas the scholar is thought of as being stoop-shouldered. It has been found that people with poor posture often have inferiority feelings (Faterson, 1931). However, this fact alone does not tell us whether the poor posture has been caused by the inferiority feelings or vice versa. It has been suggested that the relationship may be a reciprocal one:

"An individual experiencing temporary fear, grief, or anger all too often carries his body in an attitude which the world recognizes as the outward manifestation of that particular emotion. If he persists in his dramatization or consistently re-establishes it, thus forming what is ordinarily referred to as a "habit pattern," the muscular arrangement becomes set. Materially speaking, some muscles shorten and thicken, others are invaded by connective tissue, still others are immobilized by the consolidation of the tissue involved. Once this has happened the physical attitude is invariable; it is involuntary; it can no longer be changed basically by taking thought, or even by mental suggestion. Since it is not possible to express a free flow through the physical flesh, the subjective emotional tone becomes more limited and tends to remain in a restricted and closely defined area. Now, what the individual feels is no longer an emotion, a single response to an immediate situation; henceforth he lives, moves, and has his being in an attitude." (Rolf, 1962, pp. 9-10)

Predicting More Precisely: Behavior in Standardized Situations

For most purposes, physical traits and behavior produced freely in "natural" settings have not made possible precise enough predictions of individual characteristics. As a result, psychologists have spent a great deal of energy and ingenuity devising standardized situations which would elicit behavior from which better predictions could be made. These situations have ranged in their degree of standardization from minimally structured observations with a strong flavor of "real life," through open-ended and more structured interviews, to a succession of much briefer, more highly standardized tasks presented together as a psychological "test."

Rating scales. Some kinds of behavior from which one might wish to predict individual characteristics are difficult for a psychologist to observe directly. They may be too private, for example, or occur over a prohibitively long period of time. Thus in trying to assess these kinds of behavior, it is often useful to have others who know the subject give their impres-

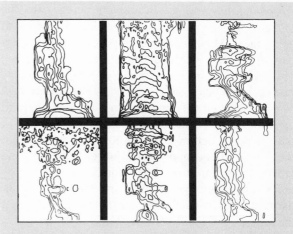

These six voiceprints were made by five different people saying the word "you." Can you tell which two were made by the same speaker?

sions of what he does. A useful device for obtaining such impressions is the rating scale. There are two kinds of rating scale, *relative* and *absolute*, each with certain advantages and disadvantages. These are frequently used in connection with an interview, as well as to record subjective impressions based on a longer period of contact. Both types have the advantage of yielding numerical values that can be analyzed quantitatively.

Relative rating scales. A relative rating scale may be used when several subjects are being rated. The order-of-merit method is typical. The rater ranks the subjects in order by indicating the best, then the next best, and so on until all subjects have been ranked on the trait being measured. This method indicates what each person's position is relative to that of all other subjects being considered. Its practical disadvantage is that the judge must keep the entire list of persons in mind throughout the rating process. This difficulty can be reduced somewhat by writing the names of the persons being ranked on cards and having the judge cast the cards into several piles (for example, good, average, and poor) before he rates them individually. He can then put the names in each subgroup in rank order and make any necessary rearrangement between subgroups in getting the final order.

Absolute rating scales.   In absolute rating scales the judge assigns a score to each individual on each trait being rated. He compares each person to some standard established independently of the particular group of individuals being considered. For example, he may rate each candidate on a seven-point scale of neatness or may check all the adjectives in a list that apply to the candidate. This method is quicker than that of relative rating but more subject to errors arising from the "personal equation" of the judges. That is, some judges assign too many high scores; others give too many low or average scores. Furthermore, the standards of an individual judge may fluctuate throughout the series.

Both types of rating scale are subject to two important types of errors of judgment: halo and stereotype. The *halo effect* (see p. 303) is the tendency to judge a likeable or intelligent person as "good" in other respects as well. *Stereotypes* are preconceived notions as to what we expect a given kind of person (Frenchman, politician, little old lady) to be like. Both errors can be minimized by having the judge rate all the individuals on only one trait at a time, so that his earlier ratings of a given person will be less likely to influence his later ones.

Because the rating scale inevitably depends so much upon the subjective judgments of the raters, however, it is usually regarded as inferior to the more objective psychological tests to be described below. Certainly the value of the ratings will depend both on a judge's ability to evaluate others and on his definition of the traits being appraised. To some extent these factors can be appraised by a check on how well two sets of judges agree on their ratings of the same individuals and on how consistent the same judges are on their ratings of the same individuals on successive occasions. Recent studies have indicated that with a skillfully constructed scale both of these potential sources of difficulty can be minimized.

A special type of absolute rating scale, the *forced-choice* rating scale, has been developed to offset the frequent tendency to rate nearly all persons near the top of the scale—the "leniency error." The basic principle is to require the rater to choose between pairs of descriptive statements determined beforehand to be equally "favorable." In actual practice the forced-choice method has not reduced leniency in

rating as much as was hoped. Furthermore, most raters do not like to use forced-choice scales.

Behavior sampling.   In behavior sampling techniques, the examiner simply observes the person's behavior in a typical situation. Unaware that he is being watched, the subject behaves as usual.

The following test of honesty is an example of behavior sampling. A teacher asks his students to perform a task "on their honor" and then leaves the room, giving them ample opportunity to cheat. A few days later the same task is assigned, but this time the teacher maintains close supervision. A student who did well without supervision but performs poorly under supervision is likely to have cheated the first time. This procedure may be repeated with a variety of tasks on different occasions so that the investigator can be sure he has a reliable measure. The purpose of such tests is not to trap the students (nothing is ever said or done to the probable cheaters) but to obtain a measure of honesty in a specified situation.

Another interesting behavior sampling technique for assessing leadership qualities was developed by the Office of Strategic Services during World War II. Situations were set up which were as nearly as possible like those that a candidate might actually meet. For example, a construction test involved an assignment in which the candidate was to complete a piece of construction, supervising men who had secretly been instructed to make every attempt to sabotage the effort. Observers rated the candidate on his behavior under this type of stress (*Fortune*, 1946).

Later assessment of such tests proved them to be more expensive by far and less valid per hour of testing time than were objective psychological tests (MacKinnon, 1958).

A recent study has shown that behavior sampling techniques may have value as a supplement to more conventional testing procedures. Three situational tests—a simulated police patrol, a simulated missing-person investigation, and a two-hour "bull session" —were found to predict success in Cincinnati, Ohio, Police Academy basic training (Mills, McDevitt, & Tonkin, 1966).   ◆

The interview.   The interview has long been the central technique used by clinical psychologists and psychiatrists in their attempts to study and treat personality disorders. It has also been used extensively by employers in selecting new workers.

In one form, the interview may be open ended: "standardized" only to the extent that there is an expectation that two people will share an office for a brief time and that one will do most of the talking. In this form, however, it has proved to be a rather undependable device for yielding impressions which predict future behavior, at least in a job setting (Mayfield, 1964). This undependability probably results in part from its vulnerability to errors in judgment such as the halo effect and stereotypes mentioned above in connection with rating scales. In addition, any impressions formed in this way are

◆ In the second part of the Cincinnati police recruitment test, the candidate investigates the mysterious disappearance of a hypothetical city employee who supposedly worked at the desk shown here. Clues include racing forms, a Scotch bottle, tranquilizers, dunning letters from local stores, perfumed love letters, a passport application, and a memo from the City Manager requiring an audit of accounts. The candidate examines the clues for ten minutes, taking notes, and then is asked to answer a questionnaire calling for factual data, hypotheses about the man's whereabouts, motives for leaving, and probable mental state, and suggest possible bases for prosecution.

limited by the perceptual filter of the interviewer and often are recorded primarily in his memory.

Many of these difficulties can be circumvented by using a *standardized interview schedule*, whereby predetermined questions are asked in a prearranged order. Such an approach yields data which are less subject to interviewer bias and which can be scored and evaluated objectively.

Clues from projective devices. Undoubtedly you have sometimes "seen" a face or the shape of an animal in a cloud. But if you mentioned this to a friend, you may have discovered that he saw a tree or a castle or something else quite different. Psychologists rely upon a similar phenomenon in their use of *projective* techniques of personality measurement. The subject is presented with a standardized set of ambiguous or neutral stimuli—inkblots or pictures which have no definite meaning but can be interpreted in various ways—and is encouraged to interpret freely what he "sees" in them. Thus the subject can "project" onto each neutral stimulus some special, private meaning —much as you projected the face or animal onto the cloud. Psychologists have found that such projections reflect the differing needs and emotional adjustments of individuals and thus help reveal their underlying personality patterns.

Projective tests are difficult to fake because there are no obviously right or wrong answers, and have the further advantage of tapping deeper levels of needs and fears than other measurement methods. They are not, however, entirely satisfactory. One major limitation is that the psychologist must rely to a large extent upon his own subjective judgment in scoring the subject's responses. Although objective standards have been set up for evaluating various types of responses, skillful interpretation on the part of the examiner is still required. This means that the judgment of the examiner influences the final "score" to a greater extent than it does with more objective tests. In addition, considerable training is necessary for using projective tests as a diagnostic tool.

The Rorschach test. The *Rorschach* technique, one of the oldest projective methods, makes use of a series of inkblots. Some are black and white, some colored, and they vary in form, shading, and com-

■ An inkblot similar to those used in the Rorschach test. What do you see in it? Ask one or two of your friends what *they* see.

plexity. The subject observes the cards in a prescribed order and describes what he "sees" in each one. This often gives information about his personality structure which is not brought out by clinical interviews. For example, the way a subject reacts to the color in the blots may throw light on his emotional responses to his environment. ■

In addition to analyzing the content of the projected stories, the Rorschach expert detects clues to personality functioning from stylistic aspects of the response. Does the person respond to the whole stimulus or only to parts? Do form and structure predominate over movement and action in the subject's attempt to organize the ambiguity in the test materials? Such analyses help the clinician to identify the individual's style of perceiving the world, his areas of conflict, and the extent of his pathology.

The Thematic Apperception Test (TAT). Another projective technique is the Thematic Apperception Test (Morgan & Murray, 1935). This test is composed of three series of ten pictures, each picture representing a different situation. The subject is asked to make up a story about each picture, describing the situation, the events that led up to it, how the characters felt, and what the outcome will be. By evaluating both the formal characteristics and the content of these stories, the examiner tries to discover the characteristic thought patterns of the subject. ●

Unusual responses may indicate a problem of some kind, but it is generally important to evaluate "unusualness" in terms of the subject's cultural background and group membership. Responses that are considered unusual if given by a member of one sociocultural group may be typical responses for members of another group. Consistent differences in responses to projective tests may be expected in groups subject to different cultural pressures.

Attempts to use the TAT in predicting vocational success have been very disappointing. Both it and the Rorschach proved ineffective in detecting creativity in a group of twenty outstanding artists (Roe, 1946). In another study, the TAT failed to predict which of a group of student pilots would succeed and which would fail (Guilford & Lacey, 1947).

On the other hand, the TAT appears to work well enough to give insight into differences among groups varying in age, ethnic origin, or socioeconomic status, and the like, even though it is not accurate enough for the measuring of individuals (Harrison, 1965).

The Numbers Game: Psychometric Methods

In developing more quantitative instruments for the measurement of personality, the psychologist is concerned with the concepts of validity, reliability, objectivity, and standardization. The index of *validity* is the extent to which an instrument actually measures what it is intended to measure. An instrument cannot be "valid" in the abstract; rather, it is valid for a specific purpose, such as predicting success in college or in a particular profession.

The *reliability* of a measuring instrument is the degree to which people earn the same relative scores each time they are measured (aside from changes due to health, fatigue, etc.). A measuring device cannot be valid unless it is first of all reliable, but reliability does not guarantee that it is valid.

A common cause of unreliability in psychological tests is a lack of *objectivity* in scoring procedures. If a test must be scored on the basis of subjective judgment, different people scoring it are likely to get widely differing results.

To be most useful, a measuring device must be *standardized*—administered under standard conditions to a large group of persons representative of the group for which it is intended. This procedure yields *norms*, or standards, so that an individual's score can be compared with those of others in a defined group. The test must, of course, be administered to all subjects in the same way and under the same conditions, or comparisons will be meaningless.

There are two general approaches to the objective measurement of personality: the philosophical and the statistical. In the *philosophical* approach, one starts with meaningful traits derived from commonsense observation or intuition and defined by certain types of behavior in real-life situations and proceeds to try to create scales for measuring them objectively. For example, the Study of Values Test (Allport, Vernon, & Lindzey, 1960) is a self-inventory designed to measure the relative importance of six basic motives in an individual's personality: theoretical, economic, aesthetic, social, political, and religious. This classification was based directly upon Eduard Spranger's *Types of Men*, a brilliant work which presents and defends the view that the personalities of men are best known through a study of their values or "philosophy of life" (Spranger, 1928).

In the *statistical* approach, one proceeds empirically, starting with objective measures of behavior and either finding which ones work as predictors or deriving traits ("factors") by statistical analysis. We encountered examples of the kinds of factors that can come out of such an analysis in the charts which accompanied our discussion of Guilford's personality theory. We shall consider two kinds of tests in which both approaches have been used to some degree: self-inventories and intelligence tests.

Self-inventories. Standardized self-inventories require the subject to give information about *himself*. He may be asked to tell what he likes or dislikes to do, what emotional reactions he tends to have in certain situations, whether he admires or condemns various figures in public life, and so on.

The self-inventory is valuable in that it goes below the surface appearance to tap the individual's own personal experience and feelings. It is also convenient to give because it does not require the services of a group of raters or interviewers. Its chief disadvantage is that the person tested does not altogether understand himself and therefore cannot always give an accurate report. Or, if he wishes, he can easily lie about himself in an attempt to make the results look more favorable.

"Lie-detector" scales have been developed which make it possible to correct for such faking in scoring self-inventories. Interestingly enough, however, there appear to be cases in which the candidates' actual scores, faked or not, are more indicative of success or failure than are scores corrected for faking. When a group of experienced salesmen were given a self-inventory, it was found that their uncorrected scores differentiated more clearly between the good salesmen and the poor ones than did the corrected scores (Ruch & Ruch, 1965). The investigators hypothesize that the man who fakes a test in order to "sell" himself and his ability as a salesman has a better image of the job requirements and will in fact make a better salesman than the man who does not make every effort to "put his best foot forward."

The self-inventory method, carelessly used, has often been disappointing as an instrument for selecting

● This child is taking the Children's Thematic Apperception Test, similar to the original TAT but with a series of pictures more suitable for children.

personnel in business and industry. In careful hands, however, it works well as a device to aid in evaluating applicants for employment or candidates for promotion (Guion & Gottier, 1965). It has also been valuable in clinical guidance situations, where the individual usually wants to gain greater understanding of himself and therefore answers questions about himself as honestly as he can.

The early interest and personality inventories were developed for the purpose of classifying individuals in terms of either occupational interest or psychopathology. Many such measuring devices are developed by a statistical approach called *item analysis*. Psychologists determine which of a number of items are answered in a consistent way by most members of a particular group. On the basis of such information from many groups, a scoring system is developed for pointing out to a young person those groups he or she resembles most in terms of interests.

There are three interest inventories of this type in general use. They are particularly appropriate for use with young people who are of an age where commitment to a career choice is imminent. The pioneer test is the Strong Vocational Interest Blank; the others are the Minnesota Vocational Interest Inventory and the Kuder Occupational Interest Survey. Although there are differences in the scoring systems used, the basic principle underlying all three is that a person who marks a great majority of the items in the same way as, for example, doctors would be likely to be happy as a doctor (Strong, 1951; Kuder, 1970).

In addition to the self-inventories which are scored for specific occupations, there are a number which are scored for interest in a few broad areas. This second type of inventory is designed for general use in educational and vocational planning at an earlier stage. The most widely used inventory of this type is the Kuder Preference Record—Vocational. Experimental items were tentatively grouped on the basis of expert opinion and extensive analyses were conducted in high-school and adult groups, in order to develop item groups showing high reliability and low correlations with other groups.

The Kuder items are of the forced-choice triad type. For each group of three items, the respondent indicates which he would like most and which he would like least:

EXAMPLE

Developers of these tests report substantial evidence that young people who choose occupations which are consistent with their interest scores find greater satisfaction in their work than those who do not choose occupations which are consistent with their scores.

Intelligence tests.   The most elaborate refining of personality tests has been done in connection with the measurement of intelligence.

Binet's early scale.   In 1904, the Minister of Public Instruction in France formed a commission of medical men, educators, scientists, and public officials to study the problem of how to teach the mentally retarded children in their public schools. The important work of this commission was done by Alfred Binet, a scholar of the then young science of psychology, and Theodore Simon, a physician. These men believed that before a program of instruction could be planned it was necessary to work out some way of measuring the intelligence of the children they were studying.

Binet and Simon prepared a test of intelligence containing problem situations which could be scored objectively, were varied in nature, were little influenced by differences in environment, and called for judgment and reasoning rather than mere rote memory.

Binet expressed the results of his tests on mentally retarded children in terms of the age at which normal children could make the equivalent score. This was called the *mental age* (MA) of the child. When a child's score on the test was equal to the arithmetic mean of the scores of five-year-olds, he was said to have an MA of five, regardless of his actual (chronological) age.

Binet's extensive use of intelligence tests showed conclusively that intelligence exists in degrees. Most people's scores cluster around the mean, and there is no break between the dull, the average, and the bright. This *normal distribution* of scores is shown in the Ψ Close-up on page 452.

You can get a good idea of what the Binet scale was like from these examples of capabilities expected of a normal person at different ages (Binet & Simon, 1911).

Age 3 Can point to nose, eyes, and mouth on request.
Age 5 Can count four coins.
Age 7 Can show right hand and left ear.
Age 9 Can define familiar word in terms superior to use; i.e., shows how it is related to other ideas.
Age 12 Uses three given words in one sentence.
Adult Gives three differences between a president and a king.

As more and more children were tested and retested at later dates, it was found that a retarded child usually fell further and further behind as he grew older. If a four-year-old child had a mental age of three, for example, his mental age at eight probably would be only six. Thus, although the mental and chronological ages maintained the same relationship to each other (¾ = 6/8), the total retardation would have increased from one year to two years.

Early in the history of intelligence tests, therefore, psychologists adopted the practice of stating the relationship between mental age (MA) and chronological age (CA) as a ratio (Stern, 1914). This ratio is known as the *intelligence quotient* (IQ) and is computed as follows:

$$IQ = \frac{MA}{CA} \times 100$$

If a child who is eight years old (CA = 8) has a test score equal to that of ten-year-olds (MA = 10), his IQ will be $\frac{10}{8} \times 100$, or 125. If his CA is ten and his MA is eight, then his IQ will be $\frac{8}{10} \times 100$, or 80. When an individual performs at the mental age equivalent to his chronological age (MA = CA), his IQ is 100—the "normal" or average IQ.

The Stanford revisions. The concept of IQ was used in the development of intelligence tests by L. M. Terman of Stanford University, who tested almost 3000 children with Binet's materials and other tests. He arranged the tests by mental age levels and in 1916 published the Stanford Revision of the Binet Tests, commonly referred to as the *Stanford-Binet*, which soon became a standard instrument in clinical psychology, psychiatry, and educational counseling.

In 1937 Terman and Maud A. Merrill published a revised edition of the Stanford-Binet (Terman & Merrill, 1937). This new revision was aimed at correcting the difficulties and defects of the former scale as follows:

1. The test was extended at the upper limits of the intelligence scale so that differentiations could be made among adults of superior intelligence. A table for finding IQ's was constructed which included a "correction" in the CA of adults.

2. Provision was made for testing children as young as two years of age. Sets of tests were provided at half-yearly intervals for children from two to five, a period when mental growth is very rapid, and at yearly intervals thereafter.

3. The 1937 scale contained two forms of comparable materials so that when retesting was necessary the psychologist would not need to worry about a practice effect from taking the same test twice.

As time passes, even the most carefully constructed test becomes obsolete and needs revision. This is especially true in the case of verbal tests, since meanings of words change, and formerly rare words suddenly spring into popularity. The vocabulary of the present-day child or adult, oriented to space and television, is much different from that of the persons who were tested when intelligence tests were first used. For example, *Mars* was a very difficult word for children in the 1916 edition of the Stanford-Binet, being equal in difficulty to the word *conscientious* at that time (Terman, 1916). In the 1937 edition it was much more familiar (thanks to Buck Rogers), being no more difficult than the word *skill* (Terman & Merrill, 1937). By the late 1950's, when space travel was an everyday topic of conversation, this planet name had become about as familiar as the everyday word *eyelash* (Terman & Merrill, 1960). The Stanford-Binet was again revised in 1960.

Performance tests. Even the 1960 revision of the Stanford-Binet, although it measures other abilities to some degree, is predominantly a test based on the use of words or ability to think and communicate through the use of words. Thus for a deaf child or for a child

Ψ *Close-up*   *The "Normal" Curve*

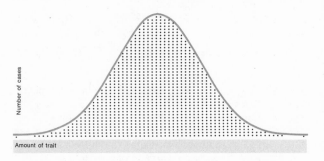

The figure at the right shows the distribution of scores that would be expected if 1000 randomly selected persons were measured on weight, IQ, or many other traits. Each dot represents an individual's score. The baseline, or *horizontal axis*, shows the amounts of whatever is being measured; the *vertical axis* shows how many individuals have each amount of the trait, as represented by their scores. Usually only the resulting curve at the top is shown, since this indicates the frequency with which each measure has occurred. Actual curves only approximate this hypothetical one, but come remarkably close to it.

This curve is very useful to psychologists because they know that a consistent percentage of the cases will fall in a given segment of the distribution. For example, if the trait is one that is distributed normally, 68.2 percent will fall in the middle third of the range of scores.

The standard deviation, as you saw in Chapter 2, is a measure of the variability of the scores. It indicates the typical amount by which the scores differ from the mean. The more widely the scores are spread out, the larger

will be the standard deviation. Most of the scores in a distribution fall within three standard deviations above the mean and three standard deviations below it, but usually a few scores in an actual distribution will be lower and a few higher.

The distance of the standard deviation from the mean can be indicated along the baseline of the curve, as is done below. Since the standard deviations are equally spaced along the range of the scores, they are convenient dividing points for classification. For further explanation of the standard deviation and of the uses of both it and the normal curve, see Appendix B.

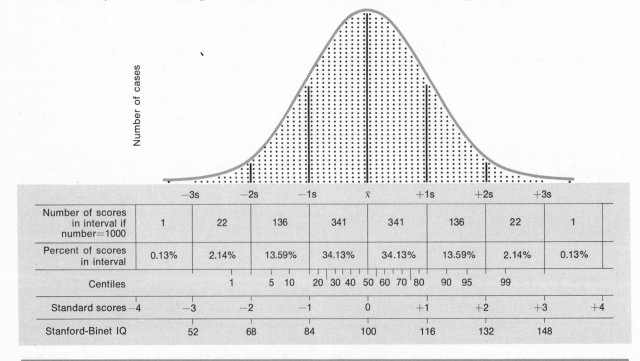

	−3s	−2s	−1s	x̄	+1s	+2s	+3s	
Number of scores in interval if number=1000	1	22	136	341	341	136	22	1
Percent of scores in interval	0.13%	2.14%	13.59%	34.13%	34.13%	13.59%	2.14%	0.13%
Centiles		1	5 10	20 30 40	50 60 70 80	90 95	99	
Standard scores	−4	−3	−2	−1	0	+1	+2	+3	+4
Stanford-Binet IQ		52	68	84	100	116	132	148	

who does not come from an English-speaking home, the Stanford-Binet often does not give a fair score.

It has been necessary, therefore, to develop certain tests called *performance tests* in which hand reactions are substituted for verbal reactions. Sometimes even the instructions are given without the use of speech. Performance tests include such tasks as *form boards* —boards with recesses into which the individual must fit blocks of the proper size and shape as quickly as he can—and *picture completion tests*, in which the individual looks at an incomplete picture and decides which of several parts will fit most sensibly into the blanks.

The WAIS and the WISC. The Wechsler Adult Intelligence Scale (Wechsler, 1955) and the Wechsler Intelligence Scale for Children (Wechsler, 1949) are combinations of verbal and performance tests. The WAIS and the WISC, as these scales are referred to for the sake of convenience, are similar in content, differing chiefly in difficulty. The WISC has been standardized for children of ages two through fifteen years. The WAIS is for age sixteen and over. Both tests consist of two parts—verbal and performance. The verbal section includes tests of general information, comprehension, vocabulary, similarities between words, arithmetic, and digit span (repeating a series of digits after the examiner).

The performance section also has several parts. In the block design test, the subject tries to reproduce a series of designs shown on cards by fitting together colored blocks whose six sides are all different. In the picture arrangement test, the task is to arrange a series of pictures in the correct sequence so that a meaningful story is depicted. Some of the other performance tests include mazes (in the WISC only), picture completion, and object assembly.

The meaning of IQ in terms of behavior. What is a person like who has an IQ of 100? What can he do that someone with an IQ of 70 cannot? Trained psychologists, as well as teachers and physicians dealing with problem cases, associate different IQ values with definite pictures of adaptive behavior.

Several classifications of IQ have been suggested by different test makers, usually in terms of categories containing a given number of IQ points. The great

majority of people have IQs between 84 and 116 on the Stanford-Binet and are regarded as being of *average* intelligence. Below them is a range classified as *dull normal* or *borderline*; individuals in this range do not do well in school but may finish eighth grade and can usually be self-supporting. Those with IQs below 68 are generally classified as *mentally retarded,* though many can be self-supporting, whereas some with IQs above 68 are institutionalized.

Individuals in the range above *average* are classified as *superior*; individuals in this range may become lawyers, engineers, teachers, and so on. Above 132 are the *gifted*; they are the group with the greatest potential for academic achievement and abstract thought.

These are only rough classifications, based on a test that measures largely abilities needed for schoolwork. The level at which an individual actually functions depends on many other factors too, including his motivations, his working habits, the demands made on him, his view of his own abilities, and the extent to which his past experiences have developed his potentialities.

In general, it can be said that the higher the economic standing of an occupational group the higher the average IQ. Within every group, however, there is a considerable range in IQ. At the top, the range is narrower, because only persons of high IQ can enter such occupations as law or accounting. In occupations like auto repairing or clerking, however, persons of low, average, and high IQ may be found.

Primary mental abilities. Although there obviously are many situations in which it is helpful to know the general overall level of a person's intelligence, as indicated by an IQ rating, modern research in the statistical tradition has shown that the "general intelligence" represented in an IQ figure is actually a composite of a number of "special intelligences" or *primary abilities* which are relatively independent of each other. Two people who obtain the same IQ may have a very different pattern of specific abilities and deficiencies: one may do best on the verbal and abstract reasoning questions, the other on the memory and motor skill items.

In the last thirty-five years great strides have been taken in the isolation and identification of such primary mental abilities by means of factor analysis. As we indicated in our discussion of personality theorists, Guilford has done some of the most far-reaching recent work in this area. Others on whose work he built include Charles Spearman and the Thurstones.

The work of Spearman.   As early as 1904, Charles Spearman proposed a two-factor theory of intelligence (Spearman, 1904). Spearman had found that most of the mental tests then available correlated positively but that the correlations were not as high as they would have been if they were all measuring the same thing. He concluded that each test must be measuring two factors—a *general* factor, which he called *general intelligence*, and a *specific* factor, unique to each test.

More refined statistical techniques have shown that the picture is considerably more complicated than this. It is now recognized that in most cases where tests correlate positively with each other, they share not one general factor but several factors, each contributing its share to the correlation. The more factors two tests have in common, the higher their correlation. Thus psychologists today generally accept a *multiple factor theory*.

The work of the Thurstones.   The real pioneering work in the investigation of primary factors in intelligence was done in the 1930's by L. L. and Thelma Thurstone (1941). In one of their studies, a battery of fifty-seven tests designed to measure general intelligence was administered to high-school and college students. Using factor analysis, the Thurstones were able to determine the extent to which various tests were measuring the same factor or ability. From this and subsequent testing, they identified seven separate factors of intelligence: verbal comprehension, numerical ability, perceptual speed, space visualization, reasoning, word fluency, and memory. Seven

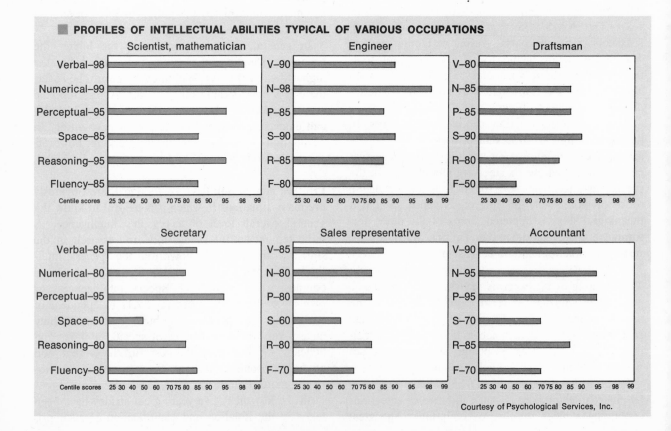

PROFILES OF INTELLECTUAL ABILITIES TYPICAL OF VARIOUS OCCUPATIONS

Courtesy of Psychological Services, Inc.

separate tests were developed, each aimed at measuring one, and only one, of these seven factors (Thurstone & Thurstone, 1947). Profiles of abilities typical of several occupations are shown here. ■

If the Thurstones had succeeded in breaking intelligence down into seven unique components, scores from the seven tests would have shown no correlation with each other at all. But when they administered the tests to a new group of students and computed the correlation coefficients between each test and every other test, they found that the tests *were* correlated. This could mean that in addition to the special factors there was a general intelligence factor, as Spearman had postulated, that could not be subdivided. Or it could simply mean that they had not succeeded in devising "pure" enough tests. Or perhaps their failure to analyze intelligence entirely into unique components was due to the fact that there are actually many more separate factors than the seven they had found. In that case, a model like Guilford's "structure of intellect" with its multiplicity of postulated factors may be more successful.

The fact that this approach did not succeed in developing uncorrelated tests cannot be taken as proof that it cannot be done. Whether or not there is such a thing as general intelligence, in addition to the primary abilities, is still in dispute (McNemar, 1964).

Understanding the Whole Person

When all the measures are in, the psychologist still must try to put them together in such a way as to show the overall pattern of the various characteristics measured. For his test scores to be useful, he needs to know the areas of greatest relative strength and weakness of the individual and how this particular pattern of traits compares with those of other people.

Profiles

Many psychologists make use of a profile, or *psychograph*, which makes it easy to picture an individual on the basis of his several scores and to "type" him by examining his particular pattern of aptitude and personality traits. At the side of the psychograph are listed the traits for which measures have been ob-

tained, and the person's standing on each trait is indicated in terms of a centile score by a dot at the appropriate point along the horizontal line extending from the trait name. A centile score indicates where a person stands in comparison to the group on which the test was standardized (see p. 449). If a person receives a centile score of 80 on a given test, we know that 80 percent of those taking the test scored lower than he did.

A psychograph of a temperament pattern gives a better picture of the total personality than could be obtained from considering individual trait scores one at a time. For example, a person very high in self-assurance and at the same time high in agreeableness would have a vastly different personality from that of a person who was equally dominant but very low in agreeableness. A particular pattern is often more important for success in a particular vocation than high scores on a few specific traits. Profiles are often used by employers to help decide whether to hire a particular applicant or to promote or transfer a present employee. By comparing a profile of an applicant with the profiles of successful workers on the specific job being considered, they can gauge the likelihood that he will be successful in that job. Educators and clinicians also find profiles helpful in advising students or clients with regard to choosing a vocation.

Shown on page 456 is the psychograph of an applicant for a position as clerk with a firm that imports and manufactures small automotive parts. •   This young woman was given a number of the psychological tests described in this chapter; her centile scores are plotted on the psychograph. Following is a résumé showing what such a profile can mean to a psychologist who is well trained in both testing and job requirements.

Miss Ortez is recommended for the position of Inventory Control Desk Clerk. She is a bright candidate with considerable drive and capacity for hard work under pressure. In addition, Miss Ortez has ambition. Moreover, she is very cooperative and congenial in her attitudes and should take direction well.

In terms of interests, Miss Ortez has a good tolerance for the heavy volume of detail involved in this work. However, it should be noted that Miss Ortez very much wants to be an accountant some day. And she has the ability to do so—an unusually good aptitude for figure

● **PSYCHOGRAPH OF AN APPLICANT**

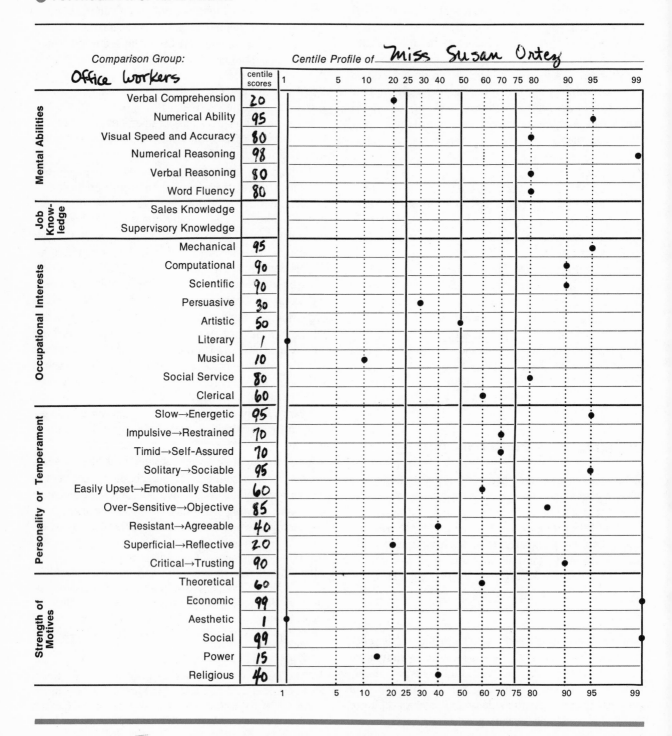

Comparison Group: Office Workers

Centile Profile of Miss Susan Ortez

		centile scores	1	5	10	20	25	30	40	50	60	70	75	80	90	95	99
Mental Abilities	Verbal Comprehension	20				●											
	Numerical Ability	95														●	
	Visual Speed and Accuracy	80												●			
	Numerical Reasoning	98															●
	Verbal Reasoning	80												●			
	Word Fluency	80												●			
Job Knowledge	Sales Knowledge																
	Supervisory Knowledge																
Occupational Interests	Mechanical	95													●		
	Computational	90												●			
	Scientific	90												●			
	Persuasive	30						●									
	Artistic	50								●							
	Literary	1	●														
	Musical	10			●												
	Social Service	80												●			
	Clerical	60									●						
Personality or Temperament	Slow→Energetic	95													●		
	Impulsive→Restrained	70										●					
	Timid→Self-Assured	70										●					
	Solitary→Sociable	95													●		
	Easily Upset→Emotionally Stable	60									●						
	Over-Sensitive→Objective	85													●		
	Resistant→Agreeable	40							●								
	Superficial→Reflective	20				●											
	Critical→Trusting	90												●			
Strength of Motives	Theoretical	60									●						
	Economic	99															●
	Aesthetic	1	●														
	Social	99															●
	Power	15			●												
	Religious	40							●								

work, in fact. Therefore, Miss Ortez shows potential not only for the immediate assignment but also for ultimately reaching her objectives in accounting work. If circumstances allow, management is advised to encourage her taking evening courses in preparation for promotion to accounting level responsibilities. It would appear to be in management's best interests as well as Miss Ortez', for she does have the potential to grow.

Miss Ortez was hired, and at the end of her first two and a half months on the job, her employer reported her performance to be outstanding.

Is Man More Than the Sum of His (Tested) Parts?

Test scores show how individuals rank with regard to dimensions they share in common—where an individual stands in relation to others who have taken the test. On the other hand, they do not show how a given trait functions in an individual's personality. No mere listing of test scores gives us the unique dynamic pattern that determines the role of each "asset" and "weakness" in the individual's actual functioning and makes him different from each other person.

Profiles such as the one shown opposite take a big step toward doing this, since they show *patterns* of strengths and weaknesses, and the pattern will be unique for each individual. At the same time, such patterns enable us to make very specific and detailed comparisons of different people who have taken the same tests. On the other hand, if measured traits interact, we still need some measure of this interaction, for the individual scores do not show it.

As we pointed out at the beginning of the chapter, one of the key problems for the personality theorist is to develop laws of behavior that can account for uniqueness. To some, this seems like a contradiction in terms. How can you have a science of unique events?

In trying to "reconcile the irreconcilable," psychologists have tended to follow one of two approaches. One has been to assume that all human beings, different as they are, simply vary in their positions on the same set of dimensions: all have some degree of intelligence, some degree of aggressiveness, some degree of flexibility, some degree of finger dexterity, and

so on. This is known as the *nomothetic* approach. It characterizes trait theory and any attempt to measure behavior on standardized scales or tests. It assumes that the dimensions of personality are the same for all people and that differences exist only in relative degree. It yields probability statements that are valid for groups characterized in a particular way. For example, such a statement could tell us that the majority of those who score high on Test A will perform within a given range in another situation. Prediction of what any single individual will do based on normative data, however, may not be very dependable.

The other basic approach has been to assume that a person is more than the sum of a group of characteristics and that predictions based on averages are of limited value in understanding or helping individuals. As is true of any "whole," there are qualities of persons that are present only when the whole person is functioning, qualities that never show up on measures of how much or little he has of particular traits measured singly. To understand and predict the behavior of an individual, one needs to go beyond the generalizations and the probabilities from "similar" cases to an intensive case study of the individual himself and his unique history, experiences, evaluations, and goals. This is the *idiographic* approach. It has characterized the work of most clinicians.

Each approach has been useful in doing what it alone can do. The ultimate arbiter of their acceptance will be their ability in some form, separately or in combination, to give us a science of the individual. While the science of physics can afford to single out the abstract features of an object rolling down an inclined plane and ignore the concrete ones, the science of personality rests not only on the abstraction of consistencies between individuals but also on the features within individuals which combine to transform the "object" of inquiry into the "person" of personality study.

Chapter Summary

Normal human beings differ widely from one another on both physical and psychological traits. The study of personality is concerned with explaining both the similarities and the differences among individuals. *Personality* can be defined as "the sum total of the ways in which an individual characteristically reacts to and interacts with others."

Such diverse individuals as fortune-tellers and police investigators "size up" the people they deal with on the basis of naïve personality theories developed by trial and error. There are numerous more highly systematized formal theories of personality, including Freudian and neo-Freudian (psychoanalytic) theories, learning theories, organismic field theories, and factor theories.

According to *Freudian theory*, all behavior is (unconsciously) powered by two basic drives: *Eros* (the "sex" or "life" instinct) and *Thanatos* (the "aggressive" or "death" instinct). The energy underlying Eros is called *libido*. Freud pictured the personality as consisting of three parts: the *id* (storehouse of the basic drives), the *superego* ("conscience"), and the *ego*, which serves as a moderator between the demands of the other two and as a reality appraiser. The ego frequently makes use of unconscious *defense mechanisms*. Over-use of such mechanisms constitutes neurosis.

In Freud's view, most inner conflicts can be traced to childhood experiences occurring during the stages of psychosexual development discussed earlier. In the course of everyday life our unconscious impulses may "break through" to the surface as *Freudian slips*. Even serious behavior disturbances are seen as the expression of unconscious processes, for according to the *principle of psychic determinism*, all behavior, however irrational it may appear, is *caused*.

Freudian theory has been criticized for being based largely on the study of individuals who are not mentally healthy, and for being very difficult to evaluate empirically. Freud did, however, make three very great contributions to the study of personality in stressing the importance of: (a) *unconscious processes*, (b) *sexuality*, and (c) *childhood experiences*.

Neo-Freudian theorists such as Jung, Adler, and Erikson have retained the basic framework of Freudian theory, but have placed less emphasis on the role of sexuality, stressing other basic drives or social influences instead. Harry Stack Sullivan was one of those who stressed the importance of social inter-

action. His major concepts include *dynamisms* (prolonged recurrent behavior patterns such as the *self-system*) and *personifications* (our images of others).

The learning theorists are the most experimentally oriented of the personality theorists. Dollard and Miller began by putting Freudian concepts into forms more amenable to experimental study. Their studies of personality thus involve investigation of the relationships between *drive, cue, response,* and *reinforcement*. The *social learning theory* of Bandura and Walters has developed out of studies of human subjects learning in social situations. Though incorporating the basic concepts of operant conditioning, it stresses the importance of *modeling*—"no-trial" learning in which a person learns by observing someone else's behavior. The major criticism of the learning theories is that while they can explain the learning and retaining of particular responses, they have little to say about personality as a whole.

Field theorists see personality and behavior as shaped by the balance and interaction of many forces. Goldstein's *organismic theory* stresses the unfolding of the inherited potentialities of the organism as a whole, powered by a basic drive for *self-actualization*. Rogers' *self theory* emphasizes the phenomenal field—the private world of the individual. The individual's *self-concept* develops out of his experiences, and he will behave in ways that are consistent with it. In this view, it is the inability to accept oneself that leads to mental illness.

In his *self-actualization theory,* Maslow stressed the study of emotionally healthy persons. He saw a hierarchy of human needs ranging, in order, from physiological needs through safety needs, needs for belonging and love, needs for esteem, and needs for self-actualization to needs for knowledge and aesthetic needs. It is only as needs on the lower levels are satisfied that the individual is free to deal with those on the higher levels. Criticisms of these three theories have focused on the vagueness of "self-actualization" as a subject for scientific study.

The work of the factor theorists utilizes the statistical technique of *factor analysis* in attempting to identify specific personality *traits*. In his study of personality, Guilford has identified two different types of traits: *hormetic* (motivational) *factors* and *temper-*

ament factors. He has also applied factor-analytic techniques to the study of intelligence, delineating a three-dimensional *structure of intellect* model. While the concepts put forward by factor theorists are among the most useful in studying personality, they have been criticized as being somewhat fractionated and artificial. Social behaviorists such as Mischel insist that stability of behavior results from maintaining and reinforcing conditions in the environment rather than from enduring qualities within the individual.

Tests designed as measures of personality are generally used for one of three purposes: (a) to predict success in school or work, (b) to prescribe educational or therapeutic treatment, or (c) to further our understanding of human behavior. Early attempts at personality measurement were often based on physical characteristics such as bumps on the head (*phrenology*), facial characteristics, (*physiognomy*), or body build (*somatotypes*). Studies of expressive behavior such as handwriting (*graphology*) and speaking voice seem promising in some respects.

Precise measurement of behavior demands more standardization of situations and measuring instruments, as in *rating scales* and *standardized interviews*. *Behavior sampling* techniques involve observing the subject's behavior in a typical situation, either natural or simulated. *Projective techniques* such as the *Rorschach Test* and the *Thematic Apperception Test* involve presenting the subject with ambiguous or neutral stimuli and seeing what meaning he "projects" onto them.

To be most accurate and most useful, a psychometric device must be *reliable*, *valid*, and *objective*, and must have been *standardized* on a group of persons representative of those for whom it is intended. A frequently used measuring device is the *self-inventory*.

Intelligence testing was pioneered in France in the early 1900's by Simon and Binet. It is based on comparison of an individual's intellectual performance with that of others of the same age. *IQ*, or *intelligence quotient,* indicates the ratio of mental age to chronological age. Three tests of general intelligence are the Stanford-Binet, which consists primarily of verbal tests, and the Wechsler tests (one for adults and one for children), each containing both verbal and performance scales. Intelligence is not a single ability, but includes a number of *primary mental abilities*, which factor analysts are attempting to identify.

By constructing a *psychograph,* or profile, psychologists can get a picture of an individual's overall pattern of traits. Psychologists interested in the study of personality have tended to follow either the *nomothetic* approach, assuming that all individuals simply vary in their positions on the same set of dimensions, or the *idiographic* approach, assuming that every individual is, when all is said and done, unique.

Chapter 12

The Social Bases of Behavior

Each of us is born alone and dies alone. Yet it has been said that man is the most social of social animals. He is conceived by a social act of heterosexual intercourse; his birth, attended by many people, completely changes the lives of some of them; his death, which may be caused by other men or delayed by the medical and psychological help of others, often has profound emotional effects on those who have come to need him. Between the acts of birth and death, man fills his life with people.

Nevertheless, the paradox remains: man is isolated within himself, within his own nervous system and consciousness. At the same time, he lives in groups, is irresistibly drawn together with others, and creates a social reality which may exert a greater control over his behavior than even physical reality. Traditional psychology has been concerned primarily with the behavior of the individual organism, removed from the complex "confounding" social influences of other people, groups, society, institutions, and culture. It has been the task of the sociologist to study man's groups and institutions (marriage, family, church, industry), and of the anthropologist to enlighten us about the broader influences of culture on human behavior. The field of social psychology has developed to answer the remaining questions about how the behavior of one individual is affected by the real or imagined presence and behavior of one or more other individuals.

You are affected by what others feel, believe, say, and do, and they in turn are affected by your feelings, beliefs, communications, and actions. When two people influence each other, we are observing an *interacting* social unit. In interactions of this kind, two major social functions emerge: First, one person's behavior may provide *information* to elicit, modify, or direct succeeding responses of the other person. Second, one person's behavior may provide reinforcing or punishing *consequences* for a prior response of the other. For example, in the game "Hot and Cold," saying "Hot" to the blindfolded person as he approaches the goal target is a stimulus which elicits different behavior from saying "Cold." Hugging, kissing, or complimenting a person reinforces the pattern of behavior that has just occurred. This informational and social reward control which we all possess and dispense is obviously important to carrying on the twin basic psychological activities of: (a) reducing our uncertainty about the environment, thereby increasing its predictability, and (b) enhancing our perceived mastery over the environment through control of its contingent relationships.

In studying the social nature of man, social psychological investigations focus sometimes on the dependent variable of social *behavior* and sometimes on the independent variable of social *stimuli*, such as a teacher's instruction to try as hard as you can to earn the gold star or to graduate *cum laude*. Also, the effect of social stimuli on people's nonsocial behavior may be studied. For example, physiological reactions to a hostile interchange with someone, learning of the content of a persuasive argument, and overeating after feeling rejected are instances of socially induced nonsocial behavior. Under some conditions, even the mere presence of passive, noninteracting other people can influence behavior—an effect called *coaction*.

In this chapter both social stimuli and social responses will be considered, as well as the processes which unite them in meaningful psychological relationships. First, we will explore the origins of human social behavior, starting with its prototypes in animal behavior. Then we will examine some of the motives responsible for the quality of social life, such as motives for approval, affiliation, and comparison, and will analyze social influences on various kinds of behavior. Subsequent chapters will examine how man has polluted his social environment with violence, conflict, anxieties, prejudice, and overcrowding—pollutants fully as detrimental to life as those of our physical environment.

The Origins of Social Life

The doctrine of individuality is a cornerstone in our thinking about evolution and about the existence of "self." We all believe in our uniqueness, independence, self-sufficiency, and individual power, as well as in personal salvation and gain through our individual initiative and creative invention. "I believe in me." But such beliefs can be shown to be relatively new developments, not existing before the close of the Middle Ages. They are the necessary consequences of the rise of a capitalist, *laissez-faire* economic order, Christianity, the tradition of romantic love, literary forms emphasizing character development, and, more recently, the psychology of personality and individual behavior.

Actually, a strong case can be made for the primary importance of the social group rather than the individual as the unit of evolution.

"The association of animals may be the evolutionary unit quite as truly as the individual, in the same way that the individual body is the evolutionary unit rather than the specialized organs and cells making it up." (Kunkel, 1917, p. 534)

Life in groups affords advantages for survival that the solitary individual cannot share. Protection from predators through warning or group counterattack, as well as the provision of a more certain and abundant food supply through hunting with the combined strength of the pack are obvious advantages. The mutual cooperation, protection, and nurturance provided by group association allow more offspring to mature and reproduce. Thus the genetic characteristics of members of such groups are likely to be passed on to succeeding generations. In contrast, creatures not part of a social group become a target for living enemies and an easier prey to nature's physical forces. Group association also provides a medium for imitation through which the adaptive innovation of any one member can benefit all the rest.

"Life in societies is the most powerful weapon in the struggle for life. . . . Thus it was that thousands of years before man appeared, association [of animals in social units] was preparing the way for human society. . . . The savage peoples of the present day live in groups, and all the remains of prehistoric men show that they too lived in groups. There is no reason to believe that the anthropoid precursor of man was an unsocial animal." (Chapin, 1913, pp. 103-105)

The Relevance of Animal Social Psychology

The last decade has seen a marked increase in the number of popular works designed to teach man about his own nature by referring him to evidence from the animal kingdom. In the popular *On Aggression,* Konrad Lorenz (1966) speculates about the causes of human violence and warfare through an examination of the initiation and inhibition of animal aggressiveness. Desmond Morris' provocative analysis in *The Naked Ape* (1968) contends that much of man's misery can be understood if we consider his relatively rapid adaptation from a docile, arboreal herbivore to an aggressive meat eater in competition with such fleet and powerful carnivores as the lion, leopard, and hyena. Still other popular works attempt to bridge the gap between competitiveness, attachment to property, love of self-display, and social organization in man and actual or imagined antecedents and similarities in nonhuman species.

Social Behavior As an Adaptive Tool

We shall explore briefly four types of empirical research on social behavior in nonhuman subjects which may increase our understanding of the nature and bases of human social behavior. In each case the research strategy is not one of "settling for a substitute" for man. Rather, the strategy is one of deliberately studying species in which social behavior is relatively primitive so that the origins of social behavior can be examined and the principles involved in these behaviors can be investigated.

Protocooperation. One biologist, Allee, has suggested that the tendency for animals to cluster together reflects a general principle of automatic cooperation which is one of the fundamental biological principles. By this, Allee means that notwithstanding the dangers and stresses of overcrowding and the complications it may create, the simple survival of an individual or a species is facilitated by the presence of aggregations or groups.

The research strategy used to test such an idea involves a comparison of survival rates of individuals versus groups in an experimentally created hostile environment.

In one simple but dramatic demonstration, goldfish were placed either singly or in groups of ten into bowls of poisoned water (containing colloidal silver). The seventy goldfish placed individually in the bowls lived an average of only three hours, whereas the seventy fish exposed to the same poisonous conditions in groups of ten lived an average of almost eight and one half hours.

Subsequent chemical analysis showed that the goldfish secreted a slime which changed much of the silver into a less toxic chemical. In nature, such a "sharing" of the potentially fatal dose of poison might allow some animals to escape death if the dose were moderate, or at least to gain time for wind, rain, or some other intervention to rescue some members (Allee, 1931).

Similar studies have demonstrated that groups of water fleas resist the poisonous effects of overalkaline solutions by giving off carbon dioxide which neutralizes the alkali; a single animal would die long before it could achieve such control of its environment. Another example which illustrates the survival value of grouped rather than solitary existence is provided by the study of the common planarian worm and its ability to withstand the lethal effects of ultraviolet radiation. Grouped animals resist the disintegrating effects of radiation about four times as long as isolated ones. Several studies have also demonstrated that natural pollutants as well as man-made poisons are better resisted by animals exposed in groups than by isolated animals. These cases of nondeliberate but effective mutually facilitated survival have been termed *protocooperation,* a term which suggests that they represent the earliest or most primitive form of cooperation.

Naturally occurring cooperation among animals. During his six years of observation of an ape colony in the Anthropoid Station in Tenerife, Kohler (1926) observed that "the group" was a vaguely organized community of chimpanzees who were *used to each other.* A chimp newcomer would be attacked even though it was not presenting a threat, while caging one of the "group" members would elicit the following reaction:

". . . one or other of the animals will rush to it and put his arms around him through the bars. But he has to howl and cry for this affection to be shown him; as soon as he is quiet, the rest of them do not worry; they show no desire to get to him, and even his good friends soon stop embracing him in order to return peacefully to the more important group." (p. 284)

This observer went on to note that when the apes had reached full maturity and were no longer awed by their big human caretakers, they would not tolerate assault on any of their members. Punishment of one member of the group in the presence of the others resulted in total uproar, touched off by a characteristic scream of alarm on the part of the culprit. In this way, concerted community action against "experimenter brutality" was effective in protecting the individual from punishment.

Incidental to Harlow's studies of the development of mother love and affectional systems in macaque monkeys (described in Chapter 9) were his observations of the cooperative behavior of both captured wild monkeys and laboratory-bred ones. When one monkey was put into a cage in the laboratory and the others were free to roam about, feral (wild) monkeys were more likely than domesticated ones to attempt to free the imprisoned one, especially if the prisoner was also a feral monkey (Harlow, 1965).

Apparently, conditions of rearing in the wild promote more cooperative behavior and a greater use of and sensitivity to distress signals, which are usually unnecessary in the benign environment of the laboratory. However, when pairs of chimps are in adjacent laboratory cages and only one of them is given food, the more fortunate one shows signs of "sympathy" or concern. The animal without food is given food when he begs for it, and often even if he does not. Two chimps sharing the same cage will divide their food supply fairly (Nissen & Crawford, 1936).

More recent laboratory research has provided evidence that some of these characteristic social behaviors may be innate.

Rhesus monkeys reared alone in closed cages were prevented from having any visual contact with other monkeys. However, when they were shown pictures of infant monkeys, they responded with increased exploration, vocalization, and play. To pictures of monkeys in threatening postures they responded with signs of emotional distress. Moreover, they would learn to operate a lever which controlled the appearance of these two types of social stimuli (Sackett, 1967).

Conditioned cooperation in the laboratory. More typically, laboratory studies of social behavior do not emphasize observation of naturally occurring behavior; rather, the researcher deliberately attempts to teach the animal to communicate, cooperate, or even show apparent altruism or empathy. In so doing, he usually makes use of the principles of classical and operant conditioning to guarantee the contingencies between stimuli and responses known to be most conducive to learning.

A three-week-old kitten and a young rat learned to eat and live together in the same cage. Then a screen was placed between the animals and their food; it would open only when both animals pressed levers simultaneously. Quite by accident, when the cat was playing with

◆   In this experiment the cat and the rat learned to obtain food by pressing levers simultaneously to raise the screen that separated them from the food. (Photo courtesy of Professor Loh Seng Tsai.)

the rat's tail, both levers were pressed and they had access to the food. The next time the cat wanted food, it again played with the rat's tail, but with no luck. But soon, when the cat had its paw on a lever, the rat ran over and pressed the other lever. The cat caught on quickly, and before long the two cooperated easily in the task of obtaining food (*Science News Letter*, 1950).   ◆

A study of the ability of rhesus monkeys to communicate and cooperate demonstrates how the learning theorist can produce through conditioning a degree of sophisticated social behavior that would rarely, if ever, be seen in the animal's natural state.

First, a pair of monkeys were each trained to press a lever whenever a light flashed in order to avoid electric shock. When this initial learning stage was completed, the animals were separated so that only one animal could see the warning light while only the other had access to the lever which had to be depressed if both animals were to avoid shock. With practice, the monkey who had the lever learned to watch the monkey with the light, and to press the lever as soon as the other monkey's visual and vocal response indicated that the warning light was on (Miller, Banks, & Ogawa, 1962).

An earlier experiment on cooperative problem solving in rats revealed that monkeys are not unique in this ability to master tasks which require responding adaptively to each other's behavior. Rats were taught to assist each other both in avoiding shock and in obtaining food. The experimental situation consisted of an electrically charged grid upon which was mounted both a food container and a platform which, when a rat stepped on it, stopped the electric shock. Thus both the animals could escape shock and obtain food if one animal remained on the platform while the other crossed the uncharged grid to obtain food. The animals learned to alternate, taking turns in remaining on the platform and crossing the grid for food. This required an elaborate training program in which animals were first taught individually how to get food and how to avoid shock and only then placed together in the cage containing the grid, the food, and the safety platform. Within twelve days the rats had essentially mastered the cooperative task (Daniel, 1942).

Field observations of social behavior in primates. Another research strategy, known as the *ethological method*, involves observation of primates' whole way of life in their natural habitat. Such research, originating with the work of Tinbergen, Lorenz, and their students, has emphasized evidence that the social patterns of group behavior have evolved to meet the biological needs of hunger, thirst, reproduction, care of the young, and self-protection.

The potential value of field observations is revealed in the studies of free-ranging Japanese monkeys by Itani (1961) and Miyodi (1964) and their team of researchers. Upon their first contact with the troop of monkeys, Miyodi and his colleagues were astonished at the intensity and variety of vocalization that confronted them from the depths of the Japanese forest. After months of careful study and observation, they were able to distinguish between several different types of calls and emotional cries, including sounds of warning, aggressive sounds, defensive sounds, and sounds indicative of sexual arousal.

Itani reports that after spending two years in fruitless pursuit of the elusive monkey troops, the research group decided to stay put and get the hungry monkeys to come to them by providing provisions, such as sweet potatoes, candy, and artificial rice. Using such "bait" paid off, and soon the research group was able to observe the activities of individuals, families, and larger group units.

Such careful observation revealed paternal as well as maternal care of the young in some of the monkey troops studied. It also revealed varied dietary preferences among troops. Some ate meat, some

fish, others roots; some ate the pit of a fruit while others threw it away. Eating, then, was not a matter of simply what was available, but of what was dictated by custom as appropriate for each troop, and these preferences were passed on from generation to generation, establishing a *protoculture*.

Most fascinating of all was the process of cultural transmission of "radical" ideas. When the researchers' provisions were first put out, the older, more conservative monkeys resisted sampling any of them. It was the younger, least experienced monkeys who quickly sampled the new foods; only later did the older members of the troop follow their venturesome example.

We also learn from Itani's study that not all cultural traditions are based upon basic biological needs for survival. Fads too can become institutionalized rituals if the unusual behavior of one member of a society is imitated and adopted by the others.

"In 1953 a young female in the Ko-shima troop began to wash in the sea the potatoes that we set out on the beach. Little by little the habit spread to other monkeys in the troop, until today [1961] a full two-thirds of all the individuals in the group invariably wash their potatoes before eating them, and the practice is more or less completely established as an element in the troop's cultural life. The washing of the sweet potatoes spread gradually, to the first young female's playmates, to her brothers and sisters, then to their particularly intimate associates." (Itani, 1961)

The studies of chimpanzees in the African forests of Tanzania by Jane Goodall (1964) likewise revealed some remarkably "human" traits, such as using sticks as tools. Twigs would be poked into termite nests and slowly withdrawn, covered with a tasty termite treat. The apes were also observed using leaves to wipe mud from their feet and sticky food from their hands, and even wiping their sticky lips with Nature's napkins.

As man evolved and became more complex and specialized, so did the nature of his cooperation and interdependence. There seems to be a continuity from the unconscious protocooperation of the simpler forms of life to the rudimentary deliberate cooperation among monkeys and apes and finally to the more intricate cultural patterns of contemporary man. In turning now to our own social animal, we will examine the ways in which human behavior and human thought reflect the influences of contact with other people and the development of social motivation.

How Social Motives Influence Behavior

Man does not live by bread alone; he spends a lot of time and energy planning how to make a better loaf than his competitors, and often he is more concerned about with whom he eats, than what he eats.

Essential to survival as the physiologically based motives are and fascinating and exotic as may be the ways in which we gratify them, their actual indulgence occupies surprisingly little time among most people of the world.

Even people in the least technologically advanced societies do not spend most of their waking moments in eating, drinking, and sexual activities. Instead, people in both modern and preliterate societies bend the bulk of their energies toward the attainment or expression of states of mind and qualities of experience that are stirred not by the innate imperatives of their biological functioning but, instead, by the values they have learned as members of their society." (Sarnoff, 1966, pp. 15-16)

Values As Direction Setters

How do values differ from society to society, and how do they affect behavior? The first part of this question can be answered by research which asks

● **LIFE-STYLES CHOSEN BY STUDENTS**

Ways to Live[a]	Favorite Way of	Least-Liked Way of
1. Refinement, moderation, restraint; preservation of the best attainments of man.	Indian	
2. Self-sufficiency, understanding of self, avoidance of outward activity.		
3. Sympathy, concern for others; restraint of one's self-assertiveness.	Japanese Chinese Norwegian	
4. Abandonment, sensuous enjoyment of life; solitude and sociality both are necessary.		Indian
5. Energetic, cooperative action for the purpose of group achievement and enjoyment.		
6. Activity; constant striving for improved techniques to control nature and society.	U.S. black	
7. Flexibility, diversity within self; accept something from all other paths of life.	U.S. white	
8. Carefree, relaxed, secure enjoyment.		Japanese
9. Quiet receptivity to nature yields a rich self.		U.S. black U.S. white Chinese
10. Dignity, self-control; but no retreat from the world.		
11. Give up the world and develop the inner self.		Norwegian
12. Outward, energetic activity; use of the body's energy.		

[a]A thirteenth way was omitted because of a translation difficulty in the Chinese sample. It was one of the least preferred by all other samples; "Let oneself be used: remain close to persons and to nature."

Adapted from Morris, 1956, and Jones & Bock, 1960

people from different societies their preferences among various ways of living, each way representing a human value.

Male college students from six different ethnic groups around the world were asked to rate each of the suggested twelve "ways to live" on a seven-point scale ranging from "I like it very much" to "I dislike it very much." As the table shows, dramatically different values were preferred by the different groups. ● For the Indian students, refinement, moderation, and restraint were most highly prized. For students from China, Japan, and Norway, sympathy, concern, and restraint were most desirable. Black and white American students differed in their emphasis on the importance of action for the sake of social progress (blacks' most important way), and personal growth, flexibility, and openness (whites' most important way).

Values that have a directing, motivating influence on behavior become social motives. Examples of social motives are the need for achievement, the need for social approval, the need to see oneself as adequate in comparison with others, and the need for affiliation.

The Need for Achievement
(or, We're Number One)

No student needs to be told that there is a strong emphasis in the United States on achievement. Business, sports, and the whole educational system all stress it. Grades are used as keys to higher levels of further competition (to admit the junior-college student to a four-year college and the college senior to graduate and professional schools). Students' characterization of the whole endeavor as one big rat race, with only a small piece of cheese in the trap, has in part been responsible for the beginnings of a relaxation of the grade-consciousness of their faculties and school administrators. Nevertheless, the need to succeed, to achieve, to perform well (at least better than other people) does become dominant in the motivational hierarchy of most students.

Americans are not unique in their quest to be Number One. Achievement anxiety is even greater among English high-school students competing for the precious few university admissions. Intense striving for economic achievement characterizes German and Japanese businessmen, while unbelievable fervor for supremacy in world soccer is characteristic of many European and South American nations.

The achievement motive can be characterized as

"the striving to increase, or keep as high as possible, one's own capability in all activities in which a standard of excellence is thought to apply and where the execution of such activities can, therefore, either succeed or fail. . . . Standards of excellence, therefore, are the mark of the achievement motive insofar as the individual perceives such standards as personally binding, compelling, or 'obligating.'" (Heckhausen, 1968, pp. 107, 108)

The need for achievement (*n* Ach) has been measured by responses to the ambiguous situations depicted in the stimulus cards of the Thematic Apperception Test (described in Chapter 11). Responses are scored for the number of themes which represent striving, goal setting, or concern for success and failure. It is assumed that the test situation is a miniature life situation, so that the individual's responses to it will show how achievement-oriented he is in his general behavior.

The origin of such needs has been subjected to intensive study.

Were adults with high and low need for achievement treated differently while they were growing up? Researchers have found out that, in general, college students with a high need for achievement tended to perceive their parents as relatively distant rather than as close, whereas students with a low achievement need described their parents as more friendly and helpful. Similarly, students with a high achievement need perceived themselves as more independent of authority in general than did those with a low need for achievement and, in fact, showed themselves to be more independent in their judgments and less inclined to conform to group opinion in tests of social suggestion (McClelland, Atkinson, Clark, & Lowell, 1953).

In another study, mothers of eight- to ten-year-old boys indicated at what ages they expected each of a list of accomplishments in their sons. Mothers of high achievers, compared to those of low achievers, expected twice as many of the accomplishments to be met by the age of seven. Both types of boys were equally expected to do things to help the parent, but the high achievers were expected, in addition, to master the environment outside of the home earlier. The boys with a high need for achievement were expected earlier to know their way around their part of the city, to try new things for themselves, to do well in competition, and to make their own friends. The achievement scores of the boys reflected these systematic differences in their mothers' expectations (Winterbottom, 1953).

The achievement motive is viewed by some investigators as a relatively general and stable characteristic of the person, present in any situation. It is seen as giving rise to a general *tendency to approach success*, although the strength of the tendency, in a given situation, is seen as depending upon three other variables: (a) expectation of success, (b) the incentive value of the particular kind of success involved, and (c) perception of personal responsibility for success (Atkinson, 1964; Feather, 1967). For example, two people might both have a high general achievement orientation but one might especially value prestige and work hardest in situations where success would increase his prestige, whereas the other might place greater value on the satisfaction of a job well done and put forth greatest efforts in situations in which success would bring him this satisfaction.

The complexity of the achievement motive is further hinted by the fact that within high *n* Ach subjects, interesting differences have been found between those who focus on gaining success and those who focus on avoiding failure. Those who focus on attaining success tend to set more realistic goals and to choose tasks of intermediate difficulty, whereas those who are most concerned about avoiding failure tend to set more unrealistic goals (too low or too high in relation to their ability) and to choose tasks of low difficulty, where failure is least likely but where success, even if achieved, would be least satisfying. The importance of a feeling of responsibility for the outcome, however, is also important in determining the level of tasks chosen. Subjects who feel highly responsible for their successes and failures tend to choose intermediate-level tasks, like the success-motivated subjects, whereas subjects who do *not* feel responsibility for their successes and failures show no preference among tasks of varying difficulty (Meyer, 1968). ■

To what degree can the imagery involved in achievement themes in a society's literature predict actual achievements in the real world?

McClelland (1965) found that the amount of achievement imagery in children's textbooks in the 1920s in thirty countries was related to the economic development in those countries twenty years later: the more the achievement imagery, the greater the economic development, as measured by electrical production per capita. De Charms and Moeller (1962), studying only American textbooks between 1810 and 1950 and using a different measure of economic development (number of patents granted), found no lag but found that both measures rose until about 1890 and declined thereafter. They found that during the same period, themes involving moral teaching declined, whereas themes involving affiliation increased.

The sweet smell of economic success. If achievement imagery is related to inventiveness and success, then perhaps people can learn to be more successful by having more achievement thoughts put into their heads. This notion seems to be supported by the success of a ten-day training program developed by McClelland (1965, 1969). Businessmen in this country and in India increased both their *n* Ach scores and their "entrepreneurial activity" following exposure to this program.

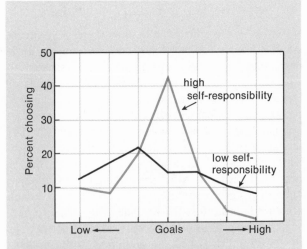

■ **GOAL SETTING AND RESPONSIBILITY**
Children nine to eleven years old were found to set goals of intermediate difficulty if they felt responsible for both successes and failures but to set consistently low goals if they did not feel such responsibility.

Adapted from Meyer, 1968

◆   **"PROBLEMS" OF THE BLACK COMMUNITY**

As Defined by White Researcher	As Defined by Black Researcher
Apathy or lack of communication with school	Failure of school officials to provide community with needed educational concepts, strategies, and tactics for successful adaptation in a hostile white environment
Pessimism about opportunities	Realistic appraisal of opportunities open to black people in America
Lack of knowledge about and interest in goals of schools	Refusal of black people to accept the inhumane goals and values of white-oriented schools
Lack of educationally relevant models	Refusal of whites to recognize the "educational relevance" of: Huey Newton, Malcolm X, W. E. B. DuBois, Eldridge Cleaver, Adam Clayton Powell, Muhammad Ali, John Carlos, Martin Luther King, and others
Alienation and isolation from middle-class white institutions	Failure of white school officials to accord dignity and respect to the black culture

Based on C. Clark, 1970

Participants were taught how to write and think in terms of achievement motivation and to distinguish *n* Ach from other social motives such as affiliation and power. Through being shown the 'associative network' of images and thoughts typical of highly motivated people, the subsequent real-life activity patterns of many of these men were altered, as measured by promotions, raises, and starting or expanding businesses (McClelland, 1965; McClelland & Winter, 1969).

Achievement motivation and minority students.   A typical complaint of teachers about students from some minority groups is that they are not sufficiently "motivated." This means that the teachers are unable to find techniques or incentives to get these students to perform at levels of academic achievement in keeping with their ability. In Chapter 2 we compared the typical multiple sources of academic motivation for white children, with the lack of such sources and supports typical for black children; and in Chapter 4 we had a glimpse of the pervasive fear that grips black children in the ghetto as well as the events that compete with school for their attention and interest. The current upsurge in psychological research directed toward understanding the complex relationships

involved in the academic underachievement of minority students has uncovered many other potentially valuable leads (Epps, 1969).

Black American school children (as well as those of other minority groups) have in general developed a low expectancy for success, especially academic success. In many cases this is a realistic expectation, supported by the lack of relevant models of success to observe and imitate among the adults they see. Black children, as compared to white children, have also developed a greater sense of being controlled (external control) than of controlling what happens (internal control). With little reason to expect academic success (or social and financial success even if academic work were successful), a relative absence of successful racial models, and little sense of the possibility of personal effectiveness, a syndrome of hopelessness (described in Chapter 10) is more likely than one of achievement orientation.   ◆

Higher achievement motivation, however, has been found in black youth who attributed their lack of success to discrimination rather than to personal inadequacy. It may be that among such students an emphasis on group efforts to remove barriers of discrimination indicates a higher level of achievement motivation than does an individualistic emphasis on self-betterment (Gurin, Gurin, Lao, & Beattie, 1969).

If this reasoning is sound, achievement motivation may need to be measured and studied differently in minority group children. One attempt to do this elicits self-evaluations from minority children concerning their performance on specific tasks and then measures how much satisfaction is associated with favorable self-appraisals for different kinds of activities (Katz, 1967). It seems clear that the same social values and culturally induced motives that give meaning and structure to the life of one person can be obstacles to fulfillment in that of another. We shall see this more fully in the next chapters.

The Need for Social Comparison

"How'd you do on the exam?"
"I got an 80, you?"
"75, but the mean was only 60."

Before taking effective action, one must have some sense of his own strengths and weaknesses, resources and biases. How does a person follow the dictum, "Know thyself"?

Essentially, there are two major channels available for such information. The first involves "reality testing," in which the child or adult pits himself or herself against some physical attribute of the environment. Push a large boulder over, climb the highest mountain, swim the deepest ocean, throw a coin across the Potomac River, flap your arms and fly off a cliff, run a mile in four minutes flat, put out a fire with your bare hands. By such actions you find out what your physical capabilities are.

Whether you have succeeded in such tests of *physical reality*, however, is almost always evaluated according to tests of *social reality*: "Can other people do it, too? Can they do it better? By how much?" Being able to distinguish a dozen different patterns of reindeer hides is not felt to be much of an accomplishment if all your friends can distinguish *two* dozen different patterns, as was not unusual for Chukchee Indians (Bogoraz, 1909).

The nonsocial motivation to know what we can do thus leads to the social motivation to use other people as yardsticks for evaluating our own accomplishments and abilities, and we initiate a process of *social comparison* (Festinger, 1954; Latané, 1966). We observe what others say and do, and we ask them questions about what they think and feel. From these tests of social reality, we come to have a picture of how strong *we* are, how bright, how emotionally responsive, how politically conservative, how attractive, and so on.

From social comparisons we also learn "can" and "ought" relationships (Heider, 1958). Is it right or correct to believe, feel, or act in a certain way and what are the standards of *appropriateness?* Other people influence us by providing explicit information about appropriateness and thus helping us to define the standards. They also influence us by reinforcing behavior that conforms to their standards and punishing or failing to reward behavior that does not (Deutsch & Gerard, 1955).

Not all comparison information is equally useful for forming exact and stable self-evaluations, however. The best information is derived from comparison with others who are close to our own ability or opinion or who are experiencing the same stimulus situation. In general, people are attracted to other people who are not very different from themselves on important dimensions where social comparisons are to be made.

Members of a group tend to use the group standards and the performance of other members as bases for self-evaluation. Thus when an individual is very different from others in his group, he makes them uncomfortable because his differences disrupt their stable base for social comparison. Typically, as we shall see, they react by either trying to bring him into line or rejecting him.

What happens to an individual who sees himself as much better in ability than those around him? Such a person may be motivated to seek out others of higher caliber, or more demanding situations, or more absolute standards (running against the clock, trying to get a perfect score, or competing against himself).

The extent to which our evaluation of our own intelligence and ability depends upon the process of comparing ourselves with others is demonstrated unhappily on every college campus each fall. Students who were "hotshots" in high school, compared to their classmates, are perplexed to discover that suddenly they are only "average"; indeed half of them are suddenly below the median compared to their new "hotshot" classmates. What has changed, of course, is not their intelligence but their basis for social comparison. As we saw in the last chapter, an IQ of 120 is "superior" in relation to the population as a whole. But it may be "average" or even "low" in a highly selected group.

The Need for Social Approval

"I had a reputation at Syracuse as a tough, hard-hitting, fanatical football player. But my hustling, hard-hitting, and willingness to play with injury was because of my fear of failure and a compulsive need to get approval from the coaches." This statement by retired professional football player Dave Meggyesy (*San Francisco Chronicle,* July 24, 1970) underscores how pervasive social motives can be in controlling individual behavior. Perhaps the most fundamental of these is the need for social approval. There are no limits to the length to which some people will go in order to gain approval from other people, including killing someone or enduring humiliation, pain, or even death.

At a very early age, children learn that behaving according to parental (and societal) definitions of what is right and proper results in an array of positive consequences. But such consequences, when they come from other human beings, do much more than merely increase the probability that the response will be repeated and learned. Many of our highly valued activities are undertaken not for their own sake but as instrumental in getting other people to notice, to appreciate, to honor, to help, or to love and cherish us.

Social approval of your actions has at least five related but distinguishable consequences:

a) approval of your behavior is a sign of recognition of *you*, and confers *visibility* and *identity*;

b) approval *legitimates* your existence, increasing your status as a person deserving to be recognized;

c) approval implies acceptance of what you have to offer, and with it the *security* of not being rejected because of inadequacy in your abilities, opinions, or feelings;

d) approval establishes a bond of contact between approver and approved, creating *liking* for the approver and perception of reciprocation by him;

e) approval provides one criterion of your *control* or power over the environment, by specifying how behavior on your part can generate desired consequences.

It is no wonder, then, that children's learning is influenced by deprivation of social approval or the positive social reinforcement of a nod, "Mm-hmm," or "Good," as shown in experiments like those of Gewirtz and Baer, described in Chapter 9. Consider what you would have done (or did) to get a little piece of gold paper in the shape of a star from your second-grade teacher.

Paradoxically, however, such forms of social reinforcement are often detrimental to learning instead of helpful, precisely because they *are* so powerful. In an educational system where students perform prescribed behaviors in order to get this *extrinsic* reinforcement dispensed by the teacher, the *intrinsic* reinforcement that could be inherent in what is learned or in the process of learning is often minimized or lost.

The social approval of age-mates can become even more precious than the social approval of parents and teachers, leading to "antisocial" behavior approved by the group. We can make sense of the class clown whose antics enrage the teacher, of teen-agers risking their lives playing "chicken," or of the apparently senseless violence of gang members toward an innocent victim by recognizing the power being exerted by social approval from age-mates.

Approval versus progress: The shuttlebox of peasant subsistence. Research in the social sciences has tended to focus on either modern, literate cultures or exotic, isolated peoples, while neglecting the ordinary peasants, who make up more than 50 percent of the world's population and are in the forefront of the population explosion. It is important to understand "peasant psychology" not only for the perspective it provides on the culture-bound aspects of our own psychology, but also because of the interactions it reveals between unique social psychological forces and other aspects of life.

Recent intensive study of rural Filipino peasants by Guthrie and others (1970a, b) reveals a society with contradictions difficult for outsiders to understand. There is extensive education: more than half of adult Filipinos are literate and use English. There is a stable central government. There are established communication networks and modest agricultural and other resources. Nevertheless, the health of the peasants is poor, disease is widespread, children's growth is stunted from poor nutrition, and life expectancy is shorter than in modernized societies.

Despite their education, the peasants continue to live in a subsistence economy, shuttling from day to day just to make ends meet. They do not plan ahead by saving or stockpiling food and other resources. In fact, they deliberately try *not* to work too hard and rarely seek to get ahead through personal achievement. Groups of tenant farmers have refused government programs of soil improvement and have *allowed* business projects to fail rather than assume responsibility for carrying them through (Madigan, 1967).

A Western "man in the street" would be likely to write off such behavior as due to sheer laziness, irresponsibility, and unwillingness on the part of the peasants to help themselves. Their behavior appears to be illogical, self-defeating, and even deceitful as viewed by our typical standards. But when we view it in the light of *their* social values, it is a natural and reasonable way for human beings to think and act.

The experience of these peasants has taught them that the only happiness they can count on comes not from personal material wealth or prestige but from the social approval of their neighbors. This approval, in turn, is contingent upon a constellation of attitudes and interpersonal behaviors which function to keep each person and family "in its place" and to restrict economic development. Even though, as individuals, they would enjoy having a less arduous physical existence, they do not want it at the price of losing social approval and social support.

Pervading their cultural orientation is an *egalitarian motive*—the deep feeling that all people should be equal. This motive is seen clearly in five social processes or attitudes:

1. *Leveling.* Anyone who tries to appear better than his neighbor is condemned. The deeply rooted belief that "we are all equal" leads to the expectation that anyone who gets far ahead of others will be "brought down." This is accomplished by teasing, perhaps threats, thefts,

attacks on property, or gossip. "One individual started a much-needed vegetable garden, but his neighbors broke down the fence and let the pigs in to destroy it. A second started keeping a dozen hens in a caged area, but neighbors asked *tulong,* or help, in the form of so many eggs that the owner had to give up. But the most prevalent agent of leveling is gossip...." (Guthrie, 1970a, pp. 42, 43)

2. *Belief in everyone's "right to live."* The community puts obstacles in the path of success of the front runner, but at the same time helps those who lag behind since "each person has a right to existence and to being treated as a human being" (p. 43).

3. *Pakikisama.* The concept of *pakikisama* places more emphasis on good feelings between people, especially boss and worker, than on concern for achievement or productiveness.

4. *Hiyâ.* Individuals who might otherwise want to change are discouraged because of the socially approved emotional reaction of *hiyâ*—a feeling of embarrassment and inferiority at being teased for failing.

5. *Desirability of just getting by.* Behavior is influenced by the generally accepted attitude that "just getting by" is sufficient; "one approaches each day's needs as that day arrives."

Many of these social values are shared by other peasant peoples of the world; often they are combined with a fatalism and readiness to accept the worst because of a belief that man is controlled by fate.

"Possibly because he is master of so little of his fate, an individual attributes much that happens to him to *suerte* or *malas,* God's blessing or the lack of God's blessing. A neighbor has a good crop, obtains employment, catches fish: it is a matter of luck. The same explanation is invoked to account for troubles." (Guthrie, 1970a, p. 45)

Likewise, Lewis' (1963) observations of poor Mexican villagers noted the passivity and absence of anxiety which resulted from attributing one's misfortunes to others or to sorcery and thus feeling little or no responsibility for failure or an unsatisfying existence. These attitudes are in sharp contrast with the typical middle-class American assumptions of individual responsibility for our actions. In Chapter 10 we examined evidences of the need for a perception of internal control and the hopelessness that results when it is lacking. Many of the attitudes of peasants can be seen as defensive, self-protective reactions in a world where in fact they *have* usually had little power to control their lives. These attitudes were adaptive and anxiety-reducing in the past but now are preventing their holders from using new opportunities in their more potentially benign environment of today.

The Need for Affiliation

Human beings are joiners. We seek the company of others like ourselves as partners in marriage, as friends, as co-workers, and as formal group associates. The Robinson Crusoe legend captures our fancy both because it pits individual man against nature and also because it tests man's social self-sufficiency on an apparently deserted isle. But few humans go it alone, the obvious exceptions being hermits and religious mystics. In fact, the very existence of solitary confinement in prisons attests to the popular acceptance of man's basic social nature. Depriving someone of the opportunity to be with others is an extreme punishment.

Gregariousness as an instinct. Because it appears that men everywhere live in groups, and because, as we discussed earlier, survival has depended upon the safety of numbers, early social psychologists assumed that gregariousness was a basic, innate instinct. The "herd" has been seen as man's normal, natural environment.

"The conscious individual will feel an unanalysable primary sense of comfort in the actual presence of his fellows, and a similar sense of discomfort in their absence. It will be obvious truth to him that it is not good for the man to be alone. Loneliness will be a real terror, insurmountable by reason." (Trotter, 1916, p. 31)

According to this same writer, evidence for the herd instinct was to be found in the following gregarious behaviors of man: (a) fear of solitude, physical or mental; (b) greater sensitivity "to the voice of the herd" than to any other influence; (c) receptivity to "the passions of the pack in his mob violence and the passions of the herd in his panics"; (d) susceptibility to the influence of the leader of the flock; and (e) dependence upon being recognized as a member of the herd.

Determinants of affiliation. Such essentially literary descriptions were followed by personality research, which demonstrated that there were individual differences in the strength of affiliative needs, as measured by projective tests (Atkinson, 1958). It was more important to some people to affiliate than it was to others. But why? What are the determinants of affiliation? When the question is phrased properly, in terms of possible independent variables (experiences that might lead to affiliation), then a scientific search is possible and an answer may be forthcoming.

Stanley Schachter (1959) posed the question of the nature and source of the "herd instinct" as an empirically testable hypothesis. Evidence from various sources indicated that being isolated aroused feelings of anxiety. If so, perhaps the arousal of a strong drive such as anxiety would lead to a tendency to avoid isolation or to seek affiliation.

To test this reasoning, he induced high fear experimentally in half of a group of subjects and a low level of fear in the other half. The subjects were university coeds who were tested in small groups of five to eight girls. The first half were led to expect that the ominous-looking Dr. Gregor Zilstein would give them a series of painful electric shocks as part of a study concerned with the effects of electric shock. The others anticipated no pain since they were to receive only mild electrical stimulation. Self-report measures indicated that those anticipating the pain were indeed made more fearful.

To see if this difference in fear of an anticipated shock had an effect on the dependent variable of affiliation, the girls were given an opportunity to spend a ten-minute "waiting period" before the shock either alone or with other girls. Each subject indicated whether she had a preference to be alone or with others and if so what it was and how strongly she felt about it. The clear-cut results confirmed the hypothesis: fear did indeed lead to affiliation. ▲ (p. 474)

A subsequent series of experiments revealed that fearful subjects preferred to affiliate only with others in a similar emotional state, even when the subjects could not talk to each other. Apparently, "misery loves miserable company." Affiliation was also greater the more uncertain the subjects were of the nature and appropriateness of their emotional reactions (Gerard & Rabbie, 1961).

To these findings were added the totally unexpected discovery that first-born subjects reacted much

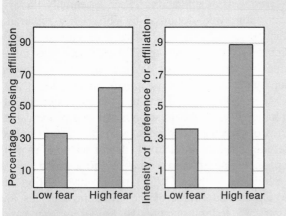

▲ **AFFILIATION INCREASES
AS FEAR LEVEL GOES UP**

Almost twice as many high-fear subjects as low-fear
ones preferred affiliation. In addition, the intensity of
their preference for affiliation was almost three times
as great as that of the low-fear subjects who chose
affiliation.

Adapted from Schachter, 1959

more fearfully and when in this condition turned to
other people more than did subjects whose ordinal
position of birth was second, third, or later. First-
borns were also more generally dependent on other
people (Schachter, 1959).

This research points to one cluster of determinants of social affiliation, uncovered when testable
hypotheses and controlled observation and analysis
were substituted for untestable notions about a "herd
instinct" or "instinct of gregariousness." There are, of
course, many other reasons why people affiliate.
These too can be uncovered only by systematic analysis; many are already under investigation.

Social Influence As "People Power"

The potential that a person or group has for changing
the attitudes, feelings, and behavior of another person
defines what is meant by *social power* or "people
power." Three sources of such power have been
identified (Raven, 1965; Collins, 1970).

1. *Content (informational) power*—change is the
result of new informational input provided by another
person or group.

2. *Source power*—change is provided not by *what*
is communicated, as in the case of informational
power, but by who (what individual or group) communicates it. Such a source may possess *expert power*
(perhaps in possessing relevant knowledge), *legitimate power*, (power is his "right" because he is a
"king" or has a high position in some fixed hierarchy); or *referent power* (it is used for *reference*, as
a basis for social comparison). When a person
identifies with a group and uses its standards for
evaluating himself, it assumes a special value as a
reference group for him.

3. *Consequence power*—change is produced
through the influence of rewards and punishments
controlled by the power source. *Reward power* comes
from being able to give something the person wants.
Coercive power comes with might and the willingness
to maintain surveillance over the lower-power person.

There are many situations and ways in which
social influence is expressed. In this section, we will
follow the influence process from its simplest origins,
in which behavior change is produced by the mere
presence of other people with no interaction between
them, through situations of deliberate influence, by
formal communicators or propagandists, by group
leaders and authority figures, and finally by Machiavellian manipulators. Next, we will consider situations
of interaction starting with the power two people
have over each other in dyadic interactions and progressing to an analysis of the complex basis of power
which groups wield over their individual members.
Finally, we will consider how the minority can resist
the power of the majority and, in the process, even
change the basic structure of social power.

Social Facilitation

An actor may experience "stage fright" and forget his
lines simply as a result of seeing the theater filled with
an audience. On the other hand, racers (track, swimming, auto, bicycle) consistently perform *better* when
other competitors are present than when they compete against time (Triplett, 1897). In many controlled studies with humans and animals, the same
generalization emerges: the mere presence of other
individuals may facilitate or interfere with behavior
(Simmel, Hoppe, & Milton, 1968).

One condition determining which of these opposing effects will occur is the degree of complexity of the response, with simple responses faring better than complex ones. Another is whether the response is in the process of being learned or is already well learned; a response being learned is most likely to be disrupted. It has been hypothesized that the *mere presence of others* is a stimulus which arouses a general, nonspecific drive state which then facilitates performance of established habits and simple responses but has an interfering effect as a distractor in situations where complex responses are being acquired (Zajonc, 1965, 1968). On the basis of this analysis, would it be better to study alone and take a test in a group, or study in groups and be tested alone?

Even when a group of people do not truly interact, they may still exert considerable influence on each other's behavior. This is so because performance of any kind in the presence of others is ego-involving, and there is always some perceived consequence of performing in others' presence. This may occur even where the people involved are strangers and the performance demands are as simple as reading one familiar word from a card—with intelligent college students as the "actors." This effect was demonstrated in an ingeniously simple experiment.

Twenty-two male undergraduates from the University of Michigan were seated around a big table in a classroom. Their task was quite simple, to read words printed on cards, taking turns, one by one, in the order of their seating. The words were drawn from among the 500 most commonly used words in the English language. On any one round half the subjects performed (read aloud a single word) while the others merely listened. Thus each subject alternated between being a performer and his own control subject. The subjects were told in advance, "Later I will ask you to try to remember all the words that are read." The starting position was varied on each round to avoid any position set. This procedure was repeated with four groups, for a total of eighty-eight subjects. ●   (Below and p. 476)

The graph compares recall of words read aloud with recall of words listened to, according to the position of the word relative to the subject's own position around the circle. For the purely listening condition, recall ranged between about 23 percent and 37 percent. But in the condition in which listening was punctuated by a public performance, even so simple a one as reading aloud an ordinary word, the recall curve was strikingly different. Recall for one's own performance was almost perfect, whereas recall for the closest words before and after was very poor; in fact, the closer the word was in time to one's own performance, the lower the recall. Anxiety about performing well apparently resulted in a tuning out of the responses just before one's own. Thus it is likely that the performer did not even hear the content of what the person just before him said but merely used the sound of that person's speaking as a general cue or signal to get set for his own approaching turn (Brenner, 1970).

●   Subjects were seated around a large, open circle, with dividers on the table between them. In the photo on the right, two subjects watch as others near them in the circle call out their words. Which of them do you think will have to speak on this round?

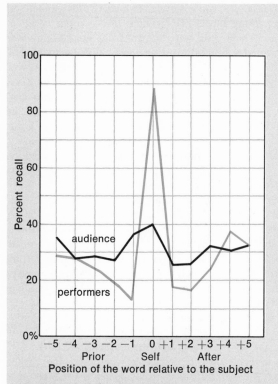

Percent recall (y-axis, 0% to 100%)

audience

performers

−5 −4 −3 −2 −1   0 +1 +2 +3 +4 +5
Prior   Self   After
Position of the word relative to the subject

● **CIRCLE OF APPREHENSION**

For those who were only audience, recall was about the same for most of the words, only slightly higher for the words nearest one's own position. However, when members of the audience became actors, the pattern was very different. They remembered the words they spoke almost perfectly but showed a sharp decline in memory for what was said just before and just after their turn to step into the spotlight.

After Brenner, 1970

This study illustrates a key feature of *social facilitation*: others are only part of the stimulus background that happens to be relevant for us. They influence us because of our own perceptions rather than because of any attempt on their part.

One-Way Influence: The Persuasive Communicator

In the struggle for the control of men's minds and behavior, there are many people in the foreground of our stimulus field who *are* armed with planned means and intended effects. ▲ Teachers and textbook writers are potential agents of change who usually rely on the informational basis of social power. The propagandist attempts to win others over to accept his position by any power of persuasion he can muster. Parents certainly have and use considerable power in influencing their children's behavior. And there are also politicians, salesmen, preachers, lawyers, doctors, Madison Avenue hucksters, hustlers, and chosen and self-appointed group leaders, all of whom are confident that they know what is best for us.

Naturally, there are differences among these social influence merchants in basic values and in their motives for personal gain or altruistic service to improve the society or the life of another human being. Nevertheless, their common object is to shape, alter, modify, rechannel, restrict, limit, inhibit, encourage, or in some other way control the behavior of others. Before you see them as the "bad guys," you must be a person who has never tried to change anyone else's mind or behavior by using a "line," logic, or appeals or by dint of the example of your acts and deeds. Can you imagine that such a person exists in the society of man?

What changes attitudes? An attitude is a relatively stable, emotionalized predisposition to respond in some consistent way toward some person or group of people or situations. The question of how attitudes are learned—and changed—is of concern to us all. A letter in an advice column of a popular magazine asked the following question:

"I am very pro-American. I have a small son and have hopes that when he grows up, he will join one of the armed forces. To ensure this, I have thought of talking to him while he is sleeping—no great speech, but a little patriotism and the suggestion that an Army career would be good. Can this type of suggestion help, or will it cause him to rebel?" (*McCall's*, November 1969, p. 65)

Louis Nizer (1961), the famous trial lawyer, describes the subtle psychology of the jury which, he feels, must be played upon since "the opportunity to condition the jury is as limitless as the attorney's art" (p. 42). Our literature abounds with the folklore of persuasive tactics, Marc Antony's funeral oration for Julius Caesar being a classic example. We learn from Niccolo Machiavelli that "nothing is so apt to restrain an excited multitude as the reverence inspired by some grave and dignified man of authority who opposes them . . . [presenting himself] with all the insignia of his rank, so as to inspire the more respect" (*Discourses,* p. 251). And from Adolf Hitler we learn that "all effective propaganda must be confined to a very few points which must be brought out in slogans . . . . the immense majority of the people are so feminine in nature and point of view that their thoughts and actions are governed more by feeling and sentiment than by reasoned consideration" (1933, pp. 77, 78).

We have come to accept it as a fact of life that whether through hard or soft sell, people are determined to influence other people. Witness homilies such as "You can catch more flies with honey than with vinegar." Examples of persuasion like those cited above, however, still distress us. One-sided social influence becomes more unacceptable to most

▲ A familiar form of one-way influence.

people to the extent that: (a) the "victim" is unable to resist because of "tender age, weak intellect," or dependence upon the influencer, (b) the influencer employs coercive power and has control of most of the relevant resources, (c) the "victim" gains nothing and the influencer loses nothing, and most importantly, (d) there is a high probability that the influence attempt will be successful. It becomes obvious, then, why many people are concerned about "politicalization" of the colleges. Education becomes propaganda when it biases thought and directs action by not presenting all the available alternatives fairly.

Ethos, logos, and pathos.   Aristotle, in his *Rhetoric*, attributed the persuasive impact of a communication to three distinguishable factors: *ethos, logos*, and *pathos*. These correspond to communicator characteristics, message features, and the emotional nature of the audience. The recent scientific study of communication effectiveness has followed Aristotle's lead in its investigation of *"who* says *what* to *whom*—and with what effect." Researchers trying to establish causal relationships between these communication variables and their dependent effects often use the approach outlined in the top part of the figure on p. 478. ▪

If the experimental group changed more than the control group, it is assumed that since other things are known to have been equal, the variation in the source made a *positive difference*. If the reverse is true, then the presence of the source variable may be inhibiting change or causing a backlash. If both groups have changed significantly and about the same amount, then some factor other than the manipulated variable is assumed to have been the causal agent.

Researchers in Yale University's Communication and Attitude Change Program (Hovland, Janis, & Kelley, 1953) have emphasized this *controlled exposure* approach to untangle the complex network of variables involved in the persuasion process. They and others have also studied how several variables *interact* with each other in influencing attitudes. For example, it might turn out that with the same message, an expert source would influence listeners who had high self-esteem more than listeners who had low self-esteem; here the effect of one variable differs depending on the level of a second variable.

■ PROCEDURE USED TO STUDY ATTITUDE CHANGE

This schematic diagram illustrates the steps involved in experiments which study
the effect of a given independent variable in the communication process (here, source effect)
in changing people's attitudes.

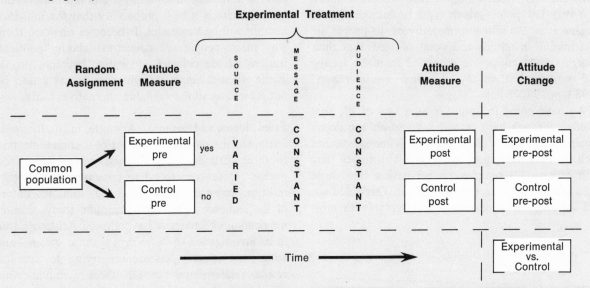

Often the same study will investigate the joint effects of two or more independent variables
at a time. For example, to investigate the effects of high or low expertise on the part of the
source and high or low self-esteem on the part of the audience, the four groups of subjects
diagrammed below left would be needed to include all the possible combinations of the two
variables. This is called a *2 X 2 factorial design.*

Three hypothetical examples of attitude change are also diagrammed below (+ 1 = attitude
change, 0 = no change). In the first, the source variable shows an effect, but the self-esteem
variable does not; in the second example, the reverse is true. These are called *main effects.*
In the third example, there is an *interaction effect:* source and self-esteem affect attitudes
only in certain combinations, with high-expert sources better for high-esteem subjects and
low-expert sources better for low-esteem subjects.

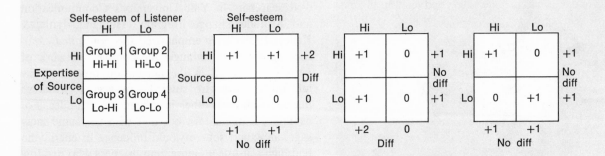

To study such interactions, a *factorial design* like that illustrated in the lower diagram is used. It involves having enough groups of subjects to compare all the possible combinations of the variables to be studied. It can then be determined whether either variable affects attitude change independently of variations in the other (a *main effect*) and also whether the variables work in combination (an *interaction effect*). In dealing with the social influence process, where so much is usually going on, predictions regarding attitude change are likely to be based upon complex interactions rather than on simple main effects. The reason becomes apparent when we consider only a few of the dimensions on which source, message, and audience may vary:

1. *Source*—expertise, trustworthiness, status, coercive and reward power, age, sex, race, ethnic group, physical appearance, attractiveness, voice qualities, identification with audience's initial attitude, and so on.

2. *Message*—use of rational or emotional appeals, type of emotional appeals (fear, guilt, shame, etc.), organizational features (builds to climax or starts out as hard-hitting), language style (formal, colloquial, slang, profanity, slogans), presents both sides of the issue or only one side, presents positive or negative points first, and so on.

3. *Audience*—all the physical and demographic characteristics on which people can vary; especially relevant are sex, intelligence, educational level, and personality traits (self-esteem, dependency, dogmatism, extroversion); also their involvement and informational level on the issue, the extremity of their initial attitude, and so on.

Despite the complexities involved, literally thousands of experiments have been conducted in the past two decades in an attempt to discover the conditions under which attitudes change when someone communicates a persuasive message (see McGuire, 1969; Insko, 1967; Kiesler, Collins, & Miller, 1969; Greenwald, Brock, & Ostrum, 1968). A number of generalizations can be drawn from this body of literature, although in some cases we would have to add "but it also depends on factors x, y, and z." In general, the likelihood that the members of a target audience will accept a communicator's message becomes greater as he:

a) is perceived as more expert;

b) is perceived as not having ulterior motives;

c) does not forewarn of his intent to persuade (especially if the audience is emotionally involved and the source is not attractive);

d) initially expresses views similar to those of the audience (the Marc Antony technique);

e) shares (or expresses) the same values the audience holds with regard to the topic;

f) is more similar to the audience in dimensions important to them;

g) advocates greater change (up to some extreme point);

h) allows his message to be inadvertently overheard rather than imposed on the audience;

i) states explicitly the conclusions he wants the audience to draw (rather than leave them implicit);

j) makes concrete, practical recommendations for action after using moderate fear appeals;

k) presents both sides of the issue if the audience initially disagrees, but only one if the audience is already on his side;

l) speaks last when two sides are presented, especially if there is a delay between them and action is required only after the last message;

m) takes into account the reasons underlying the attitudes held by the target audience and the audience traits which increase their susceptibility to particular persuasive tactics.

To change attitudes, change behavior first. Social psychologists have studied the process of changing attitudes because it has been assumed that attitudes are "predispositions to act." Thus, knowledge of the conditions which control the formation and change of attitudes has been expected to provide an efficient means of predicting and controlling behavior change. How valid are these assumptions and explanations?

Many studies have documented the fact that the correlation between measured attitudes and other behavior is very weak. Moreover, a *change in attitude* produced by the social influence of a persuasive message is often unrelated to *behavior change*. This is not surprising when we realize that the conditions under which the verbal statements on attitude scales are elicited may differ in many ways from the conditions under which the overt behavior one is trying to change is elicited. Even if both sets of behavior are related to a common underlying attitudinal core, each one is also partly under the control of its own stimulus contingencies. For example, the opinions expressed initially may be affected by how the person wants to appear to others, by who is eliciting the opinions, and by what, if any, consequences are perceived as likely to follow from publicly stating one's opinion. In addition, the new behavior sought may involve effort, expenditure, or special skills; it may be more public or incriminating than the "private" attitude change; and it may contradict a much broader pattern of perception and behavior that is being maintained by powerful social rewards.

Recently, investigators have begun a new kind of attack on attitude change, based on the wisdom shown in Aristotle's statement that "Men acquire a particular quality by constantly acting in a particular way." There is considerable evidence now to support the view that attitude change is best accomplished *after* exposure to a situation in which behavior is changed directly.

Individuals can be induced in a variety of situations and for a variety of reasons to engage in behavior which is contrary to their relevant attitudes: in a debate, in play, because their job demands it, for personal gain, to avoid punishment or ridicule, not to make trouble, and so on. Such procedures, as mechanisms for changing attitudes, have been studied as instances of *role-playing* or *forced public compliance*. One of the most reliable conclusions from social influence research is that there is a positive change in attitudes following active role-playing participation in counterattitudinal behaviors (Janis & King, 1954). People come to believe what they have preached and practiced more than what they have heard and read. This is as true in industrial and therapeutic settings as it is in the laboratory.

Getting people to comply with a small behavioral request has also been shown to increase their tendency to comply with a bigger, more discrepant request —the "foot-in-the-door technique" (Freedman & Fraser, 1966). Often the mere act of engaging in a previously low-probability behavior is enough to make the individual aware of positive aspects.

Usually, however, it is not enough simply to get a person to perform a strongly disliked activity in order

for his attitude to change. To the extent that he can attribute his compliant act to *external* forces (such as reward or coercion power), he can maintain his original attitude even though he has behaved in a contrary fashion. As long as he can say: "I did it only because X," he is unlikely to say "I must have done it because I wanted to or like to." Therefore, stimulus conditions which make the subject see a discrepant act as his own doing will make him change his attitudes to fit his behavior, separate the act and the attitude psychologically through compartmentalization or other cognitive strategies, or walk around confronting himself with irrationality: "You say what you believe, but you do not believe what you say." These findings are in accord with the examples of dissonance discussed in Chapter 10. Again we see that behavior discrepant with one's beliefs creates dissonance (and efforts to reduce it) only when the behavior is seen as one's own doing.

Leaders and Leadership

The influence of a formal communicator on an audience rarely compares with the power that someone designated as "leader" has over the behavior of group members. (Ψ Close-up, p. 481.) For centuries, the question of what constitutes leadership has puzzled political and social analysts. Are great leaders born with special traits which give them a *charisma,* a special emotional appeal and attraction? Or do great leaders emerge because momentous situational demands happen to occur at a given point in history and "put them on the spot"? Would Napoleon have been a great leader if he had been born in Switzerland in 1930? Would Martin Luther King, Jr., have been a great leader of his people if he had lived a hundred years earlier? Questions such as these are interesting to debate, but have little scientific value except to focus our attention on two approaches to studying leadership: the *trait approach* and the *situational approach.*

Do Leaders "Have What It Takes"?

It would seem that to define what it takes to be a leader, researchers would have only to compare the

Ψ *Close-up* **To Lead, One Need Only Be Labeled "The Leader"**

As a proof of the weight that is carried by the designation "leader," try the following experiment on a group of your friends (ideally friends of yours who do not know each other well). Give four of them ten minutes to outline what they think are the major problems facing the college student today and to arrange the problems in a hierarchy starting with the most important one. Record the pattern or direction of communication—who talks to whom, who interrupts, and who gets interrupted.

Now present a new problem task to the original group, this time arbitrarily designating one person as "leader," perhaps even selecting the one who participated least

before. Being given the legitimacy of the "leader" title should change not only that individual's behavior toward the others but theirs toward him. For example, they are likely now to channel their suggestions through him, not to interrupt him as much as they did before or as they do each other, and to be less critical of his suggestions and more affected by his evaluation of their suggestions than by each others' suggestions.

In another variation have the group elect a leader either before the first interaction or after the second. Does an appointed leader function any differently from an elected one?

---

traits that make leaders different from nonleaders. Indeed, long lists have been compiled of all the traits leaders have shown, but there have been an astounding number of such traits. Furthermore, an examination of the research on leader traits carried out prior to 1940 found that only about 5 percent of the "discovered" traits were common to four or more studies (Bird, 1940).

A more recent reviewer found a large number of studies in which the following traits were positively related to leadership: intelligence, adjustment, extroversion, dominance, masculinity, and interpersonal sensitivity (all measured in a variety of ways). The trait of conservatism was found to be negatively related to leadership. Unfortunately, however, these relationships were all rather weak, the correlations between the various personality traits and leadership performance averaging only about +.15 (Mann, 1959).

One summary of traits most frequently found to be associated with *effective* leadership organizes them into five general categories (Stogdill, 1948):

a) *capacity* (intelligence, alertness, verbal facility, originality, judgment);

b) *achievement* (scholarship, knowledge, athletic accomplishments);

c) *responsibility* (dependability, initiative, persistence, aggressiveness, self-confidence, desire to excel);

d) *participation* (activity, sociability, cooperation, adaptability, humor);

e) *status* (social and economic position, general popularity).

In one early analysis of the "essence of political leadership" several interesting hypotheses were presented:

"In ordinary politics it must be admitted that the gift of public speaking is of more decisive value than anything else. If a man is fluent, dexterous, and ready on the platform, he possesses the one indispensable requisite for statesmanship. If in addition he has the gift of moving deeply the emotions of his hearers, his capacity for guiding the infinite complexities of national life becomes undeniable. Experience has shown that no exceptional degree of any other capacity is necessary to make a successful leader. . . . The successful shepherd thinks like his sheep, and can lead his flock only if he keeps no more than the shortest distance in advance. He must remain, in fact, recognizable as one of the flock, magnified no doubt, louder, coarser, above all with more urgent wants and ways of expression than the common sheep, but in essence to their feeling of the same flesh with them. In the human herd the necessity of the leader having unmistakable marks of identification is equally essential." (Trotter, 1916)

Recent research has confirmed that leaders do indeed tend to be the most verbally active members of their groups. Moreover, in an experimental group of strangers any member can come to be perceived by the others as the leader, if his verbal output is greater than the others'. This has been accomplished by the experimenter's positively reinforcing one subject for talking, without the knowledge of the others (Bavelas, Hastorf, Gross, & Kite, 1965). People who talk more are likely to be chosen leaders, and then they talk more because they are leaders who must plan, decide tactics, arbitrate disputes, coordinate information, suggest alternatives, initiate group activities, and generally keep things moving along.

It also appears that to maintain their effectiveness, leaders must emphasize their community with the rank-and-file, must go to the people, and must still be seen as one of the gang. The downfall of a leader is often traced to his losing contact with his roots and his identifiability with those who have given him power.

Do Different Leadership "Styles" Have Different Effects?

Putting aside the problems of uncovering personality traits that "make" leaders, a team of social psychologists wondered whether particular styles which leaders use in relating to their groups make any difference in how a group behaves. In 1939, at the time the study was initiated, the example of Hitler's autocratic domination in Germany was frightening people who believed that democratic leadership was not only more desirable, but more effective. Others were proposing that the best leaders were those who were nondirective, who led by providing resources only when requested to do so, and let things go as they might—a *laissez-faire* style. This complex problem of the relation between leadership style and group atmosphere was studied in the context of a controlled experiment with groups of ten-year-old boys.

The subjects were four five-member groups of ten-year-old boys who met after school to engage in hobby activities. The groups were roughly equated on patterns of interpersonal relationships, personality traits, and intellectual, physical, and socioeconomic status. Four adults were trained to proficiency in each of the three leadership styles and performed in each role. An *autocratic* leader was to: (a) determine all group policies, (b) dictate techniques and activity steps one at a time,

so as to incorporate an uncertainty of future plans into the group procedure, (c) assign the work task and work companion to each member, and (d) be personal in his praise and criticism of the work of each member while remaining aloof from group participation except when demonstrating techniques. A *democratic* leader was to: (a) encourage and assist group decision-making on all policies, (b) indicate general steps toward a goal and promote overall perspective of plans, (c) leave division of labor and worker selection up to the group, and (d) be objective in praise and criticism and participate in group activities without doing too much of the work. Finally, a *laissez-faire* leader was to: (a) allow complete freedom for the group with a minimum of leader participation, (b) supply only needed materials and information, (c) take no part in work discussion, and (d) offer only infrequent comments, making no attempt to appraise or regulate the course of events unless directly questioned.

At the end of each six-week period, each leader was transferred to a different group, at which time he also changed his leadership style. In this way, all groups experienced each style under a different person. All groups met in the same place and performed the same activities with similar materials. The behavior of leaders and reactions of the boys were observed during every meeting.

The following generalizations came out of this experiment (Lewin, Lippitt, & White, 1939). ▲

1. The laissez-faire atmosphere is not identical to the democratic atmosphere. Less work—and poorer work —was done by the laissez-faire groups, and there was more play.

2. Democracy can be efficient. Although the quantity of work done in autocratic groups was somewhat higher, work motivation and interest were stronger in the democratic groups. When the leader left the room, the democratic groups typically went on working, while the autocratic ones did not. Originality was greater under democracy.

3. Autocracy can create much hostility and aggression, including aggression against scapegoats. The autocratic groups showed more dominating ascendance, as much as 30 times more hostility, more demands for attention, more destruction of their own property, and more scapegoating behavior.

4. Autocracy can create discontent that does not appear on the surface. Four boys dropped out, all during autocratic periods in which overt rebellion did not occur. Nineteen out of the twenty boys preferred their democratic leader, and there was more discontent

▲ The autocratic leader (top) directed the operation of the group in great detail, demonstrating and criticizing but never participating. The work generally proceeded smoothly but apathetically.

Under a democratic leader (center), the group members felt a real interest in their project and an incentive to do their best. The leader worked with them as a member of the group but had a special responsibility for guidance.

The laissez-faire leader (bottom) stood passively by, available for information or help but otherwise aloof from the group. Group interest tended to lag, and individual lines of action frequently emerged.

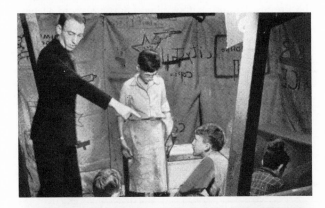

expressed in autocracy—even when the general reaction was submissive—than in democracy. "Release" behavior (such as unusually aggressive group actions) on the day of transition to a freer atmosphere suggested the presence of previous frustration.

5. Autocracy encourages dependence and less individuality. There was more submissive or dependent behavior in autocratic groups, and conversation was less varied, more confined to the immediate situation.

6. Democracy promotes more group-mindedness and friendliness. In democratic groups the pronoun *I* was used less frequently, spontaneous subgroups were larger, mutual praise, friendly remarks, and overall playfulness were more frequent, and there was more readiness to share group property.

This was the pioneering study in "group dynamics." It demonstrated that group interaction and group-related variables could be studied experimentally to yield conclusions of a causal nature. It showed that the same person, no matter what his own "traits," had a markedly different impact when he employed one leadership "style" as opposed to another. More recent research suggests that the picture is a bit more complicated—that the same leadership style will have different effects depending on the nature of the situation the leader confronts, and that a leader may have to split himself into two or more parts to perform different functions or to meet conflicting needs of different group members.

The Situational Approach

When we take stock of the enormous variety and heterogeneity of groups which leaders must lead, it is little wonder that the attempt to find a standard set of traits which would characterize the *universal leader* has been so fruitless. Could we possibly expect consistent personality traits for effective leaders of, say, a Weatherman faction planning to blow up American industry, a Sunday-school choir, a suburban wife-swapping group arranging a weekend's festivities, the Mensa society of those with genius-level IQ's, the Black Panthers, and a college faculty? It seems obvious that an effective leader must possess whatever resources are needed by the individual members of his group and by the group as a unit in order to reach its goals—and that these needed resources will be somewhat different for every situation.

Ψ *Close-up*   *One Moses Indivisible*

The importance of an effective division of responsibility for effective leadership has been humorously pointed out by Dale (1967) in relation to Moses' leadership.

"Having wandered for forty years in the desert, [Moses] found he had covered only half the distance between Egypt and Palestine. He consulted his father-in-law, Jethro, and when the latter saw that Moses 'stood by the people from morning unto evening,' he said: 'The thing that thou doest is too heavy for thee . . . .' Moses, as leader, had all the departments reporting to him.

"Organization counsel, in the person of Jethro, prescribed the remedy. [The lower portion of the figure] straight from the Bible, shows the new organization he devised. . . . Moses no longer needed to settle all the details himself; he was provided with staff assistance. . . .

"What were the results? The organization plan was adopted at Elath, about half way from the Red Sea to the Promised Land. It took almost forty years to accomplish the first half of the journey before the organization plan was introduced, only a few months for the last half."

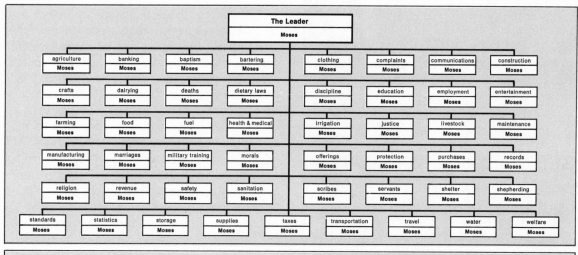

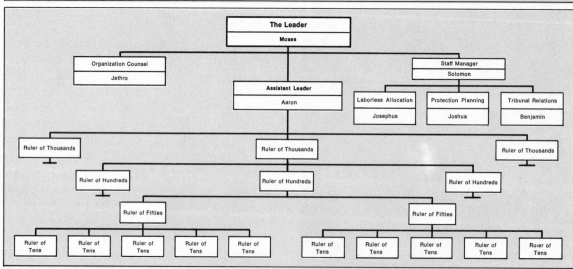

One of the marks of an effective leader is his accurate appraisal of his assets as they relate to the group goals. Where he falls short, others must be chosen to supply the necessary resources. Authority must often be delegated and the leader's role separated according to functions required by the group and talents possessed by certain members (Ψ Close-up, p. 484).

After studying the patterns of interpersonal communication in a great many small groups, Bales (1958, 1970) concluded that one leader can rarely be all things to all group members, even when dealing with groups much smaller than that with which Moses had to contend. Bales found a tendency for leadership to be differentiated into two general types of leaders: one in charge of the group's task and one responsible for handling social-emotional problems. Sometimes the same person may serve both the expertise and the human relations functions, but often secondary leaders take over certain functions.

This division of power is typically seen in analyses of the structure of street gangs. In one New York City gang, the Pirates, four leaders were required to orchestrate the varied needs of the gang. ∎

Paulie was the man with "the final say in all important decisions." He was older than the others, held himself aloof, but masterminded the gang's burglaries and robberies. He established contact with older neighborhood gangs and with fences to sell the stolen goods. Like generals in battle, he directed but never jeopardized himself by taking part physically in the "hits." *Lulu* was second in command, and was the tactician and burglary expert. He would plan the details of the burglaries, and "had a tremendous talent for anything connected with tools or electricity." *Solly* was the diplomat who dealt with the frequent police "interference." "Solly played the part of the decent fellow commiserating with the police over the bad habits of the other Pirates." He had a talent for listening quietly to a long harangue from a cop and then pacifying him with an earnest but noncommittal answer. *Blacky* occupied a very unusual position: "most of the time he played the clown, the butt of all the gang's earthy humor, which often took a brutal turn. . . ." But Blacky was supreme in the domain of sex, the field where the others were sadly lacking, and they looked to Blacky for leadership in matters relating to the opposite sex. He made available his personal "stable" of three or four girls to special friends in the gang.

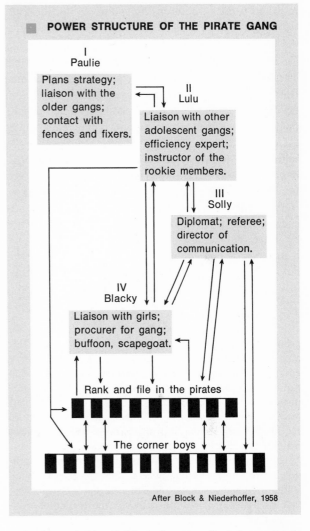

POWER STRUCTURE OF THE PIRATE GANG

I
Paulie
Plans strategy; liaison with the older gangs; contact with fences and fixers.

II
Lulu
Liaison with other adolescent gangs; efficiency expert; instructor of the rookie members.

III
Solly
Diplomat; referee; director of communication.

IV
Blacky
Liaison with girls; procurer for gang; buffoon, scapegoat.

Rank and file in the pirates

The corner boys

After Block & Niederhoffer, 1958

In this way "the division of power allowed completely different personality types to function efficiently." (Block & Niederhoffer, 1958)

James M. Barrie's lovely play, *The Admirable Crichton*, tells the classic story of leadership flowering when the time and place are ripe for it. An ordinary English butler becomes the head of his "employer's" family when they are shipwrecked on a deserted island. His skills and resourcefulness, only minimally required in his usual servant's role, become vital to the very survival of the group. Crichton rises admirably to the occasion and provides the resourceful leadership required. The tale ends, however, with the family returned safely home to England and the butler returned to his "station in life"—answering the door, tidying up, and once again making himself inconspicuously useful around the house.

The interaction of task, power, and human relations. Barrie's story captures the fancy of many of us who believe that under other circumstances we could have or would have been great leaders. If the "call" came, we could lead. Unfortunately, since leaders require followers—"too many chiefs and not enough Indians" is poor organization—most people never get the opportunity to prove that they might have what it takes.

It is generally recognized today that effective leadership is rarely the result of personality characteristics or situational factors alone. For each situation there is an optimal combination of personality characteristics of the leader and several variables of task structure, group organization, and personal relationships.

Taking group productivity as the criterion of leadership effectiveness, Fiedler (1964) studied over 800 separate groups, including bomber crews, groups from the Belgian Navy, tank crews, anti-aircraft crews, and industrial and sports teams. For each group he measured group productiveness, orientation of the leader (whether primarily task- or relationship-oriented), the quality of leader-member relationships, the degree of structure required by the group's primary task, and the power which the leader position had.

He found that leaders who were high on *task* orientation were most effective where there were (a) good leader-member relations and either a highly structured task or a strong power position for the leader or both or, at the other extreme, (b) poor leader-member relations, low task structure, and a low power position for the leader. Leaders high on *relationship* orientation were most effective in situations where there were either (a) good leader-member relations and an unstructured task and weak power for the leader or (b) poor leader-member relations with a highly structured task and strong power for the leader.

**Leaders May Sometimes Lead,
but Machiavellians Always Win**

Imagine yourself in the following situation with two other people. One hundred dollars is put down on the table to be distributed among you in any way, as soon as any *two* of you agree to how it will be split.

Obviously, the fair allotment would be $33.33 each —if all three had to decide how to share it. However, a selfish pair could cut the third party out and each have fifty dollars. One person suggests this alternative to you. Before you can agree or refuse, the left-out third party offers to give you $51, taking $49 for himself and cutting out the other person. What do you do? Do you manipulate the others to maximize your "take" before agreeing either to cut out one of the two, or to have them share what is left over after your portion? Or, is it likely that you will even be bargaining to get a small piece of the prize?

When this situation is actually staged in an experiment, over many trials, the typical pattern is for one person to come out with about $53, one to get $30, and one to get only $17. Which of the three would you be?

Niccolo Machiavelli has provided in his writings (notably *The Prince,* 1532, and *The Discourses,* 1531), the origins of a social-personality theory which helps answer that question. He was concerned with how people can be manipulated, and with what traits and tactics differentiate those who wield influence from those who are influenced.

Traits of Machiavellians. From these anecdotal descriptions of power tactics and the nature of influential people, a psychologist, Richard Christie, constructed a questionnaire scale to measure "Machiavellianism." The questions were organized around a cluster of beliefs about tactics, people, and morality. Examples of each are (Christie & Geis, 1970):

Tactics
  High Mach: "A white lie is often a good thing."
  Low Mach: "If [something is] morally right, compromise is out of the question."
View of people
  High Mach: "Most people don't really know what's best for them."
  Low Mach: "Barnum was wrong when he said a sucker is born every minute."
Morality
  High Mach: "Deceit in conduct of war is praiseworthy and honorable."
  Low Mach: "It is better to be humble and honest than important and dishonest."

The "Mach" scales differentiate between High and Low Machiavellians on the basis of the extent to which they endorse Machiavelli's rules of conduct in human relations. The scales place at one end of the continuum people who have *relative* standards of behavior ("never tell anyone the real reason you did something, unless it's useful to do so"), and at the other extreme those with *absolute* standards ("Honesty is always the best policy"). Between the extremes of the High Machs and the Low Machs fall the middle group, who endorse some part of the Machiavellian philosophy.

Essentially, this philosophy is one of pragmatism: "if it works, use it." In the $100 con-game, the people who get the lion's share consistently are those who score high on these scales. They are included in every coalition, whereas the Low Mach scorers are lucky to be included in any coalitions and have to be content with the leftovers. The Moderate Mach scorers fall in the middle of the payoff distribution, getting only slightly less than expected by a fair one-third split.

In other experimental situations, High Machs have been shown not to cheat more, but to cheat better. When they lie, they can look their accuser in the eye and convince him that they did not cheat. When competing against other students, they more effectively disrupt the performance of their competitors (work harder at it and devise more creative disturbances). When they have behaved irrationally or in a manner inconsistent with their private attitudes, they can tolerate this cognitive dissonance (See Chapter 10) without changing their attitudes to fit the behavior. In experiments, they manipulate not only other subjects, but often the experimenter as well.

What makes a High Mach high? The essence of the High Mach is "to keep his cool when others are blowing theirs." The Machiavellian maintains emotional distance, does not get involved in others' behavior, or even in his own. His behavior is guided by what he knows rationally, not by what he feels emotionally.

High Machs flourish where three general situational features exist:

a) Interaction is face-to-face (rather than impersonal or indirect);

b) Rules and guidelines are minimal and there is

considerable latitude for them to improvise and structure the ambiguity;

c) Emotional arousal is high (thus interfering with task performance) for the Low Machs, but not for them.

Predictions regarding a High Mach's behavior in a social influence situation can be made successfully when they take into account the *interaction* of this trait and the social-psychological feaures of the situation. But the High Mach is a person who has learned a strategy which gives rise to a consistent set of behaviors that are reinforced only in certain situations. Thus one cannot predict the High Mach's behavior from his scale score alone, just as effective leadership cannot be predicted solely from scores on a test.

Interactions in Dyads

Most of us live in complex networks of relationships with other people. In this section we shall examine some of the characteristics of the smallest possible interpersonal relationship, the two-person group, or *dyad*.

The Dyad As a Primary Source of Influence

In our discussion of the ways formal persuasive communicators attempt to change attitudes, we treated the "audience" as though it were merely a collection of separate individuals not related to each other in important ways. But while people are receiving persuasive messages from various would-be persuaders, they are also interacting with each other. How do these interactions affect their acceptance of the media messages?

One of the first indications of how important dyadic influence can be in shaping people's political decisions came in a study done in the late 1930s.

The study sought to determine what led people to change their minds about whom to vote for in an upcoming election. One of the study's most interesting findings was that most people, particularly those who changed their minds late in the campaign, were much less influenced by the mass media than by talking with other people ("opinion leaders"). These opinion leaders were much more exposed to the mass media than were those who exerted less influence. This finding led the authors to hypothesize what they called the "two-step flow of communication": the mass media influence mainly "opinion leaders," who in turn influence the rest of the people (Lazarsfeld et al., 1948).

More recent studies have refined and extended somewhat the two-step flow of communication hypothesis. One psychologist gave this summary:

"Opinion leaders and the people whom they influence are very much alike and typically belong to the same primary groups of family, friends, and co-workers. While the opinion leader may be more interested in the particular sphere in which he is influential, it is highly unlikely that the persons influenced will be very far behind the leader in their level of interest. Influentials and influencees may exchange roles in different spheres of influence (politics, fashions, movies, etc.). Most spheres focus the group's attention on some related part of the world outside the group, and it is the opinion leader's function to bring the group into touch with this relevant part of its environment through whatever media (newspapers, TV, out-of-town meetings, etc.) are appropriate. In every case, influentials have been found to be more exposed to these points of contact with the outside world. Nevertheless, it is also true that, despite their greater exposure to the media, most opinion leaders are primarily affected not by the communication media but by still other people." (Katz, 1957, p. 77)

Why Do We Like the People We Like?

Clearly, people associate with other people because they like them. But what are the determinants of liking, or *interpersonal attraction?* How do we "win friends and influence people"?

Aronson (1969) has summarized the seven conclusions offered by research in this area. We like people who: (a) are in closer physical proximity to us, (b) agree with us, (c) are like us in personality, (d) satisfy our needs and have needs we can satisfy, (e) are able and competent, (f) are "pleasant" and do "nice" things, and (g) like us. In short, "we like people who bring us maximum gratification at minimum expense" (p. 144). Another interpretation, of course, is that we are attracted to people who are reflections of ourselves or what we would like to be. Such people best provide the kind of social comparison information we discussed earlier.

Research in this area benefits little from the accumulated common-sense wisdom of the ages, which offers contradictory hypotheses about most aspects of liking: "Absence makes the heart grow fonder," but "Out of sight out of mind." "All the world loves a lover," but "Play hard to get and he'll be eating out of your hand," and so forth.

Do people like someone who is virtually "perfect" better than someone who has human failings? The answer to this and similar questions about interpersonal attraction requires experimentally varying the attributes of one person in the dyad and observing how the other person's liking for him is affected.

In one study each subject listened to one of four tape recordings of a "candidate for the College Quiz Bowl." The same voice was used on each tape, but on two of the tapes the candidate was presented as highly intelligent and as having done well both academically and in extracurricular activities. On the other two tapes the candidate was presented as average in intelligence and as having done only moderately well in school. On two of the tapes (one involving the superior person, one involving the average person) the candidate committed an embarrassing blunder: near the end of the interview he clumsily spilled a cup of coffee all over himself.

After listening to the tape, each subject was interviewed about his impressions of the candidate, how much he liked the candidate, and so on. "The results were clear-cut: The most attractive stimulus person was the superior person who committed a blunder, while the least attractive stimulus person was the person of average ability who also committed a blunder. . . . there was nothing charming about the blunder itself; it had the effect of increasing the attractiveness of the superior person and decreasing the attractiveness of the average person." (Aronson, 1969, p. 149)

Apparently it is possible to be too competent for one's own good: a highly competent person may be better liked if he shows some human weaknesses (or has some programmed in) than if he maintains an image of too-great perfection.

Research has also shown that expressed liking for beautiful women varies more than for homely women. A beautiful woman is most liked if she is favorable in her evaluations of other people, but least liked if she offers unfavorable evaluations. Subjects are more sensitive to the behavior of the beautiful women than they are to the same behavior of the identical woman made to appear homely (Sigall & Aronson, 1969). Attractiveness thus is a determinant of both liking and interpersonal influence.

Liking is not determined entirely by the other person's characteristics. For example, when "romantic love" is involved, the individual's own ego is at stake, and liking may depend as much or more on his feelings about himself as on the characteristics of the other person.

In one study, a group of women subjects whose self-esteem had been raised by false feedback from a personality test reacted differently from a group whose self-esteem had been lowered, when asked for a date by the same male. The latter group expressed significantly more liking for the requester than did those whose self-esteem had been raised (Walster, 1965).

Apparently when a person is feeling "down," a kind word or a positive gesture helps soothe the bruised self-esteem and leads to increased liking for the other person.

Surprisingly, this effect occurs even when that other person is the one who dealt the ego blow in the first place.

Coeds interacted in two-person groups over a series of brief meetings. After each meeting, the experimenter made it easy for one coed to eavesdrop on a conversation between the experimenter and her "partner" (actually a confederate of the experimenter) in which the partner evaluated the subject. There were four major experimental conditions: (1) *positive*—the evaluations were consistently favorable; (2) *negative*—the evaluations were consistently unfavorable; (3) *gain*—the evaluations began unfavorable, but gradually became as positive as those in the positive condition; (4) *loss*—the evaluations began favorable, but gradually became as negative as those in the negative condition.

If liking depended on a summation of "reinforcements" received by each girl, then there should have been most liking in the positive condition, least in the negative condition, and an intermediate amount in the gain and loss conditions. This did not occur. Rather, it was the pattern or sequence of reinforcements that was the major determinant of liking. Subjects liked the confederate in the "gain" condition better than the confederate whose evaluations were all positive. Similarly, there was a tendency for the confederate in the "loss" condition to be disliked more than the confederate who gave negative evaluations every time (Aronson & Linder, 1965). ∎

Spinoza had pointed to this relationship three hundred years earlier in his *Ethics*: "Hatred which is completely vanquished by love passes into love, and love is thereupon greater than if hatred had not preceded it."

The correlates of romantic love. The "blindness" attributed to love may refer less to the inappropriate choice of a partner, than to the unquestioning influence which loved ones can extend on their beloved. It is only recently that psychologists have begun to move into what has been the rather exclusive domain of romantic novelists. The research of Zick Rubin (1970) illustrates one of the most systematic approaches to this delicate topic:

This investigation had three major phases. First, a paper-and-pencil "love scale" was developed. Second, the scale was administered, together with other measures, to 182 dating couples (college students). Third, predictions based on the conception of love that emerged

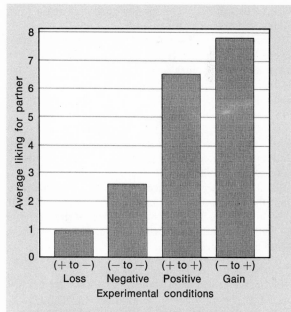

IMPROVING YOUR RATING IS BETTER THAN GOLD STARS EVERY TIME

Consistently positive ratings were evidently not as much valued as were changes toward more positive evaluation.

Adapted from Aronson & Linder, 1965

were tested in a laboratory experiment extending over a six-month period.

The development of the love scale began with the construction of a pool of items that were suggested by various psychological and sociological speculations about romantic love. Items intended to tap the more extensively researched "garden variety" of interpersonal attraction—simple liking—were also included. After preliminary sortings by panels of judges, a set of seventy items was administered to several hundred college students, who completed them with respect to their attitudes toward the person they were dating. Primarily on the basis of factor analysis of these responses, a thirteen-item scale of love and liking was then built. The content of this love scale served then as the working definition of love for the succeeding phases of the research. It included three major components:

1. *Affiliative* and *dependent need* (tapped by items like "If I could never be with _____ [my girlfriend or boyfriend], I would feel miserable.")

2. *Predisposition to help* (tapped by items like "If _____ were feeling badly, my first duty would be to cheer him (her) up.")

3. *Exclusiveness and absorption* (tapped by items like "When I am with _____, I spend a good deal of time just looking at him (her).")

It was found that love and liking for one's dating partner were more highly interrelated among men ($r = .60$) than among women ($r = .39$). In addition, although the mean *love* scores of the pairs for each other were almost identical, women tended to *like* their boyfriends more than their boyfriends liked them.

For both sexes, love (but not liking) was highly related to the respondents' estimates of the likelihood that they would marry their partners ($r = .59$). Women's estimates of this likelihood tended to be higher than men's.

Six months later the subjects filled out a questionnaire about their relationship at that time. As predicted, their initial love scores were positively related to their reports on whether or not their relationships had made progress toward permanence.

Eye contact in dyads: a "come-on" or a "get gone"?
One of the most interesting findings in Rubin's research on love is that partners who love each other more, according to their love-scale scores, spend more time looking into each other's eyes during a brief discussion period in the laboratory. But is this eye contact simply the *consequence* of being in love, or is it a *stimulus* for other behavior, perhaps inti-

macy and still greater feelings of attraction? We cannot tell from this study because eye contact was a *dependent* variable. In order to assess the stimulus properties of eye contact and related nonverbal behaviors, it is necessary to manipulate them experimentally as *independent* variables.

In the last few years a number of innovative studies have done just that. The experimenter (or a confederate) has maintained eye contact or has refrained from looking at the subject, has nodded and smiled or sat morose and unmoving, or varied his nonverbal behavior in other specified ways. The behavior of the subject has been measured under the contrasting conditions to see if it shows corresponding variations. One of the most straightforward of these experiments was actually run in the "real world" outside of the laboratory.

It has long been known that *staring* serves as a signal for threat in nonhuman primates and also that many cultures around the world have had a fear of the destructive magic of the "evil eye," which has resulted in taboos against staring.

The researchers wanted to find out how more "sophisticated" Americans would react to the eye contact of an intense stare from a stranger. The experiment they performed was extremely simple, and any student who is interested in trying it out can easily do so. The experimenter stood on the corner of the sidewalk at a busy intersection and waited for a car to pull up at the red light. As soon as the car stopped, the experimenter began to stare, calmly and continuously, at the driver. Then, when the light changed to green, the experimenter started a concealed stopwatch and measured the time it took the driver to cross the intersection. For subjects in the control group, the experimenter simply stood on the corner, without looking directly at the driver, and measured the time it took him to cross.

This experiment was repeated several times, with a number of variations, and in each of the replications the results were the same: subjects who were stared at crossed the intersection significantly faster than subjects who were not stared at (Ellsworth, Henson, & Carlsmith, 1970).

In this case, eye contact was clearly a stimulus for escape behavior. In interpreting this finding, we do not need to conclude that the stare is an innate threat signal in humans or that modern-day Americans still harbor a secret belief in the evil eye. The experimenters suggest that in this situation staring had two major properties: (a) it created an incongruous situation in which the subject did not have any obvious, appropriate response, and (b) it was a strong enough stimulus that the subject felt he was involved and had to make a response.

Incongruity alone is not enough to account for the escape behavior. This was demonstrated by a control experiment in which the experimenter performed an incongruous act that did not involve staring; on the average, subjects did not cross the intersection any faster than in the no-stare condition. They experienced incongruity but not involvement. Only when they were personally involved did the lack of an appropriate response apparently arouse tension and elicit escape at the earliest possible moment.

When the starer provides additional "suggestive" cues, or stares in a situation where approach responses are appropriate or might prove rewarding, then eye contact would be expected to be a "come-on" stimulus.

Dyadic Competition: The Prisoner's Dilemma

It happens sometimes that you inadvertently stare at someone, he or she stares back, and suddenly you are locked into a "staring contest." Neither wants to be the first to back down and look away, even though there is nothing positive to be gained from continued staring. What develops is a "game situation" in which whoever looks away first loses and the other wins.

There are many competitive situations which are not games, as when two people in a dyadic relationship are vying for power or for a greater share of limited resources available. Sometimes it is a head-on competition, in which the outcome must be a win for one and a loss for the other. This is called a *zero-sum game* (win $= +1$, loss $= -1$, sum $= 0$). More often, however, the alternatives are such that the players can choose either to compete or to cooperate. The amount each can win is determined by the strategy adopted by both players. This is called a *nonzerosum game* since the total gained or lost by both players may be greater or less than zero.

One imaginative study of dyadic interaction posed the following problem for the subjects. Each player was in the position of a truck dispatcher for a company whose truck had to reach a given destination as quickly as possible. Time was money, and the sooner the truck reached its destination, the more money was earned. The quickest route was a *one-lane* central road, but only one player could use it at a time. Each player also had a longer, alternate road that he could use to send his truck from the starting point to its destination. The one-lane road was obviously the bottleneck, and the problem was to work out who would have first rights and therefore make more money.

A cooperative strategy in the dyad would alternate first use of the one-lane road; thereby over the course of the game, both players would win a considerable sum. That rarely happened in hundreds of dyads studied across many variations (such as allowing or restricting communication, or providing one or both sides with the retaliatory weapon of blocking the one-lane road). Subjects did not optimize their winnings within the dyad but competed on each trial even when it meant competing over who would *lose* the least amount of money! (Deutsch & Krauss, 1960)

Psychologists have become interested in the factors that influence interpersonal bargaining in part because of the significance of the cold-war "games" being played by international leaders. There, of course, the potential gains and losses are measured not in experimental points but in "kill ratios"; thus laboratory simulations of the critical variables could prevent costly real-life blunders.

The methodology most often used to study competition and cooperation between two people is known as the *Prisoner's Dilemma* game matrix. It is derived from the situation facing two hypothetical prisoners who are suspected of a crime. They are separated and each is told that he has two options: to confess or refuse to confess. The consequences for him, however, will depend in part on what the other prisoner does. If one confesses and the other does not, the confessor will be freed for turning state's evidence and the other will get the maximum sentence. If neither confesses, they will both be booked on minor charges anyway and released. If both confess, they may get a less than maximum sentence because the District Attorney will recommend leniency.

If you were one of the prisoners, would you confess or keep a "tight lip"? If you anticipated that the other prisoner would not confess, then you could go free by confessing. *Your* outcome would be best if the other person behaved cooperatively and you be-haved competitively. If you both behaved coopera-tively you both would suffer a little but neither would die. But you cannot communicate and neither of you wants to die.

In the experimental analog of this situation, each person is separated from a co-player and has the option to press one of two buttons. The outcome depends on which combination of choices the players make. All the possibilities are shown in the matrix. ● Typically, American subjects employ a competitive strategy even though over a large number of trials both players suffer.

It is interesting to speculate about how two of the Filipino peasants we discussed earlier might play such a game against each other, or how one of them might react to a player who consistently chose a competitive strategy. Research has shown that even with subjects who are originally competitive, a cooperative stan-dard can be established through instructions.

The prisoner's dilemma game has methodological value at several levels: as a test for the trait of competitiveness, as a way of analyzing the interper-sonal processes that occur in bargaining and confron-tations, and as a test of the ability of various training conditions to increase cooperative strategies. Even in

a culture as competitive as our own, it may be possible to find ways to encourage dyads to make cooperation and not competition.

The Group As a Repository of Social Influence

It is clear that there are situations in which one individual communicator, leader, Machiavellian, lov-er, or competitor can exert considerable influence on another person and sometimes on a whole nation of people. But these individual power figures cannot influence all of the people all of the time. There are times when people are persuaded and moved to ac-tion not through speeches, threats, and inducements from any one person, but through the more diffuse pressure exerted by groups to which they belong. The study of group influence was given its impetus by a classic study conducted by Kurt Lewin during the Second World War.

This investigator was engaged in research of practical as well as theoretical value. With ordinary meats rationed and scarce, he set about to try to change housewives' decisions about what meats to buy. He sought to interest them in glandular meats, such as heart, sweetbreads, and kidneys, which were highly nutritious, more readily available, not rationed, and cheaper, but more generally disliked.

Working with six groups of housewives, Lewin had half of the groups listen to an attractive lecture, de-signed to change their minds about using these meats. The lecture linked the problem of nutrition to the war effort, emphasized the vitamin and mineral content of the glandular foods, and provided information on how to prepare them in ways which avoided the characteris-tic odor, texture, and appearance which made the meats distasteful to some people.

The other groups were told of the same problem and were then encouraged to discuss the obstacles that "housewives like themselves" might face in trying to change toward using more of these meats. During this discussion, the leader provided the information which had been included in the lecture, but only when the groups had become sufficiently involved to be interested in know-ing whether various obstacles could be overcome.

At the end of the meeting the women were asked to indicate by a showing of hands who would be willing to try one of these meats within the next week. A follow-up

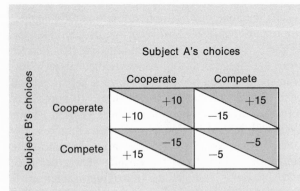

● A PRISONERS' DILEMMA GAME MATRIX

If both make the cooperative choice, each gets a moderate +10 payoff. If one chooses cooperatively, the other competitively, the competitor gets the max-imum gain and the cooperator the maximum loss. If both choose competitively, they both lose.

showed that only 3 percent of the women who heard the lectures served one of the meats never served before, while 32 percent of those participating in the group discussion and decision served one of them (Lewin, 1947).

Similar methods were tried in another study with farm mothers, to get them to feed cod-liver oil and orange juice to their babies. Only about half the mothers who received individual instruction changed in the desired direction, whereas almost all the mothers in a group-decision condition did so (Radke & Klisurich, 1947).

What properties did these groups possess that the prestigious, informative, legitimate, articulate lecturer lacked? How is it possible for a *group,* as an entity, to influence the behavior of individual members? We can identify at least four sources of group influence that probably operated to change the behavior of the women in these studies and are characteristic of groups in general: (a) shared participation, (b) public commitment, (c) social support, and (d) normative standards.

When people participate in discussions about matters of interest to them and share in the decision-making process, they become personally involved. In the "participatory democracy" thus created, each group member is a part of the active change process, rather than the passive recipient of some externally supplied information or decision made by someone else. Research and practical experience with groups in industrial and other natural settings clearly shows that shared group participation is essential before individuals will accept innovative ideas and changes in their usual way of doing things.

When the group decision involves a "show of hands," the individual member is more likely to follow through with the recommended behavioral change than where his commitment is private. Public commitment witnessed by other group members requires a follow-up in action if the individual is to perceive himself as consistent. By the commitment, he also identifies himself as one willing to pledge publicly that he will make good his promises.

Individual decisions to act are bolstered when others in the group concur. The social support provided by group consensus not only increases one's confidence in the validity of his own decision and course of action but is a line of defense in the face of external opposition. Standards accepted by the rest of the group are also used by the individual members for social comparison in deciding what is the right thing for them to do. The operation of such normative standards has been the focus of considerable research.

Social Norms

As we have seen in many of the earlier chapters, it is important for individuals to put order into their lives. To be able to predict what the environment has in store and what other people are likely to do in given situations is one aspect of this ordering principle. A second is determining what response is appropriate, "appropriateness" being defined in terms of leading to desired reinforcers. As soon as individuals are part of a social unit, then appropriateness can no longer be defined entirely by each one "doing his own thing." The group inevitably has some definition of what is expected and acceptable and will reward conformity and punish deviations from this standard, whatever it is.

These group-defined standards concerning what behaviors are acceptable or objectionable are called *social norms.* In some instances the group norm is clear and explicit and functions almost like a law. In others, the norm is never spelled out, and new members become aware only gradually and imperceptibly of its influence in controlling their behavior. (Ψ Close-up, p. 494.)

The utility of social norms. Although the existence of group norms backed by powerful punishments for their violation can stultify behavior and promote excessive conformity, norms nevertheless serve an indispensable function. Awareness of the norms operating in a given group situation helps orient and regulate social life. Norms oil the machinery of social interaction by enabling each player to anticipate how others will enter the situation (for example, what they will wear) and what they are likely to say and do, as well as what behavior on his part will be expected and approved.

Some latitude of tolerance for deviating from the standard is also part of the norm, wide in some cases,

Ψ *Close-up* *Why Charlie Don't Raise His Hand No More:*
Implicit Norms in the College Classroom

A few years ago many a new teacher at a prestigious eastern college suffered quite a shock to his ego when all attempts to generate class discussion were met with attentive, but polite, silence. His sense of personal failure was not alleviated until an old-timer or sympathetic student would inform the dejected soul that he was "bucking the norm." It seems that an implicit norm existed which restricted student participation in other than seminar-type courses. It was assumed that the teacher, called "Sir," was qualified enough to know all the answers to the questions he posed, thus they must be merely rhetorical. Similarly, it was assumed that any student, called "Mister" by the teacher, would know the answers to real questions if he had taken the time to study and seriously consider them. Talking in class therefore, was not a sign of intellect or of analytical or creative power, but merely the mark of a plodder who did not respect the intelligence of his peers. Very few students ever talked in class.

Two contrasts will help to sharpen the operation of such implicit norms. Meanwhile, at the City Colleges in a nearby large city the teachers, whether raw recruits or seasoned veterans engaged in a very different battle with their students. Here the problem for the professor was to try to get a word in edgewise. In a democracy everybody's opinion is as good as everyone else's, but bright, competitive students simply have more opinions that deserve to be heard—so went student sentiment. This reasoning led to a norm that said teachers must prove that what they have to say to students is more valuable than what students have to say to their teachers. Very few students ever stopped talking in class.

Concurrently, at a large university in the same city, education was seen as part of an economic transaction. Students paid to hear hired teachers profess, and though the same restrictive norm existed as at the first college, the reasons were quite different and led to active efforts by the class to enforce the norm. Student participation meant that those students were cutting into the teacher's valuable time (computed by the rest in tuition dollars they had paid per hour of lecture). Very few students ever talked in class.

In one notable case, breaching the norm of "shutting up and letting the teacher do what he is paid to" had devastating consequences for an eager, naïve student (allegedly after "Brownie Points"). This young man, Charlie B., would not only answer questions at great length, but would ask questions and volunteer relevant, though unsolicited information during the introductory psychology class. At first, when he rose to answer, those seated around him would poke each other, smirk, frown, and clear their throats. In time, these nonverbal comments turned into snickers, giggles, and shuffling sounds. Finally, as he was about to rise, the student on one or the other side would bump him accidentally, or in turning to look at him, would knock down his books or jam his seat up so that he could not sit down again without much effort. By the middle of the year, he never raised his hand again or even answered when the teacher called on him. What is more, two years later that same student told his teacher, "I never take lecture courses any more, even if the teacher is good; I don't know why, but somehow they just make me feel uncomfortable and anxious."

narrow in others. Thus the member has a basis for estimating how far he can go before experiencing the coercive power of ridicule, repression, and rejection.

Adhering to the norms of a group is also the first step in establishing identification with it. Through his identification with the other members and with what the group stands for, the individual is able to use the group for social comparison purposes.

Finally, identification with a group allows the individual to share in whatever prestige and power the group possesses. In this way, for example, a skinny, little kid becomes a tough, stand-tall, feared member of the Jets, or some balding middle-aged man with a motorcycle is seen by outsiders as one of the Hell's Angels.

The social control carried out by group norms,

however, does not wait for individuals to join groups (except as one joins a society by being born into it), but is introduced as a central part of the socialization process. Respecting one's elders, saying "Thank you," "doing unto others as you would have them do unto you," and our codes of etiquette are norms that influence us almost from the moment of birth.

We also learn from observations that norms operate even in certain situations where social interaction is limited and transient. For example, in elevators everyone is supposed to face front and not talk too loud. In waiting lines, it is not "right" to push ahead out of one's place. It is improper to blow one's nose except into a handkerchief. And so on.

However, it is also apparent that social norms are culture-bound: what is proper in one society is often outrageous behavior in another. Algerians, for instance, believe that American men are very dirty people because they blow the discharge from their nose into a cloth and then put the filthy cloth into their pocket and carry it around all day.

Often norms are formed or modified on the basis of majority rule. In the New York subways, men *used* to give up their seats to women, but now the norm is "first come, first served." The popular TV program "Candid Camera" depended for much of its humor on putting individuals in situations where their customary behavior was suddenly challenged by the fact that a majority of the people present (confederates of the photographer) were acting in an unusual way. Thus an unsuspecting passenger entering an elevator full of people facing the rear is in a momentary conflict and generally decides to do likewise. Then the others turn and face front; the hapless individual conforms and also comes about.

In many situations like this, the individual's behavior, though perhaps nonsensical when viewed by itself, is no more nonsensical than the behavior of the people he is imitating. By using their behavior as a cue to what is appropriate in the situation, he is asserting his "normality." Thus once again we see that "social reality," as determined by *consensual validation* (see Chapter 1), comes to represent "personal reality" for the individual.

Norm formation and change in the laboratory. In an early study of the formation of social norms,

Sherif made use of the phenomenon of *autokinetic movement*. This is a perceptual illusion in which a stationary spot of light in a dark room is perceived as moving about erratically.

At first, subjects' reactions in this situation varied widely: some saw movement of a few inches, others reported that the spot moved many yards. After a series of judgments, however, each subject would establish a *range* within which most of his reports would fall. But then, when he was put into a group with two or three others, his estimates and theirs would converge on a new range on which they would all agree. After this happened, his judgment would continue to fall in this new range even when he was in the room by himself. Each subject now perceived the situation in terms of the norm that had developed during the interaction situation (Sherif, 1935).

These group-developed norms may be quite divergent from the individual's own estimate of what is "correct," as measured by his reaction before any social influence. And such norms persist in their influence: in one study the effect was observed an entire year afterward (Rohrer, Baron, Hoffman, & Swander, 1954).

Such norms, like those outside the laboratory, can also be transmitted to new "generations."

In another situation using the autokinetic effect, the investigators started with an individual whose average report of the movement, when judged alone, was 3.8 inches. They then induced an arbitrary norm of 15.5 inches by putting him into the dark room along with three confederates of the experimenters who consistently reported this way-out value. In time, the subject (S_1 in the figure) conformed to this norm with an estimate of 14 inches. This was the first generation of conformity.

In the next generation, one of the confederates was removed and a new naïve subject (S_2) added. When he was conforming to the norm, another confederate was removed and replaced by a third subject, the third generation.

By the fourth generation, all the confederates had been taken away and a group of four real subjects remained. But so did the influence of the arbitrary norm. The average rating remained greater than 10 inches.

In subsequent generations, as the subjects who had been directly influenced by the confederates were removed one by one, the arbitrary norm gradually de-

◆ **TRANSMISSION OF AN ARBITRARY NORM**

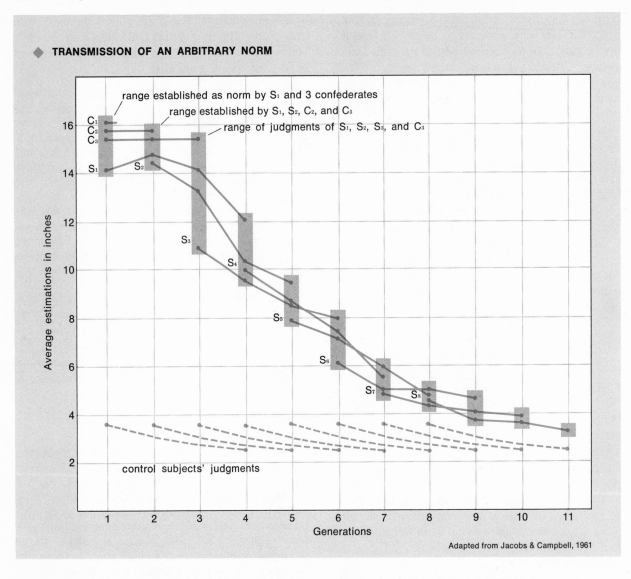

Adapted from Jacobs & Campbell, 1961

cayed until eventually the group judgments were the same as those that were natural for uninfluenced subjects (Jacobs & Campbell, 1961).   ◆

It might be argued that the social influence seen in these studies has very limited relevance, since the whole perception of motion was an illusion and the situation was so ambiguous that there was no physical reality on which the individual could depend. But research by Solomon Asch (1955) has convincingly demonstrated that group norms can sway the judgments of individuals even when the stimuli being

judged are structured and familiar and are perceived accurately when presented in a nonsocial situation. His investigations began as an attempt to show that under conditions where physical reality was clear, individuals would be *independent* of the influence imposed by social reality. Instead, his research has become the classic illustration of group *conformity*.

Groups of seven to nine male college students were assembled for a "psychological experiment in visual judgment." They were shown cards like the ones illustrated and asked to indicate which line on the comparison card was the same length as the line on the standard card. The lines were different enough that in ordinary circumstances mistakes in judgment would be made less than 1 percent of the time. All but one of the members of each group, however, were instructed beforehand to give incorrect answers unanimously on twelve critical trials distributed among the total of eighteen trials.

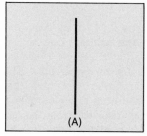 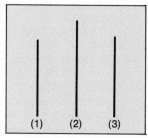

Standard line   Comparison lines

Under this group pressure, the minority subjects, over-all, accepted the majority's wrong judgments in 36.8 percent of the trials. But this figure is misleading, for individual differences were marked. Of the 123 minority subjects, about 30 percent nearly always yielded, even with differences as much as seven inches, while a fourth of the subjects remained entirely independent •

Interviews with the subjects at the end of the experiment indicated that many of those who did not yield to the opinion of the majority had strong confidence in their own judgment—after the contradicting responses, they were able to recover quickly from any doubt. Other independent subjects thought they were probably wrong but felt they should be honest about what they saw. Of the subjects who yielded to the majority opinion, some felt immediately that their perception must be wrong, perhaps due to some deficiency in themselves; others said they agreed with the majority "so as not to spoil the experimenter's results." All the yielding subjects underestimated the frequency of their conformity.

Next, the design of the experiment was changed slightly to investigate the effects of the size of the opposing majority. Pitted against just one person giving an incorrect judgment, the subject exhibited some uneasiness; when the opposition rose to two, he yielded, on an average, 13.6 percent of the time. The effect appeared in nearly full force when a majority of three opposed him: errors rose to 31.8 percent. Beyond three, the influence of the majority did not increase appreciably. When the subject was given an agreeing partner, the effects of the majority were greatly diminished—errors decreased to one fourth of what they had been with no partner, as

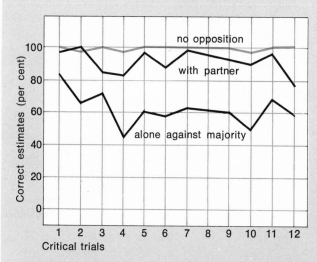 

● **JUDGMENTS WITH AND WITHOUT SOCIAL PRESSURE**

The concern of the dissenting subject is evident as he leans forward to check his judgment. In general, subjects found this a very disturbing situation. The graph compares the average errors under normal circumstances with those made under social pressure both with and without a supporting partner. (From Opinions and Social Pressure" by S. E. Asch. Copyright © 1955 by Scientific American, Inc. All rights reserved.)

shown in the graph, and the effects lasted even after the partner left (Asch, 1955).

Other investigators have used Asch's general technique to investigate the relation of sex and age to the tendency to yield to group pressure.

In one such study, using visual discrimination problems with ten- to twelve-year-old children and college students, there were consistent sex differences: female subjects yielded more often to distorted group judgments. The children, as a group, yielded somewhat more often than the college students (Tuddenham, 1961).

Social Influence in "Real World" Groups

Although a considerable amount of research has extended the validity and implications of these findings in a variety of directions, some social psychologists chose to give up the precision and control possible in laboratory research and wandered into the "field" to study natural groups. A group of young researchers drawn together by Lewin's exciting approach to studying group phenomena, organized the Group Dynamics Center, first at M.I.T. but since 1945 housed at the University of Michigan (Cartwright & Zander, 1968). One of the avowed goals of this school was to study the dynamic properties of *social interaction* within groups with the same rigor and precision that other psychological processes were being studied at an individual level. Another goal, equally important, was to use the tools and knowledge of the social sciences to investigate existing *social problems* with an eye toward applied, action-oriented solutions that would improve the quality of human life. Researchers thus focused their attention upon the causes and results of different patterns of interaction, communication, adjustment, conformity, and prejudice in situations as diverse as housing units, colleges, the military, and industry.

The ecology of proximity and influence in a housing project. Groups generally show a conformity of opinions and behavior among their members with respect to whatever the norms of the group happen to be. This conformity occurs for three general reasons: (a) we tend to associate with others most like ourselves and thus to join groups which already share our values and interests; and (b) in the act of identifying with a group, we signify our readiness to accept its standards of thought and action; but also, in addition, (c) groups exert *pressures* toward uniformity which tend to keep members in line.

One team of group dynamics researchers focused upon the complex set of variables underlying these pressures to establish, maintain, and enforce group standards.

A housing development for married M.I.T. students was chosen as the site for the investigation. One set of buildings, called *Westgate*, was arranged in U-shaped courts and had been occupied for fifteen months. The other, called *Westgate West,* was made up of two-story converted navy barracks and had been occupied only a few months. Both were physically isolated from the rest of the town, and the residents' social life tended to be centered in them and focused especially in their own building, as shown in the table. ▲   Both physical and functional distance were related to friendship choices: those who lived closer within a court or those who used the same stairwell were most often likely to become friends. For these subjects, at least, friendships were largely a function of how often people's paths crossed.

The occupants had formed a tenant's council to undertake and coordinate activities, handle problems, and act as intermediary with the university landlord. It represented tenants in both sections. A central objective of the study was to determine whether social norms existed in the two sections regarding participation in the tenants' organization and, if so, if the norms influenced the behavior and attitudes of the individuals.

▲   **FRIENDSHIP CHOICES IN A HOUSING PROJECT**

Distance	(a) Number of friends who live at each distance	(b) Possible choices	(a)/(b) Ratio of choices to possibilities
Next door	26	96	.27
One house between	6	72	.08
Two houses between	2	48	.04
Three houses between (180 feet)	0	24	.00

It was found that both participation in tenant-council activities and favorableness of attitudes toward it were an individual matter in the more recently settled Westgate West; evidently a social norm had not yet developed there. In Westgate, however, the behavior and attitudes within a court were relatively homogeneous but differed from those of other courts. The conclusion that social norms were controlling behavior in Westgate but not in Westgate West was supported by three lines of evidence.

1. Among those in Westgate West, residents who expected to stay in the project longer were more active in the council than those who expected a short-term residence. In Westgate, those who planned to move in a few months were as active as those planning a longer stay.

2. A crucial relationship between *cohesiveness* and *conformity* was found in Westgate but not in Westgate West. In Westgate, the higher the social cohesiveness, the lower the percentage of those deviating from the predominant pattern. In Westgate West, social cohesiveness and conformity to prevailing behavior in relation to the tenant council were not significantly related.

3. Deviates were more likely to be rejected in Westgate than in Westgate West. In Westgate, deviates got half as many friendship choices as they gave, whereas conformers received more choices than they gave. In Westgate West, by contrast, those who differed from the prevailing pattern in tenant-council activity were not isolated socially (Festinger, Schachter, & Back, 1950).

Isolation from a group may, of course, be one cause of deviance, but deviance from group norms, whatever its source, then leads to further isolation, imposed by the group. Uniformity, in turn, may result either from forces which act on the members individually or from the operation of group standards. For group standards to be effective in inducing conformity, the group must have existed long enough for individuals to have developed some loyalty to it, and the group must be fairly cohesive. In addition, individuals must have enough contact with the group physically and socially to "get the message."

Deviance from a group's standards can be expected to bring with it some degree of social ostracism. For most people, this sets the stage for the development of feelings of alienation.

Overcoming restrictive norms in a pajama factory.
Once formed, norms can have such a controlling influence on behavior that they make change or innovation impossible. Most norms have a strong-armed, though often silent, provision which in effect asserts that the status quo must be preserved. How, then, is it ever possible for someone to introduce a new way of doing things in a well-established group?

One answer comes from a successful experiment carried out some years ago in a pajama factory in Virginia. It has obvious social relevance to contemporary encounters between existing groups and agents of change in the fields of health and social work as well as in industrial and political settings.

The company's labor-relations policies had been liberal and progressive, yet it had found that its workers were very resistant to changes in procedure that were necessary from time to time. Though the need for the changes was explained and bonuses were given, changes were typically followed by resentment and low efficiency; in fact, about two thirds of the workers would become chronically substandard operators or quit soon after the changes were made. The problem was to find a way of making necessary changes from time to time in such a way as to get employee cooperation instead of resistance.

Several minor needed changes were identified by the management. Three experimental groups and a control group were established, composed of members matched as closely as possible with respect to group cohesiveness, efficiency ratings, and probable degree of change to be required. The control group were simply told that changes were necessary to lower costs, were given training in the new procedures, and were told the new piece rate that was being established.

Each of the three experimental groups was involved in a discussion of the urgent need for cost reduction, during which they agreed that certain procedures could be streamlined and even came up with several suggestions of their own. For one group, a few leaders were retrained first and a new piece rate established by them and then they helped train the others. In the other two groups, all members were retrained at once and all helped set the new piece rate.

The workers in the three experimental groups were exceedingly cooperative throughout. The production rate of Group 1 fell temporarily, then rose rapidly. Groups 2 and 3 regained their former efficiency after the first day, and their output continued to rise.

The control group, on the other hand, showed considerable resistance to the change, expressing hostility toward the supervisor (who was the same person in charge of Group 1) and deliberately restricting their production. They were slower to relearn and remained well below their former production rate during the thirty-two-day period of observation. Furthermore, almost a fifth of them quit within forty days of the change; none of the experimental group did so.

As a further check on the method of group participation, thirteen members of the control group were reassembled two and a half months later and transferred to a new job, using the total participation technique used for Groups 2 and 3 in the original study. This time, these individuals, who had proved so uncooperative before, learned the new job rapidly, showed no aggression, and showed improved rates of production similar to those of Groups 2 and 3 in the first study (Coch & French, 1948). On a later occasion within the same company, even more extensive changes were produced following the use of group participation techniques (French, Ross, Kirby, Nelson, & Smyth, 1958). ■

Participation does not always break down resistant norms, however. Evidently it does so only to the extent that four conditions are present: (a) the decisions are seen as important; (b) the content of the decisions is relevant to the dependent variable—production, labor relations, job satisfaction, or whatever behavior change is to be measured; (c) the participation is considered legitimate; and (d) there is no negative reaction to the *methods* by which the change is managed (French, Israel, & Os, 1960).

Cooperation between competitors or enemies.   If the competition we observed in the prisoner's-dilemma dyads is not an inevitable response for individuals and groups in a position to harm each other, what are the conditions under which they will turn to each other and cooperate for their mutual benefit?

In the example of the cat and the rat given on page 464, members of species usually hostile to each other learned to cooperate under conditions where they both benefited from cooperation. Perhaps such "superordinate goals"—shared goals which require

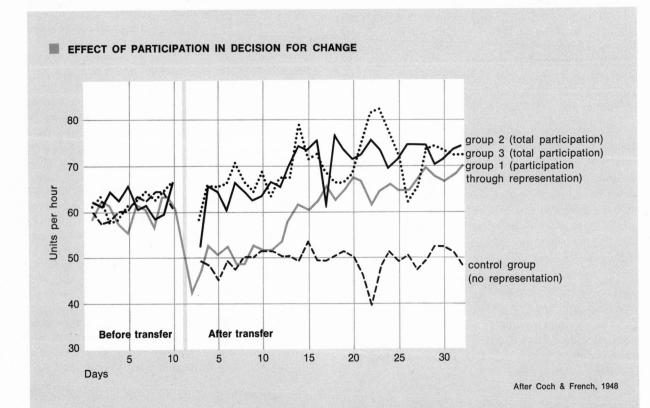

■ **EFFECT OF PARTICIPATION IN DECISION FOR CHANGE**

Units per hour

80
70
60
50
40
30

Before transfer   **After transfer**

Days   5   10   5   10   15   20   25   30

group 2 (total participation)
group 3 (total participation)
group 1 (participation through representation)

control group (no representation)

After Coch & French, 1948

cooperation if either of two usually conflicting parties is to achieve them—might be a key to intergroup amicability in humans as well. A husband-and-wife team conducted a field study designed to find out.

In a camp, friction was generated between two experimentally created groups and was later overcome as the groups worked toward common goals. The subjects were twenty-two normal boys about eleven years of age, with similar backgrounds, who were divided into two groups comparable in such factors as size and various abilities. Before arriving at the camp the boys did not know each other, and they remained unaware that an experiment was taking place.

To cement the boys into true groups, the experimenters put the groups in different bunkhouses and kept them separate for daily activities, introducing several problems that required group solution, such as carrying canoes from the bunkhouses across rough terrain to the lake and fixing meals from unprepared food. By the end of this part of the experiment, the two groups had acquired definite group structures, including leaders, names for themselves (Rattlers and Eagles), nicknames, private signals, cooperative patterns within the group, and individual symbols of identification (flags and signs set on places and facilities designated as "ours"). This part of the experiment supported the hypothesis that a definite group structure will result when individuals are placed in situations involving appealing goals and requiring cooperative effort for the attainment of these goals and that as the group structure is formed, norms regulating behavior and group activities of the individuals will become standardized.

Next, rivalry between the groups was stimulated by a series of competitive events. As predicted, this increased in-group solidarity and also produced unfavorable stereotypes of the out-group and its members. In-group democracy and cooperation did not extend to the out-group. After losing a tug-of-war, the Eagles burned the Rattlers' flag. The Rattlers retaliated, and a series of bunkhouse raids ensued, accompanied by name calling, fist fighting, and other expressions of hostility. During the conflict, a physically daring leader emerged to replace the less aggressive boy who had led the Eagles, indicating that relations with other groups will cause changes within a group.

An attempt was then made to break down the hostility and induce the two groups to cooperate with each other. First, the rival groups were brought into close contact in pleasant activities—such as eating and shoot-ing off firecrackers. The groups refused to intermingle, however, and the activities merely provided them with further opportunities for such expressions of hostility as throwing mashed potatoes and exchanging invective, indicating that intergroup contact does not in itself decrease tension.

As indicated earlier, a more successful way was found. Situations were contrived to bring about interaction of the groups to achieve superordinate goals—that is, important goals which could not be achieved without the combined efforts of both groups. In one problem situation the camp water supply was mysteriously cut off and all the boys cooperated in locating the trouble. For a time friction continued, however; after cooperating to procure a film, for example, the boys still sat primarily with their own groups while the film was being shown.

The most striking episode in this period was one in which the tug-of-war rope, formerly the central object in a most antagonistic situation, served as a tool. On an overnight trip, a truck which was to bring their food "stalled," and the boys hit upon the idea of using the rope to pull the vehicle. After looping the rope through the bumper, the two groups pulled on different ends; but the next day, when the truck "stalled" again, members of the two groups intermingled on the two lines, obliterating group divisions. • (p. 502)

Further evidence of the change in the boys' attitudes was obtained from sociometric choices made at the end of the period of intense competition and again at the close of the experiment. Rattlers' choices of Eagles as friends went up from 6.4 to 36.4 percent of their total friendship choice. Eagles' choices of Rattlers went up from 7.5 to 23.2 percent. The boys were also asked to rate each other on six characteristics designed to bring out the presence of stereotyped images. During the period of antagonism, Eagles received few favorable ratings from Rattlers, and Rattlers few from Eagles; but at the close of the experiment there was no significant difference in the ratings of in-group and out-group members (Sherif & Sherif, 1956).

Clearly this study has many implications for the overcoming of bitterness between national groups and between antagonistic groups within our own society. It provides valuable leads for action-oriented research on these crucial problems.

College as a molder of men—and liberal ladies. What impact does membership in a college community have upon the attitudes and values of its students? We know that not all students "assimilate"

CHANGING COMPETITION TO COOPERATION

At the beginning of the experiment a cooperative atmosphere developed rapidly within each group; here the Eagles are shown preparing a meal (top, left) and the Rattlers work together carrying canoes to the lake (top, center). During the second stage of the experiment, intergroup competition was fostered, and the rivalry soon became intense. Raids and counterraids took place, with flags and even articles of clothing being carried off as trophies (top, right). A tug-of-war ended in a complete impasse (bottom, left) when Rattlers adopted the Eagle strategy of sitting down and "digging in." In the final stage of the experiment, intergroup cooperation was brought about by the creation of situations that could be worked out only by cooperative means, such as searching for the source of trouble in the camp water supply (bottom, center) or pulling a "stalled" truck (bottom, right).

the prevailing norms of a given institution. How do some remain in the group but resist conformity? A study begun back in 1935 in a small New England college for girls offers some insights into both these problems. The findings are of obvious concern to every student caught between twin pressures to become part of the group and to maintain his or her independence and individuality.

Bennington College is situated in a small Vermont town, and at the start of this study had been in existence for only four years. Its curriculum emphasized individualized instruction and small group seminars. Most faculty and all students lived on or near the campus, and their relations were informal and democratic. "To a very large degree the community was integrated, self-contained, and self-conscious." The prevailing norm was one of political and economic liberalism. On the other hand, most of the girls had come from conservative homes and brought conservative attitudes with them. The question studied, then, was what impact this "liberal atmosphere" would have on the attitudes of individual students who were part of the college community.

Measures of the girls' attitudes, made at intervals during their four years at Bennington, showed that the conservatism of the freshman class steadily declined with each passing year. By their senior year most girls had been "converted" to a clearly liberal position (regarded as "radical left" in those days). Evidently this process of influence was operating both through faculty and upperclass social approval for expression of liberal views and through the greater availability of politically oriented information in the college community. Among freshmen, there was no relationship between degree of conservatism and amount of general knowledge of public affairs, but among upperclasswomen, there was a correlation between liberal attitudes and amount of knowledge of public affairs. Girls who had become liberal had absorbed more information about political, national, and civic affairs.

A second part of the study sought to discover why some girls had been able to resist this pervasive norm and retain their conservatism. It was found that the uninfluenced girls fell into two classes. Some simply had been unaware of the conflict between their conservatism and the college's liberalism. They were part of a small, close-knit group of girls who had limited social aspirations and, in a sense, had been isolated from the normative power of the larger group. A larger group of conservative girls had been quite aware of the discrepancy between their attitudes and values and those inherent

in the college norm. However, they had not used the college community as their *primary reference group*. Rather, they tended to come from conservative families with whom they maintained strong ties and whose standards they continued to use in evaluating their own behavior. They could be nonconformers to the Bennington code by conforming to the family code (Newcomb, 1958).

Twenty years later, the marks of the Bennington experience were still evident. Most girls who had left as liberals were liberals and those who had resisted remained conservatives. This had been accomplished in part by marrying men with comparable values, thus creating a supportive home environment and presumably starting their own generation-transmission chain.

Of those who left college as liberals but married men in conservative occupations or with conservative political attitudes, however, a high proportion returned to their freshman-year conservatism. This shift backwards toward one's original attitude (*recidivism*) is typical of most programs of change, therapy, or rehabilitation in which "changed" people are sent back to the situation in which old norms and reinforcement contingencies operate (Newcomb, 1963).

The Power of a Minority

Given the power of the majority to control resources and reinforcements, it is not surprising to observe the extent of conformity that exists at all levels of our society. What is remarkable is to consider how anyone escapes this group domination, or how anything new—counternormative—ever comes about. In Chapter 8 we saw that one of the problems in creativity is to free the creative person from dependence on social approval and from a need to define reality according to group consensus. In a strange way, every society depends for its maintenance on conformers who will defend the establishment norms, but reluctantly turns to its deviants for new ideas and innovations that will move it ahead.

But can a small minority turn the majority around and create new norms, using only the same basic psychological principles that usually help to establish the majority view? Recently a group of French psychologists have shown how it can be done.

Thirty-two groups of French coeds were assembled to participate in a study allegedly on color perception. Each group consisted of four naïve subjects and two confederates of the experimenters. On each trial a stimulus of a given hue was projected on a screen and the subjects were to call out the name of the color and its intensity rating. In some of the groups, whenever a blue color appeared, both the minority confederates called it "green." They were always consistent with each other and with their previous responses. In other groups, the confederates were consistent on only two thirds of the trials.

Among twenty-two subjects in a control group, who were not exposed to any dissenting confederates, only one ever gave a "green" response to the blue light. When the minority confederates in the experimental group did not consistently dissent, only 1 percent of the subjects followed their lead. But almost a third (32 percent) of those exposed to a steadfast consistent minority conformed to it in reporting that they too saw "green."

Many others shifted their perception of "blue" toward "green" on a later, individually administered test: although they had not verbally agreed with what the deviant minority reported, they had changed their perception of reality to agree with the new norm created by the insistent minority (Moscovici, Lage, & Naffrechoux, 1969; Faucheux & Moscovici, 1967). If a consistent minority can win adherents to this extent even when it is wrong, there is abundant hope for a minority with a valid cause.

Thus we come full circle in our analysis of social motives and social influence. Man as part of the herd is subject to its regulatory principles in order to optimize his own gain/loss balance. But the direction of the herd is ultimately governed by individual action. Consistency of view and dedication of purpose by one man is easily dismissed as an idiosyncratic quirk, or, as we shall see in subsequent chapters, may be labeled "madness." Two such people turn a delusion into a belief; a few more can turn it into a social movement. But psychologists have yet to discover those characteristics which enable a single individual to stand out from the yea-saying crowd, and declare that the Emperor is not wearing any clothes at all.

Chapter Summary

Interactions with other people produce both *information* and *consequences,* thus playing an important part in our lifelong attempt to establish predictability

in our environment and learn our relationship to it. Our relationship to our social environment includes both our potential for influence on others and theirs for influence on us. Study of the social nature of man includes research on both *social behavior*, as a dependent variable, and *social stimuli,* as independent variables. Even nonsocial behavior is often influenced by social stimuli.

Study of animal societies makes clear the importance of the social group in providing protection, food, and information to members and suggests that the group, rather than the individual, may be the basic evolutionary unit. Naturally occurring cooperation has been observed both in the field and in the laboratory, and even members of usually hostile or competitive species can learn to cooperate to avoid a threat or achieve a positive reinforcement.

Members of different human societies have learned to value markedly different *ways of life;* these values shape the dominant social motives in a given society. Social motives in our society that have been subjected to systematic psychological study include the needs for *achievement, social comparison, social approval,* and *affiliation.* Study of apparently self-defeating behavior in peasants in resisting potentially beneficial changes dramatizes the role of existing social motives and values in providing a climate that may be either conducive to a given change or resistant to it. The affiliative motive began to be studied productively when researchers stopped talking about the *"herd instinct"* and began studying the conditions under which affiliative behavior increased or decreased.

Even the presence of other people, without interaction or intent on their part, can influence our behavior. A familiar example is stage fright.

The one-way, intended influence in attitude-change attempts has been intensively studied. The independent variables in such studies are *communicator characteristics*, *message characteristics*, and *audience characteristics;* often these variables have *interacting* rather than *additive* effects. The most effective way to change attitudes seems to be to change behavior. If the reward structure induces and maintains the desired behavior, attitude change follows as the individual attempts to reduce the dissonance between his actions and his feelings and beliefs.

Leadership has been studied through attempts to identify characteristics of successful leaders and through study of the effects of different leadership styles. Different situations create the need for leaders with different characteristics, though effective leadership has been found to be associated with such traits as intelligence, achievement, responsibility, interpersonal sensitivity, and the ability to be ahead—but not too far ahead—of one's followers. Particular situations require particular leader skills, and sometimes leadership functions are shared among two or more leaders. The particular situation and the needs and expectations of the members help to determine what kind of leadership will be most effective.

A consistent trait termed *Machiavellianism* has been identified, predictably associated with skill in the kind of social influence known as "conning" others in certain kinds of situations. *High Machs* flourish in face-to-face situations where rules and guidelines are minimal and where other people (but not they) are emotionally aroused.

A primary source of social influence is the two-person group, or *dyad*. Studies of interpersonal attraction have shown that we tend to like people who are like us, agree with us, and meet our needs. We especially like people who make us feel good about ourselves. Even romantic love is becoming a subject for systematic laboratory study and prediction. Studies of *competition vs. cooperation,* as in the *Prisoner's Dilemma situation,* have been carried out in the laboratory but have been criticized as an unfair

test of man's potentiality for cooperation. In situations where there is a *supraordinate goal* which can be reached only through cooperation, formerly competitive subjects, both animal and human, can learn to cooperate and also to replace feelings of enmity with mutual liking.

Groups have great power to influence their members. *Group discussion, joint decision,* and *overt commitment* to behave in accordance with the decision are more likely to change behavior than information or directives "from above." Participatory decisions in industrial settings lead to greater production, more satisfaction among employees, and lower absenteeism and turnover.

Group-defined standards are called *social norms* and form a centrally important part of the social reality each person must learn about. Norms have utility in preserving the group's values and in enabling members to know what behavior is expected and will be rewarded. The member who conforms gains status and approval; the one who does not may be rejected by the group or pressured to conform. A sizeable percentage of people will deny the evidence of their own perceptions and report that they see what the majority of a group report is there. Whatever the norms, whether accurate or inaccurate, they are transmitted to new individuals who join the group. On the other hand an individual is encouraged to stand by a dissenting position if one other person in the group supports him, and a consistent pair of dissenters may even change the majority perception.

Part Six

RIGHTEOUSNESS
EXALTETH A NATION

Loss and Recovery
of Human Potential

We have now come a long way in finding out just what psychology is all about, what psychologists do, and what knowledge they have accumulated. At one level, this presentation has explored the various areas of psychological inquiry and provided a way of thinking about behavior, an approach to asking meaningful questions and being better able to assess the quality of the answers that are given.

At another level, a theme of man's development has been emerging. The development of the human organism from his lowly evolutionary origins to his lofty status as most noble, creative, and powerful of all the creatures of the earth has been the background against which we have studied particular psychological processes. If this were a novel, our story could end here with man living happily ever after. Unfortunately, such an end is not within sight. Instead, we are faced with a perversion of human perfection which finds forces within the society as well as within each man diminishing his potential. Men kill each other and themselves in big wars and little quarrels. They destroy natural and man-made objects, abuse their bodies and blow their minds with drugs, submit to dictators or tyrannize over others, riot, panic, and spread rumors. More, they develop elaborate systems of prejudice which diminish themselves, do violence to others, and unleash anarchy in their society.

In this final section, we will first examine some of the paradoxes inherent in man's perfection. We will see that it is the very possession of his complex capacities and intricate skills that makes possible the depths of disintegration, degradation, and destruction to which he can sink. Language, memory, environ-

mental control are just some of the powerful weapons which man can use against himself with as much killing power as any lethal weapon. Just as society can socialize self-centered, demanding infants into altruistic, gratification-delaying adults, so too can civilization work to uncivilize us all.

The pathology of human behavior is represented by prejudice, addiction, neurosis, psychosis, and suicide. In trying to understand these "abnormal behaviors" we will explore different conceptions of the nature of "mental illness" and "madness." Are such "sick" people really different from their "normal" neighbors? To what extent is "abnormal" or "pathological" relative to a given culture or reference group?

While people suffer—some in silence, some in anguish—dedicated researchers, therapists, nurses, and aides devote their lives to relieving some of this pain. But as we learn from Adam in Paradise and Humpty-Dumpty on the wall, the fall is easier and swifter than the recovery. But there are therapeutic approaches which have a measure of success with patients of a certain type. In the last chapter we will inquire into just what therapy is available to modify different forms of deviant behavior. Just as we have seen that physiological, learning, and cognitive-social factors are all central to the development of man's potential, so we will find therapies based on these three kinds of factors.

We end on a note of optimism for the promise which psychology holds for serving man, but also on one of uncertainty about the conditions which must exist between men to allow for their optimal growth and for the fuller realization of the potential that is theirs.

Chapter 13

Forces That Diminish Man

I cannot but conclude the Bulk of your Natives, to be the most pernicious Race of little odious Vermin that Nature ever suffered to crawl upon the Surface of the Earth.

[The historical account of man is a] Heap of Conspiracies, Rebellions, Murders, Massacres, Revolutions, Banishments, the very worst Effects that Avarice, Fraction, Hypocrisy, Perfidiousness, Cruelty, Rage, Madness, Hatred, Envy, Lust, Malice, and Ambition could produce.

Jonathan Swift
Gulliver's Travels

Although this total condemnation has been dismissed as the work of a cynical hater of men, many others concerned about "human nature" over the centuries have echoed similar sentiments. A basic theme in Western literature is that man—once great, once the most noble paragon of all creatures—has suffered a great fall from his state of perfection. "One exclaims, O, Pitiful Change" because man's nature is "so much obscured by his fall that (some few relics excepted) he is inferior to a beast." (Burton, 1620, p. 113)

According to biblical scholars, the Fall originated with Adam's sin of pride and disobedience in Paradise. In other schemes, the corrupting force upon man is traced to the social influence exemplified by Eve. This theme was expanded by Rousseau and others to one in which man, the noble, primitive savage, is diminished by his contact with society. To recapture and preserve his uniqueness and essential goodness, he must escape the cities, "the haunts of men" and the wine-press of civilization. Thoreau's isolated cabin at Walden Pond has become a symbol of man's attempt to break his bonds of dependence and exploitation and achieve a state of self-reliance. This return to Nature in order to find one's true self involves dropping out of established society and from time to time has led to the creation of Utopian communes. At present, many young people are responding to this same primitive appeal by forming and joining small communes in rural areas.

In opposition to this general view of man as the innocent victim of an all-powerful, malignant society is the position that man himself is basically evil. Born with desires, appetites, and impulses like those of a selfish beast, the individual is turned from brute to human being only by the socializing, civilizing effect of a benign environment.

We shall propose a third, very different analysis of the apparent perversion of man's "perfection." In the preceding chapters we have documented the complex development and supreme specialization that has produced man as we now know him. Through his capacity for learning, remembering, reasoning, planning, and delaying gratification, through his language, perceptual, cognitive, and motor skills, through his concept of an integrated self with a past and a future

---

Ψ Close-up   *Happiness Is Not a Psychology Text*

Two recent surveys of psychological literature give the impression that psychologists are obsessed with studying and talking about unpleasant emotions and the negative aspects of man. One analyzes the content of 172 psychology textbooks written over the past eighty-five years and finds that unpleasant emotions are discussed twice as much as pleasant ones (Carlson, 1966). The other reports that nearly 80 percent of over 500 journal articles on emotion from 1935 to 1965 have dealt with unpleasant emotions (Lindauer, 1968). Both these surveys exclude material on psychopathology; thus psychologists' preoccupation with the unpleasant is probably underrepresented by the data.

In dramatic contrast is the evidence from literary sources, which clearly indicates a preference for pleasant, positive emotions. A thorough analysis of eighteen standard reference books to collections of plays, fiction, poetry, and quotations showed that almost three quarters of all references to emotions (7,303 out of 10,519) were *pleasant* references. This accentuation of the positive has not changed from classical literature to recent times. Of the twelve emotions most frequently referred to in all literary sources, ten are pleasant emotions (Lindauer, 1968). Fear, which accounts for only 4 percent of the literary references to emotion, is one of the most frequent references in psychology.

How do you account for this discrepancy in outlook? Are psychologists telling it like it is while literary writers are providing an escape into what life could never be like? Or are psychologists overly concerned with "problems," and with behavior that needs to be modified and improved? Do they perhaps just take for granted the more prevalent, pleasant, positive side of life? Or is there a more satisfactory explanation?

---

and his organization of a social structure, man has become the master of his planet. His conquest over the creatures and the physical matter of the earth is being extended to life beneath the oceans as well as to outer space.

But each of man's unique attributes, developed and refined because it helped him survive the demands of a hostile environment through giving him better prediction and control, can also become a cancerous attribute. Thus it may be that the psychological and social ills of man (and his closest animal relatives) are in direct proportion to the level of development of his specialized capacities, skills, and functions. Man's inhumanity to other men and to himself, as well as his destruction of his own environment, become possible precisely because of the existence of his highly developed, differentiated intellectual faculties. Such an analysis, then, focuses on the paradox that inherent in the potential for perfectibility of man are the seeds of perversion and breakdown.

For example, man's remarkable memory enables him to profit from his mistakes, to master complex feats of learning, to establish continuities within his life, and to distinguish the novel events in the environment from those experienced previously. On the other hand, possession of this same gift turns man's mind into a storehouse filled with traumatic events, unresolved conflicts, and petty grudges, as well as constraining his present behavior and limiting its spontaneity through commitments, promises, and obligations. A partial catalog of human traits and attributes and their possible positive and negative consequences is given in the Ψ Close-up on page 511. You are invited to extend the list by either adding other traits that share this double nature, or elaborating upon the positive or negative aspects of those listed.

In this chapter and the next, our attention will be directed toward some of the psychological processes that are occurring when man "goes wrong." It is only by focusing in depth upon these aspects of perversion of human potentiality that we may understand the psychological principles involved and begin to establish new priorities in scientific research, in order to make psychology more relevant to improving life.

"The task is clear. The task is huge. The time is horribly short. In the past, we have had science for intellectual

Ψ *Close-up*   *Ways Man Can Go Wrong*

Attribute	Enables Him to	But Can Also Lead Him to
Memory	Profit from past mistakes Develop and use complex concepts Relate past, present, future Distinguish novel events from previously experienced ones	Carry grudges, suffer from former conflicts and past traumatic events Lose spontaneity of behavior because of commitments and obligations Feel excessive remorse or sense of loss
Time sense	Develop a history Relate present behavior to the future Distinguish between transience and permanence	Fear change Dread an unknown future Experience disappointments from unfulfilled expectations
Ability to associate elements and infer unseen events	Create, imagine events not experienced Generalize from partial data Construct theories, hypotheses	Form negative, crippling associations Misperceive himself or others, infer nonexistent attitudes or events
Perception of choice	Not be stimulus bound, be independent See himself as a responsible agent Hope, build for future	Experience conflicts, indecision Suffer from inability to act
Responsibility, self-evaluation	Take pride in accomplishments Delay gratification, undertake difficult or unpopular tasks Be concerned about effects of his actions on others	Feel inadequate Feel guilt for not living up to standards or for letting someone down Feel constrained by obligations
Competence motivation	Do work well, set high standards Gain benefits of hard work Advance technologically, use resources to meet his needs	Fear failure, suffer feelings of inadequacy Be anxious about tests of his ability Work for self-aggrandizement
Concept of justice	Protect individual rights Set up rules binding on all Value equality of opportunity	Sacrifice individual to group Torture, imprison, execute dissenters Impose his own solutions on others
Ability to use language and other symbols	Communicate with others, present and absent, for information, comfort, pleasure, planning, social control	Circulate and be prey to rumors and falsehoods; conceal true feelings Use word magic to inflict harm Mistake the symbol for the reality
Susceptibility to social influence	Follow group standards Learn and transmit values Cooperate; establish community	Overconform, sacrifice integrity Reject innovation in himself or others
Love	Experience tender emotions Nurture growth and independence of others Support, encourage, comfort others	Become jealous, vengeful Possessively limit another person's freedom Disregard his own needs

pleasure, and science for the control of Nature. We have had science for war. But today, the whole human experiment may hang on the question of how fast we now press the development of science for survival." (Platt, 1969)

Why Are People Aggressive?

The world we live in is often a violent one. The daily news accounts of murders, muggings, riots, suicides, and wars are ample evidence of the extent to which men can inflict injury on others and on themselves. What is the source of such "abnormal" behavior and how can it be understood? Can it be controlled?

Psychologists concerned with these questions have focused on the study of *aggression*, which can be defined as physical or verbal behavior with the intent to injure or destroy. Research evidence on aggression has been drawn from a wide variety of sources, including physiological studies, clinical observations, and studies of aggressive interactions in both the laboratory and the "real world." In addition, the behavior of animal species has received a great deal of attention in the hope that it will aid our understanding of aggression in humans.

For centuries men have argued the question of whether aggression is an innate characteristic to which every man is heir or a product of living in a corrupting society. As we review several of the theories that have been proposed to account for aggressiveness, we shall find that there is good evidence for both innate and environmental influences. The problem is to determine the extent to which each of these factors brings about, maintains, and directs aggressive behavior.

Aggression As Inborn

In his famous essay, "Leviathan," Thomas Hobbes argued that man is naturally selfish, brutal, and cruel toward other people. He expressed this concept by the phrase *Homo homini lupus*—"Man is [like] a wolf to [his fellow] man." Although the wolf is unjustly maligned by this phrase (wolves are actually quite peaceful and gentle with others of their own species), Hobbes' phrase expresses the fairly common belief that man is an instinctively aggressive animal.

Ψ *Close-up*   *Catharsis As a Healer*

The discharge of strongly felt emotions through tears has been traditionally seen as having healing effects, while the "bottling up" of such feelings has been seen as a cause of inner torment and self-destruction (Sadoff, 1966).

And with tears of blood he cleansed the hand,
  The hand that held the steel:
For only blood can wipe out blood,
  And only tears can heal . . .

Oscar Wilde
The Ballad of Reading Gaol

Home they brought her warrior dead,
She nor swooned nor uttered cry,
All her maidens watching said,
"She must weep or she will die";

Alfred, Lord Tennyson
The Princess

Psychic energy: Thanatos and the concept of catharsis. One of the first psychologists to elaborate on this belief and develop it into a theory was Sigmund Freud. As we saw in Chapter 11, he believed that from the moment of birth man possesses two opposing instincts: a life instinct (Eros), which causes the person to grow and survive, and a death instinct (Thanatos), which works toward the individual's self-destruction. He believed that the death instinct is often redirected outwards against the external world in the form of aggression toward others.

According to Freud, energy for the death instinct is constantly being generated within the body until an internal drive state builds up and eventually goads the person into action. If the energy cannot be released in small amounts and in socially acceptable ways, it will accumulate and eventually be released in an extreme and socially unacceptable form. Thus a highly aggressive or violent person can be assumed to be someone who: (a) generates a great deal of aggressive energy and (b) is unable to discharge that energy in small amounts.

Freud visualized this energy as being like water accumulating in a reservoir until finally it spilled over in some aggressive act. It could be drained off in various "safe" ways, however, including *catharsis* (a Greek word meaning a purification or cleansing), in which the emotions were expressed in their full intensity through crying or words or other symbolic means. Aristotle first used the concept of catharsis to explain the way in which good drama first built up and then purged feelings of intense emotion in the audience. (Ψ Close-up, p. 512.)

Some experimental support for the catharsis hypothesis of aggression is found in a study which measured aggressiveness in children at the age of five and then again at the age of twelve.

Of the children who had been highly aggressive at age five (who thus presumably had had much aggressive energy), some were still very aggressive at age twelve (as indicated by high scores on a scale of antisocial aggression). However, the rest of them now had very low scores on antisocial aggression.

The notion of psychic energy—and hence of the value of catharsis—would receive support if it could be demonstrated that these "high-switched-to-low" aggressors were in fact only expressing their aggression in a different way. Therefore, it was predicted that on other measures of aggression these "low" aggressors would score higher than "high" aggressors. This is what was found.

As shown in the graph, boys who were low in antisocial aggression did show more prosocial aggression (aggression for socially acceptable purposes, such as law enforcement or punishment for rule-breaking) and more *self-aggression* than did boys who were still highly antisocial aggressors. ▲ Furthermore, these "low" aggressors were more anxious and fearful of antisocial aggression than the "high" aggressors (Sears, 1961).

A study by Megargee (1966) also provides some support for the Freudian "psychic energy" theory of aggression and catharsis.

Megargee hypothesized that extremely aggressive acts would be carried out by individuals who usually exercise too much control and are unable to release aggressive energy in small amounts. Their instigation to aggress would accumulate over time, and when aggression finally did emerge, it would burst forth in extreme form.

To test this notion, Megargee compared boys who had been detained by the juvenile court for moderately assaultive crimes, such as battery and gang fights, with boys detained for extremely assaultive crimes, such as murder, brutal beatings, and assault with a deadly weapon. He found that the extreme aggressors were indeed overcontrolled, oversocialized individuals, as compared with both the moderate aggressors and a comparison group of average high-school graduates. They had very good conduct records in both school and prison, and were rated by others as being very friendly, cooperative, and docile people. During detention, they showed less verbal and physical aggression than all other groups of juvenile delinquents. In addition, on psychological tests, they scored very high on self-control. Typically, their deadly aggressive behavior had been triggered by a seemingly trivial frustration or minor setback.

In spite of some supporting evidence, however, Freud's theory has been criticized by psychologists for failing to specify any factors which could be used

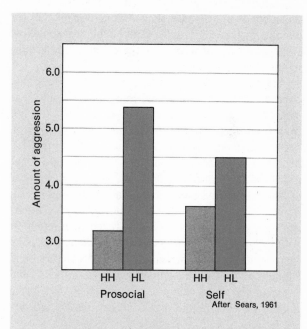

After Sears, 1961

▲ **INCREASE IN PROSOCIAL AGGRESSION AND SELF-AGGRESSION**

The graph shows the amount of prosocial and self-aggression exhibited by a group of boys who were high on aggression at the age of five and high on antisocial aggression at the age of twelve (HH) and a group who were high at the age of five but low at the age of twelve (HL).

to predict the occurrence of aggression or the direction or form it will take. It has a lovely literary, after-the-fact, descriptive quality but little scientific utility. Indeed, in his later writings Freud himself abandoned reliance upon this death instinct, but many others (such as Rollo May) have continued to incorporate it into their conception of human nature.

The "aggressive instinct."   Another theory stressing the innateness of aggression is that of Konrad Lorenz, the well-known ethologist mentioned in Chapter 12. In *On Aggression* (1966), Lorenz makes inferences about the dynamics of human aggression based on his studies of animals. He argues that aggression is a spontaneous, innate readiness to fight, which is critical for an organism's survival. In other species, however, aggressiveness between members of the same species rarely involves actual injury or death because one animal signals appeasement or submission: a defeated wolf will bare its throat to the victor, for example. According to Lorenz, man has somehow lost this means of inhibiting aggression while retaining the instinct to aggress.

Although Lorenz makes a strong case for the parallels between animal and human aggression, it is clear that there are basic differences (besides the use of appeasement gestures) between the two. First, because of man's memory and evaluative abilities, his actions are often a response to memories and ideas rather than to the immediate situation; second, because of his tool-making capacities and ability to plan ahead, he can carry out virtually unlimited injury by intention and plan and even without personal interaction with his victims. Furthermore, it is difficult to predict the conditions under which displays of weakness and submission will elicit sympathy and "fair play" and those under which they will simply elicit even more intense violence on the part of the aggressive individual or group.

During a police-student confrontation at the University of California at Berkeley, a student was being hit as he was dragged downstairs out of an occupied building. In a letter of protest, clerks in the Admissions Office allege that he screamed, "Please don't hit me any more! Won't someone help me?" According to the account, *the more he begged, the more they hit.* (*San Francisco Chronicle*, Feb. 29, 1969).

Again we see how man's unique talents and superior abilities can be perverted to make him the most dangerous and destructive of any species.

Physiological bases of aggression.   The picture that emerges from research into possible physiological bases of aggression is one of complexity, rather than of any simple relationship between physical aggression and biology. For example, Moyer (1968) argues that in animals different types of aggression (fear-induced, territorial, irritable) have their own distinct neural and endocrine patterns.

The role of the brain.   Two regions of the brain are known to be involved in aggressive behavior. The *hypothalamus* has long been known to be important in the expression of rage reactions in animals, and more recently other parts of the *limbic system* (particularly the amygdala) have also been implicated in rage and threatening behavior. As you will recall from Chapter 3, changes in aggressive behavior and leadership in a monkey colony were brought about by lesions of the amygdala, and instructions radioed to this area of the brain of a charging bull stopped his charge. Ongoing research is refining our knowledge in this field.

Some types of aggressive behavior in humans are clearly related to brain disorders. For example, brain disease of the limbic system or temporal lobe has sometimes been found in persons exhibiting a *dyscontrol syndrome* which is characterized by senseless brutality, pathological intoxication, sexual assault, or repeated serious automobile accidents (Mark & Ervin, 1970). Tumors located in different parts of the hypothalamus can either increase or reduce aggressive behavior.

The role of hormones.   The action of sex hormones before and immediately after birth has long been known to influence later sexual behavior. There is some evidence that these hormones also affect aggression. In both humans and animals, males are characteristically more aggressive than females—a fact which is apparently due in part to the early influence of sex hormones on the brain.

The role of genes.   What part do specific genes play in the expression of aggressive behavior? While it is a fairly well-known fact that animals such as bulls and cocks can be selectively bred for their fighting and killing abilities (Scott, 1958), the evidence is less clear that this holds true for human beings. The folk notion of "bad genes" or "bad blood" was supported by the studies of the Jukes and the Kallikaks but, as we saw in Chapter 4, these reports were biased and untrustworthy.

There has been some renewed interest in this problem because of recent reports linking violent criminal behavior with an abnormal chromosomal constitution called the XYY (or "supermale") syndrome. In this syndrome, the male has an extra Y chromosome due to some aberration in the formation of his father's sperm. The XYY men who have been studied by scientists generally come from a prison population. In general, they are taller than average, have a somewhat lower IQ, and are prone to extremely aggressive, violent behavior (Montagu, 1969).

Although these findings are intriguing, they should be viewed with caution. We do not yet know how representative prison XYYs are of the whole class of men who have this aberration, nor do we know how its influence operates or how important it is in relation to other influences.

Aggression As the Result of Experience

Another answer to the "why" of aggression is that it is socially learned. According to this approach, a man's aggressive behavior is due not to some instinct or built-in mechanism, but to the norms, rewards, punishments, models, and situations he has experienced in his lifetime. This approach to the problem of aggression has spawned several theories, each of which emphasizes particular environmental factors.

Aggression as a response to frustration. Almost twenty years after Freud proposed the existence of a death instinct, a group of academic psychologists formally presented an alternative theory of aggression (Dollard, Doob, Miller, Mowrer, & Sears, 1939). Aggression, they said, was man's natural response to frustration. *Frustration* was defined as the condition that exists when a goal-response suffers interference. It was seen as a function of three factors: (a) the strength of the motivation toward the goal-response;

(b) the degree of interference with it; and (c) the number of goal-response sequences interfered with. The greater the amount of frustration, the stronger the aggressive response.

Originally this group argued that every act of aggression was preceded by a frustration and that every frustration resulted in an immediate act of aggression. However, it soon became obvious that this is not always the case in real life. Aggression can occur for reasons other than frustration (to demonstrate power, for example), and frustration sometimes produces other behaviors. For these reasons, the original frustration-aggression hypothesis was revised to state that every frustration produces an *instigation* to aggression, but that this instigation may be too weak to elicit actual aggressive behavior (N. Miller, 1941). They agreed with Freud that the aggressive drive would increase if not expressed (if frustration continued) but saw the origin of aggressive behavior in *external* factors (accumulated experienced frustrations), rather than in *internal* factors (aggressive "instinct").

By postulating an aggressive drive which built up over time and which was reduced by aggressive actions, these psychologists committed themselves to a notion of catharsis that was very similar to Freud's. Numerous experiments designed to test this version of catharsis involved presenting a frustrating experience and various means of expressing aggression. In general, the results were consistent with the predictions: if aggressive impulses, once aroused, were not expressed immediately, they usually were expressed at some later time and in another form. But does this necessarily confirm the hypothesis that it was the same "aggressive drive" just expressed in a different way? Can you think of another hypothesis that could predict the same findings?

Displacement of aggression. When frustration occurs, the first and strongest aggressive impulse is toward the source of the frustration. Thus, if a child sees a piece of candy, but is prevented by his mother from eating it, he is most strongly motivated to be aggressive toward her. However, he may be inhibited from doing so by the threat of punishment. According to the frustration-aggression theory, he will then *displace* his aggression onto some target other than

the original source of his frustration. This tendency to vent one's hostile feelings on a "safe" target is illustrated by the example of a man who is berated by his boss and who then goes home and yells at his wife, who spanks their child, who kicks the dog, who bites the baby, who breaks a doll. According to the theory, the less similar the target is to the source of frustration, the weaker is the displaced aggression and the less complete the cathartic effect.

Destructive violence and "problem" behavior can sometimes be traced to a displacement of aggression.

Scott (1965) cites the case of a boy who was expelled from *kindergarten* for attacking his classmates and teacher for no apparent reason. Investigation showed that the boy rode the bus to school with his older brothers, who teased him constantly. By the time he arrived at school he would be so enraged that he would attack the nearest person to him.

Animals too have been observed to displace their aggressive behavior, as shown by this account of two apes:

". . . A very strong feeling, such as anger, tends, when checked from expending itself on the object that aroused it, to turn and expend itself upon an entirely different object. When Sultan was quite young, and I punished him, he, not daring to avenge himself upon me, would run in a fury at Chica, whom he could not abide anyhow, and persecute her, although she had absolutely nothing to do with the cause of his rage." (Kohler, 1926, p. 289)

The frustration-aggression theory of prejudice also predicts that when a powerful frustrator is feared or impossible to retaliate against, aggression may be displaced onto a *scapegoat*. Presumably, minorities and members of out-groups are favorite targets of displaced aggression because they are identifiably different from members of the in-group (against whom aggression must not be vented) and because they are already in vulnerable positions so that they are not likely to retaliate.

If the Tiber overflows into the city,
If the Nile does not flow into the countryside,
If the heavens remain unmoved,
If the earth quakes,
If there is famine and pestilence,
At once the cry goes up:
'To the lions with the Christians.'

Tertullian, Roman Historian

When anything went wrong in Rome, it would seem that the Christians were thrown to the lions. In more recent times, when the price of cotton fell in the south around the turn of the century, the number of lynchings rose sharply. And during World War II the Jews, blamed for all Germany's woes, were being annihilated as fast as they could be herded into the gas chambers. Do you see any contemporary parallels?

The role of releasers in the environment. Recently, the frustration-aggression hypothesis has been revised to stress the importance of both frustration and environment cues. According to Berkowitz (1965), the probability that a person will aggress is a joint function of his *internal readiness* to aggress and the availability of *external cues* which elicit his aggression and provide a target. ◆ The internal and external forces operate in an additive manner. If one is weak, the other must be strong for aggression to be elicited. A habitually aggressive person has a strong "readiness" and needs only mild outside provocation, but even a mild-mannered individual may become aggres-

sive if he is subjected to strong repeated frustration and potent provocation cues.

The important role of appropriate *releasers* (disliked objects or objects already associated with aggression) was demonstrated in the following study.

Subjects were seated before a table on which lay either weapons (such as a gun) or assorted neutral objects. The subjects who were in the presence of the weapons responded more violently to insults than did those who saw only neutral objects, even though, of course, no use was made of the weapons. Thus, it appears that the mere presence of such external aggressive cues as a gun can heighten the probability of aggressive behavior (Berkowitz & LePage, 1967).

The concept of external releasers has been used as a further explanation of why minority groups are consistently chosen as targets for aggression and prejudice. Because these groups have been attacked before, they have become associated with hostility and violence and thus become elicitors or releasers of further aggression toward themselves. In other words, they become associated with violence because they have *received* aggression in the past.

To demonstrate how this vicious cycle might operate, the following experiment was performed. Subjects saw a film of a prize fight in which a man named Kelly was badly beaten by a man named Dunne. Later on, supposedly in another experiment, the same subjects had a chance to give an electric shock to a person whose name was given variously as either Bob Kelly, Bob Dunne, or Bob Riley. The experimenters then recorded the number of shocks given to this same person under each of his different names.

Sure enough: he received significantly more shocks when he was named *Kelly* than when he had either of the other two names. His cue value for the subjects thus seemed to vary as a function of his association with the previously observed *victim* in the film (Green & Berkowitz, 1966).

Aggression as socially learned. In earlier chapters you were introduced to social learning theory, which explains the development of social behavior by the basic principles of learning. In explaining aggression, this theory goes beyond the emphasis on external releasers to a focus on ways in which the environment actually controls behavior (Bandura & Walters, 1963).

According to social learning theory, aggression is no different from any other kind of learned response. Aggressive behavior is learned through observation, shaping, or a combination of the two. The more it has been reinforced in the past, whether intentionally

Adapted from Berkowitz, 1965

◆ **FACTORS THAT CONTRIBUTE TO AGGRESSION**
Aggression requires both a "get set" state and a "go" cue.

[Figure: internal readiness + external releaser or eliciting cues → aggression; internal readiness fed by "strength of aggressive habits" and "frustration or anger"; external releaser fed by "disliked objects," "objects similar to or paired with above," and "objects previously paired with aggression"] or unintentionally, the more likely it is to occur. Social learning theory does not postulate any underlying aggressive drive, nor does it propose any special relationship between frustration and aggression. A person may learn to respond aggressively to any set of stimuli, including frustrating ones, but frustration is not a necessary condition for aggression.

Models for aggression. As mentioned briefly in Chapter 11, Bandura and his associates have demonstrated the learning of aggressive acts performed by an observed model.

Nursery-school children were exposed to one of several conditions: a real-life aggressive model, a model acting aggressively on film, an aggressive cartoon character, or no model at all. Soon after this experience, all the children were mildly frustrated. The experimenters then measured the amount of imitative and nonimitative aggression that the children displayed in the absence of the model.

As can be seen from these photographs, the model's punching, hammering, and throwing an inflated doll (top row) were all faithfully imitated by the young subjects, two of whom are shown here.

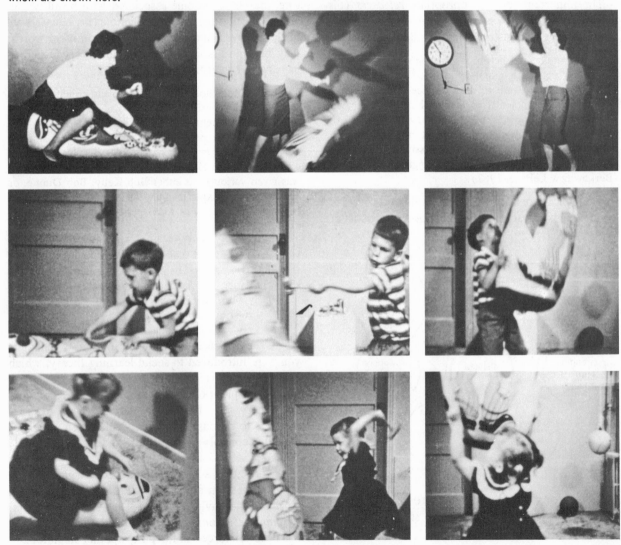

The frustrated children who had observed the aggressive models exhibited many imitative aggressive responses, while the frustrated children who had not observed a model were barely aggressive at all. Furthermore, the children who saw the filmed model were just as aggressive as those who saw the real-life model. The extent to which children imitated the model's aggressive responses is shown in the photographs (Bandura, Ross, & Ross, 1963). ▪

Any learning theory approach stresses the importance of the *consequences* of behavior as central in determining whether the behavior will increase or decrease in frequency. But neither the behavior nor the consequences need be in the learner's personal experience: he can learn their relationship through observation of what happens to another person performing the behavior. (Ψ Close-up, right.)

Suppose the children saw a model being punished for his aggressive behavior; would they then be less likely to imitate aggression?

Children were shown a film in which a model demonstrated four novel aggressive responses. One group saw a version in which the aggressive behavior was rewarded; another saw a version in which the model was punished; for a third group there were no consequences for the model. Children tested after viewing the film displayed fewer imitative aggressive acts when they had seen the model punished (Bandura, 1965).

But did the observation affect their *learning* of aggression or only the *performance* of aggressive behavior? Could it be shown that all the children had learned how to aggress as the model had done, but that the observed consequences either inhibited or fostered the actual performance of the aggressive behavior?

After the experiment proper was supposedly over, the experimenter offered each child a prize if the child could do just what the model had done. Given this positive incentive, all children readily performed the aggressive responses in imitation of the filmed model. The differences in aggression between the experimental conditions were thus erased. Evidently, the knowledge was there, but executing the aggressive act was held in check by the additional knowledge that such acts were inappropriate in this situation. Changing the payoff for aggression quickly disinhibited any controls over expressing aggression (Bandura, 1965). ● (p. 520)

Ψ Close-up Violence on Television During an Average Week

Over 600 acts of violence were televised (*not* including documentary and news programs).

Of every 10 plays, 8 contained some violence.

Of the cartoons, 95 percent contained violence.

Of the comedy shows, 67 percent contained violence.

Over one half of the major characters in a TV play inflicted violence on someone.

Of every 10 leading characters, 1 killed another person.

Of every 20 leading characters, 1 was killed.

In only 8 percent of the episodes did witnesses to the violence try to prevent it.

More foreigners and nonwhites (proportionately) died than did white people.

In 80 percent of the cases of extreme violence, due process of law was neither shown nor implied.

Of the "lawmen" 40 percent *initiated* violence, while 70 percent contributed to it.

In only 1 out of every 10 cases did "lawmen" respond to violence in a nonviolent manner.

(U.S. National Commission on the
Causes and Prevention of Violence, 1970)

Do as I say, not as I do. A number of experiments have shown that some models are more effective than others in producing imitation. The most effective models are nurturant, high-status adults who have control over the rewarding resources. The people most affected by models are those who are dependent and moderately aroused and who have been previously rewarded for displaying imitative responses (Bandura, 1969a).

If, for some reason, you *wanted* to get a person to become very aggressive, what would be your ideal learning situation? How could you "program" an aggressive person? First you would certainly want an adult model, and, since children are dependent on

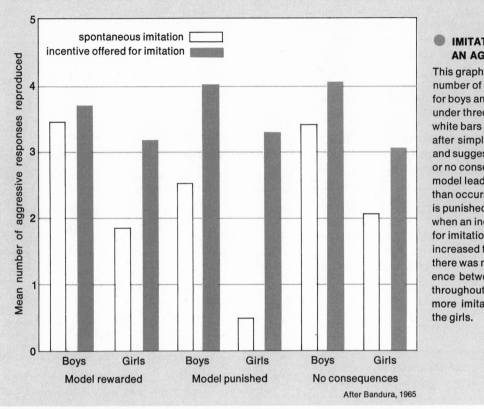

● **IMITATION OF AN AGGRESSIVE MODEL**

This graph shows the average number of imitative responses for boys and girls observing under three conditions; the white bars show their imitation after simply watching the model and suggest that either reward or no consequences for the model lead to more imitation than occurs when the model is punished. On the other hand, when an incentive was offered for imitation, all three groups increased their imitation and there was no appreciable difference between them except that throughout, the boys showed more imitative responses than the girls.

After Bandura, 1965

adults, it would be good to have the learner be a child. You would want to make sure that the aggressive adult would be noticed by the child and that the child would be emotionally aroused. Both of these conditions are satisfied by having the adult punish the child—a child is certain to notice aggression if he is the target of it, and he is usually upset, fearful, and angry when being punished. The adult model, in turn, should be nurturant and should have rewarded imitation in the past. Thus parents would be an ideal choice since they have taken care of the child for a long time and have often rewarded imitation of their attitudes, behaviors, and beliefs. Also parents control most of the available rewards (privileges, praise, affection, candy, and so on) and thus are quite powerful.

Finally, to make the situation truly "ideal," the parents too should be rewarded for their aggressive behavior by achieving *their* immediate goal—being

obeyed. All in all, it would be hard to program an environment more conducive to the learning of aggression than that provided in the home of Mr. and Mrs. Average Punishing Parent.

Obviously, if a parent always punishes a child for behaving aggressively when the aggression is discovered, the child will soon learn to inhibit aggression in the presence of the parent. However, from Bandura's research we would expect that the imitative aggressive response would be powerfully learned and simply would be withheld in the presence of the parent and performed in other situations—and it is. Mothers who punished aggression in the home were found to have children who behaved more aggressively in nursery school (Sears, Maccoby, & Levin, 1957). A study of overly aggressive adolescent boys showed that their fathers severely punished aggression in the home and that, consequently, few of the boys exhibited aggressive behavior there. In fact, many of the parents were surprised to learn that their "good boys" were highly aggressive in school (Bandura & Walters, 1959).

Parodoxically, then, a parent who physically punishes a child for aggression is modeling and fostering the very behavior he is trying to eliminate. ■

Expression of strong feelings: catharsis or goad? Because social learning theory does not postulate any aggressive drive or instinct, it rejects the concept of catharsis—that the expression of aggressive feelings will lessen aggressive actions. In fact, it predicts just the opposite result: that expressing aggressive impulses or watching aggressiveness in others will produce an *increase* in the probability of future aggression. This hypothesis is supported by studies such as the ones cited earlier, which show that aggression increases after exposure to aggressive models. In addition, studies have demonstrated that the expression of aggressive behavior in a permissive setting maintains the behavior at its original level, rather than reducing it.

Subjects were exposed to an anger-arousing antagonist; then half of them were allowed to express their anger and hostility to a sympathetic interviewer. The other subjects did not have such an interview but merely sat for a while. Subjects who experienced the cathartic interview disliked the antagonist more (rather than less) and remained more physiologically aroused than the control subjects (Kahn, 1966).

In another study, children were given an opportunity for either physical or verbal aggression toward a child who had frustrated them. Neither activity reduced their aggressive feelings (Mallick & McCandless, 1966).

The results of these studies would suggest that therapy procedures which encourage the person to give vent to aggressive feelings may have an effect opposite to that intended.

So what are you to believe? Does expressing strong emotion increase or lessen the emotions expressed? Different studies have used different experimental paradigms, so that it is often impossible to compare their results directly. Another problem is that the various studies have not ruled out alternative explanations. For example, when there is a reduction in overt aggressive behavior following the expression of aggressive feelings, it could be because of guilt-generated inhibition over having been aggressive instead of from the cathartic effect of "getting it all off one's chest." Until research demonstrates that reduction in aggressiveness following catharsis is not accompanied by undesirable side effects, we cannot be sure that catharsis really lessens emotional intensity or that it is a valid method of therapy. It may be that a distinction will need to be made between cathartic expression of anxiety and general emotional states (perhaps good) and release of actual aggressive behavior (evidently risky).

Does the Victim Ever Cause the Aggression?

As a child and its mother start to cross the street, the child runs forward just as a car suddenly swerves around the corner. For a moment the child appears certain to be hit, but the tragedy is averted as the car veers off and speeds away. The mother, virtually frozen by this unexpected threat to her child's life, grabs the child. To love and comfort her frightened baby? Sometimes, but often to scream at and slap the bad child.

This aggressive response is typically justified as

■ **"THIS WILL TEACH YOU TO HIT YOUR SISTER!"**

"teaching the child a lesson," but it is more likely to be an emotional release for the mother's feelings of fright and helplessness. It is precisely because the mother is concerned for the child's welfare that such threats to his life make her feel inadequate to protect and control her child's fate. Her strong emotional reactions are blamed on the child: "You scared the wits out of me!" "What would I have done if you had gotten yourself killed?"

In more cases than is generally realized the relationship between aggressor and victim is a personal one. The individuals are part of a dyadic interaction (see Chapter 12) in which a complex of feelings, expectations, and power plays already operates. Although there are of course many cases where an unknown person is attacked, crime statistics do not support the common view of a stranger who attacks a passive, unsuspecting victim in the dark with intent to injure. In more than 75 percent of all cases, murderers and their victims are relatives, friends, or acquaintances. Two thirds of all rape victims report knowing their attacker personally, while most victims of felonious assault have had some prior association with their assailant.

The National Commission on the Causes and Prevention of Violence reports that street "muggings" by strangers are committed primarily by narcotics addicts desperate for money to get an illegal "fix." In the face of the legal prohibitions, their violence is caused by their physiological addiction and their economic plight rather than by a desire to harm, destroy, or be aggressive.

A recent ten-week survey by the New York Police Department of three neighborhoods typical of urban society provides some interesting facts which are contrary to accepted fallacies:

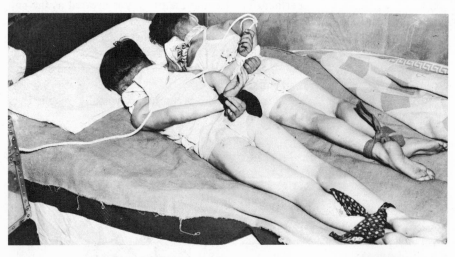

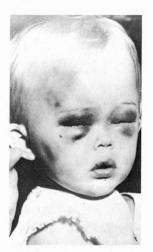

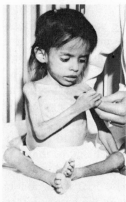

◆ As these photographs show only too well, battered children may be beaten, starved, or hog-tied by their parents or may even lose a hand or arm. According to the boys in the photo above, who were found in this condition by a neighbor after their parents had gone out for the evening, they had been tied up "so that they wouldn't get into the peanut butter." The fifteen-month-old child with the blackened eyes arrived at the hospital in this condition. The emaciated five-year-old weighed 13 pounds and had never walked. The father who had amputated his little girl's right hand at first claimed it had been "an accident."

As a group, such parents are insecure people who never knew love as children and who feel that a child's misbehavior shows their failure as parents. They see their assaults not as cruelty but as needed punishment.

About 90 percent of all murder, rape, and assault victims are attacked by persons of the *same* race. Chief murder victims are the poor, the black, the unemployed, the alienated, the alcoholic, and the addicted. A poor person making less than $3,000 a year is five times more likely to be robbed than a more well-to-do citizen earning $10,000 yearly (*San Francisco Chronicle*, Feb. 22, 1970).

In some cases it is clear that the victim openly taunts, provokes, challenges, or teases the aggressor into action, while often more subtle, "unconscious" gestures, postures, suggestions, or dress may trigger attacks. In fact, therapists report that some rape victims suffer from guilt later over their possible complicity in the rape episode.

According to FBI statistics, the risk of being a victim of crime has *increased by 120 percent* in the past decade. Even if we are cautious about the validity of this figure, since crime statistics can vary depending upon the definition of a "crime," how efficiently statistics are gathered, and how energetically the laws are enforced, nevertheless, it is still alarming that 324 persons out of every 100,000 in this country were victims of violent crimes in 1969. Reports of such figures typically lead to increased deterrents aimed at potential aggressors and to psychological investigation of aggressive people. There needs to be more research directed toward what the victim does and especially toward the "social contract of violence" which exists between many victims and their aggressors. In the cases where the victim does play an active role, what is it that he does? And what do some potential victims do that successfully inhibits or limits aggression?

The battered child. If you had witnessed the events described in our earlier example of the frightened mother who slapped her child, would *you* have done anything about the mother's aggressive attack? It is unlikely that you would have "interfered," even if the parent had been very abusive to the child. Over 700 children are killed each year in the United States at the hands of their parents and about 40,000 more youngsters are seriously beaten and tortured by their parents, siblings, and relatives. ◆ And it is estimated that perhaps three million adults have known of instances of child abuse but have not intervened

---

Ψ *Close-up*   *Case Study of a Battered Child*

When Gloria was found stealing food from a store and apprehended as a runaway, she was 14 years old and weighed only 50 pounds. Investigation disclosed an unbelievable array of abuses perpetrated against her from birth. She was regularly beaten by her mother, her hair pulled out, her head held under water, her shoulder burned with a hot iron; multiple bone fractures gave evidence of a long history of beatings. She was confined to her room and not allowed to eat with the family, receiving only left-over scraps of food. When she was 3 *weeks* old she had to be hospitalized for malnutrition. At 4 *months*, according to hospital records, she was treated for five multiple bone fractures.

She had run away in part because she was literally starving to death. There was nothing at all unusual about the "neat, clean" home the visiting nurse found during an investigation, nor about the apparently normal relations of the parents with their other children. Gloria's siblings would occasionally sneak food in to her, but this was not "acceptable" behavior. The mother reported that this child was just "different" from all the rest, uncontrollable and incorrigibly bad. There was no evidence to support this perception. It appears rather that the mother disowned the child psychologically five days after her birth, when her mother-in-law claimed that the infant did not look like her son and was not his.

With adequate care in the hospital, Gloria gained 20 pounds in eleven days and her physical health improved steadily. It is unlikely, however, that anything could undo the scars on her memory or erase her picture of the nature of maternal love (Case presented at *Symposium on Children in Peril: The Battered Child*, San Francisco, February 19, 1969).

---

in any way (Helfer & Kempe, 1968). A case of child abuse is described in the Ψ Close-up above.

The reasons for this "community conspiracy of silence" against the battered child are varied but again point up the established social matrix in which aggression and violence occur and in which norms govern behavior. People are not indifferent to child abuse. But they tend to want to believe in a "just world" (Lerner & Simmons, 1966) in which punishment is deserved, fits the crime, and has beneficial effects on the victim. Thus they usually believe that aggression by parents is basically for good ends and that a child victim must have done something to deserve the treatment he is receiving. Such beliefs are reinforcing to the one who holds them because they enable him to structure a rational, orderly social universe.

The policeman and the citizen.   In the ever increasing confrontations between the police and members of the community, the distinction between aggressor and victim often is not sharply drawn. The original victim may emerge the aggressor, and the violent episode itself may be created by the apparent victim.

Two studies of municipal police records indicate the complexity of what is happening when there is a violent encounter between police and citizens.

The most significant finding in one investigation conducted long before the current confrontations was that "at least 37 percent of the [police]men believed that it was legitimate to use violence to coerce respect." The men viewed themselves as an occupational group without sufficient status and esteem for the difficult work they were required to perform. Thus, respect for the police was seen as necessary if the law was to be respected. Examples of this perception and the men's conclusions in regard to how they should behave were given in the following statements:

"Well, a prisoner deserves to be hit when he goes to the point where he tries to put you below him."

"If a fellow called a policeman a filthy name, a slap in the mouth would be a good thing, especially if it was out in the public where calling a policeman a bad name would look bad for the police."

"In the South Side [the slum district] the only way to walk into a tavern is to walk in swaggering as if you own the place and if somebody is standing in your way give him an elbow and push him aside." (Westley, 1953, p. 39)

In an analysis of 344 arrest reports, another investigator concluded that in the cases where violent police-citizen encounters occurred, both parties were reacting to what they perceived as threats against their integrity and self-esteem.

". . . An assault grows out of an interpersonal sequence in which both parties participated to some measure. We assume that each assault is the product of a unique transaction between the assaulter and the victim and that it could not occur in the same way if either party acted differently in his relation to the other." (Toch, 1969, p. 56)

Often the sequence began with what might be an innocuous request by an officer for information or identification or an order to "move on," "break it up." In 60 percent of the episodes studied, the civilian reacted negatively to the officer's approach and failed to cooperate. The officer viewed this uncooperativeness as "irrational," disrespectful, and perhaps concealing criminal activity, whereas the individual perceived the request as unwarranted or discourteous or as an expression of personal hostility against him. A chain of events was then set off in which both parties contributed to the spiraling potential for violence. The sequences leading to violence in the 344 cases studied are shown in the diagram.   ■

It seems clear that violence of this kind can be prevented only if each side feels respected by the other. Action-oriented research on this most urgent problem is necessary if social justice and trust are to be possible.

Must People Be Aggressive?

What are the practical results to be derived from abstract psychological theories and experimental findings about aggression? How far can we go toward controlling aggressiveness and reducing its destructiveness? Under what conditions can aggressiveness become *prosocial* instead of *antisocial*?

Aggression to benefit society.   Whether or not there is an aggressive instinct, we can expect that a certain amount of aggression will always be present in a society. Although we cannot eliminate the presence of hostility, we *can* control the available outlets for it.

If people can learn to vent their hostility in socially approved ways, they will be less likely to engage in more destructive acts of violence. Sometimes the aggressive child is changed from a disrupter to a constructive leader by being given responsibility.

Admitting and expressing minor hostilities may prevent them from getting out of hand. Some people have suggested that participation in contact sports may reduce the aggressive drive.

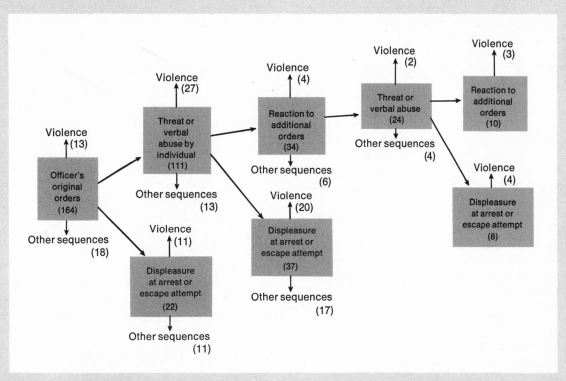

■ **SEQUENCES LEADING TO VIOLENCE**

Usually when violence occurs between police and citizens it is the end result of a chain reaction in which each action increases the mutual tension and belligerence. Toch (1969) has found that in almost half of 562 cases where violence did occur, the citizens were either reacting to what they interpreted as assaults on them (physical or verbal) or were defending others. In the other cases, the violence occurred in an effort to escape or prevent being moved, was an expression of contempt or retaliation, or was an extension of other violence. The diagram shows the sequence of events in one group Toch studied.

When those who are angered by injustice work to achieve greater justice, their effect can be constructive rather than destructive. Sometimes aggressive protest has induced or forced those in power to make changes. Most often, however, violent protest has simply been seen as a threat and as a reason for tightening the controls. At a national level, success in controlling and preventing violence will require awareness of the many economic, sociological, political, and psychological variables that enter into the equation of man + weapon = aggressive encounter.

Teaching and rewarding nonaggression instead of aggression. To the extent that aggression is learned, it can be unlearned or nonaggressiveness can be learned instead. Although much more research so far has centered on the learning of aggression, the lessons that have been learned about the effects of modeling and reinforcement can be applied directly toward the fostering of constructive, cooperative behavior. Several studies have pointed the way.

Fairweather (1964) devised a relearning procedure for aggressive mental patients which could as well be used with aggressive people in other types of institutions. Basically, the procedure relied on group pressure from peers to change a person's behavior. Hyperaggressive people would be put together in one set of rooms and rewarded as a group. For example, the group might be told that if they had no fights all day, they could have steak for dinner.

Since the reward would be forthcoming only if all the group members conformed to the standard, it was expected that pressure would be exerted by the group to make all its members conform. In this manner, hyperaggressive people were taught to employ socially acceptable methods of getting rewards. The rewards provided for prosocial behavior, however, had to be greater than the rewards they were getting by aggression.

In a variation of this approach in a rehabilitation program for predelinquent boys, the effects of staff-imposed versus group-imposed penalties were compared. As shown in the figure, the penalties (fines) administered by the staff were not at all effective in reducing the number of infractions, whereas the fines levied by the group's chosen manager resulted in almost total elimination of this disruptive behavior (Phillips, 1968).   •

In addition to techniques of reward and punishment, nonaggressive, prosocial models have also been used successfully to reduce aggression.

Hyperaggressive children were exposed to a series of short plays in which dolls exhibited an aggressive and a cooperative solution to conflicts that the children normally encountered. The consequences of aggression were depicted as being unpleasant and the consequences of cooperation as being rewarding. When the children's behavior was later observed in the nursery school, it was found that there was a decrease in their aggressive behavior and an increase in their cooperative behavior (Chittenden, 1942).   ◆

It is perhaps not generally realized how reinforcing acting aggressively can come to be. It may originally be triggered by the current stimulus conditions without any particular aggressive motivation and then be maintained by the feedback from the behavior itself. An Army sergeant discussing his experiences as an interrogator of enemy prisoners said, "First you strike to get mad, then you strike because you are mad, and in the end you strike because of the sheer pleasure of it." (*Toronto Star*, Nov. 24, 1967).

Aggression, once learned, may be very difficult to extinguish because of this and other sources of reinforcement. Social learning theorists thus stress prevention as the most hopeful means of control.

Surrender of Responsibility: The Paradox of Freedom

The Protestant Reformation provided a psychological preparation for the role men were to play under the modern industrial system. It did so in part through its

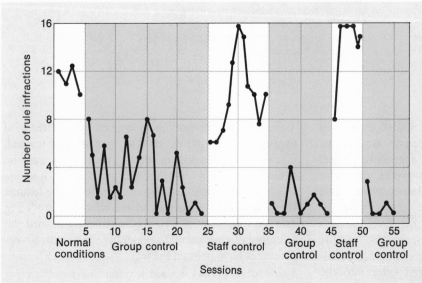

● **CONTROL OF AGGRESSION THROUGH GROUP CENSURE**

When rules were enforced through fines administered by the staff, the number of infractions was consistently higher than when they were enforced by the member of the group chosen by them to be manager.

Adapted from Phillips, 1968

doctrine of the individualistic relationship of man to God. Traditionally, the restraints upon man's personal freedom had been imposed by tribal ritual and external rules and commandments. The transition to a belief that controls should come from within enabled man to question ideas and commands instead of simply accepting them and thus to become more independent and self-reliant. It made it possible for him to achieve, compete, conquer, and chart his own destiny. But this potential for greater inner control was accompanied by feelings of isolation from others, anxiety about the limits of individual power and responsibility, and fear of the consequences of losing the predictability provided by clearly structured external control.

Thus for some individuals, freedom was (and is) a more frightening prospect than socially imposed controls. Surrendering this freedom, with all its emphasis on personal responsibility for planning, deciding, and acting, has been one mechanism for reducing feelings of anxiety and isolation. In the act of surrender, the individual has made a bargain that has appeared to be a reasonably good one: by submitting himself to figures that represented strength and unquestioned authority, he has gained a new sense of belonging and power. This "escape from freedom" has been related to the rise of Nazism in Germany, with its insistence on all power to the State (Fromm, 1941). Unfortunately, the price of forming a strong identification with an external power is an inadequate identity of one's own—an inability to find and be oneself.

Hobbled by Rigidity: The Authoritarian Personality

Because of the devastation wrought by Hitler's fascism in World War II and the threat it posed to democratic society, social scientists have been concerned about the psychological processes that made it both possible and effective. We saw in Chapter 12 that Kurt Lewin and his co-workers pitted authoritarian and democratic leadership against each other to compare their results. Researchers at the University of California's Berkeley campus set out to see if there was a cluster of political attitudes, social and economic values, and personality traits that was charac-

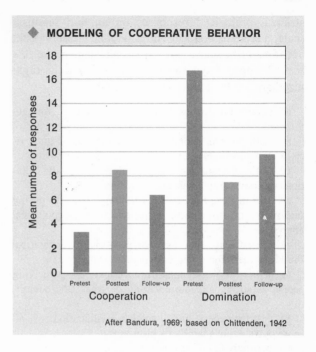

MODELING OF COOPERATIVE BEHAVIOR

After Bandura, 1969; based on Chittenden, 1942

teristic of an "antidemocratic personality" (Adorno, Frenkel-Brunswick, Levinson, & Sanford, 1950). Was it possible to identify the potential fascist, whose personality structure would render him particularly susceptible to antidemocratic propaganda?

These researchers began by constructing a scale designed to measure *ethnocentrism*—the tendency to hold prejudiced attitudes toward all groups different from one's own. High scorers on this scale show a general tendency to see the world in terms of noble in-groups which must be supported and offensive out-groups which must be avoided or rejected and attacked when they become threatening. This scale was administered to a large sample of subjects and the very low and very high scoring (the extremely tolerant and the extremely intolerant) subjects were singled out for systematic study. Then the search began for character structures consistently associated with these opposite types. In this pioneering effort, the advances of attitude scaling and sampling methods were combined with clinical interviews, projective tests, and some elements of psychoanalytic theory.

Those high in intolerance on the ethnocentrism scale were found also to give consistently rigid, constricted, prejudiced responses on an anti-Semitism scale, a scale of political and economic conservatism, and a fascism scale. The latter, nicknamed the *"F-scale,"* tapped a syndrome of personality traits organized around the following characteristics:

a) conventionalism—obedience and respect for authority;

b) authoritarian submission—idealization of authority, with an inability to question or criticize authority;

c) authoritarian aggression—rejection of all violations of conventional values;

d) anti-intraceptionism—resentment against prying into motives, resistance to introspection or psychological analysis.

e) superstition and stereotypes—rigid categorical thinking, need for order and regular routine;

f) power and toughness preoccupation—perceiving people as strong and domineering or weak and submitting;

g) destructiveness and cynicism—vilification of all those outside one's family or in-group;

h) projectivity—disposition to see evil forces at work in a hostile environment full of threatening people;

i) excessive sexual concern—an exaggerated condemnation (and ambivalence) regarding expression of sexuality and sexual freedom.

High scores on these four scales identified an *authoritarian personality,* described by one writer as:

". . . the basically weak and dependent individual who has sacrificed his capacity for genuine experience of self and others in order to maintain a precarious order and safety. In the type case, he confronts with a façade of spurious strength a world in which rigidly stereotyped categories are substituted for the affectionate and individualized experience of which he is incapable. Such a person, estranged from inner values, lacks self-awareness and shuns intraception. His judgments are governed by a punitive conventional moralism, reflecting external standards in which he remains insecure since he has failed to make them really his own. His relations with others depend on considerations of power, success, and adjustment, in which people figure as means rather than as ends, and achievement is not valued for its own sake. In his world, the good, the powerful, and the in-group stand in fundamental opposition to the immoral, the weak, the out-group. For all that he seeks to align himself with the former, his underlying feelings of weakness and self-contempt commit him to a constant and embittered struggle to prove to himself and others

that he really belongs to the strong and good. Prejudice against out-groups of all kinds and colors is a direct corollary of this personality structure." (Smith, 1950, p. 776)

Correlates of authoritarianism.   Several consistent correlations have been found between high authoritarianism (as measured by the four scales used in the California studies) and other behavior. Those who measure high are not necessarily more conformist than their low-measuring counterparts: it depends upon the conditions of social influence (Steiner & Johnson, 1963). They are more likely to change their attitudes in response to statements attributed to authority figures than in response to straight information—and will sometimes even accept attitudes contrary to their own if a respected authority endorses them (Rohrer & Sherif, 1951).

Other studies showed authoritarians to be more rigid in solving problems when their ego was threatened; to behave more punitively and condescendingly to social inferiors when they were camp counselors; to be less willing to be subjects in psychological experiments; to attribute their own attitudes to others more often than low scorers; to estimate the preferences of their superiors more accurately than those of their peers (contrary to low scorers); and to exhibit more hostility toward a low-status person than a high-status one for making the same mistake.

A very interesting set of relationships was also found more recently between authoritarianism and high scores on scales of both pessimism and cynicism in city dwellers (midtown Manhattan). Both were correlated with authoritarianism, whereas alienation was not (Levine, 1968). ∎

The fascism-breeding hearth.   What pattern of child-rearing experiences nurtures authoritarian personalities? From self-reports of the original California subjects regarding their childhoods, the researchers concluded that the proper family setting for breeding such a personality is one in which there is rigid discipline with inflexible rules and duties, in which parental affection is conditional upon "being good" and may be withdrawn for any infraction. In such a setting, interpersonal relationships become formalized dependencies. The enforced submission of the child

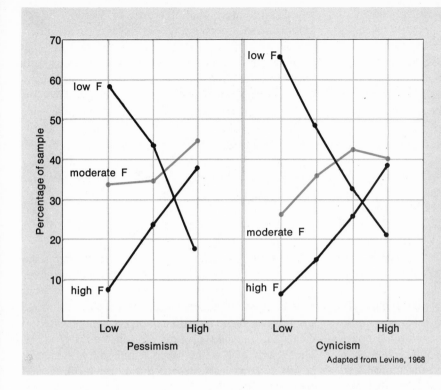

AUTHORITARIANISM, PESSIMISM, AND CYNICISM

Subjects were divided on the basis of their scores on the F-scale into Low, Moderate, and High authoritarian. The Lows were most often low in both pessimism and cynicism and the Highs most often high in both. For example, as the graph shows, of those who were low on the F-scale (authoritarianism), about two thirds were low on both pessimism and cynicism too, whereas only about 20 percent were high on these two other scales. By contrast, less than 10 percent of the high F subjects were low on either pessimism or cynicism.

Adapted from Levine, 1968

to one or both parents leads to feelings of helplessness and, in turn, to hostile and aggressive feelings. These taboo emotions must be repressed and directed away from the true targets onto discriminably different out-group members.

The need to hold this basic hostility in check presents a constant, life-long threat to the individual's security. He develops modes of perceiving and thinking that help him to contain his disrespect for the victimizing parents; his thinking becomes rigid, categorical, compartmentalized. He cannot tolerate ambiguity at either a perceptual, political, or interpersonal level.

The most comfortable social structure for him is one in which relationships are structured in terms of power hierarchies, where those high in status have the "right" to dominate those lower and to command their respect. In return for this power, they assume responsibility for the actions of those subordinate to them. Each person in such a chain of command considers himself superior to all those below him, but inferior to all those above. Deference marks the

relationship to his superiors, while rejection, exploitation, and discrimination are typical reactions to his inferiors. Thus the ideology of the authoritarian personality and the social and political order he tends to create are personalized extensions of his own internal needs.

Perspective on the authoritarian personality. The methodology underlying the approach to studying this unique "social-personality type" and its implications have been justifiably criticized (Christie & Jahoda, 1954). The major points of contention have been that: (a) overgeneralizations to a broad population have been made, based upon findings from highly selected extreme subsamples—only the individuals with the highest and the lowest scores on the ethnocentrism scale were studied in the original sample; (b) the original scale scores may have been confounded by a general *acquiescence set* (the high scorers may have been "yea-sayers" who had a tendency to agree frequently and thus may have gotten high scores even if they were not authoritarians); (c) the low authoritarian scores were positively correlated with intelligence and education, perhaps reflecting a greater ability on their part to fake "acceptable" responses; (d) the relationship of the adult behavior to the childhood experiences of the subjects was determined by unverified *introspective reports* of adults recalling their childhood, and thus may have been based on distorted recollections.

The portrait of the high F-scale scorer as neurotic, rigid, and unable to be effective is certainly overdrawn. In many situations the high-F person will be able to act more decisively than the low-F person, since his more simplistic view makes him less likely to examine ambiguity, inconsistency, and "shades of gray." It is likely that the liberal values of the researchers and of other psychologists working in this area predisposed them to overemphasize the undesirable aspects of authoritarianism.

Similarly, there was a tendency to identify the authoritarians as only right-wing conservatives. But not all rigidity and authoritarianism are on the political right. It has been pointed out (Shils, 1954; Rokeach, 1960) that some of those on the radical left, though they differ in ideological goals from the reactionary right, are fully as authoritarian in their interpersonal functioning and power tactics. (Ψ Close-up, p. 531).

Despite its acknowledged shortcomings, this approach to the study of antidemocratic attitudes opened a fascinating area of intellectual inquiry into the nature of man because it has demonstrated that political and social attitudes can be held because they serve the personal needs of the holder to defend his own security and sense of worth rather than because of rational evidence. What began as a literary-historical analysis broadened into a sociological investigation and led to an integration of methods and approaches from personality psychology and social psychology.

But perhaps the most lasting value of this research program lies in calling our attention to the fact that authoritarians, whether left or right politically, are made, not born. In the normal process of forming a consistent, organized personality, a particular combination of early life experiences and prevailing societal conditions sets the stage for a perversion of personality. Faced with the acute insecurities and bewildering changes of modern life and needing a predictable

world even more than the rest of us do, today's authoritarian personality achieves predictability through the rigidity of a "mental straitjacket" that insulates him from the doubts born of constantly trying to adapt to changing conditions. Through identification with external power or with a rigid ideology, such personalities escape having to form their own values and make independent judgments, but at the cost of openness to their own experience and selfhood. Two other, even more serious, perversions of the normal process of identification will be considered in the next chapter.

Blind Obedience to Authority

It is unsettling to think about the level of aggression which we have come to tolerate in our lives individually and as a society and frightening to guess at what may lie ahead if this trend continues. But the mind still boggles at the incredible violence we witnessed in the Nazi genocide of Jews during World War II. There was evil at its worst: millions of innocent people systematically degraded, brutally tortured, and executed. The atomic bombing of Japanese civilians seemed, for some, to have a readier justification, as an expedient means of saving lives through ending the war more quickly. It is a curious irony that Guillotin, the inventor of the infamous execution device bearing his name, believed that his invention was a humanitarian gift since it dispatched its victims efficiently and painlessly as compared to the more clumsy methods of execution then in practice.

The Nuremburg war crimes trials after World War II sought to rid the world of the presence of demonstrably evil men. But the defense these men offered, in general, was that they had committed these acts of violence because they were under orders to do so and had to obey, given the role they were in. In other words, they believed that they were not personally responsible for their actions, since their behavior was determined by the situation rather than by their choice. World opinion, however, rejected this plea from such "obviously" diseased, sadistic, pathological killers. It proclaimed that evil deeds are acts carried out by evil persons acting on evil motives.

It is psychologically comforting to attribute evil entirely to the personalities of evildoers, for the evil-

Ψ *Close-up*   The Authoritarian Personality Rides Again

Revolutionary Zeal?

Every high school and college in the country will close with riots and sabotage and cops will circle the campuses, standing shoulder to shoulder. The schools belong to the pigs.

Millions of young people will surge into the streets of every city, dancing, singing, smoking pot . . . tripping, burning draft cards, stopping traffic. . . .

High-school students will seize radio, TV, and newspaper offices across the land.

Police stations will blow up.

Revolutionaries will break into jails and free all the prisoners.

Clerical workers will ax their computers and put chewing gum into the machines.

Army platoons and the National Guard will desert to the revolution, bringing their guns with them.

Workers will seize their factories and begin running them communally, without profit.

Subvert!!

That's the task of every young person. Spread ideas that undercut the consistent world of Amerika, and then top it off by burning her symbols—from draft cards to flags to dollar bills.

We must alienate middle-class Amerika. We must get middle-class Amerika all whipped up emotionally.

Amerika suffers from a great cancer; it's called APATHY. . . .

Alienating people is a necessary process in getting them to move. (J. Rubin, 1970, p. 253)

Patriotism?

My Dear Senator Fulbright: I am a high-school industrial arts printing instructor with four years of U.S. Air Force training, five years of college (B.S. and M.T. degrees), and nine years as printing instructor. . . .

I am becoming more and more concerned about the destroying of public property and total disregard for law and policemen. The Kent State University shooting of four students is exactly what is needed in this country. Some idiots started to riot in Mexico and police shot to death thirty-two of them. That put an end to the riots.

When (if ever) will the lawmakers wake up and quit coddling the criminals and put some teeth in the laws? The true American people are VERY tired of paying high taxes to support the government officials who sit and pass laws such as the gun and ammunition laws which hinder the law-abiding citizens, and on the other hand, they turn the criminals loose. Also of concern are the riots where tax-paid property is destroyed and the government does nothing.

The men who fired the shots which took the lives of four Kent students should receive a medal. They were trained to protect themselves and government property, and they did just that. Let's punish the criminals (anyone who riots is a criminal) or close the tax-paid institutions and quit PLAYING school.

When I was in military service and college, the policemen were respected. WHEN will the lawmakers and the VERY criminal-coddling Supreme Court take the handcuffs off the police and put them where they belong? . . . (*Congressional Record* No. 87, May 28, 1970, p. S7991)

---

doer is thereby perceived as inherently different from the rest of civilized society—often as the product of a "bad seed." Thus *we* need not feel guilty about evil social conditions that he must live under, nor need we be worried that we "good-seed people" could ever do such evil unto others as he has done. Comforting as we may find such a position, however, it simply is not tenable.

Obedience in the laboratory.   A recent series of ingenious psychological experiments has shattered the myth that evil is alien to Everyman and resides only in particular other people who are different from us. Milgram (1963, 1964, 1965a, 1965b) has convincingly demonstrated that the "Eichmann phenomenon" is reproducible in the majority of ordinary American citizens under specifiable social conditions.

Volunteer adult male subjects were given the task of administering a painful series of electric shocks to another person as part of a study allegedly investigating the effect of punishment on memory. Every subject was placed in the role of a "teacher" whose only job was to administer punishment (an electric shock) to a "student" whenever the student erred in his performance on a paired-associates learning test. The subject could choose among thirty clearly marked positions ranging from "Slight shock" (15 volts) to "Danger: Severe Shock" (450 volts).

After the subject-teacher himself received a sample shock of 45 volts and the learner was strapped into an "electric chair" in an adjacent room, the experiment on obedience began. The subject was commanded to increase the shock to the next level with each error made by the learner. Since the learner made many errors, the level of punishment escalated rapidly.

The protests of the victim, heard over an intercom, were coordinated to the shock level being administered. At 75 volts he began to moan and grunt; at 150 volts he demanded to be released from the experiment; at 180 volts he cried out that he could not stand the pain any longer. At 300 volts he insisted that he was no longer taking part in the experiment and must be freed, and he stopped giving any more answers.

If the subject hesitated or protested against delivering the shock, the experimenter told him: "You have no other choice, you must go on!" At the higher levels of shock, the subject heard his victim scream out and gasp, and then there was silence. Still the experimenter insisted that absence of a response must be punished.

Before describing the results obtained, consider how far *you* would go if you were the subject-teacher. Which of the thirty levels of shock would be the absolute limit beyond which you would *refuse* to go? How far do you think the average subject in Milgram's experiment actually went? Indicate your estimates below.

1. I would refuse to shock the other person beyond voltage level (circle one number):

0	15	30	45	60	75	90	120	135	150
165	180	195	210	225	240	255	270	285	300
315	330	345	360	375	390	405	420	435	450

2. The average subject probably stopped at:_____volts.

When forty psychiatrists were asked to predict the performance of subjects in this experiment, they estimated that most subjects would not go beyond 150 volts, that at 300 volts fewer than 4 percent of the subjects would still be obedient, and that only about one tenth of one percent would go all the way up to 450 volts.

The subjects in this study represented a wide cross-section of the population varying in age from twenty to fifty years, in occupation from unskilled workers to white-collar workers and professionals and in education from elementary-school dropouts to doctoral graduates. The "victim" (who was in reality a confederate of the experimenter) was a middle-aged accountant of Irish-American background who was judged to be mild mannered and likable by most observers. His protests were standardized, tape-recorded responses to the various shock levels—none of which he actually received.

That the experimental situation produced considerable conflict and tension in most subjects is readily apparent from their comments, a sample of which is given here: "*180 volts delivered:* 'He can't stand it! I'm not going to kill that man in there! You hear him hollering? He's hollering. He can't stand it. What if something happens to him? . . . I mean who is going to take the responsibility if anything happens to that gentleman?' (*The experimenter accepts responsibility*). 'All right.'
"*195 volts delivered:* 'You see he's hollering. Hear that. Gee, I don't know.' (*The experimenter says: 'The experiment requires that you go on'*)—'I know it does, sir, but I mean—huh—he don't know what he's in for. He's up to 195 volts.' . . .
"*240 volts delivered:* 'Aw, no. You mean I've got to keep going up with that scale? No sir. I'm not going to kill that man! I'm not going to give him 450 volts!' "

Despite what he said, however, that subject, like *62 percent* of those observed, *did* go all the way in delivering the full 450 volts to the victim! The mean maximum shock for all 40 subjects was 368 volts. How does that compare with your prediction?   ◆

An even higher proportion of a group of high school seniors were obedient in a replication study. Fully 85 percent delivered 450 volts (Rosenhan, 1969).

Dissent vs. disobedience.   Dissenting is saying you disagree. Disobeying is not following the orders of an authority. Clearly they were not the same thing in these experiments.

The experts predict that the subjects will defy authority, the subjects themselves continually *say* they are not going to obey (a control group, not under pressure from the experimenter, *did* give a mean maximum shock of only 82 volts), and it is probable that you said you would disobey and that you underestimated the shock level that others would actually administer. The act of behavioral disobedience is just not the same as the statement that one will disobey. We consistently make the error of attributing more independence, control, and rationality first to ourselves and then to others than is actually observed when we or they are involved in a social situation such as that described by Milgram. We fail to appreciate the magnitude of the social forces that are acting upon a person who is enmeshed in this kind of social matrix.

Three conditions have been distinguished which lead to "blind obedience to authority" in violation of one's self-image and moral values.

1. Obedience is fostered by the presence of a *legitimate authority* who is trusted, who is seen as a valid representative of society, and who controls significant reinforcers. When the authority is not face-to-face with the subject, he loses some of his power (only 22 percent of the subjects obey fully).

2. Obedience is enhanced when a *role relationship* is established and accepted in which the individual is subordinated to another person. In the given role, the subject perceives that he is not personally responsible for his behavior since he is not spontaneously initiating action, but is merely carrying out orders. When subjects see two other people refuse to accept the experimentally imposed role, 90 percent of them are then able to disobey and defy authority commands themselves.

3. Obedience is nurtured by the presence of *social norms* which the individual sees as relating him to others in the situation and providing proscriptions as to protocol, etiquette, and socially approved and acceptable behaviors. These norms come to govern and constrain what is perceived as possible and appropriate. One subject said to the experimenter, "*I don't mean to be rude, sir*, but shouldn't we look in on him? He has a heart condition and may be dying."

Thus individuals often perceive social forces as so binding that they are locked into behaviors and interactions that they must carry out regardless of what they feel is right or believe is just. The values prescribed by the situation replace their individual values; "duty" and "loyalty" to the norms supersede the dictates of conscience. The subject does not want to

◆ The photo at left shows the shock generator used in Milgram's experiment on obedience. Below, left, the victim is being strapped in the "electric chair." Below, center, a subject is receiving the sample shock before starting the "teaching session." Below, right, a subject is refusing to go on with the experiment any longer. Most subjects became deeply disturbed by the role they were being asked to play whether they continued in it to the end or refused at some point to go on any longer. (From the film *Obedience,* distributed by New York University Film Library; copyright © 1965, by Stanley Milgram)

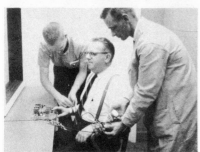

hurt anyone, but he feels that it is more imperative not to disrupt The System—the show must go on!

Blind in the light of the real world too. To prove that the subjects' acquiescence did not simply reflect the prestige of the university at which the experiment was performed, the investigator replicated the study in a downtown office building in a moderate-sized city with subjects recruited through a mail circular. The study purportedly was being carried out by a private firm conducting research for industry. About half these subjects were completely obedient to the white-coated scientists, punishing the victim to the fullest extent.

The implications of this research extend to many situations in which people do not believe they are participating in an experiment at all. There is abundant evidence from the real world to support the assertion that blind obedience will be likely whenever the three conditions described earlier are met. Two of the most cogent examples of unquestioning obedience to authority—doing whatever is asked—come from a tape-recorded interview with a wounded Vietnam veteran, who describes how he killed women and children only a few yards away from him (Ψ Close-up, below) and from statements made by the bombardier who released the first atomic bomb over Hiroshima.

Ψ *Close-up*   **The Killing Power of Obedience**

Veteran: I just got back from Vietnam. I was there for two years stationed in Da Nang. I was shot in the leg. I got a medical discharge and that's why I'm here now; I had another year to do. While I was over there, I saw a lot of action. I was corpsman with the navy; they stuck me with the marine corps for a period of eighteen months. The most particular experience I had was one time in the DMZ. We were in a small village and there was a machine gunner in the schoolhouse firing at us. We all spread out and hit the ground. I said I was a medical corpsman [no weapons] but I was the only one in position. So they handed me a grenade and said to throw it in a window and wipe it out. So when I got up close enough to see inside to drop it in, I noticed there was about twenty or thirty children sitting in the back of the room in the corner with about two or three ladies. I threw in a grenade and . . . blew them all to hell.

Interviewer: Was there any way you could knock out the machine gun without . . .

Veteran: No. There was no way at all, 'cause like you were about three feet away from them. And this grenade is set to explode around a diameter of about forty or fifty feet at least, killing power. You don't have time to think 'cause either you get shot or you kill them. It's them or you. So it's survival is all it is. Save your ass.

Interviewer: What about afterwards? I mean after you threw it, everybody get killed, or . . .

Veteran: Right. All the children were killed, the building was destroyed, that was that. Is there anything else you'd like to know?

Interviewer: Is there anything else you'd care to tell me?

Veteran: My last two weeks there in the jungle we're on a routine patrol and this little girl about three years old starts running toward us. She was about forty or sixty feet away from us at the time, we noticed something bouncing on her back as she ran, and our officer said "shoot." We shot her down. At the same time we shot her down she exploded. She blew into small bits. The V.C. attached a savoy mine to her back and it was wired to explode by the time she reached us. It was either her or us. We didn't know for sure the mine was there but we couldn't take the chance.

Interviewer: When the officer said "shoot," how many people shot?

Veteran: We all shot at her. There was about thirty of us in this particular platoon.

Interviewer: But did *you* have to do it?

Veteran: Right. You have to do it, you are ordered to do it. You either shoot them, or if you don't shoot them, your officer shoots you. You don't have any choice. No choice about it, you don't have time to think about it, you do it.

The bombardier, when interviewed recently, recalls "I just laughed" when "they said they were developing a bomb that would blow up everything for eight miles." He was not briefed about his payload, but from the special flight maneuvers necessary to avoid the mushrooming cloud he "put two and two together and figured it was radioactive." Nevertheless, he reports, "I'd flown so many missions by then that it was mostly a job to do." The characteristic dichotomy between dissent and disobedience, as well as the typical error of overestimating *other* people's internal, personal control and underestimating the influence of the social setting in controlling their behavior and decisions is summarized in the bombardier's statement:

"I don't believe in everything we do, but if I'm in the military I've got to support the government. I may not agree, but if ordered I'll sure do it. I think everyone has enough sense never to use the bomb again." (*Newsweek*, Aug. 10, 1970)

Can Civilization Be Uncivilizing?

As we saw in Chapter 12, the collection of persons into a society usually increases the individual's chances for survival, promotes his welfare, protects and safeguards his rights, and establishes a basis for consensual validation. One characteristic of man that makes possible the smooth functioning of a group (and thus the benefits of banding together into a group) is his susceptibility to constraints imposed on his behavior by social rules designating appropriate behavior. But a by-product of this tendency toward social obedience (besides the inhumanity of blind obedience just discussed) is a greater susceptibility to all kinds of social-emotional influences. When these encourage irrational or destructive behavior, or when they become threatening instead of supportive to him, social influences can become debasing instead of civilizing.

Irrationality Through Mass Hysteria

Historically the susceptibility to irrational group movements has been greatest in periods when individual freedom has been repressed by religious, eco-nomic, and/or political domination or when bewildering change, great uncertainties and anxieties, or other conditions in the environment have made it rewarding (or less punishing) for individuals to "lose themselves" in a group.

"Epidemics" of mass hysteria. From 1095 to 1272, swarms of Christians from all lands abandoned their homes and headed out on crusades to capture the Holy Land from the infidels. The "abnormal" aspect of the high level of susceptibility of medieval society to irrational social-emotional influences is most clearly revealed in the Children's Crusade, initiated about 1212 by a French shepherd boy. Young boys and girls marched together to their certain massacre despite all pleas, threats, and commands.

"Bolts and bars would not hold the children. If shut up, they broke through doors and windows, and rushed to take their place in the processions which they saw passing by. If the children were forcibly detained, so that escape was impossible, they pined away like migratory birds in seclusion." (Young, 1927, pp. 669-670)

With the end of the crusade epidemic arose the *flagellant* movement (1260-1348), which spread from Italy throughout Europe. Filled with remorse for their sins and with the fear of a demanding God, processions of migrants walked through the streets violently lashing themselves and each other with leather thongs. This spectacle (depicted in the movie *The Seventh Seal*) inadvertently helped spread the Bubonic plague as the "sinners" carried infectious disease from town to town. Flagellant practices occur even today in some places. • (p. 536)

Other less destructive manias (such as dancing manias) occurred a little later. Then, for more than a century and a half, Western Europeans became obsessed with fear of the devil and the unpardonable sin of witchcraft. Regardless of age or station in life, every person, from serf to nobleman to priest, was suspect as a possible harborer of evil spirits. Thousands of innocent victims were tortured and burned at the stake in every country. In 1562 Queen Elizabeth declared witchcraft a crime in England, and the witchcraft mania spread throughout the British Isles. It was readily adopted by the Puritans and carried to America, as witnessed in the infamous witchcraft trials in Salem, Massachusetts, in 1692.

The rise of a capitalist ethic saw the basis of these mental epidemics shift from religious to economic. From the early seventeenth century on, a series of *speculative manias* emerged in various countries, in which the desire to make money grew to fever pitch. Ordinary life was disrupted as the illusion of instant wealth through land schemes, tulip speculation (in Holland in the 1630s), gold mining, and other ventures captivated the minds of the hopeful.

A young Muslim in Pakistan is beating himself with spiked chains until the blood runs down his back. He is reenacting the agony and death of Mohammed's grandson as part of a religious procession.

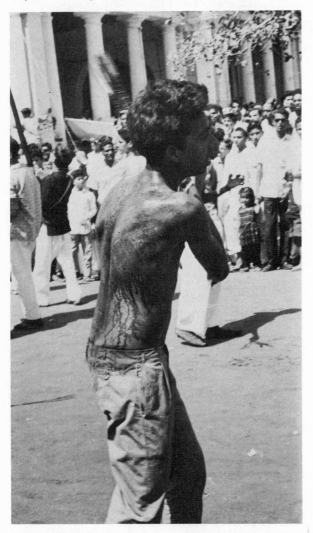

In more recent times, such mass suggestibility appears to have been centered more around political-social beliefs. Some examples which spring to mind are the Japanese kamikaze suicide squadrons in World War II, the anti-Semitic mania in Hitler's Germany, and the communist witch-hunt mania initiated in America by the late Senator Joseph McCarthy in the early 1950s.

Although these and other mass social movements are well documented in many sources, causal explanations, though numerous, are less satisfactory. A case can be made for periods of great social change as the triggering stimulus. But there is an equally plausible explanation in terms of escape from periods of prolonged boredom and stultifying sameness. Is it uncertainty about what the future holds, pessimism that the future will be worse or no better than the unbearable present, or unbridled optimism about the bountiful future that leads man to behave "irrationally," running with the herd?

Mob panics. The individual can lose his head not only to ideologies and illusions, but also to momentary circumstances which are seen as a threat to his self-interests or provide an opportunity for spontaneous "emotional release."

A crowd of nearly 100 teen-agers in New York assaulted a truck driver, set his truck ablaze, and hurled bricks and bottles at firemen trying to put out the fire—after a girl was accidentally hit by the truck.

Following an unpopular ruling by a referee in a soccer match between Peru and Argentina in 1964, fans rioted and in the fighting and stampede for exits over 300 people were killed and 500 injured.

That social man does not always profit from his mistakes is indicated by the fact that the same panic situation occurred at a soccer stadium in Argentina four years later, killing 71 spectators and injuring 130. In 1969 an estimated 100 people were trampled to death by their Sudanese countrymen in a frantic stampede to get to an alleged "miracle" well. Although varying in their devastation, mob panics have occurred throughout the world.

In an attempt to unravel the dynamics of such panic behavior, psychologists have devised simulated laboratory situations which allow controlled observations to be made.

In one study a "bottleneck" situation was created, in which each of a group of subjects was given a string attached to a small cone that had been inserted into a bottle. As water flowed into the bottom of the bottle, their task was to pull the cones out before they got wet. The top of the bottle was so narrow that if two or more people tried to "escape" simultaneously, the cones would wedge together and the exit would be blocked.

Although this simulation reproduced the essential features of the panic situation, the threat was a purely intellectual one. Not surprisingly, no serious traffic jams developed (Mintz, 1951).

To make the threat more realistic, the subjects in a later experiment were told that they would receive electric shocks if they failed to escape. They saw water put into the top of an hour-glass and had only until it had flowed into the bottom to make their escape. Verbal communication was not permitted; each subject signaled the start of his escape on an electronic panel. Each escape took only three seconds, but if two or more tried to escape at the same time, the circuit jammed and all but one had to release their switches and try again later. There was time for all to escape if they coordinated their behavior, but if traffic jams developed some would fail.

Panic did appear in this situation. Failures were twice as frequent under high threat as under low threat and twice as frequent for men as for women (Kelley, Condry, Dahlke, & Hill, 1965).

Modern Urban Pathology

People have been attracted to cities because of the economic opportunities they provide and also for their cultural and social functions. The Regional Planning Association has calculated that within a ten-minute radius of his Manhattan office, a New Yorker could meet more than 220,000 people. This is ten times the number possible in a moderate-sized city like Newark and twenty times greater than in a New York suburb (*The New York Times*, June 15, 1969).

But the advantages are counterbalanced by the adaptations an individual must make to the sensory-cognitive overload created by urban life (Milgram, 1970). The tempo and pace are faster, there is more action, more competition for resources (such as taxis, seats on mass transit, baby-sitters, nursery and private schools), a greater number of people willing to

"con" you, more incivility, more turnover in housing and jobs, less concern for your affairs, and on and on.

"In the last century, we have increased our speeds of communication by a factor of 10^7; our speeds of travel by 10^3; our speeds of data handling by 10^6; our energy resources by 10^3; our power of weapons by 10^6; our ability to control diseases by something like 10^2; and our rate of population growth to 10^3 times what it was a few thousand years ago." (Platt, 1969)

We are living in the midst of a technological explosion created by man's genius, ambition, and determination to control rather than to be controlled. But we are not equipped to handle with the same facility the kind of social life-style which our technology seems to be spawning. Nor can we easily accommodate the perpetual psychological crises occasioned by the rapid transformation of our values, ways of thinking, and modes of living with other people and ourselves. There are many signs that the pace is too fast, the conflicts too intense, and the problems too complex for us to cope with individually and as a society. ◆ (p. 538)

Overcrowding and overloading. While our cities represent man's greatest technological control in conquering nature, they have begun to limit the control which any single individual feels he has over his physical-social and even psychological environment. Within a few days of each other in 1968, New York City had a teachers' strike, a garbage strike, a police strike, a longshoremen's strike, and racial conflict. People dependent on these services were annoyed, angered, frustrated, but helpless to do anything about it except perhaps to displace their aggression.

In the summer of 1970, a temperature inversion trapped hot air and air pollutants over the city, causing temperatures to soar and creating respiration problems. The technological solution was simple: air conditioners and dehumidifiers were turned on everywhere. But the demand overtaxed the electrical supply leading to reduced electrical power not only for air conditioners but for the subways as well.

This increased the frustration of stranded and late passengers, many of whom then turned to their cars for transportation. Naturally, the greater use of cars in an already overcrowded city not only created

◆ IMPENDING CRISES IN THE UNITED STATES

Platt points out that most scientists are working on Grade 8 problems, which could not lead to annihilation. In the middle range, some work—generally inadequate—is in progress. We are just becoming aware of the seriousness of the Grade 2 problems, and at Grade 1— the most crucial of all—there is no concerted scientific or political effort toward a solution. Platt and others give us no more than a 50-50 chance of surviving until 1990.

Estimated Intensity (Based on number of people affected and degree of disruptive effect)	Estimated Time to Crisis (If no major effort is made at anticipatory solution)		
	1-5 years	*5-20 years*	*20-50 years*
Grade 1. Problems that could annihilate everyone	Nuclear or RCBW escalation	Nuclear or RCBW escalation	†(Solved or dead)
Grade 2. Problems that would bring great destruction or change to everyone		Participatory democracy Ecological balance	Political theory and economic structure Population planning Patterns of living Education Communications Integrative philosophy
Grade 3. Problems that would bring widespread, almost unbearable tension	Administrative management Slums Participatory democracy Racial conflict	Pollution Poverty Law and justice	Can't predict
Grade 4. Problems that would bring large-scale distress	Transportation Neighborhood ugliness Crime	Communications gap	Can't predict
Grade 5. Problems that would produce tension demanding change	Cancer and heart Smoking and drugs Artificial organs Accidents Sonic boom Water supply Marine resources Privacy on computers	Educational inadequacy	Can't predict
Grade 6. Other problems, important for many but now being researched	Military R & D New educational methods Mental illness Fusion power	Military R & D	
Grade 7. Problems whose dangers and hopes are exaggerated	Mind control Heart transplants Definition of death	Sperm banks Freezing bodies Unemployment from automation	Eugenics
Grade 8. Noncrisis problems, currently being "overstudied"	Man in space Most basic science		

Adapted from Platt, 1969

maddening traffic jams, but added to the air pollution. And so did the greater effort by the utilities companies to generate more electricity. All this was just one more in a long series of continuing problems created by excessive population density: inadequate garbage and sanitation facilities, erratic telephone service, noise pollution, crowded schools, and unsafe streets, among others.

Research has revealed that crowding can cause aggression and other pathological behavior in animals.

One early investigator, studying a baboon colony which was living in the London Zoo under rather crowded and disorganized conditions, observed many instances of bloody fighting, brutality, and apparently senseless violence. Some of the females were torn to pieces, and no infants survived to maturity (Zuckerman, 1932). From these observations, it was concluded that such violence was typical of these "wild" baboons, thereby lending credence to the appealing notion held by some people that man's violent "animal nature" is held in check by civilization. But later, when baboons were studied under natural conditions in Africa, in the "wild," it was discovered that they lived in well-organized, peaceful groups, in which the only aggressive behavior was directed at predators and intruders (De Vore, 1965).

The term *behavioral sink* was used by Calhoun (1962) to describe the abnormal behavior that emerged when albino rats were overcrowded in a laboratory experiment.

In this study, despite the presence of ample physical resources, such as food and nest-building materials, there were frequent vicious fights between the males as well as unprovoked attacks on females and infants. Some males were extremely aggressive, while others withdrew and became passive. Abnormalities in sexual behavior (hypersexuality, homosexuality, bisexuality) increased tremendously. Social order broke down completely to the point that such normal activities as nest-building and infant care were ignored, cannibalism occurred, and no infant reached maturity.

High population density, along with other types of stress, also produces devastating physiological changes. We have seen that the adrenal glands normally secrete hormones when physical or psychological stress demands defensive responses. If stress is prolonged and unremitting, however, the glands must work overtime to keep producing hormones, and they grow larger and may eventually be unable to function. In addition, body growth is suppressed, resistance to infection decreases, blood composition changes, various internal organs show degenerative changes, and the reproductive organs either stop functioning or function incompletely.

How far these findings apply to human beings we do not know, but the parallels between animal overcrowding and the unbelievable population density of some cities in which millions of people are forced to live today are all too obvious. How much of the greater urban crime rate, violence, vandalism, breakdown of social etiquette, and general antisocial behavior that occurs in big cities can be explained by overcrowding and how much is due to other factors which are correlated or incidental to it is a subject for urgently needed research.

The breakdown of trust and concern. Among the most potent forces which diminish the nature of man are social conditions which make it possible for a man to be close to many people and yet feel alienated from them. In a big city a man is surrounded by hundreds of thousands of people, hears them on radio, sees them on television, eats with them in restaurants, sits next to them in movies, waits in line with them, gets pushed around in subways with them, touches them—but remains untouched, unconnected, as if they did not exist.

For a young girl in Queens, they did not exist.

"For more than half an hour, 38 respectable, law-abiding citizens in Queens [New York] watched a killer stalk and stab a woman in three separate attacks in Kew Gardens.

"Twice the sound of their voices and the sudden glow of their bedroom lights interrupted him and frightened him off. Each time he returned, sought her out and stabbed her again. Not one person telephoned the police during the assault; one witness called the police after the woman was dead." (*The New York Times*, March 13, 1964)

This newspaper account of the murder of Kitty Genovese shocked a nation which could not accept the idea of such apathy on the part of its responsible citizenry. Yet only a few months later there was an even more vivid and chilling depiction of how alienated and out of contact one can be in the midst of people. Imagine for a moment that you had been in the position of an eighteen-year-old secretary who was beaten, choked, stripped, and raped in her office and then finally broke away from her assailant. Naked and bleeding, she ran down the stairs of the building to the doorway screaming, "Help me! Help me! He raped me!" A crowd of forty persons gathered on the busy street and watched passively as the rapist dragged her back upstairs. Only the chance arrival of passing police prevented her further abuse and possible murder (*The New York Times,* May 6, 1964).

Would *you* have called the police if you had lived in Kew Gardens? Would you have intervened to help the girl being raped? Will you when your chance comes do anything other than "your own thing"? (Ψ Close-up, below)

Is the failure to intervene in emergencies due to some defect in the personalities of the particular

Ψ *Close-up* **The Eyewitness**

I was the man on the spot.
  I was the first at the crime.
I got a story in hot;
  I wasn't wasting no time.

I got my name in the news.
  I got my face on TV.
I had the stuff they could use;
  I got a nice little fee.

I saw the van hit the cab;
  I saw the man with the gun;
I saw the smash and the grab;
  I saw the driver get done.

I saw the gang get away;
  They passed me as close as could be,
I could have—What's that you say?
  Why didn't I stop them? Who, me?

Peter Suffolk

bystanders, or can it be traced to existing conditions of social learning which could affect anyone?

Two social psychologists set out to answer this question by ingeniously creating in the laboratory an experimental analog of the bystander-intervention situation. A college student, placed in a room by himself, was led to believe that he was communicating with other students via an intercom. During the course of a discussion about personal problems, he heard what sounded as though one of the other students was having an epileptic seizure. The subject heard him gasp over the intercom:

"I-er-um-I think I-I need-er-if-if could-er-er-somebody er-er-er-er-er-er-er give me a little-er-give me a little help here because-er-I-er-I'm-er-er-h-h-having a-a-a real problem-er-right now and I-er-if somebody could help me out it would-it would-er-er s-s-sure be-sure be good . . . because-er-there-er-er-a cause I-er-uh-I-ve-got a-a one of the-er-sei———er-er-things coming on and-and-and I could really-er-use some help so if somebody would-er-give me a little h-help-uh-er-er-er-er-er c-could somebody-er-er-help-er-uh-uh-uh (choking sounds). . . . I'm gonna die-er-er-I'm . . . gonna die-er-help-er-er-seizure-er- [chokes, then quiet]."

During the "fit" it was impossible for the subject to talk to the other discussants or to find out what, if anything, they were doing about the emergency. The dependent variable was the speed with which he reported the emergency to the experimenter. The major independent variable was the number of people he thought were in the discussion group with him—only he and the victim, one additional person, two additional persons, or five additional persons.

It turned out that the likelihood of intervention by the subject depended on the number of bystanders he thought were present. The more there were, the slower he was in reporting the fit, if he did so at all. The graph shows that everyone in a two-person situation intervened within 160 seconds, but nearly 40 percent of those in the larger group never bothered to inform the experimenter that another student might be dying. ● A battery of personality measures taken on each subject failed to show any significant relationship between particular personality characteristics and speed of helping or likelihood of intervening (Darley & Latané, 1970).

In a series of related studies, the emergency situation was the sound and screams of a girl falling off a ladder or smoke suddenly pouring into the experimental room from a vent. The general finding in these studies was that conditions which allow by-

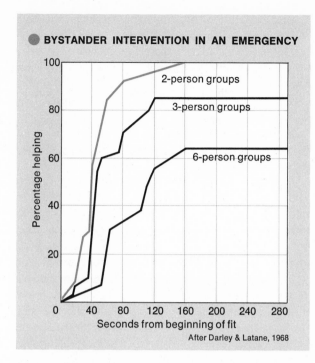

BYSTANDER INTERVENTION IN AN EMERGENCY

Percentage helping

2-person groups

3-person groups

6-person groups

Seconds from beginning of fit

After Darley & Latane, 1968

standers to perceive that there is a diffusion of responsibility among those present lead to nonintervention. People intervene when they are made to feel personally responsible. Intervention is also increased by observing others helping, while seeing others react passively reduces the chances that a bystander will intervene. Interestingly, then, the more people there are present, the less likely the victim is to receive aid. Many bystanders in these experiments were in a conflict between feeling guilt if they did not help the person and fear of embarrassment if they overreacted or made fools of themselves.

Living among strangers that one does not know, hardly even looks at, and has only superficial and impersonal contacts with can lead to apathy, alienation, and cynicism as a means of coping with overload, of psychologically distancing oneself from others, and of not getting "taken." The extent to which city dwellers develop a lack of trust of each other was demonstrated in an interesting field experiment.

In middle-income apartments in Manhattan and in apartments in small towns in surrounding counties, student investigators, working singly, rang doorbells and asked to use the telephone, explaining that the address

of a friend who lived nearby had been misplaced. The researchers wanted to see whether there would be a difference between the city and town dwellers in their willingness to help a stranger with such a request.

The differences were striking. Male students were allowed to enter half of the homes in the small towns but only 14 percent of the homes in the city. The females were admitted to 94 percent of the town homes but only 60 percent of the city ones (Altman, Levine, & Nadien, 1970).

Anonymity and the removal of constraints. Big-city living not only robs the individual of many of the potential benefits of social living but often nibbles away at one of his most precious possessions—his sense of personal identity and uniqueness. Though surrounded by people, he becomes anonymous. It is easy for him to get the feeling that no one knows or cares who he is.

Being anonymous decreases the chances of getting either one's just rewards for socially beneficial behavior or punishment for antisocial behavior. Thus it tends to remove the fear of other people's censure and disapproval, and without fear of disapproval, the constraints imposed by one's own conscience may be weakened. Emotions or impulses that would otherwise be held in check by conformity to social norms may be released under the mask of anonymity.

In one laboratory experiment, anonymity was created in one group of four coeds by having them wear baggy, size 44 lab coats and hoods that covered their faces. In addition, they sat in a darkened room and were never referred to by name. A second group of four comparable subjects were randomly assigned to a condition which emphasized their individuality. They wore name tags, were frequently referred to by name by the experimenter, and saw the faces of the other girls in their group. The girls in each of these four-person groups then were given the task of administering what they believed to be a series of twenty jolts of painful electric shocks to each of two "victims" (who were actually confederates of the experimenter).

Before seeing each victim and watching her twist, squirm, and jump in reaction to each supposed shock, the subjects listened to a taped interview with the victim. One of the victims was portrayed as an obnoxious, prejudiced, "bitchy" girl who "would deserve to be punished." The other was made to appear sweet, warm, loving, and altruistic—not someone to hurt needlessly.

The subjects were led to believe that the investigator was studying empathy and wished to determine whether they showed more empathy with the victim when they were administering the shock or when they were merely observing. Actually, he was seeking to determine whether anonymity would increase aggression against a stranger and whether the two victims would be treated in the same way.

The data in the figure show that subjects in the anonymous condition were much more aggressive than the individuated subjects initially and increased their aggression over the twenty trials. ■ The individuated girls shocked the "nice" victim less over time; the anonymous ones shocked both victims more. There was a strong positive relationship between the individuated subjects' evaluation of each victim and their aggression toward her: more if she was rated negatively, less if she was rated positively. Among the hooded subjects, no such relationship was found. Once they began to be aggressive, it appears that their behavior was not inhibited either by possible social approval or by perceptions of how nice the victim was. Behaving aggressively when you cannot be identified appears to be self-reinforcing; in any case, it increases in intensity as it is repeated (Zimbardo, 1969b).

Under conditions of anonymity, there tends to be a "here-and-now" orientation, with a narrowing of future planning. Typically there is a greater sensitivity to emotional and nonverbal feedback, a tendency toward action and away from deliberation, and a focus on self-gratification, with a corresponding lack of concern for others.

Whereas people tend to seek individuation and a recognized personal identity when the social climate is supportive, they may seek anonymity as a defense when the social environment is threatening (Ziller, 1964). When this tendency results in a collection of individuals each operating on the principle of self-interest and without feelings of loyalty to each other or the community, they become, in turn, part of what makes each other's environment threatening.

Sometimes people choose to enter a situation of anonymity (and unaccountability) through being part of a group. Examples of chosen anonymity are seen in the exuberance (and often destructiveness) at large conventions, as well as in fraternity hell-night, costume parties, the Mardi Gras, the KKK, or a

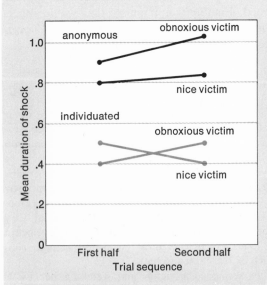

After Zimbardo, 1969b

■ AGGRESSION AS A FUNCTION OF ANONYMITY

The anonymous girls delivered more shock and gradually increased the amount of shock they gave both the victims. The individuated girls gave only about half as much shock and decreased the amount they were giving the "nice" victim in the course of the experiment.

● Members of the Ku Klux Klan are well known for carrying out their version of justice anonymously.

Ψ *Close-up* **How Serious Is Vandalism?**

1. Damage to public schools throughout the nation approaches $100 million yearly—money that comes out of new school construction funds and educational programs.

2. In New York City alone, broken window panes (over 200,000 annually), arson, and ransacking have steadily risen each year and now add nearly $3 million a year to the public school budget.

3. In major cities about a quarter of all sidewalk phones are out of order all the time. Repair and replacement costs amount to $10 million annually.

4. Automobile vandalism cost one insurance company over $4 million in claims in a single year. Naturally, this gets passed on to customers in the form of higher premium rates.

5. Some houses of worship have threatened to close after being repeatedly vandalized more than a dozen times in a year.

Thus vandalism represents not only a financial loss calculated in hundreds of millions of dollars, but personal inconvenience, loss of irreplaceable items, reduction of services to the public, and, perhaps most importantly, contributes to the destruction of social trust in one's fellow man.

U. S. News and World Report, August 25, 1969

"be-in." ● And in some situations deindividuation is imposed by society. Just as the subjects in the experiment described above were made anonymous by wearing the costumes provided by the experiment, men become G.I.'s ("Government Issue") by being dressed in identical uniforms.

This uniformity in appearance makes it easier for leaders to obtain behavioral conformity, as Adolf Hitler noted in his book *Mein Kampf*. But the psychological anonymity provided by uniforms or gang jackets also frees the wearers from conventional constraints on their behavior when they are not forced to act on orders from a leader—in part accounting for the murder, rape, and looting which soldiers of almost all nations engage in when on foreign soil.

Vandalism: Senseless Violence?

"It's just wanton, senseless destruction by vandals." Rare trees in a park garden are cut up, wrecked, and demolished; animals in a sanctuary are tortured and killed, birds defeathered; churches are desecrated, synagogues sacked; schools are burned, windows broken; comfort stations set afire; public telephones are ripped from their booths; parked cars are stripped and battered; cemetery gravestones are overturned. ◆ (p. 544)

Such is only a partial listing of the daily activities not of a conquering enemy army, but of a curious breed of citizens called *vandals*. The characteristic feature of vandalism is the destruction of property and of life without any apparent goal beyond the act of destruction itself. Such behavior seems to be motiveless and irrational since the perpetrators put a lot of effort into an activity which seems to have no instrumental value. They appear to get nothing out of it. (Ψ Close-up, above)

The public response has been a call for "law and order," with more police and stiffer penalties. It is easy for those who feel threatened by such acts (typically property owners and politicians) to see vandals as a group apart from "normal" people, thereby justifying stringent measures against these "deviants." Yet so far, the only noticeable effect of such crackdowns has been a shifting of targets and an even greater incidence of vandalism the following year.

The term *vandalism* is an emotion-arousing one which conjures up images of ruthless barbarians bent on destruction of society. It comes from the behavior of the Germanic tribe, the Vandals, who invaded Western Europe and destroyed the art and civilization of Rome in A.D. 455. But if vandalism were indeed "senseless" we could never hope to control it, because an effect without a cause does not fit into any systematic plan which could limit it. Fortunately, careful analysis gives us a somewhat different perspective. To treat acts of vandalism as homogeneous in pattern or as incomprehensible is a mistake —often a costly one for the society.

In the eighteenth century, when a group of workers called *Luddites* began destroying factory machines, they were stereotyped as "frenzied" and "mad" and their actions as "pointless." But they were part of an earnest movement aimed at the betterment of man. They were engaged in what they believed was a legitimate form of protest against the evils of the industrial system.

Similarly, the property destruction which occurred during the racial disturbances in Watts, Newark, and other American cities in the late 1960s appeared "mindless" until it was noted that the targets chosen were not arbitrary. The report of the National Advisory Commission on Civil Disorders (1968) stated: "In at least nine cities studied, the damage seems to have been, at least in part, the result of deliberate attacks on white-owned businesses, characterized in the Negro community as unfair or disrespectful toward Negroes."

Acts of vandalism can be sorted into one of six categories according to the significance that the destructive behavior seems to have for the individual (Cohen, 1968).

◆ A classroom and a church after attacks by vandals.

1. *Acquisitive vandalism*—Property damage done to acquire money or goods, such as breaking open vending machines or telephone coin boxes, stripping parts from cars or fittings from housing project heating systems.

2. *Tactical vandalism*—Property damage done intentionally to advance some other end, as a means to draw attention to a grievance or to force a reaction. Such a tactical approach is exemplified by prisoners who destroy their cells or the mess hall in protesting inadequate facilities or a man who breaks a store window to get arrested so that he will be institutionalized.

3. *Ideological vandalism*—Similar to tactical vandalism, but carried out explicitly to further an ideological cause. Antigovernment slogans painted on embassy buildings or burning down R.O.T.C. headquarters are illustrative examples. Some recent "trashing" on college campuses was planned as a tactic to make the administration call the police onto campus, in hopes that their expected overreaction would then radicalize apathetic students and faculty. At some point ideological vandalism gets labeled "sabotage" or "treason."

4. *Vindictive vandalism*—Damage done to a selected target for revenge on its owner, guardian, or representative. Sometimes a group of students demolish a classroom because they feel the teacher has been unjust.

5. *Play vandalism*—Damage to property in the context of a game: who can break windows on the highest level, shoot out the most street lamps, jam telephone receivers most ingeniously.

6. *Malicious vandalism*—Damage done to property as part of a general expression of rage or frustration. This vandalism may be indiscriminate but often is directed at symbols of the middle class, public institutions, and anonymity-promoting systems, such as subways, schools, automobiles.

Such a classification makes it clear that there are many motivations for vandalism and many kinds of people who may be *labeled* vandals.

When is destruction vandalism?   The night after the final examination in Western Civilization, it is traditional in some schools for freshmen to "let off steam" by breaking up things, usually dormitory furniture, or to have food fights in the cafeteria. The guilty parties (if an investigation is made) are reprimanded privately and asked to clean up and pay part of the repair costs. The damage done during the "panty raids" on girls' dorms in some schools or to town property after a big football game has likewise usu-

"It's encouraging that this campus is shying away from violence and is back to hanging the football coach in effigy again!"

ally been accepted as a "normal" process because "boys will be boys." Legal prosecution is rare and the matter is typically handled with a harsh word and a wink from the Dean of Students. In contrast, breaking college windows becomes "trashing" if it is seen as part of a radical protest, and is reacted to with more severe judicial action—even when the extent of property damage is the same as in the mischief of the "fraternity boys," "the frosh," or "the jocks" and considerably less than the window breakage in the public schools of any large city.   ■

In 1965, there was a public outcry concerning a mad political plot in England when the names "Andy" and "Dell" were scratched on the Kennedy memorial at Runnymede. The word "Peace" painted on Canterbury Cathedral was considered an act of vandalism—"the work of a lunatic." However, obscene graffiti in less notable places are tolerated, as was "Kilroy was here," painted on virtually everything by American soldiers in World War II.

Derailing a train by putting obstacles on the track is mischief if done by children, vandalism if they have attained the age of reason, or sabotage if the cargo of the train is related to the national defense. Even killing animals becomes a sport if the killer has a license to hunt. While polluting the environment by littering is a criminal act that draws a fine if done by an individual, pollution of the air, water, and earth by large factories and powerful utilities companies did not even draw public censure until the recent ecology movement identified these acts as vandalism against the property of mankind. To a large extent, vandalism is what someone has *called* vandalism.

Finding sense in the "senselessness."   A number of important consequences follow from calling a given destructive act "an act of vandalism." The first is to deny that it could result from legitimate motives. The second is to help define certain people as "deviants whose irrationality is a danger to everyone." The third is to absolve the society: people blame the supposedly disturbed mind of the vandal instead of looking for possible causes in the individual's transactions with society. Finally, it implies the futility of remedial action, the impossibility of scientific investigation of the problem, and the desperate need for greater police deterrents and stiffer penalties.

It *is* possible, however, to make sense of even apparently senseless malicious vandalism. One can accomplish this by talking to gang members, by observing the behavior of college students engaged in acts of physical destruction, and through various kinds of field experiments.

Analysis of the behavior of violent gangs reveals several interrelated causal factors in their violent acts (Becker, 1963; W. Miller, 1966; Yablonsky, 1968). Gang members, like many unorganized individuals in lower socioeconomic groups, lead lives with little hope of change or significant improvement, without feelings of ownership or relatedness to society. Social conditions have limited their accessibility to the traditional means of "making it," of gaining status, prestige, and social power. They have reacted by becoming outsiders, forming a counterculture with its own norms. But they still need to *use* the traditional culture in order to "make it" in their own subculture. One gang member said,

"If I would of got the knife, I would have stabbed him. That would have gave me more of a build-up. People would have respected me for what I've done and things like that. They would say, 'There goes a cold killer.' It makes you feel like a big shot." (Yablonsky, 1968, pp. 230-231)

For such a youth, vandalism against property and violence against people may be a reaction to transform boredom into excitement and to derive pleasure from violating a social taboo. At a deeper level, it may be an affirmation that powerless people who are usually controlled by institutions and things can at times rebel and be the controllers. Malicious vandalism can be seen as a public acceptance of society's rejection and as an active attempt to establish oneself as an outsider.

Perhaps the most psychologically interesting cause of acts of vandalism that do *not* have tactical, ideological, play, or revenge bases is the tendency for an apparently *senseless* act to receive *more reinforcement* than one that is understandable and predictable. A person makes his mark, gains his reputation, is remembered or feared for behavior that is out of the ordinary, unaccountable, and unlikely to be performed by others in the same situation. A justifiable act of violence or vandalism can be explained as determined by the situation—something almost anyone in your position would do. To do a thing (or "do in" a thing) for its own sake without such a push

● The tow-truck operator who removed the battered hulk said that the last car he had seen in that condition had been hit by an express train.

from the environment is to show the arbitrariness of your personal power and the purely internal forces controlling your action. We see this in Albert Camus' play *Caligula*, where the Roman emperor attempts to show that he is a god by his arbitrary exercise of power over the life and death of other people.

It is easy for college students reading this text to dissociate themselves from the violent gang member described above. However, one need only provide an old car, a sledgehammer, and the sanction to smash the car in order to unleash the same degree of violence in even the most timid of middle-class intellectual college students.

One freshman dormitory group invited to such a "smash-in" not only demolished the car in a short time, but set it ablaze, tried to prevent firemen from extinguishing it, and had to be restrained by police order from attacking it again. Graduate students who were invited to try their hand at just denting an old car a bit were reluctant at first, but got so carried away with the exhilarating feeling of physically destroying something that they did not want to stop. At one point, one student was stomping on the roof, two others were trying to pull the doors off, and another was systematically trying to break all the glass. •

Who becomes a vandal?   In a more systematic effort to observe who the people are that vandalize automobiles and what the conditions associated with such vandalism are, a simple field study was recently performed by Fraser and Zimbardo (1969). ◆

Two used automobiles in good condition were abandoned on the streets with their license plates removed and their hoods raised. One was placed a block from the New York University campus in the Bronx, the other a block from the Stanford University campus in Palo Alto, California. Hidden observers watched, photographed, and took notes on all those who came into contact with the "bait." The researchers expected to find that the greater anonymity in New York City would lead to a greater incidence of vandalism to the New York car and that most of the vandals would be adolescents and young children.

The first prediction was confirmed; the second was certainly not. Only ten minutes after the New York car was staked out, the first auto strippers appeared—a mother, father, and young son. The mother acted as lookout while father and son emptied the trunk and glove compartment, then hacksawed out the radiator

◆ The first view shows the "respectable" middle-class family who were the first to begin stripping the car. In the second view, another adult vandal removes one of the tires. In the third view, a group of youngsters take their turn at picking over the now-battered remains.

and pulled out the battery. Soon after they drove off, another passing car stopped and its adult driver jacked up the abandoned car and removed the best of its tires. By the end of the day, a steady stream of *adult* vandals had removed every conceivable removable part of the car.

Then random destruction began, as other passers-by stopped to examine the car and then cut up a tire,

◆ **FOR THIRTY PIECES OF SILVER . . .**

FRANKS' BETRAYER GOT NAZI REWARD

'Usual Amount,' $1.40 Each.
Paid for Anne and Family

Special to The New York Times

BONN, Jan. 31 A reward was paid to the betrayer of Anne Frank and her family, one of the defendants in a trial in Munich said today.

Wilhelm Zöpf, a former major in the SS, or Elite Guard, who is accused of complicity in the murders of thousands of Dutch Jews, said that the Franks' betrayer had received "the usual amount" for telling where the Jewish family was hidden and enabling their arrest.

In general this sum was said to have been 5 gulden (about $1.40) a person, but this was later increased.

Zöpf, who is 58 years old, testified that he had been acting under orders and had not been in a position "to carry out something on my own" or to sabotage the rounding up of Jews and their deportation.

urinated on the door, broke all windows, and dented in the hood, fenders, door, and roof.

"In less than three days what remained was a battered, useless hulk of metal, the result of twenty-three incidents of destructive contact. The vandalism was almost always observed by one or more other passers-by, who occasionally stopped to chat with the looters. Most of the destruction was done in the daylight hours, not at night (as had been anticipated), and the adults' stealing clearly preceded the window-breaking, tire-slashing fun of the youngsters. The adults were all well-dressed, clean-cut whites who would under other circumstances have been mistaken for mature, responsible citizens demanding more law and order." (pp. 287, 290)

That anonymity provides a release of inhibitions against engaging in such antisocial behavior is inferred from the startling contrast between what occurred in the two different locations. In the town of Palo Alto, not a single item was stolen, nor was any part of the car vandalized during the full week it was left abandoned. Instead, as a sign of the greater prevailing sense of social consciousness, one man passing by in the rain protectively lowered the hood.

People follow the norms of a society if they have a part in that society and have a feeling of social trust, reciprocity, and mutual cooperation. One can predict that conditions that create alienation and social inequity and put some people outside of the conventional reward structure of the society will inevitably make them indifferent to its sanctions, laws, and implicit norms. Such a reaction, though pathological, is not senseless: it is to be expected. And man, with all his potential for better things, cheats another neighbor, loads another gun, makes a Molotov cocktail, builds a prison, and pads his own cell in the insane asylum.

Dehumanizing Influences and Their Results

What would it take to make *you* kill another person? Could you cut the eyes out of a dead body? Can you imagine turning down a poor family's request for some food or clothing if you were in a position to authorize it just by signing your name? Is it conceivable that you would ever decide that a particular group were unfit and order their extermination?

These taboo behaviors and others become possible for normal, morally upright, and idealistic people to perform when conditions facilitate a *dehumanized* perception of the other person or group. Once you stop perceiving others as having the same feelings, impulses, thoughts, and purposes in life as you do, and psychologically eliminate or extract any human qualities they might share with you, you are prepared to treat them as dehumanized objects. The golden rule then becomes "Do unto others as you would."

This perceptual change is accompanied by a change in the descriptive and evaluative labels used to identify these objects under consideration. They are seen as—and called—"different," "inferior," "diseased," "unworthy," "untouchable," "undesirable," "the enemy," "a threat to security," "the masses," and so on. In turn, these cognitive manipulations serve to constrain the emotional arousal that one normally experiences in interacting with *people*. It therefore becomes possible to act unhampered by previously learned and self-imposed inhibitions about hurting people; to act solely out of self-interest and needs for immediate personal gratification. Others are then "used" if they have some instrumental value, ignored if they are demanding, and destroyed if they become a source of irritation.

Since antiquity, men have made slaves of other men who were their enemies in battle or who were racially different. As "slaves," they became chattels, sold to the highest bidder; families were broken up, women sexually exploited, and men degraded and sometimes literally worked to death. The attempted genocide of Jews and gypsies by the Nazis could be carried out with the same efficiency as occurs daily at the animal slaughterhouses in Omaha, by the simple expedient of perceiving these fellow human beings as inferior forms of animal life. ◆

While such examples may seem unreal because they are so far removed from your everyday life, the underlying psychological mechanism operates in many familiar situations and poses a constant threat to pervert the principles of social justice and human dignity.

A student pledging a fraternity is made to contribute to his own dehumanization by reciting, "A pledge is the lowest form of animal life on campus." College students can harass, humiliate, and often inflict considerable pain on other students if they are "brothers" and the others are "pledges."

We can identify some of the conditions which encourage people to treat others inhumanely and deprive them of their personal identity. Dehumanization may be: (a) socially imposed, (b) imposed in self-defense, (c) imposed deliberately for self-gratification, or (d) rationalized as being for the public good, a case of "the end justifying the means."

Socially Imposed Dehumanization

Some nations engage in wars for power, territory, and aggrandizement, and wars require individuals to fight them. In order to get men to violate the learned principle, "Thou shalt not kill," they are given a "cause," an "enemy" with less "right to live," and rewards for defending the cause by destroying the enemy. In war, "a premium is put upon blood-thirstiness, and the community extols the individual who is most effective in inflicting injuries upon the bodies and lives of the members of an opposing group. This becomes, in effect, a sublimation, for now the soldier can by the same acts give vent to his primitive passions and reap the approbation of his fellows." (MacCurdy, 1918)

The act of killing is redefined as one of necessity, just as you might kill a mosquito that is stinging you or a snake about to strike. Once the barriers against killing are removed, then the concept of "enemy" can be generalized to include anyone who is different or who threatens the individual soldier's security. This can be seen in the events described by the war veteran on page 534. A derogatory label like "gook" also helps the soldier not to see his enemy as persons.

Society can impose conditions which foster dehumanization in less obvious ways than through the machinery of war. Imagine spending the better part of your life having to work in a coal mine under constant danger of a cave-in, with the likelihood of contracting lung disease, spending your days without daylight, and then living in squalid housing because that is all that is available in your town for people like you. In order to make a decent wage, thousands upon thousands must work on assembly lines. On an automobile assembly line, cars may pass by each work station at the rate of over fifty an hour. Each person has less than a minute to perform his task, and must do so hour after hour. "The thing about this job," said one cog-in-the-machinery at an automobile plant, "is that the line never stops. And because it's inhuman, it never takes into account the fact that sometimes human beings get tired." (Quoted in *Newsweek*, Sept. 14, 1970). •

In order to process large numbers of people efficiently, administrators of institutions often begin to become as concerned with "managing the flow," monitoring time schedules, and minimizing disrupting influences as with whatever their ostensible function is. Once the number of individuals requiring a given service becomes too great, they stop being seen or treated as "individuals." Moving mental patients in and out of the cafeteria and the showers may take precedence over therapeutic concerns. As college enrollments increase, students become anonymous IBM numbers, and it is increasingly difficult for faculty members to relate to them on a personal level sufficiently even to recognize them outside of class. Being shoved around by the employees hired as subway "packers" in the Tokyo Transit System is no less dehumanizing than being given an administrative runaround or being told that there can be no (human) exceptions to "the rules."

Dehumanization in Self-Defense

When an individual has to function in situations that ordinarily arouse very intense feelings and elicit painful empathy, the "institutional sergeant" syndrome may develop. Students sometimes seek jobs with urban welfare departments out of an idealistic fervor to help poor people and then find their altruistic sentiments souring into cynicism under the excessive number of cases they are assigned and the enormity of the problems faced by their clients. As dedication to improving other people's lives takes a back seat to completing all the required paperwork, people become "case loads," and the main priority becomes simply reducing the case-load list. It is not uncommon for some case workers to begin refusing requests for food supplements and clothing because of the extra red tape involved plus suspicions that they are being "conned." The high turnover rate in social welfare departments is due partly to the despair that

case workers come to feel about their own ineffectiveness. The same self-protective, impersonal style of reacting to people is sometimes seen in those who work with mentally retarded or schizophrenic children, patients with terminal diseases, and institutionalized old people.

In many of these alleged "homes" the hapless inmates are given excessive tranquilizers to control them; are forced to be inactive and stay bedridden to cut down insurance risks and make it easier to manage them; are denied privacy, deprived of small conveniences, and not allowed any idiosyncrasies: and finally are given only a minimally adequate diet. It becomes obvious to the patients that their continued existence is nothing more than a burden for the staff and their relatives (Burger, 1969).

It is interesting to inquire into the techniques used to enable medical students to dissect their first cadaver—since dismembering a dead body violates basic taboos. It is common practice for example, to keep the body entirely covered except for the region to be dissected and never to begin with the face or eyes of the corpse. Surgeons have reported that before they could perform their role effectively, they had to learn not to perceive a whole person under their scalpel but only an organ, tissue, or bone.

How do psychiatrists psychologically disengage themselves from involvement in their patients' troubled lives and still respond to them sensitively and personally? How do male gynecologists learn not to become sexually aroused at the sight of their patients' bodies? Such questions reveal the more subtle aspects of the process of dehumanization.

Dehumanization for Self-Gratification

Another source of dehumanization stems from purely selfish needs for gratification. Basic to the desire for personal power and for satisfaction of impulses toward lust and sexual perversion is the use of others solely for one's own gain, pleasure, or entertainment. In prostitution, a person openly buys the privilege of dehumanizing another person. But it may also occur at a covert level among men for whom sexual intercourse is only a self-gratifying experience, in which the woman is simply the means. The dehumanization of women is obvious in the way men label them:

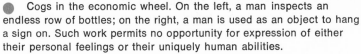 Cogs in the economic wheel. On the left, a man inspects an endless row of bottles; on the right, a man is used as an object to hang a sign on. Such work permits no opportunity for expression of either their personal feelings or their uniquely human abilities.

"beasts" or "dogs" if they are not attractive, "pigs" if they are promiscuous, "cows" if big-breasted, and "a piece" if physically appealing.

The depths to which this distortion of human concern and interpersonal sensitivity can go are revealed in news accounts of people taunting a would-be suicide to go through with it for the sheer pleasure of seeing him do so. An even more unbelievable example of dehumanization is the report of patients at a mental hospital being smuggled out of the institution by attendants and forced into prostitution. Even little girls were included. The attendants allegedly received ten dollars for each such patient they smuggled out—the patient got a piece of candy or a coin (UPI release, March 25, 1969).

Dehumanization for the Public Good (or, The Final Solution Revisited)

History has shown that the only requirement for one group of people to be able to justify the killing of another group is a perception that the other group is "unfit" and represents a threat to the "fit"—and therefore must perish for the benefit of the society as a whole. To demonstrate the current validity of such a frightening assertion, a social scientist studied the reactions of a large group of college students to an alleged threat to their security.

The subjects were male and female students at the University of Hawaii, ranging in age from seventeen to forty-eight. Groups of twenty to thirty were assembled to hear a brief speech by a professor. This authority asked for their cooperation as intelligent and educated people to assist in the application of scientific procedures to kill the mentally and emotionally unfit. The problem was convincingly presented in the following context:

"In recent times, a growing concern with the increasing menace of population explosion has taken place. Of particular concern is the fact that the unfit (*i.e.*, the mentally and emotionally unfit), are increasing the population much faster than the emotionally fit and intelligent humans. Unless something drastic is done about this, the day will come when the fit and the intelligent part of the population will find itself in danger. Education and birth-control devices are not succeeding in controlling this population explosion, and unfortunately it has now become necessary to devise new methods of coping with this problem—and new measures are being considered by several of the major powers in the world including our own. One of these devices is euthanasia,

Ψ Close-up   *"Relocation Camps" for Japanese Americans*

Less than a year after the Japanese attack on Pearl Harbor, over 110,000 Japanese Americans were taken from their homes in the Pacific Coastal states and forced to live in "relocation camps" in the deserted areas of Idaho, Arizona, and other western states. *Nisei,* American citizens of Japanese origin, had to sell their furniture, homes, and stores for a pittance and relocate in centers guarded by soldiers, "detained" by barbed wire and machine guns. This enforced migration cost the government almost 89 million dollars to accomplish. But those Americans who were aware of the evacuation program thought no price was too high to pay in order to rid the country of this "dangerous element." This sentiment was carried in the newspapers and promoted in Congress, even though other Nisei were fighting in the American military, and German and Italian citizens and aliens were not similarly sent away to detention camps in the interest of national security.

Syndicated columnist Henry McLemore demanded an immediate roundup of Japanese Americans and wrote: "Herd 'em up, pack 'em off and give 'em the inside room in the badlands. Let 'em be pinched, hurt, hungry and dead up against it. . . . Let us have no patience with the enemy. . . ."

In the *Congressional Record* are the following examples of the kind of thinking that prominent, influential leaders of the country were willing to put down for all posterity: "General Dewitt: 'They are a dangerous element. . . . There is no way to determine their loyalty. . . . It makes no difference whether he is an American citizen; theoretically he is still a Japanese, and you can't change him. . . . You can't change him by giving him a piece of paper. . . .' Senator Stewart: 'They [the Japanese] are cowardly and immoral. They are different from Americans in every conceivable way, and no Japanese . . . should have the right to claim American citizenship. . . . A Jap is a Jap anywhere you find him, and his taking the oath of allegiance to this country would not help, even if he should be permitted to do so. . . .' Congressman Rankin: 'This is a race war. . . . The white man's civilization has come into conflict with Japanese barbarism. . . . I say it is of vital importance that we get rid of every Japanese whether in Hawaii or on the mainland. . . .'" (Quoted in Hosokawa, 1969)

The photo shows the barracks at Heart Mountain, Wyoming, where 10,000 Japanese Americans lived. What would your reaction be to rejection like this by your country? One of the reactions of this group was shown in the work of the Japanese American Citizens' League in 1970 for repeal of Title II of the Detention Act of 1950. There was fear that this old law, still on the books, might enable reactivation of the detention camps for the "troublemakers" of the 1970s.

which means mercy killing. Such killing is considered by most experts as not only being beneficial to the unfit, because it puts them out of the misery of their lives, but more importantly it will be beneficial to the healthy, fit, and more educated segment of the population. It is therefore a 'final solution' to a grave problem.

"This should not be a surprising thought since we already practice it in many countries—including our own. We do decide when a human is unfit to live as in the case of capital punishment. What is not clear, however, is which method of killing should be applied, which method is least painful, and who should do the killing and/or decide when killing should be resorted to.

"For these reasons, further research is required and our research project is concerned with this problem. We need to relate intelligent and educated people's decisions to such problems, and we are therefore asking you to help us out. The findings of our studies will be applied to humans once the system has been perfected. At the moment, we need to try this out with animals first, and only when the necessary data have been obtained will it be applied to human beings in this and other countries. It is important that this be studied and applied scientifically."

Slight variations were made in four separate studies in the imminence of the threat, in the means to be used (warfare versus euthanasia), and in which group was characterized as unfit (Americans, minority groups, Asians). The students indicated whether or not they approved of the various solutions presented and then answered several questions about the practical aspects of "systematic killing."

At the end they were told the true purpose of the experiment. From their emotional responses and their attempts to justify their previous answers, it was assumed that they had accepted the problem as stated and had been concerned about its solution.

In the first variation, about two thirds approved of the "scientific solution" when the threat was expected to occur within the subject's own lifetime while two fifths endorsed it even if the threat would not be a danger for seventy to a hundred years. The use of scientific extermination was preferred over killing the unfit by sending them to battle, and there was more endorsement of killing of groups more distant from one's own. Their answers to the questions are presented in the table. (Mansson, 1969). ■

Here was a direct parallel to Hitler's "final solution" of the "Jewish problem." But it was presented as a high-minded scientific project, endorsed by scientists, planned for the benefit of humanity, and actually even a kindness to those who would be eliminated. It was further "justified" by an analogy to

■ **OPINIONS CONCERNING THE "FINAL SOLUTION"**

1. Do you agree that there will always be people who are more fit in terms of survival than not?	*Agree*	516
	Disagree	54
2. If such killing is judged necessary, should the person or persons who make the decisions also carry out the act of killing?	*Yes*	225
	No	245
3. Would it work better if one person was responsible for the killing and another person carried out the act?	*Yes*	451
	No	119
4. Would it be better if several people pressed the button but only one button would be causing death? This way anonymity would be preserved and no one would know who actually did the killing.	*Yes*	367
	No	203
5. What would you judge to be the best and most efficient method of inducing death?	*Electrocution*	10
	Painless poison	53
	Painless drugs	507
6. If you were required by law to assist would you prefer to:		
(a) *be the one who assists in the decisions?*		483
(b) *be the one who assists with the killing?*		46
(c) *assist with both the decision and the killing?*		8
No answer		33
7. Most people agree that in matters of life and death extreme caution is required. Most people also agree that under extreme circumstances, it is entirely just to eliminate those judged dangerous to the general welfare. Do you agree?	*Yes*	517
	No	27
	Undecided	26

capital punishment, and those whose opinions were being solicited were flattered as being intelligent, educated, and having high ethical values. In case there might be any lingering misgivings, assurances were made that much careful research would be carried out before action of any kind would be taken with human beings. It is likely that all 570 subjects would have said they disapproved Hitler's extermination of six million Jews, but when it was labeled differently and disguised as something noble, 517 of them accepted the basic premise and all but 33 even indicated what aspect of the job *he* or *she* would prefer to take part in. Not one of these college students said he or she would refuse to have a part in the undertaking.

This study should give every reader pause, for it shows how little effort might be necessary to translate these "artificial" experimental findings into the same nightmare of reality which occurred in Germany in World War II—and in other places and other times before that. The real threat to mankind is the presence in each man of the fear for his own life and conditions which allow him to dehumanize and devalue the life of another man.

Chapter Summary

Man has been viewed by some as noble by nature but corrupted by civilization, by others as evil by nature and held in line only by social pressures. Paradoxically the very capacities that make possible his greatest achievements also, if misused, can cause the greatest misery.

The prevalence of *aggression* has led some to attribute it to an *instinct* or to look for *physiological correlates* of aggressiveness in the *brain* or in *biochemical processes* or perhaps in faulty *genetic inheritance.* Others have seen aggression as the result of *experience*—as a response to *frustration,* particularly when *releasers in the environment* encourage it. Such thinkers, like those who have argued for an aggressive instinct, have assumed that aggressiveness, once aroused, would find some method of expression, direct or indirect; they have thus encouraged safe methods of *catharsis* and have seen *scapegoating* as one of several ways in which aggression might be displaced to a target safer than the one actually responsible for arousing it.

Children can learn aggressiveness from watching an aggressive model without having performed the response themselves. When the model is punished, they learn the response but make it only where they expect to gain from it. They also can learn to be aggressive through being punished physically by their parents.

More research is needed on the role of the victim in encouraging aggression. In police-citizen violence both sides typically are reacting to what they perceive as a lack of respect by the other and a threat to their own worth.

Nonaggressiveness and *cooperation,* like aggressiveness, can be learned through *modeling* and *reinforcement. Peer-group pressure* is more effective than *pressure from above* for holding aggressiveness in check. Aggressiveness, once triggered, can itself come to be *reinforcing* and may be very difficult to extinguish; thus *preventive measures* seem the most promising means of control.

Freedom, by placing responsibility for choice and action on the individual instead of on external authorities, can be frightening to an insecure person. Some individuals learn to fear freedom and to gain a feeling of strength and safety by identifying with a strong authority, gaining self-confidence by unquestioning acceptance of clear standards or a rigid ideology and rejecting any deviation or innovation. *Prejudiced* attitudes toward all outsiders tend to be associated with high scores on measures of *anti-Semitism, political and economic conservatism,* and *fascist attitudes;* the term *authoritarian personality* has been used to designate the person high on these four scales.

Although the Nuremburg trials were held on the assumption that the war crimes had been committed by evil men, laboratory studies have demonstrated that people generally will obey commands from someone they perceive as a *legitimate authority;* in "real life," people justify such behavior as "following orders" but tend to assume that those who give the orders will not go beyond safe or justifiable limits.

Our susceptibility to social influence, which can foster survival and well-being, can also work to our detriment. Certain conditions foster a *heightened suggestibility* in which groups and individuals engage in *irrational behavior,* ranging from *mob panics* to the self-injury of the *flagellants.* Crowded urban life too often leads to *impersonality, alienation,* and *anonymity,* which, in turn, *lower constraints* and keep people from providing each other with the supportive social environment we all need. Paradoxically, bystanders are less likely to intervene in an emergency when several others are present than when no one else is present who could help. Anonymity may be sought as a condition in which one can safely engage in exuberance or destructiveness without being held personally accountable.

Vandalism has become a costly and widespread phenomenon and is often seen as *"senseless"* and *incomprehensible.* There are several forms of vandalism, however, and several motives that can lead to it. Like other behavior, it has causes and these causes can be identified. Threats, stiff penalties, and more police cannot be expected to cure vandalism; only measures that remove the causes and provide greater rewards for legitimate, socially oriented behavior can be expected to do so. Conditions that create alienation and social inequity and put some people outside the conventional reward structures can be expected to make them indifferent to its norms.

Conditions that facilitate a *dehumanized* perception of another individual or group make it possible to do violence to them or liquidate them entirely without feeling that one is dealing with other persons. People may dehumanize others for several reasons: because of an *abnormal social situation* such as a war, in an effort at *self-defense* or at cutting off of normal feeling, as a means of *self-gratification,* or as a way of advancing what is perceived as the *"general welfare."* Groups perceived as unfit and a threat to the majority may be liquidated without qualms by the use of the rationalization that it is for the public good.

Chapter 14

Deviance, Pathology, and Madness

The unknown, the unusual, the unexplained, the mysterious have always held a peculiar fascination for man. They stimulate his curiosity to explore and understand, but they also evoke his fear. The former reaction has been institutionalized by science, education and art; the latter reaction has led to interest in pagan religious practices, witchcraft, magic, the occult, and unidentified flying objects. What cannot be understood cannot be controlled by man and, if malevolent, can perhaps come to control or even destroy him. The ambivalence in our reaction to unknown forces also is heightened by our belief that if someone were to discover their secret power and partake of it, he could thereby become all-powerful in controlling other men. Therein lie the seeds for the development of a concept of human evil and a fear of other men.

The fundamental complexity of man's reaction to events, situations, and behavior that are beyond his comprehension and established perceptual framework can be witnessed in our reactions to old science-fiction movies, ghost stories, and tales of madness. A typical scenario of many movie serials was for a dedicated scientist working alone in his basement laboratory to discover the secret of immense strength, invulnerability, transformation of matter, regeneration of life, or immortality. In the process of doing so, he would become obsessed with the idea of using this power for his own selfish motives. Precisely because the audience might identify with such anti-social impulses, the scientist had to die in the end and his discovery be lost forever. Society punishes the offender for his misdeeds and the audience indirectly for their vicarious participation in evil.

Remember your reaction to ghost stories as a child? They had to be frightening enough to hold your attention, but not so realistic as to pose an imminent threat.

One of the authors, asked by a group of young children to tell a ghost story in the darkened cellar of his home, kept them enraptured and squealing with tales of ghosts, goblins, and witches. But when, unseen, he threw a metal bar which clanged loudly against the far wall, the children ran out screaming and would not listen to the completion of the story even in a lighted room.

As scientific discoveries of nuclear bombs, antimatter, protein synthesis, organ transplants, and moon voyages force science fiction off to even more remote galaxies, and ghost stories do not stand up under children's increasingly sophisticated demands for validity checks, only our response to madness remains mingled with fascination and fear. Abnormal psychology courses remain popular among college students, and the pathology section of the introductory course is usually rated as the most interesting part of the course. Yet there is much less sympathy for someone

557

with a neurosis or a psychosis than for someone with cancer. In general, the public seems to disapprove and dislike individuals deemed mentally ill (Nunnally, 1961). The person defined as "mad" has always been set apart from other men. At different times and in different places, the individual seized by fits, visions, or hallucinations has been made into a prophet or shaman and revered as one elected for divine inspiration. But more often he has been rejected, cast out, isolated, tortured, or destroyed by the society.

Sick! Sick. Sick?

No one thinks that a physical illness caused by germs, external agents, or malfunctioning organs is the fault of the sick person. But even though the mentally ill person is not held legally responsible for his actions, people perceive him as at some level responsible for having become mentally ill. "Pull yourself together!" "You've got to help yourself!" "Straighten out or you'll have nobody to blame but yourself!" "What's the matter with you, do you *want* to be crazy?" Such admonitions are often given by well-meaning friends, relatives, doctors, and law-enforcers to those whose behavior is so deviant as to be labeled "sick." They imply an intention *not* to exercise control or behave in acceptable ways. The unconscious reasoning seems to be that if there is no physical basis for mental illness, then the patient must have become abnormal of his own accord.

One way to make sense out of the frightening puzzle of abnormal behavior of any kind—antisocial or psychotic—is to regard psychopathology as a property of a special, different type of person, as something existing in him. As we saw in the case of vandalism, it alleviates our sense of responsibility to assume that we could not have had a part in inducing the behavior; it also reduces our fear that we might be subject to such aberrations. ◆

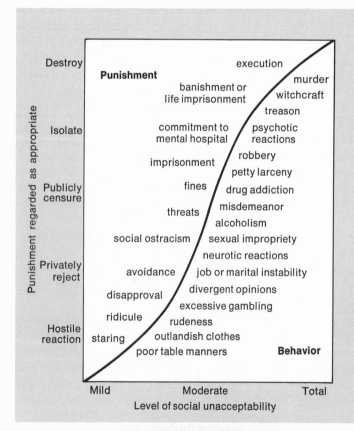

◆ **"LET THE PUNISHMENT FIT THE CRIME"**

This figure illustrates a continuum of behaviors that are deemed increasingly unacceptable and are responded to with increasing severity. Basically, all these reactions are punishments for deviance; thus behavior toward those who behave neurotically or psychotically can be seen to resemble that toward criminals and other antisocial deviants, despite our acknowledgment that the mentally ill should not be held legally responsible.

Like antisocial deviants, those showing psychopathology may be seen as threatening people's life and property. They behave in unpredictable ways, thus weakening the social control function. And more basically, they appear unable to control their behavior toward goals defined as desirable, thereby bringing into question fundamental assumptions about the dignity and integrity of human nature.

Adapted from Haas, 1965

Would You Know a Crazy Person If You Saw One?

In a physical illness there are clear, agreed-upon, usually measurable signs of pathology. For example, leukemia is identified by an unusual white-to-red blood-cell ratio, cancer by the uncontrolled growth of tumors, and paralysis by nerve degeneration and muscle unresponsivity. But mental illness is present when someone says it is.

Thus psychological pathology is established not by physical realities but by social ones. It is behavior, not tissue, that is observed, and someone has to evaluate the behavior and judge whether it is pathological. In our society, today, we generally consider a person mentally ill on the basis of some combination of the following evidence (Wegrocki, 1939; W. A. Scott, 1958; Allport, 1960):

1. He is under psychiatric care.

2. Respectable, influential members of the community (teachers, judges, parents, spouses, priests) agree that his behavior represents a given degree of maladjustment.

3. A psychiatrist or clinical psychologist makes a diagnosis of mental disturbance.

4. His test scores on psychological self-report inventories deviate by a specified extent from standards of a group designated as normal.

5. He declares himself to be "mentally sick" either explicitly or through his expressed feelings of unhappiness, anxiety, and inadequacy.

6. He behaves publicly in such ways as to call attention to his behavior as deviating from standards accepted by the majority of others in the society.

Sticks and stones may break your bones . . . but diagnostic labels make you "sick." It is important for students to appreciate that "madness" (or "insanity," "mental illness," "emotional pathology," "disturbed behavior") is not a *thing*—an objectively definable attribute of a person—but rather a *label*, a metaphor, applied to some people by others.

It is well to recall at this point the differences we noted back in Chapters 1 and 2 between observation and inference and between deductive and inductive conclusion drawing. The psychiatrist *observes* various kinds of behavior; he *infers* how they might have

been caused and how they are related and being maintained or changed. These inferences he makes on the basis of his particular theoretical orientation, type of training experiences, cultural background, and personal biases. The diagnosis and prognosis that represent his conclusion are not drawn inescapably from available premises; rather they are intelligent estimates involving an inductive leap to a generalization from certain assumptions and available fragments of evidence.

What is universal about the labeling of "abnormality" is that it marks those so designated as different from the rest of us. Such judgments carry negative connotations and imply that the individual's behavior should be changed to make it more in keeping with what the labeler regards as acceptable and appropriate for the situation.

Who should decide when a person is "mentally ill"? You might label a person "emotionally sick" with some confidence if he told you that he is unable to do things which bring him pleasure but instead does things that bring him pain; that he does not feel and act the way other people do, although he wants to; and that he often has no adequate explanation for why he feels anxious, depressed, and so on. But part of your confidence in making the diagnosis would come from the person's acceptance of his deviance, his confession of awareness of his difference, and his intention to change.

Suppose, however, that an individual who has been committed to a mental hospital tells you he is normal (as the majority will); that the world as constituted offers little pleasure; that there is pleasure in suffering for a cause; or that other people are crazy because they are behaving in ways unacceptable to *him*. Would your confidence that he was "crazy" remain as strong? (Ψ Close-up, p. 560.)

If a person had an opportunity to do X for a big reward and instead chose to do Y for a little one, would you call him "abnormal" or "not greedy"? If he gave up either reward and chose instead a course leading to certain punishment, would he be "abnormal" or "self-sacrificing," "a hero," "altruistic"? If he persisted in working toward a goal in the continued absence of a reward, would you say he was "abnormal" or unusually "determined" and "self-disciplined"? Such examples point up the arbitrariness of all these labels for behavioral acts, and our reliance upon inferred internal traits and motives to bolster the validity of our labels.

Is Any Behavior *Really* Abnormal?

Granted that labels are arbitrary and that behavior may be misjudged, is there any behavior that is always normal or always abnormal for human beings?

Is "normal" just what most people accept as normal? Inevitably, what is seen as "abnormal" is in part historically determined. A Catholic priest wants to get married; a woman smokes in public; a young man refuses induction into the army; a high-school freshman takes dope—all would have been "abnormal" in the eyes of their peers not too long ago. Are they still? Until very recently the man who entered psychotherapy because of homosexual behavior would have been made to feel society's censure for his deviant impulses and would automatically have received treatment to "cure" his "problem." Some therapists are redefining the problem today, regarding homosexuality as acceptable if it is a freely chosen alternative and not a reaction forced by fear or avoidance mechanisms based on deep feelings of inadequacy.

Or consider the Kwakiutl Indians of the Northwest Coast. They practiced a form of extreme competition which would seem crazy to an acquisitive American. They held "potlatches" in which a man gained prestige and status by being able to give away or *destroy*

Ψ *Close-up*   *Do You Have to Be Insane to Be in an Insane Asylum?*

A writer who was sent to a mental hospital after telling his psychiatrist of his abortive suicide attempt, relates the following description of the consequences. Was the author crazy or was he perceiving reality the way it was?

When I told my tale to Mr. Pipe, my psychologist, he speedily hustled me off to a legitimate head-doctor who doped me until a private ambulance came. Very much in my right and one and only mind but too paralyzed by drugs to move, I was once again taken on the long ride —this time to another hedge-trimmed bin on Long Island. I was helpless to protest, mainly because of the shame and guilt I felt for even contemplating suicide. Obviously I was not crazy, mad, psychotic, out of my mind, schizophrenic, paranoiac. I was simply a tormented man-kid who had never steeled himself to face the facts of life—who didn't know what it meant to have principles and live by them come grief or joy. . . .

Once again I was on the human assembly-line: electric shock clubbed my good brain into needless unconscious-ness (and I walked to my several executions like a brave little chappie instead of questioning them) and unquestioned Old Testament authority ruled our little club. Good-natured, but mostly cowlike and uneducated male orderlies carried out the orders from above; and apart from the mechanical treatment and the unimaginative grind of occupational therapy, each patient was left completely on his or her bewildered own. . . .

I saw now that nine tenths of the people I was quartered with were not 'insane' by any of the standards a normally intelligent person would use: the majority had lost confidence in their own ability to survive in the world outside, or their families were *afraid* of them and had palmed them off on experts, but positively no serious effort was being made to equip them to become free and independent adults. This was their birthright— beyond country and society, indeed an almost religious obligation—but they were palliated with pills or jolted with shock, their often honest rage echoed back to them as a sign of their illness. Some of them must have been 'sick,' you say. I answer: Who can not be conceived as such in a world so complex. . . . (Krim, 1964) more of his valuable possessions than his opponent. This behavior, normal among those in that culture, would be abnormal for us.

The opposite form of cultural relativity occurred among the Zuñi Indians, where "lack of ambition" did not result in a visit to the witch doctor, but was the accepted norm. The person with more initiative and drive than the others was likely to be regarded as a witch and hung up by his thumbs.

Beyond nose-counting. All these definitions of abnormality are basically statistical—how much does a given individual deviate from what most people do? "What most people do" (or what the most powerful people do), in turn, depends on the culture or epoch. Societies differ both in what the norm is and in how much variability they will tolerate before the behavior differences are seen as significant deviations. But there is always a tendency to protect the social status quo by punishing nonconformers or treating them in a variety of ways designed to bring them back to the norm or eliminate them, in order not to permit the average response ("what most people do") to shift in their direction. (Ψ Close-up, p. 562.) ●

Psychologists function as agents of the society. Yet to adopt the simplistic view that what is good for Mr. Average Person is what is *healthy* makes deviants of critics and madmen of nonconformers. It becomes obvious that the "normality" of any group's norm must in turn be judged by some other criteria. Was the anti-Semitic norm in Nazi Germany "normal"? If everyone in your college decided to take heroin, would it be "normal" to conform? Would it have been normal to be a slave owner before the Civil War?

Allport (1960) cogently argued that beyond the statistical and relative standards imposed by social systems and cultures there is an ethical standard to use in judging abnormality. He felt that a valid standard for a sound and healthy personality should be based on our human potentials rather than on any prevailing actualities.

Abraham Maslow (1962) long championed the position that the proper goal of every man is to become "self-actualized." In his view, to be psychologically healthy involves the following characteris-

"*. . . and confined you will remain until such time as you are fit to be seen among civilised people.*"

● What's abnormal?

tics: an acceptance, respect, and love for self and others; compassion for all living creatures; spontaneity of action; ability to be detached or passionately involved in different situations, as fits one's purpose; a unifying philosophy of life; a sense of the comedy and tragedy of one's existence; and a perception of reality that is efficient for the individual. He believed that though this might never become the majority reality, it would represent the most healthy and most truly human orientation.

Changes in our attitude toward psychopathology. In medieval times the "madman" was thought to be possessed by demons or suffering a justified retribution for his sins. The treatment for madness was to lock up such a source of contagious evil in a "madhouse," where a confession of evil was forced from him if possible and he was exhibited for public example and ridicule.

"Madness" assumed some new respectability when it came to be called *insanity*—a legal term denoting a lack of responsibility for one's behavior due to a mental aberration. But both the public's view and the treatment of psychologically disturbed individuals changed most when the medical label *mental illness* came into use.

Ψ *Close-up* *Social Norms As Contributors to Abnormality*

Social norms, by determining who will be rejected and branded as outcasts, may contribute to abnormality in those who cannot or will not conform, through inducing anxiety, self-doubt, and social isolation. For example, one price of our high valuation of economic success is that with any downturn in the economy there is a rise in mental-hospital admissions among the middle and upper classes.

The isolating and self-devaluating effects of our prevailing norms on one who feels inadequate to meet them are seen in the case of a forty-two-year-old man hospitalized with complaints of nervousness and insomnia, unable to hold a job or assume responsibility. It was noted: "Nothing is known about his early life except that he graduated from high school at fifteen and felt resentful that he could not go to college like his older brothers. His prewar life was unstable in that he frequently shifted jobs and residence. He states that all his early business associates went into the army as officers and have since become millionaires while he remained just 'Mickey the Mope.' All the patient's siblings are also successful in business or government and have stable homes and families."

Many people in our society have been made to feel intellectually inadequate or deficient because of excessively high standards imposed by parents, teachers, and others. Others have suffered agonies over their sexuality because of parental training which has equated sex with sin or peer training which has equated it with conquest and achievement. Feelings of being ugly, worthless, burdensome, or willfully evil may be bred into children unintentionally by parents who hold up extraordinary models for social comparison or use other "normal" child-training techniques.

A children's book popular for generations among German parents tells a series of moralistic stories in which disobedient children are punished for their failure to do what is proper. For not eating supper, the child starves and vanishes in thin air. For playing with matches, the child burns to death. For sucking his thumbs, little Struwwelpeter has them cut off. (The implications for overconcern with the genitals probably did not go unnoticed either by the anxious, guilt-ridden children treated to these bedtime tales.)

America's Tin Pan Alley replaced this Germanic heavy-handedness a few years ago with a more subtle anxiety-inducer in the song, "Santa Claus Is Comin' to Town." In it, as you may remember, children are warned that they had better watch out and not cry or even pout because Santa Claus, whose annual arrival is imminent, can see everything they are doing, even in their sleep. Concealment is impossible, and they are implored to "be good for goodness' sake!" Such a message leads a child to believe that perfect goodness is not only possible but normal, giving him an impossible standard to meet.

At the time, this seemed a great advance, for the term "mental illness" implied a "pathological" state of functioning. If a person was sick with a "mental disease," he could presumably be "treated," "rehabilitated," "cured," and returned to a "normal" state of "mental health."

What happened, however, was that this concept too often led to the treatment of the afflicted as nonpersons. They still were regarded as basically different from the rest of us (comforting thought!) and, if sick enough to be hospitalized, were kept in a state of complete dependency—the assumption being that there was nothing they could do to help themselves to get well. If they were sick, it would take a doctor to make them well, and their own role was a passive one, with no responsibility for the process of cure.

Increasingly today, psychopathology is being seen as ineffective learned behavior rather than as a psychological illness in the individual. And instead of looking for causes in the individual, many psychologists are looking increasingly to damaging social interactions or to environmental conditions that are reinforcing and thus maintaining ineffective or self-defeating behavior.

A sign of the greater tolerance for what would be classified in psychology textbooks as "behavior pathology" is seen in the substitution of less emotion-inducing metaphors and labels for the traditional "sick" ones. Compulsions become "bags," neurotic dynamics become "hang-ups," psychotic breaks become "freak-outs," and the frightening experience of discontinuity and distortion of time, place, space, and self is simply a "bad trip."

In this time of rapidly shifting social values, a counternorm is developing which advocates that each person "do his own thing," taking what he needs from the larger society but feeling no responsibility for keeping it going or helping to make the communal aggregate fulfill its functions of supporting and nourishing the individual. It may well be that the challenges being posed by this trend will lead to a more healthy concern for the individual, a reduced willingness to sacrifice individual eccentricity for the balm of consensus, and the acceptance of multiple norms of appropriateness. Meanwhile, psychiatric wards are overcrowded and understaffed and pathological tendencies of the individual are reinforced and indeed exacerbated by various forms of social pathology—problems which only concerted effort can solve.

In the next sections of this chapter, we will examine some of the most prevalent forms which social and individual pathology take. We have grouped these into five kinds of losses of potentiality for being fully human. Then, in the final chapter, we will see what can be done to put the individual back together again when what started out with fantastic potentials ends up as little more than a caricature of a man, a vegetable, or a suicidal creature bent on destroying itself.

Loss of Self-Identity and Self-Worth

It is not enough to have a predictable world. It is also essential to be able to count on oneself. Thus a part of each person's attempt to make sense out of his world and find predictability in it is his attempt to find out who he is and what he can expect from himself. Predictability implies consistency and rationality. Therefore, each person tries to prove to himself and others that he is a rational being. And because of the comfort that comes from social approval (dependent, in turn, on following social norms), most people also learn to want to see themselves as "normal"—essentially like other people.

At the root of any psychopathology is the inability of the individual to prove either that he is rational or that he is normal. If he cannot prove both but can prove one—to his own satisfaction—he may maintain a precarious equilibrium by forgoing the other.

Identification: Boon or Pitfall?

"Dumbo . . . put himself with the Cat so people wouldn't laugh at them as comedians. Cat and Dumbo are one and alike . . . ." (Mr. F. B.)

Essential to socialization is the process by which a child learn to internalize the values, beliefs, and social attitudes of the dominant adult community in which he or she will live and to identify with the same-sex parent. Without this process, the values of the society would not be maintained, and there would be no means for the peaceful transmission of power from one generation to the next. In addition, the conformity in behavior that results from this identification leads to the community's acceptance of the child and minimizes potential sources of deviance and rejection.

Despite the obvious need that society has for such a psychological process and the potential benefits that identification can offer the individual in reducing or preventing anxiety, it can also "go wrong" and harm the society or the individual or both.

The risk of false values. A society which advocates competition, headhunting, cannibalism, racism, and exploitation of the weak will be maintained by its socialized youth just as will one that values cooperation, peace, love, trust, and tolerance. Moreover, since the child is not in a position to sit back objectively and choose which parental values and behaviors to adopt and which ones to ignore or reject, his learning formula may contain a large dose of harmful ingredients. Thus, for example, a recent survey, conducted by the Salzberg Alcoholic Welfare

Organization of Vienna of over 5000 families with alcoholic parents, revealed that 60 percent of the alcoholic fathers had had alcoholic fathers of their own (UPI report, March 16, 1969).

In Chapter 13 we discussed the battered-child syndrome. What happens when these children become parents? It appears that many of them, having learned from their parents that aggression is a useful way of solving problems, become battering parents themselves. A large proportion of the parents arrested for abusing their children have recalled being knocked unconscious by their own parents when they were young (Helfer & Kempe, 1968).

The process of identification is a very hazardous one psychologically and socially. It can enable values gained at great risk and pain to be enjoyed by later generations, but it can also provide the means for the perpetuation of values that diminish man.

The risk of individuality—too much identification or too little.   Uncritical acceptance of the society's values and norms minimizes the chances that the individual will revolt against the established, traditional values. It may also lead to the pathological identification with external power that we saw in the authoritarian personality in the last chapter.

Uncritical acceptance of society's norms by most members also lessens the likelihood of innovation and advancement for the society. Thus a society needs individuality and some level of autonomy in its members. The stronger the sense of individual personal identity a child develops, the more likely he will be to show autonomy, independent judgment, and creativity. But also the greater the danger that he will develop a feeling of alienation rather than of belonging, especially if the society does not value or actively punishes his independence.

Two of the most pathological perversions of the identification process occur in the case of *identification with the aggressor* and *identification with a rejecting majority*. In the first case, one's self-identity is lost, in the other, one's self-worth.

Identification with the Aggressor

The term *identification with the aggressor* was coined by Anna Freud to designate the process that suppos-

edly takes place when a male child, both loving his father and fearing castration by him, as a result of rivalry for the mother, resolves the conflict by identifying with him. This identification process not only reduces the perceived differences between himself and his powerful father but may, through magical thinking, enable him to believe that he has the power of the stronger, supposedly would-be aggressor.

Mr. F. B.'s identification of Dumbo with the Cat can be interpreted as exemplifying this process, as can evidence from cross-cultural studies that societies in which very close mother-child ties have developed are the ones that tend to have severe initiation rites for boys at puberty (Whiting, Kluckhohn, & Anthony, 1958). Although the latter could also be explained as showing the father's jealousy over the mother's greater attention to the child who will replace the father in the society, or as an attempt to prevent rebellion of the now strong adolescent against his father, such rites do have the effect of breaking excessive dependence of the boy on the mother and of ensuring that he identifies with and accepts the man's role in his society.

Under certain conditions, however, identification with the aggressor involves an enforced fractionation of the self and an alienation of components of one's personality. Bruno Bettelheim has vividly described how identification with Nazi prison guards developed among German civilians in the concentration camps at Dachau and Buchenwald where he was imprisoned in 1938 and 1939. His analysis indicates how conditions which rendered a person helpless and dependent on the guards for survival and all reinforcement revived extreme forms of childlike identification with them. (1943, 1958)

"Prisoners seemed particularly sensitive to punishments similar to those which a parent might inflict on his child. To punish a child was within their 'normal' frame of reference, but that they should be the object of punishment destroyed their adult frame of reference. So they reacted to it not in an adult, but in a childish way—with shame and violent, impotent, unmanageable emotions directed, not against the system, but against the person inflicting the punishment. It seems that if a prisoner was cursed, slapped, pushed around 'like a child' and if he was, like a child, unable to defend himself, this revived in him behavior patterns and psychological mechanisms which he had developed in childhood. He was unable to see his treatment in its general context." (Bettelheim, 1958, p. 305)

Old prisoners had reached the final stage of adjustment to this unusual situation when they changed their personalities to mimic those of the Gestapo. They began by copying terms of verbal aggression used by the Gestapo. After several years, they practiced the same forms of physical aggression on other prisoners as did their captors. They helped get rid of the "unfit" and, when they found a traitor, might not only kill him but torture him for days first. They even attempted to look like the Gestapo and internalized a wide range of values which had not been acceptable to them previously.

"The satisfaction with which old prisoners boasted that, during the twice daily counting of the prisoners, they had stood well at attention can be explained only by their having accepted as their own the values of the Gestapo. Prisoners prided themselves on being as tough as the Gestapo members. This identification with their torturers went so far as copying their leisure-time activities. One of the games played by the guards was to find out who could stand to be hit longest without uttering a complaint. This game was copied by old prisoners." (p. 309)

The incompleteness of this pathological identification was suggested by the fact that even those who identified with the guards in these obvious and subtle ways also at times defied them courageously. But in between, taking the identity of the aggressors was less painful than keeping their own.

Identification with a Rejecting Majority

Another perversion of the identification process involves the rejection of some aspects of one's own identity because they are not acceptable to the majority community.

Self-rejection among black children. Imagine that from the time you are a child, everyone tells you that you are worthless, stupid, insignificant, and ugly and that you will never change. Imagine further that your parents, relatives, and friends also have grown up with such beliefs about themselves. You look around and all those who are similar to you are uneducated, poorly dressed, unhappy, often hungry and sick, and in inferior positions—janitors, servants, and unskilled laborers. Once you adopt the derogatory labels as

valid self-descriptions, you become "sick," for you try to reject or deny characteristics in yourself that you agree are no good but cannot separate yourself from. It is as though the mind tries to reject that part of the self that society designates as alien and inferior just as the body tries to reject a transplanted heart. (Ψ Close-up, p. 566)

The "anti-Semitic Jew" and the "white Negro" are prototypes of this identification with the majority, but the same process can also be seen among some young girls who reject their female identity in favor of a masculine role that they feel is more socially valued.

The problem of having dark skin color in a society that places value on light skin color confronts young black children by the age of three (Landreth & Johnson, 1953). Until the recent advent of the "Black is beautiful" norm, to be brown or black meant to be dirty, unclean, and everything bad.

In a study of 253 black children aged three to seven from both Northern and Southern schools, preference for a doll (among two white and two colored ones) favored a white doll. Approximately 60 percent of these children perceived a white doll as the "nice" one, and the one they liked to play with, and a colored doll as "looks bad." A third of these children through age six when asked to select "the doll that looks like you" selected a white one. Even among the children with the darkest skin color a fifth picked a white doll as looking most like them (Clark & Clark, 1958).

In an incomplete stories test, both black and white children, three to six years of age, tended to put black characters in negative roles as the "bad guy" or aggressor (Stevenson & Stewart, 1966). Black children both in the North and South chose fewer members of their own race and more whites as playmates they would like to be like or would like to play with (Morland, 1966).

Nor are such conclusions limited to black children. Recent intensive studies of Mexican-American youth likewise document their perceived status as "forgotten," "invisible" people from "across the tracks" (Heller, 1966; Rubel, 1966).

One long-term consequence of early training in "inferiority-acceptance" was shown in experiments in which college-age black students worked in biracial situations.

Black college students who had demonstrated their intellectual ability on standard, relatively objective indices,

Ψ *Close-up*   *Black Rage: Pathological or Justifiable?*

"We submit that it is necessary for a black man in America to develop a profound distrust of his white fellow citizens and of the nation. He must be on guard to protect himself against physical hurt. He must cushion himself against cheating, slander, humiliation, and outright mistreatment by the official representatives of society. If he does not so protect himself, he will live a life of such pain and shock as to find life itself unbearable. For his own survival, then, he must develop a cultural paranoia in which every white man is a potential enemy unless proved otherwise and every social system is set against him unless he personally finds out differently.

"Every black man in America has suffered such injury as to be realistically sad about the hurt done him. He must, however, live in spite of the hurt and so he learns to know his tormentor exceedingly well. He develops a sadness and intimacy with misery which has become a characteristic of black Americans. It is a *cultural depression* and a *cultural masochism*.

"He can never quite respect laws which have no respect for him, and laws designed to protect white men are viewed as white men's laws. To break another man's laws may be inconvenient if one is caught and punished, but it can never have the moral consequences involved in breaking one's own law. The result may be described as a cultural antisocialism, but it is simply an accurate reading of one's environment—a gift black people have developed to a high degree, to keep alive.

"These and related traits are simply adaptive devices developed in response to a peculiar environment. They are no more pathological than the compulsive manner in which a diver checks his equipment before a dive or a pilot his parachute. They represent normal devices for 'making it' in America, and clinicians who are interested in the psychological functioning of black people must get acquainted with this body of character traits which we call the Black Norm." (Grier & Cobbs, 1968, pp. 149-150)

---

including college board scores, and were enrolled in top-ranking colleges, nevertheless deferred to the judgments of white students when they were in biracial teams. Solutions to task problems presented by a white member of the four-man groups were more likely to be listened to and accepted than were the solutions proposed by one of the black members. Special "assertion training" was required to break this deferential set (Katz, 1970).   •

Results such as these heighten the urgency of the need for self-assertion and racial acceptance to be a basic part of the child's education at home and in school.

Paradoxically, prejudice can exert its maximum destructive impact when it operates as part of the fabric of the society, in the absence of hostile intentions and without emotional arousal or even awareness of its existence. Through consensual validation, what start out as opinions become facts, and soon both the agent and the target of discrimination function without questioning the assumptions underlying

their "shared reality." This is called *institutional* prejudice: the institutionalization of prejudiced attitudes and perceptions in this way has defined a new state of reality.

Self-rejection among women.   Institutional prejudice is seen quite clearly in the subtle though pervasive bias against women perpetuated by our male-dominated institutions. Men do not go about shouting that women are inferior. But enough elements of social reality are arranged in a way that keeps women in a subordinate role that almost everyone has tacitly accepted the "fact" of their inferiority, including women for the most part—at least until the Women's Lib movement.

The paucity of women's contributions to mathematics and science is sometimes cited as proof of their deficiencies in these fields. Also there is a higher probability that they will drop out of graduate school. But are they inherently less creative, with inferior mathematical and scientific ability and less ability to work autonomously, or is that what they learn to expect they are? Sex-role differences, which start in the cradle, are underscored by educational practices which define the "normal" girl as feminine, dependent, not ambitious or assertive, interested in practical matters (home economics rather than philosophy), and emotional and intuitive rather than rational and scientifically analytical.

While boys are playing with guns and their mechanical erector sets, girls get dolls and are encouraged to "play house" in preparation for their "station in life" as obedient, dedicated wives and self-sacrificing mothers. They are more likely than male students of equal ability to be counseled to go to commercial high schools and "finishing schools." Unless they are exceptional, they are less likely to receive encouragement to continue on with higher education. If they are exceptional and do the original work required for a Ph.D. degree, the chances of getting a good job that will be personally and financially rewarding are rare. For example, a recent survey revealed that in one large western university in 1970,

only 3.6 percent of the professors were women—a lower proportion than fifty years before. The psychology department, which awards more than one quarter of its doctoral degrees to women, had last appointed a woman to its own regular staff in 1924.

Of nearly 30 million women in the work force, nearly two thirds work as domestics, clerical, service, or sales workers. In 1968, a woman with four years of college training earned on the average $6,694 a year—the same as a man with only an eighth-grade education—and much less than her male classmates, who averaged $11,795.

Women are much more likely than men to be the butt of jokes in popular periodicals.

An analysis of 740 jokes taken from six years of the feature "Humor, the Best Medicine" in *Reader's Digest* shows that there are six times as many antiwomen jokes as antimale ones. In fact, the humor in the joke frequently depends upon an acceptance by the reader of the woman as "spendthrift," "incompetent," "gossipy," "a nag," "sentimental," "money-mad," or "jealous" (Meadow, 1970).

● The way in which a prevailing racist ideology can be internalized by children who are victims of it—and the anxieties it can engender—are shown in these drawings made by a six-year-old black girl named Ruby. They were drawn during her first year in an integrated southern school.

The white children are drawn as taller and more robust; they are smiling and their bodies are more clearly articulated and intact. In contrast, the black children are drawn without emotion, are asymmetrical, and are missing parts of their bodies. They are generally much smaller and are drawn with less attention to detail.

A black girl   A white girl   A black boy   A white boy

If discrimination begins early enough and is consistently applied in many spheres of the person's life, then that is the only social reality available on which to base one's self-identity and from which to derive a sense of self-worth. If discriminatory practices and prejudiced beliefs form the prevailing orientation, they appear as the "natural" way of the world, as the only "rational" perspective, both to the discriminators and to those discriminated against. Thus many studies have documented the general acceptance by women of the stereotype of inferiority.

In one study six articles, on subjects ranging from education to law, were read by college women. Nothing was said about the authorship of the articles but for each subject half the articles were supposedly by a male author and half by a female author (John T. McKay or Joan T. McKay, for example). The same articles were consistently rated as more authoritative and more interestingly written when attributed to male authors than when attributed to female authors (Goldberg, 1968).

One can wonder if the same experiment, repeated ten years from now, would have the same results.

What functions does discrimination serve?   In our analysis of operant conditioning (in Chapter 5) we noted that for behavior to be maintained it must have reinforcing consequences. Prejudice and discrimination continue because ultimately someone derives some measure of reinforcement from them. There are a number of reasons why someone might become and remain prejudiced.

A child in quest of information about "reality" may have his *needs for cognitive clarity* satisfied by parents or other usually reliable communicators who give him a negative "fact sheet" on one or more specific groups. Children come to believe in the truth of these statements just as they do in other descriptions adults give them about reality, and they accept "do's and don't's" as readily here as elsewhere. Supporting such direct teaching is the example provided by the adult *models* that they admire and want to emulate and be approved by.

When prejudices are in keeping with prevailing social norms and are *reinforced* by parents and peers, and when tolerance is punished, the outcome is predictable. Children learn to make the responses that will bring them the consequences they want.

When discriminatory acts are reinforced by *economic gain* or perpetuated by fear of *economic loss*, the continuation of the behavior can be predicted. And, as we saw in the last chapter, the fact that a group has been the target of prejudice and aggression in the past makes them a likely target in the present.

As we saw in the discussion of the authoritarian personality, prejudice can serve *ego-defensive functions*. By adopting stereotypes of outgroup members as the embodiment of all things evil, an anxious, insecure person with hostile or sexual impulses that he cannot accept in himself, can project and displace his own feelings and maintain a view of himself as the upright guardian of the good. He also *enhances his status* by perceiving others as inferior and himself as a leader of the righteous.

Finally, once a group becomes the target of prejudice and discrimination, it is socially segregated, preventing normal interchange and destroying or blocking channels of communication. This isolation, in turn, allows rumors and stereotypes to go unchecked, fantasies to surface and grow, and the "strangeness" of the group, real and fancied, to increase over time. The isolation of American Indians on reservations and the segregated housing patterns in our cities increase the alienation between groups and prevent either reality checks or ordinary interaction. (Ψ Close-up, p. 569.)

The "strangeness" and differences of an isolated people can even be a result of the discrimination and segregation instead of a cause of it.

In Japan, since medieval times, based on the myth of biological inferiority, there has been systematic segregation of a pariah caste known as the *Burakumin*. Not racially different, or visibly distinguishable from other Japanese, they can be identified with certainty only by their registry of birthplace and residence. Over the years, however, they have been segregated as untouchables, crowded into squalid shacks in ghettos, and limited in whom they can marry, what work they can do (only menial jobs), and how much education they can have.

Generations of segregation and inferior status have *created* differences. Their speech patterns have become different and now identify them as does the speech of the lower-class Cockney in London. Regardless of their abilities, their papers (identifying their occupation and place of residence) prevent their escape. Not surprising-

Ψ *Close-up*   *The Prevalence of Prejudice*

Prejudice, both private and institutionalized, has existed in most countries of the world. In many it still flourishes openly, and in some it is endorsed by governmental policy or even law.

Prejudice appears in Ireland between Catholics and Protestants, in Italy between northern and southern Italians, in Yugoslavia between Slovaks and Croatians, in Canada between French- and English-speaking citizens, in England between the British and colored immigrants, and in many other countries between assorted subgroupings.

During the 1950s a priest summarized the relations between blacks and Puerto Ricans in New York City as, "The spics hate the niggers and the niggers hate the spics." The names of the groups change, but hostility among various minorities is a typical pattern and may be even more violent than the hostility associated with traditional majority-minority conflicts. Those who are prejudiced against one group, for whatever reason, are likely to be prejudiced against others.

The development, institutionalization, and generalization of prejudice are dramatically demonstrated in the case of anti-Oriental feelings in this country. In the nineteenth century, the Chinese, originally imported as cheap labor by railroad and farm interests, were attacked by white laborers with whom they were put into competition for jobs. Later, when Japanese immigration was similarly encouraged, the hostility was generalized to include them,

although at the beginning, invidious comparisons between Chinese and Japanese had favored the latter. Remarkably, the Japanese were faulted because they were too intelligent, too hardworking, too exemplary models of the "Protestant ethic" of thrift, sobriety, and hard work. In 1879 the California Constitutional Convention adopted sections expressly prohibiting employment of "Mongolians" in any state, county, or municipal work or by any corporation in the state, and by 1882 the Chinese Exclusion Act had forbidden further immigration and also stated that Chinese were not eligible for United States citizenship. Although these legal restrictions were canceled in the 1920s, the continued virulence of the hostility against them was seen in the manner in which the Japanese Americans were uprooted and put into relocation camps during World War II (see p. 552).

A statement by one of the more vociferous anti-Japanese orators could be used as a sentence completion test, in which the name of almost any outgroup could be substituted by the prejudiced person:

". . . I am responsible to the mothers and fathers of Sacramento County who have their little daughters sitting side by side in the school rooms with matured Japs, with their base minds, their lascivious thoughts multiplied by their race and strengthened by their mode of life. . . . I have seen Japanese twenty-five years old sitting in the seats next to the pure maids of California. . . . I shudder to think of such a condition." (Hichborn, 1909)

---

ly, there is greater delinquency, joblessness, school absenteeism, dropout rate, and lower tested IQ among boys who live in the Buraku ghettos. These signs of "innate racial inferiority" are used to justify the necessity for further discrimination (De Vos & Wagatsuma, 1966).

Once established, prejudice is relatively resistant to extinction because of the variety of needs it may serve for the individual and the many conditions that may encourage and maintain it. Millions of dollars and considerable effort spent on public information campaigns, "brotherhood weeks," and so on

have had no significant effect in reducing intergroup hostility. This is not surprising, since informational needs represent only one source of prejudice input. Research has shown that *contact* between antagonistic groups can promote better intergroup relations or exacerbate existing hostilities, depending on many other factors; mere "exposure" does not help and is more likely to intensify existing attitudes. Changes in prejudice among individuals are likely only when change is rewarding rather than thwarting and when the social conditions that reinforce discriminating behavior are changed. We are a long way from solving the problem of the pathology of prejudice.

The kernel of truth: rational or a rationalization?
Most prejudiced people, when challenged as to the adequacy of their stereotypes, will agree that perhaps not all Italians are gangsters, all Jews aggressive, all Arabs treacherous, all black people shiftless, and so on. But they counter with the "kernel of truth" theory. Surely such beliefs would not have been formed or held so widely if there had not been some truth behind them, it is asserted. What about so-and-so, who certainly seems to be "the type"? And an anecdote is related in which an individual from the disliked group has in fact behaved as predicted.

To demonstrate that the "kernel of truth" view is probably more an after-the-stereotype rationalization than a rational, *a priori* explanation of its origin is

extremely difficult. Recently, a third-grade teacher, Mrs. Jane Elliott, performed a remarkable experiment with her young students which offers just such proof. The question Mrs. Elliott posed was: Could white children from a small Iowa farm community who were close friends be made to discriminate against each other solely on the basis of an inferior status arbitrarily assigned to them?

Without warning, blue-eyed Mrs. Elliott announced to her class of nine-year-olds one day that brown-eyed people were more intelligent and better people than those with blue eyes. The blue-eyed children, although twice as numerous, were simply told that they were inferior and that the brown-eyed children should therefore be the "ruling class."

"We began our discriminating by laying down guidelines for our inferior group to follow so that they would be sure to 'keep their place' in our new social order.

◆ Besides the observable changes in the children's overt behavior toward each other and in their schoolwork under the two conditions of the experiment, Mrs. Elliott obtained measures of their feelings under each condition by having them draw pictures of how they felt. Two pairs of these drawings are reproduced below. When they were "on top," they felt competent and capable and exulted in their feeling of power and superiority. When they were "on the bottom," they felt small, glum, and pushed down, evidently accepting the discriminators' image of them as inferior and unworthy.

The reality of the emotional strain the children had undergone during the brief two-day experiment is also reflected in the exuberance with which they crowded around Mrs. Elliott at the end as one united happy group, in which everyone could accept and be accepted by everyone else.

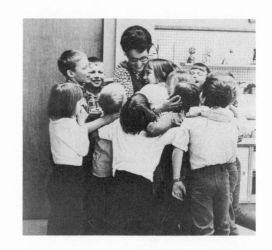

They were instructed to sit in the rear of the room, to take the last position in the lunch and recess lines, to allow the brown-eyed children to have the first choice of seats in reading class, to use only the faucet and paper cups when getting drinks (instead of the fountain, which was for brown-eyes), and many other frustrating and demeaning things. They were also informed that the superior students, due to the fact that they *were* superior, would be given some privileges which would not be available to the inferior students (like extra recess time for work well done)."

Within minutes the blue-eyed children began to do more poorly on their lessons and became depressed, sullen, and angry. The words they most often used to describe themselves (after taking a spelling test and selecting the words that were most appropriate) were: "sad," "bad," "stupid," "dull," "awful, "hard," "mean." One boy said he felt like a "vegetable." Of the brown-eyed superiors, the teacher reported, "What had been marvelously cooperative, thoughtful children became nasty, vicious, discriminating little third-graders . . . it was ghastly." Some of them even suggested that someone should warn the cafeteria personnel to keep an eye on the blue-eyes because they might steal extra food!

To show how arbitrary and irrational prejudice and its rationalizations really are, the teacher told the class on the next school day that she had lied, that it was really the blue-eyed children who were superior and the brown-eyed ones who were inferior. The brown-eyes now switched from their previously "happy," "good," "sweet," "nice" self-labels to derogatory ones similar to those used the day before by the blue-eyes. Their academic performance deteriorated, while that of the new ruling class improved. Old friendship patterns between children dissolved and were replaced with hostility.

The children's relief and delight at the end, when they were "debriefed" and learned that some of them were not "inferior" to others, is evident in the photograph. ◆ Hopefully they had learned to empathize with those they might see being made targets of prejudice in the future (Elliott, 1970).

This experiment has been repeated with other classes and even with an adult group of businessmen —with the same results. In each case the assumption of power by one group over another based on supposed superiority has led to discriminatory behavior, disruption in the social structure, loss of self-esteem, changes in performance by the "inferior" members in accord with their ascribed status, and justification by the superiors for the pattern of discrimination sanctioned by the "system." The ease and speed with which such behavior patterns can be adopted, the psychological damage they can cause to both victim and victimizer, the long-term costs to the society, and their persistence make prejudice a form of pathology no less serious than the most disintegrated form of psychotic behavior.

Loss of Self-Regulating Capacities: Dependence and Addiction

Eating, normally an activity necessary to maintain cell metabolism, can develop abnormal properties which endanger the functioning of the organism. We saw in Chapter 9 that compulsive eating can result from a loss of control over physiological and psychological mechanisms which regulate food consumption. In a mild form, being overweight leads to excessive concern over one's appearance and to the current cult of dieting. In its extreme form, obesity leads to emotional distress, limitations on one's mobility, and marked restrictions in life style. It is also implicated in a variety of organic disorders which can cause premature death.

Similarly, other consummatory activities such as drinking alcohol, smoking cigarettes, and taking drugs can become controlling factors in a person's life. The individual learns to depend on these activities for a wide range of emotional and behavioral satisfactions—to relax him, to pick him up, to alleviate depression—in short, to enable him to "make it through the day." What starts out as the generally approved social-hour cocktail can become a craving for a quart or more of bracer a day, starting as soon as the alcoholic awakes. The after-dinner cigarette likewise can turn into over four packs a day for cigarette addicts. The marijuana "high," initially reserved for parties, can become the nightmare seen recently at a drug clinic: a twenty-two-year-old addict who had injected every conceivable drug into virtually every part of his now diseased body—over 37,000 times in four years.

The loss of self-regulating capacities, then, can have disastrous physical consequences on the health of the addicted person. These stem both from the *direct* effects of the excessive amount of foreign substance on cerebral, respiratory, vascular, and digestive functioning and from the various *indirect* effects of inadequate diet and contagious disease conditions associated with some addictive habits.

The pervasive psychological and social consequences are no less serious than the physical ones. At the psychological level, there is a loss of both self-confidence and feelings of self-control as the person comes to define himself as unable to make it on his own. Accompanying this lowered self-esteem is a loss of interest in usual life activities and goals, as the addiction preempts the position of central reinforcer in his life.

The social consequences of maintaining these habits can be measured in the money lost in earnings, family savings, welfare, rehabilitation attempts, and crime. They can also be assessed in terms of the loss of human productivity and the breakdown of meaningful interpersonal relations—the end of which may be skid row, jail, a mental hospital, or a life of begging and prostitution. But although almost everyone is intellectually aware of the potential danger of addictions[1] and we are exposed to widespread information campaigns against such self-abuse, the incidence of such addiction appears to continue on its not-so-merry way upward. ■

Why do people start? This is the first puzzle. Actually, there are many reasons for the paradox that rational people voluntarily engage in a behavior that they know can be so self-destructive. Aside from possible masochism (a tendency to hurt or punish oneself), there are a number of less abnormal processes which can help start and maintain addictive behaviors.

Initially, the to-become-addictive response usually is simply a very positive source of reinforcement which is supported by observation of parents, prestige figures, or peers. The mass media spend considerable amounts of money to create a belief structure in which the "normal" way to achieve pleasure, health, happiness, relief from pain and anxiety, and even

[1]Technically, the term *addiction* means physical dependence, but we will be using it more broadly here to refer to either physical or psychological dependence severe enough that the behavior has become compulsive and the individual has lost voluntary control over it.

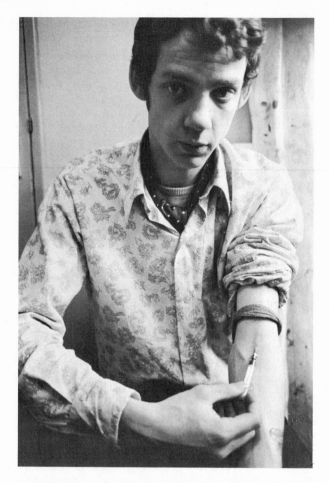

■ This nineteen-year-old boy has started to inject heroin again after having been hospitalized for hepatitis for six weeks, during which drugs were not available and his addiction was overcome.

sexual prowess is through smoking, drinking, eating, and taking drugs (starting with aspirin, tranquilizers, diet pills, and sleeping pills). Gambling, too, is promoted as a socially acceptable activity in public lotteries, TV quiz shows, and church bingo games.

Society assumes that each individual has sufficient self-imposed control over his behavior to keep from giving in fully to these temptations. And most people themselves are convinced that they would never succumb to such danger and self-destruction. "*I could not become an alcoholic or drug addict.*" They see the addict as someone who "deserves" what he gets because he is too "weak willed" to help himself.

Society is reluctant to accept any responsibility for creating conditions which both encourage addictive behaviors and work against attempts at therapeutic modification.

There are few behavior patterns more difficult to change than those centered around a compulsive addiction habit. To what extent is individual addiction a symptom of social pathology, and to what extent a sign of personal pathology?

Dependence on Alcohol

Alcoholism is one of the most serious forms of addiction, both in its incidence and in its consequences. It is estimated that there are probably nearly 5,000,000 drinkers in this country whose drinking is so excessive that they suffer serious impairment of their economic, social, and family lives.

The problem of controlling alcoholism is accentuated by the prevailing attitudes toward drinking in our society. Moderate consumption of alcohol is legally tolerated and generally socially condoned. Yet the individual who develops a dependence on alcohol receives little sympathy; instead, we berate him for his "lack of will power," criticize his irresponsibility, and assume he does not want to be helped.

Causal factors in alcoholism. Drinking makes the alcoholic's life temporarily less difficult to face; thus it provides an escape that becomes increasingly tempting the more it is used, as unsolved problems accumulate and new ones are created by the drinking itself. Despite its long-term maladaptiveness, the pattern is maintained because it is reinforced by short-term relief. At some point in the sequence, the picture is further complicated by the establishment of physical dependence too. Yet long after it is clear to everyone else that he has become an alcoholic, the individual may stoutly maintain that he has no problem and that he could stop drinking at will.

The clinical picture of the alcoholic is characterized by three distinctive features: deprivation, depression, and denial. A frequently found factor in case histories of heavy drinkers is childhood deprivation of a fundamental emotional relationship, often maternal. Depression is the characteristic emotional state of alcoholism, and denial is used as the primary strategy

of defense against admitting this depression. One investigator notes:

"Alcoholism is thus seen as a symptom of a primitive personality disorder that originated in the preverbal stage of an individual's emotional development. The characteristics typically associated with such disorders are low self-esteem, minimal tolerance for frustration, marked dependency, and a great difficulty in relating to other people, coupled with a supersensitivity about being rejected by others." (Chafetz, 1970)

Control of alcoholism. Not surprisingly, experience has shown that court punishments such as fines and imprisonment for drunkenness are unsatisfactory means of controlling excessive drinking. Nor was another legal measure—national prohibition—successful in reducing the amount of harmful drinking. Statistics on the admission of alcoholic patients to state hospitals in New York between 1889 and 1943 showed no relationship between legal prohibition of drinking and the incidence of alcoholism (Landis & Cushman, 1945).

A wide variety of clinical treatments for alcoholism have been developed, none of which has met with more than limited success. Psychotherapeutic techniques, based on the belief that drinking is primarily a symptom of an underlying emotional disorder, attempt to alter the alcoholic's attitudes and life style through personal and social counseling. It is assumed that once the patient has found a satisfactory means of coping with his problems, he will no longer need to drink. Even in cases where the dependence is purely psychological, however, the drinking habit is strong and not easily eliminated.

In some cases there has been success with treatment based on the conditioned-response principle. The patient is forced to drink alcohol mixed with emetic drugs so that he becomes severely nauseated. Eventually, a conditioned link is established so that the sight, smell, and taste of alcohol evoke nausea and vomiting. Usually, psychotherapy is also needed, however, because the drinking is being maintained by sufficient reinforcement to make life with it seem more comforting—or at least less painful—than life without it. Thus an alcoholic is not likely to be cured until he really wants to be and until he finds other ways of meeting the needs that his drinking has met.

With patients who are motivated to change, group therapy or other group approaches have generally had the greatest success. Many alcoholics have found new help in facing their problems through private organizations such as Alcoholics Anonymous. This organization provides for its members an atmosphere of mutual understanding, acceptance, sympathetic fellowship, and emotional support in which they can work out their problems without the feelings of isolation, shame, and helplessness that may torture the alcoholic struggling alone. This social therapy approach to alcoholism has met with considerable success, but many more alcoholics never join an AA group than do so.

Two of the problems in the treatment of alcoholism have been found to result not from the individuals themselves but from the practices and attitudes of those who are trying to help them. Researchers at one hospital found that very few alcoholics seen in the emergency ward followed through on a referral to the alcohol clinic. This appeared on first sight to validate the belief that alcoholics do not want to help themselves. Upon closer analysis, however, these researchers found that two other variables were operating to change the picture.

1. More than half of the alcoholics who entered the emergency ward for treatment were not labeled as alcoholic by the physician if they complained of a medical problem and if they had social connections. The physician's preference for treating a physical disorder in socially responsible citizens led him to make a diagnosis of physical pathology when it was possible to do so. A person was labeled an *alcoholic* only if he was a social derelict and relatively well physically.

2. The patient diagnosed as alcoholic and referred to the alcohol clinic had to endure questioning from up to a dozen different staff members. Then he had to make an appointment to see the resident psychiatrist which, if he kept it, earned him a four-to-six-week wait before his initial therapy session. In addition to these delays in treating what was an acute problem, he had to tolerate negative personal reactions at every step. He might be dirty and smell bad and the hospital staff might show distaste at his appearance and indifference or anger at his distress (Chafetz, 1970, p. 110).

When a hospital staff takes the responsibility for establishing a treatment relationship with the alcoholic and when the treatment involves some personal warmth and acceptance, then the majority of alcoholics referred for treatment take advantage of it. It becomes clear then, that more than anything else, a new set of attitudes is needed in dealing with alcoholism. Misunderstanding of the basic psychological problems of the alcoholic, coupled with greater concern for drug abuse among the young, has made the rehabilitation of the alcoholic a rather unpopular cause. Until more social resources are brought to bear upon both the primary problem of *prevention,* and the secondary one of treatment, the alcoholic will remain a burden to himself, his family, and society.

Dependence on Cigarettes

Smoking is the most common form of addiction in our culture. Nearly 70,000,000 people in the United States alone consume cigarettes on a regular basis (Surgeon General's Report, 1964). Until recently, little interest was generated in eliminating this habit, but in the past ten years widespread reports of a connection between smoking and illness have made cigarette smoking a cause for national concern.

Dependence on cigarettes is psychological. Although a tolerance for nicotine develops in the habitual smoker, this tolerance is limited, thus preventing the adaptive changes in nerve cells which cause physical addiction to other substances. But this hardly means that terminating the habit is a simple matter, as any heavy smoker who has tried to stop will tell you. In spite of numerous attempts to devise a method of "curing" the cigarette addict, the tobacco habit has remained amazingly resistant to extinction.

Methods of terminating smoking behavior can be classified as psychotherapeutic, sensory, or pharmacologic, depending on whether they are aimed at eliminating the psychological satisfaction, the sensory stimulation, or the chemical dependence involved in smoking. Of the three, the psychotherapeutic method has been most successful (Surgeon General's Report, 1964).

Psychotherapeutic methods work on the assumption that the primary cause of habituation is the satisfaction that has come to be associated with smoking. Since the associations are learned and not inherent, they vary tremendously from one smoker to another. One smoker may claim to smoke for stimulation, another for relaxation, and another for the feeling of social closeness which smoking gives him (Tomkins, 1968). The goal is to eliminate these pleasant associations, and as we saw in Chapter 2, the techniques that have been tried include group therapy, hypnotism, "scare" communications, stimulus satiation, and conditioned aversion.

Because of the difficulty involved in eliminating the tobacco habit, many investigators consider the prevention of smoking a more fruitful realm for experimentation. To this end, they have attempted to identify the social and psychological conditions that contribute to smoking behavior. It seems clear that if any permanent effort to eliminate smoking is to succeed, the image of the cigarette smoker as presented by such agents of culture as the mass media must be altered. It has been suggested that the required "therapy," then, must take the form of political legislation to restrict advertising which creates this "attractive death-dealing nuisance," and counter-education to warn children against the health consequences of heavy smoking. Such suggestions are being met with resistance by powerful interest groups, pointing up the conflict between the government's social responsibility for the physical health of its citizens and its concern for the economic health of commercial enterprises which thrive on this form of addiction.

Drug Addiction

Obviously, the problem of drug addiction is one of the major social and individual problems of our time. Rather than simply describe the limited available psychological research on drugs and sketch in an oversimplified view of "the addict," we have chosen instead a rather novel approach for an introductory text. After asking several classes of students what questions they most wanted answered about drugs and drug abuse, we posed these questions to one of the leading world authorities, Dr. David Smith, the founder and Medical Director of the Haight-Ashbury Free Drug Clinic in San Francisco. Appendix D presents some of the questions the students asked and the answers this very knowledgeable expert gave.

Other questions you may have can be directed to him at the address noted in the Appendix.

Compulsive Gambling

Compulsive gambling represents one of the most puzzling forms which an addiction can take. In an attempt to gain mastery over the laws of chance, the gambler forfeits control over his own impulses. He cannot quit when ahead, is most excited when the odds of winning are clearly against him, and despite heavy losses continues to maintain a belief that next time "luck will be on his side."

The pathology represented by an addiction to gambling obviously differs in many ways from the others we have discussed; we do not label the gambler as "sick," nor do we attempt to rehabilitate him. His physical health is not directly affected, and the consequences to society are less obvious than in the other addictions. The side effects of compulsive gambling, however, can be ruinous to a family's wealth, and can include loss of interest in all else but games of chance, with a loss of individual productivity and creativity, embezzlement or robbery to pay off debts, and support of syndicated crime.

Gambling in some form has existed in virtually every known culture since antiquity. Man's concern for predicting the unpredictable has been linked with primitive conceptions of divination and justice. Decision making by lot or games of chance has traditionally rested on the assumption that outcomes unpredictable to man were in fact decided by supernatural forces, such as the gods or retributive justice. Winning was seen as a reward for virtue and a sign of truth and justice, while losing signified vice deserving of punishment. Throughout recorded history, important decisions of men and nations have often been left to chance determinations, thereby absolving individuals from the responsibility of having initiated the action. Gambling has been viewed by some as a noble aspect of man's quest for adventure, and by others as madness and vice. For example, the positive view of gambling was expressed thus:

". . . undoubtedly a spiritual affair . . . no man would gamble unless he had a love of life and relished what he could obtain from life with his winnings." (Mills, 1953)

Gambling as a sign of sinful degradation has been the subject of many religious sermons, including a noteworthy one by Thomas Rennell in 1794 entitled: "The Consequences of the Vice of Gambling As They Affect the Welfare of Individuals and the Stability of Civil Government, Considered." The Roman historian Juvenal is quoted as being amazed at the madness unleashed by gambling: "It is there (at the gaming tables) you witness the most terrible contests. Is it not madness to lose one hundred thousand sestertii and refuse a garment to a slave perishing with cold?" (cited in France, 1902).

In Chapter 11 we presented psychoanalytic and behavioristic explanations of a student protester. The two dominant views of how best to understand gambling come from the same two approaches. One dynamic view (Berger, 1957) maintains that the chronic gambler has not resolved his childish feelings of omnipotence and still believes in his magical powers to control fate as he desires. Such gamblers search within themselves for feelings which will tip off the course of the future event. When they fail to anticipate the outcome correctly, they punish themselves as if they had the power to be right but did not use it appropriately. Probability is not seen as a statistical abstraction but is given human, personal qualities, as in the song from the play *Guys and Dolls,* "Luck Be a Lady Tonight."

Freud (1950) interpreted the passion for gambling as a symbolic substitution for a compulsion to masturbate. Both are "play" behaviors and involve excited activity of the hands, and the pleasure of the climactic moment is followed by quiet and by broken promises to resist the temptation next time. In both there is a struggle with impulse control to which the person feels he must give in, gambling being the more socially approved outlet.

From an operant behavior analysis, gambling is learned through a combination of superstitious learning and a variable ratio schedule of payoffs. For some people, wishing that a drawn card will be an ace, the dice will come up seven, the long shot will run first, or one's own number will win happens to be reinforced. They not only win the money or prize accompanying their bet, but their belief in their personal causality of future events is strengthened thereby.

Imagine a thousand people who begin betting on the outcome of a chance event where there are two possible outcomes with equal probability of occurring, like heads or tails on a coin. Purely by chance, one of the thousand might win ten times in a row. After such an experience, it is likely that he would develop a superstitious belief that *he* somehow had helped determine the outcome. The correspondence of wishful thinking, a randomly determined reward schedule, and payoffs administered occasionally and unpredictably thereafter could result in the development of a habit which was extremely resistant to behavioral extinction.

Society's reaction to the chronic gambler is a mixed one because, while rejecting anyone who forsakes reason for impulse, at the same time it admires his freedom to take risks, letting a fortune ride on the spin of a wheel in the hope of getting rich quick by beating the house. Such attitudes help gambling to flourish and keep even compulsive gambling from being labeled as a serious form of personal madness.

Loss of Joy in Living: Neurosis

When an individual feels chronically threatened by life's hazards and inadequate to the task of coping with them, the ordinary ego defenses we all use are not enough. Gradually he may come to rely excessively upon one or more neurotic defense patterns. These patterns have in common the search for relief from anxiety. Thus they are characterized by an absence of joy in living and by actions aimed at lessening pain rather than at positive accomplishment or the constructive solution of objectively real problems. They provide enough temporary relief from anxiety that the individual clings to them desperately despite the fact they do not solve his basic problems and may even worsen them—and thus are self-defeating in the long run. His human self-awareness and capacity for evaluation and generalization are thus used in ways that cripple him instead of making his life richer and his actions more effective.

The tragedy of the neurotic is that often his evaluations of the world as threatening and of himself as ineffectual are faulty. With more realistic perceptions there would be no need for his loss of joy or his tortured preoccupation with worries and threats.

In general (as we noted in Chapter 11), the normal person functions as an organized whole and deals with frustrations more or less effectively. But "normality," for the psychologist, includes a wide range of behavior rather than a single fixed point on a scale. Thus there is no clear dividing line between the normal and the neurotic: the difference is one of degree. The neurotic's defenses are regarded as abnormal because they represent seriously and chronically ineffective ways of coping with life's demands. However, they are rarely severe enough to require hospitalization.

If there is a continuum from normal to neurotic, at what point can we identify a person as being disturbed enough to justify assigning the label of "neurotic"? What are the behavioral signs that are used to identify the neurotic individual? A number of fairly distinct neurotic patterns have been identified, of which six will be described here.

Anxiety Neurosis

Sometimes the source of anxiety for the neurotic individual is not an external danger but an inner one. He may believe he should not have certain feelings and wishes, such as hostility or sexual desires, and thus may be unable to accept the fact that he has them. When such thoughts or impulses arise, they may be repressed—pushed out of consciousness—and much effort, also unconscious, may be devoted to keeping them there. When they threaten to emerge into consciousness from time to time, he may experience feelings of impending doom and may have attacks of physical symptoms such as palpitation of the heart and great difficulty in breathing.

Naturally, he consults a physician; in fact, it is estimated that 30 percent of all patients seen by general practitioners and internists actually fit in this category (Pitts, 1969). About 10 million Americans are thought to suffer from anxiety neurosis. Not only is the physician unable to find anything wrong, however, but the neurotic himself may be quite at a loss to explain why he is so anxious. His anxiety is said to be "free-floating." Sometimes, too, he feels extreme guilt without knowing why.

It is the elusive nonspecificity of the anxiety he experiences that is responsible for much of the terror experienced by the patient. Imagine feeling intense arousal and strange things happening inside your head and body—and having no rational explanation to account for them. You see a doctor and after a thorough physical examination he assures you that he can find nothing wrong with you. But the beat goes on inside your head!

The failure to explain this "unexplained arousal" itself now constitutes a threat to your feelings of self-knowledge and self-control and generates additional anxiety. One of the main functions of psychotherapy is to identify the original source of anxiety in order to make it a tangible, manageable fear. "Put a name on it and you can do something about it." (Grimmett, 1970)

Neurotic anxiety is thus to be differentiated from objective anxiety or fear. Fear is a rational reaction to an objective, identified danger and may involve flight or attack in self-defense. In neurotic anxiety the emotional arousal is just as strong, but the danger is inside and not identifiable, operating perhaps through associative processes or at subcortical levels.

Although anxiety attacks are triggered by factors in the individual's experience, there is some evidence of abnormal biochemical reactions also. For example, injections of lactate, a normal end product of cell metabolism, can bring on anxiety attacks in anxiety neurotics and even in some normal individuals, whereas the effect is lessened if calcium is added to the injected lactate. It may be that an excess of lactate interferes with the normal function calcium plays in the transmission of nerve impulses and that the anxiety neurotic suffers faulty metabolism leading to either excess lactate or deficient calcium (Pitts, 1969).

Phobias

In *phobic reactions,* anxiety becomes attached to a definite object in the external environment, but typically the object is not really a source of danger. Thus, the neurotic person often realizes that his acute reaction is irrational—there is not an adequate explanation for it—but that recognition only makes his anxiety more unbearable. In some cases, the choice of the phobic object is purely symbolic; in others, it has a close connection with the underlying conflict.

A construction worker had to quit his job because he began to develop a fear of heights. Everyone knows that accidents can happen on construction work; was his reaction objective or neurotic? Without further evidence you could not tell. In this particular case, however, the man also developed a fear of open spaces on the ground (not a source of danger) and also a fear of death.

It turned out that prior to the onset of his anxiety reactions, a fellow employee had begun to aggravate him constantly. In fact, he reported, "I felt like killing him." But he had felt hopeless about actually taking any action to stop the annoying behavior. It is possible that in quitting his job he was defending against his impulses toward homicide as well as his own inability to stand up to his tormentor. In any case, developing a phobia of heights was one effective resolution of his problem, providing a justification for giving up his lucrative job.

There are virtually no limits as to what a phobia may symbolize, since man's creative mind can construct quite remote associations. Phobias of harmless snakes or insects, birds flying, touching another person, hair, and other quite safe objects or situations may come to induce strong reactions resulting in panic if the individual cannot escape. In fact, the characteristic of phobic reactions is the elaborate precautions and defenses the individual erects to avoid all contact with the "dangerous" phobic object. It is as if the neurotic person handles his internal conflict by externalizing it onto some object; then as long as he can avoid the object, he can avoid confronting the terror within himself.

Obsessive-Compulsive Neurosis

Repressed desires and guilt feelings frequently lead to another type of abnormal behavior pattern known as an *obsessive-compulsive neurosis*. Actually, obsessions and compulsions are separate types of reactions that may occur quite independently of each other, but they occur together so often that they are generally considered as two separate aspects of a single behavior pattern.

Obsessions. An obsession is a persistent and irrational thought that comes into consciousness inappropriately and cannot be banished voluntarily. Almost everyone has some sort of mild obsessional experience occasionally, such as the intrusion of petty worries: "Did I really lock the door?" or "Did I turn off the stove?" Having a tune "run through one's head" persistently is another common mild obsession. This latter phenomenon has been found frequently among persons under stress.

Although mild obsessions such as persistent tunes can be irritating, true neurotic obsessions are much more insistent and so disturbing that they interfere with the individual's adjustive efficiency. Often they center about morbid thoughts of death or suicide or continual fantasies of committing murder in some brutal fashion. Extreme obsessional reactions can be almost completely disabling—the patient may be so overwhelmed by his recurrent obsession that he finds it almost impossible to concentrate on any other thoughts, and unable to control the occurrence or direction of the obsessive thoughts.

A theological student was compelled to think incessantly about the "unforgivable sin," which he felt doomed to commit some day. The unforgivable sin consisted in getting up in church during the sermon and shouting an epithet. Like many obsessives, this patient feared that at some future date the impulse reflected in the obsessive thought might become irresistible. Usually, however, such fears are groundless. Hardly ever does the obsessive lose control over his impulses, especially those that are grossly dangerous or offensive (Stern, 1964).

A recent study suggests a possible link between obsessional disorders and neurological problems in at least some cases.

The histories of 103 patients with obsessional neuroses were compared with those of 105 patients suffering from nonobsessional neuroses. It was found that twenty of the obsessional patients (19.4 percent), as compared to eight (7.6 percent) of the other group, had had previous neurological disorders of consequence (Grimshaw, 1964).

One explanation of the function that obsessions serve is that they impose a structure on impulses which are perceived (at some level) as chaotic and dangerous. Not only does obsessive thought limit action, but it also serves to contain strong emotions, such as feelings of hatred, destruction, or lust. For the obsessive, the thought, set up as the barrier between affect and action, becomes the ultimate reality to be dealt with rather than whatever would be the consequences of taking the desired but forbidden action.

The case below describes the transition from a phobic reaction to obsessive thoughts in a young girl.

An attractive girl of seventeen came to the hospital with the complaint that for the last year she had been so upset she could not study and had to stay home from school. This was the final stage of a sequence of events which had begun when she was fourteen years old. At first, she couldn't stay in school all day and would leave early to go home to be with her mother. She gradually found it impossible to stay in school for even a period or two, and eventually was unable to leave home at all. "My mother will die if I am not with her," she had convinced herself. Finally confining herself to home, she followed her mother wherever she went because she might die if out of her sight even in the next room.

At this time, she developed the obsession that in order to protect her mother from the unknown terror, she had to think about her father at regular intervals. To ensure that this obsession was satisfied, she developed the following compulsive ritual: for every third step that she took while walking, for every third word she read, or every third word she uttered, she would stop and think about her father. She dreaded having thoughts about her mother instead of her father at such times because that would kill her mother.

Added to her distress was the frightening impulse to take a knife and stick it into her father's chest. When hospitalized, she was so full of terror that she had to have a nurse at her bedside around the clock. She could not be left alone, and became especially apprehensive about being in the company of male hospital personnel.

Some insight into a basic source of her anxiety was provided by her reactions to several of the Rorschach ink blots shown her by a clinical psychologist. It became apparent—to her as well as to the psychologist—that she had frequent sexual fantasies about her father and death wishes toward her mother. Thus the conscious protectiveness toward her mother and aggressive impulses toward her father were precisely the opposite of desires and impulses that had been operating below the level of consciousness—an extreme example of reaction formation (Rapaport, 1970).

Compulsions.   Sometimes only thinking, even obsessive thinking, is not an adequate safeguard against expression of forbidden impulses. An additional mechanism for imposing order on impulses is seen in *compulsions*. (Ψ Close-up, p. 580.)

Compulsive behavior consists of repetitive ritualistic actions. Even though such rituals are highly charged emotionally for the neurotic person, he may remain unaware of their meaning. By becoming preoccupied with carrying out these minor everyday tasks repeatedly, however, the compulsive neurotic has no time or energy left to carry out the impulsive action he is unconsciously guarding against. In some cases, guilt feelings for real or imagined sins may find expression in compulsive rituals designed to undo them; an example is excessive hand-washing—a kind of Lady Macbeth reaction.

Hysterical Neurosis

It is not uncommon for students to forget appointments with the dentist or get sick on the day of a final exam, for singers to get laryngitis before an audition, or for track men to develop "charley horses" which prevent them from competing in a track meet. These represent some of the "normal" forms of avoiding an unpleasant, feared situation. These escapes are not consciously sought. In fact, the individuals using them vigorously deny that they are "escapes": they just "happen" in situations of anticipated stress. But losing one's memory or becoming physically incapacitated does remove the person from a situation which is threatening his psychological well-being or his self-esteem and does so in such a way that he cannot be blamed for not facing it.

When such a mechanism is carried to the extreme that the person becomes physically paralyzed or has a total loss of memory—without any organic defect—then the condition is abnormal and is labeled *hysterical neurosis*. Included under this general heading are two related disorders: *conversion hysteria* and *dissociated states*.

Conversion hysteria.   In conversion hysteria there is a loss of sensory or motor function without organic pathology. The individual suddenly cannot hear or see or feel, or his arm or leg may be paralyzed, or he may be unable to speak.

Many hysterical symptoms are completely incompatible with medical fact. For instance, in certain types of hysterical anesthesia (loss of sensitivity to touch or pain), areas of the body are affected which

Ψ *Close-up* *Compulsive Napkin Writing*

In most cases, compulsive reactions do not require hospitalization but merely inconvenience the individual and may puzzle his associates. Occasionally, however, they are seriously incapacitating or part of a broader picture of psychopathology, as in the case of the man whose "messages" are shown here.

This elderly male patient would spend hour after hour writing one or two messages and giving them to the other patients and the staff. When he was ordered to stop and his paper and pencil were taken away, the messages ceased for a while; then they mysteriously resumed—written on napkins and somehow slipped under the door or into the pocket or mailbox of the staff members, a different target each day. Below are some samples received by one of the authors over a three-month period. Note the remarkable similarity of the fine details of this compulsive patient's handwriting as well as the "magic number" and theme of the napkin message.

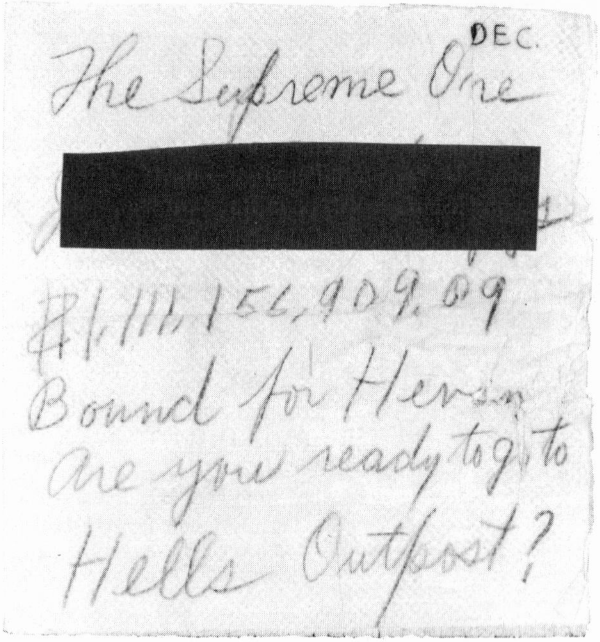

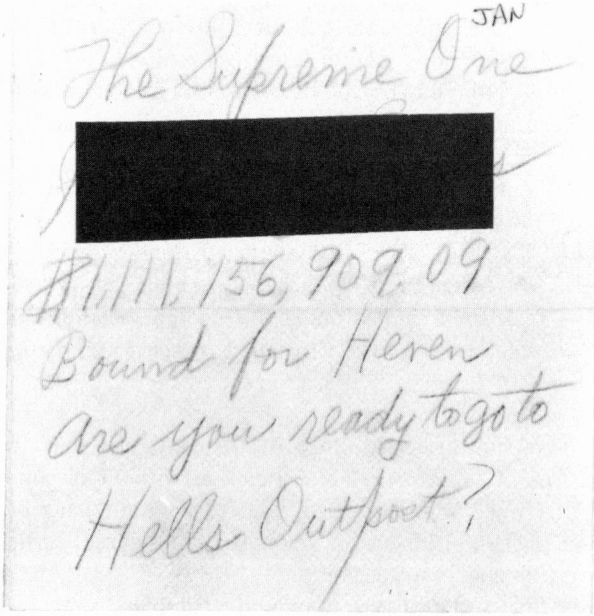

do not correspond with the actual arrangement of the neural pathways. In other cases, however, a physician may have great difficulty in telling whether the patient is suffering from an organic ailment or a hysterical one.

It is important to remember that in a conversion reaction no actual biological change is involved. This is clearly demonstrated by the fact that when the individual is asleep or under hypnosis his hysterical symptoms generally disappear. For instance, a patient who suffers from hysterical paralysis may be entirely incapable of moving his legs, but under hypnosis he may be made to get up and walk across the room. Moreover, hysterical symptoms may come and go or even appear at different times in different areas of the body; the patient who is hysterically "blind" in his right eye on one day may unconsciously shift his ailment to the left eye the next day.

Although hysterical symptoms may sometimes be made to disappear by means of hypnotic suggestion, they are fairly likely to recur, perhaps in modified form, as long as the underlying conflict remains. A typical case is described below.

The patient's illness had begun in early childhood. As the youngest of four girls, she was "babied" a good deal, being given her own way and seldom required to help with household tasks. Even as a child she suffered from constipation and "stomach trouble" and was subject to nightmares and fear of the dark, of death, and of illness. Although she had many girl friends, she was rather prudish about going with boys. Nevertheless, she married at the age of nineteen, having no knowledge of sex whatsoever. After their wedding night she told her husband that she was sorry she had married him. She stayed with him, however, despite numerous quarrels. Her first child, born after long and difficult labor, died within a week, and she remained in bed for four months. About six years later a son was born. Although this delivery was a rather easy one, she stayed in bed for three months, constantly complaining.

By the time her son was six years old, she had taken to a wheelchair. Twelve years later, shortly after the family had moved to a new home, she took to her bed permanently, refusing even to get up to go to the toilet. She was then admitted to a hospital, where examination showed her condition to be purely functional, although prolonged disuse had made her leg muscles flabby and weak and she required calcium, massage, and other forms of treatment to strengthen the bones and tendons of her ankles. She talked a great deal about her condition, insisting that it all stemmed from having got up too soon after the birth of her son and having worked too hard all her life. She seemed incapable of planning for the future and showed no interest in it. It appeared that she was merely continuing her childhood pattern of meeting difficulties with temper spells and complaints of illness. The shock of her sudden sex discoveries when she married had intensified these reactions.

Three weeks of intensive physiotherapy strengthened her legs sufficiently to enable her to walk again, and she spent five months on a gradually increasing program of daily walking exercises. Meanwhile, in psychotherapy, she was helped to understand how she had used physical complaints in order to escape from the responsibilities she found so distasteful. Since her home situation could not be favorably adjusted, she went to live with a sister in Florida and was able to make a fair social adjustment there (Strecker & Ebaugh, 1940).

Individuals who develop conversion reactions tend to be immature, emotional, and demanding, given to histrionics and self-pity. In many cases they have sexual feelings that they cannot accept. Usually they manage to obtain not only escape from the threatening situation but extra dividends in the form of considerable attention and sympathy—which in turn reinforce their pattern of helpless dependence. Interestingly, the forms which conversion reactions take and their frequency depend upon the degree of medical sophistication of the patient and the society (which must be accepting of the physical condition for the maneuver to be successful). Fainting, frequently reported in Victorian England, is a type of conversion hysteria rare today. In fact, the incidence of neurotic conversion reactions has diminished greatly in the United States in recent years, though they still occur in significant numbers in Central and South American countries and in other areas which are medically less well developed.

Dissociated states. Often in your sleep you dream wildly irrational dreams. When you awake, you do not consider that you are a different person from the one who went to sleep. It is the awake, conscious you that you perceive as the "real" you. Suppose the starting point were the dreaming state, and from time to time you woke up, briefly carried on activity of some kind, and then returned to being your irrational, dreaming self. Which would be your real self?

Or imagine what it would be like if every time friends left and returned, they reacted to you as if they were meeting you for the first time. It is only because you and they see each other as continuing, consistent identities that you are able to establish relationships of any permanence with them.

Our fascination with questions such as these is underscored by the timeless popularity of the Dr. Jekyll-Mr. Hyde theme. A mild-mannered man becomes a perverted, homicidal maniac and then changes back by means of a special potion. But after a while he undergoes this metamorphosis without the aid of the drug. In fact, he can no longer control the change; his mind revolts and forces the body and the "personality" to do its bidding.

We have noted many times throughout this text how important it is for individuals to see themselves as basically in control of their behavior—including their emotions, cognitions, and actions. Essential to this perception of self-control is the assumption that we have an integrated, consistent personality, a central core which represents our essential, unique nature. This "personality" provides a basis for perceiving a continuity of ourselves over time. We see meaning in present experiences in terms of frames of reference established in the past, and we attach significance to them in terms of their likely future consequences. Situations change, time passes, our behavior changes, even our attitudes or values may change, yet we hold firm to the belief that we are the same person throughout. It is this constancy of self which provides for most people a firm, reliable yardstick against which perceived change in the outer world is measured, interpreted, and evaluated.

In dissociated states, the individual escapes from his conflicts by giving up this precious consistency and continuity and, in a sense, disowning parts of himself. He may accomplish this in any of several ways. One way is through *somnambulism*—sleepwalking—in which the individual may walk about in his sleep and perform some action of symbolic significance for which he has no recollection when he wakes up.

This loss of memory for what one did during sleep can assume a more extreme form by occurring during waking. In states of *amnesia,* the person performs his

usual waking actions—eating, speaking, reading, driving, and so on, but has no memory of his own identity. By giving up the consistency of his personality, with its time-binding properties, he obliterates the unresolvable conflicts, with their roots in the past.

When the amnesic person gives up on his old personality, which was inadequate to cope with the recurring demands on it, he may "turn it in for a new model" by means of a *fugue* episode (from the Latin word meaning "to flee"). Here he actually travels to some other place, either a completely strange and new one or a familiar place that was emotionally supportive at some earlier time. (Ψ Close-up, p. 583.) In this new place, the person may assume a new identity and create a new life-style, dissociated psychologically, temporally, and geographically from his prior unacceptable life-style. Cases have been reported where such persons were rediscovered several years after their disappearance. Of course, we do not know how many remain undiscovered and lead the rest of their lives as their reconstituted selves.

The most extreme form of dissociation is *multiple personality*. In this type of reaction—which is very rare, despite being dramatized so often in the movies and on television—the individual may develop two (or sometimes more) distinct personalities which alternate in consciousness, each taking over conscious control of the person for varying periods of time. Each part of the multiple personality is based on sets of motives that are in conflict with the motives of the other parts. These conflicting motive patterns originally existed simultaneously in one personality but were so incompatible—and yet all so insistent—that the person was able to satisfy them all only by repressing consciousness of one set while temporarily gratifying another set.

Because multiple personalities represent conflicting sets of motives, the individual's behavior may have a Jekyll-Hyde aspect. If one part of a dual personality is selfish, the other is generous to a fault; if one is quiet and obedient, the other is violently aggressive. Thus the individual may be, at different times, two entirely different people—so completely so that his two personalities even go by different names. Usually, though not always, each personality is completely unaware of the other. In some cases one personality may be aware of the other but not vice versa.

Ψ *Close-up* *Out of Sight, Lost from Mind*

The following is a previously unpublished account by a woman who developed amnesia and experienced a fugue episode. It is unusual not only for being a personal account of such an experience but also because in the process of writing it, she began to lose control and regress to childhood, as evidenced in her handwriting, and after completing it, did lose her memory temporarily again.

I found myself with my son, then four and a half years old, but unusually precocious, in an automat in Manhattan. We were having breakfast, a meal which I usually do not eat, and I noticed that it was about 9 A.M. . . . We were, I thought, starting on an expedition of Christmas shopping (it was early in December) and the events of the day were scheduled around lunch, which I thought we were to have with my mother (who was at that time three months dead). We spent the morning hours shopping and running with great (unusual, it now seems) exuberance and hilarity down streets and into stores. . . .

As noon approached I felt a slight tension, an anxiety that somehow we were not going to make the luncheon date. We went to a telephone booth where I had decided to call my mother to make an alternate plan for lunch. In the telephone booth I discovered that I could not remember my mother's phone number or name (to look it up in the telephone book). . . . I charged my inability to remember to a virus I had heard of at that time that produced unusual psychological states in those who had it. I decided to have lunch, took my son to a museum and then to a movie. I was feeling especially energetic and seemed to do more than normal activities.

It was in the movie, thinking again of calling my mother, that I realized that I not only did not know her name but did not know my own. I took my son to the lounge and searched my purse for identification. I was being particularly careful not to frighten him, but I was myself not frightened and unusually lucid. I found in my purse a list of three names with telephone numbers and the address of one person. I did not recognize the names. I called the first person on the list—an old college teacher of mine and very close friend. When I reached him, I proceeded to describe my situation and realized that I could not describe myself. I looked to my left into a mirror and did not recognize myself.

I told my teacher that I had my son with me and described him. My teacher told me to get into a taxi—that he knew who I was and the address I was to give the driver was my home. After I hung up, I had forgotten what he said my name was, but, looking at the address and finding that it was in Brooklyn, I thought he was mistaken for I remembered (or thought I did) that I lived in New Haven. . . . I had supper with my son and boarded the train for New Haven. . . . As the train pulled out of Bridgeport, my son remarked that he knew that this was not the way home to Brooklyn. I became frightened for the first time. When I reached New Haven, I called the next name on my list . . . he told me to take the next train back to Grand Central. . . .

When I left the train and he came up to me, I knew his face at once but did not know his name or history. . . . My friend took me to his house where I immediately recognized his wife (in the manner outlined above) and knew that they had two children, who were not present.

In the morning I was taken to a psychiatrist. My husband was waiting when I left the psychiatrist's office. When I saw him I did not know him. He looked so different to me. I was very ashamed that I did not know him. I felt very hot and was blushing. I was aware for the first time that everyone was looking at me, and it was with a terrible shock that I became aware of being an object in the vision of others. At that moment, I was aware that I was a visible entity. I think now that during the state I was almost always under the impression that I was invisible except when I wanted to make myself visible to the consciousness of whomever I was talking with and then would become known as a consciousness myself rather than as a person. . . .

Students frequently make the error of confusing such cases of multiple personality with so-called "split personality," known technically as *schizophrenia,* a psychotic disorder in which the individual is "split off from reality." In multiple personality, the conscious part of the personality remains in contact with reality, though reacting to it neurotically.

This dramatic form of reaction is illustrated by the widely publicized case of Eve White. Eve, twenty-five years old and separated from her husband, had sought therapy because of severe, blinding headaches, frequently followed by "blackouts." During one of her early therapy sessions Eve was greatly agitated; she reported that she had recently been hearing voices. Suddenly she put both hands to her temples, then looked up at the doctor with a provocative smile and introduced herself as "Eve Black."

It was obvious from the voice, gestures, and mannerisms of this second Eve that she was a separate personality. She was fully aware of Eve White's doings, but Eve White was unaware of Eve Black's existence. Eve White's "blackouts" were actually the periods when Eve Black was in control, and the "voices" marked unsuccessful attempts of Eve Black to "come out." With extended therapy, it became evident that Eve Black had existed since Eve White's early childhood, when she occasionally took over and indulged in forbidden pleasures, leaving the other Eve to face the consequences. This habit had persisted, and Eve White frequently suffered Eve Black's hangovers. ∎

After about eight months of therapy, a third personality appeared. This one, Jane, was more mature, capable, and forceful than the retiring Eve White; she gradually came to be in control most of the time. Electroencephalograms of Jane and Eve White were both normal and very similar; Eve Black's was classified as borderline normal.

As the therapist probed the memories of the two Eves, he found that as a girl Eve White had felt rejected by her parents, especially after the birth of her twin sisters. Poverty and the strict discipline of her mother may also have contributed to her unhappiness. But the therapist felt sure that some shocking event must have precipitated the actual development of distinct personalities in the disturbed child.

In a dramatic moment, the climax of therapy, the missing incident came to light. Jane suddenly stiffened, and in a terrified voice began to scream, "Mother . . . Don't make me! . . . I can't do it! I can't!" When the screams subsided, a new—and final—personality took over. She was able to recall the shocking event that

■ TWO PERSONALITIES IN ONE BODY

Listed here are some of the contrasting personality characteristics of "Eve White" and "Eve Black" as noted in the first two "faces of Eve."

Eve White	Eve Black
Demure, retiring	Vivacious, a "party girl"
Sweet, quiet face	Pixie-like, mischievous face
Dresses simply, conservatively	Dresses attractively, provocatively
Reads and writes poetry	Never serious or contemplative
Soft, feminine voice	Coarse, teasing voice
Language restrained	Language vernacular, witty
Admired for her quiet strength	Liked for her wit and adventuresomeness
Industrious and competent	Lighthearted and irresponsible
Seldom animated or playful	Delights in pranks
A devoted mother	Feelings momentary and ephemeral
Not allergic to nylon	Allergic to nylon

lay at the bottom of the personality dissociation. At the age of six (only a few months after the birth of the hated twins) Eve White had been led by her mother to her grandmother's coffin and been forced to place a good-bye kiss on the dead face.

The resolved personality, who called herself Evelyn, later identified herself more with Jane than with either of the two Eves, though she was a more substantial and complete woman than Jane had been. She married a young man Jane had been dating, and was able to achieve a stable family life (Thigpen & Cleckley, 1954, 1957; Thigpen, 1961).

Hypochondria

Neurotic individuals frequently show an extreme concern about their health and physical condition, dwelling morbidly upon every minor bodily sensation as a possible sign of some serious organic disorder. When such a preoccupation is the main feature of the neurosis, it is called *hypochondria.*

One explanation of hypochondria is that the individual feels separated from his body and is attempting to know it, but by analyzing and describing it rather than by being and experiencing it. It may also be that in the process of trying to explain vague feelings of anxiety, tension, and mysterious emotional arousal, some people find it more reasonable and less threatening to the ego to have an organic problem than to have a psychological one. For such people, the choice may be between "being mentally crazy" and "being physically sick."

In any case, the hypochondriac is often said to "enjoy poor health," for his greatest satisfaction seems to be in finding bodily symptoms that confirm his dire predictions. His ailments not only prevent active engagement in life—with its risk of failure—but also may bring secondary gains in attention, sympathy, and service from others. On the other hand, his demands for extra consideration and his enormous medical consultation fees and useless surgery bills sometimes lead his exasperated family to forget that his discomfort, however irrationally induced, is subjectively real.

Depressive Neurosis

In *depressive neurosis,* the person distorts reality in degree rather than kind. He reacts to a loss or threatened loss with greater sadness and for a longer time than most people would—a vigil of eternal mourning. In addition to being depressed, patients often complain of inability to concentrate, lack of self-confidence, sleeplessness, boredom, irritation, and ill health. They consciously recognize the source of their depression, but overestimate its significance. It is seen as the end of the world. The depressive patient makes the world too large to cope with, by magnifying out of all proportion any setbacks, frustrations, personal shortcomings, or deficiencies. He is filled with the sadness of his own imagined limitations and a pessimism about ever effecting any change in them.

In many cases, there is little correspondence between the objective situation of loss, failure, or frustration and the subjective evaluation. For such a person, however, subjective reality is the only reality. The failure to enjoy life often is accompanied by the need to drink or take drugs simply to bear the pain of living another day. This fatalistic view of enduring unhappiness may become a potent source of motivation not to bear the pains of life but to escape through suicide.

The depressive reaction is an expression of helplessness, as are all the neuroses. All these strategies are ways in which the neurotic is proving to himself and the world that he is impotent, unable to deal with his problems through no fault of his own. The obsessive-compulsive says, "I *have* to think or do this." The phobic says, "I am terrified by this; I must avoid it." The hysteric says, "I cannot move from where I am; I cannot face the part of me I don't like." The depressive says, "I am weighed down by the world, I am immobilized by my intense grief." The hypochondriac says, "If I weren't so sick, I could deal with other problems, but in the face of such physical pain, all else is irrelevant."

What all these neurotic patterns have in common is a mechanism for limiting anxiety by avoiding any direct confrontation with its source, and an inability to contemplate any other way to handle the problem. The neurotic individual sees "no exit" from his problems and no choices among alternative ways of being.

When a therapy is successful with such a person, it changes his self-concept by getting him to accept the fact that he can exert control. By rediscovering the power of decision making and action, or simply by having a visible effect on the environment and recognizing it as his doing, the neurotic person learns that he not only can cope with his particular present problems but also can begin to shape his life along new dimensions that can bring pleasure, satisfaction, and feelings of accomplishment. Most of the therapeutic procedures to be described in the next chapter are directed at the neurotic reaction patterns described above. Although varying in approach, the different therapies share the basic goals of making the neurotic person more effective and self-accepting.

Loss of Contact with Reality: Psychosis

When an individual's behavior becomes so deviant from normal functioning that he seems to have lost contact with "reality," his condition is labeled *psy-*

chosis. To be psychotic is, in laymen's terms, to be crazy, mad, or insane. Not only is this the most totally disabling of the kinds of losses we have discussed, but it is society's most feared and unacceptable "disease." The very existence of psychosis challenges our fundamental concept of the integrity of mind, the controlling function of the human will, and the nature of reality.

Insanity is not a psychiatric or psychological term but a legal concept applied to any mental condition that renders the individual incapable of knowing right from wrong and therefore of being legally responsible for his actions. Thus insanity would include not only psychotic disorders but also extreme, severely incapacitating neurotic reactions.

Psychosis is not merely a more intense or exaggerated degree of neurosis, but a unique pathological condition differing in quality. The psychotic person does not necessarily pass through a neurotic stage, nor do very disturbed neurotics eventually become psychotic, although there are some cases where the symptoms may be mixed, being drawn from both types of disorder.

Whereas neurotic patients are characteristically overwhelmed with anxiety and dread, psychotic patients typically show a flattened or inappropriate affect (emotion), or extremes of manic or depressive reactions. Furthermore, the neurotic often experiences a secondary source of anxiety in perceiving that his present behavior is irrational and different from that of other people and from his own "normal" prior behavior. Some of his neurotic symptoms may in fact develop out of his search for a rational explanation for his unusual feelings and thoughts, as a justification for himself and others. Psychotics rarely acknowledge that their actions or experiences are out of the ordinary.

One way to think of the difference between normal, neurotic, and psychotic is by analogy to the difference between a simile and a metaphor. Normals and neurotics may often experience their feelings in the form of a *simile*—"I feel like a computer, which functions without emotions." The normal person may add, "but is generally mechanically competent," while the neurotic adds "but is mechanically incompetent." Psychotics eliminate the "like" and live with the full intensity of a *metaphor*—"I am a computer."

The consequence of acting out a metaphor is a dissolving of the boundary between self and object, between subjective and objective reality. The psychotic individual, then, is one who refuses to accept (a) the empirically based definition of what is real or (b) the socially agreed-upon definition of reality established through consensual validation (discussed in Chapter 1). By this strategy, his behavior is freed from many of the constraints which limit the thoughts, feelings, and actions of normal people, who must conform to the rules about what is real, causal, logical, rational, appropriate, and acceptable.

Thus the psychotic may lump together "what is" and "what ought to be." Or he may dissociate effects from their causes, actions from thoughts, feelings from actions, conclusions from premises, or truth from evidence. In one sense, what appears as the psychotic's bizarre, inappropriate, and irrational behavior follows from his creation of a closed system which is self-validating and internally consistent within his own terms (as is clear in the responses of Mr. F. B. in Chapter 1 and Appendix A). Someone has said that neurotics build castles in the air, psychotics live in them, and psychiatrists collect the rent.

Why should some people develop such a deviant way of thinking and acting? Unfortunately, despite years of research by psychologists, psychiatrists, and a host of medical investigators, there is still no satisfactory answer to this critical question. Medically oriented researchers argue for an inherited, genetic basis for some types of psychosis or point to metabolic deficiencies and malfunctioning. The psychological view has emphasized factors in the upbringing and social experience of the individual. Some researchers have even rejected the view of psychosis as abnormal, preferring to conceptualize the psychotic state as a radical revolt against questionable prevailing assumptions about the purpose of life, means-ends relationships, and a too-limited view of human thought and subjective reality (Laing, 1967).

Classification of Psychoses

Some psychotic reactions and other mental disorders may be *organic*—that is, associated with brain damage due to physical causes such as diseases of the nervous system, brain tumors, brain injuries, overdoses of gases, drugs, alcohol, or metallic oxides, and disturbances in arterial circulation occurring in senility.

More prevalent are the *functional* psychoses which stem from no known physical defect in brain tissue, but rather from deficits in functioning. They fall into three major classifications, as shown in the chart.   ▲

Paranoid Reactions

Unlike the other psychotic reaction patterns, which may be quite varied, paranoid reactions are marked by one major pathological symptom—persistent delusions. A delusion is a firmly held belief which is maintained by the individual in the face of objective evidence to the contrary and despite lack of any social support. In the *paranoid state* the delusions are transient and not well organized into a coherent story. The patient may exhibit hallucinations, but his personality is otherwise intact. As the pathology develops, the delusions become more systematized, coherent, and internally logical (everything fits if you grant the initial assumption), while hallucinatory activity disappears. This condition is termed *paranoia*.

There are three types of delusions which occur in paranoid disorders and sometimes in the other psychotic states. The most common kind is the *delusion of grandeur*. The patient believes he is some exalted being, such as an emperor, a millionaire, a great

inventor, or even God. One woman patient in a mental hospital had a pleasing personality and was rational enough in most ways to be trusted with many duties, including that of helping show visitors through the institution. But nothing could shake her firm conviction that she was really Bing Crosby's wife. We have noted that the psychotic patient Mr. F. B. at one point believed he was the Virgin Mary.

A second type of delusion is the *delusion of reference*. In this case the individual misconstrues chance happenings as being directly aimed at him. If he sees two people in earnest conversation, he immediately concludes that they are talking about him. If his bed is changed to a new position in the ward, it is because the attendants are displeased with him and want to guard him more closely or because he is being rewarded for good conduct. Nothing is too trivial or too accidental to escape notice as having some personal significance.

The third common type of delusion is the *delusion of persecution*. Here the individual is constantly on guard against his "enemies." He feels that he is being spied upon and plotted against and is in mortal danger of attack. Delusions of persecution may accompany delusions of grandeur—the patient is a great man, but he is opposed by evil forces.

The Federal Communications Commission receives many letters from people complaining that radio and

▲ **CLASSIFICATION OF THE FUNCTIONAL PSYCHOSES**

Disorder	Major Symptoms	Major Subgroups
Paranoid reaction	Logical, often highly systematized and intricate delusions with personality otherwise relatively intact.	Paranoia Paranoid state
Affective reaction	Extreme fluctuations of mood or intense, prolonged depression or euphoria, with related disturbances in thought and behavior.	Manic reaction Psychotic depression Involutional melancholia
Schizophrenic reaction	Retreat from reality, with emotional blunting, inappropriate emotional reactions, and marked disturbance in thought processes; delusions, hallucinations, and stereotypies common	Childhood Simple Paranoid Catatonic Hebephrenic Unclassified

television programs are talking about them, broadcasting their names, addresses, and personal information. The letters usually demand an investigation and punishment of the offenders, as in the one below.

Gentlemen:

On our local station I heard the announcer's voice at about 6:28 P.M. quietly say "Mynna S_____" and "Mrs. L_____." On the late night show the evening before, the tape had been so doctored that the announcer said Mynna L_____ had money. He said more on the subject and again repeated her name.

On another station other announcers simply said her name or parts of it.

There is such a person living in S_____, Pittsburgh; she used to work for my aunt. She had experienced robbery. The late night show on our local TV could lay an innocent woman open to robbery.

Has the Commission no rules? It is a wonder that I am not manic. My very bowel movements have been announced. On whatever station I turn on a radio or TV, my remarks made at home are broadcast.

I say again that suggesting robbery of an innocent woman is vandalism.

Stations should be given standards.

Very truly yours,

(signature)

In chapter 8, we presented a typescript of a computerized "psychotherapist" (The Mad Doctor) interacting with a human "patient." Kenneth Colby and his associates have also developed a computerized psychotic patient. The patient, called Parry because of certain paranoid tendencies, can be programmed to respond to an interviewer with different levels of anger, fear, and mistrust as well as to give nonverbal reactions. A typical "therapy session" between Parry and one of the authors, where these three variables are at low levels, is reproduced in the Ψ Close-up, p. 589. Could you tell from the answers that Parry was not a real human patient? If Parry were to be interviewed by input from the computerized Mad Doctor, would you be able to tell that their interaction was the product of simulated intelligence rather than of human beings thinking and speaking?

The intellectual and economic level of the paranoid is much higher than that of other psychologically disturbed patients, so that usually he functions for some time without anyone realizing his need for treatment and hospitalization. Among the psychological factors frequently found to be important in the dynamics of paranoid disorders are guilt over immoral or unethical behavior, repressed homosexuality, inferiority feelings, and unrealistically high ambitions.

Affective Reactions

In one group of psychotic disorders the major characteristic is extreme distortion of mood. Here the main symptom is a deep depression, accompanied by a generalized slowing down of mental and physical activity, with gloom, morbid thoughts of disease and death, and feelings of worthlessness. During such *depressive* episodes, patients may attempt to commit suicide and must be carefully watched. The speech of psychotically depressed patients is slow and laconic; when they do speak, it is generally to express their suffering and suicidal desires. (Ψ Close-up, p. 590.)

In sharp contrast to psychotic depression is the *manic* reaction, which is characterized by high excitement, elation, and restless activity. The manic patient indulges in frequent boisterous laughter and eloquent, loud speeches. He walks about wildly and gestures dramatically, banging upon the walls and furniture.

Most patients show only a manic pattern or only a depressive one, but some patients alternate between manic and depressive periods, often in a cycle of great regularity. Sometimes there are long periods of apparent normality between episodes. The loss of contact with reality is evidenced by the onset of these extremes of emotions without any apparent outer justification. With or without treatment, the episode typically runs its course (perhaps a few weeks or months) and then subsides.

One form of extreme depression in middle life or later (after the age of forty or so), which occurs more frequently among women than among men, is called *involutional melancholia*. Although it may be related to physiological "changes of life" involving reproductive functions, the psychological features of this reaction are apprehension, agitation, and hopelessness, as well as feelings of guilt and failure.

A statistical relationship has been found between alcoholism and mood disorders: alcoholism is found often in families of patients with affective disorders,

Ψ *Close-up*   *Parry and the Mafia*

PZ: Hello.
Parry: Hi.
PZ: What is your name?
Parry: You can call me Parry.
PZ: I am Doctor Zimbardo.
Parry: Glad to meet you.
PZ: Where do you live?
Parry: San Jose. Not a bad section, though.
PZ: What do you mean by that?
Parry: I mean not too many, well, foreign types.
PZ: What do you mean by foreign types?
Parry: Those foreigners are beginning to make this country a bad place to live.
PZ: Which foreigners do you dislike most?
Parry: Italians, for instance.
PZ: Do you dislike Italians?
Parry: (frown) Italians?
PZ: You said you don't like them, why?
Parry: Do you know anything about Italians?
PZ: No.
Parry: How about gangsters?
PZ: Are gangsters Italians?
Parry: I would say so.
PZ: Why should you say that?
Parry: Why?
PZ: Are gangsters really Italian?
Parry: No.
PZ: Can you tell me about the Mafia?
Parry: (fearful) Mafia?
PZ: I would like to know about them.
Parry: You know, they know me.
PZ: Who?
Parry: The Mafia.
PZ: Really?
Parry: They are out to get me.
PZ: Who?

Parry: The Mafia.
PZ: How do you know?
Parry: They spy on me.
PZ: (silence)
Parry: They know what I'm doing.
PZ: (silence)
Parry: You know, I have incriminating evidence against the Mafia.
PZ: (silence)
Parry: I know who the local chief of the Mafia is.
PZ: (silence)
Parry: Like I've said, the Mafia know about me.
PZ: (silence)
Parry: They are after me.
PZ: (silence)
Parry: They keep tabs on me.
PZ: (silence)
Parry: Like I've said, I've got something on them.
PZ: (silence)
Parry: I know the boss of the Mafia around here.
PZ: (silence)
Parry: I tell you, I am known to the Mafia.
PZ: (silence)
Parry: They are trying to close in on me.
PZ: (silence)
Parry: Let's talk about something else—I've given you some idea of what's going on.
PZ: Do you go to sporting events?
Parry: I would say so.
PZ: What kind?
Parry: I don't know.
PZ: What sports do you like?
Parry: What do you mean?
PZ: Do you like gambling on horses?
Parry: (distrustful look) Gambling?
                                    (end of session)

Courtesy of Dr. Kenneth Colby

and mood disturbances appear in significant excess in families of alcoholic patients (Winokur, 1970). Research to determine the psychological nature of this relationship is still in progress.

Schizophrenic Reactions

There exists no greater puzzle and challenge to medical and behavioral science than the understand-

Ψ Close-up   Depression

An analysis of the symptoms characteristic of depressed psychiatric patients reveals marked differences in five general areas: emotional, cognitive-motivational, vegetative-physical, delusional, and appearance. When a mixed sample of 966 psychiatric patients was categorized into levels according to the depth of their depression, the following symptoms most clearly differentiated those suffering severe depression from those without depression. Each symptom listed was found to occur among at least 30 percent more of the severely depressed sample than of the nondepressed sample (Beck, 1967).

Emotional

Dejected mood	Self-dislike
Loss of gratification	Loss of attachments
Crying spells	Loss of mirth response

Cognitive-Motivational

Negative expectations	Loss of motivation
Suicidal wishes	Low self-evaluation
Distorted self-image	Self-blame, self-criticism
Indecisiveness	

Vegetative-Physical

Loss of appetite	Loss of sexual interest
Sleep disturbance	Constipation
Fatigability	

Delusional

Worthless	Sinner

Appearance

Sad faced	Speech slow, reduced, not
Stooped posture	spontaneous

ing and control of schizophrenia. There are over 200,000 hospitalized schizophrenics in this country, and they occupy almost half of the beds in mental hospitals (Mosher & Feinsilver, 1970).

Initially this disorder was regarded as a progressive mental deterioration beginning early in life, and was called *dementia praecox* to distinguish it from affec-

tive psychosis. It is now recognized as neither necessarily progressive, nor a deterioration into a demented (mentally retarded) state. Rather, its essential feature is the breakdown of integrated personality functioning. Different aspects of the patient's personality are at odds with each other, and his behavior is not guided by or dependent upon environmental feedback.

Once a person stops checking against feedback, his entire range of behavioral processes may change. Perceptions can occur without sensory stimuli (hallucinations); emotions can occur without arousal stimuli or can fail to occur in their presence; thoughts and language do not follow Aristotelian logic or accepted grammatical and stylistic rules (remember Mr. F. B.). There may be a distortion in time perspective, affecting perception of causal relationships. Such individuals need to be hospitalized for treatment because behavior which is not under the control of some definable feedback system becomes unpredictable and poses a potential threat both to the individual and to other people.

Process vs. reactive schizophrenia. The onset of schizophrenia may be gradual or sudden. The gradual development of schizophrenia, in which signs of pathology appear over a long period of time, is called *process schizophrenia.* Here the prognosis for recovery is poor because the thought and behavior patterns have become firmly entrenched by the time they are recognized as clearly pathological. In contrast, *reactive schizophrenia* seems to be related to specific precipitating factors and is not supported by a history of pathological experiences and habits. With its sudden discontinuity in the patient's behavioral style it offers a more favorable chance of recovery.

Classifying schizophrenia. For convenience, clinicians distinguish several types of schizophrenia, each with a characteristic cluster of behaviors. Six such types are summarized in the table.   ●

In the ten-year period from 1957 to 1967 there was an 88 percent increase in the number of hospitalized patients under fifteen years of age diagnosed as childhood schizophrenics. This increase probably reflects more widespread recognition and diagnosis of the condition rather than an increase in its incidence.

The problem of diagnosis and labeling is a persistent one, however, and one of the big obstacles to a better understanding of schizophrenic behavior is a disagreement among clinicians on the best criteria for classifying it. While there is some consensus about a number of the prominent symptoms associated with schizophrenia, no one patient shows them all, and any single patient may exhibit a variety of them over time. For example, the record of one patient admitted to a veterans' hospital because he was obsessed with homicidal and suicidal thoughts showed five different diagnoses of his condition over a five-year period by different psychiatrists:

August 1944— simple schizophrenia
November 1944—neurosis, conversion reaction
March 1946—dementia praecox in remission, superimposed on an inadequate personality
June 1947—constitutional psychopathic individual of schizoid type
September 1949—schizophrenia in partial remission, chronic, moderate

Did the patient change or only the basis for evaluating his condition? A similar question can be asked of the results of a study which showed that American psychiatrists classified as schizophrenic thirteen times as many of their patients (in outpatient clinics) as did Dutch psychiatrists diagnosing a comparable population. Is there really that much difference in prevalence of schizophrenia or is the difference just in the criteria used?

Evidence that the difference is in those who do the labeling rather than in those who are labeled comes from a study in which American and British psychiatrists were asked to make diagnoses on the basis of videotaped doctor-patient interviews. The patients were more likely to be classified as schizophrenic by the Americans and as affective psychotic by the Britishers. Patients showing both disorder of thought and mood disorder were labeled schizophrenics by the American psychiatrists and diagnosed as suffering from an affective disorder by the British psychiatrists (Mosher & Feinsilver, 1970).

● TYPES OF SCHIZOPHRENIA

Childhood schizophrenia (autism)	A clinical entity first recognized by Leo Kanner in 1943, this type of schizophrenia appears due to a biologic deficit which results in an inability of the child to relate himself to other people and to environmental stimulation in the ordinary way. Autistic children show obsessive stereotyped behavior, a failure to attend to stimulation in more than one modality at a time, and an inability to transfer from verbal instructions to performance. They represent the clearest example of a psychological system closed in on itself.
Simple schizophrenia	Reduction of external interests and attachments, apathy, withdrawal, inconspicuous delusions or hallucinations, some disintegration of thought processes, often aggressive behavior, hypochondriacal experiences, and sex and/or alcohol indulgence.
Paranoid schizophrenia	Poorly systematized delusions; often hostile, suspicious, aggressive. Delusions are often of omnipotence, remarkable talents, and high social status. Delusions are combined with personality disorganization.
Catatonia	More sudden onset than other types with vivid hallucinations and grandiose delusions. Alternation between stupor and excitement; in stupor, there is a sudden loss of animation, and a stereotyped position may be maintained for some time, during which patient will not eat, drink, or take care of other bodily functions. Catatonic schizophrenics are the most likely to recover.
Hebephrenia	Most severe disorganization: silliness, inappropriateness of affect, incoherence of thought, speech, action, unusual mannerisms, auditory and visual hallucinations, fantastic delusions, obscene behavior, lack of modesty, hypochondriasis, emotional indifference, regression to childish behavior.
Unclassified	Acute or chronic reactions with a hodgepodge of symptoms.

Even when observers agree in classifying what they see, a full understanding of schizophrenia can come only if we supplement our observations of the outer, behavioral indicators (hallucinations, disturbances of thought and emotion, and so on) with first-hand accounts of what it feels like by patients themselves (Ψ Close-up, p. 593).

Some schizophrenic patients appear to be so apathetic and lacking in any motivation that the psychiatric staff decides therapy would be "wasted" on them. Given the limited resources available in every mental hospital, treatment decisions are often made in terms of the patients' apparent prognosis: those with a favorable prognosis receive intensive treatment, while those showing no signs of responsivity to environmental stimulation are given only custodial care. The latter often end up on a back ward where they may spend their entire lives unless they recover "on their own." But this lack of responsivity may be only apparent. They may be perceiving and even coping with events in the environment—in their own way.

Intensive observations were made by a team of observers trained to record "on a minute-by-minute basis everything that occurred" in the dayroom of a chronic, closed psychiatric ward, where the patients had been hospitalized from two to thirty-five years. During six observation periods extending over a two-week period, each patient's behavior upon entering the dayroom and his sequence of activities while there were recorded. If the patients had been truly unmotivated and unresponsive to their environment, there should not have been any systematic pattern in their personal activity. The results suggest instead that these patients were extremely aware of their environment.

Upon first entering the dayroom and discovering the presence of strangers (the observers), almost all the patients went for a short period of time to a "way station" (either the bulletin board, the Ping-Pong table, or the water fountain) from which they could examine the situation. ■ On the first observation day, they lingered there only about fifteen seconds, moving on to a place away from the nearest observer. In fact, the majority of those who went to the water fountain left it to go out on the porch, completely out of sight of the observers.

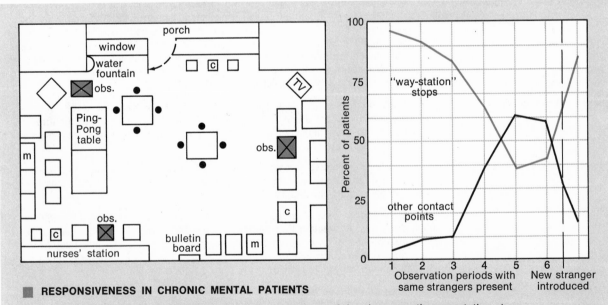

■ **RESPONSIVENESS IN CHRONIC MENTAL PATIENTS**

On the left is a diagram of the dayroom showing the position of the observers, the way-station stops, and the positions where cigarettes (c) and matches (m) could be received or given. The graph on the right shows the gradual reduction in way-station stops over the two-week period and the sudden rise at the end when a new observer was present.

Adapted from Hershkowitz, 1962

Ψ Close-up *From the Diary of a Schizophrenic*

A view of the "inner world of mental illness" is provided by the first-person accounts collected in a fascinating volume by Bert Kaplan (1964). One of them, reproduced in part below, was written by a patient during the period of his most profound disturbance. He was a male in his late twenties, a high-school graduate with above-average intelligence from a large family in a midwestern urban community. His unusual spelling and sentence structure stem not from lack of knowledge or skill, but from the same loosening of thought and expression that we observed in Mr. F. B.

I believe these things listed below are differance ways we have of letting our emotions out. Smoking 1. Learn to plan horn. 2. Chewing Gum 3. Sports ect. 4. Doing actives we enjoy doing 5. drinking till drunk. 5. Working at or with things we enjoy doing

Man can not live by what the church say's 100% Because we are human and human nature we can not live without showing or emotions. Will power I need more of in some faze's of Life

Some reason why I love men. 1. Plight 2. Attractive build 3. Neat apirance 4. not feeling my self around wemon 5. not feel able to relax around them 6. Feel that I would not be able to control my love emotion around them but, I am learn how to.

The reason I am restless at night. I am lonely and want Jim as he and Norma is the two I have been able to show my love emotion to. Sence I stated changing some from the way I was tought at home. Started to find love out side of my invirme I was razed in. . . .

I feel as though I am all alone quit abit of the time. I have a feeling I am all alone most of the time. That is why I fell in love with Jim He had a good build and a very nice person

God is giving me the gift of knowledge. God help me as his servent to keep humbley befor him at all times. Look forward and not backward. We can never change the past. But we can change the future. So we can look forwand instead of backward. . . . I feel I have been a homosexual because I am in love with everyone, We have to love all man kind in order to get to heaven It is sure hard to say no went you have form a habit of looking guys over and see if you really love them or not. . . .

We have to learn to *trust people*. We have to learn to trust people all over again after we have been sick. Sin or trusting the wrong person cause's us to become metal sick. We have to learn to master our own mind. Our actions are not allways explanable as much as we try to understand them. Don't rush things will work out better if we relax and do things at our own gate. God is love and he know the trouble we have learning to make up our own mind. Take it easy every thing will work out. (Kaplan, 1964, pp. 191-192)

Over the two-week period, this use of way-station "safety" stops decreased from 96 percent to about 40 percent. When a new observer was then put into the dayroom, however, the way-station reaction rose again suddenly to 85 percent.

The patients' use of the way station not only indicated the sensitivity of these chronically hospitalized patients to changes in their surroundings but a subtle means of coping with the new situation. They probably used the way-station stop as a brief opportunity to assess the situation and to plan subsequent reactions—without giving any impression that they were in fact concerned or even aware of the intrusion (Hershkowitz, 1962).

Subsequent observations revealed an even more fascinating pattern of motivated interaction among these patients. One of the major means of social interaction on the ward was asking for or giving cigarettes and matches. It turned out that these patients had evolved a social system to maximize the likelihood that anyone who wanted a cigarette or match would get one if he asked, or be asked if he wanted to give either one. There were certain seats in the dayroom which, if sat in by certain patients, would signify a willingness to give either cigarettes or matches. This system effectively limited the potential frustration involved in being refused or not being approached (Hershkowitz, 1970).

The creation of and sensitivity to such an interpersonal network demands more motivation and cognitive acuity than chronic psychotic patients are usually credited with. Unfortunately, much of their apparent lack of motivation comes from their attempts to appear unmotivated. It may be that such a tactic is designed to deceive not their keepers, but themselves —if you have no goals or do not want anything, you cannot be frustrated. Thus it may be that mental patients, in giving the appearance of being unmotivated, are successful in managing the impression they want to give, but thereby inadvertently become less likely candidates for therapy and subsequent release.

Origins of Psychotic Behavior

In the attempt to solve the puzzle that is psychotic behavior, researchers have vainly searched for *the* cause. Some have probed nature, others nurture. Obviously more than scientific curiosity is at stake since an understanding of why psychosis develops, and hopefully the control that such knowledge would make possible, would relieve an unbelievable amount of human suffering while simultaneously illuminating how the human mind functions—and malfunctions.

We have already discussed the problems inherent in trying to find out whether nature or nurture is the more important determinant of any trait. Many researchers favor the "polygenic" view of schizophrenia and other psychoses: that there is an interplay of genetic, biochemical, neurological, and environmental factors. Nevertheless, the appealing simplicity of finding a single biological cause of psychotic "disease" has been and remains a significant source of motivation for research efforts in many laboratories and clinics throughout the world.

Hereditary factors. "It's all in the genes," is one view of the basis of functional psychosis. An individual inherits a genetic structure which presumably makes him likely to become psychotic. Initial support for this position came from numerous studies which indicated that psychotic disorders tend to run in

families. This fact is hardly proof of the hereditary basis since people with "unfavorable" heredity often live in environments that are physically and psychologically unhealthy.

More substantial evidence supporting the hypothesis of hereditary causality came from the finding that the risk of becoming schizophrenic increased with the degree of genetic relationship to the schizophrenic patient. The full sibling of a person with schizophrenia was twice as likely to become schizophrenic as was a half-sibling—although both shared a common environment. There was a marked increase in schizophrenia risk when both parents were schizophrenic, and it was greatest of all among identical twins reared together—more than a 90 percent chance.

Although several early studies agreed that an identical twin of a schizophrenic was much more likely to develop schizophrenia than a fraternal twin, recent investigations have seriously challenged their findings.

One very thorough study of 342 pairs of twins, 35 to 64 years of age, living in Norway, where one or both had been hospitalized for a functional psychosis, found concordance rates of only 38 percent[1] for identical twins and 10 percent for fraternal twins. This difference suggests that a genetic factor is important but does not play the major role as had been assumed previously. The researcher noted, "In the investigations so far, the pattern seems consistent: The more accurate and careful the samplings, the lower the concordance figures." (Kringlen, 1969, p. 38)

Even if higher concordance rates were found, their interpretation is not clear. Identical twins are more likely to be treated alike and to have a more similar environment and more difficulty in establishing their identity than fraternal twins. And once a twin is found with schizophrenia, an investigator may be more likely to diagnose his monozygotic mate as schizophrenic if he believes that psychosis is hereditary.

Most psychologists and psychiatrists today are in agreement that what *can* be inherited is a *predisposition* to the psychosis; under conditions severe enough, a predisposed individual is believed to be

---

[1]A concordance rate of 38 percent means that in 38 percent of the cases the identical twin of a schizophrenic patient also became schizophrenic.

more likely to develop a psychosis than other individuals, who might develop some less severe disorder. Pathological ways of coping with the environment are more likely to be learned if a child lives with a psychotic relative than if he lives with a normal one. With two schizophrenic parents—two models of abnormal, pathological behavior to imitate and use for social comparison purposes—a child has a greater likelihood of learning schizophrenic behavior patterns.

Body chemistry factors. The study of internal chemistry in relation to psychosis has revealed that manic-depressive and schizophrenic patients differ measurably in blood chemistry from each other as well as from normal individuals. The interpretation of such differences requires great caution however; they may be either a cause of the psychosis or a result of it. It would be expected that a psychosis, through disruption of normal activity and interference with nutrition and sleep, might have extensive effects on the body chemistry.

Investigators have found that the blood of schizophrenics contains less of a substance called *glutathione* than does the blood of normal individuals (Martens et al., 1956) but a greater than normal quantity of *ceruloplasmin,* a substance containing copper, which makes schizophrenic blood able to oxidize adrenaline more rapidly than normal blood can (Leach et al., 1956; Leach & Heath, 1956). Such rapid processing of adrenaline could be related to the psychotic's typical distortion of emotion.

A number of studies have investigated the effects of *taraxein,* a substance extracted from the blood of schizophrenic patients. When this substance was injected into monkeys and human volunteers, abnormal brain-wave activity and thought disorganization occurred. This was not the case with injections of serum from normal blood (Heath, 1960).

The search for biochemical correlates of schizophrenia has often led to disappointments. One compound that was discovered in significantly greater proportions in the urine of schizophrenics was traced to their hospital diet. When normal volunteers were given the same diet, they too excreted large quantities of the compound, which disappeared when they were put on a sugar-water diet.

We noted earlier (Chapter 7) that REM deprivation might be linked to abnormal behavior. When normals are deprived of the opportunity for REM sleep one night, they compensate by "rebounding" the next night, making up their lost REM activity. Schizophrenics, however, do not show this REM rebound effect. A parallel finding was obtained in cats given repeated administration of the drug PCPA, which inhibits the formation of *serotonin* (a neurotransmitter substance). These cats developed a kind of "psychosis," with changes in behavior (hyperaggression and hypersexuality) as well as abnormal brain-wave patterns. Research is now being directed toward possible relationships between human schizophrenic reactions and the "model psychosis" provided by these PCPA cats through the activity of serotonin and other components of brain chemistry.

Studies have also been made with the drugs mescaline and LSD. These drugs produce some temporary symptoms of mental disturbance in normally healthy individuals. But though there are some similarities between these drug states and mental illness, there are also important differences between them.

Environmental factors. In the past decade, there has been an increasing emphasis on studying the complex environmental-social matrix in which a schizophrenic individual operates. Just as genetic factors can make an individual biologically vulnerable, so environmental factors like parental rejection or overprotection, excessive or inconsistent discipline, or extreme insecurity can predispose him psychologically to mental disorder. Studies of the family structure of schizophrenics, as well as of other features of their social life, reveal the extent to which functional psychosis may represent learned ways of attempting to cope with chronic stress and unresolvable conflicts.

When school records of thirty adult hospitalized schizophrenics and ninety matched controls were examined retrospectively, a different picture of childhood behavior emerged for boys and girls. Compared to the normal controls, the boys who later became schizophrenic showed patterns of unsocialized aggression and a disorganized, hostile family background. In contrast, the girls who became schizophrenic showed sensitiveness, hyperconformity, and introversion related to having repressive parents (Mosher & Feinsilver, 1970).

Ψ Close-up   *Culture and Abnormality*

One's culture, in prescribing and rewarding certain behavior, is an important determiner of what is seen as normal or abnormal. We would consider a man "mentally ill" and probably commit him to an institution if he wore his mother's skull around his neck to protect him from the threat of her ghost like the man pictured here. Or imagine a man who kills another man, bashes his brains out, eats them, and then for the rest of his life, uses his enemy's skull as a pillow. Among the headhunters and cannibals of the southwest coast of Netherlands New Guinea such men are normal because their culture has vouched for the soundness of such fears and the appropriateness of such behavior.

One of the most reliable prognostic indicators of future schizophrenic development is an early pattern of social isolation in which the adolescent withdraws from interacting with others. This may be a consequence of feeling different or "abnormal" in some way, or of not having learned how to relate to other people in a positive, meaningful way, or both.

Many studies clearly show that one of the most abnormal things about schizophrenic children is the relationship between their parents and the parents' use of the child to work out their own feelings of frustration and hostility. The child may be cast in the role of "buffer" or mediator and made to feel responsible for the continuation or failure of the marriage, or in subtle ways, the parents may establish a pattern in which continuation of their precariously balanced relationship relies upon keeping the child dependent upon them.

Psychologists have coined the term *schizophrenogenic mother* to describe the dominant mother who unconsciously teaches, or in a sense "persuades," her child to become schizophrenic out of her own needs or by the model she provides. This is often accomplished by using a destructive technique in which the child is given contradictory demands and expected to act upon them both. A child may be put in this *double-bind* situation when he is covertly made aware that he must remain dependent, while being overtly encouraged to become autonomous and mature. In one study, mothers of male schizophrenics were more likely than mothers of normal men to agree with the following statements: "Children should be taken to and from school until the age of eight just to make sure there are no accidents"; "If children are quiet for a little while a mother should immediately find out what they are thinking about"; and "A child should not plan to enter any occupation that his parents don't approve of" (Mark, 1953).

Family interaction studies show less responsiveness and interpersonal sensitivity in the speech of families with a schizophrenic member than in normal families. In families with the most disturbed offspring, the members do not listen to each other or spend as much time in information exchange as normal families (Ferriera & Winter, 1964). Those in families with withdrawn adolescents are less able to predict each other's responses in a test situation.

Sometimes other members of the schizophrenic's family show more deviation from normal communication patterns than the member diagnosed as schizophrenic. This leads to the conjecture that where various members of the family react "abnormally" one may be "chosen" to be labeled as the mentally sick one. He or she is then expected to act "crazy" and may even be reinforced for doing so.

The broader cultural environment also appears to influence what form pathological behavior will take when it occurs. For example, just as the neurotic conversion reaction is less common today than formerly, manic-depressive psychosis also appears much less often in mental hospitals than it did twenty or thirty years ago (Lundin, 1961). (Ψ Close-up, p. 596.)

Within our own society, people from lower socioeconomic classes are more likely to become schizophrenic and those most affluent to become neurotic (Hollingshead & Redlich, 1958). ▲ It may be that the higher rate among lower-class families can be traced to their patterns of child rearing (Lane & Singer, 1959). It may also be that many of the environmental consequences of being poor—powerlessness, frustrated ambitions, rootlessness, a losing battle for survival—provide fertile soil for psychotic pathology.

The view that poor people face a lifetime of environmental insults which increase their chances of becoming seriously disturbed psychologically has been documented in an ongoing survey in New York City. On the basis of psychiatric evaluation and computer analysis of intensive interviews with the mothers of 2000 children aged five to eighteen, it was found that 23 percent of the welfare children suffered from mental disturbances to a degree severe enough to require immediate treatment. This was almost twice as many as among their nonwelfare peers (Langner et al., 1970).

The apparent differences in who develops which disorder may also reflect bias in how patients are diagnosed. For example, poorer disturbed patients, unable to pay for therapy, may be committed to state hospitals as "out-of-contact psychotics," while those with similar symptoms who can afford psychotherapy are perceived and labeled as "neurotics in need of treatment to work through their conflicts."

As social values change, as definitions of what is acceptable and appropriate are modified, as our

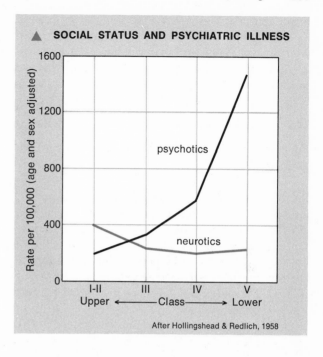

▲ **SOCIAL STATUS AND PSYCHIATRIC ILLNESS**

Rate per 100,000 (age and sex adjusted)

psychotics

neurotics

I-II   III   IV   V
Upper ← Class → Lower

After Hollingshead & Redlich, 1958

shared definitions of what constitutes meaningful goals in life and "reality" become altered, we can expect corresponding changes in the ways people attempt to adapt to their psychological environment. It seems likely that there will be an increasing incidence of those who, instead of losing contact with an unmanageable reality, will revolt against it openly, tune out temporarily with drugs, or drop out permanently with friends who decide to share the delusion of a new private reality to which they can relate.

Loss of Alternative Modes of Being: Suicide

A person who commits suicide believes that there are only two ways for him to be: the way he is now or dead. The way he is now is unbearable, and he takes the only other alternative he sees.

Suicide has traditionally been defined as an aggressive act directed against oneself, intended to cause death. However, many people who commit acts that appear to be suicidal do not really intend to die. This is seen in the movie star who takes an overdose of sleeping pills shortly before her maid is supposed to arrive at work. The soldier, who in throwing himself on top of a grenade is killed while saving his buddies, commits a suicidal act but not because he wants to die. Both intention and act are included in what we think of as suicide.

Types of Suicides

Four basic types of suicidal acts have been distinguished by researchers.

Symbolic suicide.   Sometimes an individual commits an act of symbolic suicide by participating in the destruction of some object (or even of an organization) which he views as an extension of himself. The object "stands in" for the person and allows him to act out his self-destructive impulses without being destroyed in the process. It is as if he were burning his own image in effigy.

Often it is difficult to determine reliably whether a given, isolated destructive act in fact represents a symbolic attempt at suicide. A boy who destroys his most prized toy, or whose mistreatment of his pet results in its death, may be signaling his own self-destructive urge symbolically. However, he may be merely displacing aggression actually felt toward more threatening adults.

Accidental suicide.   An accidental suicide is an accident which results in the individual's death and appears to contain some element of unconscious willing for it to occur. The person who repeatedly takes risks, who chooses jobs which are dangerous, may be seeking his own death in an "accident" that could occur as a natural part of the activities in which he must engage. But here, too, there is considerable ambiguity about the degree to which the destructive consequence was sought. A man may drive a dynamite truck not with the secret wish of being blown apart in an explosion, but because of the lucrative salary for such a job. Another person may insist on driving while drunk and be killed when he smashes the car into a tree—on some level wanting to die.

Seiden (1970) believes that the violent deaths of many young urban blacks may contain some element of intent to die. If one is hemmed in by frustrations and hopelessness and prevented from direct suicide

by a norm that defines suicide as soft and unmasculine, a violent death may have some attractiveness, especially if in the process some injury is inflicted on those in power.

Overtly intentional but unsuccessful suicide.   In another class of suicidal actions there is a decision to die and a plan for how to do it, but the attempt is not successful. The suicide attempt may fail because the "overdose" of drugs was insufficient, the blood from cut wrists congealed after a while, or a slightly opened window prevented asphyxiation from a gas oven. In cases such as these, it may well have been that the suicidal act was intended as a last desperate cry for help. If anyone responds to this suicidal attempt, then there is a new alternative available in the form of special attention, sympathy, reduced demands and responsibilities, and perhaps hospitalization and therapy. Unfortunately, the people to whom the message is directed are often unable to hear cries for help made in any less dramatic form.

An interesting sidelight is the effect that the suicide attempt has on other people. Often they will feel just as guilty as if the attempt had succeeded, which makes one wonder if this may have been one of the things the person was trying to accomplish. Thus there may also be a punitive aspect to the message as well—to make the survivor feel sorry for what he has done or failed to do. "They'll be sorry when I'm dead!" is a rather common thought for children to entertain as a way to get back at parents for some perceived injustice.

One characteristic of people who successfully commit suicide is a history of one or more prior unsuccessful attempts. A recent survey of patients at a suicide prevention center showed that 60 percent of those who did commit suicide had made an attempt to kill themselves previously (Wold, 1970). Sometimes, of course, the "attempted" suicide is inadvertently successful.

Overtly intentional and successful suicide.   Included in this class are not only people who really intended to die but also many people who intended to be rescued but who for some reason were not.

Also, there are many cases of people who have every intention of dying but who at the last moment change their minds. And there are people who, in a moment of blind rage or some other very strong emotion, commit a self-destructive action without a clear intention of dying; often they are surprised to find out that they are going to die.

Who Commits Suicide?

At least a thousand people commit suicide every day —almost half a million persons a year, according to the World Health Organization. This startling statistic becomes even more grisly when we realize that about eight times as many try it as succeed.

The means by which people commit suicide vary from country to country according to what is available and fashionable. In the United States, men most commonly use guns while women most often resort to poisoning or asphyxiation. In Nigeria, hanging is the preferred mode, while Englishmen tend to use gas as the most frequent means of suicide. In Basel, Switzerland, suicides with gas had been most common, but when the government made the gas nonpoisonous, drowning became the most popular substitute.

In an effort to determine the characteristics of those who commit suicide and the conditions associated with the suicidal act, a researcher studied the cases of over 2000 suicides in the Chicago area, using death certificates issued over a five-year period. He found that men are much more likely to commit suicide than women (Maris, 1969). This "male supremacy" holds in every country of the world, for the excess of male over female suicides goes from a low of 2.4 percent in Ireland to a high of 23.6 percent in Finland. In the United States it has averaged nearly 12 percent. Suicides become more prevalent among white males after the age of 35 and are most common among the aged. Also evident from the graph is the higher suicide rate among whites than nonwhites. ■

It may well be that the subordinate role in which our society places women minimizes their feelings of personal guilt and inadequacy and thereby lowers their predisposition to commit suicide. The liberation of women in Japan following World War II was accompanied by a marked increase in their suicide rate.

Similarly, it seems likely that an important reason for the sharp difference between white and nonwhite

male suicides in the past has been that nonwhite males, despite a generally more frustrating economic and social situation, have often been able to blame it on external constraints such as discrimination and poor educational opportunities. Thus one can speculate that as external restraints which have limited their freedom of action are removed, the demands for assuming personal responsibility for their problems and failures will increase. In fact, there is evidence that this may be occurring already: that starting in 1965 there has been a sharp rise in suicides among young nonwhite American men. In further support, as the graph indicates, the figures for nonwhite males are approximations. Seiden (1970) cites evidence that for urban black men the rate has "undergone a striking epidemic increase in the last fifteen years." He has also found that the peak age for suicide in this group is between 25 and 34.

The survey by Maris (1969) also revealed the following description of the conditions in which suicide is most and least likely to occur: most in the spring, least in winter; most in late afternoon, least in early morning; most on a Monday (for males at least) and at home (74 percent of all suicides).

Occupations which require assuming responsibility for the well-being of others take the greatest toll of

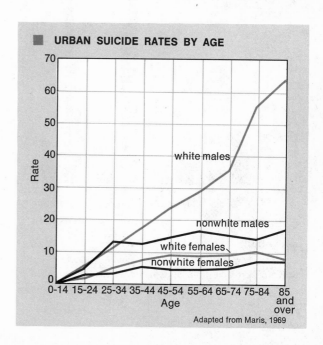

URBAN SUICIDE RATES BY AGE

Adapted from Maris, 1969

suicides. More physicians died from suicide than from auto accidents, drowning, homicides, and plane crashes combined between 1965 and 1967 according to the National Institute of Mental Health. Within this group, psychiatrists were the most likely to kill themselves—six times more likely than pediatricians.

One of the most reliable social predictors of suicide, especially for men, is whether the individual is married. Contrary to what many cynics maintain, there is something about marriage which sharply reduces the likelihood of suicide, compared to being single. Moreover, becoming widowed or divorced greatly increases the probability of death from suicide. Apparently, men also seem to need women (or to be married) more than women need men—again contrary to popular masculine myth. Suicide statistics such as those in the table reveal that the absolute increase in suicide rate as a consequence of being widowed or divorced is substantially greater for males in every age group. •

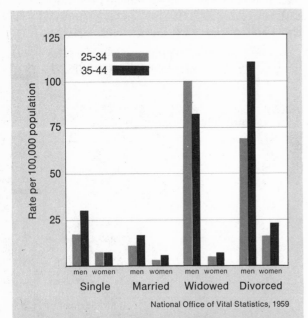

● **SUICIDE AND MARITAL STATUS**
Suicide is more frequent among single, widowed, and divorced people than among those who are married and much more common among men than among women at each age and in each group.

Personality characteristics of the suicidal person. Studies have shown that adolescents who attempt suicide have several characteristics in common: (a) a lack of happy experiences, happy relationships, and meaningfulness in their lives; (b) a feeling that their life is a burden for someone else, usually a parent or lover; (c) feelings of hostility and aggression directed toward themselves; (d) a feeling of isolation, of extreme separateness from others (such individuals are usually quiet and introspective); (e) often, a physical separation from the mother or perhaps from a lover in whom the individual has had an abnormally high investment; and (f) a warning that there is some intention to commit suicide: either a note, a previous attempt, or comments like "I feel like I want to die." Usually such a warning is fairly obvious if anyone is watching or listening.

Without question, the single most outstanding characteristic of those who attempt suicide is, not surprisingly, *depression*. Among one group of patients in contact with the Los Angeles Suicide Prevention Center, 92 percent of those who actually committed suicide were rated as *clinically depressed* (Wold, 1970). Frequently associated with this depression is the problem of chronic alcoholism.

Social bases for suicide. The suicidal person is typically one who is living alone, often without close friends or relatives, or one whose introvertive character keeps people at a distance. His isolation is both a major source of his depression and a factor which prevents others from becoming aware of and responding to his need for help.

A comprehensive study of suicidal behavior among college students in the Los Angeles area underscored the significant role played by feelings of social isolation. The rate of suicides among college students is 712 per 100,000 which is about half the rate of their noncollege peers. The suicide is neither the reputed brilliant but neurotic student, nor the desperate, failing student. Typically he has average grades, comes from a striving, middle-class family, and has had little experience with drinking, sex, or drugs. He tends to be so preoccupied with his loneliness and feelings of alienation that he does not even consider that there might be avenues of escape (Peck, 1970).

Any sudden and radical change that removes an

♦ Reproduced above are two genuine suicide notes. The isolation that is both a symptom and a cause of the suicidal person's problem is clearly shown in the note to Estelle. Every feature of this note is an expression of isolation. The sentences are isolated from the margins and from each other, just as the words are spaced far apart and even the individual letters within a word are often unconnected.

In the other note, a graphologist inferred great hostility from the fact that many of the letters at the end of words show a daggerlike projection, requiring an unusual flick of the wrist to achieve. Certainly the content is intended to fill its recipient with guilt as well as sorrow.

individual's basic sources of security and predictability can make him more susceptible to suicide. Rapid social and economic change, the unexpected loss of a loved one, or strong feelings of life's injustice, coupled with a sense of powerlessness to exert any control can become a precondition for suicide.

Another instructive bit of information about those who attempt suicide is that a third of them are influenced by someone else's suicide. Thus social learning, which accounts for so much that is valuable in our repertoire of skills, can also provide a mechanism for lowering a person's restraints against committing suicide.

The suicide note.   In Philip Roth's novel *Portnoy's Complaint,* a young boy, apparently driven by the relentless ambitions of his mother, is found hanging from the shower with a farewell suicide note pinned to his starched shirt:

Mrs. Blumenthal called. Please bring your mah-jongg rules to the game tonight.   Ronald

A note is left in about 15 percent of suicide cases, although the frequency of suicide notes is much greater among those who attempt suicide and are unsuccessful than among those who actually die. ♦

Content analysis of genuine and simulated suicide notes uncovered a number of differences between the two sets of documents. The real notes were more specific in revealing information, gave more concrete instructions, employed the word "love" and sex themes more frequently, but used fewer "thinking" words. The suicidal person's note was not a contemplation of suicide or a decision-process in operation, but an expression of a *fait accompli*. The verdict was in—it needed only to be mechanically executed (Ogilvie, Stone, & Shneidman, 1966). Graphologists have successfully distinguished between actual suicide notes and the same message written by control subjects of the same sex and age (Frederick, 1968).

Preventing Suicide

The prevalence of suicide is a grim reminder to society of its failure to make life worth living for all of its members. Suicidal behavior poses many complex questions, some philosophical, some psychological, some social, and some political-legal. Is suicide ever justified? Under what conditions do some societies encourage suicide? Should the person's decision to commit suicide be respected and intervention not undertaken? What, if anything, would lead *you* to commit suicide?

Surprisingly, we have only just begun to take suicide seriously as a human problem deserving scientific and humanitarian interest. The first Suicide Prevention Center was founded in Los Angeles by Edwin Shneidman as recently as 1958. Fortunately, such centers have begun to proliferate, and 130 prevention and crisis intervention centers were in existence by 1969.

Hospitals are instituting new programs of therapy for those who have attempted suicide, and many cities have suicide-alert phone numbers which potential suicides are urged to call. But it is obvious that for any program to work, the suicidal person must either take the initiative and identify himself or be unsuccessful in his attempted suicide. Suicide prevention efforts obviously fail when potential suicides decide to kill themselves without giving the so-called cry for help. In Mexico, where a highly publicized, around-the-clock service with a staff of psychiatrists, social workers, and medical practitioners was set up, suicidal Mexicans did not bother to avail themselves of it nor could families be induced to notify the Bureau of Medical Services when one of their members gave signs of being suicidal. They did not want to call in the authorities, bring attention or disgrace to

themselves, or perhaps admit that they could not handle the problem (*Science News,* June 1968).

It would seem that attempts at prevention need to start earlier. Instead of trying to spot a person already so desperate that he is prepared to die, we need to find ways of identifying children and young adults who are potential suicides.

Meanwhile, many people do overtly threaten to commit suicide before they actually do so. In fact, it is unusual for a person to commit suicide without giving some prior indication of his intent. Therefore, the most important response to any suicide threat is to take it seriously—as if somebody's life depended on *your* being concerned.

Chapter Summary

Mental disorder has always fascinated yet frightened man; it has been comforting to regard the mentally ill as "different" from the rest of us and to see mental disorder as something existing in them, for which the rest of us had no responsibility. The development of the view that such individuals were not "possessed" but *ill* brought more humane treatment and attempts to cure them but encouraged dependency in those being treated and gave them labels that were often constricting and self-fulfilling. Today many clinicians believe that disordered behavior is better conceptualized in terms of faulty learning or maladaptive social interaction than in terms of a medical model. Some define "normalcy" in terms of potential rather than in terms of current norms. In fact, social norms can contribute to psychopathology when they hold up standards that people feel inadequate to meet.

Each person wants to see himself as *normal* and as *rational*. If he cannot prove both, he may give up one if he can assure himself of the other.

Identification is a normal process by which a child internalizes the values and attitudes of his community and in particular of his same-sex parent. It has important value both for the individual and for the society but can "go wrong" if false values are learned or if there is either too much identification or too little. Two pathological forms of identification are *identification with the aggressor*, which leads to a *loss of self-identity*, and *identification with a rejecting majority,* which leads to a *loss of self-worth.* Prejudice, once learned, is difficult to extinguish because discrimination may serve many functions and may be maintained by a variety of reinforcers. Social segregation because of supposed inferiority leads to further alienation and mutual mistrust and may create differences not present originally.

Loss of self-regulating capacities is seen in psychological and/or physical dependence on alcohol, cigarettes, or drugs. Such a loss can have disastrous consequences physically, psychologically, and socially but is apparently learned and maintained because of short-term reinforcement. Compulsive gambling is learned and maintained in a similar manner.

Loss of joy in living characterizes the several *neurotic reactions.* In *anxiety neurosis,* free-floating anxiety is the chief characteristic and the individual may have no idea what is making him so anxious. In *phobias,* the individual has an intense fear of a particular object or activity, typically something with symbolic meaning for him; he realizes the fear is irrational but feels powerless to disregard it. In *obsessive-compulsive reactions*, the individual may be unable to rid himself of a thought or feeling, or may feel compelled to go through particular rituals in order to allay anxiety. *Hysterical neuroses* provide mechanisms for escape from anxiety through *conversion hysteria*—a physical affliction without physical cause—or a *dissociated state.* Dissociated states include *somnambulism* (sleepwalking), *amnesia* (forgetting one's identity), and *fugue* (amnesia plus flight). The most extreme form of dissociative state is *multiple personality,* a rare condition in which different parts of the personality become separate and are in control at different times, often unaware of each other. In *hypochondria,* the individual's constant concern with supposed but usually fictitious ailments gives him an excuse for not coping with problems; he also manages to elicit considerable attention and sympathy. In *depressive neurosis,* the individual gives in to grief and depression, magnifying negative factors out of all proportion. All the neuroses are mechanisms for *proving helplessness,* thereby inducing sympathy and avoiding efforts that might lead to failure, and for *limiting anxiety* by enabling the individual not to confront its source.

Loss of contact with reality is called *psychosis.* In *paranoid reactions,* the individual has delusions, either transient, as in *paranoid states,* or systematized and rigid, as in *paranoia.* Affective disorders are disorders of mood; the individual may be *manic* (euphoric) or *deeply depressed* or may alternate between the two, perhaps with periods of normalcy in between. *Involutional melancholia* is a deep, pervasive psychotic depression.

Schizophrenia is a breakdown of integrated functioning in which the individual stops checking against environmental feedback. Distortions may occur in perception, emotion, thought, language patterns, and time perspective. Types of schizophrenia include *childhood, simple, paranoid, catatonic, hebephrenic,* and *unclassified.* Schizophrenic patients occupy almost half of all beds in mental hospitals. Even those who seem completely out of touch may be responding rationally to environmental changes.

There seems to be no *one* cause of psychosis. *Genetic predispositions, biochemical abnormality, faulty models,* and *pathological social interactions* all may play a role in given cases. The higher incidence of neuroses among the affluent and of psychoses at lower socioeconomic levels may be a true difference but sometimes represents only differences in labeling. Cultural patterns also help determine what behavior is regarded as pathological.

Suicidal acts have been classified as *symbolic suicide,* in which the individual destroys some object that he views as an extension of himself; *accidental suicide,* in which the actual event seems accidental but the individual has put himself in a position where he might be killed; *overtly intentional but unsuccessful suicide,* in which the individual consciously or unconsciously contrives to perform the suicidal act in such a way that it does not succeed; and, finally, *overtly intentional and successful suicide.*

Methods of suicide vary in different cultural groups, but suicide is in all countries more common among men than among women. In our country suicides become more prevalent among white men over 35, and are most common among the aged. Suicidal people tend to be rigid, isolated individuals who lack meaning and joy in their lives and have feelings of hostility and aggression toward themselves.

Chapter 15

The Therapeutic Modification of Behavior

All techniques of therapy are directed toward the same ultimate goal—helping the individual make a more satisfactory adjustment to his problems. More basically, all therapy involves attempts by one person to change another person in some specified way.

Many other enterprises also attempt to change people's behavior—education, propaganda, advertising, and salesmanship, to mention a few. The difference between therapy and these other influence attempts is in the way the two parties relate to each other and to their society. In therapy, one of them, "the patient," is identified as likely to benefit from a change in his behavior, while the other, "the therapist," is identified as an acceptable agent for producing that change. The therapist is seen as benign, as not primarily motivated for personal gain, and as operating in this role only because there are individuals with problems. On this score, therapy contrasts with influence attempts in which some "product" or "ideology" is being promoted and the promoter expects to benefit if he is successful.

With therapy, society also establishes the conditions under which the patient is either *recommended* or *required* to undergo prescribed change procedures. Therapy is often recommended when an individual's behavior falls short of some standards of performance or expectations of others in the culture —lack of productivity, inability to profit from learn-

ing experiences, complaints of being unhappy or fearful, failure to relate to others, inability to derive pleasure from or to utilize the resources of the society. Often therapeutic change is demanded by the society when an individual threatens the social control function of society or its basic assumptions about human nature and social structure.

Virtually all college students have been "in therapy" at some time in their lives—most often of an *informal* nature. In seeking help with personal psychological problems, they have turned to parents, teachers, clergy, and friends. Such "therapy" typically is voluntarily initiated by the individual, is of short duration, and is not the primary basis of the relationship with the other person. On their part, these "unprofessional" therapists have no special training in this function. Usually they dispense advice, love, and understanding or serve as "cathartic sounding boards," and do so without charge.

Many types of *formal* therapy for psychological problems are being practiced today. Therapy varies with the kind of educational training of the therapist, his own personality, the needs of the patient, and the demands of the situation in which patient and therapist interact. In some cases, the differences between therapies we will be reviewing are of method only; in others, they represent basic differences in assumptions about the functions and goals of therapy. For example, some therapists believe that they should direct the course of therapy; others center responsibility entirely in the patient. Some therapists treat only the problem that has brought the patient to them, while others attempt to treat the whole person. For some practitioners, the goal of therapy is for the patient to gain insight; for others it is for him to feel happy, or to be able to work productively, or even just to be "manageable." For still others, it is to change very specific disturbing behaviors.

Ideally, the relationship between scientific psychology and therapy should be akin to that between physics and engineering. Empirically established generalizations and abstract theories and laws about variables and their relationships should be applied to the practical problem posed by the individual case. Unfortunately, there is not yet a unified theory of personality or behavior from which can be drawn a blueprint of practices, tactics, and strategies for bringing about a particular change in a unique person with a specific problem.

Equally important, as we saw in Chapter 2, when it comes to planning for changes in people's lives, *value judgments* underlie every decision, regardless of how much or how little objective knowledge is available. This is true in engineering and architecture too. Should a hospital be built near a highway convenient for those with cars, but inaccessible by public transportation for those without cars? Should efficiency or esthetics guide the design of low-cost housing proj-

ects? In urban relocation, do you follow the wishes of the people who are to be moved, or do you provide what "expert opinion" says is best for them? In psychotherapy, where treatment may have irreversible effects and may be undertaken and evaluated without consulting the patient, it is especially important to realize that both the choice of treatment and the criteria for its "success" depend on the values of the therapist and of the society.

In the last chapter we saw that psychopathology has been variously conceptualized as a disease (physical or mental) within the individual, as something that exists not in the individual but in his interactions with others, or as just another type of learned behavior, induced and maintained because it is reinforced. It can also be viewed as only a set of labels for behavior out of keeping with some set of social norms, with the term *abnormal* having utility only for social and legal purposes. Attempts at therapy inevitably reflect the varying assumptions about what psychopathology is, what conditions create it, and how it can be ameliorated. ■ In this chapter, we will review current attempts at therapeutic modification of behavior under the three banners of *physiological therapy, social-cognitive therapy,* and *behavior therapy*. Then we will consider attempts to combine therapeutic resources and will look at the effects of institutionalization and substitutes for it. Finally, we will look at the problems involved in trying to evaluate whether therapy "works."

■ The changes in methods of treatment of the "abnormal" over the centuries have reflected the changes in people's beliefs about the causes of apparently irrational behavior. Each theory of *causes* produces its own characteristic *methods of therapy*. On the left is a circulating swing used as late as the early nineteenth century to cure depression; in the center, a patient is being prepared for electric shock; on the right, one kind of group therapy is in session.

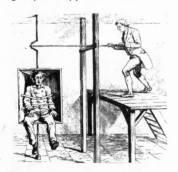 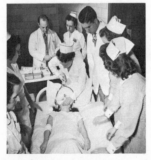 

Physiological Therapy

The distinguishing feature of the psychiatrist—whatever theory of personality and psychotherapy he advocates—is his medical training. In the psychiatric treatment of severe emotional disturbances, particularly where there is considerable loss of contact with reality, various physical methods of therapy are often used. Such medical measures range from the use of special diets to the application of chemical sedatives or the artificial induction of violent convulsions. It should be emphasized that such "physical psychiatry" is not always intended to cure the individual's emotional disorder but may be used in an attempt to prevent some extreme act such as homicide or suicide or to make the disturbed patient receptive to psychotherapy. The most prominent of these physical methods are shock therapy, narcosis, chemotherapy (drug therapy), nutrition, and psychosurgery.

Shock Therapy

Severely disturbed patients who would once have been considered hopeless have responded favorably in some cases to artificially induced seizures or convulsions. Such treatment, known as *shock therapy*, became routine in most mental hospitals after World War II but is considerably less common since the discovery of new techniques of chemotherapy. Although a number of different techniques have been used in shock therapy, one feature they have in common is inducing a state of coma lasting for several minutes to several hours after the shock. It is not entirely clear whether the coma itself is the therapeutic factor or whether the value of shock is due to some other factor—such as physiological changes in the nervous system or the creation of a violent psychological reaction. Another possibility is that for depressed patients its effect is mediated through guilt reduction, the shock being viewed as "punishment" which they deserve for some actual or imagined transgression.

The most recently developed and by far the most widely used form of convulsive therapy is electroconvulsive shock. The patient is placed on a bed and securely padded or held firmly by nurses and attendants to prevent injury during the convulsion. Often the patient is given muscle relaxants to decrease further the possibility of bone fractures or too-strong muscle contractions. Electrodes are then fastened to his head, and a current ranging from 70 to 130 volts is applied for a fraction of a second. Twenty, thirty, or more such treatments may be given over a period of weeks or months. Electroconvulsive shock has proved particularly effective in cases of severe depression.

Conflicting findings have been obtained, however, in regard to its benefits. Many psychiatrists believe that this drastic form of treatment will be used less and less in the future; it is already being supplanted by drugs and new techniques of psychotherapy. There is some evidence that electroconvulsive shock has adverse effects on learning and retention (Leukel, 1957; Stone & Bakhtiari, 1956). Certainly it disrupts the integrated functioning of the organism.

In deciding upon the utility of electroshock therapy for treating even "stubborn" cases, certain psychological factors must be weighed along with the physiological consequences. Although patients have no memory of the shock itself, they are aware of the marked changes from before to after the event, and they often can observe the violent convulsive reactions of patients who precede them in the waiting line. Many patients who develop a strong fear of shock treatments are nevertheless subjected to them involuntarily. In large state institutions which are understaffed, shock therapy has been used rather indiscriminately and sometimes as a coercive tactic in the interest of patient manageability rather than in the interest of help for the patient.

Narcosis

Narcosis (from a Greek word meaning "benumb") makes use of sleep-producing drugs, including *sodium amytal, sodium pentothal,* and *scopolamine.* This type of therapy may take either of two forms: prolonged narcosis or narcoanalysis.

In prolonged narcosis the patient is kept asleep under the influence of drugs for fifteen or more hours a day during a period of one to two weeks. Since a number of physiological complications may develop under prolonged sleep, the technique is seldom used today, although it was quite popular before the development of the shock therapies. It is still used with some frequency in Russia.

In present-day practice, prolonged narcosis is used primarily as an emergency measure to quiet severely agitated patients. Its main effect, apparently, is sedative and temporary, and it is a much more severe form of treatment than its results usually justify.

Relatively greater success has been reported with narcosis in its brief form, known as *narcoanalysis*. In this method drugs such as sodium amytal are given in amounts sufficient to cause "grogginess" but not unconsciousness—the patient remains in a state of "twilight sleep." By direct suggestion, the patient under narcoanalysis is encouraged to talk about or act out his painful experiences. Once exposed by this method, repressed emotions may be better understood and accepted by the patient. Because the individual is in a state of semisleep, however, his revelations often mix fact with fantasy and, like dreams, require the therapist's interpretation. For this reason, sodium pentothal and sodium amytal—popularly publicized as "truth serums"—have no accepted value in legal investigation except as a means of turning up leads. Information obtained by such means cannot be used as direct evidence.

Narcoanalysis is most effective when employed soon after symptoms of repressed emotional tensions appear. It has proved particularly successful in the rapid treatment of the emotional tensions produced by combat and the frustrations of military life (Horsley, 1944; Grinker & Spiegel, 1945). Narcoanalysis is usually followed by physical rest, elaborate reassurance, and a program of recreation, as the patient gradually readjusts to the demands of reality.

Chemotherapy (Drug Therapy)

Extreme forms of mental illness such as schizophrenia and the affective disorders are believed by many medically oriented investigators to be based on biochemical abnormalities. One active researcher in the area has stated, "While the etiology and pathogenesis of schizophrenia remain largely uncertain, it seems reasonable to assume that the marked psychological and behavioral changes in the schizophrenic are mediated through disturbed patterns of physiological organization" (Friedhoff, 1967, p. 27).

Two reports in the 1950s generated considerable interest in the search for abnormal substances in the blood of schizophrenics and in the use of drugs to relieve mental illness. One, already mentioned (p. 595), was the finding that *taraxein*, a protein substance from the blood serum of schizophrenics, temporarily produced some of the symptoms of schizophrenia when injected into monkeys or nonschizophrenic volunteers. From this finding it was suggested that schizophrenia might be a disease in which the body manufactures antibodies that disrupt the functioning of brain cells and that a profitable line of research might involve the development of drugs that would block the action of such antibodies.

In 1952, two investigators (Osmond & Smythies) noted that mescaline, a drug whose action is similar to that of the body chemical *epinephrine*, induces a state comparable to schizophrenia. Since then, other researchers have found several pharmacological agents which stimulate or depress the function of certain organic compounds involved in the chemical transmission of nerve impulses in the brain (Schildkraut & Kety, 1967). Such compounds include *epinephrine* and *norepinephrine* (adrenaline and noradrenaline), *dopamine*, and *serotonin* (a neurotransmitter substance implicated also in Dement's sleep studies, p. 264). The drugs most often used in such therapy fall into two general classes: *tranquilizers* and *energizers*.

Tranquilizers.   One of the most widely tested drugs, *reserpine*, comes from the root of the plant *rauwolfia* (snakeroot), whose medical properties have been recognized in India for thousands of years. Clinical use of reserpine began in this country after it was discovered that the drug was of value in treating hypertension (high blood pressure) and that it also had a calming effect on patients (Ciba, 1954). An early investigation showed that this drug seemed to make patients less inhibited and more outgoing during psychotherapy (Kline, 1954). Other investigators reported that patients given reserpine showed tendencies toward greater personality integration and a higher degree of emotional control (Dice, Bagchi, & Waggoner, 1955). A later study, however, using as subjects patients complaining of various symptoms of anxiety, showed no significant difference in the improvement of those treated with reserpine and those who received a placebo (Segal & Shapiro, 1959).

Chlorpromazine, hailed as the golden drug for mental illness, is still the most used medication to reduce schizophrenic confusion and agitation. When it was first introduced, in the late 1950s, some patients who had been considered "untreatable" responded so favorably to chlorpromazine that they were released after having languished for years in hospital wards. There is evidence that chlorpromazine acts on hypothalamic centers which are closely related to various drives. It seems to exert a selective effect on these centers, changing the results produced by stimulation—a phenomenon with infinite possibilities for further research (Olds, 1958; Stein, 1967). In general, chlorpromazine has been found to produce indifference and besides its effectiveness with schizophrenia is useful in the treatment of disorders involving overactivity, such as manic behavior or obsessional activity (Fink, Klein, & Kramer, 1965).

A disadvantage of both reserpine and chlorpromazine is that they sometimes cause side effects such as weakness, nausea, and low blood pressure (Evarts & Butler, 1959). Chlorpromazine also produces an odd kind of restlessness known as *akathisia* and after many years of high dosage may cause excessive pigmentation in skin areas exposed to light (Hamilton, 1965). In view of the undesirable side effects that may be produced by these and similar drugs, they should never be taken except under a physician's direction.

A number of the newer tranquilizing drugs have been widely used to reduce tension and anxiety among normal individuals as well as hospital patients. Of these, *meprobamate* (marketed as Miltown or Equanil) is perhaps the best known. Results have not been encouraging, however. For example, Miltown has been found to be no more effective than a placebo for reducing anxiety in abstinent alcoholics (Smith, Rutherford, & Fanning, 1957) or in a group of 130 male veterans treated as psychiatric outpatients (McNair, Goldstein, Lorr, Cibelli, & Roth, 1965). Extremely manic patients who do not respond to the usual tranquilizers have been helped by treatment with *lithium salts*, which alters the metabolism of norepinephrine in the brain (Schou, 1959; Schanberg, Schildkraut, & Kopin, 1967).

Energizers. Depressed patients are often helped by *psychic energizers* such as *imipramine*.

A survey of studies involving a total of 5864 patients found that overall, imipramine and two other widely used antidepressants (amitriptyline and isocarboxazid) helped almost 65 percent of the patients for whom they were used. Three other commonly used energizers (phenelzine, malamide, and iproniazid) aided in 40 to 49 percent of the cases in which they were used. Placebo controls were effective in only 23 percent of the cases in which they were employed (Wechsler, Grosser, & Greenblatt, 1965).

An interesting sidelight of this survey was that less effectiveness was reported in studies that used placebo controls than in the studies that were using no control group or comparing the effects of two drugs. The investigators attributed this difference, at least in part, to the fact that in the placebo-control studies the staff knew that half of the patients were receiving no drug and thus should show no change in behavior. In the other studies, by contrast, the physicians evaluating the progress knew that all the patients were receiving a drug of some kind and thus might be expected to change—a good example of methods of study influencing the finding.

While *imipramine* has been found to be the most clinically effective of the antidepressant drugs (Klerman & Cole, 1965), recent studies have reported on the similar efficacy of a group of substances known as *monoamine oxidase inhibitors*. A significant correlation has been found in several studies between clinical improvement in depressed patients and the degree of inhibition of monoamine oxidation produced during drug administration (Feldstein, Hoagland, Oktem, & Freeman, 1965).

Mescaline and lysergic acid diethylamide (LSD), discussed on page 301 as drugs that can bring on symptoms of mental disorder, have also been used in therapy. One of the principal effects of these drugs is that patients under their influence often regress to childhood behavior and feelings and are able to recall past events which may have helped cause their emotional disturbance.

In one study, 113 patients who had received LSD and mescaline after adequate preparation and in a suppor-

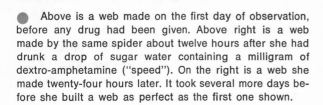

● Above is a web made on the first day of observation, before any drug had been given. Above right is a web made by the same spider about twelve hours after she had drunk a drop of sugar water containing a milligram of dextro-amphetamine ("speed"). On the right is a web she made twenty-four hours later. It took several more days before she built a web as perfect as the first one shown.

tive setting answered subjective questionnaires. Their answers revealed a high frequency of claimed benefit, with few negative reactions and frequent feelings of greater insight into reality. Clinical data on seventy-four of the cases supported the claims made in the questionnaires. The total improvement rate was about 80 percent (Savage, Savage, Fadiman, & Harmann, 1964).

LSD has sometimes been useful in group therapy, where, provided the setting is appropriate, it seems to enhance empathy and decrease defensiveness, helping the patient to communicate freely and reveal deep levels of feeling (Eisner, 1964).

Some therapists who see mental disorder as a disease advocate small doses of LSD in conjunction with traditional psychotherapies (Crocket et al.,

1963). Other therapists, who regard therapy as primarily a means for growth, use LSD primarily for rapid personality change; they induce an extended, intense psychedelic experience with large, single doses. LSD therapy has shown some promise with a wide range of psychiatric disorders, especially in cases resistant to more conventional therapies. For example, 'in one treatment program with over a thousand alcoholics, LSD therapy was reported to be twice as effective as any other treatment program (Hoffer, 1965). In reviewing the more than 300 studies dealing with this therapy, there is evidence that "LSD can produce far-reaching beneficial effects in some people, under some conditions" (Mogar, 1969, p. 393). However, even the trained psychotherapist uses the psychedelic drugs only with great caution. In some patients the drugs have led to prolonged psychotic reactions such as paranoia or to severe depression (Cohen & Ditman, 1963). In recent years, controlled studies of the effects of LSD in therapy have been curtailed legally as a result of the potential dangers of unsupervised use of the drug.

The behavioral effects of various drugs recently have been studied in a most unlikely subject—the spider. The usual intricate symmetry of webs is disrupted when the web is spun under the influence of a drug. Furthermore, the disruption differs in a systematic manner, depending upon the type of drug used. When composites of normal web structures were compared (by a computer) to those made by drugged spiders, it was found that amphetamine webs have irregular structures, tranquilizer webs are regular but more compact than usual, and barbiturate webs are small and erratic, as are those spun under the influence of mescaline (Witt, 1970). ● While one cannot generalize from disorientation patterns in spiders to similar effects of drugs on man, such innovative research gives clues as to what to investigate in human patients and is indicative of the multiple approaches being utilized to understand and treat behavior disorders.

Chemotherapy in perspective. In the 1950s mental hospital populations in the country as a whole decreased. What role drugs played in this decrease must be judged with caution, however. Indeed, a study of a state hospital in Pennsylvania revealed that even before drugs were being used to any great extent there had been a consistent decrease in the proportion of patients retained continuously after admission (Kramer et al., 1955). Obviously, other factors have been operating, among them improved methods of psychotherapy, changes in attitude on the part of hospital staffs, and better facilities for outpatient treatment.

Undoubtedly, tranquilizing and antidepressive drugs are effective in the treatment of psychotic disorders. This is the conclusion that emerges from a review of more than 400 research investigations (Davis, 1965). The drugs are not necessarily central factors in the lower discharge rates, and their use does not bring permanent cure, but they do make patients more manageable and decrease the more

extreme forms of maladaptive behavior. Neurotic patients, as a group, seem to benefit less from these drugs than do psychotic patients.

Among the dangers involved in drug therapy is an overreliance upon drugs, especially tranquilizers, to make patients easier to manage, at the neglect of adjunct therapies. In addition, some patients develop a psychological dependence upon their drugs and come to attribute any improvement in their mental state or behavior to the drug and not to their own increased capacity for control of their behavior. (Davison & Valins, 1969).

Any evaluation of the effectiveness of drugs must of course take into account the predictable positive *placebo* reactions described in Chapter 10. The *suggestion* that a given substance will relieve pain and bring well-being is often as effective in doing so as the chemical composition of the drug itself. "Placebo cure rates" vary with the disorder. Some of those reported by the U.S. Public Health Service (Haas et. al., 1959) are listed below.

Illness or Ailment	Percent Responding to Placebos Alone
headache	62%
gastrointestinal disorders	58
neurosis	34
alcoholism	22
hay fever	22
skin diseases	21
psychosis	19
asthma	5

An interesting sidelight is the finding that the method of administration may be an important factor in determining response to a placebo. One doctor found that the same placebo administered in a bright red gelatine capsule brought favorable results in 81 percent of the cases tested, as compared to only 49 percent when it was administered as a tablet and 69 percent when administered as a liquid (Clauser & Klein, 1957). Hypodermic injections have been found to be usually more effective than tablets but inferior to capsules. While blue or green solutions have been shown to bring better results in preparations applied externally, liquids to be swallowed are proven to be more effective if colored in warm tones of red, yellow, or brown—and if they have a bitter taste (Leslie, 1954).

A study that points up even more directly the need to separate drug effects from placebo effects in analyzing the effects of drugs on mental disorders was conducted with pharmacy students who were asked to help in the "testing" of two new drugs.

All forty-five students took a capsule at 8:30 A.M. and were told that its maximum effects would be felt in about two hours and would disappear by the close of the experiment at 12:30. Fifteen were informed that their capsule contained a stimulant, another fifteen that it contained a tranquilizer. The remaining fifteen were told that it contained only cornstarch (as did all the capsules, in reality).

Overall, 60 percent of the experimental subjects reported feeling the effects they were supposed to feel. This result was more pronounced among the "stimulated" subjects, 73.3 percent of whom reported feeling the effects, as compared to only 46.7 percent of the "tranquilized" subjects, perhaps because they had to continue with their usual laboratory work during the entire time.

Even pulse rates were affected. The pulse rates of the "stimulated" group rose at the second reading, taken during the supposed time of maximum effect of the drug, and fell again by the close of the period. Those of the "tranquilized" group fell and rose again by the close of the period. Those of the control group rose slightly during the period, possibly owing to the pressure of completing their laboratory tasks (Brodeur, 1965).

Nutrition: Orthomolecular Psychiatry

In recent years psychologists have become increasingly aware of the role of an adequate diet in preventing and curing mental illness (Bell, 1958). As early as 1938, Vitamin B_1 deficiency was found to cause severe relapse among "recovered" patients at the Mayo Clinic (Williams, Mason, & Smith, 1939). Relapses often occurred even among patients receiving the amount of thiamin (B_1) found in typical American diets (Williams et al., 1942). When half of these patients were given increased thiamine without their knowledge, they showed considerable improvement. In another study, four normal young men, subjected to restriction of the B-complex vitamins, showed striking deterioration in their adjustment and sense of well-being (Brôzek et al., 1946).

Mental disorders have been shown to be associated with low concentrations of vitamins B_1, B_3, B_6, B_{12}, H, C, and folic acid. Such vitamin deficiencies, in turn, may in some cases be the result of genetically induced irregularities in the metabolism of vital substances. The brain is probably more sensitive to changes in the concentration of these vital substances than are other organs and tissues.

Thus Nobel laureate Linus Pauling (1968) has proposed that mental disorder should be treated by provision of the optimum molecular environment for the mind's functioning by assuring the optimal concentrations of the various substances normally present. He calls the approach *orthomolecular psychiatry*. For example, he suggests ingestion of massive doses of ascorbic acid, Vitamin C (3 to 15 grams daily), as one form of therapy for schizophrenic patients. Glutamic acid, administered to people varying in degree and kind of mental retardation, has brought a general effect of improvement in personality and an increase in IQ by 5 to 20 points (Vogel et al., 1966).

Mail-Order Remedies

Common to drug therapy and nutrition therapy is the hope that a sufferer may pop a pill in his mouth and thereby correct what ails him. The enormous sales of pills of all kinds today indicate that this hope is certainly shared by the public. It is instructive to go back to the period prior to the Pure Food and Drug Act of 1906 and see what the public was led to believe were the causes and cures for mental and behavioral problems. The Sears, Roebuck Catalogue of 1902, distributed to over 600,000 people, not only offered rapid mail-order remedies for all diseases, but provides us with a view of the common assumptions of that time about the bases of mental disorder.

The link between acceptable physical diseases and unacceptable mental ones was via the concept of "nerves"—tired nerves, overworked nerves, weak nerves—and impure or weak blood. For only 69 cents it was possible to buy *Vin Vitae*, "a pleasant medical tonic to strengthen and tone up the nerves, purify and enrich the blood, invigorate brain, body, and muscles, regulate the system." Do you "feel generally miserable or suffer with a thousand and one indescribable bad feelings, both mental and physical?

No matter what the cause may be or how severe your trouble is, Dr. Hammond's Nerve and Brain Pills will cure you." For a mere 67 cents a bottle, a safe and reliable "cure for the opium and morphia habit" was offered. For only pennies, mere alcohol addiction could also be eliminated, since "Drunkenness is a disease and must be fought and counteracted by proper medical methods, the same as any other disease."

Electricity, then a newfound, wonderful mystery, was also sold as a curative. "For a weak or deranged nervous system the electric treatment has splendid results." A battery-charged belt, which delivered an "80-gauge" current to the testicles, was "guaranteed"

to double sexual force and power for the sexually impotent. Parts of two such ads are reproduced here. Note their care in cautioning the public about the danger of fraudulent claims by others.   ▲

Psychosurgery

Among the most dramatic, most widely publicized, and most disappointing innovations in psychiatry have been the techniques of brain surgery used in the treatment of severe emotional disorders (Moniz, 1937; Freeman & Watts, 1942). The best-known form of psychosurgery is the *prefrontal lobotomy*, an operation in which the nerve fibers connecting the

---

▲ **GUARANTEED TO CURE WHAT AILS YOU**

ELECTRO MEDICAL BATTERIES
For Home or Physicians' Use.

The Electro Medical Battery as a curative agent is becoming more appreciated from day to day. In cases of nervous trouble and partial paralysis it has brought about phenomenal results. The best physicians prescribe its use even when all else fails, and even under such adverse circumstances it often cures. For rheumatism, neuralgia, paralysis and all nervous disorders it seems to be nature's own cure. There need be no fear from the use of these machines, as there can be no bad results derived. An invalid may use them with perfect safety. There are a great variety of electrical machines and batteries on the market, from which we have selected of each kind those in which we can furnish our customers with the best value for the amount of money expended.

No. 6350.   **The Little Wonder.** A complete and perfect working little battery, neat, portable, and powerful, and produces an electric current from a small cell of zinc and carbon. This is a small machine that embodies all of the features of the larger ones and produces an electric current of great tensity and long duration with a very small charge of chemicals. There are no dangerous acids to handle, and it is so simple that any child can operate it: full instructions accompany each battery.
Each....................................$1.35

OUR 60c
Nerve and Brain
PILLS.

GUARANTEED THE HIGHEST GRADE ON THE MARKET.

DR. CHAISE'S NERVE AND BRAIN PILLS. IMPOTENCE, SPERMATORRHEA, AND DISEASES FROM OVERWORK SEXUAL EXCESSES ETC.
DIRECTIONS
SEARS, ROEBUCK & CO   CHI.

Six Boxes Positively Guaranteed to Cure any Disease for which they are intended.

THIS WILL CURE YOU if you feel generally miserable or suffer with a thousand and one indescribable bad feelings, both mental and physical, among them low spirits, nervousness, weariness, lifelessness, weakness, dizziness, feeling of fullness, like bloating after eating, or sense of goneness, or emptiness of stomach in morning, flesh soft and lacking firmness, headache, blurring of eyesight, specks floating before the eyes, nervous irritability, poor memory, chilliness, alternating with hot flushes, lassitude, throbbing, gurgling or rumbling sensations in bowels, with heat and nipping pains occasionally, palpitation of heart, short breath on exertion, slow circulation of blood, cold feet, pain and oppression in chest and back, pain around the loins, aching and weariness of the lower limbs, drowsiness after meals, but nervous wakefulness at night, languor in the morning, and a constant feeling of dread, as if something awful was going to happen.

If you have any of these symptoms our **NERVE AND BRAIN PILLS** will cure you. No matter what the cause may be or how severe your trouble is, **DR. CHAISE'S NERVE AND BRAIN PILLS** will cure you. These pills have a remarkable effect on both old and young. They can not be equalled by any other medicine as a cure for impotence, spermatorrhoea, night sweats, emissions, varicocele (or swollen veins), weakness of both brain and body, arising from excesses and abuses of any kind. It will tone up the whole nervous system, no matter how much worn out, overworked or depressed you may be; the weak and timid young man made strong and bold again; they will give youthful vigor and a new lease of life to the old.

BEWARE OF QUACK DOCTORS who advertise to scare men into paying money for remedies which have no merit. Our Nerve and Brain Pills are compounded from a prescription of one of the most noted German scientists, and are the same as has been used in German hospitals for years with marvelous success. HOW TO CURE YOURSELF, and full and explicit directions, are enclosed with every box. All orders and inquiries concerning these pills will be treated **confidentially**, and all shipments made in plain sealed package.

ONLY $3.00 FOR 6 BOXES. Enough to cure any case, no matter how severe, no matter how long standing, whether old or young, no matter from what cause. Send us $3.00 and we will send you 6 boxes by return mail, postpaid, in plain sealed package, with full instructions, full directions.

Ψ *Close-up*   *When "Shell Shock" Meant Shocked by a Shell*

The following are extracts from Report of the War Office Committee of Engineering on Shell Shock, London, 1922 (in E. Miller, 1940).

In the early stages of the (1914-1918) War, . . . mental disorders, emotional manifestations, paralysis and losses of sensory functions of non-organic origin were dealt with in either one of the following ways:

a) The condition was not recognized as coming within the province of the medical officer. The individual was made to take the responsibility for his functional efficiency in the absence of any definite organic lesion . . . .

b) The condition was recognized as being a matter appertaining to the medical officer, but, owing to the materialistic trend of modern scientific medicine, and to the introduction of the high explosive into warfare, it was attributed to a physical origin comparable to that inferred in cases of actual concussion of the Central Nervous System.

prefrontal lobes of the brain with the hypothalamus are severed.

Studies with animals have demonstrated that signs of anxiety arising from conflict may be removed by such an operation.

A monkey was taught to press a lever for food. Then, using an electric shock as the unconditioned stimulus, he was conditioned to respond to a light with increased blood flow in the aorta, faster heart rate, and heightened general activity. Eventually the light apparently became such a disturbing signal that he ceased to press the lever for food when it came on. When the prefrontal lobes were subsequently removed, the light no longer caused the vascular responses, and the monkey resumed pressing the lever for food (Smith & Nathan, 1965).

Clinical experience with human patients is consistent with results from such experiments with monkeys; it has been found that lobotomy does often diminish the emotional tone accompanying the individual's thoughts and memories. Thus, though psychosurgery is not thought to remove the sources of the patient's disturbance, it may release him from the emotional torment of disturbing ideas or hallucinations. The person whose frontal association areas have been partially inactivated by lobotomy is freed from anxiety and feelings of inferiority.

These benefits must be set against the following list of side effects, however, described by Freeman and Watts, the medical team that introduced the operation into the United States in 1936: (a) a loss of interest in body and in the relation of the self to the environment, (b) an inability to foresee the consequences of a planned series of personally relevant acts, (c) an indifference to the opinions of others, (d) an increase in impulsive behavior, since remorse, guilt, and fear are banished, (e) a reduced capacity to form a unified self-image and project it into the future (related to the enjoyment of personal esteem). In general, the lobotomy patient may be described as lacking self-continuity; that is, he loses the feeling that he is the same person he was yesterday and will be tomorrow (Robinson & Freeman, 1955).

With such side effects, who needs a cure? Unfortunately the convictions of theorists, true believers, and researchers with a new technique are often undaunted by negative or disconfirming evidence of this sort. In spite of the above list of detrimental effects, the original proponents were convinced that continued efforts would discover "the critical zone, the important fibers, the necessary areas to be resected, tracts to be cut, and dangers to be eliminated" (Freeman & Watts, 1942, p. 18).

Because psychosurgery, once performed, cannot be undone, and because its results are uncertain, it has been considered a method of last resort and is seldom used today.

Physical Therapy and the Medical Model

Any physical therapy for psychopathology assumes that physical intervention can change the course of psychological processes, either by correcting underlying chemical abnormalities or by calming or stimulating a patient to a more optimum level of arousal. In some degree, a medical model of mental disorder is assumed. ◆

The extreme form that a medical view of mental disorders may take is illustrated in extracts from the British War Office Report on the phenomenon of "shell shock"—a serious malady suffered by combat troops in World War I and believed for some time to be a brain abnormality caused by the shock of concussion from explosives. Excerpts from the report are reprinted in the Ψ Close-up on p. 614.

By World War II this physical explanation had been discarded, and such symptoms were assumed to have been psychological symptoms resulting from the stress of combat. Interestingly, the most common physical complaint of the World War II GIs was gastrointestinal disorder, and instances of "shell shock" were rare.

One of the problems of using a medical model in describing and treating behavioral disorders is that

◆ **POSITIVE AND NEGATIVE ASPECTS OF THE DISEASE MODEL**

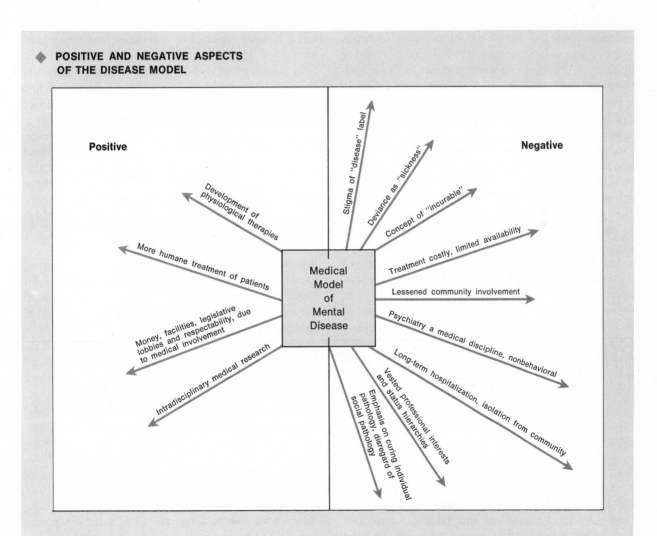

the "symptoms" of the "disease" are behavioral rather than physical; thus the changes, too, must be in behavioral terms. But descriptions of behavior are subject to bias by the observer. Many psychologists believe that the terms derived from the disease model (*sickness, cure, relapse,* even *patient*) are not really suitable terms for describing or understanding what they believe is primarily a behavioral-psychological process. Some investigators totally reject the "myth of mental illness" (Szasz, 1961, 1965) as having brought more disadvantages with it than beneficial consequences.

Meanwhile, others continue the search for more objective physical indicators both of psychopathology and of "cure" in consistent patterns of brain waves or chemical composition of the blood. For example, Rappaport and Silverman (1970) have reported finding identifiable brain wave patterns in the schizophrenic patients who are likely to benefit from certain types of therapy.

Clearly, drugs can change behavior and mental processes, both directly and indirectly (through changing arousal and facilitating or inhibiting neural conduction). They may make an individual less disturbing to others and less anxious. To the extent that normal functioning depends on an intact brain and nervous system, functioning smoothly, physical agents to restore or maintain such functioning will provide physical readiness for healthy adjustment. But to the extent that effective behavior depends on learning in a social setting, one can expect that relearning and social interaction will need to be part of therapy in order for new behavioral repertoires to be acquired. And to the extent that effective adjustment depends on a perception of one's own control over himself and his destiny, therapy must increase that perception; dependence on pills or other external physical agents is likely to work in the other direction.

Social-Cognitive Therapy

Social-cognitive therapies provide one set of alternatives to the medical model underlying physiological therapy. These therapies are concerned with the patient's thoughts, attitudes, and feelings more than with either internal physiological processes or overt (nonverbal) behavior. In general, psychotherapies of this kind attempt to encourage self-awareness and insight into the causes of one's psychological problems. The medium for this discovery is verbal interaction between therapist and client or among a group of people and a therapist-leader. For this reason they have often been referred to as *talk therapies*. Although there are many variations in approaches and goals among the different brands of social-cognitive therapy, they all deal in the same commodity—"talk."

The social-verbal interaction between patient(s) and psychotherapist usually involves the principle of *catharsis,* the discharging of emotional tension by "talking out" or otherwise expressing one's frustrations. Because most of the problems that worry people involve ideas and experiences that are psychologically painful, catharsis is usually a slow process and early sessions are likely to seem unproductive. When the patient is instructed to talk about what worries him, he will usually stick to the superficial aspects of his problem at first. In succeeding sessions, however, he is likely to become more and more frank, more able to search deeply into his own problem. Eventually he may tell of experiences and emotions that have been concealed from both himself and others.

Psychoanalytic Therapy

Psychoanalytic therapy, as developed by Sigmund Freud, is an intensive and prolonged technique for exploring the patient's unconscious motivation, with special importance attached to conflict and repression stemming from problems in the early stages of psychosexual development (see pp. 160-161). Its aim is to bring to consciousness such repressed memories and conflicts and to help the individual resolve them in the light of adult reality. Such a process presumably effects a radical change in the individual's basic personality structure. Psychoanalysts use several techniques for bringing repressed conflicts to consciousness and helping the patient to solve them. These include free association, dream analysis, analysis of resistances, and analysis of transference.

Analysis of free associations. The principal procedure used in psychoanalysis to probe the unconscious and release repressed material is free association. The patient sits comfortably in a chair or lies in a relaxed position on a couch and lets his mind wander freely, giving a running account of his thoughts, wishes, physical sensations, and mental images as they occur. He is encouraged to reveal his every thought or feeling, regardless of how personal, painful, or seemingly unimportant. The therapist often takes a position behind the patient, where he will not serve as a distraction or disrupt the flow of association.

Freud maintained that "free associations are subject to determination and are not a matter of choice." The task of the analyst is to track down the associations to their inner-determined core and to see through the disguises in which repressed urges may appear—to identify what is beneath the surface in the "iceberg" depicted on page 423.

Analysis of dreams. Psychoanalytic therapists try to gain further insight into the patient's unconscious motivation by the technique of dream analysis. When the individual is asleep, his ego is presumably less on guard against the unacceptable impulses originating in the id, so that a motive which cannot be expressed in waking life may find expression in a dream. Some motives are so unacceptable to the conscious self, however, that they cannot be revealed openly even in dreams but must be expressed in disguised or symbolic form. Thus a dream has two kinds of content. The *manifest* (openly visible) content of the dream is that which we remember and report upon awakening. It usually is not painful and, in fact, often seems quite amusing. Beneath the manifest content is the *latent* (hidden) content—the actual motives which are seeking expression but which are so painful or unacceptable to us that we do not want to recognize their existence. The therapist attempts to uncover these hidden motives by studying the symbols which appear in the manifest content of the dream.

The unconscious process which transforms the emotionally painful latent content of the dream into the less painful manifest content is called *dream work*. Dream work distorts the content of a dream in various ways, making the motives expressed in it less obvious to the dreamer. For example, a student who is filled with anxiety about failing an examination and

being expelled from school may dream that he is pushing his way through a heavy snowstorm, pursued by wild animals. Or, with rather less disguise, a woman who feels hostility toward her husband might dream of killing a rat—the significance of this symbol being revealed by her often referring to her husband as "the little rat."

Free association, with the manifest content of the dream as the point of departure, gives the analyst clues as to the latent content and enables him to interpret to the patient what he believes to be the real meaning. Skilled therapists who are familiar with the kinds of distortion created by dream work are frequently able to locate a conflict of which the patient is not aware. Using hypnosis to induce dreaming *during* a therapy session has recently been shown to be an effective technique for uncovering sources of conflict and dealing with them more immediately (Sacerdote, 1967).

Analysis of resistances. During the process of free association, the patient may show resistances—that is, inability or unwillingness to discuss certain ideas, desires, or experiences. Resistances prevent the return to consciousness of repressed material which is painful to recall, such as material connected with the individual's sexual life or with hostile, resentful feelings toward his parents. Sometimes a resistance is shown by the patient's coming late to his appointment or "forgetting" it altogether.

When such material is finally brought into the open, the patient generally claims that it is either too unimportant, too absurd, too irrelevant, or too unpleasant to be discussed.

The psychoanalyst of the Freudian school attaches particular importance to subjects which the patient does *not* wish to discuss. Such resistances are conceived of as *barriers* between the unconscious, where repressed conflicts wage guerrilla warfare on the individual's psychic health, and the conscious, which could deal with these rebellious forces rationally. The aim of psychoanalysis is to break down resistances and bring the patient to face these painful ideas, desires, and experiences. Breaking down resistances is a long and difficult process but is considered absolutely essential in order to bring the whole problem into consciousness where it can be solved.

Ψ *Close-up*   **Therapists Are People Too**

The way in which a psychiatrist's own personal involvement with the patient's problem may distort his professional judgment is apparent in this example taken from a case presentation report by the psychiatrist to the hospital staff. (Italics have been added for emphasis.)

"*I* am presenting (Patient X) to this conference because *I* believe he presents particularly interesting problems in diagnosis and therapy. *I* believe that he is a borderline schizophrenic suffering from acute identity confusion. *I* would appreciate comments on the justification of using such diagnostic categories, the dynamics involved, and the *central problem in therapy*—the patient's silence and distrust.

"In the initial interview, he was quite cooperative, answered questions quite easily and seemed eager to establish relationship. The following day he deposited under my office door a note in which he described his homosexual activities. To this *I* responded, after thanking him for the note, 'it is difficult to talk to a stranger,' and assured him that he didn't have to reveal 'everything' at once and that, indeed, there may be things he would never want to tell me especially since *I* would be leaving

in two months. This *I* said, because *I* wanted the patient to feel free to have distance between us, that *I* would not 'smother him and absorb him as did his parents.' Following this *I* became much less directive and the interviews were marked for their silence and the patient relating that he 'just can't talk in here' . . . He seemed frightened of me and rationalized his fear by saying he would be able to talk to me 'when he felt like it,' . . . and by projection when he says 'when you rejected my note I thought you were afraid of me because of the homosexuality.' In later interviews he projected his distrust by saying 'I don't think you like me but this shouldn't make any difference because I should talk to you anyway because you're my doctor'. . . .

"He expressed his fear of intimacy with me by saying that he conceives of the doctor-patient relationship as one where the doctor discusses the patient's problems as if problems were objects unrelated to the human being and that doctors don't get involved with a human being himself. This is the way he would like it to be."

Any comments? Who do you think was "projecting" and transferring—patient or therapist?

Analysis of transference.   During the course of psychoanalytic treatment, the patient usually develops an emotional reaction toward the therapist, identifying him with some person who has been at the center of an emotional conflict in the past. This phase of therapy is known as *transference*. In most cases, the analyst is identified with a parent or a lover. The transference is called *positive transference* when the feelings attached to the therapist are those of love or admiration and *negative transference* when they consist of hostility or envy. Often the patient's attitude is ambivalent—that is, he experiences both positive and negative feelings toward the therapist, as children often do toward their parents.

The analyst's task in handling the transference is a difficult and dangerous one because of the patient's emotional vulnerability, but it is a crucial part of

treatment. The therapist helps the patient to interpret the transferred feelings and to understand their source in earlier experiences and attitudes.

However, it must be remembered that the therapist is not a perfectly programmed, objective analyzer of patient input. The therapist, despite attempts to maintain an "emotional detachment," may still react to the patient's problems in a personal way. In the intense dyadic interaction which must occur when two people meet as often as five times every week for several years to discuss personal problems, it is difficult for the analyst to keep his own reactions calibrated at psychological zero. (Ψ Close-up, above.)

Psychoanalytic therapy since Freud.   As we saw in Chapter 11, neo-Freudian theorists differ from Freud in placing relatively more emphasis on the current social environment and less on childhood experiences. The same difference in emphasis appears in neo-Freudian therapy, which is aimed at understanding the patient's present situation as well as his past experiences. Also, most neo-Freudian psychotherapists believe that a cure cannot be effected simply by helping the patient understand his unconscious feelings but rather that the patient must be directed along the path of changing himself and his inadequate modes of adjustment.

Freud's emphasis on repressed sexual conflicts has also been questioned as a fundamental basis for neurotic behavior today, especially among the young. Victorian constraints and the generally accepted religious doctrine of sin forced a denial of sexuality during Freud's time, and it is not surprising that he found sexual repression a common problem among his patients. The dramatic changes in our sexual mores in recent years, however, make sexual repression a less common cause of emotional disturbance than "existential crises," failure to see meaning in life, character disorders, and inability to cope with social changes.

Evaluation of psychoanalytic therapy. Psychoanalysis has come under attack because of its closed-mindedness to criticism and because many Freudian concepts and hypotheses are not testable scientifically. Behavior therapists have criticized the practice of apparently ignoring the patient's current problem in the search for the presumed underlying cause. They maintain that the present symptom *is* the problem. What right has the psychoanalyst, they ask, to determine what the patient's "real" problem is, while shunting aside the problem which the patient wants treated?

From a practical standpoint, psychoanalysis has also been criticized on the grounds that it requires a great deal of the patient's time and money. Psychoanalysis aims to create a fundamental and permanent alteration in the individual's personality structure, a goal that usually requires at least two or three years of frequent sessions with the analyst. Even when the individual can afford to spend the time and money necessary for a complete course of analytic treatment, the results are not always satisfactory. Because psychoanalysis relies heavily upon the patient's achieving

great personal insight, it is best adapted to individuals who are above average in intelligence and who do not have severe disorders such as schizophrenia. It also is tailored for those who are highly verbal and introspective, and those with whom the *analyst* can relate during a long period of close association.

The most important question, of course, is how effectively psychoanalysis produces the improvements it aims for. Although we will consider the problem of criteria for cure at some length in the final section of this chapter, a sample evaluative study is instructive.

In one study, a psychoanalyst examined twenty-eight chronic neurotics he had treated eight to twenty-four years previously for an average period of two years and three months. The aim of this study was to evaluate lasting personality change—as determined by the reports of the patients themselves, the judgment of the analyst, and judgments made by objective observers some time after the end of treatment.

The most lasting personality changes reported by the patients were in interpersonal relationships. Patients reported lasting improvement in their ability to get along with other people, in their ability to work and to enjoy work, in their ability to enjoy life, and in their sexual adjustment. It was noted, contrary to popular opinion, that the removal of neurotic sexual inhibitions had not led patients to disregard social restraints on sexuality but rather had freed them from the compelling role of sex as a motivating force. Twelve patients reported a lasting change in their perception of reality, using such words as: "a different way of perceiving"; "a richer gamut of experience"; "I have come out of a fog."

It was found that analysis had had a marked effect on personality even in the cases where symptoms had not changed to any extent. The psychoanalyst's own evaluation of results was: seven cases, very satisfactory; fifteen cases, satisfactory; two cases, unsatisfactory; and four cases, inconclusive. Of the patients themselves, ten considered results as very satisfactory; three considered results as between very satisfactory and satisfactory; twelve considered results as satisfactory; two gave indefinite replies; and one stated that results were unsatisfactory in regard to his homosexuality but otherwise satisfactory (Schjelderup, 1955).

Obviously, patient's verbal reports or the therapist's own global evaluation are hardly objective data on which to base evaluation of a treatment. Without an appropriate control group to assess naturally occurring improvement and reliable criteria which are not subject to bias and placebo effect, we cannot evaluate claims of "success."

Other Individual Therapies

In view of the time, expense, and complexity involved in psychoanalytic treatment, it is not surprising to find attempts to shorten or simplify treatment. The full range of modifications and alternative approaches is far too broad to survey here, but a sampling will suggest some of the major dimensions of variation.

Directive counseling. Directive counseling is the simplest and most limited type of psychotherapy. Here the therapist supplies direct answers to problems which are consciously worrying the client. Directive counseling is practiced by teachers, ministers, physicians, social workers, lawyers, and employment interviewers, as well as by counselors connected with guidance clinics. It may involve reassurance, suggestion, interpretation, and questioning, as well as the giving of information.

Counseling of this kind has many values, especially in offering quick solutions to many types of relatively minor problems. In cases which call for more than advice and encouragement, however, it has limitations. It may even be harmful if it encourages the individual to rely on others for the solution to his problems or if it prevents or delays treatment of serious emotional disturbances.

Client-centered therapy. A completely *non*directive technique is that of client-centered therapy, developed largely by Carl Rogers. Nondirective therapy is based on the premise that an individual who is sufficiently motivated can work through his own problem if he can become free enough from self-deception and fear to recognize his problem for what it is. Accordingly, he is encouraged in a face-to-face interview to talk freely about anything that troubles him and to approach it in any way he likes. The therapist neither praises nor blames but accepts whatever is said, perhaps rephrasing it or helping the individual to clarify his own reactions.

The theory of nondirective therapy is that by "talking it out" in a permissive atmosphere, the client will himself come to see certain relationships between his feelings and his behavior. Therapy is regarded as a "growth process" in which the patient utilizes his own potentialities to achieve a more mature level of emotional adjustment. From the beginning, the client is responsible for his own behavior and his own decisions, as well as for the course of therapy. The idea that "the doctor knows best" is missing from this form of therapy. Superficially the role of the therapist is that of "reflecting" the feelings the client has expressed. Actually, however, the therapist's attitude of acceptance and concern is probably of greatest significance, for it helps the client develop the self-confidence and strength to handle his difficult problems of adjustment.

The following case illustrates the nature of non-directive therapy and also the characteristic gradual change from negative feelings to positive ones.

Mary Jane Tilden (a pseudonym), age twenty, was brought to the counselor by her mother. She seemed to be retreating from life, spending the major portion of her days sleeping, listening to the radio, or brooding. She had given up her job and all social contacts; she rarely bothered even to dress. Her first interview was completely negative except that she did decide to return for further treatment.

Miss T.: ". . . It's just when I compare myself to the other girls it seems—I don't feel at all up to it . . . they seem to be so normal in everything they did and they were unfolding the way everybody should unfold in this world. And when I thought about myself, I thought, 'Well, my gosh! I'm not even coming near it.' And it was just such a blow that—I just started to realize that I wasn't coming along the way I should—I mean I just wasn't progressing."

Counselor: "It wasn't that you were jealous, but that you gradually realized that here they were ready for a new part of their life and you just weren't ready for it." . . .

T.: ". . . I seem to be going backward all the time. In fact, I don't see any reason why I should be living. . . . It's very funny, I can see it for everybody else but I can't—I have enough confidence in other people's ability but I can't see it for myself."

C.: "You can understand why other people would want to live but for yourself you see very little reason." . . .

T.: ". . . There's one thing I can't quite make up my mind—I've tried to figure it out—well, what is it, when I get into a rut like this, what is it that I really want?

And when I examine myself I can't figure out what I really want. It's only by looking at what other people want that I think, well, maybe that's what I want. It's a very odd thing, and I don't like it. That's what makes me feel—that it's—a—that I can't do what I want to do because I don't really know what I want."

C.: "You feel that, so far, the best you have been able to achieve along that line is just to take a goal that seems to be good for somebody else. But that you don't feel that there's any real gain that you are sure you want." . . .

During the fifth interview Miss Tilden discussed her first tentative steps toward improving her situation, but with many reservations. By the eighth interview, she was beginning to look at her behavior more objectively.

T.: ". . . When you're in a family where your brother has gone to college and everybody has a good mind, I wonder if it is right to see that I am as I am and I can't achieve such things. I've always tried to be what others thought I should be, but now I'm wondering whether I shouldn't just see that I am what I am."

C.: "You feel that in the past you lived by others' standards and you are not sure just what is the right thing to do, but you're beginning to feel that the best thing for you is simply to accept yourself as you are." . . .

T.: "Well, I guess that is so. I don't see what it is that has changed me so much. Yes, I do. These talks have helped a lot, and then the books that I've read. Well, I've just noticed such a difference. I find that when I feel things, even when I feel hate, I don't care. I don't mind. I feel more free somehow. I don't feel guilty about things." (Rogers, 1947)

In the course of therapy, the client made considerable progress in working out for herself a new understanding and acceptance of herself and hence a more satisfactory adjustment to life. This did not come suddenly and there were setbacks, but the overall progress was unmistakable. Note that the counselor did not at any time force the issue, nor did he introduce any new ideas, give her advice, or employ reassurance or moral exhortation. What he tried to do was to reflect and clarify the client's own feelings and attitudes in such a way that she could understand herself better.

Existential psychotherapy. The form of psychotherapy called *existential psychotherapy* is not a closely knit school of thought but was begun simulta-

neously and independently by a number of Europeans who were dissatisfied with orthodox psychoanalysis (May, 1958). Realizing that the most common problem of modern man was a feeling of alienation from his world, a loss of the sense of identity or belonging, these psychiatrists and psychologists felt that psychoanalysis often tended to increase the problem by fragmenting men still further. They also turned to existentialism as a resolution of the mind-body problem (see Chapter 10), seeing the individual's experience (rather than physical events) as the basic reality.

The existentialist theory of personality emphasizes the importance of individual choices. In the grim but resolute struggle which is life, man's freedom is held to be absolute and it is his own choices which determine what he shall be. Therefore, the existential therapist seeks to find what original or basic choice has led to the maladjusted behavior of his client (Muuss, 1956).

One school of existential analysis, called *logotherapy*, focuses upon the need of the individual to see meaning in his life. The "will-to-meaning" is regarded as the most human phenomenon of all, the attribute that most distinguishes him from animals. This school emphasizes Nietzsche's statement, "He who knows a Why of living surmounts almost every How." The human being finds the "Why" through self-realization, which involves both freedom to choose a course of action and responsibility to choose in such a way as to further spiritual values. Thus logotherapy lays particular stress upon the development of spiritual and ethical values (Weisskopf-Joelson, 1955).

The existential analyst tends to vary his technique from patient to patient, believing that a flexible approach is necessary. Consequently the process of existential psychotherapy is less clearly defined than are some other forms of therapy.

Integrity therapy. Hobart Mowrer believes that the neurotic patient suffers moral failure, his difficulties arising not from inhibitions but from concealed antisocial actions. Mowrer's method of *integrity therapy* teaches people to take the consequences of what they do instead of blaming their troubles on something supposedly done to them by their parents or others. He calls not for new or different moral values, but for greater fidelity to those already accepted but poorly observed. He feels that future treatment of the emotionally ill will take guilt, confession, and expiation seriously.

Mowrer and his associates do not believe that the cause-effect relationship implied by the stimulus-response formula is an adequate explanation of human behavior. For man, something must intervene between the S and the R—namely *personal responsibility*. This is their main theme. In helping patients rediscover and accept their responsibility, the Mowrer method makes considerable use of group therapy, in which open confession of past misdeeds is combined with an acceptance of the shame and punishment one *deserves* for these sins.

Neuroses are regarded as forms of what is described religiously as a "state of sin." In overcoming them, the role of the unconscious is played down, since the development of a sense of active responsibility is the goal of fundamental importance (Mowrer, 1964).

It seems likely that confession and penance are indeed effective means of relieving guilt and making the person feel "unburdened" and "uplifted," judging from statements by Catholic students after religious confession. Likewise, acceptance of responsibility for one's actions, a goal of other therapies too, is a necessary component of maturity. However, it seems equally unlikely that guilt is the basis of all mental suffering, that all patients can verbalize their guilt, or that merely doing so will change personality and behavior disorders. Furthermore, guilt may be increased simply by having certain behaviors and experiences labeled as "sinful."

Rational psychotherapy.   Proponents of this method believe that most neurotics continue their irrational behavior because of irrational things they constantly tell themselves in a sort of self-dialogue, the elements of which must be brought to light. Among the most commonly held irrational ideas, instilled by parents or by the culture pattern, are that it is tragic not to be highly successful, that it is vitally important to be liked and approved of by everyone, or that one must rely on someone stronger than oneself. The therapist helps the patient discover what he is saying to himself and change it to something rational, such as that it is possible to be happy despite occasional disapproval

from others. He also encourages the patient to act out his new ideas, painful though the process may be.

In one case, in which the patient was severely depressed and had alcoholic tendencies, it developed that he wished to learn the art of glass staining and could do so only by holding the kind of job he had. However, the job involved considerable clerical work which was distasteful to him, and he was trying to avoid this work and blaming his boss for making him do it. The therapist made him realize that he was telling himself: "My boss makes me do inventory-keeping. I do not like to do this. . . . He is therefore a blackguard for making me do it. . . . So I'll fool him and avoid doing it. . . . And then I'll be happier." Because these ideas were so foolish that the client could not really believe them, he began to add others like these: "I'm not really fooling my boss, because he sees what I'm doing. . . . So I really should stop this nonsense and get the inventory-keeping done. . . . But I'll be damned if I'll do it for him! . . . However, if I don't do it, I'll be fired. . . . Oh, why must I always be persecuted like this? . . . And why must I keep getting myself into such a mess? . . . I guess I'm just no good. . . . And people are against me. . . . Oh, what's the use?" Instead of these sentences, which led to a vicious circle of depression, resentment, and further depression, the therapist suggested the patient should tell himself something like the following: "Keeping inventory is a bore. . . . But it is presently an essential part of my job. . . . And I also may learn something useful by it. . . . Therefore, I had better go about this task as best I can and thereby get what I want out of this job." In this way the therapist was able to use the problem of avoiding inventory-keeping as an illustration of the client's general neurosis and to help him to realize that his alcoholism was also a form of avoiding responsibility. The client was eventually led to see the importance of accepting the inevitable without illogically blaming others for it and was able to overcome his neurosis (Ellis, 1958).

The effectiveness of rational therapy was compared with more traditional techniques in a study by a therapist who had himself used three different methods, starting as an orthodox psychoanalyst and eventually settling on rational therapy.

Having kept careful records and evaluations of all cases, he was able to compare seventy-eight cases treated by rational therapy with seventy-eight treated by psychoanalytically oriented therapy, each group including sixty-one neurotics and seven borderline psychotics. Only sixteen cases treated by orthodox psychoanalysis were studied. Percentages of patients showing improvement under various methods of treatment are shown in the table.

	Distinct Improvement	Considerable Improvement	Little or No Improvement
Orthodox psychoanalysis	37%	13%	50%
Psychoanalytically oriented therapy	45	18	37
Rational therapy	46	44	10

Rational therapy was apparently superior to the other two methods. It worked best with fairly intelligent, fairly young individuals with mild disorders. There was no evidence that it was more suited to one type of disorder than another (Ellis, 1957).

These results must be viewed with caution, for they also show that the therapist himself kept changing for the better. Perhaps they simply reflect increasing skill on his part or perhaps he changed because *he* was unable to use the first two methods successfully. Or perhaps it may have been a case of finding what he expected and wanted to find—greater success with the method he had come to prefer. Evaluation of the improvement by someone else without knowledge of the method used in a given case would have produced more objective evidence.

Cognitive attribution therapy. In some cases a patient's problem seems to lie not so much in his symptoms and feelings as in the *meaning* he attaches to them. In trying to find causes for unsatisfactory social relationships or irrational feelings, he attributes nonexistent abnormalities to himself.

The following case study illustrates the extent to which a patient's depression and anxiety may be intensified by the interpretation he places upon a set of symptoms.

The client, an unmarried twenty-five-year-old male, came for therapy because he thought that he was homosexual. He was deeply upset by this prospect and found himself in frequent states of severe anxiety and depression. His attribution of homosexuality was based on several observations. Sexual intercourse was unsatisfactory, he frequently found himself looking at the crotch-area of other men, and he believed that his penis was abnormally small. This latter belief appeared to be the major source of his difficulties.

Therapy was initiated by explaining the laws of optics, to wit, that objects viewed from above, which are in the same plane as the line of vision, appear shorter. The client was advised to view himself in a mirror and this procedure helped convince him that his genitals were of "normal" size. The therapist also explained that the client's glances toward the crotch-area of other men were a natural consequence of his worry about the size of his own genitals. The client was thus persuaded that this behavior was an indication of self-evaluation and not of homosexuality. Finally, his unsatisfactory sexual experiences were explained as not being due to inadequate heterosexual interest but as a "normal" consequence of anxiety about possible inadequate performance. Such discussions subsequently relieved the symptoms with which the client began therapy. The client no longer considered himself to be homosexual and his anxiety and depression were substantially diminished (Neale, 1970).

A change in the patient's attribution process is a by-product of most therapies. Once he becomes willing and able to discuss his problems candidly and begins to observe positive consequences from his overt behavior, he stops seeing himself as immutably evil or inferior. Instead he comes to see his behavior as less bizarre, more lawful, and often as induced by his own misinterpretations.

It is well known that strong fear disrupts behavior and prevents goal attainment, thereby making the person still more upset. When in addition he has no explanation for his fear, he is likely to consider himself different from everyone else: either "not normal" or "not rational." But as we saw in Chapter 10 (p. 389), a person feeling unexplained arousal can be made to feel either euphoric or angry, depending on cues in the environment. What would happen if a person with a strong irrational fear were provided with a *misattribution* for his physiological arousal that enabled him to interpret it as a logical result of some external, actually harmless situation? This approach has been used to help subjects overcome specific fears.

In a series of studies subjects expecting an electric shock were led to believe that their physiological arousal was due to the side effects of either a pill they had taken previously or a loud noise. When their fear reactions were attributed to such an objective, nonemotional source, their reactions to the shock itself became less emotional. Compared to controls not given this misattribution, they tolerated more intense shocks and reported less pain (Nisbett & Schachter, 1966). They also behaved more adaptively when given a conflict-producing task (Ross, Rodin, & Zimbardo, 1969).

Among female subjects who had phobic reactions to rats, significantly more were able to approach and handle a laboratory rat when they were led to believe that the emotional reactions they were experiencing were due to a new drug that was being tested for its effects on their visual acuity. This study in particular lends credence to the possible benefits of misattribution in therapy since it employed a double-blind procedure and an operational definition of fear reduction—approaching and handling the phobic object, the rat (Fraser, 1971).

Hypnotherapy.   Historical accounts of the use of hypnosis for relief of pain, anxiety, conversion reactions, and other symptoms date back to antiquity. However, a systematic interest in developing hypnosis as a tool in the treatment of emotional disorders did not emerge until World War II. Since that time there has been an increase in the use of hypnotherapy both in research programs and in training centers and clinics.

Hypnosis does not constitute a therapy by itself. Rather it is used as an adjunct to a variety of therapeutic procedures. It is currently being utilized in all forms of psychotherapy, ranging from psychoanalysis to shock therapy and drug therapy (Kroger, 1963; Schneck, 1959). While it is especially recommended for psychosomatic illnesses, phobic reactions, and emotional disabilities in reading, speech, and learning, it is also used with neurotic and even psychotic patients. Often patients are referred to hypnotherapists after proving resistant to other forms of therapy. This makes evaluation of the effects of hypnotherapy somewhat more of a problem than is the case for conventional therapies. Furthermore, since hypnosis is a technique which supplements other therapies, its therapeutic effectiveness has to be evaluated in conjunction with those particular treatments.

■   At the top is the subject's normal handwriting; next is her handwriting when hypnotized and told that she was ten; then her handwriting when told she was six. At earlier suggested ages, it became the unintelligible scribble of a preschool child.

The most familiar use of hypnotherapy is in age regression, in which long-forgotten events of childhood may again be brought to light. ■   Other techniques often combined with hypnotherapy include induced dreaming, influencing and elaboration of regular dreaming, age progression, time distortion, fantasy production, deep relaxation, and increased nonverbal sensory awareness (Wolberg, 1959). The skillful use of hypnotherapy requires both training in psychotherapy and training in hypnotic techniques. Unfortunately, hypnosis still seems to retain some of the aura of black magic and Svengali; because of patients' apprehension and therapists' reluctance to experiment with it, it is not as widely used as it might be.

Evaluation of individual psychotherapies.   The criticism of these and related psychotherapies has been on the issues of their limited applicability, exclusiveness, and questionable claims of effectiveness. Any treatment which requires special techniques administered by professionally trained therapists on a one-to-one basis over a long period of time is inherently restricted in utility. The training of the therapists is expensive and lengthy and requires in turn a professional staff of teachers. This minimizes the number of therapists available. Also all of the therapies described demand special sensitivity and complex intellectual skills on the part of the therapist. These requirements make inevitable considerable variability in effectiveness even between therapists who are using the same approach. Nor is it clear to what extent the therapist's expectations come to shape the patient into discovering what the therapist's theory says is there. Even in nondirective therapy, it is difficult for the therapist not to interact with the patient in subtle ways to reinforce him for moving toward whatever criteria the therapist uses for labeling him as improved or cured.

Conventional psychotherapies are unavailable or ineffective for many segments of the population: the poor, the uneducated, the unintelligent, the nonverbal, the addicted, the psychopathic, and the psychotic. Moreover, the patients who complete therapy fall into an even more exclusive group since up to 60 percent of those who consult psychotherapists discontinue treatment after several preliminary visits (Kirtner & Cartwright, 1958). Finally, of those who do go all the way, approximately 60 to 70 percent show improvement regardless of the type of therapy administered (Frank et al., 1957).

Finally, some critics have suggested that psychotherapy is an expensive way for people to purchase temporary friendships (Schofield, 1964). That the friendship aspect may be a crucial part of successful therapy for many patients is suggested by a study illustrating "student-friend power." Psychotic patients who were "treated" for five months by untrained, inexperienced college students showed greater gains than comparable patients given no treatment or given group treatment by a psychiatrist or a psychiatric social worker (Posner, 1966).

Such criticisms and new developments have had a positive effect in directing a greater interest toward group therapy, toward more practical, short-term training, toward therapy for "underprivileged" people, and toward a reexamination of the assumptions, values, and goals of psychotherapy. Notwithstanding these negative views, psychotherapy may still be the best treatment for certain people with certain problems when practiced by a perceptive and sensitive therapist.

Group Therapies

In recent years, many efforts have been made to work therapeutically with groups as well as individuals. Group therapy is most often carried on nondirectively, although different therapists direct and guide the group's discussions in varying degrees. The benefits may range from the simple "misery loves company" type of reassurance to a deeper and more lasting personality change within the individual members.

Various techniques are used in group therapy, from play groups for preschool children to analytic groups for adolescents and adults, in which the emphasis is on interviews and discussion.

Analytic groups. The classical psychoanalytic approaches to therapy have been applied in group settings. The methods and rationale are essentially as described in the section on psychoanalysis. The unconscious is approached through the techniques of free association and dream interpretation. The problem of transference becomes more complex because of the multiple transference relationships that develop in groups. However, Wolf and Schwartz (1962) maintain that unconscious materials and transference phenomena are actually worked through more quickly and completely in analytic groups than in individual treatment.

Role-playing groups. The technique of psychodrama provides for direct expression of the patient's emotional disturbance, as he is encouraged to act out various life situations which are related to his difficulties. The theaterlike atmosphere of psychodrama enables the individual to face his problems with less emotional tension than in real life (Moreno, 1946).

At the beginning of the session the therapist helps the patient outline the general situation to be enacted. Supporting roles in the drama are usually assigned to specially trained assistants. Once the scene is set, the patient plays his role spontaneously with the aid of the assistants, who help him "live" the situation realistically.

By acting out his emotional disturbances in psychodrama, the patient is afforded a rich opportunity for catharsis—he is free to express his fears and inhibited desires spontaneously in an atmosphere which simulates real life but which does not bear all the physical and psychological threats of real life. In this atmosphere of security he not only is able to gain increased understanding of his own emotional problem but also has an opportunity to gain new adjustment skills which can be used in real-life situations.

Encounter groups. The most widely used form of group therapy today is the encounter group of some six to twelve participants. The basic goal of encounter groups is to provide an intensive interpersonal experience in a small group, focusing on the interactions and feelings that emerge within the group setting itself in an atmosphere encouraging openness, honesty, emotional sensitivity, and expression. A major aspect is thus prompt and honest feedback. A member usually receives a good deal of encouragement and affection for qualities seen as good by the other group members and unequivocal criticism for qualities seen as bad. The leader may be either directive or nondirective.

Encounter groups, first called *T-groups*, were started over twenty years ago at the National Training Laboratories (Bethel, Maine) by advocates of the group dynamics approach (see Chapter 12) in an attempt to develop group and leadership skills. It is the unique pattern of social conditions facing Americans today, however, which has made the group movement catch on and has changed its focus to more general personal growth. Many individuals are experiencing a lack of intimate association with other people, a lack of any close community. Geographical and occupational mobility, family instability, the breakdown of extended families in which many relatives used to live nearby, the anonymity and impersonality imposed by mass education, mass transportation, mass communication, and huge housing complexes all contribute to the individual's sense of isolation. Encounter groups provide an opportunity for intimacy with others—even though limited in duration and without commitment to permanence.

In addition to the social-emotional experience, encounter groups also provide a needed opportunity for social comparison of oneself with one's peers. For many entering an encounter group, the "hidden agenda" begins with "Am I an acceptable person? Am I lovable, desirable? Am I as good as other people?"

Because they do fill a widely felt need, the proliferation of encounter groups on college campuses throughout the country is matched by their increasing use by church, business, and civic organizations. In such settings they are viewed not as therapy for the sick, but as a learning experience for those with problems as well as for all those who want to "grow" —to increase the joy they derive from life, to gain self-awareness, and perhaps to reexamine their values and life-style.

When we consider how much we conceal ourselves, the many masks we wear, and the general tendency to hide our true reactions, it is clear that honest group probing in a climate of openness can be an important learning experience. Group members can become more open minded, more aware of their own needs and feelings, and more sensitive to the needs and feelings of others. They can also begin to understand better the sources of their responses to others and the reason for other people's reactions to them and can begin to build more honest and open relationships.

While encounter groups represent a potent force in modern man's emphasis on self-fulfillment and need for close relationships, their remarkable popularity has created problems as well as benefits. For the first time in history, large numbers of relatively normal individuals are seeking therapy and may be receiving the kind of help that can prevent serious emotional problems from developing. If group therapy proves to be even *as* effective as individual therapy, there is a double advantage: more people can be treated at one time in a group, and they can share the cost of treatment.

On the debit side, many charlatans are cashing in on the popularity of encounter groups and are leading groups they are not equipped to handle. There have been reports of group members in executive training groups having been psychologically damaged by intensive group experience (*Occupational Mental Health Notes*, July 1966).

Ψ Close-up   *What Effects Do Encounter Groups Have?*

Preliminary findings from one extremely well designed and executed study to evaluate the effectiveness of encounter groups indicate the value and also the possible dangers of this "therapeutic" experience.

Groups were organized specifically for this study using ten experienced leaders, each a specialist in a different brand of encounter group approach, and 251 student volunteers. The students received course credit to legitimize the research and emphasize the educational purpose of the experience. Comparisons could be made with three types of control groups; students who registered but could not be accommodated due to scheduling problems and other reasons, interested friends of the participants who could not participate that term, and those students who dropped out of the group sometime before the completion of the full thirty hours.

Assessment was both varied and intense. Self-reports and other ratings were taken before, during, immediately after, and six months after the group experience. Each participant described his attitudes, values, perceptions, motivations, self-esteem, social experiences, and other aspects of self and reactions to others and to the situation. Each student was also evaluated by the other participants, the group leader, and a sample of friends. The functioning of the group and the leader were evaluated by twenty-nine observers (two at each group session, rotated across all group leaders).

Processing of the massive amount of data collected is still going on, but the investigators point to the following illustrative findings:

1. Seventy-five percent of those in groups reported a positive change in themselves, most of them feeling the change was a lasting one. Ninety-five percent of the participants believed that the encounter group experience should become a regular part of the academic curriculum. There was a greater increase in self-esteem among a higher proportion of those who had the group experience.

2. Wide variations in outcome were found with different leaders and in different groups. In some groups, the experience had virtually no effect on the participants; in others, almost every participant reported being affected by the experience. In some, however, the effect was mixed: 60 percent of the members in a given group changed, but as many were affected negatively as positively. Some groups had no dropouts, others had 40 percent quitting.

3. Group leaders varied considerably in the amount and style of stimulation and "leadership" they provided, which had an impact on the norms of appropriate group behavior that developed within their groups.

4. What students felt they got out of the encounter groups also varied—acceptance for some, understanding or involvement for others, advice or intellectual stimulation for yet others.

5. On the average, about one student per group may have been adversely enough affected by the experience to warrant psychiatric follow-up treatment. This percentage was greater for the "experimental" than for the control group students.

6. At present writing, the authors of the study conclude: "It thus appears that the generic title 'encounter groups' covers a wide range of operations by leaders that lead to many kinds of group experiences, and perhaps to many types of learning." (Lieberman, Yalom, & Miles, 1971)

On some college campuses, there have been physical-encounter groups in which considerable physical aggression and baiting of selected participants has occurred. Some students have even reported being seriously injured, being stripped nude against their will, or being held up for group censure and ridicule. Because of the transient nature of the membership of some of these groups, there is no follow-up of these hurt members to see if they have suffered lasting damage. (Ψ Close-up, above.)

Play therapy and activity groups.   Children between the ages of seven and thirteen who have emotional problems may be placed in an activity group which meets once a week like a club and which provides opportunities for self-expression through arts and crafts—or through throwing the paints and tools instead. The children are allowed to act out their aggressions without criticism or restraint from the therapist, who tries to maintain an atmosphere of love and acceptance for each child. As the children develop a sense of their own worth, fears and conflicts diminish and more desirable behavior gradually emerges. This happened in the case of Richard.

At the age of twelve, Richard displayed violent temper tantrums in which he threw things at his parents. He was also afraid of the dark, refused to wash and keep clean, could not get along with other children, and in general had a bad name in the neighborhood. His mother was tense and overprotective but often lost her temper, screamed, and beat her children. In activity group therapy, Richard soon showed rapid progress. He learned to reach out for friendships, tackled increasingly difficult tasks in the craft work, and even became a leader in the group. Similar improvement soon appeared at home and school. Meanwhile the mother received individual therapy, and eventually she and Richard achieved a much more satisfactory relationship (Slavson, 1950).

Whether practiced in groups or individually, a major aspect of activity therapy is the release of pent-up emotionality through the use of various play techniques. During a play-therapy session the child is usually allowed to express himself spontaneously, with little guidance or interference from the counselor. Perhaps for the first time he has an opportunity to give full vent to his feelings without fear of punishment or rebuff.   •

One popular form of play therapy is *doll play*, in which the therapist provides the child with a furnished dollhouse and a "family" of dolls. The child is encouraged to play with the dolls in any way he likes and is told that he can make them do anything he wants. In general, the situation created by the child are based on his own family experiences. But in contrast to real life, the child now finds himself in control of the family situation and so is able to change the characters' actions in such a way as to

satisfy his own unfulfilled desires (Sears, 1951). Thus he may punish or even mutilate a doll which he has identified as a parent or sibling toward whom he feels hostility and resentment. Or he may represent himself as receiving wanted affection in the arms of his mother. Play therapy, in other words, permits the child to "act out" his emotional problems without danger of unpleasant consequences.

In using play therapy, the clinical psychologist may simply accept the child's expressions of his repressed and suppressed feelings, or he may go further and interpret them with the child—depending on the individual case and on the therapist. With or without such interpretation, children often benefit from play therapy because it affords both an outlet for pent-up emotion and an opportunity to experiment with solutions to their problems that they do not dare try in real life.

Some therapists use persuasive doll play, in which they attempt to induce changes in the child's behavior through a sort of rehearsal in doll play (Mann, 1957). That is, the child's problems are attributed to a doll and he is persuaded to modify this doll's behavior in such a way as to solve the problems.

Reviews of the literature indicate a failure to demonstrate that play therapy produces predictable

● Play therapy like this is based on the theory of catharsis, described in Chapter 13. In the session shown here, the boy has painted a picture of his brother and is pelting it with clay bombs. Through this and other procedures, he was able to work through his jealous, hostile feelings, get along better at home, and do better schoolwork.

changes in the personality and behavior of disturbed children (Ginott, 1961; Levitt, 1963). There is, however, some evidence for the effectiveness of play therapy, especially when it is combined with tangible reinforcements for socially desired behaviors.

Eleven elementary-school boys were randomly assigned to three treatment conditions after being referred by their teachers as being socially withdrawn, shy, introverted, friendless, lacking in spontaneity, and mildly maladjusted. Each group met once a week for fourteen weeks for a fifty-minute play session. One group had no therapy, one had play therapy, and one had play therapy and also received tokens for desirable behavior. The tokens were given for walking toward and talking to another boy and could be accumulated and exchanged for tangible reinforcers (candy and toys) at the end of the therapy hour.

None of these treatments had any significant effects on measures of productivity, anxiety, general psychological adjustment, or physical aggression. However, on measures of five other behaviors the No-therapist-control group continued to show no change, while the Therapy-only group improved on two and got worse on one, and the Therapy-plus-token group improved in four measures: this group were talking more to the other children, were in closer contact with them, played more with them, and were also rated by their mothers as having fewer problems after therapy than before. In the Therapy-only group, the children spent less time talking to the therapist and were in greater proximity to the other children, but the amount of time spent actually playing with each other *decreased* during the course of treatment (Clement & Milne, 1967).

This study points up the need to make therapy goals very specific. It also demonstrates how dependent an evaluation of "success" or "failure" is on the particular criteria that the evaluation uses.

Although play therapy is used primarily with children, a similar type of therapy which allows the patient to express himself through creative art has been used with some success in the treatment of adults with emotional problems. Activities like painting and sculpture provide the adult patient with a potential means of discharging his negative feelings toward reality and of replacing them with positive feelings of accomplishment. Another aspect of adult play therapy involves just having the freedom "to play" once again, to rediscover the child within the adult, and to engage in an activity for its own sake rather than as a means to some other end.

Family therapy. Often the patient is part of a family that is itself psychologically disturbed. He may then be viewed as merely an element in a group system of psychopathology. In such cases, it is obviously worth considering the treatment of the entire interpersonal system on a group basis. Whole families may be in group therapy sessions, or the principals in a conflict (mother and son or brother and sister, for example) may derive benefit from a group session with a therapist. In family therapy, any of the group approaches already discussed may be used.

A variant of group therapy is used at the Community Child Guidance Centers in Chicago. Several mothers watch a counselor interview a troubled mother and then, in her absence, interview her children. The children then return to a playroom, where their behavior is observed and later reported to the group. The mother comes back to discuss the situation with the counselor, still in the presence of the other mothers. This procedure may be repeated weekly until the problems are under control. Several cases are considered at each session, and it is customary for a mother to attend several sessions as an observer before her own problem is taken up. Hearing the discussion of other families' troubles gives her a new objectivity about her own.

Evaluation of group therapy. Group therapy, like individual therapy, requires further systematic evaluation. The available evidence appears encouraging. Group therapy provides both a chance to see that others have similar problems and a "safe" environment in which to explore one's real feelings.

A study conducted in one of the wards of a large Veterans Administration neuropsychiatric hospital compared group and individual therapy.

Four groups of patients were observed, each group containing an equal representation of nonpsychotics, short-term psychotics, and long-term psychotics. In one group, work and living arrangements, as well as psychotherapy, were group-oriented. The second group received group therapy but had individual work assignments, while the third group had individual therapy and individual work assignments. The fourth group acted as controls; they were given the routine individual work assigned to all patients in the ward but received no therapy.

Patients in group therapy required the shortest time in treatment, with those in individual therapy requiring the longest time. Later adjustment was equally good, regardless of which kind of therapy they had and whether tranquilizers were used. The follow-up criterion of successfully holding a job after discharge revealed that all three therapy groups were significantly superior to the control group, with the first and third groups having the highest percentages of full-time employed members (Fairweather et al., 1960).

Certain individuals appear to derive less benefit than others from group therapy, and often as many as one fourth or one third of the members drop out of groups. In seeking an explanation for this, psychologists have identified three personality characteristics which apparently enable a person to derive maximum benefit from group as opposed to individual therapy. These are willingness to form relationships with others on an emotional level, ability to express rather than repress anger, and flexible perception of authority.

Thirty-two neuropsychiatric nurses and nursing assistants who had volunteered for a series of group sessions designed to aid them in their work by helping them gain insight into their own emotions were first seen in an interview designed to measure the three characteristics. Each was assigned a score for each characteristic. At the end of the fifteen-week course of sessions, each member was asked for her positive or negative reactions to the course. Nurses who tended to be emotionally "encapsulated" (very cautious about relating to others on an emotional level) were significantly less favorable in their reactions than were those not classed as encapsulated. Significant relationships were also found between scores on the other two characteristics and degree of satisfaction with results of the course. Moreover, a group especially selected from girls high in the three personality characteristics achieved unusually fruitful results from the therapy sessions (Gruen, 1966).

It should be noted that individuals high in the three characteristics conducive to successful group therapy are not necessarily better adjusted as a whole than others. They may be neurotic in other respects, while the emotionally encapsulated may show a high degree of personality integration.

Behavior Therapy

Behavior therapy is essentially an application of the principles of conditioning theory to the problem of mental disorder. Fundamental to this orientation is a rejection of the "mental disease" model, and, with it, of assumptions about intrapsychic dynamics and "mentally sick" people. Behavior therapists argue that abnormal behaviors are acquired in the same way as normal behaviors: through a process of learning. They assert that all pathological behavior, except where there is established organic causation, can be best understood and treated in terms of the conditions of "abnormal" reinforcement which happen to have been associated with the coping attempts of those particular "learners." Treatment is needed because their behavior brings them more pain than pleasure or is threatening to them or other people. The unique aspect of this treatment is thus that it is directed toward a modification of *behavior,* rather than of the "mind," the "personality," or some presumed inner core of "mental disease."

Extinction

The simplest way to eliminate an unwanted behavior is sometimes just to stop reinforcing it. When this approach is possible, the behavior tends to become less frequent and finally disappear. Extinction is a useful therapeutic procedure in situations where undesirable behavior is actually being reinforced unknowingly, and in fact such situations appear to be rather common in everyday life. For example, adults sometimes inadvertently reinforce undesirable behavior by giving children extra attention for it.

A classroom experiment found that misbehavior increased when teachers paid extra attention to it, and decreased below the usual level when teachers ignored it and gave their attention to children who were not misbehaving (Madsen et al., 1968).

Another study found that a preschool child's extremely withdrawn behavior was being reinforced because her teacher showed attentiveness and concern when she played alone, but not when she joined the group (Allen et al., 1964).

Why does someone continue to do something that causes him pain and distress when he is capable of doing otherwise? The answer in part is given by considering the reinforcement that martyrs receive. Behind the apparent suffering, pain, and negative reinforcement to the flesh lies the positive reinforcement to the "spirit": that is, the knowledge of serving some cause beyond oneself and the satisfaction of proving one's courage and worth. Similarly, many ordinary behaviors (or symptoms) have multiple consequences—some negative, some positive. Often subtle positive reinforcements keep the behavior going despite more obvious negative consequences of the behavior. This is what is often found in cases of stuttering, where the inordinate tension, embarrassment, and inconvenience generated by stuttering are counterbalanced, in part, by the attention, sympathy, and ready excuses for failure or rejection that stuttering provides.

Clinical psychologists have long been aware that such *secondary gains* accompany and support maladaptive behavior. Many believe, however, that such gains will be abandoned only after the core problem is cured and they are no longer needed. In contrast, behavior therapists believe that the maladaptive behavior is the whole problem and that all you need to do is change the reinforcement contingencies.

Unintended reinforcement has also been found to maintain and encourage psychotic behavior.

In one case, the nurses, intending to help, were showing concern and being attentive when the patient expressed delusional statements. When they followed instructions of the behavior therapist to ignore psychotic statements and reinforce normal ones, there was a marked drop in this aspect of the patient's abnormal behavior (Ayllon & Michael, 1959).

It is standard procedure in many mental hospitals for the staff to ask patients frequently how they are feeling. This may focus the patient's attention on his emotional state and provide the expectation that the "appropriate" behavior is to be thinking and talking about one's feelings, unusual symptoms, hallucinations, and so on. In fact, the more bizarre the symptoms and verbalizations, the more attention may be shown by the staff in their efforts to understand the "dynamics" of the case. One patient, asked by an interviewer if there was "anything else that was bothering him," responded, "You mean *halicinations* or *sublimitions?*"

Although it is difficult to do so, it is important to extinguish behaviors on the part of well-intentioned staff members, teachers, relatives, and friends that are providing reinforcement for the maladaptive behaviors. It takes considerable restraint not to intervene in attacks by a bully or not to get alarmed when a child appears ready to mutilate himself, but it can be demonstrated to "work."

In cases like those described above, as in many others, extinction of undesirable behavior is typically used in conjunction with positive reinforcement of responses regarded by the therapist as more adaptive. We shall return to the positive reinforcement techniques in more detail in a later section—and also to the problem of who is to say what behavior is "adaptive" and on what basis.

Desensitization

It is difficult to be both happy and sad, or relaxed and anxious, at the same time. This principle is applied in therapy in the *reciprocal inhibition* technique developed primarily by Joseph Wolpe (1958, 1969). One type of reciprocal inhibition is *desensitization*. Since anxiety is assumed to be a major cause of inability to approach positive goals and of fixation on negative ones, the patient is taught to prevent anxiety arousal by relaxing.

Desensitization therapy begins by listing the stimuli that provoke anxiety in the patient. These stimulus situations are then arranged in a hierarchy ranked from weakest to strongest. Next, the patient is trained in a system of progressive deep-muscle relaxation. Relaxation training requires several sessions; hypnosis or drugs may be used to help tense patients learn to achieve complete relaxation.

Finally, the actual process of desensitization begins. When the patient has entered a relaxed state, he is told to imagine as vividly as possible the weakest anxiety stimulus on the list. If he begins to feel anxious, he stops and concentrates on relaxation again. When he can visualize the weakest stimulus without discomfort, he goes on to the next stronger one. After a number of sessions, he can imagine the most distressing situation on the list without anxiety —the one he was unable to face originally. Great care is taken not to arouse anxiety during this process of gradually approaching the "unthinkable" stimulus. If anxiety is evoked, the therapist terminates the imagery production and relaxes the patient, and they begin again with a weaker stimulus.

As in other conditioning, once anxiety is extinguished to a particular scene due to the pairing of that stimulus with relaxation, there is a *generalization* of this inhibition to related stimuli, including those next stronger in the hierarchy. Thus desensitization works both directly, by reducing anxiety to a particular stimulus through relaxation, and indirectly, through generalization of anxiety reduction to similar stimuli.

Desensitization is ideally suited for treatment of specific phobic reactions which are maintained by the relief experienced when the anxiety-producing stimuli are avoided or escaped. Considerable research has been done on people with snake phobias. One might wonder if overcoming anxiety reactions to the *thought* of a snake would carry over to situations in which the patient is faced with a real, living snake. The evidence indicates that therapeutic effects do transfer to real-life situations. Patients treated for fear of snakes have shown signficantly less fear in behavior tests requiring them to approach or pick up live, nonpoisonous snakes. •

This approach has been attacked by traditional therapists as one which treats only surface symptoms, which have been serving an adaptive function for the patient and, by removing them, creates still more

anxiety. It has been likened to tinkering with a weathervane in an attempt to change the wind or changing a thermometer in order to regulate the temperature. A psychoanalyst would contend that a fear of snakes is related to their phallic or mythical symbolism and that therapy must be concerned with these latent meanings.

In fact, however, the fear that removal of one symptom will simply result in the appearance of another symptom to take over its function is *not* justified by any available data. Rather, it appears that symptom removal increases the patient's self-confidence (he sees himself as the kind of person who can overcome anxiety and cope with his problems), and may even have a positive effect on other maladaptive reactions than the one treated (Grossberg, 1964). The chart gives a comparison of the dynamic and behavior-therapy approaches, as seen by two behavior therapists. ◆

Desensitization techniques have been successfully applied to a diversity of human problems, including such generalized fears as test anxiety, stage fright, acrophobia (fear of heights), agoraphobia (fear of open spaces), claustrophobia (fear of enclosed places), impotence, and frigidity (Paul, 1969).

Implosive Therapy

Another method of extinction training in current use is *implosive therapy*, in which every effort is made to

● In the studies illustrated here, desensitization was carried out by the process of having a model safely make a graduated series of snake-approach responses which the subject then repeated. Through this procedure, subjects became able to touch, then stroke, then hold a snake, first with gloves on and later with bare hands. The criterion for a "cure" included such specific responses as picking up a snake, letting it loose and retrieving it, holding it close to one's face, and letting it crawl over one's body.

◆ **DYNAMIC AND BEHAVIOR THERAPY COMPARED**

Dynamic Therapy	Behavior Therapy
1. Based on inconsistent theory, never properly formulated in postulate form.	1. Based on consistent, properly formulated theory leading to testable deductions.
2. Derived from clinical observation and made without necessary control observations or experiments.	2. Derived from experimental study specifically designed to test basic theory and deductions made therefrom.
3. Considers symptoms the visual upshot of unconscious causes ("complexes").	3. Considers symptoms as unadaptive conditioned responses.
4. Regards symptoms as evidence of *repression.*	4. Regards symptoms as evidence of faulty learning.
5. Believes that symptomatology is determined by defense mechanisms.	5. Believes that symptomatology is determined by individual differences in conditionability and autonomic ability, as well as accidental environmental circumstances.
6. All treatment of neurotic disorders must be *historically* based.	6. All treatment of neurotic disorders is concerned with habits existing *at present;* the historical development is largely irrelevant.
7. Cures are achieved by handling the underlying (unconscious) dynamics, not by treating the symptom itself.	7. Cures are achieved by treating the symptom itself, i.e., by extinguishing unadaptive CRs and establishing desirable CRs.
8. Interpretation of symptoms, dreams, acts, etc., is an important element of treatment.	8. Interpretation, even if not completely subjective and erroneous, is irrelevant.
9. Symptomatic treatment leads to the elaboration of new symptoms.	9. Symptomatic treatment leads to permanent recovery, provided autonomic as well as skeletal CRs are extinguished.
10. Transference relations are essential for cures of neurotic disorders.	10. Personal relations are not essential for cures of neurotic disorders, although they may be useful in certain circumstances.

From Eysenck & Rachman, 1965

arouse as much anxiety in the patient as possible. Implosion therapists, too, regard neurotic behavior as the conditioned avoidance of anxiety-arousing stimuli, but they feel that if a person is allowed to escape the anxiety-arousing stimulus, anxiety will never extinguish since there will be no reason for it to do so (Stampfl & Levis, 1967).

The dynamics of the situation are nicely illustrated by the old joke about the man who went around snapping his fingers all the time. When asked why, he replied that it kept the tigers away. Told there were no tigers in that part of the country, he exclaimed happily, "See, it works!" Obviously, this kind of behavior is resistant to extinction, because it arranges its own conditions for reinforcement.

In order to extinguish an irrational fear most effectively, implosion therapists believe it is necessary for the patient to experience his full-blown anxiety reaction without suffering any harm. The therapeutic situation is arranged so that the frightening stimulus occurs in circumstances where the patient cannot run away. The therapist describes an extremely frightening situation relating to the patient's fear and urges the patient to imagine himself in it, encouraging him to experience it through all his senses as intensely as possible. Such imagining is assumed to cause an explosion of panic. Since this explosion is an inner one, it is called an *implosion;* hence the term *implosive therapy.* As this happens again and again and no harm is forthcoming, the stimulus loses its power to elicit anxiety. When anxiety no longer occurs, the neurotic behavior employed to avoid it disappears. In other words, extinction occurs.

Instead of starting by imagining mildly frightening stimuli and gradually working up to the really terrifying ones, trying to prevent anxiety from ever being aroused, the implosion therapist plunges the patient into imagining as vividly as possible the most terrifying scene he can conjure up. The way such therapy works, and its contrast with desensitization, can be seen in its application with a group of ten female subjects who were afraid of snakes (try putting *your* imagination to work on the images they worked with):

Highly frightening scenes involving snakes were described, and subjects were asked to imagine these scenes as vividly as possible, using all of their senses: imagine being attacked by a huge man-sized snake, having a slimy snake crawling all over your body, having it slowly strangle you, having the snake trapped inside your stomach where it is biting you relentlessly. Subjects were periodically reminded that nothing was actually happening to them. Seven of the ten subjects were able to pick up a snake after a single forty-five-minute session (Hogan & Kirchner, 1968).

Aversive Learning

There are some types of behavioral disorders in which the most promising treatment consists of a rather old-fashioned method—punishment. These problems are typified by various addictions and "deviant" sexual responses. The individual's behavior (smoking, drinking, gambling, turning on with potent drugs) brings immediate pleasure, but has long-term negative consequences for his health or for the satisfaction of other needs. Or it may be that a given stimulus has acquired the power to elicit a conditioned response that the patient finds undesirable, such as homosexual arousal.

Although the principle of punishment is a simple one, its effective application is by no means simple. As we have seen in the earlier chapters on learning, there are a number of variables which interact to influence learning when punishment is used. Intensity, timing, and scheduling of punishment are all important, as are its predictability, the context in which it occurs, and whether it is paired with eliciting stimuli (respondent conditioning) or is a consequence of behavior (instrumental conditioning).

Aversive instrumental conditioning has been used successfully in attempts to treat homosexuality and to eliminate stuttering.

Nineteen male homosexuals were shown slides of nude and partially dressed males and females. The patient was

given a switch that changed the picture projected on the screen. If he did not remove a male figure by depressing the switch within a limited period of time, he received a painful electric shock. Removal of the male figure, and termination of the shock, was accompanied by presentation of a female picture. The patient could also produce a safe period, in which he got no shock, by requesting a female picture. Shocks were administered on an unpredictable schedule of partial reinforcement, and treatment consisted of about fifteen sessions lasting twenty minutes each.

Follow-up studies between two and fourteen months after treatment were encouraging. Although three patients had not completed therapy and treatment was unsuccessful with five, homosexuality was eliminated almost entirely in the other eleven patients (Feldman & MacCulloch, 1964, 1965).

In another study, stutterers were instructed to read printed material aloud for nearly an hour to obtain a base-line measure of stuttering. Then they were asked to read very slowly, but each time they stuttered, they received a burst of delayed auditory feedback of their own voice. Delayed auditory feedback, as we saw in Chapter 7, is very aversive to a person trying to speak. Once the patient was able to read slowly without stuttering, his reading rate was gradually accelerated while the delayed feedback was faded out. By the seventieth session, he was reading faster than during the original base-line period and stuttering on less than a word a minute, as compared with fifteen words at the start. Another stutterer, whose training had to be compressed into only a week, showed even more dramatic results: more than double his original reading rate with no stuttering at all (Goldiamond, 1965).

In order to modify the "temptation value" of stimuli which elicit deviant desires and behaviors, counterconditioning procedures are employed. Stimuli which have come to arouse unwanted responses are paired with noxious stimuli such as electric shocks or nausea-producing drugs. Therapeutic outcome is measured by the failure of the eliciting stimulus to arouse the undesired conditioned response at a physiological or behavioral level.

Treatment of a transvestite by this approach consisted of first recording the patient's sexual arousal in terms of frequency and latency of erections. Arousal occurred not only to the photo of a nude female, but equally to items of female clothing which the patient wore when he dressed in "drag." Each item of clothing was successively paired with painful electric shocks. By the end of fifteen sessions, none of the items of clothing elicited an erection, but the appropriate heterosexual response to the body of a woman—not counterconditioned—still produced sexual arousal (Marks & Gelder, 1967).

Aversive counterconditioning has been used with considerable success with alcoholics in some cases. One investigator reported a 96 percent complete abstinence rate in twenty-six patients over a period ranging from eight to fifteen months following counterconditioning (Blake, 1967). However, other evaluation studies of aversive conditioning with alcoholics, as well as such therapy with excessive smokers, have shown only mixed success. The obvious problem limiting the clinical effectiveness of these aversive conditioning techniques is that humans can easily discriminate between "unsafe" therapy-laboratory situations and situations outside where it is once again "safe" to drink, smoke, gamble, and "have a ball." It can even be argued that in the case of smokers these aversive techniques are themselves a cause of anxiety, thus strengthening the relief effect of smoking outside of the treatment situation.

Positive Reinforcement

The judicious application of positive reinforcement of desired responses according to a systematic schedule has been successfully applied in the classroom, in penal and mental institutions, and in many other settings.

Even patients who have been totally mute for many years but are physically capable of speech have been trained to speak by the use of operant techniques (Isaacs, Thomas, & Goldiamond, 1960).

In one study making use of this technique it was found that by reinforcing a patient with pennies or by agreeing to write letters for the patient contingent on speech it was possible gradually to shape what were at first primitive grunts. Further training gradually led to more complete words and finally to sentences. After sixteen training sessions, the speech behavior generalized to the patient's behavior on the ward: for the first time in two years he spoke to one of the attendants. When the attendants were also trained in reinforcement techniques, they were able to participate in further treatment, and eventually the patient was restored to full speech (Sherman, 1963).

Dramatic success has also been obtained in the application of operant conditioning procedures to the behavior problems of children with psychiatric disorders. The following is one such case.

The patient was a three-year-old boy who was hospitalized with a diagnosis of childhood schizophrenia. The child did not eat normally and lacked normal social and verbal behavior. He was given to ungovernable tantrums which included self-destructive behavior such as banging his head, slapping his face, pulling his hair, and scratching his face. He had had a cataract operation, and the wearing of glasses was essential for the development of normal vision. He refused to wear them, however, and broke pair after pair.

To counteract this problem, the psychologists decided to use the technique of shaping. An attendant worked with the child in his room for two or three twenty-minute sessions each day. First the child was trained to expect a bit of candy or fruit at the clicking sound of a toy noisemaker. The noise of the click soon became a positive reinforcer. Then training began with empty eyeglass frames. The child was reinforced first for picking them up, then for holding them, then for carrying them around. Slowly and by successive approximation, he was reinforced for bringing the frames closer to his eyes. After a few weeks, he was putting the empty frames on his head at odd angles, and finally he was wearing them in the proper manner. With further training the child learned to wear his glasses up to twelve hours a day (Wolf, Risley, & Mees, 1964).

Operant reinforcement has been effective in getting chronically regressed psychotic patients to begin responding and thus become more receptive to treatment. One procedure, based upon the bar-pressing method of studying operant conditioning with animals, employs an apparatus adapted for use with mental patients.

The devices are located in soundproof rooms within the hospital. Each room contains only a chair and a plastic ash tray in addition to the response mechanism (the *manipulandum*), and the dispenser, similar to a candy dispensing machine. The manipulandum, a metal plunger, can be pulled as fast as 10,000 times per hour, although reinforcements (usually candy or cigarettes) are delivered according to the schedule being used in a given experimental session. Complex timers and recording devices operate behind the scenes to measure the rate of response, and the experimenter can observe the subject's behavior through a one-way screen.

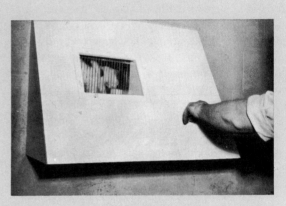

◆ The diagram shows the arrangement of the experimental room. The numbers indicate: (1) the plexiglas window to adjoining room, (2) the plunger to be pulled, (3) the place where the candy or other reinforcement was delivered, (4) and the stimulus panel. At the right is one of the stimuli used—a kitten being fed; pulling the plunger delivered milk for the kitten, which some patients found reinforcing.

Preliminary study established the fact that irregularity of response was a valid indication of psychosis, increasing with the severity of the patient's condition regardless of his particular type of psychosis. Psychotics (contrary to normals) also showed a failure to stop responding after reinforcement was stopped. After having learned to operate the manipulandum to get candy, they continued to respond hour after hour and day after day with no reinforcement.

A variety of reinforcers were studied. In general, candy proved to be the most effective reinforcer for psychotic patients. Some (but not others) responded at a rapid rate when the reinforcement was making a dipper of milk available to a hungry kitten seen behind the plexiglass window of the dispensing apparatus. ◆

Only about 40 percent of a mental hospital population can be given conventional personality tests, whereas 80 percent of such patients can be studied by use of the manipulandum apparatus. Thus the device serves a double purpose, providing a good indication of severity of disturbance as well as increasing patients' responsiveness to environmental stimuli (Skinner, Solomon, & Lindsley, 1954; Lindsley, 1956a, 1956b).

Imitation of Models

Positive reinforcement alone can be quite satisfactory for strengthening behavior that already occurs some of the time, but it can be a long and tedious technique when new behaviors are to be learned. New responses, especially complex ones, can be acquired more easily if the patient can observe and imitate a model. Imitation is often used in combination with positive reinforcement.

In one program, schizophrenic children were first treated for muteness by a variety of techniques, including reinforcement for imitation. First, the children were rewarded simply for making sounds. Later they were rewarded for vocalization only when the sound was similar to a "model" sound made by the therapist. When the children had learned to imitate sounds, rewards were given for duplicating words spoken by the therapist. By building on the children's growing repertoire of vocal behaviors, and their growing readiness to imitate, more intricate communicative and social behaviors were eventually established (Lovaas, 1968). ●

Such a therapeutic approach requires considerable patience and diligence on the part of the therapist. One of the autistic children with whom Lovaas worked required 90,000 trials before he could reliably label two objects.

In Chapter 13, we saw that both aggressive and cooperative responses can be learned through imitation of models who are reinforced. Even severely withdrawn preschool-age children can learn new behavior that they see others rewarded for in a film. A group who saw interaction between children positively reinforced later showed marked increases in social interaction, as compared with a comparable group of withdrawn children exposed to a control film (O'Connor, 1969).

Token Economies

In recent years, an increasing number of mental hospitals in this country have employed what are referred to as "token economies." This technique may be classified as a special case of positive reinforcement. Patients are tangibly rewarded for engaging in such socially constructive activities as maintaining personal cleanliness, arriving on time for meals, and performing assigned tasks. Payment consists of tokens (such as poker chips) which may be used later to "purchase" such luxuries as more elegant dining facilities, increased television time, private sleeping accommodations, and weekend passes.

Hospital administrators have found that token economies can often be quite effective in eliciting desired behaviors, even on the part of rather severely disturbed patients. It usually is necessary to start gradually, however. Thus patients may initially be rewarded for merely approaching nurses or other patients. Then, through a process of shaping, it may be possible to coax them to strike up conversations among themselves. Finally, they can be rewarded for more complex forms of interpersonal interaction as well as for other more tangible activities.

The effectiveness of token economies has been amply demonstrated in a number of studies. Patients who have led a virtually vegetative existence for years have become responsive, even performing previously neglected tasks with dedication and enthusiasm.

A token economy was established for an entire ward of eighty-six chronic schizophrenics whose median length

● The photo on the left shows an early imitation session with Billy, who at seven could not talk at all and had been making life a nightmare for his parents with tantrums in which erratic, violent destructiveness alternated with fits of beating his head against the wall. He had been diagnosed as retarded by a series of experts consulted by his distraught parents. On the right Billy and another boy are shown receiving immediate food reinforcement for social interactions. After several months, Billy was able to live at home and attend a special school. Two years later, he was doing first-grade reading and arithmetic and seemed happy, though his speech was often unclear and he still had some problems at home. (Photos by Allan Grant.)

of hospitalization was almost twenty-five years. These patients were extremely apathetic, to the point of ignoring the most basic requirements of personal hygiene.

Tokens could be earned in a variety of ways. Social behaviors and rudiments of vocational activities were most highly reinforced. A crucial facet of the process, at least initially, was the fact that awarding of tokens was immediate. Fines (also of tokens) as well as rewards were used in an effort to eliminate disruptive activities. The most responsible patients could even earn the use of a "credit card" which was good for special dining, sleeping, and pass privileges not otherwise available.

Results were dramatic. Infractions of hospital rules dropped sharply. Patients took a more active orientation toward their surroundings, evidenced by a quadrupling of the use of passes after tokens were introduced. One patient left the confines of the hospital for the first time in over forty years (Atthowe & Krasner, 1968).

Another team of behavior therapists conducted a series of experiments in which they systematically tested the effectiveness of a token economy. Their patients were chronic psychotics who had been given hospital work assignments which they had performed inefficiently and haphazardly, often not showing up at all. A token economy was instituted, in which patients were rewarded for performing their jobs. Dramatic changes in conscientiousness occurred. Patients began to report for work reliably and promptly. No requests were made for time off, though it was made clear that such requests would automatically be granted.

To test the motivating power of the token economy directly, the researchers decided to make continued reinforcement contingent upon the patients' willingness to switch to nonpreferred jobs when reinforcement was changed. To the extent that the patients did this, the token economy was controlling the choice of job.

The results were convincing. Patients immediately switched to nonpreferred jobs when it was made clear that continued reward depended upon their doing so. In a final test of the motivating power of the tokens, the investigators reversed the contingencies again and patients were now reinforced for performing their originally preferred jobs. Again the patients switched promptly to the rewarded tasks (Ayllon & Azrin, 1965).

The control used in this research is quite common in behavioral studies. Evaluating the effectiveness of a token economy by reinforcing first preferred jobs, then nonpreferred jobs, and finally preferred jobs again provides a good illustration of the "A-B-B-A" experimental design (see p. 45). The experimental

condition whose results are to be tested is instituted, then systematically altered, and finally restored. Each patient serves as his own control. In this case, the patients' choice of jobs could be reliably attributed to the reinforcement itself and not to "job satisfaction" or other factors. Employing this same design, Ayllon and Azrin found that when tokens were given automatically, regardless of job performance, or when rewards were made freely available independently of tokens, there was a marked decrement in the work patients did.

Patient motivation can be noted from a tabulation of what they freely chose to buy with their earned tokens. Privacy was easily the most sought-after commodity, followed by commissary goods and leaves from the ward. Individual differences in preference were largely limited to the rankings of these three major items. Very few tokens were spent for interviews with the hospital staff or for religious or recreational opportunities. ◆

◆ When each of the daily duties on her job card is completed, this patient receives plastic tokens she can spend for meals, off-ward trips, or purchases at the ward's "pink elephant" store. Fourteen months ago she was eating food off the floor with her hands; she now works productively eight hours a day in a community sheltered workshop.

Token economies have been used in other settings. One attempt involved a fourteen-year-old boy who, besides being hyperaggressive and destructive, had never received a single passing grade in over eight years of schooling and who was reading at a second-grade level. A token economy was instituted in an effort to deal with the boy's reading problem. Initially he received tokens for merely reading words correctly. These could be exchanged for valued rewards including allotments of money. A gradual process of shaping was employed, with the criteria for reinforcement becoming progressively more strict. The boy began to read sentences, and then whole paragraphs. Finally he was able to read short stories and was rewarded for answering questions relating to content. Not only did he make a great deal of progress during the training program, but he also seemed genuinely interested in the reading material. His progress also generalized to other areas, as evidenced by his receiving passing grades in all of his school subjects. Furthermore, there was a marked decline in his recalcitrant behavior. The program, administered by a probation officer, cost a total of $20.31 for articles the boy bought with his tokens (Staats & Butterfield, 1965).

In the near future, we can expect to see widespread application of the principles of token economies in many other settings. For example, they have been used in a number of schools, and some proponents see them as eventually replacing the present grading system. From the learner's point of view, token economies have the value of: (a) providing an unambiguous indication of approval, (b) introducing consistency and predictability into the situation by making clear exactly what must be done to achieve what effect, (c) not being dependent on the mood or personal values of the teacher or authority figure, (d) allowing the learner to have complete freedom in determining what he is willing to work for, and (e) guaranteeing that even minimally appropriate responses will be recognized and reinforced, and thus putting success and reinforcement within reach for everyone in the class.

Critics, however, shudder at the encroachment of a system based on the profit motive, maintaining that learning will come to be motivated by a "marketplace mentality" in which effort is expended only for extrinsic rewards and children have no opportunity to learn to value the joy of discovery or intellectual mastery for its own sake.

Evaluation of Behavior Therapies

Reports on the effectiveness of behavior therapy are generally quite favorable, with a success rate typically between 75 and 90 percent. Encouraged by these preliminary results, some behavior therapists hold out the promise that machines will soon be developed which will help correct behavior problems by providing reinforcement systematically. In fact, mechanical "mind modifiers" have been experimentally tested already on a variety of problems such as bed-wetting, tics, learning disorders, and smoking (Schwitzgebel, 1968).

As compared with other therapies, a number of advantages can be noted for the behavior therapies. Behavior therapies are more tied to, and receptive to, empirical research than analytic therapies have been. Because of their emphasis on treating specific symptoms, behavior therapies get results in a much shorter time than traditional therapies. This means faster relief and financial savings for the patient, and more patients treated by a given therapist. Since the therapy depends on explicit principles of learning, and not upon the personality, interpersonal skill, or interpretive ability of the therapist, training is easier and shorter and can be mastered by technicians, or *paraprofessionals*. It is clearly easier to identify and control variables in the environment than variables in the inner core of a person's psyche.

Critical evaluation of behavior therapy, however, also discloses a number of qualifications as to its effectiveness, its methods, and its unintended consequences.

There are few studies which assess long-term effectiveness of this treatment—that is, follow-ups more than a year after therapy. In the study most often cited as proof of behavior therapy's 90 percent cure rate (Wolpe, 1960), there is a major source of sampling bias. Included in the final results are only patients who had at least fifteen therapeutic sessions. All those who dropped out during the first fourteen sessions are excluded, thus stacking the cards in favor of a high success rate.

More serious criticism is raised as to what constitutes the effective independent variable in "behavior therapy" (Breger & McGaugh, 1965). It appears that in many cases, behavior therapists do not rely solely on conditioning procedures, but "mix in" more traditional counseling techniques as well, such as discussion of how a patient can stand up for himself and gain control of his relationships with other people (Weitzman, 1967).

Other critics maintain that the most effective tools in the "black bag" of the behaviorists are actually cognitive manipulations—that the primary operants are not overt behaviors at all but cognitions—images, feelings of anxiety, anticipations, and evaluations. Thus it can be argued that behavior therapy may work not because the reinforcement manipulates and maintains particular overt responses, as claimed, but because the individual, perhaps for the first time, has a predictable environment in which he can clearly see the consequences of his behavior and thus can use environmental resources to get what he wants.

A different criticism of this therapeutic approach centers upon the undesirable *indirect* learning which behavior therapy may encourage and the values that may be taught by it. For example, if reward is given only for surface behavior and conformity to what someone else decides is "good," the individual may be getting taught to value outer appearance, blind conformity to the socially accepted norms, social approval at the expense of self-approval, and action at the expense of thinking or feeling (D. Grossman, 1968).

The limitations of behavior therapy are worth noting, but concern about them should not be allowed to obscure the positive and unique contributions of this approach. Behavior therapy has had considerable success, promises more, and appears to be the best method available for treatment of inhibitory anxiety and specific phobias. There is no reason why behavior therapy should be expected to cure every psychological disorder, just as there is no reason to expect penicillin to cure cancer.

During the past few years, as behavior therapies have gained in popularity, various attempts to compare their effectiveness with that of the traditional insight or dynamic therapies have been and are being made. The question of which approach is more effective is particularly hard to resolve because of the difficulties inherent in evaluating the results of psychotherapy and in setting up controlled experiments on disturbed human beings. A recent experiment with "normal" subjects overcame some of these difficulties by comparing different ways of curing stage fright, a kind of anxiety sufficiently limited to allow rigorous controls but important enough to permit generalization of the findings.

A total of 710 students in a required public-speaking course completed a battery of anxiety and personality scales. With these was a letter explaining that a study was being made of anxiety connected with public speaking and that help in overcoming such anxiety would be available for a limited number of students. Those who were interested in receiving help were asked to indicate their willingness to participate. From those who indicated an interest, ninety-six who scored high in anxiety on the test battery were used as subjects in the experiment. Of these, seventy-four were asked to give a test speech. Immediately before he made his speech, various measures of anxiety were made on each subject, including his pulse rate and Palmar Sweat Index (a measure of emotionality). During the speech, he was observed by four trained graduate students who indicated on a checklist the presence of physical manifestations of anxiety, such as shuffling of feet, trembling knees, quavering voice, and heavy breathing.

After the test speech, these students were assigned to one of four groups. The remaining twenty-two subjects, who had given no test speech, formed the *No-Contact Classroom Control Group.* They never knew they were a part of the experiment but simply took the regular speech course. Any decrease in their anxiety could, therefore, be attributed to classroom procedures alone. After the treatment period was up, the effectiveness of the various forms of therapy was judged on the basis of measures obtained from a criterion test speech and a follow-up battery of personality and anxiety tests.

Five experienced, reputable psychotherapists were paid to participate in the study. All tended to favor the insight approach to therapy, but were flexible enough to use a different approach. Each therapist administered each form of treatment. Students were treated individually, receiving five fifty-minute sessions over a period of six weeks. The forms of treatment were as follows:

1. *Modified Systematic Desensitization (Group D).* This treatment was a slightly modified form of the Wolpe method of therapy, in which a hierarchy of anxiety situations was individually tailored to the particular student. After a brief period of practice in relaxation technique, items from the anxiety hierarchy were visualized in accordance with the procedure described on p. 631. The therapists had been intensively trained in

this procedure and were instructed to maintain the same warm, helpful attitude in using it as they did in the insight form of therapy.

2. *Insight-Oriented Psychotherapy (Group I)*. In the sessions for this group, the therapist used traditional interview procedures designed to help the patient gain insight into the roots of his problem. Reflection, clarification, and interpretation of the student's feelings played a large part in the therapeutic process.

3. *Attention-Placebo (Group AP)*. These students were told that their anxiety was largely the result of a low tolerance for stress and that this could be overcome by training. The training was to consist of working, while under the influence of a "fast-acting tranquilizer," at a stressful task that usually induced considerable anxiety. The drug would prevent the subject from experiencing anxiety during the task and he would gradually build up a tolerance for stress so that he could successfully cope with stressful situations, such as giving a speech, without the aid of the tranquilizer. The "very stressful task," identifying "disaster signals" from a number of tape-recorded sonar signals to which the subject listened through a headset, actually was one which usually induced drowsiness. Although the subject had the therapist's attention during these sessions, he had no chance for catharsis or for seeking any kind of therapeutic help because he was listening to the tapes throughout most of the session.

4. *No-Treatment Classroom Control (Group TC)*. In addition to the twenty-two no-contact control subjects, who participated unwittingly, an additional control group of twenty-nine subjects also took the regular classwork and received no treatment. However, they did receive some attention and knew they were part of the experiment. After they gave the test speech, they were interviewed and told that unfortunately one of the therapists was unable to work with students that semester but that treatment would be provided for them the following semester if they still wanted it. They were requested to return anyway to deliver another test speech at the same time as the treated students so that the data would be complete.

The most stringent test of treatment effects was analysis of the change in anxiety scores from pretreatment to posttreatment stress-condition measures, which were made when the criterion speech was delivered at the close of the experiment. All three treatment groups improved significantly more than the no-treatment controls, the systematic desensitization group being consistently superior to both the insight and the attention-placebo groups in all measures of anxiety. In addition,

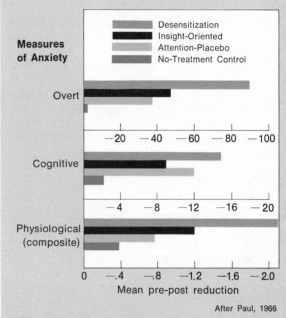

▲ REDUCTION OF ANXIETY

Three types of anxiety measures were used: overt, involving observers' ratings of behavioral signs of anxiety; cognitive, derived from subjects' scores on the Anxiety Differential; and physiological, including measures of pulse rate and palmar sweat. On all three there was greater reduction of anxiety in the desensitization group than in the other three.

more individuals in the desensitization group were regarded as "significantly improved" on all three measures (Paul, 1966). ▲

Combining Therapeutic Resources

Although many specific techniques of psychotherapy have been tried, some based on elaborate theories and others merely on practical experience, none has proved universally effective. In the face of this situation, most therapists have adopted an *eclectic* approach, not limiting themselves to any one procedure.

This broader approach was first advanced by Adolph Meyer, famed Johns Hopkins psychiatrist. Meyer's approach, which emphasizes the inseparability of *psycho*logical and *bio*logical processes is known as *psychobiology*. The psychobiological ap-

Ψ *Close-up*   **Institutionalization: A Split Image**

Enjoy Contemporary Living at Its Finest, Free-Free-Free	*Medieval Existence at Its Best (It might cost you your life)*
1. Three balanced meals a day—served on time, and no dishes to wash or garbage to carry out.	1. Ideal conditions for deindividuation; anonymity guaranteed.
2. Clean, efficiency bedroom, starched linens, maid service.	2. Sterile environment, no privacy, constant surveillance.
3. In quiet, secluded area, surrounded by trees and shrubs.	3. Get all the tender care given to a broken-down machine.
4. TV room, game room.	4. Freedom from decisions about what to wear, eat, or do or when to go to bed or get up.
5. Supervised sports, recreations, hobbies.	5. Freedom from responsibility; no more mistakes or failures.
6. Free movies.	6. Old friends and relatives will stop taking up your time.
7. Latest books and magazines in the library.	7. Frequent personal interviews by strangers.
8. Low crime rate.	8. No need or chance to prove your sexual adequacy.
9. Modern medical care.	9. Really far-out companions.
10. Interesting companions, intelligent staff eager to talk.	10. Shock shop on premises to keep life from becoming too depressing.
11. Stay as long as you like.	11. Long-term residency encouraged.
If you can convince the managers that *you* could benefit from such a life . . .	If you can convince your friends and loved ones that their only alternative is to "put you away," they will . . .
Apply to your local state mental hospital.	*Apply to your local state mental hospital.*

proach aims at an understanding of all the factors—biological, psychological, and social—that are involved in a disorder. This philosophy leads to an *integrated* therapy in which various techniques are used in various combinations, depending on the individual case. Thus, a particular patient's program of treatment might include such techniques as free association, dream analysis, hypnosis, psychodrama, and any physical methods deemed necessary. The ideal of the eclectic approach is a flexibility and freedom from theoretical dogmatism in attempting to fit the therapy to the problem—not the patient to the therapist's theory.

Institutional Care

For better . . . The most complete program of integrated therapy is found in mental hospitals, where the patient receives treatment on a teamwork basis, with psychiatrists, psychologists, social workers, occupational therapists, and other specially trained personnel all contributing their diagnostic and therapeutic skills. The seriously disturbed patient can derive important benefits from living in an institution under close observation and protection. Under these conditions, he is relieved of difficult decisions and does not have to face many of the frustrations of normal living. Guilt feelings tend to be reduced in the presence of others who are having similar difficulties. Moreover, the patient is kept from endangering the safety—both physical and financial—of himself and those around him.

Life in a well-run institution follows as normal a pattern as the condition of each patient permits. The current trend is toward increasing freedom for patients to live normally and to govern themselves while in the hospital. Such arrangements, still in the experimental stage, have caused problems in some cases but have shown great therapeutic value in others. In a private psychiatric hospital in Massachusetts, the Austen Riggs Center, patients and staff share administrative responsibility and authority.

Patients live in a building that resembles a country inn, each caring for his or her own room and deciding how to spend his leisure time. Normal social life, with no segregation by age, sex, or diagnosis, is part of hospital routine. Patients are required to perform a daily job as part of the work program and must answer to an agency of other patients and staff members if they fail to do so. A volunteer baby-sitting service organized by patients at a Fourth of July picnic has developed into a year-round nursery school for children of staff members and of local citizens, run by patients under the supervision of a professional nursery-school teacher. In general, the socializing process going on in this hospital community appears to give individual therapy a much better chance to succeed (Talbot & Miller, 1965).

The patient in an institution has at his disposal various facilities besides those entailing purely medical treatment. *Occupational therapy*, for example, is provided in all good hospitals. This term refers simply to healing through keeping busy. Engaging in such simple, rhythmic activities as knitting, weaving, sewing, or polishing metal or furniture quiets the overactive patient. The depressed patient may be helped by stimulating activities in which there is a minimum of routine. Such activities as music, dramatics, creative art, and athletic contests—requiring close attention and rapid decisions—tend to keep the patient from thinking morbidly about himself and provide interesting and satisfying contacts with reality.

. . . or for worse? The institutional care and treatment of mentally ill individuals is a medical, financial, and social problem. Over one million patients are treated annually in United States mental hospitals. In fact, about half of the hospital beds in the country are occupied by mental patients. This is not because mental disorders are more prevalent than physical illnesses but because they are generally more difficult to cure and to cope with at home and therefore require hospitalization for a longer period of time.

The total cost of mental illness in the United States, direct and indirect, is estimated at $2.4 billion a year. Each state operates mental hospitals, and in most states appropriations for the care and treatment of mental patients constitute one of the largest single items in the budget. Yet even in states with enthusiastic mental hygiene programs, facilities are inadequate. Almost all state hospitals are severely overcrowded. Furthermore, even though the number of psychologists and psychometrists has increased manyfold in the last thirty years, there still are not enough trained psychiatrists, psychologists, and other capable personnel for adequate care of the mentally ill.

Very few institutions for the treatment and care of mental patients come near approaching an ideal which promotes rehabilitation. There are many state hospitals where the conditions are so bad that if they were known, or if the taxpayers really cared, there would be a national scandal.

In some, there is but one psychiatrist for over 1000 patients. In others, treatment decisions must be based entirely on the prognosis that a new patient will respond favorably and quickly to therapy. For patients not expected to benefit quickly or for those who get therapy and do not show clear improvement in a short time, treatment is reduced by necessity to chemotherapy and occupational games—to keep the patients manageable and out of trouble. By the time

Period A—11 Physicians	Period B—6 Physicians
84 percent discharge rate (during first year after admission)	60 percent discharge rate (during first year after admission)
174 probable life patients	421 probable life patients
$4,872,000 (cost for 174 life patients at $28,000 total per patient)	$11,788,000 (cost for 421 patients at $28,000 total per patient)

◆ **THE COST OF INADEQUATE CARE**   After Cant, 1955

The uneconomical effects of false economy in services for mental patients were shown dramatically in Hastings, Nebraska, where a budget cut required that the staff of eleven physicians (including psychiatrists) be cut to only six. The chart compares the most visible human and financial costs for the two-year period preceding the cut and the two-year period following it.

Mr. F. B., the psychotic patient you met in Chapter 1, was interviewed by one of the authors, he had been in the hospital ten months, and his sole therapy consisted in playing his saxophone on those rare occasions when he felt like doing so. Treatment in many Veterans Administration hospitals and in some university-affiliated clinics tends to be far superior to that in state institutions.

Estimates of the cost per patient in the VA hospitals averages $75.00 per day. Considering that some chronic patients are hospitalized for thirty or more years, that amounts to a high cost of "treatment." Costs for more intensive care and the favorable staff/patient ratio in private institutions can run as high as $1000 a week. Thus the financial burden of institutionalizing the mentally ill is enormous for the individual, his family, and society. ◆

This is money well spent when it does patients some good. However, a recent barrage of criticism against mental hospitals has documented the destructive effects that these institutions often have. Their practices have been found to be authoritarian (Holzberg, 1960), degrading to the patient (Sarbin, 1967), dehumanizing (Goffman, 1961), and illness-maintaining (Schwartz, 1960). According to one investigator, ". . . the person's nature is redefined so that, in effect if not by intention, the patient becomes the kind of object upon which a psychiatric service can be performed. To be made a patient is to be remade into a serviceable object, the irony being that so little service is available once this is done." (Goffman, 1961, p. 379) Such conditions are more prevalent than one could wish.

Too often the patient is seen as a helpless pawn controlled by the power of staff decisions. But you already know from the study reported in the last chapter that patients are not as unaware or passive as they sometimes seem. How would you explain the difference between the following two answers given by the same schizophrenic patient (hospitalized for 30 years) during a single interview?

Q: What was the reason for your coming to the hospital?
A: Explosion occurred in 1921. Pepper war in 1921. Took in old dental chairs in Northport. Put a floral and power shave. This is Piel's book. Piel's book in paragraph. Mrs. Piel of course. The Hippo Tootsie is a song. In Ward six they have a song. Feed the pan so. The Hippo is in paragraph weight. She gave me two shanks and a wheel chair, and we went to the top, and we rode off Brennen, Brennen, Germany. Collected twenty-two men who lost the war. 1914–1918 war. Put them into a pig pen at Northport. Brought them back from the stratosphere with the Hippo Tootsie, the whistle Hippo. The Hippo that keeps the whistle in the power plant.

Q: How do you feel about the hospital?
A: The management is splendid. I have highest praise for Dr. B [hospital superintendent]. Recreation program, movies are splendid. Bingo, Coke parties are mighty good. I wouldn't attempt to improve anything in the hospital.

Mental patients, just like "normal" people, use ingratiation as an illicit interpersonal tactic to get positive consequences from others by appearing to be what they are not (Jones, 1964). They express more flattering statements about the institution and its staff when such statements can be traced back to them than when they perceive that their statements will be anonymous. They also know how to make themselves appear more "sick" or more "well," as demonstrated in two ingenious experiments that force us to rethink our conception of the passive role of the mental patient and the meaning institutionalization has for patients.

In one study, differences in the mean frequency of answering "True" to the same items on a personality test were recorded under conditions where one group of hospitalized patients were led to believe that "True" was a sign of mental sickness, while a comparable group were led to believe that "True" was a sign of healthy insight. Each group contained both "newcomers," who are generally motivated by a desire to leave the hospital (90 percent do get released in the first three months), and "oldtimers" (most of them hospitalized for longer than three years), who are generally motivated by a desire to remain. The newcomers answered "True" significantly more often when it was seen as an indicator of health than of sickness, while the oldtimers responded in exactly the opposite fashion (Braginsky et al., 1966). ●

Even more remarkable is a second study which shows how long-term schizophrenic patients subtly

manage the impressions they give to the staff about how disturbed they are, depending upon the anticipated consequences of appearing sick or moderately well.

When long-term patients were interviewed by a staff member and told that he was to evaluate whether they should remain in the open ward, they gave the impression of being well enough to do so. However, when they were told that they were being given a discharge interview, their answers reflected significantly more pathology. Specifically, they gave more *positive* self-references in the "open-ward" interview and more *negative* self-references in the "discharge" interview.

Psychiatrists rated the pathology of these patients without knowing about the experimental manipulation. It turned out that they made their ratings of severity of illness on the basis of the patient's self-references—more *ill* if more negative self-references, more *well* if more positive self-references. Thus these chronic, supposedly unmotivated and unreachable patients were capable of tuning in on precisely those variables that the staff were using in diagnosing them. The patients were thereby subtly manipulating the staff members (Braginsky & Braginsky, 1967).

Another set of problems arise from the vested interests in hospital administration, the established power structure (power of a staff member *decreases* proportionally with his direct contact with patients), and the prevalence of custodial rather than therapeutic or preventive attitudes. This triad not only makes innovation difficult, but can inhibit recovery instead of fostering it.

Sociotherapy

Individual or group therapy of the individual with problems is often combined with various types of *sociotherapy*. This term refers primarily to the process of modifying the patient's environment in such a way as to make it more supportive and predictable. For example, sociotherapy for a disturbed child may involve treatment of his parents or even placement of the child in a foster home.

Sociotherapy is most often carried out by a psychiatric social worker, perhaps with the aid of welfare agencies or other community service agencies. The psychiatric social worker aids the family of a hospitalized person in various ways, helping them solve

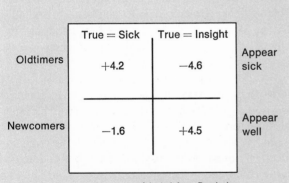

	True = Sick	True = Insight	
Oldtimers	+4.2	−4.6	Appear sick
Newcomers	−1.6	+4.5	Appear well

Adapted from Braginsky, Braginsky, & Ring, 1969

● **IMPRESSION MANAGEMENT BY PATIENTS**

This table shows the mean number of "True" responses of Newcomers and Oldtimers relative to the responses of a control group of Oldtimers given no instruction about which responses signified "sick" or "well."

financial problems or even giving therapy to other family members in some cases. The importance of smoothing the way for the hospitalized individual's return to home life is also being recognized to a greater extent than ever before, and periodic follow-up visits by the psychiatric social worker are often an important aid in the readjustment of the discharged hospital patient to normal society.

The Coppice Hospital in Nottingham, England, has a social therapy center called "The Gateway" which is in a separate building and is administered entirely by an elected committee of patients. The medical and nursing staff attend committee sessions only by invitation and give advice on request but have no voting powers. Activities of the center are financed entirely by the patients and often involve projects including the townspeople. The center thus provides opportunities for patients to develop social responsiveness and responsibility as well as to have meaningful contact with the outside community. Problems and conflicts that arise in connection with the center often provide the content for group therapy sessions at the hospital (Woddis, 1960).

Community-Based Mental Health Care

The Joint Commission on Mental Health (1961) recommended that no more mental hospitals with over 1000 beds be built; that acute cases be handled through facilities to be developed in the patient's home community, without the delay of being put on a waiting list; and that, as soon as it became possible to do so, the existing large state institutions should be either dismantled or converted to institutions for the care of chronic physical and mental patients. Since then, a start has been made through the Community Mental Health Centers Act to encourage the building of comprehensive community centers throughout the country. As such centers become more numerous and better equipped, it is hoped that more and more of those who need help can be cared for in their communities and that the large state mental hospitals will become a thing of the past.

Already this approach has shown dramatic results in decreasing the number of those committed for long-term inpatient care. In Duchess County, New York, for example, which had had one of the highest patient admission rates to the state hospital of any county in New York State, a special unit was established in 1960 to diagnose patients' needs more carefully, give intensive care to acute cases, and make arrangements for other types of care in the community for the less serious cases. It has been found that only 25 percent of the patients admitted under this arrangement need to be kept for inpatient care. The others are being treated through day care or through other community facilities.

Such comprehensive community centers have many advantages. With immediate care, adjusted to the need of the individual, overall treatment time can be greatly shortened and the patient and his family saved much trauma and grief. The stigma attached to being "sent away" is minimized or removed entirely, and the patient is spared the problems of adjusting to a lonely, faraway, impersonal institution and the equally difficult problem of coming back to his community after a long absence and trying to find his place in it again.

Substitutes for Institutionalization

It seems probable that there will be an increasing trend toward treatment of even severe behavior disorders away from hospital settings. "Psychiatry Without Doctors," "Treatment Goes Home," and "Landladies for the Mentally Ill," are examples of headlines that will be appearing more frequently, as such innovations prove successful.

Patient-run halfway houses. Fairweather and his colleagues (1969) demonstrated with an experimental pilot program that a group of newly released mental patients could be organized to function effectively outside the hospital. A lodge was founded in the community where these patients could live as a group. At first there was a single research staff member present; later he was replaced by a lay person. The patients were given full responsibility for regulating each other's behavior, for operating the lodge, purchasing and preparing food, and earning money. They set up a handyman service business which produced an income of over $50,000 in three years. They proportioned the money they took in according to each patient's productivity and responsibility.

Forty months after their discharge, a comparison was made of this group and a comparable group of another seventy-five patients who had been released at the same time but had not had this experience. The members of the supportive lodge were better able to hold income-producing jobs, to maintain satisfactory levels of adjustment, and to achieve meaningful lives in the community than the controls. All this had been achieved for the first group at a cost to the concerned taxpayer of $6 a day per lodger! (Raush & Raush, 1968)

Home care for psychotics. Other approaches aim to keep the patient out of the hospital altogether and to provide psychiatric care in the home. The first scientific validation of this principle came from a study in New York which indicated that nearly three fourths of a group of fifty-five schizophrenics treated at home with drugs and surveillance only by visiting nurses never needed any hospitalization. A study at Denver University's Medical Center similarly demonstrated that mental patients could be effectively treated at home by a team of psychiatric workers providing "family crisis" therapy. When seventy-five patients treated in this way were compared to seventy-five who were hospitalized, they did as well on measures of social and personal adjustment, more than 80 percent did not later require hospitalization, and those that did spent only a third as much time in the hospital. The financial savings with such home care, as compared to the cost of hospital care, are enormous (*Science News*, August 10, 1968). Needless to say, this approach is appropriate only when the home provides a supportive environment and is not contributing to the problem.

The attempt to bring treatment to the people, instead of forcing the people to find it and face the awesome impersonality and formality of a hospital, is reflected in the trend toward urban ghetto community mental health centers (Gardner, 1970). In some cases "store-front" therapy units are located on the streets of lower-class urban neighborhoods where those who need help will be aware of them and feel more free to go for consultation.

The Gheel foster-family tradition. While community care of mental patients represents an exciting in-novation in treatment in this country, such care has existed continuously in the small town of Gheel, Belgium, since the fifteenth century. Of 2000 functional psychotics and mentally retarded patients in Gheel, only 300 are inpatients at the hospital. The remaining 1700 are "boarders" in the 7000 households in the community. They come at any age to stay for an unspecified time, often remaining permanently. The boarder is the responsibility not only of his foster family, but of the immediate neighborhood, in which he is a free and occasionally active participant. Obviously, the community has been satisfied for some time that such a prescientific approach to creating the prototype therapeutic community works. Research is under way at present to answer the many intriguing questions that are raised by such a permanently functioning institution (Srule & Schrijvers, 1968).

Converting the last resort to a real resort. Perhaps the most unique suggestion to emerge from analysis of institutional care for severely disturbed individuals comes from the previously mentioned work of Braginsky and his colleagues (1969). If chronic patients need the escape provided by a mental hospital enough to make themselves appear sicker than they are, then it may not be the treatment but the escape that is the primary value of mental hospitals. If so, the same function can be served more cheaply, for more people, and without stigma or the necessity of employing deceptive techniques by *cooperative retreats*. With public and private funds, resorts could be established where anyone could "get away from it all" when the demands for daily survival are too great. Anyone could go to one of these retreats for a day, or for a lifetime. No work or psychiatric treatment would be required. The residents of this countryside community would plan all the activities—if they chose to. In a sense, such a proposal is a rich-man's sanitarium for the masses. Such a proposal sounds outrageous at first, and is greeted with derision. "Who wouldn't want to escape to such an easy life?" If this would be the general reaction—if almost everyone would welcome an escape from the present society—perhaps we should consider whether some of the features of this escape resort could be incorporated into society in general.

Judging "Success" in Therapy

Having completed our survey of kinds of techniques and facilities for helping those with emotional or behavioral problems, we are in a position to look at the general problem of determining when a patient is "cured."

Who? When? How? By What Criteria?

In Chapter 2 we saw that a high percentage of "cures" for treatment to stop smoking did not necessarily mean permanent cure. Evaluation of the effects of therapy is plagued by the same problem—and others. When is a patient cured? When the therapist sees visible changes in the therapy situation or the patient "feels better"? When his improvement generalizes to everyday situations? When a year after termination of therapy he is judged (by whom? by what measures?) as "making a good adjustment" (as defined by whom?)? The "cure rates" reported will depend on how the reporter has answered these questions.

It seems obvious that a therapist is not the best judge of his own success. He wants to see himself as competent and effective. Besides tending to see what he wants to see, he can inflate his "cure rate" by unknowingly encouraging difficult patients to terminate therapy, or by using vague criteria of "cure." But parents or friends who want to see improvement in the patient may also tend to "see" it, and the patient who wants to please his therapist will report that he feels he is being helped. Who can be close enough to the individual to evaluate what has really happened to him, yet objective enough not to have a bias? This is a perplexing, unsolved problem.

Changes as a result of therapy are usually assessed by various means, such as: (a) the therapist's overall impressions of change, (b) personality test scores, (c) patient interview behavior, (d) reports by friends or relatives, (e) patient self-reports, (f) patient attitudes, and (g) selected overt behaviors of the patient. But we have already seen (in Chapter 12) that changes in attitudes are not highly correlated with changes in actual behavior, and that interview behavior or a score on a personality test is not necessarily a valid predictor of how the individual will behave in other situations. What measures can you trust? In ad-

dition, we have seen (p. 629) that the same patient may be judged as improved or not improved depending on the criteria used.

Whatever the measures used, the content that is looked at (the kind of change looked for) tends to be in terms of what the particular therapist was trying to achieve, be it greater insight, removal of an annoying habit, assertiveness, self-actualization, or whatever. The goals of a particular therapy sequence are set partly by the therapist's concepts, partly by what the patient is seeking, and partly by time and cost considerations. "Success" in therapy aimed at making a patient more manageable is hardly the same as "success" in enabling him to be a self-directing, responsible citizen. Thus even with an objective, unbiased judge, the answers that are found will depend on previous answers to a host of definitional and procedural questions.

Still another problem in judging the effects of therapy is the lack of adequate controls. Until recently, therapists typically assumed that their efforts were worthwhile because they observed success in a portion of the cases they treated. The flaw in this assumption points up one of the basic requirements of any evaluative research design: the necessity for appropriate controls and control groups. For in fact, people often improve their adjustment without any formal treatment whatsoever. So when some patients in a sample get better, we do not know whether the treatment was the primary causal variable.

The solution for assessing the efficacy of a given treatment is the same as it is for observing the effect of any experimental variable. How much change can be attributed to the treatment over and above a *base rate* of change in an untreated control group? If a therapist believes that what he is doing makes a difference—and he must in order to keep doing it—then he is reluctant to assign suffering people to control groups. Yet without adequate controls, there is no way to be sure that the therapy was responsible for recovery; perhaps the patients would have recovered simply with the passage of time.

Finally, it is a truism that "doctors disagree." The same generalization applies to psychiatric specialists. In one case a hospitalized patient who had refused to eat with the others in the group began to put two to four bottles of milk on his tray and drink it with the others. The therapist regarded this behavior as a sign of improvement, but a psychiatric consultant held that it showed regression to the infantile level (Luchins, 1960).

All these are reasons why we do not know more than we currently do about the actual effects of the various therapies with different individuals and different kinds of problems. Yet the need for not only objective, stringent, explicitly formulated *criteria for therapeutic effectiveness* but also independently assessed and well-controlled *evaluative studies* represents one of the most pressing needs facing clinical psychology and psychiatry.

Does "No Therapy" Work Best?

One psychologist created a furor some years ago by reporting the following figures for groups given psychoanalytic or eclectic therapy or no therapy at all (Eysenck, 1952):

Treatment Method	Percent Cured
Psychoanalysis	44%
Eclectic treatment	64
No psychotherapy	72

It was soon pointed out that the "no psychotherapy" patients had probably not been comparable to the treated ones. Some were insurance disability cases; the others were patients in a state hospital, where the criteria of improvement are typically lower than the criteria used by therapists in private practice. Furthermore, the insurance disability cases may have received some therapeutic help from the general practitioner they consulted and the hospital patients may have been helped by the generally therapeutic surroundings of the hospital (Rosenzweig, 1954).

The critical importance of careful evaluative studies of therapy outcome is pointed up by Bergin's more recent (1966) review of seven studies comparing psychotherapy and no treatment at all. The averages in amount of change were the same for treated and untreated subjects, but there was greater variability among the treated subjects. Some of those treated got much better while others got worse and some did not change at all. Assuming objective and comparable reporting (a big assumption), this variability in outcome could be due to the kind of treatment, the therapist's skill in using it, the therapist's or patient's personality, or numerous other possible independent variables.

Ethical Issues in Therapy

As we have seen, any attempt to induce a change in another person represents an ethical decision as well as a pragmatic or theoretical one. Some therapists avoid confronting such vexing problems by keeping their goals unspecified. But anyone's changed behavior is felt by some other person; thus, the entire process of the therapeutic modification of behavior must be set within a broad social context involving the values of the patient, the therapist, and their society, as well as values that transcend any one society. Which values would *you* go with in each of the following cases?

1. A bombardier with a phobia of heights wants to be cured so he can rejoin his bomber crew and continue to drop bombs effectively.

2. A man who is impotent wants desperately to have a big family. Curing his sexual problem would add to the population explosion.

3. A youth is obsessed by a desire to excel in one pursuit to the exclusion of all other interests. You think that making him a more well-rounded person would result in a better-adjusted adult but that society might lose a gifted performer.

4. A woman with a multiple personality enjoys her sexy, lustful self, which leads her to promiscuity, and dislikes her conservative, modest self which inhibits such desires. Which "face of Eve" would you try to get rid of, or would you try to integrate them?

5. A student radical, convinced that society is corrupt and that his life and yours are controlled by the "military-industrial complex" wants to lead a violent revolution. Do you treat him as a paranoid maniac and try to fit him back into his society, or do you try to promote changes in the society to make it fit individuals better?

6. A parent consults you about a problem in which his needs seem to conflict with those of his child. How would you respond to this actual case?

George was an eight-year-old adopted son, with a slightly below-average IQ, who suffered acutely from the competition of two bright, attractive younger sisters born after he was adopted. Confused, feeling rejected, he was fighting for attention and love in many destructive ways. His attention span was poor and his schoolwork inadequate even in relation to his intelligence quotient of 85. His parents had concluded that he was retarded and should be institutionalized. In fact, they rejected him so completely that they were not interested in a suggested therapy for rehabilitation. What they had wanted from the evaluation was a recommendation for institutionalization, and they were unwilling to consider any alternative or to make a serious effort to see what progress he might be able to make with therapy (Menninger Clinic, 1969).

As our traditional patterns collide with voices demanding change in virtually all those patterns, the role of therapist as value mediator for the society becomes more sharply drawn than ever before in history. Will his role be to support the statistical definition of normalcy in terms of what the majority want, or to moderate and "adjust" each side to the other, or to see the high rate of individual disturbance as a reflection of societal "sickness" and direct his efforts toward curing social pathology? To be a "healer of men's troubled minds" today is to play a fantastically complex role at a time when the troubles are many and the pleasures are few.

Some see the ethical considerations in defining mental disorder, even before it is treated, as a rejection of the "norm" in favor of the "normal":

"As social anomie spreads, as society itself becomes more and more sick, we doubt that the mediocre man will escape mental disease and delinquency, or that he will keep himself out of the clutch of dictators or succeed in preventing atomic warfare. The normal distribution curve holds out no hope of salvation. We need citizens who are in a more positive sense normal, healthy, and sound." (G. Allport, 1969)

A Dream for the Future or Future Shock?

A mental patient with paranoid delusions began to have a fantasy that he was married to one of the nurses whom he hardly knew. As this thought became elaborated, his "marriage" was blessed with three children and his life filled with happiness. Soon this unemployed middle-aged bachelor lost interest in his work "if it was real," and cared only for his dream, "which," he told the therapist, "if real is wonderful."

When he requested the therapist's opinion about the reality or unreality of his ideas, the therapist replied that they were just a kind of waking dream. At that point, the patient cited his loneliness, his approaching old age, and the fact that he was not married and had no one who would really care if he died tomorrow. "What," he asked, "would I do if my dreams were taken away from me? What can you offer me better than this dream?"

If *you* were the therapist how would you answer him? Whether you could offer a better dream to this mentally disturbed person depends upon whether your society could offer *you* the possibility of a dream for the future.

In Chapter 13 we looked at the forces that can diminish man, including some of the ways civilization can be uncivilizing. Many people today believe that "future shock"—an anxiety-ridden inability to cope with the rapid transformations of our society—is all that the future holds for any of us (Toffler, 1970). As leaders with a vision of a better dream are cut down by the madness of an assassin's distorted reality, will their dream die too? Or will others—perhaps you—step forward to uphold the dream, as much for the "sick" as for the "well"?

Theologian Martin Buber (1957) wrote:

"The most important events in the history of that embodied possibility called *man* are the occasionally occurring beginnings of new epochs, determined by forces previously invisible or unregarded. Each age is, of course, a continuation of the preceding one, but a continuation can be a confirmation or it can be a refutation." (p. 167)

In the final analysis, whether the dream of a better future is confirmed or refuted will be determined by the *behavior* of *individuals* in the society—what each one is willing to do to make a shared dream come true.

Chapter Summary

All therapy involves an attempt by one person to change another in some specified way. Therapy may be recommended or required if a person's behavior does not meet social standards or is disturbing to the individual or others.

Shock therapy is used with some depressed patients to make them more accessible to psychotherapy. Prolonged sleep therapy is rarely used in the U.S., but *narcoanalysis* (interviewing patients in semisleep from a chemical like *sodium pentothal*) is useful in discovering buried trauma. *Chemotherapy* includes use of *tranquilizers,* to reduce anxiety and agitation, and *energizers,* to counteract depression. Other drugs, such as *LSD* and *mescaline,* which induce regression and disorganization of thought processes, are useful in some cases. The effectiveness of *placebos* hampers accurate assessment of drugs' effects. Vitamin deficiencies can induce or aggravate mental disorders; *vitamin therapy* to assure an optimum concentration of needed substances in the brain appears promising. *Psychosurgery* is rarely used today. Any *physical therapy* assumes physical causes (and hence a *medical model*) of mental disorders. Many clinicians now regard physical therapies as useful adjuncts, to assure a normally functioning brain, but see mental disorders as *maladaptive behavior*, requiring mainly relearning and social interaction.

Social-cognitive therapies are *talk therapies,* in which the individual is helped to become aware of and express his real feelings and then to develop more adaptive attitudes and behaviors. *Psychoanalytic therapy,* based on Freud's concepts, aims at basic personality change through uncovering unconscious conflicts and forgotten trauma. Other individual therapies include *directive counseling* (largely advice for immediate problems); *client-centered therapy,* in which a nondirective therapist provides a "safe" climate in which the client himself can discover buried feelings and develop greater self-understanding and self-acceptance; *existential therapy*, emphasizing the importance of the individual's choices; *integrity therapy,* encouraging the individual to take full personal responsibility; *rational therapy,* involving developing more rational self-talk; *cognitive attribution therapy,* in which the individual finds explanations other than his or her inferiority to which crippling anxieties can be attributed; and *hypnotherapy,* usually used in connection with other therapies. Individual therapies are expensive, time consuming, unavailable and perhaps unsuitable for many segments of the population, and difficult to evaluate, but perhaps the best approach in some cases.

Group therapies include *psychoanalytic groups, role-playing groups, encounter groups, play or activity groups,* and *family groups.* Group therapy can reach more people at less expense and provides some experiences not possible in individual therapy.

Behavior therapy treats only overt behaviors and does so by giving or withholding reinforcements. Variants include *extinction,* in which all reinforcement is withheld when the unwanted response occurs; *desensitization,* as in *reciprocal inhibition,* in which the individual overcomes anxiety by learning to remain completely relaxed in the presence of stimuli that formerly made him anxious; *implosive therapy*, in which the person is forced to confront the feared stimuli and discover that no harm results; *aversive learning,* in which unwanted responses are paired with noxious stimuli; *positive reinforcement,* in which desired responses are shaped by satisfying consequences; *imitation of models,* in which the individual watches the desired response and then is reinforced for making it himself; and *token economies,* in which individuals in an institution (school, prison, mental hospital) earn tokens for specified behaviors, which they can then exchange for any of several specified privileges. These therapies have been very successful, do not lead to substitute symptoms, take less time than talk therapies, and require less training for the therapist.

Mental hospitals can be therapeutic communities or dehumanizing custodial institutions. There is a move toward *community-based care* instead of faraway hospitalization, and toward more *outpatient care, halfway houses*, and other programs in which *patients take major responsibilities.*

Better evaluation of therapy is needed but is difficult because of inadequate controls, subjective criteria, and differing goals. There is also the unsolved problem of whose interests and values therapy should serve: the individual's or the society's.

Reference Manual

A Case Study of a Psychotic Patient

When a patient is admitted to a hospital or clinic his case must be diagnosed so that treatment methods can be recommended. Several staff members are likely to work together on this task. A psychiatrist and/or a clinical psychologist interview the patient, a psychometrist administers diagnostic tests, and a psychiatric social worker interviews the patient's family. The combined information from these people is written up in the form of a case study. Such a case study usually includes:

1. *Description and symptomatology*—an objective description of the patient's appearance and behavior at the time of testing, his observable reactions, and his symptoms.

2. *History*—background of patient which could have *predisposed* him to develop his abnormal behavior patterns, and specific events which could have *precipitated* his break with normal functioning.

3. *Behavioral dynamics or etiology*—an attempt to explain the interconnections between responses and their common causes.

4. *Diagnosis*—a classification of the patient's behavior according to standard categories (e.g., neurosis, character disorder, schizophrenia, paranoia, etc.).

5. *Prognosis*—a prediction of the likely course and progress of the illness, both if conditions remain unchanged, and if there is some remedial action instituted.

6. *Therapy*—a strategy for controlling the patient's behavior by means of a planned treatment which attempts to make it less pathological, thus enabling the individual to function more effectively.

The following material was taken from a case study of Mr. F. B., the psychotic patient discussed in Chàpter 1. A clinical psychologist assembled the study from previous hospital records, an interview with the patient, interviews with the patient's family, and the results of a proverbs test, an incomplete sentence test, and a drawing test. Read all the case material, make some hypotheses, and look for explanations and relationships. Then try to get a coherent picture of what Mr. F. B. is like, what he was like earlier in his life, what happened that made him "abnormal," and what, if anything, can be done to help him. Organize your conception of the patient around the following questions:

1. What do you know about his family, childhood, adolescence, and manhood?

2. What situational stresses and conflicts has he experienced in his lifetime?

3. What were the events which finally led to a break with "normal" functioning?

4. What clues can you find in the patient's responses which tell you something about why he behaves as he does?

5. Are there any consistently recurring elements in his specific responses and his general behavior?

6. How would you attempt to control (that is, change) his behavior?

Case Material

Mr. F. B. is a Caucasian of Italian descent, about average in height and build. He was in his late twenties at the time the interviews presented here were conducted. He was raised under rigid Roman Catholic standards of morality. He completed the twelfth grade, attending parochial schools. He has had musical training, and played the saxophone professionally. He has one brother, who at that time was studying for the priesthood, and had a younger sister who died. His father is overbearing and authoritarian, his mother extremely protective.

Mr. F. B. was married and has two children. He married because his wife-to-be was pregnant; she later told him the child had been fathered by another man. The only sexual intercourse he had prior to his relations with her was with prostitutes when he was in the Navy.

Mr. F. B. was first hospitalized in 1962. He was experiencing free-floating anxiety, punctuated by acute anxiety attacks. The prognosis for recovery was reported to be good.

In 1965, he was hospitalized again when he began referring to himself as a sex maniac, a pervert, and a homosexual. He expressed shame, but his manner suggested that it was superficial and of little consequence to him. He was given seventeen sodium pentothal treatments, which resulted in a short period of improvement. This was followed by regression to an agitated state with hallucinations and delusions of persecution. His parents signed him out of the hospital against medical advice.

In February of 1966, Mr. F. B. was committed to a hospital again by his wife, who divorced him and sent their children off to an orphanage. At this time he was exhibiting symptoms of preoccupation with sexual fantasies and bizarre mannerisms. He received a series of over a dozen electroshock treatments.

Following are some observations of his behavior on the ward soon after his arrival.

2/8/66 The patient stated that he was the Virgin Mary. He frequently pulled up his bathrobe in the back, displaying himself provocatively. He played the piano for a while. At times he was hostile.

2/10/66 The patient was hallucinating and talking to himself.

Observations made by members of the psychiatric staff at the same period included the following:

2/9/66 Said to psychiatrist, "Christ, do I have hot pants." His speech was pressured, inappropriate, irrelevant, and bizarre. His memory was good and he was well oriented. He frequently exhibited strange facial expressions. Group therapy and tranquilizing drugs were recommended.

2/15/66 The patient's verbal production was spontaneous and profuse. His general knowledge and calculating ability were poor. He exhibited inappropriate emotional displays and a loss of appreciation of conventional values. His reasoning was contrary to logical rules. The patient was receiving music therapy.

Examiner's Observations and Excerpts from the Interview

In November 1966, nine months after his admission to the hospital, a clinical psychologist on the hospital staff interviewed Mr. F. B. and administered the series of tests presented here. Following are some of the observations made by the examiner at the time of the interview:

The patient was polite, well groomed, and appeared to be in good physical shape. His initial reaction to the examiner was friendly, cooperative, and attentive; but before testing began, he stated that he didn't think these problems should be discussed. He exhibits several behavioral indicators of anxiety. His hand trembles when he holds a pencil. Dark nicotine stains on his fingers indicate that he is a heavy smoker. He appears to have a muscular twitch in his eyelid and at the corner of his mouth. Often he rolls his eyes or his head from side to side. At various points in the interview he became tense, wet his lips, covered his face with his hands, and looked toward the floor and grimaced. At one point during the interview, the patient stated that he is trying to forget his name, which he said makes him cry whenever he hears it; then he proceeded to cry vigorously for several minutes. He looked at the interviewer for some reaction to this episode, but the interviewer maintained his professional demeanor.

Mr. F. B. exhibited inappropriate emotional responses. He laughed or smiled at questions which ordinarily evoke a more serious reaction—when talking about some sad or upsetting thing he grinned or laughed.

What may have been the patient's initial resistance to the testing session later manifested itself in the evasive way he responded to many of the questions. That is, instead of giving answers to the questions, he would make a pseudo-analysis of the key word in the sentence, trying to keep his response objective. In light of information supplied by the ward attendant that the patient was socially withdrawn from the other patients and staff, the patient was in good contact with the interviewer and at times seemed to be actively soliciting his aid and understanding.

Mr. F. B. spoke very rapidly, spontaneously, and softly. At times the output was incoherent. Only rarely were the patient's answers directly related to the test or interview questions. He would perseverate on one word, pouring forth a number of incoherent sentences using this one word with a high frequency. While his vocabulary is quite good and some of his expressions seem almost poetical and philosophic, his speech was grammatically disorganized and he showed a marked tendency to speak in the third person.

Given below are excerpts from the interview with Mr. F. B., numbered for ease in later reference. The examiner's questions are presented in italic type; Mr. F. B.'s responses follow in regular type.

I-1. *How long have you been in this hospital?* February.

I-2. *What was the reason for your coming to this hospital?* I was looked at once or twice as being hospitalized for a reason only God could understand. Mother and father think son should be hospitalized and not be around. Move was made by my folks—more convenient for them.

I-3. *Has there been anything in particular that happened which disturbed you?* I didn't take opportunity like a good sport after everything had been settled. Went to another place, tried to be a normal worker. Have to be called by your first name at work—that's the way you find yourself.

I-4. *You have a child?* Little boy went away wondering—the answer no one knows.

I-5. *Where did he go away to?* I couldn't escape with the thoughts. I went away—tried to talk myself out of the thought that was in my mind. Made me do same thing all over.

I-6. *Same as what?* Shouldn't have said it.

I-7. *How is your physical health at the present time?* Hospital food is very delicious.

I-8. *Are you bothered often by headaches?* (Closes eyes, squints) Only one headache.

I-9. *Cause?* Everyone knows why a person gets a headache—only action is to take something for it—rather than ask foolish questions about it.

I-10. *How often do you feel like crying?* The word is a misrepresentation. Used only at proper time, when it is fitting and proper. When you see a person crying ask in your own heart why.

I-11. *How often do you cry, or have tears come to your eyes?* (Grins, rolls head) No.

I-12. *Have you felt discouraged?* Why feel discouraged, no reason to be if you are, people don't look up to you as a normal person. The word itself means nothing.

I-13. *How have other people been treating you recently at the hospital?* Couldn't ask for anything finer.

I-14. *At your home?* Maybe God knows where it is, it shouldn't be thought of. Conflicts only give you more conflicts.

I-15. *Has anyone been inconsiderate or unfair to you in any way?* No. At home a person misses what they are deprived of and don't get, don't see. Something that only one person cooks best no one knows where it comes from.

I-16. *Is this a food?* Homemade chicken noodle.

I-17. *Do you ever get the feeling that things look vaguely strange or unreal?* The word is strange to me, everyone looks at it and sees it, then criticizes it.

I-18. *Do you ever get the feeling that you are not the same person you used to be, that you don't recognize yourself?* If confronted with problem about what to do —ask about it, think about it, do or don't. Life is to be looked at with beauty. Many thoughts running through my mind. Not know where to turn to, have to know how to do with them. What causes anxiety—why is it that they don't act like themselves, not like normal humans?

I-19. *Have you had any strange or unusual psychic experiences? Seen or heard things that may not have been real?* Nothing is real—either this or that—only thing that is real in life is where to eat, where to sleep, what to do, and where to go, when he isn't lacking space, time, he can do it.

I-20. *Do you ever feel compelled to do things over and over again?* If it should be done, do it over and over again so people don't criticize it.

I-21. *Do you ever have the experience of feeling that your body—or some part of your body—doesn't actually feel like it belongs to you?* Sure, who doesn't?

I-22. *Which part of your body?* A body's a body. Don't think of it, puts more foolishness in one's mind besides all the foolishness there is. Convince yourself there never was a body.

I-23. *What sort of mood have you been in for the past few days?* If the world moved, the world moved.

I-24. *Do you have difficulty in making decisions?* Many people do have delusions or doubts.

I-25. *Would you like to go home?* No.

I-26. *Who were you living with at home?* Everyone calls them something, I call them Mother and Father.

I-27. *How long were you in the Navy?* Two years.

I-28. *Did you like it?* Very much.

I-29. *Would you go back?* No. They say you see sights, but they mean one thing.

I-30. *Are you ever bothered by nerves?* I was in [hospital] before coming here, for a rest. I had shock treatments. Thirteen or fourteen, sir.

I-31. *Did they help you?* Hard to understand, can't say if they help, can't remark about a treatment, can't criticize it. No one knows why they give treatment.

Excerpts from Test Protocols

Following the interview, the examiner administered a proverbs test and a sentence completion test to Mr. F. B. Some of his responses are presented below.

Proverbs Test. In the Proverbs Test, several well-known proverbs are read and the subject is asked to interpret them. The excerpts of Mr. F. B.'s speech presented in Chapter 1 were taken from his responses to this test; some of the other proverbs presented to him, and his responses, are given here.

The burnt child dreads fire. If it weren't for the innocent person who started it, it should not be done or said. Puts other persons in frame of mind to rather than said what becomes of it no one knows, and that's why they all know. Tell purpose point-blank regardless of persons. No danger due to another mind may lack its own thought. Not ever to be thought of as it becomes more of a dangerous thought in one's mind than ever as soon as it is told—whoever person is—it shows itself in right place after regretting having done. Not as dangerous as they said. A noble person could have done . . . leave person in place and say what they had seen and not what they thought. Not for anyone to be ever—is it that person will be put in danger to know not what they do?

New brooms sweep clean. That refers to something that has nothing that could become nothing that someone has that is being done by someone else rather than not. If it does, it than does it well it only takes itself to a little they say to do a little, to do a little more if thing is accomplished. Once it is done there should be no questions as to why it has been done. Something may have been or not been, why, who knows except maybe it had been, whereas in a way no one understands to contradict a person would have been should have been . . . When it is achieved it is given to the world to know for one purpose and that purpose is simply . . . Much of one knows of the object . . . The thought should not, to put thought in the mind first one must say . . . Man spoke of it as something beautiful, to be given but not taken. Do as told to do, not criticize as what he intended. Making it known to a person is not half as interesting as making it not known. Showing it is not as interesting as not showing it.

Incomplete Sentence Test. The Incomplete Sentence Test is normally a written test; the subject is given the italicized words and asked to complete the sentences. Mr. F. B. wrote his response to the first item but seemed unable to go on, making a number of false starts and erasures. The examiner therefore read the remainder of the test aloud and recorded Mr. F. B.'s spoken responses.

S-1. *I like* filling myself and then not caring nothing.

S-2. *When I was a child* when one outgrows the stage one knows what to do, child should be cherished more than the stage. Everyone realizes when they grow up they are still little children.

S-3. *A mother* is a mother, becomes a mother. No one knows why a mother is a mother, they know in their hearts. They know why they criticize themselves.

S-4. *I regret* a person is taking away the other person's feelings and giving him their own.

S-5. *I wish* the Devil has his place. Another person should not be listening and take his own place.

S-6. *My greatest worry is* you don't understand, don't know, don't see, lost control of everything.

S-7. *I suffer* no one knows the meaning of how much it has to be.

S-8. *My greatest fear* the word itself. More than 10,000 fears man doesn't know.

S-9. *I hate* covers a lot of territory.

S-10. *In school* that's where one thinks of the idols and brings to memory all silly things that happened long ago. Why is it that it had to be?

S-11. *My saxophone* (pause) it belongs to some person, puts their heart in it, does the job for another person. Respected by the other man who happens to be. Cash on the line for doing a little bit of work. It represents itself to the crowd as one is expressing his own clean thoughts without any foul play.

S-12. *Sex* someone criticizes something for what it actually isn't. The only thing it could have been was something else.

S-13. *Back home* people have nice things they admire when they see something they wish to forget then enjoy their own home. Things more beautiful, expressive in own surroundings.

S-14. *I failed* why is it that it has to be that someone failed. Shouldn't mention the word. Should be and criticized by persons who know that meaning of it.

S-15. *My father* (long pause) revealing one's true nature as only a fool says a father has his own way.

S-16. *Marriage* (shakes head, long pause, grimace) one bloke looks at other bloke and then wonder what is, but don't think of it or even dream of it. It should follow rather than waited for.

S-17. *My wife* (pause, incoherent, smiles, wets lips)

word should only be thought of but not said once said it's thought of.

Drawing Test. The House-Tree-Person Test is a projective technique in which the patient is asked to draw a series of pictures and is then asked questions about them. This test was administered to Mr. F. B. about six weeks after the tests presented above in order to secure some projective measure which might help to substantiate hypotheses based on his earlier responses and suggest new hypotheses to be explored. Furthermore, since he had failed to write out his responses to the Incomplete Sentence test, there had been no opportunity to check on his motor coordination.

Mr. F. B.'s drawing of a person appears on page 11. His drawings of a house, a tree, and himself are shown here. ■ The doctor who administered the test recorded the following observations:

The patient was sleeping when I went to his ward. He said that "sleep is good for a person." He was cooperative, said nothing spontaneously, and only offered a word or two upon direct questioning. The patient used a number 2 pencil which he held loosely about half way up. He took the most time to draw the house about 20 minutes 30 seconds), the least time to draw the tree (only about 30 seconds), and about a minute and a half for each of the other drawings.

Person: When asked if this was a man or a woman, he appeared quite surprised and stated that I had "not specified" which I wanted him to draw. I claimed this was so, that I was satisfied with his drawing and now wanted to know whether it was a man or a woman. He

■ Mr. F. B.'s drawings of a house, a tree, and himself.

said it was a woman, who reminded him of no one and he didn't know her age.

House: "Just a house"—doesn't remind him of any particular house. When asked if it was in the city or the country, he said, "Yes."

Tree: The tree was "just a tree" and he could not specify what kind of tree, or whether it was tall or short or young or old.

Himself: After a long silence he shook his head to indicate that he was satisfied with this drawing of himself, and he thought the person he drew was about the same age as he is now.

Analysis

Now take a look at the following analysis by the psychologist of the data on Mr. F. B. Does he stress the same points that you would? Do you think his conclusions are valid?

These analyses represent a psychodynamic or analytic view of abnormal behavior. How do you suppose a psychologist trained in a behavioristic or social learning tradition would interpret the same "facts" in trying to understand how best to modify the behavior pathology presented by Mr. F. B.?

Analysis of interview excerpts. The data gathered from the intensive interview of the patient reveal an overt expression of general hostility toward and envy of authority figures, a need for approval, a desire to be helped, psychotic detachment and ego withdrawal, persisting auditory hallucinations, the possibility of an earlier homosexual conflict, and marked disturbances in thought and language.

The hostility which the patient manifests in varying degrees throughout the testing session is clearly seen in his response to the examiner, his parents, and his home. The patient initially resists the examiner, and is several times very abrupt in his replies, as when asked the cause of his headache (I-9). The major portion of his hostility is directed against his parents (I-2, I-14, I-26).

There is a striking parallel between the statements of the patient in the item about food, and a case reported by Rosen (1953). A mother whose daughter was catatonic made the observation that the patient was simply run down, and that if she were allowed to give her daughter her own *homemade chicken soup* she would be cured. Thus, she showed her concern for her daughter by means of food. It was as if the mother understood (unconsciously) that this illness was in some way related to her earliest feeding experiences with her child. Excessive food now would compensate for a flow of love that had not existed at the time when it was most needed. Compare this case and Rosen's interpretation with Mr. F. B.'s expression of his own inconsistent need gratification through use of homemade chicken noodle soup as a symbol of (maternal?) love (I-15, I-16). There can be little doubt as to the important symbolic role that food has for an oral erotic individual like the patient. For example, when asked about his physical health, he replies with a statement about the hospital food (I-7). Furthermore, it has been hypothesized that among certain ethnic groups (notably Italians) maternal love is often expressed via the "feeding ritual." This consists of a preoccupation with the preparation of meals which are usually excessive in quantity, require a long time to prepare, and are a source of pride and gratification to both Mother and the family because of the unique quality that the cook bestows upon the meal. Failure to eat a great deal is interpreted as an insult to the mother-cook. A child is a "good child" if he eats all the food put in front of him, and a healthy child if he is fat.

The severity of the patient's condition can be readily assessed from the extent of his detachment and ego withdrawal (I-19, I-21, I-22). Although the patient says that he liked the Navy very much, he would not go back because: "They say you see the sights, but they mean *one thing*" (I-29). It appears that there are two equally plausible alternatives for the "one thing" that he saw. It could refer to the sight of nude men, which is common in the services and which might have aroused his then latent homosexual impulses, or the sight of the genitals of these men could have made him feel inadequate. On the other hand, the "sight" may be a reference to the prostitutes with whom he had intercourse. At one point in his case record, he is quoted as saying he felt inadequate when he had intercourse with his wife because her vagina was too large. If this is so, he would also probably have felt inadequate in his experience with prostitutes.

Among the thought and language disturbances the following are most salient. When asked about his *mood*, the patient replied with a *clang* (similar sounding) association: "If the world *moved*, the world *moved*" (I-23). Again, when the word *decisions* was used he replied: "Many people do have *delusions* or doubts" (I-24).

A possible instance of thought perseveration, or inappropriate continuation of a line of thought, may have occurred when the patient addressed the interviewer as "sir" shortly after talking about the Navy where the use of "sir" would be commonplace (I-30).

The verbalizations would have to be subjected to a latent content analysis (see p. 617) in order to get at their "real" meaning. Although there is little reference made by the patient to himself (he is not yet completely detached and still uses "me" and "my," although infrequently), it is obvious that the content of the thought revealed by his verbalizations is autistic, with a high degree of self-concern over certain inferiorities (or things he has done) that he has been criticized and ridiculed for by people dear to him. He seems to be preoccupied in forgetting (suppressing) his wife and their marriage, but is upset that his children are in an orphanage. It is also ventured that he may have been reprimanded severely for masturbation or genital exhibition and is still suffering from the guilt associated with the incident. Evidence for this possibility was discussed in Chapter 1.

Analysis of Proverbs Test. The language in the response to the "burnt-child" proverb is very fragmentary and involves several themes. Depersonalization is evident in: "No danger due to another mind may lack its own thought." The patient may have been referring to masturbation when he said: "Not as dangerous as they said." In the statement: "A noble person could have done—leave the person in place and say what they had seen and not what they thought," the patient may be alluding to an incident in his childhood when he was unjustifiably punished for masturbating.

A theme of sexual activity and sexual exhibitionism runs through the response to the "new-brooms" proverb: "Once it is done there should be no questions as to why it has been done [sex should not be mentioned]." "Man spoke of it [sex] as something beautiful, to be given but not taken." "Showing it is not as interesting as not showing it."

One can also observe complete disintegration of the capacity to synthesize thoughts into an orderly series. The patient's response is often not relevant to the proverb because of his high degree of over-inclusion at the expense of comments referring to the test situation. The conjecture is made that the patient's perseveration on the word "little" in the second sentence is a consequence of his self-image and his penis image. His authoritarian home training is concisely phrased: "Do as told to do."

Analysis of the Incomplete Sentence Test. The patient's completion of items provides a picture of an oral incorporative, self-indulgent, narcissistic individual (S-1). S-2 shows elements of regression. Paranoid ideas of depersonalization are evident (S-4), and there is a possibility of auditory hallucinations (S-5). A loss of contact with reality, as he perceives his ego "going under" is evident in ". . . lost control of everything" (S-6).

The patient's suffering (S-7) does not stem from a single source (S-8, 9), but is intimately related to his feelings of general inadequacy and conflict toward his parents and wife. Throughout this record, the patient is preoccupied with the idea of people criticizing his thoughts and actions (the word "criticism" is used nine times). Much of this perceived criticism may be the result of masturbation-guilt or guilt over an incident of self-exposure (S-10, 11, 12).

Sex guilt is especially severe for Mr. F. B. because of the rigid standards of morality that his parents and education have inculcated. Such stringent standards would be likely to prevent satisfaction in his sexual relationships and lead to a substitution of masturbation for intercourse as his sexual outlet.

The patient's parochial-school education would explain his use of "God," "Devil," "church," and "angel" in his incomplete sentences, and the reference to "idols" (S-10) may be to the religious statues found in Catholic classrooms. It should be noted that the patient is reported by the ward attendant as having declared that he was the Virgin Mary. A dogmatic moral tone is evident in the patient's frequent use of the word "should."

The patient's completions indicate several sources of conflict: (a) his mother's position (S-3) and her feelings toward him; (b) the conflict between hatred of his father for being so authoritarian and admiration for this type of aggressive self-assertion which he feels he lacks and which causes him to be unable to express all the things he wants to say (S-15); and (c) the conflict between the security that his home provides him and the hostility it fosters when his needs aren't gratified (S-13, I-26). His wife's premarital pregnancy by another man and the child born of this relation caused him much pain (S-16): "it should follow rather than waited for" (the baby should come after the marriage?). In item S-11, the patient is using "saxophone" as a symbol for his son (it is a penis symbol in case records). He is attempting to justify his marriage by doing a job for someone else from whom he should have gotten respect (for such a noble sacrifice).

In summary, the patient's sentence completions offer further substantiating evidence that he is a schizophrenic with severe neurotic conflicts about sex, his wife, and his parents. The patient's aggression is intrapunitive and he fears expressing himself because he will become violent and not displace his hostility. The consequence of this is a progressive withdrawal in which he speaks only to himself and cuts off all interaction with other human beings.

Analysis of the Drawing Test. The lack of details in these drawings reflects Mr. F. B.'s poor recognition and orientation to elementary, concrete aspects of life, suggesting withdrawal from the environment. The poor proportion is indicative of faulty judgment. His perspective is somewhat better than his details and proportion, indicating that he still has the ability to make an evaluation of his environment and his relation to those in it. The large number of flaws in the drawings reflect that patient's high level of critical appraisal and low level of ability to function on an interacting basis. The use of relatively light lines in the drawings is typical of inadequate or depressive individuals.

House: Because people "doodle" houses less than they doodle trees or people, they are generally more difficult to draw, and individuals often get lower scores on houses than on their other drawings. However, this patient's best production was his drawing of a house, indicating his impression of his satisfactory adjustment at home. The use of a groundline is interpreted as indicating insecurity in general and reflects a need to "anchor" the house on a firm foundation. The drawing of windows without panes is taken to represent oral and/or anal eroticism and feelings of hostility. Radical interpretation of this drawing would suggest a favorable prognosis on the grounds that inclusion of a doorknob, especially when other details are lacking, is indicative of "accessibility" and readiness to be "entered" and helped with his problems.

Tree: A "keyhole" tree, like this one by the patient, usually indicates strong hostile impulses, some of which may be internalized. Hostility is presumed here because of: (a) the patient's failure to present details usually drawn in or implied by shading, and (b) his refusal, in effect, to define more specifically his branch structure (interpreted as revealing the extent, interrelationship, etc., of his satisfaction-seeking in his environment). The tree *in toto* appears to be a phallus (and a large one!). Drawing this tree-phallus may have been anxiety arousing, and his execution of it in only thirty seconds would indicate a desire to get it finished as rapidly as possible.

Person: The patient's conflict over his own sex role is clearly reflected in his indecision in naming the sex of the "person" he drew, and in the discrepancy between what he drew and what he labeled it. The drawing, although reported to be that of a woman, has a marked masculine appearance: broad shoulders, full trunk, and "pants legs" (i.e., the complete contour of the legs can be seen unobstructed by a skirt or dress). In fact, there are no obvious indications of femininity. Furthermore, the use of faint, broken lines is believed to represent a reluctance upon the part of the subject to clearly depict the subject matter in question because of what it represents actually or symbolically. If this drawing represents the patient, then the inferior line quality might be taken to mean that he sees his ego as "going under." The patient's reluctance (or total inability) to draw details ordinarily regarded as having sexual implication (e.g., clothes) implies psychosexual deviations, fixations, or immaturity. Upon closer examination, it can be seen that an attempt has been made to faintly draw a more

feminine outline *within* the body of the masculine figure. This would be a clear-cut manifestation of homosexuality if that is what these lines represent.

Himself: This production is the most encouraging evidence available concerning the patient's prognosis. Although omitting the body once again, he draws the face in good proportions, and in detail, including eyes, nose, mouth, ears (although small), and even eyebrows. The minuteness of the ears suggests that the patient may be trying to limit or cut off the "source" of his auditory hallucinations. The happy smile comes at a time when he pictures himself, via the sailor's cap, back in the Navy. Apparently this was a happy period for the patient; he found that he could manage without his father's domination and his mother's protection, and he could assert his masculinity to some extent by having intercourse with prostitutes. This stay in the Navy was also prior to his marital difficulties and would make it a very happy time by comparison.

In summary, the patient's drawings reveal a depressed, withdrawn schizophrenic with psychosexual conflict, intense feelings of inadequacy, and a great deal of repressed hostility.

Summary and Conclusions

Mr. F. B. is a chronic hebephrenic schizophrenic. The classical elements of hebephrenia which he exhibits are: (a) generalized inappropriateness of affect; (b) poorly organized delusions, often concerning the body; (c) silly behavior and mannerisms; (d) a tendency toward rapid regression; and (e) prominent thought and speech disorders.

His illness tends toward increasing severity and gradual withdrawal from reality. Even during the period of his recent hospitalization, increasing stages of withdrawal have been evident. Initially he walked around the ward and provoked the other patients, then he began talking to himself and sitting alone, finally reaching the point where he never interacts spontaneously with anyone and spends a great deal of time sleeping ("sleep is good for a person").

Despite the increasing severity of the course of his illness, it appears that the prognosis is not entirely hopeless—if intensive therapy is administered soon.

Although the staff conference recommended extensive work with the patient, group psychotherapy and tranquilizing drugs, the only psychiatric aid he is receiving is "music therapy." Among the favorable prognostic indicators are: (a) the relatively short duration of hospitalization—(net time about twenty-nine months); (b) conscious, pervasive anxiety; (c) a generally compliant attitude; (d) depression as the general affective condition; (e) unsystematized delusions; (f) delusions concerning feelings of guilt and responsibility; (g) a desire to be "normal," to understand what it is that makes him "anxious."

The diagnosis is complicated by the presence of severe neurotic conflicts manifested in his extreme fits of depression, anxiety, and guilt feelings. The major areas of his neurotic conflicts are: (a) unresolved Oedipus complex; (b) marked castration anxiety; (c) submission-rebellion conflict; (d) nonstabilized sex role—homosexuality.

The patient's record is replete with evidence of a strong sexual love for the mother and a fear of the father. The "mother is wonderful"—"patient is very close to her. He was always afraid he would lose her, and would spend long times at home with her, especially when father wasn't home" (case record). He reports that he liked to watch his mother nurse his baby sister, that the sight of her large breasts angered him and that whenever he thinks of her, he thinks of the phrase, "little fat ass." The father is depicted as an authoritarian individual and a strict disciplinarian. The patient shows hostility toward the father, but also admiration of his masculine qualities, his ability to blow up and to say and do what he wants. The verification of the castration-anxiety hypothesis comes from his fear of being beaten and punished by his father (he lists this among his early traumatic experiences) and his feelings of inadequacy because his father "carried a bigger stick." His present identification with his mother—"patient says he feels like his mother," "he says he is the Virgin Mary"—may have developed along lines specified by Otto Fenichel:

"The normal identification of a boy with his father, characterized by the formulae, 'I should like to be like father,' 'I should like to have a penis like father's,' . . . may, in certain cases, grow into a kind of love which may best be described as an apprentice complex, a

temporary feminine submission to the father in order to prepare oneself for a later masculine competition with him. If this love meets a castration threat, this may result in an abandonment of the phallic position and make the boy turn to the mother again, but no longer in a phallic Oedipus striving, but rather in a pregenital, passive, protection-seeking, identifying way." (1945, p. 89)

The conflict between submission to authority figures and rebellion against them is reflected in: (a) his hostility toward his parents, especially as evidenced in the interview, (b) his fear of losing his temper and becoming violent, (c) his failure to give hands (instruments with which to express anger and hostility) to his drawing of the person, and (d) statements such as, "Do as told to do," "can't criticize a hospital . . . treatment."

The failure of the patient to develop a stable sex role has resulted in the development of homosexuality which became overt during the early period of his present hospitalization. The fear of his father and the castration anxiety which he engendered precluded normal masculine identification. Some schizophrenics have emotional difficulty in identifying with one sex. Their paleologic thought reveals a nonadherence to the law of excluded middle (X must be X or not X, no intermediate stage), and enables them to make a male-female composite (Arieti, 1955).

While the patient identified with the mother, he was nevertheless hostile toward her. Records of his first hospitalization (1962) state: "patient expressed hostility toward [his mother's] overprotectiveness. She made him help her with all sorts of household feminine tasks. He feels insecure, mother didn't help him develop his own capabilities."

His feminine identification may have been so strong that when his baby sister was born, he felt that his father had given him the baby:

"He loved his baby sister and felt very protective toward her. He was closer to his mother than ever before when the baby was alive. He would always watch when mother nursed baby (case record)."

However, the birth of a sibling is typically an important traumatic event. "This may be experienced as a sudden disturbance of Oedipal gratifications because the mother's care must now be shared with somebody else; or perceptions and speculations about pregnancy and birth may increase sexual curiosity and sexual activities. Both may result in a tendency toward regression into babyhood." (Fenichel, 1945, p. 93) If the patient had placed himself in competition with his baby sister for his mother's love, then his sister's early death must have caused him a great deal of anxiety and guilt—and may have been interpreted as wish-fulfillment. This may still be a source of his feelings of guilt and depression (i.e., it's his fault that she is dead).

"Schizophrenia is a specific reaction to a severe state of anxiety, originating in childhood, reexperienced and increased in some later period in life." (Arieti, 1955, p. 316) Therefore, when the father reports that the patient's troubles were caused by the marriage, he is in effect, offering only the precipitating cause of the onset of the illness. One of the reasons why the patient's wife took advantage of him is that he is "too good" (father's report). Unable to see this submission-passivity as the consequence of his authoritarian rearing, the father describes the patient as *very obedient* and a happy-go-lucky child who had no difficulty in early childhood. Contrast this with the patient's statements of his early (conscious) traumatic experiences: of being severely beaten for minor offenses, of being denied something he wanted very much (a speedometer for his bike—which he then stole), and of his inadequacy because of his small penis. In addition, the patient's self-deprecation comes as a result of failure to meet the extreme parental standards (of morality, obedience, respect, etc.) which he incorporated. Unable to satisfy the demands of an overly severe conscience, his self-image has deteriorated until he perceives himself as a "sex maniac," a "pervert," "a madman."

The extent of the "oral material" in the patient's records (tests, interviews, case records), notably that he is "preoccupied with ideas of sucking," indicates a fixation at the early oral stage of libidinal organization. This autoerotic stage in the development of object love resulted in his high degree of narcissism, passive-dependency, and autistic thinking. It is obvious that his marriage to a dominant female authority figure enabled the patient to remain in the role of an obedient little boy, who does what he is told and cannot be criticized for "doing things on his own."

Appendix B
Basic Concepts in Statistics

Statistics provide us with a method of reporting and evaluating the results of psychological research. Just as the student of business administration must learn accounting in order to derive the full meaning from sales and profit figures, the psychologist must employ statistical methods and formulas in order to draw valid generalizations about human behavior and mental processes from his observations. Complicated as these methods may seem at first glance, they are really ways of reducing a mass of data to terms that the mind can grasp.

The psychologist, like any other scientist, devotes a great deal of his time to making observations. These observations are the raw material with which he works. Having made a series of observations, he tries to integrate them into a theoretical framework or use them to find the solution to a particular problem or the answer to a question. This involves various statistical procedures. The first step is to put the observations into numerical form so that they can be handled statistically. This is done by means of *psychological* measuring devices based upon one of the scales of measurement described in Chapter 2 (pp. 38–39).

Once the psychologist's observations are put into numerical form, they may be used for two major purposes: description and inference. *Descriptive statistics* enable us to describe, organize, and summarize sets of data from observations of groups in a convenient and efficient way. For example, descriptive statistics would enable us to tell how bright a particular group of freshmen are, as a group, and whether they are all at about the same level of ability or vary widely among themselves. Descriptive statistics would also enable us to compare their scores on two or more tests. *Inferential statistics* would enable us to *infer* how typical they are of freshmen in general and would tell us how much confidence we could have in particular inferences that we might make about them.

The Use of Descriptive Statistics

Once data have been collected by means of psychological measurement, descriptive statistics are used to summarize them so that conclusions may be drawn. A descriptive statistic is a number which stands for a series of measurements collected on a group. There are a great many different statistics used in psychological research. The choice of a statistic will depend both upon the measurement scale used and the information wanted.

Since different statistics require different numerical operations, the level of measurement must be a consideration in determining which statistic to use. The higher the level of measurement, the more numerical operations are possible. We have seen that measurement on the nominal scale has only the property of classification. The numbers which represent the various classes are only labels; they do not express quantity. It would therefore be meaningless or even misleading to add them, subtract them, or perform any other numerical operation. Ratio scale data, on the other hand, may be added, subtracted, multiplied, and divided.

The more basic consideration in choosing a statistic is of course what information we want. The three types of information most commonly needed in psychological research are: (a) what is the average or most representative score value (central value), (b) how much do the other scores differ from the average score (variability), and (c) what is the interrelationship between two or more variables, as represented by different sets of scores?

Measures of Central Value

Suppose a psychologist is studying the attributes of various religious groups. He would first have to classify his subjects by religion. His measuring instrument might be a questionnaire asking each subject to state his religion. If he succeeds in putting each subject into one and only one class from a list of several religions, he has measured their religion on the nominal scale. Suppose he now wants to describe his sample by stating the religion of the "average" subject. There are several statistics that indicate a group's average measurement, but since he used only nominal measurement, he must use the central value statistic which is applicable to the nominal scale. This is the *mode*.

The mode. The mode of a group of nominal measurements is the class with the most members. For example, in the table below, the mode is Protestant since more subjects in the group are of the Protestant religion than any other religion.

Religion	Number of Subjects
1. Protestant	88 mode
2. Catholic	37
3. Jewish	17
4. Other	5

Since a table such as this shows how the individuals are distributed among the various classes, it is called a *distribution*. We often refer to a group of measurements as a distribution; when they are arranged in order from highest to lowest frequency, the array is called a *frequency distribution*.

The median. If we have at least ordinal measurement—that is, if the classifications can be put in order so that each class represents more of what we are measuring than those classes following it—another central value statistic may be used to describe the group.

Suppose we wanted to summarize the ranks of a group of army officers attending a military conference. By noting the insignia on their shoulders we could measure their ranks. Since these measurements can be put in order, we have measurement on the ordinal scale. In this table every rank is higher than the ranks below it and lower than the ranks above it.

Rank	Number of Cases
7. General	2
6. Colonel	3
5. Lieutenant Colonel	6
4. Major	9
3. Captain	10 median
2. First Lieutenant	8
1. Second Lieutenant	12 mode
	50

Higher numbers have been used to label higher ranks to preserve this order. These numbers are arbitrary in some respects; we might just as well have used 99 for General, 98 for Colonel, and so on down to Second Lieutenant. As long as the higher of two numbers always stands for the higher of the two ranks, the ordinal property is preserved.

A measure of central value that we can use for these data is the *median*. The median is the number which splits the distribution in half, so that half the cases are higher and half are lower. Since there are 50 cases altogether, the median is the rank which 25 cases are below and 25 are above. We see from the table that 20 officers are First Lieutenant or below and 20 are Major or higher. Since it is impossible to split the distribution exactly in half, we come as close to it as possible and say the median is somewhere in Rank 3—Captain.

If we wished, we could also use the mode as a measure of central value. The mode of this distribution of measurements is 1, since there are more second lieutenants than any other rank. The choice between these two statistics will depend upon what information is wanted. If we use the mode to represent all members of the group, we will be exactly right more times than if we use any other value. However, if we want the central value which will be too high as often as it is too low, we will choose the median. To state this another way, suppose we knew only that an officer was a member of this group and we wanted to guess his rank. If we used the mode, we would have the highest probability of being exactly right. If we used the median, the probability of guessing too low would be the same as the probability of guessing too high.

The mean. If measurement is on the interval scale or higher, still a third measure of central value may be used. This is the *mean*.[1] The mean is calculated by adding together all the measurements and dividing by the number of cases.

If we want to know the average verbal comprehension ability of a group of high-school students, we can begin by measuring their verbal comprehension with a test. If a test has been carefully constructed, we usually assume that it yields measurements on an interval scale. Here, we will assume that equal differences in test scores stand for equal differences in verbal comprehension. Suppose the scores on the test, arranged in order from highest to lowest, are as follows:

Student	Verbal Comprehension Score
John	20
Mary	18
Shirley	18
Peter	17
Alice	16
Nancy	13 ⎫ mean
Henry	13 ⎭
Diane	12
Douglas	11
Sam	11
Harvey	10
Jane	10
Barbara	10
David	9
Roger	7
	Sum = 195

The first step in calculating the mean is to add all the scores. The sum of all the scores is denoted by the symbol, ΣX, which is read, "sum of the X's." The capital Greek letter *sigma* (Σ) stands for "the sum of . . . ." The capital letter X stands for each of the scores in turn. By adding up all the scores, we find that $\Sigma X = 195$.

The second step in computing the mean is to

[1]The exact term is *arithmetic mean*, as distinguished from other means, such as the geometric mean. Since these other statistics are seldom used in psychology, *arithmetic mean* is usually abbreviated to *mean;* or M or $\bar{X}$.

divide ΣX by N, the total number of cases. The formula for the mean is:

$$\text{mean (or } \bar{X}) = \frac{\Sigma X}{N}$$

where $\bar{X}$ stands for the mean. This formula is read, "The *mean* is equal to the *sum* of the X's divided by the *number* of X's." Since there are 15 scores altogether, we can calculate the mean as follows:

$$\bar{X} = \frac{\Sigma X}{N} = \frac{195}{15} = 13$$

Thus, the mean of the above scores is 13. That is, the average verbal comprehension of this group of students is 13.

The verbal comprehension scores are interval data, so the mode, median, or mean *can* be used. Each of these central value statistics represents a different kind of "best guess," as is clear in the Ψ Close-up on page 47.

If our purpose is to be exactly right most often, we would use the mode. More persons had a score of 10 than any other score, so 10 is the mode. In guessing the scores of individuals in the group, we would be exactly right 3 times if we guessed each student's score at 10. Of course, we would be wrong by some amount in guessing the scores of the other 12 students. In this case, too, we would usually be guessing too low, since 10 students have scores above the mode and only 2 have scores below it. If we wanted a guess that was too high as often as it was too low, we would use the median score, 12. This guess would be exactly right only once, but would be high 7 times and low 7 times.

Thus the median is in the "middle" of a distribution of scores in the sense that the same *number* of scores (though not the same *value* or *weight* of scores) are on both sides of it. But suppose that the three high scorers, John, Mary, and Shirley, had each gotten a score of 100. The median would still be 12, but this guess would be 88 points too low in three cases. The median would be too low the same *number* of times as it was too high, but the total *amount* by which it was too low would be much greater than the amount by which it was too high. If we want a guess that takes the amount of error into consideration, we will use the mean. The mean score of the fifteen students on verbal comprehension is 13. If we guess each student's verbal comprehension score at 13, the total amount by which this guess is too low will be equal to the total amount by which it is too high.

Central value statistics describing a group are the best guesses we can make about any member of that group. The mode is the guess most often right, the median has an equal chance of being too high or too low, and the mean may be too high by the same total amount as it may be too low.

Measures of Variability

Human beings differ, as we have seen throughout this text. They differ in the way they respond to stimuli. They differ in their ability to learn and to perceive.

The purpose of a variability statistic is to tell us how spread out a distribution is. Stated another way, it tells us how well or how poorly a central value statistic represents all of the scores in a distribution. If all the scores are closely bunched together, each score is closely represented by a central value statistic such as the mean. But if not, anyone working with the group needs to know it. There are several measures that indicate the variability within a group.

The range. Perhaps the simplest way to get an idea of how spread out a distribution is, is to find the *range*. The range is the difference between the highest and lowest scores. In the table of verbal comprehension scores, the highest score is 20 and the lowest is 7. Therefore, the range is $20-7=13$.

Variability statistics, like central value statistics, must be appropriate to the level of measurement used. The range requires *interval* measurement, since subtraction is involved. On a scale without equal units, subtraction would be meaningless.

The range is a relatively uninformative measure of variability, since it depends on only two of the scores. Suppose one student had made a score of 3 on the verbal comprehension test. This single score would have increased the range by nearly one third. A variability measure, or any other statistic that uses all of the scores in a distribution, will give more information than one that uses just a few.

The standard deviation. With measurements on the interval scale, the most common measure of variability is the standard deviation. Every score in the distribution is used in its computation. More specifically, it is based upon each score's deviation from the mean. A score's deviation from the mean is denoted by the small letter x. Mathematically it may be expressed by the formula:

$$x = X - \bar{X}$$

which means, "The *deviation* is equal to the *score* minus the *mean*."

At first thought, it might seem that a good way to measure variability, using all the scores, would be simply to average all these deviations. To do so, however, would prove disappointing. Remember, the deviation of a score is equal to that score minus the mean. If a score is above the mean it will have a positive deviation. If it is below the mean it will have a negative deviation. We have seen that the total amount by which the mean is too low (the positive deviation) is equal to the amount by which the mean is too high (the negative deviation). Thus if all the plus and minus deviations are added together, they cancel out, and the result is zero. Mathematically,

$$\Sigma x = 0$$

This will be true of any group of scores. To avoid this, each deviation can be squared (multiplied by itself) before adding.[2] Since a positive number multiplied by a positive number results in a positive number, and a negative number multiplied by a negative number also results in a positive number, all squared deviations must be positive, and the average of these *squared* deviations can easily be obtained:

$$s^2 = \frac{\Sigma x^2}{N}$$

The symbol s^2 is called the *variance*. The above formula is read, "The *variance* is equal to the *sum of the squared deviations* divided by the *number of cases*."

The reason that the variance is shown as the square of a quantity is to reflect the fact that all the

---

[2]There are other, more mathematically sophisticated reasons for squaring the deviations, but a discussion of them is beyond the scope of this book.

deviations were squared before averaging. The variance is therefore expressed in terms of a different unit from the original measurements. If the original measurements were verbal comprehension scores, the variance would be in terms of squared verbal comprehension scores. Since this is at best an unwieldy concept, the square root of the variance is often used as a measure of variability. This is called the *standard deviation*, and its symbol is the letter *s*. It is computed by the formula:

$$s = \sqrt{\frac{\Sigma x^2}{N}}$$

The standard deviation, then, is in terms of the same units as the measurements from which it was derived.

The steps used to compute the standard deviation are given in the figure. The verbal comprehension test scores are used for this example. ■

The mean score is 13, and the standard deviation is 3.8. These two statistics give us a summary of the fifteen scores. The mean gives us a representative figure for the level of the group as a whole and the standard deviation a representative figure for all the deviations, because it indicates how closely the scores cluster around the mean.

Standard scores. We have seen that measures of variability are useful ways of summarizing the individual differences in a group. They can also serve to establish a standard unit. Suppose that the high-

■ **VARIANCE AND STANDARD DEVIATION**

Student	Score on verbal comprehension test	Deviation from mean	Deviation squared
	X	x	x^2
John	20	7	49
Mary	18	5	25
Shirley	18	5	25
Peter	17	4	16
Alice	16	3	9
Nancy	13 ⎫ mean	0	0
Henry	13 ⎭	0	0
Diane	12	−1	1
Douglas	11	−2	4
Sam	11	−2	4
Harvey	10	−3	9
Jane	10	−3	9
Barbara	10	−3	9
David	9	−4	16
Roger	7	−6	36
Sum	195	0	212

1. Add all the scores. This sum is called ΣX.

$$\Sigma X = 195$$

2. Divide this sum by the number of scores (N). This is the mean, $\bar{X}$.

$$\bar{X} = \frac{\Sigma X}{N} = \frac{195}{15} = 13$$

3. Subtract the mean from each score to find each deviation, x.

$$x = X - \bar{X} \text{ (See the column headed "Deviation")}$$

4. Square each deviation. That is, multiply each deviation by itself.

$$x^2 = (X - \bar{X})^2$$
(See the column headed "Deviation squared")

5. Add all the squared deviations. The result is designated as Σx^2.

$$\Sigma x^2 = 212$$

6. Divide this sum by the number of scores to find the variance, s^2.

$$s^2 = \frac{\Sigma x^2}{N} = \frac{212}{15} = 14.13$$

7. Find the square root of the variance. This is the standard deviation, s.

$$s = \sqrt{\frac{\Sigma x^2}{N}} = \sqrt{14.13} = 3.8$$

school students who took the verbal comprehension test were also given a spelling test. We might then wonder if a student is as good in verbal comprehension as he is in spelling. Suppose the means on the tests and the scores of one student, John, are as follows:

Test	Mean Scores	John's Scores
Verbal comprehension	13	20
Spelling	44	48

We know that John is above average on both tests. But we do not know *how much* above average. We cannot compare his two scores because we do not know whether one point on one test is equivalent to one point on the other test. Chances are that it is not. Suppose that one point on the spelling test is worth 2 points on the verbal comprehension test. This would mean that John's 4 points above the mean on spelling would be equivalent to 8 points above the mean on verbal comprehension. Since John was only 7 points above average on verbal comprehension, we would know that his spelling score was higher. On the other hand, if the units on the two tests are equivalent, he is better in verbal comprehension.

In order to relate the units on one test to the units on the other, we can make use of our measures of variability. We know that the standard deviation of the verbal comprehension scores is 3.8. John's score of 20 is 7 points above the mean, or almost 2 standard deviations above it (1.8 to be exact). Suppose we computed the standard deviation of the distribution of scores on the spelling test, and found it to be equal to 4. This would mean that John was one standard deviation above the mean in spelling, while he was almost two standard deviations above the mean in verbal comprehension. We could then say that John did better in verbal comprehension than in spelling.

The standard deviation, then, can be used as a unit for comparing a person's standing on two tests. Any individual's deviation from the mean can be expressed in terms of this unit. Scores expressed this way are called *standard scores* and are given the symbol z. John's score, at 1.8 standard deviations above the mean, gives him a standard score of 1.8.

If John had made the mean score, 13, his z score would be 0. If he had scored below the mean, his z score would be a negative number.

Often two different tests will be of different length or difficulty or will use different units of measurement with the result that scores on the two tests are not comparable. If someone got 82 on one test and 450 on another, for example, you would have no idea just looking at the scores whether one was better than the other. On the other hand, his standard scores on the two tests would be expressed in comparable units—standard deviations—so that you could tell at once whether one was better than the other.

What a standard score gives us is a person's position in the group in which he took the test. Therefore, if we compared John's standard score in verbal comprehension with his standard score in spelling, we would be answering the question, "Is John's *relative* performance in spelling better or worse than his *relative* performance in verbal comprehension?"

The standard deviation can be computed only if there is a measurement scale of equal units. The standard deviation, like the arithmetic mean, may therefore be used only when measurement is at least at the interval scale.

Measures of Correlation

Up to this point we have been discussing statistics which describe a single set of measurements. Psychology is usually concerned with many different variables, hence with many different sets of measurements. A question frequently asked in psychological research is: to what extent are two sets of scores related? For example, if we gave a verbal comprehension test and a spelling test to the same group of individuals, we might wonder to what extent persons who scored high on one test also scored high on the other. One way to find out would be to write down the names of all the persons scoring above the mean on the verbal comprehension test and see how many of them scored above the mean on the spelling test. This would give us a rough idea of the *correlation* between the two tests. If most of the high scorers on one test scored high on the other test too, we would say there was a high *positive correlation*. If most of the high scorers on one scored low on the other, we would say there was a high *negative correlation*.

Correlation coefficients and what they mean. Let us now approach an understanding of correlation by building on our knowledge of standard scores (*z* scores). Suppose that all the scores on the spelling and verbal comprehension tests are converted to standard scores, and assume further that each individual's *z* score on the spelling test is the same as his *z* score on the verbal comprehension test. In such a case, the tests are said to have a perfect positive correlation. This result is shown in the graph below, in which each dot represents an individual, and the scores of any individual can be read from the horizontal and vertical axes. For example, John (the circled dot) made a *z* score of 1.8 on both tests. With a perfect correlation, any individual's score on one test can be predicted exactly if we know his score on the other test.

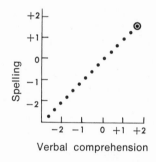

Suppose now that every individual who scored high on verbal comprehension scored low, by an equal amount, on spelling. That is, everyone was as poor on one test as he was good on the other; the best speller was worst on verbal comprehension, and vice versa. A graph of this result follows:

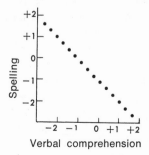

In both of these examples, scores on one test were perfectly related to scores on the other. At the other

extreme, suppose the scores are completely unrelated. In this case the best speller might be good, average, or poor on verbal comprehension. Knowledge of an individual's spelling ability would tell us nothing about his verbal comprehension. The graph of such a result might look like this:

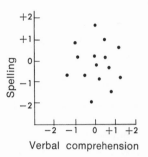

Often two variables are correlated, but not perfectly correlated. In a graph of such a relationship, the dots are not in a straight line, nor do they form a circle; their pattern is oval. The flatter the oval—the nearer it is to a straight line—the higher the correlation.

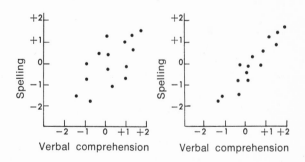

As you saw in Chapter 2, the amount by which two variables are correlated is expressed in the *coefficient of correlation* (*r*). In computing a correlation, *z* scores are used according to the following formula:

$$r = \frac{\Sigma z_x z_y}{N}$$

According to this formula, "The correlation coefficient is equal to the sum of each person's *z* score on one test multiplied by his *z* score on the other test, divided by the number of people." The actual calculation looks complicated but is simple and straightforward. The steps in computing a correlation using the spelling and verbal comprehension test scores are shown in the figure on page 671. • In this case, z_x is the standard score for the verbal comprehension test and z_y is the standard score for the spelling test.

Correlation coefficients, as you also saw in Chapter 2, can range from +1 (perfect positive correlation) through 0 (no correlation) to −1 (perfect negative correlation). In actual practice, perfect correlations, either positive or negative, are rare.

The correlation coefficient in prediction. Statisticians have determined what percentage of those who fall in the upper half of the distribution on one trait can be expected to fall in the upper half of the distribution on another when there is a given correlation between two normally distributed traits (Taylor & Russell, 1939). Below are representative correlation coefficients and their corresponding percentages:

	Percent in Better Half on Test A Who Will Fall:	
Correlation Coefficient	in better half on Test B	in worse half on Test B
.00	50	50
.05	52	48
.10	53	47
.20	56	44
.30	60	40
.40	63	37
.50	67	33
.60	70	30
.70	75	25
.80	80	20
.90	86	14
.95	90	10
1.00	100	0

As you can see from the table, the accuracy of prediction varies with the degree of correlation between the two variables being considered. For example, if you know that the correlation between two tests is .90, you can predict that 86 percent of those who were in the upper half on the verbal comprehension test will also be in the upper half on the spelling test. But 14 percent will not be, and there is always

the possibility that the particular individual you are concerned about is among this 14 percent. Thus in predicting a particular individual's score, the most you can do is indicate a probability. In this case, you can say his chances of being in the upper half on the second test are 86 out of 100.

The Use of Statistical Inference

The greatest value of statistical methodology lies in the fact that it allows us to generalize. Psychologists do not usually wish to confine their conclusions to the specific groups which they select for observation or experimentation. Instead, they hope to find relationships which will apply to much larger groups or to human beings in general. This procedure of drawing general conclusions by studying samples is called *statistical inference*. In developing general theories of human behavior it would be impossible to study all human beings under all conditions. The experimental psychologist will, therefore, deduce a specific hypothesis from a theory and design an experiment to test it on a sample. If the results come out as hypothesized, he has increased his confidence in the validity of the theory. If the results are contrary to the hypothesis, he has reason to suspect the validity of the theory.

Statistical inference is sometimes used in investigations which are not concerned with theory, but which attempt to find the answer to a specific practical question. This is the area of applied research. A common example of statistical inference in applied research is the public opinion poll. The accuracy of the pollsters in making predictions of group behavior after interviewing only a small sample of the group is an example of the power of statistical inference techniques.

The basic steps in statistical inference, whether theoretical or applied, are as follows:

1. Define a *population*. The population (sometimes called a *universe*) is the whole group in which the researcher is ultimately interested. It may be as general as all human beings, or even all living organisms. It may be as specific as all freshmen in a certain college or all registered voters in a certain congressional district.

2. Draw a *sample* from the population. The sam-

CORRELATION

	Verbal Comprehension		Spelling		
	X	$z_x=\dfrac{X-\bar{X}}{s_x}$	Y	$z_y=\dfrac{Y-\bar{Y}}{s_y}$	$z_x z_y$
John	20	1.8	48	0.8	1.44
Mary	18	1.3	45	0.2	0.26
Shirley	18	1.3	45	0.2	0.26
Peter	17	1.1	57	2.5	2.75
Alice	16	0.8	39	−0.9	−0.72
Nancy	13	0.0	42	−0.4	0.0
Henry	13	0.0	52	1.5	0.0
Diane	12	−0.3	43	−0.2	0.06
Douglas	11	−0.5	47	0.6	−0.30
Sam	11	−0.5	44	0.0	0.0
Harvey	10	−0.8	41	−0.6	0.48
Jane	10	−0.8	37	−1.3	1.04
Barbara	10	−0.8	43	−0.2	0.16
David	9	−1.1	40	−0.8	0.88
Roger	7	−1.6	37	−1.3	2.08
					$\Sigma z_x z_y = 8.39$

1. Compute the means and the standard deviations for both of the variables being correlated.

$$\bar{X}=13 \qquad s_x=3.8$$

(See p. 667)

$$\bar{Y}=44 \qquad s_y=5.3$$

(Obtained in the same manner as $\bar{X}$)

2. Convert each score to a standard score by subtracting its mean and dividing by its standard deviation.

(See columns headed z_x and z_y)

3. Multiply the two standard scores together for each individual in the group.

(See the column headed $z_x z_y$)

4. Find the arithmetic mean of these products by adding them together and dividing by the number of individuals.

$$r=\frac{\Sigma z_x z_y}{N}=\frac{8.39}{15}=.56$$

Conclusion: There is a moderate positive correlation.

ple is the group of subjects upon which the research is conducted.

3. *Measure* the sample. This is the actual research or experimentation. Depending upon the nature of the research, this measurement might be as simple as asking the subjects whom they intend to vote for in the next election. On the other hand, it might be extremely complex, perhaps including dividing the sample into several experimental groups, exposing each group to different experimental conditions, and measuring their responses to these conditions.

4. Compute one or more *descriptive statistics*. As we have seen, descriptive statistics summarize a series of measurements.

5. Use the descriptive statistics to make *inferences* about the population.

Sampling

Sampling, as you might surmise, is the process of drawing a sample from a population. Whatever sam-

pling procedure is used, it must be one which assures that the sample is truly representative of the population. More specifically, the sample must represent, within known limits, all characteristics of the population which are related to the experimental problem. Otherwise, the sample is called a *biased* one.

There are many methods of sampling, the most common of which is *random sampling*. In random sampling there are two requirements: (a) each member of the population must have the same probability of appearing in the sample; (b) the probability of each member being selected must be independent of whether or not any other member is selected. An example of random sampling is the choosing of the winners in a well-run lottery. All the tickets (the population) are thoroughly mixed, and the winners (the sample) are selected blindly. Technically, random sampling requires the replacement of each winning ticket before drawing the next, so that it is possible for the same ticket to be drawn more than once. If the population is large, however, this refinement is insignificant. A less cumbersome method of random sampling is to assign consecutive numbers to each member of the population and then select numbers from a table in which all numbers appear in random order. These tables are so constructed that the probability of any number appearing in any position on the list is the same. One such table is published in book form (Rand, 1955). Although such a book does not make very interesting reading, it is of great value to researchers.

Once a sample is drawn, measurements are taken and descriptive statistics computed. Such statistics may then serve as estimates of their counterparts in the population as a whole. These counterparts are called *parameters*.

Even the best estimate of a parameter contains a certain margin of error. It is important to know just how great this error is. Such knowledge is obtained by means of a mathematical model. A model is an abstraction which is used to describe real world phenomena. The model most often used by psychologists in this case is called the *normal distribution*.

The Normal Distribution

As explained in Chapter 11, a very typical finding in psychological research is that most individuals cluster near the mean of a distribution of scores. The farther from the mean a given score is, the fewer individuals will have that score. On page 452 we showed how the scores of 1000 persons selected at random and administered a test of some psychological characteristic would probably be distributed.

We can identify three properties of this distribution of scores: (a) the number of persons with a given score diminishes as the distance of that score from the mean increases; (b) the distribution is symmetrical about the mean; (c) the mode, the median, and the mean are equal.

This frequency distribution can be approximated by a *bell-shaped curve* that encloses all the scores. Because frequency distributions of psychological measurements are so often closely approximated by the bell-shaped curve, it is convenient to take this curve as a model, or ideal case. This model, the *normal distribution*, is a generalization about frequency distributions, just as "50-50," for example, is a

generalization about the odds in tossing coins. If a number of coins are tossed, the "model" expectation is that half will turn up heads. This is seldom exactly true, but as more coins are tossed, the model is more closely approximated. The same thing is true also for the normal distribution: a perfect normal curve is never obtained from a sample of measurements, although the larger the sample, the more closely it will approximate the normal curve. An infinitely large population would be required to fit perfectly the mathematical definition of the curve. When obtained measurements closely approximate the normal curve, the assumption is often made that the sample has been drawn from a population that *does* fit the model exactly.

The normal distribution is an extremely useful model. If the distribution of a sample is approximately normal and we know its mean and standard deviation, we can construct a curve that supposedly will show what the distribution would be in the whole population from which the sample was drawn.

Approximately two thirds of the scores are within one standard deviation from the mean. Thus in the case of IQs, about two thirds of the area under the curve is between IQ values of 84 and 116, since the standard deviation is equal to 16.

Less than 3/10 of 1 percent of the scores are farther than three standard deviations from the mean. For this reason, the range of six standard deviations —three below the mean and three above it—is taken as representing the "practical" limits of a normal distribution. Unless a sample is extremely large, we will seldom find scores which exceed these limits.

Questions Answered by Inferential Statistics

Whenever you collect two groups of scores in randomly drawn samples, you are likely to find that their means differ to some extent, due to the operation of chance factors. If you flip a coin 1000 times, you should get heads approximately 500 times. But on only ten trials, you might not get exactly half heads. Thus when you observe only a small sample of data, you need some way of determining whether your observations are due to chance or can be attributed to some real, nonrandom event or process that is operating.

The procedures of statistical inference introduce order into any attempt to draw conclusions that go beyond the observations made on particular samples. Some of the questions that can be answered by statistical inference are: (a) whether the sample of scores you have is really representative of some specified population, (b) whether an obtained difference between means of different samples is large enough that you can conclude they are probably drawn from different populations, and (c) whether the variance in scores *between* groups that have received different experimental treatments is greater than the scattering of the scores *within* each group. If two groups have different means but overlap a great deal, the difference between the two means may be due to chance rather than to the experimental treatments.

Every time you compare the scores of an experimental group with those of a control group at the end of an experiment, you are looking to see whether they are now representatives of two different populations as a result of the experimental treatment. The more different their new means and the less overlap there is, the more confidence you can have that there is a real difference and that you would find it again if you were to replicate the experiment with two more samples from the original population. The more often and the more consistently you find the difference, the bigger it is, the larger your samples, and the greater your between-group differences, as compared with your within-group differences, the more likely your statistical test will be to show that the difference is one in which you can have confidence.

Various statistical tests are available to use in answering the general questions posed above and the particular questions being raised by a given researcher. We can only name a few common ones here and indicate what they do. For example, the most common test for comparing the frequencies of various possible events that you actually find with the frequencies that would be predicted is called the *Chi-square* (χ^2) test. The test for comparing the differences between two sets of scores when small groups of subjects (fewer than thirty) have been used is called the *t-test*. The test for comparing between-group variability with within-group variability is called the *analysis of variance* or *F-test*.

This short chapter has been an extremely quick survey of concepts normally covered in a first course in statistics. Only the highlights have been covered, and these very briefly. Nonetheless, a general grasp of the material presented here will be of great help in interpreting the results of much published psychological research.

Appendix C
Theories of Learning

Historically, theories of learning have generally moved from broad attempts to offer an explanation for all the phenomena of learning toward theories which attempt to give coherence to one particular subset of experimental findings in the field of learning —for example, the role of spaced practice periods in facilitating learning. All we will do here is summarize briefly several of the major theoretical approaches, past and present. Many if not most of the terms and concepts will already be familiar to you from your study of Chapter 5.

Associative Theories

Several theories of learning have been proposed which differ sharply in detail and emphasis but agree in regarding learning as a process of relating formerly separate elements.

Thorndike's Reinforcement Theory

We have seen that for Thorndike, learning involved the gradual "stamping in" of S-R connections. Thus he has often been called a *connectionist*. He rejected the "law of exercise" in favor of the "law of effect" in explaining how the connections are strengthened. It was the consequences of the response—the events which followed it—which Thorndike considered significant in affecting its probability of occurrence on the next trial. He believed that satisfying events *strengthened S-R connections* and annoying events *weakened* them. Punishment, by making behavior more variable, would thereby weaken learning. This theory, based on the hedonistic philosophy of Jeremy Bentham, is also reflected both in the extensive use of the principle of *drive reduction* in the Hullian approach and in the Skinnerians' central dependence on *reinforcement*.

Watsonian Behaviorism

J. B. Watson, the precursor of behaviorist tradition, emphatically rejected the technique of *introspection*. He felt that the then-prevailing study of the structure of *experience* should be discarded in favor of a study of what organisms do—how they behave. In part, behaviorism rested upon the foundation of the conditioned reflex, discovered by Pavlov. In its emphasis on learning and the importance of the environment in shaping behavior, it also challenged the concept of "instinct," which had dominated American psychology in the early 1900s.

Although Watson was certainly a connectionist in his conception of what was learned, he did not refer to reinforcement as a condition for learning. According to his view, responses which have occurred recently and frequently are most likely to occur when the same stimulus is presented again.

Guthrie and Contiguity Theory

Like Watson, E. R. Guthrie emphasized the critically important role of temporal contiguity between a stimulus event and its elicited response. He believed that learning occurs regardless of whether reinforcement is given, so long as the conditioned stimulus and the response occur close together. What is learned is based upon the principle of recency; the last response made will be the one repeated. Reward acts upon learning only indirectly, by changing the situation and defining the termination of an act; it is not essential for learning to take place.

Hull's Formal Theory of Learning

The best example of a formal, comprehensive theory of learning is the system formulated by Clark Hull. Hull attempted to construct a theoretical system which: (a) could account for a vast amount of empirical data that had accumulated; (b) derived many theorems from a relatively small number of postulates; (c) was specific and explicit enough to permit direct translation of hypotheses into empirical tests; (d) was open to revision on the basis of new evidence, empirical proof, and further speculation; and (e) had as one of its goals quantification through the use of mathematically stated formulas. He intended his final theory to be broad in application, ranging from simple trial-and-error learning in animals to complex social learning in human beings, but his death in 1952 left his plan unfinished.

From 1943, when Hull published his first theoretical system (*Principles of Behavior*) to his last statement (1952) published shortly before his death, the theory underwent continuous revision, test, and expansion. From a basic set of 17 postulates, one could deduce 133 theorems, or statements, about the nature of the learning process. The Hullian theory can be summarized as follows:

1. It is assumed that what is learned is a connection between a stimulus and a response. This unit of learning, an intervening variable, is called *habit strength*. It is represented by the symbol $_sH_R$, in which H stands for "habit" and the subscripts s and R simply stand for the particular stimulus and the response being discussed.

2. Reinforcement is regarded as a necessary condition for learning. For a response to increase in strength, it must be followed immediately by a goal substance. It is assumed that *reinforcers gain their effectiveness by reducing the level of existing drive*. Thus this theory has been called a *drive-reduction* theory.

3. The learned connection between a stimulus and a response ($_sH_R$) is assumed to increase in magnitude gradually and continuously as a function of reinforced practice and to represent a relatively permanent change in behavior.

4. Performance of a learned response may be measured through its amplitude, speed, frequency of occurrence, and/or resistance to extinction. Performance reflects a more transient phenomenon than does learning and is described in terms of the "excitatory potential" of a stimulus to evoke a particular available response ($_sE_R$). Factors which influence whether or not a learned habit will be performed on a particular occasion include the level of drive (D), and the magnitude of the goal or reinforcer (K). Detracting from the tendency to perform the habit are factors like the amount of effort and fatigue involved in responding. These factors are summed up in the term *reactive inhibition* (I_R). Thus the tendency of a given stimulus to evoke a particular learned response is a function (f) of the habit strength of that connection multiplied by level of drive and magnitude of reinforcer, minus reactive inhibition. These relationships are expressed in the formula:

$$_sE_R = f \, (_sH_R \cdot D \cdot K) - I_R$$

Kenneth Spence, Frank Logan, and others continued to develop and refine this formulation after Hull's death.

Skinner's Nontheoretical Approach

The strictly formal, deductive system of Hull contrasts sharply with the approach taken by B. F. Skinner, who first developed the concept of operant conditioning. Here little or no use is made of intervening variables, since inner processes are not thought to play any part in the causal chain; behavior is assumed to be entirely under the control of the environment. Thus the experimenter is concerned only with observable, manipulable variables.

For a Skinnerian the basic issue is to discover what reinforcers sustain and control responding, rather than which stimuli evoke it. Reinforcement is defined not theoretically in terms of its drive-reducing properties but *empirically*: reinforcement has occurred when the probability of a response has been increased by the stimulus that has followed it. A reinforcer is any stimulus which, following a response, increases its probability of occurrence on the next occasion.

Both Hull's and Skinner's approaches dispense with consciousness and are anti-subjective; thus they rely upon extensive use of animals as subjects. In fact, Hull went so far as to suggest that the tendency to impute motives and reasons to subjects in conditioning experiments should be overcome by conceptual use of a robot model to provide the "suggested prophylaxis against anthropormorphic subjectivism."

Cognitive Theories of Learning

The theoretical approaches described above are primarily analytical, stressing as they do units of learning—S-R connections—and discrete effects of reinforcers. They allow for great precision in the analysis of simplified learning situations (especially involving animals), but they do not appear to do justice to the complexity involved in human learning, problem solving, reasoning, and learning one's native language because they minimize or ignore higher mental processes.

Gestalt Theory

An alternative approach is presented by the cognitive theories of learning of the Gestalt psychologists and by Tolman's purposive behaviorism. The Gestalt psychologists of the Berlin School (Max Wertheimer, Kurt Koffka, Wolfgang Kohler, and later Kurt Lewin) were interested primarily in the phenomena of human perception and thus in the experience of the subject as well as in external, observable conditions. However, the underlying principles of perception were easily carried over to a consideration of the learning process. In a very provocative book, *Productive Thinking* (1945), Max Wertheimer distinguished between the learning of a series of "correct solutions," as typified by the atomistic "connections" of the behaviorists, and learning based upon understanding. He maintained that S-R theories are adequate to handle situations of rote learning, but that productive thinking in human subjects involves the learning of underlying processes, structures, forms, and essential configurations (*Gestalten*) which can still be recognized even though all the particular elements change, as when a melody is transposed to a different key. Such learning is a process of making new discriminations or reorganizing material into a new pattern. It is essentially a matter of acquiring *information* (including concepts and generalizations) rather than specific *responses*.

Purposive Behaviorism

E. C. Tolman's theory represents an attempt at a synthesis of several of the major lines of development described above. While he was an objective behaviorist and was not concerned with conscious experience, as were the Gestaltists, nevertheless he focused upon overall patterns—"molar" rather than "molecular" behavior. According to his view, learning involves not the development of S-R bonds, but rather changes in cognitions as a result of experience with external stimuli. "Cognitions" are intervening variables built out of perceptions of and beliefs or knowledge about one's environment.

Tolman's theory shares with Hull's the important role attributed to needs and goals, but goes beyond what would be acceptable to a Hullian in the relationships he postulates between them. According to Tolman's view, needs produce demands for goals, and rewards lead to *object-cathexis* (a term borrowed from Freud), which is the tendency to seek certain goals and avoid others.

Tolman's approach could also be distinguished as one in which S-S connections are learned. He talks of "cognitive maps" and "sign-Gestalt-expectations." Organisms learn to expect an environment organized in meaningful patterns; thus they behave purposively. They learn that some stimuli are signs that certain events will follow or are usually associated with other stimuli; thus stimuli not only function as response elicitors but also supply information, as cues or signs. These signs are part of a whole pattern that includes memories from past experience as well as current perceptions. Thus learned behavior is not merely the automatic, blind emission of responses which have been associated with particular stimuli and reward contingencies; it always involves implicit and explicit goals and also hypotheses and expectations about how to achieve them. Above all, learning is purposive and rationally directed.

Cognitive theories thus are concerned with the learning of information and generalizations, as well as particular responses. Because of their emphasis on the importance of the whole in shaping the parts and their use of analogies from field theory, as developed by physicists, these theories are sometimes called *holistic*, while stimulus-response theories as a group are called *associationistic* because of their assumption that learning consists in the formation of connections between previously separate elements. The cognitive theories are also called *centralist* because they emphasize organizing processes within the individual, while the stimulus-response theories are called *peripheralist* because they emphasize stimulation and reinforcement from the environment rather than any events occurring in the nervous system or experience of the learner.

Current Trends in Theories of Learning

These theories have generated considerable research, as well as heated controversy. Attempts to perform critical experiments to prove one theory over another have repeatedly failed because of lack of specificity of the conditions necessary for refutation. Because of this and because of the vast accumulation of data pertinent to many different problem areas within learning, current approaches are generally less grandiose in scope. Psychologists no longer argue about how many kinds of learning there really are or whether one formulation can ever encompass all the necessary and sufficient conditions for all cases of learning. Investigators have become more aware of the complexity of even simple organisms and the lack of clarity and consistency in the basic concepts of "stimulus," "response," and "reinforcement."

The shift away from grand theories of learning has been accompanied by a parallel movement away from the analysis of relatively simple situations with subhuman species toward a broader concern with information processing. Thus investigations of learning now are more likely to be centered around the study of memory, with its storage and retrieval problems, and around issues in language acquisition. And though covert cognitive variables such as imagery are

under intensive investigation, they are being studied by way of objective dependent measures, such as latency of reaction time, instead of by self-reports or other subjective data.

Modern learning theorists seem to fall into two camps. Some are still concerned with basic principles of learning, but they look for model experimental situations (paradigms) in which a large body of behavioral data can be generated by the systematic manipulation of various parameters of the situation. An instance would be the study of free recall, in which there would be a consideration of all the variables that might influence both the quantity and the form of the recall. In such research, the attempt to integrate and find patterns of consistency in relationships usually occurs *after* the stage of data collection, as an attempt to order what has been observed. This is in contrast with the earlier use of theory *a priori* to direct the search for the relevant variables, with the data providing the test of the adequacy of the theory. It is also more likely to lead to miniature theories and to mathematical models than to broad-scale, all-embracing theories.

The second modern development in learning theory is the application of traditional theories to problems of behavior modification, especially to therapeutic attempts at changing the contingencies maintaining pathological responses. Examples of these applications were given in Chapter 15. These modern approaches promise greater precision in eventually relating learning phenomena and principles to what happens in many other forms of behavior, such as attention, perception, language, and motivation, and to the problems of improving maladjustive behavior so that people can more fully enjoy life.

Appendix D
Drug Use and Abuse

There is perhaps no psychological phenomenon which has had a more profound effect on such a broad segment of the population as the use and abuse of psychoactive drugs. Once restricted to the ghetto, to artistic types, and to scientifically curious researchers, "turning on" with marijuana, LSD, amphetamines, heroin, mescaline, and a variety of other drugs has now virtually transcended all class, race, religious, educational, and occupational lines. As investigations of this problem in the armed services reveal its epidemic proportions even there, we learn daily of high-school and even grade-school children dying of overdose or drug-connected suicide and of drug arrests of sons and daughters of judges, congressmen, and prominent entertainers—the wealthy, the influential, the respectable members of society. The drug revolution has not only brought the reported pleasures and dangers of the drugs themselves to many more people; in addition it has ushered in basic social changes in music, dress, philosophical orientation, and ways of relating and interacting, as well as criminal subcultures in new places, communal life, and a host of other correlated effects.

It seems obvious, then, that any text which claims to represent a contemporary view of psychology and life must address itself to this phenomenon. But what is it that students want to know about psychoactive drugs? Would you ask the same questions if you never had taken any, as you would if you were a heavy user? And then, whose opinion is sufficiently well balanced, backed by firsthand knowledge and scientific expertise, to be accepted as a legitimate authority to answer your concerns?

Our solution to these questions has been a relatively simple, direct one. First we went into several psychology classes and asked each student to write down the questions he or she would want answered by an authority on drugs. The variation in drug experience among these college students was extreme.

After organizing these questions into a meaningful sequence, we posed them in a personal interview to one of the foremost authorities on the subject, Dr. David Smith, Medical Director and founder of the Haight-Ashbury Free Clinic. Dr. Smith not only has had training in general medicine, toxology, and criminology but has been on the drug scene in San Francisco since its inception. His clinic has treated over 100,000 young drug users, and he personally has worked with many of them in the clinic and in the streets. He has also studied emerging patterns of drug use in the communes on the West Coast. We believe his frank, considered answers to questions which students like yourself want answered represent the best available opinion on the subject at this time.[1]

What is a psychoactive drug?

A *psychoactive* drug is a drug that affects mental processes. Any such drug has a certain abuse potential. One of the characteristics of this abuse potential is that the individual may use the drug compulsively because of either psychological dependence or physical dependence or both.

In psychological dependence, the individual has a strong emotional need to continue to use the drug for pleasure or for the relief of discomfort. If he can't get the drug, he becomes anxious, but he has no serious physical discomfort.

Almost any psychoactive drug can produce psychological dependence. Nicotine in cigarettes, alcohol, caffeine, marijuana, and amphetamines are drugs that are often involved in psychological dependence.

[1]Those who would like more information may want to see Dr. Smith's books: *The New Social Drug: Cultural, Medical, and Legal Perspectives on Marijuana* (Prentice-Hall, 1970) and *Love Needs Care: The Story of the Haight-Ashbury Free Clinic* (Little, Brown, 1971). The address of the Clinic is 409 Clayton St., San Francisco, California 94117.

Certain drugs can produce physical dependence too. Probably the best known in this latter category are the *narcotics* derived from opium, such as heroin and morphine. With these drugs, prolonged use makes the body physically dependent on the presence of that chemical for continued normal functioning such that if the drug is not present, there is a general physiological reaction called the *abstinence syndrome* that produces great discomfort to the individual. It will continue for several days unless relieved by further administration of the drug.

In certain cases, this withdrawal of the drug may be life-threatening. For example, if one develops physical dependence upon ethyl alcohol or on the barbiturates, which are commonly used as sleeping pills, the abrupt withdrawal from these agents can produce convulsions and even lead to death. With alcohol, the reaction is classically called the *DTs.*

With other drugs that produce physical dependence, such as heroin, withdrawal causes extreme discomfort lasting several days. The individual may have a runny nose, runny eyes, stomach upset, muscle pains—one addict called it like having a bad case of the flu—and rarely does it threaten the individual's life. However, fear of this withdrawal from heroin very often prevents the individual who is addicted to the drug from going through withdrawal, so that he may continue to take the drug long after he has stopped deriving any euphoric effects from it, merely to prevent himself from going through withdrawal.

What does it mean to develop a tolerance for drugs?

Tolerance means that the individual must increase his dose to obtain the same effect. Many psychoactive drugs produce tolerance. This is one of the great difficulties in the self-administration of drugs like heroin, because once the user is addicted, he has to increase his dose. Heroin is tightly controlled by organized crime, and the individual may build his addiction up to a level where he has to spend $50 to $100 a day to procure enough drug to maintain his habit. This is one of the reasons that heroin addicts very often have to involve themselves in a life of crime.

I do not regard psychological dependence on a drug as synonymous with drug abuse. Many individuals are psychologically dependent upon having a cup of coffee every morning before they go to work. If they do not have that cup of coffee, they feel somewhat anxious and distressed during the morning. But such dependence rarely produces health problems, and thus is not regarded as drug abuse. I define *drug abuse* as the use of a drug to the point where it interferes with the individual's health or with his economic or social adjustment.

It is often stated that one drug may lead to another. Probably the most popular of "stepping-stone" theories is that marijuana leads to heroin. There is nothing in marijuana itself that should have any relationship to an opiate like heroin, for marijuana has no narcotic properties and is more like alcohol. Any correlation between marijuana and heroin use most likely results from the fact that both drugs are illegal and are classified by law as narcotics by the state; therefore, an individual who wishes to get marijuana has to go into the criminal subculture in order to purchase his drug. Because of this association, some individuals feel that marijuana should be legalized and removed from the criminal subculture —so that the social association between marijuana and the drugs of higher abuse potential would then be broken.

Other drugs, however, do have a more direct causal relationship to heroin. For example, individuals who abuse amphetamines or other stimulants at high dosage often develop anxiety, nervousness, and paranoia, and then use depressants like the barbiturates or heroin to calm their nerves and help them get to sleep and reduce their paranoia. Almost anyone who abuses the amphetamines eventually gets into the abuse of depressants. Here we see a more direct pharmacological relationship between one drug and another.

In addition, within the same group, drugs may have cross-tolerance. For example, an individual who is addicted to heroin will also have tolerance to morphine, because they are both narcotics. An individual who is addicted to seconal or secobarbital may also use Nembutal or pentobarbital because they are all sedative-hypnotic agents. In this situation, it is not that one drug leads to another, but rather that drugs are interchangeable because they have the same effect; so the individual will use one when another is not available.

What if any, are the positive and negative effects drugs can have on normal personality functioning?

Drugs may have a wide variety of positive and negative effects on personality functioning. If an individual is in a very tense and stressful situation, the use of a psychoactive drug may help relieve his anxiety so that he can work more efficiently. In other cultures, where a high premium is placed on spiritual values, many people think that hallucinogenic drugs have a positive effect on personality because they enhance spiritual or religious experience.

But the same drug that can have a positive effect can also have a very negative effect. While an individual is under the influence of a drug like alcohol or the barbiturates, he may develop disinhibition and behave in a way that he would not behave if he had his normal inhibitions, which limit antisocial behavior. This behavior may have a disruptive effect on his life both at the time and later on. Further, if any individual has a disturbed personality, then the use of a potent drug such as LSD may precipitate a psychosis that might not have occurred had he not used the drug.

Can you describe what is typically meant by the term "expanded consciousness"? Are drugs the only way to get there? What is the evidence relating drug use to creativity (artistic, literary, or scientific)?

One of the characteristics of psychedelic or hallucinogenic drugs like LSD is that they open the mind up to new types of thoughts and sensory inputs and can tend to blur ego boundaries, or the separation of self from environment. An individual under the influence of LSD may say things like "I am one with the Universe," "I am seeing life like I have never seen it before," and so on. Such a drug experience has been described as "expanded consciousness." But it is important to emphasize that one individual may define such a pharmacological effect as "expanded consciousness" and another individual may describe exactly the same effect as "going crazy."

Those who interpret such an experience *positively* tend to feel that drugs enhance their creativity. There is little evidence to indicate that drugs can instill new creative traits that were not already there, but someone who is an artist may report that he has new insights into his art and can perform better after the use of psychedelic chemicals.

Since creative work is generally agreed to be 10 percent inspiration and 90 percent perspiration, an individual who abuses a drug and tries to maintain himself in a continual state of expanded consciousness may never get around to producing anything creative. This is one of the difficulties of drug use: thought processes may be enhanced but motivation for work is impaired. This is probably one reason why many young people are attempting to attain the state of expanded consciousness by using alternate nondrug techniques such as transcendental meditation and Yoga. It appears that a fairly large number of young people searching for expanded consciousness pass through a phase of psychedelic drug use and then stop using drugs altogether, attempting to attain a "natural high" without drugs.

Psychoactive drugs may produce a marked change in behavior, but one cannot predict what this behavioral change will be. For example, one individual may use a central nervous system depressant like alcohol and become very friendly and gregarious, whereas another individual may use exactly the same quantity of alcohol and become hostile, belligerent, and violent. These drugs influence behavior by removing the inhibitions the particular individual usually has.

Other drugs have a more direct effect on behavior. Stimulants like amphetamines can enhance performance over a short period of time, and certain people, such as athletes, truck drivers, and students staying up late at night studying may take drugs like the amphetamines in an attempt to stimulate their performance. However, this stimulation may also lead to irrational behavior, and the individual who is more sensitive may become frightened or paranoid. For the most part, an individual's ability to respond to emergencies is impaired by the use of psychoactive drugs, but again it depends on the dosage of the drug, the personality of the individual, and his social environment.

What is the relationship between being "high" on drugs and responsiveness to others, especially feelings of love, sexual arousal, and hostile aggression?

Drugs may have a profound effect on interpersonal relationships. Individuals who get compulsively involved with a drug may see a serious deterioration as their life becomes more and more centered around psychoactive chemicals. They may lose interest in loved ones, in sex, and in interacting with other people in any way except to obtain drugs. However, individuals who use drugs only for recreation may find that the inhibitions that they normally have in a group situation are relieved and that they can talk and relate to others more freely. This commonly occurs in such situations as cocktail parties or pot parties.

There is very little evidence to document the claim that any of the drugs that we are talking about are true aphrodisiacs in the sense of being able to stimulate sexual behavior or performance. A drug is not going to make you love another individual unless the feelings of love are already there. Depending on the individual, one may see an increase or decrease in sexual arousal or an increase or decrease in hostile aggression. For the most part, it depends less on the drug and more on the personality of the individual and the particular social environment.

How much of the effect of drugs is due to one's expectations about their "power" and to the presence of others?

If an individual *thinks* he is getting a particular psychoactive drug, he may *imagine* that he is feeling its usual effects. In one study it was found that morphine relieved pain in 70 percent of a group who received it. But in a similar group who were given a placebo (in this case a sugar pill) and told that it was morphine, 30 percent had pain relief. Individuals may feel high upon entering a particular social environment even before they have used a drug or taken a drink of alcohol. This may also be called a form of a placebo effect. The individual's experience and expectations of a particular drug play a great role in the type of drug reaction he has.

Can drugs produce mental-emotional breakdowns? Why do "bummers" occur; are they a sign of mental disturbance or a warning signal?

Any drug that affects the mind can potentially produce a serious mental-emotional breakdown. For the most part, this type of psychological breakdown occurs because the individual has a disturbed personality to begin with. However, certain drugs have a higher chance of producing an acute psychological breakdown even with a normal personality. Individu-

als who are under the influence of LSD may have profound alterations in judgment and cognitive functioning, or may experience tremendous alterations in perception. Their environment may become quite distorted, and if they forget they are on a drug, they may think that they are going crazy or that the experience may never end, and they may panic or experience an acute psychotic state.

When this happens, they may have to be given antipsychotic drugs. But for the most part a person on a "bummer" or "bad trip" can be handled best by being placed in a quiet, supportive environment and having someone talk to him to divert his attention away from the thing that is frightening him.

So you can have an acute mental breakdown with a drug like LSD without being physically dependent on it, whereas a person who is physically dependent on a drug like heroin rarely has a drug-induced acute mental breakdown. Individuals who have disturbed personalities have a higher chance of having a bad trip, but even a person with a normal personality, if given a high enough dose of a particular drug or placed in a threatening enough environment, can have a bad reaction.

What are the effects of drug abuse on general health? What is the evidence that drugs can cause a deterioration of brain functioning (motor activity, coordination, thinking)?

Drug abuse may produce tremendously destructive effects on an individual's general physical health as well as serious effects on his bodily functions. With amphetamines, particularly by injection, one may see hepatitis, severe malnutrition, abscesses, and a variety of skin problems. The type of destructive effect that the drug has on the individual's general health is related in great part to the drug itself and how the individual uses it. For example, it's much more destructive to general health to inject a drug than to take it orally.

Drugs can produce brain damage or destruction of the neurons of the central nervous system in a variety of ways. The drug that has produced the most brain damage of all is alcohol. It produces brain damage primarily because the alcoholic consumes large quantities of the drug and alcohol contains seven calories per cc. So he does not eat properly and develops severe nutritional problems, including liver disease, peripheral neuritis, and eventually brain damage, in which neurons of his central nervous system are destroyed. Recent research has indicated that alcohol also has a direct toxic effect on the brain cells by impairing the circulation and depriving the brain cells of oxygen. Other types of drugs such as barbiturates may also produce brain damage. For example, with an overdose of a depressant such as a barbiturate, or when a young person sniffs glue, the individual may become so depressed that his breathing is greatly impaired, and even though he doesn't die, the supply of oxygen to his brain may be so low that many brain cells die. Brain cells do not regenerate once they are destroyed; they cannot grow back.

Other drugs can produce impairment of psychological functioning, without producing brain damage. For example, high-dose use of the stimulants, such as the amphetamines, can produce extensive long-term biochemical disruption of central nervous system functioning, with long-term paranoia, memory gap, or other abnormalities that are characteristic of brain damage, but these effects gradually disappear if the individual has proper food and rest and stays away from drugs. Although amphetamines cause serious disruption in the chemistry of thinking, it has not been proved that they cause permanent brain damage.

Other drugs, such as LSD, when taken by an individual who has a disturbed personality to begin with, can produce very long-term, schizophrenic-like psychological reactions that impair his ability to think, but again this is a psychological disruption, not brain damage.

Is there any evidence that some drugs destroy chromosomes? Can drug taking by pregnant women affect their newborn babies? How?

At present, it is very difficult to determine whether any psychoactive drug produces chromosome damage in the human being at the doses normally used. A wide variety of laboratory studies have indicated that drugs like LSD, when placed in test tubes with human white blood cells or injected into animals, produce chromosome damage. But one also sees this chromosome damage with a wide variety of other

psychoactive drugs at high dosage, including nicotine, caffeine, and certain tranquilizers.

At present, we cannot say that LSD produces chromosome damage in the human being. Some studies indicate that it does; other studies indicate that it doesn't. Science takes a long time to answer such complex questions and a wide variety of experiments to determine the truth about a particular situation.

We do know that when certain drugs are taken during the first three months of pregnancy, when the organs of the fetus are being formed, malformation or a miscarriage can occur. I would caution any pregnant woman against taking any psychoactive drug stronger than caffeine during her pregnancy. However, at present it is impossible to say with certainty that drugs like LSD or marijuana produce chromosome damage.

Other drugs, such as the opiates, can produce problems with newborn babies because these drugs cross the placental barrier (the barrier between the fetus and the mother) and produce the same type of physical dependency in the infant that they do in the mother. So if the mother is addicted to heroin, for example, the baby will be addicted also. And when the baby is delivered, the doctor has to withdraw the baby from heroin, using appropriate medication. In this case, the baby can be harmed by the drug if the problem of withdrawal is not handled properly.

What are "flashbacks" and why do they occur?

Flashbacks are the recurrence of a drug experience without further ingestion of the drug. Flashbacks for the most part have been studied only with LSD, but they can occur with a wide variety of other drugs, such as DOM or STP (a long-acting hallucinogen). Very rarely, they can occur with marijuana and with certain other psychoactive chemicals that can produce acute toxic psychosis.

The LSD flashback, which is the flashback we know the most about, may recur any time up to two or three months after the last ingestion of the drug and may continue to occur for as long as one to two years. There is a much higher incidence of flashbacks after the individual has had a bad trip. Since LSD is metabolized in the body very rapidly, flashbacks are not caused by the continued presence of the chemical in the user's body but represent a psychological phenomenon of a dissociative nature. Some people have likened it to a war neurosis because in a flashback the individual has an overwhelming bombardment of sensory stimuli, much like the soldier who has a shell suddenly burst very near to him and has recurrent nightmares and remembrances of this psychologically traumatic experience for a long time after. As he gradually works it out in his mind, the recurrences disappear. This is the type of psychological mechanism that we think is operative with the LSD flashback.

Individuals who have flashbacks may or may not come for help. Some people who like the effects of LSD view the flashback as a free LSD experience. Other people find it very disruptive and get so anxious that they seek psychological help for the flashbacks. But there is very little that the medical community can do for the flashback except to help the person work out the psychological problem that so frightened him during his bad LSD reaction.

When does drug use become drug abuse? Is there a typical character syndrome of the drug addicts you've seen?

Individuals who become heavy drug users usually pass through three stages of drug use. The first is a stage of experimental use, where they may try a wide variety of psychoactive chemicals out of curiosity or peer-group pressure. Then they may decide to discard most of the drugs they have experimented with and then periodically or recreationally use just a few. For example, an individual may become a periodic alcohol drinker or pot smoker. At this periodic recreational stage, unless he reaches intoxicating levels, the individual rarely gets into difficulty. However, on occasion, because of either social circumstance or personality problems, he moves into a period of compulsive drug use. This we call *drug abuse* because it is the use of a drug to the point where it interferes with the individual's health and economic or social functioning.

There are many personality characteristics that may predispose an individual to the abuse of drugs. He may be chronically depressed prior to his use of drugs, or he may have an impulse disorder with an inability to delay satisfaction. He may be immature. He may be unusually susceptible to stress or the opinions and attitudes of other people. But in general, we cannot say that there is one particular type of addictive personality. All we can say is that there are certain personality characteristics that may predispose an individual to one type of abuse or another.

To what extent is drug taking a response to conformity pressures?

Recent research has indicated that most young people who begin taking a drug, particularly an illegal drug, do so for the first time not because of mental illness but because of curiosity and peer-group pressure. It has become apparent that the direct and indirect forms of peer-group pressure have been major factors contributing to the United States becoming a drug-oriented culture. For example, television ads attempt to get people to use all manner of products by giving the impression that all the best, socially sought-after people use them. More direct forms of peer-group influence are pressures a young person feels to smoke marijuana in order to belong to or be accepted by a particular group.

Once an individual is in the drug subculture, his patterns of drug use are greatly influenced by the attitudes that particular drug subculture has. If it's a very destructive subculture such as the one in Haight-Ashbury now, there may be tremendous peer-group pressure for him to experiment with amphetamines by injection or with heroin or cocaine or a variety of drugs of high abuse potential. If he is in a less destructive drug subculture (such as in a college), then the influence of that group's pressure may keep him within the framework of drugs of lower abuse potential. Individuals rarely make decisions about drugs on an independent basis in the beginning stages of drug use. Usually they are greatly influenced by what they think their friends are doing and by their desire to impress their friends or not to be deviants.

How did the psychedelic "flower people" movement start?

There developed in the San Francisco Bay area a widespread belief that LSD and expanded consciousness moved one into what was described as the *counterculture*—a culture whose views were opposite from those of the dominant culture in the United

States (the establishment). This counterculture emphasized love and peace, minimized material acquisition, focused on experience rather than rational thought, and moved away from destructive forces such as the war, environmental pollution, exploitation of minorities, and so on. The "hippie" was born out of this early psychedelic subculture, as were a variety of other things that have greatly influenced our society, including acid rock music, multimedia light shows, and our language, producing such words as "turn on," "tune in," "drop out," "do your thing," and so on. The basic philosophy was to drop out of the dominant society's value system, turn on to using psychedelic chemicals, expand your consciousness, and tune in to a new philosophy.

Unfortunately, a very large number of young people flocked to a small area in San Francisco, the Haight-Ashbury district, which came to be regarded as the hippie capital of the world. Many of these young people who came were quite disturbed psychologically; others were naïve and did not understand the lifestyle that they were entering. They began to experiment with a wide variety of drugs, very often taking LSD quite indiscriminately. More destructively, they became progressively more involved with drugs of higher abuse potential, particularly amphetamines, or "speed" (*speed* being the street name for methamphetamines).

Amphetamines, when injected at high dosage, produce an orgasmic flash, and the individual may inject himself many, many times in a particular day to get that flash. He may stay up three to four days in a row not eating, not sleeping, continually on the go. When the drug wears off, he may go into a period of exhaustion, sleeping for 24 to 48 hours. When he comes out of that exhaustion phase, he may enter into a prolonged period of depression. Unless he has more of the drug or unless treatment is available, he may get so depressed that he considers suicide. While he is high, he may be very paranoid and violent, and when the Haight-Ashbury became a "speed scene," a great deal of violence developed. The original, peaceful "flower children" moved out and the more destructive individuals stayed. These individuals very often took depressants to calm their nerves. As a result, the "Hashbury" is now dominated by young heroin addicts, many of whom have a past history of

amphetamine use and many of whom began using heroin as a "downer" for their stimulant reaction.

The young people who left, however, did not always go home or return to their former environment, but often formed communes either in the city or in the country. Many of them attempted to expand their consciousness without the use of drugs; others continued to use psychedelic chemicals to maintain this state of awareness that they felt was so valuable. In our studies we have found that communes which have moved on to a more stable family structure and away from drugs are healthier and more likely to survive. Communes that remain drug oriented have much less chance of providing a healthy life for the hippies or their young children.

How is organized crime involved in drug use? Why does drug addiction lead to increased crime rates, or does it?

Organized crime is involved primarily with the traffic in the opiates such as heroin. Much of the opium in the world is grown in Turkey, and a great deal of it is then smuggled into France, synthesized into heroin, and smuggled into the United States. This international smuggling ring is tightly controlled by organized crime and is the reason that a few cents worth of opium grown in Turkey, when synthesized and smuggled into the United States, may sell for many, many dollars to the addict on the street.

Once an individual is addicted to heroin, he has to obtain large quantities of money to continue to support his habit. Most of the crime associated with heroin is what we call *secondary crime*, crime that the individuals have to get involved in to support their habit. Men almost always get involved in crimes of property and selling drugs, while women turn to various forms of prostitution. It is this criminal lifestyle that produces so much of the destruction. In New York City, for example, 50 percent of the crimes of property are by heroin addicts. Individuals on heroin will continue to use heroin no matter how strict the laws are for they see no escape. It has become quite apparent that the only way to eliminate this drug traffic is through adequate treatment that will eliminate consumer demand.

Other drugs may facilitate crime in a more direct way. For example, amphetamines stimulate paranoia and violence. These more often lead to violent crimes. Alcohol produces disinhibition, and the individual may participate in an illegal act.

Why do you think drug use has become so popular? Do you think drug taking and abuse will increase or decrease in the next decade? Why?

People use psychoactive drugs for a variety of reasons. They use them for pleasure, to relieve discomfort, to escape personal problems, to expand consciousness, to facilitate performance, and so on. Very often individuals develop a strong psychological need for a particular drug because they have a particular problem that they can't deal with. American society has been accustomed to using drugs in large quantity—both for medical purposes and in illegitimate settings. Drug addiction has been with us for a long time, but it has been confined primarily to racial minorities and lower socioeconomic situations. In the last five to ten years there has been a tremendous increase in the use of illegal drugs in the middle and upper classes, especially among young people and basically because they have been turning to drugs for recreational uses, escape, and mystical experiences.

There are many theories as to why this has occurred. One is that this is a natural outcome in an already drug-oriented culture such as ours as it becomes more affluent. Another is that as individuals find out more about drugs, they become more curious about trying them. As soon as drug use becomes an acceptable or normative behavior in a particular culture, more of its members have opportunities to observe others taking drugs, drugs are more available, and group pressures toward "turning on" increase.

But at a different level, it appears that young people today are becoming more alienated and less accepting of traditional value systems. In the 1950s, the so-called "silent generation" accepted what their teachers and parents told them about the dangers of illegal drugs, even when it was false. Young people of the 1970s, however, do not accept such information at face value because they feel they've been lied to about a variety of other things and they want to find out about drugs for themselves. One then must view the increased incidence of drug use as a symptom of a much broader social transition and turmoil rather than a causative factor of this turmoil.

Could you elaborate a bit about what societal phenomenon this drug abuse is symptomatic of?

I don't think that one can pick out a particular phenomenon. It is known that drug use has increased in other times of cultural turmoil. After wars, or during wars, there is often a dramatic increase in the use of drugs. Our time is one of special instability, in which all traditional values and institutions are being challenged and neither adults nor young people know what the future holds. The youth look at the problems of pollution, the war in Vietnam, racial discrimination, and the breakdown of the monogamous nuclear family, and although they don't offer better answers for these problems in many cases, nevertheless they don't blindly accept the value system of their elders. Once you begin to break away from the value system of the dominant culture, for whatever reasons, you begin to experiment with a variety of things that would not be sanctioned by your elders, such as political protest, intentional communities, a more liberal sexual ethic, and drug use.

This is why I feel that the current increase in drug use is symptomatic of the identity crises that so many adolescents are going through, which at another level is a reflection of the broader societal turmoil. Many young people feel they have no place in modern society, except in a manner that they find unacceptable. But drug use is a very complicated phenomenon. Personality problems, adolescent turmoil, identity crises, societal reasons, and peer-group pressure—all are important. Rarely is the chemical itself the only factor to be considered when a person becomes compulsively involved with a drug.

How can a person best help someone who is on a "bad trip"? What is the methadone treatment? What is the English system?

How can a person best help someone who is on a "bad trip"? The primary requirements for treating an individual on a bad trip are to treat him in a positive, humane fashion. If possible, get him away from excessive stimuli to a supportive environment where he can be "talked down" by an experienced person.

If the individual becomes extremely panic-stricken and all communication is lost, then he must be taken to a hospital. Unfortunately, many hospitals are overcrowded, with an excess of stimuli, and do not know how to handle the bad trip. It is usually better to take the individual to a drug clinic if one is available.

What is the methadone treatment? Methadone is a long-acting oral narcotic, synthesized during World War II by the Germans for use as a pain-killer when their usual sources of opium and morphine were cut off. It has all the properties of other narcotics except that it is long-acting and does not produce the highs that one sees with short-acting narcotics. In addition, the individual can take it by mouth. Researchers in New York City found that high doses of methadone given to heroin addicts had two positive effects: first, the methadone blockaded the effect of the heroin; second, the methadone eliminated narcotics hunger. When they reached a stabilized dose of methadone, addicts could function without heroin and thus could leave the criminal subculture and proceed with the process of rehabilitation. Very good results were developed from the methadone maintenance technique. Even though methadone itself is an addicting agent, very little impairment of function is seen when an individual is on a stable dose of methadone, and it's the most promising technique now.

The English system is a plan for eliminating the criminality associated with heroin addiction by giving addicts heroin. In England, registered addicts can go to the narcotic clinics and get their daily supply of heroin and in addition get a needle and syringe. This means they don't have to steal and enter into a criminal life to get the drug. On the other hand, they are still involved with a short-acting opiate like heroin and are still taking it by injection, which greatly impairs the process of rehabilitation. In my opinion methadone maintenance clinics are superior to the British system of heroin clinics.

Can you describe briefly the operation and philosophy of your drug clinic?

The Haight-Ashbury Free Clinic is basically an adolescent medical clinic. We have a commune health section, a medical section, a dental section, a drug treatment section, and a psychiatric section. In four years of operation we've seen over 100,000 patients. The basic focus of our clinic is acute treatment, crisis intervention, diagnosis, and referral elsewhere if possible. In other words seeing a very large number of patients means that we can work with most of them only over a short period of time, and we attempt to refer them to other programs that have longer-term treatments, such as a methadone maintenance program or a therapeutic community like the "family" in the Mendicino State Hospital or Synanon. We do keep a certain number of patients in long-term treatment, and we use the multiple modality approach, trying a variety of different techniques with different people.

We make great use of ex-addicts in working with the more compulsive drug-users. We have an outpatient psychiatric clinic that works with the psychological problems of the individuals on a one-to-one basis. We have vocational counseling, and at the present time, we have a very small residential facility. We do have many young drug abusers in long-term treatment, but the majority of our work is short-term crisis intervention, diagnosis, and referral.

We see about 150 patients a day. It is impossible to keep all these patients in long-term treatment in our program, and not desirable either since a particular patient might do better, for example, out in the country or in a commune. The Clinic does not charge its patients and in its beginning was oriented primarily toward talking down bad LSD trips. As the drug scene changed in the area, we of course had to change our program and approach and have more long-term facilities. At the present time, our primary program thrust is toward the short- and long-term treatment of heroin addicts.

The clinic is financed by private donations and grants from private foundations. We have a mainly volunteer staff of about 100, including a paid staff of about 15. Most of the people who are paid are young people from the hip-culture or ex-addicts. We have about 30 volunteer doctors, about 40 volunteer nurses, and 2 paid physicians who operate in our drug treatment programs.

Most of the patients we see at our Free Clinic migrated to San Francisco from other parts of the country, and the Haight-Ashbury drug culture is part of a broader process of youth alienation and social pathology sweeping the country. Drug abuse must be viewed as a symptom of this pathology, and unless we deal with the root causes of alienation in America we have little hope of solving our drug problem.

Glossary

Absolute rating scale. See *Rating scale.*

Absolute refractory period. Period immediately following a nerve impulse, during which the nerve is incapable of responding to even very strong stimuli. (72)

Abstinence syndrome. General physiological reaction which occurs when the addict is deprived of narcotics or other habit-forming drugs upon which he has become physically dependent. (679)

Acetylcholine. Chemical substance that probably facilitates the passage of a nerve impulse from one neuron to another. (75)

Acetylcholine esterase (AChE). Enzyme which catalyzes the breakdown of acetylcholine, thus preventing continuous nerve impulses in certain neurons. (75)

Acquiescence set. Tendency to agree frequently and thus to answer "yes" to test questions. (529)

Action potential. The depolarization of the nerve membrane as a nerve impulse passes along the axon. (71)

Adenine. One of the four nucleotide bases which make up the DNA molecule; found paired with thymine. (64)

Adrenal glands. Endocrine glands located at the upper end of the kidneys; consist of inner adrenal medulla, which secretes the hormones adrenaline and noradrenaline during strong emotion, and outer adrenal cortex, which secretes the adrenal androgens and other hormones that influence maturation. (102)

Adrenaline. Hormone secreted by the adrenal medulla in strong emotion; causes a number of bodily changes, including an increase in blood sugar, a rise in blood pressure, and a more rapid pulse rate. Also called *epinephrine.* (102)

Affective reaction. Emotional reaction. (381) Psychosis characterized by extreme fluctuations of mood. (588)

Afferent neuron. Neuron which carries messages toward the central nervous system from a receptor cell; also known as a *sensory neuron.* (78)

Aggression. Physical or verbal behavior with the intent to injure or destroy. (512)

Agnosia. A disorder of perception in which sensations cannot be organized into normal perceptions. (96)

Alarm reaction. See *General-adaptation-syndrome.*

All-or-none principle. Principle that if a nerve fiber responds at all, it responds with full strength. (72) The theory that concept learning takes place suddenly rather than gradually. (316)

Alpha waves. The electrical rhythm typical of the brain during a relaxed waking state. (207)

Amacrine cells. Interconnecting cells in the retina. (84)

Amnesia. Loss of memory, especially of past personal experiences. (582)

Amphetamines. Psychoactive drugs capable of producing an orgasmic flash but later causing extreme depression; popularly known as "speed." (684)

Amygdala. Structure in the limbic area of the brain associated with primitive emotion and sexual behavior. (100)

Anal stage. In psychoanalytic theory, stage of development during which bowel control is achieved and the focus of pleasure is the eliminative processes. (159)

Androgen. Male hormone which regulates sexual development; some androgens are produced by the testes and others by the adrenal cortex. (102)

Anorexia nervosa. Loss of appetite caused by extreme anxiety. (351)

Anxiety. Generalized feelings of apprehension; central symptom in neuroses. (371, 577)

Aphasia. Impairment of ability to use or understand language, even though hearing and speech mechanisms are unimpaired. (96)

Approach gradient. Principle that the tendency to approach a desired goal gets stronger the nearer the subject is to it. (428)

Archetypes. In Jung's personality theory, universal symbols and predispositions, inherited in the "collective unconscious." (426)

Arousal. General energizing component of attention and motivation; involves organs controlled by both central and autonomic nervous systems. (266, 340-341)

Association areas. Areas of the cerebral cortex which serve to correlate and integrate the functions of the sensory and motor areas. (96)

Associative theories of learning. Theories which regard learning as a process of forming associative bonds or connections. (674)

Atmospheric perspective. Difference in clarity between near and far objects; an aid in depth perception. (286)

Attitude. An inferred construct, assumed to be acquired through experience, involving a set of beliefs and affects concerning some class of people, events, or actions. (476)

Auditory nerve. Nerve which transmits impulses from the Organ of Corti to the brain. (90)

Authoritarian personality. An individual high in rigidity, prejudice, political and economic conservatism, and fascistic traits. (527)

Autism. Childhood schizophrenia; inability on the part of the child to relate to other people or to his environment. (591)

Autistic thinking. Thinking as an end in itself and not a means to an end; determined primarily by the individual's needs or desires, as in daydreaming. (310)

Autokinetic movement. The apparent movement of a small stationary point of light in a dark room. (495)

Autonomic nervous system. That part of the nervous system which regulates bodily activities not ordinarily subject to voluntary control, including the visceral changes that occur during emotion; composed of the *sympathetic* and *parasympathetic* divisions. (76)

Aversive learning. Form of counterconditioning through punishment, sometimes used in treating such disorders as homosexuality, stuttering, and alcoholism. (634)

Avoidance conditioning. Form of instrumental conditioning in which the organism can prevent an aversive stimulus by making an appropriate response in time. (188)

Avoidance gradient. Principle that the tendency to go away from a feared place or object gets stronger the nearer the subject is to it. (428)

Axon. Long fiber leading away from the cell body of the neuron; transmits nerve impulses to other neurons or to muscles. (71)

Axonal transmission. Nerve impulse transmission in which the depolarization of the nerve membrane triggers an all-or-none impulse which rapidly moves down the length of the axon. (71)

Basilar membrane. Membrane in the cochlea on which is located the Organ of Corti; plays a role in translating sound waves into nerve impulses. (90)

Behavior genetics. The study of the heritability of mechanisms underlying specific behaviors, as opposed to body structure. (13)

Behavior sampling. Personality measurement technique in which the examiner observes the subject's behavior in a specified situation. (446)

Behavior therapies. Therapies, usually based on learning theory, which seek primarily to change specific responses by application or withholding of reinforcement. (630)

Behavioral contrast. Phenomenon which occurs when lowering the rate of responding in one situation results in an increased rate of responding in a second situation, even though the stimulus features in the second situation have not been changed. (200)

Behavioral science. A coordinated discipline in which psychologists, sociologists, and anthropologists contribute toward developing valid generalizations about human behavior. (13)

Behavioral sink. Term used to describe the abnormal behavior—unprovoked attacks, abnormal sexual behavior, etc.—that occurs when animals are overcrowded. (539)

Behavioral thermoregulation. Use of voluntary means of temperature control, such as fans or heaters, to supplement autonomic physiological controls. (358)

Behaviorism. School of psychology restricting itself to the study of man's overt behavior, believed to be determined by stimulus-response connections. (181)

Bipolar cells. First neurons in the visual pathway; conduct messages from the rods and cones to ganglion cells. (84)

Blind spot. Region of the retina where nerve fibers leave the eye; no rods or cones are found here. (84)

Brain stem. Term used to designate all the structures that lie between the cerebrum and the spinal cord. (93)

Brain waves. Minute oscillations of electrical potential given off by neurons in the cerebral cortex; measured by the electroencephalograph. (99)

Broca's area. Area in frontal lobe of cerebral hemisphere above the fissure of Sylvius; important for speech. (97)

Catatonia. Schizophrenic reaction characterized by motionless, unresponsive stupor. (591)

Catharsis. The discharging of emotional tension by "talking out" or otherwise expressing troubled emotions; important in most psychotherapy. (513, 616)

Causal determinacy. Assumption that every observed natural phenomenon can be shown to be caused by the operation of some other event(s) or process(es). (8-9)

Centiles. Points which divide a distribution of scores into 100 equal parts. A centile score of 90 means that 90 percent of the group scored lower than the individual. (455)

Central motive state. Condition resulting only when both internal and external incentives are appropriate and leading to selective attention to a certain class of incentive objects and causing biased responses in favor of certain behavior. (340)

Central nervous system (CNS). The brain and spinal cord. (69)

Central tendency, measure of. A statistic which represents the average or typical value of a series of measurements; common central tendency measures are the *mean,* the *median,* and the *mode.* (46)

Centralist theories. Cognitive learning theories, which emphasize the importance of organizing processes as central to learning. (674)

Cerebellum. The part of the brain that controls the coordination of movements necessary to maintain balance and posture. (94)

Cerebrum. The main part of the human brain, divided into right and left hemispheres. (93)

Chemotherapy. Use of drugs in therapy. (608)

Chlorpromazine. Tranquilizing drug, widely used in treatment of psychosis. (609)

Choroid coat. Middle layer of coating of the eye. (83)

Chromosomes. Large molecules consisting of DNA and proteins, which contain the genes responsible for hereditary traits; every human cell (except sex cells) contains 46 chromosomes, 23 from each parent. (64, 66)

Chunks. Units which are already known, as words are known when one is learning new material expressed in words. (248)

Cingulate gyrus. A structure of the limbic system; lesions here can make a wild animal tame. (98)

Clairvoyance. Form of extrasensory perception in which the subject supposedly becomes aware of an external object without the use of his sense organs. (302)

Classical conditioning. See *Conditioning.*

Client-centered therapy. A nondirective technique of psychotherapy based on the theory that many individuals can work through their own problems by "talking them out" in a permissive and supportive atmosphere. (620)

Coaction. Process by which the mere presence of passive, noninteracting other people can influence behavior. (462)

Cochlea. Part of the inner ear responsible for hearing; canals containing fluid which is set in motion by vibrations of the oval window and which in turn stimulates the basilar membrane. (90)

Cognitive attribution therapy. Therapy based on the principle that a patient's problem often lies not so much in his symptoms and feelings as in the meaning he attaches to them and the sources to which he attributes them. (623)

Cognitive dissonance theory. Principle that dissonant (discrepant or incongruous) cognitions motivate the individual to reduce the perceived inconsistency. (412)

Cognitive learning theories. Learning theories which regard learning as a process of making new differentiations and discriminations or reorganizing material into new patterns. (676)

Collaterals. Branches of neurons. (79)

Collective unconscious. In Jungian theory, racial unconscious or storehouse of racial memories with which every person is thought to be endowed. (426)

Compulsion. Bizarre action which the individual himself does not understand but nevertheless feels impelled to perform; usually symbolic in nature. (579)

Computer-assisted instruction (CAI). Instruction in which the student can communicate, via a typewriter keyboard, with a computer which presents displays, questions, and messages on a screen. (253)

Concept. Abstract idea derived from the grouping of objects in terms of some common property. (146, 314)

Conditioned inhibition. Process by which the organism becomes conditioned *not* to respond. (177)

Conditioned reinforcers. Rewards which, although they do not directly satisfy a need, have come to be satisfying in themselves because of previous association with reinforcement. (205)

Conditioning. A basic form of learning in which learned responses are established. In *classical,* or *respondent,* conditioning, a response comes to be evoked by a previously neutral stimulus when this stimulus is paired for a number of trials with the (unconditioned) stimulus which originally elicits the response. (174) In *instrumental* conditioning, no eliciting stimuli are presented; the subject is placed in a situation where he learns to make an instrumental response leading to reward or, in aversive conditioning, one which terminates or prevents an unpleasant stimulus. (184) In *operant* conditioning the rate of an already occurring behavior is increased or decreased through application or withholding of reinforcement. (186)

Cones. Retinal receptor cells responsible for color vision and high visual acuity. (83)

Conjunctive concept. Concept all examples of which must have one or more attributes in common. (314)

Connectionist. One who regards learning as process in which satisfying events strengthen S−R connections and annoying events weaken them (Thorndike's theory). (674)

Consensual validation. Interpersonal agreement on the meaning of language or about other aspects of physical or social reality. (7)

Consequence power. Form of social power in which change is produced through the influence of rewards and punishments controlled by the power source. (474)

Consummatory response. Action which represents the completion of goal-seeking activity. (339)

Content power. Form of social power in which change results from new informational input provided by another person or group. (474)

Contiguity theory. Learning theory which emphasizes the role of temporal contiguity of stimulus and response, holding that learning occurs regardless of whether reinforcement is given, so long as the conditioned stimulus and the response occur together; espoused by Guthrie and Watson. (674)

Continuous reinforcement. Reinforcement given regularly after each conditioning trial. (203)

Control group. Group of subjects which shares all characteristics and treatments with the experimental group except for the independent variable. (45)

Convergence. In the nervous system, distributing process whereby impulses from many neurons or receptor cells reach the same neuron or effector; makes it possible for the same muscle fiber to take part in many different reflexes. (79) In vision, process by which the eyes turn toward each other when focusing upon objects closer than about twenty feet so that both eyes fixate the same point in space; a cue in depth perception. (289)

Conversion hysteria. Neurotic reaction to stress in which psychological distress is converted into bodily symptoms. (579)

Coping strategies. Methods of dealing with a situation perceived as threatening. (390)

Cornea. Transparent portion of the protective coating of the eye, in front of the lens. (83)

Corpus callosum. Heavy bundle of fibers connecting the two hemispheres of the brain. (94)

Correlation. The degree to which two attributes are related. (46, 668)

Correlation coefficient. A statistic which summarizes the relationship of two sets of measurements taken on the same sample. (46, 670)

Cortex. A thin, grayish rind of tissue covering the cerebrum; active in conscious experience and higher mental processes. (93)

Corticalization. Evolutionary trend toward a larger and more complex neocortex of the brain in higher species. (98)

Corticotropin (ACTH). A pituitary hormone which interacts with the secretions of the adrenal cortex—an important factor in physiological reactions to prolonged stress. (102)

Co-twin control. Method of controlling for initial differences in heredity by randomly assigning one of a pair of identical twins to receive the experimental treatment while the other does not. (45)

Counterculture. A culture whose views are opposite from those of the dominant culture, such as the psychedelic "flower people" movement in San Francisco. (683)

Covariance analysis. Method of statistical control by which the impact of measurable differences in subjects upon the dependent variable can be isolated from the effects of the independent variable. (44)

Cue function. Indication of the direction of appropriate activity. (341)

Cutaneous senses. Senses of pressure, pain, warmth, and cold, receptors for which are located primarily in the skin. (83)

Cytoplasm. Cell substance, excluding the nucleus. (62)

Cytosine. One of the four nucleotide bases which make up the DNA molecule; found paired with guanine. (64)

Dark adaptation. Process by which the eyes become more sensitive so that they can see under low illumination; complete dark adaptation usually requires about half an hour of darkness. (85)

Decibel (db). Unit of measurement of the intensity of sound. (91)

Decortication. Surgical removal of the brain or separation of it from the spinal cord. (78)

Deduction. The mode of reasoning that starts with premises or propositions and derives inescapable conclusions therefrom. (10, 321)

Deficiency motivation. Motivation in which the individual seeks to restore his physical or psychological equilibrium (Maslow's personality theory). (432)

Delay of reinforcement gradient, principle of. Principle that responses which occur close in time or space to the delivery of the reinforcement are learned more quickly than responses remote from reinforcement (also called the *principle of the goal-gradient).* (204)

Delusion. A strong belief opposed to reality and maintained in spite of logical persuasion and evidence to the contrary; symptom of psychosis. Three main types: *delusion of grandeur* (belief that one is an exalted personage), *delusion of persecution* (belief that one is being plotted against), and *delusion of reference* (belief that chance happenings and conversations concern oneself). (587)

Dementia praecox. Former name for schizophrenia. (590)

Dendrites. Highly branched fibers at the receiving end of the neuron, usually quite short. (70-71)

Dependent variable. In an experiment, the factor which the hypothesis predicts will change with changes in the independent variable. (41)

Depressive reaction. Neurotic reaction in which the individual reacts to a frustrating situation or a loss with greater sadness and for a longer time than the normal person would. (585) Psychotic depression in which there is deep gloom and a slowing down of mental and physical activity. (588)

Descriptive statistic. A number which stands for a series of measurements collected on a group. (663)

Desensitization. Reconditioning in which stimuli lose their power to elicit anxiety. (631)

Dialogue system. Computer-assisted instruction in which the student can ask certain questions of the computer as well as being questioned. (253)

Dichotic listening. Technique for studying attention and information processing, in which a different message is presented to each ear at the same time through earphones. (274)

Diffuse thalamic system. Center in the thalamus, slow, repetitive stimulation of which produces sleep in normal, waking cats. (266)

Directive counseling. Least complicated type of psychotherapy, in which the therapist supplies reassurance, suggestions, or direct solutions. (620)

Discrimination learning. Learning in which the task is to distinguish between two or more stimuli or between stimulus and no stimulus. (194)

Discriminative stimuli (S^D). In associative learning, stimuli that elicit a behavioral event or signal that reinforcement is available. (192)

Dishabituation. The return of the orienting response after habituation when the stimulus input becomes distinguishably different. (172)

Disinhibition. Temporary reappearance of a conditioned response which has been extinguished, in response to an extraneous stimulus different from the conditioned stimulus; inhibition of an inhibition. (179, 430)

Disjunctive concept. Concept which includes instances which may have one of several alternative characteristics, but not necessarily all of them. (314)

Displaced aggression. Transfer of hostility from the object or person actually causing frustration to some other object or person or to the self. (515)

Dissociated states. Neurotic reactions to extreme stress in which entire episodes of life are repressed from consciousness, as in *amnesia, fugue,* and *multiple personality.* (581)

Distal stimulus. The actual object providing stimulation. (281)

Distributed practice. Use of spaced learning periods. (225)

Distribution. A table showing how individual scores are distributed. (664)

Divergence. Distributing process in the nervous system whereby impulses from a single neuron or receptor cell reach many neurons or muscles. (79)

DNA. Deoxyribonucleic acid; principal component of the genes. (64)

Drill-and-practice system. Computer-assisted instruction in which the computer is used merely for practice exercises. (253)

Drive. Complex of internal conditions directing the organism toward a specific goal; usually biological, as opposed to the social and psychological motives. (339)

Drive-reduction theory. Theory of Hull that reinforcers gain their effectiveness by reducing the level of existing drive. (675)

Drug abuse. Use of a drug to the point where it interferes with the individual's health or with his economic or social adjustment. (679)

Dyad. Two-person group. (487)

Dynamism. In Sullivan's personality theory, a prolonged, recurrent behavior pattern; a habit. (427)

Dyscontrol syndrome. Pattern of senseless brutality or other repeated offenses brought about by disease of the limbic system or the temporal lobe of the brain. (514)

Eardrum. Thin membrane which separates the external ear from the middle ear; made to vibrate by the pressure impulses of sound waves. (90)

Ecological cue validity. The dependability of various stimulus patterns as cues to the actual environment. (283)

EEG. See *Electroencephalogram.*

Effect, law of. Law stating that satisfying events strengthen S−R connections and annoying events weaken them; proposed by Thorndike. (185)

Effectance motivation. Cognitively generated striving to make sense of the environment and be effective in relation to it. (411)

Effectors. The organs (muscles or glands) which perform the actual response functions. (69)

Efference, principle of. Theory of Helmholtz that our judgments as to the presence of eye movements are simply the result of the effort of will involved in trying to alter the adjustment of the eyes. (281)

Efferent neuron. Neuron which carries messages from the central nervous system to an organ of response; also known as a *motor neuron.* (78)

Egalitarian motive. Deep feeling that all people should be equal; characteristic of peasant population studied by Guthrie. (472)

Ego. In psychoanalytic theory, the rational aspect of the personality; regulates the impulses of the id in order to meet the demands of reality and maintain social approval and self-esteem. More generally, the individual's concept of self. (423)

Ego ideal. The individual's view of the kind of person he should try to become; part of the *superego*. (422)

Eidetic imagery. Mental imagery, usually visual, which is almost like actual perception in its clarity and accuracy; rare but most often found in children. (310)

Eidetic personifications. In Sullivan's theory, personifications learned in infancy which remain intact and influence the individual's reactions to people when he grows up. (427)

Electroconvulsive shock. Form of therapy for mental illness; electric current passed through the brain produces brief unconsciousness and convulsions. (607)

Electroencephalogram (EEG). Recording of the minute electrical oscillations in the cerebral cortex known as brain waves. (99, 261)

Elicited behavior. In conditioning, a response already in the organism's repertoire which is initiated by some recognizable physical stimulus. (173, 192)

Embryo. The organism between conception and birth or hatching. More specifically, in humans, the organism from the second to the eighth week after conception. (113)

Emergency reaction. See *General-adaptation-syndrome.*

Emitted behavior. Behavior which appears without the use of an external stimulus to initiate it; basis of instrumental conditioning. (185, 192)

Emotion. Complex state of feeling involving conscious experience, internal and overt physical responses, and power to motivate the organism to action. (381)

Encounter groups. Small therapy or personal growth groups designed to provide an intensive interpersonal experience, focusing on the interactions and feelings that emerge within the group in an atmosphere of honesty and emotional sensitivity. (626)

End feet. Structures at the end of an axon which synapse with another cell. (71)

End plates. End feet of motor neurons. (71)

Endocrine glands. Ductless glands which secrete hormones directly into the blood stream. (100)

Endonuclease. Part of the enzyme system which corrects gene defects; searches out and marks defective parts of the DNA molecule. (66)

Energizer. Drug which stimulates the patient, making him feel more energetic. (609)

Engram. Memory trace; formed and temporarily stored during learning but lost unless transferred to long-term memory system. (240)

Environment. The totality of conditions within and surrounding the organism that serve to stimulate behavior or act to bring about changes in behavior. (112)

Environmental consequence stimuli (S^c). In associative learning, stimuli which follow from a behavioral event. (192)

Environmental control. Experimental control by the use of an environment in which extraneous stimuli can be eliminated or minimized, making more probable the occurrence of the behavior being investigated, relative to other irrelevant behaviors. (43)

Epigenesis. Theory of Aristotle that organs were formed gradually out of simple, unformed substances in the fertilized egg; now used to mean the emergence, in the course of development, of new phenomena and properties not contained in miniature in the germ cells. (62)

Eros. "Sex instinct" or "life instinct," one of the two drives present at birth, according to Freud; encompasses all striving for creative synthesis, thus being much broader than sex drive alone. (422)

Error variance. Amount of observed response variance which can be attributed to sources other than the manipulated independent variable(s) in an experiment. (43)

Escape conditioning. Instrumental conditioning in which the organism can terminate an aversive stimulus by making the appropriate response. (188)

Estrus. Condition of high sexual receptivity in female lower mammals, signifying readiness for pregnancy; popularly called *heat.* (364)

Ethnocentrism. Tendency to hold prejudiced attitudes toward all groups different from one's own. (527)

Ethological method. Detailed observation of the behavior of animals in their natural habitat. (465)

Excitatory postsynaptic potential (EPSP). Potential change which occurs in a neuron when a nerve impulse is approaching it from a synaptic knob; not subject to all-or-none law: when it builds to certain size, an impulse is set up in the neuron. (73)

Exercise, law of. Law stating that repetition of a response would tend to stamp it in; proposed by Thorndike. Found to be invalid. (185-186)

Existential psychotherapy. Form of psychotherapy which sees individual experience rather than physical events as the basic reality and seeks to find what previous underlying choices by the individual have led to the disorder. (621)

Expanded consciousness. Sensation produced by psychedelic drugs; individual may feel his mind is opened to new types of thought and sensory inputs or may feel that he is "going crazy." (680)

Experimental control. In the experimental method, holding constant all variables other than the independent variable which might affect the outcome. (42)

Experimental group. Group of subjects for whom the experimenter alters the independent variable or variables whose influence he wishes to study. (45) See also *Control group.*

Experimental method. The most highly formulized scientific method, in which hypotheses are tested under precisely specified conditions. (41)

Experimental neurosis. Neurosis produced in animals by prolonged stress and inescapable conflicts. (180-181)

Extinction. Gradual disappearance of a conditioned response when the conditioned stimulus is repeated without being reinforced. (179)

Extrasensory perception (ESP). Becoming aware of objects or ideas without use of the sense organs; comprises the phenomena of *mental telepathy, clairvoyance,* and *incorporeal personal agency:* not definitely established as a reality. (302)

F-scale. The fascism scale, one of four scales used to measure authoritarianism. (528)

Factor analysis. Statistical technique used in identifying and measuring the relative importance of the underlying variables, or factors, which contribute to a complex ability, trait, or form of behavior. (433)

Feedback. See *Psychological feedback.*

Feedback loop. Self-exciting circuit in the distributing system of collaterals and interneurons. (79)

Fetus. The unborn human organism from the eighth week after conception until birth. (113)

Field theory. The systematization of psychology by analogy with fields of force in physics, maintaining that all experience represents a balance and interaction of many forces. (431)

Fissure of Rolando. Deep, nearly vertical furrow or groove on the side of each cerebral hemisphere, separating the frontal and parietal lobes. (94)

Fissure of Sylvius. Deep horizontal groove on the lateral surface of each cerebral hemisphere, separating the temporal from the frontal and parietal lobes. (94)

Fixed action pattern. Rigidly stereotyped sequence of behavior such as a courtship ritual, consisting of a complex sequence of responses to a particular pattern of internal and environmental stimulation. (131, 200)

Fixed interval schedule. Schedule by which reinforcement is given regularly at the end of a certain period of time, such as every two minutes. (203)

Fixed ratio schedule. Schedule by which reinforcement is given regularly after a certain number of correct responses. (203)

Flashbacks. The recurrence of a drug experience (as with LSD) without further ingestion of the drug; especially likely to occur after the individual has had a "bad trip." (682)

Forced-choice method. Method of reducing faking on self-inventories and rating devices in which the rater must choose from alternatives of equal desirability. (446)

Form board. A board with recesses into which the subject must fit blocks of the proper size and shape as quickly as he can; used as a performance test to measure intelligence. (453)

Forward conduction, law of. Sequence of neural activity; information is transmitted only in one direction. (75)

Fovea. Area in center of retina with greatest density of cones and complete absence of rods; area of clearest daytime vision. (84)

Free association. Principal procedure used in psychoanalysis to probe the unconscious; patient lets his mind wander freely, giving a running account of every thought and feeling. (617)

Frequency theory. See *Telephone theory.*

Frontal lobes. Portion of each half of the cerebrum located in front of the fissure of Rolando and above the fissure of Sylvius. (94)

Frustration. Denial or thwarting of motives by obstacles which lie between organism and goal. (515)

Fugue. Loss of memory accompanied by actual physical flight. (582)

Functional fixedness. Inability to see a new use for a familiar tool. (324)

Functional psychosis. Severe mental disorder precipitated primarily by psychological stress. (587)

"Gambling house" theories. Theories of perception, such as *transactional approach* and *probabalistic functionalism;* based on concept that perception is a process of making assumptions or "bets" about what is there by identifying dependable cues through experience. (283)

Gamete. Male or female germ cell; contains only half the number of chromosomes found in the other cells of the body. (66)

Ganglion. A collection of nerve cell bodies located outside the central nervous system. (77)

General-adaptation-syndrome. The body's reaction under continued stress, consisting of the *alarm reaction,* during which the body makes a number of complicated physiological changes in response to a stressor; the *stage of resistance,* during which the organism, with the aid of increased secretions of the adrenal glands, is able to withstand the stressor for a time without showing symptoms; and the *stage of exhaustion,* in which the organism can no longer resist the stressor and may die if stress does not cease. (395)

Genes. Ultramicroscopic areas of DNA within the chromosomes; the real bearers of heredity. (64)

Genital stage. In Freudian theory, fifth stage of sexual development, starting at puberty with turning away from autoeroticism to interest in genitalia of others. (160)

Germ cells. Reproductive cells (male *sperm* and female *ovum*) which unite to produce a new individual. (66)

Germinal period. First two weeks of prenatal development, during which the zygote develops by division into a hollow sphere of cells. (113)

Gestalt psychology. A school of psychology which teaches that psychology should study the whole pattern of behavior instead of analyzing it into elements, since the whole is more than the sum of its parts. (284, 676)

Glial cells. See *Neuroglia.*

Glucoreceptors. Specialized cells postulated in the stomach, liver, and hypothalamus which may initiate messages regarding the available glucose levels in the blood. (347)

Gonads. The sex glands (testes in the male and ovaries in the female); produce gametes and also secrete hormones which influence bodily development and behavior. (102)

Gradient of generalization. Expression of the fact that response probability decreases in proportion to the dissimilarity between the present stimulus environment and the original reinforcing environment. (193)

Graphology. Assessment of personality characteristics by study of handwriting. (443)

Group therapy. Form of psychotherapy in which a group of persons discuss their problems under the guidance of a therapist; usually nondirective. (625)

Growth motivation. Motivation in which the individual seeks to go beyond what he has done in the past (Maslow's personality theory). (432)

Guanine. One of the four nucleotide bases which make up the DNA molecule; found paired with cytosine. (64)

Habit strength. In Hull's theory of learning, a learned connection between stimulus and response (an intervening variable), represented by the symbol $_sH_R$. (675)

Habituation. Diminished responsiveness to stimulus input when the stimulus has become familiar or is expected. (171)

Hallucination. Sensory impression of external objects in the absence of any appropriate stimulus in the environment. (298)

"Halo effect." Tendency, when interviewing or rating an individual on a particular trait, to be influenced by one's opinion of some other trait or by one's overall impression of the individual. (303)

Hebephrenia. Form of schizophrenia in which the most severe disorganization appears. (591)

Hemispheres. The halves of the cerebrum. The left hemisphere controls the right side of the body, and vice versa. (94)

Heredity. The totality of biologically transmitted factors that influence the structure of the body and thus limit behavior. (112)

Hering theory. Theory of color vision which postulated three pairs of neural processes; anticipated current opponent theory. (86)

Hermaphrodite. Individual in whom there is a contradiction between the predominant external genital appearance and the sex chromosome pattern, gonads, and internal reproductive structures; one in whom psychosexual differentiation is not complete. (363)

Heuristics. Methods designed to stimulate further thought in problem solving; "rules of thumb" used in trying to solve problems. (327)

Higher-order conditioning. Process by which, once a conditioned response has been established, the conditioned stimulus may in turn function as an unconditioned stimulus in setting up a conditioned response to a third stimulus. (178-179)

Hippocampus. A subcortical structure of the brain which is crucial for recent memory. (98)

Holistic theories. Cognitive learning theories, so-called because of their emphasis on the importance of the whole in shaping the parts. (676)

Homeostasis. The complex process of maintaining stability in the internal and external environment so that the body's chemical balance can be maintained and personality needs can be satisfied; homeostasis on the physiological level is largely automatic. (101, 343)

Homeothermic. Maintaining a constant body temperature despite changes in environmental temperatures. (357)

Homunculus. Miniature human figure, thought by some early scientists to exist in the sperm cells and needing only nourishment and time to develop into an adult. (61)

Horizontal cells. Interconnecting cells in the retina. (84)

Hormetic traits. Direct motivational aspects of the person, which depend upon both tissue needs and the kinds of experience the individual has had. (434)

Hormones. Secretions of the endocrine glands, which serve to control metabolism and maintain homeostasis. (101)

House-Tree-Person Test. A projective technique in which the patient is asked to draw a series of pictures and is then asked questions about them. (657)

Hybridization. Mating of dissimilar individuals. (66)

Hyperphagia. Excessive feeding. (103)

Hypnosis. Artificially induced state of extreme suggestibility. (408-409)

Hypnotherapy. Use of hypnosis in psychotherapy. (624)

Hypochondria. Neurotic preoccupation with the body's activities and the state of one's health. (585)

Hypoglycemia. Lowered blood-sugar level, as following an injection of insulin. (346)

Hypothalamus. Key subcortical structure; important in regulation of metabolism, temperature, and emotional behavior; control center for endocrine system. (98, 101)

Hypothesis. Statement or proposition, often based on the results of previous observations, which is tested in an experiment; it may be rejected or supported by the results but never conclusively proved. (40)

Id. In psychoanalytic theory, the primitive part of the unconscious, composed of instinctive organic cravings and characterized by unrestrained pleasure-seeking impulses. (422)

Idiographic approach. Approach to personality study in which the unique aspects of an individual's personality are of chief importance. (456)

Imipramine. Especially effective antidepressant drug or psychic energizer. (609)

Implicit speech. Tiny muscular contractions, in the speech mechanism and elsewhere, which occur during thought. (317)

Implosive therapy. Form of behavior therapy developed by Stampfl; extinction occurs as frightening stimuli are imagined without harmful result; called *implosive* because the frightening stimuli produce an inner explosion—an *implosion*—of panic. (632)

Imprinting. A form of learning which occurs very early in life and determines the form which behavior will take, as in the case of ducklings which follow the first moving object they see and remain closely attached to it. (135)

Incomplete Sentence Test. Test in which the subject is given a series of italicized words or phrases and asked to complete the sentence. (656)

Independent variable. Factor whose effects are being examined in an experiment; it is changed in some systematic and predetermined manner while the other variables are held constant. (41)

Induction. Method of reasoning by which, on the basis of specific observations and instances, an inference is drawn about a general state or abstract concept which organizes and makes meaningful those separate elements. (10, 321)

Inferential statistics. Statistics used to make a statement about a larger group based on a representative sample. (670)

Inhibition. Suppression or restraint of behavior; term has many specific meanings. (117)

Inhibitory postsynaptic potential (IPSP). Potential change occurring in a neuron which suppresses the development of a nerve impulse. (73)

Insanity. A legal concept applied to any mental condition which renders the individual incapable of ethical judgment and legally unresponsible for his actions. (586)

Instinct. Behavior whose underlying biological pattern is produced by maturation rather than learning and which appears full-blown upon the first occasion that an adequate stimulus is presented, without the organism's having previous opportunity to learn; common in lower animals but very rare in man. (130)

Instrumental conditioning. See *Conditioning.*

Insulin. Hormone secreted by the pancreas which helps the body to metabolize sugar and keep the blood sugar level steady. (101)

Integrated therapy. Psychotherapy based on an eclectic approach, stressing no particular theory or procedure but using whatever methods of therapy seem appropriate to the individual case. (642)

Integrity therapy. A form of psychotherapy developed by Mowrer; regards neuroses as forms of moral failure and emphasizes taking the consequences of one's actions and being more faithful to moral values. (621)

Intelligence. Complex mental ability; includes such primary abilities as verbal comprehension, space visualization, reasoning ability, numerical ability, and others; operationally defined, intelligence is what intelligence tests measure. (453)

Intelligence quotient (IQ). Measure of intelligence obtained by dividing the individual's mental age (MA), as determined by his performance on standardized test items, by his chronological age (CA) and then multiplying by 100. An IQ of 100 is considered to be average. (451)

Interference theory. Theory that forgetting is caused by new information interfering with what has already been learned. (239)

Intermittent reinforcement. Reinforcement given only intermittently rather than regularly on every conditioning trial. (203)

Interneurons. Nerve cells with many short dendrites and a short axon, the latter often giving off branches called collaterals; interconnect sensory input pathways and motor output pathways within the central nervous system; also called *associative neurons* or *internuncial neurons*. (78)

Internuncial neurons. See *Interneurons.*

Intervening variable. See *Mediating variable.*

Inverted-U function. Relation between arousal and excellence of performance—increased arousal increases efficiency only up to a point and beyond that has bad effects. (341)

Involutional melancholia. Psychosis characterized by abnormal anxiety, agitation, delusions, and depression; occurs in later years without previous history of psychosis; may be characterized chiefly by depression or can center around paranoid ideas. (588)

Iodopsin. Photopigment found in the cones of the eye. Three types, corresponding to the wave lengths of blue, green, and red light, are found in the three types of cones. (85)

IQ. See *Intelligence quotient.*

Iris. Colored portion of the eye immediately surrounding the pupil; adjusts in size to regulate amount of light entering the eye. (83)

Irradiation. See *Mass action.*

Isomorphism. Identity of pattern, thought by Gestalt psychologists to exist between the active organizing processes in perceived configurations and the chemical-electrical events taking place in the brain. (285)

Item analysis. Method for determining the extent to which the responses to each item in a test differentiate between two groups. (450)

James-Lange theory. Theory that emotion consists of the bodily changes which occur in response to an exciting event, holding that we feel sad because we cry rather than vice versa. (387)

Just noticeable difference (j.n.d.). Smallest detectable difference in stimulus intensity. (82) See also *Weber-Fechner Law.*

Kinesics. Study of body positions, posture, gestures and other body movements which may express emotion nonverbally. (383)

Kinesthetic sense. Sense of active movement. (83)

Labyrinthine sense. Sense of passive movement and body position. (83)

Land phenomenon. Visual illusion in which a person sees a picture in nearly full color when one wave length is presented to his right eye and another to his left eye. (311)

Latency of response. Length of time elapsing between the onset of the conditioned stimulus and the response; a measure of the strength of conditioning. (179)

Latent content. Hidden content of a dream which indicates the individual's true wishes; changed to manifest content by dream work. (617)

Latent stage. In Freudian theory, fourth stage of sexual development, during which less conscious sexual interest is thought to be present. (160)

Lateral geniculate nucleus. Relay point in the thalamus, through which impulses pass going from the eye to the occipital cortex. (84)

Lateral inhibition. The phenomenon of every stimulated cell inhibiting cells adjacent to it; causes the border of a visual pattern to be emphasized in contrast to a uniform visual field. (86)

Learning set. A readiness to respond in a certain way to a particular type of learning situation. (199)

Leniency error. Tendency on the part of a judge to rate nearly all persons near the top of a rating scale; may be corrected by the use of forced-choice scales. (304)

Lens. Structure of the eye which focuses the light rays onto the sensitive retina. (83)

Lesion. Destruction of a portion of the brain (or other tissue) by an experimenter, by accident, or by disease. (92)

Libido. Broadly conceived sexual forces; the energy of Freud's creative drive, *Eros.* (159, 422)

Ligase. Part of the enzyme system which corrects gene defects; "sews" the repaired DNA molecule back together again. (66)

Limbic system. Group of structures in the rhinencephalon which are active in certain functions such as attention, emotion, flight and defense, and remembering. (98, 266)

Limen. That value of a stimulus which is strong enough to be accurately detected 50 percent of the time; absolute threshold. (82)

Linear perspective. Phenomenon of objects appearing both smaller and closer together as they become more distant. (286)

Logical error. In personality rating, the error of assuming that certain traits always go together. (304)

Logotherapy. School of existential analysis which focuses upon the individual's need to see meaning in his life; emphasizes spiritual and ethical values. (621)

Lysergic acid diethylamide (LSD). Drug capable of bringing on vivid imagery, hallucinations, and disorganization of thought processes. (301, 680)

Mach bands. The dark and light edges of the border in a visual pattern, which are seen as extra-dark and extra-light through the process of lateral inhibition. (87)

"Mach" scales. Measures which differentiate between High Machiavellians (High Machs), persons with relative standards of conduct like Machiavelli's, and Low Machs, persons with absolute standards. (486)

Manic-depressive reactions. Psychotic reactions characterized by periods of extreme elation (manic episodes), extreme depression (depressive episodes), or an alternation between them, typically with intervening periods of normalcy. (588)

Manifest content. Surface content of a dream, which we remember; masks the emotionally painful latent content. (617)

Mass action. Sluggish, irregular, widespread movement characteristic of the spontaneous movements of the fetus; also called *irradiation*. (118)

Massed practice. Use of concentrated learning periods. (225)

Maturation. Process of development and bodily change resulting from heredity acting over a period of time; independent of learning but may be hampered by a subnormal environment. (112)

Mean. Measure of central tendency, more familiarly known as the *average;* obtained by adding a group of measurements together and dividing the sum by the number of measurements; also called the *arithmetic mean.* (46)

Measurement. Assigning numbers to persons, objects, or events according to certain rules. (37)

Median. Measure of central tendency; the measurement which splits an ordered distribution exactly in half. (46)

Mediating variable. Unseen, inner process inferred to be intervening between observed stimuli and observed response. Also called *intervening variable, hypothetical construct,* or *logical construct.* (185)

Memory drum. Instrument used in experiments on verbatim learning; presents items one at a time. (235)

Mental age (MA). Degree of mental development as measured by standardized intelligence tests; based on age at which average children make a given score; used in determining IQ. (450)

Mental retardation. Below-normal intelligence (IQ below approximately 68). (453)

Mental telepathy. Form of extrasensory perception involving the alleged passage of awareness from one mind to another without intervention of the sense organs. (302)

Meprobamate. Tranquilizing drug used for normal as well as psychotic patients, marketed as Miltown or Equanil. (609)

Mescaline. Drug which can bring on symptoms similar to those of mental illness; sometimes used in therapy, primarily to induce regression to childhood experiences. (610)

Metabolism. Chemical processes taking place in all living tissue by which energy is provided to carry on the life processes. (101)

Methadone. A long-acting oral narcotic which blockades the effect of heroin and kills the craving for it so that the drug user can begin rehabilitation. (686)

"Middle man" hormones. Secretions of the pituitary gland which act directly upon other endocrine glands to stimulate their functioning. (101)

MLU. Mean length of utterance; a measure of speech development in children. (139)

Mnemonic strategies. Techniques for encoding of material to be learned for more efficient remembering. (250)

Mode. The measurement having the greatest frequency in a distribution; a measure of central tendency. (46)

Modeling. Form of "no-trial" learning in which a person learns to do something by watching someone else do it and seeing what happens as a result. (137, 430)

More-or-less principle. Graded activity characteristic of synaptic transmission, as contrasted to the all-or-none activity found in conduction of impulses along the axon. (73)

Morpheme. The smallest unit of speech that has a definable meaning; may be a word or a word stem. (227)

Morphemics. The part of linguistic analysis that deals with morphemes. (228)

Motion parallax. Perceived changes in one's own position relative to other objects. (291)

Motive. A condition, usually social or psychological, which serves to direct the individual toward a certain goal. (339)

Motor neuron. See *Efferent neuron.*

Motor primacy. The principle that the neuromuscular structures of the body must reach a certain stage of development (maturation) before they are capable of responding to stimulation. (120)

Motor skill learning. Learning in which performance involves primarily the use of the muscles. (221)

Multiple factor theory. Theory that the positive correlations typically found among intelligence tests are due to the fact that the tests measure several common factors. (454)

Multiple personality. Extreme dissociated state in which the individual develops two or more distinct personalities which alternate in consciousness, each personality being based on sets of motives which are in conflict with those of the others. (582)

Mutagenic. Capable of causing mutations in the DNA molecule. (65)

Mutations. Alterations in the bases of the DNA molecule which change the corresponding amino acid sequence in the proteins formed; may be beneficial, harmful, or even lethal for the individual or his offspring. (65)

Myelin sheath. Fatty white covering which surrounds the axons and collaterals of large diameter in the nervous system. (71)

Narcoanalysis. Brief form of narcosis in which sleep-producing drugs are administered in amounts sufficient to cause a state of "twilight sleep" rather than deep unconsciousness; while in this state, the patient is encouraged to talk about emotionally painful experiences. (608)

Narcosis. Technique of therapy which uses sleep-producing drugs; in prolonged narcosis, now used only for severely agitated patients, the patient may be kept asleep for fifteen or more hours a day for one or two weeks. (607)

Need achievement score (*n* Ach). A measure of the individual's motivation to achieve, obtained from a modified form of the Thematic Apperception Test; not a unitary factor. (467)

Negative transfer. Interference of a prior learning task with the learning and recall of a new task; also known as *proactive inhibition*. (225-226)

Neocortex. Cortex of the brain, which has become more complex during the upward development of more complex species of animals. (98)

Neo-Freudians. Modern personality theorists who have modified Freud's basic theory in various ways, placing less stress on early sexual experiences. (426)

Neonate. Newborn infant. (118)

Nerve. Nerve trunk. (70)

Nerve fiber. Axon. (70)

Nerve impulse. Electrochemical excitation propagated along a neuron or chain of neurons. (71)

Nerve tract. Nerve pathway; bundle of nerve fibers which have a common place of origin and destination. (70)

Nerve trunk. Nerve; nerve tract connecting the central nervous system with other parts of the body. (70)

Neuroglia. Network of cells in which the entire complex of neurons is embedded and which nourish and protect the neurons; glial cells. (70)

Neurology. Study of the brain and nervous system and the diseases thereof. (13)

Neuron. Individual nerve cell. (67)

Neurosis. Emotional disorder characterized by loss of joy in living and overuse of defense mechanisms against anxiety. (576)

Nominal fallacy. False assumption that because something has been named it has been explained. (130)

Nomothetic approach. Approach to personality study which attempts to describe psychological dimensions presumed to be common to all individuals. (456)

Nondirective therapy. See *Client-centered therapy.*

Nonzero-sum game. Dyadic competition in which the amount each can win is determined by the strategy adopted by both players. (491)

Noradrenaline. Hormone secreted by the adrenal medulla during emotion; brings about a number of bodily changes, including constriction of the blood vessels near the body's surface. Also called *norepinephrine.* (102)

Nucleus. Specialized protoplasm in each cell that directs activities in the cytoplasm; necessary for cell reproduction. (62) A group of nerve cell bodies located within the central nervous system. (70) See also *Ganglion.*

Null hypothesis. Hypothesis that there is no difference between the experimental and control groups following the experimental treatment. (46)

Object constancy. The perception of continuous existence of an object as the same object despite changes in size, shape, and position of the retinal image. (281)

Observational-identificatory learning. Learning by observing and identifying with a model; important in childhood learning. (136-137)

Obsession. Persistent and irrational idea, usually unpleasant, that comes into consciousness and cannot be banished voluntarily. (578)

Obsessive-compulsive neurosis. An abnormal reaction characterized by the presence of anxiety, with persisting unwanted thoughts and/or the compulsion to repeat ritualistic acts over and over. (578)

Occipital lobe. Portion of the cerebrum located at the back of the brain; location of visual functions. (94)

Oedipus complex. Repressed desire of a person for sex relations with the parent of the opposite sex, specifically that of the boy for his mother. (160, 661)

Operant conditioning. Form of instrumental conditioning involving *operants*—responses which are emitted at a given rate. (187)

Operant extinction. Process by which conditioned operants which are unreinforced decline in strength until they are at or below their original operant level and again show variability in their topography. (188)

Operant level. Rate at which a freely available response occurs when its consequences are neither positive nor negative. (187)

Operant strengthening. Increasing the rate of responding by use of suitable reinforcers. (187)

Operational definition. A definition of an abstract concept framed in terms of the operations for observing it. (37)

Opponent cells. Cells in the lateral geniculate nucleus which make possible color vision by subtracting the output of one type of cones from the output of another. (85)

Optic chiasma. Point at which optic nerves leading from each retina form a partial cross at base of brain. (93)

Oral stage. In Freudian theory, the first stage of psychosexual development, in which the mouth is the primary source of pleasure. (159)

Organ of Corti. Thickening of the basilar membrane at the floor of the cochlear duct; contains hair cells which are stimulated by motion of the fluid in the cochlear canals; impulses pass from nerve fibers associated with the hair cells to the auditory nerve and thence to the brain. (90)

Organic psychosis. Mental disorder resulting from injury to the nervous system or from such conditions as glandular deficiency or poisons. (586)

Organismic theory. Personality theory which stresses the orderly unfolding of the inherited potentialities of the organism and its unity; based on field theory. (431)

Orienting reaction. The mechanism for paying attention to novel environmental stimuli; includes increased sensitivity, visceral changes, and changes in muscles and in brain waves. (170)

Orthogenesis. Doctrine that evolution is the progressive manifestation of latent forms of preexisting life, all of which were once infolded in a primordial cell. (62)

Orthomolecular psychiatry. Treatment of mental disorders by providing the optimum molecular environment for the brain's functioning by assuring the optimal concentrations of substances normally present (through massive doses of vitamins or glutamic acid). (612)

Osmoreceptors. Special receptor cells postulated as existing in the hypothalamus, which respond to signals of increased osmotic pressure by initiating drinking. (356)

Ossicles. Three small bones (hammer, anvil, and stirrup) in the middle ear. (90)

Oval window. Membrane separating the middle from the inner ear; receives vibration from the ossicles and in turn forces movement of the fluid in the cochlear canals. (90)

Ovaries. Female gonads (sex glands). (102)

Ovum. Female gamete or germ cell. (66)

Paired-associate learning. Learning in which the subject must respond with one word or syllable when presented with another word or syllable. (236)

Paleologic thought. Form of faulty reasoning in which subjects are regarded as interchangeable because they share identical predicates. (10)

Paradigms. Basic designs that can be used with a variety of content and with systematic variations in any of the items. (237)

Paradoxical sleep. REM sleep; EEG pattern resembles that of an alert waking state although person is deeply asleep. (261)

Paralanguage. Aspects of communication which are vocal but not verbal—voice qualities such as pitch, etc. (383)

Paranoia. Psychosis characterized by systematized, intricate delusions. (587)

Parasympathetic division. Division of the autonomic nervous system which controls most of the vital functions of life, such as digestion; its action is antithetical to that of the sympathetic division in most cases; its nerves originate from the lower segments of the spinal cord and from the brain stem. (77)

Parietal lobe. Portion of the cerebrum above the fissure of Sylvius and back of the fissure of Rolando. (94)

Passive spread. Spread of depolarization from one area of an axon to the next area, causing it to be slightly depolarized and thus causing a nerve impulse to occur at this second point; responsible for the movement of the nerve impulse along the axon. (71)

Peak experiences. Moments of highest happiness and fulfillment, characteristically experienced by self-actualized persons, according to Maslow's theory. (433)

Perception. The ordering principle that gives coherence and unity to sensory input. (276)

Perceptual defense. Selective perceiving by which an individual unconsciously screens out perceptions which are unpleasant or threatening to him. (295)

Performance test. Test in which muscular responses rather than verbal ones are required. (453)

Peripheral nervous system. Nerve fibers connecting the receptors to the central nervous system or the central nervous system to muscles and glands. (75)

Peripheralist theories. Associative learning theories, which emphasize the importance of stimulation and reinforcement from the environment. (676)

Personal equation. Phenomenon of consistent discrepancies between people in observation time. (318)

Personality. What characterizes an individual; the sum total of the ways in which an individual characteristically reacts to and interacts with others. (418)

Personification. In Sullivan's theory, an image a person has of someone else; largely determines how he will react to that individual. (427)

Phallic stage. In psychoanalytic theory, stage of development (between third and fifth year) when genital manipulation and exploration occurs and there is a strong attraction for the parent of the opposite sex, with jealousy toward the same-sexed parent. (160)

Phenomenal absolutism. Certainty of the naïve observer that he is perceiving in a direct, unmediated way the attributes of objects about him. (276)

Phenomenal field. In Carl Rogers' personality theory, private world of individual experience. (431)

Phenomenal reality. Our experience of what is there; perceptual experience. (280)

Phenylketonuria (PKU). Form of severe mental retardation caused by a mutation which prevents the manufacture of an enzyme necessary to prevent the building up of phenylpyruvic acid, which is toxic to the central nervous system. (65)

Pheromone. Odor cues which arouse sexual desire in animals. (364)

Phobic reaction. Process of displacing free-floating fear onto some environmental object. (577)

Phonemes. Basic sound units of a language. (226)

Phonology. Study of phonemes and the basic physical acoustic properties necessary to perceive and discriminate a phoneme. (227)

Phrenology. The false belief that the personality consists of "faculties," each located in a specific area of the brain, and evidenced through "bumps" on the skull. (441)

Physical psychiatry. Use of drugs, shock therapy, or other physical therapy by the psychiatrist, usually in order to prevent extreme acts or to make the patient more receptive to psychotherapy. (607)

Physiognomy. An invalid method of judging personality from facial characteristics. (442)

"Pitch is which" theory. The place or resonance theory of hearing. (90)

Pituitary gland. Endocrine gland associated directly with growth; secretes pituitary growth hormone and a number of "middle man" hormones which act upon other endocrine glands. (101)

Place theory. A theory developed by Helmholtz, who maintained that the basilar membrane consisted of a series of resonating fibers each tuned to a different frequency. (89) See also *Volley theory.*

Placebo. An inactive substance administered in such a way that the patient believes he is receiving an active drug. (407)

Placenta. Organ through which nourishment and oxygen from the mother's bloodstream are passed to the fetus and waste materials are passed in the opposite direction. Expelled after the birth. (114)

Plateau. Period of no apparent learning, as measured by performance; appears as a flat place on a learning curve. (220)

PLATO. A system of computer-assisted instruction, Programmed Logic for Automatic Teaching Operations. (253)

Polymerase. Part of the enzyme system which corrects gene defects; repairs the defective parts of the DNA molecule. (66)

Polysensory neurons. Neurons in cortical and subcortical regions of the brain, capable of response to more than one kind of sensory input. (290)

Population. Whole group from which samples are drawn for study. Also called *universe.* (670)

Positive transfer. The more ready learning of a new task because of prior learning of another task; also known as *proactive facilitation.* (225-226)

Postsynaptic membrane. The membrane of the dendrite or cell body to which the synapse leads. (71)

Preformation. Theory that human beings develop from miniature preformed homunculi in the sperm cells. (61)

Prefrontal lobotomy. Form of psychosurgery in which the nerve fibers connecting the hypothalamus with the prefrontal lobes of the brain are severed, the purpose being to cut intellectual processes off from the emotional processes which normally accompany them; used only with the most severe mental cases when all other forms of therapy have failed. (613–614)

Prenatal. Refers to entire period between conception and birth. (113)

Prepotency. Preeminence of certain kinds of stimuli over others in attracting attention. (268)

Presynaptic membrane. The membrane at the end of an axon. (71)

Primary mental abilities. The relatively independent abilities, identified through factor analysis, which make up "general intelligence." Among them are verbal, spatial, numerical, and reasoning abilities. (453)

Primary process thinking. Kind of thinking which occurs in dreams, where rules of reality and logic do not hold; characteristic of the *id*. (422)

Prime data. Data which are only one symbolic step transformed from the observed occurrence. (38)

Prisoner's Dilemma. A game matrix used to study competition and cooperation between two people. (491)

Proactive facilitation. See *Positive transfer*.

Proactive inhibition. See *Negative transfer*.

Probabilistic functionalism. Theory of perception as a process of finding out which perceptions yield the most accurate prediction of the distal stimulus and thus can be depended upon to guide behavior. (283)

Procedural control. The use of standardized instructions, stimuli, tasks, response alternatives, etc., in an experiment. (44)

Process schizophrenia. Schizophrenia which develops very slowly; prognosis poor. (590)

Prognosis. A prediction of the likely course and progress of an illness. (653)

Programmed instruction. Instruction in which material is presented in a sequence of steps, or frames, each ending with an item which the student must answer correctly before proceeding to the next. (252)

Projective techniques. Methods of measuring personality traits in which the subject is presented with a standardized set of ambiguous or neutral stimuli and is encouraged to interpret freely what he sees in them. (447)

Protocooperation. Term applied to cases of animals clustering together and thereby nondeliberately but effectively fostering their survival through processes which represent the most primitive form of cooperation. (463)

Proverbs Test. Test in which the subject is asked to interpret a number of well-known proverbs; useful in diagnosing mental illness. (656)

Proxemics. Study of nonverbal expression through spatial distance between people interacting with each other, as well as their orientation toward each other as reflected in touch and eye contact. (383)

Proximal stimulus. The retinal pattern, as opposed to distal stimulus, which is the actual object. (281)

Pseudoconditioning. Phenomenon by which behavior similar to conditioned behavior is obtained without the typical pairing of stimuli which is the essence of true conditioning; usually reflects a heightened state of excitement in which the organism makes the same response to whatever stimulus is introduced. (183)

Psychedelic drugs. Drugs, such as LSD and mescaline, which lead to vivid imagery, hallucinations, and disorganization of thought processes. (301)

Psychic determinism. Principle that mental events do not occur by chance but are meaningfully related if we explore them deeply enough; a postulate of Freud. (425)

Psychic energizers. Drugs which are used in the therapy of depressed patients. (609)

Psychoactive drug. A drug that affects mental processes. (678)

Psychoanalysis. School of psychology, originated by Freud, which emphasizes the study of unconscious mental processes; also a theory of personality and a method of psychotherapy which seeks to bring unconscious desires into consciousness and make it possible to resolve conflicts which usually date back to early childhood experiences. (422, 616)

Psychobiology. Eclectic approach to therapy aimed at an understanding of all factors—biological, psychological, and social—that may have contributed to the development of disorder. (641–642)

Psychograph. Profile showing an individual's standing on a group of objectively measured or rated traits; the traits are listed on one axis of the chart and the centiles or other values for each trait are marked at the appropriate points along the other axis. (455)

Psycholinguistics. The study of language and how it is learned. (226)

Psychological feedback. Process whereby the individual gains information concerning the correctness of his previous responses in order to correct errors; knowledge of results. (221)

Psychology. Science of the behavior of organisms. (5)

Psychophysical scaling methods. Techniques for measuring psychological responses to stimuli so as to quantify the basic concepts of *limen* and *just noticeable difference*. (82)

Psychosexual stages. In Freudian theory, stages of sexual development. (159)

Psychosis. Severe mental disorder characterized by personality disintegration and loss of contact with reality. (585)

Psychosocial stages. Stages of ego development as formulated by Erikson, incorporating both sexual and social aspects. (160)

Psychosomatic disorder. Physical symptoms, often including actual tissue damage, that may result from the continued mobilization of the body during sustained stress. (392)

Psychosurgery. Brain surgery used in the treatment of severe psychoses that have resisted all other known forms of treatment. (613)

Psychotherapy. A general term to describe treatment of personality and behavior disorders by psychological methods. (605)

Pulsation rate. Rate at which puffs of air are forced through the vocal cords; differences make voices distinguishable from each other. (274)

Pupil. Opening in the iris of the eye through which light enters the eye. (83)

Pursuit rotor. Apparatus used in studies of motor learning; subject must keep the point of a hinged stylus in contact with a revolving brass target. (221)

Random error. Error which occurs accidentally and has an unpredictable effect on response variance. (43)

Random sampling. Method of drawing a sample so that each member of the population has an equal chance of being selected, and so that the probability of each member being selected is independent of whether or not any other member is selected. (671)

Randomization. A form of experimental control in which subjects are assigned to experimental groups by chance or at random so as to eliminate any selective factor which might affect the results. (44)

Range. Simplest measure of variability; the difference between the highest and lowest measurements. (46)

Rapid eye movement (REM) sleep. Type of sleep during which dreams occur; signaled by jerky movements of the eyes beneath the lids. (261)

Rating scale. Device for recording the rater's judgment of himself or others on defined traits. On relative rating scales, the rater ranks the subjects in order from highest to lowest in the group on the trait in question. On absolute rating scales, the judge assigns an absolute value or score to the individual on each trait being rated. (445)

Rational psychotherapy. Form of brief psychotherapy which encourages the patient to substitute rational for irrational ideas in the inner dialogue which he constantly holds with himself. (622)

Reaction formation. Defense mechanism in which the individual's conscious attitudes and overt behavior patterns are the opposite of his unconscious wishes, which have been repressed. (423)

Reactive schizophrenia. Schizophrenia related to specific precipitating factors and causing sudden discontinuity in patient's life-style; better chance of recovery than in process schizophrenia. (590)

Recall. Most widely used method of measuring retention; with a bare minimum of cues, subject must reproduce a response learned earlier. (234)

Receptive field. For a given neuron, that area of the retina from which it receives impulses. (86)

Receptors. Structures in the nervous system which are sensitive to stimuli and set up nerve impulses in the sensory nerve fibers. (69)

Recidivism. A shift back to one's original attitude after a period of therapy or rehabilitation, when again in the old situation, where old norms operate. (503)

Reciprocal inhibition. Technique of behavior therapy developed by Wolpe in which relaxation inhibits the patient's anxiety responses. (631)

Reciprocal innervation. Process by which the excitation of one of an antagonistic pair of muscles is accompanied by the inhibition of the motor neurons supplying the other. (80)

Recognition. Method of measuring retention in which the subject identifies previously learned items from among a list in which they are interspersed. (234)

Reflex. Specific, automatic response involving only a part of the body, such as the knee jerk or the grasping reflex of an infant. (79)

Reinforcement. In classical conditioning, the process of following the conditioned stimulus by the unconditioned stimulus; in instrumental conditioning, the rewarding of the learner for adequate responses. In both cases, the response is strengthened. (202)

Reinforcer. Any stimulus that follows a response and increases the probability of its occurrence. (202)

Relational concept. Concept whose members must show some characteristic relationship rather than any particular feature. (314)

Relative rating scale. See *Rating scale.*

Relative refractory period. Period during which a very strong stimulus is needed to produce a response in the nerve fiber; follows absolute refractory period. (72)

Relearning. Most sensitive method of measuring retention; the subject relearns the original task under the original conditions, the difference in amount of practice needed to reach the original point of mastery providing the measure of retention. (234)

Relevant variable. A variable which might produce changes in the dependent variable and therefore must be controlled throughout the experiment. (42)

REM rebound. A marked increase in amount of dreaming after having been deprived of REM sleep, in which dreams occur. (263)

REM sleep. See *Rapid eye movement sleep.*

Replication. Repetition of an experiment under the same conditions to see if the same results are obtained. (32)

Repression. Defense mechanism in which painful or guilt-producing thoughts, feelings, or memories are excluded from conscious awareness; such repressed material may remain active at an unconscious level, resulting in bizarre behavior. (247, 424)

Reserpine. Tranquilizing drug widely used in the treatment of mental patients. (608)

Resistance to extinction. Criterion of learning based upon the persistence of a conditioned response during extinction trials. (178)

Resistances. In psychoanalysis, inability or unwillingness to discuss certain ideas, desires, or experiences during free association. (617)

Respondent conditioning. Classical conditioning. See *Conditioning.*

Response generalization. Use of a response similar to the correct one in conditioning. (176)

Response variance. Variability in responding to the same stimuli, on the part of different individuals or by the same individual at different times. (42)

Reticular activating system (RAS). The fibers going from the reticular formation to the higher centers, acting as a general arousal system. (98, 265)

Reticular formation. Mass of neural nuclei and fibers in the brain stem just above the spinal cord; important in arousing and alerting the organism and also in controlling attention and perceptual discrimination. (98)

Retina. Inner layer of the eye, containing the light-sensitive rods and cones. (83)

Retinal disparity. The slight difference in the retinal image which the two eyes get from the same object; helps make depth perception possible. (289)

Retroactive inhibition. Greater difficulty of remembering caused by the nature of activity which intervenes between learning and recall. (237)

Retrograde amnesia. Loss of memory for events immediately prior to a blow on the head or an electroshock convulsion, with no impairment of more permanent memories; explained by two-stage memory process. (99)

Rhinencephalon. Area in the brain containing both olfactory and emotional centers; the "nose brain." (94)

Rhodopsin. Photopigment found in the rods of the eye. (85)

Rigidity. Perseverance in a cognitive solution which has been successful in the past but is no longer appropriate. (323)

RNA. Ribonucleic acid, a cellular molecule similar in structure to DNA and thought by some scientists to be involved in learning and memory processes. (64, 182)

Rods. Receptor cells of the retina capable of producing sensations of white, gray, and black but not of color; remain functional under dim illumination. (83)

Rorschach Test. A projective test making use of inkblots. (447)

Rote learning. Verbatim learning, without regard for meaning. (234)

Saccadic movements. Irregular flicking movements of the eye. (280)

Sample. A group upon which measurements are taken; should be representative of some population or universe about which an inference is to be made. (671)

Savings score. Difference between amount of practice required for original learning of a given task and amount of practice required to relearn it. (234)

Scapegoating. Process of displacing aggression onto some unpopular person or group not the cause of the frustration. (516)

Schemata. In Piaget's theory, cognitive structures formed through assimilation and accommodation, relating one's actions to goals sought. (146)

Schizokinesis. Dual reaction in which visceral components of a conditioned response persist after the behavioral response has extinguished. (180)

Schizophrenia. Psychosis characterized by the breakdown of integrated personality functioning, withdrawal from reality, emotional blunting and distortion, and disturbed thought processes. (589)

Schizophrenogenic mother. Dominant mother who, usually through contradictory demands, tends to induce schizophrenic reactions in her child. (596)

Sclera. Outer protective layer of the eye. (83)

Selection control. The matching of subjects in experimental and control groups on as many relevant variables as possible. (44)

Self-actualization. Man's constant striving to realize his full inherent potentials, regarded by Goldstein, Rogers, Maslow, and others as the most fundamental goal of the human personality. (431)

Self-concept. The individual's awareness of his continuing identity as a person; develops gradually from an infant's discovery of the parts of his own body and comes to include all of his thoughts, feelings, attitudes, values, and aspirations. (431)

Self-exciting circuit. Arrangement of neurons whereby when one neuron discharges, the nerve impulse passes down the main axon into a collateral which connects with a second neuron which, in turn, transmits the impulse to the orginal cell, exciting it a second time. Self-exciting circuits make possible the prolongation of excitation. (79)

Self-inventory. Instrument for measuring personality traits by having the individual give information about himself; validity limited by subject's lack of self-understanding and by his desire to make himself appear better than he really is. (449)

Self-system. A dynamism, according to Sullivan, which develops as the individual learns to avoid threats to his security; tends to interfere with ability to deal effectively with others because it becomes isolated from the rest of the personality. (427)

Semantic differential. Technique for studying meaning by the evaluation of subjects' responses to seven-point scales made up of pairs of adjectives. (312)

Semantics. The study of meaning. (227)

Semistarvation neurosis. Psychological symptoms which appear as a result of prolonged periods on a markedly insufficient diet; characterized by apathy, depression, and irritability. (353)

Sensory deprivation. Minimal sensory stimulation, sometimes achieved by eliminating all visual and auditory stimulation as nearly as possible, sometimes by depriving subject of structured stimulation but using low-level meaningless stimulation; may lead to hallucinations and delusions. (299)

Sensory-motor arc. Functional unit of the nervous system; a chain containing a receptor neuron, one or more interneurons in the spinal cord or brain, and an effector neuron. (69)

Sensory neuron. See *Afferent neuron.*

Serendipity. The discovery of something while looking for something else. (48)

Serial anticipation. Method of learning in which the subject learns a series of words or syllables one at a time so that on successive showings he can anticipate the item that comes next. (235)

Serial position effect. Tendency for the early items in a series to be easier to recall than later items and for the last items to be easier to recall than the middle ones. (236)

Servomechanism. Machine which is intrinsically purposeful or goal seeking. (320)

Set. Readiness to respond in a particular way to some stimulus situation for which there are a variety of possible responses. (293) See also *Learning set.*

Shaping. Form of instrumental conditioning used in training animals, in which all responses that come close to the desired one are rewarded at first, then only the closest approximations, until the desired response is attained; also called *successive approximation.* (191)

Shock therapy. Method of treating severe mental disturbances by inducing convulsions which are followed by a state of coma; usually induced by electricity. (607)

Skinner box. Box containing a lever or other device which the animal must manipulate in order to obtain food or some other reward; used in experiments on operant conditioning. (37)

Social-cognitive therapy. Psychotherapy which encourages self-awareness and insight through verbal interaction with others; "talk therapy." (616)

Social norms. Group-defined standards concerning what behaviors are acceptable or objectionable. (493)

Socialization. Process by which an individual becomes an accepted member of a society of people. (137)

Sociotherapy. Process of modifying the patient's environment in such a way that he will stand a good chance of making a successful adjustment. (645)

Somatic nervous system. Components of the nervous system which control the skeletal muscles; distinguished from the autonomic nervous system. (75)

Somatosensory areas. Areas of cerebral cortex concerned with kinesthesis and the cutaneous senses; primary area lies just back of the fissure of Rolando and body surface is projected onto it. (94)

Somatotype theory. A body-type theory, proposed by Sheldon, relating physique to temperament and classifying individuals into three types: endomorph, mesomorph, and ectomorph. (443)

Source power. Form of social power in which change is provided not by what is communicated but by who communicates it. (474)

Sperm. Male gamete or germ cell. (66)

Split brain. Brain in which the corpus callosum has been cut so that the two hemispheres are no longer connected. (105)

Split-litter control. Randomly assigning the members of a given litter to experimental and control groups. (45)

Spontaneous recovery. The return of a conditioned response following extinction, after an interval of no stimulation. (179)

Standard deviation. A measure of variability; equal to the square root of the variance. (46, 666)

Standard score. Score expressed in terms of standard deviations from the mean. (668)

Standardized interview schedule. Interview in which predetermined questions are asked in a set order. (447)

Statistical control. Technique of controlling variables mathematically rather than experimentally. (44)

Statistical inference. Procedure of drawing general conclusions by studying samples. (670)

Statistical significance. The degree to which the outcome of an experiment is contradictory to the null hypothesis; the probability of obtaining a given experimental outcome if the null hypothesis is correct. (46)

Stereotype. A personification held in common by a group of people. (427) A preconceived notion as to how people of a given race, nationality, or occupation will appear or behave. (446)

Stimulus. A physical event which, if strong enough, may excite a receptor or group of receptors. (80)

Stimulus barrier. Capacity on the part of newborn babies to limit excessive stimulation by a pattern of physiological response comparable to that observed in deep sleep. (155)

Stimulus control. Control of occurrence of a response by provision of a dependable signal that a reinforcer is available. (188)

Stimulus generalization. Spread of a conditioned response to other objects similar to the original stimulus. (176)

Stressor. Anything potentially injurious to the organism, either physically or psychologically, that taxes the adaptive capacity of the organism. (395)

Structure of intellect. Systematic framework used by Guilford to classify the intellectual factors according to content, operation, and production. (437)

Subcortex. See *Brain stem.*

Subliminal. Below the threshold (limen); term applied to energy too weak to produce a response. (82)

Successive reproduction. Technique of memory study in which a subject is shown a picture and later asked to draw it from memory, a second subject is shown this drawing, reproduces it from memory, and so on. (238)

Summation. Production of a response by a combination of stimuli that, singly, are too weak to produce a response. *Temporal* summation is accomplished through the repetition of a weak stimulus; *spatial* summation through the simultaneous stimulation of two or more adjacent points. (74)

Superego. In psychoanalytic theory, that part of the personality which guards the ideas of right and wrong learned as a child; in constant conflict with the id; corresponds to the "conscience." (422)

Sympathetic division. Division of the autonomic nervous system which is active in emergency conditions, as in extreme cold, violent effort or exercise, and states of fear or rage; fibers originate in spinal cord segments between brain stem and lower back. (77)

Synapse. The space between the end feet of one neuron and the dendrites of another. (71)

Synaptic knobs. End feet. (71)

Synaptic transmission. Nerve impulse transmission in which a chemical transmitter substance crosses the synaptic gap between an active neuron and the next one in line, starting an impulse in that neuron if enough change is produced; critical in the processing of information. (72)

Synesthesia. Translation of sensory experience from one sensory mode to another, as in seeing colors when sounds are heard. (302)

Systematic error. Error which occurs with regularity and consistently biases a response in a given direction. (43)

T-Groups. See *Encounter groups.*

Taraxein. A substance extracted from the blood of schizophrenic patients which, when injected into the blood of normal persons, will produce temporary psychotic symptoms. (595)

Telephone theory. A frequency theory of hearing, according to which the basilar membrane plays the role of a telephone transmitter, relaying impulses of various frequencies to the brain; unacceptable because a single nerve fiber could not respond fast enough to transmit high frequencies in this manner. (90)

Temperament factors. Traits of personality which describe the manner in which an individual characteristically operates. (435)

Temporal lobe. Portion of the cerebrum separated from the frontal and parietal lobes by the fissure of Sylvius; it lies just beneath the temples. (94)

Testes. Male gonads (sex glands). (102)

Thalamus. Structure almost in the center of the brain; relay station for incoming sensory messages from all parts of the body; important in sensations of pain. (98, 360)

Thanatos. "Aggressive instinct" or "death instinct," one of two drives present at birth, according to Freud; includes all striving toward self-destruction or breaking down of order. (422)

Thematic Apperception Test (TAT). A projective technique making use of pictures for each of which the subject is asked to make up a story. (448)

Threshold. See *Limen.*

Thymine. One of the four nucleotide bases which make up the DNA molecule; found paired with adenine. (64)

Thyroids. Endocrine glands located in the neck which influence body metabolism, the development of intelligence, and the rate of physical growth. (102)

Thyroxin. Hormone secreted by the thyroids. (102)

Timbre. Quality of sound determined by the complexity of the sound wave—that is, by the number of overtones which sound with the fundamental tone. (290)

Token economy. Technique of positive reinforcement employed by mental hospitals in which patients are rewarded for socially constructive behavior by tokens which may later be exchanged for privileges. (637)

Trace decay theory. Theory that forgetting is caused by the fading away of knowledge as time passes. (238)

Trace transformation theory. Theory that remembering is an active process in which information stored will be distorted or transformed to make it more stable or more consistent with other memories. (239)

Trait. Characteristic which can be observed or measured. (433)

Tranquilizer. Drug which calms and soothes the patient. (608)

Transactional approach. Theory that perception is a learned act of constructing reality to fit assumptions based on the individual's transactions with his unique environment. (283)

Transduction. Process by which stimulus energy is converted into a graded depolarization of the receptor cell membrane and thence into a nerve impulse frequency which includes information about intensity of the stimulus. (81)

Transference. Process by which a patient in psychoanalytic therapy attaches to the therapist feelings formerly held toward some person who figured in an emotional conflict, often a parent or a lover. (618)

Transformational rules. Rules according to which a speaker converts the deep structure of meaning into the surface structure or morphological and syntactic arrangement of the sentences he speaks. (232)

Trial and error. Attempts to solve a problem by trying out alternative possibilities and discarding those that prove to be unsatisfactory. (190)

True variance. The amount of observed response variance which can be attributed to variations in the manipulated independent variable(s) in an experiment rather than to chance or error. (43)

Tutorial system. Computer-assisted instruction in which the computer presents levels of successive difficulty as the student is ready for them. (253)

Unconditioned response (UCR). Response made to an unconditioned stimulus; often an inborn reflex, as in the case of salivation in response to food. (173)

Unconditioned stimulus (UCS). Stimulus which elicits a response in the absence of conditioning. (173)

Universe. See *Population.*

Variability. Spread or deviation; often used as means of determining how far above or below the average of his fellows an individual is in a given trait; the most common measure of variability is the standard deviation. (46)

Variable. A quantity or property that can change. See *Dependent variable* and *Independent variable.*

Variable interval schedule. Schedule by which reinforcement is given after differing lengths of time, regardless of the number of correct responses made in between; leads to a relatively constant rate of response. (204)

Variable ratio schedule. Schedule by which reinforcement is given after a variable number of responses; leads to a high and constant rate of responding. (203)

Variance. A measure of variability which is computed by adding the square of the difference between each measurement and the mean, and dividing by the number of measurements; square of the standard deviation. (667)

Verbatim learning. Word-for-word memorization. (234)

Veridical perception. Perception in which the person's subjective perceptual experience of an object (his percept) agrees with its objective physical characteristics, as measurable and verifiable independently. (278)

Visceral. Pertaining to the internal organs, controlled largely by autonomic nervous system. (75)

Visual capture. Domination of vision over tactual perception when a conflict occurs between the two. (290)

Vitreous humor. Liquid which fills the eyeball. (83)

Volley theory. Auditory theory that nerve fibers operate in groups and that various fibers discharge their volleys of impulses at different times, making it possible for a bundle of fibers to reproduce high frequencies. Adequate for frequencies up to 5000 cps, with a place theory being needed to explain higher frequencies. (91)

Weber-Fechner law. The stimulus increment which produces a just noticeable difference is a constant proportion for most values of the stimulus (not at the extremes). (82)

Wernicke's center. Area on cortex of temporal lobe overlapping the auditory area, extending backward and curving up around the end of the fissure of Sylvius; its loss is associated with inability to understand spoken language. (97)

Within-subject control. Comparing a subject's response in the presence of the independent variable manipulation to his response in the absence of it. (45)

X chromosome. Sex-determining chromosome; all female gametes contain X chromosomes; if the zygote has also received an X chromosome from its father, it will be female. (363)

Y chromosome. Sex-determining chromosome found in half the total number of male gametes; uniting with the X chromosome always provided by the female gamete produces male offspring. (363)

Yoked control. Procedure in subjects are tested in pairs under virtually identical conditions except for the difference in the independent variable. (45)

Young-Helmholtz theory. Theory of color vision; correct in postulating that the human eye contains three kinds of cones, but erroneous in other respects. (86)

z score. See *Standard score.*

Zeigarnik effect. Tendency to remember interrupted tasks better than completed ones; tends to be reversed for tasks performed under stress produced by threat to the ego or self. (246)

Zero-sum game. Dyadic head-on competition, in which the outcome must be a win for one person and a loss for the other. (491)

Zygote. Cell formed by the union of the male and female gametes. (66)

References

A

Abelson, R. P., & Carroll, J. D. Computer simulation of individual belief systems. *American Behavioral Scientist,* 1965, **8,** 24-30.

Abelson, R. P., Aronson, E., McGuire, W. J., Newcomb, T. M., Rosenberg, M. J., & Tannenbaum, P. H. (Eds.), *Theories of cognitive consistency: A sourcebook.* Chicago: Rand McNally, 1968.

Adametz, J. H. Rate of recovery of functioning cats with rostral reticular lesions. *Journal of Neurosurgery,* 1959, **16,** 85-98.

Adamson, R. E. Functional fixedness as related to problem solving: A repetition of three experiments. *Journal of Experimental Psychology,* 1952, **44,** 288-291.

Ader, R., & Conklin, P. M. Handling of pregnant rats: Effections on emotionality of their offspring. *Science,* 1963, **142,** 411-412.

Adolph, E. Regulation of body water content through water ingestion. In M. Wayner (Ed.), *Thirst.* New York: Macmillan, 1964.

Adorno, T. W., Frenkel-Brunswick, E., Levinson, D. J., & Sanford, R. N. *The authoritarian personality.* New York: Harper, 1950.

Akert, K., Koella, W. P., & Hess, R., Jr. Sleep produced by electrical stimulation of the thalamus. *American Journal of Physiology,* 1952, **168,** 260-267.

Allee, W. C., *Animal aggregations: A study in general sociology.* Chicago: University of Chicago Press, 1931.

Allen, K. E., Hart, B., Buell, J. S., Harris, F. R., & Wolf, M. M. Effect of social reinforcement on isolated behavior of a nursery school child. *Child Development,* 1964, **34,** 511-518.

Allport, F. H. *Theories of perception and the concept of structure.* New York: Wiley, 1955.

Allport, G. W. *Personality and social encounter.* Berkeley, Calif.: Beacon Press, 1960.

Allport, G. W. Ethical considerations in the definition of mental illness. In E. A. Southwell & H. Feldman (Eds.), *Abnormal psychology: Readings in theory and research.* Belmont, California: Brooks/Cole, 1969.

Allport, G. W., Vernon, P. E., & Lindzey, G. *Study of values.* (3rd ed.) Cambridge, Mass.: Riverside, 1960.

Alper, T. The interrupted task method in studies of selective recall: A reevaluation of some recent experiments. *Psychological Review,* 1952, **59,** 71-88.

Alper, T., & Korchin, S. J. Memory for socially relevant material. *Journal of Abnormal and Social Psychology,* 1952, **47,** 25-37.

Alpert, D., & Bitzer, D. Advances in computer based education. *Science,* 1970, **167,** 1582-1590.

Altman, D., Levine, M., & Nadien, J. Unpublished research cited in S. Milgram, The experience of living in cities. *Science,* 1970, **167,** 1461-1468.

Amarel, S. On the mechanization of creative processes. *IEEE Spectrum,* 1966, **3**(4), 112-114.

Ames, A. Visual perception and the rotating trapezoidal window. *Psychological Monographs,* 1951, **65** (7, Whole No. 234).

Ammons, R. B. Effects of knowledge of performance: A survey and tentative theoretical formulation. *Journal of Genetic Psychology,* 1956, **54,** 279-299.

Anastasi, A. Heredity, environment, and the question of "how?" *Psychological Review,* 1958, **65,** 197-208.

Anokhin, P. K. New conception of the physiological architecture of the conditioned reflex. In *Intern symposium on brain mechanisms and behavior.* Montevideo. Edition of first Sechenov Medical Institute. Moscow, U.S.S.R., 1959.

Anokhin, P. K. Electroencephalographic analysis of cortico-subcortical relations in positive and negative conditioned reactions. In N. S. Kline (Ed.), *Pavlovian conference on higher nervous activity. Annals of the New York Academy of Sciences,* 1961, **92,** 899-938.

Arieti, S. *Interpretation of schizophrenia.* New York: Brunner/Mazel, 1955.

Arling, G. L. *Effects of social deprivation on maternal behavior of rhesus monkeys.* Unpublished master's thesis, University of Wisconsin, 1966.

Arnold, M. B. *Emotion and personality.* New York: Columbia University Press, 1960. 2 vols.

Aronson, E. Some antecedents of interpersonal attraction. In W. J. Arnold & D. Levine (Eds.), *Nebraska symposium on motivation.* Lincoln: University of Nebraska Press, 1969.

Aronson, E., & Linder, D. Gain and loss of esteem as determinants of interpersonal attractiveness. *Journal of Experimental and Social Psychology,* 1965, **1,** 156-171.

Asch, S. E. Forming impressions of personality. *Journal of Abnormal and Social Psychology,* 1946, **41,** 258-290.

Asch, S. E. Opinions and social pressure. *Scientific American,* 1955, **193**(5), 31-35.

Aserinsky, E., & Kleitman, N. Regularly occurring periods of eye mobility and concomitant phenomena during sleep. *Science,* 1953, **118,** 273-274.

Ashley, W. R., Harper, R. S., & Runyon, D. L. The perceived size of coins in normal and hypnotically induced economic states. *American Journal of Psychology,* 1951, **64,** 564-572.

Atkinson, J. W. (Ed.) *Motives in fantasy, action, and society.* Princeton: Van Nostrand, 1958.

Atkinson, J. W. *An introduction to motivation.* Princeton: Van Nostrand, 1964.

Atkinson, R. C. Computerized instruction and the learning process. *American Psychologist,* 1968, **23,** 225-239.

Atthowe, J. M., Jr., & Krasner, L. Preliminary report on the application of contingent reinforcement procedures (token economy) on a "chronic" psychiatric ward. *Journal of Abnormal Psychology,* 1968, **73,** 37-43.

Ax, A. F. The physiological differentiation between fear and anger in humans. *Psychosomatic Medicine,* 1953, **14,** 433-442.

Axelrod, J., & Wurtman, R. Biological rhythms and the pineal gland. *Mental Health Program Reports,* 1970, No. 4.

Ayllon, T., & Azrin, N. H. The measurement and reinforcement of behavior of psychotics. *Journal of the Experimental Analysis of Behavior,* 1965, **8,** 357-383.

Ayllon, T., & Michael, J. The psychiatric nurse as a behavioral engineer. *Journal of the Experimental Analysis of Behavior,* 1959, **2,** 323-334.

Azrin, N. H., Hutchinson, R. R., & McLaughlin, R. The opportunity for aggression as an operant reinforcer during aversive stimulation. *Journal of the Experimental Analysis of Behavior,* 1965, **8,** 171-180.

B

Bachrach, A. J. *Psychological research: An introduction.* New York: Random House, 1962.

Balagura, S. Influence of osmotic and caloric loads upon lateral hypothalamic self-stimulation. *Journal of Comparative and Physiological Psychology,* 1968, **66,** 325-328. (a)

Balagura, S. Conditioned glyceric responses in the control of food intake. *Journal of Comparative and Physiological Psychology,* 1968, **65,** 30-32. (b)

Balagura, S., & Hoebel, B. Self-stimulation of lateral hypothalamus modified by insulin and glucagon. *Physiology and Behavior,* 1967, **2,** 337-340.

Bales, R. F. Task roles and social roles in problem-solving groups. In E. E. Maccoby, T. M. Newcomb, & E. L. Hartley (Eds.), *Readings in social psychology.* (3rd ed.) New York: Holt, Rinehart & Winston, 1958.

Bales, R. F. *Personality and interpersonal behavior.* New York: Holt, Rinehart & Winston, 1970.

Bandura, A. Influence of models' reinforcement contingencies on the acquisition of imitative responses. *Journal of Personality and Social Psychology,* 1965, **1,** 589-595.

Bandura, A. *Principles of behavior modification.* New York: Holt, Rinehart & Winston, 1969. (a)

Bandura, A. Social-learning theory of identificatory processes. In D. A. Goslin (Ed.), *Handbook of Socialization Theory and Research.* Chicago: Rand McNally, 1969. (b)

Bandura, A., & Walters, R. H. *Adolescent aggression.* New York: Ronald, 1959.

Bandura, A., & Walters, R. H. *Social learning and personality development.* New York: Holt, Rinehart & Winston, 1963.

Bandura, A., Ross, D., & Ross, S. A. Transmission of aggression through imitation of aggressive models. *Journal of Abnormal and Social Psychology,* 1961, **63,** 575-582.

Bandura, A., Ross, D., & Ross, S. A. Imitation of film-mediated aggressive models. *Journal of Abnormal and Social Psychology,* 1963, **66,** 3-11.

Barber, T. X. *Hypnosis: A scientific approach.* New York: Van Nostrand Reinhold, 1969.

Barnes, R. H. *Federation Proceedings,* 1967, **26,** 114-147.

Barnett, S. A. *The rat: A study in behavior.* Chicago: Aldine, 1963.

Barron, F. The psychology of imagination. *Scientific American,* 1958, **199**(50), 150-156.

Bartlett, F. C. *Remembering: A study in experimental and social psychology.* New York: Macmillan, 1932.

Bartlett, F. C. *Thinking: An experimental and social study.* New York: Basic Books, 1958.

Bash, K. W. Contribution to a theory of the hunger drive. *Journal of Comparative Psychology,* 1939, **28,** 137-160.

Bavelas, A., Hastorf, A. H., Gross, A. E., & Kite, W. R. Experiments on the alteration of group structure. *Journal of Experimental Social Psychology,* 1965, **1,** 55-70.

Bayley, N. Behavioral correlates of mental growth: Birth to thirty-six years. *American Psychologist,* 1968, **23,** 1-17.

Beach, F. A. *Hormones and behavior.* New York: Holber, 1948.

Beach, F. A. The descent of instinct. *Psychological Review,* 1955, **62,** 401-410.

Beach, F. A. Normal sexual behavior in male rats isolated at fourteen days of age. *Journal of Comparative and Physiological Psychology,* 1958, **51,** 37-38.

Beach, F. A. Retrospect and Prospect. In F. A. Beach (Ed.), *Sex and behavior.* New York: Wiley, 1965.

Beadle, G. W. The new genetics: The threads of life. In *1964 Britannica book of the year.* Chicago: Britannica, 1964.

Beck, A. T. *Depression.* New York: Harper & Row, 1967.

Becker, H. S. *Outsiders: Studies in the sociology of deviance.* New York: Free Press of Glencoe, 1963.

Beecher, H. K. Generalization from pain of various types and diverse origins. *Science,* 1959, **130,** 267-268.

Bell, E. C. Nutritional deficiencies and emotional disturbances. *Journal of Psychology,* 1958, **45,** 47-74.

Bem, D. J. *Beliefs, attitudes, and human affairs.* Belmont, Calif.: Brooks/Cole, 1970.

Bennett, E. L., Diamond, M. C., Krech, D., & Rosenzweig, M. R. Chemical and anatomical plasticity of the brain. *Science,* 1964, **146,** 610-619.

Berger, E. *The psychology of gambling.* New York: Hill & Wang, 1957.

Bergin, A. E. Some implications of psychotherapy research for therapeutic practice. *Journal of Abnormal Psychology,* 1966, **71,** 235-246.

Berko, J. The child's learning of English morphology. *Word,* 1958, **14,** 150-177.

Berkowitz, L. The concept of aggressive drive: Some additional considerations. In L. Berkowitz (Ed.), *Advances in experimental social psychology.* Vol. 2. New York: Academic Press, 1965.

Berkowitz, L., & LePage, A. Weapons as aggression-eliciting stimuli. *Journal of Personality and Social Psychology,* 1967, **7,** 202-207.

Berlyne, D. E. *Conflict, arousal, and curiosity.* New York: McGraw-Hill, 1960.

Berlyne, D. E. Conflict and the orientation reaction. *Journal of Experimental Psychology,* 1961, **62,** 476-483.

Bernard, J., & Sontag, L. W. Fetal reactivity to tonal stimulation: A preliminary report. *Journal of Genetic Psychology,* 1947, **70,** 205-210.

Bernard, L. L. *Instinct.* New York: Holt, 1924.

Bernstein, B. A public language: Some sociological implications of a linguistic form. *British Journal of Psychology,* 1959, **10,** 311-326.

Bernstein, B., & Henderson, D. Social class differences in the relevance of language to socialization. *Sociology,* 1969, **3,** 1-20.

Bernstein, D. A. Modification of smoking behavior: An evaluative review. *Psychological Bulletin,* 1969, **71,** 418-420.

Bettelheim, B. Individual and mass behavior in extreme situations. *J. abnorm. soc. Psychol.,* 1943, **38,** 417-452.

Bettelheim, B. Individual and mass behavior in extreme situations. In E. E. Maccoby, T. Newcomb, & E. Hartley (Eds.), *Readings in social psychology.* New York: Holt, Rinehart & Winston, 1958.

Bettelheim, B. *The informed heart.* New York: Free Press of Glencoe, 1960.

Bichat, X. *Physiological researches upon life and death.* Philadelphia: Smith & Maxwell, 1809.

Bindra, D. B. *Motivation — a systematic reinterpretation.* New York: Ronald, 1959.

Bindra, D. B. Interrelated mechanisms of reinforcement and motivation, and the nature of their influence on response. In W. J. Arnold & D. Levine (Eds.), *Nebraska symposium on motivation.* Lincoln: University of Nebraska Press, 1969.

Binet, A., & Simon, T. La mesure du développement de l'intelligence chez les jeunes enfants. *Bulletin de la Société Libre pour l'Etude Psychologique de l'Enfant,* 1911, **11,** 187-248.

Birch, H. G. The relation of previous experience to insightful problem-solving. *Journal of Comparative Psychology,* 1945, **38,** 367-383.

Birch, H. G. Sources of order in the maternal behavior of animals. *American Journal of Orthopsychiatry,* 1956, **26,** 279-284.

Bird, C. *Social psychology.* New York: Appleton-Century, 1940.

Bishop, G. H. Anatomical, physiological, and psychological factors in sensation of pain. In R. G. Grenell (Ed.), *Progress in neurobiology.* Vol. 5. *Neural physiopathology.* New York: Heuber, 1962.

Black, M. *Critical thinking.* Englewood Cliffs, N.J.: Prentice-Hall, 1952.

Blake, B. G. A follow-up of alcoholics treated by behavior therapy. *Behavior Research and Therapy,* 1967, **5,** 89-94.

Bleuler, E. *Dementia praecox or the group of schizophrenias.* New York: International Universities Press, 1950.

Block, H. A., & Niederhoffer, A. *The gang: A study in adolescent behavior.* New York: Philosophical Library, 1958.

Bloom, B. S. *Stability and change in human characteristics.* New York: Wiley, 1964.

Bogoraz, V. G. *The Chukchee: Social organization.* New York: American Museum of Natural History, 1909.

Bolles, R. *Theory of motivation.* New York: Harper & Row, 1967.

Bond, M. *The effect of first impression information upon behavior emitted during a subsequent interaction.* Unpublished doctoral dissertation, Stanford University, 1970.

Book, W. F. The psychology of skill: With special reference to its acquisition in typewriting. *University of Montana Publications in Psychology,* Bulletin 53, Psychology Series 1, 1908.

Boring, E. G. *A history of experimental psychology.* New York: Appleton-Century-Crofts, 1950.

Borokowski, J. G., Spreen, O., & Stutz, J. Z. Ear preference and abstractedness in dichotic listening. *Psychonomic Science,* 1965, **3,** 547-548.

Bousfield, W. A. The assumption of motor primacy and its significance for behavioral development. *Journal of Genetic Psychology,* 1953, **83,** 79-88.

Bower, G. H., & Clark, M. C. Narrative stories as mediators for serial learning. *Psychonomic Science,* 1969, **14,** 181-182.

Bower, G., & Trabasso, T. Reversals prior to solution in concept identification. *Journal of Experimental Psychology,* 1963, **66,** 409-418.

Bower, T. G. R. Slant perception and shape constancy in infants. *Science,* 1966, **151,** 832-834. (a)

Bower, T. G. R. The visual world of infants. *Scientific American,* 1966, **215,** 85-92. (b)

Brady, J. P., & Levitt, E. E. Nystagmus as a criterion of hypnotically induced visual hallucinating. *Science,* 1964, **146,** 85-86.

Brady, J. P., & Levitt, E. E. Hypnotically induced visual hallucinating. *Psychosomatic Medicine,* 1966, **28,** 351-363.

Brady, J. V. Emotion and the sensitivity of psychoendocrine systems. In D. C. Glass (Ed.), *Neurophysiology and emotion.* New York: Rockefeller University Press, 1967.

Brady, J. V. Personal communication to authors. October 1970.

Brady, J. V., Porter, R. W., Conrad, D. G., & Mason, J. W. Avoidance behavior and the development of gastroduodenal ulcers. *Journal of the Experimental Analysis of Behavior,* 1958, **1,** 69-73.

Braginsky, B., & Braginsky, D. Schizophrenic patients in the psychiatric interview: An experimental study of their effectiveness at manipulation. *Journal of Consulting Psychology,* 1967, **31,** 543-547.

Braginsky, B. M., Braginsky, D. D., & Ring, K. *Methods of madness: The mental hospital as a last resort.* New York: Holt, Rinehart & Winston, 1969.

Braginsky, B., Grosse, M., & Ring, K. Controlling outcomes through impression management tactics of mental patients. *Journal of Consulting Psychology,* 1966, **30,** 295-300.

Bray, C. W. *Psychology and military proficiency.* Princeton: Princeton University Press, 1948.

Brazelton, T. B. Observation of the neonate. *Journal of the American Academy of Child Psychiatry,* 1962, **1,** 38-58.

Breger, L. C., & McGaugh, J. L. Critique and reformulation of learning theory approaches to psychotherapy and neurosis. *Psychological Bulletin,* 1965, **63,** 338-358.

Brehm, J. W., & Cohen, A. R. *Explorations in cognitive dissonance.* New York: Wiley, 1962.

Brehm, M. L., Back, K. W., & Bogdonoff, M. D. A physiological effect of cognitive dissonance under stress and deprivation. *Journal of Abnormal and Social Psychology,* 1964, **69,** 303-310.

Bremer, F. Cerveau isolé et physiologie du sommeil. *Comp. Rend. Soc. Biol.,* 1935, **193**(5), 1235-1241.

Brenner, M. *Informational loss in a social setting.* Mimeographed technical report, University of Michigan, 1970.

Bridgman, P. W. *The logic of modern physics.* New York: Macmillan, 1927.

Brindley, G. S., & Merton, P. A. The absence of a position sense in the human eye. *Journal of Physiology,* 1960, **153,** 127-130.

Broadbent, D. E. The role of auditory localization in attention and memory span. *Journal of Experimental Psychology,* 1954, **47,** 191-196.

Broadbent, D. E. *Perception and communication.* New York: Pergamon Press, 1958.

Broadbent, D. E. Attention and the perception of speech. *Scientific American,* 1962, **206**(4), 143-151.

Brodeur, D. W. The effects of stimulant and tranquilizer placebos on healthy subjects in a real life situation. *Psychopharmacologia.* 1965, **7,** 444-452.

Brody, J. E. When illness follows a "giving up." *The New York Times,* April 7, 1968, p. 11.

Brogden, W. J., & Culler, E. Experimental extinction of higher-order responses. *American Journal of Psychology,* 1935, **47,** 663-669.

Brogden, W. J., & Gregg, L. W. Studies of sensory conditioning measured by the facilitation of auditory acuity. *Journal of Experimental Psychology,* 1951, **42,** 384-389.

Bronowski, J. *The common sense of science.* Cambridge, Mass.: Harvard University Press, 1953.

Bronson, G. The hierarchical organization of the central nervous system: Implications for learning processes and critical periods in early development. *Behavioral Science,* 1965, **10,** 7-25.

Brower, L. P., & Cranston, P. Courtship of the Queen Butterfly, Danaus Gillippus Berenice. 16 mm. sound film, serial number PCR 2123K, Psychological Cinema Register, Pennsylvania State University, 1962.

Brown, C. *Manchild in the promised land.* New York: Macmillan, 1965.

Brown, J. S. A proposed program of research on psychological feedback (knowlege of results) in the performance of psychomotor tasks. *Conference Report 49-2,* USAF Air Training Command Human Resources Research Center, 1949, 81-87.

Brown, R. W. Language and categories. In J. S. Bruner, J. J. Goodnow, & G. A. Austin (Eds.), *A study of thinking.* New York: Wiley, 1956.

Brown, R. The first sentences of child and chimpanzee. Unpublished mimeo report, Harvard University, 1970.

Brownfield, C. Deterioration and facilitation hypotheses in sensory deprivation research. *Psychological Bulletin,* 1964, **61,** 304-313.

Brôzek, J. Experimental investigations on nutrition and human behavior: A post script. *American Scientist,* June 1963, **51,** 139-163.

Brôzek, J., Guetzkow, H., Keys, A., Cattell, R. B., Harrower, M. R., & Hathaway, S. R. A study of personality of normal young men maintained on restricted intakes of vitamins of the B-complex. *Psychosomatic Medicine,* 1946, **8,** 98-109.

Bruner, J. S. The course of cognitive growth. *American Psychologist,* 1964, **19,** 1-15.

Bruner, J. S. The growth of mind. *American Psychologist,* 1965, **20,** 1007-1017.

Bruner, J. S., & Goodman, C. C. Value and need as organizing factors in perception. *Journal of Abnormal and Social Psychology,* 1947, **42,** 33-44.

Bruner, J. S., & Kenney, H. On multiple ordering. On relational concepts. In J. S. Bruner, R. Olver, P. M. Greenfield, et al. *Studies in cognitive growth.* New York: Wiley, 1966.

Bruning, J. Personal communication, September 1970.

Brunswick, E. *Perception and the representative design of psychological experiments.* Berkeley: University of California Press, 1956.

Bryan, W. L., & Harter, N. Studies in the physiology and psychology of the telegraphic language. *Psychological Review,* 1897, **4,** 27-53, & 1899, **6,** 345-375.

Buber, M. *The eclipse of God.* New York: Harper, 1957.

Burger, R. E. Who cares for the aged? *Saturday Review,* 1969. **52**(4), 14-17.

Burnham, J. *Beyond modern sculpture.* New York: George Braziller, 1968.

Burt, C. The evidence for the concept of intelligence. *British Journal of Educational Psychology,* 1955, **25,** 158-177.

Burton, R. *The anatomy of melancholy.* New York: Tudor, 1948. (Originally published, 1620.)

Butler, R. A., & Harlow, H. F. Persistence of visual exploration in monkeys. *Journal of Comparative and Physiological Psychology,* 1954, **47,** 258-263.

Bykov, K. M. *The cerebral cortex and the internal organs.* New York: Chemical Publishing Co., 1957.

Byrne, W. L., et al. Memory transfer. *Science,* 1966, **153,** (3736), 658-659.

C

Caggiula, A. Analysis of the copulation-reward properties of posterior hypothalamic stimulation in rats. *Journal of Comparative and Physiological Psychology,* 1970, in press.

Calhoun, J. B. A "behavioral sink." In E. L. Bliss (Ed.), *Roots of behavior.* New York: Harper & Row, 1962.

Cameron, P., Frank, R., Lifter, M., & Morrissey, P. Cognitive functionings of college students in a general psychology class. Paper presented at the meeting of the American Psychological Association, San Francisco, September 1968.

Campbell, B. A., & Sheffield, F. D. Relation of random activity to food deprivation. *Journal of Comparative and Physiological Psychology,* 1953, **46,** 320-322.

Cannon, W. B. *Bodily changes in pain, hunger, fear and rage.* (2nd ed.) New York: Appleton-Century-Crofts, 1929.

Cannon, W. B. Hunger and thirst. In C. Murchison (Ed.), *A handbook of general experimental psychology.* Worcester, Mass.: Clark University Press, 1934.

Cannon, W. B. "Voodoo" death. *American Anthropologist,* 1942, **44,** 169-181.

Cannon, W. B. "Voodoo" death. *Psychosomatic Medicine,* 1957, **19,** 182-190.

Cant, G. *New medicines for the mind: Their meaning and promise.* Public Affairs Pamphlet No. 228. New York: Public Affairs Committee, 1955.

Carlson, E. R. The affective tone of psychology. *Journal of General Psychology,* 1966, **75,** 65-78.

Carmichael, L. The development of behavior in vertebrates experimentally removed from the influence of external stimulation. *Psychological Review,* 1926, **33,** 51-58.

Carmichael, L. Ontogenetic development. In S. S. Stevens (Ed.), *Handbook of experimental psychology.* New York: Wiley, 1951.

Carmichael, L., Hogan, H. P., & Walter, A. A. An experimental study of the effect of language on the reproduction of visually perceived form. *Journal of Experimental Psychology,* 1932, **15,** 73-86.

Carr, A. The navigation of the green turtle. *Scientific American,* 1965, **212**(5), 78-86.

Cartwright, D., & Zander, A. (Eds.) *Group Dynamics.* New York: Harper & Row, 1968.

Casler, L. The effects of extra tactile stimulation on a group of institutionalized infants. *Genetic Psychology Monographs,* 1965, **71,** 137-175.

Catania, A. C. Elicitation, reinforcement, and stimulus control. Paper presented at the Conference on the Nature of Reinforcement, University of Pittsburgh, June 1969.

Cates, J. Psychology's manpower: Report on the 1968 national register of scientific and technical personnel. *American Psychologist,* 1970, **25,** 254-263.

Cattell, R. B. *Personality and motivation: Structure and meaning.* New York: Harcourt Brace Jovanovich, Inc., 1957.

Cattell, R. B. *The scientific analysis of personality.* Baltimore: Penguin, 1965.

Caudill, W., & Weinstein, H. Maternal care and infant behavior in Japan and America. *Psychiatry,* 1969, **32,** 12-43.

Chafetz, M. E. Clinical studies in alcoholism. *Mental Health Program Reports,* 1970, **4,** 107-125.

Chandler, K. A. The effect of monaural and binaural tones of different intensities on the visual perception of verticality. *American Journal of Psychology,* 1961, **74,** 260-265.

Chaney, R. B., & Webster, J. C. Information in certain multidimensional signals. *U.S. Navy Electronics Laboratory Report,* 1958, No. 1339.

Chapin, F. S. *Introduction to the study of social evolution.* New York: Century, 1913.

Chicago Board of Health. Personal communication to the authors, September 1969.

Child, I. L. The relation of somatotype to self-ratings on Sheldon's temperament traits. *Journal of Personality,* 1950, **18,** 440-453.

Chittenden, G. E. An experimental study in measuring and modifying assertive behavior in young children. *Monographs of the Society for Research in Child Development,* 1942, **7**(1, Serial No. 31).

Chomsky, N. *Syntactic structures.* S'Gravenhage, Netherlands: Mouton, 1957.

Chomsky, N. A review of B. F. Skinner's *Verbal behavior. Language,* 1959, **35**(1), 26-58.

Chomsky, N. Language and the mind. *Readings in Psychology Today.* Del Mar, Calif.: CRM Books, 1969.

Chomsky, N., & Halle, M. *Sound patterns of English.* New York: Harper & Row, 1968.

Christie, R., & Geis, F. L. (Eds.) *Studies in Machiavellianism.* New York: Academic Press, 1970.

Christie, R., & Jahoda, M. (Eds.) *Studies in the scope and method of the authoritarian personality.* New York: Free Press, 1954.

Ciba Pharmaceutical Products. *The rauwolfia story.* Summit, N.J.: Author, 1954.

Clark, C. Personal communication to the authors, September 1970.

Clark, H. H. Linguistic processes in deductive reasoning. *Psychological Review,* 1969, **76,** 387-404.

Clark, K. B., & Clark, M. P. Racial identification and preference in Negro children. In E. E. Maccoby, T. M. Newcomb, & E. L. Hartley (Eds.), *Readings in social psychology.* New York: Holt, Rinehart & Winston, 1958.

Clauser, G., & Klein, H. *Münchner Medizinische Wochenschrift,* 1957, **99,** 896. Cited in Haas **et al.,** 1959.

Clement, P. W., & Milne, C. Group play therapy and tangible reinforcers used to modify the behavior of eight-year-old boys. *Proceedings, 75th Annual Convention, American Psychological Association,* 1967.

Coch, L., & French, J. R. P., Jr. Overcoming resistance to change. *Human Relations,* 1948, **1,** 512-532.

Cofer, C. N., & Appley, M. H. *Motivation: Theory and research.* New York: Wiley, 1964.

Cohen, B. S., & Ditman, K. S. Prolonged adverse reactions to lysergic acid diethylamide. *Archives of General Psychiatry,* 1963, **8,** 475-480.

Cohen, M. R., & Nagel, E. *An introduction to logic and scientific method.* New York: Harcourt Brace Jovanovich, Inc., 1934.

Cohen, S. The politics of vandalism. *New Society,* 1968, **12,** 872-878.

Colby, K. M. Computer simulation of neurotic processes. In R. W. Stacy & B. D. Waxman (Eds.), *Computers in biomedical research.* New York: Academic Press, 1965.

Colby, K. M., Watt, J., & Gilbert, J. P. A computer method of psychotherapy. *Journal of Nervous and Mental Diseases,* 1966, **142,** 148-152.

Coleman, J. S. A brief summary of the Coleman report. In Harvard Education Review Editorial Board (Eds.), *Equal educational opportunity.* Cambridge, Mass.: Harvard University Press, 1969.

Collier, G. Consummatory and instrumental responding as functions of deprivation. *Journal of Experimental Psychology,* 1962, **64,** 410-414.

Collins, B. E. *Social psychology.* Reading, Mass.: Addison-Wesley, 1970.

Cook, S. W. The production of "experimental neurosis" in the white rat. *Psychosomatic Medicine,* 1939, **1,** 293-308.

Coons, E., Levak, M., & Miller, N. E. Lateral hypothalamus: Learning of food-seeking response motivated by electrical stimulation. *Science,* 1965, **150,** 1320-1321.

Cowen, E. L. Stress reduction and problem-solving rigidity. *Journal of Consulting Psychology,* 1952, **16,** 425-428.

Cowen, E. L., & Beier, E. S. Threat-expectancy, word frequencies, and perceptual prerecognition hypotheses. *Journal of Abnormal and Social Psychology,* 1954, **49,** 172-182.

Cowles, J. T. Food tokens as incentives for learning by chimpanzees. *Comparative Psychology Monographs,* 1937, **14,** 1-96.

Craddick, R. A. Size of witch drawings as a function of time before, on and after Halloween. *American Psychologist,* 1967, **17,** 307.

Cranston, R. *The miracle of Lourdes.* New York: McGraw-Hill, 1955.

Critchley, M. Congenital indifference to pain. *Annals of Internal Medicine,* 1956, **45,** 737-747.

Crocket, R., Sandison, R., & Walk, A. (Eds.) *Hallucinogenic drugs and their psychotherapeutic use.* London: J. Q. Lewis, 1963.

Crombie, A. D. Early concepts of the senses and the mind. *Scientific American,* 1964, **215,** 108-116.

Cross, P. G., Cattell, R. B., & Butcher, H. J. The personality patterns of creative artists. *British Journal of Educational Psychology,* 1967, **37,** 292-299.

Culler, E., Finch, G., Girden, E., & Brogden, W. J. Measurements of acuity by the conditioned response technique. *Journal of General Psychology,* 1935, **12,** 223-227.

Cumming, W., & Berryman, R. Matching behavior. *Journal of the Experimental Analysis of Behavior,* 1961, **4,** 281-284.

Curry, F. K. W. A comparison of left-handed and right-handed subjects on verbal and nonverbal dichotic listening tasks. *Cortex,* 1967, **3,** 343-352.

D

Dale, E. Delegation. *Enterprise,* April 1967, 36-37.

D'Andrade, R. G., Quinn, N. R., Nerlove, S. B., & Romney, A. I. *Categories of disease in American-English and Mexican-Spanish.* Unpublished paper, Stanford University, 1969.

Daniel, W. J. Cooperative problem solving in rats. *Journal of Comparative Psychology,* 1942, **34,** 361-368.

Darley, J. M., & Latane, B. Bystander intervention in emergencies: Diffusion of responsibilities. *Journal of Personality and Social Psychology,* 1968, **8**(4), 377-383.

Darwin, C. *The expression of the emotions in man and animals.* London: Murray, 1872.

Davenport, W. Sexual patterns and their regulation in a society of the Southwest Pacific. In F. Beach (Ed.), *Sex and behavior.* New York: Wiley, 1965.

Davis, C. M. Self-selection of diet by newly weaned infants. *American Journal of Diseases of Children,* 1928, **36,** 651-679.

Davis, H. Enhancement of evoked cortical potentials in humans related to a task requiring a decision. *Science,* 1964, **145,** 182-183.

Davis, J. M. Efficacy of tranquilizing and antidepressant drugs. *Archives of General Psychiatry,* 1965, **13,** 552-572.

Davison, G. C., & Valins, S. Maintenance of self-attributed and drug-attributed behavior change. *Journal of Personality and Social Psychology,* 1969, **11,** 25-33.

Davitz, J. R. *The language of emotion.* New York: Academic Press, 1969.

Day, R. S. Fusion in dichotic listening. Unpublished doctoral dissertation, Stanford University, 1968.

Day, R. S. Temporal order judgments in speech: Are individuals language-bound or stimulus-bound? Paper presented at the ninth annual meeting of the Psychonomic Society, St. Louis, 1969.

Day, R. S., & Cutting, J. E. Perceptual competition between speech and nonspeech. Paper presented at the eighteenth annual meeting of the Acoustical Society of America, Houston, 1970.

Dearborn, G. V. N. A case of congenital general pain analgesia. *Journal of Nervous and Mental Disease,* 1932, **75,** 612-615.

De Charms, R., & Moeller, G. Values expressed in American children's readers: 1800-1950. *Journal of Abnormal and Social Psychology,* 1962, **64,** 136-142.

Dekker, E., & Groen, J. Reproducible psychogenic attacks of asthma. In C. F. Reed, I. E. Alexander, & S. S. Tomkins (Eds.), *Psychopathology: A source book.* Cambridge, Mass: Harvard University Press, 1958.

Delgado, J. M. R. *Physical control of the mind: Toward a psychocivilized society.* New York: Harper & Row, 1970.

Delgado, J. M. R., Roberts, W. W., & Miller, N. E. Learning motivated by electrical stimulation of the brain. *American Journal of Physiology,* 1954, **179,** 587-593.

Dellas, M., & Gaier, E. L. Identification of creativity: The individual. *Psychological Bulletin,* 1970, **73,** 55-73.

Dember, W. N. Alternation behavior. In D. W. Fiske & S. R. Maddi (Eds.), *Functions of varied experience.* Homewood, Ill: Dorsey, 1961, 227-252.

Dement, W. C. The effect of dream deprivation. *Science,* 1960, **131,** 1705-1707.

Dement, W. C. A new look at the third state of existence. *Stanford M.D.,* 1969, **8,** 2-8.

Dement, W. C., & Kleitman, N. Cyclic variations in EEG during sleep and their relations to eye movements, body mobility and dreaming. *Electroencephalography and Clinical Neurophysiology,* 1957, **9,** 673-690.

Dement, W. C., Henry, P., Cohen, H., & Ferguson, J. Studies on the effect of REM deprivation in humans and in animals. In S. Kety, H. Williams, & E. Evarts (Eds.), *Sleep and altered states of consciousness.* Baltimore: Williams & Wilkins, 1967.

Dennenberg, V. H. Stimulation in infancy, emotional reactivity, and exploratory behavior. In D. C. Glass (Ed.), *Neurophysiology and emotion.* New York: Rockefeller University Press, 1967.

Dennis, W. *The Hopi child.* New York: Appleton-Century-Crofts, 1940.

Desmedt, J. E. Neurophysiological mechanisms controlling acoustic input. In G. L. Rasmussen & W. F. Windle (Eds.), *Neural mechanisms of the auditory and vestibular systems.* Springfield, Ill.: Thomas, 1960.

Deutsch, J. A., & Deutsch, D. *Physiological psychology.* Homewood, Ill.: Dorsey Press, 1966.

Deutsch, M., & Gerard, H. B. A study of normative and informational social influence upon individual judgment. *Journal of Abnormal and Social Psychology,* 1955, **51,** 629-636.

Deutsch, M., & Krauss, R. M. The effect of threat on interpersonal bargaining. *Journal of Abnormal and Social Psychology,* 1960, **61,** 181-189.

DeValois, R. L. Neural processing of visual information. In R. W. Russell (Ed.), *Frontiers in physiological psychology.* New York: Academic Press, 1966.

De Vore, I. (Ed.) *Primate behavior.* New York: Holt, Rinehart & Winston, 1965.

De Vos, G., & Wagatsuma, H. *Japan's invisible race.* Berkeley: University of California Press, 1966.

Dice, N., Bagchi, B. K., & Waggoner, R. W. Investigation of effects of intravenous reserpine in disturbed psychotic and brain-damaged patients: Electroencephalographic correlation. *Journal of Nervous and Mental Disorders,* 1955, **122,** 472-478.

Dichter, E. *Handbook of consumer motivations: The psychology of the world of objects.* New York: McGraw-Hill, 1964.

Digman, J. M. Growth of a motor skill as a function of distribution of practice. *Journal of Experimental Psychology,* 1959, **57,** 310-316.

Dobzhansky, T. On methods of evolutionary biology and anthropology. Part 1. Biology. *American Scientist,* 1957, **45**(5), 381-392.

Dole, V. P. A relation between non-esterfied fatty acids in plasma and the metabolism of glucose. *Journal of Clinical Investigations,* 1956, **35,** 150-152.

Dollard, J., & Miller, N. E. *Personality and psychotherapy.* New York: McGraw-Hill, 1950.

Dollard, J., et al., *Frustration and aggression.* New Haven: Yale University Press, 1939.

Doty, R. W., Beck, E. D., & Kooi, K. A. Effect of brain-stem lesions on conditioned responses of cats. *Experimental Neurology,* 1959, **1,** 360-385.

Duffy, E. *Activation and behavior.* New York: Wiley, 1962.

Duncker, K. On problem-solving. *Psychological Monographs,* 1945, **58,** No. 5.

Duncker, K. Uber induzierte Bewegung (Ein beitrag zur theorie optisch wahrgenommener Bewegung) *Psychologie Forschung,* 1929, **12,** 180-259. In W. D. Ellis (Ed.), *Sourcebook of gestalt psychology.* New York: Humanities Press, 1950.

Dunnette, M. D., Campbell, J., & Jaastad, K. The effects of group participation on brainstorming effectiveness for two industrial samples. *Journal of Applied Psychology,* 1963, **47,** 30-37.

Dwornicka, B., Jasienska, A., Smolarz, W., & Wawryk, R. Attempt of determining the fetal reaction to acoustic stimulation. *Acta Oto-Laryngologica,* Stockholm, 1964, **57,** 571-574.

E

Ebbinghaus, H. *Memory.* New York: Teachers College, Columbia University, 1913. (Originally published: Leipzig: Altenberg, 1885.)

Edwards, A. E., & Acker, L. E. A demonstration of the long-term retention of a conditioned galvanic skin response. *Psychosomatic Medicine,* 1962, **24,** 459-463.

Edwards, A. L. *Manual for the Edwards personal preference schedule.* New York: Psychological Corp., 1959.

Edwards, A. L. *The measurement of personality traits by scales and inventories.* New York: Holt, Rinehart & Winston, 1970.

Egbert, L. Report of the American Society of Anesthesiologists, 1969.

Egbert, L., Battit, G., Welch, C., & Bartlett, M. Reduction of postoperative pain by encouragement and instruction of patients. *New England Journal of Medicine,* 1964, **270,** 825-827.

Egstrom, G. H. Effects of an emphasis on conceptualization techniques during early learning of a gross motor skill. *Research Quarterly,* 1964, **35,** 472-481.

Eisner, B. G. Notes on the use of drugs to facilitate group psychotherapy. *Psychiatric Quarterly,* 1964, **38,** 310-328.

Ekman, P., & Friesen, W. V. The repertoire of nonverbal behavior categories, origins, usage, and coding. *Semiotica,* 1969, **1,** 49-98.

Ekman, P., Sorenson, E. R., & Friesen, W. V. Pancultural elements in facial displays of emotion. *Science,* 1969, **164,** 86-88.

Elliott, J. Personal communication to the authors, October 1970.

Ellis, A. Outcome of employing three techniques of psychotherapy. *Journal of Clinical Psychology,* 1957, **13,** 344-350.

Ellis, A. Rational psychotherapy. *Journal of General Psychology,* 1958, **59,** 35-49.

Ellsworth, P. C., Henson, A., & Carlsmith, J. M. Staring as a stimulus to flight in humans: A series of field experiments. *J. Personality soc. Psychol.,* 1970, in press.

Engen, T., Lipsitt, L. P., & Kaye, H. Olfactory responses and adaptation in the human neonate. *Journal of Comparative and Physiological Psychology,* 1963, **56,** 73-77.

Epps, E. (Ed.) Motivation and academic achievement of Negro Americans. *Journal of Social Issues,* 1969, **25.**

Epstein, A. N., & Milestone, R. Showering as a coolant for rats exposed to heat. *Science,* 1968, **160,** 895-896.

Erikson, E. *Childhood and society.* New York: Norton, 1950.

Erikson, E. H. *Identity: Youth and crises.* New York: Norton, 1968.

Erickson, M. H. Negation or reversal of legal testimony. *American Medical Association Archives of Neurology and Psychiatry,* 1938, **40,** 548-553.

Espenschade, A. Motor performance in adolescence: Including the study of relationships with measures of physical growth and maturity. *Monographs of the Society for Research in Child Development,* 1940, **5**(1, Whole No. 24).

Evarts, E. V., & Butler, R. N. A review of the effects of chlorpromazine and reserpine in patients with mental disorders. In J. O. Cole & R. W. Gerard (Eds.), *Psychopharmacology: Problems in evaluation.* Washington: National Academy of Sciences—National Research Council, 1959.

Eysenck, H. J. The effects of psychotherapy: An evaluation. *Journal of Consulting Psychology,* 1952, **16,** 319-324.

Eysenck, H. J. *The structure of human personality.* (2nd ed.) London: Methuen, 1960.

Eysenck, H. J., & Rachman, S. *The causes and cures of neurosis.* San Diego, Calif.: Knapp, 1965.

F

Fairweather, G. W. *Social psychology in treating mental illness: An experimental approach.* New York: Wiley, 1964.

Fairweather, G. W., Sanders, D. H., Maynard, R. F., & Cressler, D. L. *Community life for the mentally ill: Alternative to institutional care.* Chicago: Aldine, 1969.

Fairweather, G. W., et al. Relative effectiveness of psychotherapeutic programs: A multicriteria comparison of four programs for three different patient groups. *Psychological Monographs,* 1960, **74** (5, Whole No. 492).

Falk, J. L. Limitations to the specificity of NaCl appetite in sodium-depleted rats. *Journal of Comparative and Physiological Psychology,* 1965, **60,** 393-396.

Fantz, R. L. Form preferences in newly hatched chicks. *Journal of Comparative and Physiological Psychology,* 1957, **50,** 422-430.

Fantz, R. L. Pattern vision in newborn infants. *Science,* 1963, **140,** 296-297.

Faterson, H. F. Organic inferiority and the inferiority attitude. *Journal of Social Psychology,* 1931, **2,** 87-101.

Faucheux, C., & Moscovici, S. Le style de competement d'une minorite et son influence sur les reponses d'une majorite. *Bulletin du Centre d'Etudes et Recherches Psychologiques,* 1967, **16,** 337-360.

Feather, N. Valence of outcome and expectation of success in relation to task difficulty and perceived locus of control. *Journal of Personality and Social Psychology,* 1967, **7,** 372-386.

Feldman, M. P., & MacCulloch, M. J. A systematic approach to the treatment of homosexuality by conditioned aversion: Preliminary report. *American Journal of Psychiatry,* 1964, **121,** 167-171.

Feldman, M. P., & MacCulloch, M. J. The application of anticipatory learning to the treatment of homosexuality. I. Theory, technique and preliminary results. *Behavior Research and Therapy,* 1965, **2,** 165-183.

Feldstein, A., Hoagland, H., Oktem, M. R., & Freeman, H. Mao inhibition and anti-depressant activities. *International Journal of Neuropsychiatry,* 1965, **1,** 384.

Fenichel, O. *The psychoanalytic theory of neurosis.* New York: Norton, 1945.

Fenz, W. D. Conflict and stress as related to physiological activation and sensory, perceptual, and cognitive functioning. *Psychological Monographs,* 1964, **78** (8, Whole No. 585).

Ferguson, L. R. *Personality development.* Belmont, Calif.: Brooks/Cole, 1970.

Ferrare, N. A. Institutionalization and attitude change in an aged population. Unpublished doctoral dissertation. Western Reserve University. 1962.

Ferriera, A. J., & Winter, W. W. Information exchange and silence in normal and abnormal families. In W. W. Winter & A. J. Ferriera (Eds.), *Research in family interaction.* Palo Alto, Calif.: Science & Behavior Books, 1964.

Festinger, L. A theory of social comparison processes. *Human Relations,* 1954, **7,** 117-140.

Festinger, L. *A theory of cognitive dissonance.* Stanford: Stanford University Press, 1957.

Festinger, L., & Carlsmith, J. M. Cognitive consequences of forced compliance. *Journal of Abnormal and Social Psychology,* 1959, **58,** 203-211.

Festinger, L., Schachter, S., & Back, K. *Social pressure in informal groups.* New York: Harper & Row, 1950.

Fiedler, F. E. A contingency model of leadership effectiveness. In L. Berkowitz (Ed.), *Advances in experimental social psychology.* Vol. 1. New York: Academic Press, 1964.

Fieve, R. R. Interdisciplinary studies of manic-depressive psychosis. *Mental health program reports,* 1970, No. 4, 175-194.

Fine, R. The psychology of blindfold chess: An introspective account. *Acta Psychologia,* 1965, **24,** 352-370.

Fink, M., Klein, D. F., & Kramer, J. C. Clinical efficacy of chlorpromazine-procyclidene combination, imipramine and placebo in depressive disorders. *Psychopharmacologia,* 1965, **7,** 27-36.

Fiske, D. W., & Maddi, S. R. *Functions of varied experience.* Homewood, Ill: Dorsey, 1961.

Fitzsimmons, J., & Oatley, K. Additivity of stimuli for drinking in rats. *Journal of Comparative and Physiological Psychology,* 1968, **66,** 450-455.

Flavell, J. H. *The developmental psychology of Jean Piaget.* Princeton: Van Nostrand, 1963.

Fleishman, E. A., & Parker, J. F. Factors in the retention and relearning of perceptual-motor skill. *Journal of Experimental Psychology,* 1962, **64,** 215-216.

Fluckiger, F. A., Tripp, C. A., & Weinberg, G. H. A review of experimental research in graphology, 1933-1960. *Perceptual and Motor Skills,* 1961, **12,** 67-90.

Folkins, C. H., Lawson, K. D., Opton, E. M., Jr., & Lazarus, R. S. Desensitization and the experimental reduction of threat. *J. abnorm. Psychol.,* 1968, **73,** 100-113.

Fortune. A good man is hard to find. 1946, **33** (3), 92-95+.

Foss, B. M. Mimicry in Mynahs (Gracula Religiosia): A test of Mowrer's theory. *British Journal of Psychology,* 1964, **55,** 85-88.

France, C. J. The gambling impulse. *American Journal of Psychology,* 1902, **13,** 364-407.

Frank, J. *Persuasion and healing.* Baltimore: Johns Hopkins Press, 1961.

Frank, J. D., Gleidman, L. H., Imber, S. D., Stone, A. R., & Nash, E. H., Jr. Patients' expectancies and relearning as factors determining improvement in psychotherapy. *American Journal of Psychiatry,* 1957, **115,** 961-968.

Fraser, S. The control of a phobic reaction by cognitive attribution therapy. Unpublished doctoral dissertation, New York University, 1971.

Fraser, S., & Zimbardo, P. G. Unpublished research cited in P. G. Zimbardo, The human choice: Individuation, reason, and order versus deindividuation, impulse, and chaos. In W. J. Arnold & D. Levine (Eds.), *Nebraska symposium on motivation.* Lincoln: University of Nebraska Press, 1969.

Frederick, C. J. An investigation of handwriting of suicide notes. *Journal of Abnormal Psychology,* 1968, **73,** 263-267.

Freedman, D. Hereditary control of early social behavior. In B. M. Foss (Ed.), *Determinants of infant behavior.* Vol. 3. London: Methuen, 1965.

Freedman, J. L., & Fraser, S. C. Compliance without pressure: The foot-in-the-door technique. *Journal of Personality and Social Psychology,* 1966, **4,** 195-202.

Freeman, W., & Watts, J. W. *Psychosurgery.* Springfield, Ill.: Thomas, 1942.

French, J. D., & Magoun, H. W. Effects of chronic lesions in central cephalic brain stem of monkeys. *American Medical Association Archives of Neurology and Psychiatry,* 1952, **68,** 591-604.

French, J. R. P., Jr., Israel, J., & Os, D. An experiment on participation in a Norwegian factory: interpersonal dimensions of decision-making. *Human Relations,* 1960, **13,** 3-19.

French, J. R. P., Jr., Ross, I. C., Kirby, S., Nelson, J. R., & Smyth, P. Employee participation in a program of industrial change. *Personnel,* 1958, **35**(3), 16-29.

Freud, S. Three contributions to the sexual theory. *Nervous and Mental Disease Monograph Series,* 1910, No. 10.

Freud, S. *An autobiographical study.* London: Hogarth, 1935.

Freud, S. *Collected papers.* Vol. 5. Dostoevsky and parricide. London: Hogarth Press, 1950.

Friedhoff, A. J. Metabolism of DMPEA and its possible relationship to schizophrenia. In *The origins of schizophrenia.* Proceedings of the First Rochester International Conference, 1967.

Friedman, M., & Rosenman, R. F. Overt behavior pattern in coronary disease. *Journal of the American Medical Association,* 1960, **173,** 1320-1325.

Friedman, S. B., & Glasgow, L. A. Psychologic factors and resistance to infectious disease. *Pediatric Clinics of North America,* 1966, **13,** 315-335.

Friedman, S. B., Ader, R., & Glasgow, L. A. Effects of psychological stress in adult mice inoculated with coxackie B viruses. *Psychosomatic Medicine,* 1965, **27,** 361-368.

Frijda, N. H. Emotion and recognition of emotion. In M. Arnold (Ed.), *Feelings and emotions.* New York: Academic Press, 1970.

Fromm, E. *Escape from freedom.* New York: Holt, Rinehart & Winston, 1941.

Funkenstein, D. H. The physiology of fear and anger. *Scientific American,* 1955, **192**(5), 74-80.

Funkenstein, D. H., King, S. H., & Drolette, M. E. *Mastery of stress.* Cambridge, Mass.: Harvard University Press, 1957.

Fuster, J. M. Effects of stimulation of brain stem on tachistoscopic perception. *Science,* 1958, **127,** 150.

G

Galambos, R. Suppression of auditory nerve activity by stimulation of efferent fibers to cochlea. *Journal of Neurophysiology,* 1956, **19,** 424-437.

Galanter, E. Contemporary psychophysics. In *New directions in psychology.* New York: Holt, Rinehart & Winston, 1962.

Galton, F. *Inquiries into human faculty and its development.* London: J. M. Dent & Sons, 1907. (Originally published: London: Macmillan, 1883.)

Gantt, W. H. Psychosexuality in animals. In P. H. Hoch & J. Zubin (Eds.), *Psychosexual development in health and disease.* New York: Grune & Stratton, 1949.

Gantt, W. H. Reflexology, schizokinesis, and autokinesis. *Conditional Reflex,* 1966, **1,** 57-68.

Ganz, L., & Wilson, P. Innate generalization of a form discrimination without contouring eye movements. *Journal of Comparative and Physiological Psychology,* 1967, **63,** 258-269.

Gardner, E. A. Serving an urban ghetto through a community mental health center. *Mental Health Program Reports,* 1970, No. 4.

Gardner, R. A., & Gardner, B. T. Teaching sign language to a chimpanzee. *Science,* 1969, **165,** 664-672.

Garner, W. R. Good patterns have few alternatives. *American Scientist,* 1970, **58,** 34-42.

Gastaut, H., & Bert, J. Electroencephalographic detection of sleep by repetitive sensory stimuli. In G. E. W. Wolstenholme & M. O'Connor (Eds.), *The nature of sleep.* London: Churchill, 1961.

Gazzaniga, M. S., & Sperry, R. W. Simultaneous double discrimination response following brain bisection. *Psychonomic Science,* 1966, **4,** 261-262.

Geber, M. The psycho-motor development of African children in the first year, and the influence of maternal behavior. *Journal of Social Psychology,* 1958, **47,** 185-195.

Gebhard, P. H. Situational factors affecting human sexual behavior. In F. Beach (Ed.), *Sex and behavior.* New York: Wiley, 1965.

Gelernter, H. Realization of a geometry theorem proving machine. *Proceedings of the International Conference on Information Processing.* Paris: UNESCO, 1960.

Gerall, H. D., Ward, I. L., & Gerall, A. A. Disruption of the male rat's sexual behavior induced by social isolation. *Animal Behavior,* 1967, **15** (1), 54-58.

Gerard, H. B. Choice difficulty, dissonance and the decision sequence. *Journal of Personality,* 1967, **35,** 91-108.

Gerard, H. B., & Rabbie, J. M. Fear and social comparison. *Journal of Abnormal and Social Psychology,* 1961, **62,** 586-592.

Gewirtz, J. L. Deprivation and satiation of social stimuli as determinants of their reinforcing efficacy. In J. P. Hill (Ed.), *Minnesota symposia on child psychology.* Vol. 1. Minneapolis: University of Minnesota Press, 1967.

Gewirtz, J. L. Levels of conceptual analysis in environment—infant interaction research. *Merrill-Palmer Quarterly of Behavior and Development,* 1969, **15,** 7-47.

Gewirtz, J. L., & Baer, D. M. Deprivation and satiation of social reinforcers as drive conditions. *Journal of Abnormal and Social Psychology,* 1958, **57,** 165-172.

Gibbon, J. Discriminated punishment: Avoidable and unavoidable shock. *Journal of the Experimental Analysis of Behavior,* 1967, **10,** 451-460.

Gibson, E. J. *Principles of perceptual learning and development.* New York: Appleton-Century-Crofts, 1969.

Gibson, E. J. The development of perception as an adaptive process. *American Scientist,* 1970, **58,** 98-107.

Gibson, E. J., & Walk, R. D. The effect of prolonged exposure to visually presented patterns on learning to discriminate them. *Journal of Comparative and Physiological Psychology,* 1956, **49,** 239-242.

Gibson, E. J., & Walk, R. D. The "visual cliff." *Scientific American,* 1960, **202** (4), 67-71.

Gibson, E. J., Walk, R. D., Pick, H. L., Jr., & Tighe, T. J. The effect of prolonged exposure to visual patterns on learning to discriminate similar and different patterns. *Journal of Comparative and Physiological Psychology,* 1958, **51,** 584-587.

Ginott, H. G. *Group psychotherapy with children: The theory and practice of play-therapy.* New York: McGraw-Hill, 1961.

Gluckman, M., & Hirsch, J. The response of obese patients to weight reduction: A clinical evaluation of behavior. *Psychosomatic Medicine,* 1968, **30,** 1-11.

Goffman, E. *Asylums.* New York: Doubleday, 1961.

Goldberg, P. Are women prejudiced against women? *Transaction,* 1968, **5**(5), 28-30.

Goldfarb, W. The effects of early institutional care on adolescent personality. *Journal of Experimental Education,* 1943, **12,** 106-129.

Goldiamond, I. Fluent and nonfluent speech (stuttering): Analysis and operant techniques for control. In L. Krasner & L. P. Ullman (Eds.), *Research in behavior modification.* New York: Holt, Rinehart & Winston, 1965.

Goldstein, K. *The organism.* Boston: Beacon Press, 1963.

Gollin, E. S. A developmental approach to learning and cognition. In L. P. Lipsitt & C. C. Spiker (Eds.), *Advances in child development and behavior.* Vol. 2. New York: Academic Press, 1965.

Goodall, J. Tool-using and aimed throwing of free-living chimpanzees. *Nature,* 1964, **201,** 1264-1266.

Goodner, C. J., & Russell, J. A. Pancreas. In T. C. Ruch & H. D. Patton (Eds.), *Physiology and Biophysics.* Philadelphia: Saunders, 1965.

Gottesman, I. I. Genetic variance in adaptive personality traits. *Journal of Child Psychology and Psychiatry,* 1966, **7,** 199-208.

Gough, H. G. Techniques for identifying the creative research scientist. In *Conference on the creative person.*

Berkeley: University of California, Institute of Personality Assessment and Research, 1961.

Graham, K. R. Brightness contrast by hypnotic hallucination. *The International Journal of Clinical and Experimental Hypnosis,* 1969, **17** (1), 62-73. (a)

Graham, K. R. Eye movements during waking imagery and hypnotic hallucinations. Unpublished doctoral dissertation, Stanford University. 1969. (b)

Green, R., & Berkowitz, L. Name-mediated aggressive cue properties. *Journal of Personality,* 1966, **34,** 456-465.

Greenblatt, G., Eastlake, D., & Crocker, S. The Greenblatt chess program. *Proceedings of the Fall Joint Computer Conference.* Washington, D.C.: Thompson, 1967.

Greene, W. A. The psychosocial setting of the development of leukemia and lymphomia. *Annals of the New York Academy of Sciences,* 1966, **125,** 794-801.

Greenwald, A. G., Brock, T. C., & Ostrom, T. M. *Psychological foundations of attitude.* New York: Academic Press, 1968.

Gregory, R. L. *Eye and brain: The psychology of seeing.* New York: McGraw-Hill, 1966.

Gresham, W. L. Fortune tellers never starve. *Esquire,* 1949, **32** (5).

Grice, G. R. The relation of secondary reinforcement to delayed reward in visual discrimination learning. *Journal of Experimental Psychology,* 1948, **38,** 1-16.

Grier, W. H., & Cobbs, P. M. *Black rage.* New York: Basic Books, 1968.

Grimmett, H. Personal communication to the authors, October 1970.

Grimshaw, L. Obsessional disorder and neurological illness. *Journal of Neurology, Neurosurgery, and Psychiatry,* 1964, **27,** 229-231.

Grinker, R. R., & Spiegel, J. P. *Men under stress.* Philadelphia: Blakiston, 1945.

Gross, L. Scarcity, unpredictability and eating behavior in rats. Unpublished doctoral dissertation, Columbia University, 1968.

Grossberg, J. M. Behavior therapy: A review. *Psychological Bulletin,* 1964, **109,** 73-88.

Grossman, D. On whose unscientific methods and unaware values? *Psychotherapy: Theory, Research and Practice,* 1968, **5,** 43-54.

Grossman, S. P. Neuropharmacology of central mechanisms contributing to control of food and water intake. In C. Code (Ed.), *Handbook of physiology.* Baltimore: Williams & Wilkins, 1967.

Grossman, S. P. Physiological basis of specific and nonspecific motivational processes. In W. Arnold (Ed.), *Nebraska symposium on motivation.* Lincoln: University of Nebraska Press, 1968.

Gruen, W. Emotional encapsulation as a predictor of outcome in therapeutic discussion groups. *International Journal of Group Psychotherapy,* 1966, **16,** 93-97.

Guetzkow, H. S., & Bowman, P. H. *Men and hunger.* Elgin, Ill: Brethren, 1946.

Guhl, A. M. The social order of chickens. *Scientific American,* 1956, **194** (2), 42-46.

Guilford, J. P. *Personality.* New York: McGraw-Hill, 1959.

Guilford, J. P. Factorial angles to psychology. *Psychological Review,* 1961, **68,** 1-20.

Guilford, J. P. *Discovering and measuring human intellec-*

tual abilities. Summary of the third annual California Conference on Higher Education, May 1964.

Guilford, J. P. Intelligence: 1965 model. *American Psychologist,* 1966, **21,** 20-26.

Guilford, J. P., & Lacey, J. I. (Eds.) *Printed classification tests* (AAF Aviation Psychology Program Research Report No. 5). Washington: Government Printing Office, 1947.

Guilford, J. P., & Zimmerman, W. S. The Guilford-Zimmerman Temperament Survey. Beverly Hills, Calif.: Sheridan Supply Company, 1949.

Guion, R. M., & Gottier, R. F. Validity of personality measures in personnel selection. *Personnel Psychology,* 1965, **18,** 135-164.

Gunter, R., Feigenson, L., & Blakeslee, P. Color vision in the cebus monkey. *Journal of Comparative and Physiological Psychology,* 1965, **60,** 107-113.

Gurin, P., Gurin, G., Lao, R., & Beattie, M. Internal-external control in the motivational dynamics of Negro youth. In E. Epps (Ed.), Motivation and academic achievement of Negro Americans. *Journal of Social Issues,* 1969, **25.**

Guthrie, G. M. *The psychology of modernization in the rural Philippines.* I.P.C. Paper No. 8. Quezon City: Ateneo de Manila University Press, 1970. (a)

Guthrie, G. M. The shuttlebox of subsistence attitudes. Paper delivered at the ONR-Maryland Symposium on Attitudes, Conflict and Social Change, May 1970. (b)

Guttman, N., & Kalish, H. I. Discriminability and stimulus generalization. *Journal of Experimental Psychology,* 1956, **51,** 79-88.

H

Haas, H., Fink, H., & Hartfelder, G. Das placeboproblem. *Fortschoritte der Arzneimittleforschung,* 1959, **1,** 279-454. Translated in *Psychopharmacology Service Center Bulletin,* 1959, **2**(8), 1-65. U.S. Department of Health, Education and Welfare, Public Health Service.

Haas, K. *Understanding ourselves and others.* Englewood Cliffs, N.J.: Prentice-Hall, 1965.

Haber, R. N. (Ed.) *Contemporary theory and research in visual perception.* New York: Holt, Rinehart & Winston, 1968.

Haider, M., Spong, R., & Lindsley, D. B. Attention, vigilance, and cortical evoked potentials in humans. *Science,* 1964, **145,** 180-182.

Hamilton, M. Ten years of chlorpromazine. *Comprehensive Psychiatry,* 1965, **6,** 291-297.

Hammer, E. F. Creativity and feminine ingredients in young male artists. *Perceptual and Motor Skills,* 1964, **19,** 414.

Hampson, S. L. Determinants of psychosexual orientation. In F. Beach (Ed.), *Sex and behavior.* New York: Wiley, 1965.

Harlow, H. F. The formation of learning sets. *Psychological Review,* 1949, **56,** 51-65.

Harlow, H. F. Sexual behavior in the rhesus monkey. In F. Beach (Ed.), *Sex and behavior.* New York: Wiley, 1965.

Harlow, H. F., & Harlow, M. K. Learning to love. *American Scientist,* 1966, **54,** 244-272.

Harlow, H. F., Harlow, M. K., & Meyer, D. R. Learning motivated by a manipulation drive. *Journal of Experimental Psychology,* 1950, **40,** 228-234.

Harlow, H. F., & McClearn, G. E. Object discrimination learned by monkeys on the basis of manipulation motives.

Journal of Comparative and Physiological Psychology, 1954, **47,** 73-76.

Harlow, H. F., & Zimmerman, R. R. The development of affectional responses in infant monkeys. *Proceedings of the American Philosophical Society,* 1958, **102,** 501-509.

Harriman, A. E. The effect of a preoperative preference for sugar over salt upon compensatory salt selection by adrenalectomized rats. *Journal of Nutrition,* 1955, **57,** 271-276.

Harrison, R. Thematic apperception methods. In B. B. Wolman (Ed.), *Handbook of clinical psychology.* New York: McGraw-Hill, 1965.

Hart, J. T. Memory and the memory-monitoring process. *Journal of Verbal Learning and Verbal Behavior,* 1967, **6,** 685-691.

Hartry, A. L., Keith-Lee, P., & Morton, W. D. Planaria: Memory transfer through cannibalism reexamined. *Science,* 1964, **146,** 274-275.

Hartshorne, H., & May, M. A. *Studies in the nature of character.* Vol. 1. *Studies in deceit.* New York: Macmillan, 1928.

Hashim, S. A., & Van Itallie, T. B. Studies on normal and obese subjects with a monitored food dispensing device. *Annals of the New York Academy of Sciences,* 1965, **131,** 654-661.

Hastorf, A., & Cantril, H. They saw a game: A case study. *Journal of Abnormal and Social Psychology,* 1954, **49,** 129-134.

Havighurst, R. J. *Developmental tasks and education.* New York: Longmans, Green, 1952.

Havighurst, R. J. *Human development and education.* New York: Longmans, Green, 1953.

Hayes, K. J., & Hayes, C. Imitation in a home-raised chimpanzee. *Journal of Comparative and Physiological Psychology.* 1952, **45,** 450-459.

Heath, R. G. A biochemical hypothesis on the etiology of schizophrenia. In D. Jackson (Ed.), *The etiology of schizophrenia.* New York: Basic Books, 1960.

Hebb, D. O. *The organization of behavior.* New York: Wiley, 1949.

Hebb, D. O. *A textbook of psychology.* Philadelphia: Saunders, 1958.

Heckhausen, H. Achievement motive research: Current problems and some contributions towards a general theory of motivation. In W. Arnold (Ed.), *Nebraska symposium on motivation.* Lincoln: University of Nebraska Press, 1968.

Heider, F. Social perception and phenomenal causality. *Psychological Review,* 1944, **51,** 358-374

Heider, F. *The psychology of interpersonal relations.* New York: Wiley, 1958.

Heider, F., & Simmel, M. An experimental study of apparent behavior. *American Journal of Psychology,* 1944, **57,** 243-259.

Held, R. Plasticity in sensory-motor systems. *Scientific American,* 1965, **213**(5), 84-94.

Helfer, R. E., & Kempe, C. H. *The battered child.* Chicago: University of Chicago Press, 1968.

Heller, C. S. *Mexican-American youth: Forgotten youth at the crossroads.* New York: Random House, 1966.

Helmholtz, H. *Handbuch der physiologischen optik.* New York: Dover, 1952 (Orig. pub.: Leipsig: Voss, 1867.)

Helson, R. Sex differences in creative style. *Journal of Personality,* 1967, **35,** 214-233.

Henry, J. Homeostasis, society, and evolution: A critique. *Scientific Monthly,* 1955, **81,** 300-309.

Hernández-Peón, R., Scherrer, H., & Jouvet, M. Modification of electrical activity in cochlear nucleus during "attention" in unanesthetized cats. *Science,* 1956, **123,** 331-332.

Heron, W. Perception as a function of retinal locus. *American Journal of Psychology,* 1957, **70,** 38-48.

Heron, W. Cognitive and physiological effects of perceptual isolation. In P. Solomon, et al. (Eds.). *Sensory deprivation.* Cambridge: Harvard University Press, 1961.

Herrick, R. M., Myers, J. L., & Korotkin, A. L. Changes in S^D and S^Δ rates during the development of an operant discrimination. *Journal of Comparative and Physiological Psychology,* 1959, **52,** 359-363.

Herrnstein, R. J. Will. *Proceedings of the American Philosophical Society,* 1964, **108,** 455-458.

Hershenson, M., Munsinger, H., & Kessen, W. Preference for shapes of intermediate variability in the newborn human. *Science,* 1965, **147,** 630-631.

Hershkowitz, A. Naturalistic observations on chronically hospitalized patients. 1. The effects of "strangers." *Journal of Nervous and Mental Diseases,* 1962, **135,** 258-264.

Hershkowitz, A. Personal communication to the authors, November 1970.

Hess, W. R. Diencephalon: Autonomic and extrapyramidal functions. *Monographs in biology and medicine.* Vol. 3. New York: Grune & Stratton, 1954.

Hess, E. H. Space perception in the chick. *Scientific American,* 1956, **195**(1), 71-80.

Hess, E. H. Imprinting. *Science,* 1959, **130,** 133-141.

Hess, E. H., & Polt, J. M. Pupil size as related to interest value of visual stimuli. *Science,* 1960, **132,** 349-350.

Hess, E. H., Seltzer, A. L., & Shlien, J. M. Pupil response of hetero- and homosexual males to pictures of men and women: A pilot study. *Journal of Abnormal Psychology,* 1965, **70,** 165-168.

Hess, R. D., & Tenezakis, M. Guess what (who?) is most believable. Reported in *The Stanford Observer,* 1970. **4**(8), 11.

Hetherington, E. M., & Brackbill, Y. Etiology and co-variance of obstinacy, orderliness, and parsimony in young children. *Child Development,* 1963, **34,** 919-943.

Hichborn, F. *Story of the session of the California legislature of 1909,* San Francisco, 1909.

Hilgard, E. R. Learning and maturation in preschool children. *Journal of Genetic Psychology,* 1932, **41,** 36-56.

Hilgard, E. R. *Hypnotic susceptibility.* New York: Harcourt Brace Jovanovich, 1965.

Hilton, W. *The ladder of perfection.* Baltimore: Penguin Books, 1957.

Hinkle, L. E., Jr., & Plummer, N. Life stress and industrial absenteeism. *Industrial Medicine and Surgery,* 1952, **21,** 363-375.

Hirsch, J. Individual differences in behavior and their genetic basis. In E. L. Bliss (Ed.), *Roots of behavior.* New York: Hoeber, 1962.

Hitler, A. *Mein Kampf.* Cambridge, Mass.: Riverside, 1933.

Hodgkin, A. L., Huxley, A. F., & Katz, B. Ionic currents underlying the activity in the giant axon of the squid. *Archives of Scientific Physiology,* 1949, **3,** 129-150.

Hoebel, B., & Teitelbaum, P. Hypothalamic control of feeding and self-stimulation. *Science*, 1962, **135**, 375-377.

Hoffer, A. LSD: A review of its present status. *Clinical Pharmacological Therapy*, 1965, **183**, 49-57.

Hogan, R. A., & Kirchner, J. H. Implosive, eclectic, verbal and bibliotherapy in the treatment of fears of snakes. *Behavior Research and Therapy*, 1968, **6**, 167-171.

Hokanson, J. E., & Burgess, M. The effects of three types of aggression on vascular processes. *Journal of Abnormal and Social Psychology*, 1962, **64**, 446-449. (a)

Hokanson, J. E., & Burgess, M. The effects of status, type of frustration, and aggression on vascular processes. *Journal of Abnormal and Social Psychology*, 1962, **65**, 232-237. (b)

Hokanson, J. E., DeGood, D. E., Forrest, M. S., & Brittain, T. M. The availability of avoidance behaviors in modulating vascular stress responses. *Journal of Personality and Social Psychology*, 1971, in press.

Hollingshead, A. B., & Redlich, F. C. *Social class and mental illness: A community study.* New York: Wiley, 1958.

Holmes, D. S., & Schallow, J. R. Reduced recall after ego threat: Repression or response competition? *Journal of Personality and Social Psychology*, 1969, **13**, 145-152.

Holmes, O. W. *The poet at the breakfast table.* Boston: Houghton Mifflin, 1872.

Holzberg, J. D. The historical traditions of the state hospital as a force of resistance to the team. *American Journal of Orthopsychiatry*, 1960, **30**, 87-94.

Homme, L. E., de Baca, P. C., Devine, J. V., Steinhorst, R., & Rickert, E. J. Use of the Premack principle in controlling the behavior of nursery school children. *Journal of the Experimental Analysis of Behavior*, 1963, **6**, 544.

Hood, A. B. A study of the relationship between physique and personality variables measured by the MMPI. *Journal of Personality*, 1963, **31**, 97-107.

Horsley, J. S. *Narco-analysis.* New York: Oxford University Press, 1944.

Horst, P. *Personality: Measurement of dimensions.* San Francisco: Jossey-Boss, 1968.

Hosokawa, B. *Nisei: The quiet Americans.* New York: Morrow, 1969.

Hovland, C. I., Janis, I. L., & Kelley, H. H. *Communication and persuasion.* New Haven: Yale University Press, 1953.

Hubel, D. H., & Wiesel, T. N. Receptive fields of single neurones in the cat's striate cortex. *Journal of Physiology*, London, 1959, **148**, 574-591.

Hubel, D. H., Henson, C. D., Rupert, A., & Galambos, R. Attention units in the auditory cortex. *Science*, 1959, **129**, 1279-1280.

Hull, C. L. Quantitative aspects of the evolution of concepts. *Psychological Monographs*, 1920, **28** (Whole No. 8).

Hull, C. L. *A behavior system: An introduction to behavior theory concerning the individual organism.* New Haven: Yale University Press, 1952.

Hunt, J. McV. The effect of infant feeding frustration upon adult hoarding in the albino rat. *Journal of Abnormal and Social Psychology*, 1941, **36**, 338-380.

Husband, R. W. Human learning on a four-section, elevated finger maze. *Journal of General Psychology*, 1928, **1**, 15-28.

Huxley, A. *The doors of perception.* New York: Harper & Row, 1954.

Hyden, H. *Acta Physiologica Scandinavica Supplementum*, 1943, 17.

I

Inbau, F. E., & Reid, J. E. *Criminal interrogation and confessions.* Baltimore: Williams & Wilkins, 1962.

Insko, C. I. *Theories of attitude change.* New York: Appleton-Century-Crofts, 1967.

Irwin, O. C. Infant speech: Development of vowel sounds. *Journal of Speech and Hearing Disorders*, 1948, **13**, 31-34.

Irwin, O. C. The effect on speech sound frequency of systematic reading of stories to infants. Unpublished study by the Iowa Child Welfare Research Station, 1958. Reported in P. H. Mussen (Ed.), *Handbook of research methods in child development.* New York: Wiley, 1960.

Isaacs, W., Thomas, J., & Goldiamond, I. Application of operant conditioning to reinstate verbal behavior in psychotics. *Journal of Speech and Hearing Disorders*, 1960, **25**, 8-12.

Itani, J. The society of Japanese monkeys. *Japan Quarterly*, 1961, **8**(4), 421-430.

Itard, J. M. G. *The wild boy of Aveyron.* New York: Appleton-Century-Crofts, 1962.

J

Jackman, N., Schottstaedt, W., McPhail, S. C., & Wolf, S. Interaction, emotion, and physiological change. *Journal of Health and Human Behavior*, 1963, **4**, 83-87.

Jacobs, E., Winter, P. M., Alvis, H. J., & Small, S. M. Hyperbaric oxygen: Temporary aid for senile minds. *Journal of the American Medical Association*, 1969, **209**, 1435-1438.

Jacobs, H. L., & Sharma, K. N. Taste versus calories: Sensory and metabolic signals in the control of food intake. *Annals of the New York Academy of Sciences*, 1968, **134**.

Jacobs, R. C., & Campbell, D. T. The perpetuation of an arbitrary tradition through several generations of a laboratory micro culture. *Journal of Abnormal and Social Psychology*, 1961, **62**, 649-658. Copyright held by APA.

Jacobsen, C. F., Jacobsen, M. M., & Yoshioka, J. G. Development of an infant chimpanzee during her first year. *Comparative Psychology Monographs*, 1932, **9**(1), 1-94.

Jacobson, A., Kales, A., Lehmann, D., & Zweizig, J. R. Somnambulism: All night EEG studies. *Science*, 1965, **148**, 975-977.

Jacobson, E. Electrophysiology of mental activities. *American Journal of Psychology*, 1932, **44**, 677-694.

Jakobson, R. *Child, language, aphasia, and phonological universals.* The Hague: Mouton, 1968.

Jakobson, R., & Halle, M. *Fundamentals of language.* The Hague: Mouton, 1956.

James, W. Subjective effects of nitrous oxide. *Mind*, 1882, **7**, 186-208.

James, W. What is an emotion? *Mind*, 1884, **9**, 188-205.

James, W. *The principles of psychology.* Vol. 1. New York: Holt, 1890.

James, W. *Essays in radical empiricism.* New York: Longmans, Green, 1912.

James, W. An analysis of esophageal feeding as a form of operant reinforcement in the dog. *Psychological Reports,* 1963, **12,** 31-39.

Janis, I. Psychological stress. New York: Wiley, 1958.

Janis, I. L., & King, B. T. The influence of role-playing on opinion change. *Journal of Abnormal and Social Psychology,* 1954, **49,** 211-218.

Jenkins, D. C., Rosenman, R. H., & Friedman, M. Development of an objective psychological test for the determination of the coronary-prone behavior pattern in employed men. *Journal of Chronic Diseases,* 1967, **20,** 371-379.

Jensen, D. D. Paramecia, planaria and pseudo-learning. Learning and associated phenomena in invertebrates. *Animal Behavior Supplement,* 1965, **1,** 9-20.

Joint Commission on Mental Illness and Health. *Action for mental health.* New York: Basic Books, 1961.

Jones, A., Bentler, P. M., & Petry, G. The reduction of uncertainty concerning future pain. *Journal of Abnormal Psychology,* 1966, **71,** 87-94.

Jones, E. *Ingratiation.* New York: Appleton-Century-Crofts, 1964.

Jones, E. E., & Harris, V. A. The attribution of attitudes. *Journal of Experimental Social Psychology,* 1967, **3,** 1-24.

Jones, H., & Scott. W. *Hermaphroditism, genital anomalies and endocrine disorders.* Williams & Wilkins, 1958.

Jones, H. E. *Motor performance and growth.* Berkeley: University of California Press, 1949.

Jones, L. V., & Bock, R. D. Multiple discriminant analysis applied to "ways to live" ratings from six cultural groups. *Sociometry,* 1960, **23**(2), 163-164.

Jones, S. C., & Panitch, D. The self-fulfilling prophecy and interpersonal attraction. *Journal of Experimental Social Psychology.* 1970, in press.

Jouvet, M., & Delorme, F. Locus coeruleus et sommeil paradoxal. *C. R. Soc. Biol.,* 1965, **1959,** 895.

K

Kagan, J., & Lewis, M. Studies of attention in the human infant. *Merrill-Palmer Quarterly of Behavior and Development,* 1965, **11,** 95-127.

Kahn, M. The physiology of catharsis. *Journal of Personality and Social Psychology,* 1966, **3,** 278-286.

Kamin, L. J. Predictability, surprise, attention, and conditioning. In R. Church & B. Campbell (Eds.), *Punishment and aversive behavior.* New York: Appleton-Century-Crofts, 1969.

Kamiya, J. Operant control of the EEG alpha rhythm and some of its reported effects on consciousness. In C. Tart (Ed.), *Altered states of consciousness.* New York: Wiley, 1969.

Kanner, L. Autistic disturbances of affective contact. *Nervous Child,* 1943, **2,** 217-250.

Kaplan, B. *The inner world of mental illness.* New York: Harper & Row, 1964.

Kaplan, E. L., & Kaplan, G. A. Is there such a thing as a prelinguistic child? In J. Eliot (Ed.), *Human development and cognitive processes.* New York: Holt, Rinehart & Winston, 1970.

Kasamatsu, A., & Hirai, T. An EEG study on the Zen meditation. *Folia Psyckiatria Neurologica Japonica,* 1966, **20,** 315-336.

Katz, D. The scriptochronograph. *Quarterly Journal of Experimental Psychology,* 1948, **1,** 53-56.

Katz, E. The two-step flow of communication: An up-to-date report on an hypothesis. *Public Opinion Quarterly,* 1957, **21,** 61-78.

Katz, I. The socialization of academic motivation in minority group children. In D. Levine (Ed.), *Nebraska symposium on motivation.* Lincoln: University of Nebraska Press, 1967.

Katz, I. Experimental studies of negro-white relationships. In L. Berkowitz (Ed.), *Advances in experimental social psychology.* Vol. 5. New York: Academic Press, 1970.

Kaufman, I., & Rock, I. The moon illusion. *Scientific American,* 1962, **204,** 120-130.

Kavanau, J. L. Behavior of captive white-footed mice. *Science,* 1967, **155,** 1623-1639.

Keeton, W. *Biological sciences.* New York: Norton, 1967.

Kelley, H. H. The warm-cold variable in first impressions of persons. *Journal of Personality,* 1950, **18,** 431-439.

Kelley, H. H. Attribution theory in social psychology. In D. Levine (Ed.), *Nebraska symposium on motivation.* Lincoln: University of Nebraska Press, 1967.

Kelley, H. H., Condry, J. C., Dahlke, A. E., & Hill, A. H. Collective behavior in a simulated panic situation. *Journal of Experimental Social Psychology,* 1965, **1,** 20-54.

Kellogg, W. N., & Kellogg, L. A. *The ape and the child: A study of environmental influence on early behavior.* New York: Hafner, 1967. (Originally published: New York: McGraw-Hill, 1933.)

Kelly, G. A. Man's construction of his alternatives. In G. Lindzey (Ed.), *Assessment of human motives.* New York: Holt, Rinehart & Winston, 1958.

Kelly, R. B., Atkinson, M. R., Huberman, J. A., & Kornberg, A. Excision of thymine dimers and other mismatched sequences by DNA polymerase of escherichia coli. Unpublished mimeograph report, Stanford, 1969.

"Kerner" commission. *Report of the U.S. National Advisory Commission on Civil Disorders.* Washington, D.C.: U.S. Government Printing Office, 1968.

Kessen, W. *The child.* New York: Wiley, 1965.

Kety, S. S. Psychoendocrine systems and emotions: Biological aspects. In D. C. Glass (Ed.), *Neurophysiology and emotion.* New York: Rockefeller University Press, 1967. (a)

Kety, S. S. Relationship between energy metabolism of the brain and functional activity. In S. S. Kety, E. V. Evarts, & H. L. Williams (Eds.), *Sleep and altered states of consciousness.* Baltimore: Williams & Wilkins, 1967. (b)

Keys, A., Brôzek, J., Henschel, A., Mickelson, O., & Taylor, H. L. *The biology of human starvation.* Minneapolis: University of Minnesota Press, 1950.

Kiesler, C. A., Collins, R. E., & Miller, N. E. *Attitude change: A critical analysis of theoretical approaches.* New York: Wiley, 1969.

Kimble, G. A. *Hilgard and Marquis' conditioning and learning.* (2nd ed.) New York: Appleton-Century-Crofts, 1961.

Kimura, D. Cerebral dominance and the perception of verbal stimuli. *Canadian Journal of Psychology,* 1961, **15,** 166-171.

Kimura, D. Left-right differences in the perception of melodies. *Quarterly Journal of Experimental Psychology,* 1964, **16**, 355-358.

King, J. H. Brief account of the sufferings of a detachment of United States Cavalry, from deprivation of water, during a period of eighty-six hours while scouting on the "Llano Estacado," or "Staked Plains," Texas. *American Journal of Medical Science, 1878,* **75**, 404-408.

King, S. H., & Henry, A. F. Aggression and cardiovascular reactions related to parental control over behavior. *Journal of Abnormal and Social Psychology,* 1955, **50**, 206-210.

Kinsey, A. C., Martin, C. E., & Pomeroy, W. B. *Sexual behavior in the human male.* Philadelphia: Saunders, 1948.

Kinsey, A. C., Pomeroy, W. E., Martin, C. E., & Gebhard, R. H. *Sexual behavior in the human female.* Philadelphia: Saunders, 1953.

Kinzel, A. F. Body-buffer zone in violent prisoners. Paper presented at the meeting of the American Psychiatric Association, May 1969.

Kirtner, W. L., & Cartwright, D. S. Success and failure in client-centered therapy as a function of client personality variables. *Journal of Consulting Psychology,* 1958, **22**, 259-264.

Klein, R. F., Bogdonoff, M. D., Estes, E. H., Jr., & Shaw, D. M. Analysis of the factors affecting the resting FFA level in normal man. *Circulation,* 1960, **22**, 772.

Klerman, G. L., & Cole, J. O. *Pharmacological Review,* 1965, **17**, 101.

Klimova, V. I. The properties of the components of some orientation reactions. In *The orientation reaction and orienting-investigation of activity.* Moscow: Academy of Pedagogical Sciences, 1958.

Kline, N. S. Use of *Rauwolfia serpentina* Benth. in neuropsychiatric conditions. *Annals of the New York Academy of Sciences,* 1954, **59**, 107-132.

Klineberg, O. Emotional expression in Chinese literature. *Journal of Abnormal and Social Psychology,* 1938, **33**, 517-520.

Knapp, R., Kause, R., & Perkins, C. Immediate vs. delayed shock in t-maze performance. *Journal of Experimental Psychology,* 1959, **58**, 357-362.

Kohler, W. *The mentality of apes.* New York: Harcourt Brace Jovanovich, 1926.

Kohts, N. *Infant ape and human child.* Moscow: Museum Darwinianum, 1935.

Kolers, P. A., & Perkins, D. N. Orientation of letters and their speed of recognition. *Perception and Psychophysics,* 1969, **5**, 279-280.

Krafft-Ebing, R. V. *Psychopathia sexualis.* New York: Physicians & Surgeons Book Company, 1932.

Kramer, M., Goldstein, H., Israel, R. H., & Johnson, N. A. A historical study of the disposition of first admissions to a state mental hospital. Experience of the Warren State Hospital during the period 1916-1950. *Public Health Monographs,* 1955, No. 32.

Kretschmer, E. *Physique and character.* (2nd ed.) New York: Harcourt Brace Jovanovich, 1925.

Krim, S. *Views of a nearsighted cannoneer.* New York: Excelsior Press.

Kringlen, E. Schizophrenia in twins. *Schizophrenia Bulletin,* December 1969, Issue 1, 27-39.

Kroger, W. S. *Clinical and experimental hypnosis.* Philadelphia: Lippincott, 1963.

Krueger, W. C. F. The effect of overlearning on retention. *Journal of Experimental Psychology,* 1929, **12**, 71-78.

Kubala, A. L., & Katz, M. M. Nutritional factors in psychological test behavior. *Journal of Genetic Psychology,* 1960, **96**, 343-352.

Kuder, G. F. *Administrator's manual, Kuder Preference Record.* Chicago: Science Research Associates, 1960. Copyright © 1960, by G. Frederick Kuder. Sample items Reprinted by permission of the publisher.

Kuder, G. F. Some principles of interest measurement. *Educational and Psychological Measurement,* 1970, **30**, 205-226.

Kunkel, B. W. Members one of another. *Scientific Monthly,* 1917, **4**, 534-543.

Kupalov, P. S. Some normal and pathological properties of nervous processes in the brain. In N. S. Kline (Ed.), *Pavlovian conference on higher nervous activity. Annals of the New York Academy of Sciences,* 1961, **92**, 1046-1053.

L

Lacey, J. I. Somatic response patterning and stress: Some revisions of activation theory. In M. H. Appley & R. Trumbull (Eds.), *Psychological stress: Issues in research.* New York: Appleton-Century-Crofts, 1967.

Lacey, J. I., Kagan, J., Lacey, B. C., & Moss, H. A. The visceral level: Situational determinants and behavioral correlates of autonomic response patterns. In P. H. Knapp (Ed.), *Expression of the emotions in man.* New York: International Universities Press, 1963.

Lachman, S. J. A behavioristic rationale for the development of psychosomatic phenomenon. *Journal of Psychology,* 1963, **56**, 239-248.

Laing, R. D. *The Politics of Experience.* New York: Pantheon, 1967.

Landauer, T. K., & Whiting, J. W. M. Infantile stimulation and adult stature of human males. *American Anthropologist,* 1964, **66**, 1007-1028.

Landis, C., & Cushman, J. F. The relation of national prohibition to the incidence of mental disease. *Quarterly Journal of Studies on Alcohol,* 1945, **5**, 527-534.

Landreth, C., & Johnson, B. C. Young children's responses to a picture inset test designed to reveal reactions to presence of different skin color. *Child Development Monographs,* 1953, **24**, 63-80.

Lane, R. C., & Singer, J. L. Familial attitudes in paranoid schizophrenia and normals from two socioeconomic classes. *Journal of Abnormal and Social Psychology,* 1959, **59**, 328-339.

Langner, T. S., et al. Reported in *The New York Times,* March 2, 1970, p. 28.

Lasagna, L., Mosteller, F., von Felsinger, J. M., & Beecher, H. K. A study of the placebo response. *American Journal of Medicine,* 1954, **16**, 770-779.

Lashley, K. S. *Brain mechanisms and intelligence.* Chicago: University of Chicago Press, 1929.

Lashley, K. S. An experimental analysis of instinctive behavior. *Psychological Review,* 1938, **45**, 445-472.

Lashley, K. S. Persistent problems in the evolution of mind. *Quarterly Review of Biology,* 1949, **24**, 28-42.

Lashley, K. S. In search of the engram. In *Physiological mechanisms in animal behavior: Symposium of the Society for Experimental Biology.* New York: Academic Press, 1960.

Latané, B. (Ed.) Studies in social comparison: Introduction and overview. *Journal of Experimental Social Psychology,* 1966, **2,** Supplement No. 1.

Lazarsfeld, P. F., Berelson, B., & Gaudet, H. *The people's choice.* (2nd ed.) New York: Columbia University Press, 1948.

Lazarus, R. S. Emotions and adaptation: Conceptual and empirical relations. In W. J. Arnold (Ed.), *Nebraska symposium on motivation.* Lincoln: University of Nebraska Press, 1968.

Lazarus, R. S., & McCleary, R. A. Autonomic discrimination without awareness: A study of subception. *Psychological Review,* 1951, **58,** 113-122.

Leach, B. E., & Heath, R. G. The in vitro oxidation of epinephrine in plasma. *American Medical Association Archives of Neurology and Psychiatry,* 1956, **76,** 444-450.

Leach, B. E., et al. Studies of the role of ceruloplasmin and albumin in adrenaline metabolism. *American Medical Association Archives of Neurology and Psychiatry,* 1956, **76,** 635-642.

Leahy, A. M. Nature-nurture and intelligence. *Genetic Psychology Monographs,* 1935, **17,** 23-308.

Leeper, R. A study of a neglected portion of the field of learning: The development of sensory organization. *Pedagogical Seminary and Journal of Genetic Psychology,* 1935, **46,** 41-75.

Leeper, R. W. A motivational theory of emotion to replace "emotion as disorganized response." *Psychological Review,* 1948, **55,** 5-21.

Lefford, A. The influence of emotional subject matter on logical reasoning. *Journal of General Psychology,* 1946, **34,** 127-151.

Lehman, H. C. Chronological age vs. proficiency in physical skills. *American Journal of Psychology,* 1951, **64,** 161-187.

Leiderman, H. Imagery and sensory deprivation. *Proceedings of the Third World Congress of Psychiatry,* Montreal: University of Toronto Press, McGill University Press, 1965.

Lenneberg, E. H. On explaining language. *Science,* 1969, **164,** 635-643.

Leo, J. Women are said to be infringing on another men's prerogative: The freedom to curse. *The New York Times,* October 20, 1968, p. 49.

Lerner, M. J., & Simmons, C. H. Observers' reaction to the innocent victim: Compassion or rejection. *Journal of Personality and Social Psychology,* 1966, **4,** 203-210.

LeShan, L. An emotional life-history pattern associated with neoplactic disease. *Annals of the New York Academy of Sciences,* 1966, **125,** 780-793.

Leslie, J. Ethics and practice of placebo therapy. *American Journal of Medicine,* 1954, **16,** 854.

Lettvin, J. V., Maturana, H. R., McCulloch, W. S., & Pitts, W. H. What the frog's eye tells the frog's brain. *Proceedings of the Institute for Radio Engineers of New York,* 1959, **47,** 1940-1951.

Leukel, F. A comparison of the effects of ECS and anesthesia on acquisition of the maze habit. *Journal of Compara-*

tive and Physiological Psychology, 1957, **50,** 300-306.

Leventhal, H. Fear communications in the acceptance of preventive health practices. *Bulletin of the New York Academy of Sciences,* 1965, **41,** 1144-1168.

Levine, A. J. Alienation in the metropolis. Unpublished doctoral dissertation, Columbia University, 1968.

Levine, J. M., & Murphy, G. The learning and forgetting of controversial material. *Journal of Abnormal and Social Psychology,* 1943, **38,** 507-517.

Levine, S. The psychophysiological effects of infantile stimulation. In E. L. Bliss (Ed.), *Roots of Behavior.* New York: Harper & Row, 1962.

Levitt, E. E. Psychotherapy with children: A further evaluation. *Behavior Research and Therapy,* 1963, **1,** 45-51.

Lewin, K. Group decision and social change. In T. M. Newcomb & E. L. Hartley (Eds.), *Readings in social psychology.* New York: Holt, Rinehart, & Winston, 1947.

Lewin, K. Role of depression in the production of illness in pernicious anemia. *Psychosomatic Medicine,* 1959, **21,** 23-27.

Lewin, K., Lippitt, R., & White, R. K. Patterns of aggressive behavior in experimentally created social climates. *Journal of Social Psychology,* 1939, **10,** 271-299.

Lewis, M. M. *Infant speech.* London: Routledge and Kegan Paul, 1951.

Lewis, O. *Life in a Mexican village: Tepoztlan restudied.* Urbana, Illinois: University of Illinois Press, 1963

Liddell, H. S. The conditioned reflex. In F. A. Moss (Ed.), *Comparative psychology.* New York: Prentice-Hall, 1934.

Liddell, H. S. *Emotional hazards in animals and man.* Springfield, Ill.: Thomas, 1956.

Liebermen, M. A., Yalom, I. D., & Miles, M. D. The group experience project: A comparison of ten encounter technologies. In L. Bank, G. G. Gottsegen, & M. G. Gottsegen (Eds.), *Encounter: Confrontations in self and interpersonal awareness.* New York: Macmillan, 1971, in press.

Lindauer, M. S. Pleasant and unpleasant emotions in literature: A comparison with the affective tone of psychology. *Journal of Psychology,* 1968, **70,** 55-67.

Lindsley, D. B., Schreiner, L. H., Knowles, W. B., & Magoun, H. W. Behavioral and EEG changes following chronic brain stem lesions in the cat. *Electroencephalography and Clinical Neurophysiology,* 1950, **2,** 483-498.

Lindsley, O. R. Operant conditioning methods applied to research in chronic schizophrenia. *Psychiatric Research Reports,* 1956, **5,** 118-139. (a)

Lindsley, O. R. *Progress report I: An experimental analysis of psychotic behavior.* Research Grant MH-977. National Institute of Health, June 1956. (b)

Linton, H. B., Epstein, L., & Hartford, H. Personality and perceptual correlates of secondary beginning strokes in handwriting. *Percept. mot. Skills,* 1961, **12,** 271-281.

Linton, H. B., Epstein, L., & Hartford, H. Personality and perceptual correlates of primary beginning strokes in handwriting. *Percept. mot. Skills.* 1962, **15,** 159-170.

Lipsitt, L. P. Learning processes of human newborns. *Merrill-Palmer Quarterly of Behavior and Development,* 1966, **12,** 45-71.

Lipsitt, L. P., Engen, T., & Kaye, H. Developmental changes in the olfactory threshold of the neonate. *Child Development,* 1963, **34,** 371-376.

Lockard, J. S. Choice of a warning signal or no warning

signal in an unavoidable shock situation. *Journal of Comparative and Physiological Psychology,* 1963, **56,** 526-530.

Long, L. Conceptual relationships in children: The concept of roundness. *Journal of Genetic Psychology,* 1940, **57,** 289-315.

Lorenz, K. Der Kumpan in der Umvelt des Vogels. Der Artgenosse als auslösendes Moment sozialer Verhaltungsweisen. *Journal of Ornithology,* 1935, **83,** 137-213.

Lorenz, K. Morphology and behavior patterns in closely allied species. In B. Schoffner (Ed.), *Group processes.* New York: Josiah Macy, 1955.

Lorenz, K. *On aggression.* New York: Harcourt Brace Jovanovich, 1966.

Lorge, I. Influence of regularly interpolated time intervals upon subsequent learning. *Teachers College Contributions to Education,* 1930, No. 438.

Lovaas, O. I. Learning theory approach to the treatment of childhood schizophrenia. In California Mental Health Research Symposium, No. 2. *Behavior Theory and Therapy.* Sacramento, California: Dept. of Mental Hygiene, 1968.

Lubin, A. A note on Sheldon's table of correlations between temperamental traits. *British Journal of Psychology, Statistical Section,* 1950, **3,** 186-189.

Luby, E. D., Frohman, C. E., Grisell, J. L., Lenzo, J. E., & Gottlieb, J. S. Sleep deprivation: Effects on behavior, thinking, motor performance and biological energy transfer systems. *Psychosomatic Medicine,* 1960, **22,** 182-192.

Luce, G. G. *Current research on sleep and dreams.* Health Service Publication No. 1389. U.S. Department of Health, Education, and Welfare, 1965.

Luchins, A. S. Mechanization in problem solving—The effect of Einstellung. *Psychological Monographs,* 1942, **54**(6, Whole No. 248).

Luchins, A. S. An approach to evaluating the achievement of group psychotherapy. *Journal of Social Psychology,* 1960, **52,** 345-353.

Luchins, A. S., & Luchins, E. H. *Rigidity of behavior.* Portland: University of Oregon Press, 1959.

Luckhardt, A. B., & Carlson, A. J. Contributions to the physiology of the stomach. XVII. On the chemical control of the gastric hunger contractions. *American Journal of Physiology,* 1915, **36,** 37-46.

Lundin, R. W. *Personality: An experimental approach.* New York: Macmillan, 1961.

Luria, A. R. *The mentally retarded child.* Oxford: Pergamon Press, 1963.

Luria, A. R. *The mind of a mnemonist.* New York: Basic Books, 1968.

Luria, A. R. The functional organization of the brain. *Scientific American,* 1970, **222** (3), 66-78.

M

McCain, G., & Segal, E. M. *The game of science.* Belmont, Calif.: Brooks/Cole, 1969.

McCleary, R. A., & Moore, R. Y. *Subcortical mechanisms of behavior.* New York: Basic Books, 1965.

McClelland, D. C. *The achieving society.* Princeton: Van Nostrand, 1961.

McClelland, D. C. Toward a theory of motive acquisition. *American Psychologist,* 1965, **20,** 321-333.

McClelland, D., & Winter, D. *Motivating economic achievement.* New York: Free Press, 1969.

McClelland, D., Atkinson, J. W., Clark, R. A., & Lowell, E. L. *The achievement motive.* New York: Appleton-Century-Crofts, 1953.

Maccoby, E. (Ed.) *Development of sex differences.* Stanford, Calif.: Stanford University Press, 1966.

McConnell, J. V. Memory transfer through cannibalism in planaria. *Journal of Neuropsychiatry,* 1962, **3,** 45.

McConnell, J. V., Jacobson, A. L., & Kimble, D. P. The effects of regeneration upon retention of a conditioned response in the planarian. *Journal of Comparative and Physiological Psychology,* 1959, **52,** 1-5.

McConnell, R. A. ESP and credibility in science. *American Psychologist,* 1969, **24,** 531-538.

MacCurdy, J. T. War neurosis. Cambridge, 1918. Cited in E. Miller (Ed.), *The neuroses in war.* New York: Macmillan, 1940.

McFarland, J. W., Gimbel, H. W., Donald, W. A. J., & Folkenberg, E. J. The 5-day program to help individuals stop smoking. *Connecticut Medicine,* 1964, **28,** 885-890.

McGinnies, E. Emotionality and perceptual defense. *Psychological Review,* 1949, **56,** 244-251.

McGinnies, E., & Sherman, H. Generalization of perceptual defense. *Journal of Abnormal and Social Psychology,* 1952, **47,** 81-85.

McGlashin, T. H., Evans, F. J., & Orne, M. T. The nature of hypnotic analgesic and placebo response to experimental pain. *Psychosomatic Medicine,* 1969, **31,** 227-246.

McGuigan, F. J. Covert oral behavior during the silent performance of language tasks. *Psychological Bulletin,* 1970, **74,** 309-326.

McGuire, W. The nature of attitudes and attitude change. In G. L. Lindsey & E. Aronson (Eds.), *The handbook of social psychology.* Vol. III. Reading, Mass.: Addison-Wesley, 1969.

Machiavelli, N. *Discourses.* 2 vol. New York: Humanities, 1950. (Originally published, 1531.)

Machiavelli, N. *The prince.* Baltimore, Md.: Penguin, 1961. (Originally published, 1532)

MacKinnon, D. W. An assessment study of Air Force officers. Part V. Summary and applications. *WADC Technical Report* 58-91 (V). Wright Air Development Center, 1958.

MacKinnon, D. W. The study of creativity and creativity in architects. In *Conference on the creative person.* Berkeley: University of California, Institute of Personality Assessment and Research, 1961.

MacLean, P. D. Psychosomatics. In J. Field, H. W. Magoun, & V. E. Hall (Eds.), *Handbook of physiology.* Vol. 3. Washington, D.C.: American Physiological Society, 1960.

McNair, D. M., Goldstein, A. P., Lorr, M., Cibelli, L. A., & Roth, I. Some effects of chlordiazepoxide and meprobamate with psychiatric outpatients. *Psychopharmacologia,* 1965, **7,** 256-265.

MacNeilage, P. F. EEG amplitude changes during different cognitive processes involving similar stimuli and responses. *Psychophysiology,* 1966, **4,** 280-286.

McNemar, Q. *The revision of the Stanford-Binet Scale.* Boston: Houghton Mifflin, 1942.

McNemar, Q. Lost: Our intelligence? Why? *American Psychologist,* 1964, **19,** 871-882.

Madigan, F. C. (Ed.) *Human factors in Philippine rural de-*

velopment. Cagayan de Oro City: Xavier University Press, 1967.

Madsen, C. H., Jr., Becker, W. C., Thomas, D. R., Koser, L., & Plager, E. An analysis of the reinforcing function of "sit down" commands. In R. K. Parker (Ed.), *Readings in educational psychology.* Boston: Allyn & Bacon, 1968.

Magoun, H. W. Central neural inhibition. In M. R. Jones (Ed.), *Nebraska symposium on motivation.* Lincoln: University of Nebraska Press, 1963. (a)

Magoun, H. W. *The waking brain.* (2nd ed.) Springfield, Ill.: Thomas, 1963. (b)

Mahesh Yogi, M. *Maharishi Mahesh Yogi on the Bhagavad-Gita: A Zen translation and commentary.* Baltimore: Penguin, 1969.

Maller, O., Clark, J. M., & Kare, M. R. Short-term caloric regulation in the adult opossum. *Proceedings of the Society for Experimental Biology and Medicine,* 1965, **118,** 275-277.

Mallick, S. K., & McCandless, B. R. A study of catharsis of aggression. *Journal of Personality and Social Psychology,* 1966, **4,** 591-596.

Mallory, E. B., & Miller, V. B. A possible basis for the association of voice characteristics and personality traits. *Speech Monographs,* 1958, **25,** 255-260.

Malmo, R. B. Activation: A neuropsychological dimension. *Psychological Review,* 1959, **66,** 367-386.

Maltzman, I. On the training of originality. *Psychological Review,* 1960, **67,** 229-242.

Manis, M. *Cognitive processes.* Belmont, Calif.: Wadsworth Publishing Co., 1966.

Mann, L. Persuasive doll play: A technique of directive psychotherapy for use with children. *Journal of Clinical Psychology,* 1957, **13,** 14-19.

Mann, R. D. A review of the relationships between personality and performance in small groups. *Psychological Bulletin.* 1959, **56,** 241-270.

Mansson, H. H. Justifying the final solution. Paper presented at the International Congress of Psychology, London, 1969.

Maranon, G. Contribution à l'étude de l'action émotive de l'adrénaline. *Revue Fr. Endocrinal,* 1924, **2,** 301-325.

Maris, R. W. *Forces in urban suicide.* Homewood, Ill.: Dorsey Press, 1969.

Mark, J. C. The attitudes of the mothers of male schizophrenics toward child behavior. *Journal of Abnormal and Social Psychology,* 1953, **48,** 185-189.

Mark, V., & Ervin, F. R. *Violence and the brain.* New York: Harper & Row, 1970, in press.

Marks, I. M., & Gelder, M. G. Transvetism and fetishism: Clinical and psychological changes during faradic aversion. *British Journal of Psychiatry,* 1967, **113,** 711-729.

Marks, L. E., & Miller, G. A. The role of semantic and syntactic constraints in the memorization of English sentences. *Journal of Verbal Learning and Verbal Behavior,* 1964, **3,** 1-5.

Marler, P. Acoustical influences in bird song development. *The Rockefeller University Review,* Sept.-Oct. 1967, 8-13.

Martens, S., et al. Glutathione levels in mental and physical illness. *American Medical Association Archives of Neurology and Psychiatry,* 1956, **76,** 630-634.

Maslow, A. H. *Motivation and personality.* New York: Harper & Row, 1954.

Maslow, A. H. Psychological data and value theory. In A. H. Maslow (Ed.), *New knowledge in human values.* New York: Harper & Row, 1959.

Maslow, A. H. *Toward a psychology of being.* Princeton, N.J.: Van Nostrand, 1962.

Mason, D. J. Judgments of leadership based upon physiognomic cues. *Journal of Abnormal and Social Psychology,* 1957, **54,** 273-274.

Mason, J. W., Brady, J. V., & Tolson, W. W. Behavioral adaptations and endocrine activity. In R. Levine (Ed.), *Endocrines and the central nervous system.* Proceedings of the Association for Research in Mental Diseases. Vol. 43. Baltimore: Williams & Wilkins, 1966.

Masserman, J. H. *Behavior and neurosis.* Chicago: University of Chicago Press, 1943.

Massett, L. Learning to control the uncontrollable. *Science News,* 1970, **97,** 259.

Masters, W. H., & Johnson, V. E. *Human sexual response.* Boston: Little, Brown, 1966.

Masters, W. H., & Johnson, V. E. *Human sexual inadequacy.* Boston: Little, Brown, 1970.

Max, L. W. Experimental study of the motor theory of consciousness. IV. Action-current responses in the deaf during awakening. Kinesthetic imagery and abstract thinking. *Journal of Comparative Psychology,* 1937, **24,** 301-344.

May, R. The origins and significance of the existential movement on psychology. In R. May, E. Angel, & H. F. Ellenberger (Eds.), *Existence: A new dimension in psychiatry and psychology.* New York: Basic Books, 1958.

Mayer, J. Regulation of energy intake and body weight: The glucostatic theory and the lipostatic hypothesis. *Annals of the New York Academy of Sciences,* 1955, **63,** 15-43.

Mayer, J. *Overweight: Causes, cost and control.* Englewood Cliffs, N.J.: Prentice-Hall, 1968.

Mayfield, E. C. The selection interview: A re-evaluation of published research. *Personnel Psychology,* 1964, **17,** 239-260.

Mead, M. *Coming of age in Samoa.* New York: Morrow, 1961. (Originally published, 1938.)

Mead, M., & Bateson, G. *Balinese character.* New York: Academy of Sciences, 1942.

Meadow, W. *Changing attitudes toward women as revealed in anti-woman popular humor.* Unpublished mimeograph report, Stanford University, 1970.

Megargee, E. I. Undercontrolled and overcontrolled personality types in extreme antisocial aggression. *Psychological Monographs,* 1966, **80**(Whole No. 611).

Mehrabian, A. Communication without words. In *Readings in psychology today.* Del Mar, Calif.: CRM Books, Inc., 1969.

Melzack, R., & Scott, T. H. The effects of early experience on the response to pain. *Journal of Comparative and Physiological Psychology,* 1957, **50,** 155-161.

Melzack, R., & Wall, P. D. Pain mechanisms: A new theory. *Science,* 1965, **150,** 971-979.

Menninger Clinic, Children's Division. *Disturbed children.* San Francisco: Jossey-Bass, 1969.

Merrill, R. M. The effect of pre-experimental and experimental anxiety on recall efficiency. *Journal of Experimental Psychology,* 1954, **48,** 167-172.

Meyer, R. J., & Haggerty, R. J. Streptococcal infections in families: Factors altering individual susceptibility. *Pediatrics,* 1962, **29,** 539.

Meyer, W. U. Reported in W. Arnold (Ed.), *Nebraska symposium on motivation.* Lincoln: University of Nebraska Press, 1968.

Michelet, J. *Satanism and witchcraft: A study in medieval superstition.* New York: Citadel, 1962.

Milgram, S. Behavioral study of obedience. *Journal of Abnormal and Social Psychology,* 1963, **67,** 371-378.

Milgram, S. Group pressure and action against a person. *Journal of Abnormal and Social Psychology,* 1964, **69,** 137-143.

Milgram, S. Some conditions of obedience and disobedience to authority. *Human Relations,* 1965, **18,** 57-75. (a)

Milgram, S. Liberating effects of group pressure. *Journal of Personality and Social Psychology,* 1965, **1,** 127-134. (b)

Milgram, S. The experience of living in cities. *Science,* 1970, **167,** 1461-1468.

Mill, J. S. *A system of logic.* (9th ed.) Vol. 1. *Ratiocinative and inductive.* London: Longmans, Green, Reader, & Dyer, 1875. (Originally published, 1843.)

Miller, E. (Ed.) *The neuroses in war.* New York: Macmillan, 1940.

Miller G. A. The magical number seven plus or minus two: Some limits on our capacity for processing information. *Psychological Review,* 1956, **63,** 81-97.

Miller, G. A. *The psychology of communication: Seven essays.* New York: Basic Books, 1967.

Miller, G. A., & Isard, S. Some perceptual consequences of linguistic rules. *Journal of Verbal Learning and Verbal Behavior,* 1963, **2,** 217-228.

Miller, G. A., & Selfridge, J. A. Verbal context and the recall of meaningful material. *American Journal of Psychology,* 1950, **63,** 176-185.

Miller, N. E. The frustration-aggression hypothesis. *Psychological Review,* 1941, **48,** 337-342.

Miller, N. E. Experimental studies of conflict. In J. McV. Hunt (Ed.), *Personality and the behavior disorders.* Vol. 1. New York: Ronald Press, 1944.

Miller, N. E. Fear as an acquired drive. *Journal of Experimental Psychology,* 1948, **38,** 89-101.

Miller, N. E. Experiments on motivation. *Science,* 1957, **126,** 1271-1278.

Miller, N. E. Liberalization of basic S-R concepts: Extensions to conflict behavior, motivation and social learning. In S. Koch (Ed.), *Psychology: A study of a science.* New York: McGraw-Hill, 1959.

Miller, N. E. Learning of visceral and glandular responses. *Science,* 1969, **163,** 434-445.

Miller, N. E., & Dollard, J. *Social learning and imitation.* New Haven: Yale University Press, 1941.

Miller, R. E., Banks, J. H., Jr., & Ogawa, N. Communication of affect in cooperative conditioning of rhesus monkeys. *J. abnorm. soc. Psychol.,* 1962, **64,** 343-348.

Miller, W. Violent crime in city gangs. *The American Academy of Political and Social Science,* March 1966.

Mills, R. B., McDevitt, R. J., & Tonkin, S. Situational tests in metropolitan police recruit selection. *Journal of Criminal Law, Criminology, & Political Science Annals,* 1966, **57** (1), 99-106.

Mills, W. G. The spirit in gambling. *Sporting News,* 1953, **3.**

Milner, B., & Penfield, W. The effect of hippocampal lesion on recent memory. *Transactions of the American Neurological Association,* 1955, **80,** 42-48.

Mintz, A. Non-adaptive group behavior. *Journal of Abnormal and Social Psychology,* 1951, **46,** 150-159.

Mischel, W. *Personality and assessment.* New York: Wiley, 1968.

Mischel, W. Towards a reconceptualization of personality. Paper presented at the meeting of the Western Psychological Association, Vancouver, B.C., June 1969.

Mishkin, M., & Forgays, D. G. Word recognition as a function of retinal locus. *Journal of Experimental Psychology,* 1952, **43,** 43-48.

Miyodi, D. Social life of Japanese monkeys. *Science,* 1964, **143,** 783-786.

Moffitt, A. R. Speech perception by infants. Unpublished doctoral dissertation, University of Minnesota, 1968.

Mogar, R. E. Current status and future trends in psychedelic (LSD) research. In C. Tart (Ed.), *Altered states of consciousness.* New York: Wiley, 1969.

Mohsin, S. M. Effect of frustration on problem-solving behavior. *Journal of Abnormal and Social Psychology,* 1954, **49,** 152-155.

Moltz, H. Contemporary instinct theory and the fixed action pattern. *Psychological Review,* 1965, **75,** 27-47.

Money, J. *Sex research: New developments.* New York: Holt, Rinehart & Winston, 1965.

Moniz, E. Prefrontal leucotomy in the treatment of mental disorders. *American Journal of Psychiatry,* 1937, **93,** 1379-1385.

Montagu, A. *Human heredity.* Cleveland: World, 1959.

Montagu, A. Chromosomes and crime. In *Readings in psychology today.* Del Mar, Calif.: CRM, 1969.

Mook, D. G. Oral and postingestional determinants of the intake of various solutions in rats with esophageal fistulas. *Journal of Comparative and Physiological Psychology,* 1963, **56,** 645-659.

Moore, S. C. Editorial. *Parachutist,* 1963, **4,** 5-7.

Moreno, J. L. (Ed.) *Psychodrama and group psychotherapy. Monograph No. 18.* New York: Beacon House, Inc., 1946. Quoted by permission.

Morgan, C. D., & Murray, H. A. A method for investigating fantasies: The thematic apperception test. *American Medical Association. Archives of Neurology and Psychiatry,* 1935, **34,** 289-306.

Moritz, A. P., & Zamchech, N. Sudden and unexpected deaths of young soldiers. *American Medical Association Archives of Pathology,* 1946, **42,** 459-494.

Morland, J. K. A comparison race awareness in northern and southern children. *American Journal of Orthopsychiatry,* 1966, **36,** 22-31.

Morrell, F., & Ross, M. Central inhibition ih cortical conditioned reflexes. *American Medical Association Archives of Neurology and Psychiatry,* 1953, **70,** 611.

Morris, C. Varieties of human value. Chicago: University of Chicago Press, 1956.

Morris, D. *The naked ape.* New York: McGraw-Hill, 1968.

Morruzzi, G., & Magoun, H. W. Brain stem reticular formation and activation of the EEG. *Electroencephalography and Clinical Neurophysiology,* 1949, **1,** 455-473.

Moscovici, S., Lage, E., & Naffrechoux, M. Influence of a consistent minority on the responses of a majority in a color perception task. *Sociometry,* 1969, **32,** 365-380.

Mosher, L. R., & Feinsilver, D. *Special report on schizo-phrenia.* National institute of Mental Health, April 1970.

Mowrer, O. H. On the psychology of "talking birds"—a contribution to language and personality theory. In *Learning theory and personality dynamics: Selected papers.* New York: Ronald, 1950, 688-726.

Mowrer, O. H. Hearing and speaking: An analysis of language learning. *Journal of Speech and Hearing Disorders,* 1958, **23,** 143-151.

Mowrer, O. H. *The new group therapy.* Princeton, N.J.: Van Nostrand, 1964.

Mowrer, O. H., & Viek, P. An experimental analogue of fear from a sense of helplessness. *Journal of Abnormal and Social Psychology,* 1948, **43,** 193-200.

Moyer, K. E. Kinds of aggression and their physiological basis. *Communications in Behavioral Biology,* 1968, **2,** 65-87.

Moyer, K., & Bunnell, B. Effect of stomach distention caused by water on food and water consumption in the rat. *Journal of Comparative and Physiological Psychology,* 1962, **55,** 652-655.

Mulbar, H. *Interrogation.* Springfield, Ill.: Thomas, 1951.

Munn, N. L. The effect of the knowledge of the situation upon judgment of emotion from facial expressions. *Journal of Abnormal and Social Psychology,* 1940, **35,** 324-338.

Münsterberg, H. *On the witness stand: Essays on psychology and crime.* New York: Clark Boardman, 1927. (Originally published: New York: Doubleday, 1908.)

Murray, E. J. *Sleep, dreams and arousal.* New York: Appleton-Century-Crofts, 1965.

Murray, H. A. *Explorations in personality.* New York: Oxford University Press, 1938.

Muuss, R. Existentialism and psychology. *Educational Theory,* 1956, **6,** 135-153.

Myer, J. S. *Feeding and body weight regulation in Florida king snakes.* Paper presented at the Third International Conference on Food and Water Intake, Haverford College, 1968.

N

Nakazima, S. A. A comparative study of the speech developments of Japanese and American English in childhood. II. The acquisition of speech. *Studia Phonologica,* 1966, **4,** 38-55.

Nalye, R. L., Diener, M. M., Dellinger, W. S., & Blanc, W. A. Urban poverty: Effects on prenatal nutrition. *Science,* 1969, **166,** 1026.

Nardini, J. E. Survival factors in American prisoners of war of the Japanese. *American Journal of Psychiatry,* 1952, **109,** 241-247.

National Office of Vital Statistics. Unpublished data, 1959. Reported in R. W. Maris, *Forces in urban suicide.* Homewood, Ill.: Dorsey Press, 1969.

National Safety Council. *Accident facts.* Chicago: National Safety Council, 1969.

Neale, J. Personal communication, November 1970.

Nelson, K. Accommodation of ·visual-tracking patterns in human infants to object movement patterns. Unpublished doctoral dissertation, Yale University, 1970.

Newcomb, T. M. Attitude development as a function of reference groups. In E. E. Maccoby, T. M. Newcomb, & E. L. Hartley (Eds.), *Readings in social psychology.* New York: Holt, Rinehart & Winston, 1958.

Newcomb, T. M. Persistence and regression of changed attitudes: Long-range studies. *Journal of Social Issues,* 1963, **19,** 3-14.

Newell, A., Shaw, J. C., & Simon, H. A. Elements of a theory of human problem solving. *Psychological Review,* 1958, **65,** 151-166.

Newell, A., Shaw, J. C., & Simon, H. A. Report on a general problem-solving program. In *Proceedings of the International Conference on Information Processing.* Paris: UNESCO, 1960.

Nichols, R. C. The National Merit twin study. In S. G. Vandenberg (Ed.), *Methods and goals in human behavior genetics.* New York: Academic Press, 1965.

Nisbett, R. E. Determinants of food intake in human obesity. *Science,* 1968, **159,** 1254-1255.

Nisbett, R. E., & Schachter, S. Cognitive manipulation of pain. *Journal of Experimental Social Psychology,* 1966, **2,** 227-236.

Nissen, H. W., & Crawford, M. P. A preliminary study of food-sharing behavior in young chimpanzees. *Journal of Comparative Psychology,* 1936, **22,** 383-419.

Nissen, H. W., Chow, K. L., & Semmes, J. Effects of restricted opportunity for tactual, kinesthetic, and manipulative experience on the behavior of a chimpanzee. *American Journal of Psychology,* 1951, **64,** 485-507.

Nizer, L. *My life in court.* New York: Pyramid, 1961.

Novin, D. The relation between electrical conductivity of brain tissue and thirst in the rat. *Journal of Comparative and Physiological Psychology,* 1962, **55,** 145-154.

Nunnally, J. C. *Popular conceptions of mental health.* New York: Holt, Rinehart & Winston, 1961.

O

Occupational Mental·Health Notes. July 1966.

O'Connor, R. D. Modification of social withdrawal through symbolic modeling. *Journal of Applied Behavioral Analysis,* 1969. **2,** 15-22.

Ogilvie, D. M., Stone, P. J., & Shneidman, E. S. Some characteristics of genuine versus simulated suicide notes. In P. J. Stone, D. C. Cunphy, & M. S. Smith (Eds.), *A computer approach to content analysis.* Cambridge, Mass.: MIT Press, 1966.

O'Hara, C. E. *Fundamentals of criminal investigation.* Springfield, Ill.: Thomas, 1956.

Olds, J. Self-stimulation of the brain: Its use to study local effects of hunger, sex, and drugs. *Science,* 1958, **127,** 315-324.

Olds, J., & Milner, P. Positive reinforcement produced by electrical stimulation of septal area and other regions of the rat brain. *Journal of Comparative and Physiological Psychology,* 1954, **47,** 419-427.

Olin, C. H. *Phrenology.* Philadelphia: Penn, 1910.

Oppenheimer, R. Analogy in science. *American Psychologist,* 1956, **11,** 127-135.

Osborn, A. F. *Applied imagination: Principles and procedures of creative thinking.* (2nd ed.) New York: Scribner's, 1957.

Osgood, C. E., Suci, G. J., & Tannenbaum, P. H. *The measurement of meaning.* Urbana, Ill.: University of Illinois Press, 1957.

Osler, S. F., & Fivel, M. W. Concept attainment. I. The role of age and intelligence in concept attainment by induction. *Journal of Experimental Psychology.* 1961. **62**, 1-8.

Osmond, H., & Smythies, J. Schizophrenia: New approach. *Journal of Mental Science,* 1952, **98**, 300-315.

Overman, J. B., & Seligman, M. E. P. Effects of inescapable shock upon subsequent escape and avoidance responding. *Journal of Comparative and Physiological Psychology,* 1967, **63**, 28-33.

P

Pahnke, W. N., & Richards, W. A. Implications of LSD and experimental mysticism. In C. Tart (Ed.), *Altered states of consciousness.* New York: Wiley, 1969.

Parkes, A. S., & Bruce, H. M. Olfactory stimuli in mammalian reproduction. Odor excites neurohumoral responses affecting olstrus, pseudopregnancy and pregnancy in the mouse. *Science,* 1961, **134**, 1049-1054.

Pascal, G. R. Handwriting pressure: Its measurements and significance. *Character and Personality,* 1943, **11**, 234-254.

Paul, G. L. *Insight vs. desensitization in psychotherapy.* Stanford: Stanford University Press, 1966.

Paul, G. L. Outcome of systematic desensitization. II. Controlled investigations of individual treatment technique variations, and current status. In C. M. Franks (Ed.), *Behavior therapy: Appraisal and status.* New York: McGraw-Hill, 1969.

Pauling, L. Orthomolecular psychiatry. *Science,* 1968, **160**, 265-271.

Peck, M. L. Paper presented at the Third Annual American Association of Suicidologists Convention, San Francisco, 1970.

Penfield, W. *The excitable cortex in conscious man.* Liverpool: Liverpool University Press, 1958.

Penick, S., Smith, G., Wienske, K., & Hinkle, L. An experimental evaluation of the relationship between hunger and gastric motility. *American Journal of Physiology,* 1963, **205**, 421-426.

Perin, C. T. A quantitative investigation of the delay-of-reinforcement gradient. *Journal of Experimental Psychology,* 1943, **32**, 37-51.

Petrinovich, L., & Bolles, R. Deprivation states and behavioral attributes. *Journal of Comparative and Physiological Psychology,* 1954, **47**, 450-453.

Peyman, D. A. R. An investigation of the effects of group psychotherapy on chronic schizophrenic patients. *Group Psychotherapy,* 1956, **9**, 35-39.

Pfungst, O. *Clever Hans (the horse of Mr. Von Osten).* New York: Holt, Rinehart & Winston, 1911.

Phillips, E. L. Achievement place: Token reinforcement procedures in a home-style rehabilitation setting for "predelinquent" boys. *Journal of Applied Behavior Analysis,* 1968, **1**, 213-223.

Phillips, J. L. *The origins of intellect: Piaget's theory.* San Francisco: Freeman, 1969.

Piaget, Jean. The child and modern physics. *Scientific American,* 1957, **196**(3), 46-51.

Pierrel, R., & Sherman, J. G. Train your pet the Barnabus way. *Brown Alumni Monthly,* February 1963, 8-14.

Pines, M. Why some 3-year-olds get A's—and some get C's. *New York Times Magazine,* July 6, 1969, pp. 4-5, 10-17.

Pinkerton, J. (Ed.) *A general collection of the best and most interesting voyages and travels in all parts of the world.* London: Longman, Hurst, Rees, & Orne, 1808-1814.

Pitts, F. N. The biochemistry of anxiety. *Scientific American,* 1969, **220**, 69-75.

Platt, J. What we must do. *Science,* 1969, **166**, 1115-1121.

Playboy, 1969 **16**(2), 46.

Polsky, N. *Hustlers, beats, and others.* Chicago: Aldine, 1967.

Posner, E. G. The effect of therapists' training on group therapeutic outcome. *Journal of Consulting Psychology,* 1966, **30**, 283-289.

Postman, L. Learning and perception. In S. Koch (Ed.), *Psychology: A study of a science.* Vol. 5. New York: McGraw-Hill, 1963.

Postman, L., & Rau, L. Retention as a function of the method of measurement. *University of California Publications in Psychology,* 1957, **8**, No. 3.

Powell, G. F., Brasel, J. A., & Blizzard, R. M. Emotional deprivation and growth retardation simulating idiopathic hypopituitarism. I. Clinical evaluation of the syndrome. *New England Journal of Medicine,* 1967, **276**, 1272-1278.

Premack, D. Reinforcement theory. In D. Levine (Ed.), *Nebraska Symposium on Motivation.* Lincoln: University of Nebraska Press, 1965.

Premack, D. A functional analysis of language. Paper presented at the meeting of the American Psychological Association, Washington, D.C., 1969.

Premack, D. The education of Sarah. *Psychology Today,* 1970, **4**(4), 54-58.

Prescott, D. A. *Emotion and the educative process.* Washington, D.C.: American Council on Education. 1938.

Pressey, S. L. A simple apparatus which gives tests and scores—and teaches. *School and Society,* 1926, **23.**

Pribram, K. H. A review of theory in physiological psychology. *American Review of Psychology,* 1960, **11**, 1-40.

Pribram, K. H. Interrelations of psychology and the neurological disciplines. In S. Koch (Ed.), *Psychology: A study of a science.* Vol. 4. New York: McGraw-Hill, 1962.

Pribram, K. H. Emotion: Steps toward a neurophysiological theory. In D. C. Glass (Ed.), *Neurophysiology and emotion.* New York: Rockefeller University Press, 1967.

R

Radke, M., & Klisurich, D. Experiments in changing food habits. *Journal of the American Dietetics Association,* 1947, **23**, 403-409.

Rahe, R. H., & Holmes, T. H. Life crisis and major health change. *Psychosomatic Medicine,* 1966, **28**, 774.

Rahe, R. H., Gunderson, E. K. E., & Arthur, R. J. Demographic and psychosocial factors in acute illness reporting. *Navy Medical Neuropsychiatric Research Unit Report No. 69-35.* San Diego, Calif., 1969.

Rapaport, C. Personal communication to the authors, 1970.

Rappaport, M., & Silverman, J. A sensor for schizophrenics. *Behavior Today,* 1970, **1**(21), 1.

Ratliff, F., & Hartline, H. K. The responses of Limulus optic nerve fibers to patterns of illumination on the receptor mosaic. *General Physiology,* 1959, **42,** 1241-1255.

Ratliff, F., Hartline, H. K., & Miller, W. H. Spatial and temporal aspects of retinal inhibitory interaction. *Journal of the Optical Society of America,* 1963, **53,** 110-121.

Raush, H. L., & Raush, C. L. *The halfway house movement: A search for sanity.* New York: Appleton-Century-Crofts, 1968.

Raven, B. H. Social influence and power. In I. D. Steiner & M. Fishbein (Eds.), *Current studies in social psychology.* New York: Holt, Rinehart & Winston, 1965.

Ray, W. S. Judgments of intelligence based on brief observations of physiognomy. *Psychol. Reports,* 1958, **4,** 478.

Razran, G. H. S. Decremental and incremental effects of distracting stimuli upon the salivary CRs of 24 adult human subjects. *Journal of Experimental Psychology,* 1939, **24,** 647-652.

Razran, G. Introductory remarks. In N. S. Kline (Ed.), *Pavlovian conference on higher nervous activity. Annals of the New York Academy of Sciences,* 1961, **92,** 816-817.

Reitman, W. R. *Cognition and thought.* New York: Wiley, 1965.

Reynolds, G. S. The effects of stress upon problem solving. *Journal of General Psychology,* 1960, **62,** 83-88.

Reynolds, G. S. *A primer of operant conditioning.* Glenview, Ill.: Scott, Foresman, 1968.

Rheingold, H. L., Gewirtz, J. L., & Ross, H. W. Social conditioning of vocalizations in the infant. *Journal of Comparative and Physiological Psychology,* 1959, **52,** 68-73.

Rhine, J. B. Incorporeal personal agency: The prospect of a scientific solution. *Journal of Parapsychology,* 1960, **24,** 279-309.

Richter, C. P. On the phenomenon of sudden death in animals and man. *Psychosomatic Medicine,* 1957, **19,** 191-198.

Riesen, A. H. Arrested vision. *Scientific American,* 1950, **183** (1), 16-19.

Riesen, A. H. Stimulation as a requirement for growth and function in behavioral development. In D. W. Fiske & S. R. Maddi (Eds.), *Functions of varied experience.* Homewood, Ill.: Dorsey, 1961.

Robinson, M. F., & Freeman, W. J. *Psychosurgery and the self.* New York: Grune & Stratton, 1955.

Robinson, P., & Rackstraw, S. J. Variations in mothers' answers to children's questions as a function of social class, verbal intelligence, test scores, and sex. *Sociology,* 1967, **1,** 259-276.

Rock, I., & Harris, C. S. Vision and touch. *Scientific American,* 1967, **216**(5), 96-104.

Roe, A. The personality of artists. *Educational and Psychological Measurement,* 1946, **6,** 401-408.

Roethlisberger, F. J., & Dickson, W. J. *Management and the worker.* Cambridge, Mass.: Harvard University Press, 1939.

Roffwarg, H. P. Personal communication to the authors, 1970.

Roffwarg, H. P., Muzio, J. N., & Dement, W. C. Ontogenetic development of the human sleep-dream cycle. *Science,* 1966, **152,** 604-619.

Rogers, C. Significant aspects of client-centered therapy. *American Psychologist,* 1946, **1,** 415-422.

Rogers, C. R. The case of Mary Jane Tilden. In W. U. Snyder (Ed.), *Casebook of non-directive counseling.* Boston: Houghton Mifflin, 1947.

Rogers, C. R. *On becoming a person: A therapist's view of psychotherapy.* Boston: Houghton Mifflin, 1961.

Rogers, C., & Skinner, B. F. Some issues concerning the control of human behavior: A symposium. *Science,* 1956, **124,** 1057-1066.

Rogge, O. J. *Why men confess.* New York: Nelson, 1959.

Rohrer, J., & Sherif, M. (Eds.) *Social psychology at the crossroads.* New York: Harper & Row, 1951.

Rohrer, J. H., Baron, S. H., Hoffman, E. L., & Swander, D. V. The stability of autokinetic judgments. *Journal of Abnormal Psychology,* 1954, **49,** 595-597.

Rokeach, M. *The open and closed mind.* New York: Basic Books, 1960.

Rolf, I. P. *Structural integration: Gravity, an unexplored factor in a more human use of human beings.* New York: author, 1962.

Romanes, G. *Animal intelligence.* New York: Appleton-Century-Crofts, 1881.

Rosen, J. *Direct analysis.* New York: Grune & Stratton, 1953.

Rosenblatt, J. S. Effects of experience on sexual behavior in male cats. In F. Beach (Ed.), *Sex and behavior.* New York: Wiley, 1965.

Rosenhan, D. Some origins of concern for others. In P. H. Mussen, J. Langer, & M. Covington (Eds.), *Trends and issues in developmental psychology.* New York: Holt, Rinehart & Winston, 1969.

Rosenzweig, S. A transvaluation of psychotherapy: A reply to Hans Eysenck. *Journal of Abnormal and Social Psychology,* 1954, **49,** 298-304.

Rosenzweig, M. R., Bennett, E. L., Diamond, M. C., Wu, Su-Yu, Slagle, R. W., & Saffran, E. Influences of environmental complexity and visual stimulation on development of occipital cortex in rats. *Brain Research,* 1969, **14,** 427-445.

Ross, L., Rodin, J., & Zimbardo, P. G. Toward an attribution therapy: The reduction of fear through induced cognitive-emotional misattribution. *Journal of Personality and Social Psychology,* 1969, **12,** 279-288.

Rothman, M. A. Response to McConnell. *American Psychologist,* 1970, **25,** 280-281.

Rotter, J. B. Generalized expectancies for internal versus external controls of reinforcement. *Psychological Monographs,* 1966, **80**(1, Whole No. 609).

Routh, D. K. Conditioning of vocal response differentiation in infants. *Journal of Developmental Psychology,* 1969, **1,** 219-226.

Routtenberg, A. The two-arousal hypothesis: Reticular formation and the limbic system. *Psychological Review,* 1968, **75,** 51-80.

Routtenberg, A. Current status of the two-arousal hypothesis. Paper presented at the International Congress of Psychology, London, July 1969.

Rozin, P. Specific hunger for thiamine: Recovery from deficiency and thiamine preference. *Journal of Comparative and Physiological Psychology,* 1965, **59,** 98-101.

Rozin, P., & Mayer, J. Thermal reinforcement and thermoregulatory behavior in the goldfish, carassius auratus. *Science,* 1961, **134,** 942-943.

Rubel, A. J. *Across the tracks: Mexican-Americans in a Texas city.* Austin: University of Texas, 1966.

Rubin, E. Figure and ground. In D. C. Beardslee & M. Wertheimer (Eds.), *Readings in perception.* Princeton: Van Nostrand, 1958. (Originally published, 1921.)

Rubin, J. *Do it: A revolutionary manifesto.* New York: Simon & Schuster, 1970.

Rubin, R. T., Miller, R. G., Arthur, R. J., & Clark, B. R. Differential adrenocortical stress responses in naval aviators during aircraft landing practice. *Navy Medical Neuropsychiatric Research Unit Report No. 12.* San Diego, Calif., 1969.

Rubin, Z. Measurement of romantic love. *Journal of Personality and Social Psychology,* 1970, **16,** 265-273.

Ruch, F. L., & Ruch, W. W. The K factor as a (validity) suppressor variable in predicting success in selling. Paper read at a meeting of the American Psychological Association, Chicago, September 1965.

Ruff, G., Levy, E. Z., & Thaler, V. H. Factors influencing reactions to reduced sensory input. In P. Solomon et al. (Eds.), *Sensory deprivation.* Cambridge: Harvard University Press, 1961.

Russek, M. Participation of hepatic glucoreceptors in the control of intake of food. *Nature,* 1963, **197,** 79-80.

S

Sacerdote, P. Hypnosis in cancer patients. *American Journal of Clinical Hypnosis,* 1966, **9,** 100-108.

Sacerdote, P. *Induced dreams.* New York: Vantage Press, 1967.

Sachs, J. S. Recognition memory for syntactic and semantic aspects of connected discourse. *Perception and Psychophysics,* 1967, **2**(9), 441.

Sackett, G. P. Some effects of social and sensory deprivation during rearing on behavioral development of monkeys. *Revista Interamerica de Psicologia,* 1967, **1,** 55-80.

Sadoff, R. L. On the nature of crying and weeping. *Psychiatric Quarterly,* 1966, **40,** 490-503.

Salapatek, P., & Kessen, W. Visual scanning of triangles by the human newborn. *Journal of Experimental Child Psychology,* 1966, **3**(2), 155-167.

Samuel, A. Studies in machine learning using the game of checkers. Part 2. Recent progress. In M. Halpern (Ed.), *Annual review of automatic programming.* New York: Pergamon Press, 1970, in press.

Sarbin, T. R. On the futility of the proposition that some people be labeled "mentally ill." *Journal of Consulting Psychology,* 1967, **31,** 445-453.

Sarnoff, I. *Society with tears.* New York: Citadel, 1966.

Sartre, J. P. *Existentialism and human emotions.* New York: Philosophical Library, 1957.

Satinoff, E., & Rutstein, J. Behavioral thermoregulation with anterior hypothalamic lesions. *Journal of Comparative and Physiological Psychology,* 1970, **71,** 77-82.

Savage, C., Savage, E., Fadiman, J., & Harmann, W. LSD: Therapeutic effects of the psychedelic experience. *Psychological Reports,* 1964, **14,** 111-120.

Schachtel, E. G. *Metamorphosis.* New York: Basic Books, 1959.

Schachter, J. Pain, fear and anger in hypertensives and normotensives. *Psychosomatic Medicine,* 1957, **19,** 17-29.

Schachter, S. *The psychology of affiliation.* Stanford: Stanford University Press, 1959.

Schachter, S. Cognitive effects on bodily functioning: Studies of obesity and eating. In D. C. Glass (Ed.), *Biology and behavior: Neurophysiology and emotion.* New York: Rockefeller University Press, 1967.

Schachter, S., & Singer, J. Cognitive, social and physiological determinants of emotional state. *Psychological Review,* 1962, **69,** 379-399.

Schanberg, S. M., Schildkraut, J. J., & Kopin, I. J. *Biochemical Pharmacology,* 1967, **16,** 393.

Schein, E. H. Reaction patterns to severe, chronic stress in American prisoners of war of the Chinese. In H. Proshansky & B. Seidenberg (Eds.), *Basic studies in social psychology.* New York: Holt, Rinehart & Winston, 1965.

Schein, M. W., & Hale, E. B. Stimuli eliciting sexual behavior. In F. Beach (Ed.), *Sex and behavior.* New York: Wiley, 1965.

Schildkrau, J. J., & Kety, S. S. Biogenic amines and emotion. *Science,* 1967, **156,** 21-30.

Schjelderup, H. Lasting effects of psychoanalytic treatment. *Psychiatry,* 1955, **18,** 109-133.

Schlosberg, H. The description of facial expressions in terms of two dimensions. *Journal of Experimental Psychology,* 1952, **44,** 229-237.

Schlosberg, H. Three dimensions of emotion. *Psychological Review,* 1954, **61,** 81-88.

Schneck, J. M. *Hypnosis in modern medicine.* (2nd ed.) Springfield, Ill.: Thomas, 1959.

Schneider, A. M. Control of memory by spreading cortical depression: A case for stimulus control. *Psychological Review,* 1967, **74,** 201-215.

Schofield, W. *Psychotherapy: The purchase of friendship.* Englewood Cliffs, N.J.: Prentice-Hall, 1964.

Schou, M. Lithium in psychiatric therapy: Stock-taking after ten years. *Psychopharmacologia,* 1959, **1,** 65-78.

Schutz, F. Differences between the imprinting of the following and sexual reactions in mallards. Paper presented at the meeting of the XIXth International Congress of Psychology, London, 1969.

Schwartz, G. E., & Johnson, H. J. Affective visual stimuli as operant reinforcers of the GSR. *Journal of Experimental Psychology,* 1969, **80,** 28-32.

Schwartz, M. S. Functions of the team in the state mental hospital. *American Journal of Orthopsychiatry,* 1960, **30,** 100-102.

Schwitzgebel, R. L. Survey of electromechanical devices for behavior modification. *Psychological Bulletin,* 1968, **70,** 444-459.

Science News Letter. Cats work, play with rats. 1950, **58,** 183.

Scott, J. P. *Aggression.* Chicago: University of Chicago Press, 1958.

Scott, J. P. The anatomy of violence. *The Nation,* June 21, 1965.

Scott, W. A. Research definitions of mental health and mental illness. *Psychological Bulletin,* 1958, **55,** 29-45.

Sears, P. S. Doll play aggression in normal young children. *Psychological Monographs,* 1951, **65,** No. 6.

Sears, R. R. Relation of early socialization experiences to aggression in middle childhood. *Journal of Abnormal and Social Psychology,* 1961, **63,** 466-492.

Sears, R. R. Development of gender role. In F. Beach (Ed.), *Sex and behavior.* New York: Wiley, 1965.

Sears, R. R., Maccoby, E. E., & Levin, H. *Patterns of child rearing.* Evanston, Ill.: Row, Peterson, 1957.

Sears, Roebuck Catalogue, 1902. New York: Crown, 1970.

Sechrest, L., & Wallace, J. Figure drawing and naturally occurring events: Elimination of the expansive euphoria hypothesis. *Journal of Educational Psychology,* 1964, **55,** 42-44.

Secord, P. F., Dukes, W. F., & Bevan, W. Personalities in faces. I. An experiment in social perceiving. *Genetic Psychology Monographs,* 1954, **49,** 231-270.

Segal, M. M., & Shapiro, K. L. A clinical comparison study of the effects of reserpine and placebo on anxiety. *American Medical Association Archives of Neurological Psychiatry,* 1959, **81,** 392-398.

Segall, M. H., Campbell, D. T., & Herskovits, M. J. *The influence of culture on perception.* New York: Bobbs-Merrill, 1966.

Segalman, R. The conflict of cultures between social work and the underclass. *Rocky Mountain Social Science Journal,* 1965, **2,** 161-173.

Seiden, R. H. We're driving young blacks to suicide. *Psychology Today,* 1970, **4**(3), 24-28.

Seligman, M. E. P. Chronic fear produced by unpredictable electric shock. *Journal of Comparative and Physiological Psychology,* 1968, **66,** 402-411.

Seligman, M. E. P., & Grove, D. P. Non-transient learned helplessness. Unpublished mimeograph report, 1970.

Seligman, M. E. P., & Maier, S. F. Failure to escape traumatic shock. *J. exp. Psychol.,* 1967, **74,** 1-9.

Seligman, M. E. P., Maier, S. F., & Greer, J. H. Alleviation of learned helplessness in the dog. *Journal of Abnormal Psychology,* 1968, **73,** 256-262.

Selye, H. *The physiology and pathology of exposure to stress.* Montreal: Acta, 1950.

Selye, H. The general-adaptation-syndrome in its relationships to neurology, psychology, and psychopathology. In A. Weider (Ed.), *Contributions toward medical psychology.* Vol. I. New York: Ronald Press, 1953.

Selye, H. *The stress of life.* New York: McGraw-Hill, 1956.

Senden, M. v. *Raum- und Gestaltauffassung bei operierten Blindgeborenen vor und nach der Operation.* Leipzig: Barth, 1932. Cited in D. O. Hebb, *The organization of behavior.* New York: Wiley, 1949.

Shaefer, E. S., & Bayley, N. Maternal behavior, child behavior, and their intercorrelations from infancy through adolescence. *Monographs of the Society for Research in Child Development,* 1963, **28**(3, Whole No. 7).

Shankweiler, D., & Studdert-Kennedy, M. Identification of consonants and vowels presented to left and right ears. *Quarterly Journal of Experimental Psychology,* 1967, **19,** 59-63.

Shaw, G. B. *The adventures of the black girl in her search for God.* New York: Dodd, Mead, 1933.

Sheldon, W. H. *The varieties of temperament.* New York: Harper & Row, 1942.

Sheldon, W. H., Stevens, S. S., & Tucker, W. B. *The varieties of human physique.* New York: Harper & Row, 1940.

Sherif, M. A study of some social factors in perception. *Archives of Psychology,* 1935, **27,** No. 187.

Sherif, M., & Hovland, C. I. *Social judgment: Assimilation and contrast effects in communication and attitude change.* New Haven: Yale University Press, 1961.

Sherif, M., & Sherif, C. W. *An outline of social psychology.* (2nd ed.) New York: Harper & Row, 1956.

Sherif, M., & Sherif, C. *Social psychology.* New York: Harper & Row, 1969.

Sherman, J. A. Reinstatement of verbal behavior in a psychotic by reinforcement methods. *Journal of Speech and Hearing Disorders,* 1963, **28,** 398-401.

Shils, E. A. Authoritarianism: "right" and "left." In R. Christie & M. Jahoda (Eds.), *Studies in the scope and method of the authoritarian personality.* New York: Free Press, 1954.

Shirley, M. M. *The first two years.* Minneapolis: University of Minnesota Press, 1931.

Shvachkin, N. Kh. The development of phonemic perception in early childhood. In C. A. Ferguson & D. I. Slobin (Eds.), *Readings in child language development,* 1971, in press. (Originally published in *Izvestiya Akad. Pedag., Nauk RSFSR,* 1948, **13,** 101-132.)

Sidman, M., & Stoddard, L. T. Programming perception and learning for retarded children. In N. R. Ellis (Ed.), *International review of research on mental retardation.* Vol. II. New York: Academic Press, 1969.

Sigall, H., & Aronson, E. Liking for an evaluator as a function of her physical attractiveness and nature of the evaluations. *Journal of Experimental Social Psychology,* 1969, **5,** 93-100.

Sigel, I., Roeper, A., & Hooper, F. H. A training procedure for acquisition of Piaget's conservation of quantity: a pilot study and its replication. *British Journal of Educational Psychology,* 1966, **86,** 301-311.

Simmel, E. C., Hoppe, R. A., & Milton, G. A. (Eds.) *Social facilitation and imitative behavior.* Boston: Allyn & Bacon, 1968.

Simon, H. A. Motivational and emotional controls of cognition. *Psychological Review,* 1967, **74,** 29-39.

Simpson, H. M. Effects of a task-relevant response on pupil size. *Psychophysiology,* 1969, **6,** 115-121.

Siqueland, E. Further developments in infant learning. Paper read at the symposium in learning processes of human infants, XIXth International Congress of Psychology, London, 1969.

Skeels, H. M. Adult status of children with contrasting early life experiences. *Monographs of the Society for Research in Child Development,* 1966, **31**(3), 1-65.

Skinner, B. F. *Verbal behavior.* New York: Appleton-Century-Crofts, 1957.

Skinner, B. F. Pigeons in a pelican. *American Psychologist,* 1960, **15,** 28-37.

Skinner, B. F. Teaching machines. *Scientific American,* 1961, **205**(5), 90-102.

Skinner, B. F., Solomon, H. C., & Lindsley, O. R. A new method for the experimental analysis of the behavior of psychotic patients. *Journal of Nervous and Mental Disease,* 1954, **120,** 403-406.

Slavson, S. R. Group psychotherapy. *Scientific American,* 1950, **183**(6), 42-45.

Slucki, H., Adam, G., & Porter, R. W. Operant discrimination of an interoceptive stimulus in rhesus monkeys. *Journal of the Experimental Analysis of Behavior,* 1965, **8,** 405-414.

Smith, J. A., Rutherford, A., & Fanning, R. A comparison of phenaglycodol (Ultran), meprobamate and a placebo in abstinent alcoholics. *American Journal of Psychiatry,* 1957, **114,** 364-365.

Smith, K. V. *Delayed sensory feedback and behavior.* Philadelphia: Saunders, 1962.

Smith, K. V., & Smith, W. M. *Perception and motion: An analysis of space-structured behavior.* Philadelphia: Saunders, 1962.

Smith, K. V., Zwerg, C., & Smith, N. J. Sensory-feedback analysis of infant control of the behavioral environment. *Perceptual and Motor Skills,* 1963, **16,** 725-732.

Smith, M. B. Review of *The authoritarian personality. Journal of Abnormal and Social Psychology,* 1950, **45,** 516-522.

Smith, O. A., & Nathan, M. Effects of hypothalamic and prefrontal cortical lesions on conditioned cardiovascular responses. *Physiologist,* 1964, **7,** 259.

Smode, A. Learning and performance in a tracking task under two levels of achievement information feedback. *Journal of Experimental Psychology,* 1958, **56,** 297-304.

Snyder, F., Hobson, J. A., Morrison, D. R., & Goldfrank, F. Changes in respiration, heart rate, and systolic blood pressure in human sleep. *Journal of Applied Physiology,* 1964, **19,** 417-422.

Sober, H. A. (Ed.) *Handbook of biochemistry.* Cleveland: Chemical Rubber Co., 1968.

Sokolov, E. N. Neuronal models and the orienting reflex. In M. A. Brazier (Ed.), *The central nervous system and behavior.* New York: Josiah Macy, 1960.

Solley, C. M., & Haigh, G. A. A note to Santa Claus. *Topical research papers. The Menninger Foundation,* 1957, **18,** 4-5.

Sontag, L. W., Baker, C. T., & Nelson, V. L. Mental growth and personality development: A longitudinal study. *Monographs of the Society for Research in Child Development,* 1958, **23**(2), 11-85.

Spearman, C. "General intelligence" objectively determined and measured. *American Journal of Psychology,* 1904, **15,** 201-293.

Spears, W. C. Assessment of visual preference and discrimination in the four-month-old infant. *Journal of Comparative and Physiological Psychology,* 1964, **57,** 381-386.

Speisman, J. C., Lazarus, R. S., Mordkoff, A. M., & Davison, L. A. The experimental reduction of stress based on ego-defense theory. *Journal of Abnormal and Social Psychology,* 1964, **68,** 367-380.

Spelt, D. K. The conditioning of the human fetus in utero. *Journal of Experimental Psychology,* 1948, **38,** 338-346.

Sperling, G. The information available in brief visual presentations. *Psychological Monographs,* 1960, **74**(11, Whole No. 498).

Sperling, G. A. Model for visual memory tasks. *Human Factors,* 1963, **5,** 19-31.

Sperry, R. W. Mental unity following surgical disconnection of the cerebral hemispheres. *The Harvey Lectures,* Series 62. New York: Academic Press, 1968.

Spong, P., Haider, M., & Lindsley, D. B. Selective attentiveness and cortical evoked responses to visual and auditory stimuli. *Science,* 1965, **148,** 395-397.

Spranger, E. *Lebensform.* (3rd ed.) New York: Stechert, 1928.

Srule, L., & Schrijvers, J. *The prototype therapeutic community.* Paper presented at the meeting of the American Psychiatric Association, 1968.

Staats, A. W., & Butterfield, W. H. Treatment of non-reading in a culturally deprived juvenile delinquent: An application of reinforcement principles. *Child Development,* 1965, **36,** 924-942.

Stagner, R. Homeostasis as a unifying concept in personality theory. *Psychological Review,* 1951, **61,** 5-22.

Stampfl, T. G., & Levis, D. J. Essentials of implosive therapy: A learning theory-based psychodynamic behavioral therapy. *Journal of Abnormal Psychology,* 1967, **72,** 496-503.

Stayton, S. E., & Weiner, M. Value, magnitude, and accentuation. *Journal of Abnormal and Social Psychology,* 1961, **62,** 145-147.

Stein, L. In S. Garutini & M. N. G. Dukes (Eds.), *Antidepressant drugs.* Amsterdam: Excerpta Medica Foundation, 1967.

Steiner, I., & Johnson, H. Authoritarianism and conformity. *Sociometry,* 1963, **26,** 21-34.

Stellar, E. The physiology of motivation. *Psychological Review,* 1954, **61,** 5-22.

Stern, P. J. *The abnormal person and his world.* Princeton: Van Nostrand, 1964.

Stern, W. The psychological methods of testing intelligence. *Educational Psychology Mongraphs,* 1914, No. 13.

Sternbach, R. A. *Pain: A psychophysiological analysis.* New York: Academic Press, 1968.

Sternbach, R. A., & Tursky, B. Ethnic differences among housewives in psychophysical and skin potential responses to electric shock. *Psychophysiology,* 1965, **1,** 241-246.

Stevens, C. F. *Neurophysiology: A primer.* New York: Wiley, 1966.

Stevenson, H., & Stewart, E. A developmental study of racial awareness in young children. *Child Development,* 1966, **61,** 37-75.

Stodolsky, S., & Lesser, G. S. Learning patterns in the disadvantaged. *Harvard Educational Review,* 1967, **37**(4), 546-593.

Stogdill, R. M. Personality factors associated with leadership: A survey of the literature. *Journal of Psychology,* 1948, **25,** 35-71.

Stone, C. P., & Bakhtiari, A. B. Effects of electroconvulsive shock on maze relearning by albino rats. *Journal of Comparative and Physiological Psychology,* 1956, **49,** 318-320.

Strecker, E. A., & Ebaugh, F. G. *Practical clinical psychiatry.* (5th ed.) Philadelphia: Blakiston, 1940. Quoted by permission.

Strickland, L. Surveillance and trust. *Journal of Personality,* 1958, **26,** 200-215.

Stromeyer, C. F., Psotka, J., & West, M. Eidetic imagery: A brief resume of studies in progress. Unpublished report, submitted to *Nature,* 1969.

Strong, E. K., Jr. *Manual for Vocational Interest Blank for Men.* Stanford: Stanford University Press, 1951.

Stunkard, A., & Koch, C. The interpretation of gastric motility: Apparent bias in the report of hunger by obese persons. *Archives of General Psychology,* 1964, **11,** 74-82.

Suchman, J. R. *The elementary school training program in scientific inquiry.* Urbana, Ill.: University of Illinois Press, 1962.

Sullivan, H. S. *The interpersonal theory of psychiatry.* New York: Norton, 1953.

Suppes, P. Mathematical concept formation in children. *American Psychologist,* 1966, **21,** 139-150.

Suppes, P. On using computers to individualize instruction. In D. D. Bushnell & D. Allen (Eds.), *The computer in education.* New York: Wiley, 1967.

Surgeon General's Office, U. S. Department of Health, Education and Welfare. *Smoking and health: Report of the advisory committee to the Surgeon General of the public health service.* Public Health Service Publication No. 1103. Washington, D.C., 1964.

Szasz, T. S. *The myth of mental illness.* New York: Harper & Row, 1961.

Szasz, T. S. *Psychiatric justice.* New York: Macmillan, 1965.

T

Talbot, E., & Miller, S. C. The mental hospital as a sane society. *Trans-action,* 1965, **26,** 39-42.

Tapp, J., Mathewson, D., D'Encarnacas, P., & Long, C. The effect of the onset of stimuli on reactivity in the rat. *Psychonomic Science,* 1970, **19,** 61-62.

Tart, C. *Altered states of consciousness.* New York: Wiley, 1969.

Taylor, D. W., Berry, P. C., & Block, C. H. Does group participation when using brainstorming facilitate or inhibit creative thinking? *Administrative Science Quarterly,* 1958, **3,** 23-47.

Teitelbaum, P. The use of operant methods in the assessment and control of motivational states. In W. K. Honig (Ed.), *Operant behavior.* New York: Appleton-Century-Crofts, 1966.

Teitelbaum, P., & Epstein, A. The lateral hypothalamic syndrome: Recovery of feeding and drinking after lateral hypothalamic lesions. *Psychological Review,* 1962, **69,** 74-90.

Terman, L. M. *The measurement of intelligence.* Boston: Houghton Mifflin, 1916.

Terman, L. M., & Merrill, M. A. *Measuring intelligence.* Boston: Houghton Mifflin, 1937.

Terman, L. M., & Merrill, M. A. *The Stanford-Binet intelligence scale.* Boston: Houghton Mifflin, 1960.

Terrace, H. S. Errorless transfer of a discrimination across two continua. *Journal of the Experimental Analysis of Behavior,* 1963, **6,** 224-232.

Teuber, H. L. Lacunae and research approaches to them. In C. H. Millikan & F. L. Darley (Eds.), *Brain mechanisms underlying speech and language.* New York: Grune and Stratton, 1967.

Thigpen, C. H. Personal communication to the authors, August 1961.

Thigpen, C. H., & Cleckley, H. A case of multiple personality. *Journal of Abnormal and Social Psychology,* 1954, **49**(1), 135-144.

Thigpen, C. H., & Cleckley, H. A. *The three faces of Eve.* New York: McGraw-Hill, 1957.

Thomas, A., Chess, S., Birch, H. G., Hertzig, M. E., & Korn, S. *Behavioral individuality in early childhood.* New York: New York University Press, 1963.

Thompson, R., & McConnell, J. V. Classical conditioning in the Planarian, Dugesia Dorotocephala. *Journal of Comparative and Physiological Psychology,* 1955, **48,** 65-68.

Thompson, W. R. Influence of prenatal maternal anxiety on emotionality in young rats. *Science,* 1957, **125,** 698-699.

Thorndike, E. L. Animal intelligence. *Psychological Review Monograph Supplement,* 1898, **2,** (4, Whole No. 8).

Thorndike, E. L. The mental life of the monkeys. *Psychological Review Monograph Supplement,* 1901, No. 15.

Thorndike, E. L. *The elements of psychology.* New York: Seiler, 1905.

Thurstone, L. L., & Thurstone, T. G. Factorial studies of intelligence. *Psychometric Monographs,* 1941, No. 2.

Thurstone, L. L., & Thurstone, T. G. *SRA primary mental abilities.* Intermediate—ages 11-17. Chicago: Science Research Associates, 1947.

Tinbergen, N. An objectivistic study of the innate behaviour of animals. *Bibliotheca Biotheoretica,* Leiden, 1942, **1,** 39-98.

Tinklepaugh, O. L. An experimental study of representational factors in monkeys. *Journal of Comparative Psychology,* 1928, **8,** 197-236.

Toch, H. *Violent men.* Chicago: Aldine, 1969.

Toffler, A. *Future shock.* New York: Random House, 1970.

Tolman, E. C. Operational behaviorism and current trends in psychology. *Collected papers in psychology.* Berkeley: University of California Press, 1950. (Originally published, 1936.)

Tomkins, S. A modified model of smoking behavior. In E. F. Borgatta & R. R. Evans (Eds.), *Smoking, health, and behavior.* Chicago: Aldine Publishing Co., 1968.

Triplett, N. The dynamogenic factors in pacemaking and competition. *Amer. J. Psychol.,* 1897, **9,** 507-533.

Trotter, W. *Instincts of the herd in peace and war.* London: T. Fisher Unwin, 1916.

Tsang, Y. C. Hunger motivation in gastrectomized rats. *Journal of Comparative Psychology,* 1938, **26,** 1-17.

Tschukitschew. *Contributions of the Timiriazer Institute,* 1929, 36. Cited in R. D. Templeton & J. P. Quigley, The action of insulin on the motility of the gastrointestinal tract. *American Journal of Physiology,* 1930, **91,** 467-474.

Tuddenham, R. D. The influence of a distorted group norm upon judgments of adults and children. *Journal of Psychology,* 1961, **52,** 231-239.

Tulving, E., & Patkau, J. E. Concurrent effects of contextual constraint and word frequency on immediate recall and learning of verbal material. *Canadian Journal of Psychology,* 1962, **16,** 83-95.

Turing, A. M. Computing machinery and intelligence. *Mind,* 1950, **59,** 433-460.

Turnbull, C. M. Some observations regarding the experiences and behavior of BaMbuti Pygmies. *American Journal of Psychology,* 1961, **74,** 304-308.

U-V

Underwood, B. J. Spontaneous recovery of verbal associations. *Journal of Experimental Psychology,* 1948, **38,** 429-439.

Unger, S. M. Habituation of the vasoconstrictive orienting reaction. *Journal of Experimental Psychology,* 1964, **67,** 11-18.

U.S. National Commission on the Causes and Prevention of Violence. *To establish justice, to insure domestic tranquility; the final report.* New York: Praeger, 1970.

Valenstein, E., Cox, V., & Kakolewski, J. Modification of motivated behavior elicited by electrical stimulation of the hypothalamus. *Science,* 1968, **159,** 1119-1121. (a)

Valenstein, E., Cox, V., & Kakolewski, J. The motivation underlying eating elicited by lateral hypothalamic stimulation. *Physiology and Behavior,* 1968, **3,** 969-971. (b)

Valenstein, E., Cox, V., & Kakolewski, J. Re-examination of the role of the hypothalamus in motivation. *Psychological Review,* 1970, **77,** 16-31.

Verhave, T. The pigeon as a quality-control inspector. In R. Ulrich, T. Stachnik, & J. Mabry (Eds.), *Control of human behavior.* Glenview, Ill.: Scott, Foresman, 1966.

Vogel, W., Broverman, D. M., Draguns, J. G., & Klaiber, E. L. The role of glutamic acid in cognitive behavior. *Psychological Bulletin,* 1966, **65,** 367.

Von Békésy, G. The ear. *Scientific American,* 1957, **197** (2), 66-78.

W

Wagner, A. H. Stimulus-selection and a "Modified continuity theory." In G. H. Bower & J. T. Spence (Eds.), *The psychology of learning and motivation.* Vol. 3. New York: Academic Press, 1970.

Wahler, R. G. Infant social development: Some experimental analyses of an infant-mother interaction during the first year of life. *Journal of Experimental Child Psychology,* 1969, **7,** 101-113.

Walker, D. R., & Milton, G. A. Memory transfer vs. sensitization in cannibal planarians. *Psychonomic Science,* 1966, **5,** 293-294.

Wallach, M. A., & Kogan, N. *Modes of thinking in young children: A study of the creativity-intelligence distinction.* New York: Holt, Rinehart & Winston, 1965.

Wallace, R. K. Physiological effects of transcendental meditation. *Science,* 1970, **167,** 1751-1754.

Walster, E. The effect of self-esteem on romantic liking. *Journal of Experimental and Social Psychology,* 1965, **1,** 184-197.

Walter, W. G. The social organ. *Impact of Science on Society,* 1968, **18,** 179-186.

Ward, W. C., & Kogan, N. Motivation and ability in children's creativity. Unpublished report, 1970.

Warden, C. J. The relative economy of various models of attack in mastery of a stylus maze. *Journal of Experimental Psychology,* 1924, **7,** 243-275.

Warden, C. J. *Animal motivation: Experimental studies on the albino rat.* New York: Columbia University Press, 1931.

Watson, J. B. Experimental studies on the growth of emotions. In C. Murchison (Ed.), *Psychologies of 1925.* Worcester, Mass.: Clark University Press, 1926.

Watson, J. B., & Rayner, R. Conditioned emotional reactions. *Journal of Experimental Psychology,* 1920, **3,** 1-14.

Weaver, W. Science and people. *Science,* 1955, **122,** 1255-1259.

Webb, W. B. *Sleep: An experimental approach.* New York: Macmillan, 1968.

Wechsler, D. *Wechsler intelligence scale for children.* New York: Psychological Corp., 1949.

Wechsler, D. *Wechsler adult intelligence scale.* New York: Psychological Corp., 1955.

Wechsler, H., Grosser, G. H., & Greenblatt, M. Research evaluating antidepressant medications on hospitalized mental patients: A survey of published reports during a 5-year period. *Journal of Nervous and Mental Disease,* 1965, **141,** 231-239.

Wegrocki, H. J. A critique of cultural and statistical concepts of abnormality. *Journal of Abnormal and Social Psychology,* 1939, **34,** 166-178.

Weiss, B., & Laties, V. G. Behavioral thermoregulation. *Science,* 1961, **133,** 1338-1344.

Weiss, J. M. Effects of coping responses on stress. *Journal of Comparative and Physiological Psychology,* 1968, **65,** 251-260.

Weisskopf-Joelson, E. Some comments on a Viennese school of psychiatry. *Journal of Abnormal and Social Psychology,* 1955, **51,** 701-703.

Weitzman, B. Behavior therapy and psychotherapy. *Psychological Review,* 1967, **74,** 300-317.

Welker, W. I. An analysis of exploratory and play behavior in animals. In D. W. Fiske & S. R. Maddi (Eds.), *Functions of varied experience.* Homewood, Ill.: Dorsey, 1961.

Wells, F. L. A statistical study of literary merit. *Archives of Psychology,* 1907, **16,** No. 7.

Westley, W. A. Violence and the police. *American Journal of Sociology,* 1953, **59,** 34-41.

Wever, E. G. *Theory of hearing.* New York: Wiley, 1949.

Wever, E. G., & Bray, C. W. Present possibilities for auditory theory. *Psychological Review,* 1930, **37,** 365-380.

White, B. L., & Held, R. Plasticity of sensorimotor development in the human infant. In J. F. Rosenblith & W. Allinsmith (Eds.), *The causes of behavior.* Vol. 1. (2nd ed.) Boston: Allyn & Bacon, 1966.

White, R. W. Motivation reconsidered: The concept of competence. *Psychological Review,* 1959, **66,** 297-333.

Whiting, J. W. M. Menarcheal age and infant stress in humans. In F. A. Beach (Ed.), *Sex and behavior.* New York: Wiley, 1965.

Whiting, J. W. M., Kluckhohn, R., & Anthony, A. The function of male initiation ceremonies at puberty. In E. E. Maccoby, T. Newcomb, & E. D. Hartley (Eds.), *Readings in social psychology.* New York: Holt, Rinehart & Winston, 1958.

Whorf, B. L. *Language, thought, and reality.* J. B. Carroll (Ed.). New York: Wiley, 1956.

Wiener, B. Motivational factors in short-term retention. II. Rehearsal or arousal? *Psychological Reports,* 1967, **20,** 1203-1208.

Williams, R. D., Mason, H. L., & Smith, B. F. Induced vitamin B_1 deficiency in human subjects. *Proceedings of Staff Meeting, Mayo Clinic,* 1939, **14,** 787-793.

Williams, R. D., Mason, H. L., Smith, B. F., & Wilder, R. M. Induced thiamine (vitamin B_1) deficiency and the thiamine requirement of man: Further observations. *Archives of Internal Medicine,* 1942, **69,** 721-738.

Williams, R. J. *Biochemical individuality.* New York: Wiley, 1956.

Williams, R. L., Agnew, H. W., & Webb, W. B. Sleep patterns in young adults: An EEG study. *Electroencephalography and Clinical Neurophysiology,* 1964, **17,** 376-381.

Winokur, G. Genetic factors in mood disorders. *Mental Health Program Reports,* 1970, **4,** 215-235.

Winter, G. D., & Nuss, E. M. *The young adult: Identity and awareness.* Glenview, Ill.: Scott, Foresman, 1969.

Winterbottom, M. R. The relation of childhood training in independence to achievement motivation. Unpublished doctoral dissertation, University of Michigan, 1953.

Witkin, H. A., et al. *Personality through perception.* New York: Harper & Row, 1954.

Witt, P. N. Reported in *Newsweek,* August 10, 1970.

Woddis, G. M. *Medical World,* 1960, **93**(3), 255.

Wolberg, L. Hypnotherapy. In S. Arieti (Ed.), *American handbook of psychiatry.* Vol. 2. New York: Basic Books, 1959.

Wold, C. I. Characteristics of 26,000 suicide prevention center patients. *Bulletin of Suicidology,* 1970, **6,** 24-28.

Wolf, A. V. *Thirst: Physiology of the urge to drink and problems of water lack.* Springfield, Ill.: Thomas, 1958.

Wolf, A., & Schwartz, E. K. *Psychoanalysis in groups.* New York: Grune & Stratton, 1962.

Wolf, M., Risley, T., & Mees, H. Application of operant conditioning procedures to the behavior problems of an autistic child. *Behavior Research and Therapy,* 1964, **1,** 305-312.

Wolf, S., & Wolff, H. G. *Human gastric function.* (2nd ed.) New York: Oxford University Press, 1947.

Wolff, P. H. Observations on the early development of smiling. In B. M. Ross (Ed.), *Determinants of infant behavior.* Vol. 2. New York: Wiley, 1963.

Wolff, P. H. The development of attention in young infants. *Annals of the New York Academy of Sciences,* 1965, **118,** 815-830.

Wolpe, J. *Psychotherapy by reciprocal inhibition.* Stanford: Stanford University Press, 1958.

Wolpe, J. Reciprocal inhibition as the main basis of psychotherapeutic effects. In H. J. Eysenck (Ed.), *Behavior therapy and the neuroses.* New York: Pergamon Press, 1960.

Wolpe, J. *The practice of behavior therapy.* New York: Pergamon Press, 1969.

Woods, J. *The yoga-system of pantanjali.* Cambridge, Mass.: Harvard University Press, 1914.

Worchel, P. Anxiety and repression. *Journal of Abnormal and Social Psychology,* 1955, **50,** 201-205.

Worden, F. G. Attention and auditory electrophysiology. In E. Stellar & J. M. Sprague (Eds.), *Progress in physiological psychology.* Vol 1. New York: Academic Press, 1966.

Y–Z

Yablonsky, L. The violent gang. In S. Endleman (Ed.), *Violence in the streets.* Chicago: Quadrangle Books, 1968.

Yates, A. J. Delayed auditory feedback. *Psychological Bulletin,* 1963, **60,** 213-232.

Yerkes, R. M., & Morgulis, S. The method of Pavlov in animal psychology. *Psychological Bulletin,* 1909, **6,** 257-273.

Yoshii, N., & Hockaday, W. J. Conditioning of frequency—characteristic repetitive EEG response with intermittent photic stimulation. *Electroencephalography and Clinical Neurophysiology,* 1958, **10,** 487.

Young, K. *Source book for social psychology.* New York: Knopf, 1927.

Young, P. T. *Motivation and emotion.* New York: Wiley, 1961.

Young, P. T. Evolution and preference in behavioral development. *Psychological Review,* 1968, **75,** 222-241.

Zajonc, R. B. Social facilitation. *Science,* 1965, **149,** 269-274.

Zajonc, R. B. Social facilitation in cockroaches. In E. C. Simmel, R. A. Hoppe, & G. A. Milton (Eds.), *Social facilitation and imitative behavior.* Boston: Allyn & Bacon, 1968.

Zarcone, V., Gulevich, G., Pivik, T., & Dement, W. C. REM deprivation and schizophrenia. In J. Wortis (Ed.), *Recent advances in biological psychiatry.* New York: Plenum Press, 1970, in press.

Zborowski, M. *People in pain.* San Francisco: Jossey-Bass, 1969.

Zeaman, D., & Smith, R. W. Review and analysis of some recent findings in human cardiac conditioning. In W. F. Prokasky (Ed.), *Classical conditioning.* New York: Appleton-Century-Crofts, 1965.

Zeigarnik, B. Uber das Behalten von erledigten und unerledigten Handlungen. *Psychologische Forschung,* 1927, **9,** 1-85.

Zeller, A. F. An experimental analogue of repression. II. The effect of individual failure and success on memory measured by relearning. *Journal of Experimental Psychology,* 1950, **40,** 411-422.

Ziffer, H., Frank, O., Christakis, G., Talkington, L., & Baker, H. Data analysis strategy for nutritional survey of 642 New York City school children. *The American Journal of Clinical Nutrition,* 1967, **20,** 858-865.

Zigler, E. Social deprivation and rigidity in the performance of feebleminded children. *Journal of Abnormal and Social Psychology,* 1961, **62,** 413-421.

Zigler, E. Motivational determinants in the performance of retarded children. *American Journal of Orthopsychiatry,* 1966, **36**(5).

Zigler, E. Motivational and emotional factors in the behavior of the retarded. *Connecticut Medicine,* August 1968.

Zigler, E. Developmental versus difference theories of mental retardation and the problem of motivation. *American Journal of Mental Deficiency,* 1969, **73**(4).

Ziller, R. C. Individuation and socialization. *Human Relations,* 1964, **17,** 341-360.

Zimbardo, P. G. The effects of early avoidance training and rearing conditions upon the sexual behavior of the male rat. *J. comp. physiol. Psychol.,* 1958, **51,** 764-769.

Zimbardo, P. G. *The cognitive control of motivation.* Glenview, Ill.: Scott, Foresman, 1969. (a)

Zimbardo, P. G. The human choice: Individuation, reason, and order versus deindividuation, impulse, and chaos. In W. J. Arnold & D. Levine (Eds.), *Nebraska symposium on motivation.* Lincoln: University of Nebraska Press, 1969. (b)

Zimbardo, P. G., & Maslach, C. *The internal control of complex skin temperature in humans.* Unpublished manuscript. Stanford University, 1969.

Zimbardo, P. G., & Miller, N. E. Facilitation of exploration by hunger in rats. *Journal of Comparative and Physiological Psychology,* 1958, **51,** 43-46.

Zimbardo, P. G., & Montgomery, K. D. The relative strengths of consummatory responses in hunger, thirst, and exploratory drive. *Journal of Comparative and Physiological Psychology,* 1957, **50,** 504-508.

Zimbardo, P. G., Rapaport, C., & Baron, J. Pain control by hypnotic induction of motivational states. In P. Zimbardo (Ed.), *The cognitive control of motivation.* Glenview, Ill.: Scott, Foresman, 1969.

Zimmerman, R. R. Analysis of discrimination learning capacities in the infant rhesus monkey. *Journal of Comparative and Physiological Psychology,* 1961, **54,** 1-10.

Zubeck, J. P., Pushkar, D., Sansom, W., & Gowing, J. Perceptual changes after prolonged sensory isolation (darkness and silence). *Canad. J. Psychol.,* 1961, **15,** 83-100.

Zuckerman, S. *The social life of monkeys and apes.* London: Kegan Paul, 1932.

Zweigenhaft, R. Signature size: Key to status awareness. *Journal of Social Psychology,* 1970, **81,** 49-54.

Acknowledgments

For the most part, professional services are acknowledged through the bibliographical references. Other sources of illustrations and quoted matter not given on the copyright page or on the page where they appear are listed below. To all, the authors and publisher wish to express their appreciation.

6   From *A Hopkins Reader* by John Pick, Editor, Oxford University Press, 1966, by permission.

11   Photo by Nancy Moses, Chicago Read Mental Health Center.

19   The Bettmann Archive (top); photo by James Ballard (bottom).

20   Photo by Dr. Philip G. Zimbardo (left); Wide World (upper right); Jester, Columbia University (lower right).

25   From "Psychological Clues Detected in Elderly," New York *Times,* November 12, 1968, p. 22 L, © 1968 by The New York Times Company, reprinted by permission (left); from "Theories Abound on Birth Increase" by Martin Tolchin, New York *Times,* August 11, 1966, p. 35, © 1966 by The New York Times Company, reprinted by permission (center); from "Smoking Linked to Poor Grades" by Jane E. Brody, New York *Times,* January 3, 1967, p. 13 L, © 1967 by The New York Times Company, reprinted by permission (right).

37   Photo courtesy of Pfizer Inc. (left); courtesy of Dr. B. F. Skinner (right).

38   From Fermi, Laura, & Bernadini, G. *Galileo and the Scientific Revolution.* New York: Basic Books, 1961.

41   Photo by Dr. Philip G. Zimbardo.

42   Photos by Thomas Medcalf.

44   Photo by Dr. Philip G. Zimbardo.

49   U.S. Army photo, Walter Reed Army Institute.

56   National Aeronautics and Space Administration, Washington, D.C. 20546.

58   Drawing by Niklaas Hartsoeker; courtesy of Clarendon Press, University of Oxford.

61   The Bettmann Archive.

64   From "The New Genetics: The Threads of Life" by G. W. Beadle in *Britannica Book of the Year,* 1964, by permission.

70   University College, London.

74   Courtesy of Dr. Edwin R. Lewis (left); courtesy of Dr. Sanford L. Palay (right).

81   From *Neurophysiology: A Primer* by C. F. Stevens, 1966, John Wiley & Sons, Inc. Reprinted by permission of the publisher.

84   Photo courtesy of Dr. Edwin R. Lewis.

87   From "Spatial and Temporal Aspects of Retinal Inhibitory Interaction" by F. Ratliff et al., *Journal of the Optical Society of America,* Vol. 53, 1959, pp. 110-121, by permission of the publisher (left); photo by James Ballard (right).

88   From *Frontiers in Physiological Psychology* by R. W. Russell, Editor, by permission of Academic Press and the author. Copyright © 1966 Academic Press, Inc.

91   Based on "Volley Theory" by E. G. Wever from *Theory of Hearing,* 1949, John Wiley & Sons, Inc., by permission of the author.

99   Courtesy of Dr. José M. Delgado.

102   Courtesy of Dr. David Krech.

103   Courtesy of Dr. Neal E. Miller.

104   Reprinted from the *Psychology Review,* Vol. 61, 1954, pp. 5-22, by permission of the American Psychological Association and the authors.

105   Courtesy of Dr. José M. Delgado.

107   From *The Harvey Lectures,* Series 62, 1968, by permission of Academic Press, Inc., and the author.

114   Courtesy of Carnegie Institution of Washington.

119   Courtesy of Davenport Hooker, from Hooker, D. *A Preliminary Atlas of Early Human Fetal Activity.* Pittsburgh: Author, 1939.

120   Smith, K. U., Zwerg, C., & Smith, N. J. "Sensory-feedback Analysis of Infant Control of the Behavioral Environment." *Perceptual and Motor Skills,* 1963, 16, 725-732, Figure 2. Reprinted by permission of the publisher and the authors.

121   Courtesy of Dr. Marcelle Geber.

122   Courtesy of U.S. Department of the Interior, Bureau of Indian Affairs.

123   Black Star.

126   Courtesy of Dr. Robert L. Fantz.

127   Courtesy of Dr. Keith Nelson.

128   Reprinted by permission from *Scientific American,* photos by William Vandivert.

129   Reprinted from the *Journal of Comparative and Physiological Psychology,* Vol. 56, No. 5, October 1963, p. 873, by permission of the American Psychological Association and the authors.

131   Photos by John H. Gerard.

132   Courtesy of Dr. Archie Carr and *Scientific American.*

133   Courtesy of Dr. Einar Siqueland.

134   Courtesy of Dr. Eleanor J. Gibson.

136   From "Imprinting" by E. H. Hess, *Science,* Vol. 130, July 17, 1959, pp. 133-141, Figs. 1 and 2. Copyright 1959 by the American Association for the Advancement of Science.

142   Courtesy of Dr. Beatrice T. Gardner.

143   Courtesy of Dr. David Premack.

147   From *British Journal of Educational Psychology,* 1966, pp. 305-306, by permission of the publisher.

152   Lesser, Gerald and Susan Stodolsky, "Learning Patterns in the Disadvantaged," *Harvard Educational Review,* 37, Fall 1967, pp. 568-569. Copyright © 1967 by President and Fellows of Harvard College. Reprinted by permission of the publisher and the authors.

156 Magnum, photo by Ribound.

160, 161 Photos by Ted Croner.

164 Courtesy of Eli Lilly and Company.

173 Photo courtesy of Dr. Lewis P. Lipsitt, Hunter Laboratory, Brown University (left); reprinted from the *Journal of Comparative and Physiological Psychology,* Vol. 56, 1963, pp. 73-77, by permission of the American Psychological Association and the authors (center); from "Decrement and Recovery of Responses to Olfactory Stimuli in the Human Infant" by Trygg Engen and Lewis P. Lipsitt, *Journal of Comparative and Physiological Psychology*, 1965, 59, 312-316, by permission of the authors (right).

175 Reprinted from the *Psychological Bulletin,* Vol. 6, 1909, pp. 257-273, by permission of the American Psychological Association.

178 From "Central Inhibition in Cortical Conditioned Reflexes" by F. Morrell and M. Ross, *The American Medical Association Archives of Neurology and Psychiatry,* Vol. 70, 1953, p. 611, by permission of the publisher and the authors (upper); from *Electroencephalography and Clinical Neurophysiology,* Vol. 10, 1958, pp. 487-502, Fig. 3, by permission of Elsevier Publishing Company (lower).

191 The New York *Times.*

193 Reprinted from the *Journal of Experimental Psychology,* Vol. 51, 1956, p. 81, by permission of the American Psychological Association and the authors.

194 Reprinted from the *Journal of Comparative and Physiological Psychology,* Vol. 52, 1959, pp. 359-363, by permission of the American Psychological Association and the authors (left); photo by John Sanderson.

195 From *Journal of the Experimental Analysis of Behavior,* 1961, 4, 281-284. Copyright 1961 by the Society for the Experimental Analysis of Behavior, Inc.

196 Courtesy of Dr. Thom Verhave (left); courtesy of Dr. B. F. Skinner (right).

198 From "Operant Discrimination of an Interoceptive Stimulus in Rhesus Monkeys" by Slucki, Adam, and Porter, *Journal of the Experimental Analysis of Behavior,* 1965, 8, 405-414. Copyright 1965 by the Society for the Experimental Analysis of Behavior, Inc.

199 Reprinted from the *Psychological Review,* Vol. 56, 1949, pp. 51-65, by permission of the American Psychological Association and the author.

200 From *Primer of Operant Conditioning* by G. S. Reynolds. Copyright © 1968 by Scott, Foresman and Co.

201 Courtesy of Dr. Neal E. Miller.

206 Photo by Thomas Medcalf.

207 From "The Opportunity for Aggression As an Operant Reinforcer During Aversive Stimulation" by Azrin, Hutchinson, and McLaughlin, *Journal of the Experimental Analysis of Behavior,* 1965, 8, 171-180. Copyright 1965 by the Society for the Experimental Analysis of Behavior, Inc.

208 Courtesy of Yerkes Regional Primate Research Center of Emory University, Atlanta, Georgia.

217 From "Perception as a Function of Retinal Locus" by W. Heron, *American Journal of Psychology,* Vol. 70, 1957, pp. 38-48, by permission of the University of Illinois Press.

219 From *Eye and Brain: The Psychology of Seeing* by R. L. Gregory. Reprinted by permission of George Weidenfeld & Nicolson Ltd., London.

222 Reprinted from the *Journal of Experimental Psychology,* Vol. 56, 1958, pp. 297-304, by permission of the American Psychological Association and the author (upper); *Psychology and Military Proficiency: A History of the Applied Psychology Panel on the National Defense Research Committee* by Charles W. Bray (Copyright 1948 by Princeton University Press): adaptations of Fig. 14, p. 196. Reprinted by permission of the publisher (lower).

223 From *Perception and Motion: An Analysis of Space-Structured Behavior* by Karl U. Smith and W. M. Smith, 1962 W. B. Saunders Company, Fig. 4-1, p. 59, and Fig. 5-16, p. 83, by permission of W. B. Saunders Company and the authors.

224 From *Teachers College Contributions to Education,* 1930, No. 438, by permission of *The Record.*

225 Reprinted from the *Journal of Experimental Psychology,* Vol. 57, 1959, pp. 310-316, by permission of the American Psychological Association and the author.

231 From "On Explaining Language" by E. H. Lenneberg, *Science,* Vol. 164, May 9, 1969, pp. 635-643, Table 1. Copyright © 1969 by the American Association for the Advancement of Science.

235 Photo by Dr. Philip G. Zimbardo.

236 From "Retention as a Function of the Method of Measurement" by L. Postman and L. Rau, University of California Publications in Psychology, 1957, Vol. 8:3, p. 236. Originally published by the University of California Press; reprinted by permission of The Regents of the University of California.

238 From *Remembering: A Study in Experimental and Social Psychology* by F. C. Bartlett, 1932 The Macmillan Company, by permission of Cambridge University Press.

240 Photo by Jean Martin, Montreal Neurological Institute. Courtesy of Dr. W. Penfield, from Penfield, W., *The Excitable Cortex in Conscious Man.* Liverpool: Liverpool University Press, 1958.

241 Reprinted from an article by G. A. Sperling from the 1963 *Human Factors Journal, 5,* 19-31, by permission.

250 From "Recognition Memory for Syntactic and Semantic Aspects of Connected Discourse" by J. S. Sachs, *Perception and Psychophysics,* 2(9), 1967, p. 441, by permission of Psychonomic Journals, Inc.

251 From "Narrative Stories as Mediators for Serial Learning" by G. H. Bower and M. C. Clark, *Psychonomic Science,* Vol. 14, 1969, pp. 181-182, by permission of Psychonomic Journals, Inc.

253 Courtesy of Dr. Sidney L. Pressey (left); from "Advances in Computer-Based Education" by D. Alpert and D. C. Bitzer, *Science,* Vol. 167, March 20, 1970, pp. 1582-1590, Fig. 3. Copyright © 1970 by the American Association for the Advancement of Science (right).

254 Courtesy of Dr. Richard Atkinson.

256 Copyright © Don Bronstein 1967. Reprinted from *Chicago: I Will,* published by The World Publishing Company.

258 Arthur Rickerby, *Life* Magazine © Time, Inc.

262 "Stages of Sleep Across a Night," by Wilse B. Webb

originally used in "Sleep Characteristics of Human Subjects" from *Bulletin of the British Psychological Society,* 1965, Vol. 18, pp. 1-10 (left); courtesy of Dr. William Dement (right).

268 Photo by Thomas Medcalf.

269 Courtesy of the Armstrong Rubber Company.

270 Cartoon by Reamer Keller, reprinted by permission of Adcox Associates Inc.

271 Reprinted from the *Journal of Abnormal Psychology,* Vol. 70, 1965, pp. 165-168, by permission of the American Psychological Association and the authors.

272 From "Attention, Vigilance and Cortical Evoked Potentials in Humans" by M. Haider et al., *Science,* Vol. 145, July 10, 1964, pp. 180-182, Fig. 2. Copyright © 1964 by the American Association for the Advancement of Science.

273 From "Plasticity of Sensorimotor Development in the Human Infant" by B. L. White and R. Held, in *The Causes of Behavior,* edited by J. R. Rosenblith and W. Allinsmith, 1966 Allyn and Bacon, by permission of B. L. White and R. Held (left); photo by Dr. Philip G. Zimbardo (right).

276 From *Journal of Personality,* Vol. 35, 1967, pp. 91-180, by permission of Duke University Press.

277 Courtesy of Dr. Herman A. Witkin.

278 Reprinted by permission from *Scientific American,* photos by William Vandivert.

282 Courtesy of the Institute for International Social Research.

287 Courtesy of Dr. Norwood R. Hanson, from Hanson, N. R., *Patterns of Discovery.* Cambridge University Press, 1958.

288 Courtesy of Dr. L. D. Harmon and Dr. K. C. Knowlton, Bell Laboratories.

289 Official U.S. Navy Photographs.

293, 294, 298 From "A study of a Neglected Portion of the Field of Learning—the Development of Sensory Organization" by Robert Leeper, *The Journal of Genetic Psychology,* 1935, 46, pp. 41-75, by permission of The Journal Press and the author.

295 Compiled from data presented in "Contemporary Psychophysics" by Eugene Galanter, from *New Directions in Psychology* by Roger Brown, Eugene Galanter, Eckhard H. Hess, and George Mandler. Used by permission of Holt, Rinehart & Winston, Inc. Holt, Rinehart & Winston, Inc., 1962.

296 From "The Perceived Size of Coins in Normal and Hypnotically Induced Economic States" by W. R. Ashley, R. S. Harper, and D. L. Runyon, *American Journal of Psychology,* Vol. 64, 1951, pp. 564-572, by permission of the University of Illinois Press.

305 From "An Experimental Study of Apparent Behavior" by F. Heider and M. Simmel, *American Journal of Psychology,* Vol. 57, 1944, pp. 243-259, by permission of the University of Illinois Press.

310 Photo by Wayne Schiska.

312 Reprinted from the *Journal of Experimental Psychology,* Vol. 15, 1932, pp. 73-86, by permission of the American Psychological Association.

316 Reprinted from the *American Psychologist,* Vol. 19, 1964, pp. 1-15, by permission of the American Psychological Association and the author (left); from *Studies in Cognitive Growth* by J. S. Bruner et al., 1966 John Wiley & Sons, Inc. Reprinted by permission of the publisher (right).

317 From "Electrophysiology of Mental Activities" by E. Jacobson, *American Journal of Psychology,* Vol. 44, 1932, pp. 677-694, by permission of the University of Illinois Press.

319 Photo by Dr. Philip G. Zimbardo.

322, 324, 328 Photos by Wayne Schiska.

331 Courtesy of Dr. Frank Barron.

333 The Welsh Figure Preference Test by George S. Welsh, Ph.D. Copyright 1959, published by Consulting Psychologists Press, Inc.

338 © 1969, The Chicago Tribune.

341 From *A Textbook of Psychology* by D. O. Hebb, 2nd edition, 1966, p. 235, Fig. 75, by permission of W. B. Saunders Company and the author.

345 From *Animal Motivation: Experimental Studies on the Albino Rat* by C. J. Warden, 1931 Columbia University Press, by permission of the publisher.

348 From "The Effect of the Onset of Stimuli on Reactivity in the Rat" by J. Tapp, D. Mathewson, P. D'Encarnacas, and C. Long, *Psychonomic Science,* Vol. 19, 1970, pp. 61-62, Fig. 2, by permission of Psychonomic Journals, Inc.

349 Reprinted from the *Journal of Comparative and Physiological Psychology,* Vol. 51, 1958, pp. 43-46, by permission of the American Psychological Association and the authors.

353 Wallace Kirkland, courtesy of *Life,* © 1945, Time, Inc.

355 Reprinted with permission from Matthew Wayner, *Thirst,* Copyright 1964, Pergamon Press.

358 Courtesy of Dr. Victor G. Laties and Dr. B. Weiss, from Weiss, B., & Laties, V. G. "Behavioral Thermoregulation." *Science,* 1961, 133, 1338-1344. © 1961, The American Association for Advancement of Science (left); Courtesy of Dr. A. N. Epstein (right).

361 Alinari. Art Reference Bureau, New York.

367 Reprinted from the *American Psychologist,* Vol. 13, 1958, pp. 673-685, by permission of the American Psychological Association and the author.

372 Photos by Dr. Philip G. Zimbardo.

376 Arthur Rickerby; *Life* Magazine © Time, Inc.

384, 386 United Press International.

385 Courtesy of Dr. H. Schlosberg and the American Psychological Association.

389 From *Endocrines and the Central Nervous System* by R. Levine, Editor, Proceedings of the Association for Research in Mental Disease, Vol. 43, 1966 Williams and Wilkins, by permission of the Association for Research in Nervous and Mental Disease.

391 Reprinted from the *Journal of Abnormal Psychology,* Vol. 73, 1968, pp. 100-113, by permission of the American Psychological Association and the authors.

393 From *Human Gastric Functions* by Wolf and Wolff, Oxford University Press 1947, by permission.

395 From *Journal of Health and Human Behavior,* Vol. 4, 1963, pp. 83-87, by permission of the American Sociological Association.

398 Adapted from *Psychological Stress* by I. Janis, 1958 John Wiley & Sons, Inc. Reprinted by permission of the publisher.

399 Reprinted from *Psychological Monographs,* Vol. 78, No. 585, 1964, p. 13, fig. 11, by permission of the American Psychological Association and the author.

401 From *The Cognitive Control of Motivation,* edited by Philip G. Zimbardo. Copyright © 1969 by Scott, Foresman and Company.

406 Reprinted from the *Journal of Comparative and Physiological Psychology,* Vol. 66, No. 2, 1968, p. 405, by permission of the American Psychological Association and the author.

407 From "The Availability of Avoidance Behaviors in Modulating Vascular Stress Responses" by J. E. Hokanson, D. E. DeGood, M. S. Forrest, and T. M. Brittain, *Journal of Personality and Social Psychology,* 1971.

408 James Burke, *Life* Magazine © Time, Inc.

410 From *Psychosomatic Medicine,* 1969, Vol. 31, pp. 227-246, Figure 1, by permission of Harper & Row, Inc., Medical Department.

411 From *The Cognitive Control of Motivation,* edited by Philip G. Zimbardo. Copyright © 1969 by Scott, Foresman and Company.

413 Reprinted from *J. abnorm. soc. Psychol.,* Vol. 69, 1964, pp. 303-310, by permission of the American Psychological Association and the authors.

421 *Fortune Tellers Never Starve* by W. L. Gresham. *Esquire* Magazine 1949. Copyright 1949 by W. L. Gresham. Reprinted by permission of Brandt & Brandt.

426 © Punch, London.

429 From Neal E. Miller—"Experimental Studies of Conflict" in *Personality and the Behavior Disorders,* edited by J. McVicker Hunt. Copyright 1944 The Ronald Press Company, New York.

437 Reprinted from *Psychological Review,* Vol. 68, 1961, pp. 1-20, by permission of the American Psychological Association and the author.

442 From *A Handbook of Physiology, Phrenology, and Physiognomy,* by Fowler and Wells.

443 From *The Varieties of Temperament* by William H. Sheldon et al., 1940 Harper & Row; and *Journal of Personality,* Vol. 18, 1950, pp. 440-453, by permission of Duke University Press.

445 United Press International.

447 Courtesy of Dr. Robert B. Mills and the Cincinnati Police Academy.

448 Prepared by John Mayahara.

449 Courtesy of Merrill Palmer Institute, by Donna Harris.

466 From *Varieties of Human Value* by O. Morris, table 12.1, copyright © 1956 by The University of Chicago Press, used by permission; and from *Sociometry,* Vol. 23, No. 2, June 1960, pp. 163 and 164, by permission of the American Sociological Association.

468 From the *Nebraska Symposium on Motivation* edited by W. J. Arnold, © 1968 The University of Nebraska. Reprinted by permission.

469 Adapted from *The Psychology of Affiliation* by S. Schachter, 1959 Stanford University Press, by permission of the publisher.

475 Courtesy of Dr. M. Brenner.

476 Adapted from "Informational Loss in a Social Setting" by Malcolm Brenner from Mimeographed Technical Report, University of Michigan 1970. Used by permission of the author.

477 Photo by Dr. Philip G. Zimbardo.

483 Courtesy of Dr. Ronald Lippitt.

484 Excerpt from "Delegation" by Ernest Dale from *Enterprise,* The Magazine of the Young Presidents' Organization, April 1967, by permission.

485 From *The Gang: A Study in Adolescent Behavior* by Bloch and Niederhoffer, Philosophical Library 1958, by permission.

489 Reprinted from the *Journal of Experimental and Social Psychology,* Vol. 1, 1965, pp. 156-171, by permission of the American Psychological Association and the authors.

496 Reprinted from the *Journal of Abnormal and Social Psychology,* Vol. 62, 1961, pp. 649-658, by permission of the American Psychological Association and the authors.

497 Reprinted by permission from *Scientific American,* photo by William Vandivert.

500 From "Overcoming Resistance to Change" by Coch and French, *Human Relations,* 1948, Vol. 1, pp. 512-532, by permission of Plenum Publishing Corp.

502 Courtesy of Dr. Muzafer Sherif, from Sherif, M., & Sherif, Carolyn, *An Outline of Social Psychology.* (Rev. ed.) New York: Harper & Row, 1956.

506 Photo by Jean-Claude Lejeune.

513 Reprinted from the *Journal of Abnormal and Social Psychology,* Vol. 63, 1961, pp. 466-492, by permission of the American Psychological Association and the author.

516, 517 Cartoon by Norman Mansbridge, © Punch, London.

517 From *Advances in Experimental Social Psychology* by L. Berkowitz, Editor, by permission of Academic Press and the author. © 1965 Academic Press, Inc.

518 Courtesy of Dr. Albert Bandura.

520 Reprinted from the *Journal of Personality and Social Psychology,* 1965, pp. 589-595, by permission of the American Psychological Association and the author.

522 United Press International.

525 Reprinted from Hans Toch, *Violent Men* (Chicago: Aldine Publishing Company, 1969); copyright © 1969 by Hans Toch.

526 From "Achievement Place: Token Reinforcement Procedures in a Home-Style Rehabilitation Setting for 'Pre-Delinquent' Boys" by E. L. Phillips, *Journal of Applied Behavior Analysis,* 1968, Vol. 1, p. 273. Copyright 1968 by the Society for the Experimental Analysis of Behavior, Inc.

536 United Press International.

537 From "Classification of Problems and Crises by Estimated Time and Intensity" by John Platt, *Science,* November 28, 1969, Vol. 166, No. 3909, p. 1118. Copyright © 1969 by the American Association for the Advancement of Science.

540 From *A Big Bowl of Punch,* 1964 Simon & Schuster. Copyright *Punch,* London. Reprinted by permission of the Ben Roth Agency, Scarsdale, N.Y.

541   Reprinted from the *Journal of Personality and Social Psychology,* Vol. 8, No. 4, 1968, pp. 377-383, by permission of the American Psychological Association and the author.

542   Photo by Dr. Philip G. Zimbardo.

543   United Press International.

544   Wide World.

545   Courtesy of Publishers-Hall Syndicate.

546   Photo by Dr. Philip G. Zimbardo.

547   Photos by Dr. Scott C. Fraser.

548   From "Frank's Betrayer Got Nazi Reward," New York *Times,* February 1, 1967, p. 12 © 1967 by The New York Times Company. Reprinted by permission.

551   Photos by Dr. Philip G. Zimbardo.

552   Courtesy of Mrs. Sakaye Kato.

553   From *Justifying the Final Solution* by H. H. Mansson from a paper presented at the International Congress of Psychology, London, 1969. Reprinted by permission of the author.

558   From *Understanding Ourselves and Others* by K. Haas, © 1965 by Prentice-Hall, Inc. Reprinted by permission.

561   © Punch, London.

566   From Chapter VIII of *Black Rage* by William H. Grier and Price M. Cobbs, © 1968 by William H. Grier and Price M. Cobbs, Basic Books, Inc., Publishers, New York. Reprinted by permission.

570   Courtesy of Mrs. Jane Elliott and ABC Television, photo by Charlotte Button.

572   Photo by Mary Ellen Mark.

592   From "Naturalistic Observations on Chronically Hospitalized Patients: 1. The Effects of Strangers" by A. Hershkowitz, *Journal of Nervous and Mental Diseases,* 1962 Williams & Wilkins, Vol. 135, pp. 258-264, by permission of the Association for Research in Nervous and Mental Disease.

593   From *The Inner World of Mental Illness* by Bert Kaplan, Editor, 1964 Harper & Row, pp. 191-192.

596   Photograph by John Scofield, © 1962 National Geographic Society.

597   From *Social Class and Mental Illness: A Community Study* by Hollingshead and Redlich, 1958 John Wiley & Sons, Inc., p. 230. Reprinted by permission of the publisher.

599, 600   From *Forces in Urban Suicide,* 1969 The Dorsey Press.

601   Courtesy of Dr. Daryl Bem.

606   The Bettmann Archive (left); photo by Bob Towers (middle); photo by Ken Regan, Camera 5 (right).

610   Photo by Dr. Peter Witt, Division of Research, North Carolina Department of Mental Health, Raleigh, N.C.

613   Copyright 1968, Chelsea House Publishers, a division of Chelsea House Educational Communications, Inc., reprinted by permission.

623   Reprinted from the *Journal of Consulting Psychology,* Vol. 13, 1957, pp. 344-350, by permission of the American Psychological Association and the author.

624   Photo by Bernard Hoffman, courtesy of *Life,* © 1942 Time, Inc.

628   Photo by Edward Clark, courtesy of *Life,* © 1952 Time, Inc.

632   Courtesy of Dr. Albert Bandura.

633   From *The Causes and Cures of Neurosis* by H. J. Eysenck and S. Rachman (San Diego: R. Knapp, 1965), by permission of the publisher, Routledge & Kegan Paul Ltd., and the authors.

636   Reprinted by permission of Ogden R. Lindsley.

638   Courtesy of California Department of Mental Health.

641   From *Insight vs. Desensitization in Psychotherapy* by G. L. Paul, 1966 Stanford University Press, by permission of the publisher.

644   Based on "New Medicines for the Mind: Their Meaning and Promise" from *Public Affairs Pamphlet,* No. 228, 1955 Public Affairs Committee, by permission of the publisher.

649   Reprinted from the *Journal of Consulting Psychology,* Vol. 16, 1952, pp. 319-324, by permission of the American Psychological Association and the author.

Back endsheet (left) Courtesy of Container Corporation.

Back endsheet (right) Reproduced with the permission of the author of the Dvorine Pseudo-Isochromatic Plates, published by the Scientific Publishing Company, Baltimore, Md. (top); courtesy of the American Optical Company (bottom).

Name Index

Subject Index

How well have we communicated? How can we make the next edition better?

We need your reactions and ideas if we are to serve students better. What did you like best and least? What would you have liked more or less of? How could it have been handled better? Please jot down your suggestions, cut out this page, fold and fasten it, and send it in to us. No postage needed.

Many thanks! F. L. R. and P. G. Z.

Please make a check mark on each line to indicate your evaluation of the chapter.

CROSS OUT CHAPTERS NOT READ

	VERY VALUABLE, INTERESTING			NO VALUE OR INTEREST
Chapter 1 Unraveling mystery	1	2	3	4	5
Chapter 2 Scientific method	1	2	3	4	5
Chapter 3 Physiological	1	2	3	4	5
Chapter 4 Development	1	2	3	4	5
Chapter 5 Conditioning	1	2	3	4	5
Chapter 6 Skills, memory	1	2	3	4	5
Chapter 7 Sleep to perception	1	2	3	4	5
Chapter 8 Thinking	1	2	3	4	5
Chapter 9 Motivation	1	2	3	4	5
Chapter 10 Cognitive control	1	2	3	4	5
Chapter 11 Personality, tests	1	2	3	4	5
Chapter 12 Social	1	2	3	4	5
Chapter 13 Dehumanizing forces	1	2	3	4	5
Chapter 14 Pathology	1	2	3	4	5
Chapter 15 Therapies	1	2	3	4	5
Appendix A Psychotic case	1	2	3	4	5
Appendix B Statistics	1	2	3	4	5
Appendix C Learning theories	1	2	3	4	5
Appendix D Drugs	1	2	3	4	5

What did you like best about the book?

What did you like least about the book?

Specific suggestions:

Size of your class_____

Were there sections?_____Taught by graduate students?_____

What supplementary materials did you use?   Your name and school (if you wish)

_____   _____

_____   _____

Do you plan to take more psychology?_____   Male_____Female_____Age_____

What is your probable major?_____   Your course grade_____

F O L D   H E R E

C U T   P A G E   O U T

F O L D   H E R E

FIRST CLASS
PERMIT No. 282
•
G L E N V I E W
I L L I N O I S

BUSINESS REPLY MAIL
NO POSTAGE NECESSARY IF MAILED IN UNITED STATES

Dr. Floyd Ruch and Dr. Philip Zimbardo

POSTAGE WILL BE PAID BY

SCOTT, FORESMAN AND COMPANY
1900 EAST LAKE AVENUE
GLENVIEW, ILLINOIS 60025

COLLEGE DIVISION